the
AMERICANA
ANNUAL

1993

GROLIER

AN ENCYCLOPEDIA OF THE EVENTS OF 1992
YEARBOOK OF THE ENCYCLOPEDIA AMERICANA

This annual has been prepared as a yearbook for general
encyclopedias. It is also published as *Encyclopedia Year Book.*

© GROLIER INCORPORATED 1993

Copyright in Canada © by Grolier Limited

Library of Congress Catalog Card Number: 23-10041

ISBN: 0-7172-0224-0

ISSN: 0196-0180

Printed and manufactured in the United States of America

Contents

Feature Articles of the Year

© Bob Daemmrich

© Andrew Reid/Gamma-Liaison

HELP WANTED
COUNTER & GRILL
NO EXPERIENCE NEEDED
WILL TRAIN

© David Wells/The Image World

© J. Langevin-T. Orban/Sygma

© Tom Craig/REA/Saba

The Alphabetical Section

Entries on the continents, major nations of the world, U.S. states, Canadian provinces, and chief cities will be found under their own alphabetical headings.

A Review of the Year 1992

© Alfred/Sipa
© Brad Markel/Gamma-Liaison

© Rick Stewart/Allsport

The year 1992 will be remembered as the year U.S. military forces helped deliver supplies to the war-torn African nation of Somalia; the Democrats—with a ticket of Arkansas Gov. Bill Clinton and Tennessee Sen. Al Gore, Jr., both of whom were born after World War II—won the presidency; and a Canadian baseball team took the World Series (*see* photos, page 6).

On the international scene, the federal republic of Yugoslavia broke up; the people of the European Community nations considered ratification of the 1991 Maastricht Treaty on European union; Israel and the Arab nations talked peace; Canada again failed to settle its constitutional problems; South Africa also wrestled with its own constitutional issues but saw continued violence; Boris Yeltsin faced severe domestic pressure as the leader of the new Russian republic, while the other former Soviet republics also coped with new independence and the resulting difficulties; conflict escalated between Hindus and Muslims in South Asia; and the United Nations increased its membership to 179 and took a new look at its peacekeeping role.

Meanwhile, Britain's Prime Minister John Major won a new term for the Tories; the president of Brazil was impeached; the emperor of Japan made a historic journey to China; a cease-fire agreement sought to end El Salvador's long-standing civil war, and Panama's former dictator Manuel Noriega was convicted and given a long prison sentence in the United States; southern Africa suffered from a horrendous drought, while an unusual number of African nations went to the polls; and a wave of neo-Nazi extremism struck Germany.

© Steve Liss/"Time" Magazine

Also during 1992, the U.S. Congress was racked by scandal; the city of Los Angeles experienced severe civil disorder; and women and members of minority groups made inroads at the ballot boxes. The United States and nations elsewhere sought to escape recession; large corporations everywhere were "downsizing." A renewed "Buy American" trend developed (*photo above*), and Canada, Mexico, and the United States reached a free-trade agreement. Hurricanes devastated parts of Florida and Hawaii. Rio de Janiero was the site of a world Earth Summit. Debate in religious circles concerned the issue of the ordination of women. The world of television said good-bye to Johnny Carson and the Huxtable family. *Murphy Brown* won new Emmy accolades and real-life newspaper headlines. Movie fans saw *Malcolm X,* and Broadway theatergoers welcomed back *Guys and Dolls.* Disney magic arrived in France, and Seville, Spain, hosted a world exposition. Jackie Joyner-Kersee, Bonnie Blair, and the U.S. basketball Dream Team were Olympic headliners. The medical community faced a tuberculosis scare in urban centers. And with the 500th anniversary of Christopher Columbus' famous journey, a 33-year-old Native American from Guatemala was awarded the Nobel Peace Prize. The year closed with George Bush on a visit to Somalia to see U.S. troops and a stop in Moscow to sign a new arms agreement, START II, early in 1993.

THE EDITORS

January

1 Egypt's Boutros Boutros-Ghali begins a five-year term as secretary-general of the United Nations.

6 The UN Security Council votes, 15–0, to support a resolution condemning Israel's decision to deport 12 Palestinians from the occupied territories.

10 U.S. President George Bush concludes a ten-day trip to Australia and various Asian countries, which was aimed at winning trade concessions to promote U.S. jobs.

The U.S. Department of Labor announces that the nation's unemployment rate was 7.1% in December 1991, the highest level in five and one-half years.

12 Algeria's new army-dominated ruling council calls off runoff elections planned for January 16. President Chadli Benjedid had resigned on January 11 after the fundamentalist Islamic Salvation Front scored an unexpected win in the first round of parliamentary elections.

15 The European Community and several individual nations recognize the independence of the breakaway Yugoslav republics of Croatia and Slovenia.

16 Representatives of the government of El Salvador and of the Farabundo Martí National Liberation Front sign an agreement ending the country's 12-year-old civil war.

17 Seven men are killed by a bomb, reportedly planted by the Irish Republican Army, in the town of Carrickmore, Northern Ireland. [An eighth man would die as a result of the attack on January 21.]

19 Bulgaria's President Zhelyu Zhelev is elected to a new five-year term. He defeated Velko Valkanov in a runoff election after no candidate received the minimum 50% of the vote in the nation's first direct presidential election on January 12.

George Bush began 1992 with a trip to the Pacific and Asia region to gain trade concessions for the United States. The president and Mrs. Bush were received in Tokyo by Emperor Akihito (rear right) and Empress Michiko on January 8.

© Harayoshi Yamaguchi/Sygma

© Haviv/Saba

23 U.S. Secretary of State James Baker announces that U.S. military planes will begin an emergency airlift of food and medicine to the Commonwealth of Independent States (the former Soviet Union). The announcement came as representatives from 47 nations were attending the second day of a conference on the aid issue.

26 The Washington Redskins defeat the Buffalo Bills, 37-24, in professional football's Super Bowl XXVI.

28 President Bush delivers the annual State of the Union address.

29 President Bush sends to Congress a $1.52 trillion budget for fiscal year 1993.

31 Leaders from the 15 nations that are members of the UN Security Council hold a summit conference at UN headquarters.

Trans World Airlines files for bankruptcy protection. The department-store chain R.H. Macy had filed for such protection on January 27.

Leaders of 15 governments, including the heads of the five permanent members of the UN Security Council, gathered at the United Nations on January 31 for the first Security Council summit. A nonbinding declaration on the future of the Council was agreed to at the meeting.

February

1 President Bush confers with Russia's President Boris Yeltsin at Camp David.

The United States begins to return thousands of Haitians to their homeland. On January 31, the U.S. Supreme Court lifted a December 1991 injunction preventing such repatriations.

Richard N. Bond is selected as chairman of the Republican National Committee, succeeding Clayton K. Yeutter, who was appointed counselor to the president in charge of domestic policy on January 31.

4 In Venezuela, forces loyal to President Carlos Andrés Pérez thwart an attempted coup.

7 In Paris, Russia's President Yeltsin and France's President François Mitterrand sign a treaty calling for political, economic, and military cooperation between their two countries.

10 Former heavyweight boxing champion Mike Tyson is convicted of rape in Indianapolis, IN.

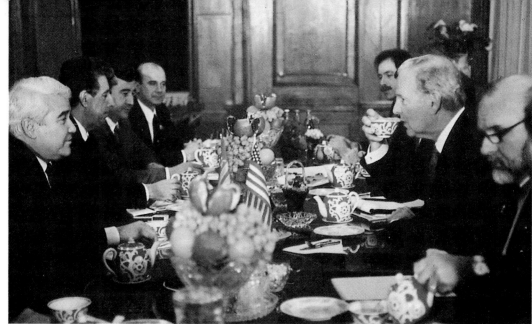

© East News/Sipa

In mid-February, U.S. Secretary of State James A. Baker 3d toured six southern former Soviet republics to initiate diplomatic relations with the newly independent governments. On February 12 the secretary (right) was in Turkmenistan for talks with President Saparmurad Niyazov and his advisers.

The U.S. presidential campaign got into full swing with the New Hampshire primary on February 18. Former U.S. Sen. Paul Tsongas of Massachusetts, below, was the first choice among the state's Democrats.

© Peter Blakley/Saba

11 Following the resignation of Ireland's Prime Minister Charles Haughey in the midst of allegations linking him to a scandal involving government wiretapping, former Finance Minister Albert Reynolds is confirmed by Ireland's parliament as Haughey's successor.

16 Sheikh Abbas al-Musawi, the leader of the Lebanese Shiite organization Hezbollah, is killed when Israeli helicopter gunships attack his motorcade in southern Lebanon.

18 The first 1992 U.S. presidential primary is held in New Hampshire. On the Republican side, George Bush and his opponent Patrick Buchanan receive 53% and 35% of the vote, respectively. Former U.S. Sen. Paul Tsongas (MA) leads the field among the Democrats; Arkansas Gov. Bill Clinton is second.

19 The United States deports Joseph Doherty, a member of the Provisional Irish Republican Army, to Northern Ireland. Doherty had fled Britain in 1981 while awaiting sentencing for his part in the killing of a member of the British army.

20 The U.S. Commerce Department announces that the nation's merchandise trade deficit dropped to $66.2 billion in 1991.

23 The XVI Winter Olympic Games conclude in Albertville, France.

24 The General Motors Corp., the world's largest industrial corporation, announces a loss of $4.45 billion for 1991. The loss is the largest in history by a U.S. company.

President Bush announces the nomination of Edward J. Perkins as the U.S. ambassador to the United Nations. He will succeed Thomas R. Pickering, who is to be named ambassador to India.

27 In San Antonio, TX, President Bush joins leaders from six Latin American nations in signing a pact calling for increased cooperation in combating drug trafficking.

March

2 Nine countries, including San Marino and eight former Soviet republics, are admitted as members of the United Nations.

3 More than 270 miners are killed in an explosion in the Turkish town of Kozlu.

6   A drought emergency is declared in Zimbabwe as southern Africa generally suffers from a severe lack of rain.

7   In Belgium, Jean-Luc Dehaene, a Flemish Christian Democrat, is sworn in as prime minister. General elections in November 1991 had failed to produce a clear victor.

9   Menahem Begin, 78, the prime minister of Israel (1977-83) who signed a peace treaty with Egypt, dies in Jerusalem.

10   Former Soviet Foreign Minister Eduard A. Shevardnadze is selected to head a newly created State Council in the former Soviet republic of Georgia.

15   The mountainous region of eastern Turkey is hit by a second earthquake within three days. Nearly 500 people are killed in the quakes.

17   Voters in South Africa approve a referendum supporting the reform program of President F. W. de Klerk, which is aimed at a new constitution through negotiations.

Nearly 500 persons were killed and many buildings were destroyed as the mountainous region of eastern Turkey was struck by earthquakes on March 13 and 15.

Many blacks in South Africa were pleased as 68.7% of those voting in a whites-only referendum on March 17 supported President F. W. de Klerk's government-reform program.

18 The Islamic Jihad, a Lebanese Shiite group, takes responsibility for a car-bomb explosion in front of the Israeli embassy in Buenos Aires, Argentina, on March 17 that killed at least 28 persons. According to the statement, the explosion was in retaliation for the February murder by Israeli commandos of Shiite leader Sheikh Abbas al-Musawi.

The U.S. Senate upholds President Bush's veto of a bill that would have placed conditions on renewing most-favored-nation trade status for China.

20 Ten of the 11 presidents of the Commonwealth of Independent States conclude a summit in Kiev, the Ukraine, without agreement on important military, economic, and political issues.

22 The Albanian Democratic Party defeats the Socialist (formerly Communist) Party in national elections in Albania.

A U.S. Air jet bound for Cleveland, OH, from New York City crashes on takeoff during a snowstorm, killing 27 persons.

23 Barbara H. Franklin is sworn in as U.S. secretary of commerce. On March 11, Andrew H. Card, Jr., had taken the oath as secretary of transportation.

25 Representatives of 25 nations from North America, Europe, and the former Soviet Union sign an ''open skies'' treaty, permitting reconnaissance flights over their territories.

Russian cosmonaut Sergei Krikalyov, who had been aboard the space station *Mir* since May 1991, returns to Earth. The political situation in the former Soviet Union had postponed his return.

30 In Jamaica, Percival J. Patterson is sworn in as prime minister, succeeding Michael N. Manley, who resigned for health reasons.

31 The UN Security Council votes to impose limited sanctions against Libya if that government refuses to extradite agents suspected by British, French, and U.S. investigators in connection with two airline bombings.

On April 2, Pierre Beregovoy, above, was named to succeed Edith Cresson as premier of France. The 66-year-old Socialist had been serving as the nation's finance minister.

April

1 Daniel S. Goldin, a 51-year-old former executive at the private aerospace corporation TRW, is sworn in as administrator of the National Aeronautics and Space Administration. He succeeds Richard H. Truly.

2 French President François Mitterrand names Finance Minister Pierre Beregovoy to replace Edith Cresson as premier.

In U.S. District Court in Brooklyn, NY, John Gotti, the reputed leader of the Gambino crime family, is convicted of racketeering, racketeering conspiracy, and ten separate counts, including murder, extortion, and tax fraud.

4 Sali Berisha, 47, is the first non-Marxist to become president of Albania since World War II.

5 Peru's President Alberto K. Fujimori imposes decrees dissolving the National Congress, suspending portions of the constitution, and imposing press censorship. The president calls the actions an attack on rebels and drug traffickers.

Thailand's five pro-military parties name Gen. Suchinda Kraprayoon, who participated in a 1991 coup, as premier.

6 In two-day general elections, Italy's four-party government coalition loses its majority.

Duke University wins the National Collegiate Athletic Association's Division I basketball championship for a second consecutive year, defeating Michigan 71-51.

8 Yasir Arafat, leader of the Palestine Liberation Organization (PLO), is rescued after his private plane is forced to crash-land during a sandstorm in a Libyan desert.

9 Great Britain's ruling Conservative Party, led by John Major, wins a majority in parliamentary elections.

In U.S. Federal District Court in Miami, FL, Gen. Manuel Antonio Noriega is found guilty of eight counts of cocaine trafficking, racketeering, and money laundering. The former leader of Panama is acquitted of two cocaine-trafficking charges.

President F. W. de Klerk is the first South African leader to visit Nigeria.

10 Three persons are killed as a bomb explodes in London's financial district. The Provisional Irish Republican Army assumes responsibility for the attack.

12 Fred Couples wins the 56th Masters golf tournament.

13 Chicago's business district comes to a virtual halt as a series of tunnels below the city ruptures, causing extensive flooding.

20 Expo '92, called the largest world's fair ever, officially opens in Seville, Spain.

23 In Myanmar, Gen. Than Shwe is named to succeed Gen. Saw Maung as head of the ruling junta. Saw Maung resigned for reasons of health.

27 The republics of Serbia and Montenegro proclaim a new Federal Republic of Yugoslavia.

Betty Boothroyd is the first woman to be elected speaker of Britain's House of Commons.

28 In Germany, Klaus Kinkel is nominated to succeed Hans-Dietrich Genscher as foreign minister. Genscher, who had held the post since 1974, had announced his resignation on April 27.

29 In Simi Valley, CA, a Superior Court jury acquits four white police officers of all but one count in the case stemming from a videotaped beating of black motorist Rodney King in March 1991. Looting and violence breaks out in Los Angeles following the verdict; a state of emergency is declared.

Sierra Leone's President Joseph Momoh is overthrown in a military coup.

© Richard Smith, Katz Pictures/Saba

Britain's Conservative Party was returned to power for a fourth consecutive time on April 9. John Major, who had succeeded Margaret Thatcher as Tory leader and prime minister in November 1990, and his wife Norma, above, voted in their constituency in Huntingdon.

On May 1, Rodney King, below, urged the people of Los Angeles to stop their rampage. Burning, looting, and violence had broken out in the city in late April after four white police officers were acquitted of all but one charge in a case resulting from the videotaped beating of King in March 1991.

© AP/Wide World

May

5 Sibghatullah Mojadedi, who became Afghanistan's interim president after the Communists gave up power in April, names a 36-member temporary cabinet.

7 The premiers of North Korea and South Korea issue a communiqué outlining a plan to reunite family members who had been separated since the Korean War.

A U.S. constitutional amendment barring Congress from enacting midterm pay increases is ratified as Michigan becomes the 38th state to approve the amendment, which was passed by Congress in 1789.

13 The U.S. Senate sustains President Bush's veto of a campaign-finance reform bill.

Lebanon's President Elias Hrawi appoints Rashid al-Solh, a Sunni Muslim, to succeed Umar Karami as premier. Karami had resigned on May 6 as nationwide riots caused by increasing inflation and the collapse of the currency continued.

After two unsuccessful attempts on May 10–11, members of the crew of the U.S. space shuttle "Endeavour" captured Intelsat VI, right, and returned the wayward communications satellite to its proper orbit.

NASA

16 The U.S. shuttle *Endeavour* completes a nine-day mission during which a wayward communications satellite was sent into proper orbit during a three-man space walk.

The United States retains yachting's America's Cup.

21 China conducts its largest-ever underground nuclear test.

22 Following a two-day meeting between President François Mitterrand and Chancellor Helmut Kohl, France and Germany agree to create a 35,000-member military force independent of the North Atlantic Treaty Organization.

Croatia, Slovenia, and Bosnia-Herzegovina—former Yugoslav republics—are admitted to the United Nations.

Johnny Carson retires as host of *The Tonight Show,* a post he had held for nearly 30 years.

24 Thomas Klestil, 59-year-old career diplomat, is elected president of Austria.

25 In Italy, members of Parliament and regional representatives choose Oscar Luigi Scalfaro as president. Francesco Cossiga had given up the post on April 25.

30 The UN Security Council agrees to impose international sanctions against Yugoslavia in an effort to end the fighting in Bosnia-Herzegovina.

June

1 For the second consecutive year, the Pittsburgh Penguins capture the National Hockey League's Stanley Cup.

8 Atef Bseiso, director of security affairs for the Palestine Liberation Organization (PLO), is killed outside a Paris hotel.

14 The UN Conference on Environment and Development (the Earth Summit) concludes in Rio de Janeiro, Brazil. Several agreements

to reconcile economic development and environmental concerns were reached during the meeting.

The Chicago Bulls win the National Basketball Association title for a second consecutive year.

16 In Washington, President Bush and Russia's President Yeltsin agree in principle to cut long-range nuclear weapons.

Former U.S. Secretary of Defense Caspar Weinberger is indicted on five felony counts of lying and obstructing a congressional inquiry in connection with the Iran-contra case.

17 More than 40 blacks are killed in a massacre in the South African township of Boipatong. Some 200 Zulu men reportedly carried out the attack.

Heinrich Struebig and Thomas Kemptner are released from captivity by Lebanese Shiite guerrillas. The two German relief workers were the last known Western hostages held in Lebanon.

18 Voters in Ireland approve the European Community's Treaty on European Union. The Danish electorate had rejected the pact—which was reached in Maastricht, the Netherlands, in December 1991—on June 2.

23 Israel's opposition Labor Party, led by Yitzhak Rabin, defeats the ruling Likud bloc in parliamentary elections.

26 U.S. Navy Secretary H. Lawrence Garrett 3d resigns amid questions about his involvement in a scandal stemming from the alleged assault of 26 women, including 14 female officers, at a 1991 convention of naval officers in Las Vegas, NV.

28 In Italy, Giuliano Amato, a Socialist, forms a new government.

Afghanistan's acting President Sibhgattulah Mojadedi steps down and governmental power is handed over to Burhanuddin Rabbani, 53-year-old leader of the Jamiat i-Islamil guerrilla group.

One person is killed as sections of southern California are hit by two powerful earthquakes.

A body unearthed from a shallow grave in southern New Jersey on June 27 is identified as that of Sidney J. Reso, an Exxon executive who was kidnapped on April 29.

29 By a 5-4 margin, the U.S. Supreme Court reaffirms the "essence" of the constitutional right to an abortion but upholds parts of a Pennsylvania law regulating access to the procedure.

Mohammed Boudiaf, president of Algeria's ruling Supreme State Council, is assassinated in the city of Annaba.

30 In the Philippines, former Defense Secretary Fidel V. Ramos, who defeated six opponents in the May 11 presidential election, takes the oath of office.

Willie L. Williams is sworn in as police chief of Los Angeles, succeeding Daryl F. Gates.

© Patrick Robert/Sygma

Yitzhak Rabin, above, cast his ballot in Israel's parliamentary elections on June 23. Rabin's Labor Party defeated the ruling Likud bloc, and the former prime minister was asked to form a new government.

© Alberto Garcia/Saba

On June 30, Fidel V. Ramos (center), 64, took the oath as president of the Philippines. The West Point graduate succeeded Corazon Aquino, whom he had served as secretary of defense.

© Vladimir Chechtcs/Gamma-Liaison

Anticipating the possible dissolution of Czechoslovakia, Václav Havel, above, the 55-year-old playwright who led the 1989 "Velvet Revolution" that overthrew the Communists in Czechoslovakia, resigned as the nation's president in a brief ceremony at the presidential summer residence outside Prague on July 20.

Immediately after Ross Perot's unexpected July 16 statement that he would not be a third-party presidential candidate, Democrats, including the below delegate to the national convention, and Republicans alike began to woo Perot supporters.

© Maggie Steber/JB Pictures

July

1 Japan's Prime Minister Kiichi Miyazawa and President Bush discuss economic issues in Washington, DC.

2 Ali Kafi, a veteran of Algeria's war of independence, is named to succeed Mohammed Boudiaf as president. Boudiaf was assassinated in Annaba, Algeria, June 29.

The U.S. Federal Reserve System reduces its key interest rates in an effort to improve the economy.

President Bush vetoes a bill that would have required states to permit citizens to register to vote when applying for driver's licenses, other licenses, and government benefits.

4 In elections in Nigeria, the left-of-center Social Democratic Party wins a majority of seats in both houses of the new National Assembly.

5 In Ecuador, Sixto Duran Ballen, the 70-year-old U.S.-born leader of the United Republican Party, is chosen president in a runoff election.

Andre Agassi wins his first grand-slam tennis title, taking the men's singles final at Wimbledon. Germany's Steffi Graf had captured the women's title on July 4.

8 Russia's President Boris Yeltsin addresses the annual meeting of the leaders of the seven leading industrial democracies (G-7) in Munich, Germany. President Bush had visited Poland en route to the conference.

9 The U.S. space shuttle *Columbia,* with seven persons aboard, completes a 14-day scientific mission. The journey established a new endurance record for the U.S. shuttle program.

10 A U.S. district judge in Miami, FL, sentences former Panamanian leader Gen. Manuel Antonio Noriega, who had been convicted of racketeering, drug trafficking, and money laundering, to 40 years in prison.

In Poland the Sejm (parliament) confirms the cabinet of Premier Hanna Suchocka. The 46-year-old lawyer, a member of the center-left Democratic Union, is Poland's first woman premier and the fifth head of government of the post-Communist era.

14 The American League defeats the National League, 13–6, in baseball's annual All-Star Game.

16 At the Democratic National Convention in New York City, Arkansas Gov. Bill Clinton and U.S. Sen. Albert Gore, Jr. (TN) accept the party's nominations for president and vice-president, respectively. . . . Texas billionaire Ross Perot announces that he will not run for the presidency as a third-party candidate.

18 John Smith is selected to succeed Neil Kinnock as leader of Britain's Labour Party.

20 Václav Havel resigns as president of Czechoslovakia, stating that his opposition to the dissolution of the federation makes it impossible for him to remain in office. On July 17 the parliament of the Slovak Republic had adopted a "declaration of sovereignty."

25 The XXV Summer Olympics begin in Barcelona, Spain.

26 Ending a three-week impasse, Iraq agrees to permit UN arms experts to inspect the agricultural ministry building in Baghdad to search for arms-related evidence.

29 Clark M. Clifford, former U.S. secretary of defense, and his protégé, Robert A. Altman, are charged by U.S. and New York state prosecutors with conspiracy, bribery, and other offenses in connection with the Bank of Credit and Commerce International (BCCI) case.

August

3   In South Africa a two-day general strike in support of ending white rule begins.

4   The last of some 2,000 U.S. Marines and other troops land in Kuwait for military exercises with Kuwaiti forces.

5   A U.S. grand jury indicts four Los Angeles police officers on federal charges of violating the civil rights of Rodney King. On April 29 a state jury had acquitted the four officers of nearly all charges in the March 1991 beating of King.

7   Members of the UN Conference on Disarmament agree on the draft of an international treaty to forbid the production of chemical weapons and destroy existing ones. The pact now must be approved by the Disarmament Conference and the UN General Assembly and signed by at least 65 nations.

11   Meeting in Kennebunkport, ME, President Bush and Israel's Prime Minister Rabin announce agreement in principle on a package of $10 billion in U.S. loan guarantees to Israel.

12   Representatives of the United States, Canada, and Mexico announce accord on a plan for free trade across North America.

13   President Bush reveals that James Baker will leave the State Department to become White House chief of staff and to oversee his reelection campaign.

The UN Security Council votes to permit the use of force if necessary to ensure that food and other relief supplies reach war-torn Bosnia-Herzegovina.

14   President Bush orders an emergency airlift of food to the famine-ridden East African nation of Somalia.

20   After renominating George Bush and Dan Quayle for the presidency and vice-presidency, the 1992 Republican National Convention concludes in the Astrodome in Houston, TX.

Early in August, international attention was focused on Serb-run detention camps in Bosnia-Herzegovina amid allegations that detainees in such camps were being tortured and executed.

© Patrick Robert/Sygma

21 Hubert A. Ingraham is sworn in as prime minister of the Bahamas. Ingraham's Free National Movement had defeated Prime Minister Lynden O. Pindling's Progressive Liberal Party in parliamentary elections on August 19.

23 In Lebanon thousands of Lebanese Christians boycott the opening round of parliamentary elections, charging that Syria is controlling the voting.

24 Hurricane Andrew strikes south Florida, causing some loss of life and extensive damage.

In a formal ceremony in Beijing, China and South Korea establish diplomatic relations.

26 The United States, Britain, and France order the Iraqi government to halt all aircraft flights over southern Iraq. The action is intended to protect Shiite Muslims in the area. [A no-fly zone had been in effect in northern Iraq since the end of the 1992 Persian Gulf war.]

Czech Premier Václav Klaus and Slovak Premier Vladimir Meciar agree that the Czechoslovak federation will be dissolved as of Jan. 1, 1993.

28 The Japanese government announces an emergency plan to inject $87 billion to stimulate the economy.

September

2 President Bush announces the sale of 150 advanced F-16 fighter jets to Taiwan.

5 A nine-day strike at the General Motors metal-stamping plant at Lordstown, OH, comes to an end. The strike had led to the temporary layoffs of 42,900 GM employees at several plants across the United States.

7 In the South African bantustan (homeland) of Ciskei, as many as 28 persons are killed and 200 are injured as soldiers fire on African National Congress marchers who are demanding the removal of the territory's military rulers.

Major League Baseball Commissioner Fay Vincent resigns after team owners request his resignation by a vote of 18-9.

8 Outside Sarajevo, the capital of Bosnia-Herzegovina, two French officers in the United Nations peacekeeping force are killed by machine-gun fire. On September 3 an Italian military plane transporting UN relief supplies to the war-torn area of the former Yugoslavia had crashed mysteriously near Sarajevo, killing four crew members.

9 Russia's President Boris Yeltsin postpones a planned visit to Japan and South Korea.

10 Iran's President Ali Akbar Hashemi Rafsanjani announces that China will provide Iran with a nuclear-power plant.

11 Hurricane Iniki slams into the western Hawaiian islands, killing at least three persons and causing an estimated $1.6 billion in property damage.

12 In Peru police capture Abimael Guzmán Reynoso, the leader of Sendero Luminoso (Shining Path)—a Maoist guerrilla organization that waged a 12-year campaign against the government.

13 Stefan Edberg of Sweden defeats Pete Sampras to repeat as the men's U.S. Open tennis champion. Monica Seles of the former Yugoslavia had defended her women's title on September 12.

20 French voters narrowly approve the European Community's Treaty on European Union (the Maastricht Treaty).

A pedestrian appears oblivious of a large poster encouraging the French to support the Maastricht Treaty on European unity. The French electorate approved the agreement in a close vote on September 20.

© Bernard Bisson/Sygma

22 One day after the opening of the 47th session of the UN General Assembly, Yugoslavia is expelled as a UN member for its alleged role in the war in Bosnia-Herzegovina.

23 In Thailand prodemocracy activist Chuan Leekpai is named premier, heading a five-party coalition that had emerged following September 13 parliamentary elections.

24 The sixth round of bilateral peace talks between the Arabs and Israelis end in Washington without an agreement over control of the Golan Heights.

25 The United States launches the Mars Observer, an unmanned spacecraft designed to orbit and study Mars.

Hurricane Iniki devastated the western islands of Hawaii on September 11. The island of Kauai, above, was hit particularly hard. Damage was estimated at $1.6 billion. Iniki was the first hurricane to strike Hawaii since November 1982.

October

1 Texas businessman Ross Perot announces that he is reversing his July 16 decision and will reenter the U.S. presidential race.

The U.S. Senate ratifies the Strategic Arms Reduction Treaty (START).

4 An Israeli El Al cargo plane crashes into an apartment complex in a suburb of Amsterdam, the Netherlands, killing some 50 people.

The opposing factions in Mozambique's 16-year-old civil war sign a peace accord in Rome.

5 The U.S. Congress overrides President Bush's veto of a bill regulating cable television. The action marks the first time that the legislature has overturned a Bush veto.

9 The second session of the 102d U.S. Congress adjourns.

12 Coinciding with commemorations of the 500th anniversary of Christopher Columbus' landing in the New World, the National Aeronautics and Space Administration begins a search of the universe for signs of intelligent extraterrestrial life.

A strong earthquake in and around Cairo, Egypt, kills some 550 persons.

16 Rigoberta Menchú, a 33-year-old Guatemalan Quiché Indian, is named winner of the 1992 Nobel Peace Prize.

18 The 14th national congress of the Chinese Communist Party concludes in Beijing following the selection of a 189-member Central Committee.

19 The last of three debates among the three U.S. presidential candidates is held in East Lansing, MI.

23 President Bush announces that Vietnam has agreed to turn over to the United States all of the documents, photographs, and personal effects that it possesses involving U.S. personnel missing as a result of the Vietnam war.

Emperor Akihito becomes Japan's first head of state to visit China.

24 The Toronto Blue Jays capture baseball's World Series, defeating the Atlanta Braves, four games to two.

26 In a referendum in Canada's ten provinces and two territories, voters reject the Charlottetown Accord, a constitutional-reform package that had been agreed upon by the nation's leaders on Aug. 28, 1992.

31 The Roman Catholic archbishop of Monrovia announces that five Catholic nuns have been shot to death in Liberia.

November

On Nov. 3, 1992, Arkansas Gov. Bill Clinton (D) was elected president of the United States and U.S. Sen. Barbara Mikulski (D-MD) captured a second term.

3 In U.S. elections, Ark. Gov. Bill Clinton is chosen as 42d president; the U.S. Congress remains under the control of the Democratic Party.

4 President Bush vetoes a tax and urban-aid bill.

In Ghana's first presidential election since 1979, military leader Jerry Rawlings is elected president.

5 Chessmaster Bobby Fischer defeats his old rival Boris Spassky with a tenth victory in the 30th game of a nine-week contest. Fischer played the exhibition series in Yugoslavia in violation of a United Nations economic embargo and despite threats that he was subject to prosecution in the United States should he return.

6 The U.S. Labor Department announces that the nation's unemployment rate dropped to 7.4% in October, down from 7.5% in September.

8 Colombia's President César Gaviria Trujillo orders a 90-day state of emergency to combat drug-related terror that has struck the nation.

9 Russia's President Boris Yeltsin and British Prime Minister John Major sign a treaty of friendship between the two nations.

11 The governing body of the Church of England votes to allow the ordination of women priests.

12 Jordan's King Hussein issues a general amnesty that frees 140 political and criminal prisoners.

13 Riddick Bowe takes away Evander Holyfield's heavyweight-boxing title.

15 In Lithuania the former Communists of the Democratic Labor Party win a solid parliamentary majority in the second round of national elections.

Voters in Panama reject a plan of 58 constitutional reforms, including a proposal that would have forbidden the nation from having a standing army.

© Martyn Mayhow/Sipa

16 The UN Security Council authorizes a naval blockade against Yugoslavia.

In Detroit, MI, two police officers are charged with murder and two others are subject to lesser criminal charges in the November 16 beating death of a black motorist.

The Roman Catholic Church issues a new catechism.

17 Nigeria's President Ibrahim Babangida announces the postponement until June 1993 of presidential elections scheduled for December 5.

19 The UN Security Council approves an arms embargo against Liberia.

20 Trade negotiators from the United States and the Economic Community agree on a plan to reduce EC agricultural subsidies to oilseed producers.

22 *The Washington Post* reports that ten women have made allegations of sexual harassment against Sen. Bob Packwood (R-OR). On November 11, Sen. Daniel Inouye (D-HI) had denied the accusations of nine anonymous women that he had harassed them sexually.

25 The U.S. Commerce Department reports that the gross domestic product (GDP) increased at a rate of 3.9% in the third quarter of 1992.

The Czechoslovak Federal Assembly adopts a constitutional amendment permitting the dissolution of the federation without a nationwide referendum, thereby removing the last roadblock to the creation of separate Czech and Slovak nations, scheduled for Jan. 1, 1993.

In parliamentary elections in Ireland, the Fianna Fail Party loses at least ten seats. Irish voters also approve two constitutional amendments making it easier for women to travel abroad to obtain an abortion, but reject a measure allowing abortions in Ireland itself.

27 In Venezuela an attempted coup—the second in ten months—against President Carlos Andrés Pérez fails.

The 14th-century St. George's Hall at Windsor Castle, some 30 mi (50 km) west of London, England, was destroyed by fire on Nov. 20, 1992. The cost of the damage was estimated at $100 million. Amid developing controversy over whether Queen Elizabeth should contribute to the castle's repair cost, it was announced that she would begin paying income taxes.

December

On Dec. 6, 1992, thousands of militant Hindus destroyed a 16th-century Muslim mosque in Ayodhya, India. The mosque is on the site the Hindus consider the birthplace of the Hindu deity Ram, and they long have insisted on building a temple there. The mosque's destruction led to extensive rioting in India, which spread to Pakistan and Bangladesh (above).

1 The German government announces the final facets of a series of measures to crack down on right-wing extremist violence against foreigners in Germany. Two Turkish girls and a Turkish woman had died in a firebombing in Mölln on November 23.

3 The Greek oil tanker *Aegean Sea* runs aground near the Spanish port of La Coruña, causing a massive oil spill.

6 Militant Hindus destroy a 16th-century Muslim mosque in the Indian city of Ayodhya, igniting religious strife across the country.

The United States recaptures tennis' Davis Cup.

9 Operation Restore Hope—a UN-sanctioned effort to provide security for famine-relief operations in the African nation of Somalia, which had descended from civil war into lawless violence—gets under way as 1,800 U.S. Marines land in Mogadishu, Somalia.

British Prime Minister Major announces that Prince Charles and Princess Diana have "decided to separate."

11 The two principal warlords in Mogadishu, Somalia, sign a peace accord that was brokered by the U.S. special envoy to Somalia, Robert Oakley.

Japan's Prime Minister Kiichi Miyazawa shuffles his cabinet.

13 The semiannual summit of the leaders of the European Community (EC) concludes in Edinburgh, Scotland. During the meeting, the leaders reached a series of agreements to move the EC closer to union.

14 The Congress of People's Deputies, the Russian parliament, elevates Deputy Premier Viktor S. Chernomyrdin to the premiership.

Acting Premier Yegor T. Gaidar, the chief architect of President Boris Yeltsin's economic-reform program, had been rejected for the post on December 9.

15 The International Business Machine Corp. (IBM) announces plans to eliminate 25,000 additional jobs in 1993.

17 Following the kidnapping and murder of an Israeli border guard, Israel deports some 400 Palestinians to Lebanese territory.

The leaders of Canada, Mexico, and the United States sign the North American Free Trade Agreement. To take effect, the pact now must be ratified by the legislatures of the three nations.

18 In South Korea, Kim Young Sam, 64-year-old former dissident who ran as the candidate of the ruling party, is elected president.

24 President Bush grants full pardon to six former members of the Reagan administration, including Defense Secretary Caspar Weinberger, in connection with the Iran-contra affair.

27 A U.S. F-16 shoots down an Iraqi fighter after it enters a no-fly zone over southern Iraq.

28 Kenya holds its first multiparty elections in 26 years.

29 The United States and Russia agree to a nuclear-arms treaty, reducing the two nations' strategic arms by two thirds.

Fernando Collor de Mello resigns as president of Brazil as the Brazilian Senate begins an impeachment trial against him. Itamar Franco is sworn in as the nation's new president.

Prime Minister Milan Panic is removed as premier of Yugoslavia. On December 20, Panic had failed to unseat Serbia's President Slobodan Milosevic in an election.

New York Gov. Mario Cuomo commutes the prison sentence of Jean Harris, who was convicted of murdering Dr. Herman Tarnover in 1980.

31 President Bush is in Somalia for a firsthand look at the nation's famine and a visit with U.S. troops.

George Bush ended 1992 with U.S. troops in Somalia. En route, the president conferred with King Fahd in Saudi Arabia.

Special Features

© Charles Steiner/Sygma

During 1992 not only was the White House marking the 200th anniversary of the setting of its cornerstone, but Republicans and Democrats of different persuasions vied for the right to live in it for the next four years. Meanwhile the U.S. employment picture was changing, and many analysts believed the job issue turned the tide away from George Bush and in favor of Bill Clinton in the presidential race. Internationally, Yugoslavia was breaking up—some of its former republics became independent nations and the area was one of horrible war *(page 25, top right)*. The 1992 spotlight also was on Spain as it was host to the Summer Olympics *(opening ceremony, bottom page 25)* and to a world exposition. The following pages offer reports on those four stories. A discussion of alternative medicine, a look at today's pro athlete, and a taste of the Disney magic as it traveled to Paris for the opening of Euro Disneyland complete the Feature Section.

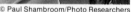

THE 1992 ELECTION

The Democrats Take Back the Presidency

By Robert Shogan

In front of the Old State House in Little Rock, shortly after midnight, Nov. 4, 1992, Arkansas Gov. Bill Clinton (D) acknowledged his election as 42d president of the United States. The president-elect was surrounded by (r-l) his wife Hillary, his daughter Chelsea, Vice-President-elect Al Gore, Tipper (Mrs. Al) Gore, and the Gore children.

The 1992 presidential election was shaped by two events which took place well before the first ballots were cast in the New Hampshire primary—the economic recession and the Persian Gulf war.

The recession, which began in the summer of 1990, President George Bush's second year in the White House, technically ended in the spring of 1991. But in actuality its impact on the economy and on the national mood was far harsher and more enduring than either economists or political analysts anticipated. The war, which culminated in sweeping military victory for the United States and its allies in February 1991, sent Bush's approval rating in the polls to record heights and led to the general assumption that he could not be defeated for re-election. But the consequent overconfidence among the president and his advisers probably contributed to his long delay in dealing with the nation's domestic problems, which eventually brought about his defeat by Arkansas Gov. Bill Clinton.

The Background and the Primaries. The pattern that the campaign would follow began to emerge in the fall of 1991 when the White House's rosy outlook for Bush's future was becoming clouded by continued sluggishness of the economy and the corresponding decline in the president's approval rating. Conservative columnist and former Nixon and Reagan White House aide Patrick Buchanan saw these conditions as an opportunity. Like other conservatives, Buchanan had become disillusioned with Bush because of his 1990 decision to break his oft-repeated "read-my-lips" 1988 campaign pledge not to raise taxes. Convinced that the president was politically vulnerable, Buchanan announced in December 1991 that he would challenge him for the GOP nomination.

He found fertile ground in New Hampshire, site of the nation's first presidential primary, where anti-Bush resentment ran deep because the state had been hit particularly hard by the recession. In the February 16 primary, Buchanan got 37% of the vote; although Bush won with 53%, Buchanan's showing was hailed in the media as a moral victory for the challenger and a setback for Bush. Two weeks later, in the March 3 Georgia primary, Buchanan got 36% of the vote, delivering another blow to Bush's prestige. This turned out to be the high-water mark for his candidacy, as the incumbent president's vastly superior resources took their toll. Nevertheless, Buchanan's challenge hurt Bush in the long run by calling attention to his weaknesses and alienating conservatives whose support the president would need badly in the general election.

The impact of the rise and fall of Bush's political fortunes also was being felt on the contest for the Democratic nomination. When Bush was riding high in the polls, most of the prominent potential Democratic contenders had taken themselves out of the race, leaving a political vacuum which a half dozen lesser-known candidates sought to fill.

Of this group, Arkansas Gov. Bill Clinton ultimately emerged as the front-runner, attracting support with a well-honed message promising economic revival. He also was aided by his anticipated ability to win electoral votes in his native South, where Democrats had been shut out in the previous three elections. Yet another factor in his favor was his espousal, as leader of the Democratic Leadership Council, of centrist doctrines deemed likely to win back middle-class voters. Though he favored some forms of government action to stimulate the economy, Clinton also stressed individual responsibility on the part of beneficiaries of government aid.

The 45-year-old former Rhodes scholar's most serious vulnerability was related to his personal life. Rumors long had been widespread in political circles that the governor with the folksy charm and the easy grin had been involved in extramarital affairs. Early in the campaign, Clinton and his wife, Hillary, sought to relegate these rumors to the past by insisting that their marriage was now on a firm basis. But in January of 1992, as polls showed him taking the lead in the New Hampshire primary campaign, the speculation about Clinton's womanizing, a concern which had forced Gary Hart to abandon his

"I accept tonight the responsibility that you have given me to be the leader of this, the greatest country in human history. I accept it with a full heart and a joyous spirit. But I ask you to be Americans again, too. To be interested not just in getting, but in giving; not just in placing blame but now in assuming responsibility . . . ."

Bill Clinton
Nov. 4, 1992

About the Author: Robert Shogan, the national political correspondent in the Washington Bureau of *The Los Angeles Times,* is the author of *The Riddle of Power: Presidential Leadership from Truman to Bush* (1991) and *None of the Above: Why Presidents Fail & What Can Be Done about It* (1982). Mr. Shogan also has been an assistant editor of *The Wall Street Journal* and a correspondent with *Newsweek* magazine.

1988 presidential candidacy, was revived by a story in the supermarket tabloid *Star*. The paper published claims by Gennifer Flowers, a nightclub singer in Little Rock and Dallas, that she had conducted a 12-year affair with Clinton; her claims were buttressed by excerpts from taped phone conversations between Flowers and Clinton. The governor denied her story, contending that the meaning of the phone conversations had been distorted. In a televised interview on CBS' *60 Minutes* on January 26, Clinton, with Hillary by his side, admitted "wrongdoing" in his marriage but accused the press of playing "gotcha" with his personal life, and challenged reporters to turn their attention to more substantive concerns.

Aides insisted the appearance had rescued his candidacy, but subsequent events showed he remained vulnerable on the overall issue of character. On February 6, *The Wall Street Journal* reported that Clinton had gotten a deferment from the Vietnam war draft by signing up for a University of Arkansas ROTC program that he never actually joined. And while many sympathized with Clinton's opposition to the Vietnam war, his explanations of his conduct seemed evasive and inconsistent and raised new doubts about his character.

The two issues—the draft and the allegations of extramarital affairs—compounded each other, raising questions about Clinton's trustworthiness. His poll ratings tumbled and he fell into second place in New Hampshire, behind former Massachusetts Sen. Paul Tsongas. Like Clinton, Tsongas had focused his candidacy on a plan for reviving the economy; he also was aided by the fact that he hailed from a neighboring New England state. Some thought Clinton's candidacy was finished, but he fought back, regaining some of the ground lost to Tsongas and finishing a respectable second. On primary night he proclaimed himself to be "the comeback kid."

Clinton floundered briefly after New Hampshire but he had amassed enough resources to maintain his candidacy in a dwindling field. One rival, Virginia Gov. Douglas Wilder, had dropped out of the race in January, pleading duties in Richmond. Two others—Nebraska Sen. Bob Kerrey and Iowa Sen. Tom Harkin, who had finished third and fourth, respectively, in New Hampshire—fell by the wayside soon afterward. Zeroing in on Tsongas, now his most formidable rival, Clinton charged that the former Massachusetts senator was biased in favor of business and contended that his proposed gasoline-tax hike was excessive. After being defeated soundly by Clinton in a series of primaries in the South and then in Illinois and Michigan, Tsongas suspended his candidacy on March 19. That left former California Gov. Edmund (Jerry) Brown, Jr., as Clinton's sole remaining foe but Clinton eliminated him as a serious threat in the New York primary on April 7.

Even though the path to the nomination was now clear, Clinton still was plagued by doubts about his character, and many Democrats were pessimistic about his chances of winning the White House. It was at this point that Clinton received what turned out to be a blessing in disguise with the shift of public attention to the prospective candidacy of Ross

Edmund B. (Jerry) Brown did not give up his quest for the Democratic presidential nomination until Governor Clinton was nominated at the Democratic Convention. During a low-budget campaign, the former California governor had urged supporters to show their support by telephoning his 800 number.

© Brad Markel/Gamma-Liaison

Texas businessman Ross Perot (at podium with his wife Margot at his side) added an interesting twist to the 1992 presidential race. After unexpectedly announcing his willingness to become a presidential candidate on the "Larry King Show," he suddenly withdrew from the contest on July 16. On October 1 he was back in the campaign—with retired Adm. James B. Stockdale (extreme left) as his running mate. On November 3 he captured 19% of the popular vote— the largest percentage by an independent since Theodore Roosevelt took 27% in 1912.

Perot. The self-made billionaire from Texas had announced on a February 20th television talk show that he would consider running if supporters would get his name on the ballot in all 50 states.

In another campaign year, Perot might have been laughed off because of his lack of political experience. But in 1992, with voters troubled by the prolonged economic slump, dissatisfied with Bush, and dubious about Clinton—the presumed Democratic choice—Perot's outsider status was an asset, abetted by his vows to confront the political establishment and to find practical solutions to the federal deficit and the nation's other long-neglected problems. By mid-May, as Perot gained rapidly in the polls, he seemed to represent Bush's most serious challenger. But then the press, digging into Perot's past, unearthed evidence of high-handed tactics he used in dealing with antagonists in his private life, in business, and in public controversies, including conducting investigations of his own children and of then Vice-President Bush. Polls showed negative impressions of Perot on the rise and his standing in the presidential competition sinking. Suddenly on July 16, in the midst of the Democratic Convention, Perot pulled out of the race, explaining that he feared his candidacy would force the House of Representatives to decide the outcome of the election and would be "disruptive to the country."

The timing was beneficial for Clinton. During the weeks that Perot had dominated the political scene, the memories of the controversies about Clinton's personal life seemed to have faded from the public mind. And Clinton had used the time to issue a four-year "putting people first" plan for the economy, vowing to spend $200 billion to spur the economy, revitalize the cities, and repair the infrastructure, but pledging to save enough from taxes on the wealthy and spending cuts to reduce the deficit. His choice of Tennessee Sen. Albert Gore, Jr., as his running mate and the opening of the Democratic Convention, which was used to provide the nation with a sympathetic

The 1992 Republican National Convention, which was held in Houston, TX, August 17–20, nominated George Bush for a second term. First Lady Barbara Bush, above, addressed the gathering on "family-values night," August 19.

Photos, © Ralf-Finn Hestoft/Saba

Presidential experience was the theme during George Bush's campaign stops. The president also attacked Bill Clinton's record as governor of Arkansas and sought to exploit the doubts about the governor's character which had been raised during the nomination process.

© Ralf-Finn Hestoft/Saba

view of Clinton's early life, gave him a welcome burst of favorable publicity. With Perot out of the race, most of the voters who had been backing him now found Clinton a reasonable alternative and for the first time the polls showed him in front of Bush, with his lead soon reaching double digits.

As for President Bush, the continued stream of bad news about the economy had kept him down in the polls. But remembering that in 1988, when Bush also had been behind, the Republican Convention had helped him turn the tide in his favor, his advisers sought to make history repeat at the GOP's 1992 convention in Houston. Their main focus at the convention was to regain the loyalty of the party's conservative base and divert the average voter's attention from the nation's economic difficulties by stressing moral themes, built around so-called traditional family values. Bush's former foe, Pat Buchanan, set the tone with an impassioned prime-time speech on the convention's opening night, August 17, in which he asserted "there is a religious war going on in our country for the soul of America." The strategy pleased conservatives. But polls showed that many nonideological voters were disturbed and irritated at the stridency of the conservative rhetoric, and the president remained well behind in the race.

The Last Campaign Days. As the final leg of the campaign got off to its traditional Labor Day start, the fundamental choice confronting voters boiled down to trust versus change —whether to trust President Bush to make the best of things, or bet on Democrat Bill Clinton to change them. With the economy still in the doldrums, the idea of change, which Clinton reiterated at every step along the campaign trail, was not hard to get across to Americans; Clinton's more difficult task was to persuade voters that he was the man to lead the country into a new political and economic era. Trying to allay concerns about the Democratic Party's traditional reliance on government intervention and spending, Clinton sought to present himself as "a different kind of Democrat," dedicated

© Brooks Karft/Sygma

© Martin Simon/Saba

New York Gov. Mario Cuomo, left, nominated Bill Clinton for the presidency and former Rep. Barbara Jordan, above, gave the keynote address at the 1992 Democratic National Convention, which was held in New York City, July 13–16.

to creating equal opportunity for all citizens rather than insistent on big spending to benefit only the poor.

As for Bush, his strategy in the campaign was to cast himself as the nation's tried-and-true helmsman while warning that the course charted by Clinton would send the ship of state crashing onto the rocks. "The question is," Bush asked in his acceptance speech in Houston, "who do you trust to make change work for you?" The president belatedly set forth his own economic blueprint, an "Agenda for American Renewal," whose centerpiece was an across-the-board cut in income-tax rates, coupled with more than $132 billion in spending cuts, along with restated versions of previous proposals for health care, job training, and education.

But Bush's strategists privately conceded that it was probably too late for him to convince swing voters that he could make the economy right again anytime soon. His chances of victory depended mainly on persuading them that Clinton would make things worse. He attacked the Democratic standard-bearer as really a liberal taxer and spender, dressed up in the campaign garb of a political moderate; his campaign commercials contended that the bite of Clinton's proposed tax increase would be felt not just among the rich, as Clinton claimed, but well down in the ranks of the middle class.

Bush denounced Clinton's record in Arkansas. And whenever he could he sought to exploit the doubts about Clinton's character and values which had been raised during his campaign for the nomination, focusing on Clinton's sometimes inconsistent answers about his draft status during the Vietnam war and on his participation in antiwar protests while he was abroad as a Rhodes scholar. To almost all of these accusations Clinton and his aides responded immediately, and often fired back charges of their own. As a result, critics complained that the campaign was reduced to a chain of attacks, rebuttals, and counterattacks, framed in hyperbolic rhetoric in which little time was afforded for discussion of the nation's problems.

(Continued on page 35.)

Immediately after the convention, the Clinton-Gore ticket conducted a bus tour from New York to St. Louis. Their basic campaign theme was that the United States needed a change in its top leadership. Governor Clinton also emphasized that he was a new type of Democrat.

© Bob Daemmrich/Sygma

CONGRESS—A Storm Center in 1992

During the stormy course of the 102d U.S. Congress' second year, Democratic House Speaker Tom Foley of Washington called it "the Congress from hell." And amid the prevailing atmosphere of acrimony and recrimination that dominated the session, that judgment was one of few points on which Democratic and Republican members of the legislative body alike probably would have agreed.

Several factors combined to turn Capitol Hill into a veritable purgatory for a good many lawmakers, particularly members of the House of Representatives. Probably the most significant was the evidence of impropriety, or at least insensitivity, which seemed to abound on all sides as demonstrated by inquiries into the operations of the House bank and the House Post Office. Another element was the anxiety among House members over the decennial redistricting following the 1990 census. Compounding all this was the sour mood of the electorate brought on by hard economic times and the failure of the gridlocked government in Washington to bring relief.

The difficult environment of 1992 was rooted in events during 1991 which cast the Congress in an unfavorable light. On the Senate side, there was the 23% pay raise senators voted themselves without giving due public notice of their intentions; the investigation of the ties of a number of senators to Charles H. Keating, a principal figure in the savings and loan scandal; and what many felt was the Senate Judiciary Committee's clumsy handling of charges of sexual harassment brought against Supreme Court nominee Clarence Thomas.

As for the House, its image problems stemmed from a 1991 General Accounting Office report that some members routinely wrote checks on the private bank maintained for them without funds to cover the checks. Reacting to the wave of public indignation, the House shut down the bank and Speaker Foley announced that the House ethics panel—the Committee on Standards of Official Conduct—would investigate the widespread bouncing of checks by scores of lawmakers.

Scandals. The House bank, which had been in existence for 155 years, became a subject of intense public interest. Like commercial banking institutions, the House bank accepted deposits and provided checking accounts. But it differed from most other banks in that it covered overdrafts by its depositors free of charge, using funds from other lawmakers' accounts, a benefit that by some estimates was worth up to $2,000 per year. These overdrafts were tantamount to interest-free loans.

On March 5, after concluding the inquiry begun the previous fall, the House ethics panel found that 335 current and former members had written nearly 20,000 bad checks. Some of the bad checks totaled into the tens of thousands of dollars. The committee recommended that the names of the 19 current and five former lawmakers who were the worst offenders be released. As for those with more limited involvement, most committee members felt it would be unfair to put them in the spotlight, reasoning that because of the bank's poor record keeping, some might be considered to be victims of the way the bank was operated.

But many citizens were unimpressed by this argument, and the demand for fuller disclosure mounted, aided and abetted by some Republicans. They saw the embarrassment to the House, which the Democrats had controlled for nearly 40 years, as yielding them a partisan advantage in an election year. In the face of this pressure, the House voted without dissent to release the names of all current and former members who had overdrafts. But Republican

Several factors—including scandals in the operation of the House of Representatives bank and Post Office, a pay raise senators had voted themselves, as well as reapportionment following the 1990 census—made 1992 a difficult year for congressional incumbents. Congress underwent a higher-than-usual degree of turnover in November.

hopes of gaining a political edge faded when it became clear that Republicans had been part of the problem. Three former Republican House members who had moved up to the Bush cabinet—Defense Secretary Dick Cheney, Labor Secretary Lynn Martin, and Agriculture Secretary Edward Madigan—admitted having bounced checks while they were in Congress. And the names of several key Republican leaders were on the list of overdrafters.

On top of furor over the House bank came allegations of irregularities involving the House Post Office. The trouble there first had come to light in the summer of 1991 with reports that federal officials were investigating allegations of embezzlement and drug dealing involving postal clerks, a probe that ultimately led to the indictment of four lower-level Post Office employees. Then early in 1992, published accounts of the investigation, including reports of complicity by higher-ups, led to charges by Republicans that the Democratic leadership was trying to cover up another scandal. By some accounts the scheme involved House members converting official expense vouchers or checks for campaign contributions into cash through transactions disguised as stamp purchases.

House Speaker Foley, already under fire for what critics charged was his lax handling of the bank scandal, came in for more unwelcome attention when it was disclosed that his wife, Heather, who also served as his chief of staff, had testified before the grand jury probing into possible obstruction of justice in the House Post Office investigation. In a closed meeting with House Democrats, Foley denied any wrongdoing by his wife and rejected the idea that she should step aside as his chief of staff.

A five-month investigation of the charges by a bipartisan House task force produced a split verdict on July 22. Democrats on the task force blamed the Post Office's managers, clearing members of any serious wrongdoing, while the Republicans put the onus on the Democrats, contending that individual members had taken advantage of special privileges. Meanwhile the U.S. attorney's office in the District of Columbia continued to press its own investigation into the charges. Three House Democrats—Ways and Means Chairman Dan Rostenkowski of Illinois and Joe Kolter and Austin J. Murphy of Pennsylvania—were subpoenaed by the grand jury. But they refused to testify, citing their 5th Amendment protection against self-incrimination and dismissing the probe as politically motivated.

But whatever the partisan fallout, it was clear that these charges hurt both parties and Congress as an institution. A Gallup Poll for *Newsweek* conducted in March found that disapproval of Congress' performance had jumped to 78% from 53% in July 1991. Asked whether members of Congress understood the problems of people like themselves, 75% of those interviewed said no. And despite attempts to minimize the significance of the House bank revelations, 88% of those polled said it that was "a big deal" that members wrote bad checks.

Departures and Reform. Concern about the darkening public mood, combined with the burden of coping with redistricting, contributed to a post-World War II record number of retirements. No fewer than 53 members quit politics, in addition to the 13 members who gave up their seats to seek higher office. And a record number of those who did not quit voluntarily were sent packing by their constituents in party primaries. All told, 20 House incumbents were beaten in primaries, exceeding the previous post-World War II high of 18 set in 1946.

On the Senate side, seven members retired and two-term Democrat Alan J. Dixon was defeated in the Illinois primary March 17 by a black woman, Carol Moseley Braun. Exit polls indicated Dixon was hurt by his vote to confirm Clarence Thomas to the Supreme Court.

The scandals gave impetus to reform efforts, both within and outside the Congress. On

© Steve Benson for "U.S. News & World Report"/Tribune Media Services

Measures to limit the terms of lawmakers were on the ballot in 14 states—including California, Florida, Michigan, and Ohio—in November 1992. Although all of the initiatives were approved by the electorate, they faced future challenges in the nation's courts. Analysts believed that the constitutionality of such measures would be questioned.

April 3 leaders of the Senate and House announced that "gift items, mementos, and souvenir items" no longer would be discounted at House and Senate stationery-supply stores and that members of Congress would have to pay $400 per year for gym privileges and $520 for medical care on Capitol Hill that previously had been free. These moves came on top of the previous announcement that the House sergeant of arms no longer would fix traffic tickets. To prevent future misconduct, the House approved legislation to bring all its nonlegislative functions under the control of a nonpartisan administrator, retired army Lt. Gen. Leonard P. Wishart. And the House and Senate created a joint committee to propose reforms in the congressional-committee system and legislative procedures with recommendations due late in 1993.

On another front, the 27th Amendment to the constitution, preventing members of Congress from voting themselves a pay raise, was adopted. Under the stricture, any pay increase Congress voted itself could not take effect until the next session. The amendment, drafted by James Madison more than 200 years earlier, had gained periodic support during times of indignation over congressional enactment of raises. In the wake of the raise which the Senate voted itself in 1991, five states ratified the amendment, bringing the total to the 38 required for it to become part of the constitution.

Election Results. Meanwhile, at the grass roots, advocates of limiting the terms of lawmakers managed to get such measures on the ballot in 14 states, including California, Florida, Michigan, and Ohio. On election day, all the measures were adopted, imposing limits of from six to 12 years on service in Congress. The initiatives could affect 181 members of the new 103d Congress from those 14 states and from Colorado, which had approved a term-limit measure in 1990. But the initiatives faced court challenges on constitutional grounds.

Given all these circumstances, it was inevitable that the November 3 election would produce a big change on Capitol Hill. The voters sent 110 new House members to Washington, and of the 348 incumbents who had survived primary challenges, 24 were rejected. The reelection of 324 sitting House members worked out to a winning percentage for incumbents of 88%—the lowest survival record in almost 20 years and sharply down from the 96% rate of two years earlier. In many cases, involvement in the banking scandal appeared to contribute to the defeat of incumbents. All but five of the defeated members had overdrawn their bank accounts and five had at least 140 overdrafts.

Another change was a striking difference in the makeup of the Congress on gender, ethnic, and racial lines. The new House would include 47 women members, an increase from 28 in the 102d Congress; 38 blacks, a gain of 13; and 17 Hispanics, an increase of seven. One reason for the gains made by minorities was the redrawing of state district maps to comply with recent Supreme Court rulings which interpreted the Voting Rights Act to facilitate the election of minority House members. Republicans had envisaged the new minority districts as helping them make gains in the House by drawing away minority votes from Democratic candidates. But the creation of the new minority districts contributed to the defeats of only three Democratic incumbents—in Alabama, Maryland, and Louisiana.

As a result of population trends reflected in the 1990 census, 19 House seats were shifted from traditionally strong Democratic areas in the East and Midwest to states in the South and West where Republicans have been strongest in recent years. But in 1992 the West was particularly hard hit by the recession, thus turning Republican voters against incumbent President George Bush and his Republican Party. For example, California, the nation's largest state, gained seven seats as a result of reapportionment, and Republicans had counted on winning at least five of these new seats. Instead, the Democrats, who had enjoyed a 26-to-19 advantage in the prereapportionment House, increased their lead to 30 to 22, a net gain of one. The overall results in the House gave the Republicans 176 seats, a net gain of only nine, against a still formidable majority of 258 Democrats and one independent.

Winds of change swept through the nearly all-white-male Senate, too. Four new women senators, all Democrats—Braun of Illinois, Barbara Boxer and Dianne Feinstein from California, and Patty Murray from Washington state—were elected; Maryland's Barbara Mikulski, a Democrat, was reelected; and Kansas' Nancy Landon Kassebaum, a Republican, had four more years to serve on her term. And Colorado voters picked Democrat Ben Nighthorse Campbell as the first Native American senator in several decades. Four incumbent senators were defeated: John Seymour, Republican of California, was beaten by Feinstein; Robert W. Kasten, Jr., Republican of Wisconsin, was ousted by Democrat Russell Feingold; and Democrat Terry Sanford of North Carolina lost to Republican Lauch Faircloth. In a runoff election in Georgia on November 24, Democratic incumbent Sen. Wyche Fowler was defeated by Republican Paul Coverdell. In North Dakota, Democrat Kent Conrad defeated Republican Jack Dalrymple in a December 4 election to fill the vacancy created by the death of Democratic Sen. Quentin Burdick. That result left the party balance in the Senate at what it was before the elections—57 Democrats and 43 Republicans.

Robert Shogan

© Ira Wyman/Sygma

It was this environment that helped revive the political ambition of Ross Perot, more than two months after he had called off his prospective candidacy. Not that Perot's interest in the presidency ever had been completely dormant. Since his supposed withdrawal he had spent nearly $4 million of his own money to finance local efforts, which had succeeded in getting his name on all 50 state ballots. After several broad hints that he was reconsidering his early decision and meetings with top leaders of both the Bush and Clinton campaigns, he announced on October 1 his decision to become a full-fledged candidate. "I thought the political parties would address the problems that face the nation," Perot said in explaining his previous reluctance to run. "We gave them a chance. They didn't do it."

Perot's first act as a candidate was to announce his running mate—retired Adm. James B. Stockdale, a senior research fellow at the conservative Hoover Institution and a former Vietnam prisoner of war. Then he plunged into his campaign, spending freely and relying heavily on television "infomercials" to tell voters about himself, his view of the nation's problems, and his proposed solutions—particularly a program to eliminate the deficit in six years through raising taxes and cutting spending, including clamping down on entitlement programs.

As it turned out, the most important aspect of Perot's campaign was the series of three television debates that pitted him against Clinton and Bush on October 11, October 15, and October 19. In these encounters, which drew huge audiences, none of the candidates committed a major gaffe, though President Bush disappointed many of his supporters by his lack

Candidates Bush, Clinton, and Perot engaged in three debates on October 11, 15, and 19. The three vice-presidential candidates debated one another on October 13. The forums drew a larger-than-anticipated television audience, with the third presidential contest gaining a Nielsen rating of 44.6.

of forcefulness during the first two. By general agreement, though, Perot benefited most. Simply being on the same stage with the two major-party candidates enhanced his status. Bush and Clinton concentrated their attacks on each other, allowing the independent candidate to relax and make his arguments forcefully and with folksy humor. In the vice-presidential debate on October 13, Perot's running mate Stockdale seemed ill-suited to the political arena. But Perot's own strong performance overcame Stockdale's weak showing, and he surged in the polls. He may have hurt his own cause, however, when ten days before the election he claimed that the real reason why he had abandoned his candidacy in July was that he had learned that the Bush campaign planned to discredit his daughter, Carolyn, with a fake photo and to disrupt her wedding. Critics pointed to this episode as another sign of Perot's quirkiness and unfitness to be chief executive.

As Perot gained in the home stretch, the margin of Clinton's lead over Bush narrowed. But it was not clear how much of this was due to his losing support to Perot, who also took votes from Bush, and how much was due to Republican voters returning to the fold after considering a vote for Clinton. Heartened by the closing of the gap, Bush campaigned furiously in the closing hours, predicting a comeback victory.

The Results. But in the end, Bush could not overcome the impact of the struggling economy, which had grown more slowly during his term in the White House than during any other post-World War II presidency. On election day, November 3, Clinton captured 43% of the popular vote and 370 electoral votes, to 38% of the popular vote and 168 electoral votes for Bush. Perot won no electoral votes but his 19% of the popular vote was the big surprise of the election, the largest share for any independent candidate since former President

© Schoor-"The Kansas City Star"/United Features Syndicate

Following the November 3 election, a cartoonist comments on a question asked of the candidates during the second debate. Economic concerns by the voters were believed to have caused President Bush's defeat and Governor Clinton's election.

"WELL, GEORGE...I GUESS THIS ANSWERS THE QUESTION ...."HOW HAS THE RECESSION AFFECTED YOU PERSONALLY ?"... "

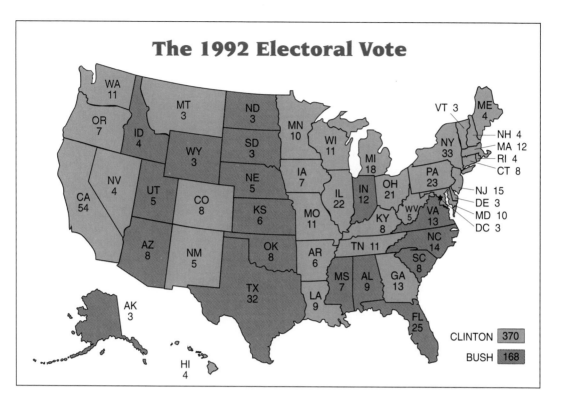

The 1992 Electoral Vote

WA 11
MT 3
ND 3
MN 10
VT 3
ME 4
OR 7
ID 4
SD 3
WI 11
NY 33
NH 4
MA 12
RI 4
CT 8
NV 4
WY 3
IA 7
MI 18
PA 23
CA 54
UT 5
NE 5
IL 22
IN 12
OH 21
NJ 15
DE 3
MD 10
DC 3
CO 8
KS 6
MO 11
KY 8
WV 5
VA 13
AZ 8
NM 5
OK 8
AR 6
TN 11
NC 14
SC 8
TX 32
MS 7
AL 9
GA 13
LA 9
AK 3
HI 4
FL 25

CLINTON 370
BUSH 168

Theodore Roosevelt, running on the Bull Moose ticket in 1992, won 27%.

Clinton carried seven of the ten biggest states—California, New York, Pennsylvania, Illinois, Ohio, Michigan, and New Jersey—while Bush won only Texas, Florida, and North Carolina. Exit polls demonstrated the profound impact of the economy on the results. More than one third of the voters felt they were financially worse off than they were four years ago and the majority of them voted for Clinton. A study of the Voter Research and Surveys exit polls by *The Washington Post* showed that Perot's candidacy had not affected the outcome of the election. The analysis, based on the second choice of Perot voters, indicated that if Perot had not been in the race, only Ohio, which Clinton carried, might have shifted to Bush, while none of the states Bush carried would have gone to Clinton.

The election brought good news for Democrats on other fronts. They not only maintained control of the Senate and House (*see* sidebar) but also won eight of the 12 races for governor, adding two to their total and giving them 30, as against 18 Republicans and two independents. From a nonpartisan viewpoint, a positive aspect of the election was the increase in turnout, which was estimated to have totaled 104 million Americans or 55% of the voting-age population, the highest since 1972 when 55.2% of those eligible voted. Most analysts attributed the turnout gain to public anxiety over the economy, but some said the televised debates and the extensive appearances by the candidates on television talk shows also contributed to the increase.

© Antoine Gyori/Sygma

The Breakup of
YUGOSLAVIA

By Robin Alison Remington

About the Author. Robin Alison Remington is Frederick A. Middlebush Professor of Political Science at the University of Missouri—Columbia. The recipient of Fulbright and the American Council of Learned Societies research grants, Professor Remington has written extensively on Yugoslavia's domestic and political developments since the 1970s. Her books include *The Warsaw Pact: Case Studies in Communist Conflict Resolution.* Professor Remington is a member of various professional societies, including the American Political Science Association and the American Association for the Advancement of Slavic Studies.

The upheaval experienced by the nations of Eastern Europe in the early 1990s had a particularly devastating impact in Yugoslavia. In 1992 the Yugoslav state established in 1918 to unite the South Slav peoples had disappeared, and its remnants were torn apart by fratricidal wars.

Since 1945 the country had been organized as a federation of six republics—Serbia, Croatia, Slovenia, Macedonia, Montenegro, and Bosnia-Herzegovina—and two autonomous provinces in Serbia, Kosovo and Vojvodina. When the League of Communists gave up its monopoly of power in 1990, struggle intensified between those republics seeking a confederal Yugoslavia community of nations and Serbian demands for an integrated federal Yugoslavia that non-Serbs feared would amount to a "greater Serbia." In mobilizing their supporters, republic politicians whipped up historic ethnic animosities resulting in outbreaks of violence.

© Christopher Morris/Black Star

The process began when Slovenia and Croatia withdrew from the federation in 1991. Slovenia, which had a relatively unmixed population, was able to disengage without too much resistance. Croatia, however, had 600,000 ethnic Serbs, who rejected the move to independence and were supported by the Serbian-led Yugoslav armed forces. Meanwhile Macedonia

(Continued on page 42.)

As 1992 ended, the state that once was Yugoslavia had become the internationally recognized independent nations of Bosnia-Herzegovina, Croatia, and Slovenia; the nonrecognized republic of Macedonia; and the Federal Republic of Yugoslavia, consisting of Serbia and its regions of Kosovo and Vojvodina, and Montenegro. Meanwhile, parts of the former federation had become horrible battlegrounds, and residents of such locales as Vukovar, Croatia, above, were forced to seek safer havens.

AUSTRIA

HUNGARY

Ljubljana

SLOVENIA

Zagreb

CROATIA

ROMANIA

VOJVODINA

BOSNIA-HERZEGOVINA

Belgrade

Sarajevo •

SERBIA

ADRIATIC SEA

MONTENEGRO

Podgorica

KOSOVO

BULGARIA

Dubrovnik

• Skopje

ITALY

MACEDONIA

0   100 mi

0   100 km

ALBANIA   GREECE

**THE FORMER
YUGOSLAVIA**

A CHRONOLOGY

◆

The Region That Was Yugoslavia

924
King Tomislav establishes independent Catholic Croatia.

1102
Croatia accepts Hungarian king, and retains limited home rule.

1331–55
The Serbian empire—including Albania, Kosovo, Macedonia, Montenegro, Serbia, parts of Bosnia, Dalmatia, and Greece—enjoys a golden age.

1389
June 28. Serbia is defeated by Turks at Kosovo, beginning 500 years of Ottoman rule.

1878
Congress of Berlin returns Macedonia to Turkey, allows Austria to occupy Bosnia-Herzegovina, and recognizes Serbian and Montenegrin independence.

1881
Croatia incorporates Serbian minority in the Military Frontier.

The assassination of Austria's Archduke Franz Ferdinand and his wife, Countess Sophie Chotez, by a Bosnian Serb in Sarajevo in 1914 led to World War I.

© Bettmann Archive

1908
Austria annexes Bosnia-Herzegovina.

1914
Archduke Franz Ferdinand, the crown prince of Austria, is assassinated in Sarajevo by a Bosnian Serb. Serbian refusal to bow to Austrian ultimatums sets the stage for World War I.

1918
The Kingdom of Serbs, Croats, and Slovenes is established.

1921
June 28. ''Vidovdan'' constitution establishes a constitutional monarchy with a Serbian king.

1928
Montenegrin deputy shoots Stjepan Radic, leader of the Croatian Peasant Party, in Parliament.

1929
Unable to establish a government, King Alexander declares a dictatorship. Croatian militant Ustashi turns to underground resistance.

Oct. 9. King Alexander, who has assumed complete control of the country, changes its name to Yugoslavia.

1931
September. A constitution, providing a basis for dictatorship, is adopted.

1934
Alexander is assassinated in France. Prince Paul heads regency for King Peter.

1937
March. Yugoslavia and Italy sign a nonaggression pact.

1941
March 25. Prince Paul joins the Axis Tripartite Pact with Germany and Italy, setting off a military coup.

April 6. Germany invades Yugoslavia.

April 10. German Chancellor Adolf Hitler installs Ante Pavelic, head of the Ustashi terrorist movement that assassinated King Alexander, as head of a token independent state of Croatia that includes most of present-day Croatia, Srem, and Bosnia-Herzegovina. Be-

tween 350,000 and 700,000 Serbs we killed or died in Ustashi death camps

1941–1945
War of national liberation is foug side-by-side with a civil war betwe Communist partisans led by Josip T and Draza Mihailovic's Chetniks su porting the Serbian monarchy.

1945
November. The monarchy is abolishe replaced by the Federal Republic Yugoslavia.

1948
June 28. Yugoslavia expulsion fro Cominform signals Soviet-Yugosl split.

1952
The 6th Party Congress adopts soci ist self-management.

1956
July 18–19. President Tito meets wi Egypt's President Gamal Abdel Nass and India's Prime Minister Jawaharl Nehru in Yugoslavia. The conferen establishes the basis for the nonaligne and later Third World movement.

1963
April 7. Under a new constitution, tl country's name is changed to the S cialist Federal Republic of Yugoslavi

June 30. The Federal Assembly elec Josip Tito president for life.

1968
Soviet-led invasion of Czechoslovak leads to the establishment of Territor Defense Forces at the republic level.

1971
Croatian national mass moveme arises. Top Croatian leadership forced to resign.

1974
Feb. 21. A new constitution calls for collective presidency consisting of president and one representative fro each of the six republics and two a tonomous provinces.

1980
May 4. Marshall Tito dies at the age 87. He is succeeded as collective pre ident by the vice-president. (The ne

president's term would be one year, and he would be succeeded by the next in line.)

1981
The Yugoslav army puts down nationalist riots in Kosovo.

1986
Slobodan Milosevic becomes head of Serbian Communist Party.

1987
Milosevic prevents police from beating Serbian demonstrators at a meeting in Kosovo Polje.

1989
Amendments to the Serbian constitution reduce the powers of the autonomous provinces of Kosovo and Vojvodina. Thirteen hundred miners in Kosovo go on a hunger strike. Some 250,000 Slovenes sign a petition protesting emergency measures in Kosovo.

May. Milosevic becomes president of Serbia.

1990
January 14. Extraordinary Party Congress gives up League of Communists (LCY) monopoly of power, but deadlocks over Slovene-proposed party reforms.

February. Government sends in federal army to stop battles between thousands of Albanian demonstrators and Serbian police.

April-May. Center-right coalition is set up in Slovenia. Franjo Tudjman wins Croatian presidential election, and Croatian Democratic Union wins parliamentary majority.

August. Serbian minority in Croatian Krajina votes 99% for self-rule.

September 28. Revisions to Serbian constitution strip Kosovo and Vojvodina of autonomous status.

November-December. Elections are held in Bosnia-Herzegovina. Leader of Muslim Democratic Party, Alija Izetbegovic, becomes the president of the collective presidency.

December 9. Slobodan Milosevic re-elected president of Serbia. His Socialist Party of Serbia (SPS) wins control of parliament.

1991
March 9. The army is used against 100,000 anti-Milosevic protesters in Belgrade.

May 15. Serbia and Montenegro block scheduled rotation of Croatian representative, Stjepan Mesic, to president of collective presidency.

June 25. Slovenia and Croatia declare independence.

June 27. The federal government's show of force backfires; shooting starts in Slovenia.

July 7. The European Community (EC) brokers truce. Fighting erupts in Croatia almost immediately.

September 25. A UN arms embargo is imposed against all Yugoslav republics.

December 17. Under German pressure, the EC announces that it will recognize the independence of Croatia and Slovenia in January 1992.

December 31. Yugoslav federal government and Serbia accept peace plan, negotiated by former U.S. Secretary of State Cyrus Vance.

1992
March 1. An overwhelming majority of Muslim and Croatian voters in Bosnia-Herzegovina cast their ballots for independence. Most of the ethnic Serb minority boycotts the election.

April 7. The United States recognizes the independence of Bosnia-Herzegovina, Croatia, and Slovenia.

April 27. Serbia and Montenegro form the new Federal Republic of Yugoslavia.

May 22. Bosnia-Herzeginia, Croatia, and Slovenia are admitted to the United Nations.

May 24. Yugoslav forces begin a withdrawal from Sarajevo, following a federal directive for Serb and Montenegrin troops to leave Bosnia. . . . The Albanian majority in the Kosovo province of Serbia holds unsanctioned elections, choosing Ibrahim Rugova as president.

May 30. The UN Security Council passes Resolution 757, imposing international sanctions on Yugoslavia to force an end to its interference in Bosnia-Herzegovina.

June 29. UN peacekeeping forces move in to take charge of the Sarajevo airport after Bosnian Serbs abandon the facility for artillery positions.

© Eastfoto
Josip Broz Tito (1892–1980), known simply as Tito, was the creator of post-World War II Yugoslavia and its absolute ruler for more than 35 years.

July 3. Ethnic Croats proclaim the independent state of "Herzeg-Bosnia," in a portion of Bosnia bordering Croatia.

July 7. Frustrated by the continued failure to win international recognition, the government of Macedonia resigns.

July 13. The 100th day of the siege of Sarajevo is marked by a renewed Serbian offensive.

July 14. The Yugoslavian parliament confirms Milan Panic, a naturalized U.S. citizen, as premier.

Sept. 22. The UN General Assembly votes to prevent the Serb-dominated Federal Republic of Yugoslavia from taking the UN seat of the former federation.

Oct. 6. The UN Security Council votes to create a war-crimes commission amidst continued reports of Serbian concentration camps and "ethnic cleansing."

Oct. 9. The UN Security Council imposes a no-fly zone over Bosnia.

November 16. The UN Security Council authorizes a naval blockade against Yugoslavia.

December 29. Milan Panic is removed as prime minister of Yugoslavia. Earlier in the month, Panic had been unsuccessful in his election bid to defeat Serbia's President Milosevic.

41

also had declared its sovereignty, and Bosnia-Herzegovina was preparing to follow suit.

EC Intervention. As 1991 drew to a close, international players took center stage in the first act of the Yugoslav war drama. Germany insisted that recognition of Slovenia and Croatia would halt Serbian President Slobodan Milosevic's attempt to create a "greater Serbia." Fearing that Bonn would act unilaterally, the European Community (EC) recognized Slovenia and Croatia as independent states in January 1992. Recognition of Bosnia-Herzegovina was made contingent upon a referendum. Macedonia was put into a holding pattern until the problem of Greek insistence that Athens had a copyright on the name Macedonia could be resolved. A request for recognition by the Albanian opposition in Serbian-ruled Kosovo was rejected. At the same time, some 14,000 UN peacekeepers moved into Croatia to maintain a cease-fire between the combatants. In the EC-mandated referendum in Bosnia-Herzegovina on February 28 and March 1, the Croats and Muslims voted for independence; the Serbs boycotted the process. Bosnian President Alija Izetbegovic appealed in vain for UN peacekeepers to defuse rising violence following the referendum. In its debates the UN was more concerned with costs and bureaucratic lines of authority than with consequences. The symbolic gesture of making Sarajevo the headquarters of the UN Yugoslavia operation did nothing to stop the march toward war.

The Bosnian War. The second act of the drama followed the lull between the referendum and recognition of Bosnia-Herzegovina by the EC and the United States, on April 6 and 7, respectively. Based on the April 1991 census, this new state

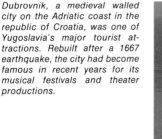

Dubrovnik, a medieval walled city on the Adriatic coast in the republic of Croatia, was one of Yugoslavia's major tourist attractions. Rebuilt after a 1667 earthquake, the city had become famous in recent years for its musical festivals and theater productions.

had a population of 4.3 million; of this, 43.7% were Muslim Slavs, 31.4% were Serb, and 17.3% Croat. Recognition without a precondition that these three groups first agree on internal political structures that would allow them to live together without resort to arms was the signal to start shooting.

As war clouds broke over Bosnia-Herzegovina, armies began to proliferate. Officially the former Yugoslav armed forces returned to become the armed forces of the new Federal Republic of Yugoslavia declared by Serbia and Montenegro on April 27. In fact, a large part of that army and much of its heavy equipment remained behind in Bosnia. On May 13 the army of the Bosnian Serbs (variously estimated at 35,000 to 70,000) was created under the leadership of Gen. Ratko Mladic, former commander of the Yugoslav army's second district in Sarajevo. Reportedly, Yugoslav officers were given a choice of returning or staying on to fight with Mladic's forces.

Just who these forces were responsible to was far from clear. Mladic's authority, and even more so that of the Yugoslav army commanders in Belgrade, over the more than 35,000 Serbian irregulars and paramilitary warlords was tenuous at best. The lines of civilian control appeared even more blurred. Was General Mladic accountable to the civilian political leader of the Bosnian Serbs, Radovan Karadzic, head of the Serbian Democratic Party (Bosnia)? Did the general have a pipeline to Milosevic's office? Were both Mladic and Karadzic in Milosevic's pocket?

On May 22, Slovenia, Croatia, and Bosnia-Herzegovina were accepted as members of the UN. Both the EC and the UN subsequently stepped up sanctions against Yugoslavia, including an oil embargo; suspension of air traffic; freezing of Serbian and Montenegrin assets abroad; and a ban on cultural,

© Haviv/Saba

Dubrovnik was left with little food, water, or electricity in the fall of 1991 as it came under attack from Yugoslav federal forces. The military offense was part of the response to Croatia's declaration of independence in June 1991.

Cyrus Vance, 75, was named United Nations mediator of the Yugoslav crisis in October 1991. As such, the former U.S. secretary of state in the Carter administration traveled frequently to the region and attended numerous peace conferences.

sports, and academic contacts. These measures, and the decision in November to use North Atlantic Treaty Organization (NATO) and West European Union (WEU) warships to prevent blockade busting, rested on the belief that Milosevic was in control of the new Bosnian Serb army and other Serbian irregular forces that were waging war in Bosnia. Undeniably, Belgrade had been the supplier and patron of those forces. But for sanctions to accomplish their objective, the question was not who had put together the Bosnian Serb war machine, but who could turn it off.

New Yugoslav State. Meanwhile, as the soldiers in politics and at war sorted out their relationship to emerging political structures, the new Federal Republic of Yugoslavia had its own birth pangs. As yet unrecognized by the international community, the "rump" Yugoslavia was a multiethnic federation with a population of 10.5 million. According to the Serbian Ministry of Information, it included 6.4 million Serbs, 1.7 million Albanians, 755,300 Montenegrins, 345,376 Hungarians, 327,158 Muslims, and 343,241 persons identifying themselves only as "Yugoslavs."

Although there was no formal transition team, new federal players were undoubtedly either Milosevic's choices or choices with whom he acquiesced. Dobrica Cosic, an internationally known novelist regarded by many as having provided the intellectual rationale for Milosevic's resurgent Serbian nationalism, became the first president of the federation. On July 14 he was joined by Milan Panic, a Serbian-American millionaire recruited as prime minister of Yugoslavia to improve Serbia's disastrous image abroad. At first dismissed by Western media, policymakers, and many Yugoslavs as the puppet of

Sarajevo, the historic capital of Bosnia-Herzegovina that hosted the 1984 Winter Olympics, was under prolonged siege from Serbian nationalists in 1992. Simultaneously, armed bands—some supporting and others opposing the government of the new independent republic—roamed the streets and engaged in sniper fire.

© Brogi/Contrasto/Saba

Troops under the auspices of the United Nations clear mines in a threatened area. By the end of 1992, a multinational force of some 22,500 military and civilian members had been dispatched to the trouble spot.

Serbian hard-liners, Panic turned out to be tougher than expected. He became his own defense minister, rejected Milosevic's militant nationalism as the politics of fear, and steadily rose above Milosevic in public-opinion polls.

Panic entered the Serbian transformation drama in the midst of a massive identity crisis, in which many Serbs were beginning to see the once-idolized Milosevic as the destroyer rather than the savior of the Serbian nation. He was blamed for savaging the economy and turning Serbia into an international outcast. Political opposition grew with the May imposition of EC and UN sanctions. A coalition of opposition groups, the Democratic Movement of Serbia (DEPOS), joined with striking university students (June 15-July 10) and organized mass protests in which an estimated 293,000 took part between June 28-July 5. Calls for Milosevic's resignation came from all sides, even from the Serbian Orthodox Church.

In response to the gruesome television display of Serbian "detention camps" and charges of Serbian genocide against Bosnian Muslims, Prime Minister Panic denounced the Bosnian Serb practice of "ethnic cleansing." He vowed to end human-rights violations and cooperated with the steering committee of the internationally sponsored Yugoslav Peace Conference set up in August, which was cochaired by UN troubleshooter, former U.S. Secretary of State Cyrus Vance, and the EC representative, Lord Owen of Great Britain. Notwithstanding major resistance to his cooperation with the Geneva Conference and open policy to end the war by negotiated solutions, Prime Minister Panic survived two no-confidence votes in the federal parliament and an attempt to rule that he was ineligible to run for the presidency of Serbia based on a residency requirement.

Slobodan Milosevic, 51-year-old Serbian nationalist and former Communist, campaigned for re-election as president of Serbia in December 1992 with the vow never to retreat from a policy of "great solidarity with the Serbian people outside Serbia." Milosevic was reelected amid charges that the voting had been rigged.

© Geeraerts Daniel/Gamma-Liaison

Throughout September and October, Panic appeared to be strengthened by the cooperation of President Cosic, who negotiated agreements with Croatian President Franjo Tudjman (September 30 and October 20) and his Bosnian counterpart Izetbegovic (October 19) to work for peace, mutual recognition, reversal of the practice of ethnic cleansing, and the right of refugees to return to their homes. However, neither Cosic, Panic, nor Gen. Satish Nambir's UN peacekeeping forces in Croatia had or was willing to use the authority to make Serbian militants in Krajina reopen the highway between Belgrade and Zagreb as agreed on October 20. This failure underlined the gap between agreement and implementation.

Bosnia's Agony. Meanwhile, Bosnia-Herzegovina had become a state in name only. Roughly 70% of its territory was occupied by Bosnian Serbs still openly practicing "ethnic cleansing"; at least some Croatian forces appeared to have allied with the Serbs in their own land grab for the "independent" Croatian Union of Herzeg-Bosnia, controlled by Tudjman's supporter Mate Boban. In December, as Bosnian Muslims were reduced to defending embattled city-states, 47 members of the Islamic Conference meeting in Jidda, Saudi Arabia, called for military intervention and an end to the arms embargo, to allow the Bosnian Muslims to defend themselves. Embargo or no embargo, Arab arms and Islamic fundamentalist volunteers joining what they saw as a holy war played an increasing role in the Bosnian conflict.

Notwithstanding the righteous rhetoric, the time lag between UN resolutions to implementation mechanisms created doubts about international commitment. As the UN approved U.S. "Operation Restore Hope" to get relief supplies into Somalia on December 3, reports from Washington suggested that the United States might seek the use of force to stop

© Noel Quidu/Gamma-Liaison

Milan Panic, 62-year-old Serbian-born native who emigrated to California in 1956 and founded a multinational drug-manufacturing company, returned to his homeland and was named premier of Yugoslavia in July 1992. Five months later he unsuccessfully challenged Slobodan Milosevic for the presidency of Serbia and later was removed as premier. During the presidential campaign, he had pledged to stop the war in Bosnia and do what he could to end the economic sanctions imposed by the UN on Yugoslavia.

Serbian commandos take over a mosque and tear down a Muslim flag in Banja Luka, Bosnia. Muslims were a particular target of the "ethnic cleansing" that occurred in Bosnia-Herzegovina.

© Haviv/Saba

Serbian flights over Bosnia, as called for by the October 9 Security Council Resolution to establish a military no-fly zone. Daily there was less hope in Sarajevo and no visible progress on deciding just what means of the "all means necessary" pledged on September 14 would be used to ensure deliveries of humanitarian supplies to besieged Bosnian cities. Of the 8,000 survivors of the Serbian camp conditions that revolted the world in July, some 6,000 remained in the camps in November for lack of any country willing to give them visas.

Serbian Elections. Increased international pressure on Yugoslavia involved suspension from the work of the UN in September, the establishment of a war-crimes investigation commission in early October, and the November toughening of sanctions enforcement against Serbia. This pressure had the effect of weakening Milan Panic's effort to capture the Serbian presidency from Milosevic in the December 20 elections. November 19 clearance by the UN for the shipment of $238,000 worth of television equipment for Belgrade's independent television station Studio One failed to break Milosevic's television monopoly.

As the elections approached, however, attention refocused on the plight of the nearly 1.7 million people that the U.S. Central Intelligence Agency (CIA) Director Robert Gates estimated were "at risk of starvation in Bosnia" during the coming winter. Amid media accounts of continued atrocities and mass rapes, U.S. Secretary of State Lawrence S. Eagleburger on December 16 named names of those Serbs and Croats that Washington considered war criminals. Slobodan Milosevic topped the list. Changing its position, the United States also gave active support to those Islamic countries calling for an end to the UN arms embargo on Bosnian Muslims. On December 17, NATO agreed that if the UN voted to enforce the no-fly zone over Bosnia-Herzegovina, NATO forces could be used to carry out the mission.

The timing of these moves appeared to be a last-ditch effort to shore up Panic in his electoral challenge to Milosevic. If so, the strategy backfired. The results of the voting gave Milosevic a decisive lead of 56%, with Panic trailing behind with 34%. A few days later Panic was removed as premier of Yugoslavia, and Milosevic opened negotiations on a new government with Vojislav Seselj, leader of the militant Serb Radical Party, which had made a strong showing in the elections.

In wake of the elections, fears on all sides intensified that the third act of the breakup of Yugoslavia would be civil war in the Yugoslav federation itself, as paramilitary groups proliferated, and violence spread to Kosovo and the heavily Muslim Sandzak regions of Serbia and Montenegro. When the 1992 curtain came down, the international community appeared divided between those moving in slow motion toward military engagement and those persuaded by Cyrus Vance's warning that to engage in military action now would mean a cutoff of relief operations and "tragic" disaster for hundreds of thousands of Bosnians.

YUGOSLAVIA SUCCESSOR STATES 1992

SLOVENIA (population 1.9 million)

Slovenes	91%
Croats	3%
Serbs	2%
Other	4%

CROATIA (population 4.7 million)

Croats	77.9%
Serbs	12.2%
Yugoslavs	2.2%
Muslims	1.0%
Other	6.7%

BOSNIA-HERZEGOVINA
(population 4.3 million)

Muslims	43.7%
Serbs	31.4%
Croats	17.3%
Yugoslavs	5.5%
Other	2.1%

MACEDONIA (population 2.0 million)

Macedonians	64.6%
Albanians	21.0%
Turks	4.8%
Romanies (Gypsies)	2.7%
Serbs	2.2%
Others	4.7%

FEDERAL REPUBLIC OF YUGOSLAVIA
(population 10.2 million)

MONTENEGRO (population 615,276)

Montenegrins	69%
Muslims	13%
Serbs	3%
Albanians	7%
Yugoslavs	5%
Other	3%

SERBIA (population 5.7 million)

Serbs	85%
Yugoslavs	5%
Muslims	3%
Montenegrins	2%
Romanies	2%
Other	3%

VOJVODINA (population 2.0 million)

Serbs	65%
Hungarians	20%
Croats	5%
Romanians	2%
Slavs	3%
Other	5%

KOSOVO (population 1.9 million)

Albanians	82%
Serbs	10%
Muslims	3%
Romanies	2%
Other	3%

THE U.S. EMPLOYMENT SCENE

By Robert A. Senser

Although the U.S. employment scene is undergoing significant change during the 1990s, Americans desire a full-time job as much as ever. Visits to an unemployment office, such as the one above, are particularly stressful.

About the Author. During a writing career spanning more than 40 years, Robert A. Senser has specialized in labor and economic subjects. After an apprenticeship as a newspaper reporter in Illinois and Wisconsin, he served as editor of *Work*, published by the Catholic Council on Working Life in Chicago, IL, in the 1950s and 1960s. He then was a labor and political officer in the U.S. Foreign Service for 22 years. His work as a freelance writer includes the book *Primer on Interracial Justice* (1962), numerous pamphlets, and articles in various national publications. He is currently a consultant to the Asian-American Free Labor Institute in Washington, DC.

Most people have a love/hate attitude toward work. A popular refrain, "Thank God it's Friday," often echoes their feelings at the end of the workweek. But on Monday they face up to reality: There *is* something much worse than having to go to work, and that is having no work to go to.

Despite widespread ambivalence, the work ethic is very much alive in the United States. At any given time, two out of three Americans more than 15 years of age either hold down a job or are looking for one. Among the major industrial nations, only the citizens of Canada and Sweden are more job-prone.

The post-World War II U.S. economy established a record of stimulating, and responding to, the demand of Americans for paid employment. Between 1950 and 1990, U.S. civilian employment doubled, far exceeding the increase in the working-age population. A high point of that labor-market expansion came in the 1959–73 period, which saw a net increase of 20.4 million persons at work. In that period annual unemployment rates averaged as low as 3.5% and almost always below 6%. No wonder that this job-creating performance won acclaim as the "Great American Job Machine."

Starting even in the late 1970s, however, that machine began to sputter from time to time in troublesome ways symbolized in the ups and downs of unemployment rates. That indicator surpassed 6% in 14 of the 18 years following 1974, reaching a postwar record of 9.7% as an annual average in 1982 and of 10.8% one month late that year. The economy's proven ability to bounce back fostered a mood of optimism, however. When President Reagan stated in his 1987 Economic

Report to Congress, "I will not be satisfied until all Americans who want to work can find a job," his words carried the ring of a realistic goal, not of a politician's farfetched promise. The unemployment indicators of 1988 and the two subsequent years were good omens when they again dipped down below 6%.

Losing Horsepower. So it was a disappointment that the rate again moved up to 6.7% in 1991 and then climbed to 7.6% in the third quarter of 1992, setting an eight-year quarterly high. But that rate, the official one calculated by the U.S. Bureau of Labor Statistics (BLS) and widely publicized in the media, tells just part of the story. It counts only unemployed persons actively looking for work (9.6 million in September), not those who work only part-time even though they want full-time employment (6.3 million that same month) and not those who want a job but have given up hope of finding one (about 1.1 million). By adding those two groups to unemployment figures, the BLS tabulates a third-quarter 1992 "comprehensive" unemployment rate of 11%.

Economists and politicians debated the long-term causes, including the net effect of international trade on U.S. jobs, but the immediate causes and effects showed up clearly as "downsizing" became the personnel policy of more and more businesses. Symptomatic was the September announcement by General Motors, a powerhouse of U.S. corporations, that it would shrink its white-collar work force by 20,000 positions before the end of 1993, a full year ahead of a previously announced schedule. That same month the International Business Machines Corporation announced that its continuing personnel cutbacks would mean an elimination of 40,000 jobs worldwide in 1992 —28,000 in the United States alone.

Nationally, private nonfarm payrolls shrank by a total of 2 million positions in the recessionary period stretching from July 1990 through September 1992. More than half of that loss came among blue- and white-collar jobs in manufacturing and extractive (oil, coal, and other mining) industries, continuing a long-term trend. It is not just that so few blast furnaces still are blasting in steel mills. Even high-tech industries lost ground because of defense cutbacks and foreign competition. The aircraft industry shed some 115,000 jobs after reaching a quarter-century peak of 719,000 employees in June 1990. As an ironic result of that trend, the number of people employed in governmental services during the spring of 1991 began to exceed those working in all manufacturing companies combined.

The performance of the private service-producing sector of the economy during this recessionary period was the major surprise and disappointment. In the past, the surging employment numbers of the services sector more than made up for employment slug-

The United States Unemployment Rate	
All Civilian Workers	
1946	3.9%
1947	3.9%
1948	3.8%
1949	5.9%
1950	5.3%
1951	3.3%
1952	3.0%
1953	2.9%
1954	5.5%
1955	4.4%
1956	4.1%
1957	4.3%
1958	6.8%
1959	5.5%
1960	5.5%
1961	6.7%
1962	5.5%
1963	5.7%
1964	5.2%
1965	4.5%
1966	3.8%
1967	3.8%
1968	3.6%
1969	3.5%
1970	4.9%
1971	5.9%
1972	5.6%
1973	4.9%
1974	5.6%
1975	8.5%
1976	7.7%
1977	7.1%
1978	6.1%
1979	5.8%
1980	7.1%
1981	7.6%
1982	9.7%
1983	9.6%
1984	7.5%
1985	7.2%
1986	7.0%
1987	6.2%
1988	5.5%
1989	5.3%
1990	5.5%
1991	6.7%
1992	7.6%*

*Third quarter 1992

Source: U.S. Department of Labor

© Ralf-Finn Hestoft/Saba

When a new hotel planned to open in Chicago early in 1992, more than 3,000 persons applied for some 1,000 jobs. Many waited outside in freezing temperatures for an interview.

gishness in manufacturing and mining. In 1983, *Forbes* magazine, reflecting a widespread view, hailed the vigorous service-driven economy as "the most advanced stage of economic development." But in the downturn that began in mid-1990, the services sector lost much of its old vitality. In contrast to previous recessions, this time the payrolls of service-sector businesses not only failed to take up the slack but even dropped more than 300,000 positions.

Not since the Great Depression did the job shortage touch such a wide range of occupations, blue-collar and white-collar, up and down the pay scale. Accountants, clerks, and other white-collar workers, overwhelmingly from the lower- and middle-income ranks, joined laborers, machinists, autoworkers, and other blue-collar workers in unemployment lines. Even executives were affected. Blue-collar workers continued to have unemployment rates about twice those of white-collar workers, but even so, because white-collar workers had become so numerous, their lower jobless percentage still made a big dent, adding 1.1 million persons to jobless ranks over two years.

Wages: Not What They Used to Be. A Census Bureau report issued in March 1992 carried a timely reminder that what counts is not just the *number* of jobs in the country but also the *kinds* of jobs—above all the size of their remunerations. "The economic well-being of most persons in the U.S. economy," the bureau wrote, "depends on their own [job] earnings or on the earnings of other family members." It also pointed out that work income makes up about 80% of total national income from all sources and that "declining wage rates can be a source of economic and social stress."

For most Americans, paychecks have shrunk in recent years. In mid-1992 full-time wage and salary workers averaged $440 per week, according to the BLS. That equaled a real (inflation-adjusted) drop of about 6% from the level of early 1979. For production and nonsupervisory workers—80% of the work force—the downward drift shows up in almost every way of tracking employment income, whether by the hour, week, or year, and whether for wages alone or total compensation costs (wages plus benefits). The significant point is that this erosion began before the 1989–92 recessionary periods.

Although men as a group still remain better paid than women, in the 1970s and 1980s men did not enjoy the kind of earnings growth that characterized the 1950s and 1960s. It has become an "age of sinking expectations" for male workers, especially for those with four years or less of high school, according to economist Lee Price of the Joint Economic Committee of the U.S. Congress. For example, the typical young male (aged 25–34) with a high-school diploma earned $19,925 in 1989, a real decline of 20% from the earnings of a male of the same age group and education in 1969.

Bigger Income Disparities. There is an even more important trend than the declines in average income—a widening of income inequality. The proportion of jobs paying low wages (less than $250 a week) expanded to about 25% in 1992 from about 19% in 1979. Drawing on a comprehensive survey of wage distribution during the past decade, economist Barry Bosworth of the Brookings Institution noted in testimony before the Joint Economic Committee: "To the extent that there has been any improvement in real-wage performance, it is concentrated exclusively in the top fifth of the wage distribution." Losing out the most were workers with only four or fewer years of high school, who comprise a little more than half of the total work force. According to a study by BLS economist Daniel E. Hecker, only about 25% of the workers without a college education were in the top 20% of the most highly paid wage and salary workers in 1990, compared with 43% in 1979. The reason, he found, is not just that millions of well-paid jobs requiring only a high-school education have disappeared, but also that an increasing number of college graduates (an estimated 17% in 1990) now hold jobs that do not require a college degree.

The Census Bureau study published in March 1992 confirmed the trend toward income inequality in the 1979–90 period. According to the bureau's findings, that gap existed even among men and women who work full-time and year-round. In 1990 there were 12.5 million men and women who, though holding regular jobs all year, had extremely low annual earnings, defined by the Bureau as below the poverty rate, or $12,195 for a family of four in 1990. That year, they comprised nearly 17% of all full-time, year-round wage and salary work-

© C. J. Higgins/Envision

Employment Counts

The U.S. government keeps track of employment and unemployment in the nation through two monthly surveys—the household survey and the establishment survey.

In the household survey, U.S. Census Bureau employees collect current work information directly from some 60,000 households across the nation and supply the data to the U.S. Labor Department's Bureau of Labor Statistics (BLS) for analysis. This survey counts persons in and out of the labor force and is the source for calculating the unemployment rate.

In the establishment survey, the BLS collects payroll information on employment, hours, and earnings from some 340,000 factories, stores, and other economic units in the private sector, excluding agriculture. This survey counts jobs rather than persons—a major reason why its results are not always completely in line with trends in the household survey, since some people hold two or more jobs.

With the job market tight, some Americans, including the educated and the well-trained, have had to resort to innovative approaches in their search for employment. The Georgian at left received national exposure and several job offers after his own ad campaign.

© Ogust/The Image Works

© Cameramann Int'l., Ltd.

© Rob Crandall/Picture Group

© Crandall/The Image Works

Today the job-search process involves some traditional as well as relatively new methods, including checking the "help-wanted" newspaper columns; consulting with various employment counselors; going to a job fair—such as the well-attended one at the Washington [DC] Convention Center, second row, left; and taking advantage of a computer job bank at a state employment-commission office.

ers, compared with 10.5% in the same poverty-level category in 1979. The year 1964, however, gives a different picture: Then the comparable rate for the same group was 20.5%. From 1979 on, however, the increase in workers with low earnings occurred in almost all segments of the work force studied by the bureau—males and females, young and old, married and single, whites and minorities. In an interview with *The Washington Post*, William Niskanen, an economist with the Washington-based Cato Institute and a member of the Council of Economic Advisers in the Reagan administration, said that a major explanation for this trend appears to be that "internationalization of the economy has [through competition] basically increased the supply of low-wage labor" available and thereby created a brake on wage increases at the low end of the skill scale. A parallel reason is that the employment shift to the service industries during the 1980s involved jobs

© Ira Wyman/Sygma

© Kevin Horan/Picture Group

© David Wells/The Image Works

© John Giordano/Saba

that paid significantly less than those lost in the declining manufacturing and mining industries.

Measures of Feelings. Altogether, how many Americans are unemployed, too discouraged to look for work, working at part-time or temporary jobs because they cannot find regular full-time jobs, earning poverty-level wages, or holding dead-end jobs well below their skill level? The government does not tabulate them, but the Economic Policy Institute did in its new report, *The State of Working America: 1992–93*, coauthored by Lawrence Mishel and Jared Bernstein. These groups, enduring a condition the coauthors call ''labor-market distress,'' add up to 36 million persons, or nearly 40% of the nongovernmental labor force.

By coincidence, at about the same time that the institute released its report in September, the editors of *Forbes* reported on the state of the United States from their own perspective in the 75th-anniversary issue of their magazine. ''We are in a golden age,'' Malcolm S. Forbes, Jr., editor-in-chief, wrote in an editorial. ''The United States is still by far the richest, most productive country in the world,'' another article correctly pointed out. In citing examples of the progress

Recent college graduates face a new challenge in looking for employment as the number of such graduates entering the work force exceeds the number of job openings requiring a college degree. The end of the Cold War has led to cutbacks in the U.S. defense budget and troop requirements and has added a strain on the employment scene. Meanwhile the service industry is one in which the job picture has been bright; for example, fast-food restaurants are attracting workers of all ages, backgrounds, skills, and training.

DECLINING OCCUPATIONS – PROJECTED 1990-2005

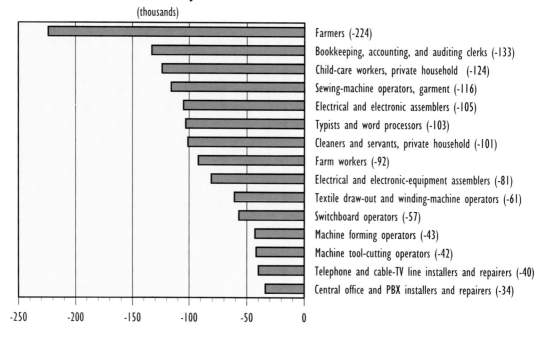

(thousands)

- Farmers (-224)
- Bookkeeping, accounting, and auditing clerks (-133)
- Child-care workers, private household (-124)
- Sewing-machine operators, garment (-116)
- Electrical and electronic assemblers (-105)
- Typists and word processors (-103)
- Cleaners and servants, private household (-101)
- Farm workers (-92)
- Electrical and electronic-equipment assemblers (-81)
- Textile draw-out and winding-machine operators (-61)
- Switchboard operators (-57)
- Machine forming operators (-43)
- Machine tool-cutting operators (-42)
- Telephone and cable-TV line installers and repairers (-40)
- Central office and PBX installers and repairers (-34)

-250   -200   -150   -100   -50   0

made, the magazine used statistical and pictorial contrasts with the 1950s and 1960s and even with the Great Depression years. Such comparisons with the past and with other countries, one article said, "should convince any open-minded person that, economically speaking, things are pretty darned good for the typical American—even if he or she does not feel particularly good about them."

Employment Outlook. The Bureau of Labor Statistics periodically peers ten or 15 years into the future to see what the U.S. labor market might be like then. In late 1991 the BLS looked ahead 15 years and made projections on how the size and shape of the U.S. work force would change between 1990 and 2005. In its most crucial projection, BLS estimated that employment would grow by 24.6 million jobs by 2005. According to the BLS analysis, the service-producing industries in the private sector again would generate the great majority of additional jobs—20 million, with nearly 4 million in health services alone, an industry that boomed in the 1990s. Another industry that did so, business services (temporary help agencies, building cleaning, guard services, data and computer processing, and the like), is expected to add 2.4 million employees as more and more firms contract out services that previously were done in-house by regular employees. Meantime, employment in manufacturing is expected to continue its long-term decline gradually, but construction will buck the job-erosion trend in the goods-producing industries by adding more than 900,000 jobs.

The BLS provided more details on its 1990–2005 projections in a series of publications, including the *Occupational Outlook Handbook,* which describes the likely job opportuni-

The 20th edition of the U.S. Department of Labor's "Occupational Outlook Handbook," the "government's premier publication in career guidance," was published in May 1992.

Occupational Outlook Handbook

1992-93 Edition

U.S. Department of Labor
Bureau of Labor Statistics
May 1992

Bulletin 2400

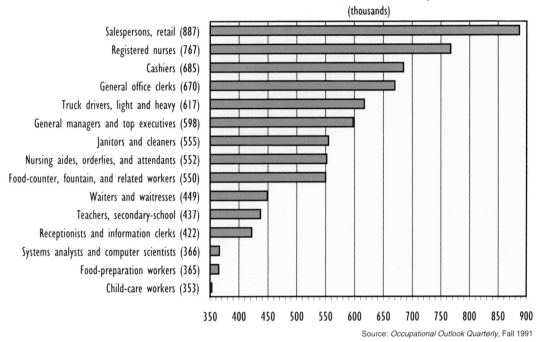

GROWING OCCUPATIONS – PROJECTED 1990-2005

(thousands)

Salespersons, retail (887)	
Registered nurses (767)	
Cashiers (685)	
General office clerks (670)	
Truck drivers, light and heavy (617)	
General managers and top executives (598)	
Janitors and cleaners (555)	
Nursing aides, orderlies, and attendants (552)	
Food-counter, fountain, and related workers (550)	
Waiters and waitresses (449)	
Teachers, secondary-school (437)	
Receptionists and information clerks (422)	
Systems analysts and computer scientists (366)	
Food-preparation workers (365)	
Child-care workers (353)	

350 400 450 500 550 600 650 700 750 800 850 900

Source: *Occupational Outlook Quarterly*, Fall 1991

ties in about 330 occupations. Some sidelights culled from those publications:

• Employment of paralegals will increase at a rate of 85%; that of retail sales workers by only 24%. But in actual jobs, retail sales will grow by 887,000 compared with only 77,000 more paralegals.

• There were 1 million jobs for computer programmers and systems analysts in 1990, but nearly 4 million jobs for janitors, cleaners, and groundskeepers. Although the ranks of those computer occupations will expand by about 70% by 2005, they still will be outnumbered nearly three to one by janitors, cleaners, and groundskeepers.

• Jobs requiring a college degree are expected to increase by 9 million, at double the rate of other jobs. However, college graduates entering the work force outnumber the job openings with college-degree requirements, and will continue to do so.

• Since most jobs become available when somebody leaves, the number of jobs or job-growth percentages in an occupation or industry do not offer the best practical guide to actual employment opportunities. Turnover creates regular job openings in businesses with large numbers of workers even if they have little or no employment growth.

Long-Term Options. In its overall employment projection to 2005, the BLS includes a total that sounds large and impressive—a 15-year net increase of 24.6 million jobs—but that translates into an employment growth rate of only 1.2% per year. It is less than half of the annual rate achieved from 1975 to 1990. The projected shrinkage is based largely on an assumption that the service-producing sector of the economy

Executive Compensation—A Discordant Trend

The title of a *Fortune* magazine article, "The Madness of Executive Compensation," capsuled how the business press viewed a new trend. That was in July 1982, when the annual pay of more and more top corporate managers started to exceed $1 million. Breaching the million-dollar barrier, in the view of a corporate director writing in the *Harvard Business Review* in 1985, was a discordant trend during a recession when many corporations were requiring workers to take pay cuts and to accept changes in work rules.

Year by year since then, as executive pay continued to grow, so did public criticism, mostly on business pages. A highly publicized trip by President Bush to the Asia-Pacific region, including Japan, early in 1992 had the accidental effect of lifting the issue to a new level of public scrutiny and criticism. In the delegation of 21 business people accompanying the president were 12 chief executive officers (CEOs) of major U.S. corporations, including the Big Three auto executives, many with complaints of unfair competition from Japan. The news stories in and out of Tokyo, however, dealt less with trade problems than with salary contrasts. For example, the average annual compensation of the 12 CEOs was about $2 million, compared with $300,000 to $400,000 paid to Japanese chief executives; and the compensation of the Big Three auto heads totaled $7 million in 1990, four times the amount received by their Japanese counterparts.

Recession-plagued 1992 was not a good year for the image of top U.S. corporate executives. Graef S. Crystal, a compensation expert and author of the 1991 book *In Search of Excess: the Overcompensation of American Executives,* became a minor media star with revelations illustrating the title and subtitle of his book. He branded the U.S. auto industry as especially remiss in failing to link executive pay to performance.

"CEO pay," noted *Business Week,* "is undermining competitiveness, fairness, and leadership in U.S. corporations." The magazine, which has been monitoring executive pay for 42 years, based its conclusions on the following data:

• Although the average CEO salary fell by 7% to $1,124,770 in 1991, the average total CEO pay, including stock options, increased by 26% to a record $2,466,292 in 1991—a year in which after-tax corporate profits fell by 4.5% and hundreds of thousands lost their jobs.

• As a result, the average income of such a CEO, which was 42 times that of a factory employee in 1980, was 104 times higher in 1991.

Possible Solutions. That gap is "obscene," said H. Ross Perot, himself a CEO and a long-time critic of U.S. management practices. U.S. Vice-President Dan Quayle, the Democratic presidential nominee Arkansas Gov. Bill Clinton, and other politicians also sharply denounced the trend, without agreeing on what should be done about it. One reform idea centers on changing the tax code. In figuring their federal taxes, corporations can deduct all salaries as a normal cost of doing business. Several proposals to limit corporate-tax deductions on executive pay died in Congress in 1992 but likely would be revived in 1993.

Many argued that the solution to the salary issue is not to increase public regulation of corporations but to improve self-governance by the corporations themselves. Institutional investors, who control on average more than 50% of the voting stock of the largest corporations, have begun to exercise their influence to link executive pay to performance. They received some support from the U.S. Securities and Exchange Commission (SEC). In February 1992 the SEC eliminated the leeway that corporations had to prohibit shareholder initiatives on executive pay from being considered at annual shareholder meetings. In October the SEC also approved new rules requiring publicly traded companies to disclose in full the earnings of their leading executives. The new regulations will make it easier for shareholders to challenge incumbent directors.

Robert A. Senser

most likely will not be able to regain its phenomenal job-creation pace of the past.

The possible margin of error in such projections is large, basically because the economy is not a job "machine" after all. Unlike a machine, a huge economy like that of the United States does not function as an integrated mechanical whole, but depends on many millions of separate and largely unpredictable choices made each hour by individuals, singly or in groups, as employees, employers, consumers, sellers, government officials, and in other roles. Consequently, any projec-

tion must rely on assumptions about the future drawn from statistical aggregates of decisions that people have made in the past. That leaves a lot of room for surprises. Three of the four projections about 1990 that the BLS made in prior years (1979, 1981, 1983, and 1985) underestimated the employment levels actually achieved in 1990 by 3% to nearly 5%. Its projections were off because its assumptions were off.

Although governmental and business decisions on monetary, fiscal, educational, trade, and industrial policies will be paramount in shaping the number and kinds of jobs Americans will have in the future, the choices of ordinary persons also will play a part. Juliet B. Schor, associate professor of economics at Harvard, explores this neglected terrain in her 1991 book, *The Overworked American: the Unexpected Decline of Leisure*. She points out that, contrary to a popular impression, the working time of Americans has not declined but has grown. According to estimates in her study, the average fully employed person is now on the job an additional 163 hours annually, or the equivalent of a 13th month each year, because of longer weekly work schedules and more weeks of work. She attributes this trend mostly to moonlighting (in 1989 more than 7 million Americans reported holding two or more jobs), a rise in overtime hours, and a reduction in paid time off.

Persons overcommitted to paid employment, in Schor's analysis, deprive themselves of needed leisure time and deprive others of work in the competitive labor market. Schor proposes a variety of reforms for "escaping the trap of overwork." In the area of employment practices, she prescribes replacing overtime hours with compensatory time off and giving part-time workers health insurance, vacation time, and other fringe benefits prorated by their hours worked (to provide an alternative for those clinging to full-time jobs only because of fringe benefits). Arguing that "excessive hours are unhealthy and antisocial, and ultimately erode the quality of life," Schor urges individuals who have attained reasonable economic security to step "off the consumer treadmill" requiring more income to acquire more material goods.

In many occupations today, a basic familiarity with computers is a big plus, if not essential. Employment in various computer-related industries is expected to grow in the years ahead.

A GROWING INTEREST IN
ALTERNATIVE MEDICINE

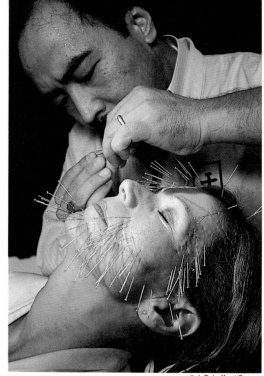

© J. P. Laffont/Sygma

By Jenny Tesar

Alternative forms of medicine—such as the ancient Chinese technique of acupuncture, above—are encountering new popularity as people express growing dissatisfaction with modern Western medicine. Some unconventional therapies are finding increased acceptance in the traditional medical community, as well.

About the Author. Jenny Tesar is a free-lance writer, specializing in the fields of science, medicine and health, and technology. She is the author of a series of books on the environment, published by Facts on File in 1991. In 1992, Ms. Tesar was devoting most of her attention to the world's wildlife, writing a collection of books on the topic as well as contributing to the preparation of a group of *Wildlife Adventure Cards* for Grolier Enterprises. A former high-school science teacher, Ms. Tesar is a computer enthusiast.

Fed up with the spiraling costs of modern medicine, frightened by debilitating side effects of drugs, disenchanted with the assembly-line atmosphere in doctors' offices, and questioning the need for many surgical procedures, a growing number of people are looking for alternatives. Instead of seeing physicians, they are seeking solutions to medical problems from a potpourri of unconventional therapies.

Cancer patients unwilling to limit treatment to drugs and radiation are practicing meditation and visualization. Sufferers of lower-back pain are visiting chiropractors instead of undergoing surgery or periodic traction. People with high blood pressure are supplementing drugs with biofeedback. Rather than pop some aspirin, headache victims are drinking herbal teas and visiting reflexologists.

Americans spend an estimated $27 billion annually on alternative therapies. In a late 1991 poll conducted by Yankelovich Clancy Shulman, nearly 30% of the respondents said they had tried some type of alternative medicine; 84% of these people said they would seek help from such therapies again.

One reason for the appeal of many alternative therapies is that they stress the importance of interactions among body, mind, and life-style. They focus on the whole person rather than on an ailment. Practitioners of this so-called holistic approach begin consultations with a patient by learning not only about any symptoms of illness but also about the person's diet, appetite, emotions, exercise regimen, and personal and family medical history. This approach differs from what many people see as a fragmentation in conventional medicine: They go to an orthopedist for back pain, an allergist for hives, a psychiatrist for depression, a gastroenterologist for digestive problems. As a result of physician specialization, some patients feel that they are viewed as a collection of parts rather than as whole beings. Another aspect of holistic medicine's appeal is its stress on the active participation of patients in making health-care decisions and in pursuing good health. This approach is attractive to people who feel that physicians are autocratic experts whose communications with their patients seem limited to handing out prescriptions.

Ancient Roots. Many alternative therapies have ancient roots. The earliest written records mentioning the use of massage to treat ailments date back 3,000 years, to China. Acupuncture—the insertion of needles into specific points on the body to stimulate and balance the flow of energy through the body—has been practiced in China for more than 2,000 years. Ayurvedic medicine—the use of natural diet, herbs, exercise, and such therapies as massage for preventive health care dependent on the individual's body type—was developed in India at least 4,000 years ago. Herbalism—the use of potions derived exclusively from plants—also has been utilized for thousands of years in China, India, and many other places. It is estimated that about 80% of the world's people still depend on herbal remedies and other "folk" medicine as the basis for their health care. In fact, acupuncture and herbalism never have ceased to be important in Chinese medical practices.

Some therapies are newcomers. Homeopathy—the treatment of a disease with small amounts of the natural substances that in a larger portion would bring on the disorder—was developed in the early 1800s in Germany. Modern chiropractic—the manipulation of the spine to treat spinal and nervous

Hypnotherapy
The patient is guided into a hypnotic state by focusing on an object or mental image. The practitioner then makes suggestions—telling the patient that he or she will feel no more pain, for example. It is theorized that hypnotherapy accesses the limbic system, linked to emotion and involuntary activities. Although symptoms are relieved, the medical condition is not altered. Hypnotherapy is used by 15,000 U.S. physicians.

Reflexology
Reflexologists claim the body is divided into ten "zones" running vertically down the body and terminating in the feet. Manipulating the part of the foot corresponding to the zone where the ailing body part is located is said to ease the problem. Manipulating the big toe, for example, should cure headache. Although reflexology was introduced in the United States in the early 1900s, its adherents say it dates back to 2330 B.C.

© Philippe Plailly/Photo Researchers

© Françoise Sauze/Photo Researchers

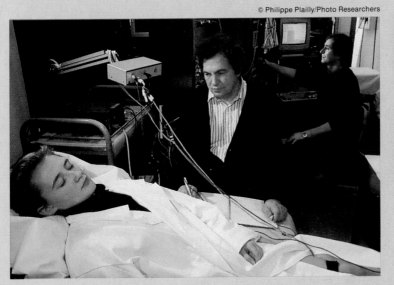

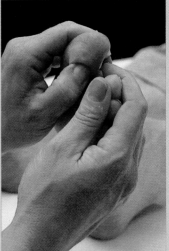

disorders—was founded by Canadian-born Iowa merchant Daniel David Palmer in 1895. Biofeedback—the self-help technique that uses feedback from specially designed equipment to detect and consciously control physiological functions —was developed in Europe and introduced in the United States in the 1960s, then refined with the help of modern computers. Guided imagery—the therapy in which patients relax and visualize their immune system battling disease—had its start in the 1970s as a technique to help athletes improve their performances. Crystal healing—the use of energy passing through quartz and other crystals to release tension and treat ailments—and bioenergetics—a type of psychotherapy that concentrates on breathing exercises and other physical workouts—are offshoots of the quasireligious set of beliefs of the New Age phenomenon of the mid-1980s.

Gradual Acceptance. The U.S. medical community long debunked unconventional treatments, dismissing them as frauds and denouncing their practitioners as charlatans. This was easy to do because the validity of the treatments was based largely on anecdotal evidence. But in recent years researchers have accumulated convincing scientific evidence to support the effectiveness of some of the therapies.

For example, studies by the RAND Corporation and others indicate that chiropractic manipulation of the spine is more

Biofeedback

In this method, the patient is hooked up to sensors monitoring body functions such as temperature or blood flow. By watching the sensors while concentrating on the desired result, patients can train themselves to alter heart rate, circulation, or muscle tension. The technique can be effective in treating chronic pain, tension headaches, and other disorders. Biofeedback is covered by most major medical insurers and is offered at many hospitals.

Acupuncture

Acupuncturists insert hair-thin needles at precise points in the skin to relieve pain. The method, which originated more than 2,000 years ago in China, views the body as a bioelectric system with energy pathways running through it. The needles are inserted at points corresponding to the body part where the pain originates, and are thought to rebalance the energy flow. Acupuncture is practiced by 2,000 to 3,000 U.S. physicians.

© Will & Deni McIntyre/Photo Researchers

© Eastcott/Momatiuk/The Image Works

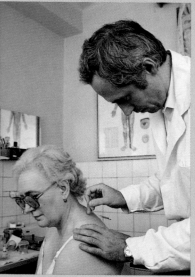

effective in treating lower-back pain than are conventional medical treatments. Other studies have reported that acupuncture can ease the pain for some patients with arthritis, rheumatism, and chronic back pain. Acupuncture also helps smokers, alcoholics, and drug addicts who are trying to end their addictions. Homeopathic remedies have been shown to be effective for treating allergies and influenza. Migraine sufferers who were taught relaxation training reduced the number of migraines by up to 40% and needed less medication to cope with the headaches they did get.

Support for holistic approaches comes from the relatively new discipline of psychoneuroimmunology (PNI), which investigates relationships among the central nervous system, the endocrine system, and the immune system. PNI researchers have found that the brain can stimulate the release of chemicals that enhance the ability of immune cells to fight disease. Activation of this process is affected by emotions, indicating that a person's mental state indeed can affect the course of an illness.

Further evidence of a mind-body connection came with a 1991 report that people who are under stress suffer from more colds than people who are not stressed. Other research found that premature infants who were given regular massages gained weight faster than babies who were left alone. And a ten-year study at Stanford University found that breast-cancer

Chiropractic	Homeopathy
Chiropractors manipulate the spine to correct "subluxations," or misalignments. They claim that problems in internal organs and other parts of the body also can be caused by spinal misalignments and can be cured through chiropractic. However, most patients visit chiropractors for relief of back pain. This is the most widely accepted alternative medicine in the United States; one in 20 Americans visits a chiropractor each year.	This is a method of treating illness by administering minuscule doses of natural substances that, if given in larger quantities, would cause the same symptoms as the disease being treated. Homeopaths believe that "like cures like." Originated by German doctor Samuel Hahnemann in the early 1800s, homeopathy has gained new popularity over the past decade. In 1988, $2.5 billion of homeopathic remedies were sold in the United States.

© Art Stein/Photo Researchers

© Brian Seed/Tony Stone Worldwide, Ltd.

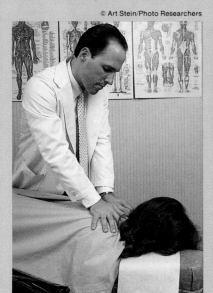

© Dion Ugust/The Image Works

One of the attractions of alternative medicine for many is its attention to the patient's whole life-style—diet, exercise, and emotional well-being—in treating and preventing illness.

patients increased their chances of survival by participating in support groups and by practicing self-hypnosis to ease pain.

As a result of such research, physicians have begun to take a few alternative therapies seriously. They are either incorporating the therapies into their own practices or referring patients to qualified practitioners. Among the most accepted alternative therapies, by both physicians and the general public, is chiropractic. Some hospitals grant chiropractors co-admitting privileges—the right to admit patients with the approval of an attending physician. In early 1992 the American Medical Association complied with a court order to reverse its antichiropractic attitudes: The association acknowledged that it is ethical for physicians to refer patients to chiropractors.

Biofeedback and acupuncture are covered by some insurance companies. Physicians are recommending biofeedback and stress-management techniques to heart patients. In New York recovering drug addicts with low income can be reimbursed from Medicaid for acupuncture treatments. Medical clinics offer hypnosis programs for people who want to stop smoking. In general, other countries have been quicker than the United States to accept alternative therapies. For example, in England, 42% of physicians make referrals to homeopaths. In France, 32% of physicians use homeopathy and acupuncture.

The importance of exercise and proper nutrition—central themes in holistic medicine—also has gained recognition among physicians. They no longer ignore the benefits of exercise and dietary changes in preventing and treating heart disease and other ailments. Still, there is much work to be done in this area. Dr. Dean Ornish, an internist at the University of California at San Francisco, estimates that at least half of the approximately $12 billion spent on heart-bypass surgery in 1990 could have been saved had people followed a low-fat diet, exercised, and stopped smoking.

Even the most far-out therapies soon may be subjected to controlled clinical trials. In late 1991 the U.S. Congress passed a bill creating the Office for the Study of Unconventional Medical Practices at the National Institutes of Health. Armed with a $2 million appropriation, the office has begun to sift through proposals to determine which unproven cures seem the most promising and most deserving of government research money.

Concerns. Such therapies as reflexology—in which the middle of the left foot is massaged to treat stomach complaints —and aromatherapy—a branch of herbalism that treats certain ailments with aromatic plant oils—find little if any favor among members of the medical establishment. The main harm physicians see in these therapies is that they may keep ill people from seeking treatment that really works. Of much greater concern to physicians are therapies with harmful side effects. For example, a significant number of people who have received chelation therapy—which involves the injection of the synthetic amino acid EDTA and which proponents claim is an effective treatment for coronary disease and cholesterol

A Glossary of Other Alternative Therapies[1]

Acupressure is similar to acupuncture but uses fingers instead of needles to apply pressure at specific points on the body.

Alexander technique aims to prevent or treat pain by improving poor posture.

Bach's flower remedies involve the oral use of 38 flowers and alcohol-based formulas made in Wallingford, England, to cure such disorders as shyness and drug dependence.

Hydrotherapy is the use of water to treat disorders. It includes hot or cold baths, compresses, steam inhalation, and mineral waters.

Hypnotherapy seeks to ease pain or treat ailments by making therapeutic suggestions while the patient is in a hypnotic trance.

Iridology involves the examination of the eye, particularly the iris, to diagnose mental and physical problems.

Kirlian photography uses special film to obtain an aura—a display of patterns and colors—around a body part, which then is used as a diagnostic tool.

Macrobiotics is a preventive health diet based on whole grains and cooked vegetables. A person needs to balance yin (passive energy) and yang (active energy).

Naturopathy has as its fundamental principle that all forms of disease are due to the same cause —the accumulation in the system of waste materials and bodily refuse.

Rolfing is the high-pressure massage and manipulation of the spine to align vertebrae with gravity.

Shiatsu is a massage from a therapist's fingers, elbows, or feet to bear down on the energy points of the body. It is used to treat such disorders as migraines and diarrhea.

Therapeutic massage uses stroking and other techniques on the afflicted part of the body to reduce pain and promote healing.

[1]Not discussed in the text.

problems—have experienced kidney damage, convulsions, and irregular heartbeat. Chelation therapy never has been shown to be effective in clinical trials.

If done improperly, chiropractic manipulation can injure the neck or spine seriously. Herbal remedies may have dangerous side effects and may be contaminated with toxic metals and other poisons. In their own defense, alternative-therapy practitioners point out that there also are numerous instances of physicians who have failed to diagnose problems correctly or have treated patients ineffectively or improperly.

In addition to concern over risks associated with alternative therapies, there is the fact that alternative medicine is largely unregulated. Herbs and other medications recommended by the healers have not met strict government criteria comparable to those that must be met by prescription drugs— criteria not only for purity and safety but also for efficacy. Practitioners of some therapies do not need to meet any licensing requirements, much less any approaching the stringent requirements for an M.D. Other alternative-medicine practitioners are licensed by the states in which they practice and meet rigid training and other qualifications established by organizations such as the American Chiropractic Association and the American Society of Clinical Hypnosis.

Practitioners of alternative therapies believe that the promise of these therapies is nowhere near fully explored. Yet most of these healers stress that alternative medicine is not a cure-all. Indeed, many prefer the term "complementary" to "alternative." They say that the therapies are not designed to replace conventional medicine but to be integrated with it. They believe that conventional and alternative practitioners have much to learn from one another. And they envision multidisciplinary practices that offer both conventional and unconventional care, to maintain good health among the healthy and to cure those who are ill.

Photos, © Gamma-Liaison

THE YEAR OF SPAIN

By George W. Grayson

As part of the celebrations of the 500th anniversary of Christopher Columbus' first voyage to the New World, the Spanish cities of Barcelona and Seville hosted the XXV Summer Olympics and the 1992 Universal Exposition ("Expo '92"), respectively. A crowd of some 65,000, including 32 heads of state, attended the Games' nontraditional opening ceremonies (above). Expo '92 was located on a 540-acre (219-ha) site on an island in the Guadalquivir River (page 65). As part of the preparations for the fair, eight new bridges were built across the river.

The world's spotlight shone on Spain in 1992. Seville, Barcelona, and Madrid were among Spanish cities that hosted spectacular events that emphasized the Iberian nation's unique contributions to the history of four continents, its cultural magnificence, its strategic position in contemporary international relations, and its hospitality to investors as well as tourists. The influx of visitors in 1992 revived a somewhat flagging economy at a time when belt-tightening, required to accommodate the country's full convergence with the European Community (EC), widened the breach between Premier Felipe González Márquez' Socialist government and the major labor federations.

The year marked the quincentenary of Christopher Columbus' first voyage to the New World. To commemorate Spain's historic role as the first major link between Europe and the Americas, replicas of the *Niña, Pinta,* and *Santa Maria* toured several U.S. ports.

Meanwhile, Barcelona was the site of the 1992 Summer Olympic Games (*see* SPORTS). In preparation for the army of athletes, journalists, and spectators who attended the festivities, the Catalán capital spent billions of dollars to revitalize its waterfront, construct a new beltway system to divert cars from traffic-choked streets, erect numerous sports-related facilities, and restore historic buildings in the city's Gothic Quarter, as well as those designed by the architect Antonio Gaudí (1852–1926). These projects became newsworthy in their own right and drew worldwide attention to the heritage of Spain's Catalonia region even before the Olympic torch arrived.

At the same time, $10 billion was lavished on Seville for the 1992 Universal Exposition. This "Expo '92" contained the pavilions of 110 nations and 22 international organizations and served as a center for the promotion of technology. The exposition's theme, "The Age of Discovery," was selected by Spain to promote its culture, traditions, and unique position as the bridge between Europe, North Africa, and the Western Hemisphere. Seville's city leaders took advantage of 1992 to revitalize and develop their city. They built new housing, parks, and facilities for a high-speed train linking Seville to the capital, Madrid.

Spain's artistic heritage also was highlighted when Madrid was designated as the "city of culture" for 1992. Accordingly, the majestic city that Philip II made the nation's capital in 1561 became Europe's unofficial cultural center. Expanding access to the treasures of the Prado—a world-class art museum with incomparable paintings by Goya, Velázquez, and

About the Author. George W. Grayson is the Class of 1938 Professor of Government at the College of William and Mary in Williamsburg, VA. A specialist in Iberian and Latin American affairs, Professor Grayson has written several books, including *The Politics of Mexican Oil, The United States and Mexico: Patterns of Influence,* and *Oil and Mexican Foreign Policy,* as well as numerous articles for newspapers, magazines, and scholarly journals. He has lectured at the Foreign Service Institute of the U.S. Department of State and has served as a member of the Virginia House of Delegates for several years.

For the many visitors to Spain in 1992, the nation's various festivals—as well as such landmarks as the Sagrada Familia (Holy Family) church, right, in Barcelona—were major attractions. The unfinished Sagrada Familia, one of Antonio Gaudi's major works, is a prime example of Catalonian architecture. Many of Spain's festivals are of a religious nature. "Giants" and ancient "coaches" (left) peculiar to Valencia have been featured at the city's Corpus Christi religious procession.

El Greco—was just one of many ways that Madrid prepared for the wave of artists, musicians, ballet dancers, and opera singers who arrived to demonstrate their artistic talents.

History. The first available records reveal that a people known as the Iberians occupied much of what is present-day Spain some 5,000 years ago. Later the Phoenicians, Celts, and Greeks established colonies and trading posts in Iberia before Carthage conquered much of the peninsula in the 5th century B.C. The Romans, who introduced the Latin language, drove out the Carthaginians only to be expelled by the Visigoths. This Germanic tribe established the first separate and independent government to rule the peninsula in the 6th century. Almost all of their kingdom, in turn, was conquered by the Muslims (Moors) who launched their invasion in 711.

Fourteen ninety-two was a landmark year in Spanish history. After a protracted conflict, Christian descendants of the Visigoths finally expelled the Muslims, who had occupied all or part of the Iberian peninsula for seven centuries. Just a few years earlier, Ferdinand II of Aragon and Isabella I of Castile merged their two kingdoms to lay the foundation of modern Spain. In addition to combating the Islamic "infidels," the monarchs sanctioned the Inquisition to persecute non-Catholics. In 1492 they banished the last of the Spanish Jews who failed to convert to Christianity. Their expulsion sprang partly from intolerance and partly from a desire to confiscate the wealth of the once-prosperous Jewish community.

Another significant event of 1492 was the sponsoring of Columbus' expedition to the Orient. Although the Genoese navigator did not reach the Far East as anticipated, he established a Spanish presence in the Western Hemisphere. His discoveries inspired expeditions by Hernán Cortés, Francisco Pizarro, Hernando de Soto, Francisco Vásquez de Coronado, and others. The success of these so-called *conquistadores* ensured Spain's role as a power in Europe for several centuries. Spain's vast American empire furnished gold, silver, and political status. Its links with the Hapsburg family and the Holy Roman Empire helped forge an empire that—at its zenith—embraced North Africa, the low countries, the French province of Roussillon, much of Italy, the lion's share of Latin America, and the Philippines and other Pacific islands.

Revolts in several territories and rivalries with other European nations drained the royal treasury and weakened the military. In 1588 the British navy—aided by bad weather and the Dutch—destroyed half of the once-mighty, 130-ship armada. Following this defeat, nobles challenged the crown, Catalonia erupted in revolt, and Portugal—ruled by Spain for 60 years—regained its independence in 1640. The Bourbons, who succeeded to the throne at the beginning of the 18th century, proved better administrators than their Hapsburg prede-

(Continued on page 70.)

Christopher Columbus' voyages to the New World were milestones in Spanish history and helped pave the way for Spain's rise as a power in Europe. An 1892 U.S. lithograph, below, depicts the navigator and a group of captive natives from the New World before the court of Ferdinand and Isabella in the spring of 1493.

© The Granger Collection

EXPO '92

Flags of the participating nations flew and fireworks were ignited as Expo '92 opened in Seville on April 20, 1992. Emilio Cassinello, Expo's commissioner general, referred to the fair as "a daring idea in its utopian pretense to squeeze humanity to an enclosure." The Bioclimatic Sphere, below, released a cooling mist into the air, and the 1.3-mi (2-km)-long, 65-ft (20-m)-high air-conditioned cable-car system included 135 cars. The fair, which was attended by more than 16 million visitors, was intended to "transform Seville and Andalusia into an economic center for the whole western Mediterranean." The locale was to be made into a research and technology park following the fair's closing.

With Seville known for its very hot summers, the European Community (EC) Pavilion, left, featured 12 cooling towers, representing the 12 EC members. Each tower was 30 yds (27 m) high and was fitted with 36 micronizers to evaporate water and lower the temperature. Expo's monorail was 2 mi (3.2 km) long and capable of transporting 4,200 passengers per hour.

Expo '92, the 1992 Seville Universal Exposition, was held on a 538-acre (217-ha) site on the Isla de la Cartuja in Seville, Spain, April 20 through Oct. 12, 1992. Expo '92 was billed as the "last and largest world's fair of the 20th century." With "The Age of Discoveries" as its theme, it commemorated the 500th anniversary of Christopher Columbus' journey to the New World. In fact, its Pavilion of the 15th Century was built within the grounds of a 15th-century monastery where Columbus reflected between his voyages.

The United States Pavilion, above, presented almost continuous sports and musical events, including a basketball show. The highly praised United Kingdom Pavilion, left, known as the "cathedral of water," offered a sheet of water 60 ft (18 m) high and 235 ft (72 m) wide, streaming down the building's facade into a pool of water.

cessors. Still, they not only witnessed the loss of all of Spain's European possessions but also were forced to yield Gibraltar and Minorca to Great Britain.

In the early 18th century, Napoleon overran Iberia and placed his brother on the Spanish throne. Even though Ferdinand VII regained his monarchy, he could not hold onto his American territories. By 1825, most of Spain's New World colonies had severed their political ties to Madrid. The Spanish-American War in 1898 further undermined Spanish power: The United States took legal or de facto control of Cuba, Puerto Rico, Guam, and the Philippines.

Even the Spanish-American War did not alert Madrid to the pitfalls of colonialism. In 1912, Spain occupied parts of Morocco. The Moroccans resisted and in 1921 killed more than 10,000 Spanish troops. Warfare continued in North Africa and strikes and civil violence spread throughout Spain until Gen. Miguel Primo de Rivera forcibly restored order in 1923. Seven years later, Primo, who as prime minister had failed to keep a promise to reestablish constitutional government, was forced to resign. Amid political polarization and acute economic distress, King Alfonso XIII fled the country in 1931. Land reform and other changes sponsored by leaders of the new republic attracted the support of liberals, socialists, and other antimonarchists. They met fierce opposition from the Roman Catholic hierarchy, wealthy landowners, the military, and other traditional elements. In 1936 hostilities erupted between the Republicans (the Loyalists) and the rebels (the Nationalists) and, for three years, Spain became a bloody proving ground for weapons that would be deployed in World War II. The Soviet Union and volunteer "International Brigades" organized by the Communists aided the Republicans. Germany's Adolf Hitler and Italy's Benito Mussolini cast their lot with the ultranationalist forces of Francisco Franco. The generalissimo, as Franco was known, emerged victorious in 1939 when Moscow withdrew its support from the Republicans.

The stern, authoritarian Franco maintained control of a military-dominated regime for three decades after World War II. The country enjoyed an economic boom during the postwar years as the dictatorial Franco, an inveterate anticommunist, crafted a military alliance that permitted U.S. air and naval bases in his country. In 1969 the aging general built a political bridge to contemporary Spain. He designated Juan Carlos, the 31-year-old grandson of Alfonso XIII, as his political heir.

Upon Franco's death in late 1975, the new king courageously impelled Spain's full transition from dictatorship to democracy. Although bequeathed unlimited authority, Juan Carlos realized that Spain's ever larger and more affluent middle class would not acquiesce to a traditional monarchy. Thus he ended Franco's curbs on political associations, replaced a conservative prime minister with the reform-minded Adolfo Suárez González, and persuaded the Cortés (the Spanish parliament) to pass a political reform law by a vote of 425 to 59—with 13 abstentions—in November 1976. Juan Carlos and

Ultraconservative and authoritarian Francisco Franco dominated the Spanish scene from the moment he came to power in April 1939 until shortly before his death in November 1975.

© UPI/Bettmann

Suárez then worked closely for legislation that ensured universal suffrage, disbanded Franco's political movement, conferred rights on trade unions that long had been persecuted, and legalized political parties.

In mid-1977, Spain's voters chose a new Cortés in the first free elections held since 1936. No party boasted an absolute majority in this body that was composed of a 350-seat Congress of Deputies and a largely ceremonial Senate of 207 members. Suárez, however, remained prime minister as head of a moderate alliance that was dominated by his own Union of the Democratic Center (UDC) and that won 165 seats in the Congress of Deputies and 107 in the Senate. The Spanish Workers Socialist Party (PSOE) finished second with 118 congressional and 35 senatorial seats; the Communists (PCE) captured 20 and 12 seats, respectively; and the conservative Popular Alliance (AP) won 16 and two seats—with the remaining positions held by Basque and Catalán regional parties. By late 1978, the Cortés had approved a new constitution that proclaimed Spain a constitutional monarchy, separated church and state, guaranteed human and civil rights, and granted limited autonomy to various regions. Even though Catalonia, Galicia, and the Basque country had elected regional parliaments by the early 1980s, Basque extremists continued to author violent acts against Madrid.

Spain's nascent constitutional democracy passed its first major test in 1981. In the face of mordant criticism from the press, opposition parties, and elements of his own UDC, Prime Minister Suárez abruptly resigned in January. This move plunged post-Franco Spain into a severe political crisis highlighted by an attempted coup d'état by dissident civilguard officers. The conspirators hoped to convert Juan Carlos to their cause and return the country to an authoritarian monarchy under the tutelage of the armed forces. Rather than capitulate, the youthful king, acting as commander-in-chief, rallied the majority of the military to the democratic regime. He quelled the insurrection, whose three ringleaders were sentenced to 30 years in prison and expelled from the service without pay.

Juan Carlos (below), grandson of Alfonso XIII, was designated by Franco as his heir. During his 17 years on the throne, the king has worked to foster democracy in Spain. He is married to Queen Sofia *(below right),* the daughter of the late King Paul and Queen Frederika of Greece.

© Nicolas-Chamussy/Sipa

Another sign of their country's growing political maturity occurred when Spaniards awarded an absolute majority (202 seats) in the Congress of Deputies to the PSOE in the October 1982 parliamentary contests. Three colonels were arrested for plotting a coup before campaigning began. Still, the country remained calm amid the Socialist victory that brought Felipe González to the prime ministership. The boyishly handsome, 40-year-old lawyer, whose slogan was "Socialism Means Freedom," committed himself to strengthening Spain's democratic institutions while modernizing a hugely statist economy that was beset by slow growth, high inflation, and mounting unemployment. His electoral triumph virtually eliminated the UDC and the Communists as serious contenders as the conservative Popular Party, successor to the Popular Alliance, emerged as the chief opposition party. Since his initial electoral success, González has led the Socialists to victories in 1986 (184 Chamber of Deputies seats) and 1990 (175 seats).

Despite intra-PSOE tensions, González was expected to be the party's standard-bearer in the general elections that must be held before October 1993.

Economics. Although the post-World War II "Spanish miracle" had expanded the country's overall wealth, Prime Minister González inherited an inefficient, inward-looking economy. It was characterized by state ownership of key industries, a sea of regulation, aging plants, an arthritic banking system, and a lack of competition among professionals who relied on associations known as *colegios* to preserve their privileges. At the apex of this highly structured system stood a huge bureaucracy spawned by Franco to accommodate centralized decision-making.

Pragmatism proved to be the watchword of González' economic strategy. When appropriate, his government resorted to nationalization. A case in point was the 1983 takeover of Rumasa, a conglomerate with activities ranging from agriculture and wine exports to shipping and real estate. Criticism of this bold action abated when the Economics Ministry revealed that the firm, which generated 1.8% of the country's gross domestic product (GDP) in 1982, engaged in fraud, mismanagement, and tax evasion. Meanwhile, Economy Minister Carlos Solchaga Catalán, a champion of free-market policies and a González confidant, restructured the bloated steel and shipbuilding industries in a move that eliminated 60,000 jobs. This action elicited a sharp outcry from the Communist Workers' Commissions and the socialist General Workers' Union, which was an important force within the PSOE.

Both González and Solchaga realized that continued political and economic modernization lay in integrating Spain with Western Europe through the European Community (EC). After months of negotiations, Spain achieved entry into the economic union on Jan. 1, 1986. Admission catalyzed a second postwar boom. As a less-developed member of the EC, Spain received billions of dollars in subsidies. At the same time, foreign investors anxious to gain a beachhead for exporting to EC countries opened factories in Spain, where wages remained among the lowest in Western Europe. By 1992 foreigners had pumped about $30 billion into the Spanish economy. The stock of U.S. investment alone mushroomed to $7.2 billion—with a 30% increase anticipated for 1993. As a result, Spain's GDP grew at a 5% average between 1986 and 1989 before sagging in 1990 (3.6%), 1991 (2.4%), and 1992 (3%). Unemployment was hovering at about 17% of the labor force, while inflation was surpassing 5.5%. Also vexing has been a central-regime deficit that totals 4.4% of GDP, complemented by red ink flowing across the ledgers of most of the 17 regional governments.

During 1992, Prime Minister González was seeking to get Spain's economy to converge with the targets set by the EC heads of government at the Maastricht, the Netherlands, meeting in December 1991. To achieve the most important goal—a unified currency by 1996—Madrid must slash its inflation by more than 3 percentage points. In April 1992, Finance

Economic development has been the key in post-World War II Spain. Today, the Spanish economy is one of the fastest-growing ones within the European Community. Auto manufacturing, below, has become a growing and leading industry.

© Kim Newton/Woodfin Camp & Assoc.

© Erica Lansner/Black Star

© Thomas Mayer/Black Star

© Frederico Mendes/Sipa

During the Year of Spain, international attention focused not only on the cities of Barcelona (top left) and Seville (left), but also on the capital, Madrid (above). Granted a municipal charter by King Alfonso VIII in 1202 and established as the nation's capital by Philip II in 1561, Madrid was designated the cultural capital of Europe for 1992. With a population of some 3 million, it is Spain's largest city. The Mediterranean port of Barcelona —Spain's second-largest city, with some 1.7 million people—is the major urban center of the nation's Catalonia region. The city underwent extensive modernization in preparation for the 1992 Summer Olympics. Located in southern Spain in the Andalusia region, Seville has been known for centuries as a city of parks, palaces, and churches. A major trading center during the 15th and 16th centuries, the city also is known as a center of Islamic architecture. Its population nears 700,000.

Minister Solchaga took an important step toward this objective when the government decreed a sweeping cut in unemployment payments, combined with an increase in the time in work required to qualify for benefits. The labor unions reacted to this measure, which could save the government upward of $4 billion, by going on strike in May and calling another for October. Undeterred, Solchaga sought to slash subsidies to the national airline and state-railway monopoly, revamp the management of the state's health-care system, and break the price-fixing and other restrictive practices of pharmacists, physicians, architects, and other professionals.

In return for its commitment to convergence, Spain was demanding that the EC comply with another protocol reached at Maastricht—namely, the creation of a compensation fund

(Continued on page 76.)

The Christopher Columbus Quincentenary

To mark the 500th anniversary of Christopher Columbus' historic voyage to the New World, monuments were built; scholars gathered for symposia; nations issued coins and stamps; and books were written. However, the most colorful celebrations took place at sea. A group of tall ships took part in a transatlantic Grand Regatta, which originated in Lisbon, Portugal, and in Genoa, Italy, *page 74*—the generally recognized site of Columbus' birth. The tall ships also led a festive Operation Sail '92 in New York City on July 4, 1992. In addition, replicas of Columbus' three ships—the *Niña,* the *Pinta,* and the *Santa María*—sailed from Spain for the Americas, following as closely as possible Columbus' route. The caravels participated in Operation Sail '92 and toured various cities, including Miami, FL, *above.* Meanwhile, various groups, especially Native Americans who felt that Columbus' discovery led to great exploitation, questioned the wisdom of the celebrations.

Spain's Mediterranean coastline, the Costa del Sol—a mecca for visitors from throughout the world—has been developed extensively with hotels, villas, marinas, and shopping centers since the 1960s.

by the end of 1993. Such a fund would provide monies for the environment and transport systems in the EC's poorest members—Ireland, Greece, Portugal, and Spain. The 12 EC members also agreed to earmark additional aid to those nations until their per-capita income reached 90% of the EC average. Failure to fulfill these pledges could lead the poorer nations of Europe to block political and monetary-union treaties.

Though it has cast its lot with Europe, Spain also has cultivated close ties with its former colonies in Latin America. These relations have taken the form of cultural exchanges, joint business ventures, trade accords, and investment—which shot up from $198 million in 1989 to $619 million during the first six months of 1991. In mid-1992, Spain hosted the second Ibero-American summit conference. It attracted representatives from 23 Iberian, Latin American, and Caribbean nations.

Outlook. Regionalism continues to be a surging force in Spain that could grow even stronger. A legacy of centralism notwithstanding, Madrid will have to devolve more power to the 17 regions to promote harmony and enhance the status of moderate local parties. Separatists already boast 16% of the vote in the Basque area, and radicals are making impressive strides in Catalonia. At the same time, Spain exhibits the essential ingredients for greater prosperity—a skilled work force, a good and improving infrastructure, ample investment monies, and enlightened leadership. Once the remaining impediments to competition in banking and the professions are swept away, Spain should leave the ranks of the "poor four" of the EC to take its position among the more affluent nations of Europe. Greater development will attract even more legal and illegal immigrants from Eastern Europe, Latin America, and Africa—unless, of course, Madrid takes effective steps to stem such an influx that has caused severe racial tensions in France, Germany, and other EC members.

See also SPAIN in the Alphabetical Section.

THE ★★★★ PRO ATHLETE *TODAY*

By Richard E. Lapchick

According to a Lou Harris survey of high-school students, a staggering 43% of black as well as 16% of white high-school student-athletes believe they will play professional sports! As drugs, gang violence, AIDS, and racial intolerance seem to rob so many teenagers of their youth, the dream of playing professional sports seems like a rainbow to ride on to escape some of the harsh realities of today's world.

Who are these pro athletes today and what makes them seem so special to young people? Some things about them make the allure seem obvious. Above all else, in a reeling economy with high unemployment rates, the salaries of professional athletes are astonishing. There are athletes making $7 million per year to play a game! Hundreds of players make more than $1 million per season. The *average* salaries in the National Basketball Association (NBA) and Major League Baseball easily surpass $1 million. Shaquille O'Neal, a 21-year-old basketball player who had yet to play in a pro game, signed a multimillion-dollar shoe contract with Reebok! Basketball's Michael Jordan reportedly earns $15 million per year in endorsements alone.

About the Author. Richard E. Lapchick is the director of Northeastern University's Center for the Study of Sport in Society. A former associate professor of political science at Virginia Wesleyan College, Dr. Lapchick is the author of seven books. The latest is *Five Minutes to Midnight: Race and Sport in the 1990's* (1991). His comments on timely sports subjects have been heard on many of the leading television news programs.

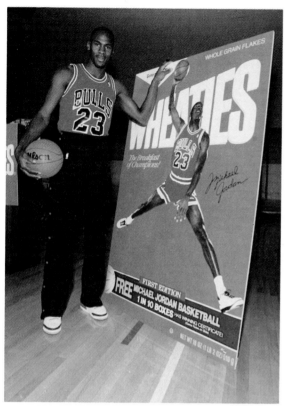

Many of today's pro athletes increase their exposure through lucrative commercial endorsements. Michael Jordan (above) has pitched several products, including Wheaties cereal.

Stories about athletes appear every day on television and in the newspapers. Pro athletes are rich and famous. Their special talents, whether "natural" or developed by hard work, set them apart. They beat the 10,000-to-one odds that a high-school player faces to make the pros. That is the snapshot that most Americans see of their athletes. The athletes' lives are much more complex.

The Past. The changes from the past are striking. My father, Joe Lapchick, was a star basketball player for 20 years with the Original Celtics, and coached St. John's University for 20 years and the New York Knicks for ten years. He was inducted into the Basketball Hall of Fame as both a player and a coach. Joe Lapchick retired in 1965, earning $12,500 annually at St. John's. He had signed the first basketball-shoe endorsement with Kinney's in 1932 for $1,200 per year!

I dragged my father to a Catholic elementary-school championship in the early 1960s to see an eighth grader whom I had gone to summer camp with the previous year. After the game, a reporter asked him what he thought of this 13-year-old. His response was resurrected more than 20 years later when Kareem Abdul-Jabbar was negotiating for sports' first $2 million contract. My father said: "Lew Alcindor [as he was known at the time] will be the most dominant player to ever play the game. I'll bet that someday he'll even make $50,000 a year." When Kareem retired, he was making $50,000 per game!

The money and the fame athletes receive today through increased exposure differ greatly from in the past. While athletes of my father's era were paid less, they were not the property of the public as much as today's pros have become. Their private lives were just that—private. Not so for the pro athlete of the 1990s.

Life in the Glass Bowl. The escalation of the public's interest in pro sports and pro athletes, ever heightened by this advanced media age, has made today's pro an automatic role model for young people. The athletes may not choose that, but the reality is that they are chosen. In the same Lou Harris survey mentioned earlier, 46% of high-school students chose athletes as their role models. With the exception of entertainers, no other category came close in terms of popular acceptance.

This, of course, places a heavy responsibility on athletes. The media seems to give daily reports on athletes having difficulty with the law or in their personal lives. Pete Rose, baseball's all-time hit leader, is banned from the game for

© S. Halleran/Allsport

gambling. Track star Ben Johnson loses his Olympic gold medal for steroid use. Steve Howe is banned for life from Major League Baseball for repeated use of cocaine. Basketball's beloved Earvin ("Magic") Johnson announces he is HIV-positive, resulting from an admitted promiscuous lifestyle prior to his marriage. Far less beloved but more wealthy, former heavyweight champ Mike Tyson goes to prison after a rape conviction.

The high finances of today's sports have added to the pressures facing the pro athlete. In tennis, many young stars, including Jennifer Capriati (center with family), have been coached and pressured by their fathers.

Mothers and fathers have begun to feel uncomfortable with athletes as role models for their kids. Many athletes respond that parents never should surrender their responsibility as role models to athletes or anyone else. Why do young people feel differently? According to the Harris Survey, "athletes are admired not nearly so much because of their star qualities in their sport, but much more as decent and generous human beings . . . It is for their off-field performance as leaders and human beings with character that athletes are most admired." When students were asked to explain why they select the pro athlete as a role model, the fact that he or she is a star player was cited only slightly more than half the time. More prevalent answers included because the athlete "is a warm human being who really cares about other people"; because the athlete is "unselfish"; because the athlete is a "real leader"; because the athlete "works with young people on programs to curb drug abuse"; and because the athlete has "a high sense of integrity."

So who knows athletes better, adults or students? Adults know only the fame, fortune, and glamour they see in the media snapshots or when they see the pro athletes on the field. Students see the athletes up close. Every pro team has a community-relations program, as do many college athletic departments. Athletes are constantly in schools talking to students

Editor's Note. Among other things, Northeastern University's Center for the Study of Sport in Society and its related National Consortium for Academics and Sports help pro athletes return to complete their college education. More than 1,000 pros, 100 Olympians, and 3,000 former college athletes who did not make the pros have participated. Nearly 2,000 have received their degrees. All join the Consortium's Outreach and community-service program in which they have counseled directly more than 1.2 million young people across the United States.

about balancing academics and athletics, and about the dangers of drug and alcohol abuse, teenage pregnancy, race relations, and not surrendering their responsibility to others. A handful of athletes are bad role models, while the overwhelming majority are positive role models.

However, in addition to a higher social consciousness, many athletes know that lucrative endorsement contracts will not be as available to them if they do not behave responsibly in public. It is in their interest, as well as the public's, for them to do so. To be sure, there are some who may not seem to care and only want to "be themselves." But they are relatively rare. The programs at Northeastern University's Center for the Study of Sport in Society have worked with more than 1,100 pros in educational programs. Overwhelmingly, these athletes are serious, family-oriented, and deeply religious.

Athletes' Expectations and What They Get. What athletes expect from their careers is often far different from what the public believes. The public sees the obvious extraordinary salaries, and virtually all athletes indeed do expect whatever the marketplace is bearing. That causes a certain resentment from the typical fan earning $25,000 per year. It makes the fan more likely to believe some stereotypical images of athletes, including the high life-styles of easy sex, drugs and alcohol, and getting everything for free.

The sports camp, administered by current or former athletes, is an example of how athletes can have a positive effect on youngsters. New York Met Dave Magadan (below) gives instructions at the Bucky Dent Baseball School in Del Ray Beach, FL.

The fan rarely sees the toll taken by the daily pressure of high performance. With an average career of only three and one-half to four years, only the superstars are secure. Most marginal pros have understudies waiting for them to fall. Even the superstars have bodies that eventually will give way: wit-

© Henry Horenstein

ness the retirements of Magic Johnson and Larry Bird in late 1991 and August 1992, respectively. The publicity and the hero worship, which can be such positive factors for athletes and the community, ultimately increase the pressure to succeed.

Today's athlete is more aware that fame and fortune rarely endure beyond their playing careers unless they are prepared for life after sport. Very few are. We occasionally read about former pros committing suicide, being homeless, unemployed, or broke. The average fan shudders sympathetically but usually believes that life after sport for most former pros is glamorous. They see Jack Kemp and Bill Bradley, potential presidential candidates, on TV and think they are typical. In truth, the transition from the pros to the real world is a very difficult one. A survey of all former National Football League (NFL) players showed that, in comparison to average men, they had higher levels of job and family instability, greater unemployment, and more defaults on loans. They also had four times the number of physical disabilities and lived an average 21 years less than the typical American man. Player associations and the pro-sport leagues now are much more conscious of the need to prepare pro athletes for life after their playing days are over.

© Larry Downing/Sygma

The Athletes' Payback. Record-setting attendance, millions of TV fans, expansion of pro sports, and the increase in women watching and competing in sport all indicate that athletes are entertaining their audiences handsomely. Such entertainment gives the fan an escape from the real world of bad economies, political turmoil, and personal problems. However, the fans, mindful that the players are rich and they are not, have become less tolerant of the hometown team losing or of the highly paid player not performing up to par. Fans boo stars. As the purchases of some of baseball's free-agent contracts demonstrate, money does not buy wins. However, it can lose fans when it does not.

Fans and the media also are ready to pounce when athletes go outside of normally accepted values or the law in their behavior. Jack Clark, a Red Sox multimillion-dollar-per-year player, won no sympathy from fans when he declared bankruptcy in 1992. It might have been different if he had been leading the Red Sox to a division championship. In 1988, Boston's Wade Boggs got months of terrible press and fan hostility after a romantic affair was publicized highly. The boos and the stories quieted when his batting average moved up among the league leaders. There were no follow-up stories on the promiscuity of other athletes. It was a Wade Boggs story and then it died.

Mike Tyson was another story completely. To those who followed his career, Tyson always seemed like a man on the edge of self-destruction. When a jury decided that it finally had happened and convicted him of rape, an avalanche of stories and fan reactions buried athletes with yet another stereotype—that athletes are more inclined toward sexual abuse of women. It was no longer a Mike Tyson story but a story

© Terry Ashe/Gamma-Liaison

Finding a successful career after their playing days have ended remains a serious problem for many athletes. Football's Jack Kemp (top) and basketball's Bill Bradley (above) joined the political arena and, respectively, addressed the 1992 Republican and Democratic conventions.

about "athletes." This was in spite of the fact that only 90 athletes were involved in any form of sexual abuse with women in 1990–91.

It was most disturbing to black athletes. Many quietly protested that whatever Mike Tyson represented, it was not them. They believed that the Tyson case fed other stereotypes about blacks. The issue of race is by no means dead in pro sports. Few blacks and Hispanics have broken into the coaching ranks. In the most recent seasons of each of the major sports in which blacks and Hispanics compete, there were only seven people of color who were head coaches. There never has been a black general manager in the NFL or in Major League Baseball. Considering that the playing field is the most integrated workplace in the United States (75% of the players in the NBA and 62% of those in the NFL are black, and 32% of baseball's major-leaguers are black or Hispanic), these failures bear even closer scrutiny.

An argument silently made behind the scenes was that white fans will not root for teams with a black coach or general manager. As the NBA, with the most black players and a few black coaches, entered a period of decline in the late 1970s and early 1980s, the silence was broken. Then David Stern took over as NBA commissioner and marketed the league, bringing it to new heights. At one point there were six NBA

© Jeff Atteberry/"Indianapolis Star"/Pool/Saba

Former heavyweight boxing champion Mike Tyson was convicted of rape and sentenced to six years in prison in 1992. The highly publicized case caused new debate about the glamour and excesses of star athletes in the United States.

Major-league baseball's growing salary structure has become a controversial issue. The listing of the game's highest-paid players is watched in the same manner as the hitting and pitching stats.

teams with head coaches who were black and five with general managers who were black. The NBA is, by far, the most open to blacks in high-level positions. Fans pay to see winning teams, no matter who is coaching or playing. Now baseball and the NFL need to follow the NBA's lead at the team level. At least there is now a consciousness of the issue that should lead to change. As for the black fans, they only go to NBA games in proportion to their numbers in society. Relatively few attend baseball or football games. Many black leaders insist this is because blacks will not support sports that will not hire blacks in leadership roles.

What Is Ahead for the Professional Athlete. Everyone says salaries of pro athletes cannot continue to rise the way they have since the early 1980s. But everyone has been saying that throughout the decade and the rise has increased each year, especially in basketball and baseball. Both have free agency. If the NFL and the National Hockey League (NHL) get free agency, then their salary structures also will go through the roof. Realistically, unless the players' associations and the leagues somehow can work closely together—as the NBA and the NBA Players' Association do—then there will be no reasonable control of salaries in the near future.

Athletes will continue to expand their social consciousness and help revive the urban communities where their teams play. Community service will become part of the game. The teams will help to better prepare their players for the transition out of the game so they can have a full life. As a consequence of both these trends, even fewer athletes will act irresponsibly off the court.

And the fans will keep attending and tuning in games as the level of play gets better and better. How can heroes be replaced? What will happen to the NBA without Larry and Magic? People asked the same thing when Dr. J's (Julius Erving's) career wound down. Will another extraterrestrial like Michael Jordan come along? Who will build on the legends of baseball's Nolan Ryan, and football's Dan Marino and Joe Montana? Stay tuned.

© Apesteguy-Reglain-Stevens/Gamma-Liaison

© Tom Craig/REA/Saba

Disney Goes Parisian

By Barbara J. Braasch

Members of the Disney cartoon family, including Minnie Mouse, above, led the festivities as the $4.4 billion Euro Disneyland opened some 20 mi (32 km) outside Paris, France, on April 12, 1992. The first Disney theme park in Europe, Euro Disneyland includes 29 attractions on five different "lands."

The year 1992 was an action-packed one for Mickey Mouse, the Walt Disney Company's lovable world ambassador. Mickey helped unveil new shows, attractions, and hotels during a yearlong celebration for the 20th anniversary of Walt Disney World in Orlando, FL. Along with a cast of other familiar characters, dazzling fireworks, and brass bands, he also was on hand to welcome visitors to his latest domain, the Magic Kingdom at Euro Disneyland Resort in Marne-la-Vallée, France. In fact, when Euro Disneyland joined the other Disney amusement parks—in California, Florida, and Japan —it meant the peripatetic mouse now extends smiling greetings to guests somewhere around the world every hour of every day.

Euro Disneyland. While the French elite sneered and termed the all-weather wonderland, just 20 mi (32 km) outside Paris, "a cultural Chernobyl," the Disney folks—with a wave of their magic wand and $4.4 billion—transformed 5,500 acres (2 226 ha) of wheat and sugar beets into Europe's largest theme park. Euro Disney is definitely an all-American amusement park. In spite of its location deep in the heart of France, the park adopts little from the country, a fact that causes much Gallic rancor. For example, despite this being a place where no meal is complete without wine, Disney refuses to serve alcoholic beverages within the park. French is the language of choice for robots, animated characters, and most patrons and staff, but subtitles make it easy for English-speaking visitors to get around. The park's 12,000 "cast members" (employees) speak languages from around the globe.

The Magic Kingdom's layout is familiar to veterans of the original Disneyland in Anaheim, CA, or Disney World. Four separate areas—Frontierland, Adventureland, Fantasyland, Discoveryland—radiate out from Main Street, U.S.A. Park visitors enter through the Disneyland Hotel, a big, pink, turn-of-the-century-style palace designed by Disney Imagineers. Covered passageways beneath the Main Street Station of the Euro Disneyland Railroad then lead visitors into Main Street. Behind the false-front buildings, glass-roofed arcades provide sheltered access to park areas during periods of inclement weather.

Many of the park's 30 major attractions are upgraded editions of crowd-pleasers in California and Florida; others, such as Alice's Curious Labyrinth and the Visionarium film, are new. In the dungeon of *Le Chateau de la Belle au Bois Dormant* (Sleeping Beauty's Castle), a fantastic Audio-Animatronics dragon thrills children when it awakens, flashes glowing eyes, snorts steam, and uncurls long talons.

Buildings and grounds outside the theme park were planned as an integral part of the resort. Around man-made Lake

About the Author. A freelance writer, editor, and editorial consultant living in central California, Barbara J. Braasch has served as associate editor of Sunset Books and staff writer for *Sunset Magazine*. The author of 11 travel guides, including *Alaska, California,* and *Gold Rush Country,* Ms. Braasch has contributed to such publications as the *San Jose Mercury News,* the *San Diego Union,* and *Better Homes & Gardens.* She was graduated from the University of Colorado and Munson's Graduate School of Business in San Francisco.

Not only did Euro Disneyland make its debut in 1992, but Walt Disney World near Orlando, FL, marked its 20th anniversary. Parades, special attractions, and a variety of travel promotions to the park were held to celebrate the occasion. Disney World, which opened in 1971, attracts some 30 million visitors annually.

Buena Vista stand five architecturally stunning hotels, a campground, a championship golf course, and Festival Disney's entertainment complex of restaurants, shops, dinner shows, and discotheques. The themed hotels, designed by such master builders as Michael Graves and Robert A. M. Stern, are playful adjuncts to the park. The shingle-style Newport Bay Club's 1,100 rooms make it the largest hotel in Western Europe. Hotel Cheyenne recreates an Old West movie set complete with lively gunfights.

Will these attractions be enough to lure the all-year crowds Euro Disney anticipates? Initial estimates indicated a slow start. Misleading reports of traffic jams, overcrowding, and mechanical problems caused many Paris-area residents to postpone visits. Only time would tell whether the park could overcome typical Gallic resistance to things American. "If they bring their children to Euro Disneyland, they'll have a good time," insisted Michael D. Eisner, chief executive officer (CEO) of the parent Disney company. If the company's past track records hold true, it was a safe statement.

The Disney Story. For more than six decades the Walt Disney Company has been the preeminent name in family entertainment. From humble beginnings as a cartoon studio in the 1920s to today's major corporation, Disney has been an "industry based on happiness." The Disney Company can trace its origins back to 1923 when Walt Disney left Missouri for California and started a storefront cartoon studio in Hollywood with his brother Roy. It was here that Mickey Mouse was born and achieved cartoon-star status when *Steamboat Willie* premiered in 1928. The "Silly Symphonies" soon followed and the first full-color cartoon of the series, *Flowers and Trees*, won the first Academy Award offered in that category. From that time through 1992, Disney pictures have picked up a total of 66 Oscars.

Born in Chicago in 1901, Walt Disney, below, moved to Hollywood in 1923 and began his career in animation. He introduced Donald, who would become the world's most famous duck, in the 1934 cartoon "The Wise Little Hen." The forever popular "Snow White and the Seven Dwarfs", below right, was Disney's first animated feature film. It was released in 1937.

© MCMLIV Walt Disney Productions

© 1937 The Walt Disney Company

Snow White and the Seven Dwarfs, Disney's first animated feature film, was a spectacular success when released in 1937. Such favorites as *Pinocchio, Fantasia, Dumbo, Bambi,* and *Cinderella* soon followed. After two Christmas television specials, Walt Disney began the Disneyland anthology series in 1954 that, with a few title changes, would remain on the air for 29 years. The Mickey Mouse Club debuted in 1955, making stars of a group of talented Mouseketeers.

Walt Disney then turned his attention to amusement parks, looking for new designs where both parents and children could have a good time. This was the genesis of Disneyland, which opened in 1955 and has become the pattern for every theme park built since that time. Walt Disney died in 1966 before his plans for Florida's Disney World could be realized. Until his death in 1971, Roy Disney oversaw the building and financing of his brother's ambitious dreams for hotel and recreation facilities that would provide a complete vacation destination for the whole family.

One of Walt Disney's last plans had been for an Experimental Prototype Community of Tomorrow (EPCOT), a combination of a future world and a showcase for world nations. This 250-acre (101-ha), constantly evolving center opened to wide acclaim in 1982. A year later, Tokyo Disneyland, the first Disney park outside the United States, opened on a 204-acre (83-ha) site 6.5 mi (10.4 km) from the heart of the city. Like its predecessors, the park was designed with five themed areas emanating from a central plaza. Some adaptations were made in deference to the different language and culture, but the park has a uniquely Disney spirit.

Mickey Mouse and his cohorts went to Japan in April 1983 for the opening of Tokyo Disneyland. More than one million persons visited the park—Disney's first outside the United States—in its first month of operations.

© Gamma-Liaison

"Pretty Woman," starring Richard Gere and Julia Roberts and released by Disney's Touchstone label, was one of the top-grossing films of 1990.

Michael Eisner (below), who became Disney's chairman and chief executive officer in September 1984, presided at the May 1989 opening of Florida's Disney-MGM Studios Park, a working movie and television studio which offers the tourist a look at filmmaking. The attractions at the Disney World complex were broadened further with the opening later that year of Typhoon Lagoon, a 56-acre (22.6-ha) water park.

For the decade after Roy Disney's death, the company was led by a management team trained by the Disney brothers. Roy E. Disney, Roy's son and Walt's nephew, resigned as a company vice-president in 1977 but helped engineer a bruising takeover battle in the mid-1980s. It was then that Michael Eisner, a 42-year-old Paramount executive, was brought in as Disney's chairman. Frank Wells, former vice chairman of Warner Brothers, became president.

Eisner and Wells pushed hard on all fronts—theme parks, movies, and merchandising—to maximize company assets. Business quickly exploded under this aggressive leadership. They began covering Disney World with hotels and convention centers, including the elegant Grand Floridian Resort. New attractions—such as Splash Mountain, Captain EO, and Star Tours—were added to the theme parks. Admission prices were increased and three new, separately ticketed attractions popped up in Florida—Disney-MGM Studios Theme Park, Typhoon Lagoon, and Pleasure Island.

Although commitment to Disney family-type movies was still evident, the company's Touchstone label released its first R-rated movie, *Down and Out in Beverly Hills,* in 1985. By 1991, Disney led other studios in box-office gross with such winners as *Three Men and a Baby* (1987), *Who Framed Roger Rabbit* (1988), *Dick Tracy* (1990), and *Pretty Woman* (1990). Lovers of Disney animation saw the reissue of popular classics and the release of *The Little Mermaid* (1989) and *Beauty and the Beast* (1991). The latter went on to break box-office records and win critical acclaim.

While the Disney Channel was successful, Eisner and Wells also pursued network television, launching such series favor-

© Kolczinski/Gamma-Liaison

© Abolafia/Gamma-Liaison

ites as *Golden Girls, Empty Nest,* and *Home Improvement.* In the consumer field, sales were tripled with the opening of more than 100 highly successful Disney Stores in shopping malls, expansion of mail-order catalog sales, and extension of licensing Disney character likenesses. The dynamic duo moved into new areas by starting Hollywood Records, acquiring the Wrather Corp. (owner of Disneyland Hotel), becoming publisher of *Discover* magazine, and debuting the first two health-conscious, fast-food restaurants, Mickey's Kitchens.

As the 1990s began, Disney was making more money than any other company in the entertainment field. Revenues tripled between 1988 and 1992, rising from $2 billion to $6.2 billion. Theme parks accounted for nearly 60% of the increase. Some 30 million people visit Disney World annually, while Disneyland clocks more than 13 million per year.

Outlook for the Future. Disney announced in mid-1992 that the opening of its second phase of Euro Disneyland, the Disney-MGM Studios Europe, would be moved back from 1995 to 1996. Does this mean that the Disney magic is flickering out? According to analysts, the delay is just a reaction to Euro Disneyland's unexpectedly low attendance figures during its initial months that resulted in a downturn in the price of Disney stock. While Disney may not experience the giant leaps forward seen in the late 1980s, there was plenty of evidence of imaginative planning that should ensure Disney's moving confidently ahead.

New parks were being considered. Disney Development has revealed plans for a second theme park adjacent to Disneyland in Anaheim. Tokyo Disneyland's success almost guarantees an expansion. An updated Swiss Family Robinson Treehouse was to open in Japan in mid-1993. The first new "land" in Disneyland in two decades, called Mickey's Toontown, was taking shape in 1992. Guests would take a zany trolley to see their favorite character's home and ride a roller coaster.

The marketing of Disney products has become a vital part of the company's financial picture. Not only are souvenir shops major attractions at the Disney parks, but Disney Stores have become a fixture at more than 100 shopping malls across the United States.

The Alphabetical Section

ARMENIA

AZERBAIJAN

BELARUS

ESTONIA

GEORGIA

RUSSIA

TAJIKISTAN

TURKMENISTAN

UKRAINE

UZBEKISTAN

KAZAKHSTAN

KYRGYZSTAN

LATVIA

LITHUANIA

MOLDOVA

© Allsport/UK Ltd.

The flag long has been a symbol of national pride, identity, and unity. With the fall of the USSR and the breakup of Yugoslavia, the community of nations grew in 1992 and the flags of the former Soviet republics and the former Yugoslav republics of Croatia, Slovenia, and Bosnia-Herzegovina—now independent nations—gained new meaning. Accordingly, the flags of the Baltic republics —Estonia, Latvia, and Lithuania—as well as those of Bosnia-Herzegovina, Croatia, and Slovenia were among those that proudly introduced their nations' delegations at the Summer Olympics. At the Summer Games, athletes from 11 republics of the Commonwealth of Independent States and from Georgia—parts of the former USSR—joined together as the Unified Team.

The flags of nine former Soviet republics as well as those of the three former Yugoslav republics gained greater significance as they began flying outside the United Nations headquarters in New York as the new states were admitted to the world body. The Baltic republics had become UN members in 1991.

BOSNIA-HERZEGOVINA

CROATIA

SLOVENIA

ABORTION

The debate over the right to abortion, waged since the U.S. Supreme Court guaranteed a woman's right to terminate an unwanted pregnancy in its landmark 1973 *Roe v. Wade* ruling, reached a turning point in the United States in 1992. Beginning in June, the Supreme Court took several steps that effectively defused this emotional issue before the November elections.

In its long-awaited June decision in *Planned Parenthood of Southeastern Pennsylvania v. Casey,* the Supreme Court disappointed both supporters of abortion rights and their opponents. Pro-choice advocates were dismayed by the court's upholding of states' rights to impose restrictions—such as parental consent and 24-hour waiting periods for women seeking abortions—that were contained in a Pennsylvania law. But the court also discouraged antiabortion forces by upholding *Roe v. Wade,* thus reaffirming a woman's right to abortion. The court's mixed signal—that women have the right to abortion but with certain restrictions, so long as they do not place an undue burden on the exercise of that right—gave something to each side in the debate, but not enough for either to claim a clear victory.

As the year drew to a close, the Supreme Court reiterated the somewhat confused message contained in *Casey* by declining to hear two cases regarding abortion rights. On November 30 the court declined to hear an appeal of a lower-court ruling that invalidated Guam's abortion law. In so doing, the court effectively killed the law, which banned virtually all abortions in the U.S. island territory. It also foreshadowed the probable demise of other highly restrictive abortion laws, passed in Louisiana and Utah, which had been struck down by federal courts. On December 7 the court declined to hear *Barnes v. Moore,* a challenge to Mississippi's requirements that women receive specific information about abortion and wait 24 hours before undergoing the procedure. That action reaffirmed the court's June ruling.

Election Campaigns. The Supreme Court's ruling in *Casey* muddied the debate over abortion rights, which had been defined largely in terms of unrestricted rights as against a virtual ban on the procedure. Faced with complicated questions regarding abortion restrictions, the 102d Congress failed to vote on the Freedom of Choice Act, a proposal that would codify the right to abortion guaranteed by *Roe v. Wade* and set uniform standards for state regulation.

By November 3 abortion figured low on the list of voters' concerns, emerging as a central issue in only a few congressional races. Despite the issue's low profile in the elections, abortion-rights advocates drew hope from the victory of Arkansas Gov. Bill Clinton, which effectively ended the 12-year dominance of anti-

abortion sentiment in the White House. Like his predecessor, Ronald Reagan, President George Bush consistently had vetoed all legislative attempts to ease strict antiabortion regulations, and the Republican platform contained a strongly worded plank opposing abortion. Although the issue never loomed large in the presidential debates, Clinton campaigned on an unequivocal pro-choice platform; he promised to overturn the executive order prohibiting abortion counseling in federally financed family-planning clinics, to appoint federal judges who believe the Constitution protects the right to abortion, and to support the Freedom of Choice Act, due to come before Congress again.

Abortion Pill. The extent to which the abortion debate had subsided by year's end was clear from reports that the European makers of RU486, the French abortion-inducing pill, again were considering applying for permission to market the controversial drug in the United States. RU486—currently sold only in France, Britain, Sweden, and China—had been used by more than 100,000 women in Europe to end unwanted pregnancies. The U.S. Food and Drug Administration (FDA) had banned its import since 1989, and the government in early 1992 seized the drug from a pregnant California woman who had tried to bring the drug into the country for personal use. Roussel-Uclaf, the maker of RU486, had not tried to sell the drug in the United States because its parent company, Hoechst AG of Germany, feared retaliation by U.S. antiabortion groups that had threatened to organize boycotts of Hoechst's other products.

But the lull in the abortion debate following the Supreme Court's June ruling in *Casey* appeared to help pave the way for U.S. women to gain access to RU486. Pro-choice advocates strongly promoted the drug as a safe, noninvasive means of terminating pregnancy, usually with fewer side effects than surgical abortion. Studies in 1992 also found the drug to be the most effective "morning-after" contraceptive pill available. Taken within 72 hours of sexual intercourse, "morning-after" pills prevent the implantation of a fertilized egg in the uterus, the point generally defined as the beginning of pregnancy. However, many opponents of abortion define conception, not implantation, as the beginning of life, and thus opposed this use of RU486 as well. An investigation into RU486's effectiveness in treating brain tumors was launched in 1992, suggesting that the drug may have other medical uses.

In the wake of these developments, 34 newly elected House members urged Hoechst to apply for permission to begin marketing RU486 in the United States, a development that President-elect Clinton said he would be willing to support.

MARY H. COOPER
"CQ [Congressional Quarterly] Researcher"

ACCIDENTS AND DISASTERS

AVIATION

Jan. 20—A French airliner en route from Lyon to Strasbourg crashes in the mountains of eastern France, leaving 87 persons dead.

Feb. 6—Sixteen persons are killed when a Kentucky National Guard military transport plane crashes into a motel filled with convention visitors in Evansville, IN.

Feb. 9—A chartered airliner carrying French tourists to a resort crashes into a marsh in southern Senegal, leaving 30 persons dead.

Feb. 23—Six loggers are killed when a helicopter flying them back to their camp crashes near Hobart Bay, AK.

March 14—A helicopter crashes in the North Sea while ferrying workers from an oil-drilling platform to their living quarters; 11 of the workers are killed.

March 22—Twenty-seven persons are left dead when a jet plane veers off a runway and rolls into a bay upon takeoff from La Guardia Airport in New York City.

April 22—A plane loaded with skydivers crashes on takeoff at Perris Vally Airport in Perris, CA, leaving 15 dead.

April 26—A transport plane traveling in rough weather crashes near Saveh, Iran, killing all 39 passengers.

June 6—Forty-seven persons are killed when a Panamanian jet crashes near the Colombian border.

July 20—An experimental military aircraft crashes at Quantico, VA, killing seven persons.

July 20—A cargo plane crashes in a suburb of Tbilisi, Georgia, killing at least 40 persons, including 30 on the ground.

July 24—All 71 persons aboard an Indonesian passenger plane are killed when the plane crashes into a hill while trying to land at Pattimura, Indonesia.

July 31—A Thai jetliner crashes in the Himalayas northwest of Katmandu, Nepal, killing all 113 aboard.

July 31—A Soviet-built Chinese airliner crashes during takeoff at Nanjing, China; 106 persons are feared dead.

Sept. 7—Twelve members of a skydiving club are killed when their twin-engine plane crashes shortly after takeoff from Hinckley, IL.

Sept. 27—A Nigerian military transport plane crashes shortly after takeoff from Lagos, Nigeria, killing all 163 aboard.

Sept. 28—One hundred sixty-seven are killed when a Pakistani jet crashes into a hillside while preparing to land at Katmandu, Nepal.

Oct. 4—An Israeli cargo jet crashes into two high-rise apartment buildings near Amsterdam, the Netherlands, killing more than 50 persons in the Netherlands' worst aviation disaster ever.

Nov. 6—A Russian military helicopter strikes the side of a cliff near the Black Sea, killing at least 30 passengers and crew members.

Nov. 24—A plane traveling to Guangzhou in southern China crashes into a mountain, killing all 141 persons aboard.

Dec. 21—A powerful wind gust blows a Dutch charter plane out of control, and it crashes while trying to land at Faro, Portugal; at least 54 persons are killed.

Dec. 22—All 157 persons aboard a Libyan airliner die when a jet traveling from Benghazi to Tripoli crashes.

FIRES AND EXPLOSIONS

Jan. 17—A natural-gas explosion in Chicago, IL, sets off a series of fires; as least three persons are killed, and 18 buildings on the city's north side are damaged or destroyed.

March 3—At least 270 miners are feared dead after a methane gas explosion rips through a coal mine in Kozlu, Turkey.

April 22—At least 190 are killed and more than 1,400 are injured when a series of sewer explosions rocks a 20-block area in Guadalajara, Mexico.

May 9—Twenty-six miners are trapped and killed in a coal-mine explosion in northern Nova Scotia.

Dec. 7—An explosion in a coal mine in southwest Virginia traps eight miners inside; all are feared dead as rescue efforts fail.

LAND AND SEA TRANSPORTATION

March 3—An express train and freight train collide near the town of Nelidovo, Russia, killing at least 40 persons.

March 8—An oil tanker collides with a ferry crowded with religious pilgrims in the Gulf of Thailand, leaving 87 dead.

March 24—A tanker truck filled with liquid ammonia explodes and burns in Dakar, Senegal, killing at least 60 persons.

April 3—Fifty-five persons are killed when a bus explodes near Yiyang, China.

April 25—Nine persons are killed and 50 are injured in a series of motorcycle accidents among fans at the 24-hour Le Mans motorcycle race in France.

May 15—A bus bursts into flames in northern Taiwan, killing 20 children and three adults.

June 17—Forty-eight persons are killed when a military bus and a fuel-oil tanker collide and catch fire near Mersa Matruh, Egypt.

Nov. 1—Fourteen are killed and at least 60 injured in Pakistan when an express train careens into a parked freight train.

STORMS, FLOODS, AND EARTHQUAKES

Feb. 1—Avalanches caused by heavy rains hit several remote villages in southeast Turkey, killing at least 170 persons.

March 10—Six persons are left dead and much damage is done when a series of severe storms strikes several Southern and Midwestern states.

March 15—The second strong earthquake in three days hits eastern Turkey; altogether, the quakes kill nearly 500 persons.

May 13—Torrential rains in Uzbekistan cause mud slides which kill at least 200 persons.

May 20—At least 36 persons are killed when an earthquake rocks northern Pakistan.

Aug. 8–12—Heavy rains and hailstorms hit northern China, causing floods and landslides that leave at least 111 dead.

Aug. 19—An earthquake strikes the Kyrgyzstan-China border, killing more than 50 persons.

Aug. 24—In what is considered the costliest storm in U.S. history, Hurricane Andrew strikes southern Florida, killing 18 persons and leaving at least 250,000 homeless.

Sept. 1—A strong earthquake off the Pacific coast of Nicaragua sets off a tidal wave, killing at least 116 persons in Nicaragua.

Sept. 4—At least 400 are killed when a flash flood strikes Gulbahar, Afghanistan.

Sept. 11—Hurricane Iniki strikes the western Hawaiian islands, causing widespread devastation and leaving four persons dead.

Sept. 18—Over the past month, devastating floods in northern Pakistan and India have killed more than 2,500 persons.

Sept. 22—Heavy rains and strong winds sweep across southern France, causing flash floods and killing 39 persons.

Oct. 12—A strong earthquake strikes 20 mi (32 km) southwest of Cairo, Egypt, killing approximately 550 persons.

Oct. 18—The second major earthquake in three days hits Colombia, killing at least ten persons.

Nov. 22—A series of tornadoes strikes many Southern and Midwestern states, leaving at least 16 dead and injuring more than 100 others.

Dec. 8—A mud slide caused by torrential rains buries at least 100 workers, and possibly many more, at a gold mine in Llipi, Bolivia.

Dec. 12—A quake measuring 7.5 on the Richter scale kills at least 2,200 persons in the Flores region of Indonesia. At least 90% of the buildings at Maumere are destroyed.

MISCELLANEOUS

Feb. 29—The roof of an Arab cafe in Jerusalem, Israel, collapses, killing at least 23.

March 19—A landslide buries part of a shantytown near Belo Horizonte, Brazil, killing 31 persons.

May 5—Thirteen persons are left dead when temporary bleachers at a soccer match in Corsica collapse suddenly.

July 23—In northern Vietnam, at least 23 persons are buried when a landslide strikes the Tra Linh district north of Hanoi.

ADVERTISING

The economic recession continued to hurt the U.S. advertising, marketing, and media industries, but the year 1992 showed a slight improvement over 1991. Executives thus were guardedly optimistic about a mild recovery.

The anticipated quadrennial ad-spending boost from the 1992 Olympic Games failed to materialize but ad spending for the presidential election campaign was up. Independent candidate Ross Perot broke new ground with his 30-minute infomercials. Most media companies and ad agencies had cut costs and pared staffs so much in 1990–91 that they were able to avoid such measures in 1992.

Controversies. Two of the leading breweries in the United States went to court over a comparative TV-advertising campaign in which Anheuser-Busch challenged Coors Brewing Company's longtime claim of using pure Rocky Mountain spring water in its products. Coors filed a $10 million damage suit against Anheuser-Busch and unsuccessfully asked for a temporary injunction against the ads. Anheuser-Busch, meanwhile, countersued to stop Coors from using the Rocky Mountain water motif in future advertising. Both suits were pending when Anheuser-Busch ran a second TV ad that again claimed Coors was diluting Coors Light.

Coca-Cola Co., meanwhile, revealed that Hollywood talent agency Creative Artists Agency, which was hired as a creative consultant in 1991, actually was creating TV commercials for its flagship brand, Coca-Cola Classic. This was the first time that commercials for a major national marketer were created and produced by anyone other than a traditional ad agency. Some in the ad industry feared that other clients might follow suit and look outside ad agencies for creative talent.

Elsewhere, adman Tom McElligott, co-founder of McElligott Wright Morrison White in Minneapolis, was the victim of an unexpected coup when his three partners attempted to oust him as chairman, chief executive officer (CEO), and creative director. McElligott fought the attempted takeover and the three partners joined other agencies. The agency lost several accounts, however.

General Motors Corp. shocked the ad industry by placing the estimated $140 million advertising account for its Oldsmobile division up for review. Leo Burnett Co. had handled the account since 1967. General Motors has not dismissed an agency on a vehicle-brand advertising assignment since 1958.

Media Moves. Time Warner President and co-CEO Nicholas J. Nicholas, Jr., was replaced by Vice-Chairman-CEO Gerald M. Levin. Nicholas had been considered heir apparent to Chairman and co-CEO Steve Ross but apparently differed with him over the future direction of the communications company. CBS emerged as the top-ranked network in the annual prime-time sweepstakes for the first time in seven years. Perennial winner NBC finished second. CBS' success was attributed to an effective marketing program, based on such hit shows as *Murphy Brown*. NBC's ratings decline continued speculation that it would be sold by General Electric Co.

Longtime *Tonight Show* host Johnny Carson retired and was replaced by Jay Leno. The move sparked new shows and heightened a running feud between Leno and rival Arsenio Hall. It also was rumored that NBC late-night star David Letterman would leave the network after his contract expires in 1993. Marketers welcomed the turmoil because it offered a new variety of advertising opportunities.

Creative. *Advertising Age* named Weiden & Kennedy, which is based in Portland, OR, as 1991's agency of the year. Barcelona-based Casadevall Pedreno SPR won the Grand Prix prize for a humorous TV spot at the International Advertising Film Festival. This was the second time in four years that a Spanish agency won the top prize.

The new managers of the Clio advertising awards hosted an orderly, professional ceremony despite limited participation by top agencies still wary of the organization's credibility.

Ad Volume and Acquisitions. The McCann-Erickson ad agency predicted in June that U.S. advertising spending would increase 5% in 1992 to $132.7 billion. This was down from a previous prediction of a 6.2% rise. Worldwide, the agency predicted growth of 5.2% to $294.5 billion. ABC, CBS, and NBC, along with Fox Broadcasting, reported $3.7 billion in sales for the 1992–93 network-TV up-front market, up slightly from the $3.5 billion spent in 1991–92.

The biggest acquisitions took place on the client side as Colgate Palmolive Co. bought privately owned Mennen Co. for $670 million and Germany's Benckiser purchased Coty from Pfizer for more than $450 million. On the agency side, Omnicom Group completed its purchase of Goodby Berlin & Silverstein of San Francisco.

Personalities. Flamboyant adman Jerry Della Femina left the agency that bears his name after selling his shares to his French partners at Euro RSCG. Della Femina first opened a restaurant on Long Island, NY, and in November began a new agency called Jerry, Inc., when he landed the *Newsweek* magazine account. . . . Charlotte Beers became the most powerful woman in the U.S. advertising industry when she was named chairperson and CEO at Ogilvy & Mather Worldwide. . . . Barry Diller surprised the entertainment industry by resigning as chairman of Fox Inc., which includes Fox Broadcasting Corp. Diller was rumored to be considering a bid for NBC.

JOHN WOLFE, *"Advertising Age"*

© Luc Delahaye/Sipa

In April 1992 rebels celebrate the fall of the former Soviet-backed regime in Afghanistan. More than 2 million Afghans were killed and some 6 million Afghans became refugees during the 13-year war between the government and the rebels.

AFGHANISTAN

After 13 years, Marxist-Leninist rule in Afghanistan ended in 1992, but the coalition government that followed was weak and divided. Instead of creating a new unity, the death of communism sharpened splits among non-Communists. In late 1992, Afghan domestic violence threatened to spill over into Tajikistan.

Political Developments. President Najib, who had ruled since 1986 thanks to Soviet support, survived in power until April. Although controlling only Kabul and a few other large towns, his forces had fought off repeated assaults by the resistance. But after the former Soviet Union shut off all aid on Jan. 1, 1992, Najib's 75,000 bureaucrats and 150,000 security forces were left without subsistence.

On March 18, Tajik forces under resistance leader Ahmad Shah Massoud cooperated with Gen. Abdul Rashid Dostam's Uzbek militia to declare autonomy in the northern provinces around Mazar-e-Sharif. The new district lay astride the main communications lines from the former Soviet Union.

Najib tried to flee the country on April 16, but General Dostam's militia, which controlled the Kabul airport, turned him back. Najib then took refuge in the UN's Kabul offices and dropped from public view. (It later was rumored that he had escaped to Russia.) Within a week the remaining government strong points outside the capital had collapsed. The resistance had agreed that an interim government of 30 field commanders, ten Islamic clerics, and ten exile representatives would take power once the Communists fell. In anticipation of a "consensus liberation" by this coalition, Massoud delayed occupying Kabul. But when his rival, Gulbuddin Hekmatyar, entered the city and tried to seize power on April 26, Massoud and Dostam joined forces to drive him out.

Sibghatullah Mojadidi, the leader of a small Pakistan-based exile political group, crossed the border into Afghanistan on April 27 and assumed the presidency. By agreement, he served for two months and was succeeded by Burhanuddin Rabbani, leader of a larger exile group, for a four-month term. The new government included two other exile leaders—Abdul Rassul Sayaf and Sayed Ahmed Gailani, as ministers of interior and foreign affairs, respectively—and Massoud as minister of defense.

Hekmatyar, who had been picked to be vice-president, now refused to join the government, protesting the Uzbek militia's former allegiance to Najib and demanding its dissolution. Indeed the militia had been notorious for its excesses against non-Communists and especially non-Uzbeks, but Hekmatyar's own ongoing collaboration with former regime officials was just as opportunistic. Forced out of Kabul in April, Hekmatyar began a rocket bombardment of the city that continued into the autumn, causing some 3,000 deaths and driving a half million Kabulis from their city.

But the government had little practical power, even in Kabul itself. Elsewhere, pro-

AFGHANISTAN · Information Highlights

Official Name: Republic of Afghanistan.
Location: Central Asia.
Area: 250,000 sq mi (647 500 km²).
Population: (mid-1992 est.): 16,900,000.
Chief Cities (1988 est.): Kabul, the capital, 1,424,400; Kandahar, 225,500; Herat, 177,000.
Government: Burhanuddin Rabbani, general secretary, People's Democratic Party (appointed June 29, 1992) and president; Fazil Haq Khaliqyar, prime minister (named April 1990). *Legislature*—bicameral National Assembly.
Monetary Unit: Afghani (50.6 afghanis equal U.S.$1, June 1992).
Gross Domestic Product (1989 est. U.S.$): $3,000,000,000.
Foreign Trade (1991 U.S.$): *Imports,* $884,000,000; *exports,* $235,000,000.

vincial centers quietly set up their own governments. Rabbani was elected to a two-year term as president in December, in a vote boycotted by several factions. He did seem to be gaining some support at year's end, however.

Socioeconomic Developments. Communism's fall meant the imposition of strict Islamic practices not only in the provinces, where they always had survived anyway, but in Kabul itself. Women went veiled and alcohol was strictly prohibited. Unfortunately, robbery, looting, and a backlash of vigilante justice also took hold. In May unknown assailants abducted, tortured, and murdered the former regime's chief justice, Karim Shadan. Simultaneously, a proclaimed amnesty for party members was suspended after atrocities by the Najib government were revealed. In September three men were hanged publicly for unspecified crimes. Unbridled vengeance threatened to outdo Communist oppression even as Hekmatyar's rockets continued to fall on Kabul.

Hekmatyar's strength lay mainly in his Pashtun origins. Before the 1979 Soviet invasion, Pashtuns were Afghanistan's largest and traditionally ruling ethnic group. The second- and third-most-numerous peoples, the Tajiks and Uzbeks, were represented by Massoud and Dostam, respectively. The Hazaras, who found political strength not in one leader but in a half dozen independent resistance groups, were a smaller but fervently ethnocentric minority.

The war sharply reduced Pashtun numbers in Afghanistan. They were overrepresented in the one third of the population that had been driven into foreign exile, and Tajiks became the largest group that remained. The main Tajik leaders, Massoud and Ismail Khan, also had attracted a following among pluralistically minded Pashtuns, but for many Pashtuns Hekmatyar's championing of their return to power outweighed all other considerations.

By the end of July, an estimated 600,000 of the 3.2 million Afghan refugees in Pakistan had come home. By mid-September, some 176,000 had returned from Iran. Pashtun numbers were increasing, but the other ethnic groups—especially the Hazaras, who were formerly at the bottom of the social scale—were resolved not to let them dominate. As early as June, more than 100 persons died when fighting erupted between Hazaras and Pashtuns in Kabul.

Afghanistan's economy was surprisingly resilient. Although the afghani varied between 1,400 and 2,000 to the dollar, food prices were lower by May, and nomads were resuming their migration patterns. Most of the violence was confined to Kabul; the rest of the country was repairing the war's devastation.

Outside Powers' Involvement. In October 1991 the United States had canceled its military aid to the Afghan resistance. In March 1992, after Russian subsidies to Kabul had ceased, Najib asked for U.S. aid, saying he would fight terrorism, drug trafficking, and Islamic fundamentalism. The request was ignored. When the interim government took power, U.S. policy was to support it, but to leave political advice to the UN. In June the United States played a role in trying to secure the release of 30–50 former Soviet servicemen held by the resistance and the return to Afghanistan of some 500 children taken to Soviet boarding schools.

Russia recognized the interim government on April 30. Moscow's main concern was the return of its soldiers captured during the war. Russian Foreign Minister Andrei Kozyrev visited Kabul in mid-May and arranged for the release of three. But in August, after Hekmatyar's rockets killed two Russian-embassy personnel and destroyed one of the planes sent to evacuate the rest, the last 50 Russian employees, including the ambassador, had to leave secretly in a plane provided by Dostam. The French, Bulgarian, and Italian embassies removed their staffs at the end of August.

Pakistan had backed Hekmatyar, but now turned away from him. Pakistan's Prime Minister Nawaz Sharif personally flew to Kabul to recognize the interim government on April 29. But Pakistani influence in Kabul was fading, and cutting the Hekmatyar link only annoyed Pakistani radicals still in favor of the uncompromising resistance leader.

India and Iran played relatively minor roles in Afghanistan. India offended many Afghans when it offered Najib asylum in April. Iran's advice to the Afghans to make peace and its proclaimed cutoff of military aid to the Hazaras did not lower the level of fighting. In fact, the huge stockpiles of weapons accumulated in Afghanistan began to play a role in neighboring Tajikistan, where political tensions were mounting. In September, Russian troops took over guarding the Tajik-Afghan border to stop arms smuggling, but were able to intercept only about one third of the weapons. As the smugglers shot at the troops, it was clear that for the Russians the Afghan war was not over.

ANTHONY ARNOLD, *Author: "Afghanistan: The Soviet Invasion in Perspective"*

AFRICA

The year 1992 was one of ballots and bullets in sub-Saharan Africa. The hopes raised by the continuing move throughout much of the region toward democracy were at times realized and at times traduced by the manipulation of sitting presidents as in Cameroon and Zaire and by the unwillingness of competing political movements to play fair as in Nigeria or to accept the decision of their peoples as apparently was the case in Angola. In other countries—especially, Somalia and Liberia—there were no elections or even internal security, only continuing civil wars with much death and destruction and no early end in sight.

Political Trends. Several of the democratic governments elected and installed in the past several years—for example, in Benin and Zambia—continued to govern and began to confront the difficult economic challenges facing them. The government of President Frederick Chiluba in Zambia successfully removed subsidies on the price of maize, which had become a major drain on the government's budget. The government of Ethiopia, taking power after defeating the army of former President Mengistu Haile-Mariam on the battlefield, promised elections in 1994 and held local elections during 1992. Difficult to organize and administer, the elections provoked accusations of fraud. Meanwhile, the government in Addis Ababa presided over an uneasy peace after three decades of internal war. Independence for the province of Eritrea after a two-year waiting period was taken for granted. However, the peace was fragile, broken by clashes between the Oromo Liberation Front—the largest of several parties representing the Oromo people, 40% of the population of the country. The economy remained weak while the government began implementing economic reforms, starting with a devaluation of the currency.

The move toward political liberalization in the region also continued, with presidential elections held in Angola, Ghana, Cameroon, Madagascar, and Kenya. A referendum on multiparty politics was expected in Malawi, a country which had been ruled by one man— Hastings Kamuzu Banda—and his political party since independence. In Zaire a national conference of Zairians from all walks of life debated the shape of the country's future political system. In Mozambique the government and the insurgency movement, Renamo, signed a peace agreement and agreed to move toward elections. And negotiations on a new constitution among the government of President F. W. de Klerk, the African National Congress (ANC), and the Inkatha movement in South Africa continued with some interruptions.

However, these continuing signs of political liberalization were not all they seemed. The election in Cameroon in October, which President Paul Biya won, was regarded widely as full of irregularities. In Nigeria, President Ibrahim Babangida canceled the results of the party primaries to choose the candidates of the two parties because of widespread fraud and vote buying. He postponed the presidential election,

In Mali, Alpha Omar Konaré, a former teacher and a key figure in the removal of President Moussa Traoré in 1991, was elected president in the second round of voting in April 1992. Several African nations went to the polls in 1992.

scheduled for December, until June 1993. The first round of presidential elections in Angola, in which President José Eduardo dos Santos gained the most votes, was followed by renewed fighting by the Union for the Total Independence of Angola (UNITA). UNITA, led by Jonas Savimbi and long supported by South Africa and the United States, had been fighting against the government of President dos Santos —head of the Popular Movement for the Liberation of Angola (MPLA), a Marxist-oriented party long supported by the Soviet Union and Cuba—since the country's independence in 1975. It appeared that Savimbi was unprepared to accept the results of the first round of voting and the possibility of defeat in a second round.

In Zaire the national conference continued to meet and politicians maneuvered for position. President Mobutu Sese Seko remained in power, lived on his yacht in the Zaire River, and printed money to finance his weakening government. Inflation in Zaire exceeded 1,000%. Nguza Karl-I-Bond—first in opposition to the Mobutu regime, then joining it, and then withdrawing—began to warn that his copper-rich province, Shaba, would not accept the political leadership of Étienne Tshisekedi, whom President Mobutu reluctantly appointed prime minister at the insistence of the national conference. Meanwhile, economic conditions continued to deteriorate in Zaire and no one was predicting when the political stalemate would be resolved.

The election in Kenya and the referendum in Malawi were the result of intense external pressure rather than the willingness of sitting presidents to liberalize their political systems and test their mandates through the ballot box. Foreign-aid donors cut off their aid to both countries until their governments agreed to open up to liberalize their political systems. It was largely for that reason that political change or the promise of change had occurred. Many outside observers worried that political liberalization under such conditions well could be manipulated by existing governments and exacerbate ethnic tension, particularly in Kenya, where President Daniel Arap Moi had expressed his view that open political competition would increase violence among peoples of different ethnic origins. There was some ethnic violence in Kenya during the year and many critics of the Moi regime alleged that the violence had been provoked by the regime itself to prove its point.

The year in South Africa was an eventful one. The white minority government there, committed to negotiations with the black majority on a new constitution that finally would provide them with political rights, lost a by-election in February to a Conservative candidate who opposed power-sharing. In a daring move, President de Klerk called for a national referendum (with only whites voting) on whether to negotiate a political settlement with the country's black majority. The result of the referendum was strongly supportive of de Klerk's continuing to negotiate with the black majority, though the wording of the referendum itself left little room for nuances or disagreements on details. The rest of the year was filled with maneuvering among the various political groups within South Africa: the more liberal whites supporting de Klerk's negotiations; the conservative whites opposing power-sharing with the nonwhite population; the ANC; Inkatha, led by Chief Mangosuthu Buthelezi and representing primarily the Zulu people; and the Pan African Congress, small but militant and vocal.

Violence in the black townships and elsewhere continued, including attacks by ANC and Inkatha members on one another and a massacre of ANC militants in Boipatong in June by local police, another massacre of ANC demonstrators against the "independent" government of the homeland of Ciskei, and accusations by the ANC that the government was provoking or at least turning a blind eye to violence against its members. The violence and political maneuvering stalled progress on negotiations on power-sharing and the establishment of an interim government.

Violence. Bullets shared the stage with ballots in much of the rest of Africa. A military coup led by a 26-year-old army captain in Sierra Leone promised an end to corruption and misrule that had characterized past regimes in that small West African country. The people cheered in the streets at the announcement of the coup, but tough challenges lay ahead for the new leaders. The little war in Rwanda, a tiny country in East Africa, ground on with the rebels—exiled Tutsis (a minority people in the country)—challenging the government of the majority Hutus. The Tutsis appeared to be supported by the neighboring Ugandan regime, while the French intervened to protect the sitting Hutu government. Midyear efforts by France and the United States at brokering a peace produced little progress.

It was also bullets that were predominant in Sudan, where a government inspired by Islamic fundamentalism ruled in Khartoum and fought with insurgency movements based in the south of the country that objected to the imposition of Islamic *Sharia* law throughout the country, Arabization, and oppressive rule from the north. The war ground on throughout the year and, together with the drought, produced many refugees and an uncertain number of deaths. Foreign relief efforts often were stymied by both sides in the conflict attempting to deprive each other of essential foods.

The worst human tragedy in Africa and perhaps in the world in 1992 was in Somalia, where warlords and their well-armed followers challenged each other for predominance. The

Nations of southern Africa were affected by horrible drought in 1992. Residents of Mozambique, left, dug for what little water they could obtain.

© Peter Magubane/Gamma-Liaison

continuing conflicts between them, combined with erratic rainfall, produced a human disaster of enormous proportions, with many thousands of Somalis dying from war wounds and above all from starvation. The worst scenes were those of young men, armed with AK-47s, beating their starving countrymen—often old men, women, and children—as the latter clamored for food from relief agencies. The armed men were believed to be stealing much of the food to feed themselves and their comrades. There were surprisingly few efforts by Somalia's neighboring states in Africa and across the Red Sea in Arabia to help resolve the conflict. And the international community responded to the spreading disaster there hesitantly, taking a long time to recognize the extent of the tragedy, until the United States (with the support of the UN) sent in troops to ensure the delivery of relief supplies.

Another conflict, on the other side of the continent, brought its measure of death and destruction. Several warring factions in Liberia for several years had been attempting to gain control of the entire country. The intervention of a force of West African soldiers, organized by the Economic Community of West African States (ECOWAS), to halt the conflict and promote election had created a political stalemate in which one of the factions, led by Charles Taylor (believed to be supported by Col. Muammar Qaddafi of Libya), resisted elections and the disarming of his troops. Taylor continued to occupy most of the country but not the capital. At the beginning of November, his forces began to attack the capital in an effort to gain power through bullets rather than ballots.

Other News. In addition to ballots and bullets, there was other news in Africa in 1992. The bad news included the worst drought on record in parts of East and much of southern Africa. In Zimbabwe the lack of rainfall resulted in a drop in maize production of 90% and a sharp decline in sugar, cotton, and soybeans as well. The government of Zimbabwe compounded its agricultural problems by passing a law permitting it to purchase land from large commercial farmers at prices set by the government. Many of the large commercial farmers are white and produce a significant proportion of the food surplus and export crops. Many Africans, permitted to farm only in specified reserves during the colonial period, aspired to own land and expected the government to provide them with that land as it had promised before it came to power in the early 1980s. Compulsory land purchase by the government had scared a number of the commercial farmers, who began to relocate to Zambia and Mozambique, taking up offers of land for cultivation from governments of those countries.

In Kenya the historically unprecedented high population growth rates—averaging 4% per year and resulting in a doubling of the population every two decades—were beginning to decline. Fertility rates (the number of births per woman in her lifetime) in the cities showed a decrease and demographers were hoping that it indicated the start of the "demographic transition" that had occurred in other parts of the developing world when families reduced the number of births due to the improved rate of child survival and their economic circumstances. In Zimbabwe there were reports of rising use of condoms, another sign that Africans were prepared to practice family planning and reduce the number of births if birth-control devices were available. A reduction in the rapid increase in population in Africa was regarded by many development specialists as essential if the standard of living of the average African was to rise, if government services ever were to reach the bulk of the peoples, and if severe environmental degradation was to be avoided.

CAROL LANCASTER
Georgetown University

AGRICULTURE

Major developments in world agriculture in 1992 included new reforms to privatize farms in Eastern Europe and the republics of the former Soviet Union; a North American Free Trade Agreement (NAFTA) affecting future agricultural trade among the United States, Canada, and Mexico; adverse weather in parts of Europe, Asia, Africa, and North America that restricted agricultural production; and continued research to improve agricultural productivity. In addition, efforts to develop new products and markets from agricultural produce continued.

World grain production resumed its upward trend after a brief interruption in 1991. However, the growth rate was slightly below the long-term average and about half as large as world-population growth. Production was restrained by the worst drought in decades in southern Africa and Australia, drought in the western United States and northern Europe, hurricane damage along the U.S. Gulf Coast, severe flooding in India and China, and freeze damage to Canadian crops. Despite weather problems, world grain and oilseed crops slightly exceeded global utilization, creating the potential for a small increase in reserve supplies to help offset future weather problems. World cotton production was slightly below the previous year's big crop, due to adverse weather in the three largest producing areas—China, the United States, and the former Soviet Union.

United States

Production and Income. U.S. and world poultry production and consumption continued to increase, reflecting consumer trends toward low-cost, healthy, and convenient foods. U.S. pork and beef supplies also rose as farmers responded to declining feed costs and slightly increased profitability. Production of fish from U.S. fish farms remained in a sharp upward trend, also adding to the nation's meat supply. U.S. catfish production from January through June rose 22% above a year earlier. Near-record cool summer temperatures in the Midwest provided adequate but slightly below-normal supplies of canning and freezing vegetables such as snap beans, sweet corn, peas, and tomatoes. Fruit production was mixed, with plentiful supplies of apples and pears, but with reduced supplies of strawberries, peaches, and pineapple. Citrus supplies expanded as California production recovered from the severe 1991 freeze.

The western one fourth of the United States remained in a serious drought situation because of below-normal snowpack and rainfall. Severely affected areas included the Pacific Northwest, California, Nevada, and Idaho.

Parts of California and Nevada were in their sixth consecutive year of drought. Agriculture, agribusiness, crop production, and farm income in those areas all suffered. Water shortages in heavily irrigated areas caused continued conflicts between farmers and urban water users.

Along the Gulf Coast of Florida and Louisiana, agriculture and agribusinesses were damaged severely in late summer by Hurricane Andrew. Crops affected included avocados, limes, vegetables, soybeans, rice, cotton, sugarcane, and nursery and ornamental crops. Hurricane Iniki caused extensive damage to the Hawaiian sugar crop and sugar mills, with some damage to nut crops, coffee, papaya, guava, and banana orchards.

U.S. farm income held about steady, with a small percentage of farm families in serious financial trouble. With better income prospects in other occupations, young people continued to leave agriculture, causing farm numbers to decline and farm sizes to increase. Declining farm populations intensified economic stress on many rural areas, particularly west of the Mississippi River where rural off-farm employment opportunities are limited. U.S. Census data indicated that the nation lost 24% of its farmers in the decade of the 1980s.

Policy and Programs. Major 1992 domestic-policy issues for U.S. agriculture included wetland regeneration, soil conservation, ground-water-contamination control, food-inspection standards and procedures, corn-based ethanol fuels, and export-enhancement policies.

The U.S. Department of Agriculture enrolled another 1.1 million acres (445 344 ha) of highly erodible and environmentally sensitive farmland in the Conservation Reserve Program (CRP), a long-term program mandated by Congress. The CRP was in its seventh year and at year's end contained 36.5 million acres (14.8 million ha), the equivalent of slightly more than one tenth of the nation's currently used cropland. It protects steep slopes from soil erosion while providing wildlife habitat and reducing surface water pollution from agricultural sources. Landowners receive annual rental payments for ten years to compensate for removing land from production.

Officials continued to develop the nation's policy for maintaining and reclaiming wetlands for wildlife habitat and water-pollution control. In 1992 the U.S. Department of Agriculture implemented a small pilot Wetland Reserve Program (WRP) in nine states. The WRP pays farmers for ten years for removing potential wetland from production and converting it to wildlife habitat. Crop farmers also implemented initial phases of soil-conservation compliance plans that must be implemented fully by 1995 for the farmers to remain eligible for government-program benefits. This program requires tillage practices that keep crop resi-

© Dirck Halstead/Gamma-Liaison

In Humboldt, SD, on Sept. 2, 1992, President Bush announced a $1 billion program to subsidize U.S. wheat sales overseas. He later promised increased aid to farmers whose crops were damaged by Hurricane Andrew and flooding in east Texas.

dues on the surface of erodible soils to slow rainfall runoff, thus reducing erosion and groundwater contamination. Other practices used to reduce erosion include strip cropping, sod waterways, and terraces.

Farmers also expanded the use of Integrated Pest Management (IPM), a system that uses professional scouting for crop pests and application of pesticides for insect, weed, and disease control only where economic-damage thresholds have been reached. IPM also uses biological controls where possible. The system reduces production costs, while helping to protect the environment.

Trade Policies. U.S. corn growers welcomed the newly negotiated North American Free Trade Agreement (NAFTA) and potentially greater access to Mexican markets. Fruit and vegetable producers, however, worried about increased Mexican competition due to lower labor costs. Livestock producers and processors anticipated greater access to a growing market in Mexico but stressed that U.S. quality and inspection standards should be maintained on food entering the United States from Mexico. The agreement, which remained to be ratified by the U.S. Congress as 1992 ended, requires products imported from Mexico to meet U.S. hygienic and pesticide-residue regulations.

U.S. farmers also gained greater access to corn-processor markets in Japan through a trade agreement with that nation. Quotas on Japan's imports of corn were scheduled to increase in 1993–94, with opportunity for U.S. agriculture to participate in growing Japanese starch and ethanol markets. U.S. beef exports to Japan continued to increase in response to trade liberalization and growing consumer demand.

International

Eastern Europe and the Former Soviet Union. Food prices in the nations of Eastern Europe and the former USSR were decontrolled and government agricultural subsidies were reduced or eliminated in the transition toward market economies. Several republics also returned land to previous owners or their heirs, as a step toward restoring private ownership of farms. Price decontrols and reduced subsidies sharply reduced livestock-product consumption and production. However, winter food shortages were much less than expected because of financial assistance from the United States, the European Community (EC), Canada, and Japan. In September the United States extended to Russia a new $1.15 billion food-assistance package covering imports in late 1992 and early 1993, along with financial assistance for other smaller republics. The United States also offered barter trade to help deal with limited credit availability.

South America. Crops were good in South America's major grain- and oilseed-exporting countries. Late in the year, Brazil sharply increased credit to its farmers to encourage increased crop plantings for the 1993 harvest. Improved crops helped support the agricultural economy of the area. Chile continued its strong growth in fresh-fruit exports. With its summer reversed six months from Northern Hemisphere nations, the country can supply fresh products for winter markets in North America, Europe, and the Middle East. Major exports include grapes, peaches, and apples. Chile placed added emphasis on market development in 1992 to diversify into exports of plums, cherries, pears, kiwifruit, and strawberries as well as fresh vegetables. It maintained competitive costs through improved and expanded irrigation, as well as efficient warehousing and refrigerated shipping.

Eastern and Southern Asia. Despite weather problems including floods, drought in some areas, and a late start to monsoon rains, the crops of the eastern and southern Asia region matched those of 1991. China continued to export corn but imported wheat. India and Pakistan remained large importers of vegetable oil, and Pakistan imported wheat. Per-capita food production in the region's largest countries remained about constant, while animal- and poultry-product consumption increased in areas with strong economic growth, including South Korea, Taiwan, Japan, Singapore, Hong Kong, and Thailand. Vietnam maintained recent large gains in rice production and continued to export rice. Indonesia was a growth market for U.S. farm products and remained an important supplier of rubber, spices, coffee, cocoa, mushrooms, and coconut oil.

Western Europe. Drought in northwestern Europe reduced grain and oilseed production, but record stocks were used to maintain large exports and domestic use. The EC lowered its price supports slightly for farm products and continued its modest land-idling policy to help control surpluses. It also moved closer to the full integration of member economies scheduled for January 1993. Unification would eliminate trade restrictions among member nations and bring common hygienic standards and inspection procedures for EC agricultural products. It would create the world's largest market for farm and nonfarm products.

Africa. Crops were good in north Africa but southern African nations experienced the most severe drought in decades, along with areas of famine and large imports even in some normally exporting countries. U.S. and EC financial aid helped cover immediate food needs of the area. Lagging agricultural production in central and parts of southern Africa also has a long-term dimension, with limited funds for investment in improved varieties, fertilizer, irrigation, reclaiming desert lands, and other yield-improving technology. In addition, government policies were limiting farm income and investment incentives. Little progress was made in dealing with these long-term African agricultural problems in 1992, although new research programs began to focus on its agricultural sector.

Research and New Product Development

Researchers and agribusiness firms worked to improve agricultural productivity and match farm products more closely with market needs. Emerging research included development of genetic-mapping techniques for corn, a joint public agency-private firm effort to develop insect-resistant crops, and efforts to create more productive crop varieties for developing countries. One project targets potatoes, pumpkins, sweet potatoes, bananas, coffee, and pineapples for development of higher-yielding varieties through conventional plant breeding and biotechnology. Research goals include improved pest and disease resistance, better adaptation of varieties to local climates, increased yield potential, and training of developing-country scientists.

Consumer and agricultural groups in the United States and Europe continued to delay adoption of the milk-production-increasing hormone, *Bovine somatotropin* (BST), to further evaluate its safety for consumers and effects on dairy cows. Research showed no adverse effects on milk, since the product is a naturally occurring hormone that dairy animals produce in their bodies. In other research developments, the U.S. Department of Agriculture released a new line of corn that is resistant to aflatoxin to seed companies for development into commercial hybrids. Aflatoxin is a carcinogen from mold that develops in cornfields under extreme hot, dry conditions. U.S. federal regulations prohibit interstate movement of corn with more than 20 parts per billion of aflatoxin since it is hazardous to livestock and humans. Commercial aflatoxin-resistant corn is expected to be available to farmers within five years.

ROBERT WISNER, *Iowa State University*

ALABAMA

The elections and governmental problems related to finances and alleged ethical misconduct dominated Alabama news in 1992.

Elections. The biggest change in Alabama's U.S. House of Representatives contingent since 1984 occurred as a result of the fall elections. The seven-member delegation was chosen on the basis of a redistricting plan approved by Republican-appointed federal judges rather than the state legislature. The assembly adopted an alternative plan on March 5 and

Surrounded by supporters and draped in chains on Jan. 23, 1992, Birmingham, AL, Mayor Richard Arlington surrendered to U.S. marshals on a contempt of court citation. The mayor was found in contempt for refusing to turn over his records to a U.S. grand jury investigating corruption charges. The mayor said that the investigation was racially motivated.

© Mike Clemmer/Picture Group

overrode a veto by Gov. Guy Hunt (R). However, on March 27 both the Justice Department and the U.S. Supreme Court rejected it.

Congressional primaries were held in June. Democratic State Sen. Earl Hilliard of Birmingham, a black, won a historic nomination —and later election—in the solidly Democratic, black-majority 7th U.S. District. Two members of the House delegation retired in 1992—Claude Harris (D) and William Dickinson (R). In other primary decisions, voters selected Democrat George Wallace, Jr., the son and namesake of the former Alabama governor, and Republican Terry Everett as congressional nominees in the 2d District and former state Sen. Spencer Bacchus to oppose incumbent Democratic Rep. Ben Erdreich in the 6th District. U.S. Sen. Richard Shelby easily won renomination in the Democratic primary.

Bill Clinton did no general-election campaigning in Alabama. However, both President George Bush and Vice-President Dan Quayle did, with good results. On November 3, Alabama remained in the GOP column in the presidential tally, giving the defeated incumbent, Bush, 48% of its vote, his successful Democratic opponent, Bill Clinton, 41%, and independent H. Ross Perot 11%.

On election day, Republicans Bacchus and Everett prevailed over Erdreich and Wallace, marking the first time a member of Alabama's premier political family had lost an election since 1958. Senator Shelby and incumbent Democratic Reps. Bud Cramer, Tom Bevil, and Glenn Browder easily retained their seats, as did Republican Rep. Sonny Callahan.

Education. The state continued to be in serious financial difficulty in 1992. Although many programs suffered, most attention was focused on schools. The legislature declined to pass a tax-reform program which, it was hoped, ultimately might provide more money for education and other needs. Meanwhile a state circuit court considered whether the state's formula for financing its schools discriminated against children in poorer areas.

The Governor. Guy Hunt again was confronted in 1992 with allegations of unethical conduct. The governor contended that he was not subject to the state's ethics law, but on May 28 a federal district court ruled that he was, and this was upheld on appeal. On July 15 an 18-member grand jury was impaneled to investigate Hunt's use of state aircraft to travel to preaching sites where offerings were taken. On September 9, Hunt acknowledged that in 1986 he had received two checks for $5,000 each (neither reported as a campaign contribution) from a real-estate developer who later was appointed to the state liquor board. On December 28, Hunt was indicted on 13 charges.

Former Governor Wallace was diagnosed on August 27 as having Parkinson's disease. On September 25 he was hospitalized again. He overcame a massive blood infection, however, and was released after a few weeks.

WILLIAM H. STEWART, *University of Alabama*

ALABAMA • Information Highlights

Area: 51,705 sq mi (133 915 km²).

Population (July 1, 1991 est.): 4,089,000.

Chief Cities (1990 census): Montgomery, the capital, 187,106; Birmingham, 265,968; Mobile, 196,278; Huntsville, 159,789.

Government (1992): *Chief officers*—governor, Guy Hunt (R); lt. gov. Jim Folsom, Jr. (D). *Legislature* —Senate, 35 members; House of Representatives, 105 members.

State Finances (fiscal year 1991): *Revenue,* $9,7671,000,000; *expenditure,* $8,855,000,000.

Personal Income (1991): $63,458,000,000; per capita, $15,518.

Labor Force (June 1992): *Civilian labor force,* 1,941,000; *unemployed,* 156,800 (8.1% of total force).

Education: *Enrollment* (fall 1990)—public elementary schools, 527,097; public secondary, 194,709; colleges and universities, 217,550. *Public school expenditures* (1990), $2,487,250,000.

ALASKA

Several environmentally-related controversies made news in Alaska in 1992. The most heated conflict focused on the continuing debate about opening the Arctic National Wildlife Refuge to oil production. In addition to the disagreements between the pro-development forces and those concerned about environmental dangers, the issue featured conflict between the Iñupiat Eskimos of the North Slope, who stood to benefit monetarily from production, and the Gwich'in Athapaskan Indians of interior Alaska, who depend upon the porcupine-caribou herd for subsistence. U.S. congressional decisions to continue prohibitions on drilling in the refuge and to allow outer-continental-shelf drilling put the debate to rest for the present.

Two unrelated incidents, discovered during perusals of U.S. government files during the year, generated concern. The first, found by a University of Alaska-Fairbanks researcher, involved evidence that the U.S. government had buried several pounds of radioactive waste in a mound at Cape Thompson in northwest Alaska during the early 1960s. While no official notice was provided to either the state government or the people of the two Iñupiat villages regularly using the location for subsistence activities, the intent of the project was to "test" whether there were adverse environmental effects caused by the leaching of the waste into the tundra and surrounding coastal waters. (Area residents long have complained of high cancer rates among the population of the two villages, and there have been persistent reports of deformed animal life.)

The second incident involved the discovery that the U.S. air force has maintained several unmanned nuclear generators in the northern interior region for several years, again without informing state or local government officials. Residents of the area requested that the equipment be removed.

Politics. Alaska voters continued the state's history of supporting Republican presidential candidates, providing incumbent George Bush with 40.5% of the vote in the November general election. They also supported independent candidate Ross Perot with 27.8% of the vote, maintaining their traditional support for independent and third-party candidates. Alaska's congressional delegation remained solidly in the Republican camp, with both incumbents, Sen. Frank Murkowski and Rep. Don Young, winning by surprisingly large margins. After a much criticized and litigated attempt at reapportionment—said to favor the Republican Party—and an acrimonious primary election that featured a GOP-only ballot and an open ballot for all other candidates, the result was little change at either federal or state levels.

The makeup of the 18th Alaska state legislature remained virtually unchanged from that of the 17th, with the Senate split evenly between Democrats and Republicans at ten seats apiece and the House of Representatives featuring 21 Democrats, 18 Republicans, and one Alaskan Independence Party representative.

Earlier in the fall, organizers submitted completed petitions to recall Gov. Walter Hickel and Lt. Gov. John Coghill, both members of the Alaskan Independence Party. The director of the Office of Elections (appointed as the appropriate authority by the lieutenant governor) then announced that the petitions would be certified in preparation for a special recall election. However, Alaska's attorney general halted that process by filing a legal action against the director for failure to accept his order to declare the petitions invalid. The issue would be decided by the courts.

Economy. The Alaska economy continued in a state of decline. Unemployment remained high in seasonal industries, and most of the major oil industries announced cutbacks for 1993. At the same time, several major retail warehouse outlets either opened or announced plans to open new stores in the state. Meanwhile, the administration of Governor Hickel continued to promote the construction of an Alaska natural gas pipeline. Alaska also continued to maintain communication and trade with the former Soviet Union.

Other. The federal government continued to manage fish and wildlife on federal lands in Alaska, given the state's inability to reach any agreement on the subsistence issue consistent with provisions for a "rural preference," as outlined in the Alaska National Interest Lands Act. A special legislative session, called when no action was taken during the regular session, was no more successful.

In January a federal appeals court ruled that Alaska Natives have the right to self-government within their villages just as do Indian tribes in the lower 48 states.

CARL E. SHEPRO, *University of Alaska*

ALASKA • Information Highlights

Area: 591,004 sq mi (1 530 700 km²).
Population (July 1, 1991 est.): 570,000.
Chief Cities (1990 census): Juneau, the capital, 26,751; Anchorage, 226,338; Fairbanks, 30,843; Sitka, 8,588.
Government (1992): *Chief Officers*—governor, Walter J. Hickel (I); lt. gov., John B. Coghill (I). *Legislature*—Senate, 20 members; House of Representatives, 40 members.
State Finances (fiscal year 1991): *Revenue,* $6,355,000,000; *expenditure,* $4,941,000,000.
Personal Income (1991): $12,015,000,000; per capita, $21,067.
Labor Force (June 1992): *Civilian labor force,* 263,400; *unemployed,* 25,200 (9.6% of total force).
Education: *Enrollment* (fall 1990)—public elementary schools, 85,297; public secondary, 28,577; colleges and universities, 29,833. *Public school expenditures* (1990), $797,811,000.

ALBANIA

During 1992, Albania made significant strides in dismantling the Communist system. The Democratic Party scored an impressive victory in the second multiparty parliamentary elections. Albanian-Serbian relations were tense, and contacts with Greece were strained over the position of Albania's Greek minority.

Political Developments. In early 1992 the government of nonparty "technocrats," installed in December 1991 and headed by Prime Minister Vilson Ahmeti, made preparations for a new round of general elections. The Socialists (formerly Communists) continued to lose support in the countryside, where they had obtained the bulk of their vote in the 1991 elections. The opposition condemned the Socialist leaders for paralyzing democratic reforms and clinging to their privileges.

In national elections in March, the Democratic Party won a landslide victory, gaining 92 out of 140 seats in the Peoples' Assembly; the ousted Socialists obtained 38 seats under the system of proportional representation. The remaining ten seats were divided among the Social Democrats, the Unity Party for Human Rights, and the Republicans. Parliament subsequently elected Sali Berisha of the Democratic Party as Albania's first non-Communist president. Aleksander Meksi became prime minister.

The new government, faced with some tough economic decisions, was unable to stimulate a rapid economic recovery. Moreover, popular expectations had been raised greatly by the defeat of communism, and a sense of public disillusionment soon began to grow with regard to the Democrats' performance. This mood was evident in the comparatively low voter turnout of 70% in the July local elections and the poor performance of the Democrats. The Socialists regained some strength in the rural districts and won 41% of the total vote (compared with 25% in the parliamentary elections), while Democrats gained a disappointing 43% (down from 65% in March). In Albania's 43 administrative districts, the Socialists won 22 mayoralties, while 19 went to the Democrats.

The Democrats also experienced some internal turmoil when Gramoz Pashko, a cofounder of the party, was expelled from the party's parliamentary group. There were indications that the party could split into distinct centrist and center-right offshoots. The Socialists themselves were not immune to factionalism, and the rift between harder-line Communists and reformed social democrats appeared to widen. Despite some setbacks the democratic reforms continued to be consolidated. Local government obtained a good measure of administrative autonomy, and the police and army largely were depoliticized.

ALBANIA · Information Highlights

Official Name: People's Socialist Republic of Albania.
Location: Southern Europe, Balkan peninsula.
Area: 11,100 sq mi (28 750 km²).
Population (mid-1992 est.): 3,300,000.
Chief City (1989): Tiranë, the capital, 238,100.
Government: *Head of state,* Sali Berisha, president (took office April 1992). *Head of government,* Aleksander Meksi, prime minister (took office April 1992). *Legislature* (unicameral)—People's Assembly, 140 members.
Gross National Product (1990 est. U.S.$): $4,100,000,000.

Economic Reform. The new government faced an uphill task in transforming the collapsing economy by cutting state subsidies, freeing prices, and stabilizing the currency to meet International Monetary Fund (IMF) requirements. Nonetheless, it successfully liberalized prices on a wide range of products and introduced preliminary legislation to stimulate private enterprise. Tiranë was intent on reducing the high rate of unemployment, estimated at more than 60% of the adult working population, and planned to cut the large unemployment benefits that drained the state budget. The private retail and service trade witnessed a dramatic growth as state controls were lifted, and agricultural production began to recover after the disastrous 1991 harvest.

Before the Democratic victory, economic decline and the easing of repressive police controls sparked riots in several Albanian towns, as poor citizens ransacked warehouses and stores for scarce products. The Democratic administration made the restoration of law and order a high priority and sought to rebuild the prestige and authority of the police.

Tiranë received IMF credits and donations from the European Community in excess of $100 million. The EC also continued to supply large amounts of humanitarian assistance. More than 70 joint ventures were established in the country, primarily in collaboration with Italian, German, and Greek corporations.

Ethnic and Foreign Relations. Frictions increased in Albania over the status and activities of the approximately 60,000-strong Greek minority, residing primarily in the southern parts of the country. Some Albanian politicians grew concerned that the Greek organization *Omonia* was pushing toward territorial and ethnic autonomy and was supported by irredentist political groups and Orthodox religious circles in Greece. The Albanian parliament barred *Omonia* and other ethnic-based parties from standing in the general elections. However, the newly formed Unity Party for Human Rights was allowed to register and gained two parliamentary seats in the heavily Greek-populated districts. Several thousand Albanian citizens left the country and took shelter in Greece, Macedonia, and Italy.

Greek minority demands for expanding their educational and cultural autonomy and Greek government claims that its population in Albania numbered more than 200,000 people also alarmed some Albanian leaders. In addition, the demands of Cam Albanians exiled in Tiranë for restoring the rights and property of this Albanian minority in northern Greece further strained Tiranë's relations with Athens. The Greek authorities denied that a Cam Albanian minority still resided on its territories.

Albania's prime foreign-policy concern remained the position of the large Albanian population in Serbia's Kosovo province. In May the Kosovar Albanians held parliamentary and presidential elections that were declared illegitimate by Serb and Yugoslav authorities. Ibrahim Rugova became Kosovo's president and was recognized formally as such by Tiranë.

JANUSZ BUGAJSKI
Associate Director of East European Studies
Center for Strategic and International Studies

ALBERTA

In December 1992 former Calgary Mayor Ralph Klein became premier of Alberta after winning a Progressive Conservative (PC) run-off leadership vote. Klein had been Alberta's environment minister in the PC government after he left municipal politics in 1989. In September, Premier Don Getty had announced that he was stepping down as premier and party leader. Getty had served nearly seven years as premier, but when his government began to run large deficits and to hike taxes frequently, his popularity quickly eroded. It was expected that Klein would call a provincial election either in late 1993 or early 1994.

In the October 26 national referendum, more than 60% of Alberta's voters rejected the Charlottetown Accord on constitutional reform.

ALBERTA • Information Highlights

Area: 255,286 sq mi (661 190 km²).
Population (September 1992): 2,568,200.
Chief Cities (1986 census): Edmonton, the capital, 573,982; Calgary, 636,104; Lethbridge, 58,841.
Government (1991): *Chief Officers*—lt. gov., Gordon Towers; premier, Ralph Klein (Progressive Conservative). *Legislature*—Legislative Assembly, 79 members.
Provincial Finances (1992–93 fiscal year budget): *Revenues,* $11,000,000,000; *expenditures,* $13,300,000,000.
Personal Income (average weekly earnings, July 1992): $543.22.
Labor Force (September 1992, seasonally adjusted): *Employed* workers, 15 years of age and over, 1,241,000; *Unemployed,* 9.2%.
Education (1992–93): *Enrollment*—elementary and secondary schools, 534,300 pupils; postsecondary—universities, 49,000; community colleges, 26,500.
(All monetary figures are in Canadian dollars.)

Budget. Provincial Treasurer Dick Johnston unveiled a C$13.3 billion budget in April that had a deficit of $2.2 billion. Under the budget, overall government spending was expected to increase by 6%, although Johnston later sponsored legislation holding spending increases to 2.5% through 1995. The budget cut Alberta's personal and corporate income-tax rates by 1%, but increased health-care premiums and user fees for driver's licenses, campgrounds, and hunting permits. For the first time since the Great Depression, Alberta was a debtor province. Its accumulated debt of about $14.5 billion overshadowed its assets, forcing the government to spend an estimated $1.23 billion yearly on interest payments on the debt, or 9.3% of its budget.

Business. In Alberta's largest government-backed financial disaster, taxpayers were shaken to discover that $566.5 million of their money invested in NovAtel Communications Ltd. had been lost. The PC government had promoted NovAtel, a cellular phone manufacturer, as a means of diversifying Alberta's economy from oil, gas, and other resources to high tech. NovAtel had been part of the government-owned Alberta Government Telephone (AGT), but when the province moved to privatize AGT, difficulties arose in selling off NovAtel. When it was finally sold in 1992, taxpayers discovered that the new owners had paid just $61 million for it, leaving a loss of $566.5 million. The company reportedly had outstanding loans of some $300 million to its clients, mainly in the United States, where substantial losses already had occurred.

Airline Takeover. Canadian International Airlines, headquartered in Calgary and with 16,000 employees throughout Canada, had to scramble during 1992 to stay in business. The nation's second-largest airline after Montreal-based Air Canada, Canadian at one point was losing as much as $700,000 per day. Canadian had tried to persuade Texas-based American Airlines to invest in it. After negotiations collapsed, it went to Air Canada to seek a merger, something it earlier had been determined to avoid. Then in November, Air Canada, which initially had wanted to take over Canadian Airlines, rejected the idea. That same month the federal government agreed to keep Canadian in business with a $50 million loan guarantee, and the airline directors made attempts to work out a new arrangement with American Airlines. Calgary Mayor Al Duerr said that if Canadian collapsed it would be a disaster for the city, with the loss of 7,000 direct and indirect jobs.

PAUL JACKSON, *"The Calgary Sun"*

ALGERIA

Parliamentary elections at the end of 1991 set the stage for a sharp confrontation between the military and the Islamic Salvation Front (FIS) that spilled blood across Algeria in 1992 —a year of violence and counterviolence. President Chadli Benjedid was forced to step down in January and his successor, Mohammed Boudiaf, was assassinated in June. The courts officially dissolved the FIS in March, but suppression of the Islamic movement did nothing to resolve Algeria's deep political cleavages.

Politics. A coalition of military and civilian leaders led by Gen. Khaled Nezzar forced Benjedid to resign on January 11 after the elections of Dec. 26, 1991, gave the FIS an insurmountable lead in the competition to control Algeria's national assembly. The FIS won 188 seats in the first round of a scheduled two-round election. The Socialist Forces Front came in second with 25 seats and the former single party, the National Liberation Front, won 16. Moreover, FIS candidates held the lead in 186 of the 198 races to be settled in the runoff which was scheduled for January 16.

President Benjedid's resignation momentarily transferred power to an advisory organ called the High Security Council, which annulled the results of the first round of elections and canceled the second round. The council then appointed a new joint executive called the High State Committee (HCE) to exercise the power of the presidency. The surprise head of the five-man HCE was Boudiaf, a leader of Algeria's war for independence (1954–62), who had been in exile in Morocco for 28 years. The other members were General Nezzar; Ali Kafi, who headed the national veterans' association; Ali Haroun, who was minister of human rights; and Tejini Khaddam, a former minister of religious affairs whose inclusion in the body hardly served to subdue the wrath of the Islamic movement.

Although the transfer of power from Benjedid to the HCE was essentially peaceful and constitutionally ingenious, the subsequent crackdown on the FIS unleashed a wave of violence. In the weeks following the coup, the military arrested some 9,000 Islamists, including Abdelkader Hachani, who had emerged as the movement's provisional spokesperson after the arrest of Abassi Madani in 1991. The arrests did little to stem the incidence of armed attacks carried out against policemen, soldiers, and security installations around the country. The government declared a state of emergency on February 9 as the death toll from clashes between Islamic guerrillas and security forces rose. Nearly 200 soldiers and police officers were killed in the first ten months of the year and more than 100 civilians were wounded when a bomb blew up at Algiers airport in August.

The most prominent victim of the breakdown of order was Boudiaf, assassinated in murky circumstances while delivering a speech

ALGERIA · Information Highlights

Official Name: Democratic and Popular Republic of Algeria.
Location: North Africa.
Area: 919,591 sq mi (2 381 740 km²).
Population (mid-1992 est.): 26,000,000.
Chief Cities (1987 census): Algiers, the capital, 1,507,241; Oran, 628,558; Constantine, 440,842.
Government: Head of state, Ali Kafi, president (took office July 1992). Head of government, Belaid Abdesselam, prime minister (appointed July 8, 1992).
Monetary Unit: Dinar (21.332 dinars equal U.S.$1, June 1992).
Gross Domestic Product (1990 est. U.S.$): $54,-000,000,000.
Foreign Trade (1990 est. U.S.$): Imports, $9,200,-000,000; exports, $10,200,000,000.

in eastern Algeria on June 29. During his five months in office, the former exile spoke out against violence and religious intolerance, but he also condemned the past regime's record of mismanagement and corruption "that had brought water to the mill of the FIS." He declared the need for "radical change," but had little leverage by which to enact his own policies. Caught in a political cross fire between the Islamists and the military, he began to question the latter's methods of dealing with the Islamic movement before his fatal trip to Annaba. A government report in July shed little light on who was responsible for the assassination.

Despite speculation that General Nezzar would take Boudiaf's place, the military remained in the background as Ali Kafi was named head of the HCE. Rheda Malek, a former diplomat and chief of the National Consultative Council, another new organ created in April as an interim parliament, was appointed as the fifth member of the HCE. Sid Ahmed Ghozali, who had been one of the civilian architects of the deposition of Benjedid, gave way as prime minister to Belaid Abdesselam in July. Industry and energy minister from 1965 until 1977, Abdesselam brought a reputation as a tough economic and political manager to the post. In mid-July, a military tribunal sentenced FIS leaders Abassi Madani and Ali Belhadj to 12 years in prison for their role in the disorders of June 1991, while those of 1992 continued unabated.

Economic and Foreign Affairs. The appointment of Abdesselam as premier was an attempt to halt the erosion of the economy. Debt, unemployment, and the reluctance of foreign investors to respond to the Ghozali government's overtures continued to plague the economy, which showed a 3.5% decline for the first quarter. Shortage of hard currency forced production cutbacks in the absence of raw-materials and spare-parts imports. Strikes further weakened the economy as workers reacted to rising food and utility prices. Abdesselam called for further austerity and a return to a strong public-sector role, but the political tur-

Supporters of Angola's President José Eduardo dos Santos of the Popular Movement for the Liberation of Angola (MPLA), right, hold an election rally. Angola's main opposition party—the Union for the Total Independence of Angola, (UNITA)—refused to accept MPLA's victory in the September 1992 balloting.

© Piero Guerrini

moil confounded his efforts much as they had those of his predecessor.

Relations with France were prickly throughout the year as French officials criticized the cancellation of the elections and the Saharan detention camps in which the Islamists were being held. Algeria moreover broke relations with Iran for its support of the Islamic movement. The return of Boudiaf from his long exile in Morocco momentarily raised expectations of a negotiated settlement to the long-standing dispute over Western Sahara. This, no less than Boudiaf's other dreams, was not to be.

ROBERT MORTIMER
Haverford College

ANGOLA

After 14 years of fighting Portuguese rule and 16 additional years of postindependence civil war, conflict-weary Angolans went to the polls in the first open, multiparty election in the country's history in 1992; postelection violence, however, seemed to threaten a resumption of civil strife.

Early in April the Angolan parliament set conditions for voter registration and estab-

---

ANGOLA • Information Highlights

Official Name: People's Republic of Angola.
Location: Western Africa.
Area: 481,351 sq mi (1 246 700 km²).
Population (mid-1992 est.): 8,900,000.
Chief City (1982 est.): Luanda, the capital, 1,200,000.
Government: *Head of state and government,* José Eduardo dos Santos, president (took office 1979); Fernando Jose Franca Van Dunem, prime minister. *Legislature*—People's Assembly.
Gross Domestic Product (1990 est. U.S. $): $7,900,-000,000.
Foreign Trade (1990 est.): *Imports,* $1,500,000; *exports,* $3,800,000.

---

lished a National Electoral Council to manage the September 29–30 national election. These arrangements were agreed upon in meetings between the ruling party—the Popular Movement for the Liberation of Angola (MPLA), the main opposition group—Jonas Savimbi's Union for the Total Independence of Angola (UNITA), and other opposition parties. United Nations monitors were invited to verify the results of the election.

More than 95% (nearly 5 million) of those who were qualified to vote registered for the September election. President José Eduardo dos Santos of the MPLA received 49.6% of the votes cast and Jonas Savimbi of UNITA, 40.1%. The MPLA also won 55% of the parliamentary vote, while UNITA received 38%. However, with 11 candidates running in the presidential race, dos Santos was just short of the majority required to avoid a runoff election. Many observers felt that a compromise government consisting of MPLA and UNITA members would be the best hope for the future stability of the country, particularly since the rival armies of both organizations then could be demobilized.

Savimbi, however, charged that the election had been rigged, despite the fact that nearly 400 official international observers maintained that it was fair and free. He left Luanda for his stronghold, Huambo, in southern Angola, and his generals withdrew from the unified security forces. MPLA supporters were forced to leave UNITA-controlled towns, and Savimbi's guerrillas launched attacks in the capital city of Luanda and elsewhere. Government forces counterattacked, thereby escalating the violence. An estimated 2,500 people were killed in the fighting, but hopes for a peaceful settlement rose when UNITA agreed to join a coalition government early in December.

PATRICK O'MEARA and BRIAN WINCHESTER
Indiana University

ANTHROPOLOGY

In 1992 anthropologists analyzed a fossil that may represent the earliest known human ancestor; two Chinese skulls offered insight into the evolution of modern humans; and contrasting evolutionary theories emerged concerning the species that immediately preceded modern humans.

Human Ancestors. A new investigation of a palm-sized skull fragment found in Africa in the mid-1960s concluded that the fossil dates to 2.4 million years ago and came from the earliest known direct human ancestor. If this assertion proves correct, it pushes the fossil record of the human *(Homo)* lineage back 500,000 years.

The fossil preserves bone from the right side of the head and around the ear opening and jaw joint, as well as part of the skull base. The position of the jaw joint and shape of the skull fragment mark it as a direct human ancestor, argued Andrew Hill and his colleagues of Yale University. However, the fossil does not contain enough information to be classified within a specific *Homo* species, Hill said.

Some anthropologists familiar with the fossil tentatively accepted Hill's conclusions. Others said the specimen may be younger than 2.4 million years old, a date derived from volcanic ash just below where it was found originally. Skeptics also questioned whether the anatomical features cited by Hill clearly place the small fossil within the *Homo* lineage.

Chinese Skulls. Excavations near China's Han River yielded two nearly complete skulls of human ancestors who lived at least 350,000 years ago, according to Li Tianyuan of the Hubei Institute of Archaeology in China and Dennis A. Etler of the University of California, Berkeley. The partly crushed skulls support the view that widely dispersed populations of *Homo erectus*—a human ancestor that lived from around 1.6 million to 400,000 years ago—displayed different anatomical arrangements that led to the independent evolution of modern humans in several areas. This view contrasts with the theory that modern humans evolved first in Africa and then spread to other regions.

The Chinese skulls, dated on the basis of extinct animal bones found in the same excavation, display flat faces much like those of modern humans and long, low brain cases with thick bones much like those found on *H. erectus* specimens. A different mosaic of advanced and primitive features characterizes the skulls of human ancestors found in Europe and Africa dating to the same time period, Etler asserted.

***Erectus* Debate.** New studies proposed clashing evolutionary views of *H. erectus*.

H. erectus existed only in Asia and met extinction on a side branch of human evolution, argued Bernard Wood of the University of Liverpool, England. In an analysis of 90 cranial, jaw, and tooth measurements taken from African *Homo* remains dating to nearly 2 million years ago, Wood identified three species, including one that in his opinion served as a precursor of modern humans.

A second theory, proposed by Milford H. Wolpoff of the University of Michigan in Ann Arbor and Alan G. Thorne of Australian National University in Canberra, held that *H. erectus* never existed. Modern humans evolved in several parts of the world beginning around 2 million years ago, according to Wolpoff and Thorne. They found that modern humans share many important anatomical features with fossils usually assigned to *H. erectus*. Thus the two investigators rejected the labeling of the older fossils as *H. erectus*.

G. Philip Rightmire of the State University of New York at Binghamton defended the traditional view of *H. erectus* as a single species that gave rise to modern humans perhaps only in Africa or Europe. He argued that fossil skulls from Indonesia show clear differences between *H. erectus* and early modern humans, contrary to the theory of Wolpoff and Thorne.

BRUCE BOWER, *"Science News"*

ARCHAEOLOGY

There were several unusually exciting discoveries in archaeology during 1992.

Eastern Hemisphere

Arabian Trading Post. Investigators announced the discovery of a nearly 5,000-year-old city in the Arabian desert that apparently once served as a major hub of the frankincense

Archaeologists discovered the tomb of Caiaphas, the high priest who presided at Jesus' trial. Twelve boxes for storing the dead, including the one below, were part of the find.

© Israel Antiquities Authority/ASAP, Jerusalem

Using ancient clues and space-age technology at a remote site in Oman, archaeologists unveiled what is believed to be the legendary city of Ubar. Known as Iram in the Koran, it was a Middle East trading center, famous for its frankincense.

trade in the Middle East and the Mediterranean. Known as Ubar, the ancient trading center was buried by shifting desert sands about 2,000 years ago.

Ancient caravan tracks leading to the desert city first turned up on sand-penetrating radar images taken by the space shuttle *Challenger* and by U.S. and French satellites. These images and ancient maps of the region guided investigators to the outpost's ruins in southern Oman. The discovery suggests that urban development in the southern Arabian desert began about 1,000 years earlier than previously assumed.

Biblical Bones. Israeli archaeologists said that the bones of a man found in an ancient burial cave in Jerusalem may be the remains of the high priest who presided at the trial of Jesus and delivered him to the Romans for crucifixion. The cave contained 12 limestone boxes for storing the dead and probably served as a family tomb. One box contained intricate decorations and the inscription "Joseph, son of Caiaphas." Joseph, usually called Caiaphas, ruled as Jewish high priest in Jerusalem from 18 A.D. to 36 A.D. The box contained the bones of a man who died at about age 60. Other evidence uncovered in the tomb, such as a bronze

coin minted in 43 A.D., places the site in the first century.

Egyptian Fleet. An archaeological excavation at Abydos, in southern Egypt, uncovered 12 ships that were buried intentionally during the third millennium B.C. Mud bricks encased each ship in a "boat-grave." Investigators found numerous ceramic offerings around the hulls of the ships, which are in good condition.

Ship burials around the base of pyramids occurred later in Egyptian history, but the origin of the practice is unknown. The Abydos boat-graves preceded the first pyramids by several hundred years. They lie next to structures once used for the funeral rituals of early pharaohs. Buried vessels may have been intended to accompany a pharaoh to the afterlife.

Gold Coins. University of Chicago archaeologists working at Ayla, an ancient Red Sea port in Jordan, discovered 32 gold coins that may have belonged to a Muslim pilgrim traveling to Mecca about 1,000 years ago. Ayla was an important port in an international trade network and a popular stop for religious pilgrims. The scientists said that 29 of the coins probably were minted at an outpost in southern Morocco that was at the center of the once-bustling gold trade. The three other coins were minted elsewhere in north Africa. All the coins date to between 976 and 1013. A trader would have carried a more diverse set of coins, so the archaeologists suspect they belonged to a pilgrim.

Greek Blades. A team of scientists concluded that skillfully fashioned stone tools found at an archaeological site in Greece date to about 100,000 years ago. Similar stone flakes and blades from the same time period have been found in central and western Europe, as well as the Middle East. The new analysis, based on dating of stone flints at the site, extends the distribution of sophisticated stone toolmaking into southeastern Europe. Both Neanderthals and modern humans apparently fashioned the sharp stones at various sites. Investigators cannot say which group made the Greek artifacts.

Early Tin. The 4,500-year-old Turkish site of Goltepe yielded clues to early tin-extraction methods. Chemical analysis of pottery fragments from Goltepe indicated that ancient metal workers first ground up rocks and stones with quartz and limestone containing a tin-oxide material. They then heated the powder between layers of charcoal in shallow bowls to encourage the formation of tiny beads of crystallized tin. Crushing and reheating of the mixture produced a liquefied tin. The findings suggest that ancient cultures used local deposits of raw materials more than has been assumed.

Western Hemisphere

Prehistoric Amazonians. The oldest known pottery in the Americas emerged from the Brazilian site of Taperinha on the bank of the Amazon River. Archaeologists dated reddish-brown pieces of bowls, which were found in an ancient refuse dump that covers 15 acres (6 ha), at between 7,000 and 8,000 years old. The discovery suggests that the tropical lowlands, usually ignored by scientists, were the cradle of civilization in South America.

The Taperinha pottery is at least 1,000 years older than the previous earliest pottery from South America, found at a Colombian site, and 3,000 years older than the first pottery produced by better-known cultures in the Andes Mountains, Central America, and southern Mexico.

Spanish Shipwreck. Treasure hunters and archaeologists explored the underwater remains of a well-preserved early Spanish sailing ship. The vessel, submerged under 20 ft (6 m) of water in the Bahama Islands, may be the oldest ever found in the Americas, dating to the early 16th century. The wooden ship also may be the first known example of a caravel, the hardy, maneuverable boats used by Christopher Columbus and other seafaring explorers. Archaeologists so far have mapped the outlines

of the vessel's surviving hull and catalogued scattered artifacts, such as guns, crossbows, swords, military helmets, coins, and pottery.

Mexican Sites. Archaeologists identified several sites along a remote canyon as part of an important "cultural corridor" linking pre-Hispanic civilizations of Mexico's central highlands with those of its southeastern coast late in the first millennium A.D. The largest site, an ancient city called Cuajilotes, lies about 100 mi (161 km) north of Veracruz on Mexico's east coast. Pyramid-shaped mounds, some 60 ft (18 m) high, dot the center of the city. Some of the mounds appear to have featured shrines on their flat tops. Investigators believe Cuajilotes was a trade center on a major commercial route between coastal and highland societies.

Maya Tomb. Excavations at the ancient Maya city of Copán in Honduras revealed a tomb that may contain the remains of a king who lived more than 1,400 years ago. Inside the tomb, a skeleton lies on a stone slab surrounded by jade jewelry, carved shells, decorated pottery, and other artifacts.

Archaeologists who discovered the tomb said it may hold one of the four kings who ruled the Copán region during the 6th century. Further work at the site will test their suspicion. The skeleton's teeth appear in good condition and indicate the individual died as a young man. The placement of the tomb and the array of items left on and around the body suggest the structure served as a royal burial.

Maya Sculpture. The largest architectural sculpture known from an ancient Maya city was discovered on the side of a pyramid among the ruins of Nakbe in Guatemala. The sculpture depicts the head of a bird 34 ft (10 m) wide and 16 ft (5 m) high. It represents a god archaeologists call the Principal Bird Deity, which according to ancient Maya belief presided over the ascension of kings to the throne. The sculpture dates to the beginnings of Maya culture, around 300 B.C. The "golden age" of Maya civilization extended from 300 A.D. to 900 A.D. Investigators say the appearance of the sculpture at a time when Nakbe underwent massive construction projects suggests that religion importantly propelled the rise of Maya civilization.

Research Center. Archaeologists digging on Roanoke Island off the North Carolina coast uncovered a research laboratory dating to the 1580s, the earliest known example of a scientific laboratory in the Americas. The facility, which was established by English colonists, apparently contained equipment for the analysis of rock and soil from nearby locations in order to see whether copper and other precious metals existed in North America. Artifacts found included remnants of a forge for melting rock and separating out its metal content and waste material formed during this process.

BRUCE BOWER, *"Science News"*

ARCHITECTURE

As architects continued to grapple with balancing an architecture that expressed its time and a growing popular interest in historic styles, new models constantly were sought. Among those brought forward in 1992 was architect Karl Friedrich Schinkel, the 19th-century German neoclassicist. Whether literally adopted or translated into more interpretive design language, borrowing from the past clearly was respectable again, after 40 years of the profession's near domination by unornamented modernism.

Design Extremes. The full rich range of current designs could be seen by comparing two projects: One was Sawgrass Mills, a 120-acre (48.6-ha) colorful shopping center of massive sheds in Sunrise, FL, designed by Arquitectonica International, relieved by playful Greek temples, modernist glass cubes, and Corbusian boxes, themselves a virtual catalogue of design styles. By contrast, a modest house in rural Vermont, designed by Brooks & Carey Architects, appeared from many angles much like the rural vernacular houses that always had been built there; only a curved wall on the back gave away its recent origins. The Mount Carmel Elementary School in Douglas county, GA, designed by Lord Aeck Sargent, Architects, represented still another extreme—the industrial esthetic of stamped aluminum siding, corrugated metal awnings in playful shapes, and exposed steel trusses inside. The Minneapolis Convention Center—designed by Setter Leach & Lindstrom, Leonard Parker Associates, and others—was fronted by brown round stone towers decorated with colored vertical insets; it resembled a building left over from an ancient civilization, although the towers were credited with breaking down the apparent bulk of the 800,000-sq-ft (74 322-m²) building.

Awards. The 1992 Pritzker Prize for Architecture went to Portuguese architect Alvaro Siza, whose buildings were described by the jury as appearing to be "natural creations" that are built according to modest local traditions with no particular plan. The American Institute of Architects (AIA) 1992 Gold Medal went to Benjamin Thompson, whose "festival marketplaces," starting with Faneuil Hall in Boston, have been noted most for the popular appeal of traditional forms decorated with colorful flags and banners. Among the ten AIA Honor Awards were the National Gallery Sainsbury Wing in London, by Venturi Scott Brown and Associates, an abstraction of the traditional forms of the original gallery building; Firestone Memorial Library expansion in Princeton, NJ, by Koetter Kim & Associates; Team Disney Building in Lake Buena Vista, FL, by Arata Isozaki & Associates; Vitra International Furniture Manufacturing Facility and Design Museum in Rhein, Germany, by Frank O. Gehry

& Associates; the Paramount Hotel in New York City, by Haigh Architects with Philippe Starck Interiors; Newark Museum in Newark, NJ, by Michael Graves, that mixes styles as diverse as 1930s modernism and the much older U.S. Southwest; and The Canadian Centre for Architecture in Montreal, by Peter Rose, a massive addition to a Victorian mansion.

Preservations. The 46th annual National Preservation Conference was held in a newly invigorated Art Deco district on Miami's South Beach. It looked at the successes (and failures) of the 1966 National Preservation Act and for ways to maintain interest in preservation, including involving minorities. Among the National Trust Awards was one for the Borne Apartments in New Orleans by The Architectural Team, a project that was meant to be a prototype for the revival of depressed inner-city neighborhoods. The architects, developer, and contractor—all minorities—rehabilitated 23 shotgun-style houses of the 19th century where freed slaves once lived, carefully salvaging as much of the historic fabric as possible. Among other distinguished renovations was that of El Capitán, a theater in Hollywood that bucked current trends by returning to a single screen. The project won another 1992 National Trust Award for the architects Fields & Devereaux. One distinguished renovation of an increasingly common type in urban centers, the conversion of industrial loft space to office use, was carried out for the United Brotherhood of Carpenters and Joiners in New York City by architects Davis Brody & Associates.

Renovation, which accounted for 28% of all construction projects of more than $1 million in 1991, was expected to account for even more in 1992. It also was expected to account for fully half of all residential construction.

Preservation Controversies. Evidence of the seriousness of architects' concerns with preservation could be found in the debates over plans to add onto a number of distinguished 20th-century buildings. Among ongoing plans blocked by controversies among architects, critics, and civic groups were: the expansion of the 1972 Kimbell Art Museum in Fort Worth by the late master Louis Kahn, according to plans by Romoldo Giurgola; New York's Whitney Museum of American Art, completed in 1966 by Marcel Breuer, to be expanded by Michael Graves (plans dropped in 1992); and the 1965 Salk Institute in La Jolla, CA, also originally designed by Kahn, with new additions proposed by Anshen and Allen. Also controversial was a plan by the Federal Reserve to demolish and replace architect Gunnart Birkerts' 1973 landmark regional branch in Minneapolis because, claimed the Reserve, it no longer met its needs.

One addition that opened in 1992 and did overcome successfully the controversy surrounding it was that by architects Gwathmey

A $13.8 million expansion of the Firestone Memorial Library at Princeton University was presented a 1992 Honor Award by the American Institute of Architects. The design was cited for its use of natural light and for building materials that corresponded nicely with the structure,which was completed in 1948.

© Courtesy of Koetter Kim & Associates, Inc.

Seigel Associates onto Frank Lloyd Wright's Guggenheim Museum, built in New York City in 1959. Nonetheless, even after the opening of the new slab-like office and gallery space behind Wright's rotunda, Charles Gwathmey was called upon to defend his design in *Architectural Record* against the criticism of Carter Wiseman. Expansions that did not create so much controversy included Hardy Holzman Pfeiffer Associates' sympathetic stone addition to Cass Gilbert's 1911 New Haven Public Library and Voorsanger & Associates' addition to The Pierpont Morgan Library in New York. Similarly, a 170,000-sq-ft (15 794-m²) "oceanarium" raised hardly a peep when it was appended by architects Lohan Associates to Chicago's neoclassic aquarium, designed in 1929 by Graham, Anderson, Probst, and White.

Architectural Diversification. There was much talk about U.S. architects' need to diversify their talents into related fields such as energy consultation and building-product development due to the decline in construction, even though the volume had begun to pick up from a 1991 low. Still, with almost as many architects due to emerge from U.S. schools by 1998 as are currently in practice, there was much puzzlement about what they all would do. One answer was to look abroad. Cesar Pelli & Associates captured two commissions and hoped for a third to design buildings in a 40-acre (16-ha) sports and entertainment complex in Fukuoka, Japan, that included a 40,000-seat domed baseball stadium and a 1,000-room hotel.

But European architects captured work in the United States too. One important building completed at the beginning of 1992 was the Alice Pratt Brown Hall at Rice University in Houston, designed by the Barcelona-based Ricardo Bofill/Taller de Arquitectura. While these architects have been noted for dramatically overscaled classic elements, Brown Hall had both the expected columns and an unexpected cubistic massing, reminiscent of Wrightian imagery.

Damage caused by Hurricane Andrew in August also promised additional work, but in the rush to rebuild, it became apparent that little new construction would be designed freshly. The best that could be hoped was that the new construction would be built to stricter codes.

Among other larger projects was a $145 million New Jersey Performing Arts Center to be built in Newark, NJ, to a plan by Skidmore Owings & Merrill and James Stewart Polshek.

Growing Regulatory Complexities. Architects faced increasingly complex regulations, ranging from the 1990 Americans With Disabilities Act—meant to give handicapped persons access to virtually every public space—to clean-air restrictions that limited the use of such products as solvent-thinned paint. Regulations that would call for the removal of long-banned lead-based paint raised the possibility that many historic elements in older buildings would have to be taken out when paint stripping proved impractical.

Charles K. Hoyt, *"Architectural Record"*

A car-bomb explosion destroyed the Israeli Embassy in Buenos Aires, Argentina, on March 17, 1992. The Islamic Jihad, a Lebanese Shiite group, took responsibility for the attack, which killed at least 28 persons.

ARGENTINA

In 1992, Argentina's President Carlos Saúl Menem was hounded by charges of corruption at almost every level of his administration; his otherwise-successful economic policy came under pressure because of its high social costs and its effect on the currency.

Politics and Government. Accused of corruption, the presidentially appointed mayor of Buenos Aires, Carlos Grosso, resigned on October 29. Bribes seemed to be an integral part of contracting for school lunches, hospital janitorial services, and meals at government facilities. Economy Minister Domingo Cavallo, architect of Argentina's highly successful economic-adjustment plan, was criticized in October for having an outside income nearly five times his salary. A number of public officials had been suspended in May during an investigation of irregularities in the issuance of identity cards and citizenship papers; the questionable recipients included suspected drug traffickers and gunrunners. Administrators in the defense area were thought to be involved in illegal arms transactions and dealings in spare parts for military airplanes. At the beginning of the year, Menem accepted the resignation of one of his private secretaries for his involvement in a scandal over the sale of tainted powdered milk to government institutions. Deputy Interior Minister Juan Carlos Mazzón was forced to resign in January after Menem was informed of his prison record.

Hopes for an independent judiciary were dashed on September 8, when President Menem dismissed his justice minister, León Arslanian, after he objected to executive-branch meddling with a list of nominees for 235 new judgeships. Arslanian contended that names had been added to the list for political reasons, rather than for their record as judges.

In a setback for Menem, Peronist Party candidate Avelino Porto lost his bid for a Senate seat representing Buenos Aires on June 28. Porto, a former minister of health, lost badly to Fernando de la Rúa, a leader of the opposition Unión Cívica Radical, who campaigned against government corruption and criticized executive preponderance over the legislative and judicial branches.

During the summer, Menem began to back away from his campaign to do away with restrictions on presidential reelection. On July 20 he announced his intention to postpone consideration of that issue, pledging to deepen free-market reforms and improve tax collection, competition, and social policies. Under the constitution, an incumbent president must wait six years before again running for that office; Menem did not have enough votes in congress for a constitutional convention to amend the provision.

Economic Policy. After providing nearly two years of growth, Economy Minister Cavallo's recovery plan was tested severely in November by a speculators' run on the dollar, to which the fully convertible peso was pegged. This forced the central bank to sell dollars and purchase pesos. A devaluation of the peso was rejected, even though, at 20% for 1992, inflation in Argentina's dollarized economy was higher than in the United States. A stable economy had attracted private investors to a sell-off of all state-owned enterprises, including oil and gas, electricity, water, and railways. A $2 billion deal announced on July 30 turned over 51% of the electricity company to Argentine, Chilean, French, and Spanish interests. Earlier in the year the government sold its telephone service for nearly $3 billion and stakes in publicly owned oil fields were sold for $1.5 billion. Controls on economic activity were reviewed, resulting in a reduction of import duties and procedures, while export duties were eliminated.

Implementation of Cavallo's economic-recovery plan cost thousands of jobs and required freezing salaries, wages, and pensions, which heightened unrest among those whose purchasing power had eroded. Representatives of 156 unions met with President Menem on February 5 to protest the labor policies of his administration. They rejected a removal of the state monopoly over social security, and the privatization of unemployment insurance and retirement plans. In June some 200,000 public-school teachers struck for higher pay—equivalent to that of municipal workers—and against plans to transfer responsibility for public education to local governments. Organized labor carried out its first general strike against the Menem government on November 9, demanding a minimum monthly wage of 500 pesos, and opposing the government's decision to negotiate salary raises on the basis of productivity instead of cost-of-living increases.

By joining the Brady Debt Reduction Plan in April, Argentina was able to reduce its $62 billion foreign debt by about $10 billion. Some $31 billion in medium- and long-term commercial obligations and interest arrears was renegotiated. Under the accord, Argentina's creditors either could exchange debt for 30-year bonds at a discount rate of 35% and backed by U.S. treasury bonds, or could exchange the loans for 30-year bonds with the same face value as the old debt, but with an interest rate starting at 4%. The arrangement was contingent upon Argentina settling its bilateral debt of $8.7 billion with Paris Club members. That agreement, providing for a 16-year payback of $2.8 billion, was reached in July. The debt settlements restored Argentine access to international lending agencies.

Foreign Relations. Argentina and Britain held talks in Buenos Aires at the end of February about developing oil resources on the continental shelf surrounding the disputed Malvinas/Falkland Islands. In July, however, the Falklands' government, based on bidding closed to Argentine companies, chose British and U.S. firms to make the preliminary studies, triggering an angry response from the Argentines.

Argentina marked the tenth anniversary of its ill-fated invasion of the British-held Falklands on April 2. President Menem assured his countrymen that the islands would be recovered from Great Britain "before the year 2000," by diplomatic means rather than force. Even though the Falklands' population was opposed as strongly as ever to living under rule by Argentines, the latter believed that democratic Argentina's gains in growth, stability, and international respectability would change the islanders' attitude. Menem was invited to make a state visit to London in 1993.

An agreement with Brazil regarding nuclear-weapons inspection and nonproliferation had been signed in Vienna on Dec. 13, 1991; it called for implementation assistance from the United Nations International Atomic Energy Agency. Argentina also committed itself to compliance with the Tlatelolco Treaty, banning nuclear weapons in Latin America.

President Menem announced in February that he would send 900 troops to join UN peacekeeping forces in Yugoslavia. This came during an official visit to Buenos Aires by U.S. Secretary of Defense Richard Cheney, who cited Argentine military participation in the Gulf war and made a gift of two cargo planes and two naval vessels to Argentina. The air force later obtained 40 used warplanes from the United States, to replace losses in the Malvinas/Falklands conflict.

The Menem government gave a high priority to Mercosur, the fledgling Southern Cone common market embracing Brazil, Uruguay, and Paraguay, as well as Argentina. Meeting in Argentina in June, chief executives of the four states worked out a timetable for the bloc to become operational by 1995. Also approved was the construction of a billion-dollar inland barge route on the Paraguay-Paraná river system that would be navigable year-round.

LARRY L. PIPPIN, *University of the Pacific*

ARGENTINA • Information Highlights

Official Name: Argentine Republic.
Location: Southern South America.
Area: 1,068,297 sq mi (2 766 890 km²).
Population (mid-1992 est.): 33,100,000.
Chief Cities (mid-1990 est., incl. suburbs): Buenos Aires, the capital, 11,382,002; Cordoba, 1,166,932; Rosario, 1,096,254.
Government: Head of state and government, Carlos Saúl Menem, president (took office July 8, 1989). Legislature—Senate and Chamber of Deputies.
Monetary Unit: Austral (9,901 australs equal U.S.$1, financial rate, Dec. 8, 1992).
Gross National Product (1990 est. U.S.$): $82,700,-000,000.
Economic Indexes: Consumer Prices (1991, 1988 = 100), all items, 216,061.9; food, 185,492.0. Industrial Production (1989, 1980 = 100), 79.
Foreign Trade (1990 U.S.$): Imports, $4,076,000,000; exports, $12,353,000,000.

ARIZONA

In the 1992 elections, Arizona voters gave their eight electoral votes to President George Bush and overwhelmingly adopted a paid holiday in honor of Martin Luther King, Jr. Two competing holiday proposals had been defeated in referenda in 1990.

Elections. With 14 propositions on the ballot, Arizona had more issues subject to public vote than any other state in 1992. By a two-to-one margin, voters rejected a measure that would have banned almost all abortions in the state. But a term-limit amendment passed as did a constitutional requirement that all new taxes and fees be approved by a two-thirds vote of the legislature. In addition, the requirement that governors be elected by majority vote was repealed. The provision had been adopted in 1988 after Evan Mecham won with 40% of the vote but then was forced into a runoff election in 1991. Voters also deemed that executions should be by lethal injection instead of the gas chamber.

Although U.S. Sen. John McCain had been rebuked by the Senate Ethics Committee for actions in behalf of Charles Keating, Jr., a thrift operator who was convicted of fraud and racketeering, he easily won a second term. In Arizona's new 6th District, state Sen. Karan English (D) defeated Doug Wead, a Christian fundamentalist. Incumbent U.S. Representative John J. Rhodes (R) was defeated by Democrat Sam Coppersmith after surviving a difficult three-way primary. Rhodes had been implicated in the House check-bouncing scandal. The state's four other congressmen—Ed Pastor (D), Bob Stump (R), Jon Kyl (R), and Jim Kolbe (R)—were reelected easily.

In the state legislature, Republicans regained control of the Senate by a margin of 18 to 12; the margin had been 17D-13R. In the House, Republicans increased their margin from 33–27 to 35–25.

Crime and Legal Issues. Former state Sen. Carolyn Walker, the only legislator implicated in a 1991 political-corruption scandal to go to trial, was convicted of conspiracy and filing a false campaign-expense report. She was acquitted on seven other charges, including bribery and money laundering.

In Prescott a U.S. District Court jury convicted former Navajo Tribal Chairman Peter MacDonald on 16 counts of racketeering, extortion, fraud, and interstate transportation in aid of racketeering and conspiracy. He still was serving time on his convictions in Navajo court.

Federal marshals seized gambling equipment on several of Arizona's Indian reservations in the absence of a gambling compact between the state and the tribes. Angry residents of the Fort McDowell Apache reservation for a time barricaded roads to prevent the equipment's removal. In late November the state agreed to allow 250 video-gambling machines.

Biosphere 2. At the Biosphere 2, a glass enclosure in which eight persons plan to stay for two years to assess the ecology of a closed system, oxygen levels were dropping after completion of the first year. The unexplained decline resulted in an atmosphere equivalent to that of an altitude of nearly 12,000 ft (3 658 m). Oxygen was being piped from the chemistry lab to the eight residents' bedrooms. The oxygen deficiency had interfered with sleep. All inhabitants also experienced significant weight loss, which led to increased use of the three-month emergency food supply. A scientific review committee—chaired by Thomas Lovejoy, a biologist from the Smithsonian Institution—criticized the Biosphere committee's overall scientific plan.

PETER GOUDINOFF
The University of Arizona

ARKANSAS

Arkansas Gov. Bill Clinton's successful campaign for the U.S. presidency kept the state in the national limelight during 1992. Campaigning in the party primaries and for the general election exposed the strengths and weaknesses of the state as never before. The governor's frequent absences brought added attention to the office of lieutenant governor and the authority of the "acting governor." His resignation sparked a lawsuit to determine the method of filling the vacancy that the Arkansas Supreme Court resolved by ruling that Lt. Gov. Jim Guy Tucker would become governor.

Government. Problems in the Department of Human Services, first over child-welfare concerns, then with problems in Medicaid reimbursement, forced the governor to call two special sessions of the General Assembly. The first, a five-day session called after a class-

---

ARIZONA • Information Highlights

Area: 114,000 sq mi (295 260 km²).
Population (July 1, 1991 est.): 3,750,000.
Chief Cities (1990 census): Phoenix, the capital, 983,403; Tucson, 405,390; Mesa, 288,091; Glendale, 148,134; Tempe, 141,865.
Government (1992): *Chief Officers*—governor, J. Fife Symington (R); secretary of state, Richard Mahoney (D). *Legislature*—Senate, 30 members; House of Representatives, 60 members.
State Finances (fiscal year 1991): *Revenue,* $9,016,000,000; *expenditure,* $7,872,000,000.
Personal Income (1991): $62,166,000,000; per capita, $16,579.
Labor Force (June 1992): *Civilian labor force,* 1,725,000; *unemployed,* 123,800 (7.2% of total force).
Education: *Enrollment* (fall 1990)—public elementary schools, 479,050; public secondary, 160,803; colleges and universities, 264,735. *Public school expenditures* (1990), $2,532,510,000.

In Little Rock on Dec. 12, 1992, Bill Clinton relinquished the governorship of Arkansas as he prepared to move into the White House, and Lt. Gov. Jim Guy Tucker, 49-year-old former state attorney general and U.S. congressman, took the oath of office as the state's chief executive.

© W. L. "Pat" Patterson/Office of Arkansas Secretary of State

action lawsuit was filed against the state, met in February and approved, along with 77 other bills, a $15 million increase in child-welfare benefits. Other key legislation included provisions for removing unconstitutional or illegal references to race from the charters of colleges and universities and a $10 million fund to assist in recruiting aerospace industries to locate in the state.

Changes in federal reimbursement practices for the Medicaid program brought legislators back into session in December. Funding for Medicaid services had plagued state officials throughout the year. In April, health-service employees were required to take a 20% pay cut in an attempt to avoid a budget shortfall. Such efforts were only temporarily successful, and by fall budget deficits forced the termination of

25 workers. The second special session provided an increase in funding.

Republican Congressman John Paul Hammerschmidt retired after a 13-term career representing the 3d District, while Beryl Anthony, Jr., a seven-term congressman from the 4th District, and Rep. Bill Alexander, a 12-term member of Congress from the 1st District, were defeated in the Democratic primary. State Sen. Max Howell, a senior member of the General Assembly, retired after 45 years. In November, U.S. Sen. Dale Bumpers was reelected with 60% of the vote. Voters also approved a term-limits amendment to the constitution.

Environmental concerns received much attention. Issues included disputes over hazardous-waste incineration, disposal of animal waste, new regulations for solid-waste disposal, a court injunction against out-of-state garbage being shipped to local landfills, timber-management practices in the Ouachita National Forest, and tests for the feasibility of commercial mining at Crater of Diamonds state park.

Social and Educational Issues. Little Rock had a record number of homicides in 1992, and attacks on personnel caused school officials in central Arkansas to adopt new security measures. . . . The school dropout rate continued to decline, reaching a low of 3.6% in 1992. . . . The State Board of Education adopted a policy of requiring a "C" average for students to participate in extracurricular activities.

Other News. Former U.S. Congressman Wilbur Mills (D-AK) and businessman Sam Walton died in 1992 . . . . Eaker Air Force base, established in 1962, was closed in March.

C. FRED WILLIAMS
University of Arkansas at Little Rock

ARKANSAS • Information Highlights

Area: 53,187 sq mi (137 754 km²).
Population (1990 census): 2,350,725.
Chief Cities (1990 census): Little Rock, the capital, 175,795; Fort Smith, 72,798; North Little Rock, 61,741; Pine Bluff, 57,140.
Government (1991): *Chief Officers*—governor, Bill Clinton (D); lt. gov., Jim Guy Tucker (D). *General Assembly*—Senate, 35 members; House of Representatives, 100 members.
State Finances (fiscal year 1990): *Revenue,* $4,511,000,000; *expenditure,* $4,223,000,000.
Personal Income (1990): $33,389,000,000; per capita, $14,188.
Labor Force (June 1991): *Civilian labor force,* 1,137,600; *unemployed,* 86,700 (7.6% of total force).
Education: *Enrollment* (fall 1989)—public elementary schools, 311,060; public secondary, 123,900; colleges and universities, 88,572. *Public school expenditures* (1989), $1,319,370,000.

ART

During 1992 exhibitions of modern art were more common than other major art exhibitions. The emphasis on modern art also was reflected in the art market. Nevertheless, there were outstanding Old Master and non-Western exhibitions as well. Although no major new museums opened in the United States, a number of renovations and new wings were completed. There were major acquisitions of art as well.

Exhibitions. The most talked-about museum show during 1992 was the exhibition entitled "Henri Matisse: A Retrospective," which opened at the Museum of Modern Art (MoMA) in New York City in late September. The first full-scale retrospective devoted to the artist since 1970, the show featured 400 selected works, including loans from the Hermitage and Pushkin museums in Russia and the Centre Pompidou in Paris.

Six Matisses also were included in the stunning show of the "William S. Paley Collection," which opened at MoMA in February. The show was at the Indianapolis Museum of Art in September and the Seattle Art Museum in December. It would move to the Los Angeles County Museum of Art, the San Diego Museum of Art, and the Baltimore Museum of Art in 1993.

Another eagerly awaited retrospective of a modern artist was that of the Belgian Surrealist René Magritte. The show of 150 paintings, drawings, and sculptures premiered at the Hayward Gallery in London in May. It moved to the Metropolitan Museum in New York in September and the Menil Collection in Houston in December. Its final stop would be at the Art Institute of Chicago in 1993.

The Russian and Soviet avant-garde, "The Great Utopia: 1915–32" exhibit stopped at the Guggenheim Museum in New York City in September after being viewed in Europe. The more than 800 works displayed focused on the development and legacy of the abstract art produced in Russia between 1915 and 1932, including works by Kandinsky, Lissitzky, Malevich, Popova, Rodchenko, and Tatlin.

The modernist interpretation of Latin American culture was the focus of a show entitled "Crosscurrents of Modernism: Four Latin American Pioneers," with 90 paintings by Wilfredo Lam, Matta, Diego Rivera, and Joaquín Torres-Garcia. It was shown only at the Hirshhorn Museum in Washington, DC, from June to September.

"Picasso & Things" was the first show to deal exclusively with the still lifes of Pablo Picasso. More than 100 works, ranging in date from 1901 to 1969, were brought together. The show opened at the Cleveland Museum in February, moved to the Philadelphia Museum in June, and closed at the Grand Palais in Paris in December. An exhibition featuring the work of

The first full-scale retrospective devoted to Henri Matisse (1869–1954) since 1970 was presented at New York City's Museum of Modern Art from Sept. 24, 1992, through Jan. 12, 1993. "Music," right, a 1939 oil on canvas from the Albright Knox Art Gallery in Buffalo, NY, was shown.

"The Son of Man," a 1964 oil on canvas from the Harry Torczyner collection, was part of a René Magritte retrospective shown in London, New York, and Houston in 1992.

a more recent modern artist was the retrospective of Richard Diebenkorn with 50 plus paintings, including early abstractions as well as examples from his Bay Area figurative period. After appearing in London, Madrid, and Frankfurt, the show was at the Los Angeles Museum of Contemporary Art from the end of March until mid-June and opened at the San Francisco Museum of Modern Art in November.

"Hand-Painted Pop: The Formative Years, 1955–62" examined the links between pop art and abstract-expressionist technique. The show opened at the Museum of Contemporary Art in Los Angeles in December and would move to New York's Whitney Museum in the summer of 1993. Shows of contemporary art included a survey of the late African-American graffiti artist Jean-Michel Basquiat, which opened at the Whitney Museum in October. Also opening at the Whitney Museum, in November, was a retrospective of the Minimalist painter Agnes Martin. The show would be on view in other museums in 1993.

Old Master retrospectives included shows by Italian Renaissance masters Andrea Mantegna and Leonardo da Vinci. The Mantegna exhibition of 130 works of prints, drawings, and paintings in grisaille by Mantegna and his school opened in London and then traveled to New York's Metropolitan Museum in early May. The Leonardo exhibition demonstrated the artist's understanding of human anatomy. Comprised of 40 drawings from the collection of Queen Elizabeth II, the show premiered at the Philadelphia Museum in September and later was to be exhibited at Houston's Museum of Fine Arts and the Museum of Fine Arts in Boston.

Two other Old Master shows included paintings by the Italian Baroque painter Guercino (Giovanni Francesco Barbieri) and the Spanish Baroque painter Jusepe de Ribera. The Guercino show opened at the National Gallery of Art in Washington, DC, in the spring after appearing in Bologna and Frankfurt in 1991. Ribera, known for his dramatic pictures of martyrdoms and penitent saints, was honored with a show of 60 works, many never exhibited outside Spain and Italy. This 400th-anniversary show of Ribera's birth made its last stop at the Metropolitan Museum in September after being exhibited in Spain and Italy.

French 18th-century mythological painting was surveyed in the show "The Loves of the Gods: Mythological Painting in 18th Century France." The 65 works included paintings by Watteau, Boucher, Fragonard, David, and others. After opening at the Grand Palais in Paris in 1991, the show arrived at the Philadelphia Museum in February and closed at the Kimbell Museum in Fort Worth, TX, in August.

Shows of U.S. artists included an exhibition of works by the 19th-century *trompe l'oeil* painter William M. Harnett. Premiering at the Metropolitan Museum of Art in March with 50 paintings, the exhibition moved to the Amon Carter Museum in Fort Worth in July, the Fine Arts Museum in San Francisco in November, and would close at the National Gallery in Washington in 1993.

A U.S. artist of more recent vintage, George Bellows of the Ashcan school, was given his first retrospective since 1957 with 65 canvases, including genre scenes as well as celebrated sporting subjects such as the boxing match between Jack Dempsey and Luis Firpo. The show opened at the Los Angeles County Museum in February; moved to New York's Whitney Museum in June and the Columbus (OH) Museum of Art in October; and would close at Fort Worth's Amon Carter Museum in 1993.

"The Century of Tung Ch'i-Ch'ang" was the first major retrospective of painting and calligraphy by this artist and critic who is of major importance because of his enormous influence on 17th-century Chinese art. More than 170 of his works were shown at the Nelson-Atkins in Kansas City in April, the Los Angeles County

Museum in July, and New York's Metropolitan Museum in October.

The highly touted "Al-Andalus: The Art of Islamic Spain" was the first comprehensive exhibition of Spanish Islamic art from the 8th through the 15th centuries. Featured among the more than 100 objects were illuminated manuscripts, ceramics, ivories, arms and armor, textiles, carpets, and architectural elements, including a magnificent domed ceiling from the famed Alhambra in Granada, Spain. The exhibit opened at the Metropolitan Museum in July after premiering at the Alhambra in March.

Significant art of the ancient world was featured in shows from ancient Egypt and the ancient Near East. "Egypt's Dazzling Sun: Amenhotep III and His World," with 100 works produced during Egypt's golden age during the reign of the 14th-century B.C. pharaoh, opened at the Cleveland Museum in July. The show would travel to the Kimbell Museum in October. The ancient Near East was represented with a show entitled "The Royal City of Susa: Ancient Near Eastern Treasures from the Louvre." It opened at the Metropolitan Museum in November, with 200 objects from the royal city of Susa in Iran, ranging in date from 5000 B.C. to 500 A.D.

"The Greek Miracle: Classical Sculpture from the Dawn of Democracy, Fifth Century B.C." premiered at the National Gallery in November and would travel to the Metropolitan Museum in 1993. With 33 bronze and marble sculptures from the Greek golden age, including the famed "Kritios Boy," the show was considered a major event in the United States in that it commemorated the 2,500th anniversary of the birth of democracy.

Museums. Perhaps the most exciting museum news during 1992 was the long-awaited reopening of Frank Lloyd Wright's Guggenheim Museum in July to rave reviews. Enlarged by Gwathmey, Siegel and Associates with a controversial tower addition, its opening exhibition featured light works by Dan Flavin for a marriage of architecture and light sculpture. Expanded galleries included selections from the permanent collection, some never seen before. Concurrently, Guggenheim Museum SoHo, designed by the Japanese architect Arata Isozaki, opened in downtown Manhattan. It will show contemporary art. Isozaki and James Stewart Polshek also were responsible for the master plan of another renovation—the west wing of the Brooklyn Museum, which opened in November and added 40,000 sq ft (3 700 m²) of gallery space to the museum.

With the completion of a ten-story addition, designed by Gwathmey, Siegel and Associates, Frank Lloyd Wright's Guggenheim Museum in New York City reopened in July 1992. The museum had undergone an interior restoration.

© Rafael Macia/Photo Researchers

Other reopenings included the Art Institute of Chicago's June unveiling of its remodeled galleries of Chinese, Japanese, and Korean art to the public after a three-year, $5 million facelift, followed by the September opening of an expanded sculpture garden at the Walker Art Center in Minneapolis. The latter was designed by Cambridge (MA) landscape architect Michael Van Valkenburgh.

The Dallas Museum of Art began construction of the Nancy and Jake Harmon Building. Designed by Edward Larrabee Barnes for an 8.9-acre (3.6-ha) site in downtown Dallas, TX, the three-story $30 million wing will add more than 140,000 sq ft (13 000 m²) for two temporary exhibition galleries. It was expected to be completed in the summer of 1993.

Six museums received grants from the Lila Wallace-Reader's Digest Fund to reinstall and present their permanent collections. Included were the Philadelphia Museum, the Minneapolis Institute of Arts, the Walters Art Gallery in Baltimore, the Isabella Stewart Gardner Museum in Boston, the Denver Art Museum, and the Mississippi Museum of Art in Jackson.

New facilities being planned included a new building for Houston's Museum of Fine Arts to be built immediately east of the museum's current location. Rafail Moreo was chosen to design the estimated $40 million, 125,000-sq-ft (11 600-m²) structure. It will double the museum's existing gallery space.

Major acquisitions included the William S. Paley Collection of nearly 80 paintings, drawings, and sculptures to the Museum of Modern Art in New York. The gift included Picasso's "Boy Leading a Horse" and Gauguin's "The Seed of the Aeroi," as well as paintings by Degas, Derain, Matisse, and Cézanne.

Changes in museum personnel included the resignation of J. Carter Brown of the directorship of the National Gallery of Art—a post he held from 1969. Earl A. Powell 3d, head of the Los Angeles County Museum of Art, was named as his successor. In October, Michael Shapiro, the chief curator of the St. Louis Museum, succeeded Powell as director of the Los Angeles Museum. Laughlin Phillips, son of the founder and director of the Phillips Collection in Washington, DC, announced his retirement after 17 years as director and board chairman. He would continue as board chairman. Charles Moffett, senior curator of paintings at the National Gallery of Art from 1987, was named the new director. Robert P. Bergman, director of the Baltimore's Walters Art Gallery, was named to succeed Evan Hopkins Turner as director of the Cleveland Museum. Jane Wilson was elected president of the National Academy of Design.

The Art Market

Auction prices for works of art during 1992 continued in the same gloomy vein as in 1991, with a few exceptions. Although many works failed to sell, high-quality works with good provenance, fresh to the market, brought excellent prices. In short, great works of art still brought great prices. Buyers in 1992 were older, wiser, and knowledgeable collectors looking for bargains who ignored estimates and bid what they considered a fair price. Speculators who drove prices up in the late 1980s were gone. The top prices went to Old Master paintings, followed by modern and Impressionist paintings. The top lot for the year was Antonio Canaletto's "Old Horse Guards, London, From St. James Park," sold for $17.8 million to Andrew Lloyd Webber at Christie's London sale in April. The highest-priced modern painting was Henri Matisse's "Harmony in Yellow." The 1927–28 painting was sold to an anonymous buyer at Christie's in November for $14.5 million, setting a record for Matisse.

The Impressionist market, along with the volatile contemporary market in general, suffered the biggest decline. The highest-priced Impressionist painting was Claude Monet's beautiful "Waterlily Basin" for $12.1 million at Christie's November sale. The top lot in the contemporary market was Andy Warhol's "Marilyn X 100," a 1962 silk screen that sold at Sotheby's November sale for $3.7 million. In the 19th-century painting market, sales were down from 1991. The top price for a European painting went to Courbet's "Flowers on a Beach," sold at Christie's for $1.54 million, a record for the artist. Private collectors were the main buyers of 19th-century U.S. art, with such artists as Childe Hassam, Winslow Homer, George Caleb Bingham, Thomas Eakins, Frederick Church, Albert Ryder, Fitz Hugh Lane, and A. F. Tait bringing the top prices. The highest price for a 20th-century U.S. painting went to Georgia O'Keeffe's "Ritz Tower, Night"; the work went for $1.2 million at Christie's November sale.

The Latin American market still was considered strong. The high roller of 1992 as in 1991 was Diego Rivera, whose "Mujer Con Alcatraces" sold for $2.8 million at Sotheby's spring sale. Other top names included Fernando Botero, Rufino Tamayo, Wilfredo Lam, Roberto Matta Echaurren, Joaquín Torres Garcia, Frida Kahlo, José Maria Velasco, and Remedios Vara.

Major gifts to museums included the William S. Paley Collection—nearly 80 paintings, drawings, and sculpture, mostly by French masters, and with major works by Picasso, Gauguin, Derain, Cézanne, Matisse, and Toulouse-Lautrec—to New York's Museum of Modern Art. New York's Metropolitan Museum collection was enhanced by paintings from Mr. and Mrs. Douglas Dillon.

MARGARET BROWN HALSEY
*New York City Technical College
of the City University of New York*

ASIA

Asia continued its remarkable overall economic performance in 1992 despite the world recession. During 1991 the region had achieved a 5.8% domestic-national-product growth rate, while the global economy languished with 0.3% negative growth. The Asia-Pacific area has tripled its share of world gross national product (GNP) since 1960, and it is estimated that the region will constitute one fifth of the world economy by the year 2000.

APEC, ASEAN, and Regional Development. Buttressing the economic expansion were significant new regional institutions directed toward political, economic, and security cooperation. Foremost among these are the Asia Pacific Economic Cooperation (APEC) forum and the Association of Southeast Asian Nations' new Free Trade Area (AFTA) plan. Formed in 1989, APEC is the only international organization to include the "three Chinas"—Hong Kong, Taiwan, and the People's Republic (PRC)—as members. The organization was focusing primarily on regional trade liberalization at a time when protectionism was on the upswing elsewhere. At its September 1992 meeting in Bangkok, Thailand, APEC members agreed to establish a permanent secretariat. Moreover, in recognition of the imminent creation of a North American Free Trade Area, APEC agreed to study the prospect for Mexico's future membership. APEC's most important achievement thus far was the establishment of regional data bases on trade, technology, tourism, human-resource development, energy, marine pollution, telecommunications, fisheries, and transportation.

ASEAN took the first steps toward the establishment of an Asian-Pacific trade bloc. At its fourth summit in Singapore, Jan. 27–28, 1992, ASEAN heads of state agreed to the creation of a free-trade area among themselves over a 15-year period. By 2008 tariffs on most agricultural products and manufacturers would be reduced to a 5% maximum. Only unprocessed agricultural commodities would be exempted, primarily at Indonesia's request. The summit also welcomed Vietnam and Laos as the latest signatories to ASEAN's 1976 Treaty of Amity and Cooperation. This action formally marked the Cold War's end in Southeast Asia and also could be seen as the first step toward Indochinese membership in a future expanded ASEAN. Finally, the summit agreed to expand its annual dialogues with major economic and political partners to discuss regional security, though the association stopped short of adding a security dimension to ASEAN's activities.

In northeast Asia, the possibility of a regional development zone in the Tumen Jiang River Valley—which flows across North Korea, China, and Russia—was being discussed by regional specialists. Three ports would be developed at the Tumen Jiang River outlet in North Korea to open entrepôt trade which would link this area to the western Pacific. Japanese and South Korean investors expressed interest in the project at a Pyongyang meeting in May 1992. However, the massive costs ($30 billion) and the political risk for investors in North Korea probably would delay its start for some time to come.

Tension. Asia's most contentious political-security flash point remained the conflict among China, Taiwan, Malaysia, the Philippines, Vietnam, and Brunei over ownership of the Spratly Islands archipelago in the South China Sea. All claimants were increasing the forces on the islands they occupy, though only China and Vietnam exchanged official protests in 1992. In February, China passed a law authorizing the use of force to implement its claim to the entire island chain. Vietnam protested; and the ASEAN states, at their annual foreign ministers' meeting, issued a Declaration on the South China Sea, which proffered an international negotiation framework. China had rejected any international forum for Spratly discussion, though Beijing indicated it was prepared to discuss its claims bilaterally and promised not to use force to settle the dispute.

The Spratlys' importance is based on its rich fisheries, undersea resources, and the fact that the islands are scattered across the major shipping lanes from the Indian Ocean to northeast Asia. A U.S. oil-exploration company was operating test rigs in an area claimed by both Beijing and Hanoi. The Denver-based Crestone Energy Corporation stated that Chinese officials had promised that the PRC navy was prepared to protect Crestone's activities.

Vietnam, desperate for hard currency to fuel its own development programs, also proceeded to sign production-sharing contracts for South China Sea oil exploration. In July, Hanoi authorized the French firm Total to begin drilling in an exploration block adjacent to the area of Crestone's China-backed operations.

Political tension mounted between the PRC and Vietnam. China seized a number of Vietnamese merchant ships on smuggling charges and staked claims on two more islets in the section of the archipelago closest to Vietnam. Analysts believe that these actions constituted a reassertion of China's historic interest in a region that had been blocked during the Cold War by the presence of both Soviet and U.S. forces. However, as the Russian Pacific fleet was leaving Southeast Asia and the United States was reducing its deployments in the region, China felt freer to flex its own political and military muscles, primarily at Vietnam's expense. The net effect, however, might be to drive Vietnam more rapidly toward ASEAN.

SHELDON W. SIMON
Arizona State University

122

ASTRONOMY

In 1992 astronomers made several remarkable discoveries: They probed structures at the edge of the universe, discovered planets around another star, and mapped the surface of an asteroid.

Cosmology. Astronomers announced in April that a satellite had detected evidence of the earliest structures in the universe. Recording minute temperature fluctuations of microwave radiation, the orbiting satellite mapped a fossil pattern that cosmologists had been searching for since 1964. The discovery gave the most persuasive confirmation yet of the Big Bang theory, which says that a minute, dense speck exploded and expanded to create today's universe. Stephen Hawking, celebrity cosmologist and best-selling author of *A Brief History of Time,* called the finding the "discovery of the century, if not of all time."

Most cosmologists see the results as supporting the idea of a universe born some 15 billion years ago at a temperature so hot that only radiation prevailed. There were immense quantities of light and heat but nothing for them to fall on—no atoms, stars, planets, or people.

Launched in November 1989, the Cosmic Background Explorer (COBE) satellite collected hundreds of millions of temperature measurements taken during its first year in orbit. What COBE found was statistical evidence for temperature variations in the so-called cosmic background, the cooled remnant of the Big Bang itself. The fluctuations are minute, averaging only 0.00003° Kelvin. Yet they indicate *density* differences that prevailed when the universe was less than a few hundred thousand years old. These density fluctuations are enough to cause matter to clump by gravitational attraction and ultimately to form the giant structures we see today in the universe— such as galaxies dotting the surfaces of "bubbles" or aligned along "walls" hundreds of millions of light-years long.

The COBE result also compounds a nagging astronomical question: What comprises the known matter that is out there but which cannot be seen, matter that makes up 90% to 99% percent of the universe? To create the bubbles and walls in only 15 billion years, there initially had to be more matter present—to act as a magnet—than can be "seen" today. On every scale—from individual galaxies, to clusters of galaxies, to the cosmic background itself—the mysterious dark matter raises its enigmatic head. Since it cannot be seen, its presence only can be inferred by its effect on what can be seen. A dramatic illustration of the matter's presence was released by U.S. astronomers in January. Their picture shows normally "round" images of distant galaxies bent into arcs by the gravitational tug of dark matter intervening along the line of sight.

New Planets. Providing what may be the first definitive evidence of planetary systems other than our own, two U.S. astronomers in 1992 announced the discovery of planets circling a star other than the Sun. In this case, two bodies were found: One circles its parent star every 66.6 days, the other every 98.2 days. The inner planet, which moves the fastest, has a mass 3.4 times that of the Earth. Its companion tips the scales at 2.8 Earth masses. (For comparison, our solar system's innermost planet, Mercury, orbits the Sun every 88 days and has a mass only 0.05 the Earth's).

The new suspected planets circle a pulsar, a relic of an exploded star. Known as PSR 1257 + 12, it rotates 161 times a second; during each rotation it sends a pulse of radiation toward the Earth. The discovery was made by timing precisely when these pulses arrive. They always occur in a strictly periodic pattern that can be interpreted as due to the gravitational pull of the planets on the pulsar. When the planets pull the pulsar toward Earth, the signals arrive early; when they pull it away, the signals arrive late. The displacement of the pulsar is not much—about 15 ft (4.5 m) each way.

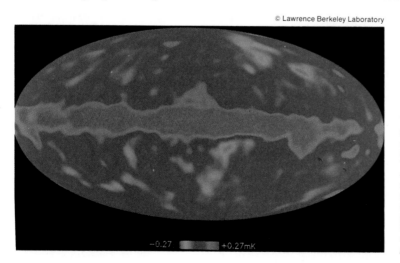

−0.27 ▮▮▮ +0.27mK

The map of the sky, left, taken by instruments aboard the Cosmic Background Explorer satellite, indicates that large wrinkles in "space-time" clumped together into galaxies. Our galaxy (the horizontal band) dominates the microwave sky. Studies performed by the orbiting satellite gave credence to the Big Bang theory, which holds that a minute speck exploded and expanded to create the universe.

© JPL

The U.S. Galileo spacecraft, traveling to the planet Jupiter, took close-up photographs of the asteroid Gaspra, above, revealing its irregular shape and various craters.

Asteroid Portrait. The Galileo spacecraft, en route to encounter Jupiter in 1995, accomplished a space first—close-up photography of an asteroid. On Oct. 29, 1991, the spacecraft passed within 1,000 mi (1 600 km) of the asteroid Gaspra, but because of a crippled antenna its pictures had to be "dribbled" to Earth. Their analysis only appeared in September 1992.

Gaspra was found to be irregularly shaped —11 x 7 x 7 mi (19 x 12 x 11 km) across—and pockmarked with craters. It appears that this asteroid was spawned some 200 million years ago during a catastrophic collision that blew apart its parent body. Bright areas on Gaspra are associated with impact craters and are thought to be freshly exposed terrain. The body's dark areas are probably low-lying sites to which old surface material has migrated. The smoothness of Gaspra suggests its surface is covered by a several-meter-deep granular layer of the mineral olivine, or perhaps pyroxine.

Comet News. In 1951, Gerard P. Kuiper proposed that a reservoir of comets exists beyond the orbit of the planet Pluto. He envisioned it to be the source of comets, like Halley's, that return to the Sun's vicinity time after time. Yet the so-called Kuiper Belt eluded detection. Finally, on Sept. 14, 1992, astronomers announced they had located an object, named 1992QB$_1$, that might be a member of Kuiper's belt. Although its orbit was not known definitely, this body presently lies about 40 astronomical units from the Sun (the Sun-Earth separation is 1 astronomical unit), matching the distance Kuiper proposed. Yet, no matter what this object turns out to be—a giant comet or an ordinary asteroid—it is the most distant object found in the solar system since Pluto was discovered in 1930.

For more than a decade astronomers had anticipated the return of Comet Swift-Tuttle, the parent of the famous Perseid meteor shower that delights stargazers each August. This comet had been seen last in 1862, and researchers only could guess at its orbit.

Unusual bursts of Perseid meteor activity in 1991 and 1992 suggested the comet might be nearby. (Comets leave many tiny particles along their track through the heavens that burn up as meteors when they strike Earth's atmosphere.) On September 26 a Japanese comet hunter picked up the long-sought object through powerful binoculars. Remarkably, calculations made soon after Swift-Tuttle's appearance indicate that there is a one-in-10,000 chance that the comet will strike the Earth at its next return in 2126. Depending on the size of the comet's nucleus and the density of its material, the resulting devastation would envelop areas at least as large as small countries. Yet the cataclysm might be worldwide, threatening civilization.

Frustratingly, it is impossible to predict whether such an impact will occur. Swift-Tuttle is an active comet that frequently spews up gas and debris from its nucleus into space. When it does so, these little "rockets" change the comet's course. Since these jolts are unpredictable, astronomers cannot estimate where the comet will be in orbit come 2126. Celestial menaces to Earth garnered the attention of the U.S. Congress only recently.

Pollution of the Heavens. For many years astronomers increasingly have been concerned about the proliferation of artificial lighting. It brightens the nighttime sky and limits the effectiveness of telescopes seeking the faintest and most distant objects in the universe. In 1984 the Carnegie Institution of Washington closed its famous Mount Wilson Observatory because of light pollution from nearby Los Angeles. And Japan's national observatory near Tokyo has seen its skies brighten sixteenfold between 1958 and 1989.

The problem of light pollution reaches beyond scientific research. It deprives everyone in urban and suburban environments of the chance to see myriads of stars and the splendor of the Milky Way, the band of light that marks the midriff of our home galaxy. So serious has the problem of light pollution become that a special conference was held in June, jointly sponsored by the Tucson-based International Dark-Sky Association, the International Council of Scientific Unions, and UNESCO. Sponsors also addressed the potentially ruinous effects from the overexploitation of radio frequencies and dangers from artificial-satellite and launch-vehicle space debris.

LEIF J. ROBINSON, *"Sky & Telescope"*

AUSTRALIA

In a year in which fiery verbal clashes were standard parliamentary fare, Australians were assailed in 1992 with the rhetoric of competing views on how to ease the malaise of domestic and international deficits and a continuing economic slump marked by official unemployment hovering around 11% with an "under-employment" level estimated at 15%-17%. Meanwhile, the political battleground was being shaped for a general election due early in 1993.

In his first year as prime minister, Paul Keating faced the political fallout stemming from ten years of Australian Labor Party (ALP) rule. With the recession's effects unabated, he undertook traditional measures of fiscal stimulus by boosting government outlays (which resulted in heavier deficit financing) and lowering interest rates. However, business confidence remained low as inflation ran at about 2.5% and gross-domestic-product (GDP) growth was scarcely 2%.

The Economy. Economic changes seen as necessary for recovery were slow to appear. A weaker Australian dollar provided some relief, but international competitiveness remained elusive in spite of some structural reform at the industry level and in transport. A major factor in the employment picture stemmed from changes within the hard-hit manufacturing sector, where job loss was driven by the need to become internationally competitive and more export-oriented. The dismantling of tariff protection continued to cause manufacturers to move offshore, with the share of domestic manufacturing sales taken by imports rising.

Stock prices drifted, reflecting the corporate sector's mediocre to poor results. Banks in particular suffered major balance-sheet problems. National savings fell to a record low, continuing a three-year decline, but there was improvement in housing construction.

For working people, average income rose marginally, while those dependent on investment returns suffered sharp declines. With the continuing slackness in consumer confidence, personal spending remained hesitant in spite of a level of sustained prosperity that defied the broader economic indicators. The hardening "rich and poor" syndrome attracted the attention of church leaders, who joined the economic fight, giving scant comfort to politicians.

Meanwhile the rural economy remained under severe cost pressure; seasonal conditions were mixed, with pastoral areas in New South Wales and Queensland suffering drought while major grain-growing regions received good rains.

Regional Performance. Arising from regional differences in economic activity, a clear dichotomy was evident between the states of Queensland, New South Wales, and Western Australia, all performing at or above the national average; and Victoria, South Australia, and Tasmania, performing below the national average. With manufacturing under a cloud, the heavy factory dependence in Victoria and South Australia accentuated problems arising from injudicious financial management. Queensland and Western Australia, with the lowest reliance on manufacturing, showed strength with the high proportion of their output from mining and rural industry. New South Wales, with a well-balanced economy and greater emphasis on the services sector (including tourism), also fared better. Only Queensland had a budget in surplus.

The Budget. The expansionary budget presented by Treasurer John Dawkins in August extended an economic statement in February that announced increases in federal funding for vocational-training programs for both young job seekers and retrenched adult workers. In a major initiative, funds were allocated for refurbishment of the rail trunk linking mainland capitals. With 1992–93 outlays of A$110 billion (up 7.1%) and projected revenue of A$96 billion (up 3.4%), the budget deficit rose to A$13.4 billion.

Politics. The state of the economy, and ways to correct its problems, dominated political argument. Most in contention was the program of change set out in the Liberal Party's "Fightback!" plan (introduced in December 1991) by opposition leader John R. Hewson—a corrective approach (including a "goods and services" consumption tax of 15% and industrial-relations-reform measures designed to strip unions of dominance by instituting "workplace agreements") that contrasted with what many judged to be Keating's political expediency. Hewson's emphasis on economic correctives, which Parliament watchers referred to as a return to "working-class oratory," left him with an image problem that the ALP exploited.

AUSTRALIA • Information Highlights

Official Name: Commonwealth of Australia.
Location: Southwestern Pacific Ocean.
Area: 2,967,896 sq mi (7 686 850 km²).
Population (mid-1992 est.): 17,800,000.
Chief Cities (mid-1987 est.): Canberra, the capital, 289,800; Sydney, 3,531,600; Melbourne, 2,965,-600; Brisbane, 1,215,300.
Government: *Head of state,* Elizabeth II, queen; represented by Bill Hayden, governor-general (took office February 1989). *Head of government,* Paul Keating, prime minister (took office Dec. 19, 1991). *Legislature*—Parliament: Senate and House of Representatives.
Monetary Unit: Australian dollar (1.4388 A$ equal U.S.$1, Nov. 9, 1992).
Gross Domestic Product (1990 U.S.$): $254,400,-000,000.
Economic Indexes (1991): *Consumer Prices* (1980 = 100), all items, 225.1; food, 211.1. *Industrial Production* (1988, 1980 = 100), 129.
Foreign Trade (1991 U.S.$): *Imports,* $38,581,-000,000; *exports,* $41,716,000,000.

The ALP dropped out of government in two states (Tasmania, in December 1991, and Victoria, in October) but retained power in Queensland's September election. In South Australia the party's federal president, John Bannon, resigned the state premiership in the face of damaging evidence presented to an official inquiry into huge losses by the state-owned bank and associated lending agencies.

The June resignation of Nick Greiner, Liberal premier of New South Wales, followed a quasijudicial inquiry into his appointment of a former parliamentarian to a government post. Greiner's apparent expediency was found to be "corrupt," and he resigned rather than precipitate a no-confidence motion in Parliament. In an appeal to the state's Supreme Court, the corruption finding was overturned.

In April the ALP was humiliated in a by-election for former Prime Minister Robert Hawke's seat in suburban Melbourne, when a left-wing populist secured 34% of the primary vote (compared with 29% for ALP and 27% for the Liberals) and won the seat on distribution of preferences.

Foreign Relations. As prime minister, Keating accented Australia's "swing to Asia/Pacific" with visits to Indonesia and Papua New Guinea and then to Japan, Singapore, and Cambodia, as part of a studied move toward strengthening regional groupings in general and trade matters. Much was made of his call for a downgrading of traditional ties with Britain. Meanwhile, reports indicated that among U.S. businessmen Australia was seen increasingly as a useful "gateway to Asia." U.S. trade policies, especially in relation to EEP (external economic policy) support for wheat, brought expressions of concern, but the U.S. alliance remained intact.

After 30 years, control of the VLF radio base for communication with nuclear-powered submarines, built at North West Cape, passed from U.S. to Australian hands.

High-Court Decisions. A legal precedent was set when Australia's High Court decided that a group of Torres Strait Islanders had a valid native title to the Murray Islands off Queensland. The decision had implications for the legal framework of property rights throughout Australia; previously the concept of *terra nullus* (inferring an unoccupied land) had prevailed ever since initial settlement in 1788, but the court ruled that "native title" could exist where such rights had not been extinguished by the government. The court's recognition of the Murray Islands claim was held to be of immense significance.

Declaring it to be an abrogation of an implied freedom of political expression, the High Court struck down a law banning electronic-media advertising during the official election campaign. Another decision threw out a case against a journalist and his newspaper over criticism of the functioning of the Industrial Relations Commission. The two judgments were seen as support by the High Court for a "bill of rights" concept (which the constitution itself implies but does not contain).

R. M. YOUNGER
Author, "Australia and the Australians"

AUSTRIA

For Austria, the year 1992 was one of moderate economic growth, political stability, and heavy involvement with refugees from Eastern Europe.

Government. The Social Democratic-People's Party coalition, headed by Socialist Chancellor Franz Vranitzky, remained in power throughout 1992. Despite several personnel changes in March, the basic political composition of the cabinet remained the same.

Elections for the six-year term as president were held on April 26. President Kurt Waldheim had announced on June 21, 1991, that he would not seek reelection. Rudolf Streicher, a Social Democrat, received 40.8% of the vote. He was followed by Thomas Klestil of the People's Party, with 37.1%; Heide Schmidt of the right-wing Freedom Party, with 16.4%; and Robert Jungk of the Green Alternative Party, with 5.7%. Since no one had achieved a 50% majority, a runoff was held on May 24 between Streicher and Klestil. Klestil received 56.85% of the votes, carrying all nine provinces.

At a meeting of the parliament on July 8, Waldheim took formal leave of office and Klestil was sworn in. In his inaugural address, Klestil promised an active nonpartisan presidency, supportive of Austrian membership within the European Community (EC) as soon as possible. Austria's application for membership in that organization dates from 1989.

Foreign Affairs. Following the diplomatic recognition of Slovenia and Croatia by the

---

AUSTRIA • Information Highlights

Official Name: Republic of Austria.
Location: Central Europe.
Area: 32,375 sq mi (83 850 km²).
Population (mid-1992 est.): 7,900,000.
Chief Cities (1991 census): Vienna, the capital, 1,533,176; Graz, 232,155; Linz, 202,855; Salzburg, 143,971; Innsbruck, 114,996.
Government: *Head of state,* Thomas Klestil, president (took office July 8, 1992). *Head of government,* Franz Vranitzky, chancellor (took office June 16, 1986). *Legislature*—Federal Assembly: Federal Council and National Council.
Monetary Unit: Schilling (10.79 schillings equal U.S. $1, Oct. 27, 1992).
Gross Domestic Product (1990 U.S.$): $111,000,000,000.
Economic Indexes (1991): *Consumer Prices* (1980 = 100), all items, 145.9; food, 135.2. *Industrial Production* (1980 = 100), 135.
Foreign Trade (1991 U.S.$): *Imports,* $50,740,-000,000; *exports,* $41,086,000,000.

On July 8, 1992, Thomas Klestil, 59-year-old career diplomat and member of the People's Party, took the oath as president of Austria. In his inaugural address, the new chief executive spoke on behalf of Austria's membership in the European Community (EC).

© P. Kurz/Contrast/Gamma-Liaison

states of the EC, Austria on January 15 also granted them recognition. The government undertook substantial economic aid for the two regions, and a popular relief fund drive raised about $36 million in additional funds over a ten-week period. As the fighting in Yugoslavia continued and spread to Bosnia-Herzegovina, the number of refugees fleeing to Austria increased dramatically, totaling 57,000 by August. The provision of basic life-support needs for these refugees imposed large fiscal burdens on both the national and provincial governments.

On March 27, President Waldheim paid a visit to Munich to receive an award from the conservative Peutinger Collegium. During his visit he was a luncheon guest of German Chancellor Helmut Kohl and Bavarian Prime Minister Max Streibl. This reception by German leaders provoked much criticism from international Jewish organizations and the Israeli government, which remained severely hostile to Waldheim because of his controversial service in the German army during World War II.

Austria and Italy finally resolved long-standing differences regarding South Tyrol. Following World War I, when Austria was required to cede South Tyrol to Italy, there were many differences relating to the treatment of Germans living there. Austria referred these differences to the League of Nations and later to the United Nations (UN). In 1969, Austria and Italy agreed to a so-called South Tyrol Package, consisting of 137 measures to safeguard the German- and Romansh-speaking groups in South Tyrol. Implementation went slowly, but on June 19, 1992, Austria informed UN Secretary-General Boutros Boutros-Ghali that the differences were resolved.

Always a strong supporter of the UN, Austria completed its second two-year term (1973–74; 1991–92) as a nonpermanent member of the Security Council. Over the years Austria has been one of the three largest contributors of personnel to the UN peacekeeping forces, with many Austrian officers serving in command positions. In 1992, Austria's ambassador to the UN, Peter Hohenfellner, headed the committee to supervise the embargo against Iraq. And at the June UN Conference on Environment and Development in Rio de Janeiro, Chancellor Vranitzky gave two major addresses.

Economy. In a meeting in Brussels on February 14, negotiators from the seven-member European Free Trade Association (EFTA) and the 12-member EC reached agreement on differences which had held up the establishment of the European Economic Area (EEA), scheduled to go into effect on Jan. 1, 1993. This pact, designed to ease trading conditions among the 19 member states, was ratified by the Austrian parliament at the end of September.

Austria, with a labor force of 3.4 million, employed 55% in the service sector, 33% in industry and small trades, and 8% in agriculture. Refugees added considerably to the number of foreign workers regularly employed. The real growth of the 1992 Austrian economy was estimated to be 2%, down slightly from 1991.

Other Events. On March 30, Austrian Air Lines inaugurated direct flights from Vienna to Chicago, its second scheduled U.S. destination (after New York).

After study at the University of Innsbruck, scientists held that the body of a man found in the Similaun Glacier of the Oetztaler Alps in September 1991 dates from the Stone Age (ca. 5000 B.C.) rather than from the Bronze Age (ca. 1800 B.C.) as originally thought. Although the body was recovered by Austrian authorities, later surveys determined that it was found on Italian South Tyrol territory. In February it was agreed that the university would turn over the body to South Tyrol by Sept. 19, 1994.

ERNST C. HELMREICH
Professor of History Emeritus
Bowdoin College

AUTOMOBILES

Spurting sales of light trucks, including increasingly popular family minivans and all-wheel-drive utility vehicles, gave the U.S. auto industry a lift in 1992 out of the recession which began in 1990.

Sales. The upswing in the truck market was welcome news to the Big Three automakers—General Motors (GM), Ford, and Chrysler Corporation. New-car sales remained sluggish and mostly unprofitable because costly incentives were required to spur sales, even for the Japanese makes. But the Big Three long have dominated in trucks by a wide margin and profits on pickups, vans and utility vehicles were quite substantial.

With new-car sales failing to recover from the disappointing levels of 1991, demand for light trucks took a record share of the total market in 1992. Truck sales amounted to 3,093,030 units in the first eight months of 1992, compared with 2,791,162 in the same period of the previous year and equal to 36.0% of the overall market. Car volume, by contrast, declined to 5,508,988 from 5,520,658.

Overall U.S. new-car and light-truck sales totaled 8,602,018 units during the first eight months of 1992, up from 8,311,820 in the same period of 1991. The 1992 sum included 6,259,955 from the Big Three, compared with 5,892,076; 2,107,835 from Japanese transplant or home plants, compared with 2,176,634; and 234,228 from Europe, against 243,110.

The domestic Big Three benefited from the fact that they accounted for 85.9% of light-truck sales in the 1992-model year, compared with 14.0% for Japanese entries. The car market, on the other hand, kept the Japanese share at 30.0% and the European slice at 4.1%, while the Big Three garnered 64.5%. Fueling the strength of the Big Three in the truck side were Chrysler's eight-year-long hold on nearly half of the minivan market, the introduction of larger utility vehicles by Ford and Chrysler, and the growing acceptance of light trucks and their offshoots by owners who once opted for station wagons or sedans as their family "second" vehicles. Chevrolet sold more trucks than cars for the first time ever.

The Japanese automakers, moreover, felt the effects of the economic downturn in the United States for the first time in new-car sales from their "transplant" factories in North America, as well as among their import units.

A strong "buy-American" sentiment hurt the Japanese in the wake of a visit by U.S. President George Bush and the chairmen of the Big Three to Tokyo in January 1992. A spate of Big Three plant closings and weak profit reports in 1991 and early 1992 aroused concerns about the ability of the U.S. auto industry to maintain its competitive edge against the Japanese and the European Community (EC).

WORLD MOTOR VEHICLE DATA, 1991

Country	Passenger Car Production	Truck and Bus Production	Motor Vehicle Registrations
Argentina	114,113	24,845	5,784,500
Australia	278,421	14,904	9,776,600
Austria	13,682	5,506	3,691,749
Belgium	253,491	84,170	4,276,737
Brazil	705,363	254,763	13,063,345
Canada	1,072,352	833,103	16,553,385
China	40,300	604,196	5,835,865
Czechoslovakia	172,726	28,587	3,508,120
France	3,187,634	423,139	28,460,000
Germany	4,809,480	390,523	38,276,274
Hungary	–	5,001	2,195,338
India	176,995	176,569	4,350,000
Italy	1,631,941	245,385	29,727,000
Japan	9,753,069	3,492,363	57,697,669
Korea, South	1,158,245	339,573	3,394,803
Mexico	720,384	268,989	9,882,490
The Netherlands	84,709	26,103	6,091,294
Poland	154,578	30,000	6,304,000
Spain	1,773,752	307,959	14,442,492
USSR	1,170,000	759,000	24,002,364
United Kingdom	1,236,900	217,141	26,301,748
United States	5,438,579	3,371,942	188,655,462*
Yugoslavia	215,789	26,126	4,439,360
Total	34,162,503	11,929,887	582,981,777**

*U.S. total does not include Puerto Rico, which has 1,527,611 vehicles.
**World total includes 444,899,624 cars and 138,082,153 trucks and buses. Other countries with more than one million vehicle registrations include Algeria, 1,250,000; Bulgaria, 1,500,000; Chile, 1,016,641; Denmark, 1,892,624; Finland, 2,217,729; Greece, 2,522,628; Indonesia, 2,591,087; Iran, 2,200,000; Iraq, 1,040,730; Ireland, 1,028,667; Malaysia, 2,426,799; New Zealand, 1,867,745; Nigeria, 1,410,000; Norway, 1,942,558; Philippines, 1,219,471; Portugal, 2,198,000; Romania, 1,100,000; Saudi Arabia, 4,500,000; South Africa, 5,200,153; Switzerland, 3,297,237; Taiwan, 2,800,000; Thailand, 2,813,865; Turkey, 2,359,738; and Venezuela, 2,184,000. *Source*: Motor Vehicle Manufacturers Association of the United States, Inc.

Management. Hardest hit of all major automakers by the profits crunch was the biggest producer of all—GM. After net losses of nearly $2 billion in 1990 and an all-time high of $4.5 billion in 1991, followed by a loss of $930 million in the first nine months of 1992, Robert C. Stempel resigned as chairman in October 1992. The resignation occurred only 27 months after he assumed the top spot in GM management. Replacing the 59-year-old Stempel as chief executive officer was John F. Smith, Jr., a 54-year-old veteran of the corporation's finance and international staffs who headed GM overseas operations during a prosperous expansion

The new Ford Probe was marketed with the young, image-conscious buyer of sports coupes in mind and offers a 16-valve, four-cylinder engine or a 24-valve, V-6 engine.

© Ford Motor Company

following the collapse of Communist regimes in Eastern Europe. Smith had been promoted to GM president and chief operating officer at the board's insistence in April 1992, as nonmanagement directors, led by former Procter & Gamble Co. Chairman John G. Smale, pressured Stempel for drastic steps to halt GM's decline. Smale, 65, became chairman upon Stempel's resignation.

Top-level management changes also were put into place at Ford Motor Co. and Chrysler Corp. with the active-duty retirements of chairmen Harold A. Poling and Lee A. Iacocca, respectively. Iacocca, the former Ford president who is credited with orchestrating a turnaround which saved Chrysler from bankruptcy in the 1980s, handed over the Chrysler chairmanship Dec. 31, 1992, to a former president of GM of Europe, Robert J. Eaton. The 68-year-old Iacocca was to stay on as chairman of the Chrysler board's executive committee. At Ford, Poling, 62, was scheduled to retire as chief executive officer on April 1, 1993. The identity of his successor was to be disclosed by the end of 1992.

Imports and Transplants. Although the U.S. market share taken by the imported and U.S.-built Japanese makes held close to 1991 levels in 1992, transplant facilities were expanded by Nissan and a capacity enlargement program was speeded up by Toyota. Nissan's Smyrna (TN) facility added production of a new Altima midsize car, replacing the Stanza. Smyrna also was building Sentra subcompact cars and pickup trucks. Toyota's Camry midsize car plant at Georgetown, KY, was on stream to double its capacity for the 1994-model year and may add production of the Lexus 300 models imported from Japan for Toyota's upscale franchise.

For the fourth year in a row, the Honda Accord produced at Marysville, OH, was leading all makes in U.S. new-car sales during 1992. But the Ford Taurus, also a midsize car,

© General Motors
In an effort to regain lost customers and improve its financial picture, General Motors redesigned several of its models, including the Cadillac Seville, above.

was running a close second to the Accord. Honda also was assembling Civic subcompact cars in Ohio and in 1992 was joined by Toyota as a Japanese automaker producing a majority of its U.S.-sold cars in transplant locations.

The 1993 Models. Highly rounded or "ovoid" styling predominated on domestic and imported model changes. Big Three cars featuring the new look included Chrysler's highly acclaimed new midsize sedans, the Chrysler Concorde, Dodge Intrepid, and Eagle Vision; Ford's Probe and Lincoln Mark VIII, and GM's Cadillac Seville and Eldorado and Pontiac Bonneville and Grand Am.

Not to be outdone, Japanese producers emitted a bevy of new models with flowing design cues. Mazda introduced four car lines with the new look—two assembled at its Flat Rock (MI) plant shared with Ford, the 626 and MX-6 in the compact segment, plus two imported from Japan, the higher-priced 929 sedan and RX-7 coupe. Restyled Toyota Corolla and Mitsubishi Mirage subcompacts joined the new vogue, as did Nissan's Altima compact.

Mazda canceled plans for an upscale Amati franchise, planned for 1994. Amati was to have joined Toyota Lexus, Nissan Infiniti, and Honda Acura in a fast-growing luxury-car group.

The truck market welcomed several newcomers. Ford's Explorer and Chrysler's Grand Cherokee got off to a fast sales start in the upscale utility-vehicle segment. Ford and Nissan jointly introduced a front-wheel-drive minivan called the Mercury Villager and Nissan Quest and built at Ford's Avon Lake (OH) plant.

GM's three-year-old Saturn small-car division, a pioneer in labor relations and marketing techniques, became a popular entry with sales in excess of 16,000 units a month. A station-wagon body style was added by Saturn for 1993. The Japanese minicompact producer Daihatsu abandoned the U.S. market.

MAYNARD M. GORDON, *Detroit Bureau Chief*
"Dealer Business Magazine"

During December 1992, Ford presented the Lincoln Mark VIII, a newly designed coupe with the company's first multivalve engine—a powerful 32-valve aluminum V-8.

© Ford Motor Company

BALTIC REPUBLICS

The Baltic nations of Lithuania, Latvia, and Estonia gained their independence from the USSR in September 1991, just three months before the final collapse of the Soviet state. It had been more than a half century since Joseph Stalin forcibly had annexed the Baltic republics to the USSR in 1940. Understandably then, 1992, the first year of freedom restored, began with high expectations. However, by year's end the mood in the Baltic region was considerably more somber, as the three countries found themselves enmeshed in problems. They all experienced varying degrees of political fragmentation, economic decline, minority conflicts, and difficulties with Russia.

Among the three, Lithuania experienced the most political fragmentation, Estonia and Lithuania the sharpest economic decline, and Latvia and Estonia the most acute minority problems; by the fall of 1992, relations with Russia had worsened for all of them. These problems compounded the difficulties of moving from Soviet authoritarianism to independent statehood and democratic government.

Lithuania's Political Shift. Lithuania had led the way to independence, proclaiming its sovereignty in defiance of the Soviet Union on March 11, 1990. Under the leadership of its president, the ardent nationalist Vytautas Landsbergis, Lithuania braved a Soviet economic embargo that spring and armed provocations by Soviet troops the following year. The recognition of Lithuanian independence in September 1991 was a victory for Sajudis, Landsbergis' nationalist party. Early in 1992 the governing group plunged into radical economic reform, intending to privatize property and marketize economic relations in quick order. By spring, however, the reforms were foundering, and Landsbergis' attempt to revitalize the process by increasing his own powers was rejected by the voters in a referendum. The decline of public confidence in his leadership and in the policies of Sajudis was reflected in the first postindependence parliamentary elections, held in October and November, when the Democratic Labor (former Communist) Party won 44% of the vote, compared with 20% for Sajudis. The former Communists, led by Algirdas Brazauskas, had campaigned on a platform that advocated slowing down and softening the impact of economic reform.

Economy. Predictably, the Baltic republics experienced economic decline as they began the wrenching process of transforming themselves from command to market economies. All three had abandoned the Russian ruble, but Estonia had the only convertible currency, the *kroon;* it also had the highest rate of inflation, reaching 47% for July and August combined. The country's leadership, intent on turning Estonia toward the West, began cutting trade ties with the former Soviet republics. This resulted in serious shortages of grain and fuel, both of which were imported from Ukraine and Russia in the past. The effect on Estonian agriculture, previously a leader in the USSR, was dramatic. The huge state and collective farms neither could operate their equipment fully nor feed their dairy and swine herds properly. Consequently, hay production was slashed by more than 75%, nearly one third of the dairy herds had to be slaughtered, and milk production fell by half. This meant that Estonia's agricultural exports nearly stopped, while the drop in milk and meat production threatened to imperil the nutritional requirements of the population.

Lithuania's economic plight, which became the main issue in the fall elections, was comparable. Dependent upon fuel from Russia, which now was jacking up its prices, Lithuania by late fall was in the midst of an energy crisis, and many people were without heat and hot water. Lithuanian agriculture was in even worse shape than Estonia's. The Landsbergis government had broken up the large collective farms rapidly and distributed the land to private farmers in small parcels, but the new small farms lacked support structures to provide credit, seed, fertilizer, and equipment.

Minority Rights. The minority-rights problem has been most acute in Latvia and Estonia, both of which include very large Russian and other nonnative populations. Latvians constitute a bare majority (52%) in their country; the Estonians are only a little better off with 60%. Understandably, protecting the historic culture of the original indigenous populations has become a matter of great concern in both countries. In both cases, the largest minority consists of Russians who migrated to the Baltics to work in the sprawling factories built dur-

---

BALTIC STATES · Information Highlights

Nation	Population (in Millions)	Area (sq mi)	(km²)	Capital	Head of State
Estonia	1.6	17,458	45 215	Tallinn	Lennart Meri, president
Latvia	2.7	24,600	63 714	Riga	Anatolijis Gorbunovs, president
Lithuania	3.7	25,200	65 268	Vilnius	Vytautas Landsbergis, president

	Estonia		Latvia		Lithuania	
Ethnic	Estonian	61.5	Latvian	52.0	Lithuanian	79.6
Breakdown	Russian	30.3	Russian	34.0	Russian	9.4
	Other	8.2	Other	14.0	Other	11.0

Concern about the treatment of Russian minorities in the Baltic nations of Estonia and Latvia led Russia's President Boris Yeltsin to cancel further troop withdrawals from the area in the fall of 1992. The action caused debate, especially in Latvia, left.

© Daniel Sheehan/Black Star

ing the Soviet period. Both Latvia and Estonia have adopted an inhospitable attitude toward their minorities. This attitude has been expressed in restrictive citizenship and electoral laws passed in Estonia and pending in Latvia. The idea has been that citizenship should be conferred automatically only on members of the titular nationality whose families were resident in the respective countries at the time of the Soviet annexation in 1940. In Estonia this excluded approximately 40% of the population, which was denied the right to vote in 1992.

Under the new Estonian legislation, noncitizens may apply for citizenship by fulfilling certain requirements, such as two years of residence followed by a one-year waiting period, and the acquisition of a basic working knowledge of the Estonian language. Meanwhile, as noncitizens, these individuals legally are prohibited from participating in property-privatization programs. Also, since Russian was the common language of the former Soviet Union, few Russians or others speak either Estonian or Latvian. Many middle-aged and older residents of Estonia and Latvia consider learning a new language a hardship.

In Latvia, where Latvians are a distinct minority in several industrial cities with large Slavic populations, the debate over the citizenship issue nonetheless has split the government. Prime Minister Ivars Godmanis has taken a restrictive approach, but the foreign minister, Janis Jurkans, adopted a more moderate attitude with an eye to Latvian-Russian relations. In the late summer, Jurkans was dismissed because of his disagreement with Godmanis, but the conflict still was unresolved. One proposal was to settle it by a public referendum, but that raised the question of who would be permitted to vote in the referendum. To the beleaguered minorities of Latvia and Estonia, the real intent of the language and other requirements for citizenship seemed to be to make them emigrate. For the Latvian and Estonian leaderships, on the other hand, the need to restore and protect the ethnic and cultural hegemony of their true indigenous populations has become a core belief of the new nationalist political faith.

Relations With Russia. Finally, the minority problem has fueled a crisis in Baltic relations with Russia, where nationalist feeling has forced President Boris Yeltsin to intervene on behalf of the Russian minorities. Yeltsin's main card has been the timing and pace of Russian troop withdrawals from the three Baltic countries. In 1990 more than 500,000 Soviet troops were based in the Baltic region, with about half the number in Latvia, the headquarters of the Soviet Baltic command. After Baltic independence was achieved in 1991, the USSR agreed to withdraw its troops. Following the collapse of the USSR, Russia agreed to continue the withdrawal; by mid-1992 more than three quarters of the troops had been evacuated. However, in the late fall, under intense pressure from domestic constituencies concerned about the treatment of the Russians now living in the region, Yeltsin suspended further troop withdrawals, linking resumption to the improved treatment of the minorities in Estonia and Latvia. (In Lithuania, which automatically had conferred citizenship on its 20% non-Lithuanian population, this was not an issue.) This left for the time being approximately 100,000 troops in the three countries, with Latvia still bearing the greatest burden in terms of numbers and military facilities. Meanwhile, the Russian government also appealed to the United Nations to extend its protection to Russian and other minorities in the Baltic states.

The three Baltic states, having turned their backs on their ties of 50 years with the former Soviet republics in 1992, have been trying desperately to reorient their politics and economics toward Western Europe; but the legacy of the past has held them back.

ROBERT SHARLET, *Union College*

BANGLADESH

Opposition to the government of Begum Khaleda Zia, the need to rebuild the infrastructure after 1991's cyclone, and refugee issues shaped events in Bangladesh in 1992. The need for economic assistance and investment continued to be top priorities for the nation.

Political and Economic Unrest. After more than one year in office, the Bangladesh Nationalist Party (BNP) and Prime Minister Zia seemed paralyzed. Besides the destruction from the cyclone, further strains were caused by an influx of more than 200,000 Muslim refugees from Myanmar (Burma), and labor and student opposition increasingly turned violent. To the government's credit, the military was kept at bay. Despite pressures for his release, former President H. M. Ershad remained in jail, serving a ten-year sentence and leaving his Jaitya Party (JP), with its considerable military support, relatively disorganized.

Without sufficient resources, recovery efforts from the cyclone were minimal. Dissatisfaction focusing on the BNP government resulted in crippling strikes early in the year by teachers, bank employees, and transportation and industrial workers. By fall, violence was so prevalent that Bangladeshi business groups and outside observers were concerned about a virtual breakdown in civic order and appealed for strong measures.

Contributing to these problems was the continuation by the BNP government, under pressure from the World Bank and other donor agencies, of the economic liberalization begun under Ershad. Privatization and deregulation had led to the closing of about 60% of all the privatized plants, and attempts by business to streamline others resulted in additional unemployment. Another 1,500 plants reportedly were ailing.

Banks also were affected. Employee unions negotiated extraordinarily high wages and perks, and intervened in management recruitment and even approval of loans. The central Bangladesh Bank, with the passage of the Banking Companies Act in 1991, had a mandate to clean up banking but was unable to do so. After several managers who resisted the unions were attacked, opposition to the unions crumbled. As a result, recovery of loans virtually stopped, irregularities abounded, and, according to the finance ministry, only 12% of the Bangladesh Bank's senior officials were selected on the basis of merit.

Student unrest also grew. University life long has been divided along partisan lines, with parties freely using students to organize demonstrations and strikes. Increasing violence among student supporters of the BNP and opposition Awami League (AL) and Jaitya Party (JP) supporters resulted in the death of two students and a passerby in August, leading the prime minister to dissolve the BNP's student wing and suspend all political activities at Dhaka University. The AL followed suit, and a code of behavior for students was to be drafted for submission to Parliament.

The AL stepped up demonstrations against the BNP and also urged action against members of the Jamaat-e-Islami Party, accused of siding with Pakistan during Bangladesh's war of independence. At issue was the election of Golam Azad as president of the Jamaat. Azad had fled to Pakistan after the war, and his citizenship had been revoked. He returned to Bangladesh in 1978 on a Pakistani passport, raising questions about his citizenship and loyalty. The AL and other groups formed a "people's court," sentencing Azad to death, but the government placed him in protective custody, promising to examine the various charges against him.

Refugee Problems. Refugees from the Arakan region of Myanmar (called Rohingyas) continued to flow into Bangladesh, with border police unable to stem the tide. Attempts to negotiate with Yangon (Rangoon) by Foreign Minister Mustafizur Rahman were not successful. Fears of disease outbreaks and potential violence between refugees and local people led to the confinement of Rohingyas in guarded camps, adding to their impoverishment and the financial burden to Bangladesh. The United Nations (UN) High Commission on Refugees agreed to $29 million in aid. Bangladesh appealed unsuccessfully to China to use its influence with Yangon. Appeals to the UN and the Association of Southeast Asian Nations were seen as more promising.

Two other refugee groups benefited from negotiations. The so-called "Biharis" (non-Bengali Muslims, often accused of siding with Pakistan) were likely to be able to migrate to Pakistan, which until recently was reluctant to absorb more refugees. Also negotiations with India resulted in the return of exiled Chakma people to the Chittagong Hill Tracts.

ARUNA NAYYAR MICHIE
Kansas State University

BANGLADESH · Information Highlights

Official Name: People's Republic of Bangladesh.
Location: South Asia.
Area: 55,598 sq mi (144 000 km²).
Population (mid-1992 est.): 111,400,000.
Chief City (1981 census): Dhaka, the capital, 3,430,312.
Government: *Head of state,* Abdur Rahman Biswas, president (took office, Oct. 10, 1991). *Head of government,* Khaleda Zia, prime minister (sworn in March 20, 1991). *Legislature*—Parliament.
Monetary Unit: Taka (39.00 taka equal U.S.$1, August 1992).
Economic Index (1991): *Consumer Prices* (Dhaka, 1980 = 100), all items, 296.4; food, 272.6.
Foreign Trade (1991 U.S.$): *Imports,* $3,408,-000,000; *exports,* $1,693,000,000.

BANKING AND FINANCE

Dramatically declining interest rates fueled record profits in the U.S. banking and savings and loan industries in 1992, which also continued to undergo a period of turmoil, consolidation, and tighter regulation.

Monetary Stimulus. The low rates resulted from the Federal Reserve Board's efforts to stimulate the economy by making it cheaper to borrow money. But, as both a cause and an effect of the steadily weak economy, the banks made relatively few new loans to businesses for most of the year, although the lowest interest rates in many years encouraged millions of homeowners to refinance their mortgages.

Instead, with long-term interest rates still high, banks bought record amounts of Treasury securities, and by May had loaned more money to the U.S. government than to businesses. Nevertheless, by the end of the year some signs emerged that what government officials had called a "credit crunch" may have begun to ease slowly. In November the Federal Reserve Bank of St. Louis reported that loans to businesses held by the nation's largest banks had increased at a 1% annual rate in the prior two months, a significant improvement from the 7% decline of the previous year.

The strongest gains occurred in areas where the local economies had been stronger than in the country as a whole, like the Southeast. Decreased lending, moreover, had slowed noticeably in other areas, except for southern California, which continued to feel the shock from plummeting real-estate prices.

Profits and Interest Rates. The institutions' record profits—commercial banks earned $15.7 billion by midyear, compared with $10.2 billion a year earlier—were largely the result of historically wide spreads between the interest rates they charged borrowers and the interest rates they paid depositors. By the middle of the year only 6.37% of the nation's banks were not turning profits, compared with almost twice as many banks a year earlier.

The low interest rates, particularly for certificates of deposit (CDs), prompted many bank customers to plow their money into mutual funds in record amounts in hopes of getting higher returns. By November one-year CDs were averaging a yield of about 3.3%, their lowest level in years, and other kinds of accounts also posted low yields. As a result, by the middle of the year investors had pulled more than $200 billion out of small-denomination CDs alone.

Many banks tried to cope with customer changes in investing patterns by offering their own mutual funds, although the laws written during the Great Depression that separate investment banking and commercial banking continued to make it more expensive for the banks to offer these services than Wall Street.

Failures. During the 1980s regulators closed 1,039 banks, more than during the prior 45 years—since the founding of the Federal Deposit Insurance Corporation (FDIC) in 1933. In 1991 they closed 124 institutions, with assets of more than $63 billion.

In 1992, however, regulators closed far fewer institutions—fewer even than they had predicted. By early November they had seized 104 banks with assets of $36.6 billion. The insurance fund that protects deposits was $5.5 billion in the red at midyear, kept afloat from a

© Jarrold Cabiuck/NYT Pictures

Albert V. Casey, the chairman of the Resolution Trust Corporation—the U.S. government agency established in 1989 to oversee the savings and loans bailout—estimated in May 1992 that the S&L bailout would cost no more than $130 billion.

large taxpayer loan approved in 1991 by Congress. Some Democratic lawmakers claimed that the Bush administration, in an election-year gambit, had delayed closing institutions in an attempt to convey the impression that the worst was behind the industry. The accusation was denied strongly by the regulators and the administration.

Nonetheless, the pace of failures was expected to increase in 1993 because of new rules requiring earlier intervention by the regulators and because of the expectation that profits would not continue to rise once interest rates stopped declining.

One sign of the industry's troubles was the failure of the First City Bancorporation of Houston, one of the largest banks in Texas, after regulators found that its two largest subsidiaries were insolvent. Federal regulators said the failure would cost the bank-insurance fund about $500 million to protect depositors in First City and its 20 bank subsidiaries, which had assets of $8.8 billion. It was the second time the insurance fund had been forced to spend heavily to deal with First City's troubles. In 1988 regulators paid an emergency infusion of $970 million toward a bailout plan in which a new owner took control of the bank.

Some weak banks used their strong earnings in 1992 to cover bad loans and shore up their capital in anticipation of new regulations —which went into effect in December and early 1993—that provide benefits to the strongest institutions and penalize the weak.

New Regulations. Under the new rules, which were required by the Federal Deposit Insurance Corporation Improvement Act of 1991, banking regulators will have to close banks and savings institutions if their capital base falls below 2%, even though they are not technically insolvent. Regulators predicted that by the end of June 1993 about 60 institutions with $25 billion of assets would fail to meet the new standards, although independent economists have estimated that twice as many banks with assets approaching $80 billion might have to be rescued.

Another new regulation requires banks and savings associations to pay annual deposit-insurance premiums based on their financial strength. The new regulation, which cut in half a proposed increase in the premiums and exempted three quarters of the industry from any increase at all, came after intense lobbying by the Bush administration and the banking industry. The premiums are intended to cover the cost of insuring depositors at failed institutions.

A third regulation flatly prohibits the weakest banks and savings associations from paying higher-than-average interest rates to attract deposits. The practice had devastating consequences for the savings and loan industry in the 1980s, as many institutions chased deposits gathered by brokers who sought high rates.

Huge amounts of this money poured into federally insured institutions, allowing them to make large and risky loans, many of which turned sour. As losses mounted and banks needed still more deposits to stay liquid, the institutions bid up interest rates. Eventually these high-cost deposits compounded the cost of the government's savings and loan bailout.

In another departure from past practice, federal regulators began to limit sharply the protection of accounts holding more than $100,000. In past years the regulators almost routinely had protected larger depositors because they maintained it was ultimately cheaper for the insurance fund—failing banks would be sold to other institutions that wanted the best customers. But the 1991 banking law took away some of the discretion of the regulators and made it harder for them to protect large depositors when less costly alternatives were available.

Regulatory Lame Ducks. The election of Bill Clinton in November's presidential voting was expected to bring a clean sweep of senior regulators in Washington and the appointment of new top officials at three of the four federal bank and savings agencies. Two of those agencies—the comptroller of the currency and the FDIC—were run by caretakers for much of the year. In August, William Taylor, the head of the FDIC, died, leaving the agency in the temporary hands of Andrew C. Hove, Jr., the vice chairman of the agency. The Senate already had declined, in May, to act on the nomination of James E. Gilleran, the top California banking regulator, to head the comptroller of the currency. He had been named to replace Robert L. Clarke, whose nomination to a second term was killed by the Senate in 1991. And during December, T. Timothy Ryan, Jr., director of the Office of Thrift Supervision, which regulates the nation's savings associations, said he would retire two years before his term expires.

S&L Bailout Costs. The savings and loan bailout stalled in March after the spending authority lapsed for the agency supervising the rescue. With at least another 100 institutions holding assets of more than $60 billion still to be seized in 1993, Congress was expected to take up a new spending measure when it convened in January. Since 1989, Congress has spent more than $100 billion on the savings bailout program, and by some government estimates, the rescue of the industry ultimately will cost taxpayers $500 billion, including interest charges, over the next 40 years.

In November it was announced that federal financial regulators had reached a $400 million settlement with Ernst & Young—one of the nation's largest accounting firms—on charges that the company improperly audited federally insured banks and S&Ls that failed.

STEPHEN LABATON, *"The New York Times"*

BELGIUM

Resolution of a cabinet crisis provoked by November 1991 elections and government efforts to reduce the budget deficit shaped Belgium's political scene in 1992.

Politics. On March 7, Jean-Luc Dehaene, 51, was sworn in as prime minister. Fifteen weeks earlier, inconclusive election results that weakened the Socialists had left former Prime Minister Wilfried Martens in charge of only a caretaker government. Martens had served as prime minister for nearly 13 years and as head of nine governing coalitions. Failures by a Flemish Liberal and a Flemish Christian Democrat to form viable cabinets preceded the successful effort by the Flemish Christian Democrat Dehaene. Known as a skilled political mediator and the man who had negotiated the formation of Martens' previous cabinet in 1988, Dehaene had served as deputy prime minister and as minister of communications and institutional reform in that cabinet.

The new center-left government consists, as did Martens', of ministers drawn from the French and Flemish wings of the Christian Democrat and Socialist parties. About half the size of previous cabinets, it counted the support of 120 of the 212 seats in the chamber in 1992. Dehaene thus had enough votes to govern, but not the two thirds necessary for constitutional changes associated with devolving power from the center to the linguistic regions.

Despite this problem, Dehaene proclaimed his intention of completing the constitutional reforms begun under Martens. Social renovation and reduction of the public debt and the budget deficit were announced priorities.

To move the devolution process forward, a "Dialogue of the Communities" was begun by nine political parties. Its prime intent was to frame proposals for the direct election of regional parliaments and to define the fiscal powers of the executives of the linguistic regions. Neither the Flemish nationalist *Vlaams Blok* nor the extreme liberals of the ROSSEM grouping were invited to participate, despite the strength they showed in the 1991 general election. Feelings against the anti-immigrant diatribes of the right-wing *Vlaams Blok* were evidenced in a large antiracist demonstration in March.

Economics. The need to address the debt issue was accentuated by the terms of the accord reached by European Community (EC) ministers at Maastricht, the Netherlands, in December 1991. It was agreed there that annual national budget deficits of no more than 3% of a nation's gross domestic product (GDP) and a national debt of no more than 60% of the GDP are prerequisites for participation in the projected EC economic and monetary union. For trading and manufacturing purposes, Belgium's participation in such a union from its inception

---

BELGIUM • Information Highlights

Official Name: Kingdom of Belgium.
Location: Northwestern Europe.
Area: 11,780 sq mi (30 510 km²).
Population (mid-1992 est.): 10,000,000.
Chief Cities (Dec. 31, 1990): Brussels, the capital (incl. suburbs), 960,324; Antwerp (including suburbs), 467,875; Ghent, 230,446; Charleroi, 206,928; Liège, 185,201; Bruges, 117,100.
Government: *Head of state,* Baudouin I, king (acceded 1951). *Head of government,* Jean-Luc Dehaene, prime minister (sworn in March 7, 1992). *Legislature*—Parliament: Senate and Chamber of Representatives.
Monetary Unit: Franc (31.08 francs equal U.S.$1, commercial rate, Oct. 23, 1992).
Gross Domestic Product (1990 U.S.$): $144,800,000,000.
Economic Indexes (1990): *Consumer Prices,* all items (1980 = 100), 160.8; food (1988 = 100), 108.9. *Industrial Production* (1980 = 100), 119.
Foreign Trade (1991 with Luxembourg, U.S.$): *Imports,* $121,369,000,000; *exports,* $118,570,000,000.

---

is significant. Also, EC calculations projected that, for 1992, Belgium would be a net recipient from the EC budget of about ecu 1.6 billion ($2 billion).

In 1991, however, the budget deficit moved to 6.3% of GDP from 5.5% in 1990; the national debt grew to 123% of GDP from 121.4% in 1990. In an effort to reverse this trend, new tax procedures were put in effect on April 1. The standard value-added tax (VAT) rate was raised from 19% to 19.5%; special top rates of 25% and 33% were ended. A freeze was placed on new defense spending and recruitment into the civil service was limited. Further reductions of social benefits were anticipated as the government strove to reduce the budget deficit to 5% of the GDP by year's end. In November the Belgian Senate approved and the king signed the Maastricht treaty which had been accepted by the lower house.

Despite budgetary and employment problems, the standard of living in Belgium remained high. According to the misery index published by the Population Crisis Committee in Washington, DC, Belgium tied with the Netherlands and ranked behind only Denmark in a composite of ten indicators of well-being.

Foreign Affairs. Belgium continued to pressure Zaire to move toward increased democracy. It also contributed airlifted supplies to the Commonwealth of Independent States (the former USSR). In July, Belgium joined 28 other nations in signing a revised version of the 1990 Conventional Forces in Europe Treaty.

In the United Nations it cosponsored a resolution imposing sanctions on Yugoslavia following bloodshed in Bosnia-Herzegovina; it also endorsed the use of force to assure delivery of humanitarian aid to that region. At the close of the year, Belgium surrendered its rotating seat on the UN Security Council.

J. E. HELMREICH, *Allegheny College*

BIOCHEMISTRY

Biochemists in 1991–92 made significant discoveries in the area of cancer research. They also discovered that an RNA, and not a protein, is the enzyme that catalyzes peptide-bond formation between amino acids during protein synthesis.

p53 Protein and Cancer. Cancer is characterized by an uncontrolled proliferation of abnormal cells. Scientists believe that progression of cancer is caused when a gene's normal growth-regulating function is impaired or stopped. Such growth-regulating genes are known as suppressor genes. An important suppressor gene is p53, which has been found to be mutated in a variety of human cancers. Research on how the normal protein encoded by this suppressor gene protects humans from cancer has been at fever pitch in recent years. In 1991, Michael Kasten and his colleagues at Johns Hopkins University found that the normal p53 protein was involved in telling the cell when to stop dividing.

How p53 protein accomplished this task became clear in 1992. Two groups of scientists working independently—one led by Scott Kerns, also at Johns Hopkins University, and the other by George Farmer at Columbia University—discovered that p53 protein binds to DNA at specific sites, and that this binding directly activates the expression of genes whose products inhibit cell proliferation. The mutated p53 protein lacks the DNA-binding ability and thus fails to activate the genes involved in cell-growth inhibition, causing the cells to become cancerous. The researchers also showed that certain tumor viruses promote cancer by inactivating the normal p53 protein in the host cell.

Ribosomal RNA (rRNA) as a Catalyst. Until the early 1980s scientists believed it was a given that all enzymes are proteins. This tidy picture began to unravel when it was established by Thomas Cech of the University of Colorado and Sidney Altman of Yale University that RNA, once thought to be a passive carrier of genetic information, can catalyze cutting, joining, and moving around pieces of other RNA molecules. The catalytic function of RNA was expanded by two reports in 1992. One study, by Harry Noller and his coworkers at the University of California (Santa Cruz), showed that a key step in protein synthesis—formation of the peptide bond linking one amino acid to the next—is catalyzed solely by RNA in the ribosome, a cell's protein-producing factories. The second report, from Cech's laboratory, reported that the previously studied RNA had the ability to make and break the bonds that join amino acids to transfer-RNA (tRNA), the molecule that carries them to the ribosome for protein assembly.

The outline of protein synthesis first was worked out in the 1960s. The genetic information for the assembly of a protein from its building blocks—amino acids—is contained in DNA. This information first is transcribed into a linear molecule called messenger-RNA (mRNA). Then the mRNA attaches to a ribosome which is composed of about 60% rRNA and 40% proteins. The ribosome moves along the mRNA and, as it does, a tRNA molecule carrying a specific amino acid reads the message in the mRNA and inserts the amino acid, which is linked to the previously added amino acid by a peptide bond. Until 1992 scientists believed the rRNA served simply as a scaffolding to hold the protein components in place while one of the proteins in the ribosome catalyzed peptide-bond formation. It was this conventional belief that was upset by Noller's group, who showed that even after all the proteins were extracted exhaustively from the ribosome, the remaining RNA still retained most of the ribosome's ability to catalyze peptide-bond formation. The new findings fueled speculation that RNA played the central role in the origin of life, since it is known to be capable of its own replication and, as demonstrated by Noller's group, of making proteins.

Prostate Cancer. Prostate cancer is the second-most-common cause of cancer deaths among men. The prostate is a small gland located at the base of the bladder that secretes fluids to nourish and transport sperm. When restricted to the prostate, a tumor grows slowly, taking years to reach a diameter of about 0.2 inches (0.5 cm). But once it metastasizes and moves to the backbone, the tumor grows rapidly and death ensues within a few years.

Marcella Rossi of the Massachusetts Institute of Technology and Bruce Zetter of Children's Hospital in Boston answered the puzzle of why the cancer cells escaping from the prostate thrive so well after they infiltrate the bone. They reasoned that the bone must contain a factor or factors that promoted the explosive growth of the tumor cells. To find the factors, they separated components from the bone marrow and searched for proteins that stimulated the proliferation of prostate-tumor cells growing in laboratory cultures. This procedure resulted in the identification of transferin, a protein that is found throughout the body but is particularly abundant in the bone marrow. Transferin aids in the transport of iron to various body cells but plays a critical function in the bone marrow, where the red blood cells continually are formed and hemoglobin (the iron-containing protein) is synthesized.

These results strongly indicated that apart from its function as a carrier of iron, transferin also may be a critical growth factor for prostatic-cancer cells. It was expected that these findings would lead to the development of therapies for the treatment of prostate cancer.

PREM P. BATRA, *Wright State University*

BIOGRAPHY

A selection of profiles of persons prominent in the news during 1992 appears on pages 137–151. The affiliation of the contributor is listed on pages 591–94; biographies that do not include a contributor's name were prepared by the staff. Included are profiles of:

BERGEN, Candice

Candice Bergen's hit television program, *Murphy Brown*, gained even more attention during the 1992 U.S. presidential campaign, when a nationwide ruckus was caused by Vice-President Dan Quayle's criticism of the high-profile show. The show's plot line had television journalist Murphy Brown, played by Bergen, bearing a baby out of wedlock. As was the show's tendency, the lines between real life and television were blurred as real-life anchorwomen starred as guests at Murphy's baby shower. Quayle claimed the show was encouraging the undermining of traditional U.S. moral values by glorifying single motherhood. Politicians from both parties and representatives of various advocacy groups entered the fray, arguing as heatedly as if Murphy were real.

In the midst of all the commotion, Bergen received renewed publicity, in August winning a second Emmy Award for her expert characterization of the riotous Murphy. (She was awarded the first Emmy in 1990.)

Background. Candice Bergen was born May 9, 1946, in Beverly Hills, CA, the daughter of famed ventriloquist Edgar Bergen and former model Frances Westcott.

Candice Bergen

© Trapper/Sygma

Candice had a wealthy but strict upbringing. Although her privileged childhood—where typical guests at family parties might include Ronald and Nancy Reagan, Fred Astaire, Rex Harrison, and David Niven—might look ideal to an outsider, it often was painful. Candice frequently felt overshadowed by her father's famous dummies, Charlie McCarthy and Mortimer Snerd.

At age 14, Bergen was sent to a Swiss boarding school, from which her parents soon withdrew her after discovering the trouble the rebellious teenager was getting into. She enrolled at the University of Pennsylvania in 1963, but failed in her junior year because she was getting so many modeling jobs. Her first film role was in Sidney Lumet's 1966 film, *The Group*.

In 1967, Bergen decided to become a photojournalist and almost immediately found work writing and submitting photography to magazines like *Life*. She also did a one-week stint on the TV show *AM America* and was offered a correspondent position on CBS' *60 Minutes*, which she refused.

Despite many television and film roles, including an Oscar-nominated role in the film *Starting Over*, Bergen was known more for her family background and patrician beauty than for any real accomplishment of her own. All that changed, however, when she took on the starring role in *Murphy Brown* in 1988. The show took off immediately and became one of the most popular shows in the United States. The role also allowed Bergen to unleash her little-used, and considerable, comic skills. The program's writers became adept at blurring the lines between real-life and sitcom characters, with frequent mentions of actual celebrities, as well as occasional guest stars playing themselves. This tendency helped the show become so entrenched in U.S. culture that Murphy seemed almost real, bringing Bergen new fame and respect in her own right as an actress.

Bergen has been married since 1980 to French film director Louis Malle. The two have one daughter, Chloe.

BLAIR, Bonnie

When speed skater Bonnie Blair won the first U.S. gold medal of the 1992 Winter Olympics at Albertville, France—in the 500-m event—she also made history. With her win she became the first U.S. woman ever to capture golds in consecutive Winter Games. With her victory in the 1,000-m race four days later, Blair earned a record of winning more gold medals than has any other woman at the Winter Olympic Games.

Blair was urged on at Albertville by a fan club of sorts composed of about 50 family members and friends, who wore matching purple jackets (designed by Blair's brother) and sang *My Bonnie Lies Over the Ocean* in unison, led by Blair's 73-year-old mother, Eleanor. This support was typical of the close-knit family. Blair's father, Charles, who died in late 1989, had told his daughter she would go to the Olympics even before she

Bonnie Blair

© Mike Powell/Allsport

dreamed she could, and she dedicated her first 1992 gold medal to him.

Background. Bonnie Blair was born March 18, 1964, in Cornwall, NY, and grew up in Champaign, IL, the youngest of six children. She began skating at age 2, encouraged by her five older siblings, who all were speed skaters. Blair learned to skate on a short track popular in Champaign. In 1979 she skated on a longer track for the first time when she went to Milwaukee for the 1980 Olympic trials. She qualified for the 1980 Winter Games in the process and discovered where her true talent lay.

In 1984, Blair went to the Winter Olympic Games in Sarajevo, Yugoslavia, as the top sprinter on the U.S. team, finishing eighth in the 500-m. In Calgary in 1988, she was considered a favorite and indeed became the only U.S. multiple medal winner, setting a world record in the 500-m with 39.10 seconds and taking the bronze medal in the 1,000-m race.

After a troubled 1990–91 season, Blair came back and won every 500- and 1,000-m race on the World Cup circuit in 1991–92, capping this achievement with the historic triumph in her third Olympics. Her coach, Peter Mueller, characterizes her as "a killer"; she is considered the world's most efficient speed skater, although small at 5'5" (1.67 m) and 130 lbs (59 kg).

Blair hoped to gain a higher profile with her 1992 victories, despite the relative obscurity of her sport. However, as she puts it, "I'm in this because I love what I'm doing." Her next goal is to become the first woman to break the 39-second barrier in the 500-m event.

The skater, who also has participated successfully in competitive cycling, enjoys softball, golf, and baking cookies in her spare time. She serves on various committees, including the National Sports Committee of the Leukemia Society of America and the Women's Sports Foundation.

BOUTROS-GHALI, Boutros

On Jan. 1, 1992, Boutros Boutros-Ghali, former Egyptian foreign minister who helped maintain the fragile allied coalition against Iraq during the Persian Gulf war, became the sixth secretary-general of the United Nations, succeeding Javier Pérez de Cuéllar. He is the first African or Arab to head the world body.

Though his qualifications as a peacemaker were formidable—he was a key participant in the Camp David peace accords between Egypt and Israel—Boutros-

Ghali had to win over skeptics on the Security Council who thought him too old, at 69, to take on the bloated UN bureaucracy. As Egypt's representative to the Organization of African Unity, he was one of that group's list of candidates for secretary-general, though many members would have preferred a black African.

To win the post he says he was "born" for, he broke with tradition, traveling the globe soliciting support from powerful friends. France, which considers the Paris-educated Boutros-Ghali an adopted son, was an enthusiastic backer, and Egyptian President Hosni Mubarak and the Saudi Arabian ambassador to the United States personally lobbied U.S. President George Bush, who provided crucial last-minute support.

Israel's leaders, though nervous at the thought of an Arab secretary-general during their volatile peace negotiations with Arab countries, did not object to the selection of Boutros-Ghali, a man they knew to be fair. When Egypt's foreign minister quit rather than go with Anwar el-Sadat on his historic trip to Jerusalem in 1977, Boutros-Ghali, then deputy foreign minister, took his place. After Camp David in 1978, he was one of the few Egyptian leaders at Sadat's side at the White House signing of the Egyptian-Israeli peace treaty in 1979.

His first official act as secretary-general was to participate in the signing of the El Salvador peace accords in Mexico on January 16. In New York the new chief, who already had disavowed a second five-year term when the first expires in 1996, stepped on bureaucratic toes as he set out to prune the Secretariat into a leaner post-Cold-War peacemaker at the cost of some high-level jobs. He also proposed that a permanent peacekeeping force be created and put at his disposal to be used to enforce UN-negotiated peace agreements in places such as Cambodia and the former republics of Yugoslavia.

Background. Boutros Boutros-Ghali was born Nov. 14, 1922, in Cairo, Egypt, into one of the country's most distinguished Coptic Christian families. His grandfather was a prime minister and his father a finance minister. He received a law degree from Cairo University in 1946 and a doctorate in international law from the Sorbonne in Paris in 1949. A tenured professor of international law and international relations at Cairo University and Fulbright scholar at Columbia University, he has written more than 100 publications and articles.

Called "exquisitely tailored" by *The New York Times,* Boutros-Ghali is well-known for his wit in three languages—English, French, and Arabic. He and his wife, the former Leah Nadler, daughter of a prominent Jewish candymaker in Alexandria, Egypt, have no children.

RICK MITCHELL

Boutros Boutros-Ghali

© Bernard Bisson/Sygma

Carol Moseley Braun

BRAUN, Carol Moseley

On Nov. 3, 1992, Carol Moseley Braun became the first black woman, and only the fourth black American, elected to the U.S. Senate, after capturing 55% of the Illinois vote to defeat Republican Sen. Rich Williamson. Her victory came at a time when voters were in an anti-incumbent mood and many women still were angry over the 1991 Senate confirmation of Supreme Court Justice Clarence Thomas.

It was, in fact, Sen. Alan J. Dixon's (D-IL) vote for Thomas despite allegations that he had sexually harassed University of Oklahoma law professor Anita Hill when she worked for him some years ago that prompted Braun, also a Democrat, to seek the Senate seat. She said that, in watching the televised confirmation hearings, she saw "an elitist club made up of mostly white male millionaires over 50." As a relative unknown, Braun ran a grass-roots campaign in her primary battle to defeat Dixon. The message she carried was "we can do better," but the political establishment paid her little heed, and even powerful women's groups gave her scant attention. Her primary campaign was funded so poorly that she could not afford television advertising until the end of the campaign. However, in March she defeated the two-term Democrat in a three-way primary fight.

After this victory, Braun achieved a kind of political-star status. Those who had snubbed her earlier now came calling. She spoke at the Democratic Convention and was wooed by influential senators. Even prominent New Yorkers, led by Braun's longtime friend and philanthropist Sherry Bronfman, raised money for her campaign. Three months after she defeated Dixon, Braun was the top fund-raiser among all Senate candidates, male or female.

Braun appealed to blacks and whites alike, even succeeding in garnering the vote from the traditionally Republican Chicago suburbs. She was viewed by many as a defiant woman who was all the stronger because of her conflict-filled background.

In being elected to the Senate, Braun joined three other women who also were elected for the first time and two women incumbents, Democrat Barbara Mikulski and Republican Nancy Kassebaum.

Background. Carol Elizabeth Moseley was born in Chicago, IL, on Aug. 16, 1947. She grew up on Chicago's South Side and attended city schools, the University of Illinois, and the University of Chicago Law School. She is a former assistant U.S. attorney and was an Illinois state representative for ten years (1979–89). From 1990 she served as the Cook county recorder of deeds.

During her life, Braun had survived beatings by her policeman father, a divorce, and the death of a brother from drug and alcohol abuse. She also politically survived 1992 allegations of Medicaid fraud involving her handling of a windfall profit paid to her 71-year-old mother from the sale of timber rights on some Alabama land. Braun is the mother of a 15-year-old son.

BRETT, George Howard

George Brett sealed his bid for the Baseball Hall of Fame when he reached a major milestone with his 3,000th hit on Sept. 30, 1992. The hit, Brett's fourth of the game, came in Anaheim Stadium against rookie left-hander Tim Fortugno of the California Angels. Brett would have preferred to produce the hit in Kansas City, where he has spent his 19-year career.

Arriving with the Royals late in 1973, two years after he was chosen in the second round of the annual draft, Brett soon became an All-Star. Drafted as a shortstop, he made his major-league mark as a third baseman. The late Charlie Lau, then Kansas City's batting coach, convinced Brett to become a line-drive hitter, while teammate Hal McRae, the Royals' manager in 1992, taught him the value of aggressive base-running.

In a career often interrupted by injury (ten separate stints on the disabled list), Brett has exceeded a .300 average 11 times and became the only player to win batting titles in three different decades (1976, 1980, and 1990). His .390 mark in 1980 stood in 1992 as the highest average since Ted Williams hit .406 in 1941. The 6' (1.8-m), 205-lb (93-kg) left-handed hitter has made the All-Star team 13 times, won Kansas City player-of-the-year honors seven times, and was the American League's most valuable player (MVP) in 1980 and runner-up in 1985.

Brett has led the league in batting, hits, triples, slugging percentage, and on-base percentage three times each, and total bases and doubles twice each. He has hit three home runs in a game twice during the regular season and once in the American League Championship Series (ALCS)—on Oct. 6, 1978. A great clutch performer, Brett has hit .340 in six ALCS appearances and

George Brett

.373 in two World Series. He holds the ALCS career record of nine home runs—one of them a dramatic, three-run, Yankee Stadium shot against Goose Gossage that gave the Royals their first pennant in 1980.

Brett has become the all-time Kansas City leader in games played and the city's most popular player. Though he won a Gold Glove at third in 1985, he moved to first two years later, then became a designated hitter after the Royals signed Wally Joyner for 1992.

Background. George Howard Brett was born on May 15, 1953, in Glen Dale, WV. The youngest of four sons born to Jack Brett, an accountant, and his wife Ethel, a bookkeeper, George moved with his family to Hermosa Beach, CA, when he was 2 years old. A baseball and football letterman at El Segundo High School, Brett later attended El Camino (CA) Junior College and Longview (MO) Community College. Brother Ken pitched in the majors, while brothers Bobby and John played in the minors.

George Brett married the former Leslie Davenport on Feb. 15, 1992. The couple, residents of Mission Hills, MO, were expecting their first child in March 1993.

DAN SCHLOSSBERG

BUCHANAN, Patrick Joseph

All through his unsuccessful campaign for the 1992 Republican presidential nomination, Patrick Buchanan pounded away at the incumbent GOP chief executive, George Bush. And when the time finally came for Buchanan to endorse Bush for a second presidential term, at the Republican National Convention in Houston, Buchanan kept pounding—only this time his target was Democratic standard-bearer Bill Clinton. As *The Washington Post* commented: "He made peace with Bush by declaring war on Clinton."

Although he was given little if any chance of actually getting the nomination himself, Buchanan's aggressive conduct of his challenge to Bush successfully highlighted conservative grievances and embarrassed the incumbent president. When announcing his candidacy in Concord, NH, on Dec. 10, 1991, Buchanan declared that he was running "because we Republicans can no longer say it is all the liberals' fault. It was not some liberal Democrat who declared: 'Read my lips! No new taxes!,' then broke his word to cut a back room deal with the big spenders."

At the Republican National Convention in Houston, some critics complained that Buchanan's address in which he heaped scorn and ridicule on Clinton and the Democrats was divisive. But others argued that it would help rally rank-and-file conservative voters behind Bush. And nearly everyone agreed that by his speech and his challenge to Bush, the militant Buchanan had positioned himself well for another run for the White House in 1996.

Background. Belligerence long has been the hallmark of Buchanan's political style, and he comes by it honestly. The Irish Catholic household in Washington, DC, into which he was born on Nov. 2, 1938, was run, he later recalled, like a "benevolent dictatorship," with his father, William, firmly in charge. The senior Buchanan used a leather belt to maintain order among Patrick and his six brothers. And he insisted that each of his boys take 400 swings at a punching bag four times a week to ready themselves for neighborhood brawls.

After attending Washington's Georgetown University and the Columbia University School of Journalism, Buchanan worked as an editorial writer for the *St. Louis Globe Democratic* for three years until 1965. Then he signed on as a presidential campaign aide to Richard Nixon and stayed on at the White House as a speech writer after Nixon's 1968 election victory. He became noted for the sharpness of his thrusts against the liberal establishment. It was Buchanan who generally was believed to have crafted Vice-President Spiro Agnew's 1969 attack on "the small and unelected elite" who Agnew charged controlled television and its power to mold public opinion.

Buchanan left the White House after Nixon was driven from office by the Watergate scandal, in which Buchanan himself was not implicated, and returned to journalism and television. He kept up his drumfire of criticism against liberals, particularly those who he deemed exerted influence on television coverage of politics, and was rewarded handsomely for his efforts. He was earning about $400,000 per year in 1985 when he gave up journalism to serve once more in the White House as President Reagan's communications director. After a two-year stint with Reagan, Buchanan returned to private life. Like many other conservatives, Buchanan found himself increasingly dissatisfied with President Bush's policies, particularly the president's reneging on his vow to oppose new taxes.

Shelley Anne Scarney, a receptionist in the Nixon White House, has been married to Buchanan since 1971.

ROBERT SHOGAN

Patrick Buchanan

BUSH, George Herbert Walker

George Bush's defeat in the November 1992 elections climaxed a presidency marked by dramatic peaks and valleys.

The 41st president got off to a strong start. His inaugural promise "to make kinder the face of the nation and gentler the face of the world" won the hearts of millions of Americans weary of the sharp ideological debate that marked the Reagan years. Bush extended the hand of bipartisan cooperation to the Democratic-controlled Congress, and vowed to kindle "a thousand points of light" to help deal with some of the nation's neglected social problems. He subsequently followed up on his campaign pledge to be "the education president" by offering a plan to raise school standards.

Critics complained that his proposals were too limited and lacked any unifying framework. But despite his lack of what he himself once referred to as "the vision thing," polls suggested that Bush's low-keyed approach matched the cautious public mood. His approval rating in the Gallup poll remained high. Any early criticism of his domestic policy soon was drowned out by the accolades for his achievements abroad, notably his handling of the Persian Gulf crisis. Bush marshaled an international coalition against the Iraqi conquest of tiny Kuwait in August 1990 and the military victory won in February

George Bush

© Peter Blakely/Saba

1991 sent Bush's Gallup approval rating soaring to a record 89%.

Greatly aided by the collapse of the Communist threat in the Soviet Union and Eastern Europe, Bush also won laurels as a peacemaker. With the end of the Cold War he was able to sign disarmament treaties that not long before would not have been thought possible and to initiate substantial cuts in U.S. defense spending. But in the midst of triumph abroad, problems had begun emerging at home as the result of an economic slowdown that started in fall of 1990. Hoping to head off a severe slump, Bush and the Democratic Congress hammered out a compromise budget plan that was supposed to trim the deficit. But to get that agreement the president had to revoke his well-remembered "read-my-lips" 1988 campaign pledge not to approve new taxes. The shift provoked bitter protests within Bush's own party and, combined with disapproval of the president's overall handling of budget negotiations, sent his poll standings into a sharp decline. Though these problems were overshadowed for a time by the Gulf war, they returned to haunt Bush in the fall of 1991 as the recovery from the recession turned out to be weaker and slower than the president had led the country to expect. As economic indicators continued to sag, so did Bush's standing in the polls; it registered only 39% in a Gallup poll released on Sept. 4, 1992, after both national conventions had concluded.

As president, Bush remained what he always had been—a man of the middle, praised by his admirers for his moderation and willingness to compromise but accused by his critics of lacking strong convictions. This profile appeared to have been shaped by the varied circumstances of his early life and the nature of his career.

Background. The roots of George Herbert Walker Bush are in New England, where he was born in Milton, MA, on June 12, 1924. His father, Prescott, served as a U.S. senator from Connecticut and like other members of the Republican Yankee elite placed great emphasis on fiscal responsibility but also gave great weight to individual rights. Bush was graduated from the Phillips Academy in Andover, MA, and attended Yale University, graduating Phi Beta Kappa in 1948.

After World War II, during which he won the Distinguished Flying Cross for his heroism as a naval aviator, and college, Bush moved to Texas. Establishing himself in the oil business and politics in the Lone Star State, he was exposed to Sunbelt economic beliefs, which were more freewheeling than in the East, and attitudes on mores and manners that were generally more restrictive. In making the adjustment from one region to another, Bush seemed to have chosen to avoid conflict by not taking firm philosophical positions, instead looking to personal relations as the center of his political career.

Another factor inhibiting Bush from taking strong stands were the jobs he held in government. With the exception of his two terms as a congressman from Texas (1976–71), Bush spent his pre-presidential public life as ambassador to the United Nations, chairman of the Republican National Committee, envoy to Communist China, chief of the Central Intelligence Agency, and then as Ronald Reagan's two-term vice-president. In all those positions he was governed by policies established by a higher authority.

Bush and his wife Barbara maintain their official residence in Washington, DC, and a voting residence in Houston, TX. They are the parents of five grown children.

See also FEATURE ARTICLE, page 26.

ROBERT SHOGAN

CAREY, Ronald R.

A new era dawned at the International Brotherhood of Teamsters on Feb. 1, 1992, when Ronald R. Carey was sworn in for a five-year term as president of the largest labor union in the United States. The union includes truckers, policemen, fire fighters, health-care workers, and municipal employees. Carey is the first popularly elected president of the Teamsters, a fact made possible by a 1989 federal lawsuit which ended with the Teamsters' executive board signing a consent decree to purge the union of corruption. Three of the union's six previous presidents were convicted of such crimes as tax evasion, jury tampering, and fraud, and a fourth died while under indictment.

In a three-way December 1991 election for the presidency of the Teamsters, Carey received 48.5% of the votes cast. His opponents—R.V. Durham, a Teamsters' vice-president and head of a North Carolina local, and Walter J. Shea, a longtime member of the union's national staff—took 33% and 18%, respectively. Only 27% of the union's 1.6 million members voted.

Background. Ronald R. Carey was born on March 22, 1936, in New York City, the second of six children. His father also was a Teamster, retiring in 1976 after being a driver for United Parcel Service (UPS) in New York City for more than 40 years. After graduating from Long Island City High School in 1953, Ronald Carey refused a swimming scholarship to St. John's University and enlisted in the U.S. Marines. After leaving the military service, he followed in his father's footsteps and became a

Ronald R. Carey

© Martin Simon/Saba

UPS driver and joined the Teamsters' Local 804. Within two years he was elected local shop steward and by 1968 he was president of Local 804, one of the largest UPS locals in the country. Carey retained the post until his election to the Teamsters' presidency.

Not part of the old Teamsters' elite, Carey has a reputation for integrity and keeping close to the interests of the rank-and-file. As president of the local he denied jobs to relatives of union officials and disallowed union credit cards, which often had been used for personal expenses. He took his local out on strike three times—over retirement benefits, the use of part-time workers, and, symbolically, to show support for workers who wanted to wear emblems other than the union pin on their uniforms.

One of his first acts as Teamsters president was to cut his own salary by $50,000 to $175,000. He also sold the Teamsters' limousine, two jets, and condominium in Puerto Rico. Also during his first year as president, Carey negotiated a contract for car haulers, saved Teamster jobs in northern California when they were threatened by a change in the operation of a large supermarket distribution center, and convinced Northwest flight attendants to stay with the Teamsters.

Ronald R. Carey is married to the former Barbara Murphy, a part-time sales clerk at Macy's. They are the parents of five grown children. The Teamsters' president continues to enjoy swimming.

CARRERAS, José

José Carreras enhanced his reputation as one of the world's leading tenors in 1992 when he appeared in his hometown of Barcelona, Spain, singing and serving as music director at the opening and closing ceremonies of the Olympic Games. Carreras, an international opera star since the 1970s, made his major debut at the Barcelona Opera House. Always proud of his native region, Catalonia, Carreras performs there as often as possible.

Also notable among Carreras' achievements of the past few years are his appearance at Barcelona in the 1989 world premiere of the opera *Cristóbal Colón*, produced to celebrate the 500th anniversary of Columbus' landing in the New World; and his 1990 televised concert with two other world-famous tenors—fellow countryman Plácido Domingo and Italy's Luciano Pavarotti—from the outdoor stage at Caracalla, Rome. This performance—*Carreras, Domingo, Pavarotti in Concert*—reached more than 1.5 billion viewers. The video and audio recordings of the concert were best-sellers as well.

José Carreras

© Swersey/Gamma-Liaison

Background. José María Carreras Coll was born on Dec. 5, 1946, the youngest of three children of José María and María Antonia (Coll) Carreras. His father, a teacher before the Spanish Civil War, was later a policeman and then in the cosmetics business. At about age 7, young José began to show an interest in music. His parents, recognizing his potential, enrolled him at the Barcelona Conservatory to begin eight years of musical studies. At age 11 he appeared at Barcelona's Gran Teatro del Liceo as a boy soprano. In his late teens he entered the University of Barcelona to study chemistry, while also taking vocal training. He soon decided on a singing career and returned to the conservatory to continue with private voice lessons.

In January 1970, Carreras debuted in Barcelona in a minor role from the opera *Norma*. Late in 1971 he made what he considers his first "real" debut, also in Barcelona, as Gennaro in *Lucrezia Borgia*. In 1972 he made his U.S. debut with the New York City Opera as Pinkerton in *Madama Butterfly*, and he first appeared with New York's Metropolitan Opera in 1974, as Cavaradossi in *Tosca*. This was followed in 1975 by his debut at La Scala in Milan in *Un Ballo in Maschera,* by which time he had become an established star.

Tragedy struck in the 1980s, and Carreras took a yearlong hiatus, during which he battled acute lymphocytic leukemia. After recovering, he made a victorious return to performing in 1988, appearing at Barcelona's Arch of Triumph in July.

Carreras performs regularly at festivals and opera houses in many parts of the world and has made many recordings. He is married, with a son and a daughter. The singer has attributed his recovery from cancer to "The wave of support from people all over the world, the love of my family, and God." He further has said, "With so many people counting on me, I felt I just couldn't disappoint them."

CLINTON, Bill

The crucial moment in Bill Clinton's drive for the 1992 Democratic presidential nomination came in the February New Hampshire primary. After his front-running candidacy was battered by controversy over his past and doubts about his character, the Arkansas governor rallied, finished a respectable second, and pronounced himself "the comeback kid." He thus managed to transform a ballot-box defeat into a moral victory. Clinton's performance in New Hampshire was another demonstration of the resiliency and tenacity that has shaped his personal life and greatly contributed to his success as a politician.

"I am a product of the middle class," Clinton proudly declared in accepting his party's nomination in July, striving to link himself to "the hard-working Americans" who "pay the taxes" and make up most of the electorate. Certainly he was not the child of privilege. Adversity sought him out early; his father, William Blythe 3d, a traveling salesman, was killed in an auto accident three months before William Jefferson Clinton was born, Aug. 19, 1946, in the little town of Hope, AR.

Background. His mother, Virginia Cassidy Blythe, left him with his grandparents while she went back to school for training as a nurse anesthetist, providing her son not only with the necessary wherewithal but also with an example of the fortitude which would serve him well throughout his life. While still a teenager, Clinton found the courage to confront his stepfather, Roger Clinton, whose name he took for his own, and warn him to stop physically abusing his mother during his bouts of heavy drinking.

Convinced that education offered his only chance of surmounting his difficult origins, Clinton threw himself into his schoolwork in Hot Springs, where he was raised. His diligence paid off, launching an academic career that carried him from Georgetown University, where he took his bachelor's degree in 1968; to Oxford, where he was a Rhodes scholar; to Yale University Law School,

Clinton won two successive four-year terms in 1986 and 1990. In gaining his 1990 victory, Clinton promised to serve out his full term, a pledge he was willing to break for the presidency.

Meanwhile through his involvement in the National Governors Association, Clinton was acquiring a national reputation as a forward-looking and practical reformer in important social areas. He was cochair of President Bush's education summit with the nation's governors in 1989. He also assisted in reaching the compromise that helped make possible congressional enactment of the welfare-reform act of 1988. He was active in the Democratic Leadership Council, which had been established to move the Democratic Party toward more centrist positions, and became its chairman in 1990. He used this position to test themes and forge a national network of political allies that would become important factors in his candidacy for the presidency, which he officially announced in October of 1991. On Nov. 3, 1992, the Arkansas governor was successful in his quest to become the nation's 42d chief executive.

Bill and Hillary Clinton have one child, a daughter, Chelsea.

See also FEATURE ARTICLE, page 26.

ROBERT SHOGAN

Bill Clinton

© Ira Wyman/Sygma

from which he was graduated in 1973. It was at Yale that Clinton met a fellow student, Hillary Rodham, who became his wife and also in many ways his partner in politics. Hillary Clinton is a prominent attorney in Arkansas and has been a leader in organizations devoted to reform in child care and education.

His schooling completed, Clinton returned to his native state and taught law at the University of Arkansas in Fayetteville (1974–76). He also entered politics, a field for which his oratorical skills and outgoing personality made him seem well-suited. His first try for elective office—a 1974 challenge to a well-established Republican congressman—ended in defeat. But once again Clinton bounced back, winning election as state attorney general in 1976. With that position as a launching pad he gained the governorship in 1978, when he was only 32, becoming the youngest of the nation's state chief executives.

Clinton arrived in the state house in Little Rock brimming with ambition and imagination, perhaps too much for his own political good. Eager to improve the state highways, he pushed through increases in the gasoline tax and auto-license fees. But those moves stirred resentment among many voters who took their revenge by turning Clinton out of office when he sought a second term in 1980. His candidacy also was hurt by the unpopularity of Democratic President Jimmy Carter, who failed to carry the state in his own unsuccessful reelection campaign against Republican challenger Ronald Reagan.

But instead of making excuses, Clinton put his energies into still another comeback, and succeeded in 1982 when he won back the governorship from Frank White, the Republican incumbent, who had defeated him two years earlier. This time Clinton made education his priority, pushing through a comprehensive plan for school reform, which included a controversial proposal for teacher testing. His efforts in education and his newfound awareness of the importance of compromise after his 1980 defeat helped Clinton consolidate his support in the state. He easily won reelection to another two-year term in 1984. And then after the state constitution was amended to double the length of the governor's tenure,

CLINTON, Hillary Rodham

It was unclear at the end of 1992 what role Hillary Clinton, wife of U.S. President-elect Bill Clinton, would play as the nation's first lady. Clinton is an outspoken woman with her own career and an agenda that is not dependent on her husband's political fortunes. Not long before the election, Clinton said she intended to take a "comprehensive" role in the White House. She did play a prominent role while her husband was governor of Arkansas, serving in 1983 as the head of an education panel which rallied support for the governor's controversial education reforms.

Clinton's success as a lawyer, her views on children's rights, and her active role as adviser to her husband all provided political fodder during the 1992 presidential

Hillary Clinton

© Ira Wyman/Sygma

campaign for traditionalists, who attacked her as a radical feminist more interested in furthering her career than in being a mother and wife. The so-called "Hillary Factor" became a catch phrase during the campaign, as Democratic and Republican strategists alike wondered whether she would help or hurt her husband's chances for election. In the end, the electorate apparently decided she was not a significant detriment and elected Bill Clinton.

Background. Born on Oct. 26, 1947, Hillary Rodham, daughter of Hugh and Dorothy Rodham, grew up in Park Ridge, a middle-class Chicago suburb. Originally a Republican, her politics became more liberal during the 1960s. She attended Wellesley College where, as president of the student government, she gave a 1969 commencement address criticizing a Nixon-administration defender; the speech made *Life* magazine. She then went on to Yale Law School, where she was an editor of *The Yale Review of Law and Social Action.* In 1974 she held a summer job on the U.S. House Judiciary Committee, which was looking into the possible impeachment of then President Richard Nixon, and later in the same year moved to Arkansas to be with her soon-to-be husband, Bill Clinton, whom she married on Nov. 11, 1975. She became a partner in a prominent Little Rock law firm, and twice was rated among the 100 most influential lawyers in the United States by *The National Law Journal.*

A champion of children's rights, Clinton was portrayed erroneously during the 1992 campaign as an advocate of children's suing their parents for the smallest of reasons. In actuality, her stance is more mainstream and concerns cases of abuse or neglect. Clinton served as chair of the Children's Defense Fund from 1986 until February 1992, and was a board member of the Legal Services Corporation (1978–81), chairing it for two years. She also served on the boards of several major corporations, including Wal-Mart, TCBY Enterprises, and Lafarge; she gave up these positions during the campaign.

Bill and Hillary Clinton have one daughter, Chelsea, born in 1980.

GORE, Albert, Jr.

No sooner had the selection of Tennessee Sen. Albert Gore, Jr., as Democratic running mate for Bill Clinton been announced just before the July 1992 Democratic Convention than critics labeled him as a "Clinton clone," chosen to underline the main features of Clinton's own political appeal. Besides being a Southerner, like Clinton, Gore was another representative of the so-called baby-boom generation and came from approximately the same sector of the national ideological spectrum as did Clinton, a point just slightly to the left of center.

But Gore contrasted with Clinton in ways that seemed at least as politically significant. Unlike the Arkansas governor, whose entire career in government had been at the state level, Gore had to his credit four terms in the House, to which he first was elected in 1976, and nearly eight years in the Senate, where he took the seat once held by his father, Albert Gore, Sr., and to which he won reelection easily in 1990. Moreover, Gore had used his time on Capitol Hill to focus on national defense, where Clinton had no practical experience; and on environmental issues, where Clinton's own record in Arkansas had been a cause for criticism.

In the national defense area, Gore made nuclear-arms control his specialty and was given a leading role in fashioning the Democratic alternative to President Reagan's reliance on heavy multiwarheaded nuclear missiles. He also was one of the few prominent Democrats to support President Bush's request to use force in the Persian Gulf war. But the environment was the subject considered closest to his heart, reflected by his focus in the Senate on the dangers to the Earth's ozone layer and by the 1992 publication of his book, *Earth in*

© Terry Ashe/Gamma-Liaison
Albert Gore, Jr.

the Balance: Ecology and the Human Spirit. The latter, which reached the best-seller lists, was attacked by Republicans during the campaign; they claimed that it proved Gore to be "an environmental extremist."

Beyond his policy accomplishments, many Democrats hoped that Gore's service in the Army during the Vietnam war and his exemplary personal life would help to offset the misgivings about Clinton's character that had been raised by allegations of draft evasion and marital infidelity raised during his campaign for the presidential nomination. In the same vein it was felt that Gore's wife, the former Mary Elizabeth Aitcheson, called Tipper, who is widely known for her battle against pornography in popular music and her devotion to her own children, might ease concerns of voters made uneasy by the outspoken feminism of Clinton's wife, Hillary. The overall political strategy of the Democrats worked as the Clinton-Gore ticket was elected on November 3.

Background. Born in Washington, DC, March 31, 1948, Albert Gore, Jr., was graduated from Harvard University in 1969 and attended the Graduate School of Religion at Vanderbilt University and Vanderbilt Law School. He worked as a journalist for the Nashville *Tennessean.* He made an unsuccessful run for the Democratic presidential nomination in 1988 but stayed on the sidelines in 1992, in part out of continued concern for his son, Albert 3d, who had been injured badly in an auto accident in 1989. The Gores have three other children—Karenna, Kristin, and Sarah.

ROBERT SHOGAN

GORE, Mary Elizabeth (Tipper)

Tipper Gore, the wife of Vice-President-elect Al Gore, is at the same time a politician's wife whose main goal is to help her husband, and a feminist who has her own aims to pursue. Unlike Hillary Clinton, President-elect Bill Clinton's wife, she never has had a long-lived career, although at one time she planned to become a child psychologist. For Gore, family and home have been the priority. In addition, however, she has been a vociferous advocate of labeling on record albums and a tireless volunteer for the homeless.

Tipper Gore first came to national attention in her own right in the mid-1980s as a crusader against pornographic and sadistic rock music. She had been shocked one day by the sexually explicit lyrics on Prince's *Purple*

© Dennis Brack/Black Star

Tipper Gore

Rain album, to which her oldest daughter was listening. Together with a group of other mothers, she formed the Parents' Music Resource Center. That group sought to warn parents about lyrics that glorified rape, suicide, sadomasochism, incest, and the occult, and successfully lobbied the Recording Industry Association of America for a rating system to tell consumers if lyrics were violent or sexually explicit.

Among Gore's other causes are the poor and homeless. She is the organizer of Families for the Homeless, a group that raised money and tried to bring attention to the homelessness issue.

Lest Gore's image come across as that of a prissy woman out of touch with the times, word was spread during the 1992 presidential campaign that she had been a drummer for an all-girl band, the "Wildcats," while she was in high school, and that in 1992 she bought the double compact disc of the Grateful Dead's *Europe '72* album. Then at the Democratic Convention, she and Hillary Clinton danced to Fleetwood Mac's "Don't Stop (Thinking About Tomorrow)." She also boogied with her husband after his acceptance speech at the convention.

Background. Mary Elizabeth Aitcheson was born in Washington, DC, on Aug. 19, 1948, and acquired the nickname Tipper as a baby. When her parents divorced in 1952, she and her mother moved to Virginia to live with her grandparents. She attended a girls' school in Washington and met Al Gore at his high-school prom in suburban Washington.

She was graduated from Boston University in 1970 with a degree in psychology, and was married to Al Gore on May 19 of that year. She worked for a time as a photographer for *The Tennessean* in Nashville, but gave that up when her husband was elected to the U.S. House of Representatives in 1976. Gore free-lanced for a while, but concentrated mostly on her family, even after she had entered the public spotlight in the 1980s. In fact, when her husband's aspiring political career put him in contention for the 1988 Democratic presidential nomination, Gore cut short a promotional tour for her book *Raising PG Kids in an X-Rated Society* to join him on the campaign trail.

The Gores have three daughters and a son. Their youngest child, Albert 3d, almost lost his life in 1989 when he pulled his hand out of his father's and dashed in front of a speeding car. His parents say they have gained a new perspective on what is important in life due to that incident and his difficult recovery.

JOYNER-KERSEE, Jackie

At the 1992 Summer Olympics in Barcelona, Spain, Jackie Joyner-Kersee became the first woman to win consecutive gold medals in the heptathlon, a seven-event discipline considered the most challenging in women's sports. By so doing, the U.S. track star enhanced her reputation as the greatest woman athlete since Mildred (Babe) Didrikson. With 7,044 points in the heptathlon, Joyner-Kersee lagged only behind her own world record of 7,291 set at the 1988 Seoul Olympics but stayed well ahead of other challengers. Of her victory, she said: "For me, it's the challenge, the challenge to try to beat myself or do better than I did in the past."

Five days after making history in the heptathlon in Barcelona, Joyner-Kersee failed in her bid to win a second consecutive gold medal in the long jump, losing to her friend and longtime rival Heike Drechsler of Germany and behind Irena Belova of the Unified Team (the former USSR). Although she admitted that she felt a "little disappointment" with her bronze-medal performance, she acknowledged that "today was Heike's day. She was the best." With such remarks, Joyner-Kersee demonstrated again that she was not only a world-class athlete but also a champion of good sportsmanship.

Background. Born on March 3, 1962, in East St. Louis, IL, Jacqueline Joyner was named after then first lady Jacqueline Kennedy at the insistence of her grandmother, who said that she would be "the first lady of something." Joyner competed in her first track meet when she was 9 years old and was leaping more than 17 ft (5 m) in the long jump by the time she was 12. In high school, Joyner quickly became a state legend, setting the high-school long-jump record of 20'7½" (6.29 m). She went on to win four consecutive National Junior Pentathlon Championships. The future Olympian also excelled academically.

Recruited by the University of California at Los Angeles, Joyner chose a basketball scholarship and continued to compete in the long jump. Bob Kersee, an assistant track coach at UCLA, saw Joyner's multi-event skills wasting and convinced Joyner to train for the heptathlon. After a four-year working relationship, Joyner and Kersee were married in 1986.

Joyner targeted the 1984 Olympic Games in Los Angeles for a gold medal but slipped to a silver because of

Jackie Joyner-Kersee

© David Madison/Duomo

an injury. She, however, took additional pride in her brother Al as he won the gold medal in the triple jump in Los Angeles. Joyner-Kersee's performance at the Olympics in Seoul was a personal best; she brought home gold medals in both the long jump and the heptathlon.

Joyner-Kersee's athletic ability is matched only by her affable style. Having won her first Olympic medal on U.S. soil, Joyner-Kersee wants to end her Olympic run with the 1996 Games in Atlanta, GA. In the meantime, she and Bob Kersee have talked about starting a family.

KEATING, Paul John

After 26 years in the Australian House of Representatives, including eight as the nation's treasurer, Paul Keating was chosen by the Australian Labor Party (ALP) caucus in December 1991 as Australia's 23d prime minister. In his first year as national leader, he faced widespread disenchantment as the nation wallowed in economic problems, many of which increasingly were seen to stem from policies he had initiated in his earlier role as treasurer. In spite of government efforts to achieve greater productivity, unemployment remained at 11%, and Keating was unable to lift the ALP's standing in the opinion polls.

In the prosperous 1980s, Keating had taken a leading role in "internationalizing" the Australian economy. His emphasis, then as in 1992, was in supporting Australia's positioning within the Asian economic sphere. His record as treasurer earned both high approval and strong disapproval. His moves to improve the climate for productive investment were praised; however, drawing criticism was inflation-driven deterioration in the cost structure facing industries. Hope for economic progress was eroded by sustained inflation and mounting overseas debt. Modest budgetary surpluses in four years were outweighed by an unprecedented level of deficit financing over the 1980s. Reliance on monetary policy in the 1980s to hold down consumer demand failed to restrain inflation until 1991, when the worst national slump in many decades brought severe unemployment. In 1992 stimulative measures initiated in Keating's first months as prime minister had a mixed reception.

Keating's political deftness in handling public issues and in dampening factional discord within the ALP was matched by criticism of his policies and of what some saw as his "Machiavellian guile." His uninhibited style in parliamentary debate brought mixed reaction.

Background. Paul John Keating was born Jan. 18, 1944, in Bankstown, a Sydney suburb, to Minnie and Matthew Keating. His father was an active Labor supporter, and Keating showed intense interest in Labor affairs even as a boy. He became a union official at age 21, and was a protégé of one of Labor's fallen idols, octogenarian John Thomas Lang, former premier of New South Wales.

Keating progressed through Labor's Youth Council and within the ALP's local branch in Bankstown. He secured nomination for the federal parliamentary seat of Blaxland, and won it at 25. After brief ministerial experience in 1975, he showed debating skill in Opposition from 1976 to 1983.

After the ALP's electoral victory in March 1983, Robert J. Hawke chose Keating as treasurer. Keating downplayed Labor's socialist goal, instead criticizing capitalism while promoting a mixture of economic progress and social reform. His growing status within the party reached the point where in June 1991 he pressed a claim to succeed Hawke; upon failing in his bid, he resigned his post. A few months later, however, a second challenge in caucus succeeded.

Married in 1974, Keating and his Dutch-born wife, Annita, have three daughters and a son.

R. M. YOUNGER

KING, Larry

During the U.S. presidential campaign of 1992, it sometimes seemed as though radio and television talk-show host Larry King was as ubiquitous as the candidates themselves. A broadcaster for more than 35 years and already popular as a radio talk-show host, King

Paul Keating

© Asikalin/Sipa

Larry King

© Sygma

gained new prominence in February when businessman (and later independent presidential candidate) H. Ross Perot used the *Larry King Live* show on CNN to announce that he would seek the presidency if his supporters put his name on the ballot of all 50 states. After this event, television talk shows increasingly became a forum for politics and politicians alike. President George Bush and his Democratic challenger, Bill Clinton, as well as the vice-presidential candidates, climbed aboard the talk-show bandwagon, appearing on King's show as well as those of the major networks. This trend, with the resultant accessibility of the candidates to the public's questions, largely was attributed to King's influence.

King is not college-educated, nor does he profess to be a true journalist. He prides himself on not preparing for interviews and not asking the hard-nosed questions expected of prime-time broadcast journalists. Instead, he asks questions he says he figures his listeners would ask, in a casual way that often results in the person being interviewed saying more than he had planned. The Perot announcement, for example, came at the end of the interview, after Perot already had said he would not run for president. But King persisted, asking, "By the way, is there any scenario . . . in which you'd say 'O.K., I'm in.' " The response was Perot's now-famous announcement.

Background. Larry King was born Lawrence Harvey Zeiger in Brooklyn, NY, on Nov. 19, 1933. His father died when he was 10; King headed for Miami at age 23 because he had heard even neophytes could get a job in radio there.

Sure enough, King's entry into radio came in 1957 when the disk jockey for the radio station where he was sweeping floors suddenly quit. By 1970, he was riding high with a local radio talk show, a TV interview show, and a newspaper column. His ego and his debts, however, also were high. In 1971 he was charged with grand larceny for misusing $5,000 of a business associate's funds. The charges later were dropped because the statute of limitations had expired. Nonetheless, King lost his broadcast and newspaper jobs, and his marriage ended in divorce.

By 1978, King had declared bankruptcy, claiming that he was $352,000 in debt, including $14,000 in gambling debts. His comeback and rise to national fame began that same year, however, when he went to Washington, DC, to launch *The Larry King Show* for Mutual radio. Since then his easygoing, populist style of interviewing has brought him TV viewers in 130 countries and more than 3.5 million radio listeners. His radio show, *The Larry King Show,* is broadcast for three hours nightly; the *Larry King Live* show airs for an hour each weeknight. Additionally, he has a weekly newspaper column in *USA Today* and has written five books.

MAJOR, John

In April 1992, when John Major led his Conservative Party to a surprisingly decisive win over the Labour Party in Great Britain's general election, *The Economist* summed up the achievement on its front cover. "Major's hour," read the simple headline, next to a picture of a smiling and relieved prime minister.

It was, certainly, a close election. As the campaign drew to an end, the political and economic situation had not augured well for the Conservatives. Britain was mired in the longest-running recession since the 1930s and polls were putting Labour up to seven points ahead. The Conservatives, however, shrewdly—and some say unfairly—attacked Labour's plans to increase the taxes of those in higher income brackets. Major took to Britain's streets, campaigning from a soapbox and pressing flesh in the style of U.S. presidential candidates. In the end, the Conservatives managed to win a majority of 21 parliamentary seats. Major and his soapbox were deemed by the pundits to be significant factors in the win, but a more significant factor was probably the un-

© Terry O'Neill/Sygma
John Major

popularity among voters of his opposite number, Labour Party leader Neil Kinnock.

Major, on the other hand, has demonstrated popularity among voters, all the more so because he is vastly different in style, if not in substance, from his predecessor, Margaret Thatcher. He is, in the view of many, ordinary almost to the point of dullness. For example, in the British television series *Spitting Image,* in which public figures are lampooned by latex puppets, Major's puppet is completely gray. Thatcher, disappointed by Major's abandonment of some Thatcherite policies, also has been quoted as describing Major as "gray." His political allies dispute the accusations of grayness, but most agree that Major is more of an administrator than a visionary. He is said to be hypersensitive to criticism, but is regarded as a highly sympathetic and loyal man who has supported political friends and foes in the face of public controversy. Many ascribe his considerable sense of fair play to his love of cricket.

Background. Unlike most British prime ministers, John Major comes from a working-class family and has no university education. He was born on March 29, 1943, to Gwen and Thomas Major. The latter was a trapeze artist and music-hall performer turned purveyor of garden ornaments. From adolescence, the future politician and his family lived in a cold-water flat in a working-class south London neighborhood. After a stint at a respected grammar school, Major ended his inauspicious academic career in March 1959, the same month in which he joined the Young Conservatives, and took a job in London's financial district as an insurance-company clerk, a job he soon traded for a better-paying one mixing cement.

In 1965 he became a bank clerk for Standard Bank (later Standard Chartered). After working his way up the career ladder to become aide to the chairman of Standard Chartered, and after two unsuccessful parliamentary bids in 1974, he entered the House of Commons as the representative for Huntingdon in 1979. A protégé of Prime Minister Thatcher, he served under her as a junior minister of social security (1986-87), chief treasury secretary (1987–89), foreign secretary (July-October 1989), and chancellor of the exchequer (1989–90). In November 1990, after a bloody battle within the Conservative Party that sent Thatcher packing, the protégé became the successor.

Major and his wife, Norma, whom he married in 1970, have two children—a son and a daughter. In addition to cricket, he also enjoys the opera.

SUZANNE CASSIDY

© Vince Heptic/Saba

Rigoberta Menchú

MENCHÚ, Rigoberta

The winner of the 1992 Nobel Peace Prize was Rigoberta Menchú, a 33-year-old Indian woman from the highlands of Guatemala. A Mayan of the Quiché tribe, Menchú had spent more than a decade denouncing human-rights violations and abuses against the indigenous people who make up more than 60% of the population of her country. Both her parents and a younger brother were killed by the Guatemalan army in 1980, and Menchú was forced to flee to Mexico.

Menchú was nominated for the award by Nobel laureates Adolfo Pérez Esquivel of Argentina and Archbishop Desmond Tutu of South Africa. In announcing the award, the Nobel committee said, "Like many other countries in South and Central America, Guatemala has experienced great tension between the descendants of European immigrants and the native Indian population. In the 1970s and 1980s, that tension came to a head in the large scale repression of Indian peoples. Menchú has come to play an increasingly prominent part as an advocate of native rights."

News of Menchú's award came during the commemoration of the 500th anniversary of Christopher Columbus' landing in the Americas, helping focus attention on indigenous peoples' complaints that Columbus brought cruelty and persecution to the New World and that inhumane treatment of the Americas' Indian populations continues today. The awards committee acknowledged that "this was a somewhat controversial prize," and said that choosing an Indian for the award in the year of Columbus' quincentennial "was not a coincidence, but it was not the only factor."

Background. The story of Rigoberta Menchú's life was told in her 1983 book, *I, Rigoberta Menchú*, which has been translated into 11 languages. Born in poverty and uneducated, she worked as a farm laborer as a small child. She spoke only Quiché, one of Guatemala's 23 Indian languages, until she was 19. Her father, Vicente, a peasant leader, was burned to death inside the Spanish embassy in Guatemala City in 1980 when he participated in a peaceful takeover of the building. The embassy was set afire by army troops despite the protest of the Spanish ambassador. Troops also burned her 16-year-old brother to death and tortured, raped, and killed her mother. Menchú fled the country in 1981; two of her sisters joined the guerrillas.

Guatemala has been fighting a small Marxist insurgency for 30 years. Up to 10,000 people have been killed in the fighting and 50,000 have "disappeared," according to human-rights groups. Menchú never openly has praised or denounced the armed struggle, but her life has been threatened repeatedly, and she has been denounced as a "Communist." The Guatemalan government did not support Menchú for the Nobel Peace Prize, and, in fact, helped propose a wealthy non-Indian social worker when Menchú's nomination was made public.

The Nobel laureate was visiting Guatemala when the award was announced, but did not say whether she planned to remain in the country. She said she intended to use the $1.2 million award to establish a foundation in her father's name to defend the rights of indigenous peoples.

RICHARD C. SCHROEDER

PEROT, H. Ross

Like the range-riding straight-shooting cowboy of yore, the blunt and tough-minded leader of business long has been a venerated figure for Americans, and few executives have fit that stereotype better than Texas billionaire H. Ross Perot. It seemed only natural that he should turn his hand to politics in 1992, when a gridlocked federal government and a sluggish economy left millions of Americans impatient with the two major political parties.

Perot's ultimately unsuccessful presidential bid for awhile overshadowed the nominees of the two established parties and threatened to test the strictures of the political system. He ended by receiving 19% of the popular vote—the highest total by a third-party candidate since Theodore Roosevelt won 27% for the Bull Moose Party in 1912. Perot's candidacy for the nation's highest office was an episode quite in keeping with the freewheeling pattern that had helped carry him to the top in the world of private enterprise.

Background. Born June 27, 1930, in Texarkana, TX, Henry Ross Perot was influenced early in life by the energetic commitment of his father, Ross, to his occupations as a cotton broker and horse trader. The young Perot started off at Texarkana Junior College, then accepted an appointment at the U.S. Naval Academy, where he met his future wife, Margot. He was graduated in 1953, twice having been elected president of his class. After four years of navy service, Perot became a salesman for IBM, then in 1962 started his own company,

Ross Perot

© Brad Markel/Gamma-Liaison

Electronic Data Systems. Aided by a computer-services boom due to the establishment of the Medicare and Medicaid programs, he soon became a billionaire.

Other business ventures over the years brought mixed results. His attempt to bail out one of the nation's largest brokerage firms at the behest of the New York Stock Exchange failed in 1970–71. In 1984 he sold his company to General Motors and attempted to streamline the automaker's bureaucratic operations. However, this effort was abandoned shortly, and Perot parted company with GM, taking with him a $700 million settlement.

Meanwhile, Perot increasingly was getting attention outside the world of business. He became an outspoken critic of the U.S. Defense Department for its alleged failure to be vigorous enough in looking into reports of U.S. prisoners of war still held captive in Vietnam. In 1979 he engineered the escape of two of his employees imprisoned by the Iranian government, a feat dramatized by a book and a TV show—both entitled *On Wings of Eagles*. And in the mid-1980s he helped push through a sweeping reform of the Texas school system.

The Perot presidential boom was touched off by a television appearance on CNN's *Larry King Live* show on Feb. 20, 1992. In response to one of King's questions, Perot offered to run for the White House, and to back his candidacy with $100 million of his own money, if volunteer supporters would get his name on the ballot in all 50 states. Swiftly gathering support around the country, by June Perot vaulted into the lead in three-way polls. A three-way split in the electoral college forcing the House of Representatives to decide the election seemed likely. But growing misgivings about Perot's aggressive tactics in pursuing both his business career and his public-policy interests began to erode his support. On July 16 he abruptly abandoned his plans to run, declaring: "I don't have any drive to be president of the United States," and expressing concern that his candidacy would be disruptive. After he changed his mind two months later and formally became a candidate, Perot had difficulty regaining the support of many of his earlier admirers. But his final vote total constituted an impressive protest by the U.S. electorate.

H. Ross and Margot Perot were married in 1956. They have five children, and reside in Dallas, TX.

See also FEATURE ARTICLE, page 26.

ROBERT SHOGAN

QUAYLE, James Danforth

For most U.S. vice-presidents in modern times the office has served as a stepping-stone which helped them climb toward the presidency. But for Dan Quayle his job as President George Bush's understudy often turned instead into a stumbling block athwart the path of his political ambition. Quayle's political career took another apparent backward step with the defeat of the Bush-Quayle ticket in November 1992.

A good part of Quayle's problems was that he got off on the wrong foot on the national scene in 1988. Bush's selection of him as a running mate caught much of the political world off guard, including, or so it seemed, Quayle himself, though he quietly had campaigned for the job. He appeared ill-prepared for the intensive scrutiny to which he was subjected by the press at the 1988 Republican convention and during the campaign, particularly about whether family influence had helped him find a spot in the national guard and thus avoid service in Vietnam. His worst moment came during the vice-presidential debate when his Democrat opponent, Texas Sen. Lloyd Bentsen, squelched him with the line: "You're no Jack Kennedy," after Quayle had tried to compare himself to the former president.

Once in office, Quayle committed a series of verbal gaffes—declaring that the United States "condones" violence in El Salvador and calling the 1991 Persian Gulf war "a stirring victory for the forces of aggression"—which provided his detractors with plentiful ammuni-

© Ralf-Finn Hestoft/Saba

Dan Quayle

tion. Then as the 1992 Republican Convention approached, he encouraged a spelling-bee contestant to misspell potato as "potatoe."

With Quayle's poll ratings in decline, some Republicans urged Bush to replace him on the ticket, but the president stood firm behind his 1988 selection. And whatever his other shortcomings, Quayle displayed tenacity and humor under fire. Referring to the Democratic ticket in his 1992 acceptance speech, Quayle said: "Well, if they're moderates, I'm a world champion speller." And Quayle built a constituency for himself among conservatives who admired his effort as chairman of the administration's Council on Competitiveness to cut back on government regulation. Conservatives also liked Quayle's provocative criticism of the television show *Murphy Brown* for, he charged, glorifying unwed motherhood.

Background. James Danforth Quayle was born on Feb. 4, 1947, in Indianapolis, IN, the grandson of the late Eugene Pulliam, conservative founder of a publishing empire that included the *Indianapolis Star*. After graduating from DePauw University and Indiana University School of Law, he entered politics in 1976, winning election to the House of Representatives. In 1980 he moved up to the Senate and won reelection in 1986. There he joined with most other conservatives in opposing gun control and federal funding for abortion and led the fight for Senate confirmation of conservative Judge Daniel Manion to the U.S. Court of Appeals. Probably his most significant achievement as a senator was the 1982 Job Training Partnership Act, coauthored with Democratic Sen. Edward M. Kennedy of Massachusetts, which was designed to help workers laid off in industries hurt by foreign competition.

Quayle and his wife, Marilyn, whom he met in law school, have three children: Tucker, Benjamin, and Mary Corinne.

ROBERT SHOGAN

RABIN, Yitzhak

Israel's Yitzhak Rabin, remembered by the public as the hero of the Six-Day War, returned to the premiership in July 1992 after a 15-year absence; he brought with him hopes for a possible breakthrough in the Arab-Israeli peace talks that began in 1991. After Rabin's Labor Party won an electoral victory over the Likud bloc on June 23, he formed a coalition government with a number of smaller parties, and immediately set about trying to breathe new life into the peace process.

Days after assuming the premiership, Rabin removed a major obstacle to progress by curtailing further Jewish settlements in the West Bank and Gaza Strip. This action

© Ricki Rosen/Saba

Yitzhak Rabin

prompted the United States to end a yearlong ban on loan guarantees for Israel. He followed this up by offering a measure of self-government to the Palestinians, and indicated a willingness to return at least some of the land seized from Jordan and Syria in the 1967 war in exchange for peace. The gains made by these concessions were endangered in October and November by a flare-up of fighting in the occupied territories and along the border with Lebanon. Meanwhile Rabin won a vote of confidence in the Knesset on November 2, narrowly averting a split in his fragile coalition.

Background. Born in Jerusalem on March 1, 1922, of Russian immigrant parents, Yitzhak Rabin grew up in British-occupied Palestine. He graduated with honors from the Kadoorie Agricultural School in Galilee, and was a member of the Haganah (the Jewish Defense Force) before World War II. After the war, in which he fought as part of the British army, his military career advanced rapidly. He commanded a brigade in the 1948 Arab-Israeli War, and became chief of staff in 1963. Rabin led Israeli forces to victory over the Arabs in the 1967 Six-Day War, and was ambassador to the United States from 1968 to 1973.

During his first stint as prime minister (1974–77), Rabin signed an interim agreement with Egypt in September 1975 that helped prepare the way for the Egyptian-Israeli peace treaty of 1979, and ordered the commando raid that rescued Israeli hostages held by Palestinian terrorists at Entebbe airport in Uganda in July 1976. He resigned in April 1977 after he was found to have committed financial irregularities.

As defense minister (1984–90), Rabin fought the Palestinian *intifada* uprising with what he described as a policy of "might, power, and beatings." But despite his record as a vigilant guardian of Israel's security, he opposed the intransigence of his Likud predecessor, Yitzhak Shamir, who was reluctant to make any compromise in negotiations with the Arabs.

RAMOS, Fidel V.

The handpicked candidate of President Corazon Aquino, Gen. Fidel V. Ramos, won the May 11, 1992, election for president of the Philippines. Because of the intense efforts to provide security in the counting of ballots, it took several weeks before the outcome was determined. In a seven-way contest—the first under a new national constitution—he received a mandate from less than one quarter of the electorate.

Ramos, 64, won without the backing of his original party or the powerful Catholic Church, and despite the intense opposition of leftist groups that remembered him as former head of the Philippine Constabulary. As

such, he had helped enforce martial law imposed by former President Ferdinand Marcos (1972–81). Ramos, however, was able to garner moderate and conservative support, because of his timely defection from Marcos following the latter's discredited election in 1986 and his steadfast support for President Aquino. Ramos served as secretary of defense during most of Aquino's six-year term and is credited with putting down six coups against her administration.

The new chief executive took office on June 30 in an inauguration ceremony quite at variance with the usual pageantry surrounding such events. The festivities, however, were consistent with the new president's message of austerity and discipline and his insistence that any display of luxury was inappropriate given the country's dire poverty.

President Ramos moved rapidly but not radically during his first 100 days in office. He retained several of Aquino's cabinet members but reduced the number of cabinet-rank positions. His new cabinet choices were drawn almost exclusively from business, a reflection of his interest in pursuing privatization. Such an objective caused his administration to be called the "corporate cabinet." Ramos also retreated from earlier administrations' rhetoric on the importance of land reform.

Strongly pro-United States, he may be in a position to repair Philippine-U.S. relations, strained following the 1991 decision to close U.S. bases in the Philippines. He, however, will have to contend with nationalists' fears and with a Congress dominated by opposition parties. As the first Protestant president in a country whose people are 85% Catholic, Ramos also has started to build bridges toward the Catholic Church. That may be difficult given the church's opposition to his efforts to accelerate population-control programs.

Background. Fidel V. Ramos was born in 1928 and was graduated from the U.S. Military Academy in 1950. He later earned a degree in civil engineering from the University of Illinois and saw military service in Korea and Vietnam. He became deputy chief of staff of the armed forces in 1981 and chief of staff in the final days of the Marcos era. He retained the latter post under President Aquino until she named him defense secretary in January 1988.

President Ramos is married and the father of five daughters. A cigar, unlit since he gave up smoking in 1987, usually is in his mouth.

LINDA K. RICHTER

SCHWARZENEGGER, Arnold

International film star Arnold Schwarzenegger in 1992 was devoting much time to his work as chairman of the President's Council of Physical Fitness and Sports— a post to which he was appointed by U.S. President George Bush in 1990. The fact that Schwarzenegger is popular enough to influence U.S. children simply by appearing at schools and lecturing about fitness is an indication of the Austrian-born former bodybuilder's rise to the top of popular culture.

Despite frequent bad reviews and jokes about his lack of acting ability, as well as limitations imposed by his physique, Schwarzenegger has become internationally well-known. The star of such action-oriented films as *Commando* (1985), *Predator* (1987), *The Running Man* (1987), and *Total Recall* (1990), Schwarzenegger also has achieved success in lighter, more comedic roles in the 1990s. Said to be one of the ten wealthiest entertainers in the United States, Schwarzenegger is a shrewd businessman and investor. Ambitious and not given to introspection, he simply goes after—and achieves—seemingly everything he desires to. His 1991 movie *Terminator 2: Judgment Day,* rumored to be the most expensive film ever made, was a tremendous financial success, accounting for more than half of all U.S. movie tickets sold during the five days after its release. As with most Schwarzenegger films, *Terminator 2* was criticized for its violence, but was very popular with fans. The actor's popularity often is attributed to the touch of

Arnold Schwarzenegger

Robin Yount

humor he manages to give to even his most violent roles. The ten films Schwarzenegger made during the 1980s grossed a worldwide total of more than $1 billion.

Background. Arnold Schwarzenegger was born July 30, 1947, in Graz, Austria, the son of Gustav, a police chief, and his wife Aurelia. Schwarzenegger and his older brother, Meinhard, were raised austerely; their father was a strict disciplinarian. Schwarzenegger believes this strict upbringing, along with his competing for attention with Meinhard—a champion boxer until his death at 23—accounts for his determination.

Schwarzenegger became fascinated at an early age with bodybuilding and with the United States. He joined the Austrian army in 1965, and after only one month in the service, won the Junior Mr. Europe title. However, he spent a year in the brig for going AWOL to participate in the competition. In 1967, at age 20, Schwarzenegger became the youngest man ever to win the Mr. Universe contest. The following year he traveled to the United States to compete again for the Mr. Universe title, remaining in the country afterward. In 1970 he won the Mr. World, Mr. Universe, and Mr. Olympia titles—an unprecedented feat.

After a final retirement from bodybuilding in 1980, Schwarzenegger received a bachelor's degree in business and international economics from the University of Wisconsin. He obtained most of the necessary credits through correspondence, having been busy running a mail-order business in fitness books and cassettes and making profitable real-estate investments.

His appearance in the film *Pumping Iron* (1977) first brought Schwarzenegger to the attention of the public, although he already had won a Golden Globe Award as best new actor for a small role in the 1976 film *Stay Hungry*. In 1982 he starred in *Conan the Barbarian,* followed by *Conan the Destroyer* in 1983. The 1984 movie *The Terminator* made Schwarzenegger a popular star.

Schwarzenegger and his wife Maria Shriver, the daughter of Eunice Kennedy Shriver, are the parents of two daughters, Katherine Eunice and Christina Aurelia. Schwarzenegger, despite his connection to the Kennedy family, campaigned for George Bush in 1988 and 1992.

YOUNT, Robin R.

Robin Yount, the longtime leader of the Milwaukee Brewers, reached the climax of his 19-year professional baseball career on Sept. 9, 1992, when he collected his 3,000th career hit. Yount's single against José Mesa of the Cleveland Indians came before 47,589 fans at Milwaukee County Stadium, where Yount made his debut as an 18-year-old shortstop in 1974. The hit made him the 17th player to reach the 3,000-hit plateau and the first since Rod Carew of the California Angels in 1985.

Although he finished the 1992 season with a .264 batting average, 24 points below his career mark, and eight home runs, his fewest since 1977, Yount helped Milwaukee stage an unsuccessful late-season bid to overcome the Toronto Blue Jays for the American League (AL) East title.

Yount always has been a team leader. In 1982, when the Brewers won their only pennant, Yount enjoyed personal peaks with 29 home runs, 114 runs batted in (RBIs), and a .331 batting average. He led the American League in total bases and slugging percentage, won a Gold Glove for his play at shortstop, and hit .414 in the seven-game World Series against the St. Louis Cardinals. Through 1992 he remained the only player to produce two four-hit games in one World Series. Yount not only won AL most valuable player (MVP) honors after that season but was named major-league player of the year by *The Sporting News*. When he repeated as MVP in 1989, Yount joined Stan Musial and Hank Greenberg as the only players to win the award at two different positions. He had shifted to center field in 1985 following off-season shoulder surgery.

Yount received additional honors after the 1989 campaign when *USA Today* named him AL player of the decade for the 1980s and Milwaukee writers elected him the Brewers' MVP for the fourth time. Playing for a small-market team, coupled with his desire for privacy, have made Yount an anonymous star outside his home city. He has made the All-Star team only three times.

Background. Robin Yount was born in Danville, IL, on Sept. 16, 1955. He was a year old when he and his older brother Larry moved to Woodland Hills, CA, with their mother, Marion, and their father, Philip, an aerospace engineer. Larry, now Robin's legal adviser, pitched for the Houston Astros in 1971 while Robin was a schoolboy star in football and baseball at Taft High School. The younger Yount, who also played American Legion ball, was named city baseball player of the year just before he was drafted by the Brewers. A first-round pick in the 1973 amateur free-agent draft, Yount reached Milwaukee after spending a single season in the minors.

Yount married the former Michele Edelstein after the 1977 season. They live with daughters Melisa, Amy, and Jenny, and a son, Dustin, in Paradise Valley, AZ. Yount's hobbies include racing cars, riding motorcycles, fishing, camping, skiing, and playing golf. He once considered leaving baseball for the pro golf tour.

DAN SCHLOSSBERG

BIOTECHNOLOGY

The year 1992 brought advances in methods designed to destroy brain cancer and skin melanoma cells, detect genetic diseases in embryos before implantation, and obtain human-gene products from farm animals.

Brain-Cancer Cells. Normally, brain cells do not divide. In fact, in a cancer-diseased brain, only the cancer cells divide. In a procedure designed to destroy brain-cancer cells, Dr. K. Culver and his colleagues at the National Institutes of Health (NIH) introduced a retrovirus, carrying the gene for the enzyme thymidine kinase, into actively dividing mouse fibroblast (connective-tissue) cells. Retroviruses only can infect and proliferate in cells that are dividing actively. The viruses also produce the enzyme thymidine kinase, which makes the cells vulnerable to antiviral drugs such as ganciclovir.

The retrovirus-containing mouse fibroblasts were injected into the brains of 14 rats suffering from brain cancers. Five days were allowed to elapse to permit the retroviruses within the infected mouse cells to reproduce, leave the fibroblasts, and infect the surrounding cancer cells. After five days, the rats were treated with ganciclovir. In 11 of the 14 rats there was a complete destruction of both the brain cancers and the transferred mouse cells. In the remaining rats, some cancerous brain tissue survived. In all 14 rats there was no evidence of destruction of any normal (nondividing) brain tissue. The NIH approved a protocol for repeating the procedure with human beings.

Embryonic-Cell Analysis for Cystic Fibrosis. A new procedure which permits one to detect a genetic disease in an embryo even before a pregnancy is initiated has been developed by Dr. A. H. Handyside and his colleagues in England. It involves the in vitro fertilization of an egg and the culturing of the developing embryo in the laboratory for three days. At the end of that time, the embryo has reached the eight-cell stage and one cell can be removed without endangering the subsequent normal development of the embryo. The single removed embryonic cell can be examined for the presence of a disease-causing gene.

In the first use of this procedure, the scientists were looking for the presence of the cystic-fibrosis gene. It was necessary for them to obtain a sizable quantity of that portion of the DNA which includes the gene. This was accomplished through the "polymerase chain reaction," which yields a large number of copies of any specified section of the cell's DNA. When this was done, the embryo was found to be free of the cystic-fibrosis gene. The embryo was placed in the mother's uterus, with the subsequent birth of a healthy child.

Human Proteins in the Milk of Farm Animals. The process by which farm animals become the source of human proteins begins with the removal of fertilized eggs from the oviducts of recently mated females. Each egg then is injected with a piece of DNA containing a human gene that is flanked by genes of the animal which are active only in its mammary glands. Subsequently, the egg is implanted in the uterus of the female. A few of the animals born carry the human gene in one of their chromosomes and are referred to as "transgenic" because they carry a gene from a foreign organism. They are able to transmit the foreign gene to their offspring.

By late 1992, the enzyme *alpha-1-antitrypsin,* which helps fight emphysema, had been obtained successfully from the milk of transgenic sheep; the enzyme *tissue plasminogen activator,* which dissolves blood clots, had been obtained from the milk of transgenic goats; and the gene for *lactoferrin,* which has bacteria-fighting capabilities, had been transferred to a bull, some of whose female offspring will inherit the gene and produce *lactoferrin* in their milk.

Injectable DNA Therapy for Skin Melanoma. A procedure to stimulate a patient's immune system to attack and destroy malignant skin cells has been developed by Dr. G. J. Nabel at the University of Michigan. It involves the introduction of the gene for a protein called HLA-B7 into cancerous cells. When the cells produce this protein, it becomes incorporated into the cells' membranes and acts to attract the T-cells of the patient's immune system to the malignant cells, which then are destroyed.

Several trillion copies of the gene for the HLA-B7 protein were injected into a tumor of a 67-year-old woman with malignant melanoma, whose life expectancy was less than a year. It was hoped that T-cells would be attracted to the skin cancer and not only would destroy the cancer cells containing the HLA-B7 protein but also would attack surrounding tumor cells that contain other abnormal proteins. If successful, this test will initiate the use of DNA as a medical drug.

Federal Regulation. On Feb. 4, 1992, the Bush administration announced a new policy governing genetically engineered organisms and their products. The basic thrust of the policy was that only if evidence is presented that there is an unreasonable risk in using a product made by altering an organism's genes will there be government regulation of the item's production and use. A comparable policy is to apply to the release of genetically altered organisms into the environment. If organisms are only slightly different from their parental strains, the genetically engineered organisms need not be regulated more than are the parental strains. The new policy is designed to reduce the expense and time required to approve genetically engineered organisms and their products for commercial use.

LOUIS LEVINE, *City College of New York*

BOLIVIA

Although little noticed in the United States, Bolivia continued its "quiet economic miracle" in 1992, with inflation held in check at about 10%, economic growth projected at 3.5% to 4.0%, and the country's structural reform program drawing praise from the World Bank and other international bodies. The year was marred, however, by growing unrest in the military and among the nation's workers over the austere conditions induced by government reforms. As the country moved toward national elections in May 1993, strains appeared in Bolivia's relations with the United States and open protest erupted over the government's cooperation in U.S.-inspired anti-drug efforts.

Labor. The year began with a strike led by the Bolivian Workers' Confederation (COB) to protest government plans to privatize more than 100 state-owned enterprises, including the state mining company, Comibol, and companies run by regional development corporations. The strike was settled on January 29 with the mediation of the Roman Catholic Church. The government promised consultation with mine workers on its privatization plans and on proposed tax increases. The dispute continued to fester, however, as the government announced plans for a 35% cut in the number of public employees. The ninth Congress of the COB, held in May, called for a popular insurrection —"a war involving the entire population"— and in July the COB mounted a 48-hour strike, accompanied by street demonstrations.

Military. Labor unrest was accompanied by similar discontent within the military over the shrinking defense budget and the government's cooperation in U.S. antidrug programs. Bowing to pressure, the government announced in July that it was withdrawing special police units and military troops from future drug-control missions and on August 1 it turned down a U.S. request to dispatch additional troops for the antidrug effort. At the same time, it withdrew diplomatic immunity from U.S. Drug Enforcement Administration (DEA) agents in field operations in the country.

Tension over the U.S.-inspired drug war mounted when a U.S.-DEA employee was arrested in Santa Cruz for the shooting of a Bolivian national in a barroom brawl. Arrested by local police, the DEA man was released to U.S. officials who quickly returned him to the United States. The shooting victim was paid compensation by the United States but in the wake of the incident demands rose for limiting the DEA's presence in Bolivia and for the extradition of any U.S. personnel accused of breaking Bolivian laws.

Politics. In March, President Jaime Paz Zamora restructured his cabinet to bolster his flagging Patriotic Accord (AP) coalition, which suffered from internal divisions and the grow-

ing protest movement. The AP coalition is made up of Paz' social democratic Movement of the Revolutionary Left (MIR) and the conservative National Democratic Action (ADN), led by former military ruler Hugo Banzer Suárez. Eight ministers were dismissed in the shuffle and nine were reconfirmed.

In July, further responding to growing political rifts in Bolivia, the country's eight largest parties agreed on a calendar for reform of the constitution, the judiciary, the electoral law, and the educational system. An all-party commission was to define the reforms by October 30 and the package was to be presented to the national Congress by November 30.

International. On January 24, Paz Zamora signed an agreement with Peru's President Alberto Fujimori, granting landlocked Bolivia access to the Pacific Ocean through Peruvian territory. In return, Bolivia agreed to work toward securing Peruvian access to the Atlantic Ocean via the river systems of Bolivia and Brazil.

In June, Paz signed an agreement with the presidents of the member countries of Mercosur—Argentina, Brazil, Paraguay, and Uruguay—for a ten-year project to develop the Paraguay-Paraná River network into a year-round *hidrovía,* providing an outlet to the Atlantic Ocean. At the meeting, Bolivia also expressed interest in joining the Mercosur pact.

RICHARD C. SCHROEDER, *Consultant to the Organization of American States*

BRAZIL

In June 1992, Brazil's President Fernando Collor de Mello basked in international admiration as he hosted world leaders at the Earth Summit in Rio de Janeiro. By the end of the year, Collor had given up the presidential office in the face of impeachment charges.

Politics. Controversy beset President Collor all year. In mid-January he lost a heated con-

Thousands of Brazilians in numerous cities took to the streets in late August 1992 to demand that President Fernando Collor de Mello be removed from office. Facing an impeachment trial, the president resigned on December 29.

stitutional battle with Congress and the Supreme Court over pension jurisdiction. The president subsequently ousted four corrupt cabinet ministers and pledged closer cooperation with the national legislature. Yet strained relations with Congress continued. In March the chief executive sacked combative Environmental Secretary José Lutzenberger and environmental agency chief Eduardo Martins. This preceded an overhaul of his 12-member cabinet and entire presidential staff.

He hoped that replacing younger technocrats with seasoned politicians would boost his abysmal public ratings and broaden legislative support. He ultimately failed on both counts. In a May 24 interview, media executive Pedro Affonso Collor de Mello accused his brother of using cocaine and profiting from high-level government corruption. The allegation of graft centered on businessman Paulo Cesar "P.C." Farias. Since serving as Collor's 1989 campaign treasurer, Farias had cultivated multiple government ties. One of his companies also challenged Pedro Affonso Collor de Mello's control over a media market. De Mello claimed that Farias was running an extortion network within the administration, with Collor's richly compensated acquiescence. The president immediately denied the story, sued his brother for libel, and ordered a police investigation. In late May, de Mello got the upper hand when Congress created a special commission of inquiry to explore the charges.

The recently liberated Brazilian press had a field day covering the three-month-long congressional probe. Witness after witness attested to high-level racketeering, tax evasion,

and influence peddling. Investigators also uncovered a Farias payoff scheme that had channeled millions of dollars to the president and several associates. Collor proclaimed his innocence and dismissed the inquiry as "political theater." Outraged citizens did not believe the chief executive and participated in huge demonstrations in favor of his impeachment. Release of the commission's incriminating 200-page report on August 24 gave impulse to his ouster. Even participants in Collor's tenuous political coalition turned against him.

On September 29 the Chamber of Deputies voted, 441–38, to impeach the president. Collor's entire cabinet immediately offered their resignations, but the president himself refused to give in. He stepped down temporarily to prepare for his Senate impeachment trial, and promised an implausible victory. However, only minutes after the Senate began the trial on December 29, Collor resigned as chief executive. Within hours, Vice-President Itamar Franco was sworn in to assume the duties of the presidency until the term expires in January 1995. Franco, 61, is a prolabor nationalist and a career politician with a spotless reputation. Franco did pledge to continue Collor's economic reforms at a much slower pace and with more concern for their social costs. In pursuit of this goal, he pieced together a "partnership" cabinet with representatives of Brazil's four largest political parties.

In October 3 national municipal elections, voters penalized those parties that had stood longest with Collor. The large Brazilian Democratic Movement Party (PMDM), which had spearheaded the impeachment drive, and the left-wing Workers Party (PT) registered strong showings. PMDM leader Orestes Quercia soon became mired in a scandal that chilled his own presidential aspirations.

Its ugliness aside, the 1992 political crisis demonstrated the strength and vitality of Brazil's young democracy. Particularly impressive were the alertness of the press, the outspokenness of the populace, and the adherence to constitutional processes and norms by legislative and executive branches. The success of institution-building was threatened by the specter of military intervention. An ominous April communiqué from a group of high-ranking army and air-force officers compared the disorder and tensions in Brazilian politics to those in coup-prone Venezuela and Peru. An emergency military-wage increase defused that crisis, but the underlying danger remained.

Economics. In January the International Monetary Fund (IMF) approved a $2.1 billion standby credit to Brazil to support Collor's economic program. To qualify for this loan, Brazil had to cut inflation and public-sector spending. Its failure to attain these IMF targets led Brazil to renegotiate with the IMF.

Economically the year started off encouragingly enough. The IMF announcement gave Collor and Economy Minister Marcílio Marques Moreira hope that a long-delayed debt restructuring with foreign commercial banks might materialize. A late-February, 14-year, $11 billion debt-financing agreement with the Club of Paris creditor nations further bolstered Brazil's prospects. Although its commitment to repay $4.1 billion to Club nations in 1992–93 was unpopular at home, Brazil's pledge was necessary to boost financial confidence abroad. Negotiators finally reached a preliminary settlement on the complex commercial-bank accord in July. Its primary aim was to reduce Brazil's outstanding $44 billion debt to the foreign commercial banks by 35% in return for increased interest payments. The pact's sec-

ondary, and perhaps more important, aim was to stabilize the Brazilian economy, attract new foreign investment, and restore credibility in Brazilian finance. The politics of impeachment, however, prevented the politicians from paying the treaty its due consideration for months. By the time interim President Franco got around to it, he deemed the repayment provisions too burdensome and urged renegotiation.

Just as the all-important commercial-bank deal suffered neglect during the crisis, so too did Brazil's domestic economy. Inflation, which had been declining steadily the first few months of the year, approached 23% per month once the crisis hit—for an annual rate of 2,000%. Unemployment also rose sharply. Political instability translated into instability in the stock market. Not only did Collor fail to cut public outlays, he fueled inflation with a summer spending spree. He allocated hundreds of millions of dollars to state governors and mayors to win their political support. While failing to save the embattled president, the handouts accelerated price increases and ballooned the federal deficit. Periodic attempts at fiscal reform also fell prey to politics. Congress became ever more reluctant to pass any of Collor's free-market initiatives as the year progressed. Even Franco retreated from his predecessor's reformist zeal and proposed a more moderate "patchwork" fiscal agenda.

Brazil recorded some economic successes as Collor auctioned off several more state-owned companies in his privatization campaign. In March a historic agreement among the government, carmakers, and trade unionists resulted in a 22% decrease in domestic auto prices. In return for pledges of job security, the unions agreed to tie wage increases to the monthly inflation index. Other positive developments included a continuing flood of foreign investment, a healthy balance of trade, a record grain harvest, higher steel output, expanded exports, and a population growth rate under 2% for the first time in 50 years. Overall, the economy registered zero growth, down from 1.2% in 1991.

Foreign Affairs. One of the few bright spots for Fernando Collor was Brazil's celebrated hosting of the 11-day 1992 UN Conference on Environment and Development, the "Earth Summit." (*See* SPECIAL REPORT/ENVIRONMENT.) Early in the year, Brazil and Argentina cemented their nuclear-nonproliferation accord to end a protracted race to become the first South American nuclear power. Yet relations remained tense on Brazil's northern frontier. Venezuela finally took military action against Brazilian gold miners who repeatedly had encroached into the nation's Yanomami Indian Reserve. Brazil did not join in the clashes on either side.

GEORGE W. GRAYSON
College of William & Mary

BRAZIL • Information Highlights

Official Name: Federative Republic of Brazil.
Location: Eastern South America.
Area: 3,286,473 sq mi (8 511 965 km²).
Population (mid-1992 est.): 150,800,000.
Chief Cities (mid-1989 est.): Brasília, the capital, 1,803,478; Sao Paulo, 10,997,472; Rio de Janeiro, 6,011,181; Belo Horizonte, 2,339,039.
Government: *Head of state and government,* Itamar Franco, president (sworn in Dec. 29, 1992). *Legislature*—National Congress: Senate and Chamber of Deputies.
Monetary Unit: Cruzeiro (11,618 cruzeiros equal U.S.$1, Dec. 31, 1992).
Gross Domestic Product (1990 est. U.S.$): $388,000,000,000.
Economic Indexes (1991): *Consumer Prices* (Sao Paulo, 1988 = 100), all items, 130,030.9; food, 122,131.7. *Industrial Production* (1980 = 100), 100.
Foreign Trade (1991 U.S.$): *Imports,* $21,010,000,000; *exports,* $31,622,000,000.

BRITISH COLUMBIA

The year 1992 saw several new policy departures by British Columbia's New Democratic Party (NDP) government. Also, 68% of the province's voters said no to a constitutional-reform plan set forth in the October national referendum.

Government and Politics. The NDP's first provincial budget emphasized the need to maintain economic stability and confidence. General-fund revenue for 1992–93 was estimated at C$16.191 billion and expenditure at C$17.98 billion. The resultant deficit was shown as C$555 million below the revised estimated deficit of C$2.344 billion for 1991-92. Tax increases included extension of the corporation capital tax base and higher personal-income tax and surtax, together with 1% increases in the general corporate-income and small-business taxes. The sales tax also was extended to legal services and nonvoice telecommunications. The basic home-owner grant increased by C$20 to C$450, but the supplementary C$430 grant was eliminated. A Working Opportunity Fund was launched.

Newly enacted legislation included the establishment of a new commissioner for resources and the environment; freedom-of-information and protection-of-privacy initiatives; tighter provisions against conflict of interest by legislative members; and extensions in the coverage of the human-rights act. In addition there was an explicit recognition of the inherent right to aboriginal self-government, and a British Columbia (BC) treaty commission was formed to expedite the settlement of aboriginal land claims. Bulk water exports were prohibited for two years, and the environmental regulation of pulp mills was to have zero tolerance of organochlorine emissions by the year 2002. New social programs included free school lunches and increased access to abortion services and funding for women's clinics. New provisions for the administration of public medicare and the capping of payments to doctors led to a major confrontation with the BC Medical Association during the year.

Long-awaited revisions to the 1987 industrial-relations act were introduced at a fall sitting of the legislature. The new Labour Relations Code was seen as a swing of the pendulum back toward organized labor.

The final episode in the Fantasy Gardens theme park controversy saw former Premier William Vander Zalm acquitted in June on a charge of criminal breach of trust. In September, Forestry Minister Dan Miller was suspended from the cabinet for three months due to a potential conflict of interest in a timber-license transfer.

Constitutional Reform. In April a legislative members' committee on the constitution recommended recognition of new areas of exclusive provincial jurisdiction and the election of members of the Canadian Senate from five designated regions. In the subsequent October 26 national referendum, British Columbians showed the highest level of opposition to the Charlottetown Accord. Concern centered on the guarantee of House of Commons seats for Quebec and on veto power over changes to national institutions, together with constitutional recognition of an inherent right of aboriginal self-government. Premier Michael Harcourt was perceived widely as not having defended provincial interests effectively.

Economy. The province experienced a renewed sense of economic confidence during 1992 as it enjoyed Canada's highest rate of population increase, fed by increasing levels of migration from eastern Canada and immigration from overseas. This growth led to increased consumer consumption and expenditures on housing and pushed service-sector economic growth to 2.8% for 1992, with a top provincial rate of growth forecast at 3.4% for 1993. The economic outlook was less optimistic for the resource sectors. Unemployment was 10.6% in September.

NORMAN J. RUFF, *University of Victoria*

BULGARIA

In 1992, Bulgaria continued its effort to convert from a socialist planned economy to a market system. The resulting high inflation and unemployment helped bring down the government of Prime Minister Filip Dimitrov in October.

Economic Affairs. Unemployment for the first half of 1992 was reported at 472,356 (15% of the work force) and was expected to reach 750,000 (25% of the work force) by the end of the year. Inflation rose by 40.7% during the first six months of 1992, prompting the Bulgarian National Bank to lower the lending interest rate from 54% to 49% in order to keep inflation in check and to maintain the stability of the lev against decreasing demand for foreign currency. In April new price limits were set for 14 basic food items, while the remainder of prices were liberalized. The first stock exchange in Sofia opened on May 19 with three companies participating and a total of 32 shares traded. The second session on May 26 was more active, with 2 million leva in treasury bonds sold.

In April the government moved to establish a privatization agency under the Council of Ministers, which would be headed by 11 members—five chosen by the ministers and six by Parliament—and an executive director. On April 23 the National Assembly passed legislation on the privatization of state and municipal property. Under the new law small firms would be sold at auction, while large enterprises would be converted into joint-stock ventures.

In mid-April the National Assembly passed an amendment to the Land Reform Law of February 1991. Restrictions previously in effect on the amount of land that could be held by private owners were abolished for individuals, and provisions were established for joint companies with less than 50% foreign ownership. Despite strong protests from the Bulgarian Socialist (formerly Communist) Party (BSP), President Zhelyu Zhelev approved the law in early April. By mid-June, 1,224,447 applications had been filed for the restitution of nearly 7.4 million acres (3 million ha) of land, prompting the government to extend the application deadline until August 4.

The Dimitrov government was at odds with labor unions throughout the year. In late March an estimated 40,000 miners went on strike, protesting the proposed discontinuation of lead and uranium mining. The government agreed to the strikers' demands, and in July authorized a 26% increase in wages for all state employees.

The International Monetary Fund (IMF) granted Bulgaria a $212 million credit for economic reform in April, on condition that the freeing of prices be continued and privatization efforts accelerated. The European Bank for Reconstruction and Development approved $52 million for upgrading the coal-burning Maritsa Iztok power plant and the reduction of coal pollution, $65 million for road improvement, and $65 million for the modernization of the telecommunications system.

In February the Kozloduy nuclear-power plant, which supplied about 40% of the country's power, was taken off-line following unsuccessful attempts to repair a pump in one of the two reactors. Power rationing ensued, with reduced power to households one out of every four hours. The European Community (EC) granted $12 million for the modernization of Kozloduy, which is considered a hazard by Western experts.

BULGARIA • Information Highlights

Official Name: Republic of Bulgaria.
Location: Southeastern Europe.
Area: 42,823 sq mi (110 910 km²).
Population (mid-1992 est.): 8,900,000.
Chief Cities (mid-1990 est.): Sofia, the capital, 1,141,142; Plovdiv, 379,083; Varna, 306,300.
Government: *Head of state,* Zhelyu Zhelev, president (took office August 1990). *Head of government,* Filip Dimitrov, prime minister (took office October 1991). *Legislature*—Grand National Assembly.
Monetary Unit: Lev (23.3 leva equal U.S.$1, Aug. 1992).
Gross National Product (1990 U.S.$): $47,300,-000,000.
Economic Index (1989): *Industrial Production* (1980 = 100), 139.
Foreign Trade (1991 U.S.$): *Imports,* $3,017,000,-000,000; *exports,* $3,835,000,000.

Politics. In the fall, political tension intensified between Premier Dimitrov's Union of Democratic Forces [UDF] and the opposition —consisting of the BSP and the Movement for Rights and Freedoms (MRF, representing the ethnic Turkish minority). Opposition deputies attacked the government for its economic policies and alleged arms sales to the warring factions in neighboring Yugoslavia, and Dimitrov became involved in a personal feud with President Zhelev, the former head of the UDF. The BSP and MRF combined to defeat Dimitrov in a confidence vote on October 28. After a two-month interval, Lyuben Berov, an economic adviser to the president, was confirmed as Dimitrov's successor in December.

Prosecutions and Purges. Legal action against the former Communist officials continued in 1992. In June the military section of the Supreme Court sentenced former head of the Bulgarian Intelligence Service General Vladimir Todorov to 14 months' imprisonment for destroying files relevant to the 1978 assassination of Georgi Markov in London. Former President Todor Zhivkov was indicted for erecting two labor camps in which 149 people died during the period 1959 to 1962. In July former Prime Minister Andrey Lukanov was among 60 former government officials arrested for misappropriation of state funds. Former Premier Georgi Atanasov was sentenced to ten years in prison for the same offense in November. Steps also were taken to purge clergy of the Bulgarian Orthodox Church—including Patriarch Maxim—tainted by their association with the Communist regime.

Foreign Affairs. In 1992, Bulgaria signed treaties of friendship and cooperation with its neighbors Greece, Turkey, and Romania, and became a member of the Council of Europe. In March, Prime Minister Dimitrov visited the United States.

VLADIMIR TISMANEANU
Foreign Policy Research Institute

BURMA. *See* MYANMAR.

BUSINESS AND CORPORATE AFFAIRS

U.S. business wrestled with problems and adjustments in 1992, seeking to find formulas for the future and finding it difficult to drop the habits and structures of the past. Solid gains were marred by dismal failures, especially among the old-line, big-name companies. Yet, there were strong signs of optimism at year's end.

Systemic Change. The nature of events led to the conclusion that U.S. business was in the midst of the most basic changes since the immediate post-World War II years. Some of the biggest names in U.S. industry—General Motors, IBM, Sears Roebuck, Digital Equipment, and R.H. Macy, among them—were compelled to make drastic changes in policies and management.

Downsizing, or cutting back on people and facilities to what was viewed as a more efficient size, was common. So was debt reduction or the exchange of debt for equity. But many other problems challenged the industrial world. The efficacy of business bigness was questioned, the evolving role and responsibilities of boards of directors were discussed, executive salaries were challenged, and accounting standards and financial-reporting requirements were reexamined. One of the most serious issues facing business was employee health-care costs—one of the array of benefits business had offered employees during two previous decades but which now were becoming unaffordable.

Problem Areas. Outside and unforeseen factors also forced boards and managers to confront a new reality, including the need to dismantle a large part of the defense machinery because of the reduced threat from abroad. United Technologies announced it would cut 14,000 jobs, or 7% of its work force, with half the cuts involving its defense and aerospace units. And Martin Marietta agreed to buy General Electric's aerospace division, not including its jet-engine unit, for $1.8 billion in preferred stock.

Some companies still were fighting for their lives in 1992. In fact, according to Dun & Bradstreet (D&B), while the rate of increase of large business failures slowed drastically during the first half of the year, small business failures were up, a delayed response to bills left unpaid by the earlier failures of large companies. During the first six months of the year, D&B recorded 1,870 nonfinancial business failures, involving liabilities exceeding $1 million, a record high.

The challenges and changes continued as the year ended. Sears reluctantly announced that it was returning to its old core of retail stores and Allstate Insurance. Insurers were reeling from the combined impact of Hurricanes Andrew and Iniki, with more than $10 billion of claims, and the disastrous impact of their real-estate investments, some of which continued to decline in value. R.H. Macy filed Chapter 11 bankruptcy. Even the big accounting firms were caught up in the problems. Ernst & Young agreed to a record $400 million settlement after conceding it inadequately audited four savings and loan associations that failed at a cost of $6.6 billion.

Positive Signs. As the year wore on it became evident that many companies had positioned themselves for the eventual upturn. After five quarters of declines in 1990 and 1991, corporate profits rose throughout the year. Making the gains more impressive was the fact

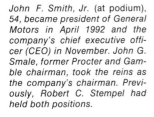

John F. Smith, Jr. (at podium), 54, became president of General Motors in April 1992 and the company's chief executive officer (CEO) in November. John G. Smale, former Procter and Gamble chairman, took the reins as the company's chairman. Previously, Robert C. Stempel had held both positions.

that they were achieved with relatively small increases in sales. In the third quarter, for example, profits of the 500 companies making up the Standard & Poor's Composite Index rose 16% higher than a year earlier, and the S&P Industrial Index recorded a 24% rise. Sales, however, were up only 5% or 6%, indicating that cost-cutting measures indeed were paying off.

Mergers and acquisitions were back in style as those with cash scooped up smaller competitors. Unlike the 1980s, however, these actions tended not to be hostile.

Disparate company earnings indicated the degree to which each had adjusted to the new economy. Philip Morris, Exxon, and General Electric earned more than $1 billion in the third quarter, but IBM, Sears, and GM lost nearly $2.8 billion, $834 million, and $753 million, respectively. GM, which was in the midst of reorganizing its vehicle-making operations, announced a 57.5 million share stock offering, the largest in U.S. history.

Shareholders and Boards. Challenges for the big-name companies came from hitherto unexpected directions, and they made the executive office a hot seat. The best efforts of some old-line managers seemed inadequate to the task of pleasing investors, directors, and critics-at-large, and some of them were gone before the year was out.

Institutional investors and individual shareholder groups, which only recently began exercising their growing shareholder power, publicly questioned the high salaries of corporate executives, especially when performance was poor. They had plenty of ammunition. Executive pay had grown four times faster during the past decade than the income of the average worker and three times faster than that of profits. Sometimes bonuses were awarded when profits were negligible or nonexistent and when managements had failed for years to turn around laggard companies. Some incomes, mainly from stock options, were so great— Leon Hirsch, chief executive of U.S. Surgical, was paid $118 million in 1991, for example— they attracted the attention of Congress, where legislation was threatened. The Securities and Exchange Commission (SEC) insisted that executive salaries be included in proxy statements for discussion and vote by shareholders. (*See also* SIDEBAR, page 55.)

New Managers. Directors also moved in on the operating executives and pressured some to resign—the most prominent being Robert Stempel, the General Motors chairman. He was replaced as chairman by John G. Smale, retired chief executive officer (CEO) of Procter & Gamble, and a member of the GM board, and as CEO by John Smith, Jr., who had built his reputation as the turnaround manager of GM's European operations. Stempel's resignation and the forced admittance of an outsider to active GM management served notice on other chiefs that great changes were under way.

So inclusive was the speculation that it included John Akers, the IBM chief. While his position seemed secure in spite of skimpy profits, an employee-termination program involving 40,000 positions in 1992 alone, and a net third-quarter loss after special charges of $2.78 billion, the speculation indicated the extent of uncertainty in a corporate America desperate to adjust to entrepreneurial challenges from smaller domestic companies and the growing intensity of global competition.

Other changes included the removal by Steven Ross, chairman of Time-Warner, of Nicholas J. Nicholas, as the company's president and CEO. Nicholas was scheduled in 1994 to become the sole CEO of the company but was replaced by Gerald Levin, who had worked his way up through Time, Inc. (Time-Warner chairman Ross died on December 20. *See* OBITUARIES.) Lee Iacocca, Chrysler chairman, was preparing to leave in a blaze of glory as the company unexpectedly reported big third-quarter profits. He was to be replaced by Robert J. Eaton, 52, a former GM executive.

Retiree Benefits. Corporations also had to face new Federal Accounting Standards—FAS 106—regulations, which required them by the first quarter of 1993 to either write off their costs for retiree benefits all at once or phase-in the cost over a 20-year period. IBM decided to take the hit immediately for a total of $2.3 billion, General Electric did also, to the tune of $1.8 billion, but it appeared that GM would work off the impact over two decades. Many other companies had not decided. While FAS 106 would not affect cash flow, it would put a dent in profits and perhaps in the way stock-market analysts valued corporate shares. What it did do was make companies more acutely aware of the relentless growth in the cost of corporate benefits, especially health care. *Fortune* magazine asked companies to help them estimate the cost of just one medical procedure —an appendectomy—and received responses that were shocking and difficult to forget. *Fortune* estimated, for example, that Dayton Hudson, a retailer, would need to sell 39,000 Ninja turtle action figures and Atlantic Richfield would have to sell 192,000 gallons of gasoline to pay for the procedure.

Scandals. Two years after he disappeared, Eddie Antar, founder of the Crazy Eddie electronic chain, was arrested in Israel and charged with numerous securities violations, including charges that he skimmed $7 million from the company and faked records to make it look like the company was growing.

Salomon Brothers Inc. agreed to pay $290 million to settle federal charges that it had submitted phony bids at U.S. Treasury auctions.

JOHN CUNNIFF, *The Associated Press*

Two new U.S. senators from California: Democrat Barbara Boxer (left), a member of the U.S. House since 1983, captured a full term; former San Francisco Mayor Dianne Feinstein (D) was chosen to fill the term of Gov. Pete Wilson.

CALIFORNIA

With the recession, cutbacks in the state's vast defense industry, and a dearth of new businesses moving into the state, a serious budget crisis affected state and local governments in California during 1992. The November election saw strong Democratic gains in the state.

Budget. Gov. Pete Wilson (R) and the legislature blamed one another for the serious budget shortfall. They finally reached an agreement a record 63 days after the constitutional deadline. It was a thin product compared with more lush days, but still a budget of more than $57 billion. With a Democratic legislature facing the uncertainties of redistricting and proposed term limits, and a Republican governor determined to rein in public spending, a general tax increase was unthinkable. Instead, large cuts were made in public health, welfare, and other funds; nearly $1 billion was "borrowed" from future school-aid funds; college and university fees were increased sharply; and $1.3 billion was taken from local property-tax revenues, in effect leaving cities and counties to raise the taxes and fees that the legislature would not. The governor used the line-item veto to cut the budget by $450 million.

The battle ended in September when legislators concluded that they had to return home to campaign in their new districts. The total cut of 5.2% was the first absolute reduction in

general-fund expenditures in more than half a century. While the haggling continued, the state had to pay its bills with IOUs—interest-bearing promissory notes—for the first time since the Great Depression. The governor warned that the state's fiscal problems had not ended. Indeed, a fourth consecutive budget shortfall loomed for 1993.

Election. The election offered few surprises. Democrats feared losses in the legislature after redistricting, but instead gained two seats in the Assembly. Bill Clinton carried the state easily, with 47% of the vote—the first time since 1964 that the Democratic presidential candidate prevailed in the state. Independent Ross Perot did better than his national average, receiving 21% of the vote.

Two women Democrats were elected to the U.S. Senate. Dianne Feinstein, former mayor of San Francisco and a moderate, easily won election to fill out the term of the seat vacated when former Senator Wilson became governor. Barbara Boxer, a veteran House member, was elected to a full term, capturing the seat vacated by Alan Cranston. The state, having gained seven U.S. House seats as result of reapportionment, sent 17 new representatives to Congress. Women taking other major offices included Yvonne Brathwaite Burke as the first black woman member of the powerful Los Angeles County Board of Supervisors and Susan Golding as mayor of San Diego.

Voters also passed the term-limits proposal for federal legislators but rejected a "right-to-die" initiative that would allow doctors to assist terminally ill patients who desired to commit suicide. Also defeated was a proposal to require employers to provide health insurance for their employees.

Workers' Compensation. California long has had one of the most expensive on-the-job-injuries programs of any state, yet with one of the lowest benefit rates. The passage of a reform measure in 1992 was caught between Democratic efforts to maximize benefits and the governor's desire to minimize premium cost. The bill was vetoed and a compromise could not be worked out.

Crime. In an ongoing investigation of legislative corruption by the Federal Bureau of Investigation (FBI), Alan Robbins of the San Fernando Valley, a state senator for 18 years, agreed to plead guilty to political racketeering and income-tax-fraud charges, to resign his office, and to accept a prison term. In other cases, two Los Angeles county deputy sheriffs were convicted of charges related to stealing some $200,000 of drug money seized in raids. A 15-year member of the Los Angeles Harbor Commission, said to be involved in major conflicts of interest, suddenly resigned, but no charges were filed. A member of a major state-tax board was required to leave office after he was convicted of filing false expense reports. The head of a Newport Beach investment company was convicted of defrauding many local governments of millions of dollars by diverting for his own use funds unused in the short term.

After a quarter of a century, California resumed use of the death penalty in April. Robert A. Harris died in the gas chamber at San Quentin for the murder of two San Diego teenaged boys 14 years earlier.

Education. Budget deficits meant drastic cuts in higher-education funds. Thousands of classes were canceled and campuses struggled to keep up with a growing student population. Meanwhile, both the University of California and the State University and College System had come under scrutiny in recent years for granting excessive pay and perquisites to top executives, sometimes secretly. Following a widely praised career as president of the University of California, David P. Gardner retired amid strong criticisms for his practice of accepting deferred salary benefits, unpublicized perquisites, and large special-pension privileges. The Regents and the new university president, Jack W. Peltason, promised a serious review and reforms of compensation for top administrators.

The superintendent of California's school system also faced problems. A state grand jury charged Bill Honig with misusing more than $330,000 in public money. The money was used to pay four school-district employees who worked for a consulting firm headed by Honig's wife.

See also GEOLOGY; LOS ANGELES.

CHARLES R. ADRIAN
University of California, Riverside

CAMBODIA

Under an agreement reached in October 1991, a large force of United Nations civilian and military officials began arriving in Cambodia in early 1992. Its mission was to disarm the warring Cambodian factions and create a neutral political climate in which free elections could be held. The UN Transitional Authority in Cambodia (UNTAC) faced many obstacles in the war-torn country. The greatest problem was the refusal of the militarily strong Khmer Rouge faction to honor the October 1991 agreement.

UN members promised $2 billion for UNTAC, to support 16,000 soldiers and 6,000 civilian administrators until elections could be held in 1993, but the money came in slowly. And by July, fewer than 4,000 UN soldiers had arrived and Lt.-Gen. John Sanderson, the Australian in charge of UN military operations, had disarmed only 12,700 of the 200,000 Cambodian soldiers in the country.

Politics. Yasushi Akashi, the Japanese diplomat who headed the civilian side of UNTAC, found it necessary to work through the Cambodian government that was in place when he arrived. But this government, which originally was installed by Vietnamese invaders in 1979, was so corrupt that some ministers even sold off government office buildings and pocketed the profits.

Moreover, after the Cambodian constitution was amended in December 1991 to allow a multiparty system, hard-line Communists in the government led by National Assembly

A member of the UN Transitional Authority in Cambodia (UNTAC) patrols a rural area. The authority's purpose was to disarm warring Cambodian factions and prepare the nation for elections. The militarily strong Khmer Rouge made UNTAC's task particularly difficult.

© Jacques Witt/Sipa

President Chea Sim began a campaign to seize power by intimidating the more moderate "reform" faction led by Premier Hun Sen. Chea Sim's group, which controlled the secret police, was believed to have ordered the killing of several moderate politicians—including Tea Bun Long, a senior official in charge of religious affairs.

Economy. Cambodians who had survived 20 years of chaos in their country hoped the UN would restore order and prosperity quickly. But much of the country's infrastructure had been destroyed. For example, many paved roads had deteriorated into muddy tracks, and most of the rolling stock on the railroads was unusable. UNTAC had to deal with basics like clearing mine fields and reforming the country's legal system.

Many of the disarmed soldiers turned to banditry because they had no experience with farming, and public order—both in the towns and in the countryside—actually declined in 1992. Because of the insecurity, only 3.7 million acres (1.5 million ha) of land were planted with rice, compared with 6.18 million acres (2.5 million ha) in the late 1960s, when Cambodia was a rice exporter. During 1992 rice had to be imported.

CAMBODIA • Information Highlights

Official Name: Cambodia.
Location: Southeast Asia.
Area: 69,900 sq mi (181 040 km²).
Population (mid-1992 est.): 9,100,000.
Chief City (1991 est.): Phnom Penh, the capital, 900,000.
Government: *Head of state and government:* Prince Norodom Sihanouk, president (named Nov. 20, 1991).

But foreign investment was beginning to revive. The government had received more than 250 applications for investment projects since 1990 and had approved 55 by early 1992. A few thousand tourists even visited Phnom Penh and the ancient ruins at Angkor Wat.

Foreign Relations. In June the Khmer Rouge faction, which ruled Cambodia from 1975 to 1979, served notice that it would not cooperate with UNTAC until all Vietnamese forces were withdrawn from the country. When UNTAC said they had been withdrawn, the Khmer Rouge demanded that all Vietnamese civilians be forced out as well, playing on the traditional enmity between Cambodians and Vietnamese. The Khmer Rouge also demanded a share of political control over the interim national government.

An effort by Thai and Japanese diplomats to negotiate with the Khmer Rouge broke down in October. The UN Security Council was ready to impose economic sanctions against the Khmer Rouge in November unless last-minute efforts by French and Indonesian diplomats persuaded the Khmer Rouge to cooperate.

The Khmer Rouge were believed to be earning tens of millions of dollars annually from the sale of gemstones mined in northwestern Cambodia and from logging operations in that region. The sales were made through Thailand, and the Thai government seemed powerless to stop them, so UN sanctions might have little effect on the Khmer Rouge. However, the UN and other Cambodian factions might decide to hold elections in 1993, and leave the Khmer Rouge in control of about 15% of Cambodia with a relatively small population.

PETER A. POOLE
Author, "Eight Presidents and Indochina"

Lavish entertainment from Parliament Hill was part of the festivities as Canada marked its 125th anniversary on July 1, 1992. Issues involving the federal constitution dominated events in Canada during its special anniversary year.

CANADA

In 1992, Canada's Confederation was 125 years old. The mood of celebration was forced. The recession entered its third year unabated, and Canadians learned that for the first time since 1983 family incomes had declined.

National life was preoccupied with the struggle to meet Quebec's demand for an acceptable constitutional offer before its deadline of Oct. 26, 1992. Two years of reports, public consultations, and negotiations culminated on August 28 when federal, provincial, and territorial governments and four aboriginal groups announced a consensus at Charlottetown, P.E.I. In a national referendum, however, the plan failed to win approval.

Politics. Entering the fourth year of his second term, Prime Minister Brian Mulroney had bleak reelection prospects. Job losses from the Canada-U.S. Free Trade Agreement and the continuing recession, the 7% goods and services tax of 1991, and the privatization or elimination of government services helped make Mulroney the most unpopular prime minister in the history of political polling in Canada.

Polls as well as economics persuaded the Conservatives to bury their election promise of a C$5.4 billion national day-care plan in favor of child-support payments to low-income families. The government could boast that instead of paying $35 per month to each Canadian child under 16, needy children could expect up to $144 a month. Family allowances, Canada's oldest universal social program, introduced in 1945, died in 1992.

Changes to Canada's Immigration Act, also designed to rally conservative supporters, allowed refugee claimants to be fingerprinted and turned away at the border instead of joining the backlog of refugee determination cases. While Ottawa continued to privatize and divest itself of responsibilities, Canadian native peoples insisted that the federal government would not escape responsibility for them. On May 4 a federally supervised vote in the Northwest Territories found 54% support for splitting the area into a predominantly Inuit territory of Nunavut and an Indian-dominated territory, Denendeh.

Constitution Making. In 1984, Brian Mulroney had pledged to bring Quebec into the Canadian constitution "with honor and enthusiasm." At the end of June 1990, the failure of his first effort—the so-called Meech Lake Accord—infuriated Quebec. Support for separation soared to 60%. A provincial commission agreed that Canada would have to come up

In a referendum on Oct. 26, 1992, Canadians rejected the Charlottetown Accord, a series of newly proposed changes in Canada's constitution. Prime Minister Brian Mulroney, right, favored the plan; Quebec separatists, left, were against it.

with a better offer by Oct. 26, 1992, or Quebecers would vote on whether they preferred sovereignty to continued Canadian citizenship. Meanwhile, Quebec's Premier Robert Bourassa boycotted all constitutional negotiations.

After more than a year of fervid public and private consultations across the rest of Canada, it was apparent that more partners would be involved in any new constitutional negotiations. Not only Ottawa and the ten provinces would have to be satisfied; so would Canada's two northern territories and no less than four native groups, including the northern Inuit, the mixed-blood métis, and both "status" and "nonstatus" Indians. (One million "status" Indians retain the privileges, protections, and constraints of the Indian Act; "nonstatus" Indians mainly have abandoned reserve life.)

Demanded by the western provinces and Newfoundland was a "Triple-E" Senate—"Equal, Effective and Elected"—to replace the existing appointed Senate; that would reduce Quebec's representation from almost one quarter of the Senate's seats to no more than a tiny province like Prince Edward Island. Native leaders insisted that their support depended on recognition of an inherent (hence nondebatable) aboriginal right of self-government. Transfer of federal powers to the provinces, with financial compensation—a basic Quebec demand and echoed by the other provincial governments—offended a majority in English-speaking Canada who favored a stronger central government. Quebec's insistence on being a "distinct society" had helped kill the earlier accord, but it remained important.

The Dobbie-Beaudoin Committee. Short of ignoring Quebec's challenge and letting Quebecers reach their October 26 decision, the Mulroney government struggled to produce a second accord. Mulroney put Joe Clark in charge of negotiations. In September 1991 a list of 28 constitutional proposals was tabled. Five stage-managed forums assembled experts and citizens and generated a more positive mood among Canada's citizens.

Again published at the end of February, the Dobbie-Beaudoin report reflected agreement by all three national parties (though not the regional Bloc Québécois nor the Reform Party). The committee accepted native self-government, a "distinct society" clause for Quebec, a "social charter" to protect economic rights, the transfer of limited federal powers to the provinces, and a Senate that would be elected, effective, but only "equitable" in representation among the regions.

Provincial Consultation. With consultation over, agreement among the premiers mattered, since the 1982 amending formula required support from at least seven out of ten premiers and, on some matters, unanimity. In March, Clark attempted his first meeting of first ministers, territorial leaders, and aboriginal representatives—17 groups in all. To help gain leverage with provincial premiers, Mulroney met a popular demand for a referendum-legislation act as a means of bypassing provincial politicians. In April, Parliament hurriedly passed an act to govern nonbinding referenda.

So armed, Joe Clark and his aides resumed vigorous shuttle diplomacy among the provincial capitals. Eager ideologically to reduce government's role, the Conservatives were happy to eliminate a federal role in housing, culture, job-training, mining, forestry, tourism, and other fields that it shared with the provinces. Premiers accepted a vague version of a social contract, conceded the deliberately vague aboriginal insistence on self-government, and split completely on demands for a Triple-E Senate. The objections were obvious. Ontario, with 10 million people, would have no more voice in such a Senate than Prince Edward Island with 130,000. Some provincial premiers—notably Wells and Alberta's Don Getty—warned that they would attack any deal that failed to assert the third E, equality, in a new Senate. Meanwhile Quebec was deliberately absent from the table but fully informed.

In federal circles there was some hope that the provinces would remain deadlocked even after the negotiations deadline had been extended to July 15. That would allow the Mulroney government to prepare an offer that Quebec could not refuse and to use a national referendum to endorse the deal and undercut the premiers. On July 8, however, Joe Clark proudly announced that the premiers had reached a consensus. Ontario's New Democratic Party (NDP) premier, Bob Rae, had yielded on the Triple-E Senate in return for reducing its powers, winning more seats in the House of Commons for the larger provinces, and persuading Alberta and other holdouts to accept the aboriginal demands. The agreement included an entrenched commitment to universal health care and other social programs and recognition of Quebec as a "distinct society," with one third of the Supreme Court's nine justices being Quebecers. But there was no agreement on a major Quebec demand, the constitutional veto that former Premier René Lévesque had sacrificed before the 1982 negotiations.

The National Consensus. Reaction to the premiers' announcement was mixed. Brian Mulroney made a poor effort at concealing his dismay, and a special cabinet meeting scolded Clark for allowing an agreement to jell that Quebec never could accept.

Yet nine provinces and Clark had agreed. Any offer to Quebec would begin from the July 8 agreement. Though denounced by nationalist politicians and media, Quebec's Bourassa ended his boycott of the discussions and attended a series of lunches and meetings during July and August. Forced by the October 26 deadline for the question to be put to Quebec, 17 participants finally reached agreement during five days of closed sessions in Ottawa in late August. The plan survived a symbolic transfer to Charlottetown, the tiny capital of Prince Edward Island, where the idea of Confederation had been born in 1864, and was released on August 28. Perhaps to their own surprise, the prime minister, ten premiers, two territorial leaders, and four aboriginal representatives had reached a historic consensus.

The "Charlottetown Accord." Principal features of the accord included:

• a "Canada Clause" as a guide to the courts in interpreting the constitution, including the Canadian Charter of Rights and Freedoms, setting out Quebec's distinctiveness, Canada's linguistic duality, and the key social- and economic-policy objectives.

THE CANADIAN MINISTRY

M. Brian Mulroney, prime minister
Harvie Andre, minister of state and leader of the government in the House of Commons
Perrin Beatty, minister of communications
Pierre Blais, minister of consumer and corporate affairs and minister of state for agriculture
Benoit Bouchard, minister of national health and welfare
Pauline Browes, minister of state for the environment
Pierre H. Cadieux, minister of state for fitness and amateur sport, minister of state for youth, and deputy leader for the government in the House of Commons
Kim Campbell, minister of justice and attorney general of Canada
Jean Charest, minister for the environment
Joe Clark, president of Queen's Privy Council for Canada and minister responsible for constitutional affairs
Mary Collins, associate minister of national defense and minister responsible for the status of women
Jean Corbeil, minister of transport
John C. Crosbie, minister of fisheries and oceans and minister for the Atlantic Canada Opportunities Agency
Marcel Danis, minister of labor
Robert R. DeCotret, secretary of state of Canada
Paul Dick, minister of supply and services
Jake Epp, minister of energy, mines, and resources
Tom Hockin, minister of state for small businesses and tourism
Otto J. Jelinek, minister of national revenue
Monique Landry, minister for external relations and minister of state for Indian affairs and northern development
Doug Lewis, solicitor general of Canada
Gilles Loiselle, president of the Treasury Board and minister of state for finance
Elmer M. MacKay, minister of public works
Shirley Martin, minister of state for transport
Marcel Masse, minister of national defense
Charles J. Mayer, minister of Western economic diversification and minister of state for grains and oilseeds
Donald F. Mazankowski, deputy prime minister and minister of finance
John McDermid, minister of state for finance and privatization
Barbara J. McDougall, secretary of state for external affairs
William H. McKnight, minister of agriculture
Gerald S. Merrithew, minister of veterans affairs
Lowell Murray, leader of the government in the Senate
Frank Oberle, minister of forestry
Thomas E. Siddon, minister of Indian affairs and northern development
Bernard Valcourt, minister of employment and immigration
Monique Vézina, minister of state for employment and immigration, and minister of state for seniors
Gerald Weiner, minister of multiculturalism and citizenship
Michael H. Wilson, minister of industry, science, and technology and minister for international trade
William Winegard, minister for science

• An elected, equal, effective Senate with six members from each province and one from each territory, with others added later to represent aboriginal peoples, with some power over key federal appointments, resource taxes, and legislation materially affecting the French language or culture.

• More seats in the House of Commons for the largest provinces to compensate for provincial equality in the Senate; Quebec was guaranteed at least one quarter of all Commons seats.

• Recognition of the inherent right of aboriginal self-government.

Other provisions included the curbing of federal spending power and federal intervention in areas of provincial jurisdiction; and federal responsibility for unemployment insurance and for national cultural institutions and programs, with culture within the provinces their exclusive responsibility. Ottawa also would grant exclusive provincial jurisdiction over forestry, mining, tourism, housing, recreation, and urban affairs; but such changes would not affect aboriginal rights or governments. Future constitutional amendments affecting the Senate, House of Commons, and amending formula would require unanimity. Territories could become provinces with parliamentary approval, but they only could acquire additional senators or a role in the amending formula with unanimous provincial and federal consent.

The Referendum Campaign. Robert Bourassa finally had a deal to offer Quebecers on October 26. Alberta and British Columbia would need constitutional referenda also, and by September 8 the Mulroney government had decided to use its new Referendum Act outside Quebec. Canadians could say yes or no to the consensus package. All three federal parties promptly agreed. Only Lucien Bouchard's separatist Bloc Québécois and a handful of Liberal and Conservative critics in English Canada were opposed.

CANADA • Information Highlights

Official Name: Canada.
Location: Northern North America.
Area: 3,851,792 sq mi (9 976 140 km²).
Population (mid-1992 est.): 27,400,000.
Chief Cities (1986 census): Ottawa, the capital, 819,263; Toronto, 3,427,168; Montreal, 2,921,357.
Government: *Head of state,* Elizabeth II, queen; represented by Ramon Hnatyshyn, governor-general (took office January 1990). *Head of government,* M. Brian Mulroney, prime minister (took office Sept. 17, 1984). *Legislature*—Parliament: Senate and House of Commons.
Monetary Unit: Canadian dollar (1.2720 dollars equal U.S.$1, Nov. 19, 1992).
Gross Domestic Product (1990 est. U.S.$): $516,700,-000,000.
Economic Index: *Consumer Prices* (1991, 1980 = 100), all items, 188.1; food, 170.9.
Foreign Trade (1991 U.S.$): *Imports,* $118,119,-000,000; *exports,* $126,833,000,000.

Across Canada, the number of critics soon grew. Furious opposition from Quebec separatists was guaranteed, and the *Non* campaign promptly acquired impressive momentum behind Bouchard, Parti Québécois leader Jacques Parizeau, and Jean Allaire, author of a Quebec Liberal report that would have left Ottawa responsible for little but national defense, currency, and equalization payments. Outside Quebec, the "no" forces ranged the political spectrum, from radical feminists to Preston Manning's right-wing Reform Party. By October the "no" side had found its aging champion, former Prime Minister Pierre Elliott Trudeau, who also had denounced the earlier deal. He denounced Quebec's leaders as "blackmailers" and the "Charlottetown Accord" as a mess that would set French-speaking Quebecers, aboriginals, and ethnic minorities above "little obscure people without rank."

Caught in the euphoria of achieving consensus and convinced that Canadians would recognize both the great achievement and the dangers of saying no, the "yes" side proved fatally slow in getting organized, tactically uncertain, and politically ineffective. Discredited by hard times and past efforts to sell such policies as the deeply unpopular Canada-U.S. Free Trade Agreement of 1989 by a mixture of hope and fear, the government sought out prominent nonpartisans to promote the "yes" cause and found them politically ineffective. Even native leaders shunned their prominent spokesman, Ovide Mercredi, on the argument that the deal cost them traditional and unspecified rights. By mid-campaign, the "no" side had a big majority in Quebec and growing support in the West.

Few realized how strong the "no" vote was until the October 26 results came in. Three small Atlantic provinces voted yes; Nova Scotia teetered to a no. Quebec's French-speaking constituencies sent a powerful message of rejection. In Ontario the major cities finally pulled the province into the narrowest of yes margins. Then, from Manitoba to the Yukon territory, "no" votes carried all but a handful of federal constituencies. By the final count, 54% of Canadians had voted no, and Quebecers were left to choose between sovereignty or the old, unacceptable federalism.

Economic Fallout. Most political experts agreed that the referendum would have gone better if the worst recession since the 1930s had shown any sign of lifting. Instead, industries continued to disappear over the border or into receivership, thousands of jobs vanished monthly, and shrinking tax revenues forced most governments deeper into debt and spending cuts. Labor unrest also was apparent. At a strikebound Northwest Territories gold mine, police reinforcements were needed to protect replacement workers, and in September a bomb explosion killed nine underground. At the Westray coal mine near Plymouth, Nova Scotia, there was no union to protect the 26 men who died in a methane explosion on May 9. A job-creation project in a county with 20% unemployment, the Westray mine had profited from huge federal and provincial subsidies and lax inspection. Charges later were brought against company officials for violations.

Law and Justice. In March, 107 years after he was tried and hanged for treason, Louis Riel was recognized by the House of Commons for his contribution to defending métis and francophone rights in 1870. In the case of David Milgaard, jailed since 1970 for a murder he denied committing, Milgaard's lawyers persuaded a majority on the Supreme Court that he should have a new trial and that, whatever the verdict, he should go free. Saskatchewan, where Milgaard had been convicted, found no reason to order the trial. In another decision, the Supreme Court decided that sleepwalking was an acceptable alibi for a man who had killed his mother-in-law. It also insisted free speech was a legitimate defense for Ernst Zundel, a Holocaust-denier convicted earlier for "spreading false news." After a Toronto mob staged a small copycat version of the Los Angeles riots, courts allowed police to seize photos, videotapes, and other media reports as evidence in the ensuing trials. Subject to strict conditions, the Supreme Court approved such seizures.

External Affairs and Defense. Gloomy Canadians had to look abroad for encouragement. A United Nations (UN) agency listed Canada as the best place in the world to live, while international financiers compared Canada favorably to the United States in controlling inflation (2.4% compared with 4.1% in the United States). The deficit as a percentage of gross domestic product fell from 8.7% at the start of the Mulroney years to 4% in 1991–92. The close relationship between Prime Minister Mulroney and U.S. President George Bush won few votes in either country, but it helped commit Canada to the proposed North American Free Trade Agreement (NAFTA) that includes Mexico, despite home-grown disillusionment with the 1989 Canada-U.S. Free Trade Agreement.

Despite drastic cuts in the defense budget and full-time troop strength, Canada continued to supply forces to every new UN peacekeeping operation from Cambodia to the Sahara. Soldiers from Canada's North Atlantic Treaty Organization (NATO) contingent were deployed to Croatia and later dodged bullets and shell fire from both sides in Sarajevo. Their commander, Maj.-Gen. Lewis MacKenzie, struggled to reopen supply routes to feed the hungry.

People. Canadians abroad who made their country feel proud included Roberta Bondar, a neurobiologist who became the 18th woman to have traveled in space when she returned from an eight-day mission on the U.S. space shuttle *Discovery* on January 30. In the Winter Olympics in Albertville, France, Kerrin Lee-Gartner from Calgary overcame serious injuries to win a gold medal in downhill skiing, and Sylvie Daigle anchored a gold-medal performance in the women's 300-m short-track speed-skating event. At Barcelona's Summer Games, Canadian women rowers won three gold medals and Mark Tewksbury, another Calgarian, won gold in the 100-m backstroke; but Canadian hearts opened to Silken Laumann, a rower from Mississauga, who won a bronze medal two and one-half months after her leg was shattered in a rowing accident.

Canadian forces were involved in various United Nations peacekeeping operations in 1992. Under the direction of Maj.-Gen. Lewis MacKenzie, Canadian troops sought to ensure the arrival of emergency relief supplies in Sarajevo, the capital of Bosnia-Herzegovina in the former Yugoslavia. The city was under bombardment from Serbs.

One sporting triumph did unite Canadians. Toronto's Blue Jays became the first Canadian-owned team to reach baseball's World Series and then defeated the Atlanta Braves in four of six games. The victory, two days before the crucial constitutional referendum, spread rejoicing coast to coast but did not translate into political consequences.

DESMOND MORTON
Erindale College, University of Toronto

The Economy

During 1992 the Canadian economy remained recession-bound. Business investment in plants and equipment plunged during the second quarter, reflecting low consumer demand, stagnant production, and weak corporate balance sheets. Retail sales fell 0.2% to C$15.5 billion in September from August, ending a three-month spurt of gains. The most significant seasonally adjusted decreases were reported by general merchandise stores and in automotive parts, accessories, and services. Seven provinces posted sales decreases in September.

Production. A drop in the output of cars and auto parts in July, followed by a 2.1% output decline in the strike-ridden British Columbia (B.C.) pulp and paper industry and a 3% reduction in steel production—the seventh in eight months—caused a 0.7% fall in manufacturing output. The economy was so sluggish that in September the value of factory shipments dropped 2.5% from August. Unfilled orders decreased 0.8%, following increases in two of the previous three months.

Similar lackluster performance of the construction sector was reflected by a fall in the value of building permits, which deteriorated from C$2.2 billion in July to C$2.1 billion in August. This could be attributed to a slump in nonresidential construction, where the August value of permits slumped 16.2%.

Other Indicators. A slight economic upturn occurred in August when the real gross domestic product (GDP) rose by 0.5%. But almost all of the increase was attributed to the end of the B.C. pulp and paper industry strike and resumption in auto-parts production following July plant shutdowns. Moreover, this output blip was too weak to lead the economy into recovery.

Trends in the labor market further confirmed the recessionary mode of the Canadian economy. The loss of 193,000 jobs during the first six months of 1992 in comparison with a gain of 64,000 jobs over the same period of 1991 brought disappointment to the unemployed, who by October numbered 1.56 million. Also the percentage of job seekers, confronted by the bleak prospects of finding a job, shrunk from 65.8% in June to 65.2% in October, as compared with 66.2% in October 1991.

Huge losses suffered by large corporations became the chief source of economic slowdown. By midyear after-tax earnings of 141 major reporting companies had dwindled by 50%. Profits in the mining, manufacturing, and services sectors fell by 32%, 38%, and 77%, respectively. Firms operating food, clothing, specialty, and department stores found their losses multiplied 60 times.

Trade. Canada's performance in the foreign-trade sector, however, was one of the few flickers of life in an otherwise stagnant economy. The seasonally adjusted value of exported merchandise rose monthly through August, except in June. After increasing by 1.3% in July, exports rose 0.7% in August to C$13 billion and were 5.3% above the level of August 1991. The largest increases were recorded for exports of forestry products, industrial goods, and automotive products.

R. P. SETH, *Mount Saint Vincent University*

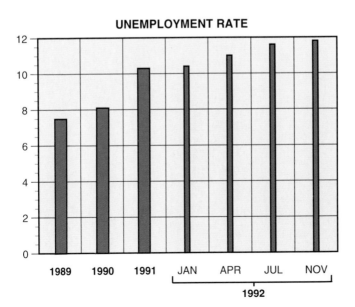

UNEMPLOYMENT RATE

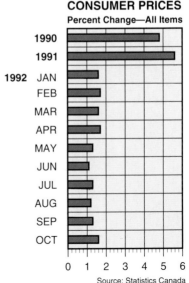

CONSUMER PRICES
Percent Change—All Items

Source: Statistics Canada

The Arts

Canada's art organizations had a bleak year in 1992 due to reduced funding and increased costs. The Art Gallery of Ontario, for example, announced that it would be closed for seven months and laid off more than half of its 445 workers because its funding from the provincial government was held at the reduced level of the previous year. Other cultural groups, such as theaters and museums, also had financial problems. The federal government was blamed by many, as its expenditure on the arts did not take into account steeply rising costs. The Canada Council, which is funded by the federal government and is the biggest source of arts grants (C$106 million in 1992), had had no increase in its funding for six years, while inflation had reduced the purchasing power of its annual grants by 20%. The two-year-old Canadian recession also caused a decline in corporate and foundation giving.

But innovative funding ideas did emerge. Attendees at the first season of the Ottawa Shakespeare Festival could pay C$2 to have their names written, beside a line from the play being performed, in a big copy of that play displayed outside the theater.

The Canadian Broadcasting Corporation (CBC), the government-owned national radio and television network and biggest employer of artists, played a major role in the country's cultural life. It also was a conspicuous bright spot that it began moving from its 24 different Toronto locations into just one. Named Broadcast Centre, the new building cost approximately C$380 million and took almost four years to build. The move was to be completed in late 1994. Meanwhile, CBC president Gérard Veilleux announced major changes designed to make CBC radio and TV more distinctly Canadian and clearly establish time slots for different types of listening and viewing. Veilleux has proved energetic and effective, but his domain, like almost all other cultural ones in Canada, was at the mercy of the dollar.

Visual Arts. A. J. Casson, the last of the Group of Seven—a band of Canadian painters who around 1920 abandoned European influence to paint strong, vigorous, modern, and thoroughly Canadian scenes—died in 1992. Casson joined the group in 1926, when their number had grown to ten. A memorial exhibition of about 30 Casson canvases was held at the McMichael Canadian Art Collection in Kleinburg, Ont., where Casson and most of the Group of Seven are buried.

There was a retrospective tour of 162 works by another Canadian painter of great influence, David Milne. Milne, who died in 1953, had a distinctive, low-key quality to his work that made it easily recognizable.

At the National Gallery of Canada, the exhibit "Painting in Quebec 1829–1850" showed 267 paintings by 70 artists and revealed much about the life of those times. Mario Béland was the exhibition's curator. In Montreal, Pierre Théberg, curator of the Montreal Museum of Fine Arts, celebrated Montreal's 350th anniversary by mounting "The Genius of the Sculptor in Michelangelo's Work." Displayed were 161 paintings, drawings, engravings, and sculp-

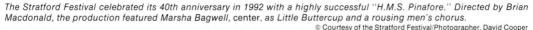

The Stratford Festival celebrated its 40th anniversary in 1992 with a highly successful "H.M.S. Pinafore." Directed by Brian Macdonald, the production featured Marsha Bagwell, center, as Little Buttercup and a rousing men's chorus.

© Courtesy of the Stratford Festival/Photographer, David Cooper

Some 30 canvases—including "Spring Laksy," right—by A. J. Casson, the last of Canada's Group of Seven painters, were featured at a memorial exhibition at the McMichael Canadian Art Collection in Kleinburg, Ont.

© McMichael Canadian Art Collection, Gift of Miss Irene Doole

tures. Patricia Ainslie of the Glenbow Museum in Calgary was curator of the very largely attended Canadian tour of "Correspondences: Jack Shadbolt." At 84, Shadbolt, an accomplished British Columbia artist, still was painting vigorously.

Performing Arts. The Stratford (Ont.) Festival celebrated its 40th anniversary with old and new plays. The old included five Shakespearean plays—the most ever in a Stratford season. The new featured Elliott Hayes' adaptation of *World of Wonders* by novelist Robertson Davies. Directed by Richard Rose, it starred Nicholas Pennell as the magician, Magnus Eisengrim. Another old favorite was *H.M.S. Pinafore,* directed by Brian Macdonald. It proved so successful that its run was extended by two weeks. The festival's longtime artistic director, David William, who was stepping down at the end of the 1993 season, staged the opening production of Shakespeare's *The Tempest,* with Alan Scarfe as Prospero, Claire Rankin as Miranda, and Ted Dykstra as Ariel. Actor and director Richard Monette was named to succeed William.

The Shaw Festival at Niagara-on-the-Lake, Ont., opened its 31st season with George Bernard Shaw's *Pygmalion.* Directed by Christopher Newton, artistic director of the festival, it starred Andrew Gillies as Henry Higgins and Seana McKenna as the Cockney flower girl, Eliza Doolittle. Gillies resisted the temptation to make Higgins appealing, and McKenna scored a triumph with her faultless handling of the changing accents. Other productions included Shaw's first play, *Widowers' Houses,* first staged in 1892, and his witty 1912 work, *Overruled.* Something which may influence the

Shaw Festival for years to come was the signing of an agreement between the festival and a Russian theater to exchange staff members and ideas. A similar arrangement was made with Poland's theaters.

In Toronto the Canadian Opera Company's production of *The Barber of Seville,* under director Anthony Besch and conductor Samuel Wong, starred Russell Brawn as Figaro, Ning Liang as Rosina, and Michael Schade as Count Almaviva. The same company also presented *Mario and the Magician,* a new opera by Harry Somers and Rod Anderson. The Elora (Ont.) Festival presented *Florence, the Lady with the Lamp,* a promising new opera by Timothy Sullivan and Anne McPherson about Florence Nightingale.

Toronto saw the National Ballet's new version of John Cranko's *The Taming of the Shrew,* starring Karen Kain and Serge Lavoie. The Canadian tour of the Royal Winnipeg Ballet's *Swan Lake* was a personal triumph for Evelyn Hart as Odette.

Film. The 16th annual Montreal Film Festival opened with *El Lado Oscuro Del Corazon* ("The Dark Side of the Heart"), written and directed by Eliseo Suiela. Dario Grandinetti starred as the poet and Sandra Ballesteros as the prostitute. In its ten-day run, Toronto's 17th Festival of Festivals showed 335 films from 42 countries. *Leolo,* Quebec director Jean-Claude Lauzon's film about a boy becoming an adult, opened the festival. The National Film Board said it anticipated releasing more than 100 titles in the 1992–93 season and had had a cumulative audience of more than 439 million in 1991–92.

DAVID SAVAGE, *Free-lance Writer*

CARIBBEAN

It was a time of political flux for the Caribbean in 1992. A wave of anti-incumbent feelings swept the electorates of the islands, and some familiar political leaders abandoned public office rather than test their sagging popularity at the polls.

The economies of the region remained generally sluggish, victims of the slowdown in growth in the industrialized countries and the slackening demand for the region's exports. In addition, there was widespread apprehension about the potential effect of the North American Free Trade Agreement (NAFTA) among Canada, Mexico, and the United States on the region's export-oriented economies.

The countries of the 13-member Caribbean Community (CARICOM), comprised of most of the English-speaking nations of the region, continued to pursue the elusive goal of economic integration. At the same time, CARICOM took steps to open trade channels and economic-cooperation mechanisms outside the region—in Central America and with Venezuela, the United States, and a consortium of industrialized countries guided by the World Bank.

Political Changes. The year began with the installation of a new government in Trinidad and Tobago. After five years as the opposition, the People's National Movement (PNM), led by Patrick Manning, had unseated incumbent Prime Minister A.N.R. Robinson of the National Alliance for Reconstruction (NAR) in elections held Dec. 16, 1991. Robinson had been wounded and held hostage by rebellious fundamentalist Muslims in an abortive uprising in July 1990. There was dismay when a Trinidad court ordered the release of 114 of the rebels in mid-1992.

In Puerto Rico in January, incumbent Gov. Rafael Hernández Colón, 55, announced his retirement from public life at the end of his term on Jan. 2, 1993. Hernández Colón had served three times as governor of the U.S. commonwealth and had led the island in a futile effort to resolve Puerto Rico's long-standing status debate over its relationship to the United States. The November 3 gubernatorial election was won by Pedro Rosselló, a pro-statehood candidate. (*See also* PUERTO RICO.)

On March 15, Prime Minister Michael Manley of Jamaica announced his resignation on the grounds of ill health. Manley, 67, had been prime minister for two terms from 1972 to 1980 and was elected again in 1989. He was succeeded by Percival Patterson, a former deputy prime minister in Manley's cabinet.

On August 19 the 25-year rule of Sir Lynden Pindling, the six-term prime minister of the Bahamas, came to an end. The 62-year-old Pindling had been under attack on charges of corruption and involvement in the drug trade.

He was defeated by Hubert Ingraham, 45, a lawyer and onetime Pindling cabinet member, who ran on an anticorruption and antidrug platform. Shortly after the election, on August 23, Hurricane Andrew swept across the Bahamian island of Eleuthera, leaving hundreds homeless and severely damaging tourist resorts.

In perhaps the sharpest transition of all, Cheddi Jagan, an avowed Marxist, was elected president of Guyana on October 5 in what was described as that country's first free election since 1964. Jagan, a 74-year-old U.S.-trained dentist, won 54% of the vote over incumbent Prime Minister Hugh Desmond Hoyte. Hoyte had been privatizing state-owned industries and had sparked an economic revival in Guyana since taking office in 1985. Jagan promised to continue many of Hoyte's free-market reforms but expressed reservations about further privatization of Guyana's rich mineral resources.

In other significant political action, there were cabinet shuffles in St. Kitts and Nevis and in St. Vincent and the Grenadines. In Antigua and Barbuda, longtime Prime Minister Vere Bird, 82, announced he would retire at the end of the current parliamentary term in 1994. St.

A large number of Haitians sought asylum in the United States in 1992. Many were returned to their homeland on the basis that they lacked the proper criteria for U.S. entry.

© Chris Brown/Sipa

Lucia bucked the anti-incumbent tide by reelecting Prime Minister John Compton, 66, to a third term on April 27.

Economy. The Caribbean Development Bank (CDB) warned in a report issued in May of a "continuation of sluggish economic activity" in the region through 1992. Real growth in the traditional Caribbean industries, especially tourism and sugar, "will either continue to decline or stabilize at the 1991 level," the Bank predicted.

Caribbean sugar producers particularly were hurt by cuts in the U.S. tariff-rate quota for sugar imports. The tariff-rate quota represents the amount of sugar that may enter the United States at low tariff rates or duty-free. The quota had been reduced by 35% in September 1991 and by an additional 11% in 1992. The leading supplier of sugar to the United States is the Dominican Republic, with 17.6% of the total U.S. sugar-import quota. Smaller amounts are sold by Barbados, Belize, Haiti, Jamaica, St. Kitts and Nevis, and Trinidad and Tobago.

While the United States lowered its sugar imports from the Caribbean, at the same time it expanded duty-free benefits available to other Caribbean products under the Caribbean Basin Initiative (CBI). In October 1991 the United States had provided new or expanded duty-free treatment for 94 Caribbean products valued at $47 million per year. In May 1992 the United States announced duty reductions on an additional 46 products worth $51.6 million.

Aid for the Caribbean was forthcoming from other sources as well. In August, Mexico and Venezuela renewed for the 12th year the so-called San José Pact, under which the two countries supply oil to Caribbean Basin countries on preferential terms. In the same month, donor countries and international organizations led by the World Bank pledged a $1 billion package of aid to the region.

CARICOM. The Caribbean Community continued to expand its ties with countries outside the region. In January, CARICOM foreign ministers met for the first time with their counterparts from the countries of Central America and signed an agreement to promote cooperation in trade and other matters. In July the 13th annual CARICOM summit met in Trinidad and gave final approval to a free-trade pact with Venezuela, which was scheduled to take effect on Jan. 1, 1993. Under the agreement, CARICOM countries would have duty-free entry to Venezuela until 1998, after which Venezuela is expected to secure duty-free entry to the CARICOM market. The CARICOM summit voted to proceed with plans to establish a regional currency and to work toward a monetary unit by the year 2000.

A special summit meeting was held in October to review the region's slow pace in setting a common external tariff for trade with areas outside the region. Other topics on the agenda of the special meeting were a massive report submitted by the West Indian Commission on further steps toward greater Caribbean unity and consideration of the possible effects of the NAFTA on the Caribbean economies. Officials expressed fear that the NAFTA would generate low-wage competition from Mexican products for Caribbean exports to the United States.

Drugs. In June the United States announced a proposed plan to reduce the flow of cocaine through the Caribbean and Central America. The scheme, tentatively approved by the U.S. National Security Council, would station armed Black Hawk helicopters in Jamaica and the Dominican Republic to intercept planes carrying drugs to rendezvous with smugglers at sea or on land.

Nobel Prize. In October, Derek Walcott, a West Indian poet and playwright, was awarded the Nobel Prize for literature. In announcing the prize, the Swedish Academy of Letters lauded Walcott as an apostle of Caribbean multiculturalism. (*See also* LITERATURE—*Overview*.)

RICHARD C. SCHROEDER, *Consultant*
Organization of American States

CENTRAL AMERICA

International agencies and much of the press have expressed two broad themes in describing Central America's developments in the 1990s—increased political stability and the beginning of economic recovery. Both characterizations had limitations, but some evidence could be found to support them. No Central American government was overthrown in 1992, although Nicaragua's was clearly in trouble. All the Central American presidents faced serious questions of human-rights violations, unemployment, or land reform, but only Nicaragua's President Violeta Chamorro was in any danger of losing her job.

The Inter-American Development Bank announced a recovery from the malaise of the 1980s, finding the first signs of a growing manufacturing sector in Central America. At the same time, however, an extremely significant development in international trade threatened Central America's new and precarious commercial progress—the North American Free Trade Agreement (NAFTA). Although the leaders of Canada, Mexico, and the United States had signed NAFTA, it remained to be ratified. The NAFTA market had impressive potential if perhaps an equal number of pitfalls. One problem, almost totally ignored, was what the huge trade confederation would do to tiny, excluded Central America, whose major trade partners are Mexico and the United States. Mexico had some bilateral trade agreements with Central American states, and the United States had for decades sponsored programs such as the Caribbean Basin Initiative to increase its trade with Central America, but there had not been any attempt to put these relationships into the NAFTA context.

On the average, two thirds of Central America's manufacturing output went to neighboring states, a relationship encouraged by attempts to revive the 30-year-old Central American Common Market (CACM). While it was more important to sell outside the region, no one had designed a means to fit the inchoate CACM into the gigantic NAFTA in 1992.

Among newer problems facing Central America was the amount of toxic waste being shipped from the United States for disposal. Since 1989 some 45 known dumping proposals were made, with 40 being rejected by Central American governments. Corruption, lax environmental laws, and the demand for jobs made such continued success in stopping the dumps problematical. In 1990 five Central American presidents had created a commission to set waste-disposal guidelines, but an official convention was not signed. Only Belize, Guatemala, and Panama maintained reasonably effective bans on importing hazardous waste.

The Agency for International Development (AID) came in for some surprising criticism in October, caused in a sense by its own success. Charged with stimulating the economies of Latin America, the agency had channeled $1 billion in U.S. funds to Caribbean and Central American states since 1980. The result was the creation of about 3,000 manufacturing plants employing 735,000 workers and exporting $14 billion in goods annually to the United States —all as part of U.S. policy to assist Central America's growth. But critics of the program noted that the Latin American workers had few benefits and earned as little as $.30 per hour. At the same time, the number of textile jobs in the United States declined as much as 42%. The Bush administration promised an investigation that likely would be handed over to the Clinton administration. During the presidential campaign, however, Gov. Bill Clinton said little about his policy toward Latin America.

Belize. With the sovereignty of Belize settled by Guatemala's diplomatic recognition in 1991, the former British colony began to acquire stature for its unspoiled tourist attractions and its great concern for the environment. Belize actively resisted efforts of other nations to use the region as a dumping ground. It carefully policed borders with Mexico and Guatemala to prevent the encroachments of squatters who destroy the forest for firewood. Assisted by funding from the National Aeronautics and Space Administration (NASA), Belize was able to pinpoint where incursions were taking place.

© D. Dancer/Sipa

Costa Rica strives to promote "eco-tourism"—using its natural wonders, such as the Rara Avis rain forest (above), to help bring about economic development for the nation.

As a partner of Guatemala in the Maya Biosphere Reserve, Belize struggled to protect its ruins and its rare rain forests. Scientists labored to learn more about Mayan life and to answer such questions as how a vast population could thrive in a rainy environment with such poor soil and so little surface water.

Private groups also were helping out. In 1992 the conservationists' "Program for Belize" bought more than 200,000 acres (81 000 ha) along the Guatemalan border, to establish a Rio Bravo Conservation and Management Area, and to keep rain forests out of the hands of developers. A program to persuade private landowners to harvest only small amounts of their timber each year for sales to pharmaceutical houses, rather than clear-cutting it, was being debated as 1992 ended. Mayans long had believed that certain plants have great value in fighting rheumatism and diarrhea.

Costa Rica. Costa Rica's economy continued to reflect the austerity program dictated by the International Monetary Fund (IMF) and such proposals as the so-called Brady Plan. Long-range results were mixed; economic growth for 1992 was estimated at 2.5% to 3%. Inflation moderated some, but still was too high; wages seemed to decline in the face of some rising prices, especially in utilities. Banana production was termed "excellent," although most of the increase in production was a result of increased acreage under cultivation, not higher yields. Some reductions were made in public-sector labor to help reduce the deficit. The government also proposed raising the tax rate on pensions to the same level as salaries, but no legislation passed. Late 1992 figures indicated that the annual trade deficit was being reduced by half.

Just as they had elsewhere in the hemisphere, environmental matters moved steadily to the forefront in 1992. Costa Rica was garnering international renown for its programs to develop parks and save its rain forests. At times the environmental consciousness originated from outside the country. In January the United States banned the importation of tuna fish from Costa Rica and other countries in retaliation for harming dolphins with tuna nets. But Costa Ricans were learning that development and preservation could go together and that it often meant profits. The national park system now was protecting 25% to 30% of the nation's territory—in private and public preserves, Indian reservations, and 15 parks.

No longer suffering abuses in commercial logging, Costa Rica continued to lose land and timber to squatters, illegal grazing, and expanding banana plantations. Some land had become so overgrazed that even cattle no longer could use it. The government continued to work closely with the U.S. pharmaceutical manufacturer, Merck and Co., to explore the forests for a growing number of medicinal plants previously unknown to modern civilization. By 1992 the renown of Costa Rica's preservation efforts had become so widespread that environmental conferences were held in the country almost every week. Some locals even were complaining about the number of tourists. Tourism had become a $300 million annual industry, providing roughly the same level of income as banana and coffee production—long the nation's chief production sources of international exchange.

Women played leading roles in Costa Rica's attempts in 1992 to cope with the new society. A group made up of some 30,000 women helped slum dwellers construct decent shelter, creating clusters of new housing across the nation. Gay-rights activists received support from a nationally known feminist lawyer whose efforts on behalf of a lesbian organization garnered considerable publicity.

El Salvador. The major question in El Salvador in 1992 seemed to be how one defines peace. The facts were clear; after 21 months of pressure from the United Nations, the El Salvador government and representatives of the Farabundo Martí National Liberation Front (FMLN) signed a peace treaty on Jan. 16, 1992, at Chapultepec Castle in Mexico City, ending a 12-year war. To enforce the agreement the UN posted 1,000 observers throughout El Salvador. The terms called for the rebels to disarm, but allowed them to transform the FMLN into a political party. The government in turn was to cut its army in half—to 31,000 men—and to replace paramilitary police with civilians, including former rebel soldiers. By September only one third of the rebel troops had demobilized, the excuse being that even this small group had not received the promised resettlement package of cash, food, clothing, and a small parcel of land. For its part the government had not disbanded the National Guard. Resident diplomats felt that President Alfredo Cristiani had delayed the process because he did not want to purge the higher-ranking officers required to leave by the treaty.

In spite of UN pressure, President Cristiani refused to do more until the FMLN turned in all of its arms; at the same time the rebels insisted upon the total "purification" of the military. The government and the FMLN agreed to new "final" terms on November 7.

The discovery in October of 38 bodies, mostly children, in a shallow grave exacerbated the peace process. The public assumed the bodies were part of a group of several hundred Salvadorans killed by the army in 1981. The government had blocked all investigations of the atrocity and would assume no responsibility for it.

El Salvador remained one of the most densely populated nations in the hemisphere. In spite of legislation that turned over property to 25% of the nation's peasants in the 1980s, most peasants still did not own their own land. During the civil war, some of the plantation owners were forced off their land. With the war over, however, some were finding that former rebels occupying the land now wanted to go to work for the former owners.

CENTRAL AMERICA · Information Highlights

Nation	Population (in Millions)	Area (sq mi)	Area (km²)	Capital	Head of State and Government
Belize	0.2	8,865	22 960	Belmopan	Minita Gordon, governor-general George Price, prime minister
Costa Rica	3.2	19,730	51 100	San José	Rafael Angel Calderón Fournier, president
El Salvador	5.6	8,124	21 040	San Salvador	Alfredo Cristiani, president
Guatemala	9.7	42,042	108 890	Guatemala City	Jorge Serrano Elías, president
Honduras	5.5	43,278	112 090	Tegucigalpa	Rafael Leonardo Callejas, president
Nicaragua	4.1	49,998	129 494	Managua	Violeta Barrios de Chamorro, president
Panama	2.4	30,193	78 200	Panama City	Guillermo Endara, president

As 1992 began, El Salvadoreans celebrated the signing of a peace treaty between their government and representatives of the Farabundo Marti National Liberation Front (FMLN). The pact ended a 12-year civil war.

© Cindy Karp/Black Star

Roberto D'Aubuissón, the former head of the Nationalist Republican Alliance (ARENA) and an important figure in the peace talks, died in February of lung cancer at the age of 48. The leader of an anticommunist crusade for many years, D'Aubuissón was blamed for the deaths of thousands who opposed the government.

The steady steps toward peace improved the economic outlook in 1992. Stores and hotels were busy and foreign investment increased substantially. Nearly $1 billion in foreign aid was expected to help rebuild the nation's infrastructure.

Guatemala. Perhaps the most unexpected news to come out of Guatemala was the awarding of the 1992 Nobel Peace Prize to Rigoberta Menchú (see BIOGRAPHY), a 33-year-old Indian woman who has been a tireless advocate for peace and human rights. She planned to use her prize money to start a fund named in honor of her father, who burned to death in 1980 during a protest against the military. Although half of her family perished in the civil war, Menchú asserted that she never had been a guerrilla. She instead has toured the world advocating human rights and condemning her government's war on the Indians. Guatemala's President Jorge Serrano Eliás acknowledged Menchú's honor without enthusiasm, and the army said the award established a victory for the guerrillas.

Since 1980, Mexico had supported a tide of Guatemalan refugees that numbered as many as 200,000 at one time. Providing aid to these refugees has been a costly burden, and Mexico shut it off in 1992. While many of the Indian refugees had found conditions in Mexican camps better than in Guatemala, most were expected to return home. However, repatriation of the 40,000 refugees still in Mexico could take two years.

At home, thousands of Indians protested against the development of a resort on Lake Atitlan, on land they claimed as their own. As a result developers promised to make some concessions. About 60% of Guatemalans are Indian peasants; yet 70% of the arable land still was owned by an elite 2% of the general population. Tensions between the government and the landless remained very high.

Poor urban-labor conditions were an emerging issue in 1992. Labor leaders in the United States supported demands of Guatemalan workers for an investigation of J. C. Penney and K Mart by the Office of the U.S. Trade Representative. Workers charged that they were paid only $2 for a 16-hour day in stifling, dirty warehouses, making clothing for the U.S.-based retailers. Second only to coffee in terms of export dollars, textile exports had reached the $100 million mark. However, Guatemala could lose its special trade advantage with the United States if the charges were substantiated.

The government and guerrilla leaders reached a tentative agreement on human-rights issues at talks in Mexico City. The government agreed to end the forceable recruitment of peasants into the army. However, the rebels continued to insist on the total disbanding of army patrols.

Honduras. In September the World Court adjudicated one of the hemisphere's longest-running boundary disputes. At issue was the line between El Salvador and Honduras in particular, the borders in the Gulf of Fonseca and its islands which also reach to Nicaragua territory. The dispute dated back to colonial times with the area being subjugated by several different Spanish conquistadores. In the 1840s the United States and Great Britain came close to war as they sought control of the gulf through their respective Central American allies. In the 20th century the border issue became more bitter with disputes over migration into Honduras, land reform, and commercial practices. The disputes led to the so-called Soccer War of 1969 and to the near destruction of the Central American Common Market. A 1980 treaty had not settled all the disputes, prompting El Salvador and Honduras to go to the World Court in 1986.

One of the five justices declared it the most complicated case in the World Court's history, requiring 50 sessions and 12,000 pages of documents dating back to colonial times. Many minor details were settled quickly; gulf residents affected by the changes were given dual citizenship. Honduras retained possession of strategic Tigre Island; El Salvador, Honduras, and Nicaragua agreed on joint control of the gulf itself. The probable impetus for a settlement was the need to revive the area's economy through the Central American Common Market.

The nation's economic reform begun in 1990 continued while the economy grew at a modest 2.2%. Agriculture performed a bit better in spite of floods and strikes at the banana plantations. The Agricultural Modernization Act, approved by the congress in early 1992, included measures that accelerated privatization, set a new labor code, and further reformed taxes. Low coffee prices also prompted the government to halve the export tax to 3.5%. While the changes would not lead to an immediate improvement in the quality of life, they were expected to encourage an increase in foreign and multinational investment. The latest census, however, showed that Honduras was still a 55% rural country, with a 27% literacy rate.

University of Pennsylvania archaeologists revealed in April that they had uncovered a tomb near Copan that could be the final resting place of a king who had ruled in the 6th century —a little-known period of Mayan history. Evidence of royalty included unusual amounts of jewelry and pottery found with the remains.

Nicaragua. February marked the second anniversary of Violeta Barrios de Chamorro's startling presidential victory. While she had made many proposals for change, a stalled economy had hindered progress. The inflation rate was reduced from the incalculable to the merely very serious; the deficit was cut down a bit. There were also signs of prosperity among elite businessmen in Managua. However, unemployment held at 50%, and exports to the United States were less than 10% of what they had been in 1980. A total of $104 million in badly needed aid from the United States was held up by U.S. demands for political reforms. To get alternative help, Nicaragua was forced to abide by the austere dictates of the IMF that limited spending and borrowing.

One result appeared to be a decline in the ideological split between Sandinistas and contras; the new split seemed to be between rich and poor. In May armed women of all political stripes blocked the roads in Ocotal and occupied city hall, insisting upon the establishment of a maternity ward and day-care center. The type of issues that sparked the demonstrations also included the meager pension of $14 per month due a war widow and the lack of medicine in the hospitals. A new law required a father to support his illegitimate child, but there have been few additional gains for women.

Traditional life-styles continue to dominate in Guatemala, as 60% of the population are Indian peasants. Labor conditions in urban centers remain poor.

Some 100 persons lost their lives and thousands were left with their homes destroyed as a tidal wave spawned by an earthquake crashed into Nicaragua's shoreline in September 1992.

© Wesley Bocxe/Sipa

At times it must have seemed to President Chamorro that all sides were arrayed against her. U.S. aid was stalled because U.S. Sen. Jesse Helms objected to former Sandinistas in high positions. Many of the Sandinistan opponents had migrated to Miami, and many had given financial support to Senator Helms. However, criticism of Sandinistas in the government also originated from within Nicaragua. Chamorro's own vice-president, the mayor of Managua, and the president of the National Assembly also disapproved of Sandinista leadership of the army and police.

While the Sandinistas warned Chamorro not to yield to pressure from Washington, she had few options. In September, Chamorro fired the Sandinista chief of police and a number of his aides. However, U.S. aid did not move south. It appeared that the conservative U.S. legislators were holding out for the removal of Gen. Humberto Ortega, brother of former President Daniel Ortega and army chief of staff. However, there was a serious question whether Chamorro could rule without the support of the general.

The geology of Nicaragua is as unstable as its politics, as evidenced by a volcanic eruption in July and a tidal wave in September that brought great suffering. The wave was spawned by an earthquake 35 mi (56 km) off the coast that sent 30-ft (9-m) waves crashing along the shore for nearly the whole length of Nicaragua. Approximately 100 lives were lost and thousands were left homeless. Several nations, including the United States, sent aid to combat the disaster.

Panama. In December 1989, the United States invaded Panama to capture dictator Manuel Noriega and to bring him to trial in Miami. The culmination of the mission took place in April when he was found guilty on eight drug and racketeering charges; in July he was sentenced to 40 years in prison. It appeared to be the first time in history that a jury in the United States had convicted a foreign head of state of criminal charges. Noriega would be eligible for parole in ten years.

In seven years the Panama Canal was to be the property of Panama. Increasingly, shippers expressed concern over the nation's will and ability to manage and protect the canal. While eight years of training is required to prepare a canal captain, the great majority of pilots still were U.S. citizens. Some shippers also worried that Panama would exploit the canal, using its receipts for social programs and neglecting maintenance. Studies also indicated that containerized shipping, using some ground transportation, soon might be competitive with canal crossings.

Security was also a problem in Panama; the nation's army was disbanded after the 1989 U.S. invasion. While Panamanians voted against the permanent elimination of defense forces, no new army was formed. The high crime rate would not allow the police to take over the defense of the country and the canal.

The Guillermo Endara government warmly welcomed U.S. President George Bush when he stopped in Panama for a visit of a few hours, but much of the public responded in a different manner. Hundreds of demonstrators pelted the welcoming ceremony with rocks, forcing the U.S. delegation indoors. Many poor Panamanians have opposed the Endara administration, and many have demanded compensation from the United States for neighborhoods damaged during the invasion.

On November 15 a large majority of voters rejected an extensive package of constitutional changes backed by the Endara administration. The two-to-one opposition vote reflected Endara's declining popularity. In 1992 unemployment continued to exceed 20%, even though Panama was resuming its role as a major money and banking center.

THOMAS L. KARNES
Arizona State University

CHEMISTRY

Developments in chemistry in 1992 included a flood of new information on the properties of hollow carbon compounds, advances in the control of chemical reactions using laser light, and the naming, at last, of the heaviest known elements.

Fullerenes. In 1992 chemists continued to report discoveries about the fascinating properties of fullerenes, a new form of elemental carbon that has captivated scientists since its discovery in 1985. Arranged in the form of hollow cages, the carbon atoms could be the building blocks for an array of new materials, including stronger plastics, catalysts in chemical reactions, and faster computer chips.

The prototype in the fullerene class is a soccer-ball-shaped 60-carbon sphere, C_{60}, named "Buckminsterfullerene" after the inventor who designed geodesic domes. A method to produce fullerenes in bulk quantities was discovered by workers in Arizona and Germany in 1990, turning these curious molecules into a serious object of study.

In 1992 chemists concentrated on how fullerenes behaved when "doped" with added metals, and found interesting electrical properties. When the alkali metals potassium, cesium, and rubidium are added to C_{60} in proper amounts, the resulting materials display metallic properties at room temperature and are superconductors—i.e., conduct current without resistance—at low temperatures.

In addition, a number of research groups have worked to place metal atoms inside the fullerene cages. C_{82} cages with as many as three scandium atoms trapped inside have been reported. And workers at Rice University reported in 1992 placing a uranium atom inside the small 28-carbon fullerene, C_{28}. The complex appears to be stabilized by covalent bonding.

The fullerenes were believed at first to be chemically inert, but it was becoming clear that they have a rich and varied chemistry. They appear to be especially reactive with free radicals, which are compounds with unpaired electron spins. C_{60}, with 30 carbon-carbon double bonds to attack, is so reactive that it has been called a "radical sponge." Du Pont chemists, for example, reported sticking as many as 34 methyl groups on C_{60}.

Scientists are interested especially in the properties of "giant fullerenes," family members with very large numbers of carbons. In 1992 examples as large as C_{330} were produced, along with claims by some that some fullerenes may form tube shapes rather than spheres. The tubes may have useful electronic and mechanical properties. Some scientists have argued that only spheres are produced under normal circumstances, and theoretical calculations indicate that normally spheres should be more stable than tubes.

In 1992 it was discovered that fullerenes can be found in nature: Both C_{60} and C_{70} were detected in samples of carbon-rich rocks from Russia from Precambrian times—the earliest era of geological history. Also, French scientists reported that C_{60} powder can be compressed to diamond, another form of pure carbon, if very high pressure is applied at a rapid pace.

Laser Studies. In late 1991, Richard Zare and his coworkers at Stanford University announced that they had induced different bonds of a modified water molecule to react. The Stanford team took heavy water molecules, in which one of the ordinary hydrogen atoms of H_2O was replaced by a deuterium atom, and selectively excited vibration of either the oxygen-hydrogen or the oxygen-deuterium bond with finely tuned laser light. When struck by an energetic hydrogen atom, the excited bond of the water molecule reacted preferentially and was cleaved. These studies extended work done earlier at the University of Wisconsin.

A team of workers at California Institute of Technology took a different tack toward reaction control by using the timing of ultrafast laser pulses to influence a chemical reaction. The Caltech team employed two sequential femtosecond (10^{-15} second) duration laser pulses to study the reaction of iodine molecules, I_2, with xenon atoms, Xe. They found that the maximum formation of XeI product took place when the laser pulses were separated by about 350 femtoseconds. This time is believed to be related to the time necessary for the I_2 bond to enlarge following absorption of the first pulse.

Other Events. The three heaviest known elements—very short-lived species with atomic numbers 107, 108, and 109—were named at a ceremony in Darmstadt, Germany. The elements were discovered in the early 1980s by workers at a heavy-ion-research facility there. While no one disputes the claim, the naming event breaks the precedent of waiting until a discovery has been confirmed independently.

Element 107 will be called nielsbohrium to honor the eminent Danish physicist, Niels Bohr. Element 108 will be named hassium after the Latin name for Hesse, the state in which the Darmstadt lab is located, and 109 is to be christened meitnerium in honor of the Austrian physicist Lise Meitner. The International Union of Applied and Pure Chemistry still must give final approval, but discoverers of elements traditionally are allowed to name them.

Chemists at Pennsylvania State University described the synthesis of a cluster of eight titanium atoms and 12 carbon atoms that is surprisingly stable. The compound appears to have a highly symmetrical shape and may lead the way to the creation of new types of catalysts and other applications.

PAUL SEYBOLD, *Wright State University*

CHICAGO

A costly underground leak from the Chicago River, the scuttling of another airport proposal, and an unusual bridge accident highlighted news in Chicago in 1992.

Flood. A flood from the Chicago River closed down the city's business district in mid-April, causing millions of dollars in business losses and damage. A slow leak from the river into underground tunnels—40 ft (12.2 m) below the city—turned into a torrent of millions of gallons of water and moved upward into building basements. City officials shut off power to the downtown Loop area. Tens of thousands of office workers were sent home; Marshall Field's department store, the Board of Trade, and other major landmarks were closed; and the subway system was shut down. It took days before the breach was plugged and weeks before the water in the tunnel system was pumped out and the downtown business community returned to normal. Damage estimates reached $1.8 billion, more than was caused by the 1871 Chicago fire.

The flood had originated in September 1991 when a dredging company punctured the tunnel while installing steel pilings into the floor of the Chicago River. Serving as a means of transporting coal in the early part of the century, the tunnel system more recently was employed to carry cable-television and electrical cables. Early in 1992 a cable-television-company crew discovered the tunnel leak and reported the problem to city officials. But the complaint apparently got buried in the City Hall bureaucracy and nothing was done to stop the water flow. On April 13 a boiler-room employee reported water pouring into the subbasement of the giant Merchandise Mart.

In the flood's aftermath, Mayor Richard M. Daley admitted there had been deceit and laziness by those in city government who could have acted to fix the problem before it was too late. He fired four bureaucrats who he said were partly responsible for the disaster. Daley announced a $7 million program to install bulkheads to prevent future leaks. But he would not have the tunnel system sealed, asserting it had an important role in carrying electrical lines and other utilities to Chicago's Loop.

Airport. For two decades Chicago has been seeking a site for a third major airport. The late Mayor Richard Daley once proposed building the airport in Lake Michigan, but dropped the idea because of costs and environmental concerns. The 1992 proposal called for a $10.8 billion airport in the Lake Calumet area on Chicago's southeast side. The current Mayor Daley and the governors of Illinois and Indiana supported the project, saying it would create 235,000 jobs. But when Illinois legislators refused to approve an airport bill, Daley abruptly grounded the proposed airport in early July.

"It's dead, it's dead," he told Gov. Jim Edgar, reacting to the failure to win legislative approval in Springfield.

Bridge Accident. Another bizarre accident on the Chicago River occurred in September when a span of the busy Michigan Avenue bridge sprang open. The accident toppled a construction crane operating on the bridge. Although the mishap did not cause any serious injury, it forced the temporary closing of foot and vehicle travel over the river at Michigan Avenue. Structural engineers blamed unbalance on the bridge span for the unusual accident.

ROBERT ENSTAD, *"Chicago Tribune"*

CHILE

A Chilean civilian government, headed by Christian Democrat Patricio Aylwin, marked its second year in office in March 1992, after 17 years of military rule, on a tide of rising economic expectations and amid growing support for the government in the international community.

Economy. The Chilean economy was undergoing a miniboom in 1992, with the annual growth of the gross domestic product (GDP) projected to exceed 7%. Exports were rising and inflation was expected to be held to 13%, below the official target of 15%. Construction activity was vigorous and consumer goods were readily available. Industrial production was 11% higher in the first quarter of the year than in the same period in 1991, and business investment was rising, reaching a level of 22% of GDP, well above the average attained during the years under military rule.

The favorable economic figures were satisfying to the Aylwin government, but some advisers, fearing an overheated economy, advised caution. In fact, the country showed signs of labor shortages in some sectors. Overall unemployment in the first half of the year dipped to 4.6%, about two percentage points

---

CHILE • Information Highlights

Official Name: Republic of Chile.
Location: Southwestern coast of South America.
Area: 292,259 sq mi (756 950 km²).
Population (mid-1992 est.): 13,600,000.
Chief Cities (June 15, 1990): Santiago, the capital, 4,385,481; Concepción, 306,464.
Government: Head of state and government, Patricio Aylwin, president (took office March 1990). *Legislature*—National Congress: Senate and Chamber of Deputies.
Monetary Unit: Peso (362.14 pesos equal U.S.$1, official rate, Nov. 2, 1992).
Gross Domestic Product (1990 est. U.S.$): $27,800,-000,000.
Economic Index (Santiago, 1991): *Consumer Prices* (1980 = 100), all items, 773.8; food, 770.6.
Foreign Trade (1991 U.S.$): *Imports*, $7,424,000,000; *exports*, $8,924,000,000.

With a formal ceremony on the South Lawn, George Bush welcomed Chile's Patricio Aylwin and Mrs. Aylwin to the White House on May 13, 1992. The two presidents discussed trade issues during their talks.

© Brad Markel/Gamma-Liaison

better than in the previous year. Construction supplied the largest part of the jobs, showing an employment increase of 13%, but commerce, transportation, and financial services also posted substantial gains.

Constitutional Reform. On May 21 the Aylwin government sent to the National Congress a package of 30 proposed constitutional reforms designed to limit the power of the military. The reforms met immediate opposition from a group of 23 high-ranking officers, led by army commander and former military President Augusto Pinochet. The reform package also was criticized by two opposition parties, the Renovación Nacional (RN) and the Unión Demócrata Independiente (UDI).

The principal reform proposals would empower the president to dismiss military commanders-in-chief and to remove less senior officers as well. The main target seemed to be Pinochet, who, under current rules, could serve until the end of 1997. Other proposed changes would limit the power of the constitutional tribunal—six of whose seven members were appointed by the former military regime—and add the civilian president of the chamber of deputies to the National Security Council to counterbalance the four service chiefs who sit on that body. The National Congress would be enlarged and the electoral rules revised.

Municipal Elections. The governing coalition, the Concertación por la Democracia, swept municipal elections on June 28, taking 53.35% of the vote against 28.9% for the right-wing opposition coalition. The municipal balloting was the first in Chile since the military seized power in 1973, and the first test of strength for the political parties since Aylwin took office in 1990. Aylwin's Christian Democrats won the largest share of any single party, with 28.97% of the vote, somewhat less than the 35% party chiefs had predicted. The Chilean Communist Party fared relatively well, taking 7%, higher than the 2% predicted.

The results confirmed widespread popular support for the Aylwin coalition, but left in doubt whether the government had sufficient support to push through its reform package. The vote also set the stage for maneuvering for position within the ruling coalition for places on the presidential slate in 1993.

Trade. During a visit to Washington in May, Aylwin was told by U.S. President George Bush that the United States intended to begin talks on a free-trade pact with Chile after the Canada-Mexico-U.S. North American Free Trade Agreement (NAFTA) was signed following the U.S. presidential elections.

White House officials said the president would notify the U.S. Congress of his intent to put free-trade talks on the same "fast-track" basis as the NAFTA accord. Chile was the first country to sign a debt-reduction pact with the United States under President Bush's Enterprise for the Americas Initiative. A free-trade agreement with Mexico that would eliminate bilateral tariffs by 1996 also was signed.

Environment. The Aylwin government introduced an environmental-protection bill and proposed new regulations requiring catalytic converters in all new cars sold in Chile in 1992. A tax also would be levied on motorists driving in downtown Santiago, one of the smoggiest cities in Latin America. In July the government was forced to close schools and factories because of excessive air pollution.

Letelier Case. An international commission in January ruled that the Chilean government should pay $2.6 million to the families of Orlando Letelier, a former foreign and defense minister in the 1970–73 government of Salvador Allende, and his U.S. associate Ronni Moffit. Both were assassinated by a car bomb in Washington, DC, in 1976. Officials of the Chilean military government were blamed for the killings.

RICHARD C. SCHROEDER, *Consultant to the Organization of American States*

© Stevens/Sipa

Emperor Akihito (right) *became the first Japanese head of state to visit China as he toured the People's Republic Oct. 23–28, 1992. The visit marked the 20th anniversary of the normalization of diplomatic relations between the two nations.*

CHINA, PEOPLE'S REPUBLIC OF

The three-year-long logjam in China's political economy brought on by the brutal suppression of the democracy movement in June 1989 finally was broken in 1992. Deng Xiaoping, China's paramount leader, who no doubt will be remembered as a consummate politician, emerged from retirement once again and, at age 87, effected a major shift in the center of gravity of the Chinese political system. Whether or not his arrangements for an orderly succession and for the preservation of his course of economic reform will hold after his death remained to be seen. Nonetheless, China's political and economic complexion at the end of 1992 looked very different from that at the beginning of the year.

Deng's "Southern Progress." In January, Deng reappeared in public for the first time in many months. He made a trip to China's southernmost province of Guangdong and to Shenzhen, a rapidly developing special economic zone located on the Hong Kong border. His comments during the trip—all of them extolling the rapid development of the coastal zones, the investment of foreign capital, the growth of the private sector, and the emergence of what he called "market socialism"—were withheld from publication for more than a month. Then, on February 23, a signed "op-ed" piece appeared on the front page of *People's Daily*,

the Communist Party newspaper. The author spoke of the virtues of capitalism and of China's need to pass through a capitalist stage as it developed a socialist economy. It was the first time such views ever had appeared in that newspaper.

Soon thereafter the national and local press were filled with articles that used a Chinese word best translated as "royal progress" to describe Deng's trip. His comments on what he saw in southern China were hyped as a major theoretical breakthrough. This media blitz was seen as an endorsement of a reinvigorated program of rapid economic liberalization. It also was taken to indicate that Deng was maneuvering actively to bring about a change of leadership at the 14th congress of the Chinese Communist Party, scheduled to be held in the fall. Soon even Deng's archconservative rival, the aged economic planner Chen Yun, was reported to have jumped onto the economic-reform bandwagon.

Charting a Future Course. Because national party congresses are held at five-year intervals, and because of Deng's advanced age, it widely was assumed that the 14th congress would be Deng's last opportunity to shape the future by influencing the appointment of his successors. It would be his third attempt to do so. His first designated successor, Zhao Ziyang, sided with the demonstrators in Tiananmen Square in Beijing in 1989, and summarily was dismissed after

© Xinhua-Chine Nouvel/Gamma-Liaison

Trading was suspended at the Shenzhen Stock Exchange, which had opened in 1990, when rioting erupted in August 1992 over the allocation of application forms for stocks.

the crackdown. His second choice, Jiang Zemin, remained in position as general secretary of the Chinese Communist Party, but had failed to make his mark as a dynamic leader and to establish the network of connections he would need to maintain his position without his patron.

Deng was given some room to maneuver in setting a new course for China's development as a result of the death of five of his elderly conservative colleagues, on whose support he had had to rely when he intervened to bring an end to "Beijing spring" in 1989. Wang Renzhong, vice-chairman of the advisory political consultative conference, died in March; Marshal Nie Rongzhen died in May; Li Xiannian, chairman of the political consultative conference, died in June; Deng Yingzhao, widow of former Premier Zhou Enlai, died in July; and conservative theoretician Hu Qiaomu died in October. Two more conservatives—Chen Yun and Wang Zhen—were reportedly too ill to appear in public.

When the new leadership eventually was unveiled at the Congress in October, there were several significant changes. Zhu Rongji, reformist former mayor of Shanghai, was not only promoted to membership in the Politburo,

but to its standing committee as well. Many regarded him as Deng's third (and perhaps last) attempt at designating a reform-minded successor. Yang Shangkun, China's president, was excluded unexpectedly from the top ranks of the leadership, and his brother was forced to resign from his position as head of the military's general political department. These changes thwarted what some had seen as an attempt by the Yangs to form a family dynasty within the party-state.

In addition to Zhu Rongji, the seven-member leading group of the party included its general secretary, Jiang Zemin, Premier Li Peng, Qiao Shi (head of the party-state's security apparatus), Li Ruihuan (former Tianjin mayor responsible for propaganda work), and Hu Jintao (governor of Tibet and, at age 50, the youngest member). Yang Shangkun's place was taken by Adm. Liu Huaqing.

Economy. In a period of world economic recession, China's economic performance in 1992 stood out unusually strongly. Overall growth for the year was estimated at 12%, with industrial-sector growth at 20% and agriculture at 8%. State-owned industry continued to grow at the relatively slow rate of 8%, while collective enterprises grew at more than 18% and the private sector topped the list with a growth rate in excess of 24%. As anticipated, these differential rates of growth resulted in the total output of the state-owned sector falling below 50% of total industrial output for the first time since the mid-1950s. Perhaps most startling was the ten-year growth of rural-based industries. By year's end there were more than 20 million so-called "township and village enterprises" employing close to 100 million workers and accounting for more than 40% of China's total industrial output.

The introduction of industry into the Chinese countryside was intended originally as a means of absorbing underemployed labor in the agricultural economy. In practice, however, many urban residents were implementing what some called, paraphrasing the government's slogan for the future of Hong Kong— "one household, two systems." They retained their contract giving them use rights to a piece of land. One family member tended to the farming, while another sought employment in a nearby factory. By so doing, the family kept access to a low-cost source of foodstuffs while taking advantage of the high wages to be earned in local industry.

Encouraged by the year's economic growth, and spurred on by Deng's obvious enthusiasm for further reform, central authorities encouraged the expansion of stock exchanges in Shenzhen and Shanghai, permitting them for the first time to sell shares to foreign investors. So popular was this form of investment that a riot broke out in Shenzhen—the first major demonstration in China since Tiananmen—

triggered by the charge that officials were monopolizing access to the scarce securities.

Price reform, stalled in 1989 in an attempt to rein in inflation, was reinaugurated cautiously. Government grain subsidies to urban residents, a long-standing perquisite that in recent years had become a drain on the state budget, were ended. The shock to urban family budgets was cushioned somewhat by means of a small wage supplement.

Housing subsidies to urban residents, another significant item in the national budget, also were scheduled for reform. Urban rents (which in 1992 consumed only about 4% of the urban family budget) were to be raised gradually, and residents were being encouraged to acquire title to their apartments from the state through an installment purchase plan.

Meanwhile schools and hospitals, finding their costs growing faster than their government budgets, were being encouraged to engage in a range of profit-making activities to supplement their income from the state. Educational and medical institutions were scrambling to open factories, to rent or sell land, to admit additional fee-paying students and patients—all in an effort to make ends meet, and often at the expense of the quality with which they carried out their primary tasks.

Among other social consequences of reform, the loosening of the system of controls that limited the geographical mobility of China's vast population resulted in a very substantial influx of workers into China's largest cities. As many as 100 million workers were moving into Beijing, Shanghai, Guangzhou, and other major cities in search of temporary or permanent employment. Locating housing, jobs, and social services often posed insurmountable problems. For that and other reasons, and despite the surging economic growth, nostalgia for Mao Zedong, the former Chinese Communist Party leader, underwent a sudden upsurge.

Foreign Affairs. China's leaders continued to attend to the business of improving their image abroad during 1992. In January, Premier Li Peng visited New York to address the United Nations and, over protests by many in Congress and the public, U.S. President George Bush met with him briefly after his speech.

Marking the 20th anniversary of normalization of Sino-Japanese relations, Party General Secretary Jiang Zemin visited Tokyo in the spring. He extended an invitation to the Japanese emperor to visit China—an invitation that was accepted and resulted in the emperor's visit to China in October. China's ongoing concern about the possible threat arising from a revival of Japanese militarism led Jiang to withhold an endorsement requested by his Japanese hosts of legislation pending before the Japanese Diet permitting the stationing of Japanese forces abroad as a part of international peace-keeping operations.

At year's end, Russian President Boris Yeltsin paid a visit to Beijing, the first such visit since his predecessor, Mikhail Gorbachev, visited the city during the height of the democracy movement in 1989. Vilified in private by the Chinese as a deserter from the socialist cause, Yeltsin was welcomed publicly as a potential customer for Chinese products and capital. Bilateral trade between China and Russia in 1992 amounted to more than $5 billion. China extended a much-needed line of credit to the Russian government and was said to have accepted nearly $500 million in military equipment as partial repayment.

In mid-December, U.S. Secretary of Commerce Barbara Franklin led a delegation of U.S. business executives on a trip to China designed to increase China's purchases of U.S. exports. Franklin was the highest-ranking U.S. government official to visit China since Secretary of State James Baker's visit more than a year earlier. The Chinese side chose to portray the visit as a sign of improvement in Sino-U.S. relations.

In many respects, however, official ties between Beijing and Washington remained strained at year's end. From the beginning of his term of office, President Bush was regarded by the Chinese as an understanding friend and as a champion of China's interests in the face of strong congressional disapproval of the country's human-rights record. His midcampaign decision to authorize the sale of F-16 aircraft to Taiwan was seen by many U.S. observers to have been motivated primarily by his interest in garnering the votes of General Dynamics employees in the hotly contested campaign in Texas. The decision was seen by many in China as a betrayal of friends and, more importantly, as the reversal of a decade-long U.S. policy and as a violation of the terms of agreements on arming Taiwan signed by the two governments in 1982.

CHINA • Information Highlights

Official Name: People's Republic of China.
Location: Central-eastern Asia.
Area: 3,705,390 sq mi (9 596 960 km²).
Population (mid-1992 est.): 1,165,800,000.
Chief Cities (Dec. 31, 1989 est.): Beijing (Peking), the capital, 6,920,000; Shanghai, 7,780,000; Tianjin, 5,700,000.
Government: *General Secretary of the Chinese Communist Party,* Jiang Zemin (chosen June 1989); *Head of government:* Li Peng, premier (took office Nov. 1987); *Head of state:* Yang Shangkun, president (took office March 1988). *Legislature* (unicameral)—National People's Congress.
Monetary Unit: Yuan (5.7055 yuan equal U.S.$1, official rate, Dec. 31, 1992).
Gross National Product (1989 est. U.S.$): $413,000,-000,000.
Foreign Trade (1991 U.S.$): *Imports,* $63,791,-000,000; *exports,* $71,910,000,000.

Deng Xiaoping, China's 88-year-old paramount ruler, continued to work for a socialist market economy in China. The plan was endorsed by the 14th national Communist Party Congress, meeting in October 1992.

© Agence Chine Nouvelle/Sipa

Regarding disagreements over trade issues that have divided the two countries, some progress was made in 1992. Pressured by the United States, the Chinese agreed to concessions over the protection of intellectual properties, particularly in the area of computer software. Although Beijing agreed to consider measures to alleviate the substantial trade deficit on the U.S. side, preliminary figures at year's end suggested that the deficit for 1992 would hit a record high of close to $20 billion.

President Bush's veto once again prevented Congress from withdrawing or attaching conditions to the renewal of China's most-favored-nation status. In opposing the special status for China, Democrats in Congress were motivated not only by an interest in pressuring China to adopt a less repressive stance toward dissidents, but also by an interest in embarrassing the Republican president. With a Democrat in the White House this dynamic was expected to change, though President-elect Clinton had not given any clear indication of his policy toward the People's Republic of China by year's end.

A generally sour relationship with the United States, a fear of the prospects of Japanese expansionism, and a sense that the British government was attempting to subvert the transfer of sovereignty over Hong Kong in 1997 created something of a siege mentality in Beijing as the year drew to a close. The siege mentality was manifested in a renewed interest in establishing a Chinese political and economic presence in the Spratly and Paracel Islands off China's southern coast—an area where exploration for oil had been under way for some years. Steps were also taken to develop the Chinese navy's capacity to support this Chinese presence against counterclaims by Vietnam, Taiwan, the Philippines, and others.

The siege mentality was manifested as well in a heightened interest in what others were coming to call "greater China." China's grow-

ing economic ties with Taiwan and Hong Kong had focused attention on the potential of those three economies working in concert to rival Japan's as the dominant force in East Asia.

Moreover, many in China had come to look upon Taiwan's experience of economic modernization under an authoritarian political system as something of a model for the mainland in the next several years. Conservatives emphasized the effectiveness of the authoritarian regime in postponing political liberalization while providing for latitude in economic development. In response, political reformers emphasized that authoritarian control eventually had given way to political liberalization in Taiwan, a process that had been spurred on, they argued, by the exercise of economic freedoms.

This new interest in the potential of Greater China as a player in the East Asian political and economic scene tended to sharpen Chinese sensitivities to issues affecting the future of Taiwan and Hong Kong. It accounted for Beijing's shrill and intransigent reaction to Hong Kong Governor Chris Patten's rather modest proposals for the democratization of Hong Kong and for going ahead with construction of a new airport in Hong Kong without prior agreement from Beijing.

It also accounted for the harshness of China's reactions to U.S., French, and German proposals to sell military equipment to Taiwan and to the proposals of opposition politicians on Taiwan for a "one China, one Taiwan" solution to the future relations between the mainland and its island province.

Paradoxically, the spokesperson chosen to enunciate these sharp and xenophobic responses in the closing months of 1992 was none other than Zhu Rongji, the individual designated by Deng Xiaoping to carry on the work of liberal reform.

JOHN BRYAN STARR
Yale-China Association

CITIES AND URBAN AFFAIRS

In 1992 urban issues were eclipsed by the presidential campaign until late April, when the bloodiest riot in the 20th-century United States broke out in Los Angeles. President George Bush and Democratic challenger Bill Clinton sparred briefly in reacting to the riots, but congressional leaders of both parties soon cooperated to pass emergency-aid legislation. Though a larger, comprehensive aid package ultimately fell victim to election-year politics, some of Clinton's proposals, if enacted during his years in office, may prove to be of great importance to cities.

A Window of Opportunity. The Los Angeles riot began in the afternoon of April 29 and raged until May 3, after 10,000 National Guard and federal troops had been mobilized to assist state and local law-enforcement officials. With the rioting declared by many to be a "wake-up call" focusing attention on pervasive unemployment, poverty, and racial tensions in inner cities, it appeared that, for the first time in 15 years, an important new federal initiative for the cities might be forthcoming. (*See also* SPECIAL REPORT.)

An estimated 6,000 businesses and 15,000 jobs were lost because of the rioting. In June, Congress passed and the president signed $1.3 billion in emergency aid that allocated $500 million for summer jobs, almost $400 million for low-interest loans and emergency grants to businesses damaged or destroyed in the riot areas, and flood relief for Chicago. Through the summer, Congress worked on a larger urban-aid bill. A version finally emerged in October. The legislation would have created 25 urban and 25 rural enterprise zones and financed "weed-and-seed" programs that combined enhanced law enforcement with job training and education programs; but in addition there were a host of tax increases and offsetting tax reductions not related to cities at all. Of the $30 billion the legislation would have cost over five years, only an estimated $6 billion would have gone to programs for cities. Though congressional leaders delayed sending the bill to the White House so that the president could sign it after the November 3 election, he vetoed it anyway, claiming it had been compromised by pork-barrel politics.

The fate of the urban-aid legislation revealed the weak political position of cities. The boost given to the urban agenda by the riots proved to be short-lived. Few congressional representatives are elected in districts located wholly within central cities. None of the presidential candidates—Bush, Clinton, or Ross Perot—highlighted urban issues in their campaigns. The subject was brought up in the second debate, and on that occasion both Bush and Clinton backed the idea of enterprise zones.

City Problems and Future Policies. Through the 1980s cities struggled with fiscal problems brought on by declining city economies and federal-aid cutbacks. By 1992 many cities had managed to adjust through a combination of tax increases and service reductions, but their fiscal health was achieved by ignoring a host of serious problems.

The two most serious problems were the presence of large numbers of unemployed people and the long-term deterioration of public infrastructure. On May 16 several mayors led a march in Washington demanding federal attention to domestic-policy problems. The U.S. Conference of Mayors proposed a $35 billion aid plan for the urban United States, with most of the money for public works, housing rehabilitation, and physical improvement.

During the campaign, Governor Clinton promised a job-training program and a universal college-loan program that recipients could pay back through payroll deduction or through national service. If his ideas were implemented, many of the unemployed in inner cities would benefit. Clinton also was expected to propose that federal enterprise zones be established to lure businesses to depressed areas through tax breaks and subsidies to businesses hiring the unemployed. Clinton also favored the idea of a local development bank that would make loans to inner-city entrepreneurs.

Public works and infrastructure development constituted the centerpiece of Clinton's economic-stimulus proposals. The reconstruction of bridges, roads, and other public infrastructure would have a significant impact on inner cities because the nation's most severely deteriorated infrastructure is located there. Many sewer and water mains in older cities are nearly a century old. Cave-ins and major leaks are becoming increasingly common. To keep their economies competitive, cities also must invest in a new generation of high-speed telecommunications and transportation.

The implementation of a universal health-care system, as proposed by Clinton, would have a significant impact on inner cities, which face a major public-health crisis. Rising infant-mortality rates and outbreaks of communicable diseases—some thought to be eradicated (such as measles)—threaten the health of urban dwellers of every social class. A national health-insurance program would improve neighborhood health clinics and public hospitals. The AIDS epidemic overloads health services in cities across the country. Clinton has promised to consolidate the federal fight against AIDS. The 1992 reappearance of tuberculosis—a disease that devastated urban populations in the 19th century—revealed the tattered state of public-health services in major U.S. cities.

DENNIS R. JUDD
University of Missouri-St. Louis

The Los Angeles Riots

The Los Angeles riots that began April 29, 1992, were one of the most significant news events of 1992. Measured by the number of deaths and injuries, property damage, and the response required to reestablish order, they stand as the United States' worst episode of civil disorders in the 20th century. Their scale, and the dramatic nature of the event that triggered them, served as a catalyst for the first meaningful attempt to implement new urban policy since the 1970s. Except for a small amount of emergency aid, however, legislation aimed at the problems of inner cities became mired in election-year politics.

The Uprising. On the afternoon of April 29, word spread through the predominantly Latino and African-American neighborhoods of south central Los Angeles that four white policemen had been found not guilty of the brutal beating of Rodney King. For months the nation repeatedly had seen the 81-second amateur video of four policemen standing over King, viciously striking him 56 blows with their billy clubs, flashlights, and boots. Not since the civil-rights demonstrations in the summer of 1963 had such a spectacle of urban violence been carried into so many living rooms through the medium of television. Even though the trial of the

four police officers had been moved to the white, middle-class suburbs of Simi Valley, a guilty verdict seemed certain. The jury's decision for acquittal generally was greeted with stunned disbelief. President George Bush called it "disappointing." Public leaders and police in Los Angeles had not considered the possibility of complete acquittal, and thus had no plan in place to quell disturbances.

The rioting abated by May 3. An air of tension lingered in many cities across the country; there also had been outbreaks of disorder in San Francisco, Atlanta, and Las Vegas. In Los Angeles the death toll reached 53, compared with 43 deaths in the 1967 Detroit riots and 34 in the August 1965 riots in the Watts section of Los Angeles. Reportedly, there were 2,383 injuries and 16,291 arrests in the first two days alone. (Later figures had the number arrested ranging from 7,000 to 18,000.) More than 5,500 fires were set, and property-damage estimates ranged up to $1 billion. Between midnight and noon of April 30, the Los Angeles fire department, aided by units from surrounding communities, received 2,102 emergency calls; 829 reported buildings on fire. Fire fighters were prevented from fighting major fires by angry mobs of youths. Of the total of 5,537 structure

After four white policemen were found not guilty of beating a black motorist on April 29, 1992, Los Angeles, CA, experienced the worst episode of civil disorders in the 20th century. Devastating fires were a common feature of the rioting.

© Simonpietri/Sygma

© Michael Schumann/Saba

In an effort to halt the extensive looting at the height of the unrest, Mayor Tom Bradley instituted a dusk-to-dawn curfew in Los Angeles on April 30. Stores owned by Korean immigrants were a principal target of the looters. A cry by some for an end to hate crimes was one result of the disorders.

© Haviv/Saba

fires reported in the first week, the fire department responded to about 500 of them. About 4,000 businesses were destroyed.

Unlike the civil disorders of the 1960s, incidents of burning, looting, and random sniping were not confined to racially segregated ghetto areas, but spread to much of the city. Early in the evening of April 29, a mob threatened to overrun the Parker Center, the police headquarters located in the downtown area. Motorists on highways passed plumes of smoke and apprehensively watched other motorists. At the height of the rioting on April 30, the smoke was so thick over the metropolitan area that for several hours air-traffic controllers were able to keep only one runway open at Los Angeles International Airport.

Attempts to Restore Order. The city was slow to respond to the disorders. Police entered large sections of south central Los Angeles hours after looting and beatings of motorists had begun. At 6:45 P.M., Police Chief Daryl F. Gates issued a tactical alert, which ordered the city's 18 police divisions to make up to half of their officers available to quell disorders. At 7:30 P.M., when demonstrators seemed on the verge of overrunning Parker Center and began attacking downtown property, Chief Gates announced a general mobilization of all officers. At 8:55 P.M., Mayor Tom Bradley declared a state of emergency. Despite Mayor Bradley's urgings, at 11:00 P.M., Chief Gates told Gov. Pete Wilson that it probably would not be necessary to call up National Guard troops. On the morning of April 30, Gates finally agreed the Guard was needed; about 2,400 guardsmen were deployed in the mid-afternoon. By Friday, May 1, 6,000 members of the Guard had been mobilized. On Fri-

day morning, President Bush announced that federal troops would be sent to the city. The 2,500 army infantry soldiers and 1,500 marines began to assist law-enforcement efforts the next day. Altogether, more than 6,000 Los Angeles police, county sheriff's deputies, and California Highway Patrol; 2,700 fire fighters; 10,000 National Guard members; and 4,000 federal troops were mobilized to restore order.

Early news reports indicated that the slow response to the riots reflected a conscious strategy by Chief Gates to show restraint, avoid confrontations between rioters and police, and thus reduce the overall level of violence. This explanation, however, was rejected by a special committee appointed by the city's civilian Police Commission. On Oct. 21, 1992, the committee, headed by former FBI and CIA director William Webster and by Hubert Williams, president of the Police Foundation, issued a report criticizing both Mayor Bradley and Chief

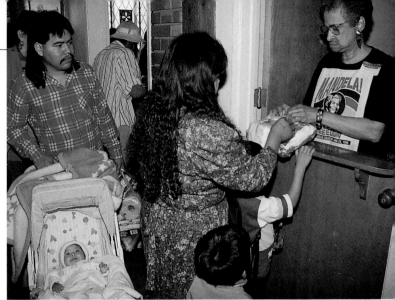

With stores closed and supplies limited, residents of south central Los Angeles received food at the African American Community Center, right.

© Lara Jo Regan/Saba

Gates. The committee noted that the mayor and the chief had not spoken directly in more than a year. The committee faulted Mayor Bradley for failing to implement a regional police-reinforcement plan on the evening of April 29, which immediately would have mobilized police reinforcements from surrounding communities. The committee's harshest criticism was reserved for Chief Gates. The commission said that Gates had misled city officials into believing that he had a plan for dealing with possible disorders. The committee found that no such plan existed.

The Webster committee issued recommendations for improving Los Angeles' response to future civil disorders. It recommended more patrolmen be assigned to patrol the street, the 911 emergency communications system be improved, a riot response plan be put in place, and coordination among public officials be improved. The committee avoided commenting on the root causes of the riots.

The Causes. On October 3 a bipartisan committee of the California General Assembly issued a report concluding that the causes of the Los Angeles riots were almost identical to the conditions that sparked the riots of the 1960s. From 1965 through 1968, there were 329 major incidents of racial violence, with 220 deaths. In its 1968 report on the violence, the National Commission on Civil Disorders wrote about widespread feelings of frustration and rage, which it traced to white racism, segregation, and poverty. The commission said the most common trigger for rioting was a confrontation with police.

For African Americans and Latinos in Los Angeles, the Rodney King verdict seemed to condone a familiar pattern of behavior by police officers. Police Chief Gates was well-known for his "get tough" approach aimed at drugs and street gangs. In the 1980s, 16 blacks died of choke holds administered by Los Angeles police officers. In April 1988, as part of "Operation HAMMER," 1,000 police officers descended upon south central Los Angeles, making 1,453 arrests, mostly for trivial offenses such as jaywalking. By 1990 police and county sheriffs had picked up 50,000 suspects. There were frequent charges of police brutality.

During 1991 another incident heightened tensions and anger. An African-American high-school honor student, Latisha Harlins, had been shot fatally in the back of the head by a Korean grocer who thought she was stealing a carton of orange juice. There was a videotape of this crime, too. The grocer was sentenced to a six-month probation.

Despite the similarities, the Los Angeles riots differed from the 1960s' riots in three respects: (1) civil disorders were not contained to a contiguous area; (2) rioters engaged in acts of violence that were targeted rather than random; (3) the rioters were multiethnic.

Rioters roamed far and wide to harass symbols of repression and authority. They attacked fire fighters. They expressed their generalized resentment toward white society by dragging people out of vehicles. One incident filmed by news helicopters showed Reginald Denny, a truck driver, pulled from his cab and brutally beaten by rioters. What news coverage failed to report immediately was that several blacks risked their lives to save him. Between April 30 and May 5, 3,498 Latinos, 2,832 African Americans, and 640 non-Latino whites were arrested by police and sheriff's deputies in the riot areas. The multiethnic composition of the rioters has led some observers to label it a "rebellion" rather than a riot.

Structural changes in the U.S. economy have affected residents of central cities everywhere. Urban economies have experienced a loss of well-paying jobs in manufacturing. A "two-tier" job market has replaced the industrial economy of the past. Most of the new jobs are in either high-technology manufacturing or services requiring years of education and training, or are minimum-wage jobs in fast-food establishments and other direct-service businesses. Most inner-city youths lack access to good schools or to job training. At least as many as half of all young black males in Los Angeles have an arrest record, partly due to the targeting of south central Los Angeles by the police, and in many areas more than half drop out of school.

The extent of looting, in Koreatown on the western edge of south central Los Angeles and elsewhere, revealed the frustrations over the economic conditions faced in the city's barrios and ghettos. Bands of angry looters and arsonists sought out businesses in Koreatown. Some Korean business owners stayed to defend their stores with a variety of weapons. Though anger was directed at public authorities and Korean businesses, economic frustrations were the basic cause of the disorders.

Policy Responses. Policy responses to the riots were complicated by election-year politics. Bill Clinton, who at the time was trying to clinch the Democratic presidential nomination, at first blamed President Bush for ignoring the cities, but soon muted his criticisms. Jesse Jackson and Congresswoman Maxine Waters of California attacked Republicans for ignoring the plight of African Americans. On May 5 the Bush administration blamed the Great Society programs of the 1960s. That day, however, President Bush proposed a $600 million emergency-aid package, composed of low-interest loans and emergency grants, mostly to devastated businesses. Later that week the president toured the riot area and proposed $19 million more for low-income housing.

In June, Congress passed and the president signed $1.3 billion in emergency-aid legislation that allocated funds for summer jobs, loans to businesses in Los Angeles, and Chicago flood relief. A larger urban-aid bill eventually was passed by the House on October 6 and the Senate on October 8, but with a host of amendments. The centerpiece was a proposal to create 25 urban and 25 rural enterprise zones, where businesses would benefit from reduced capital-gains taxes and subsidies for workers. There were also provisions for "weed and seed" programs in inner-city neighborhoods. Congressional leaders decided to delay sending the bill to the White House until after the November 3 election. It was vetoed on November 4. There was a consensus, however, that even if it had been approved, the legislation would have had little effect in solving the problems that led to the Los Angeles riots.

DENNIS JUDD

COINS AND COIN COLLECTING

Anniversaries and special events made 1992 a boom year for coin collectors.

Before 1992 all U.S. paper money was produced by the Bureau of Engraving and Printing in Washington, DC. During the year, the Bureau released into circulation the first $1 bills printed at its new satellite facility in Fort Worth, TX.

The 200th anniversary of the establishment of the U.S. Mint was celebrated on April 2. To the disappointment of hobbyists, the anniversary was marked not with a commemorative coin, but with a medal. And the Mint did not turn to its staff of talented sculptors/engravers for an original tribute. Instead, it chose the medal's design through a competition among its employees. The obverse design, based on a painting by John Ward Dunsmore, *Inspecting the First Coins*, shows George and Martha Washington examining the first products of the Philadelphia Mint; the reverse features a collage of popular U.S. coins.

Proving popular with collectors, however, was the silver dollar issued for the bicentennial of the White House. The mintage of 500,000 pieces sold out in the pre-issue ordering period.

The Winter Olympic Games in Albertville, France, and the Summer Olympics in Barcelona, Spain, brought a multitude of commemorative coins from the host nations as well as many participating countries. Among the latter was a coin from Estonia, which in 1992 struck its first circulating coins in more than 50 years.

The 1992 U.S. Olympic commemorative coins interpret climactic moments on the road to victory—a gold $5 portrays a sprinter, a silver $1 shows a baseball pitcher, and a copper-nickel half dollar depicts a gymnast in motion. Surcharges on each coin were earmarked for the training and financing of U.S. athletes.

The International Olympic Committee (IOC) introduced a five-year, 15-coin series honoring the first century of the modern Olympic movement. Beginning in 1992, one gold and two silver proof coins will be issued each year by a different national mint—Canada, Australia, Austria, France, and Greece.

Coins, paper money, medals, and tokens relating to Christopher Columbus and his voyages have been popular in the United States since the World's Columbian Exposition in 1893. The quincentennial of the explorer's landing in the New World led to many numismatic tributes. The most innovative design on the three U.S. commemorative coins dedicated to Columbus is on the reverse of the silver dollar. The work of the newest U.S. Mint sculptor/engraver, Thomas D. Rogers, Sr., it depicts a split image of the *Santa Maria* and the U.S. space shuttle *Discovery*.

MARILYN A. REBACK
American Numismatic Association

COLOMBIA

The popularity of President César Gaviria Trujillo was affected adversely in 1992 by a persistent shortage of electricity throughout Colombia and the prison escape of former drug czar Pedro Escobar. In addition, recently enacted tax reform—although watered-down from the government's initial proposals—caused resentment among Colombians who found themselves paying an additional 2% value-added tax as well as being forced, in some situations, to buy compulsory government bonds. Meanwhile, the war between the government and the guerrillas continued with Gaviria imposing a 90-day state of emergency in November.

Politics. The growing disenchantment was demonstrated in the March municipal elections, when abstention rates topped 65% of the electorate. Nonetheless there were some significant results. A new coalition formed of the Conservative Party and the ADM-19 succeeded in winning the mayoral races in Calí and Medellín, two of the three largest cities in the country. The Liberal Party of President Gaviria won in Bogotá and in 18 of the 30 most populous cities. In an attempt to bolster his dwindling popularity—and with it the fortunes of the Liberal Party—President Gaviria announced a shake-up of cabinet positions on July 30. One half of previous cabinet members were replaced.

The government also was hurt by continuing electricity shortages and blackouts ranging from nine to 15 hours per day and by a weeklong strike by communication workers protesting the privatization of the government-owned telephone company in late April.

The Escobar Escape. Most damaging to the government was the escape by the former kingpin of the Medellín drug cartel, Pablo Escobar, from the luxurious Envigado prison on July 22. While imprisoned, Escobar was believed to be running the cartel, and that—coupled with revelations of complete government confusion and its inability to recapture Escobar—produced an extremely adverse public reaction.

The Economy. Through it all, the Colombian economy continued to function as one of the soundest in South America. It was estimated in October that the gross domestic product (GDP) for the year would grow at a rate of 2.5% to 3%, up considerably from previous estimates of 2.1%. Industrial production was up 8.3% over 1991, while construction rose by almost 15%. Agricultural production lagged, with a decrease of 2.3% from the previous year, although coffee production maintained a high rate of growth for the year. Inflation for the 12 months ending Aug. 31, 1992, was 28.1%, down slightly from the 31% of the previous 12 months. The producer's price index, a leading indicator, was even lower at 19.9%.

COLOMBIA • Information Highlights

Official Name: Republic of Colombia.
Location: Northwest South America.
Area: 439,734 sq mi (1 138 910 km²).
Population (mid-1992 est.): 34,300,000.
Chief City (Oct. 15, 1985): Bogotá, the capital, 3,982,941.
Government: *Head of state and government,* César Gaviria Trujillo, president (took office Aug. 1990). *Legislature*—Parliament: Senate and Chamber of Deputies.
Monetary Unit: Peso (618.80 pesos equal U.S.$1, Dec. 30, 1992).
Gross Domestic Product (1990 est. U.S.$): $43,000,000,000.
Economic Index (1991): *Consumer Prices* (1980 = 100), all items, 1,108.6; food, 1,215.8.
Foreign Trade (1991 U.S.$): *Imports,* $4,967,000,000; exports, $7,269,000,000.

Unemployment was up slightly to 11.2% in September versus 10.4% in September 1991. Foreign investment continued to increase at a moderate rate, with 50% concentrated in the Colombian oil industry.

Foreign Affairs. Colombia continued its leadership role in the Andean Group, a loose economic association of the countries of the west coast of South America, with a call for lowered tariffs in a wide variety of manufactured goods. President Gaviria created consternation during his late September visit to Washington, when he requested that serious consideration be given to the inclusion of Colombia in the proposed North American Free Trade Agreement among the United States, Canada, and Mexico.

ERNEST A. DUFF
Randolph-Macon Woman's College

COLORADO

The 1992 election saw Bill Clinton become the first Democratic presidential candidate to carry Colorado since Lyndon Johnson's 1964 sweep. But voters also imposed strict tax and budget limitations and passed a statewide anti-gay-rights measure.

Elections. Clinton won Colorado's eight electoral votes with a popular vote of 628,199, or 40.1%. Republican George Bush finished with 561,473, or 35.9%, and independent Ross Perot received 364,793, or 23.3%, as 78% of the state's registered voters cast ballots.

Democrats kept outgoing Tim Wirth's U.S. Senate seat as Ben Nighthorse Campbell won with 51.8% of the vote to Republican Terry Considine's 42.8%. Campbell would become the only Native American in the Senate. Republican Scott McInnis captured Campbell's former congressional seat from the 3d District, defeating Democratic Lt. Gov. Mike Callihan. McInnis' win gave Republicans a four-to-two edge in the House delegation as GOP incumbents Wayne Allard (4th District), Joel Hefley

(5th District), and Dan Schaefer (6th District) easily won reelection, as did Democrats Patricia Schroeder (1st District) and David Skaggs (2d District).

Republicans kept undivided control of the Colorado legislature with a 19–16 edge in the Senate and 34–31 in the House of Representatives—down by four votes in each chamber from the previous GOP majority.

The ballot was packed with ten voter-initiated measures. Amendment 1, which limits both tax and budget increases for state and local governments unless voters approve increases, was the ninth such measure on the ballot since 1966 and the first to succeed. Amendment 2, which overturned existing gay rights ordinances in Denver, Boulder, and Aspen and prohibited state and local governments from including homosexuals in future civil-rights legislation, passed 811,479 to 707,525. Opponents of the measure, backed by the American Civil Liberties Union, swiftly filed suit to have it declared unconstitutional.

Voters—who approved limited-stakes gambling in Central City, Black Hawk, and Cripple Creek in 1990—overwhelmingly defeated four 1992 ballot proposals—Amendments 3, 4, 5, and 9—that would have extended gambling to other cities, and approved a measure that gives local communities a veto over new gambling sites. Amendment 6, backed by Democratic Gov. Roy Romer, would have increased the state sales tax by 1% to maintain and increase state aid to public schools. Voters rejected it 825,226 to 650,548. A rival educational proposal to authorize state vouchers averaging $2,100 to students attending private schools, Amendment 7, was crushed, 1,008,651 to 502,877. Voters okayed Amendment 8, earmarking lottery profits to parks, and passed Amendment 10, restricting the hunting of black bears.

Economy. The U.S. Department of Energy announced plans in July to stop making plutonium triggers for nuclear weapons at its Rocky

© Peter Turnley/Black Star

As a result of the 1992 elections, Colorado Democrat Ben Nighthorse Campbell will be the first Native American in the U.S. Senate since 1929. A member of the Cheyenne tribe, Campell was born on April 13, 1933, in Auburn, CA. After dropping out of high school, he served in the Air Force and worked his way through college. A former rancher, jewelry designer, and Olympian, the senator-elect had served in the U.S. House of Representatives since 1987 and was a member of the agriculture and interior committees.

Flats plant northwest of Denver. The move would reduce the plant's 8,000-member work force by about 4,100 workers by 1995, with many of the remaining workers involved in cleaning up environmental problems at the site.

On October 9, President Bush signed a law drafted by Representatives Schroeder and Allard to convert the Rocky Mountain Arsenal into the nation's largest urban wildlife refuge, while ensuring the cleanup of polluted portions of the 70-sq-mi (44-km²) site northeast of Denver.

Work on the $3.1 billion Denver International Airport project continued throughout 1992 as contractors raced to meet its scheduled Oct. 29, 1993, opening date. The state Department of Labor and Employment reported that the unemployment rate in Colorado dropped to 5.5% in September, and the Center for Business and Economic Forecasting in Denver predicted that the state would end 1992 with a net gain of 30,000 jobs.

BOB EWEGEN, *"The Denver Post"*

COLORADO • Information Highlights

Area: 104,091 sq mi (269 596 km²).
Population (July 1, 1991 est.): 3,377,000.
Chief Cities (1990 census): Denver, the capital, 467,610; Colorado Springs, 281,140; Aurora, 222,103; Lakewood, 126,481.
Government (1992): *Chief Officers*—governor, Roy Romer (D); lt. gov., C. Michael Callihan (D). *General Assembly*—Senate, 35 members; House of Representatives, 65 members.
State Finances (fiscal year 1991): *Revenue,* $7,863,000,000; *expenditure,* $6,992,000,000.
Personal Income (1991): $65,365,000,000; per capita, $19,358.
Labor Force (June 1992): *Civilian labor force,* 1,774,100; *unemployed,* 120,900 (6.8% of total force).
Education: *Enrollment* (fall 1990)—public elementary schools, 419,929; public secondary, 154,284; colleges and universities, 227,131,114. *Public school expenditures* (1990), $2,639,671,000.

COMMONWEALTH OF INDEPENDENT STATES

The Commonwealth of Independent States (CIS), a loose association of ten former Soviet union republics, replaced the USSR at the end of 1991. As its name indicates, the new Commonwealth is composed of independent states. The initiative to create the CIS and simultaneously terminate the existence of the USSR originated in December 1991 with the presidents of the three Slavic republics, Russia, Ukraine, and Belarus. The most influential founder of the CIS was President Boris Yeltsin of Russia—by far the largest, most populous and most powerful of the former Soviet republics. Soon after its inception, the five former Soviet Central Asian republics as well as Moldova and Armenia joined the CIS. Although Azerbaijan and Georgia did not join, they maintained an observer status at the meetings or "summits" of the CIS. The three former Soviet Baltic republics of Latvia, Lithuania, and Estonia, which had gained full independence earlier in 1991, chose not to join the CIS, but maintained relations with most of its members through treaties and trade agreements.

The CIS was perceived by its founders as a bridge institution or a transitional arrangement designed to achieve three objectives—bring a peaceful end to the tottering Soviet Union, liberate the nations long dominated by the Communist Party-state, and assist the newly independent countries in developing their statehood and establishing their economies in a coordinated manner. The latter refers to the fact that it was felt that the ties that bound the republics for more than 70 years politically, socially, and economically—especially the economic ties of a formerly centrally planned economy—could not be cast off in a day.

The first two founding objectives were achieved, although at the time the Central Asian republics were less enthusiastic than the others in ending their Soviet status and gaining independence. The last objective was of course longer-range, and while some progress had been made in the first year of the CIS, the prognosis was not hopeful for the future. The stronger Ukraine, enjoying its long-sought independence from Russia, was showing an inclination to go its separate way, while the weaker Central Asian states tended to cling to Russia in a dependency relationship which dated from their colonization by Russia in the pre-Soviet period.

Overall Problems. In virtually all of the CIS and affiliated states, the post-Soviet political systems were in disarray, the economies in shambles, and the societies deeply troubled, with most individuals fearful of an uncertain future and anxious about the turbulent times in

© Peter Blakey/Saba

In December 1992, Russia's Congress of Peoples Deputies selected Viktor K. Chernomyrdin, 54-year-old deputy prime minister in charge of fuel-energy, as the new prime minister.

which they were living. All of the states described themselves as emerging democracies and were attempting market reforms. Given the absence of any relevant historical experience in the region, it should not surprise anyone that the enormous dual undertaking of trying simultaneously to build democracy and create capitalism showed only marginal gains in 1992.

While democratic forms were in place nearly everywhere (elections, legislatures, lobbying, and party activity), the executive, in the Soviet tradition, tended to dominate political life, often in a benevolent authoritarian manner. Similarly, market reforms were launched by these governments, but frequently in a haphazard and inconsistent way, leaving the former economies in ruins without fashioning new ones. In both politics and the economies, the shadow of the Soviet past could be seen in the way some of the former republic and local Communist parties redefined themselves as democratic institutions and clung to power, while former Communist cadres frequently managed to privatize the choice properties for their personal gain. In turn, many of the societies of the new nations were riven by ethnic conflict, with at least six small-scale civil wars being fought within or on the frontiers of the CIS. Finally, the great difficulties of the transitional period, especially surging inflation, pushed the vast majority of the populations of the new states below the poverty line. All of these problems were transnational, spanning the territory of the former USSR, with the political, economic, and social chaos of Russia in particular spilling across borders and adversely affecting life in all of the post-Soviet states.

Political Developments. Russia's first tumultuous year of independent existence since 1917 was one of extremes—from harmony to discord, from optimism to pessimism, and from hope to despair. By the eve of the December session of the Congress of People's Deputies, the Russian supraparliament, Yeltsin's victories from the final stormy year of the Soviet Union were fading from public memory. Much of the political capital he had earned from defeating first the coup plotters and then his archrival Mikhail Gorbachev had been spent during 1992 on the economic-shock-therapy program for capitalist development imported from the West. The program which had been launched with such unity of purpose, optimism, and high hopes in January had gone awry by summer, and by year's end had plunged Russia into a deep economic crisis. Beset by elite discord and public despair, President Yeltsin, in spite of his electoral mandate, was governing largely on the strength of his charisma.

The origin of Russia's economic crisis, which was having a deleterious effect on the neighboring economies, was rooted clearly in politics. Persuaded by Western academic economists to apply shock therapy immediately as the quickest route to the desired goal of creating a market system, the new Russian leadership left unresolved fundamental questions of power. The old rules of the game, based on the Communist Party's monopoly of power, had been cast aside, but no agreement had been reached on the shape and configuration of power within the new constitutional system. Russia, like most of the other states, had inherited from Gorbachev's partially reformed USSR a cumbersome and conservative split-level legislative system (the Congress and its smaller working body, the Supreme Soviet), an executive presidency directly elected and imperfectly grafted onto the dual parliament, a weak and less than independent judiciary (capped in Russia by a new and untested constitutional court), and the old familiar centralized Soviet-period bureaucracy scaled down but no longer kept in line by the parallel Communist Party hierarchy. To complicate matters, most of these institutions each had been set up separately within the past one to three years and did not mesh well into an efficient and effective governing system. With variations, similar conditions existed in other CIS states, with most sharing the common dilemma of a lack of coherence among governing bodies operating mostly in a vacuum, without the necessary underpinning of supportive democratic political and legal cultures.

The leading political figures in this environment (in addition to Yeltsin) were people such as Presidents Leonid Kravchuk of Ukraine, former chief ideologist of the Ukrainian Communist Party; Nursultan Nazarbayev of Kazakhstan, the former leader of Kazakhstan's Communist Party; and Islam Karimov of Uzbekistan, also a former party leader.

Throughout much of the CIS, commissions were hard at work in 1992 drafting post-Soviet constitutions that would accommodate new public values, institutions, and social forces within a stable framework for political discourse and public policy. The task looked easier than it turned out to be—witness Russia's constitution-drafting efforts. The two areas of greatest dispute were how to divide power be-

Russia's President Boris Yeltsin (left) is greeted by China's President Yang Shangkun in Beijing in December. Several agreements were signed during Yeltsin's three-day visit.

Azerbaijan's deputy foreign minister and Armenia's acting foreign minister joined Iran Foreign Minister Ali Akbar Velayati (center) in Tehran in March 1992 to sign a draft agreement to bring about a cease-fire in the fighting between the two former Soviet republics. The pact did not take hold and hostilities continued.

© AP/Wide World

tween the legislative and executive branches, and between the Russian central government and its restless ethnic minorities within the federation. The first fault line pitted President Yeltsin, who favored a strong executive, against Ruslan Khasbulatov, speaker of the Russian parliament, who pressed for legislative supremacy; the second problem set Moscow against such ethnic minorities as the Chechens and Tartars, who sought independence, as well as other national enclaves insisting on greater autonomy within the Russian Federation. Failing to achieve a political consensus on a new constitution, the Congress of People's Deputies amended the already patchwork Russian constitution 204 more times.

Between the spring and December sittings of the Russian Congress, the main political event was the constitutional court's seven-month deliberation on the "Communist Party Case." The case arose from a conservative legal challenge to Yeltsin's decrees of 1991 banning the Communist Party and nationalizing its vast property holdings. The court joined this challenge with a counterpetition from the liberal side, which questioned the historical constitutionality of the party. The Constitutional Court thus became another venue in the ongoing political struggle between Yeltsin's reformers and their conservative parliamentary opposition. The court's chairman, Valery Zorkin, steered carefully through this highly charged political case, issuing a Solomonic decision giving something to each litigant on the day before the December Congress convened.

President Yeltsin emerged from this Congress battered and with his reform cabinet only nominally intact. Commanding the support of only 20% of the 1,041 deputies and facing a larger opposition bloc, Yeltsin lost key roll calls when the centrist Civic Union voted with the opposition. As a result he failed in an attempt to obtain special powers over the economy; saw Yegor Gaidar, his reformist prime minister, voted down; and fruitlessly bargained away his appointment power over certain key posts in the government. The selection of a new prime minister, Viktor Chernomyrdin, signaled Russia's retreat from economic shock therapy, but did nothing to alleviate the country's underlying political conflict.

Ironically, politics in Russia were relatively calm compared to other CIS and neighboring states. In Moldova a civil war was under way between the Romanian-speaking majority and the Russian-Ukrainian minority, which had proclaimed its region a separate state within Moldova. Armenia, and Azerbaijan continued their bloody struggle over the Nagorno-Karabakh region of Azerbaijan claimed by both countries. Georgia's civil wars spilled over into the Russian Caucasus region, where a civil conflict broke out between the Ingushi and the North Ossetians. By year's end, Tajikistan was engulfed in a civil war which already had made refugees of nearly 10% of the population.

Economic Developments. Soon after the fall of the Soviet Union, Russia and the CIS states continued or accelerated market reforms to varying degrees. Early 1992 was a time of heady optimism in the economic boardrooms of the former USSR. It was also a period of illusion and wishful thinking for the new elites. Indeed, it was acknowledged that the public would experience some social pain during the transition, but it confidently was felt that its duration would be short and the impact on the most vulnerable groups mitigated by various offsetting financial adjustments. By the end of the year, few illusions were left, the road to market looked longer and steeper, and widespread social pain was nearly universal with vulnerable groups such as the aged, the poor, and the disabled most affected.

In the beginning, the necessary steps to marketization were clear. CIS governments relied heavily on the experience of the capitalist democracies, interpreted for them by Western academic economists called to Moscow, Kiev, and other CIS capitals. Some of these theorists already had practiced their craft in post-Communist Eastern Europe, which had had prior market experience within contemporary memory. In contrast, Russia and the CIS states had little significant market experience.

The initial step in the market model was to decontrol prices, which historically had been set artificially in the Soviet system, letting them rise and fall with supply and demand. Next was the need to stabilize the currency and begin the passage to convertibility, meaning the past policy of fixing the ruble's value arbitrarily had come to an end. Third was the need to demonopolize and privatize the elephantine Soviet industrial enterprises. Fourth was the task of privatizing agricultural land by converting or breaking up the large Soviet collective and state farms. Finally, the cumulative impact of this strategy was expected to be ameliorated by hard-currency investment in, and Western aid to, the emergent economies, provided they met the conditions set by the International Monetary Fund (IMF) for reducing large budget deficits based on heavy state subsidies. Such was the economic transition in theory.

The reality of 1992 was quite different. Yeltsin took the lead in decontrolling prices, anticipating some social discomfort but projecting positive results by fall. There was little consultation or coordination with Russia's CIS partners. Several of the CIS states (especially Ukraine), as a result of being in the ruble zone, were forced to release their own prices prematurely without adequate preparations. Predictably, prices soared but the opportunity for profit also drew abundant supplies of food to the farmer's markets in the cities, alleviating shortages. So far so good, although all but the basic foodstuffs became very expensive for pensioners and others on fixed incomes. The promised social protection of these groups unfortunately lagged behind the price increases.

The value of the currency was freed and the ruble began to float against the dollar within the CIS. The West had promised a large financial package to buffer and stabilize the ruble during the transition, but for various reasons—recession in the United States and Europe, the U.S.

elections, and increasing Western uncertainty that Russia and its CIS partners had the political will to carry through the reforms—the money was slow and late in coming and arrived in smaller amounts than expected, to Yeltsin's chagrin. Disappointment was even greater in Ukraine and other CIS countries, which felt neglected as they witnessed Russia getting most of the attention. The ruble, which several years earlier had been priced artificially at $1.60, not unexpectedly fell against the dollar, passing two cents and a penny along the way. The CIS governments increased salaries to compensate (most people were still on the public payroll), but the plunging ruble dramatically devalued the vast overhang of personal savings owned by consumers. When goods were scarce, this deflationary outcome would have been deemed positive, but now it became a problem.

The third step of demonopolization and privatization was harder. In spite of considerable downsizing of the giant ministries which traditionally ran nearly every aspect of Soviet economic life, bureaucratic habits and ways of operating remained entrenched, slowing the process of decentralizing large enterprises, not to mention privatizing them, which moved at a snail's pace in 1992. As a consequence, enterprising managers and private entrepreneurs often met with red tape and administrative resistance. Conversely, loss-making enterprises continued to receive state subsidies. Of course, there were individual successes at the industrial level and certainly more so at the local and retail level of the economies, where privatization made the greatest progress during the year. The city of Nizhnii Novgorod (formerly Gorky), Russia, was a prime success story. In a bid to show the increasingly disgruntled population that there was a payoff in market reform, a plan was announced to issue vouchers worth 10,000 rubles to every man, woman, and child. These vouchers could be used in bidding for state enterprises and property put up for sale at public auctions. In Ukraine the privatization process was even more sluggish; in other CIS states fraught by armed conflict, other priorities understandably prevailed.

The issue of land privatization was perhaps the most difficult step to the market under con-

COMMONWEALTH OF INDEPENDENT STATES · Information Highlights

Nation	Population (in Millions)	Area (sq mi)	(km²)	Capital	Head of State and Government
Armenia	3.3	11,506	29 801	Yerevan	Levon Akopovich Ter-Petrosyan, president
Azerbaijan	7.1	33,400	86 400	Baku	Ebulfez Elcibey, president
Belarus	10.2	80,154	207 599	Minsk	Stanislav Shushkevich, president
Kazakhstan	16.5	1,048,000	2 714 320	Alma-Ata	Nursultan A. Nazarbayev, president
Kyrgyzstan	4.3	76,641	198 500	Bishkek (Frunze)	Askar Akaev, president
Moldova	4.3	13,012	33 701	Chisinau (Kishinev)	Mircea Snegur, president
Russia	147.4	6,592,000	17 073 280	Moscow	Boris Yeltsin, president
Tajikistan	5.1	55,251	143 100	Dushanbe	Rakhman Nabiyev, president
Turkmenistan	3.5	188,455	488 098	Ashkhabad	Saparmurad Niyazov, president
Ukraine	51.7	233,089	603 700	Kiev	Leonid M. Kravchuk, president
Uzbekistan	19.9	172,591	447 011	Tashkent	Islam Karimov, president

sideration during 1992. In Russian history, land was controlled feudally or held communally by the peasant village. Privatization of land was begun only on the eve of World War I. The war interrupted the process and later the Bolsheviks reversed it, favoring collective agriculture which built on the communal tradition. Since the first year of the Russian Congress in 1990, Yeltsin had been urging amendment of the constitution to permit private ownership of land, to no avail. Finally, in December 1992, a limited reform was enacted. Heretofore under Russian statutory law, individuals could engage in land transactions only with the state. The constitution now permitted landowners to sell to individuals and corporations, but restricted any change in usage of the land. Unconditional private property in land, therefore, remained beyond reach in 1992.

By late fall, Russia's soaring inflation (30% per month) was being exported to its CIS partners through interstate trade, while the ruble had fallen to more than 400 to the dollar, inflicting further damage on neighboring economies still in the ruble zone. Where privatization was making progress, the best deals often were going to members of the old Soviet bureaucracy, who pulled strings and used inside connections; in the countryside, entrepreneurship remained hobbled by the restrictive right of land ownership. In the cities of the CIS, services worsened, crime raged, and, while a minority grew rich through commodity brokering and currency speculation, the standard of living worsened for the majority.

Foreign Affairs. Although the former USSR fractured into 15 states, Russia saw itself as the main diplomatic and military successor, controlling most of the former Soviet nuclear arsenal and armed forces, and taking over the USSR's seat on the UN Security Council. In turn, the world outside the CIS looked upon Russia as the major international actor in Central Eurasia. The major issues between the CIS and the West during 1992 were the strategic nuclear arms on CIS territory and the former Soviet debt. Presidents Bush and Gorbachev thought they had settled the first issue in 1991 when they signed a treaty to eliminate long-range weapons, but the breakup of the USSR reopened the question. The United States had to renegotiate the agreement with each of the four states possessing these arms—Russia, Ukraine, Belarus, and Kazakhstan. Ukraine, however, held out, implicitly linking implementation to the flow of more Western aid. In regard to the debt, Russia assumed full responsibility so far as foreign creditors were concerned, but as domestic economic problems mounted, fell behind in debt service and had to request rescheduling.

Yeltsin's personal diplomacy during the year carried him to the United States, Britain, South Korea, and China. The visits to Washington and London did not yield much additional aid for the sorely pressed Russian economy as the West, distracted at home, drew back from Russia and the CIS' problems. A planned trip to Japan was canceled because of nationalist pressure not to yield the Russian-occupied Kuril Islands to the Japanese.

Within the CIS and on the territory of the former USSR, the main foreign-policy issues were the division of Soviet military hardware among the states, the question of the withdrawal of Russian troops from neighboring countries, and the treatment of the Russian minorities who found themselves in a new diaspora outside of the Russian Federation. On the first problem, the main conflict was over division of the Black Sea fleet and facilities between Russia and Ukraine, and was resolved partially by an agreement reached in August. On the troop-withdrawal issue, Russia felt the greatest pressure from Lithuania, Estonia, and Latvia, but other states expressed concern as well. Moldova protested that the Russian 14th Army based on its territory was intervening in the local civil war on behalf of the Russian minority. Georgia also claimed Russian meddling in one of its civil wars, and elsewhere, in the major fighting in Tajikistan, the Russian garrison tried to avoid getting caught in the cross fire. Finally, Russian nationalists took up the plight of their ethnic kin who, with the end of the Soviet Union, found themselves marooned in foreign and, in some cases, hostile countries. Uneasy about their future in distant places, Russians were emigrating from the hot spots of Central Asia to their Russian homeland, contributing to the formidable refugee problem. Still other Russians were beginning to organize along ethnic lines within the new states. Greatest offense was given by Latvia and Estonia, which were making the acquisition of citizenship very difficult for the large numbers of Russians and others living among them. Russian politicians and military leaders declared their intention of protecting Russians living abroad, possibly an ominous sign for the future peace and stability of the region.

The first year of the Commonwealth of Independent States was not an auspicious one for its future. At best, a fragile partnership was achieved between two thirds of the former USSR's successor states. At worst, the CIS was torn by intrastate and interstate tensions with political leaderships inexperienced and often divided, economies plummeting, social tensions rising, and all of this feeding a series of brushfire wars along and within borders. Making matters worse, by year's end Russia, whose troubles affected all of Central Eurasia, was in a profound constitutional crisis between president and parliament.

See also BALTIC STATES; GEORGIA, REPUBLIC OF.

ROBERT SHARLET, *Union College*

COMMUNICATION TECHNOLOGY

In 1992 communication technology continued to take new directions, with digital systems steadily replacing analog, the introduction of light-wave systems of fiber-optic cables and photonic amplifiers, and new modes of switching and transmission becoming the base for broad-band, high-speed international channels. The incorporation of computers in these systems enhances the capabilities of the "Intelligent Network" to provide new services and results in greater control by the network user.

Transmission and Switching Technology. The international development of personal communication systems moved a step closer to reality in 1992 when decisions of the World Administrative Radio Conference resulted in worldwide frequency allocations for mobile radio and other wireless land-based and satellite systems. Such systems would enable users to reach each other directly with pocket-size, lightweight telephones capable of operating anywhere, in or out of buildings, and free from fixed wiring. It has been estimated that personal communication networks will serve more than 50 million people in the United States and 150 million worldwide by the year 2000, with each user having a personal telephone number.

In 1992 digital techniques began to replace the older analog mobile radio systems in major U.S. cities. In digital systems, voice and data signals are converted to a series of pulses and spaces (ones and zeros) for transmission, and reconverted to their original format at the receiving terminal. This results in a threefold increase in the number of users who can be accommodated on a radio channel and provides improved quality and freedom from noise.

IBM, GTE, and nine large cellular telephone companies announced plans to use digital technology to develop methods for sending data—like facsimiles and electronic mail— over the cellular telephone network. Greater efficiency in the use of the radio channel will be achieved by interspersing streams of data signals into the digitized voice stream, utilizing the idle intervals in speech for bursts of data.

Early in 1992 the TAT-9 transatlantic fiber-optic cable system owned by AT&T and 39 other companies and national telephone administrations was put into service, carrying voice, data, and video signals between the United States, Canada and Great Britain, France, and Spain. The 5,586-mi (8 988-km) system operates at a transmission rate of 560 megabits per second over each of two optical fiber pairs. It can carry 80,000 simultaneous phone calls, twice the capacity of earlier transoceanic communication systems. TAT-9 will link up to undersea fiber-optic systems reaching Italy, Greece, Turkey, and Israel.

Field tests of a record-breaking experimental light-wave system operating at 6.8 billion bits per second (gigabits/s) for a distance of more than 520 mi (837 km) of optical light guide were conducted in Roaring Creek, PA, by AT&T. With twice the capacity of any earlier system, the transmission was accomplished with four lasers and spliced-in optical amplifiers using a technique known as wavelength-division multiplexing. Four different wavelengths, or colors of light, are used, one for each 1.7-gigabit channel; the four are combined at the receiving end. Such a system could carry about 100,000 simultaneous telephone conversations, or an equivalent amount of digital data.

The Federal Communications Commission (FCC) authorized the use of a portion of the radio spectrum for two-way interactive video and data services by way of an attachment to the home TV receiver. Information exchanges for banking, ordering of products and services, and access to libraries and other information sources will become readily available from the home or office. Other interactive information systems have had trials over the past several years in the United States and Europe, but with limited success. Suppliers of the new system believe that the lower cost and increased flexibility of their technology will appeal to millions of potential users.

In 1992 several companies made available new families of broad-band switches to meet the need for connecting local-area networks (LANs) which may be separated widely. This computer-controlled technique, known as frame relay, breaks up the channel data stream into short bursts called packets, each one carrying its own destination address. The stream is reconstructed and redirected at the receiving end, having used the channel at maximum speed and efficiency. Frame relay is capable of handling data approximately 30 times faster than other switching systems. At such speeds, the contents of a 500-page book could be transmitted in one second.

Microelectronics and Microprocessors. The world's smallest semiconductor laser was produced by AT&T Bell Laboratories. It is a tiny pinhead-shaped device only 5 millionths of a meter (5 microns) in diameter and one-tenth of a micron in thickness. The key factor in its construction was the use of successive reflections around the circumferential edge of the head instead of the bulky mirrors normally used in lasers to reflect light internally.

IBM produced a lateral bipolar transistor capable of operating at a maximum frequency of 20 gigahertz (GHz), more than three times the speed achieved with earlier bipolar transistors. The new device utilizes both positive and negative charge carriers and owes its increased speed to lower capacitance and resistance in the structure.

M. D. FAGEN
Formerly, AT&T Bell Laboratories

COMPUTERS

Consumers continued to benefit during 1992 from intense competition within the personal-computer (PC) market. Businesses that have come to depend on local area networks (LANs) saw improvements in these systems. And the advent of pen-based computers promised to expand the computer market to people who view keyboards with fear and loathing.

Effects of Price Wars. With a wide range of technologically similar models to choose from, consumers bought on the basis of price. Industry giants found they could not depend on the strength of brand names to make a sale. Instead, they had to enter into a fierce price war as new competitors flooded the market with in-

expensive clones assembled from standardized parts. Between mid-1991 and mid-1992, PC prices plunged 50% or more. An extreme example was seen in the price of IBM's laptop computer. When IBM introduced its laptop in 1991, the price was $5,900. By mid-1992 the machine was selling for $1,600.

But while some potential customers held off in hopes of even lower prices, industry watchers cautioned that there was a limit to how far prices could fall. Already, there were indications that some manufacturers were keeping costs low by using substandard parts in their machines.

Free-falling prices, coupled with the recession, severely affected companies' bottom

The Tiny Personal Computer

When IBM entered the U.S. notebook computer market in March 1992, it acknowledged a trend already recognized by almost every other computer manufacturer: When it comes to selling personal computers (PCs), small is in. While the market for desktop PCs has been growing at an estimated 8% annually, the market for pint-sized machines is booming. Industry analysts reported in 1992 that sales of notebook PCs were increasing 20% to 25% annually.

When the first portable computers came on the market in the early 1980s, some people nicknamed them "luggables." These bulky machines often weighed more than 20 lbs (9.1 kg) —fine for people with strong arm muscles but hardly enticing to on-the-go salespeople and executives. Next came the slimmer and sleeker laptops, most of which weigh in at 8 to 12 lbs (3.6 to 5.5 kg).

In contrast, most models in the current crop of notebooks weigh 7 lbs (3.2 kg) or less, including the battery and transformer. They run for two to three hours on the battery before it must be recharged. (Alternately, they can be plugged into an electrical outlet, like larger computers.) They typically feature a 386SL or 486 CPU and a 60- to 120-megabyte hard disk drive. Both monochrome and color models are available.

Improvements have been so rapid that one year's state-of-the-art model is likely to be sold as a closeout special the following year. This trend was expected to continue as machine weight decreases, battery life increases, and optional features become standard. In June 1992 the Dell Computer Corporation set a new pace when it introduced the Dell 320SLi, which weighs only 3.5 lbs (1.6 kg).

© Courtesy, IBM

The trend to tiny PCs has been fueled by a broad range of technological advances. Microprocessors have become more powerful, hard disk drives have shrunk in size, displays are brighter and easier to read, and plastics are replacing heavy metal frames and casings. For example, since 1991, notebooks have been available with 2.5-inch (6.35-cm) hard disk drives. Even smaller 1.8-inch (4.57-cm) drives began appearing in some 1992 models.

A number of companies are designing smaller-than-notebook computers called palmtops. Palmcom International Ltd. of Hong Kong introduced its Palmcom 286 to the international market in 1992. This fully IBM-compatible computer weighs only 1.1 lbs (.5 kg) and is operated by just two AA batteries that provide at least 40 hours of operation.

In June, Hewlett-Packard introduced a 1.3-inch (3.3-cm) disk that holds up to 21.4 megabytes of information (the equivalent of 14,389 typed pages). Hewlett-Packard shrunk the drive's housing, too, so that the entire package measures only 0.4 inch by 2 inches by 1.44 inches (1.02 cm by 5.08 cm by 3.66 cm).

Miniaturization does have limitations. At a certain point it becomes necessary to sacrifice full-size keys on the keyboard and to restrict the size of the display severely. But for people who consider easy portability a key criterion, these days mark but the infancy of the tiny PC.

JENNY TESAR

lines and led to mergers, acquisitions, and strategic alliances. A few examples: IBM announced that it was joining with Toshiba and Siemens to develop memory chips capable of storing 256 million bits of data each. (Today's most advanced memory chips store 16 million bits of data.) Toshiba and Apple were working together to develop a CD-ROM-based multimedia player. IBM and Apple formed a joint-venture software company, Kaleida, to create multimedia products. Apple and Microsoft, whose relationship had been marked by a lawsuit and derogatory advertisements, announced that they would work more closely on software development.

Local Area Networks. Several developments spurred growth in the number, size, and efficiency of LANs. For companies that have several disparate networks, microprocessor technology called the intelligent hub translates signals from one kind of LAN into signals understandable by other LANs. This allows users on one LAN to obtain data or use peripherals on other LANs.

Novell, which has about 65% of the LAN market, introduced its Netware Management System during 1992. These products are designed to help network administrators manage, audit, monitor, and troubleshoot networks. For example, the Network Services Manager lets an administrator view a network from a single PC and zero in on each component within the network, obtaining detailed information.

Initially, laptop computers could not be plugged into networks. This drawback has been rectified. Laptops now come with expansion slots so that special adapters can be inserted. A person can take a laptop and an appropriate adapter and plug into any network. This capability provides numerous benefits, but it also raises serious concerns about privacy and network security.

Electronic mail (E-mail)—sending electronic memos from one person to another on the same network—is an extremely efficient means of communication and has become very popular. But E-mail users have no guarantee that their communications will remain private. At one level, this is unavoidable. To maintain a LAN properly, a network administrator must have access to all data on the network. But at other levels, the situation is murkier, with people disagreeing on a company's rights to read messages on its network.

Network security is maintained by limiting access through the use of passwords. Passwords can be assigned to log on to the network itself or to access specific data files or programs. But the system is not foolproof, and threats to data security multiply as more and more machines can tap into a LAN.

Pen-Based Computing. Though pen computers still were in their infancy in 1992, research suggested that they might form the hottest

Photographer, Dave Martinez/ © Courtesy, Apple Computer, Inc.

In 1992, Apple Computer demonstrated its first PDA (Personal Digital Assistant) using the Newton technology. It will assist in capturing, organizing, and communicating ideas.

computer market during the rest of the decade. Instead of communicating with the computer via a keyboard or mouse, users enter data by writing or drawing on the screen; they call up data by pointing to icons on the screen.

Today's models recognize neatly printed words. Many are being used by salespeople, inventory takers, meter readers, and other mobile workers.

The most eagerly awaited pen computer is Apple's Newton, which Apple officials unveiled in 1992 and said would be on the market in 1993. Newton, which will weigh about 1 lb (.45 kg) and sell for less than $1,000, will be able to convert handwritten notes into computer documents that can be stored or sent via wireless communications to fax machines, electronic mailboxes, and other computers. Sharp Electronics, which worked with Apple on Newton, also promised to introduce a pen computer in 1993, as did a number of other competitors.

There are still major technical problems to be solved before pen computers live up to user expectations—and manufacturer hype. The most important challenge is designing software that can recognize handwriting. However, some companies are focusing their efforts on an alternate strategy. Instead of designing software that can convert handwriting into computer data, they are creating software that simply stores notes and sketches for later retrieval. The chore of comprehending the input thus is left up to people.

JENNY TESAR
Free-lance Science Writer

199

CONNECTICUT

Democrat Bill Clinton, with 42% of the vote, won Connecticut's eight electoral votes in the November 1992 presidential election. Republican incumbent George Bush got 36% of the vote, and independent Ross Perot had 22%. Bush, who was reared in Greenwich, had carried the state in the 1988 presidential balloting.

Democrat Christopher J. Dodd won a third U.S. Senate term, defeating Republican newcomer Brook Johnson. The state's U.S. representative delegation in Washington remained evenly divided politically as all six incumbents were reelected. They were Democrats Barbara B. Kennelly, Sam Gejdenson, and Rosa DeLauro and Republicans Christopher Shays, Gary Franks, and Nancy L. Johnson. The Democrats kept control of the state legislature. An expected voter backlash against incumbent Democrats who had supported the 1991 enactment of a state income tax failed to materialize.

Legislature and the Economy. The 1992 session of the General Assembly adopted a record $8.08 billion budget, a 6.12% increase over the prior fiscal year's budget.

The state's economy remained under stress in 1992. Regulators reported 13 banks and thrifts failed, compared with 21 in 1991. Hartford-based insurers Travelers Corporation and Aetna Life & Casualty took steps to reduce expenses by starting layoffs that would affect about 5,000 jobs at each company over a two-year period. In September, Travelers said Primerica Corporation, a New York City financial firm, would invest $722.1 million in the insurer in exchange for 27% of Travelers stock. Travelers has been troubled by bad commercial real-estate loans made in the 1980s.

United Technologies, the state's largest private employer, continued to lay off employees, particularly at its Pratt & Whitney jet-engine division. Business there has suffered because of U.S. Defense-Department cutbacks and a decline in sales to commercial airlines. In March, Colt Manufacturing Company, the gun maker, filed for protection from creditors under Chapter 11 of the U.S. Bankruptcy Act. In September, G. Fox & Company, a retailing chain founded in 1847, announced it would close its flagship store in downtown Hartford in early 1993. Its remaining 13 stores would drop the G. Fox name on Jan. 30, 1993, and become part of Boston-based Filene's. About 1,000 G. Fox jobs would be lost because of the merger and store closing. G. Fox and Filene's are owned by May Department Stores of St. Louis, MO. Troubled Society for Savings, a 174-year-old Hartford bank, announced it would merge with Boston's Bank of Boston.

Other News. Benno C. Schmidt, Jr., president of Yale University for six years, resigned in the spring to head a private project that would develop a national alternative to public schools. Trustees of the debt-ridden University of Bridgeport gave up control of the school to Professors World Peace Academy, a unit of the Rev. Sun Myung Moon's Unification Church.

Connecticut Gov. Lowell P. Weicker, Jr., proposed major spending cuts, including in social programs, in his State of the State Address to the legislature on Feb. 5, 1992. One year earlier, the governor had unveiled a state income tax.

CONNECTICUT · Information Highlights

Area: 5,018 sq mi (12 997 km²).
Population (July 1, 1991 est.): 3,291,000.
Chief Cities (1990 census): Hartford, the capital, 139,739; Bridgeport, 141,686; New Haven, 130,474; Waterbury, 108,961.
Government (1992): *Chief Officers—governor,* Lowell P. Weicker, Jr. (I); lt. gov., Eunice Groark (I). *General Assembly*—Senate, 36 members; House of Representatives, 151 members.
State Finances (fiscal year 1991): *Revenue,* $9,816,000,000; *expenditure,* $11,115,000,000.
Personal Income (1991): $85,642,000,000; per capita, $26,022.
Labor Force (June 1992): *Civilian labor force,* 1,742,000; *unemployed,* 124,700 (7.2% of total force).
Education: *Enrollment* (fall 1990)—public elementary schools, 347,396; public secondary, 121,727; colleges and universities, 168,530. *Public school expenditures* (1990), $3,553,400,000.

Former Waterbury Mayor Joseph J. Santopietro and six Republican associates were convicted in April of dozens of charges of taking illegal payments from developers, tax evasion, and embezzlement. Santopietro was sentenced to nine years in federal prison.

The first legal gambling casino in Connecticut opened February 15 in Ledyard on the Mashantucket Pequot Indian reservation. Owned and operated by the tribe, Foxwoods High Stakes Bingo and Casino is open every day, around the clock.

Parts of Connecticut were devastated by a December storm, which caused four deaths in the state. Severe flooding struck coastal areas; heavy snows hit interior sections.

ROBERT F. MURPHY
"The Hartford Courant"

CONSUMER AFFAIRS

Surveys during 1992 revealed the hesitancy and lack of confidence felt by U.S. consumers about their economic well-being. Cutbacks in consumer spending and the paying off of debts had an impact on the economy. Sales of new cars were down. For the first time in decades, more used cars were sold than new cars. Retail sales just were holding their own.

Consumer Legislation. In October 1992, Congress overrode President Bush's veto of a bill to regulate cable-television companies. (*See* SPECIAL REPORT/TELEVISION, page 529.) After three decades of attempts by consumer advocates, a truth-in-savings bill was passed in late 1991. This act requires banks to tell depositors exactly how much an account is earning using a standard measure—annual percentage yield. Interest must be paid on all savings on deposit and not just part of the deposit as allowed before. Low-balance accounting no longer would be possible because interest must be paid on the full amount of principal in the account each day. Financial institutions now are required to calculate interest rates on savings in a uniform, easily understood way.

On Dec. 20, 1991, President Bush signed into law the Telephone Consumer Protection Act. This law is a victory for every consumer whose dinner has been interrupted by unwanted, machine-generated telephone solicitations. The Federal Communications Commission (FCC) has the responsibility to set up and manage ways to control unsolicited mechanical calls. The FCC also is to come up with a way for consumers not willing to receive telemarketing calls to make their wishes known.

Credit Cards. There was much activity in the credit-card business during 1992. The Federal Trade Commission (FTC) put increasing pressure on the three major credit-reporting companies (TRW, Trans-Union, and Equifax) to be more accurate in their records of the millions of credit-card users and to make reports to those persons who believed that their records were in error. Credit-card interest rates represented an interesting phenomenon. Many rates were still between 19% and 21%, while other credit rates were dropping to 16%, and some fell as low as 14%.

The big credit-card news was the introduction in late 1992 by General Motors of its GM MasterCard. About 30 million applications were mailed, supported by a massive advertising campaign to encourage persons to apply. This is a no-fee card with an interest rate about 16%. But the real promotional aspect of it was that for every dollar charged one would receive a credit of five cents toward the purchase of a GM car. So, if one charged $10,000 over a period of time, that person would receive a $500 discount on a new GM car. One may accumulate the discount over a seven-year period.

Nutritional Labeling. After a year's delay, the U.S. Department of Agriculture issued a food pyramid to communicate the roles different foods have in a balanced diet. The original pyramid was opposed by meat- and dairy-industry lobbyists, who complained that the illustration placed their products in an unfavorable position. The Bush administration gave food processors a one-year reprieve from regulations requiring new nutrition labels on meat and poultry products. Consumer activists denounced the labeling delay.

Medical Ads. A study by University of California at Los Angeles researchers reported that 61% of 109 medical ads analyzed were found to be inaccurate, misleading, and even dangerous, and should have been rejected by the Food and Drug Administration (FDA). The FDA did report that more than 400 over-the-counter medication ingredients do not do what they claim and ordered marketers of thousands of products containing the ingredients to change their labels.

STEWART M. LEE, *Geneva College*

CRIME

In the 1988 presidential campaign, the Republican camp, headed by George Bush, capitalized on public fears of violent crime by running advertisements featuring furloughed prisoner Willie Horton. But in the 1992 race for the White House, law-and-order issues were muted largely because Bill Clinton (D), like George Bush, supported the death penalty.

And, in a break with the past, the GOP lost its lock on the crime issue. In a poll taken shortly before the 1992 election, 38% chose Clinton when asked who could do the best job of dealing with crime. Bush trailed at 32%, followed by independent Ross Perot at 13%. Politics notwithstanding, crime was still a major topic for the news media throughout the year.

A sweeping anticrime bill that would have set a five-day waiting period for buying a handgun, expanded the federal death penalty to more than 50 additional crimes, and provided harsher sentences for gun crimes died at the close of the Senate session under a White House-endorsed filibuster. Republicans said the measure was inadequate because it did not include Bush's proposals to deny successive appeals to death-row inmates and let police seize evidence without a warrant.

Drug smuggling continued to be a major concern. In October police in Colombia said they had killed the head of the Medellín drug cartel's army of assassins in a shoot-out outside his hideout. Police said Brances Muñoz had been wanted for the bombing of a Colombian airliner in 1989 which killed more than 100 people. But the head of the Medellín cartel, Pablo Escobar, and two others who had escaped with him from prison in July, were still at large as the year drew to a close.

Auto Theft. Carjacking, the latest version of auto theft, in which a thief steals a car at gunpoint, caught U.S. attention in 1992 with thieves striking in inner cities and the suburbs. The death of a Washington, DC, area woman dragged for 2 mi (3.2 km) when her car was stolen spurred passage of a federal law that makes armed carjacking a federal offense. Congress, despite being unable to agree for more than two years on a broad anticrime bill, passed legislation to impose federal sentences of 15 years to life imprisonment for such carjackings. The bill also makes owning or operating so-called chop shops that specialize in dismantling stolen autos for their parts a federal crime punishable by up to 15 years in prison. Also, repair shops selling or installing used parts on a car are required to call a toll-free number and check the identification numbers against a Federal Bureau of Investigation (FBI) database of stolen-vehicle numbers. Officials estimate that about half of the 1.5 million cars reported stolen each year in the United States are stripped for their parts.

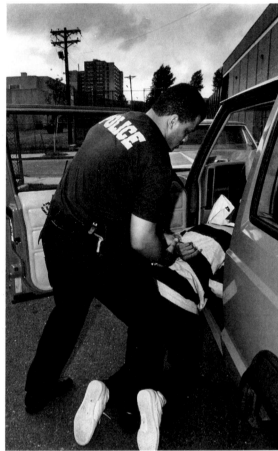

© Nina Berman/Sipa

The number of carjackings—armed automobile robberies—increased in 1992. According to an FBI study, more than 60 such crimes were committed daily in the United States.

Major Crimes. In New Jersey, Arthur D. Seale and his wife, Patricia, pleaded guilty to federal charges in the kidnapping death of Sidney J. Reso, 57, president of Exxon Company International. Reso had disappeared in April after leaving his Morris Township home for his office. Seale said he and his wife abducted the Exxon executive in a plan to demand $18 million in ransom from the company. He said Reso was shot accidentally during the kidnapping and died four days later after being deprived of food and water in a locked wooden box in a rented public storage unit.

In Wisconsin, Jeffrey Dahmer admitted killing 15 people. He was given 15 consecutive life sentences and also was sentenced to life in prison for a killing in Ohio. Although he pleaded insanity, he was ruled to be sane. Among his victims were Konerak Sinthasomphone, 14, who died in May 1991. Dahmer had convinced police the boy was his adult lover and the two had had a spat. The officers led the boy back to Dahmer's apartment, where months later they found human skulls, severed heads, and other body parts.

Seven young men, described by a judge as a "pack of jackals," were given harsh sentences in New York City for the 1990 killing of a Utah tourist. The victim, Brian Watkins, 22, was stabbed fatally on a subway platform in front of his family. The defendants must serve at least 25 years in prison before they are eligible for parole. They used money they stole from the Watkins family to pay the $15 admission to a dance hall. Sentenced were Yul Gary Morales, who allegedly did the stabbing; Anthony Anderson; Ricardo Lopez; Ricardo Nova; Johnny Hincapie; Emiliano Fernandez; and Pascal Carpenter.

An Egyptian immigrant was sentenced to seven and one half to 22 years in prison in connection with the 1990 assassination in New York City of militant Jewish Rabbi Meir Kahane, the former head of the Jewish Defense League. The defendant, El Sayyid A. Nosair, was convicted of gun possession, assault, and coercion, but was acquitted of murder. Kahane was shot fatally after giving a talk at a midtown Manhattan hotel. Some jurors said they had doubts because prosecutors did not produce any witnesses who said Nosair fired the fatal shots.

In Austin, TX, a rape suspect who wore a condom at the woman's request was indicted after an earlier grand jury refused to bring charges. Joel Rene Valdez, 27, was accused of breaking into the victim's home and holding a knife on her. But he said she consented to sex and that offering him a condom proved it. The woman said she was trying to protect herself against sexually transmitted disease. The initial refusal to indict prompted protests by women's groups.

The Justice Department said it would investigate the killing of New York City rabbinical student Yankel Rosenbaum after Lemrick Nelson, a black teenager, was acquitted of murder in the case. Rosenbaum was stabbed fatally in 1991 during racial violence in the Crown Heights section of Brooklyn, NY.

Matthew Stuart pleaded guilty and was sentenced to three to five years in prison in connection with the 1989 Boston murder of his brother Charles' pregnant wife. The death of Carol DiMaiti Stuart led to heightened tension between blacks and police when Charles Stuart claimed a black mugger shot her and himself.

Crime Rates. Some experts were surprised by the latest FBI crime statistics. The agency said the amount of crime reported to police declined 2% in the first half of 1992 compared with the same period the previous year. Perhaps most startling was a 3% decrease in the number of murders, along with a 1% decrease in robberies. But the FBI said the number of forcible rapes rose 4% and aggravated assaults jumped 6%. The increased reporting of rape led to speculation that women, in the wake of the highly publicized Anita Hill-Clarence Thomas

sexual-harassment case, may be more willing to come forward. But federal officials claimed that rape continued to be underreported compared to other crimes. A government-financed survey released in April estimated that 683,000 adult women were raped in 1990, more than five times the number of sexual assaults the Justice Department had reported.

According to the latest six-month FBI report, covering the first six months of 1992, property crime dropped 3%—including a 4% decline in burglary, a 3% decline in larceny-theft, and a 2% dip in car theft. Arson increased 6%, the only rise among property crimes when compared with the same period the previous year. The FBI statistics are based on reports from some 16,000 law-enforcement agencies. It is believed that less than 40% of the crimes in the United States are reported to police.

Another federal study, conducted by the Justice Department's Bureau of Justice Statistics and based on interviews with about 83,000 people, said crime rates appear to be holding steady. The report said U.S. residents 12 years or older experienced 34.7 million crimes in 1991, a relatively slight increase from 34.4 million in 1990. The rates of robbery, aggravated assault, and household burglary showed no significant changes from 1990 to 1991, the bureau said. Its study did not tabulate murders.

Meanwhile, as the number of adults arrested for murder declined, the number of boys under 18 charged with homicide climbed. A study by the National Crime Analysis Project found that the number of 15-year-old boys arrested for murder soared 217% between 1985 and 1991. For 17-year-olds the number climbed 121%, and even for those 12 and under the number rose 100%.

The Death Penalty. The pace of executions in the United States increased in 1992. Ten months into the year, the total reached 26—already more than that of any year since 1962, when 47 inmates were put to death. The death-row population nationwide also continued to climb, with more than 2,600 people awaiting execution. Death-penalty opponents said capital punishment has become so costly it is draining financial resources from measures more likely to deter crime.

In California, Robert Alton Harris was put to death in the gas chamber in that state's first execution in 25 years. Harris was convicted of killing two teenage boys in 1978. His impending execution touched off an intense legal battle in April as the U.S. Supreme Court, throughout a night of extraordinary maneuvering, repeatedly canceled a series of stays. Harris won in lower courts. Since the Supreme Court reinstated capital punishment in 1976, 36 states have passed laws authorizing the death penalty. California became the 20th state actually to execute someone since the reinstatement.

DNA "Fingerprinting"

By 1992, the use of deoxyribonucleic acid (DNA) "fingerprinting" to identify the source of biological evidence in criminal cases was in widespread use, although it remained controversial. In violent crimes such as rape and murder, biological evidence—hair, blood, and semen—often can be obtained from the victim, suspect, or crime scene. Traditionally, tracing of such evidence to an individual has been approached by studying constituent polymorphic proteins using an analytical technique called electrophoresis. Polymorphic proteins exist in multiple forms in the population and are forensically useful genetic markers, since individuals can be differentiated based on their observed types (phenotypes).

Recently, however, increasing attention has been paid to the use of DNA for individualization purposes in criminal cases, primarily because DNA is so stable in physiological stains, and because it is extremely polymorphic and therefore highly informative. The human genome that contains more than 3 billion nucleotide subunits and that provides the information required for the synthesis of some 100,000 proteins is unique for each person. The introduction of DNA-profiling methods for individualization purposes has been most exciting for law-enforcement personnel.

Method of DNA Profiling. In 1985 a novel method of individualization was described, based on analysis of hypervariable, "mini-satellite" DNA segments found in the human genome. Mini-satellite DNA, also known as variable nucleotide tandem repeats (VNTRs), consists of short core sequences comprised of about 15–30 bases. The core sequence, which can be repeated up to 100 times, is arranged in a tandem array. Each is present in only a relatively small number of people in the population, but the genome of each person contains many different VNTRs.

DNA profiling is performed by first separating genomic DNA from proteins and other cellular components. A portion of the isolated DNA is tested for its quality and quantity. If a sufficient amount of undamaged DNA has been isolated, a "restriction" enzyme is used to cleave the DNA at specific sites, producing numerous fragments of varying length. The fragments are separated by size using gel electrophoresis. The gel is placed into a denaturing solution to produce single-stranded DNA and then is placed onto a "Southern" blotting apparatus to transfer the strands to a more durable nylon membrane. After the DNA has been bonded to the nylon, an isotopically labeled VNTR-specific probe is added. This hybridiza-

tion procedure is followed by washing away unbound probe. The membrane now is placed in contact with a sheet of X-ray film. The developed film reveals the position, size, and number of bands for each sample. Each probe produces a one- or two-band pattern. The visual determination of a match between two samples is confirmed by computer-image analysis. The membrane can be analyzed repeatedly with other probes, thereby generating additional information without requiring more sample.

The significance of two samples matching is calculated by establishing the frequency of the banding patterns in the relevant population. For mixtures of probes that recognize five independent loci simultaneously, the chance of a match between two randomly chosen individuals is minuscule.

There is general scientific agreement that DNA analysis produces reliable and accurate results. Both the Eighth U.S. Circuit Court of Appeals [*United States v. Two Bulls,* 1990] and the Second U.S. Circuit Court of Appeals [*United States v. Jakobetz,* 1992] have approved the admissibility of DNA-profiling evidence.

Controversies. DNA fingerprinting has been the focus of many controversies in courtrooms, in the popular media, and in scientific journals. Some issues involve the interpretation of the banding patterns. For example, in a phenomenon called bandshifting, two samples of DNA from the same source produce patterns that are similar but not identical, due to differential migration of some DNA fragments. Most of these issues have been resolved as better-quality control methods have been employed and as the technology has evolved and improved. The most controversial issue that remains is the method of determining the statistical significance of a match.

In 1990 the U.S. Congress' Office of Technology Assessment published a report concluding that DNA testing is both valid and reliable. And in April 1992 the National Research Council of the National Academy of Sciences issued a report entitled "DNA Technology in Forensic Science." This report calls for setting national standards for DNA testing, for accreditation of crime laboratories, and for proficiency testing of DNA analysts. Significantly, it also recommends that the method of calculating the probability of a match be made in a more conservative manner, thus producing a more reasonable and acceptable statistic.

LAWRENCE KOBILINSKY

A demonstrator shows his support of California's decision to reinstate the death penalty in 1992. In April, Robert Alton Harris was the first person to be executed in California in 25 years. Nationwide some 30 persons were put to death during 1992—the highest total since 1962, when 47 inmates were executed.

© Darcy Padilla/NYT Pictures

In Virginia, Roger Keith Coleman was electrocuted in May, still proclaiming his innocence in the 1981 rape and murder of his sister-in-law. A vigorous legal and public-relations drive was mounted in his behalf, claiming Coleman's guilt was established in a process flawed by his inexperienced trial lawyers and widespread presumption he committed the crime.

Gun Control. The fight over gun control was put on hold in 1992. The so-called Brady bill was shelved when Congress failed to agree on a broad anticrime measure that contained the bill's requirement for a five-day waiting period for prospective firearms purchasers. The measure is named for James S. Brady, former President Ronald Reagan's press secretary, who was shot in the head during an assassination attempt on Reagan.

There was increasing alarm in the United States over evidence that guns are becoming more prevalent in the schools and among young people on the streets. Studies by the American Medical Association and the federal government showed that gunshot wounds are the second leading cause of death among all high-school-age children in the nation. The studies also said that in domestic fights, the use of firearms makes it 12 times more likely that a death will result than does the use of other weapons.

There also were some indications that in the aftermath of the Los Angeles riots, more people were buying guns out of fear that police might not be able to defend them adequately. In California alone, 50% more people bought guns in the first 11 days of May than had purchased them during the same time in 1991.

In a Baton Rouge, LA, suburb, Japanese exchange student Yoshihiro Hattori was shot to death by Rodney Pearis outside Pearis' home when the youngster did not understand a command to "freeze." The boy and a friend had gone to the home by mistake, believing it was the location of a party.

White-Collar and Organized Crime. Charles Keating, Jr., convicted in December 1991 in Los Angeles on federal fraud and racketeering charges stemming from the collapse of Lincoln Savings & Loan, was sentenced to ten years in prison in April on state charges. The S&L case stuck taxpayers with a $2.6 billion bill.

The ten-year federal prison sentence of junk-bond financier Michael Milken was reduced by U.S. District Court Judge Kimba Wood, because Milken cooperated with federal authorities and tutored prisoners. He now was eligible for freedom early in 1993.

Washington lawyer Clark Clifford, 85, and his partner, Robert Altman, were indicted on federal and New York state charges in the Bank of Credit and Commerce International (BCCI) scandal. They were accused of deceiving regulators about BCCI's ownership of the largest bank in the nation's capital. BCCI pleaded guilty to federal racketeering charges and agreed to forfeit $550 million in assets.

In the year's major organized-crime case, John Gotti was convicted in federal court in New York of racketeering and five murders, including the killing of former mob boss Paul Castellano. Gotti, reputed head of the nation's most powerful crime family, was sentenced to life in prison as nearly 1,000 of his supporters protested outside a Brooklyn courthouse.

JIM RUBIN, *The Associated Press*

CUBA

The population of Cuba, its activities controlled as tightly as ever by the ubiquitous state-security apparatus, suffered greater economic hardships in 1992 than in the preceding year, and the government of President Fidel Castro did not promise improvements anytime soon. Neither did it indicate that moves toward democratization, hinted at earlier by some officials, would be put into effect in 1993. Despite signs of tension, Castro's 33-year-long rule seemed secure and diplomats in Havana, who had predicted the imminent fall of Cuba's Communist regime after the 1989 collapse of the Soviet bloc, were revising their predictions. A new wave of Cuban refugees fled for the United States.

Economy. Cubans were learning how to live with less. As imports were slashed because of the lack of foreign exchange and food shortages were more acute, thousands of city workers were sent to the fields to harvest vegetables and other products. With less petroleum available, power outages darkened entire neighborhoods across the country. To save electricity, streetlights were off; TV and movie programming was cut back; and newspapers had fewer pages because of the scarcity of newsprint. People walked or rode bicycles to work as public transportation was cut by 50%. The life was somewhat easier in the provinces than in Havana, where 2 million of the country's 10.5 million people live.

The 1992 sugar harvest of 7 million metric tons was considerably higher than expected, but that commodity's low world-market price added little to the country's depleted hard-currency reserves. Cuba was trying to expand Western investments. To attract foreign tourism, it offered inexpensive travel packages to visitors from Western Europe, Canada, and Latin America.

Trade. In 1992, Cuba quadrupled its sales of nickel, of which it has large reserves, to the West. Canada reportedly was planning to invest $1.2 billion in the country's production of nickel and cobalt. The country also benefited

© Mel Rosenthal/JB Pictures

A Cuban carries a portrait of Fidel Castro, who marked his 33d year as Cuba's leader in 1992. Although most Communist regimes had fallen, Cuba remained under Communism.

by exporting medicines and offering luxury drug and physical-therapy rehabilitation clinics to patients who could pay with foreign currency.

U.S. companies, already barred from trading with Cuba by a 30-year-old U.S. economic embargo, were restricted further by the "Cuban Democracy Act" passed by Congress in October, which prohibited their foreign subsidiaries from doing business with the Castro government and ships trading with the island from entering U.S. ports for six months. The law, opposed by dissidents in Cuba and by the Roman Catholic Church, was supported by important segments of the Cuban exile community in the United States. But it was criticized by Canada and West European and Latin American countries, including the staunchly pro-U.S. Britain and Argentina, which regarded the act as an infringement on their sovereignty. Cuba responded by launching a vigorous anti-U.S. campaign, saying that the new U.S. sanctions ruled out any immediate possibility of political compromise with Washington. The United Nations also rebuked the United States and called for an end to the embargo. Playing a nationalist card, Cuba attacked the Miami-based exiles, portraying them as a white oligarchy, eager to reclaim their confiscated properties and restore a capitalist system of racial discrimination and inequality.

CUBA • Information Highlights

Official Name: Republic of Cuba.
Location: Caribbean.
Area: 42,803 sq mi (110 860 km²).
Population (mid-1992 est.): 10,800,000.
Chief Cities (Dec. 31, 1989 est.): Havana, the capital, 2,096,054; Santiago de Cuba, 405,354; Camagüey, 283,008; Holguín, 228,053.
Government: *Head of state and government,* Fidel Castro Ruz, president (took office under a new constitution, December 1976). *Legislature* (unicameral)—National Assembly of People's Power.
Gross National Product (1990 est. U.S.$): $20,900,000,000.
Foreign Trade (1989 U.S.$): *Imports,* $8,100,000,000; *exports,* $5,400,000,000.

Cuban-Russian Ties. In 1992 the full impact of cutbacks in trade with the former Communist countries was felt for the first time. Although Cuba signed commercial exchange agreements with most of the former Soviet republics, it imported 50% fewer goods, including oil, from that area than in 1991, and no longer received a preferential price for its main export, sugar. In the past, "socialist friendship" was the basis for Havana's economic ties with Moscow, which annually covered Cuba's large trade imbalances. But the former Soviet republics, with deep economic problems of their own, looked for cash and relegated relations with Havana to a low priority. How deeply Cuba was affected became clear when Castro announced the construction stoppage of a nuclear-power plant in Cienfuegos, built with Soviet technology and assistance, which was to save millions of tons of imported oil.

After lengthy discussions, Havana and Moscow agreed that about 2,000 Soviet troops stationed on the island would return home by mid-1993, although the Russian-manned electronic listening installation at Lourdes, west of Havana, and the Russian-operated submarine and maintenance naval station in Cienfuegos would remain operational. Although cooled, Cuban-Russian relations were expected to continue. Some independent republics of the former USSR needed Cuban sugar and citrus fruit and did not want to forgo the repayment of the island's $15 billion debt, the largest among all the Soviet debtors.

Constitutional Changes. In July, Cuba's National Assembly of People's Power, the country's parliament, made minor changes in the constitution, including the adoption of direct secret elections. The changes indicated a small move toward a more mixed economy, but preserved the ruling role of the Communist Party in that only one party would offer candidates. There were some changes within the party, which with 612,000 members holding top positions in the administration and the armed forces, was the mainstay of the Castro regime. In October, Carlos Aldana, the party's main ideologue and regarded as Cuba's number 3 man after Fidel Castro and his brother Defense Minister Gen. Raúl Castro, was expelled from the party, its Politburo, and Central Committee because of unspecified "errors." At the same time, Ricardo Alarcón Quesada, former ambassador to the United Nations and recently appointed foreign minister, was made a member of the Politburo, as was José Ramon Balaguer, who replaced Aldana in some of his functions. In June, Fidel Castro fired his son, Fidel Castro Díaz Balart, from his position as chief of the country's nuclear-energy program, citing "inefficiency" in the work of the 43-year-old scientist.

GEORGE VOLSKY
University of Miami

CYPRUS

Once again Cyprus in 1992 remained *de facto* divided into two parts, just as it has been since 1974 when Turkey invaded, taking about 37% of the island in the north. That territory—recognized only by Turkey—was headed by Turkish Cypriot Rauf Denktash as president. The other territories of the Republic of Cyprus were under President George Vassiliou and his internationally recognized administration. The UN Peacekeeping Force in Cyprus (UNFICYP) remained on the island as it had since 1964 when intercommunal fighting first erupted. Major questions revolved around Turkish Cypriot minority rights, the restoration of residential rights for Greek Cypriots driven from their homes in the north by the invasion, the repatriation of Turks brought to the north from the mainland, and the withdrawal of Turkish forces.

Rapprochement Attempts. In early April 1992, UN Secretary-General Boutros Boutros-Ghali warned that UNFICYP might be withdrawn, given the lack of progress toward an agreement between the two communities. The UN Security Council that same month reaffirmed that Cyprus should remain a single sovereign state with its territorial integrity intact. Working with a "set of ideas" proposing a settlement that would change Cyprus into a bizonal federation, Boutros-Ghali conferred separately at the UN with Vassiliou and Denktash, then in June brought the two men together for their first meeting since March 1990. Discussions resumed (July to August 1992) between the two sides under UN auspices, but no settlement ensued. The Security Council on August 26 unanimously passed a resolution supporting the "set of ideas" and the concept of a federal state with two zones. At the UN in October the intercommunal talks recommenced, but the outcome was fruitless. In November negotiations were suspended, to be resumed in March 1993.

EC Application. Building on past efforts, President Vassiliou continued throughout 1992

CYPRUS • Information Highlights

Official Name: Republic of Cyprus.
Location: Eastern Mediterranean.
Area: 3,571 sq mi (9 250 km²).
Population (mid-1992 est.): 700,000.
Chief Cities (1982 census): Nicosia, the capital, 48,221; Limassol, 74,782.
Government: *Head of state and government,* George Vassiliou, president (took office Feb. 1988). *Legislature*—House of Representatives.
Monetary Unit: Pound (0.480 pound equals U.S.$1, July 1992).
Gross Domestic Product (1990 U.S.$): $5,300,-000,000.
Economic Index (1991): *Consumer Prices* (1980 = 100), all items, 169.0; food, 183.9.
Foreign Trade (1991 U.S.$): *Imports,* $2,621,000,000; *exports,* $952,000,000.

to work for Cyprus' entry into the European Community (EC) as a full member. (At the time, Cyprus was an associate member.) In early summer the government expressed its pleasure that the EC had decided to consider the Cypriot application separately from that of Turkey.

Serb Influx. Fighting in the fragmented former Yugoslav state caused a number of Serbs and Serbian companies to move to the Greek Cypriot-dominated part of Cyprus, bringing criticism from abroad concerning the Serbs' use of island connections to help bypass UN sanctions currently in place against Serbia because of the Balkan war. In October the Central Bank in Cyprus tightened regulations that would affect transactions with both Serbia and Montenegro.

Release of Sampson. In late April, Nicos Sampson was released provisionally from prison for compassionate reasons two years before his 20-year sentence for military conspiracy ended. On a prior medical release, he had gone to France and only returned after a long lapse of time. In 1974, Sampson, a Greek Cypriot, illegally had seized the presidency of the island for eight days after a coup had overthrown the government of the lawful president, Archbishop Makarios III.

The University. The University of Cyprus, founded by the Cypriot House of Representatives in 1989, opened in Nicosia.

GEORGE J. MARCOPOULOS, *Tufts University*

CZECHOSLOVAKIA

The year 1992 turned out to be the final year of Czechoslovakia's existence. By Jan. 1, 1993, it was slated to be divided into two separate countries—the Czech Republic and the Slovak Republic.

Elections of June 1992. Soon after the collapse of Czechoslovakia's Communist regime in 1989, the union beween the Czechs and Slovaks, always fragile, began to show signs of strain. The final stage for the breakup of the 74-year-old country was set by the outcome of elections for the Federal Assembly and the Czech and Slovak National Councils held on June 5–6, 1992. The 85% of eligible voters who took part in the elections had to choose among as many as 42 parties and party coalitions, but only 13 of these managed to obtain the required 5% to 15% of the votes needed to secure seats in the legislatures. The decisive winners among them were the liberal-conservative Civic Democratic Party (ODS) in the Czech Republic (with 33.9% of the votes), and the left-leaning nationalist Movement for Democratic Slovakia (HZDS) in Slovakia (with 33.5% of the votes). Second place both in the Czech and the Slovak republics (with more than 14% of the votes in each) was won by former Communists, running

as the Left Bloc in the Czech Republic and as the Party of the Democratic Left in Slovakia. None of the other parties whose candidates qualified to be elected got more than 9% of the votes.

Thus it was up to the two victorious parties, the ODS and the HZDS, to form the new government and to draw up plans for Czechoslovakia's future. That, however, turned out to be an impossible task. The ODS, led by federal Finance Minister Václav Klaus, insisted resolutely on the preservation of a truly "functional" federal system, with a strong central authority. The HZDS, headed by former Communist Vladimír Mečiar, remained adamantly committed to loosening Slovaks' ties to the Czechs, proclaiming Slovakia's sovereignty, getting it recognized internationally, and converting Czechoslovakia into a much looser confederation, with only a bare minimum of powers left to the confederation's government.

Furthermore, a major controversy developed between the two victorious parties about Czechoslovakia's economic reform. The Czech leadership kept pushing for the speediest possible transition to a free-market economy even if it created hardships in the form of rising prices, unemployment, and bankruptcy for enterprises unable to pay their way without government subsidies. The Slovaks, on the other hand, became more and more critical of Klaus' "shock therapy," which created more difficulties and hardships in Slovakia than in the Czech lands. This was due mainly to the fact that a much larger proportion of Slovakia's plants than of those in the Czech Republic were engaged in the kind of large-scale and grossly inefficient heavy industrial production which became the prime target of the economic reform. As a result, unemployment was more than three times higher in Slovakia than in the Czech lands, providing more fuel for Slovak nationalist attacks on "Prague centralism" and "Czech colonialism."

In a number of postelection meetings, negotiators for the two republics failed to settle their differences or find an acceptable compro-

---

CZECHOSLOVAKIA • Information Highlights

Official Name: Czech and Slovak Federal Republic.
Location: East-central Europe.
Area: 49,371 sq mi (127 870 km²).
Population (mid-1992 est.): 15,700,000.
Chief Cities (Dec. 31, 1990 est.): Prague, the capital, 1,215,076; Bratislava, 444,482; Brno, 390,986.
Government: Head of state president, vacant, Head of government, Jan Strasky, premier. Legislature —Federal Assembly.
Gross National Product (1990 est. U.S.$): $120,300,000,000.
Economic Indexes (1991): Consumer Prices (1980 = 100), all items, 195.7; food, 184.1. Industrial Production (1980 = 100), 100.
Foreign Trade (1991 U.S.$): Imports, $9,957,-000,000; exports, $10,859,000,000.

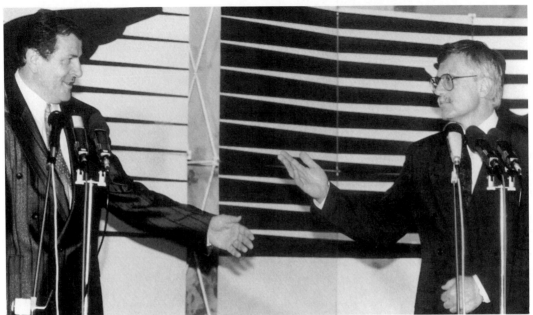

On June 20, 1992, Václav Klaus (right) and Vladimír Mečiar—the two leading figures of the Czech and Slovak regions—agreed on the transformation of Czechoslovakia into two separate nations. The division occurred on Jan. 1, 1993.

© Brauchli/Sygma

mise solution of the crisis. Finally, on June 20, Klaus and Mečiar signed a nine-point political agreement calling for a "constitutional division" of Czechoslovakia into "two fully independent states."

Interim Government. A ten-man caretaker federal Council of Ministers was set up to guarantee a proper functioning of the country in the postelection period, contribute to resolving questions concerning the constitutional setup of Czechoslovakia, and prepare conditions for a smooth functioning of "two sovereign states with international status." When the newly elected Federal Assembly convened in July to elect a new federal president, Slovak deputies blocked the reelection of President Václav Havel, and he resigned prior to the expiration of his term of office. Since no other candidate managed to obtain the required majority of votes, the presidency remained vacant and its functions devolved on the federal Council of Ministers. In August the Slovak National Council proclaimed Slovakia's sovereignty and adopted a new Slovak constitution. A number of subsequent measures defined various aspects of the separation. The republics agreed to remain in a customs union and (temporarily at least) in a monetary union as well, and to coordinate their foreign, defense, and economic policies. As the year approached its end, however, they already were beginning to act as independent states. The new Slovak constitution went into effect on October 1, and the Federal Assembly voted itself out of existence on November 25.

The Economy. The forthcoming split-up of Czechoslovakia notwithstanding, the transition to a free-market economy kept moving forward through its planned stages. Having virtually completed the auctioning off of smaller publicly operated enterprises such as restaurants, hotels, and retail stores, the government followed through with scheduled "large privatization" by converting larger state-owned enterprises, such as factories and assembly plants, into joint-stock companies and selling its shares to private investors. During the year some 8.5 million Czechs and Slovaks bought government vouchers which they could trade for shares of enterprises made available for this purpose during several rounds of the "large privatization."

The problems and difficulties accompanying the economic reform from its inception remained much the same in 1992. The gross domestic product (GDP), national income, industrial production, and exports to former Communist countries continued to drop. Two thirds of agricultural enterprises registered losses. New taxes, including a value-added tax, were enacted, resulting in additional increases in the cost of living. But inflation slowed down, unemployment remained low (except in Slovakia), and foreign-exchange reserves rose. Meanwhile, Slovakia became embroiled in a quarrel with Hungary over the Gabcikovo hydroelectric project, which involved diverting the course of the Danube River along the Slovak-Hungarian border. Hungary withdrew from the project for environmental reasons, but the Slovaks went ahead with their part despite Hungarian objections. Both sides agreed to mediation of the dispute by the European Community in October.

EDWARD TABORSKY
University of Texas, Austin

The New York City Ballet was among the companies that celebrated the 100th anniversary of Tchaikovsky's "The Nut-cracker." The work, which premiered in St. Petersburg in December 1892, long has been a Christmastime favorite.

DANCE

Uncertainty hovered over the dance world in 1992. Financial setbacks, a large number of deaths in the field, and an apparent drift of artistic purpose raised questions about the survival of U.S. dance organizations.

Symptomatic of this disarray was the crisis faced by American Ballet Theatre (ABT), whose future suddenly seemed in doubt. Jane Hermann, who had succeeded Mikhail Baryshnikov as artistic director in 1990, did not renew her contract, which expired on August 31. Although she had reduced the annual budget, the company's accumulated deficit remained at $5 million. Hoping to expand its base of support, ABT considered a merger with the Joffrey Ballet that both groups eventually decided was unfeasible. Kevin McKenzie, a former ABT principal dancer, was named artistic director in October but would be obliged to operate with a reduced budget.

Hard-pressed to pay off debts, many U.S. companies scaled down their seasons or production values. Even the New York City Ballet, more solvent than others, stipulated that leotards and no scenery be used when 11 choreographers were invited to create new works for its Diamond Project.

The absence of a dominant esthetic in this series and elsewhere suggested that even established choreographers were searching for something new.

Ballet. The Diamond Project, named after a major donor (the Aaron Diamond Foundation), was the idea of Peter Martins, the City Ballet's artistic director, who hoped to stimulate new choreography.

Among the most successful premieres were David Allan's *Reunions*, featuring the brilliant young dancer Ethan Stiefel, and Richard Tanner's *Ancient Airs and Dances*. The other works were Martins' *Jeu de Cartes*, William Forsythe's *Herman Schmerman*, Miriam Mahdaviani's *Images*, Lynne Taylor-Corbett's *Mercury*, John Alleyne's *Bet Ann's Dance*, Robert LaFosse's *I Have My Own Room*, Bart Cook's *Flötezart*, Alexandre Proia's *Refractions*, and Toni Pimble's *Two's Company*.

Martins' other premieres during 1992 were *Zakouski* and *Delight of the Muses*, set to a commissioned score by Charles Wuorinen.

ABT, despite financial constraints, presented new productions and premieres. Michael Smuin's ingenious version of Prokofiev's *Peter and the Wolf* used celebrity narrators like Dudley Moore, Victor Borge, and Bobby McFerrin. Ulysses Dove's *Serious Pleasures* and Mats Ek's *Grass* offered studies in alienation. Agnes de Mille's *The Other* recycled a "Death and the Maiden" theme. Novice John Selya, a dancer in the troupe, presented two sketchy premieres—*Moondance* and *Jack and Jill*.

The company also presented the first U.S. production of *Symphonic Variations*, by the British choreographer Frederick Ashton, and a new authoritative staging by Nicholas Beriozoff of Michel Fokine's *Firebird*.

ABT invited Rudolf Nureyev, who embarked on a conducting career at the age of 54, to lead its orchestra at the May 6 performance of Kenneth MacMillan's *Romeo and Juliet*. The title roles were danced by two French guests, Sylvie Guillem and Laurent Hilaire. Thin and weak, Nureyev looked pleased with the ovation he received after conducting the Prokofiev score at the Metropolitan Opera House. In October, British newspapers repeatedly stated, without confirmation, that Nureyev was ill with AIDS. (He died early in 1993.)

The Joffrey Ballet skipped a costly season in New York City and canceled its engagement in May in Los Angeles in the wake of the riots there. But it toured nationally with a major revival of Léonide Massine's 1933 ballet, *Les Présages*.

Feld Ballet/NY featured two acclaimed premieres by Eliot Feld—*Evoe* and *Endsong*. Other new Feld ballets were *To the Naked Eye, Clave,* and *Wolfgang Strategies*.

Twyla Tharp recruited guests from the City Ballet (Robert LaFosse) and the Paris Opera Ballet (Patrick Dupond, Isabelle Guérin, Lionel Delanoé, Stéphane Elizabé, Delphine Moussin) for her new company, Twyla Tharp and Dancers. A highly successful New York season offered exuberant Tharp premieres: *Octet, Sextet, Men's Piece,* and *Grand Pas: Rhythm of the Saints*.

Tharp disbanded the group and formed another to tour *Cutting Up*, a collection of disparate numbers for a few of the same dancers, herself, and Baryshnikov. The new tour, which left out New York, received mixed reviews, but proved popular as a novelty vehicle for Baryshnikov, still a ballet superstar at the age of 44, and Tharp, 51.

Baryshnikov's other guest appearances included the City Ballet, where he danced George Balanchine's *Duo Concertant* and Mark Morris' solo *Three Preludes*.

Modern Dance. Morris, who returned to the United States with his troupe from three years in Brussels, enjoyed both popularity and controversy. Those who idolized or criticized him singled out his campy wit, which colored *The Hard Nut*, a comic-strip version of *The Nutcracker*, at the Brooklyn Academy of Music. Morris premieres in his Manhattan Center season were *Polka, Beautiful Day, A Lake,* and *Behemoth*.

Merce Cunningham won acclaim with new works—*Beach Birds, Loosestrife,* and *Change of Address*, a dynamic ritual. The Martha Graham Dance Company revived an excerpt from *Panorama*, a 1935 Graham social-protest work. The 33 women in the piece stunned viewers with their energetic militant spirit. Graham's 1943 *Salem Shore* was revived with the actress Claire Bloom reciting a text onstage on opening night as Terese Capucilli portrayed a sea captain's wife.

After Graham's death in 1991, company members were encouraged to create new works. Two were presented in 1992: Pascal Rioult's *Naramaya* and Donlin Foreman's *. . . . ing*.

The Bill T. Jones/Arnie Zane Dance Company offered provocative pieces by Jones that often focused on love and AIDS. The premieres were *Love Defined, Aria, Last Night on Earth,* and *Fête*. AIDS was a key motif in David Rousseve's ambitious dance-theater piece *Urban Scenes/Creole Dreams*.

Paul Taylor's new *Oz* and Christopher Gillis' *Andalusian Green* both were danced by Taylor's company, which revived his 1957 *Epic*. Other premieres included *Aurora*, Murray Louis' *Blue Streak* and *A Fine Line*, and Lar Lubovitch's *Waiting for the Sunrise*. The Alvin Ailey American Dance Theater premieres were Dwight Rhoden's *Frames;* Donald Byrd's *Folk Dance;* and Billy Wilson's festive tribute to Dizzy Gillespie, *The Winter in Lisbon*.

Foreign Companies. The Royal Danish Ballet delighted audiences and critics in Copenhagen with the romantic works of August Bournonville at the second Bournonville Festival. A few of the new productions later were seen in Costa Mesa, CA, and Washington, DC. Les Ballets de Monte Carlo made a debut at the Spoleto Festival in Charleston, SC, and the Netherlands' Scapino Ballet offered contrasting pieces in New York.

The Kirov Ballet from Russia returned with a controversial *Swan Lake*. Oleg Vinogradov, the Kirov director, retained set pieces of choreography but was criticized for his confusing ending and new dances. The corps looked fine in *La Bayadère*, but the Kirov soloists failed to grasp the style of Western choreographers in Antony Tudor's *The Leaves are Fading* and Jerome Robbins' *In the Night*. An unexpected success was the revival of the 1940 *Romeo and Juliet*, in which Leonid Lavrovsky fused mime and dance.

Experimental works that stood out were *Achterland*, with innovative movement by Anne Teresa de Keersmaeker from Belgium, and *Dah-Dah-Sko-Dah-Dah*, marked by the robotic rhythms of Saburo Teshigawara from Japan.

Folk groups from abroad included Mazowsze from Poland, Lado from Croatia, Red Star Red Army Chorus and Dance Ensemble from Russia, Ballet Folklórico from Mexico, and Gypsy Passion from Spain.

Obituaries. Among the personalities who died in 1992 were the modern-dance pioneer Hanya Holm, the British choreographer and former Royal Ballet director Kenneth MacMillan, the designer Rouben Ter-Arutunian, the dancer and choreographer Clark Tippet, the tap star Charles (Honi) Coles, and Andrès Bossard, cofounder of the mime group Mummenschanz.

ANNA KISSELGOFF, *"The New York Times"*

DELAWARE

A long election campaign and a continuing weak economy dominated events in Delaware in 1992.

Elections. Wilmington voters made history when they elected James H. Sills, Jr., a member of the Democratic Party, as the first African-American mayor of Wilmington, the state's largest city. Sills, a University of Delaware professor and state legislator, defeated incumbent Daniel Frawley in an upset victory in the September 12 Democratic primary. He then received 91% of the November vote, with only token opposition from third-party candidate Beatrice Patton Carroll.

As a result of the November balloting, Rep. Thomas R. Carper (D) and Gov. Michael N. Castle (R) would switch jobs in January 1993. Castle, who was barred from seeking a third gubernatorial term, ran for the lone Delaware seat in the U.S. House of Representatives, defeating former Lt. Gov. S. B. Woo (D). In the gubernatorial contest, Carper, who had served five terms in the U.S. House following three terms as state treasurer, received 65% of the vote to defeat B. Gary Scott (R).

State Sen. Ruth Ann Minner was elected lieutenant governor, defeating Philip Cloutier (R), the president of the New Castle County Council. Democrats retained their 15–6 margin of control in the state Senate, while Republicans retained control in the state House of Representatives by a margin of 23-18. The state's three electoral votes were won by Bill Clinton, thus retaining a tradition in which the state's voters have supported the winning presidential candidate for 11 consecutive elections.

The 1992 election culminated a three-year effort by the Democratic Party to restructure itself and win the most important statewide office. For the Republicans, divisive primaries and an inability to field strong candidates in several important races showed a party in need of renewal.

Economy. Delaware's economy remained weak, although conditions were not as bad as in surrounding states. Employment growth was negative in 1991 and the first half of 1992. There was hope that the second half of 1992 would begin to show signs of a slight rise in employment. A 1.5% drop in unemployment over the previous year was seen in the 5% rate of June 1992, but this lower rate was attributed to workers leaving the labor force rather than to job growth.

The 1.8% decline in Delaware's employment level in 1991 was slightly more than the nationwide decline but better than the 3.3% decline in the Mid-Atlantic region. The state showed relative strength in holding its loss of manufacturing jobs at 2.2%, a rate below both the regional and national averages of 5.6% and 3.9%, respectively. Another blow came in December when General Motors announced it would close its Wilmington plant in 1996. The possibility of further job losses in chemical manufacturing also remained.

Legislative Session. The economy, a tight state budget, and politics dominated the second session of the 136th General Assembly. The legislature, however, did enact a new healthcare system for children, establish an economic-stimulus package, and provide a small pay increase for state workers and teachers. Dealing with reapportionment and an investigation into the activities of the state insurance commissioner produced the most political heat. As the end of the legislative session approached on June 30, a late increase in revenues allowed lawmakers to balance the budget with relatively little pain and even provide funding for some favorite projects.

JEROME R. LEWIS, *University of Delaware*

DENMARK

In a June 2, 1992, referendum, by a surprising vote of 50.7% to 49.3%, Danes rejected ratification of the 1991 Maastricht Treaty that sought a more centralized European Community (EC), including a single European currency. Denmark's various political parties and the government generally had favored the treaty. Prime Minister Poul Schlüter stated afterward that the government would consider calling for a second referendum at a later date. Denmark's Folketing (Parliament) in June tightened Denmark's rather lax entry laws for noncitizens, the so-called Foreigners' Law.

Foreign Affairs. Queen Margrethe II and Prince Henrik, along with Foreign Minister Uffe Ellemann-Jensen, made a state visit in July to the Baltic nations of Estonia, Latvia, and Lithuania. In June the royal couple had celebrated their silver wedding anniversary.

In May representatives of the Nordic Council and the three Baltic states in a meeting at

© Hornbak-Christensen/Sipa

Posters in Copenhagen publicize Denmark's June 2 referendum on the Maastricht Treaty on European unity. Denmark's rejection of the agreement caused an upheaval in the European Community. Danes were to vote again on the pact in 1993.

Palanga, Lithuania, agreed to a number of items that would strengthen their cooperation. The agreement covered such items as the purity of Baltic waters, security, culture and education, communications, and the withdrawal of foreign forces, as well as trade and the restructuring of agriculture. A Baltic Council involved in these and similar matters had been established in Copenhagen in March.

Pressed by members of the Progressive Party and three other parties in the Foreign Affairs Committee, Parliament called a special session in September to agree to send 100–150 Danish soldiers as part of an expanded United Nations force in Bosnia-Herzegovina.

During the year, Denmark and Finland arrived at a compromise in their dispute over the passage of oil-drilling platforms under the suspension bridge being built across the Great Belt, the waters between the Danish islands of Sjaelland and Fyn. Finland had demanded that a narrow section of the bridge be opened so that the tall platforms, exceeding in height the level of the bridge above the water's surface, could proceed through the internationally trafficked Great Belt. Denmark rejected Finland's demand; after this, Finland agreed to mount the "legs" of the platforms after passing under the bridge. Denmark agreed to pay Finland compensation of 3 million finnmarks (about $700,000).

Economic Affairs. Inflation was less of a problem in Denmark than elsewhere in Europe. In September the rate of inflation was 2.1%, a record of sorts. Wages generally had kept ahead of inflation by about 1% during 1991. Denmark's rate of unemployment was among Europe's highest, however, having grown 50% in four years to about 11% by midsummer. The rate of exchange of the Danish krone had lost 53% of its world market value since 1980.

A prolonged period of drought affected farmers and spelled ruin for much agriculture as well as cattle breeding. While farmers faced formidable problems, fishermen benefited to some extent because fish stocks, especially around the island of Fyn, had sought deeper waters where it was possible to make huge catches with the use of trawlers.

Through May 1992, Denmark had produced about 3.3 million tons of oil from the ocean bottom.

The Faroe Islands. The Faroe Islands, enjoying extensive home rule, became the last area in Western Europe to impose a sales tax, effective Jan. 1, 1993.

ERIK J. FRIIS
"The Scandinavian-American Bulletin"

DENMARK · Information Highlights

Official Name: Kingdom of Denmark.
Location: Northwest Europe.
Area: 16,629 sq mi (43 070 km²).
Population (mid-1992 est.): 5,200,000.
Chief Cities (Jan. 1, 1990 est.): Copenhagen, the capital, 1,337,114 (incl. suburbs); Århus, 261,437; Odense, 176,133.
Government: *Head of state,* Margrethe II, queen (acceded Jan. 1972). *Head of government,* Poul Schlüter, prime minister (took office Sept. 1982). *Legislature* (unicameral)—Folketing.
Monetary Unit: Krone (6.0490 kroner equal U.S.$1, Dec. 16, 1992).
Gross Domestic Product (1990 U.S.$): $78,000,-000,000.
Economic Indexes (1991): *Consumer Prices* (1980 = 100), all items, 181.7; food, 166.0. *Industrial Production* (1980 = 100), 133.
Foreign Trade (1991 U.S.$): *Imports,* $32,257,-000,000; *exports,* $35,812,000,000.

DRUGS AND ALCOHOL

Despite strong indications that the U.S. drug situation had not improved by 1992, the "war on drugs"—first declared in 1971—was a conspicuous nonissue in the 1992 presidential campaign. This developed despite a series of 1992 reports indicating that cocaine and heroin use, drug smuggling, and international opium and cocaine production were increasing and that drug-related crime in the nation's large cities remained a deadly problem.

Drug Production and Use. Drug use in general, primarily casual use among the middle class, had been declining steadily since the mid-1980s. But drugs—particularly crack cocaine and heroin—continued to cause damaging social and public-health ills among the poor in U.S. inner cities, despite a $70 billion federal antidrug effort since the early 1970s.

In October 1992 the federal government's Drug Abuse Warning Network reported a 34.8% annual increase in cocaine-related visits to hospital emergency rooms in the first three months of 1992 and a 17.8% yearly increase in heroin-related emergencies. "This shows [that] the hard-core [drug] problem is as bad as ever," Terence J. Pell, chief of staff of the White House Office of National Drug Control Policy, said when the data were released.

The annual U.S. State Department report on global drug production, released in February, found that the production of opium (heroin's main ingredient) increased by 8% in 1991, and that—despite a drop in the cultivation of coca in South America—worldwide cocaine production significantly increased. "There's no indication anywhere that there's less cocaine coming out of South America than there was coming out three years ago," said Stanley E. Morris, a former official in the Bush administration's drug-control-policy office.

The annual survey compiled for the federal government by the University of Michigan's Institute for Social Research, released January 27, found that some 13.8% of the high-school seniors interviewed reported using marijuana in 1991. That compared with a high of 36.5% in 1979. But other surveys—including a report issued by the Federal Centers for Disease Control in September and the annual report by the Parents' Resource Institute for Drug Education in October—indicated that the use of drugs such as marijuana, cocaine, and LSD and other hallucinogens increased slightly among teenagers and young adults in 1991.

The Antidrug Effort. There was criticism throughout 1992, primarily from Democrats, about the effectiveness of the administration's antidrug effort, which in 1992 had a budget of some $12 billion, about 68% of which was spent on domestic law enforcement and on international interdiction and control programs. Critics complained that more of the budget should have gone into drug treatment and education programs.

Bob Martinez, the former Florida governor who directs the Office of National Drug Control Policy, defended the administration's approach, saying many drug addicts do not accept treatment and others can get off drugs without federal programs. Martinez himself drew criticism in 1992 for not being a forceful administrator and for losing bureaucratic battles with other federal agencies and within the White House. Democrats also complained that Martinez was "politicizing" his office and spending an inordinate amount of time campaigning for President Bush. Martinez dismissed the charges. "This is nothing more than politics masquerading as principle," Martinez said in September after the Senate approved a measure banning federal drug officials from taking part in political campaigns.

Michael M. Baylson (left), the U.S. attorney for the Eastern District of Pennsylvania, tours an area of Philadelphia with Sister Carol Keck, executive director of the city's Norris Square Neighborhood Project. Baylson was instrumental in formulating the Bush administration's antidrug initiative—Operation Weed and Seed. Under the "weed" part of the plan, there would be an effort to clear drug trafficking out of 50 depressed areas in the United States, and under the "seed" portion, new social and educational services would be provided in the involved areas.

Alcohol. There was less contention over alcohol, a substance health officials consider to be the nation's most abused drug. Although national surveys indicated that the number of alcohol-related traffic deaths continued a steady ten-year decline, alcohol remained a significant public-health problem, especially among teenagers and young adults. The Federal Centers for Disease Control reported in September, for example, that a series of 1991 surveys revealed that 46% of high-school students reported that they had used alcohol at least once in the previous 30 days.

U.S. Surgeon General Antonia C. Novello released a Department of Justice study in April reporting that alcohol consumption was associated with 27% of all murders, 31% of rapes, 33% of property offenses, and 37% of robberies committed by young persons. The surgeon general lobbied throughout 1992 for clearer labeling of alcoholic beverages and tougher enforcement of underage-drinking laws. She also called on the alcoholic-beverage industry to refrain voluntarily from targeting young persons in advertising and promotions.

MARC LEEPSON, *Free-lance Writer*

ECUADOR

In 1992, Ecuador carried out its fourth consecutive constitutional change of government as President Rodrigo Borja of the Democratic Left Party transferred the presidency to Sixto Duran Ballen of the Republican Unity Party. This milestone in the country's democratic history also was marked, however, by a dramatic shift to the right and increasing ungovernability.

Antidrug Action. Borja ended his term making progress on two fronts—the struggle against drug trafficking and the incorporation of militant indigenous groups. Drug raids carried out in June led to the seizure of more than $100 million in assets and the arrests of 51 peo-

ple, including the head of the Reyes drug ring, the under secretary of defense, the police commander of Guayaquil, and the director of a bank owned by the armed forces.

Indian Land Agreement. In May the government's negotiations with CONAIE, the organization representing the country's large Indian population, concluded with a controversial agreement to set aside 3 million acres (1.2 million ha) in Ecuador's eastern province of Pastaza for about 20,000 Achuar, Shiwar, and Quichua Indians. While the agreement gave title of the land to the communities, it included guarantees of continued residence for non-Indians and free access for the military in the territory, which includes a disputed border with Peru. The government won the right to continue oil exploration in the area and to keep any proceeds from its finds, although the Indian communities won the right to veto ecologically damaging forms of oil production and other future development in the region.

Borja's Economic Program. The Borja government continued its gradual approach to placating business interests: Export licensing procedures were streamlined, and the labor code of 1938 was modified to limit union activity. These measures further alienated Borja's center-left base of support while failing to spark economic recovery. Inflation remained high at around 50%, and economic growth was sluggish.

Shift to the Right. In the first-round presidential elections in May, both of the candidates who advanced to the runoff came from parties of the right that had called for accelerated economic liberalization; the candidate of Borja's party received only 8.3% of the vote. In the July runoff election, the pro-business Duran Ballen defeated Jaime Nebot Saadi of the Social Christian Party. Duran abandoned Borja's reluctance to pursue economic union with the other countries of the Andean Pact and pulled out of OPEC in order to increase foreign-exchange earnings by dropping the cartel's production quotas.

In September the new president announced a program of radical economic liberalization, which included freeing prices and interest rates, allowing the sucre to float, freezing public-sector hirings, cutting public spending by 4%, and raising utility rates and gas prices.

Antigovernment Protests. While the plan did contain some cushions for the poor, it met with strikes and massive protests led by CONAIE, student groups, and the Frente Unitario de Trabajadores (FUT) labor federation. These were accompanied by vandalism and a wave of bombings by a group calling itself Grupo Libertad. Troops were called into Guayaquil to control the situation, and the government vowed to repress future illegal strikes.

MICHAEL COPPEDGE
Johns Hopkins University

ECUADOR • Information Highlights

Official Name: Republic of Ecuador.
Location: Northwest South America.
Area: 109,483 sq mi (283 560 km²).
Population (mid-1992 est.): 10,000,000.
Chief Cities (1990 census): Quito, the capital, 1,100,847; Guayaquil, 1,508,444; Cuenca, 194,981.
Government: *Head of state and government,* Sixto Duran Ballen, president (took office August 10, 1992). *Legislature* (unicameral)—Chamber of Representatives.
Monetary Unit: Sucre (1,706.02 sucres equal U.S.$1, floating rate, Oct. 27, 1992).
Gross Domestic Product (1990 U.S.$): $9,700,000,000.
Economic Index (1990): *Consumer Prices* (1981 = 100), all items, 2,835.2; food, 4,007.2.
Foreign Trade (1991 U.S.$): *Imports,* $2,399,000,000; *exports,* $2,125,000,000.

EDUCATION

After almost a decade of serious attention to education reform in the United States, policymakers and educators in 1992 began to see that systemic changes would be needed. Piecemeal efforts—in teacher training, curriculum reform, assessments, or through the examples of lighthouse-type schools—were too fragmented and isolated to produce the impact wanted. As the big picture emerged, particularly among state policymakers, the unifying theme was a focus on outcomes—on paying attention to what students know and can do rather than how many courses they have taken.

The U.S. presidential campaign showed that job training and retraining would be major education priorities for whatever administration was in power. The reauthorization of federal research in education remained to be settled, and Congress was looking ahead to fundamental changes in Chapter I when it considers reauthorization of that program in 1993.

Federal and National Initiatives. According to the Education Commission of the States, systemic reform means: a common mission; high standards stated in terms of desired results; coherent, integrated policies; a long-term perspective; and implementing even incremental change in the context of a comprehensive strategy. Early in the year the National Council on Standards and Testing integrated systemic reform into its report "Raising Standards for American Education." Panel members included governors, members of Congress, educators, researchers, and other policymakers; they were charged by Congress to advise on the desirability and feasibility of national standards and tests and to recommend policies to implement them. The council concluded that high national standards, tied to assessments, were desirable. It also said states must assure that "the tools for success" are available to students. These conclusions became known as school delivery standards, covering such elements as facilities, well-trained teachers, and access to high content.

For most of the rest of its session, Congress focused on shaping legislation embodying the standards and testing recommendations of the council, along with school-improvement initiatives. The Bush administration proposed a bill for elementary and secondary education; this essentially was a choice plan that would have allowed parents to use vouchers at nonpublic schools. Primarily because the final bill included federal support for school delivery standards but not for the voucher plan, the bill lost bipartisan support. However, it set a pattern for the development of an overall plan for school reform at the federal level. Because of the pressure for the federal government to fund the development of standards and new forms of assessments, the issues were sure to be brought up again when the new Congress convenes in 1993. Further, because of strong support for the inclusion of school delivery standards in any legislation funding higher curriculum standards, equity concerns would become part of such reform legislation. Sure that school delivery standards would remain an important policy consideration, the National Governors' Association was preparing a report on them, with policy recommendations, for its 1993 annual meeting in August.

Despite the failure of legislation supporting the development of standards and assessments, federal research money launched efforts to develop higher curriculum standards in history, language arts, science and math, and geography. The prototype is the set of standards developed by the National Council of Teachers of Mathematics and adopted by that group in 1989. One strategy being used was to fund states or state consortia for the development of new curriculum frameworks, following the lead of California and Connecticut.

The attention to systemic reform showed up in another national effort—the competition for grants from the New American Schools Development Corporation. A privately financed initiative proposed by President Bush to encourage the development of "break-the-mold" schools, the competition attracted almost 700 applications. The corporation awarded only 11 grants, about one third the number originally anticipated, because it had raised only one fourth of its intended $200 million kitty. The 11 winners received one-year grants to develop designs; a smaller number of grantees would receive implementation grants. Despite its moderated goals, the corporation stimulated innovative thinking among leaders of individual schools, school systems, institutions, and groups. According to an analysis by the RAND Corporation, the competition finalists did not propose totally new ideas. Rather, they put ideas together in a systemic way. The common elements among the winning designs exemplified systemic reform. Their plans would require high standards and new assessments; changes in curriculum and instruction; changes in staffing, staff training, and staff development; different school organizations and governance; integration of technology; and integration of social services with school programs.

Student Achievement. Assessment results from international studies generally underscored the concern about low curriculum standards in the United States. A new comparison of math and science items conducted by the International Assessment of Educational Progress placed U.S. students at or below the average of other developed nations. In reading, U.S. students ranked among the highest scorers, and they were on a par with students in geography. However, analysts noted that the

Benno C. Schmidt, Jr. (right) resigned as president of Yale University—a post he held since 1986—to become president and chief executive officer of the Edison Project. The plan, which was conceived by Christopher Whittle (left), the chairman of Whittle Communications, seeks to build 1,000 for-profit, technologically advanced schools that will be models for "revolutionary" changes in U.S. education.

© Joyce Dopkeen/NYT Pictures

skills assessed in reading and geography were very basic and did not require higher-order thinking skills.

These test results were highlighted in the second "report card" issued by the National Education Goals Panel. With little new data on student performance or the other indicators being used for the annual reports from the panel, the 1992 report focused on the global context for seeking higher standards. It emphasized that U.S. students are not exposed to the same high-difficulty content as students in many other countries. For example, U.S. eighth-graders are less likely to be taught algebra than are students in other developed countries. Also, parents in other countries have higher academic expectations for their children. This satisfaction with the status quo also extended to the workplace. U.S. workers, according to one study, were much more likely to believe their current skills would be adequate five years from now than were workers in Germany or Japan.

Assessment Reform. As for national initiatives on developing new assessments, the report of the National Council on Education Standards and Testing quelled any demand for a single national test. The report instead recommended a national system of tests to include state-of-the-art assessments of individual students and a national large-scale sample, all of which would be linked to higher curriculum standards. The development of such tests would take time and much expertise, and the federal government was expected eventually to be a major, or sole, funder of the effort.

Meanwhile, the New Standards Project began pilot-testing performance assessments in math and literacy in several states. This pioneering effort expected to develop assessments in all core subjects and for grades four, eight, and ten. It is a joint project of the University of Pittsburgh's Learning Research and Development Center and the National Center on Education and the Economy. The latter proposed an "exit" exam for all students in which they would need to demonstrate mastery of certain skills by age 16. Those passing the exam would proceed to options that could include school-to-work transitions or college-preparatory courses. This idea fit with a 1992 report from the Secretary's Commission on Achieving Necessary Skills (SCANS) describing how schools should go about integrating its recommendations for new skills into the regular curriculum. Rather than a vocational approach, SCANS, an activity of the U.S. Department of Labor, calls for mastery of basic skills but also for competency in higher-order skills and group decision-making, as well as instruction provided through real-life situations.

State and Local Reforms. Complementing national attention to standards and assessment, state leadership in 1992 took systemic approaches to change, despite severe budget cutbacks. Average teacher salary increases among the states, for example, were the lowest in many years, and at the end of the year local school districts from Maryland to California were struggling with the loss of state funding. Nevertheless, some state legislatures and state boards stepped up reform efforts.

Pennsylvania became the first state to adopt outcome-based frameworks as graduation requirements. This would mean that high-school students in that state would be measured on their mastery of specific skills rather than on the number of courses they took. Almost a dozen other states were developing outcome-based frameworks, but by late 1992 none had made this system a requirement.

About 30 states were working under grants from the National Science Foundation to create systemic support for improvement of math and science instruction. California became the second state to authorize the establishment of charter schools. Its plan is much more significant than that of Minnesota, where up to eight charter schools may be approved on a pilot basis. The California legislation allows for up to 100 charter schools which may be proposed by anyone so long as 10% of the teachers in the district or 50% of the teachers in the school approve of the conversion to charter status. Charter schools must meet certain requirements, including agreed-upon outcomes, but otherwise would be exempt from laws governing school districts.

Individual school districts also exhibited an innovative spirit during 1992. The LaCrosse, WI, district approved a plan to use family income rather than race to balance school enrollment. Five school districts in the Minneapolis, MN, area came together to form the Metropolitan Learning Alliance, which would create educational programs for K-12 students in the nation's largest shopping mall in Bloomington. With strong support from the business community, Cincinnati, OH, reorganized by cutting central office staffing in half, putting all management under a vice-president for business, and grouping schools into clusters with a lead principal reporting to the superintendent.

Despite unfavorable reviews of the takeover in 1989 of the Chelsea, MA, school district by Boston University, Baltimore, MD, placed nine schools—eight elementary and one middle school—in the hands of a for-profit Minneapolis firm. The schools opened in September under a cloud of protest from personnel transferred out of the schools, but there also were compliments from remaining teachers. Education Alternatives, Inc., had a five-year contract to manage the schools, retrain teachers, and produce gains in student achievement.

The privatization of schools made headlines when Benno Schmidt, Jr., president of Yale University, announced that he would leave his post in order to head up the Edison Project, a nationwide system of innovative private schools sponsored by Whittle Communications. Schmidt was expected to be a major fund-raiser for the effort, which would need up to $3 billion for development. Whittle said the first 200 of a projected 1,000 schools would open in 1996.

School-Board Restructuring. All of these various restructuring initiatives finally brought about a review of education governance. Consequently, the nation's school boards came under criticism in 1992. Often sidelined by the policy-making and reform ferment of the 1980s, school boards received partial blame for the lack of rapid improvement of schooling, especially in urban areas. Starting a substantive debate on school-board leadership was a report from the Task Force on School Governance, sponsored by the Twentieth Century Fund and the Danforth Foundation. Finding that school boards too often stand in the way of school reform, the task force recommended that boards focus exclusively on policy. Its report also called for a gradual transition to appointed school boards in big cities, stronger ties to other levels of government, and true coordination between schools and other service-providing agencies within communities.

In October the Institute for Educational Leadership (IEL) released a report on school boards which included self-assessments indicating school-board members did not believe they were taking strong leadership in meaningful ways. The IEL report was even more emphatic about cross-agency collaboration. A third report was expected to be released early in 1993, based on a study of school governance by the Committee for Economic Development.

Student Subgroups. Certain subgroups of children and young people received special attention during 1992. Census data and other sources confirmed the increase in child poverty, now affecting one in five children, due primarily to an increase in single-parent families. The National Education Goals Panel, admitting that it did not have adequate data about preschool-age children, decided upon a set of indicators, the Early Childhood Assessment System, that would be used for future annual reports. The assessment, to be taken several times during the kindergarten year, covers physical well-being and motor development, social and emotional development, attitudes toward learning, language usage, and cognition and general knowledge. The panel avoided the use of earlier indicators, such as birth weight, access to health services, or day-care experiences, which early-childhood experts had urged be adopted.

While the graduation rate for black students improved considerably during the 1980s, according to the U.S. Census Bureau, it remained static among Hispanic students. Almost one half of Hispanics dropped out of school before graduating, but Hispanic dropouts tended to have higher rates of employment than did black dropouts. Young Hispanic children were much less likely to be enrolled in preschool programs than were other racial groups, and Hispanic adults were about eight times as likely to be illiterate. Also, the National School Boards Association released a report showing that segregation of Hispanic students in public schools had been growing steadily for two decades, especially in urban areas.

One group singled out for attention in 1992 previously had been mostly in the background, as far as research and interest were concerned. However, an American Association of University Women (AAUW) report, "How Schools Shortchange Girls," addressed the issue of gender bias directly. Summarizing more than 100 sources of data and information, the report found that teachers, the curriculum, and the social atmosphere of schools work against the self-esteem of girls. While starting out at least on a par with boys, girls gradually fall behind, particularly in such areas as science and math. One half of girls who drop out of school do so because they become discouraged and believe they lack ability, according to the AAUW study. It recommended a number of solutions, including strengthening of Title IX, better staff development and curricular materials, better counseling, and attention to bias in testing.

Higher Education. The major happening in higher education was the five-year reauthorization of the Higher Education Act, with negotiations primarily focused on student aid. The new legislation set up one formula for determining student need and allowed families to borrow for college expenses regardless of family income. Although there were hopes that there would be a better balance between aid distributed through grants and aid through loans, the legislation wound up favoring loans. Limits on borrowing for loans were increased significantly.

Meanwhile, the National Education Goals Panel adopted recommendations for measuring the quality and outcomes for higher education, a breakthrough on assessment in this area. It decided the federal level should collect data about higher-education completion rates, including by minority status, and develop a national sampling of indicators of the ability of college or occupational training graduates to use their knowledge skillfully.

ANNE C. LEWIS
Education Policy Writer

EGYPT

In 1992, Egypt marked the 40th anniversary of the revolution that overthrew the monarchy and established the republic. Many of the problems that precipitated the revolution continued to plague Egypt, including a population explo-sion, a deteriorating economy, and clashes between the government and Islamic fundamentalist factions.

The Economy. Although the rate of population increase fell from 2.8% to 2.5% during the year, resistance to government-promoted birth-control measures remained; more than 1.4 million people were added to the country's 56 million, about 100,000 fewer than the increase in 1991. Prior to the revolution, population density in the Nile Valley was 1,400 per sq mi (540.5 per km²); by 1992 it reached 4,000 per sq mi (1 544.4 per km²). In the 40 years since the revolution, Cairo's population had grown from 2 million to 14 million. Despite export of laborers to the oil fields of the Persian Gulf, unemployment was 20%; at least half the 400,000 people entering the work force in 1992 did not find jobs.

The country's debt remained among the largest in the Third World—more than $30 billion. Defense expenditures continued to devour 30% of the government spending, more than three times the percentage before the revolution. Education, which before 1952 accounted for 12% of government expenditures, now received only 6%.

Egypt remained dependent on foreign assistance to keep its economy afloat, although the United States warned that it might have to cut its annual aid package, which in 1992 was about $2.5 billion. Even with lifting controls on agriculture, the country has to import about $4 billion in food annually. The government barely met International Monetary Fund (IMF) and World Bank requirements for assistance. A major goal established by the IMF was to cut back the number of employees in the public sector, which has increased from about 1 million to 4 million since the 1960s.

Inflation was cut from 27% to 18% in 1991, and the Egyptian pound was floated ahead of the February 1992 deadline set by the IMF. These and other austerity measures led the European Community (EC) to offer Egypt support with annual grants of $280 million between 1992 and 1996.

EGYPT • Information Highlights

Official Name: Arab Republic of Egypt.
Location: Northeastern Africa.
Area: 386,660 sq mi (1 001 450 km²).
Population (mid-1992 est.): 55,700,000.
Capital: Cairo.
Government: *Head of state*, Mohammed Hosni Mubarak, president (took office Oct. 1981). *Head of government*, Atef Sedki, prime minister (took office November 1986). *Legislature* (unicameral)— People's Assembly.
Monetary Unit: Pound (3.3195 pounds equal U.S.$1, free-market rate, Nov. 16, 1992).
Gross Domestic Product (1990 est. U.S.$): $37,000,-000,000.
Economic Index (1991): *Consumer Prices* (1980 = 100), all items, 571.5; food, 639.0.
Foreign Trade (1991 U.S.$): *Imports,* $7,754,000,-000; *exports,* $3,617,000,000.

© Thomas Hartwell/NYT Pictures

Muslim worshipers overflow into the street outside a Cairo mosque during a Friday prayer service. Clashes between the Egyptian government and Islamic fundamentalists became more common during 1992, resulting in more than 50 deaths.

Political Affairs. Clashes between government authorities and Islamic fundamentalist factions caused more than 50 deaths in 1992. Violence between Muslim groups and Egypt's 7 million to 8 million Coptic Christians also resulted in a number of fatalities.

The country was shocked in June when Muslim fundamentalists assassinated one of Egypt's foremost political columnists, Faruq Foda, age 49. He was shot on a Cairo street a few hours after announcing plans to form a new interreligious movement. Fundamentalists regarded his books attacking Islamic zealots and other right-wing groups as sacrilegious. In an attempt to maintain a balance between zealots and mainstream Islamic groups, such as the Muslim Brotherhood, the government took action against another writer, Alla Hamed, whose latest novel contained material offensive to pious Muslims. The author, publisher, and distributor of the book were sentenced to eight years in prison.

In response to calls from the security forces for wider powers to deal with terrorism, the People's Assembly passed new legislation imposing the death penalty on anyone convicted of engaging in a terrorist act. For merely belonging to a "terrorist" group the punishment became five years in prison. "Terrorist leaders" and anyone supporting their activity financially would be sentenced to hard labor for life.

Human-rights groups, including Amnesty International and Middle East Watch, reported that 1991 was one of the worst for abuses, including torture and rape, in Egyptian prisons. They blamed this record on continued use of emergency legislation imposed after President Anwar el-Sadat's assassination in 1981.

Earthquake. In October, Egypt's worst earthquake in modern times struck the Cairo area, killing some 550 people, injuring nearly 10,000, and leaving more than 100,000 homeless. Demonstrators in Cairo denounced the government for failure to respond quickly enough to the crisis. Many victims accused the authorities of nepotism, favoritism, and maladministration in distribution of relief funds. In contrast, several Islamic groups responded quickly with rescue efforts and by providing assistance to victims after the disaster.

Foreign Affairs. President Hosni Mubarak continued his role as intermediary between Israel and Arab parties in the Middle East peace negotiations. Relations with Israel were eased after the Labor Party won control of Israel's government in July. In the same month, Israel's new premier, Yitzhak Rabin, visited Cairo, and Mubarak praised Rabin's freeze on construction of new Jewish settlements in the occupied territories.

DON PERETZ
State University of New York, Binghamton

ENERGY

U.S. energy policy took an unusual turn in 1992. It was a year of exceptional calm in the energy sector, with no significant disruptions in supplies or changes in prices of the major sources of energy. Yet Congress, which historically has been spurred to action only by major energy crises, chose 1992 to pass a massive energy bill—the first in more than a decade—that addressed virtually every aspect of the energy sector.

Despite the apparent lack of concern over energy supplies in the United States, the world's most voracious energy consumer, there was growing political support for congressional action. Although the 1991 Persian Gulf war had ended in victory for the United States and its allies and resulted in little change in oil supplies and prices, the conflict served as a reminder to Americans of their heavy dependence on oil from the Middle East and prompted calls to wean the United States from its appetite for foreign oil. Shortly after the conflict ended, the Bush administration had released its long-awaited National Energy Strategy, a broad prescription for improving U.S. energy supplies that provided a ready blueprint for congressional action.

National Energy Strategy. Congress had considered, but failed to pass, energy legislation in 1991. After removing controversial elements of the bill, lawmakers finally agreed to a compromise measure in early October 1992. President Bush signed the Energy Policy Act into law on October 24. The new law's main objective was to decrease U.S. dependence on foreign oil by increasing the production of domestic energy resources. To this end, some of the measure's key provisions encouraged greater competition in the electric utility industry, gave tax relief to independent oil and gas drillers, promoted the use of non-gasoline fuels for cars, and facilitated the licensing of nuclear-power plants.

Oil. The principal source of energy in the United States, oil accounted for 41% of the energy consumed in 1992. Of the almost 17 million barrels Americans consumed each day, nearly half came from overseas, largely the Persian Gulf. Because domestic oil production had been declining for several years, the country was expected to continue to depend on foreign oil for years to come. An important reason for oil's continuing dominance of the energy sector was its price. Despite a temporary disruption of oil supplies from the Middle East caused by the Persian Gulf war, the price of oil wavered little and remained stable throughout 1992 at about $20 per barrel. At that price, low by historical standards, there was little incentive for Americans to save fuel by cutting down on their driving or buying more fuel-efficient cars. As a result, the warning provided by the war only a year earlier fell on deaf ears in 1992, and oil consumption continued virtually unchanged.

As a way to boost domestic oil production and reduce the country's dependence on oil imports, the Bush administration, backed by the domestic oil industry, had asked Congress to open Alaska's Arctic National Wildlife Refuge to oil drilling. But the refuge, one of the last potentially rich sources of domestic petroleum reserves, also is a fragile ecosystem, and environmentalists convinced Congress to drop the drilling provision from the new law. Another controversial measure called for tighter gasoline-mileage standards for cars, a step supporters said could save 2 million barrels of oil per day. Because transportation accounted for more than 11 million barrels of oil consumed in the United States each day, greater fuel efficiency would reduce both the demand for oil and the release of pollutants into the atmosphere produced when cars burn gasoline. But in the struggle over this measure, environmentalists lost out to U.S. automakers, who claimed the design changes required to meet tighter fuel standards would be too costly and further would undermine the beleaguered industry's ability to compete with foreign automakers.

Coal and Natural Gas. Of the three fossil fuels, oil remained the most heavily used but the least abundant in the United States. The other two fossil fuels, coal and natural gas, each accounted for just less than a quarter of U.S. energy consumption. Because both were in abundant supply, the United States was self-sufficient in coal and gas and was expected to remain so for the foreseeable future.

The push for cleaner air opened new avenues for natural-gas use, especially as an alternative fuel for automobiles. Although it emits fewer pollutants than gasoline when burned and is about half as expensive, natural gas fueled only one car in 6,000 in the United States in 1992. Because there was not yet a solid market for natural-gas vehicles and few gas stations sold natural gas at the pump, most of the existing natural-gas vehicles in operation were fleet vehicles—such as delivery vans, taxicabs, and buses—that tended to have a limited travel range and could refuel at a common site. But the market for natural-gas-powered vehicles was expected to grow steadily, especially in California and other states that had imposed stiff clean-air regulations due to go into effect over the decade.

Coal retained its place as the cheapest fossil fuel and was the leading energy source for electric-utility plants and industrial facilities. But coal is the dirtiest fuel, emitting particles that contribute to urban smog and that cause the acid rain which has killed trees and aquatic animals in parts of the Midwest and the East. To improve the efficient use of coal and enhance its value as an export commodity, the Energy Policy Act contained provisions aimed at improving "clean coal" technologies, seeking ways to make coal useful as a transportation fuel, and boosting exports of this abundant resource.

Conservation Efforts. As the population continued to grow, so too did demand for electrical power, the fastest-growing energy sector. Demand for electricity was expected to increase by 40% in the 1990s, and utilities in many parts of the country were considering plans to expand their capacity by adding new coal-fired plants. But many utilities resisted adding expensive new power plants to meet the growing demand for electricity. The year saw further advances in an electricity-conservation trend that began in the late 1980s, when some electric utilities discovered that helping their customers save electricity could be cheaper than adding new plants to generate it. Entering into partnerships with industries, utilities were able to help some of their biggest customers reduce their consumption of electric power by as much as a third by offering rebates for investments in energy-saving technology.

Despite their usefulness to customers and the utilities, these partnerships generated complaints from companies that had cut their energy consumption on their own. They charged that the utilities gave an unfair advantage to their competitors, who benefited from the partnerships. Because the legal challenges were only beginning to arise during the year, it was unclear how the conflict of interest between competitiveness and conservation would be resolved. In a nonbinding ruling in one such case, a New York administrative judge in December ruled in favor of conservation by recommending that all industrial customers should help pay for an upstate utility's conservation program, just as they already had contributed to the power company's other costs.

Nuclear Power. Once considered an ideal energy source because of the almost inexhaustible supply of uranium, the fuel used to drive nuclear-power plants, nuclear power hit the skids after 1979. That year the Three Mile Island nuclear-power plant near Harrisburg, PA, underwent a partial core meltdown, leading to a halt of new nuclear-power facilities in the United States. Opposition to nuclear power continued to build with the accumulation of radioactive waste from the country's 110 operating atomic power plants and peaked after the disastrous explosion in 1986 of the Chernobyl nuclear-power plant in the Ukraine.

Opposition to nuclear power continued to prevent the expansion of this sector of the energy industry. Moreover, in June demolition crews tore down a lasting vestige of the once-booming nuclear industry, the Shoreham nuclear plant on Long Island, NY. Approved by the Nuclear Regulatory Commission in 1985, the $5.5 billion facility had operated for only 30 hours before local governments and New York state blocked its operation out of concern for the plant's emergency evacuation plans.

Despite continued opposition from environmentalists and fearful citizens who refused to live near them, nuclear-power plants provided about 20% of electricity consumed in the United States during 1992. The Energy Policy Act sought to ease the industry's plight by simplifying the licensing procedure for new nuclear-power plants. The law enabled utilities to obtain a combined construction and operating license for such a plant, replacing the two-step licensing procedure previously in effect. The law also authorized research-and-development programs to commercialize advanced reactor technologies.

Alternative Energy Sources. Experts agreed that the best way to avoid the problems of dependence on foreign energy sources and environmental degradation related to the consumption of traditional energy sources was to turn as much as possible to energy sources other than fossil fuels and nuclear power. By harnessing the energy stored in flowing water, wind, subterranean steam, and sunlight, the United States could obtain the energy it needs without destroying the environment or placing its economic viability in the hands of foreign countries. Despite the obvious allure of alternative energy sources, however, they have been slow to penetrate the U.S. market, providing barely 8% of the total demand for energy in 1992.

The two most widely used renewable energy sources were hydropower and biomass, which together accounted for 93% of the renewable-energy market. Hydropower, the generation of electricity by about 49,000 dams around the country, was the only renewable energy source that had been exploited almost to capacity: By the 1990s there were few remaining river sites suitable for profitable dam construction. Biomass, the other renewable source that was used widely, involves the burning of wood, agricultural wastes, and municipal garbage to generate heat and electricity. A fairly recent addition to the renewable-energy industry, biomass held the promise of being a viable source of electricity for many communities that had yet to build facilities to burn it.

The other renewable energy sources, which together provided just 7% of the energy from renewable sources during the year, offered enormous potential for future development. Wind farms, which use wind-driven turbines to generate electricity, appeared largely to have overcome the technical problems that had hobbled their initial development in the early 1980s. The cost of wind-driven electrical power fell from about 40 cents per kilowatt-hour (kwh) in 1980 to less than 9 cents by 1992, and was expected to fall below a nickel by 1995.

Confined largely to a few mountainous sites in California, wind farms offered a cheap, clean source of energy that provided more than 1,600 megawatts (MW) from about 18,000 turbines during the year. But 16 other states, mostly in the Great Plains, were thought to be even more suitable for wind-farm development. Although current wind-driven turbines could meet 10% of U.S. demand for electricity, they have a major drawback: When the wind dies down, they cease producing electrical power. For this reason, utilities, accustomed to having a continuous supply of electricity from their coal-fired plants, continued to balk at purchasing these facilities.

Twenty years after it first was proposed as the answer to gasoline shortages, solar energy had made relatively little headway. The main obstacle remained cost: Power from photovoltaic cells, which convert the energy in sunlight to electricity, cost 30 cents per kwh in 1992. That was only one tenth its cost 20 years earlier, but still was four to six times the cost of power from fossil fuels. Another drawback of solar energy was its confinement to the Southwest and a few other parts of the country that receive enough intense sunlight to make it an efficient energy source.

Geothermal energy, obtained by tapping into underground reserves of superheated water and steam, provided electricity for 3 million households during the year, almost all of them in California. While the cost was competitive, at about 4 to 8 cents per kwh, the potential for further development of geothermal energy was limited by the geographical remoteness of most known resources. Technical problems also appeared to limit its use: The Geysers, a vast geothermal field located near San Francisco, underwent a sudden drop in steam pressure as production increased, jeopardizing the prospects for future production in this $3.5 billion facility.

Clinton Election Impact. With the election in November of Arkansas Gov. Bill Clinton as U.S. president, the link between energy policy and environmental policy seemed likely to grow stronger. Clinton called repeatedly during the campaign for reducing oil imports and tightening auto fuel-efficiency standards. He also chose as his running mate Tennessee Sen. Al Gore, a well-known environmentalist who strongly endorsed the development of alternative fuels and energy conservation.

Clinton sent another signal of his intention to focus more heavily on conservation than on production of energy with his selection of Hazel R. O'Leary to head the Department of Energy. O'Leary, an executive at the Northern States Power Co. in Minneapolis and formerly an energy official in the Ford and Carter administrations, was involved with energy-conservation efforts both as a utility executive and government official. Commenting on the issue

© Ira Wyman/Sygma

Hazel R. O'Leary, 55-year-old energy company official who had served in both the Ford and Carter administrations, was named secretary of energy by President-elect Clinton.

of government regulation of energy, O'Leary pointed out at the time of her appointment to the cabinet that she had "regulated the [energy] industry broadly" in the public sector and had seen such regulation from the view of the private sector as well. She noted that "in the private sector, I've been forced to live with those regulations and, perhaps more importantly, I've seen how these regulations if not carefully crafted and balanced can impact jobs and lives and economies of people who expected and hoped for better from government."

President-elect Clinton's pick to head the Department of the Interior, former Arizona Gov. Bruce Babbitt, also signaled a new emphasis on conservation. The Interior secretary would have influence over the use of federal lands for private use, including oil drilling. While Babbitt promised to continue "making available the natural sources" of federal lands to support local economies, his strong record in conservation gained him the endorsement of environmental groups.

Both O'Leary and Babbitt were confirmed to their cabinet positions by the Senate and were sworn into office on Jan. 22, 1993.

MARY H. COOPER
"CQ (Congressional Quarterly) Researcher"

ENGINEERING, CIVIL

The most heroic civil-engineering efforts of 1992 saved downtown Chicago, IL, from almost complete immersion during a major flood on April 13. In other developments, engineers introduced futuristic technologies to road travel and repair; buildings of fabric construction were becoming more popular, safer, and economical; and engineers were trying new methods to clean up hazardous waste sites.

Chicago and Other Water Projects. About 24 buildings and Chicago's subway system were flooded when a breach in a 90-year-old, 50-mi (80-km)-long underground freight-tunnel system caused water to seep throughout the downtown area. More than 70 buildings lost power and companies sent thousands of workers home. Initially, engineers attempted to plug the tunnel hole by pouring material into the Chicago River at the point of the breach. When this method did not work, engineers drilled access shafts throughout the tunnel system and dropped sandbags from a bucket loader. Once the flow abated, crews constructed more substantial concrete plugs and eventually drained an estimated 130 million gallons of floodwater from the tunnel system. By May 22 the area had been dewatered and crews began to construct permanent concrete bulkheads in the tunnel system. (*See also* CHICAGO.)

The U.S. Army Corps of Engineers completed a major overhaul of the Mississippi River in 1992. Corps engineers installed 13 bendway weirs along the river's Dogtooth Bend, about 160 mi (258 km) south of St. Louis. Bendway weirs are totally submerged rock structures that are directed upstream at a 30-degree angle to the main river flow. The weirs give engineers a new method of improving navigation channels and preserving the river environment. In effect, they deceive the river into flowing in a straight channel. Currents no longer are directed downward to dig the channel deeper and sediment is captured between the bendway weirs rather than building up as a sandbar.

Award-Winning Bridge. The West Seattle Swing Bridge was awarded the 1992 American Society of Civil Engineers Outstanding Civil Engineering Achievement Award. The $33.5 million structure is the only double-leaf, hydraulically operated, concrete swing bridge in the world. Its swing motion relies on oil hydraulics in a pressure and friction application. The hydraulic system lifts and rotates two 413-ft (126-m) bridge leafs, each weighing 7,500 tons, in just four minutes.

Fabric Structures. In 1992 construction using fabric framework made advances in structural engineering. Although these structures have been built worldwide since the 1970s, only recently have they become a safe and economical, as well as aesthetic, building alternative.

The Atlanta Falcons football team moved into the Georgia Dome in September. The dome is covered by a 748-ft (228-m), lightweight Teflon-coated fabric roof. While many such covers are supported by mechanically blown air, the Georgia Dome roof is supported by a complex truss system of poles suspended from cables at the top of the structure that does not block spectator views.

The largest cable-supported fabric roof in the United States covers the main terminal of the Denver International Airport, which was set to open in 1993. The $18 million roof covers a 1.45 million-sq-ft (134 705-m^2) area. Seventeen tent-like modules spaced 60 ft (18.3 m) apart are supported by two rows of masts spaced 150 ft (45.7 m) apart. Most of the masts rise 104 ft (31.7 m) above the main floor. Two groups of four masts each located at the borders between three terminals are 125 ft (38.1 m) high. The fabric membrane extends beyond the periphery of the walls, which are glass.

Transportation. Highway engineering saw the $150 million Strategic Highway Research Program (SHRP) come to the end of its five-year authorization. The program worked toward new developments in asphalt, concrete, and highway operations and maintenance, and included a $41 million Long Term Pavement Performance program. It created more than 50 products and performance tests. One such product, a robotic pavement-crack sealer, may save states significant time and money in road maintenance. According to SHRP, 37 states spent almost $50 million on highway-pavement-crack sealing in 1991. The researchers believed that the crack-sealing robot system might slash those costs substantially.

The prototype, under field trial in 1992, uses a combination of video-imaging and electronic-range scanning to identify, locate, and map routed cracks of 0.9 inches (2.29 cm) with an accuracy of better than 0.5 inches (1.27 cm). The system consists of a lead vehicle towing a robot arm that transports generators, computers, sensor-processing hardware, controllers, and a video camera. The system then returns to the crack and fills it with sealant material. Officials estimated the system would cost approximately $100,000, with $75,000 in annual operating and maintenance costs.

After ushering in the era of freeway travel, people in the Los Angeles area were seeing the completion of the area's last major thoroughfare, the $2.2 billion Interstate 105 Glenn Anderson Freeway. Sometimes known as the Century Freeway, it has been under construction since the early 1980s and includes high-occupancy vehicle lanes, a light-rail-trolley line, and stations in the median. Sensors embedded in the pavement will transmit traffic information to an operations center.

Waste Treatment. Civil engineers continued to search for innovative technologies that could

© Ralf-Finn Hestoft/Saba

Workers in Chicago, IL, fill in a retaining wall in the Chicago River that collapsed in April 1992, causing flooding in the city's underground tunnel system. Many downtown buildings with access to the tunnels were forced to close.

clean contaminated soil and groundwater. In 1992 the U.S. Environmental Protection Agency (EPA) approved the first North American application of a cleanup technology known as soil washing. The method, in use in Germany and the Netherlands for some ten years, was being tried at an undisclosed site in the "Superfund" cleanup program. Soil washing removes almost 100% of heavy metals and semivolatile organic chemicals often found in contaminated soils. The tainted soil is washed with a special detergent that separates contaminants from the soil. The clean soil then is returned to the site.

European methods also were entering the wastewater-treatment field. Sludge treatment and disposal became an issue in the 1970s, when the advent of secondary wastewater treatment produced twice as much sludge as did primary treatment. Many municipalities in Canada and the United States were turning to European-style sludge digesters—structures that mix sludge until it breaks down, leaving about half as much to dispose of. The large, egg-shaped digesters cost more to build but are much more efficient than the typical North American flat, cylindrical tank models.

TERESA AUSTIN, *Free-lance Writer*

ENVIRONMENT

Politics and economics played a role in many of 1992's environmental highlights—from clean-air protection to endangered birds.

Ozone Holes. The year brought further signs of a deterioration in Earth's protective stratospheric ozone layer—a high-altitude band of gas that shields out biologically damaging ultraviolet rays from the Sun. As during every Antarctic spring since 1987, scientists detected a worsening "hole"—zone of thinned ozone—in the southern polar skies. By September 23 the hole spanned 8.9 million sq mi (23.1 million km²), an area nearly as large as North America and 15% larger than 1991's hole.

There were other worrisome signs elsewhere. In February, ozone thinning over North America averaged a record 15% above normal, according to experiments of a National Aeronautics and Space Administration (NASA) team of 80 international scientists. And while many researchers initially had downplayed the likelihood of an Arctic hole ever forming, the new data suggested such a hole should now be expected within ten years.

Responding to the new data, U.S. President George Bush announced in February that the United States would expedite its phaseout of chlorofluorocarbons by Jan. 1, 1996, four years earlier than called for under the Montreal Protocol. On November 25, representatives of more than half the world's nations agreed to revise that treaty, matching the new U.S. phaseout for chlorofluorocarbons and initiating regulations of three new ozone-destroying pollutants.

Erosion. In late March the United Nations released the first global survey of soil erosion and degradation. Its data showed that since World War II, human activities have damaged more than 3 billion acres (1.2 billion ha) of agricultural land so badly that reclaiming the acreage would prove difficult or impossible. Affected regions totaled an area greater than China and India together.

Almost 22 million acres (8.9 million ha) no longer can support vegetation, the survey found. Some 740 million acres (299.5 million ha) more require restoration efforts greater than most developing nations can afford—even though these degraded lands reside predominantly in developing countries. Approximately 35% of the degradation was attributed to overgrazing by livestock, 30% to deforestation, and 28% to bad farming practices such as overfertilization or abandoning fallow cycles.

Air Pollution. The U.S. Environmental Protection Agency (EPA) issued a flurry of new air-pollution news and regulations in the weeks directly preceding the presidential election. On October 19 the agency released its annual urban-air-trends report, confirming overall progress in reducing the six pollutants for which EPA has issued primary air-quality standards: smog, lead, sulfur dioxide, carbon monoxide, particulates, and nitrogen dioxide.

On October 26, EPA announced phased-in final rules aimed at cutting allowable sulfur-dioxide emissions from electric-power plants. By 1995 the biggest coal-burning utilities must begin lowering their emissions. Smaller utilities must initiate stricter sulfur controls by 2000. The result: By 2010 sulfur-dioxide emissions from these plants should total 10 million tons—just half the level they emitted in 1980.

The next day, EPA issued rules to cut nitrogen-oxide emissions from electric-power plants. Two days later, on October 29, it released the first proposed "air toxics" rule called for under the Clean Air Act. The new regulations were expected to limit the chemical industry's air emissions of volatile organic chemicals by up to 80%. Not only are many of these toxics suspected of causing cancer, but they also contribute, along with sulfur dioxide and nitrogen oxide, in fostering the production of smog in urban air.

On October 30, EPA required the initial dispensing of specially blended automotive fuel. By increasing the oxygen content of fuels sold in the 39 most polluted metropolitan regions, EPA hoped to cut carbon-monoxide emissions from cars and trucks by 15% to 20%.

Pollutant Trading. In May the Chicago Board of Trade received federal authority to launch a futures market in sulfur dioxide. Under 1990 revisions to the Clean Air Act, companies that emit less of this smog-and-acid-rain-fostering pollutant than normal can sell to other companies some share of their "right" to pollute. Within a week, three coal-burning utilities negotiated emissions "swaps." Wisconsin

Power and Light agreed to sell at least 15,000 allowances (rights to 15,000 tons of sulfur-dioxide emissions) to Duquesne Light Co. of Pittsburgh and another 10,000 allowances to the Tennessee Valley Authority.

Pesticide Costs. Roughly 2.5 million tons of pesticides are sold globally each year at a retail price of about $20 billion. An estimated 500,000 tons of those—worth $4.1 billion—are used in the United States each year. Overall, U.S. farmers save about $4 worth of crops for every $1 of pesticides they apply. However, a recent study by David Pimentel and others of Cornell University calculates the additional environmental and social costs of pesticide use—from farm-worker poisonings to deaths of beneficial insects and a growing resistance of crop pests to chemical poisons—at more than $8 billion annually.

Pesticide users directly pay about $3 billion of these extra costs, and then pass them on to consumers. Society pays the remaining $5 billion through higher insurance, medical, and social-service fees, the researchers observed.

In August, EPA issued new rules to protect farm, forest, and greenhouse workers from pesticides—the first revision of these standards in 18 years. For the first time, all workers using pesticides not only must be assigned personal protection equipment—such as rubber gloves and gas masks—as needed, but also must have access to soap, water, towels, or other means of cleaning off accidental contamination. The new rule also established "restricted entry intervals" for all pesticides—periods when workers may not enter newly treated areas.

Gulf War Update. Severe oil pollution attributable to the 1991 Persian Gulf war appeared to have been restricted primarily to the Saudi Arabian coast, within 248.5 mi (400 km) of the spill sites, a group of Monaco-based marine scientists with the International Atomic Energy Agency (IAEA) reported in August. Outside these heavily affected zones, the IAEA survey detected less oil contamination than had been seen prior to the war. The researchers attributed this change to a war-related shutdown in the area's usual oil production and transport operations.

However, another international team of researchers, headed by Naser Sorkhoh of the University of Kuwait, found very little natural recovery within the heavily oiled ecosystems. On many oiled beaches, for example, formerly common crustaceans were dead or gone. But the scientists did witness an unexpected and dense growth of blue-green microbial mats atop oil soiling the Saudi coasts, which was felt to represent "the first sign of self-cleaning activity in this polluted region . . . [and] the only living things in this environment."

Wetlands. In recent years, farming and urban development have destroyed huge tracts of native wetlands, areas that provide not only

© B. Nation/Sygma

The U.S. logging industry and environmentalists continued to come into conflict in 1992. The interests of the lumber industry versus preserving the endangered northern spotted owl was a trouble spot and subject of government study.

breeding grounds for birds, fish, and shellfish but also a significant filtering, or cleansing, of water contaminated with pesticides and other pollutants. In August the Bush administration proposed a "redefinition" of wetlands that would have eliminated federal protection from vast expanses of these lands.

The Vice-President's Council on Competitiveness proposed defining wetlands as regions remaining wet all year. Ecologists, by contrast, designate as a wetland any area that stays wet several months per year. In October a federal survey of wetlands protected under the Clean Water Act indicated that at least half the 106 million acres (42.9 million ha) would not meet the new definition. The environmentalists' outcry was so great that the Bush administration never adopted the redefinition.

Condors, Spotted Owls, and Murrelets. In mid-January, Xewe and Chocuyens—two zoo-bred California condors—moved into the wilds, the first attempt by federal conservationists to reintroduce this nearly-extinct animal back into its native habitat. In 1987 the last known wild condor was trapped and brought to join eight others in captivity. By 1992 zoos had bred 52 condors from these captive wild birds.

Also in January a U.S. District Court temporarily barred the Department of the Interior (DOI) from selling rights to log timber from old-growth forests where northern spotted owls had been seen. The decision escalated tensions between logging communities and a group of more than 25 environmental organizations.

A DOI scientist had argued as early as November 1987 for his agency to list the owl as threatened or endangered with extinction—a ruling that should have ended logging of prized timber in many coastal, old-growth forests of Washington, Oregon, and California. But DOI, which also sells timber leases on federal lands, sided with loggers and fought the courts to sell timber rights in forests where the owl lived. In 1990, DOI finally designated the bird as threatened—but refused to protect the owl's habitat, violating the Endangered Species Act (ESA).

When DOI finally issued a draft recovery plan for the owl in May 1992, it tailored the bird's protection to exclude 1.5 million acres (600 000 ha) of forests that scientists had reported was critical to the owl's survival. The limited range would allow breeding pairs to drop by almost 25%—to just 2,300.

While judges, DOI officials, and Congress debated the legality of the recovery plan, scientists began arguing that a neighbor of the owl —a seabird known as the marbled murrelet— needed similar ESA protection of its habitat. However, DOI ignored a series of deadlines to rule on the murrelet's protection, prompting a September U.S. District Court order to act on the murrelet immediately. When DOI refused, the judge banned logging where the murrelet lived—coastal old-growth forests of the Pacific Northwest. By year's end, the issue of federal protection for neither bird was resolved.

JANET RALOFF
Environment/Policy Editor, "Science News"

Earth Summit

From June 3 to June 14, 1992, some 35,000 visitors swarmed into Rio de Janeiro, Brazil, to commemorate the 20th anniversary of the 1972 Stockholm conference—the first United Nations (UN) meeting on the environment. More than 1,000 of the celebrants in Rio were diplomats attending the United Nations Conference on Environment and Development (UNCED), the first formal follow-up to the Stockholm meeting. Better known as the Earth Summit, this gathering drew 118 world leaders, the most ever assembled for a meeting in history.

Most of the remaining visitors attended a parallel environmental conference known as the Global Forum. Amid an at-times Mardi Gras atmosphere, forum participants danced, listened to music, marched in parades, attended lectures, and formed partnerships between nongovernmental groups that spanned oceans and traditional economic differences.

One of the big changes between the Rio and Stockholm conferences was the importance participants placed on dealing with poverty. People who struggle to find food or work have little time or energy to focus on preserving the health of plants and animals around them, a 1987 report to the UN by the World Commission on Environment and Development observed.

And by the opening of the UNCED, that view became doctrine. "Although at Stockholm only lip service was given to the notion that economic development was the solution to environmental degradation in the Third World, this idea was the bedrock of the Rio conference," wrote Edward A. Parson of Harvard University

and his coworkers in the October 1992 issue of *Environment.*

Indeed, argued UNCED's organizer Maurice F. Strong of Canada, the meeting's aim—to develop "integrated strategies to prevent further degradation of the global environment"—made the summit "the most important conference in the history of humanity." He added, however, "People can't allow their leaders to forget what they promised here."

Chief among those promises were commitments to ratify two new treaties.

Climate Change. Details of the first treaty, a Convention on Climate Change, actually were drawn up prior to the Rio summit.

In 1990 the UN created an Intergovernmental Negotiating Committee (INC) to draft a proposed treaty, based on the scientific findings and policy recommendations offered by a panel of selected experts. But INC deliberations quickly bogged down in debate over the urgency with which nations must begin imposing costly limits on their releases of greenhouse gases such as carbon dioxide.

An accumulation of these gases in the atmosphere could trigger a serious, long-term warming of Earth's climate. Such a warming would shift rainfall patterns, threaten many agricultural belts with drought, melt polar ice, and flood coastal cities.

Along with the 12-nation European Community, several countries had argued strongly for a need to limit carbon-dioxide releases to 1990 levels by the turn of the century. The United States not only contended that such limits were premature, but also that any emis-

© Cham-Mendes/Sipa

Amid much ceremony, some 35,000 delegates from more than 170 nations attended the United Nations Conference on Environment and Development (UNCED)—commonly known as the Earth Summit—in Rio de Janeiro, Brazil, June 3-14, 1992.

France's President François Mitterrand adds his signature to indicate his presence at the Earth Summit and his concern with environmental issues.

© Cham/Sipa

sion controls should extend to all warming gases, not just the leader: carbon dioxide.

At a May 9, pre-Rio negotiating session in New York City, INC chairman Jean Ripert of France drafted a compromise. This new document—ultimately signed by 153 countries in Rio, including the United States—gave the United States much of what it had asked. Instead of setting binding limits on greenhouse gases, the document merely committed industrialized countries to adopting policies that reduce releases and enhance absorption of greenhouse gases.

Biodiversity. Delegates representing 153 nations signed a second proposed treaty at Rio —this one aimed at protecting plants and animals in their native habitats. The United States was notable for its refusal to back this pact.

U.S. President George Bush explained the U.S. position, saying that provisions in the document "threaten to retard biotechnology and undermine the protection of [patentable] ideas." He also predicted that overall U.S. "efforts to protect biodiversity itself will exceed requirements of the treaty." Because several other wealthy nations also had threatened not to sign the proposed treaty, negotiators worked throughout the summit to reach a compromise. The final proposal asked ratifying nations to develop strategies for not only the conservation of but also the sustainable use of animals and plants. Countries that are home to a species also deserve to reap some unspecified "fair" share of profits or technology (such as a cancer treatment) based on that species, the document said. Finally, the convention called for nations to begin inventorying the plants and animals threatened with extinction.

Legislatively, the Convention on Climate Change must be ratified by 50 countries and the Biological Diversity Convention by 30 in order to become treaties. Such ratifications could take several years.

Agenda 21. The summit also yielded an 800-page plan for charting and galvanizing international cooperation on environmental protection and sustainable development. Known as Agenda 21, this broad-spectrum charter— or "agenda for action"—was the only UNCED document that attempted to marry environmental protection and economic development through coordinated goals and priorities. Its recommendations ranged from eradicating poverty and combating deforestation to limiting the illegal traffic in toxic chemicals and developing legal means for prosecuting "environmental crimes"—such as the deliberate destruction of large-scale ecosystems.

The Follow-up. By November two new institutions had been created to encourage the implementation of goals endorsed at UNCED. The first was a new UN agency, the Sustainable Development Commission. Designed to monitor how governments follow through on the promises they made at UNCED, it requires that nations regularly report on their progress in achieving measures outlined in Agenda 21. The 53-member governing board also will accept reports from nongovernmental agencies —providing a court, of sorts, through which outside critics can point out notable failures or successes. Strong helped set up one such new nongovernmental agency, an Earth Council, headquartered in Costa Rica.

The biggest impediment to effective follow-up, most UNCED observers said, probably would be financing. Projections of the cost to carry out Agenda 21's goals exceeded $120 billion. At Rio, however, funding pledges from developed nations totaled only about $3 billion to $5 billion.

JANET RALOFF

ETHIOPIA

With the unity of the one-year-old government unraveling, Ethiopia was beset by civil strife in 1992. Meanwhile, Western nations, whose attention was focused elsewhere, reduced their aid to a trickle despite the onset of yet another extraordinary drought.

Civil Strife. Just one year after the transitional government of Meles Zenawi took power under the banner of unity and democracy, the government coalition disintegrated. In January opposition to the Christian and Tigrean domination of the government erupted in the Muslim Oromo regions of Arusi and Wallega. The Oromo Liberation Front (OLF) maintained that President Meles' domination of the Ethiopian People's Revolutionary Democratic Front (EPRDF) was skewed in favor of Tigrean Christians. The Oromos are the junior partner in the government, representing about 40% of the population, while the EPRDF is the senior partner. Government troops fought skirmishes in both regions and, in addition, had to contend with violence perpetrated by former members of the army who were made destitute when the Marxist government of Mengistu Haile Mariam was overthrown in 1991.

In early June 1992 elections were held to select representatives to 14 regional assemblies. The OLF boycotted the elections, accusing the government of manipulating the vote. The New York-based African-American Institute, which had sent electoral observers, also claimed widespread fraud and abuse. A few days after the election, the OLF withdrew from the government coalition, raising the prospect of another civil war. Indeed, one member of the government maintained he could "see civil war ahead." Even with the defection, however, the EPRDF maintained its control of the government.

Reduced International Aid. Despite its efforts at creating a democracy, Ethiopia's government had to contend with vastly reduced economic aid from the United States. The reduction came for several reasons. Not only was there a certain amount of election-year hostility to foreign aid in the United States but there also was a great focus on problems in Russia and the states that once made up Yugoslavia. Additionally, Ethiopia was in arrears in its debt payments to the United States and there were legislative prohibitions on providing aid to foreign governments that are in arrears. For these reasons, the $60 million in economic aid that the Bush administration earmarked for Ethiopia in 1992 did not win congressional approval.

The World Bank, however, organized a $672 million aid program to help Ethiopia rebuild after two decades of civil war and Marxist rule. The monies, approved in February, were to be used for medical aid and the construction of roads, bridges, and schools.

Famine. The United Nations Food and Agriculture Organization (FAO) and the World Watch Institute, an environmental group based in Washington, DC, maintained in March that eastern Africa from South Africa to Egypt was in the grip of the worst drought of the century. The drought, which began in 1992, could cause chaos in Ethiopia, where food shortages already existed and, according to the FAO, millions urgently needed food assistance. The potential for civil war and insufficient Western concern portended an alarming famine crisis.

Domestic Affairs. Meles committed Ethiopia to a free-market economy in 1992. The trucking and transportation industries were being turned over to private ownership, along with many service industries. A new investment law offered tax breaks in food processing and civil aviation.

The remains of former Emperor Haile Selassie I—who died mysteriously in 1975, one year after being toppled by Marxist revolutionaries—were found in February in a grave on the grounds of the Imperial Palace. His remains were reinterred in Trinity Cathedral on July 23, the 100th anniversary of his birth.

A new Patriarch of the Eastern Orthodox Church, Abuna Paulos, was selected in July. A Tigrean, Paulos had been imprisoned for seven years by Mengistu's government.

Eritrea. Efforts were under way to establish Eritrean independence firmly after 30 years of rule by Ethiopia, which had annexed the former Italian colony in 1962. Although the occupation army was routed in 1991, a referendum on the issue was not scheduled until 1993.

The provisional government had to contend with an antiquated infrastructure, severe drought, and a light manufacturing sector that was destroyed almost completely by war. Nonetheless, the government was pushing forward and refugees who had fled to Sudan during the years of fighting were returning home.

PETER SCHWAB
State University of New York at Purchase

ETHIOPIA • Information Highlights

Official Name: People's Democratic Republic of Ethiopia.
Location: Eastern Africa.
Area: 471,776 sq mi (1 221 900 km²).
Population (mid-1992 est.): 54,300,000.
Chief Cities (1988 est.): Addis Ababa, the capital, 1,686,300; Asmera, 319,353; Dire Dawa, 117,042.
Government: *Head of state,* Meles Zenawi, transitional president (took office 1991). *Legislature*—Council of Representatives (transitional; established 1991).
Monetary Unit: Birr (2.07 birr equal U.S.$1, May 1992).
Gross Domestic Product (1989 est. U.S. $): $6,600,000,000.
Economic Index (Addis Ababa, 1991): *Consumer Prices* (1980 = 100), all items, 209.0; food, 211.2.
Foreign Trade (1990 U.S.$): *Imports,* $1,076,000,000; *exports,* $294,000,000.

ETHNIC GROUPS, U.S.

The position of many ethnic groups in U.S. society was getting better and growing more frustrating simultaneously in 1992. Expanded political clout was counterbalanced by continuing inequities in prosperity and opportunity. The frustration over these inequities was seen in violent confrontations.

Politics. Sixty-eight people who are members of various minority groups were elected to the U.S. Congress (including nonvoting delegates) in 1992. This was the largest ethnic representation in history and included 40 blacks, 19 Hispanics, eight Asians/Pacific Islanders, and one Native American.

President-elect Bill Clinton's choice of civil-rights leader Vernon Jordan to cochair his transition team signaled new access to the White House for blacks and other minorities. Democratic Party National Committee chairman Ron Brown; Jesse Brown, a black Vietnam veteran; Mike Espy, a black U.S. congressman; energy-company executive Hazel O'Leary, a black; and former San Antonio Mayor Henry Cisneros and former Denver Mayor Frederico Peña, both Hispanic Americans, were named to the cabinet. In all a record number of members from minority groups were expected to be part of the administration.

Redistricting, tighter enforcement of the Voting Rights Act, and demographic shifts all combined to change the ethnic composition of the U.S. Congress. Most of the congressional victories by minority members came in newly drawn, gerrymandered districts. This had critics worried that segregation would be perpetuated and that multicultural interests would be ignored by minorities and whites. Four southern states elected blacks to the U.S. House for the first time in the 20th century, and Illinois Democrat Carol Moseley Braun (*see* BI-

OGRAPHY) became the first black woman to be chosen for the U.S. Senate.

Hispanic political influence increased with the election of 17 voting members to Congress —including Republican Henry Bonilla of Texas; Lucille Royball-Allard (D-CA), the first Mexican-American woman in Congress; Nydia Velázquez (D-NY), the first Puerto Rican woman in Congress; and Luis Gutierrez (D-IL), who benefited from a newly drawn Hispanic-majority district. For the first time since 1929 there would be a Native American in the U.S. Senate as of January 1993. Ben Nighthorse Campbell, a Cheyenne and three-term Democratic member of the U.S. House of Representatives, won election in Colorado. Redistricting put new Asian candidates on the ballot in California, and such Asian groups as Filipinos and Koreans moved into politics in unprecedented numbers. Jay Kim (R-CA) became the first Korean American elected to Congress.

Ethnic-group representation in government also increased on the state and local levels. This increase shifted the center of minority political gravity away from blacks alone and toward multiethnic coalitions and potential interethnic competition.

In other developments, Mayor Tom Bradley announced in September that he would not seek reelection as mayor of Los Angeles, a post he had held since 1973. Following devastating riots in Los Angeles (*see* SPECIAL REPORT/CITIES) the mayor had replaced controversial white police chief Daryl Gates with Willie Williams, a black from Philadelphia. In Philadelphia, Mayor W. Wilson Goode, a black, retired in January after two terms. In February, Benjamin Hooks, NAACP executive director for 15 years, announced his retirement.

Economic Issues. Heightened political activity grew in part from interethnic conflicts, such

Ronald H. Brown, the chairman of the Democratic National Committee since 1989, was one of four blacks to be selected for President-elect Bill Clinton's cabinet. The 51-year-old lawyer was designated to be secretary of commerce.

as the Los Angeles riots. In the aftermath of the riots, the Bush administration proposed opening up urban enterprise zones, The year's major urban-aid bill, authorizing such zones, passed Congress in October but was vetoed by President George Bush. The president claimed the legislation had been compromised by politics.

U.S. Census Bureau information released in 1992 underscored a structural problem within urban black communities—a lack of black entrepreneurship. Most minority firms had $5,000 or less start-up capital and neighborhood reinvestment had declined. Meanwhile, the federal General Accounting Office reported that black applicants are less likely than whites to receive benefits under Social Security disability programs. In September the federal government for the first time formally accused a mortgage lender of racial redlining. On a positive note, the Federal Bureau of Investigation agreed to change its procedures for promoting and transferring blacks. To counter racism, the Ad Council and the Leadership Conference Education Fund presented a series of television commercials emphasizing the need for tolerance and intergroup cooperation.

Reports by several government agencies and the Children's Defense Fund (CDF) showed that, even though income disparities between whites and most ethnic groups had narrowed during the 1980s, ethnic groups did not benefit proportionally from the economic gains of the period. In 33 states, child poverty rates actually increased.

The CDF report, issued in July, showed that in 1989, 39.8% of all black children, 38.8% of all Native-American children, 32.2% of all Hispanic children, and 17.1% of all Asian-American children lived in families with incomes below the federal poverty line, compared with 12.5% of white children. American Indians suffered especially because federal housing programs are designed for urban areas and thus ignore housing needs on reservations.

Education. Reports on educational progress for ethnic groups showed mixed results. The American Council on Education reported that during the late 1980s blacks and Hispanics made modest gains in college enrollment, while Asians nearly doubled their enrollment. A National Center for Education Statistics study showed that dropout rates for both black and white students age 16 through 24 fell between 1972 and 1991. Hispanics, however, left school at a rate nearly triple the national average.

Although minority-student enrollment was up nationally, the National Education Association reported that minorities remain underrepresented in the teaching profession. One third of public-school students are members of minority groups but only 8% of public-school teachers are black, 3% Hispanic, and 1.4% Asian.

Educational disparities among different Asian groups are narrowing, according to census data. High-school and college graduation rates exceeded those for other groups. Newer Asian immigrants were approaching Japanese Americans and Chinese Americans in high-school and college graduation rates. But class differences divide the groups. Overall nearly 13% of adult Asian Americans have less than a ninth-grade education, compared with a U.S. national average of 10%.

Court Ruling and Federal Policy. The South has become the nation's most desegregated region, in part because of an increase in busing and school consolidation. The future of court-ordered busing, however, was shaken in April when the Supreme Court ruled, 8–0, that school districts did not have to adopt busing or other "heroic measures" to avoid "resegregation" if population shifts cause single-race schools. The Supreme Court also clouded the future of black public colleges with its June ruling that such schools in Mississippi were kept separate and inferior unlawfully.

After the U.S. Department of Education charged that university and law-school admission policies that gave special treatment to minority candidates violated federal law, the law school of the University of California at Berkeley agreed to end the practice of having minority candidates compete against each other rather than the general applicant pool.

Native Americans. Indians continued to protest efforts to take artifacts and bones from reservations. That was the case in May when the Cheyenne River Sioux tribe of South Dakota claimed rights to a dinosaur skeleton on Sioux land. Old treaty rights also were pressed. The Catawba Indians in South Carolina agreed to accept a $50 million payment and an expansion of their reservation in lieu of a suit to recover 144,000 acres (58 300 ha) taken illegally in an 1840 treaty. The federal government proposed in late November that 400,000 acres (161 943 ha) of public land in Arizona be ceded to the Hopi Indians to settle a more than 100-year-old land dispute between the Navajos and Hopis.

In July, Seneca Indians in New York blocked highways and set fires to protest state efforts to collect sales taxes from reservation stores. The issue of taxation threatened to explode everywhere because of a February U.S. Supreme Court ruling allowing states and counties to collect property taxes on privately held Indian land on reservations.

The "fashion" of whites to claim Indian heritage in filing census data expanded when college and university officials seeking diversified enrollments allowed students to declare their ethnicity or race without proof. At the University of Michigan newly declared American-Indian students received financial aid and other benefits reserved for Native Americans. By the fall 1992 semester, Native-American students were asked to declare an affiliation with a specific tribe. Schools in Arizona, Oklahoma, and Colorado also worked to reduce the number of fraudulent claims.

RANDALL M. MILLER
Saint Joseph's University, Philadelphia

EUROPE

The year 1992 was one of disappointment and, in places, of tragedy in both Western and Eastern Europe. The continuing recession exacerbated disagreement over moves to further integration and on enlargement of the European Community (EC). In Eastern Europe and the former Soviet Union, the hopes for sudden prosperity and political harmony following the end of Communist rule in 1989-91 were dashed as production plummeted, currencies inflated, and ethnic hatreds brought vicious fighting from Yugoslavia to Georgia. Refugees fleeing these conflicts joined the thousands of economic refugees from outside Europe, provoking concern and occasional violent xenophobia.

Recession in Western Europe. The high cost of unification of West and East Germany in

Britain's Queen Elizabeth visited Brandenburg Gate in Berlin during her fall visit to Germany. Both Britain and Germany suffered from economic difficulties during 1992.

© Terry Fincher/Gamma-Liaison

1989 was the principal reason for Europe's renewed economic recession from mid-1991. Net transfers from Western to Eastern Germany were expected to be between $78 billion and $98 billion in 1992. Unwilling to impose large tax increases, the government resorted to borrowing, forcing up interest rates and raising credit costs in other EC countries. Economic growth remained low or even negative. Western Germany expected to achieve only 1.5% growth, and the EC as a whole was unlikely to exceed even its 1991 figure of 1.3%. As a result, the Community made no progress in reducing its high unemployment. Britain, with a negative growth rate of 2.4% in 1991–92, had 2.6 million unemployed. Even France, with low inflation and continuing growth, saw its unemployment rise to above 10%. West European voters became increasingly disgruntled. In both national and regional elections, the ruling parties either were defeated or suffered humiliating loss of support. France's Socialist Party won only 18% of the vote in regional elections on March 22. In two regional elections in Germany on April 5, the voters showed their disapproval of Chancellor Helmut Kohl's economic policies and his failure to stem the tide of immigration by giving his Christian Democratic Party its lowest vote in 20 years. In national elections in Italy on April 5 and 6, the Christian Democrats received only 29.7%, their worst showing ever. The unpopularity of the Conservative Party in Britain was so great that it was regarded as an electoral surprise when Prime Minister John Major led it to a narrow victory in parliamentary elections on April 9 with a majority of 21 seats.

Maastricht Treaty Under Attack. In Maastricht, the Netherlands, in December 1991, the European Council, EC's 12 heads of state or government, had approved a treaty for creation of monetary unity and common currency of those members meeting rigid standards of ''convergence'' of their economies. Implementation could be delayed until 1999 if less than seven countries met these standards. The EC was to establish common foreign policies, and to consider ''the means to the eventual framing of a common defense policy, which might in time lead to a common defense.''

Public suspicion of the treaty surfaced in June when the Danes rejected the treaty in a referendum by 50.7% to 49.3%. Although the treaty was ratified easily by a referendum in Ireland in June, the campaign in France was fought hard. On September 20 the French voted in favor of the treaty by only 51% to 49%. When on November 4, Major presented the treaty to Parliament for a preliminary vote, he won a majority of only three. With such lukewarm support, British ratification was postponed until 1993, to permit Denmark's demand for special treatment under the treaty to be met.

© Alain Nogues/Sygma

French farmers marched in the streets of Paris and threw grain into the Seine River in November 1992 to protest General Agreement on Tariffs and Trade (GATT) negotiations on further reducing European Community (EC) subsidies to farmers.

Progress continued toward creation of a completely integrated Community by Dec. 31, 1992. By the Single European Act of 1986, the EC had agreed to streamline voting procedures in the Council of Ministers, to increase the powers of the European Parliament, and to carry out about 170 detailed changes to abolish the remaining barriers within the EC, not only for industrial and agricultural trade, but for other sectors such as banking, insurance, and services. By November the percentage of the required harmonizing laws passed varied between 64% in Belgium and 90% in Denmark. Abolition of frontier controls over the movement of people within the EC proved more difficult. Because of the refusal of Britain, Ireland, and Denmark to abolish passport controls on travelers from other EC countries, France, Germany, Belgium, the Netherlands, and Luxembourg signed an agreement at Schengen, Luxembourg, in June 1990, to abolish passport controls for travel between them, and Spain, Portugal, Italy, and Greece later joined. Implementation of the plan was delayed until at least mid-1993 by the failure of several national parliaments to ratify the agreement.

Enlarging the Community. In October 1991 the seven-member European Free Trade Association (EFTA)—Austria, Finland, Iceland, Liechtenstein, Norway, Sweden, and Switzerland—agreed to form with the EC a European Economic Area (EEA), which would be the world's largest trading bloc. Within the EEA, most industrial goods, workers, capital, and services were to move freely from 1993, while the EFTA countries would contribute $2.4 billion to aid the poorer countries of the EC.

Seven countries sought full membership in the EC. Turkey had applied in 1987, Austria in 1989, Malta and Cyprus in 1990, and Sweden in July 1991. Finland followed in March 1992, but in a December referendum, the voters of neutral Switzerland—who approved membership in the World Bank and the International Monetary Fund in May 1992—refused to join EEA. While all EC members were determined to postpone admission of such relatively poor countries as Turkey, Cyprus, and Malta, they were divided on admission of the wealthy EFTA members. At the European Council in Lisbon on June 26–27, negotiation of the entry of EFTA applicants was postponed until the stalled talks on the EC budget could be resolved and the Maastricht Treaty had been ratified by all 12 EC members. In a major currency crisis in September, Sweden maintained the Swedish krona in parity with the European Currency Unit (ecu) through draconian temporary interest hikes, whereas Britain and Italy both were compelled to drop out of the Exchange Rate Mechanism (ERM) because of their governments' inability to support the value of their currencies. As a result, it appeared that a "two-speed" Europe was emerging, in which the stronger economies like the French and German would accept full monetary union, while weaker economies like Britain's would be allowed to opt out. An emergency summit meeting in Birmingham, England, of the European Council on October

16 made little progress in solving the Community's divisions, although an effort was made to make the Commission's activities more comprehensible to the general public.

A new crisis, however, had arisen over the General Agreement on Tariffs and Trade (GATT) talks, which had been stalled primarily by France's refusal to accept the U.S. demand for further reduction of EC subsidies to farmers. When the United States on November 5 announced it would impose heavy import taxes on such European farm products within 30 days unless agreement on subsidies was reached, the French found themselves isolated within the EC but, faced by violent demonstrations by their farmers, the government warned it might risk world disapproval by vetoing a compromise agreement on subsidies reached between EC negotiators and the United States. At the EC meeting in Edinburgh on December 11–12, the members agreed to allow Denmark to hold another referendum on the Maastricht Treaty and appeared to be near a solution on the aid issue.

Fears and Hopes for Eastern Europe. The collapse of communism in Eastern Europe and the former Soviet Union continued to present enormous challenges to the West, but also some hope for a more prosperous and secure future. The process of ending the military confrontation of the Cold War continued. The 52-nation Conference on Security and Cooperation in Europe (CSCE), meeting in Helsinki on July 9–10, created the office of a high commission for national minorities, with the duty of examining possible new ethnic conflicts that could turn violent. New procedures for arbitrating disputes were to be drawn up. Individual countries or organizations such as the North Atlantic Treaty Organization (NATO) could be called to act for CSCE to provide humanitarian relief or to monitor cease-fires. A Forum for Security Cooperation was to improve security relations between national armies. The states of the former Soviet Union agreed in May on the amount of conventional forces they each would maintain within the limits of the Treaty on Conventional Forces in Europe (CFE) signed in 1990, making it possible for the treaty to come into force provisionally. In June, Russian and U.S. negotiators agreed to reduction of their nuclear warheads from 22,500 to 7,000. NATO continued to reduce the size of its forces and cut back its command structure, while it undertook a new role by enforcing in collaboration with the Western European Union a UN-imposed naval blockade of Serbia in the Adriatic Sea.

Western economic aid for Eastern Europe and the former Soviet Union proved slow and grudging. In April most of the countries of the former Soviet Union were offered membership in the International Monetary Fund (IMF) and the World Bank, while the Western powers reaffirmed their intention of supplying Russia with $24 billion in aid, with the first $1 billion to be paid shortly after the G-7 summit meeting in Munich in July. The only other concession offered by the summit, however, was a promise to consider deferral of repayment of Russia's debt to the West.

The EC proved incapable of ending the civil war in Yugoslavia that had begun with fighting between Serbs and Croats in Croatia in mid-1991 and spread into even bloodier conflict in Bosnia-Herzegovina in 1992. After Lord Carrington, the EC mediator, failed to halt the fighting, in May the EC imposed trade sanctions on Serbia. In August, the EC joined with the United Nations in sponsoring a peace conference on Yugoslavia in London, which sketched out proposals for a Bosnian settlement. In November the Western European Union, composed of nine EC members, agreed to work with NATO in enforcing a naval blockade on Serbia in the Adriatic Sea. (*See also* Feature Article/The Breakup of Yugoslavia, page 38.)

Immigration Problems. The Yugoslav fighting sent a flood of refugees seeking safety. By September there were 2 million refugees within the former Yugoslavia itself, while Germany had received 220,000 Yugoslav refugees. The number of refugees entering Germany in 1992 was expected to reach 500,000, bringing its overall total to 1.4 million. All countries of Western Europe, however, were facing a growing pressure of would-be immigrants, who in 1991 numbered 800,000 from Eastern Europe; 900,000 migrant workers, mostly from North Africa; and 600,000 asylum-seekers from the rest of the world, especially from sub-Saharan Africa.

F. Roy Willis
University of California, Davis

FAMILY

The changing definition of family became a political theme in 1992 as U.S. presidential candidates and even the television comedy *Murphy Brown* raised the issue. Also of great importance—both in the United States and worldwide—were the ongoing concerns over poverty, health, and children's rights.

Politics and the Changing Family. In the Republican Party, the traditional view of family as a household unit of mother, father, and children predominated, with Vice-President Dan Quayle setting the tone in May when he attacked the title character of *Murphy Brown* for her decision to bear a child out of wedlock. Quayle said such a decision mocked the importance of fathers and condoned questionable morals. At the GOP convention, President George Bush had his own extended family, from wife to grandchildren, join him on stage.

The Democrats' view of the family was more inclusive, as presidential candidate Bill Clinton spoke of his "faith in an America that includes every traditional family and every extended family, every two-parent family, every single-parent family, and every foster family."

Such disagreement came at a time when only 26% of U.S. families fit the traditional mold of a married couple with one or more children under age 18. Additionally, one fourth of all U.S. children were born out of wedlock and more single fathers were raising children. Even for childless couples, the definition of family was changing, with the U.S. Census Bureau recognizing "unmarried partners." Heeding this trend, a number of employers began offering such benefits as health insurance to unmarried partners.

There were continuing increases in single-parent families, with 26% of children living with just one parent. Increasingly, fathers were this parent. The Census Bureau reported that single dads headed 14% of the nation's single-parent households. An estimated 380,000 of these men never had been married.

The decade-long decline in marriage rates accelerated sharply in 1991. The Census Bureau reported that one out of every four Americans over age 18 never had been married. Interracial marriages nearly had tripled since 1970. There were 1 million married couples of different racial backgrounds.

Child and Elder Care. Family-oriented legislation made little headway on the federal level in 1992. For the second year in a row, a family-leave bill, providing up to 12 weeks of unpaid leave to care for newborns or sick relatives, was vetoed by President Bush. Although the Senate amassed enough votes to override the veto, the House of Representatives could not. A number of states and even one county— Dade county, FL—adopted such legislation, however.

Private industry also took steps to help employees cope with the competing demands of family and work. A coalition of 137 companies and organizations, the American Business Collaboration for Quality Dependent Care, formed in September with plans to fund 300 programs nationwide to care for employees' children and elderly relatives.

The Labor Department reported that at least 57% of women with children under 6 years old were working outside the home, and the Families and Work Institute said that about 40% of workers expect to care for aging parents.

Economics. With a lack of child support continuing to be a problem, Congress began looking into overhauls of the system. Legislative proposals were expected to be introduced in 1993. Only half of the estimated 5 million women who are entitled to child support get it, according to the Census Bureau. Another quar-ter get less than they are due, and the remainder get nothing. Lack of child support contributes to such problems as escalating welfare rolls and children living in poverty.

A Children's Defense Fund study released in April put the child poverty rate at 40%. The same study showed that the median family income in 1990 had dropped by 6.7% since 1973. The loss of well-paid blue-collar jobs and increases in single-parent and minority families were blamed.

Poverty was not a problem for a select group of Americans—those 660,000 whose incomes exceeded $310,000. An estimated 60% of the growth in after-tax income between 1977 and 1989 went to this group, whose average income climbed to $559,800, according to Congressional Budget Office data. On the other end of the economic scale, the bottom 40% of taxpayers—those with average 1989 incomes of $20,100 or less—saw their pretax income decline by up to 9%.

Health. The American Health Foundation reported during the year that children were less physically fit, more prone to disease, and increasingly likely to die from murder or AIDS than in the mid-1980s. Decreases were seen, however, in smoking and drug and alcohol abuse.

Worldwide, the rapid spread of AIDS and a resurgence of malaria and cholera threatened children's health. By the end of the 1990s, as many as 10 million children will be infected by the AIDS virus, said the United States Agency for International Development. The agency also stated that one third of the children born annually in the developing world are malnourished and that 13 million children die each year from avoidable diseases.

In Russia, where data about social problems just was becoming public, only 14% of children were said to be in good health.

Adoption and Custody. The number of children placed for adoption declined. Only 3% of babies born to unmarried white women were given up for adoption between 1982–88, down from 19% in the years before 1973. Among unmarried black women, a 2% figure remained constant.

Infertile couples were stymied further in their efforts to become parents by the enactment of laws in 18 states sharply restricting surrogate motherhood. A New York state Department of Health report estimated that 4,000 infants had been born to surrogate mothers in the United States.

Questions of parental rights emerged during the summer when a 12-year-old boy legally severed his ties with his biological mother so that his foster parents could adopt him. Gregory Kingsley, who changed his name to Shawn Russ, was seen as an example of how the foster-care system can fail children.

KRISTI VAUGHAN

FASHION

Fashion in 1992 was a bizarre blending of reality and fantasy. Younger designers, competing in a tight economic market, created exaggerated costume looks that owed more than a little to 1960s hippie looks. More-established names went theatrical by ultra accessorizing their designs or juxtaposing salon fashion with hip-hop or ''grunge'' street style.

Hemline lengths dominated the fashion news as Karl Lagerfeld declared the short skirt passé and dropped his hems to mid-calf and the ankle. Designers everywhere followed his lead but cautiously included knee-length hems to ease the shock or offered pants, a safe option.

This new stress on pants gave rise to the single most important trend of the year—the ''dandy'' look. Based on menswear looks but put together with a distinctly feminist stamp, its most adept practitioner was Ralph Lauren. Returning to his menswear roots, he inspiringly assembled a collection of severe but natty trouser suits in flannel and chalk stripes and accessorized them with vests, derbies, canes, ties, and watch fobs. He also stretched the vest into dress looks and pin-striped cashmere knits for day, while adding sequined stripes to gray chiffon for evening pants.

Another proponent of the pure menswear look was Donna Karan, who offset her masculine collection with feminine accessories, such as chiffon scarf ties and wide-brimmed hats.

Other important pants looks were Calvin Klein's bloused-at-the-ankle knits; Giorgio Armani's wider, cuffed tweed trousers; and Christian Lacroix's cropped above-the-ankle styles in menswear checks. More-fanciful versions included see-through wool voiles worn over thigh-high stockings at Chanel, wide black-chiffon pajama looks at Thierry Mugler, as well as Gianni Versace's exaggerated bell-bottoms and Yves St. Laurent's cigarette-leg velvets. The single most important pant shape seen in every collection, however, was the classic five-pocket jean. It was shown in denim and twill in basic blues, as well as in a wide range of bright colors and a variety of prints. Sophisticated versions surfaced in black velvet or satin, while gold lamé or beaded styles were for evening galas. Showstoppers were Marc Jacob's red snakeskin jeans and those at Vivienne Westwood in denim, photoprinted with blowups of Marlene Dietrich's face. But the most popular and profitable jean was in black or brown leather.

Although hemlines dropped to mid-calf or lower, the longer skirts were designed to look anything but dowdy. They mainly were narrow, body-hugging styles done in knits or woven fabrics with stretch fibers and featuring high slit openings, or with zipper or button closures that were meant to be left undone to show the leg. There were versions in see-

© Brian Willer

Important fashion news of the year was reflected in the dropped hemlines of the long narrow skirt that featured high slits, buttons, or zippers for exposing the leg.

through fabrics like tulle, chiffon, or openwork lace and crochet, while others sported loose fabric strips or panels for maximum exposure.

The influence of the 1960s was seen in peasant skirts like the tiered dirndls in soft gauzy cotton and rayon fabrics; and in the revival of the ''broomstick'' skirt—named after the hippie fad of drying the skirt by tying it to a broomstick handle, with the result a pattern of random vertical wrinkles and ridges.

Military looks, an offshoot of the menswear trend, epitomized the blend of practical fashion and costume fantasy that was seen on the runways. Past and present uniforms provided inspiration for plain and fancy jackets, coats, and suits. There were wearable, authentic-looking officer's coats and pea jackets done in loden, melton, or leather; then there were the fanciful versions like the brass-buttoned, braid-bound Sergeant Pepper bandleader jackets at Perry Ellis or Emanuel Ungaro's ''epauletted,'' cropped majorette look. Rifat Ozbek used Custer cavalry jackets and West Point tails in his wild and witty collection, and Complice's ringmaster outfits had sequined lapels and cuffs or frog closures.

© Barthelemy/Sipa

The menswear look for women was a major trend. Pants suits were shown in traditional men's fabrics and cuts and with masculine-style ties and other accessories.

Twin sweater sets continued to be strong and ranged from the Gap's price-conscious cotton duo to the luxurious cashmere pairings seen at St. Laurent and Oscar de la Renta. The skinny ribbed "poor-boy" pullover was another important sweater look that was teamed with the longer, narrow skirts or stretched to mid-calf for the must-have dress look of the year.

Colors. Black—basic and recession-proof—was the color that dominated most major collections, closely followed by gray, navy, and dark brown. Red—ranging from vivid rose to flame orange—was the only major bright color seen and was used most effectively for the evening looks that provided the dazzling finales at Chanel and Anne Klein. The only major designers bucking the black trend were Armani and Calvin Klein, both of whom continued using their trademark neutrals.

The year's print direction was definitely animal: The stripes and spots of wild and tame species—leopards, zebras, ponies, dalmatians—were duplicated on everything from soft silks and woolens to sheer chiffon, leather, and vel-

vet. Reptile prints and snakeskin were the other natural patterns prevalent in clothing and accessories. Retro prints, like patchwork and ethnic patterns, and mini-florals evoked Woodstockian moments.

Accessories. The most important accessories were those related to the "dandy" look. The vest and the crisp white shirt were items that easily and inexpensively transformed many traditional suit looks into a menswear mode and were, by far, the most popular wardrobe additions. Neckties and ascots, suspenders, and pocket handkerchiefs were other choices as were pocket watches, watch fobs, and stick pins in jewelry. There were even spats.

Peace-symbol pendants, ethnic medallions, bangles, earrings, and "love beads" were items related to the 1960s nostalgic trend; and stone-studded or enameled animal pins echoed the stripes and spots in ready-to-wear. Stoles, ponchos, and shawls were back in everything from tweeds to chiffons, and belts were important waist definers for the long sweaters and trousers. The newest handbags looked like boxy beauty cases from the 1940s, but the cleverest were Isaac Mizrahi's satchels and totes built into his leather jackets, or the skirts with pouch pockets with coin-purse openings.

The newest shoes covered the instep; styles ranged from flat menswear oxford looks, to demiboots with several heel heights, to Louis XVI-heeled, bowed or buckled pumps. Platform shoes were a strong look in pumps, and chunky-heeled lace-up granny boots set the 1960s footwear direction.

The beret was still the preferred hat shape, although many preferred sterner shapes. There were Ralph Lauren's bowlers and Rifat Ozbek's oversized "Mad Hatter" toppers. At Chanel, Karl Lagerfeld replaced hats altogether, using papier-mâché wigs in vivid brights.

Menswear. With women's wear preempting their traditional looks, designers of menswear moved toward a more relaxed, dressed-down, uncomplicated dress code. Fabrics were lighter, softer, and more drapable; jackets were boxier, less constructed, and designed to be layered over colorful vests, bulky boxy sweaters, and fuller trousers. The most popular coats were three-quarter length and patterned after casual outerwear like barn jackets, parkas, and duffles. Car coats and bomber jackets in leather shearling and suede were also popular. The Western look was strong, with authentic cowboy gear from Levi and Lee competing with pricey designer versions.

In footwear, Chelsea boots and versions of lug-soled hikers' footwear carried through the dress-down attitude. Wide, rough leather belts with bold brass buckles and narrow, silk knit ties were minimalist accessories of the year.

ANN ELKINS, *"Good Housekeeping"*

FINLAND

In 1992, Finland commemorated the 75th anniversary of independence. Finland had been a Russian grand duchy from 1809, and prior to that was a part of Sweden for many centuries.

Elections. Local elections were held throughout Finland on October 18. The Social Democrats received 27.1% of the vote, a clear lead over the Center Party with 19.2%. In 1991 parliamentary elections, the Center Party had won 25% and the Social Democrats 22.2%. The Swedish People's Party did not do as well in the local elections as in 1992.

Political and Foreign Affairs. Upon the USSR's breakup, Finland's was the first Western government to enter into political agreements with Russia. A friendship treaty, replacing one with the USSR in force since 1948, was signed in Helsinki on January 20. Another treaty dealt with trade and commerce, while a third concerned cooperation in the border regions.

There was strong disagreement within and among the political parties, as well as among Finland's citizens, as to whether the country should become a member of the European Community (EC). Following a bitter controversy in parliament, the EC backers won out and the government submitted an application for membership on March 18. The Finns felt that prior to the signing of a final treaty, measures to protect Finnish agriculture would have to be adopted. It was not expected that Finland would become a full-fledged member until 1997. At the end of October the parliament voted in favor of joining the European Economic Area (EEA).

Although not a member of the North Atlantic Treaty Organization (NATO), the Finnish government decided to send an observer to the June meeting of the NATO Cooperation Council. A summit meeting of the Conference on Security and Cooperation in Europe was held in Helsinki on July 9–10. Fifty-two heads of state attended. After months of competitive bidding, Finland decided to purchase 64 Hornet F/A-18 fighter planes from the U.S. firm McDonnell-Douglas.

Economic Affairs. The increasing role played by women in Finnish affairs was well-illustrated by the Bank of Finland, headed since April 5 by a woman president, Dr. Sirkka Hämäläinen. The shaky position of Finnish banks in general, due to the economic situation, was abated by the government's establishment of a fund totaling 8 billion Finnish marks (about $1.6 billion) to aid the banks with their payment problems and assure their stability.

In August the government finalized its national budget for 1993. At first set at 175 billion marks (about $35 billion), the budget proposal included a gasoline-tax increase and reduced unemployment support, as well as a reduction in agricultural export subsidies and a 4% reduction in the salaries of state and local public employees.

TVK, one of Finland's large labor unions, went bankrupt in August and was dissolved.

Following the devaluation of the Finnish mark in late 1991, it was decided in September to allow it to float. This resulted in an immediate decrease in its value of 16%–18%, but subsequently devaluation was halted at 14%.

Unemployment was a scourge throughout 1992, with the total number of people out of work at 377,000 at the end of September.

ERIK J. FRIIS
"The Scandinavian-American Bulletin"

FLORIDA

In 1992, Florida reeled from Hurricane Andrew (*see* sidebar), a lingering recession, and the deadlock between Gov. Lawton Chiles and a legislature reluctant to enact his economic-reform package. The state gained additional seats in the U.S. House of Representatives.

The Economy. While a slowdown in housing construction hampered the state's economy, Florida's share of international trade increased by 10%, and it led the nation in attracting new businesses. The rebuilding of south Dade county in the aftermath of Hurricane Andrew gave the state's economy a boost. The state, however, remained reluctant to undertake the economic reforms considered essential by Governor Chiles and many financial experts.

Politics. Florida lost significant clout in the U.S. House of Representatives with the retirement, effective in January 1993, of several powerful members of its delegation. The year also brought court-enforced redistricting of U.S. congressional and state legislature seats and the creation of four new seats in the House of Representatives, three of which were for fast-growing southeast Florida.

FINLAND • Information Highlights

Official Name: Republic of Finland.
Location: Northern Europe.
Area: 130,127 sq mi (337 030 km²).
Population (mid-1992 est.): 5,000,000.
Chief Cities (Dec. 31, 1990 est.): Helsinki, the capital, 492,400; Tampere, 172,560.
Government: *Head of state,* Mauno Koivisto, president (took office Jan. 27, 1982). *Head of government,* Esko Aho, prime minister (took office April 1991). *Legislature* (unicameral)—Eduskunta.
Monetary Unit: Markka (5.088 markkaa equal U.S.$1, Dec. 16, 1992).
Gross Domestic Product (1990 est. U.S.$): $77,300,-000,000.
Economic Indexes (1991): *Consumer Prices* (1980 = 100), all items, 199.6; food, 187.4. *Industrial Production* (1980 = 100), 121.
Foreign Trade (1991 U.S.$): *Imports,* $21,711,-000,000; *exports,* $23,111,000,000.

© Walker/"Palm Beach Post"/Sygma

Hurricane Andrew

A 1992 hurricane that carved out a 25-mi (40-km) area of devastation in southeast Florida ushered in a new record for the most expensive natural disaster in U.S. history. On August 24, Hurricane Andrew hit hard just south of Miami after sweeping across the Bahamas. With winds of up to 164 mph (264 km/h) and an 8-ft (2.4-m) tidal surge, the storm topped the weather charts as a Category 5 hurricane. Andrew left an estimated 250,000 people homeless and many more without food, water, telephones, or electricity. The storm was blamed directly for 18 deaths. It was five weeks before power was restored to all affected areas.

By August 27, federal officials had deployed between 2,000 and 5,000 troops to distribute food and clothing, set up tents, and control looting. However, state and local officials criticized civilian assistance as sluggish and disorganized. The Federal Emergency Management Agency (FEMA) took heat for its bureaucratic morass. Others blamed Gov. Lawton Chiles for failing to assess fully the extent of damage and delaying in requesting assistance. Meanwhile, a cascade of private and ad hoc relief teams formed. Donation boxes calling for supplies appeared across the nation.

Damage estimates varied widely, with loss figures ranging from $10 billion to $20 billion.

FLORIDA • Information Highlights

Area: 58,664 sq mi (151 939 km²).
Population (July 1, 1991 est.): 13,277,000.
Chief Cities (1990 census): Tallahassee, the capital, 124,773; Jacksonville, 672,971; Miami, 358,548; Tampa, 280,015; St. Petersburg, 238,629.
Government (1992): *Chief Officers*—governor, Lawton Chiles (D); lt. gov., Buddy MacKay (D). *Legislature*—Senate, 40 members; House of Representatives, 120 members.
State Finances (fiscal year 1991): *Revenue,* $25,754,000,000; *expenditure,* $25,168,000,000.
Personal Income (1991): $252,146,000,000; per capita, $18,992.
Labor Force (June 1992): *Civilian labor force,* 6,591,100; *unemployed,* 559,900 (8.5% of total force).
Education: *Enrollment* (fall 1990)—public elementary schools, 1,369,934; public secondary, 491,658; colleges and universities, 538,389. *Public school expenditures* (1990), $8,885,235,000.

In the presidential contest, George Bush carried Florida and won its 25 electoral votes by a margin of less than 100,000. Democratic U.S. Sen. Bob Graham won a landslide reelection victory over Republican Bill Grant. Elections to the state legislature led to a deadlocked Senate with the two political parties holding 20 seats apiece; the Democrats maintained a solid majority in the House. Florida became one of 14 states to pass an amendment calling for term limits for officeholders.

Governor Chiles and the legislature engaged in a struggle over the budget, with the governor vetoing two budgets before reluctantly accepting a third, which contained only a small portion of his economic-reform proposals.

Crime. Yahweh Ben Yahweh, leader of the Nation of Yahweh, and several of his followers

© Najlah Feanny/Saba

© John Berry/Gamma-Liaison

Initial reports by one insurance-industry group said firms could expect to pay at least $7.3 billion in claims. Hurricane Hugo, which ravaged the South Carolina coast in 1989, had held the record for the costliest storm with an estimated $4.5 billion in insurance costs and $10 billion in damages overall.

In September, Congress passed and President George Bush signed an $11.1 billion disaster aid package for Florida, Louisiana, Hawaii, and Guam. The measure included grants, rebuilding funds, and a variety of loan guarantees, with most of the money going to Florida.

Several months after Andrew hit, the lives of many Dade county residents seemed unalterably changed. With entire communities demolished, more than 10% of the area's population had to seek temporary homes. An estimated 65,000 jobs were lost, at least temporarily. Because of the sudden housing shortage, rents rose precipitously; with a new ban on mobile-home building, many lower-income residents lost the only viable choice they had for homeownership. And, with the abrupt rise in unemployment, the county government was faced with a fiscal crunch that could force it to delay several construction projects.

were convicted of conspiracy in a U.S. district court. Aileen Wuornos, a suspect in the murders of seven men along Florida highways, was convicted of one murder and sentenced to death.

Former Miami Beach Mayor Alex Doud was convicted on one count of accepting a $10,000 bribe from a drug dealer. In a trial under way at year's end, four judges were being tried in federal court in Miami on charges of bribery, extortion, and money laundering. It was one of the largest judicial-corruption trials in recent U.S. history.

A rash of sniper attacks and rock-throwing on Interstate 295 near Jacksonville halted after two youths were arrested in November.

Environment. Federal Judge William M. Hoeveler ordered farmers, the state, and the

federal government to begin a $400 million cleanup of the polluted Everglades National Park and Loxahatchee National Wildlife Refuge. The state created a 34,700-acre (14 042-ha) artificial marsh to act as a filter between the Everglades and nearby farmland.

Sports. The University of Miami Hurricanes football team enjoyed another excellent season after sharing the Division I national championship for 1991.

While baseball's Florida Marlins prepared for their inaugural season in 1993, supporters of a major-league franchise in the Tampa Bay area were disappointed when baseball owners blocked the proposed move of the San Francisco Giants to the area.

PAUL S. GEORGE
Miami-Dade Community College

FOOD

Important food developments in 1992 included a worsening famine in southern Africa and reduced animal-product consumption in Eastern Europe and the former Soviet Union. In an effort to help U.S. consumers make better food choices, the U.S. Department of Agriculture redesigned its dietary-guidelines chart, while the food industry prepared for new labeling requirements.

In the European Community (EC), governments modified food regulations in anticipation of economic unification on Jan. 1, 1993. Leaders of the United States, Mexico, and Canada agreed to a North American Free Trade Agreement (NAFTA), which was intended to encourage unrestricted movement of food and farm products across the borders of the three countries. Under the pact, imports to the United States must meet U.S. health standards.

U.S. food prices had the smallest rise in 25 years and consumers included a greater variety of rice and bakery products in their diets, as well as tropical fruits and specialty vegetables. Increased supplies brought record U.S. and world consumption of chicken and turkey and expanded pork consumption. A rise in U.S. food prices was restrained by large supplies, a recovery in California fruit and vegetable production after severe freeze damage in 1991, and low inflation in marketing costs. U.S. away-from-home food expenditures continued to rise, surpassing 50% of total food costs.

Assistance. Food-assistance programs remained important for many. Developing nations, Eastern Europe, the former Soviet Union, and southern Africa relied on assistance from the United States, the EC, and Japan, while a record number of Americans received food stamps. The Agriculture Department reported that 25.8 million, or about one in every ten Americans, received food stamps in July. Including other programs for the elderly, schoolchildren, infants, and women, an estimated 50 million Americans received assistance.

Labeling. The U.S. food industry and government agencies prepared for a new food-labeling system, to be effective in 1993. Designed to reduce confusion on the nutritional aspects of food products, the changes would expand and standardize nutritional labeling. Fiber and cholesterol information would be listed as well as the more traditional information. Implementation of the changes, which was delayed by a late-in-the-year government dispute, was estimated to cost $2.8 billion.

Production and Supplies. New research techniques showed that dairy cows eventually might produce milk with little or no fat and with naturally occurring characteristics for improved health such as blood-clot-dissolving agents to lower the risk of heart attacks. In seafood production, research focused on increasing supplies from fish farms at lower cost.

The U.S. government's announcement that it would not require specific testing or labeling for a number of genetically engineered food products made it likely that such products would be on the market by late 1993 or early 1994. Proponents of such food argued that it would help increase production while decreasing the use of chemicals. Opponents feared unknown long-term effects.

Global food supplies grew slightly less than world population in 1992, with production restricted by drought in Australia, northern and eastern Europe, the former Soviet Union, and parts of Africa. Consumption in the former Soviet Union fell with rising inflation and unemployment as well as reduced funding for imports. Food supplies were critically short in southern Africa, due to severe drought and political instability. From a global perspective, however, supplies were adequate and permitted more varied diets in rapidly developing and industrialized countries.

ROBERT N. WISNER
Iowa State University

The Food Guide Pyramid

In late April 1992 the U.S. Department of Agriculture released revised nutritional guidelines, including a Food Guide Pyramid, right. The pyramid depicts five basic food groups and shows the recommended number of daily servings from each group. Fats, oils, and sweets are atop the chart and are not classified as a food group. As such, they should be consumed "sparingly."

Fats, oils, sweets
Use sparingly

Milk, yogurt, and cheese
2 to 3 servings

Meat, poultry, fish, dry beans, and eggs
2 to 3 servings

Vegetables
3 to 5 servings

Fruits
2 to 4 servings

Bread, cereal, grains, and pasta
6 to 11 servings

FOREIGN AID

Foreign-assistance programs enjoyed little public attention in the United States during 1992, as voters' concerns over job security, the federal budget deficit, and other pressing domestic concerns dominated the yearlong campaign debates. Despite the dominance of domestic issues, Congress approved the first foreign-aid appropriations bill in two years as the November 3 election day neared.

Changing Priorities. The foreign-aid bill for fiscal year 1993, which President George Bush signed into law on October 6, earmarked $26.3 billion for a wide range of international-assistance programs. The bill's spending priorities reflected the remarkable transformation of the global power balance resulting from the end of the Cold War that had pitted the United States and its North Atlantic Treaty Organization (NATO) allies against the Soviet-dominated Eastern European bloc. Despite many lawmakers' reluctance to provide help of any kind to the United States' former adversary, the foreign-aid package included $417 million in economic and technical assistance for Russia and 11 other republics that once comprised the Soviet Union. A separate measure authorized $800 million to help the former Soviet republics dismantle the Soviet nuclear arsenal. Congress placed some strings on aid to Russia by making payments contingent on "significant progress" in the removal of former Soviet troops from the three Baltic states — Estonia, Latvia, and Lithuania.

To help Russia build from scratch an economy based on private enterprise, Congress appropriated a $12.3 billion increase in the U.S. contribution to the International Monetary Fund (IMF), which lends money to Russia and many other countries for economic development. Many critics of direct aid to Russia favored funneling U.S. assistance through the IMF because it enforces strict economic-performance standards on countries that receive its loans. Critics of this approach, including a bipartisan group of 32 senators, urged that the multilateral agency suspend its strict conditions for Russia, warning that deteriorating economic conditions could favor the return of authoritarian rule there.

The end of the Cold War brought about a decrease in assistance to some of the United States' military allies. Greece, Portugal, and Turkey, fellow members of NATO, no longer would receive military grants to help build their defensive capabilities. Congress replaced those grants with low-interest loans.

Middle Eastern Aid. The changing international landscape left unscathed Congress' longstanding practice of reserving the biggest portion of foreign aid for U.S. allies in the Middle East. The bill provided $3 billion in military and economic aid to Israel and $2.1 billion to Egypt, making those two countries by far the main beneficiaries of U.S. largess.

The foreign-aid appropriations bill also included a five-year program of guarantees for $10 billion in loans for Israel, to build housing for tens of thousands of Jewish immigrants from the former Soviet Union. The loan guarantees had been placed on hold by President Bush to curb former Prime Minister Yitzhak Shamir's policy of aggressively expanding Jewish settlements in territories occupied by Israel. Labor Party leader Yitzhak Rabin, elected in June, promised to limit the growth of some settlements.

AID Under Fire. At the same time that Congress approved funding for foreign-aid programs, the Agency for International Development (AID), the administering agency for those programs came under attack for mismanagement. AID, a semiautonomous branch of the State Department that dispensed $7.7 billion in nonmilitary foreign aid to 80 countries in 1992, long has been accused of wasting funds. In 1992, as public support for foreign programs waned amid growing concern over domestic economic problems, the criticism mounted, and AID even was accused of jeopardizing U.S. jobs. During the 1992 vice-presidential debate, Sen. Albert Gore, Jr. (D-TN) charged that AID had encouraged U.S. manufacturing plants to relocate to Central America, a charge that Vice-President Dan Quayle heatedly denied. The charge stemmed from earlier coverage of this issue by CBS' *60 Minutes* and ABC's *Nightline*. AID came under further scrutiny after Sen. David Boren (D-OK) charged that the agency's program in Mozambique had enabled the African country to purchase $55 million in non-U.S. products. One of the conditions of U.S. foreign assistance is that recipients favor goods and services from the United States over other imports whenever possible.

Some foreign-aid experts said the television reports criticizing AID may have been unfair. But the agency seemed destined for a radical overhaul and was already the focus of a presidential commission, which later recommended that Congress redefine the agency's mission in a changed international environment.

New Directions? It remained unclear what impact the November 3 election of Bill Clinton as president would have on foreign aid. Clinton's repeated campaign charge that his opponent had concentrated excessively on foreign affairs to the detriment of pressing domestic issues may portend the beginning of a less activist period in U.S. foreign policy. On the other hand, Clinton supported the bill providing aid to Russia and the loan guarantees to Israel, the most controversial elements of the foreign-aid appropriations for 1993.

MARY H. COOPER
"CQ [Congressional Quarterly] Researcher"

FRANCE

With his gaze turned increasingly to the history books and his place in them, France's President François Mitterrand envisioned 1992 as the year the French people, under his guidance, would come to the rescue of the European Community's (EC's) ambitious but faltering project for European union. Instead, the traditionally pro-Europe French gave Mitterrand—76 years old and 11 years in power—a scare, by approving a September referendum on the EC's proposed Maastricht Treaty for European union by only the narrowest of margins. The vote, 51.05% for and 48.95% against, confirmed Europeans' cooling to the Community's federalist integration project and revealed a France which, like many of its European neighbors, was turning increasingly in oh itself, estranged from its elected leaders, frightened of economic prospects in a stagnant international economic climate, and more prone to building protective walls around itself than bridges for stronger economic and political links with its neighbors.

The referendum result, interpreted by analysts as the French "yes, but" on Europe, was the country's central event of the year, substantiating the existence of a "French malaise"; revealing a France divided along economic, educational, and urban rural lines; and pointing to the difficulties lying ahead for French leaders. The year left the French in a cranky and pessimistic mood, and there was no indication by year's close that anything—not even the promise of parliamentary elections in March 1993—was up to lifting the clouds.

Domestic Affairs. France had greeted 1992 on an upbeat note, with all eyes turned to the Alpine city of Albertville, in the Savoie region, where the Winter Olympics were held from February 8–23. Putting on the games cost well more than $2 billion, more than two thirds of which was picked up by the French government. Critics, many from outside France, charged the Albertville organizers with destroying the area's delicate ecology for the sake of a show, but the French public appeared to support the government position that the spending on new infrastructure, including some dubious winter-sport installations, would boost an isolated area's economic development.

But the high spirits did not last long, with a series of public scandals dominating attention and fixing the public mood for the rest of the year. First, persistent inquiry by an investigating judge in Rennes, Renaud Van Ruymbeke, kept a spotlight on the questionable financing of Mitterrand's Socialist Party and the illegal financial relations between the party and a private consulting firm. Unsubstantiated reports began surfacing in January that top Socialist officials were being investigated. But in July a bomb exploded with reports that Henri Emmanuelli, former Socialist Party treasurer and current president of the National Assembly, would be indicted in the affair; this finally occurred in September. Mitterrand proposed a revision of campaign financing that would exclude private businesses from making contributions, but the idea was rejected even by his own party. The affair marked the final fall for a party first elected to power in 1981 on the wings of public hopes for more ethical government.

Public dismay over the party financing scandal paled, however, compared with reaction to continuing revelations—which first surfaced in October 1991—that public officials knowingly distributed for transfusion and other emergency use blood contaminated with the HIV virus. Before tainted blood products were removed definitely from circulation, they were used to treat more than 2,000 hemophiliacs—275 of whom died. Hundreds more developed AIDS. In October a Paris court convicted three health officials in the case. Michel Garretta, former head of the National Center for Blood Transfusions, went off to four years in prison claiming he was paying for "the state" and for higher government officials who ultimately

© J. Witt/Sipa

The regions of Vaucluse—including the village of Bédarrides, right, which is at the junction of two rivers—and Ardèche in southeastern France suffered from torrential rains in September 1992.

were responsible, but who were hiding behind a convenient scapegoat.

Regional elections in March revealed the degree of public disenchantment with the ruling Socialists. The Socialist Party took 18% of the vote, down from 30% in like elections in 1986. But the beneficiary of the Socialists' collapse was not the traditional right—down itself to 33% from its 1986 score of 41%—but rather several newer, nontraditional political forces: two ecologist parties (14%) and the far-right National Front (14%). The elections placed France among other Western democracies where traditional political parties recently have experienced identity crises and loss of public support.

The elections also were seen as a new low for disastrously unpopular Prime Minister Edith Cresson. Less than one year after naming the country's first woman head of government—with the idea of energizing and wooing the electorate before legislative elections set for March 1993—Mitterrand dismissed Cresson on April 2 and immediately named Finance Minister Pierre Bérégovoy to take her place.

Bérégovoy, a longtime Mitterrand confidant and architect of France's successful low-inflation and strong-currency economic policies, was assigned to tackle the country's 10% unemployment—a task in which he had made no notable headway by the end of the year. But one of the new prime minister's first actions was to announce full suspension for 1992 of France's nuclear testing on possessions in the Pacific—a decision aimed at wooing France's growing ''green'' political movement into an electoral accord with the Socialist Party.

The Bérégovoy government was no sooner in place than it barely survived a no-confidence vote by the National Assembly over approval on May 21 of a new European Community Common Agricultural Policy (CAP). The reform, designed to cut the EC's skyrocketing farm-support costs—which topped $80 billion in 1992—was attacked by French farmers as the death blow to rural France. Facing sporadic anti-CAP violence throughout the summer, the government decided—while holding one eye to the spring 1993 national elections—to stand against any further compromises in a bitter U.S.-EC dispute on international farm trade.

When the United States and EC reached an agreement on November 20 on cutting agricultural subsidies, French leaders attacked the accord as unacceptable. But with Mitterrand staking his reputation on construction of a more cohesive Europe, any French recourse to veto of the agreement seemed unlikely.

Catastrophe struck in May at the stadium of Furiani, Corsica, when a temporary set of bleachers collapsed only minutes before the beginning of the semifinal game of the French soccer cup, leaving 13 spectators dead and more than 1,200 injured. An investigation re-

© Pigi Cipelli/Sipa

In 1992, French President Mitterrand named a new premier, faced a close vote on the Maastricht Treaty on European union, and went to Sarajevo in Bosnia-Herzegovina, above.

port found that the temporary bleachers, built to accommodate 10,000 additional spectators, had been unsafe. A number of stadium and local soccer officials were convicted of manslaughter or neglect. Another disaster, this time in the form of torrential rains, struck the regions of Vaucluse and Ardèche in southeastern France in September. By the time the rains stopped, 39 people had been killed, 20 of them in the ancient Roman settlement of Vaison-la-Romaine. Many of the victims were campers staying in trailers along the normally tranquil Ouvèze River. An investigation was launched to determine if, as some local observers claimed, a failure to enforce existing building and development codes contributed to the disaster's toll.

In June, Mitterrand responded to Denmark's surprise ''no'' vote in a referendum on the EC's Maastricht Treaty by announcing France would hold its own referendum. A number of opposition political leaders attempted to turn the September 20 vote into a referendum on Mitterrand himself, but surveys showed most of the public voted on the issue of Europe. Public discussion was widespread and animated, and the referendum appeared to rekindle, at least temporarily, French interest in political questions.

But public discontent with institutional authority remained widespread, as was evident in a wildcat protest movement organized by truck drivers in late June to protest implementation of a new point system, based on driving infractions, for revoking driver's licenses. Ten days of truck blockades on some of France's busiest freeways left many tourists and shippers stranded. The blockades were raised after police intervention in some areas, and after agreement on a review of the new system, which was modified by a doubling of the number of ''points'' allowed before license revocation.

A ten-day strike by French truckers protesting strict licensing rules led to more than 160 blockades on France's busiest highways at the beginning of the summer tourist season.

© Alexandra Boulat/Sipa

In September, just more than one week before the referendum on the Maastricht Treaty, Mitterrand was rushed to a Paris hospital for prostate surgery. Doctors announced during the president's six-day hospital stay that he had prostate cancer, but that it appeared to have been caught early enough to allow full recovery. With rumors flying of a possible Mitterrand resignation, however, both Prime Minister Bérégovoy and later the president himself emphasized that Mitterrand intended to remain at the Élysée presidential palace until the end of his mandate in 1995.

With a cold winter setting in, the police chose a late October morning to move in on 200 homeless families of immigrants from Mali, who had set up a camp in a Paris park to protest their inability to locate decent, affordable housing. The families, in some cases separated in the confusion, were loaded on buses and taken to various temporary lodgings—hotels, hospitals, barracks—in the Paris suburbs. Many working adults among the uprooted immigrants complained that the operation took them to lodging that in some cases was two hours or more from their job, and often without access to public transportation. But the operation reflected the public authorities' worries about health conditions during the wet winter months, as well as the French urbanization pattern of reserving the stylish inner cities for the wealthy, and drab, high rise suburbs for the poor and working class.

On November 1 a new antitobacco law took effect, severely limiting the time-honored French right to smoke wherever one pleased. The law—which bans smoking in all enclosed public places, restricts smoking on the job, and requires restaurants and cafés to provide non-smoking areas and sufficient ventilation in smoking areas—was considered revolutionary in a country where 40% of the adult population smokes. The law, which provides for fines of up to $250 for individuals smoking in a non-smoking area and up to $1,200 for businesses found in violation, was attacked by owners of the country's thousands of small restaurants and cafés as antibusiness and undemocratic, but France nevertheless appeared to be following the Western mainstream in pressing nonsmokers' rights.

By the end of the year anticipation of a conservative victory in the March parliamentary elections was so strong that a public debate raged over how Mitterrand would respond to a second political "cohabitation," after his first sour experience with a conservative prime minister in 1986–88. Both former President Valéry Giscard d'Estaing and Paris Mayor and former Prime Minister Jacques Chirac insisted that a second cohabitation was out of the question—suggesting that a conservative victory should lead Mitterrand to resign and call an early presidential election. But squabbles between the two conservative leaders, both of whom have their sights on the presidency, made it perfectly clear that a united conservative front in the next presidential election, whenever it oc-

FRANCE • Information Highlights

Official Name: French Republic.
Location: Western Europe.
Area: 211,208 sq mi (547 030 km²).
Population (mid-1992 est.): 56,900,000.
Chief City (1987 est.): Paris, the capital, 2,152,423,000.
Government: *Head of state,* François Mitterrand, president (took office May 1981). *Chief minister,* Pierre Bérégovoy, prime minister (took office April 1992). *Legislature*—Parliament: Senate and National Assembly.
Monetary Unit: Franc (5.3725 francs equal U.S. $1, Nov. 16, 1992).
Gross Domestic Product (1990 est. U.S.$): $873,500,-000,000.
Economic Indexes (1991): *Consumer Prices* (1980 = 100), all items, 189.9; food, 190.0. *Industrial Production* (1980 = 100), 114.
Foreign Trade (1991 U.S.$): *Imports,* $230,786,-000,000; *exports,* $213,299,000,000.

curred, would be hard to come by. In the face of the right's internecine fighting, Mitterrand painted a serene picture of himself and let the word filter out through aides that he was not the least frightened by prospects for a second cohabitation period. Mitterrand had said he would choose a new prime minister following the elections from the party receiving the largest share of the vote, and at year's end speculation focused on Edouard Balladur, a former finance minister and member of Chirac's Gaullist party, Rally for the Republic (RPR).

Foreign Affairs. In February, Mitterrand received Russian President Boris Yeltsin in a state visit, a year after having snubbed the Russian leader during another Paris visit as a subordinate threat to Soviet leader Mikhail Gorbachev.

At a Franco-German summit in La Rochelle, France, Mitterrand and German Chancellor Helmut Kohl created the first Franco-German army corps, which is to include up to 45,000 soldiers and to be operational by 1995. Touted by the French as the embryo of a future European Community army, the corps's creation was received frostily by the United States—even though the summit's communiqué stipulated, largely at German insistence, that the corps "will contribute to the reinforcement of the Atlantic alliance."

In June, Mitterrand made a surprise visit to Sarajevo, the Bosnian capital engulfed in the Balkans war, to express his solidarity with a besieged population and to attempt to force a break in the blockade of the city's airport. The airport reopened briefly the day after Mitterrand's visit and the president enjoyed a brief rise in his low standing with French public opinion. In August, Mitterrand ruled out any French military intervention in the war, saying, "Adding war on top of war would resolve nothing." By the fall the war seemed almost forgotten; the government declined, along with other Western countries, to take in any appreciable number of soldiers being released from Serbian prison camps, and except for the presence of 1,350 French troops in Bosnia, escorting humanitarian convoys, Mitterrand's bold diplomacy of June seemed far away.

The Economy. France in 1992 enjoyed one of the very best economic performances of all the Western industrialized countries, registering a 2.4% growth in gross national product (GNP) in the second trimester of the year, above Japan, the United States, and Germany. The rate of inflation remained well below Germany's, a key test of France's competitiveness. And in September the French central bank, with solid assistance from the German Bundesbank, effectively resisted speculative attacks against the French franc. If France won a battle against forced devaluation that Britain and Italy could not, it was because "a deval-

© Jon Levy/Gamma-Liaison

A storekeeper adjusts price tags on French wines. A trade dispute led the United States in 1992 to impose sanctions, tripling the price of some Western European wines.

uation of the franc had absolutely no economic justification," said Finance Minister Michel Sapin in an October speech before the National Assembly's economic council. According to Sapin, "France has more growth than Germany, less inflation, public finances under better control, and a balanced current account. One does not devalue a stable and solid money, and the franc is stable and solid."

Despite the bright statistical picture and official discourse, other signs indicated the economy might be in for a further slowdown in early 1993. An October survey of thousands of company leaders showed widespread pessimism, with many worrying that the country could slip into recession. The gloom reflected falls in both retail sales and industrial production over the preceding quarter. In addition, unemployment continued to hover just above 10%, affecting nearly 3 million people.

Cultural Invasion. In 1992, France was shaken by the arrival in March of Mickey, Donald, Snow White, and all the other Disney characters at the new Euro Disneyland entertainment park 20 mi (32 km) east of Paris. Anti-Disney fever ran high among a cadre of French intellectuals. Employees publicly chafed at their new company's strict dress code. After a slow and sometimes disorganized start, however, the park picked up steam and steadily growing numbers of French visitors, to surpass the 7 million attendance point by the end of September. Disney officials put off the park's programmed expansion by a year, but France's cartoon invaders appeared set to take up long-term residence. (*See also* FEATURE ARTICLE, page 84.)

HOWARD LAFRANCHI, *Paris Bureau*
"The Christian Science Monitor"

GARDENING AND HORTICULTURE

"Gardening in America," a study by National Family Opinion Research, commissioned by *Organic Gardening* magazine, revealed that there were a total of 60,559,000 gardeners in the United States in 1992.

International Floral Exhibitions. Two international floral extravaganzas were staged during 1992. The first-ever U.S. international exhibition, AmeriFlora '92, was an official quincentenary celebration of Christopher Columbus' arrival in the New World. It was held in Franklin Park, Columbus, OH, from April 20 through October 12. More than 500,000 flowers and plants were exhibited on an 88-acre (35.6-ha) site. The fair ended with a giant chrysanthemum festival. (*See also* pages 74–75.)

Floriade 1992 opened April 15 in Zoetermeer, the Netherlands, on 200 acres (81 ha) of parkland. An internationally recognized garden festival, the Floriade occurs once a decade. The show continued until October 11.

Award Winners. The All-America Selections (AAS) judging committee named four new cultivars, two flowering annuals, and two vegetables as its 1993 winners.

Verbena "Imagination" was presented the AAS Flowering Annual Award. It exhibits fine lacy foliage and intense violet blue or magenta flower color. Unlike other verbena, "Imagination" shows tolerance of drought, heat, and severe weather, making it suited for hot, dry locations. It also received the award from Fleuroselect, the AAS European counterpart, and is available from Ernst Benary Seed Growers Ltd. of Germany. "Mont Blanc" Nierenbergia also received the AAS Flowering Annual Award. It is the first white nierenbergia from seed. The plant flowers prolifically throughout the season, producing star-shaped, pure white blossoms on a low-growing, spreading plant. "Mont Blanc" also exhibits tolerance for heat, drought, and severe weather. It is available from American Takii Inc., Salinas, CA, and also received the European Fleuroselect Award.

The AAS vegetable winners were Tomato "Husky Gold" and Pumpkin "Baby Bear." "Husky Gold" is the first tomato to be presented an AAS award in nine years of testing. It produces a gold-color, 7- to 8-oz (198.4- to 226.8-g) fruit with outstanding flavor on a dwarf, indeterminate plant. "Husky Gold" tomato is available from Petoseed Co., Inc., Saticoy, CA. "Baby Bear" pumpkin is a scaled-down version of the jack-o'-lantern pumpkin weighing 7 to 8 oz (198.4 to 226.8 g). Each plant can produce eight to nine pumpkins or more. "Baby Bear" is available from Johnny's Selected Seeds, Albion, ME.

There were four All-America Rose Selections (AARS) award winners for 1993. The hy-

© Floriade World Horticulture Exhibition

Colorful tulips were on view for the enjoyment of visitors to Floriade 1992, an international flower show in Zoetermeer, the Netherlands, April 15–Oct. 11, 1992.

brid tea "Rio Samba," hybridized by the late William Warriner and introduced by Jackson and Perkins, Medford, OR, was honored because of its brilliant yellow flowers shaded into orange. The 25- to 30-petal flower is gently perfumed; its flowers grow one per stem, making it excellent for cutting. "Solitude" is a radiant orange grandiflora with orange-gold reverse. The scalloped outer petals provide an elegant, old-fashioned look. "Solitude" was hybridized by Pernille Poulsen Oelsen and Mogens Oelsen of Poulsen Poser Aps. "Sweet Inspiration," a floribunda with exceptional form, was honored for its pink flowers on a compact and dense plant. "Sweet Inspiration" also was hybridized by the late William Warriner and introduced by Jackson and Perkins. "Child's Play," a miniature rose introduced by Nor'East Miniature Roses Inc. and hybridized by F. Harmon Saville, was awarded honors because of its flowers that open with classic pointed bud form, displaying white petals edged with pink. The miniature rose plant grows to 2 ft (0.61 m) in height and produces a dense, well-branched bush.

RALPH L. SNODSMITH
Ornamental Horticulturist

GENETICS

The year 1992 saw continued progress in understanding the roles of genes in disease, behavior, populations, and evolution.

Gene Amplification. Myotonic dystrophy (MyD), a muscular degenerative disease, is an inherited disease which, when passed through succeeding generations of a family line, occurs at a progressively younger age and causes increasingly more severe symptoms. The MyD gene is located on chromosome 19 and the disease is inherited as a dominant trait.

A number of geneticists have discovered that one section of the gene increases in size (gene amplification) as it passes from grandparents to parents to grandchildren, with an accompanying increase in severity of the disease. Dr. J. D. Brook and colleagues at the Massachusetts Institute of Technology reported in 1992 that the increase in the gene's size is the result of an increase in the number of copies of a particular sequence of three nucleotides (triplet), abbreviated as CTG for the initials of their chemical names (cytosine, thymine, guanine). The number of copies of the triplet can increase from ten in a normal gene to 2,000 in the abnormal gene of a severely affected individual. What causes the CTG sequence to increase progressively in its number of copies in certain family lines remained undetermined late in 1992.

Genetics of Corn (Maize) Evolution. Corn, more properly called maize, has been cultivated for more than 7,000 years. The presumed ancestor of corn is believed to have resembled closely a wild and weedy plant called teosinte, which can be found in Mexico. Whereas ears of modern corn plants contain hundreds of kernels arranged in at least eight rows, teosinte plants produce an ear with only two rows of interwoven kernels. Despite this and other differences, teosinte and modern corn plants are crossed easily and produce fertile offspring.

In a study designed to estimate the number of gene changes that must have occurred in the cultivation process which transformed teosinte-type plants into modern corn plants, Dr. J. Doebley and colleagues at the University of Minnesota crossed the two types of plants, thereby obtaining hybrid plants which they then crossed with each other. Among the offspring of the hybrid plants were found all the possible combinations of traits that characterize both types of plants. The scientists concentrated their study on nine major traits and found that the pattern of association of these traits indicated the predominant role of five genes which account for between 50% and 80% of the difference between teosinte and modern corn. The relatively small number of genes involved supports the theory that the cultivation process was quite rapid and might have required as little as 1,000 years.

Genetics of Homosexuality. Drs. R. C. Pillard of Boston University and J. M. Bailey of Northwestern University in Illinois reported on their studies of both male and female homosexuals. Each person studied had either a twin or an adopted sibling of the same sex. In the case of the twin pairs, the scientists were able to identify those who were identical and those who were nonidentical. They studied 110 male twin pairs and 115 female twin pairs. In both groups roughly half of the twin pairs were identical and half were nonidentical. In addition, 57 pairs of adoptive brothers and 32 pairs of adoptive sisters were studied.

The findings in both groups were very similar. In about 50% of the sets of identical twin pairs, both brothers or both sisters were homosexual. This frequency decreased to about 25% in both sets of nonidentical twin pairs and declined further to about 13% in both adoptive groups.

A pattern in which a decrease in the frequency of a trait parallels a decrease in the degree of genetic relatedness of individuals is what one expects if the trait is, to a significant extent, genetically determined. The lack of complete correspondence of sexual orientation between identical twins demonstrates that there is also a considerable environmental factor in the development of this behavior.

Gene Elimination in Flour Beetles. Dr. R. W. Beeman and colleagues at the U.S. Department of Agriculture reported that members of many populations of the flour beetle, *Tribolium castaneum*, contain a mutant gene called Medea. If a female is heterozygous for Medea (M/+) and her mate is M/+ or +/+, the offspring that are +/+ die. If a female is +/+ and her mate is M/+ or +/+, the offspring that are +/+ survive. If either mate is M/M, all offspring survive.

It seems clear that the eggs produced by an M/+ female contain a lethal chemical compound. It also is apparent that during embryonic development, the Medea gene can neutralize the effect of this otherwise lethal compound. If a Medea gene is introduced into a new population, it eventually will become homozygous in all individuals, resulting in the elimination of the normal (+) allele of the gene from the beetle population.

U.S. Army's "Genetic Dog Tag" Program. The U.S. Army has begun collecting and storing blood and tissue samples of new recruits. This will permit pathologists to cross-match the DNA of tissue specimens of otherwise unidentifiable individuals to that of stored samples. The army hopes to collect specimens from all service members by the year 2000.

See also SPECIAL REPORT/CRIME—DNA *"Fingerprinting."*

LOUIS LEVINE
Department of Biology
City College of New York

GEOLOGY

Earthquakes and volcanoes claimed their fair share of destruction for 1992, with major quakes in California, Turkey, and Egypt. Oceanographers drilled deeper into the Earth's crust in hopes of better understanding ocean plates. And paleontologists discovered a new type of deadly dinosaur.

Earthquakes. California's largest earthquake in 40 years struck near the town of Landers in the Mojave desert on June 28. Measuring magnitude 7.5 on the Richter scale, the powerful quake killed only one person because it hit in a relatively unpopulated region. From a scientific standpoint, the Landers event may prove to be the most important earthquake ever; many state-of-the-art seismometers recorded the event in extreme detail.

The Landers jolt apparently raised the risk that a major quake soon would strike along the San Andreas fault. In the 1980s seismologists warned that the southern end of the San Andreas is ready to produce a tremor of magnitude 7.5 or larger. The Landers earthquake apparently increased seismic strain in the area.

Researchers particularly were surprised that the Landers earthquake triggered swarms of smaller tremors in regions up to 750 mi (1 206 km) from the main quake's epicenter. The triggered swarms were detected in northern California, southern Nevada, southern Utah, western Idaho, and even as far away as Yellowstone National Park. Scientists were not sure how the main earthquake could have set off seismic activity so far away.

A magnitude 6.8 earthquake hit eastern Turkey on March 13, devastating the town of Erzincan and killing 479 persons, according to reports. The earthquake occurred along the North Anatolian fault, caused by a collision between the Arabian plate and the Eurasian plate.

On October 12, only a few miles from the pyramids and 20 mi (32.2 km) southwest of Cairo, Egypt experienced a shock of 5.9 magnitude. An estimated 550 people were killed with thousands more injured. Major monuments were unharmed, but Cairo was marked by pockets of collapsed buildings.

At least 116 people were killed in Nicaragua on September 1 by large tsunami waves, triggered by an offshore earthquake. The quake, which measured magnitude 7.2, occurred about 35 mi (56.3 km) off the coast of central Nicaragua. Shaking from the quake was not severe enough to cause major damage, but it created waves as high as 25 ft (7.6 m).

A deadly earthquake struck the Tien Shan mountains in Kyrgyzstan, central Asia, on August 19. At least 60 people were reported dead in the wake of the magnitude 7.4 shock that destroyed several villages and set off landslides. Quakes in this area occur because India is crashing slowly into the Asian continent.

Volcanoes. Mount Pinatubo in the Philippines erupted several times in 1992, although none of the blasts equaled 1991's eruption, which was one of the century's largest. Scientists studying the aftereffects of 1991's eruption from Pinatubo said it has altered weather around the Earth. Sulfur particles from the eruption have spread throughout the atmosphere, blocking sunlight and leading to a global cooling of almost 0.5° C.

The volcanic debris from Pinatubo and from the eruption of Mount Hudson in Chile in 1991 also worsened the Antarctic ozone hole in 1991. The ozone hole is caused by chlorine and bromine pollution in the atmosphere. But volcanic particles in the atmosphere allowed these chemicals to attack ozone both higher in the atmosphere and lower in the atmosphere than they normally do.

Alaska's Mount Spurr erupted several times during the summer, repeatedly blanketing Anchorage in volcanic ash and closing down the Anchorage airport. The volcano first erupted on June 27, sending ash to a height of 50,000 ft (15 240 m). On August 18 another large eruption occurred. Mount Spurr is one of eight volcanoes in south-central Alaska.

Oceanographers diving at the bottom of the Pacific Ocean in a tiny submersible discovered a spot where a volcanic eruption just had occurred a few weeks earlier. The lava flows had covered over a community of tube worms and other animals living around vents of superheated water. The eruption was so recent that scavengers had not yet arrived on the scene to eat up the newly killed animals. Although underwater volcanoes generate about three quarters of all eruptions on Earth, scientists never before have happened on the site of such a recent eruption.

Paleontology. Geologists believe they have identified a crater left by a meteorite that struck Earth 65 million years ago. This cataclysm is believed to have wiped out the last remaining dinosaurs as well as many other forms of life. Scientists first raised the impact theory in 1979, but they despaired of ever locating the scar from the proposed crash. In 1991–1992 attention began to focus on a large circular structure buried about .62 mi (1 km) below the northern end of Mexico's Yucatán Peninsula. Scientists suspected the structure was a crater but they did not know its age. In 1992 researchers reported the proposed crater formed 65 million years ago, at the same time as the famous extinctions. While it strengthens the case that a meteorite or comet caused some of the extinctions, other creatures are believed to have disappeared 2 million years before the impact.

Paleontologists in South Dakota discovered one of the best-preserved examples of a *Tyrannosaurus rex,* the infamously ferocious dinosaur. But despite its reputation for inflicting pain on other creatures, this *T. rex* apparently

Geologist Ken Hudnut inspects a raw ridge of rock stirred by the earthquake that struck Landers, CA, in June 1992. The quake, the state's largest in 40 years, triggered many smaller tremors and became the subject of extensive study.

suffered several diseases and injuries itself. Abnormal scars on a rib and on the skull suggest the animal was bitten several times by other *T. rex*. Growths on the leg bones indicate that the specimen also broke both of its legs at separate times during its life.

Paleontologists working in Utah found a new type of vicious, meat-eating dinosaur that they named Utahraptor. The animal, which lived about 125 million years ago, sported claws that would have been 15 inches (38 cm) long, capable of slicing open the bellies of its prey. Utahraptor would have reached an estimated 20 ft (6.1 m) in length and would have weighed almost a ton. This newfound dinosaur is the largest and oldest member of the dromaeosaurid dinosaur family, which included some of the most savage predators to have walked the Earth.

Australian researchers uncovered a tiny fossilized tooth that could alter radically a long-standing theory about the evolution of marsupial mammals in the land down under. Marsupials carry newborn young in an external pouch, in contrast to the more familiar placental mammals that carry their young to term inside the body. On all continents save Australia, marsupials largely were wiped out by placental mammals millions of years ago. Researchers attributed marsupial survival in Australia to the separation of the continents before placental mammals could reach there. But the new discovery overturns that theory because it shows that placental mammals indeed did reach Australia before it became an island, calling into question the old assumption that marsupials are inferior creatures.

Plate Tectonics and Inner Earth. Geophysicists made advances in understanding what happens to ocean floor when it gets recycled back into the Earth. Ocean crust is created at volcanic ridges and then carried conveyor-belt fashion to great trenches where it dives down into the Earth, a process called subduction. For 20 years scientists have debated whether the subducted ocean floor sinks all the way down to the core, or whether it gets trapped in the upper part of Earth's mantle, a thick region separating the core from the crust. Researchers now have used earthquake waves passing through the Earth much like a medical CT scanner machine to "peer" inside the planet. They find that the sinking pieces cannot make it easily through the barrier between the upper and lower mantles. The barrier is depressed in several places, indicating that the sinking slabs have run into the boundary and slowed down or stopped completely.

Oceanographers have drilled their deepest hole in the ocean floor, and have come very close to reaching the lowest layer of the crust. Researchers had been drilling this hole near the Galápagos Islands on and off for 12 years. It reached 1.25 mi (2 km) below the ocean floor in 1992. Studying the inside of this hole will help scientists understand seafloor spreading—the process that creates new ocean plates.

RICHARD MONASTERSKY, *"Science News"*

GEORGIA

Sports and politics captured Georgians' attention during 1992, but economic activity and racial unrest also were discussed.

Sports. Tomahawks adorned Atlanta skyscrapers, as the Atlanta Braves captured baseball's National League championship for the second consecutive year. Excitement abated only when the Braves were defeated in the World Series by the Toronto Blue Jays. Atlantans saw the model for an Olympic Stadium, the new home for the Braves in 1997. The Atlanta Falcons football team played in their new home, the Georgia Dome. Seating 70,000 and with 15 restaurants, 532 television sets, and luxury suites which rent annually for $120,000, the dome is the second-largest in the world. It will host the 1994 Super Bowl and the 1996 Summer Olympic Games. The Atlanta Olympic mascot, a computer-generated blue morph called "Whatizit," was introduced.

Politics. Georgia voters in November elected the state's first black congresswoman, Democrat Cynthia McKinney. In a November 24 runoff election, Republican Paul Coverdell, a former Peace Corps director, defeated the incumbent Sen. Wyche Fowler. Although George Bush failed to carry the state in the presidential election against Democratic challenger Bill Clinton, Georgia sent four Republican representatives to Congress, including House Whip Newt Gingrich.

In attempts to further racial progress, two plans were submitted to, and approved by, the U.S. Justice Department. One, a redistricting plan, created three majority black congressional districts; the other phased out elections for superior-court and state-court judges, allowing for minority and female attorneys to fill vacancies in rural as well as urban judgeships. Gov. Zell Miller, who gained national attention when he addressed the Democratic Convention in July, also proposed the removal of the Confederate battle flag from the Georgia state flag.

In other political news, the General Assembly established a state-lottery commission, created a fund to clean up hazardous dumps, proposed license suspension for all DUI (driving under the influence) offenders, and defeated legislation that would require instant background checks for gun purchases.

Racial Issues. Young black people, outraged over the Rodney King case in Los Angeles in April, rampaged through downtown Atlanta, smashing windows and looting stores. National Guard troops were ordered but not deployed.

At Spelman College, the largest donation ever made to a black college, $37 million, was bequeathed by the founder of *Reader's Digest*.

Economic Activity. Governor Miller announced layoffs for state employees during the year. He also called for plans to raise motorist fees and submitted an amendment for a state-

wide lottery that was voted on and passed during the general election. Delta Airlines cut part-time jobs, and Georgia Power Company reduced its work force. Georgia outperformed the national economy in terms of job growth—led by retail, housing construction, and small service businesses. The housing market also showed improvement, and nearly 200 companies announced plans to create new and expanded manufacturing facilities in the state.

People. Atlanta Mayor Maynard Jackson underwent bypass surgery, but returned to work within weeks. . . . Former President Jimmy Carter announced the Atlanta Project, a major initiative to help cure inner-city social ills.

KAY BECK, *Georgia State University*

GEORGIA, Republic of

Of all the new nations that emerged from the collapse of the USSR, Georgia had the most tumultuous transition year in 1992. The country's first democratically elected president was driven from office by an armed opposition, former Soviet Foreign Minister Eduard Shevardnadze was chosen to lead the new government, and a second interethnic civil war broke out between the Georgians and one of the country's national minorities. By the end of the year, Georgia was an armed camp, the economy was in turmoil, and political stability remained elusive.

Gamsakhurdia's Presidency. The Soviet Republic of Georgia declared its independence in April 1991, some eight months before the final breakup of the USSR. The following month, Zviad Gamsakhurdia, a former nationalist dissident, was elected president by an overwhelming majority. Gamsakhurdia's militant Georgian nationalism aroused opposition among the Ossetians, an ethnic minority in Georgia's South Ossetian Autonomous Province, where a separatist movement already had

A large crowd surrounded Eduard Shevardnadze and Mrs. Shevardnadze as they voted in the Republic of Georgia's first post-Soviet parliamentary elections in October 1992. The former Soviet foreign minister was chosen speaker of parliament, a post equivalent to president.

© Georges de Keerle/Sygma

begun to develop. Fearful of losing their autonomy, the South Ossetians demanded the right to unite with their compatriots in North Ossetia, which lay across the border in the territory of the Russian Federation. After an exchange of constitutional salvos, the Georgian-South Ossetian conflict degenerated into a small-scale civil war.

Meanwhile, Gamsakhurdia was becoming increasingly authoritarian and intolerant of opposition, bridling the press and arresting his political opponents. When Russia and other Soviet republics established the Commonwealth of Independent States in December 1991, Georgia declined to join.

Interim Government. By the end of 1991, Gamsakhurdia's high-handed tactics had provoked his Georgian opposition into armed rebellion. Fighting raged around the principal government buildings in Tbilisi until the opposition militia prevailed; Gamsakhurdia fled the country in early January 1992. In March, Shevardnadze, who had led the Georgian Communist Party before becoming the USSR's foreign minister, was invited to return to his native Georgia to head the State Council of the republic's provisional government. A skilled Soviet politician in Moscow and a master of international diplomacy, Shevardnadze soon found himself entangled in the extremely complex and intensely passionate politics of post-Soviet Georgia.

GEORGIA • Information Highlights

Official Name: Republic of Georgia.
Location: Western Asia.
Area: 27,000 sq mi (70 000 km²).
Population (mid-1992 est.): 5,500,000.
Chief Cities (Dec. 1989 est.): Tbilisi, the capital, 1,460,000.
Government: *Head of state,* Eduard A. Shevardnadze, speaker of Parliament (elected Oct. 11, 1992). *Head of government,* Tengiz Sigua, prime minister. *Legislature*—Parliament.

Abkhazi Revolt. In July the Abkhazian Autonomous Republic in western Georgia declared its independence, and large-scale fighting broke out between Georgian forces and the Abkhazi secessionists. Abkhazis constituted less than 20% of Abkhazia's population; Georgians made up 45%; Russians and other nationalities comprised the remainder. Georgia's second interethnic civil war became part of the larger pattern of ethnic unrest in the Caucasian region of the former USSR. Caucasian volunteers as well as Russians fought alongside the Abkhazis.

Shevardnadze turned to President Boris Yeltsin of Russia to mediate the conflict and discourage the volunteers from the Russian Caucasus. Yeltsin, worried that successful secession in Georgia might stoke the smoldering secessionist fires of various national minorities within the Russian Federation, tried to negotiate a political solution to the conflict, but to no avail. By year's end, a truce had been negotiated in South Ossetia, but fighting continued in Abkhazia.

Economy. Predictably, with the breakdown in public order, Georgia's economy went into a tailspin. Inflation approached 50% monthly, industrial production had fallen by two thirds since 1990, and unemployment was estimated at 20%. Many large factories, dependent upon Russia for spare parts as well as orders, became victims of the economic disarray in Russia. Complicating the situation, Abkhazi fighters cut off rail service to Moscow and to neighboring Armenia. Food remained plentiful, but nearly everything else was in short supply.

Elections. Parliamentary elections in the fall produced a huge plurality for Shevardnadze, who became speaker of the new parliament. However, whether his enhanced legitimacy would help him resolve the country's problems remained to be seen as 1992 ended.

ROBERT SHARLET
Union College

The arrival of some 500,000 foreigners seeking asylum in Germany led to marches (left) and attacks by the right wing and neo-Nazis. In turn, Turks in Mölln (right) decried the November killing of two Turkish girls and a grandmother.

GERMANY

In 1992, Germans continued to struggle with the enormous task of putting their nation back together. After 40 years of division, most Germans realized, the true unification of their country could not be accomplished by the signing of a few treaties and the passage of new laws. The social and economic integration of East and West, it became clear, would take far longer and cost far more than was imagined in the heady days following the formal unification of the country. The economic, political, and psychological differences between the formerly divided states hardly diminished in 1992 and in some respects grew even larger.

But unification was by no means the only problem confronting Germany. Long a leader in the movement toward a united Western Europe, the Federal Republic was criticized strongly by some of its European neighbors for its high interest rates, which provoked a crisis in the European Monetary System (EMS) and slowed progress toward a common European currency.

A more serious problem was the influx of more than 500,000 foreigners seeking asylum. Their arrival sparked a wave of extremist right-wing and neo-Nazi violence in both the eastern and western regions of the country. By year's end authorities had registered more than 1,800 attacks on foreigners with a death toll of 17. Right-wing extremists and neo-Nazis also desecrated Jewish cemeteries and set fires at two former concentration camps. The attacks on asylum-seekers and the weak response of German political leaders and police forces reminded many observers of the country's darker past. Criticism of Germany abroad reached levels unheard of since the Third Reich.

Politics. For Chancellor Helmut Kohl and his ruling Christian Democrats (CDU) 1992 was a difficult year. In April his party lost votes in two state elections and at year's end was the major governing party in only one of the ten western states. In eastern Germany CDU's support in 1992 polls dropped from almost 40% to 20%. In March, Kohl's defense minister was forced to resign after a scandal over illegal arms shipments to Turkey. The German weapons were used by the Turks in their attacks on rebel Kurds. Kohl's problems continued in June when the Christian Democrats were outvoted in the parliament for the first time since 1982. The issue was a new abortion law for the unified nation. A coalition of Free Democrats, opposition Social Democrats, and dissident Christian Democrats formed to pass a "pro-choice" law. At year's end the legislation was before Germany's supreme court.

The Social Democrats (SPD) under their leader and probable chancellor candidate at the next national election, Björn Engholm, moved steadily back into the center of the political spectrum during 1992 and were closer to returning to power than at any time since the early 1980s. The new look of the Social Democrats was illustrated dramatically in late August when Engholm together with 14 members of the party's "Germany 2000" committee abandoned their previous opposition to any change of Article 16 of the Constitution, which grants an unconditional right to political asylum. Such an amendment long been had sought by the CDU, but given the two-thirds majority required for any amendment, it needed Social Democratic support. On December 5 leaders of the three main parties agreed on the outlines of a new, comparatively restrictive law, scheduled for enactment in early 1993.

Engholm also pushed through a change in the party's policy toward the deployment of German military forces outside the North Atlantic Treaty Organization (NATO) region. The SPD leadership accordingly proposed that the party support another constitutional amendment, one that would permit German participation in United Nations-sponsored military operations.

The Free Democratic Party (FDP), the junior partner in the governing coalition, managed to hold its own in polls and elections throughout the year. In April the party's titular leader and foreign minister of the Federal Republic, Hans-Dietrich Genscher, resigned after 18 years in office. The party was divided over the question of who should be its new leader. The favorite was Klaus Kinkel, Genscher's successor in the foreign ministry. At the same time, the FDP, sensing that the Kohl government was a sinking ship, continued to explore the possibility of again aligning itself with the Social Democrats. The June abortion vote marked the first time the two former partners had cooperated since their "divorce" in 1982.

In spite of their absence from the Bundestag, the western German Green Party enjoyed near double-digit support in most polls. With the party's Realist wing firmly in control, the Greens had gone quietly about the business of governing in a record three state governments —Lower Saxony, Hesse, and Bremen. Their counterparts in the former East Germany, whose ranks also include the remnants of the revolutionaries of 1989–90, the Alliance 90, were represented in the Bundestag and participated in the coalition that governs the state of Brandenburg. In 1992 the parties reached agreement on their own unification for the 1994 national election. The new party will present a common program and electoral lists. There is little doubt that the current leadership would support (the electorate permitting) a coalition with the Social Democrats. In October the party was shocked by the death of one of its founders, Petra Kelly. The peace activist was shot and killed by her companion, a former army general, who then took his own life.

At the two state-level elections in 1992 antiforeigner right-wing parties made sharp gains. In April the Republican Party, led by a former SS sergeant, won 11% of the vote in the western state of Baden-Württemberg; another rightist party, the German Peoples Union, won 6.3% in Schleswig-Holstein. Neither party had been represented previously in the state legislature.

Economy. The recession-plagued world economy, dwindling domestic consumption, and the costs of unification took their toll on Germany's economic performance in 1992. Real growth was only 1.5%, the lowest level since 1982; in the former East Germany the growth rate was only 7%, far less than needed if this part of the country is ever to reach parity with the West. Inflation for the year averaged 4%, a high level by German standards.

In western Germany a mild recession began in 1992. Unemployment rose to almost 6%. Many companies announced large-scale layoffs and "downsizing" programs. Daimler-Benz, the famous automobile maker, announced the largest work force cuts in its history.

In April about 2.6 million public-service workers in western Germany went on strike over pay. The strike, which lasted ten days, brought into sharp focus the question of how the huge costs of unification will be divided between government, business, and labor. The union charged that the Kohl government, allied with business, wanted to pay for unification at the expense of the average German worker. In 1992 unification cost the average western German household about $120 per month in increased income and social security taxes. Lower income groups, according to some studies, had paid a proportionately higher amount for unification than had more affluent Germans.

German Chancellor Helmut Kohl (extreme left) and French President François Mitterrand held a two-hour "minisummit" in Paris in September. The two leaders continued in 1992 to work together for a unified Europe.

© Regis Bossu/Sygma

Transportation workers in western Germany were on the picket lines—frequently in front of empty buses or at vacant railroad stations—in the spring as some 2.6 million public-service workers staged a ten-day strike over salary issues.

In the East about 40% of the work force remained unemployed, housing was in short supply, and rents had tripled since 1990. A major hindrance to economic development was the question of property ownership. Almost 1.5 million claims had been made on property confiscated either by the Nazis after 1933 or by the Communists after 1945. An estimated $65 billion of investment in the former GDR was being held up because of unresolved ownership. The final unification treaty in 1990 had set forth as a general principle that the "restitution of property to its former owners takes precedence over monetary compensation." This provision was proving difficult to implement and had led to a huge backlog of court cases. In 1992 supplementary legislation was passed by the parliament, which was designed to speed up the legal process and encourage new investment in the region.

In March, Detlev Dalk, a member of the Bundestag from the Alliance 90/Green Party, committed suicide, apparently to protest this ownership policy. In a letter to Chancellor Kohl, Dalk wrote that he saw no other way of arousing public concern about the "disastrous consequences" of the policy than his "public death." The prospect of losing their homes through no fault of their own had left many eastern Germans anxious and depressed.

Unification and Germany's Neighbors. The linkage between the unification process and Germany's relations with its European neighbors was demonstrated dramatically in September when high German interest rates precipitated a crisis in the European Monetary System (EMS). To pay for the expenses of unification, which in 1992 amounted to more than $100 billion, the government turned to the financial markets. But to attract investment capital and to rein in the inflation that accompanied the unification expenditures, Germany's powerful and independent central bank (Bundesbank) increased interest rates to almost 10%. Required by the EMS to keep their currencies within a narrow exchange-rate band, weaker European economies like Britain's and Italy's struggled to stay tied to the mark by applying their own high interest rates. Unfortunately, the damage to their own economies was greater than the benefits of staying in the system, and both countries withdrew. The incident set back efforts to move toward a common European currency by the end of the century.

Communist Legacy in Eastern Germany. Germans in 1992 began the long and sometimes painful process of coming to terms with the injustices and human-rights abuses of the 1949–89 Communist dictatorship in the former East Germany. In January a former high-ranking administrator in the Protestant church and the current prime minister of the state of Brandenburg, Manfred Stolpe, revealed that he had had extensive contacts with the hated secret police, or Stasi. Stolpe, who came under heavy criticism for this alleged collaboration, maintained that he had had to deal with the regime in order to protect the church. Throughout the year further evidence of church cooperation with the Communist regime became public. In some cases church officials had informed on dissident pastors and parishioners.

Other prominent eastern Germans also had to confront their past. In January the Christian Democratic leader of one of the new eastern states, Thuringia, resigned after disclosures that he had collaborated with the Communist government. In February, Katrin Krabbe, the world-champion sprinter and a national idol in the former East Germany, was suspended by the German Olympic Committee for manipulating drug-testing procedures. The extensive use of drugs was apparently commonplace in the Communist-run Olympic program. In March a new legislative commission, headed by a leading dissident in the former East Germany, was established to conduct a sweeping investigation of the Communist dictatorship, and in July, Erich Honecker, the 79 year-old former East German Communist Party leader, was returned to Germany from Moscow to stand trial on manslaughter charges in connection with the shooting deaths of East Germans attempting to flee the regime. Many Eastern Germans, however, believed that Western criticism of prominent "Ossies" (Easterners) was a further attempt to deprive them of their pride and identity. They accused Western Germans of applying a double standard in dealing with the Communist past. They contrasted West Germany's lax prosecution of Nazis after 1945 with its zeal in pursuing Communists after 1989.

Foreigners and Right-Wing Violence. In August the fire-bombing of a hostel for asylum-seekers in the eastern port city of Rostock set off a wave of antiforeigner violence, which continued through the year. In November three Turkish women were killed when their house in the small western city of Mölln was fire-bombed. The national government, citing the emergency provisions of the constitution, assumed control of the police investigation. A few days later several suspects were arrested and charged with the killings. One extremist right-wing group was outlawed. A new special police unit to combat right-wing violence also was announced. The unit will have the task of observing and penetrating the right-wing groups and will take over investigations of particular incidents when local police departments need assistance.

Police forces in eastern Germany in many cases were unable to cope with right-wing extremist violence. Understaffed, and poorly trained and equipped, they were charged with protecting a society with which they themselves were still unfamiliar.

Critics charged Kohl with a lack of leadership on the antiforeigner violence issue. Instead of facing up to the problems and taking practical steps to deal with them before they reached the level seen in Rostock, Kohl, they charged, played domestic politics, blaming the Social Democratic opposition for making action impossible.

The great majority of the country's 80 million citizens deplored the violence, and in November and December hundreds of thousands took to the streets in Berlin, Munich, and elsewhere to demonstrate against right-wing extremism. But until these rallies, many Germans seemed more concerned with reducing the number of foreigners allowed into the country than with protecting those already there from right-wing violence. About one fourth of the adult population stated in opinion surveys that it had some "understanding" for the resentment felt by unemployed young people against foreign asylum-seekers.

Germany's 60,000 Jewish residents were especially sensitive to the antiforeigner outbursts. Polls in October found that one third of Germany's Jews felt threatened by rising anti-Semitism, and about 75% said that the government was not doing enough to combat right-wing extremism.

Foreign Policy. In January, Germany was able to persuade all the members of the European Community (EC) to recognize the independence of the former Yugoslav republics of Slovenia and Croatia. Germany's decision to press for recognition despite the opposition of the United States and the UN was seen by some observers as signaling a new assertiveness in the Federal Republic's foreign policy.

In February, Germany forgave half of the $5.5 billion debt Poland owed to the Federal Republic. Because most of the debt was amassed in the 1970s by the Communists, Germany considered the partial forgiveness as an expression of support for Poland's new democracy. Bonn also continued to be by far the largest Western contributor of aid to Eastern Europe and the former Soviet Union.

In September the Federal Republic informed the United Nations General Assembly that it would like a permanent seat on the Security Council. The Kohl government also proposed a constitutional amendment that would allow German military participation in UN military operations. In spite of its domestic problems, Germany was prepared to take a role in world politics commensurate with its economic power.

DAVID P. CONRADT, *University of Florida*

GERMANY • Information Highlights

Official Name: Federal Republic of Germany.
Location: North-central Europe.
Area: 137,931 sq mi (356 910 km²).
Population (mid-1992 est.): 80,600,000.
Chief Cities (Dec. 31, 1989 est.): Berlin, the capital, (1990 est.), 3,400,000; Hamburg, 1,626,220; Munich, 1,206,683, Leipzig, 530,010; Dresden, 501,417.
Government: *Head of state,* Richard von Weizsäcker, president (took office July 1, 1984). *Head of government,* Helmut Kohl, chancellor (took office Oct. 1982). *Legislature*—Parliament: Bundesrat and Bundestag.
Monetary Unit: Deutsche mark (1.5715 D. marks equal U.S.$1, Dec. 14, 1992).
Gross Domestic Product (1990 U.S.$): $1,157,200,-000,000.
Economic Indexes (1991): *Consumer Prices* (1980 = 100), all items, 134.0; food, 127.0. *Industrial Production* (1980 = 100), 126.
Foreign Trade (1991 U.S.$): *Imports,* $382,050,-000,000; *exports,* $391,295,000,000.

GREAT BRITAIN

In Britain in 1992 the more things changed the more they stayed the same. Former Prime Minister Margaret Thatcher was ennobled, becoming Baroness Thatcher, but she seemed to interpret noblesse oblige as an obligation to make life more miserable for her successor, John Major (*see* BIOGRAPHY). The economic recession deepened, becoming Britain's longest-running recession since World War II, but voters in April's general election returned Major and his Conservative Party anyway. And work progressed on the Channel Tunnel, but its opening was put off twice, to December 1993. The delay was apt indeed, for it seemed that Britons themselves wanted to maintain their distance from the rest of Europe.

Domestic Politics. When the year opened, things could not have looked worse for Major and the Conservatives. Norman Lamont, chancellor of the exchequer, spoke repeatedly of an economic recovery being just around the corner, but an upturn remained elusive. It was not until March that Major announced that the general election would be held on April 9, although the campaign already had been under way when the year began. For the opposition Labour Party, 1992 seemed to offer the best hope for a return to power in more than a decade. Led by Neil Kinnock, the party attacked the Conservatives for their failure to get the economy moving and for allowing unemployment to soar. In one of the main themes of the Labour campaign, the party also accused the Tories of underfunding the country's cherished National Health Service and of preparing it for wholesale privatization. For their part, the Conservatives set about trying to convince the electorate that a Labour government would mean higher taxes and a return to the days when the nation's business was slowed by union strikes. On the fringes of the fray were the Liberal Democrats, a centrist party led by Paddy Ashdown, that had hopes of holding the balance of power in the event of a hung Parliament.

Going into March the Labour Party had a slim majority in the opinion polls, though the polls also showed that the voters were not wildly enthusiastic about either the Conservatives or Labourites. That same month, John Smith, the shadow chancellor of the exchequer, revealed that the Labour Party, if elected, would increase revenues for child benefits and state pensions by increasing the tax burden of those earning more than 21,000 pounds (about $33,000). Smith's plans were seized on by the Conservatives, who launched a highly damaging campaign to instill in voters a fear of Labour's tax plans. With the end of March came the most bizarre episode of the campaign: the so-called "War of Jennifer's Ear," which raged around a Labour television commercial that assailed Conservative funding of the health service. The advertisement was discredited and Labour was left with egg on its

John Smith, who was elected leader of Britain's Labour Party in July 1992, joined Margaret Beckett, a Labour spokeswoman, at the party's annual congress in the fall. Smith, 54, had been shadow chancellor of the exchequer since 1987.

© Matthieu Polak/Sygma

face, a feeling that Major was to experience more literally a week later when he took to the British streets on a soapbox and was pelted with an egg. In the end, though, the soapbox and Conservative criticism of Labour's tax plans won the day, with the Tories pulling off a last-minute win. Christopher Patten, Conservative Party chairman and one of Major's closest political allies, lost his parliamentary seat; his reward for the Conservative victory came later with his appointment as governor of Hong Kong. Several days after the election, Kinnock announced that he was stepping down after nine years as Labour leader; he was replaced in July by John Smith, the shadow chancellor and a Scottish lawyer.

After the summer came a tumultuous September. David Mellor, one of Major's closest friends and the secretary of state for national heritage, was forced to resign after revelations that he had had an extramarital affair and had accepted an expenses-paid family vacation from the daughter of a Palestine Liberation Organization (PLO) official. The Mellordrama, as some of the British newspapers put it, was nothing compared to another of the month's political crises: turmoil in the financial markets, fueled by uncertainty over an impending French referendum on the Maastricht Treaty for closer political and economic union within the European Community (EC), left the pound sterling at its lowest rate against the *deutsche mark* since Britain joined the community's Exchange Rate Mechanism (ERM) in 1990. On September 16 the pound plummeted still further and Chancellor of the Exchequer Lamont, desperate to prop it up, raised interest rates twice, while the Bank of England plundered its reserves to buy sterling. By the end of the day the battle was lost, so Lamont pulled the pound out of the ERM. Angry Conservative members of Parliament called for Lamont's resignation. What should have been a triumphant Conservative Party conference in October was instead one of the most rancorous in recent memory. And an article by Thatcher in, ironically, *The European* newspaper, which called for Britain to abandon the Maastricht Treaty and membership in the ERM, did nothing to heal divisions.

In October, Major's embattled government announced that 31 of Britain's 50 coal mines would close between then and March, tossing some 30,000 coal miners onto the already burgeoning unemployment rolls. The announcement struck a chord in the normally placid British, some 150,000 of whom took to the London streets in protest. The ferocity of the public reaction forced Major to make an embarrassing volte-face: He trimmed the proposed closures to ten. In December the British High Court declared that both the original pit closure plan and the subsequent compromised plan were unlawful. In November the prime minister had averted political death when Parliament narrowly voted to proceed with a bill to ratify the Maastricht Treaty.

Economy. The gloom was unremitting on the economic front in 1992. Throughout much of the year, Britain was mired in a landscape of business closures, sweeping layoffs, a widening trade gap, diminishing manufacturing output, a stalled housing market, and high and long-term unemployment. Indeed, as the year was ending, unemployment was approaching the 3 million mark. Pleas from monetarists for devaluation of sterling and pleas from the retail and construction industries for a reduction in interest rates went unheeded by Major and Lamont, who remained committed until the last to keeping inflation low by keeping the pound tied to the *deutsche mark* within the ERM.

In July the National Economic Development Office predicted that the construction industry's output would drop by 6.5% in 1992; recovery was not expected until 1994. That same month six monetarists, including Sir Alan Walters, Thatcher's former economic adviser, wrote to *The London Times,* warning that recession could last well into 1993, and even longer, unless Britain abandoned the ERM. In August *The Economist* reported that the number of people unemployed for one year or more had risen to its highest level since July 1988. In September the EC finance ministers met in Bath, England, to discuss the growing pressures on the ERM currencies. That same month the debate over British membership in the ERM was rendered moot by the sterling crisis, which forced the pound out of the mechanism. A week later, Lamont cut base interest rates by 1% to 9%. At the Conservative Party conference in October, Lamont said low inflation would continue to be a key facet of government economic policy, but he said that Britain would not be rushing back into the ERM. On October 12, *The Financial Times* reported the steepest decline in British business confidence in three years. According to *The Independent on Sunday,* Major and Lamont were considering "a fundamental shift" in economic policy in order to stimulate employment and a recovery. On October 16, as the EC met for a one-day summit in Birmingham, Britain lowered its interest rates by a further 1% to 8%. That same month *The Economist* reported that September saw the 29th successive monthly rise in unemployment.

Northern Ireland. As new civil wars broke out in Europe, the terrible conflict in Northern Ireland entered its 21st year. The year opened with the Irish Republican Army (IRA) conducting a ferocious bombing campaign in London and Belfast. On January 10 an IRA bomb, stashed in a briefcase between two parked cars, exploded in London, just down the street from the ministry of defense.

That same week another IRA bomb killed eight civilian workmen on a bus in Northern

Spotlight on Scotland

Scotland is a small area rich in natural resources. Its position on the North Sea makes it a prime producer of oil; its rivers brim with salmon; its highland glens and peaks attract visitors from around the world; its Scottish whiskey is also world-renowned. But in spite of all its traditional tartan trappings, Scotland, politically part of the United Kingdom of Great Britain and Northern Ireland, is a modern country afflicted with all of the accompanying social problems.

As of June 1992, unemployment in Scotland stood at 9.4%. According to Shelter, the national campaign for the homeless, homelessness in Scotland has more than doubled since the mid-1980s. In Dundee and, particularly, Edinburgh, the abuse of heroin and associated opiates has led to worrying rates of HIV infection, which causes AIDS. Scotland, however, has been less hard hit than other parts of Britain by the nation's longest-running recession since the 1930s. That is largely because Scotland had less distance to fall. It did not experience to the same extent the 1980s boom that sent property values rocketing in southeast England. Things, however, hardly have been easy and many Scots blame Prime Minister John Major's Conservative government.

As 1992 opened, and a major British steel mill at Ravenscraig planned to close, Scots began to consider with renewed fervor the question of independence from Britain. As plans were made for Edinburgh to host a European Council summit at the end of the year, many Scots concluded that Scotland should be freed from its union with Britain to pursue its own interests as the 13th independent nation of the European Community (EC). Scottish nationalism, a force of varying strength since the union with Britain came into being in 1707, was given even more urgency as Britain's April general election approached. In a poll conducted for *The Scotsman* newspaper and Independent Television News, 50% of those interviewed expressed support for full independence, the highest percentage since polling on the question began. In many polls, independence won the most favor among young people.

In an interview, Kevin J. Pringle, research officer for the Scottish National Party (SNP), claimed that Scots were tired of the "colonial type" rule of the Conservative Party, which held just 11 of Scotland's 72 parliamentary seats following the April balloting. The Westminster government, asserted Pringle, squanders Scotland's resources and gives its industry short shrift.

The SNP wants the question of independence to be put to the people. In a 1979 refer-

© Rex Features, USA

Alec (Alexander A. E.) Salmond, above, *37, became the leader of the Scottish National Party (SNP), which advocates Scottish "independence in Europe," in 1990. A former energy economist for the Royal Bank of Scotland, Salmond has been a member of the British Parliament since 1987. Although the SNP lost two seats in the 1992 election, he was one of three party members to win a parliamentary seat. Prior to the voting, Salmond had said that change for Scotland now was "inevitable."*

endum on a proposed independent legislature for Scotland, a majority of those who voted approved the proposal, but the measure failed because it did not win 40% of the total electorate. The SNP now wants a referendum that gives voters three choices—status quo, devolution, or independence. Others say that the 1992 election was, in effect, a referendum on Scotland's future. If the Scots really wanted independence, they say, they would have voted for the SNP. In fact, the SNP lost two of its parliamentary seats and the Conservatives gained one.

Peter Jones, Scottish political editor of *The Scotsman,* said in an interview that the election "certainly stalled" the independence movement. He does not believe, however, that the issue of home rule or independence "is going to go away." Jones is of the opinion that the Conservative government, which is opposed to the breakup of the union, will tinker with the "machinery of government" to appease the Scottish public.

SUZANNE CASSIDY

Ireland. Several hours after the bombing, Peter Brooke, secretary of state for Northern Ireland, appeared on a late-night talk show in the Republic of Ireland and was cajoled into singing a song. Unionist politicians were outraged that Brooke apparently should be gallivanting in Dublin while families grieved in Ulster, and demanded that he resign. He offered his resignation to Major, who turned it down. Later that month a former intelligence officer for the British Army in Northern Ireland pleaded guilty to terrorism charges; the government dropped two murder charges against him, thereby averting a trial that some believed would have revealed collusion between the army and loyalist terrorists. When the violence continued into February, Major sought to take matters into his own hands, inviting the leaders of the four main political parties in Northern Ireland to a meeting at No. 10 Downing Street.

On February 20, Joseph Doherty was deported from the United States and was returned to the Belfast prison from which he escaped in 1981. Doherty, a former IRA guerrilla who was involved in the 1980 shooting of a British Army captain, spent nearly nine years in U.S. jails, fighting off extradition. In February's final week, the Labour Party accused the government of misusing the Prevention of Terrorism Act, which gives the police powers to detain people for up to seven days without charging them. According to Labour, terrorist charges were brought against just four of the 153 people detained under the act in 1991.

On February 28 another IRA bomb exploded during the morning rush hour at London's London Bridge railway station, wounding 28. The following day still another exploded near the London law courts; no one was injured seriously. In March the violence subsided somewhat as attention turned to the general election campaign. Three days before

the election, however, a small IRA bomb went off in central London. It was a harbinger of things to come.

On April 9, Gerry Adams, leader of Sinn Fein, the IRA's political wing, lost his parliamentary seat to the Social Democratic and Labour Party. It was estimated that 2,000 Protestants voted for the nonviolent, mostly Catholic SDLP to unseat Adams. The day after the election a massive IRA bomb, hidden in a van, exploded in London's financial district, killing three people, wounding 91, and causing widespread damage. A second car bomb exploded about four hours later, damaging buildings and bridges at a northwest London intersection.

A ray of light appeared in June with the announcement that for the first time in 19 years representatives of the Irish government would meet in London with officials of both Catholic and Protestant political parties from across the border. The meeting, chaired by Sir Patrick Mayhew, who succeeded Brooke as secretary of state for Northern Ireland after the general election, was to discuss, among other issues, the Republic of Ireland's constitutional claim to Northern Ireland. In a major breakthrough, the participants agreed to hold formal talks in hopes of establishing some form of devolved government for Northern Ireland. As the year drew to a close, the IRA's mainland bombing campaign still had not been thwarted. Some 64 people were wounded in two bombings in Manchester on December 4.

Foreign Affairs. An old controversy reemerged at the beginning of the year, as a parliamentary committee heard testimony from a man who had helped to design a long-range cannon, or "supergun," for Iraq in the late 1980s. Christopher Cowley asserted that British officials had known of the project for at least two years before components intended for the weapons were seized by customs officials. Major called the assertions "nonsense." However, later in the year it was revealed that officials of the Thatcher government had approved sales of products with military uses to Iraq, despite a 1985 ban on such exports. Major ordered an independent judicial inquiry.

At the end of January, Russian President Boris Yeltsin visited Britain; in a joint declaration, Russia and Britain agreed to be "friendly states and partners within the international community." Yeltsin would visit London again in November to appeal for help with Russia's burden of debt and to address a joint session of both chambers of Parliament. An Anglo-Russian treaty pledging cooperation between the two nations was signed.

In June, Britain assumed the six-month presidency of the EC. At the end of the month, it agreed reluctantly to an EC commitment to support the use of UN force to get humanitarian aid through to Sarajevo in the war-torn for-

---

GREAT BRITAIN · Information Highlights

Official Name: United Kingdom of Great Britain and Northern Ireland.
Location: Island, western Europe.
Area: 94,525 sq mi (244 820 km²).
Population (mid-1992 est.): 57,800,000.
Chief Cities (mid-1990 est.): London, the capital, 6,794,400; Birmingham, 992,800; Leeds, 712,200; Glasgow, 689,200; Sheffield, 525,800.
Government: *Head of state,* Elizabeth II, queen (acceded Feb. 1952). *Head of government,* John Major, prime minister and First Lord of the Treasury (took office November 1990). *Legislature—* Parliament: House of Lords and House of Commons.
Monetary Unit: Pound (0.6394 pound equals U.S.$1, Dec. 14, 1992).
Gross Domestic Production (1990 U.S.$): $858,300,-000,000.
Economic Indexes (1991): *Consumer Prices* (1980 = 100), all items, 199.7; food, 173.7. *Industrial Production* (1980 = 100), 118.
Foreign Trade (1991 U.S.$): *Imports,* $210,019,-000,000; *exports,* $185,212,000,000.

mer Yugoslavia. Meanwhile, reports of alleged Serbian and Croatian atrocities began to filter into Britain. Baroness Lynda Chalker, Britain's overseas development minister, spoke of Serbian ''ethnic cleansing of the most thorough proportions.'' Despite the reports, Chalker and other British officials balked at suggestions that Britain should open its doors to more refugees from the conflict. David Owen, a former British foreign secretary, argued that the North Atlantic Treaty Organization (NATO) should enforce an immediate cease-fire. In an interview with *The New York Times,* Lord Owen said that ''when faced with concentration camps and sealed trains, we have done nothing. We made that mistake with the Jews in the second World War.'' Major countered that it would be impossible to ''unite the international community'' behind a military solution. Later, Major appointed Owen as a peace negotiator in the region. And in August the British government dropped its objections to military intervention, agreeing to commit up to 1,800 ground troops to help escort relief convoys carrying food and medicine to Bosnia-Herzegovina. On the same day, Britain announced that it was prepared to send warplanes into southern Iraq to form an allied ''no–fly zone'' to protect Shiite Muslims from Iraqi air attacks. At the end of August, Major cochaired a major conference in London on the crisis of the former Yugoslavia. In December he met with President Bush in Washington. The two leaders agreed to press for a new UN resolution to enforce Serbian compliance with a UN no-fly zone for Bosnia.

Closer to home, relations with Germany sank to a new low, as Lamont publicly criticized the German Bundesbank during the sterling crisis and Conservative politicians stoked British fears about German economic dominance. Fear of a strong and reunified Germany was seen as one element of Britain's reluctance to throw its fortunes in with those of the EC. Relations deteriorated, too, with China as Hong Kong Gov. Christopher Patten pressed for more democracy for the colony.

Royalty. What should have been a glorious year for the British monarchy—the year when Queen Elizabeth II celebrated the 40th anniversary of her accession to the throne—turned out to be the worst in a string of bad years for the royals. January offered a mere taste of what was to come. First, photographs, showing the Duchess of York cavorting on vacation with the son of a Texas oilman, were found in a London apartment and passed on to the press. Then a British television program castigated Buckingham Palace for the lack of members of ethnic minorities on its staff. Then followed the publication of a book by Phillip Hall that made a serious case for requiring the monarchy to pay income tax. In February there was some much-needed positive publicity as the Prince of Wales launched a new institute of architecture

in London. And the British press leaped to the queen's defense when Australia's Prime Minister Paul Keating broke protocol and put his arm around the waist of the queen, who was visiting Australia. But in March the trouble began in earnest when, after days of intense speculation, Buckingham Palace announced the separation of the Duke and Duchess of York after five and one-half years of marriage. In April another royal marriage broke up as Anne, the princess royal, filed for divorce from her husband of 18 years, Capt. Mark Phillips.

There was a brief respite from the turmoil in May when the queen traveled to Strasbourg, France, to speak for the first time before the European Parliament. But June brought the most damaging controversy to date. That month, *The London Sunday Times* began publishing excerpts from a new biography of the Princess of Wales, *Diana: Her True Story,* by Andrew Morton, a former tabloid reporter. Morton's book, whose sources included some of Diana's closest friends, claimed that the princess, locked in a loveless marriage, had developed bulimia and had attempted suicide five times. It painted Prince Charles as a cold, aloof husband and father who cared more for polo and old friends than for his wife and family.

If June was a cruel month, August was crueler still. First, photographs of a topless Duchess of York cavorting with her Texas financial adviser at a plush resort, were splashed across the world's tabloids. Then, days later, came the release of a taped telephone conversation between, allegedly, the Princess of Wales and a male intimate. On the tape, the woman was heard to complain about her husband. The man was heard exhorting her to blow kisses into the telephone. In a statement that was hardly a ringing expression of support for Diana, Buckingham Palace said the tape was ''inconclusive in terms of voice quality.''

In November the *Daily Mail,* the British newspaper that broke the story of the rift between the Duke and Duchess of York, predicted that a formal announcement acknowledging that the marriage of the Prince and Princess of Wales was ''over in all but name'' would be made by the end of the year. Separate living arrangements already were being negotiated, the newspaper claimed. Buckingham Palace duly announced the separation on December 9. In the meantime, adding to the royal disasters, part of the state apartments at Windsor Castle went up in flames, causing hundreds of millions of dollars' damage. The queen, submitting to public pressure, subsequently volunteered to pay an income tax. In a private ceremony in Scotland on December 12, Princess Anne took a second chance at marriage, wedding Timothy Laurence.

SUZANNE CASSIDY
Free-lance Journalist, London

The Arts

Arguably, the most significant thing that happened to the publicly funded arts in Britain in 1992 occurred neither on a stage nor on a canvas. It was the resignation in September of David Mellor as secretary of state for national heritage, the Cabinet position responsible for arts, broadcasting, and the press. A passionate arts supporter who was expected to fend off demands from Conservatives for a radical reorganization of the British Broadcasting Corporation (BBC), Mellor was replaced by Peter Brooke, a former secretary of state for Northern Ireland who was unknown to arts leaders.

Theater. For the West End, 1992 was something of a reprise of the previous year as the economic recession hit hard at box-office receipts. Even John Osborne's eagerly awaited sequel to his 1956 classic, *Look Back in Anger,* failed to stir the malaise. *Déjà Vu,* a look at Osborne's most famous character, Jimmy Porter, as an angry aging man, closed less than two months after it opened. Despite the bleak commercial atmosphere, some acclaimed plays won deserved transfers to the West End from the fringe and subsidized theater, among them a revival of Brian Friel's *Philadelphia, Here I Come!* and John Guare's *Six Degrees of Separation,* a Broadway import starring Stockard Channing.

A new play, *The Rise and Fall of Little Voice* by Jim Cartwright, transferred after a smash run at the Royal National Theatre. For the National Theatre, 1992 was a particular triumph—despite the recession, a new production of J. B. Priestley's *An Inspector Calls,* Alan Bennett's long-running *The Madness of George III,* and Tony Kushner's new play, *Angels in America,* drew capacity crowds.

At the Royal Shakespeare Company, the curtain went down early on the world premiere of Richard Nelson's *Columbus,* but the company won praise for Sam Mendes' production of *Richard III* and artistic director Adrian Noble's imaginative staging of *The Thebans,* Sophocles' Oedipus trilogy. Other notable plays included Frank McGuinness' Broadway-bound *Someone Who'll Watch Over Me,* a poignant, powerful drama about an Irishman, Englishman, and American held hostage together in a Beirut cell.

Music. For the Royal Opera House, 1992 was itself something of a tragic opera. In October two separate reports criticized the Royal Opera management for inefficiency and fiscal imprudence. One of the reports, prepared for the Arts Council, the quasigovernmental body that channels public cash to arts organizations, urged the Royal Opera to shelve its £200 million (c. $340 million) redevelopment project. By October the Royal Opera's accumulated deficit was put at nearly £4 million (c. $6.8 million). By contrast, the mood at the English National Opera could not have been brighter. In April the company announced that it had purchased the freehold of the London Coliseum to secure the historic building as the company's permanent home.

Despite the offstage turmoil, the Royal Opera had a fine year musically. In September, Luciano Pavarotti gave five performances in the leading role of Puccini's *Tosca.* In October the acclaimed Glyndebourne Festival production of Gershwin's *Porgy and Bess,* directed by Trevor Nunn, had its Covent Garden premiere. That same month, conductor Georg Solti celebrated his 80th birthday by conducting Kiri Te Kanawa and Placido Domingo in Verdi's *Otello.*

© Catherine Ashmore

With Damon Evans as Sportin' Life, Willard White, center, as Porgy, and Cynthia Haymon as Bess, George Gershwin's "Porgy and Bess" opened at Covent Garden in October 1992.

At the English National, there were new productions of Verdi's *The Force of Destiny* and Gilbert and Sullivan's *Princess Ida*. For pop-music aficionados, the year held two important milestones—in June former Beatle Paul McCartney turned 50, while October marked the 30th anniversary of the Beatles' first release, "Love Me Do."

Visual Arts. The Victoria and Albert Museum opened the year with an exhibition devoted to "The Art of Death." Filled with memento mori from over the centuries, the exhibition had been delayed because of the Persian Gulf war. Memories of the Gulf war were revived by another exhibition, that of the works of Britain's official Gulf war artist, John Keane, at the Imperial War Museum. It was met with a storm of criticism from patriots who took umbrage at one of Keane's paintings, "Mickey Mouse at the Front," which shows Mickey Mouse sitting on what looked to be a toilet next to a shopping cart crammed with antitank missiles. The Imperial War Museum, unruffled by the controversy, purchased the painting and several other drawings for £15,000 (c. $25,000).

In April art lovers mourned the death of painter Francis Bacon at age 82. The following month, London's Hayward Gallery opened a much-talked-about exhibition of the works of the Belgian surrealist artist René Magritte (*see* ART). Other notable exhibitions included a Tate Gallery exhibition of the works of the late German realist Otto Dix; a Royal Academy of Arts retrospective of the works of Alfred Sisley; and a Rembrandt exhibition at the National Gallery's Sainsbury Wing.

Dance. The Royal Ballet's troupe of rising stars, notably Darcey Bussell and Viviana Durante, dazzled balletomanes in performances of Kenneth MacMillan's *Romeo and Juliet* and *Manon* and Anthony Dowell's acclaimed production of *Swan Lake*. In May and June the Royal Ballet visited Japan on a four-week, 11-city tour. In April the Sadler's Wells theater welcomed Mikhail Baryshnikov's and Mark Morris' White Oak Dance Project. And in October the Birmingham Royal Ballet staged Kurt Jooss' 60-year-old drama, *The Green Table*, guided by Jooss' daughter, Anna Markard.

Film and Television. The British film industry, demoralized by scant funding, still produced some major films in late 1992. Among them were *Chaplin*—Sir Richard Attenborough's film about the life of Charlie Chaplin, which starred Robert Downey, Jr.—and Peter Kosminsky's *Emily Brontë's Wuthering Heights,* a British-American coproduction that starred Ralph Fiennes and Juliette Binoche. In November, Kenneth Branagh's *Peter's Friends,* with Emma Thompson and Stephen Fry, premiered at the London Film Festival.

On the small screen, the picture was clouded by fears about the future of British

© Catherine Ashmore

Irek Mukhamedov and Viviana Durante danced the parts of Romeo and Juliet in the Royal Ballet's "Romeo and Juliet." Kenneth MacMillan was the choreographer.

television. In February the profits versus programming debate was sparked by the forced resignation of David Plowright, the executive chairman of Granada Television Ltd., one of Britain's most respected commercial television companies, whose hits included *Brideshead Revisited* and *The Jewel in the Crown*. Plowright had balked at demands for increased profits that he thought would compromise the quality of his company's programming.

In September, Michael Grade, chief executive of Channel 4, a commercial television station, accused the management of the BBC of setting the nation's public television company on a course of "terminal decline" by implementing overly market-oriented reforms, abandoning popular entertainment for the elitist high ground, and "appeasing" the Conservative government. Marmaduke Hussey, chairman of the BBC's board of governors, told *The London Sunday Times* that Grade was "making an emotional and nostalgic pitch for the BBC in the 1980s." The realities of broadcasting in the 1990s demanded that the BBC make some changes, Hussey said.

SUZANNE CASSIDY

GREECE

During 1992, Prime Minister Constantine Mitsotakis' New Democracy Party retained control of the Greek Parliament with a slight majority. Andreas Papandreou and his Panhellenic Socialist Movement (PASOK) continued to be the main opposition.

Political Life. In January, after a ten-month trial, former Prime Minister Papandreou was acquitted of charges that he took part in embezzlement schemes connected with the Bank of Crete. He also was cleared of accusations that he had taken bribes; however, two former socialist ministers on trial with him, George Petsos and Dimitris Tsovolas, were convicted of improper governmental activities. Then, in May, Parliament voted to drop wiretapping charges that had been brought against Papandreou. Separately, George Koskotas, former chairman of the Bank of Crete and Papandreou's chief accuser, was convicted of forgery and sentenced to five years in prison.

On July 31, Parliament—by a vote of 286 of the 300 deputies—ratified the Maastricht Treaty on European unity, showing the commitment of both New Democracy and PASOK to the European Community.

Macedonian Issue. Macedonia became a tense issue in 1992. During the medieval and modern eras, control of Macedonia, with its mixed ethnic populations, had been contested by Greeks, Turks, Serbs, and Bulgarians. Following the Balkan Wars of 1912–13 the area had been divided among Greece, Serbia, and Bulgaria, with Greece receiving the major port city of Thessaloniki. After World War I the Serbian part was absorbed into Yugoslavia, and after World War II it became the republic of Macedonia within the Yugoslav federal union. In 1992, with the crumbling of Yugoslavia, the federal republic of Macedonia sought international recognition as an independent state.

In Greece there was strong opposition to the use of the name Macedonia for this inde-

© AP/Wide World

During 1992, Greek Prime Minister Constantine Mitsotakis faced the tense issue of Macedonia, worked to improve the Greek economy, and made historic trips to Iran and Israel.

pendent state; the Greeks referred to it as the republic of Skopje, after the capital city. Basically, Greek resistance was based on fear that an independent Macedonia would seek to expand into Greek Macedonia, and that the new state was trying to capture the glories connected with Alexander the Great of Macedonia, whom the Greek government, the parliamentary opposition, the Greek church, and the population in general considered an integral part of Hellenic civilization. Greek fears were exacerbated when the self-designated republic adopted as the symbol on its flag the 16-point star of the ancient Macedonian dynasty. Further problems arose when maps were produced in the new state that showed parts of Greece being incorporated into an enlarged Macedonian entity. Under these circumstances the government of Prime Minister Mitsotakis worked throughout the year to prevent both the European Community and the United States from recognizing the new state formally until it adopted a name that would be at least a variant of Macedonia.

Foreign Affairs. Objecting to Foreign Minister Antonis Samaras' endeavors in the Macedonian issue, Mitsotakis summarily dismissed him in April and assumed that ministry until handing it over to Michalis Papaconstantinou when the cabinet was reshuffled in August. Samaras, meanwhile, resigned from Parliament.

During the year, Prime Minister Mitsotakis conferred with many foreign leaders, including U.S. President George Bush, Albanian President Sali Berisha, Serbian President Slobodan Milosevic, Turkish President Turgut Özal, and Prime Minister Suleyman Demirel of Turkey. Though efforts were made to improve Greek-Turkish relations, these remained strained because the two countries had sharp differences

---

GREECE • Information Highlights

Official Name: Hellenic Republic.
Location: Southeastern Europe.
Area: 50,942 sq mi (131 940 km²).
Population (mid-1992 est.): 10,300,000.
Chief Cities (1981 census): Athens, the capital, 885,737; Salonika, 406,413; Piraeus, 196,389.
Government: *Head of state,* Constantine Karamanlis, president (took office May 1990). *Head of government,* Constantine Mitsotakis, prime minister (took office April 1990). *Legislature*—Parliament.
Monetary Unit: Drachma (213.75 drachmas equal U.S.$1, Dec. 30, 1992).
Gross Domestic Product (1990 est. U.S.$): $76,700,-000,000.
Economic Indexes (1991): *Consumer Prices* (1980 = 100), all items, 681.7; food, 680.6. *Industrial Production* (1980 = 100), 109.
Foreign Trade (1991 U.S.$): *Imports,* $21,582,-000,000; *exports,* $8,653,000,000.

about air and sea rights in the Aegean Sea and because of the unresolved Turkish occupation of part of Cyprus.

When Mitsotakis went to Iran for high-level talks in 1992, he became the first prime minister of any EC member country to visit since the Iranian revolution of 1979. His trip to Israel in May marked the first time a Greek prime minister had visited that country since its independence.

Economy. The Mitsotakis government continued an austerity program it had started in 1990 to strengthen the economy through such measures as controlling inflation, improving the balance of payments, privatizating government-run businesses (such as buses), reforming the social-security system, and imposing new taxes. The result during much of 1992 was widespread discontent manifested at various times by chaotic strikes and work stoppages in many sectors of society, including banks, post offices, transportation, and law firms. Mitsotakis found that the policies of Minister of National Economy and Finance Ioannis Paleokrassas and his successor, Stefanos Manos, who took office in August, were criticized strongly by Andreas Papandreou and PASOK. Indeed, even some important members of the New Democracy Party held that Manos' goals were laudable but the methods used excessive.

In July, Paleokrassas escaped an assassination attempt when a rocket was fired at his automobile, killing one bystander and injuring others. A statement issued apparently by November 17—a shadowy, underground organization—claimed responsibility and condemned the austerity program.

GEORGE J. MARCOPOULOS, *Tufts University*

HAITI

More than a year after the member countries of the Organization of American States (OAS) imposed an embargo on Haiti and launched diplomatic efforts to force the return of ousted President Jean-Bertrand Aristide, the situation remained hopelessly deadlocked as 1992 drew to a close.

Officials of the United States and the other nations of the 34-country OAS said in October that they had not given up hope of securing concessions from the military-dominated Haitian government but admitted that the intransigence of all sides, including Aristide's followers, was blocking efforts to reach a compromise solution.

Embargo. As the stalemate persisted, the economic embargo proved only partly effective. Supplies of food, fuel, and medicines were reduced sharply, adding to the suffering of Haiti's already impoverished masses. The country's small elite thrived, however, by dealing

---

HAITI · Information Highlights
Official Name: Republic of Haiti.
Location: Caribbean.
Area: 10,714 sq mi (27 750 km²).
Population: (mid-1992 est.): 6,400,000.
Chief City (1987 est.): Port-au-Prince, the capital, 797,000 (incl. suburbs).
Government: *Prime minister*, Marc Bazin (took office June 19, 1992). *Legislature*—suspended.
Monetary Unit: Gourde (5.0 gourdes equal U.S.$1, buying rate, July 1991).
Gross Domestic Product (1990 est. U.S.$): $2,700,-000,000.
Economic Index (1990): *Consumer Prices* (1980 = 100), all items, 191.1; food, 177.3.
Foreign Trade (1991 U.S.$): *Imports*, $374,000,000; *exports*, $103,000,000.

---

on the black market in smuggled goods. Repression by the military and paramilitary goon squads continued, particularly in the countryside beyond Port-au-Prince, the capital.

Refugees. Meanwhile, thousands of Haitians sought to escape the violence and poverty of their country. In the year following the Sept. 30, 1991, coup, more than 38,000 Haitians fled, many in overloaded, rickety boats. Many of the craft capsized or sunk and hundreds of Haitians drowned.

U.S. Response. In May, U.S. President George Bush ordered the U.S. Coast Guard to intercept boats leaving Haiti and return their occupants without benefit of a hearing to determine their eligibility for refugee status. The president's order directed Haitians seeking asylum to submit applications to the U.S. Embassy in Port-au-Prince. On July 29 a U.S. Court of Appeals ruled that the president's order violated rights guaranteed by U.S. immigration law. Three days later the U.S. Supreme Court stayed the Appeals Court order, and on October 7 the Supreme Court agreed to review the administration's forcible-repatriation policy.

Diplomatic Struggle. A tripartite accord was signed February 23 by representatives of the Haitian parliament, Aristide, and an OAS special envoy. The agreement would have ended the embargo, installed an interim prime minister approved by Aristide, and granted a general amnesty to police and soldiers involved in Aristide's overthrow. The Haitian parliament took no action on the agreement. On April 14 installed a new cabinet which, in turn, was replaced on June 19 by a cabinet headed by Marc Bazin, a political moderate and former World Bank economist. Aristide refused to accept Bazin, prolonging the stalemate.

Observers. In September the Haitian government agreed to accept a token force of OAS observers to monitor human-rights compliance in the country. The OAS had sought admission of 500 observers, but the government accepted only an 18-person team.

RICHARD C. SCHROEDER, *Consultant*
Organization of American States

HAWAII

Hawaii, still reeling from a costly September 1992 hurricane, was swept by a political tide in November, when Democrats won most national, state, and local elections.

Politics. Frank F. Fasi, Republican mayor of Honolulu, was the only major Republican officeholder to survive the voting onslaught. Fasi was elected to a sixth four-year term, narrowly defeating Democratic challenger Dennis O'Connor, a former state legislator and city councilman. It probably will be the last time Honolulu has a six-term mayor as voters approved a two-term limit on the post.

Political analysts believed that Fasi's victory was due in part to his public support, late in the campaign, of U.S. Sen. Daniel K. Inouye, the veteran Democratic candidate who was accused of sexual improprieties by Inouye's Republican opponent Rick Reed. Although Reed lost to Inouye by more than 100,000 votes, he retained his seat in the state Senate, in which he has another two years; his impact there, however, likely would be minimal, since the Democrats easily retained senate control. (They hold 22 of the 25 seats.) Inouye, a World War II hero, began his sixth term in January 1993. Hawaii's two incumbent U.S. representatives—Democrats Neil Abercrombie and Patsy Mink—also won reelection against weak opposition. In the presidential race, Arkansas Gov. Bill Clinton (D) carried the state with 48% of the vote.

Republican strength in the 73-member state legislature fell to an all-time low. The party retained three Senate seats but lost two seats in the House (retaining four), leaving only seven party stalwarts in both houses. The legislature also had a change of leadership. Both Democratic Senate President Richard Wong and Democratic House Speaker Daniel Kihano retired. One of the new elected Democratic state senators is Matt Matsunaga, son of the late U.S. Sen. Spark Matsunaga.

The September balloting reduced the ranks of Hawaii's women mayors from three to two, when Mayor Lorraine Inouye of the Island of Hawaii lost in the primary to former councilman Stephen Yamashiro. Democrat Yamashiro went on to win in the general election. The other women mayors—JoAnn A. Yukimura, Democrat of Kauai, and Linda Crockett Lingle, Republican of Maui—were at midterm in their offices.

Hurricane. The political campaigning was waged in the aftermath of Hurricane *Iniki,* which struck Hawaii on September 11, with winds clocked as high as 227 mi (365 km) per hour. The storm, which caused five deaths, did an estimated $1.6 billion damage to tourist-oriented Kauai, where telephone and electricity services were knocked out for weeks. The island's population of about 50,000 residents, plus some 7,500 tourists on the island when the hurricane struck, had to scramble for essentials such as food and water until the National Guard and emergency services moved in from other islands.

Property damage on the island of Oahu, 100 mi (161 km) southeast, was estimated at $2.5 million, with an additional $10 million damage to crops, principally sugar cane. No hotels were damaged on Oahu, although some Waikiki beach resorts had slight wave intrusion.

Mass Transit. Honolulu's hopes of easing transportation woes received a bitter blow in midsummer when the City Council voted down a $1.7 billion tax-financed mass-transit plan.

CHARLES H. TURNER
Free-lance Writer, Honolulu

HAWAII • Information Highlights

Area: 6,471 sq mi (16 759 km²).
Population (July 1, 1991 est.): 1,135,000.
Chief Cities (1990 census): Honolulu, the capital, 365,272; Hilo, 37,808; Kailua, 36,818; Kaneohe, 35,448.
Government (1992): *Chief Officers*—governor, John D. Waihee III (D); lt. gov., Benjamin J. Cayetano (D). *Legislature*—Senate, 25 members; House of Representatives, 51 members.
State Finances (fiscal year 1991): *Revenue,* $4,916,000,000; *expenditure,* $4,510,000,000.
Personal Income (1991): $24,045,000,000; per capita, $21,190.
Labor Force (June 1992): *Civilian labor force,* 566,100; *unemployed,* 25,900 (4.6% of total force).
Education: *Enrollment* (fall 1990)—public elementary schools, 122,840; public secondary, 48,868; colleges and universities, 53,772. *Public school expenditures* (1990), $838,143,000.

HONG KONG

Hong Kong's return to China would not happen until 1997, but change was well under way in 1992. In April, for example, the Hong Kong police force took over the patrol of the China-Hong Kong border from the British Army and in September a British battalion began its withdrawal, the first of many.

Politics. The British still controlled the government and Christopher Patten replaced Lord Wilson as the 28th, and potentially last, governor of Hong Kong in July. In October, Patten, a former Conservative Party chief and close ally of British Prime Minister John Major, announced a series of political changes. The proposals, which did not violate Hong Kong's Basic Law, called for more voters to participate in local elections by increasing the base of "functional constituency elections." Lawyers, trade unionists, and other businessmen vote for legislators in such balloting. The Chinese denounced the plan since they were not part of its formation.

In other political matters, the Chinese government in March appointed 44 Hong Kong ad-

Hong Kong Gov. Christopher Patten visited China Oct. 20-23, 1992, for discussions regarding his political-reform program. Throughout the trip, he was snubbed by China's Premier Li Peng. Nevertheless the program was approved by the Hong Kong legislature in mid-November.

© Susan Williams/Agence France-Presse

visers to "facilitate mutual understanding" between China and the territory. This was seen by many as an attempt to build a second, unelected power base in Hong Kong as most of the advisers were prominent pro-Beijing or conservative figures. Beijing interests lost out in July, however, when the legislature voted down the multiseat single-vote plan the pro-Beijing advisers favored.

Economy. The value of the Hong Kong Exchange Fund was disclosed for the first time, showing that Hong Kong's foreign-currency reserves of $28.9 billion were 12th-largest in the world. Hong Kong now was the world's 19th-largest exporter with textiles, clothing, and consumer electrical and electronic products leading the way. A 5% growth in gross domestic product (GDP) was expected in 1992.

The rising cost of building the Chek Lap Kok Airport was a problem, beginning with the disclosure that its April cost was almost 14% higher than that of July 1991. The cost probably would continue to rise because of inflation.

Chinese influences were seen everywhere, including in publishing. The Sino-United Published (Holdings) Ltd., formed by the merger of three large Beijing publishing companies, had assets of $128 million and controlled a newspaper, printing company, and about 30 publishing houses and book stores.

In January, China-based World Wide Electronic Co. leased an 8.4-acre (3.4-ha) site at the Tai Po Industrial Estate for a planned $312 million semiconductor plant. Other Chinese-backed companies were involved in everything from banking and insurance to transportation and retailing. Their cumulative investment was estimated at about $78 billion.

Hong Kong Park, built on the former estate of the British commander in the Central District, opened in March. Tourism continued profitable, earning $641 million in 1991.

Migration. About 60,000 people emigrated in 1992. As of February, about 3,700 principal beneficiaries and their 7,300 dependents had been registered as British citizens under the British Nationality Scheme. An agreement was reached in May with the Vietnamese government, allowing the forced return of Vietnamese migrants who were not deemed to be fleeing persecution. By June, more than 22,000 of 55,000 Vietnamese migrants had been screened out as nonrefugees.

DAVID CHUENYAN LAI
University of Victoria, British Columbia

HOUSING

The U.S. housing market staged a moderate recovery in 1992, bouncing back from the lowest level of activity since World War II. The recovery was concentrated in the single-family component of the market, as the multifamily component languished at the depressed 1991 level.

The 1992 housing recovery was aided by the U.S. Federal Reserve (Fed), which guided interest rates to the lowest levels in two decades through management of monetary policy. However, the George Bush administration and Congress were unable to agree on a fiscal-stimulus package for housing and the economy, as political gridlock developed during the presidential-election year. In fact, several key tax incentives for housing expired during the year, setting back efforts to deal with the major housing problems that had been growing in the United States since the early 1980s. These problems involved barriers to affordability for first-time home buyers, shortages of decent and affordable rental housing for low-income people, and a growing number of homeless families —particularly in inner-city areas.

The credit crunch that had been squeezing the producers of housing since the end of 1989 persisted in 1992. The Bush administration and the Fed publicly decried the credit crunch at thrift institutions and commercial banks as an unwarranted constraint on small businesses in general and homebuilders in particular. In the fall, the federal regulators of thrifts and banks approved a uniform and reasonable system of real-estate lending standards, for implementation early in 1993. Furthermore, the financial condition of thrifts and banks improved dramatically in 1992, placing these depository institutions in a better position to support loan growth in the future.

The new Democratic administration of President-elect Bill Clinton would inherit a housing sector with major pluses and minuses. On the plus side, the single-family-housing market would enter 1993 with lean inventories of unsold stock, a substantial amount of pent-up demand, and historically low interest rates. On the minus side, the multifamily market still was fundamentally weak, with overbuilt rental markets in many areas as well as major supply-demand imbalances in the condo market.

The Clinton administration also would inherit a growing divergence between the housing "haves" and "have-nots" in the United States, a divergence also showing up in measures of income and wealth distribution. During the 1992 presidential campaign, Clinton's prescriptions for change included a series of measures designed to address key U.S. housing problems.

Struggling Toward Recovery. Total housing starts rose 18% in 1992 to 1.2 million units, up from a post-World War II low of 1.015 million units in 1991. Single-family starts rose by 22% to 1.03 million units, while multifamily starts remained at 175,000 units, virtually identical to the depressed performance of 1991. The overall housing recovery was the weakest of the post-World War II period.

The single-family-housing recovery occurred in the face of low levels of consumer confidence and stagnant job growth for most of the year. A large volume of pent-up housing demand had built up during the 1990–91 period, providing the raw material for recovery in 1992.

Falling interest rates enticed some of this potential into the market during 1992. The cost of fixed-rate-mortgage credit fell to the lowest level since the early 1970s, and the cost of adjustable-rate-mortgage credit fell to the lowest level on record. Management of monetary policy by the Fed was crucial to this pattern, and the Fed lowered its short-term interest-rate targets to 3% by midyear.

The multifamily-housing sector was flat throughout 1992, at a level of activity around 25% of the volume posted in the mid-1980s. Despite years of low production of multifamily units, rental vacancy rates remained at historically high levels as the demand for rental units was held down by the 1990–91 economic recession and a period of stagnant economic growth that ran through 1992. Furthermore, production of rental units for low-income families was affected adversely late in the year as the Low-Income Housing Tax Credit program expired and political gridlock prevented passage of tax legislation that would have extended this critical production incentive.

The condominium component of the multifamily housing sector—i.e., ownership units in multifamily structures—also languished in 1992 at a depressed level. The Northeastern region of the United States, where the condominium market historically has been concentrated, remained in economic recession, and excess supplies of condominium units weighed heavily on the market.

The credit crunch facing the homebuilding industry continued to be a constraint on construction and land development in 1992. The multifamily sector was particularly hard hit because of the relatively high risk of lending for this type of housing. Indeed, permanent multifamily mortgage financing was difficult to get, in addition to the very tight conditions in the markets for housing-production credit.

Deepening Housing Problems. The United States in 1992 was facing a variety of interrelated housing problems that had spread and

Total housing starts in the United States rose by 18% during 1992. The single-family-housing market, in particular, gained new strength. This recovery was due largely to the pent-up demand that had accumulated during the 1990-91 recession.

deepened since the early 1980s. Many first-time home buyers lacked the resources to cover down payments and closing costs. Some owners continued to occupy run-down homes because their incomes were not sufficient to finance either home improvements or a move. Most low and moderate-income renters paid an unreasonable share of their incomes to live in housing that often was inadequate. High rents, combined with little or no savings, put many renters one paycheck away from eviction and homelessness.

A Census Bureau report showed that 91% of all renters could not afford to purchase the median-priced home in their region of the country, and 86% could not afford even a more modestly priced home. The Census Bureau's analysis showed that the overwhelming reason that most potential first-time home buyers cannot afford to purchase is the lack of cash to cover down payments and closing costs. Many renters and newly formed families who could afford monthly mortgage payments could not overcome the upfront cash hurdle without assistance. The research performed by the Census Bureau suggested that 660,000 renters could afford to buy a home if they had an extra $2,500 and 1.5 million could afford to buy with an extra $5,000.

Families whose aspirations for ownership are blocked must compete in the rental market with those who need or prefer to rent, and this leaves poor renters with fewer choices and higher rents. The Joint Center for Housing Studies at Harvard University, in its 1992 "State of the Nation's Housing" report, found that more than three quarters of the poor and unsubsidized renters were paying more than half their incomes for housing. Furthermore, since the mid-1980s, there had been a net loss of about 500,000 units from the low-cost rental-housing stock, as continually undermaintained apartments became uninhabitable.

The lack of decent and safe housing had become most evident in the distressed areas of U.S. central cities. Through a series of disinvestment decisions by public and private entities, the social, infrastructure, and housing nexus of some central-city neighborhoods had deteriorated to the point where civil disorder threatened those remaining, and their property. Riots in Los Angeles crystallized these deepening problems in 1992.

Clinton Policy Approach. Discussion of housing issues during and after the 1992 presidential campaign revealed an apparent sensitivity of the incoming Clinton administration to the United States' housing problems. Furthermore, discussions stressed that housing problems are interrelated, and that addressing one set of problems can ease strains in other areas. In particular, there was realization that increasing first-time homeownership opportunities and removing barriers to buying a home also can help those seeking decent and affordable rental housing, as those families obtaining homeownership make way for others who are competing for the often short supply for good units that families with modest incomes can afford.

Thus a housing-policy priority of the Clinton administration was to be down-payment assistance for moderate-income, first-time home buyers. A revitalized Federal Housing Administration mortgage-insurance program was discussed as a vehicle for delivering low down-payment housing credit for first-time buyers.

The Clinton dialogue also stressed that the dual problems of fewer units to rent, and more people paying higher portions of their incomes toward rent, required a dual approach to solving the low-income rental-housing problems. The Clinton program stressed that government-assisted production of affordable rental housing should complement programs (such as housing vouchers) designed to help people meet rent payments. Housing policies in the 1980s focused on income supplements and sharply reduced the federal government's support for production of rental housing. Reinstatement of such support was a part of Clinton's "Rebuild America" plan.

It also was noted that private-sector efforts to produce affordable housing have been complicated by government restrictions that unnecessarily increase the final cost to the buyer or renter. Restrictive zoning requirements, burdensome processing time and fees, layered bureaucratic requirements, and a host of other requirements have crept into the building process and driven the cost of housing up enough to prevent low and moderate-income families from buying or renting in some areas. These problems were documented by a special commission established in 1991 by Jack Kemp, President Bush's secretary of the U.S. Department of Housing and Urban Development. The commission recommended that the federal government should step in to stop the actions that some communities have used to prevent others from moving in.

Implementation of Clinton's housing-policy priorities would be constrained by the U.S. federal budget deficit. Bold new initiatives that require tax incentives or budgetary outlays to help first-time buyers or low-income renters might have to be financed by cutbacks in other components of federal support to housing. Housing provisions delivering substantial support to higher-income individuals might be prime candidates for cutbacks. The home-mortgage-interest deduction and the one-time capital-gains exclusion for taxpayers aged 55 years or older are big-ticket items that would be reconsidered by the new administration.

See also UNITED STATES—*The Economy.*
KENT W. COLTON and DAVID F. SEIDERS
National Association of Home Builders

HUMAN RIGHTS

While the priority of human rights has gained the official recognition of more and more nations in recent decades, many important holdouts remain. Freedom House, a New York City-based human-rights group, in early 1992 identified 13 countries as the "worst violators of human rights"—seven were in Asia (Afghanistan, China, Iraq, North Korea, Syria, Vietnam, and Myanmar, formerly Burma), four in Africa (Equatorial Guinea, Libya, Somalia, and Sudan), and two in the Caribbean (Cuba and Haiti). In March the UN Human Rights Commission cited a record 22 nations for human-rights abuses. The commission also said that it would continue its surveillance of a number of other nations.

Although not on any such "worst violators" list, various Southeast Asian nations have formed a de facto coalition resisting Western pressures to take a stand against human-rights violations in the region. At a Manila meeting in July between foreign-ministry officials of Southeast Asian and Western nations, U.S. Undersecretary of State Robert Zoellick singled out the military regime of Myanmar for gross human-rights violations. Rejecting advice to apply sanctions against Myanmar, representatives of the Association of Southeast Asian Nations (ASEAN) defended the Myanmar junta as being "legitimate" and "legally constituted." Because of this and other disagreements, the European Community (EC) declined to renew its economic-cooperation agreement with ASEAN.

Breakthroughs. During 1992 the United States formally ratified the International Covenant on Civil and Political Rights (ICCPR), which was drafted by the United Nations in 1966 and set forth universal standards for the protection of basic civil and political rights. The U.S. Senate gave its consent to ICCPR in April and President Bush signed the instrument of ratification in early June. More than 100 nations, including Canada and EC members, also have ratified the covenant.

The World Bank set a human-rights precedent in May. Along with leading Western donor nations, the Bank froze most of its economic aid to the government of Malawi for 1992 and 1993 because of worsening repression in the African one-party state. The World Bank previously had abstained from linking economic aid with a country's human-rights record.

Levi Strauss & Co., a U.S.-based firm with $5 billion in jeans sales in 1991, took the initiative of making sure that its far-flung operations around the globe follow practices "not incompatible with our values." It now requires its contractors and suppliers to commit themselves to "terms of engagement" on labor conditions they can control, including a safe and healthy work environment, no employment of children or forced labor, no corporal punishment, and a normal workweek of less than 60 hours. Levi Strauss also adopted broader criteria under which "pervasive violations of basic human rights" would bar a country as a production source. Myanmar became the first country to lose Levi Strauss contracts.

Anxious to protect its $200 million-per-year export trade in the face of rising criticism, the All-India Carpet Manufacturers Association announced a plan to halt the illegal practice of using child and bonded labor in the hand-knotted carpet industry. India has several hundred thousand children, some as young as 6, working long hours in carpet weaving. The association also favored the adoption and promotion internationally of a "child labor free" label on rugs. However, only 300 of the 2,000 rug exporters in India subscribed to the association's voluntary reform plan. The partial breakthrough against child labor in India came as a result of a campaign led by the London-based Anti-Slavery International and various nongovernmental organizations.

According to Laura S. Wiseberg, director of the Montreal-based International Human Rights Documentation Network, there has been an "astronomical growth" of human-rights groups recently on all continents. The Network has more than 5,000 such groups listed in its database, not counting many thousands of unions, professional associations, churches, and other private groups that devote some of their resources to human-rights issues. Because of their monitoring, "human cruelty can no longer be hidden in dark and distant corners of the planet," as the 1992 Human Development Report of the UN Development Program pointed out.

Challenges. The People's Republic of China continued to be the major target of such exposure, especially in regard to the use of forced labor for exported goods. Meanwhile, human-rights groups also kept up pressure on less-publicized abuses elsewhere. In their 1992 reports, Amnesty International and Human Rights Watch both highlighted evidence that many governments are letting their security forces get away with murder, kidnapping, torture, and detention without charges or trial. Such human-rights violations continue unabated, Amnesty stated, largely because persons who commit them seldom are held accountable and so have little fear of punishment even when their guilt becomes public. Amnesty attributed the deaths of more than 500 persons to torture or inhuman prison conditions in some 40 countries in 1991. During a mission to Turkey, Lois Whitman, deputy director of Helsinki Watch, a branch of Human Rights Watch, was told by Turkish lawyers that police torture 80% to 90% of political suspects and 50% of ordinary criminal suspects, including children.

ROBERT A. SENSER

HUNGARY

In 1992, Hungary experienced stresses and strains resulting from its unsteady political balance and its ailing economy; the country was involved in a dispute with its northern neighbor, Slovakia, but bolstered its relationships with the European Community, Russia, and the United States.

Politics. Hungary's coalition government, consisting of the Hungarian Democratic Forum (HDF), the Independent Smallholder's Party (ISP), and the Christian Democratic People's Party (CDPP) remained intact despite internal opposition and constant constitutional debate. The first test of the coalition's survival came in February when Jozsef Torgyan, leader of the ISP, announced his party's withdrawal from the coalition government. Torgyan cited the ISP's inability to influence decisions of the coalition as the reason for his action. Torgyan had had frequent differences of opinion with Prime Minister Jozsef Antall (HDF). However, his attempt to lead the ISP out of the coalition was prevented by a rebellion among his own followers. On February 22, 33 out of the 45 ISP deputies in the legislature repudiated Torgyan and declared their support for the coalition.

More political tension arose from disputes between the prime minister and the president of the republic, Arpád Goncz, concerning the future of Hungarian Radio and Television. In late spring, Csabar Gombar and Elemer Hankiss were scheduled to be dismissed from their positions as presidents of Hungarian Radio and Television, respectively. Both had been prominent dissidents during the Communist years, and had since opposed the efforts of the present ruling coalition to influence the media. They were supported in their endeavor to maintain an independent press by the other two prominent opposition parties, the Free Democrats (Goncz' party) and the Young Democrats. When Antall asked President Goncz for the dismissal of these men, Goncz refused, even after

several requests for action. The president also opposed a law aimed at the prosecution of former Communist officials, which was voided by Hungary's constitutional court on March 3.

In August, Istvan Csurka, a right-wing HDF leader, created a furor when he published an article blaming the country's ills on foreigners and Jews. Antall tried to smooth over the resulting controversy, which again threatened the coalition's survival.

Economy. Despite optimistic predictions, the Hungarian economic plan failed to meet the expectations for a smooth transition to a market economy. In January the government predicted a budget deficit of 69.8 billion forints (about $900 million), a growth in gross national product (GNP) of 1%-2% and an inflation rate of 20%-25%. By June substantial modifications were being made in this economic plan. Industrial production was up only slightly, unemployment rose to 9.7%, and the economy continued to shrink. Inflation remained high as predicted. As a result, the budget deficit had to be raised to about $2.3 billion, and hopes for substantial GNP growth were disappointing.

Much of this decline in the economy has been the result of a new law passed in September 1991 requiring businesses to declare bankruptcy in the event of being unable to pay bills for a period of 90 days. As a result, by May 1992, 5% of all Hungarian businesses had declared bankruptcy. This caused a loss of taxes for the government and was a major reason for the increased budget deficit. It was expected that many more businesses would continue to fall into bankruptcy; the number of private entrepreneurships had doubled since 1988.

On March 13 the first automobile rolled off the assembly line at the new General Motors Opel-Hungary Plant in Szentgotthard. The Opel Astra would be the first passenger automobile produced by a Western company in Eastern Europe. The plant expected to produce 15,000 automobiles annually. In October a Suzuki automobile plant in Esztergom also opened.

In January 1992 parliament approved legislation mandating the privatization of all agricultural and industrial cooperatives in Hungary; in June a company was set up to administer state property in the hope of speeding the privatization process and increasing economic recovery. The government also allowed commercial banks to buy and sell hard currency freely instead of turning all hard-currency reserves over to the Hungarian National Bank. All these measures were part of Hungary's attempt at establishing a viable market economy.

Foreign Affairs. On February 6 a ten-year bilateral treaty of cooperation and friendship was signed with Germany. The German government pledged to assist Hungary in obtaining full membership in the European Council and to aid in its transition to a market economy.

HUNGARY • Information Highlights

Official Name: Republic of Hungary.
Location: East-central Europe.
Area: 35,919 sq mi (93 030 km²).
Population (mid-1992 est.): 10,300,000.
Chief Cities (Jan. 1, 1991): Budapest, the capital, 2,018,035; Debrecen, 213,927; Miskolc, 194,033.
Government: *Head of state,* Arpád Goncz, president (elected August 1990). *Head of government,* Jozsef Antall, prime minister (took office May 1990). *Legislature* (unicameral)—National Assembly.
Monetary Unit: Forint (82.05 forints equal U.S.$1, Dec. 30, 1992).
Gross National Product (1990 est. U.S.$): $60,900,-000,000.
Economic Indexes (1990): *Consumer Prices* (1980 = 100), all items, 374.1; food, 339.5. *Industrial Production* (1980 = 100), 102.
Foreign Trade (1990 U.S.$): *Imports,* $8,764,000,000; *exports,* $9,707,000,000.

In March, Hungary was granted "most favored nation" status by the Bush administration and received a visit from U.S. Gen. Colin Powell, chairman of the Joint Chiefs of Staff, who discussed military cooperation with Hungarian leaders. On a visit to Budapest in May, British Prime Minister John Major gave support to Hungary's aim of becoming a member of the European Community (EC) by the end of the decade.

Also in May, the government repudiated a 1977 agreement made by the Communist regime with Czechoslovakia for a joint hydroelectric project on the Danube River. Despite protests from Hungary, which was concerned about the environmental impact of the project, the Slovak government went ahead with its part of the plan. Both parties agreed to EC mediation of the dispute in October. Another point of contention between Hungary and Slovakia (an independent country as of January 1993) concerned the rights of the 600,000 ethnic Hungarians living in Slovakia, which Hungary sought to guarantee.

During a visit to Hungary by Russian President Boris Yeltsin in November, he and Prime Minister Antall held talks aimed at restoring the trade links between their two countries.

World's Fair. In March it was announced that Budapest would be host to a 1996 world's fair. Plans for the fair, however, had to be subsequently downsized due to the lack of economic resources.

VLADIMIR TISMANEANU
Foreign Policy Research Institute

ICELAND

For Iceland, 1992 was characterized by economic slowdowns, most resulting from declining fishing catches. The nation strengthened its ties with Europe with the signing at Oporto, Portugal, in May of an agreement to form a European Economic Area, bringing hopes of increased trade with Europe and better terms for Iceland's vital marine-product exports.

Prime Minister Davíd Oddsson made a state visit to Israel in February, only to face Israeli claims that a former Estonian who had lived in Iceland for more than 40 years was guilty of war crimes and should be brought to trial. President Vigdís Finnbogadóttir agreed to continue as Iceland's head of state for another four-year term, which she said would be her last. She addressed the UN Conference on the Environment in Rio de Janeiro in June. In September, Norway's King Harald V and his wife Queen Sonja paid an official visit to Iceland.

Economy. Although inflation remained at an all-time low of 1% to 1.5% annually, continuing high interest rates were blamed for the recession plaguing the country. Lower prices for marine exports exacerbated the problems, and

---

ICELAND • Information Highlights

Official Name: Republic of Iceland.
Location: North Atlantic Ocean.
Area: 39,768 sq mi (103 000 km²).
Population (Dec. 1, 1991 est.): 259,581.
Chief City (Dec. 1, 1991 est.): Reykjavík, the capital, 99,653.
Government: *Head of state,* Vigdís Finnbogadóttir, president (took office Aug. 1980). *Head of government,* David Oddsson, prime minister (took office April 1991). *Legislature*—Althing: Upper House and Lower House.
Monetary Unit: Króna (57.87 krónur equal U.S.$1, selling rate, May 1992).
Gross Domestic Product (1990 U.S.$): $4,200,-000,000.
Foreign Trade (1991 U.S.$): *Imports,* $1,720,000,000; *exports,* $1,554,000,000.

---

most fish-processing industries reported operating losses of 5% to 10% for the year. Unemployment, at 1.5% or less for almost a decade, grew to almost 4% in the autumn. Economic growth declined, with the gross domestic product declining by 2.7%, while foreign-currency earnings dropped by 4%.

Attempting to reduce a large budget deficit, the government introduced an austerity campaign in the public sector. Education and health services were cut back severely, university fees were introduced, and the portion of health care and pharmaceutical costs paid for by public health insurance was reduced. Several government industries were sold off and widespread plans for further privatization of public enterprises were in the pipeline.

Marine scientists painted a bleak picture of the situation of the cod-fishing stocks, which had been declining steadily over the past five years. Minister of Fisheries Thorsteinn Pálsson announced that cod-catch quotas for the 1992–93 fishing year would be reduced by about 25%. Since cod accounts for almost half the export income from marine products in Iceland, and these supply 65% to 75% of total export revenues, the cutbacks caused widespread difficulties. Efforts were made to compensate by raising quotas for other fish stocks. Attempts were made to purchase fishing quotas elsewhere and to supplement the catch by fishing for deep-sea stocks in international waters.

After nearly four years of negotiations with Atlantal—an international consortium of three aluminum producers from the United States, Sweden, and the Netherlands—talks on the proposed building of an aluminum smelter in southwest Iceland were concluded without result. The parties reported economic factors made the building of a new smelter unfeasible at this time. They said discussions might be revived later under more favorable conditions. This conclusion left the national power company, Landsvirkjun, with a huge power surplus and heavy interest payments to meet on foreign loans taken to build new facilities.

KENEVA KUNZ, *University of Iceland*

IDAHO

Idaho bucked national trends in 1992's November general election, providing President George Bush with a wide margin of victory for the state's four electoral votes, giving Republicans a three-to-two majority in its federal congressional delegation, and returning both chambers of the state legislature to unqualified Republican control. Voters rejected an initiative rolling back property taxes to 1% of market value, approved a constitutional amendment outlawing casino gambling, and elected Boise Mayor Dirk Kempthorne (R) to succeed retiring Sen. Steve Symms (R).

Election. Arkansas Gov. Bill Clinton's electoral sweep reached into the intermountain West on election day, but not into Idaho. Bush claimed 43% of the state's nearly 475,000 votes, with independent Ross Perot, at 28%, doing nearly as well as Democrat Clinton, who had 29%. In addition, voters rejected 2d District Democratic Rep. Richard Stallings' attempt to move to the Senate, giving Mayor Kempthorne an easy victory. In the race to succeed Stallings, Republican Mike Crapo, president pro tem of the state Senate, soundly defeated state auditor J. D. Williams. In the 1st District, however, incumbent Democrat Larry LaRocco kept his seat, turning back an underfinanced challenge from former state Sen. Rachel Gilbert of Boise.

The reapportioned state Senate, evenly divided between Democrats and Republicans since 1990, returned to solid Republican control, with the Republicans taking 23 seats to the Democrats' 12. The House remained overwhelmingly Republican, by a 50–20 margin. The hardest-fought ballot issue, the 1% initiative, was defeated by a 2–1 margin in the face of assertions that it would gut schools and local governments, the sole recipients of Idaho's property tax.

Crime. Three people died in an August 21–22 shootout during an 11-day siege by authorities at the backwoods home of Randy Weaver and his family near the northern town of Bonners Ferry. Weaver, a 44-year-old follower of the Christian Identity movement that sometimes is associated with white separatists, and Kevin Harris, 25, gave themselves up after the shooting deaths of a U.S. marshal and Weaver's wife and teenage son. Both awaited trial on charges of murder, conspiracy, assault, and firearms violations. Weaver originally was sought for failure to appear in court in February 1991 on a firearms charge.

Natural Resources. Following the National Marine Fisheries Service's listing of three Snake River salmon runs under the Endangered Species Act, the U.S. Army Corps of Engineers experimentally lowered the river's Lower Granite reservoir below levels acceptable for barge traffic to the port of Lewiston for a month, beginning in March. Although future drawdowns proposed by Gov. Cecil Andrus (D) to help rescue the fish runs were unpopular in northern areas dependent on river transportation, they were received better in southern Idaho, where upper Snake River water could provide an alternative means of flushing juvenile salmon downstream. The year ended amid uncertainty over future efforts to save one sockeye and two chinook runs.

In August wildfires in Idaho caused Governor Andrus to declare a state of emergency. The blazes in central Idaho charred more than 235,000 acres (95 101 ha).

JIM FISHER
"Lewiston Morning Tribune"

ILLINOIS

Illinois voters made political history in 1992 when they elected the first black woman, Carol Moseley Braun (*see* BIOGRAPHY), to the U.S. Senate. Otherwise, Republicans managed to overtake Democrats in state legislative races.

Election. Braun, a lawyer and liberal Democrat from Chicago, was a little-known Cook county recorder of deeds until she toppled incumbent Sen. Alan Dixon in a three-way Democratic primary in March. She went on to win the Senate seat in November with 55% of the vote, compared with 45% for her Republican opponent, Richard Williamson, a former White House aide who was making his first try for elective office. Her election was not the first time Illinois voters have made history. In 1928, Illinois voters elected Oscar DePriest to Congress as the first black from a northern state in the House of Representatives.

In 1992 House elections, Chicago voters chose Luis Gutierrez (D), a city alderman who once delivered newspapers to the mayor's office, as the first Hispanic from the state to be elected to Congress. He was chosen in a gerrymandered Chicago district that was drawn to give Hispanics a congressional seat from Illi-

---

IDAHO • Information Highlights

Area: 83,564 sq mi (216 432 km²).
Population (July 1, 1991 est.): 1,039,000.
Chief Cities (1990 census): Boise, the capital, 125,738; Pocatello, 46,080; Idaho Falls, 43,929.
Government (1992): *Chief Officers*—governor, Cecil Andrus (D); lt. gov., C. L. Otter (R). *Legislature*—Senate, 42 members; House of Representatives, 84 members.
State Finances (fiscal year 1991): *Revenue,* $2,584,000,000; *expenditure,* $2,305,000,000.
Personal Income (1991): $15,935,000,000; per capita, $15,333.
Labor Force (June 1992): *Civilian labor force,* 512,700; *unemployed,* 31,500 (6.1% of total force).
Education: *Enrollment* (fall 1990)—public elementary schools, 160,097; public secondary, 60,743; colleges and universities, 51,881. *Public school expenditures* (1990), $686,819,000.

Bobby L. Rush, surrounded by his wife Carolyn (left) and daughter Kacy, acknowledged his election to the U.S. House of Representatives from Illinois' 1st District on Nov. 3, 1992. The 46-year-old Democrat, a leader of the Black Panthers in the 1960s, had been a member of the Chicago City Council since 1983.

nois. Also elected was Bobby Rush (D), a former member of the Black Panthers, who would represent Chicago's South Side.

In the presidential race, Democrat Bill Clinton handily carried the state with 48% of the vote. President George Bush received 35%, while independent Ross Perot received 17%. In state races, Republicans overcame the Democratic sweep of Clinton and Braun at the top of the ballot to win control of the Illinois Senate for the first time in 18 years. The change in Senate leadership was expected to diminish the influence of Mayor Richard M. Daley and other Chicago Democrats in Springfield.

Democrats retained control of the 118-seat Illinois Assembly. Nonetheless, Republican Gov. Jim Edgar said it was a major victory for his party to win control of the Senate in a state that for years has had a Republican governor and Democratic-controlled legislature. Republicans hoped that their new majority in the Illinois Senate would mean that more state funds would be funneled to the suburbs.

An exit poll of Illinois voters showed that most of those voting—49%—thought the condition of the nation's economy was "not so good." Forty-two percent said their family's financial situation was about the same as four years earlier, while 37% said it was worse. On the issue of more women in the U.S. Senate, 39% said it was very important, another 39% said it was somewhat important, while 21% said it was not important.

In other election results, Illinois voters narrowly defeated a constitutional amendment that would have required the financially strapped state treasury to provide the majority of funding for public schools. The state presently was providing 33%. Proponents said the measure would have reduced the tax burden for property owners. Opponents claimed it would have benefited Chicago schools at the expense of suburban communities and increased Illinois' income tax.

Gambling. Illinois legislators grappled with the efforts of Mayor Daley to win state approval of a $2 billion casino and entertainment complex in Chicago. Democrats generally favored the proposal, while Republicans and Governor Edgar opposed it. The debate was expected to run into 1993. Daley and his allies claimed the casino would create jobs and bring in $125 million annually in gaming taxes.

Edgar maintained that any new revenues from the casino would be at the expense of the state lottery, the pari-mutuel horse-racing industry, and the fledgling riverboat gambling in Illinois.

Other. A Macon County Circuit Court judge found an 8-year-old boy guilty of rape in connection with the 1991 gang rape of a 10-year-old girl.

Ownership of the East St. Louis City Hall was returned to the city by an appeals court which overturned a lower court ruling granting the building to a man who suffered permanent brain damage as the result of a beating by a fellow prisoner in the city jail. The impoverished city had lacked the funds to pay the $3.4 million settlement.

ROBERT ENSTAD, *"Chicago Tribune"*

ILLINOIS • Information Highlights

Area: 56,345 sq mi (145 934 km²).
Population (July 1, 1991 est.): 11,543,000.
Chief Cities (1990 census): Springfield, the capital, 105,227; Chicago, 2,783,726; Rockford, 139,426.
Government (1992): *Chief Officers*—governor, Jim Edgar (R); lt. gov., Bob Kustra (R). *General Assembly*—Senate, 59 members; House of Representatives, 118 members.
State Finances (fiscal year 1991): *Revenue,* $25,092,000,000; *expenditure,* $24,619,000,000.
Personal Income (1991): $239,293,000,000; per capita, $20,731.
Labor Force (June 1992): *Civilian labor force,* 6,219,900; *unemployed,* 536,900 (8.6% of total force).
Education: *Enrollment* (fall 1990)—public elementary schools, 1,309,640; public secondary, 511,767; colleges and universities, 729,246. *Public school expenditures* (1990), $7,917,549,000.

INDIA

India experienced another year of political instability and economic crisis, as well as ethnic, sectarian, and other forms of turmoil—especially in Punjab and Kashmir. The country also was rocked by a major financial scandal and by widespread violence occasioned by the razing of an ancient Muslim mosque by Hindu militants in the state of Uttar Pradesh. The ruling Congress(I) party, headed by P. V. Narasimha Rao, took important steps to democratize its organization, and it finally obtained a bare majority in the Lok Sabha (lower house of Parliament). Rao's economic liberalization program continued, but at a slower pace. The year also saw a marked weakening in government and society and in national confidence and morale.

Politics. After months of preparation, a special session of the Congress(I) party in mid-April drew 50,000 participants to Tirupati, Andhra Pradesh, to consider longstanding proposals for party reform. The session was the first high-level party convention in seven years, the first without the leadership of the Nehru-Gandhi dynasty, and the first to feature delegates elected at local levels. Members of the highest policy-making body, the Working Committee, also were elected for the first time in 20 years.

Prime Minister Rao remained in firm control in spite of some opposition within his party and some loss of public support. In August he managed to put together a slim majority in the Lok Sabha with the merger of a faction of the Telegu Desam of Andhra Pradesh with the Congress (I). His position also was strengthened by divisions in the two leading opposition parties—the Bharatiya Janata Party (BJP) and the Janata Dal (JD).

In the face of an unusual amount of opposition, the Congress(I) was victorious in the presidential election. On July 13, Shankar Dayal Sharma, the outgoing vice-president, was chosen to succeed R. Venkataraman as president of India. K. R. Narayanan, a prominent educator and former ambassador to the United States, later was elected vice-president by a near-unanimous vote. He was the first member of the scheduled caste to be chosen for the nation's second highest post.

Rao's failure to deal decisively with some serious domestic crises was partially responsible for a loss of popular support. One controversy that divided Hindu and Muslim fundamentalists involved Hindu demands to build a temple on the site of an ancient mosque in Ayodhya, Uttar Pradesh, believed by orthodox Hindus to be the birthplace of the god Rama. The controversy flared up into a major political, religious, communal, and social crisis in December, after Hindu militants demolished the mosque and began to lay the foundations of

© Bartholomew/Gamma-Liaison

P. V. Narasimha Rao, 71, marked his first anniversary as prime minister of India on June 21, 1992. During the year, Rao saw his Congress(I) party win the nation's presidential election, continued to push his economic-reform program, and witnessed increased tensions between Muslims and Hindus as Hindu militants destroyed a Muslim mosque in Ayodhya. On the international front, he visited Japan.

a Hindu temple on the precise site. This action led to violent riots throughout India. It also led to the exacerbation of Hindu-Muslim tensions and violence, the resignation of the chief minister of Uttar Pradesh, and mounting criticisms of Prime Minister Rao for his failure to prevent the destruction of the mosque and for his alleged indecision in dealing with the Hindu militants who had sparked a national crisis. Many Indians considered the crisis to be the most serious since the partition of the Indian subcontinent in 1947.

Another crisis involved the continuing violence and disruptions in Punjab and Jammu and Kashmir. The situation in these two Indian states—the former the breadbasket of India and the homeland of the majority of Sikhs, the latter a state with a Muslim majority and a divided border in a strategic location—was so serious as to threaten disruption of the entire Indian nation.

Sikh militants, many of whom demand complete independence from India, held Punjab in a virtual reign of terror. On February 19, the first state elections in nearly five years were held. The Congress(I) won a majority, but the elections largely were boycotted, even by the party of moderate Sikhs, the Akali Dal, and only 22% of the eligible voters went to the polls. The Congress government, headed by Chief Minister Beant Singh, was able to make some headway in restoring law and order with the backing of some 150,000 army troops and 50,000 paramilitary personnel. The Sikh militants were weakened by clashes with these forces, but remained in virtual control of much of Punjab. Government sources placed the death toll for the first seven months of 1992 at 1,377 civilians and 1,637 militants.

In Kashmir, Muslim militants took advantage of the growing alienation of the state's Muslim majority and blundering policies and actions by the Indian government, and used terroristic tactics to create chaos in this perpetually troubled border state. Under these conditions, the tourism industry, a major source of income, virtually dried up. Figures for the first ten months of the year showed only 7,000 foreign tourists—less than 10% of the normal number—visiting the Vale of Kashmir, a main tourist attraction. The loss of revenue left the state's economy in shambles. At the same time, the political situation was unstable and dangerous. Many Kashmiris blamed the government of India for their plight. Some even advocated separation from India, preferring either independence or union with Pakistan.

The Economy. In his address to the budget session of Parliament on February 17, President Venkataraman emphasized the need to make "hard decisions to overcome the grim economic situation confronting the country." The determination of the Rao government to make some of these hard decisions was evidenced in the proposed central budget for fiscal year 1992–93 (beginning on April 1). Central objectives for the budget were to continue the sweeping economic reforms that had been initiated by the Rao government soon after it as-

sumed power in June 1991, and to remove some of the inequities in the existing tax structure as well as some of the barriers to foreign trade and investment. The budget estimated that revenues would amount to about $45.8 billion, with expenditures to exceed this figure by $1.4 billion, and that the revenue, fiscal, and budget deficits would be reduced. Finance Minister Manmohan Singh also proposed making the rupee—India's main currency unit—partially convertible and expressed the hope that it could be made fully convertible within a few years. The budget was approved by Parliament on April 20, after prolonged and acrimonious debate.

In the meantime, the eighth 'five-year plan' (1992–97) for economic development had been launched formally on April 1. The plan placed greater emphasis on improving the nation's infrastructure and its social services. The estimated total expenditure over the five-year period was approximately $288 billion. About $160 billion would come from the public sector. The plan targeted an annual growth rate of 5.6%, but this goal was probably unrealistically high since the growth rate in 1991–92 was only 2.5%.

India's foreign debt was among the largest of any nation on the globe; in March it was set at about $70 billion. The need for massive international aid remained great, and this dependence continued to be a big concern both in India and abroad.

International assessments of India's economic condition and future prospects were mixed, although the assessments had been more favorable since the Rao government initiated its economic-liberalization program. In 1992 the World Bank issued a lengthy report on India's economic situation and needs that predicted that the nation could become "one of the most dynamic economies in the latter half of the 1990s and beyond." However, the World Bank was not confident that India would take the steps necessary to achieve this exalted status. The report recommended continued aid to India, through the Aid India Consortium, at about the same amount as the previous year—approximately $6.7 billion. At its June meeting, the consortium approved a slightly higher amount.

In addition to the reductions in deficits planned in the 1992–93 budget, the government also made special efforts to reduce the rate of inflation. When the budget was presented in late February, inflation was running at an annual rate of more than 13%. By the end of the year, the rate had been reduced to about 10%, which still inflicted severe hardships on India's poorer people and jeopardized India's credit rating and foreign trade and investment prospects. The nation's balance-of-payments and foreign-trade positions continued to be precarious. A rise in foreign-exchange reserves was a

---

INDIA • Information Highlights

Official Name: Republic of India.
Location: South Asia.
Area: 1,269,340 sq mi (3 287 590 km²).
Population (mid-1992 est.): 882,600,000.
Chief Cities (1991 census): New Delhi, the capital, 294,149; Bombay, 9,909,547; Calcutta, 4,388,262.
Government: Head of state, Shankar Dayal Sharma, president (elected July 1992). Head of government, P. V. Narasimha Rao, prime minister (sworn in June 21, 1991). Legislature—Parliament: Rajya Sabha (Council of States) and Lok Sabha (House of the People).
Monetary Unit: Rupee (28.571 rupees equal U.S.$1, official rate, Dec. 3, 1992).
Gross National Product (1990 est. U.S.$): $254,000,000,000.
Economic Indexes: Consumer Prices (1991, 1980 = 100), all items, 268.0; food, 272.3. Industrial Production (1990, 1980 = 100), 210.
Foreign Trade (1991 U.S.$): Imports, $19,931,000,000; exports, $14,149,000,000.

heartening—but inadequate—development. By the end of fiscal year 1991–92, these reserves had risen to approximately $5.5 billion.

During the first five months of fiscal 1992–93, exports increased by 4.6%, but imports rose by 22.2%. Exports to countries of the former Soviet Union and other rupee-payment countries dropped by 54.65%, but exports to other nations increased by 9.39%.

Financial Scandal. During the year India was rocked by the biggest financial and securities scandal in the nation's history. The scandal involved manipulation and other illegal practices by a "cozy nexus between public-sector companies, banks, and brokerage houses," which combined to raise huge amounts for speculative investment in financial markets and reaped huge profits before the roof fell in. Some Indian government officials and even the Reserve Bank of India and a few large foreign banks, including Citibank and the Bank of America, reportedly were involved. More than $1 billion was thought to be missing from the banks; losses by small investors were catastrophic.

When the scandal surfaced, the Bombay stock market fell by 1,500 points. Some of the worst offenders, mostly brokers, were arrested and brought to trial. Minister of Commerce P. Chidambaram, who generally was regarded as one of the ablest members of Rao's government, resigned under considerable pressure. He was not charged with being involved directly in the scandal, but he did accept responsibility for the criminal involvement of some of his top assistants and for his failure to recognize the escalating scandal until it had been exposed by the Indian media.

The scandal was investigated by two high-level committees. The first was an in-house investigation called by the governor of the Reserve Bank of India. In three separate reports this committee presented damning revelations in meticulous detail, but it declined to fix responsibility. A multiparty nonpartisan parliamentary committee, headed by Ram Nivas Mirdha, a prominent Congress(I) representative, deliberated for weeks on the scandal and its political as well as economic implications; but this committee also failed to make recommendations for punitive actions.

Foreign Affairs. Prime Minister Rao made a five-day official visit to Japan in June. He led the Indian delegation to the nonaligned summit in Jakarta in September-October. In May, President Venkataraman spent six days in China on an official visit. It was the first such visit by an Indian head of state, but it was marred somewhat by China's test explosion of its largest nuclear device while the Indian president was still in the country. During the year, India took part in joint naval exercises in the Indian Ocean with the United States and several Asian countries.

India's relations with its South Asian neighbors, especially Pakistan, continued to be ambivalent and often strained. Several rounds of talks between high-level representatives of India and Pakistan were evidence of the continuing efforts to improve relations; but differences over nuclear proliferation in the subcontinent, and Indian charges that Pakistan continued to assist Muslim and Sikh militants, blocked any real reconciliation. The presence of large numbers of Tamil militants from Sri Lanka in India, mainly in the state of Tamil Nadu, was an irritant in relations with Sri Lanka. India's forced evacuation of thousands of refugees from Bangladesh created new strains in relations with that country.

The collapse of communism in the former Soviet Union and Eastern Europe, and the subsequent emergence of 15 independent republics in what had been the Soviet Union, forced India to reassess its foreign policy interests and priorities. India had been heavily dependent on the Soviet Union in defense and trade matters and for overall support in foreign affairs. Trade with the new republics was far below the previous levels of Indo-Soviet trade. India gave special attention to developing relations with the republics, signing a five-year trade agreement with the Russian Federation in early May and similar agreements with the other republics. When Defense Minister Sharad Pawar visited Ukraine in October, Ukrainian officials proposed "long-term cooperation between India and Ukraine" in defense matters.

Both India and the United States termed their relations as excellent in 1992. However, there were sharp differences on such issues as trade, nuclear nonproliferation, missile curbs, and human rights. Some U.S. actions created bitter feelings in India. On April 29 the U.S. trade representative, Carla Hills, put India back on the "special 301" trade-restrictions list, claiming that the nation had not satisfied U.S. concerns about patent protection for U.S. intellectual property. On May 11 the United States imposed sanctions against India and Russia for proceeding with a $250 million rocket-engine venture in spite of U.S. objection. The United States remained India's largest trading partner and its most important source of direct foreign investment and new cooperative enterprises. Unofficial estimates indicated that bilateral trade would total approximately $6 billion in 1992, with a $1.5 billion surplus in India's favor.

During the year, Thomas Pickering, former U.S. representative to the United Nations, became U.S. ambassador to India, while Siddhartha Shankar Ray, former chief minister of West Bengal, became India's ambassador to the United States.

NORMAN D. PALMER
Professor Emeritus
University of Pennsylvania

INDIANA

Election year l992 produced few surprises in Indiana.

Spring Contests. With the presidential nominations practically determined and only one statewide election a serious contest, the May 5 primary generated little interest or turnout. In the primary's one close race, Attorney General Linely E. Pearson decisively won a hard-fought, three-way competition for the Republican gubernatorial nomination. The major surprise of the primary was Michael Bailey's victory over the party-backed candidate for the Republican congressional nomination in the 9th District. Bailey won national notoriety for his graphic antiabortion television ads during the primary and during his unsuccessful run against Lee Hamilton.

Election Results. In state and local elections, Democratic Gov. Evan Bayh won reelection by the largest margin in modern times, and Republicans added two seats to the majority they enjoyed in the previous state Senate, while Democrats added three seats to their majority in the state House of Representatives. The two other statewide races—superintendent of public instruction and attorney general—were contested widely, with the GOP candidate winning the former and the Democrat the latter.

In elections for federal offices, the Bush-Quayle ticket carried Indiana with a substantial six-point plurality, and Republican U.S. Sen. Dan Coats easily defeated Indiana Secretary of State Joseph H. Hogsett. All but one of Indiana's ten congressmen won reelection—incumbent James Jontz was defeated narrowly by Republican Steve Buyer, a veteran of the Persian Gulf war, in the 5th District. The election left the Hoosier state with two Republican senators, and seven Democratic and three Republican congressmen.

The general campaign likewise aroused little interest because the two major races, for governor and U.S. Senate, were never close.

Bayh had a huge poll lead over Pearson, while Coats had a commanding lead over Hogsett. The absence of any scandals or mismanagement by the governor, the mildness of the recession in Indiana, the governor's huge campaign-fund advantage, and Pearson's generally poor strategy all led to Bayh's record majority of 62%. Coats' decisive victory was probably due to ideology.

Economy. Indiana was only moderately affected by the national recession of the early l990s because of the economic restructuring that took place after the recession of the early 1980s. Most state economic indicators were better than the national averages in l992, and agriculture, overall, enjoyed a good year. Corn, the state's major crop, was expected to achieve a record harvest, with production up 65% from the previous year. Production of soybeans, the state's number-two crop, was up an anticipated 10%, but wheat production dropped 22%.

News Events. The Mike Tyson rape trial in Indianapolis drew extensive national attention. The former heavyweight boxing champion was convicted of raping Desiree Washington, a beauty pageant contestant, and was sentenced to a six-year term in the Indiana Youth Center. . . . The crash of a C-130 military cargo plane brought disaster to Evansville on Feb. 6, 1992. The Kentucky Air National Guard plane was practicing "touch-and-go" landings when it went down between a restaurant and a hotel. The five-man crew and 11 on the ground were killed. . . . Legendary Butler University basketball coach Paul Daniel "Tony" Hinkle, a man respected for his character as well as his record, died on September 22 at the age of 92.

THOMAS E. RODGERS
University of Southern Indiana

INDIANA • Information Highlights

Area: 36,185 sq mi (93 720 km²).
Population (July 1, 1991 est.): 5,610,000.
Chief Cities (1990 census): Indianapolis, the capital, 741,952; Fort Wayne, 173,072; Evansville, 126,272.
Government (1992): *Chief Officers*—governor, Evan Bayh (D); lt. gov., Frank L. O'Bannon (D). *General Assembly*—Senate, 50 members; House of Representatives, 100 members.
State Finances (fiscal year 1991): *Revenue,* $12,288,000,000; *expenditure,* $11,548,000,000.
Personal Income (1991): $96,365,000,000; per capita, $17,179.
Labor Force (June 1992): *Civilian labor force,* 2,855,400; *unemployed,* 192,400 (6.7% of total force).
Education: *Enrollment* (fall 1990)—public elementary schools, 675,887; public secondary, 278,694; colleges and universities, 283,015. *Public school expenditures* (1990), $4,323,743,000.

INDONESIA

As Indonesia's economy continued its 20-year growth pattern, the attention of the nation focused on the political arena where President Suharto was expected to stand for his sixth term in 1993.

Domestic Politics. Indonesia's fifth national election since Suharto's New Order Government came to power in 1966 took place in June 1992. The election, held every five years, was for the 400 seats in Indonesia's House of Representatives. These popularly elected members, together with 100 appointed military members, comprised half of the 1,000-man 1993 People's Consultative Assembly that would elect a president and vice-president for five-year terms. More than 90% of the country's 108 million registered voters went to the polls. The government-sponsored party of functional groups (GOLKAR) won 68% of the vote, down from 73% in 1987. The Muslim-

Large tuna lined the main street of the town of Maumere on the island of Flores after a tidal wave swept through the Indonesian island. A Dec. 12, 1992, earthquake that registered 7.5 on the Richter scale and killed some 2,200 people caused the tidal wave. Most of Maumere's buildings were destroyed.

© Reuters/Bettmann

based Development Unity Party received 17.5%, and the Indonesian Democratic Party, a coalition of three secular parties and the Protestant and Catholic Christian parties, captured 15% of the vote.

The question of presidential succession continued to dominate the political landscape, with much attention focused on the possible vice-presidential nominee as a designated successor in 1998. Conventional wisdom said that the next president had to be ethnically Javanese, an Army general, and a Muslim. As such, speculation centered on the current military chief, Gen. Try Sutrisno. The rapid advancement of General Wismoyo, Suharto's brother-in-law, suggested a different scenario.

There was no indication that the Indonesian military had any intention of constitutionally abandoning its social and political role. Suharto, in response to rising calls for greater democratization, raised the possibility in his August National Day address that the number of military members appointed to parliament could be reduced.

INDONESIA • Information Highlights

Official Name: Republic of Indonesia.
Location: Southeast Asia.
Area: 741,097 sq mi (1 919 440 km²).
Population (mid-1992 est.): 184,500,000.
Chief Cities (Dec. 31, 1983 est.): Jakarta, the capital, 7,347,800; Surabaya, 2,223,600; Medan, 1,805,500; Bandung, 1,566,700.
Government: *Head of state and government,* Suharto, president (took office for fifth five-year term March 1988). *Legislature* (unicameral)— House of Representatives.
Monetary Unit: Rupiah (2,036.54 rupiahs equal U.S.$1, Oct. 21, 1992).
Gross National Product (1990 est. U.S.$): $94,000,-000,000.
Economic Index (1991: *Consumer Prices* (1980 = 100), all items, 123.0; food, 118.3.
Foreign Trade (1990 U.S.$): *Imports,* $21,837,000,000; *exports,* $25,675,000,000.

Economy. A May 1992 World Bank report stated that Indonesia was ready by the end of the decade "to become a solid middle-income country." Its record of an annual 6% to 7% growth in gross domestic product (GDP) is based on a rapidly diversifying economy in which gas and oil revenue as a percentage of export earnings has been halved to 40% in a decade. There also has been a surge in foreign investment, with more than twice as much approved ($26 billion) in the four-year period 1988–91 than in the previous 20 years. Despite a planned $85 billion investment, Indonesia's infrastructure remained a problem. Corruption, too, was an issue.

Foreign Affairs. In September 1992, Indonesia hosted the summit meeting of the Nonaligned Movement (NAM). As leader of the 108-nation grouping, Suharto set forth a new agenda which focused on economic relations. He also took what was called the "Jakarta Message" to the United Nations.

But the luster of the September NAM summit was diminished by international concern over Indonesia's policy in East Timor, the former Portuguese colony annexed in 1976. More than 50 people had died in a November 1991 confrontation between army troops and Timorese youths. Indonesian dislike of the linking of human-rights concerns to economic relations resulted in the disbanding of the Intergovernmental Group on Indonesia, the Hague-based 24-year-old aid consortium. In June the U.S. House of Representatives refused to provide U.S. funds for the training of Indonesian military officers as a protest against alleged human-rights abuses. Questions raised by Timor also impeded the conclusion of an economic treaty between the Association of Southeast Asian Nations (ASEAN) and the European Community (EC).

DONALD E. WEATHERBEE
University of South Carolina

INDUSTRIAL PRODUCTION

Industrial countries remained mired in recession in 1992. While production floundered in the West, output continued to fall sharply in the countries formed in the wake of the dissolution of the USSR and Communist Eastern Europe.

Shipment of Complete U.S. Aircraft					
	1988	**1989**	**1990**	**1991**	**1992**
Total Units	3254	3675	3486	2934	2444
Large Transports	423	398	521	589	567
General Aviation	1143	1535	1144	1021	780
Rotorcraft	383	515	603	571	460
Military	1305	1227	1218	753	637

United States

U.S. industrial production grew by 1.5% in 1992, following a 1.9% fall in 1991. Among product categories, output of defense equipment continued to drop, down more than 8%. But the declines of 1991 were reversed elsewhere. Production perked up in basic steel and mill products, which saw a 6.3% increase. Motor-vehicle and parts output gained 7.8%. Tire output advanced 14% and household appliances had a 4.8% increase. Hardware and tool manufacturers showed a 4.2% growth, paint output was up nearly 17%, and drug and medicine manufacturers raised output in excess of 7%.

Transportation. U.S. consumers had their choice of 618 separate passenger-car and light-truck models, offered by 31 domestic and foreign manufacturers. Combined auto and light-truck sales increased 4.8%. Increasingly, consumers chose light trucks. While car sales barely budged, light-truck sales rolled up a 14% gain. Reaching 4.7 million units, pickups, vans, sports utility, and multipurpose vehicles made up more than 36% of the 12.9 million cars and light trucks sold in 1992, up nearly 3% from 1991. Domestic car sales increased 2.7%, to 6.3 million units, while imports dropped 6.7% to 1.9 million. Medium-truck sales rose 8% in 1992, to 132,000, and heavy-truck sales increased 15%, to 114,000.

Japanese-affiliated auto firms had seven plants operating in the United States in 1992. Four were wholly owned, and three were joint ventures with the Big Three. These seven plants turned out 1.6 million cars in 1992, about 200,000 of them assembled with or for the Big Three. Japanese productivity travels well: It took these Japanese facilities 3.27 final-assembly production workers one day to turn out one car, compared with the Big Three's average of 4.29 workers.

The aerospace industry was hit by defense cuts, global economic weakness, and strong foreign competition in 1992. Shipments posted a record $129.9 billion in 1991, but dropped 2.2% in 1992. Adjusting for price changes, the drop was an even steeper 6%. Order backlogs declined in 1992, as one airline after another canceled or delayed deliveries. McDonnell Douglas delayed its launch of its new MD-12 wide-body jet.

General aviation—which includes business transport, recreation, specialized uses, and regional airline service—has been in a slump for a decade, in part because of high liability costs for owners and manufacturers of small airplanes.

Computers. The U.S. computer industry was hardest hit by layoffs as restructuring efforts designed to cut costs and increase efficiency continued. Employment dropped 5% to 224,000.

© Steve Kagan/NYT Pictures

At the Toyota Motors Corporation factory in Georgetown, KY, cars are manufactured under what has been dubbed "lean production"—i.e., a smaller number of workers, capable of performing a variety of functions. No longer is a worker limited to a single task. It is believed that the Toyota system can produce products with less inventory, less investment, and less error.

U.S. Industrial Production

	Percent Change 1990–1992	Index (1987 = 100) 1992 level*	Percent* Change 1991–1992
Total Production	−1.9	108.6	1.5
Mining	−1.4	98.9	−2.3
Utilities	0.8	108.1	−0.7
Manufacturing	−2.2	109.6	1.9
Consumer Goods	0.2	109.9	2.2
Business Equipment	−1.2	124.3	2.2
Defense and Space Equipment	−6.4	83.4	−8.4
Durable Goods Manufacturing	−4.0	108.6	1.3
Lumber and Products	7.0	98.5	4.7
Furniture and Fixtures	6.4	101.1	2.0
Clay, Glass, and Stone Products	−10.1	96.3	5.0
Primary Metals	−8.0	103.5	3.9
Fabricated Metal Products	−5.1	101.7	1.3
Nonelectrical Machinery	−2.4	127.2	10.7
Electrical Machinery	−1.2	112.4	2.2
Transportation Equipment	−6.3	97.0	−1.9
Nondurable Goods Manufacturing	0.1	110.8	2.7
Foods	0.9	109.8	1.1
Tobacco Products	1.1	101.5	1.7
Textile Mill Products	−0.2	105.8	5.3
Apparel Products	−2.7	98.5	2.4
Paper and Paper Products	−0.3	106.9	1.8
Printing and Publishing	0.3	113.7	1.3
Chemicals and Products	0.6	116.1	4.7
Rubber and Plastics Products	−0.1	117.3	6.5
Leather and Products	−11.8	83.3	−5.4

* Preliminary Estimate
Source: Board of Governors of the Federal Reserve System

Although shipments of computers and peripherals were up 4% to $60 billion, there was not much profit to show for it. Price reductions were drastic and competition fierce, as product life cycles shortened to just one year. They had been as long as five years a decade earlier. Bargain prices led to a 9% rise in personal-computer shipments to 11 million units, but that still fell short of the double-digit growth rates of the 1980s. With some 60 million personal computers installed, half in households, the U.S. market may be becoming saturated.

Notebooks—computers weighing 3 lbs (1.4 kg) to 9 lbs (4 kg)—are gaining market share, with suppliers introducing more than 200 models in 1992. In an effort to excite the consumer electronics market, the industry also introduced a wide array of personal digital devices. One such device functions as a portable electronic reference library. Other small devices have no keyboard and rely on a special pen-driven interface. They serve as portable electronic organizers, personal computers, and electronic drawing pads. (See also COMPUTERS.)

Metals. As motor-vehicle and home-appliance business improved, so did shipments of steel-mill products. After dropping 7% in 1991 to 78.9 million short tons, steel-product shipments grew 4% to 82 million short tons in 1992. Massive industry restructuring and investment in new technology over the last decade have

made the U.S. steel industry one of the low-cost producers among industrialized countries. Pretax production costs were lower than in any other steel-producing country, except Great Britain.

Among other metals, aluminum ingot and product shipments rose 2.5% to a record 16.5 billion lbs (7.5 billion kg), as the transportation sector expanded output and used more aluminum per vehicle. Copper production rose 1%, while lead-mine production dropped 14%. For lead, the storage battery is the main market. Lead for gasoline, which once accounted for 20% of the demand, dropped out of the picture completely in 1991 when Du Pont closed the last TEL plant in the United States. Titanium shipments increased 2% to 15,600 metric tons. Offering strong competition worldwide are Russia and Ukraine with a combined production capacity of 52,000 metric tons per year.

Fuels. Crude-oil production in the United States declined to 7.2 million barrels per day (mb/d). With exploration activity dwindling and development costs rising, crude production in the United States was sliding toward levels last seen in 1955, the last time production was below 7 mb/d. Coal output increased 4% in 1992, to 1.015 billion tons. Output of low-sulfur coal west of the Mississippi was accounting for 41% of total production. Coal-mining produc-

Value of New Construction Put in Place in the United States
(Billions of 1987 dollars)

	1991	1992	Percent Change
Total new construction	358.6	373.2	4.1
Private construction	499.9	535.8	7.2
Residential buildings	141.3	162.6	15.1
Nonresidential buildings	118.3	108.4	−8.4
Industrial	20.0	19.4	−3.0
Office	20.6	16.1	−21.8
Hotels and motels	5.6	3.4	−39.3
Other commercial	22.8	18.7	−18.0
Religious	3.1	3.1	0
Educational	3.5	3.6	2.8
Hospital and institutional	8.2	8.6	4.9
Miscellaneous buildings	3.8	3.7	−2.6
Telecommunications	7.8	8.2	5.1
Railroads	2.4	2.6	8.3
Electric utilities	9.3	9.8	5.4
Gas utilities	5.5	5.7	3.6
Petroleum pipelines	0.5	0.5	0
Farm structures	2.3	2.3	0
Miscellaneous structures[1]	2.9	2.9	0
Public construction	99.0	102.2	3.2
Housing and redevelopment[2]	3.1	3.2	3.2
Federal industrial	1.6	1.7	6.2
Educational	21.3	21.7	1.9
Hospital	2.4	2.4	0
Other public buildings[3]	16.8	18.0	7.1
Highways and streets	27.2	28.0	2.9
Military facilities	1.7	1.7	0
Conservation and development	4.3	4.5	4.6
Sewer systems	8.8	8.6	−2.3
Water supply facilities	4.6	4.8	4.3
Miscellaneous public[4]	7.2	7.6	5.5

Source: Bureau of the Census. Preliminary.
[1] Includes amusement and recreational buildings, bus and airline terminals, animal hospitals, and shelters, etc. [2] Includes privately owned streets and bridges, parking areas, sewer and water facilities, parks and playgrounds, golf courses, airfields, etc. [3] Includes general administrative buildings, prisons, police and fire stations, courthouses, civic centers, passenger terminals, postal facilities. [4] Includes open amusement and recreational facilities, power generating facilities, transit systems, airfields, open parking facilities, etc.

The use of the computer at U.S. steel plants has helped improve productivity to the point where the U.S. steel industry again is competing in the world market. U.S. production of basic steel and mill products increased 6.3% in 1992.

© Keith Williams/NYT Pictures

tivity rose rapidly throughout the 1980s, and gained 6.8% in 1991.

New Plant and Equipment. Investment in new plant and equipment totaled $547 billion in 1992, an increase of 5.3%. In 1992 investment dropped by 0.8%. Manufacturing industries increased investment by 5.2%, to $185 billion. Durable-goods producers as a group raised capital spending by 2.7%. While even motor-vehicle manufacturers switched from a 12.7% drop in 1991 to a 6.2% gain in 1992, aircraft manufacturers cut capital spending by 21.6%.

Nondurable-goods manufacturers increased capital outlays by 7.2%, to $109.5 billion. In 1991 they reduced spending by 5.5%. All industries upped expenditures, with the largest increases made by food producers—9.4%, and by textile manufacturers—11.4%.

Mining-industry outlays increased 7.8%, following a 7.7% decline. Among transportation industries, railroads raised spending by 7.4%, following a 16.2% increase in 1991. Capital outlays in air transportation dropped 10.9%, on top of a 4.8% decline in 1991. Public utilities increased spending by 12.8%, after a 9.9% growth in 1991. Commercial-sector outlays were up by 4.3%, following a 9.1% boost in 1991.

Productivity. Manufacturing productivity in the United States improved considerably in 1992, reflecting the combined effects of output gains and employment cuts. Compared with a 1.9% gain in 1991, the output per hour of all persons in the manufacturing sector increased 2.6% in the first nine months of 1992 over the comparable 1991 period. Preliminary data indicated a strong fourth-quarter performance.

Fairly strong productivity gains were throttling employment growth in goods production. Manufacturing jobs peaked at 20.3 million in 1980. They have dropped three years in a row: 1.7% in 1990, 3.5% in 1991, and 1.3% in 1992. The entire goods-producing sector has shrunk, from the high of 26.6 million jobs reached in 1979 to 23.5 million jobs in 1992.

Construction. Construction activity recovered mildly, posting a 4% gain for 1992. However, the volume fell 10% short of the record reached in 1986. Housing starts reached 1.2 million, up from 1 million in 1991. Private nonresidential construction declined by 8%, reflecting high vacancy rates for commercial buildings and tighter lending standards. Remodeling and repair work showed faster gains than new construction. New construction probably accounted for less than 60% of the industry's business in 1992. Construction ac-

Industrial Production: International Overview
1985 = 100

	1985	1986	1987	1988	1989	1990	1991	1992*
Industrial Countries	100	101	104	110	114	117	116	115
Australia	100	105	101	105	111	111	114	116
Austria	100	101	102	106	113	121	123	125
Belgium	100	101	103	109	114	118	115	116
Canada	100	99	106	112	112	108	101	100
Denmark	100	108	104	106	108	108	112	111
Finland	100	101	106	110	114	113	103	102
France	100	101	103	107	111	113	114	114
Germany	10C	102	102	106	111	117	121	119
Ireland	100	102	111	123	128	144	149	152
Italy	100	104	108	114	118	118	115	NA
Japan	100	100	103	113	120	125	128	121
Luxembourg	100	103	103	115	125	125	124	125
Netherlands	100	102	103	103	105	107	107	114
Norway	100	103	111	117	128	130	133	141
Spain	100	102	107	111	117	116	115	114
Sweden	100	100	103	104	108	105	97	92
Switzerland	100	104	104	111	117	120	121	120
United Kingdom	100	102	106	110	110	109	106	105
United States	100	101	105	110	113	114	112	114

*Preliminary Estimate
Source: International Monetary Fund

Employees on Nonagricultural Payrolls
(in thousands)

	1991	1992*	Percent Change
Goods-producing industries	23,830	23,470	−1.5
Mining	690	640	−7.8
Construction	4,685	4,610	−1.7
Manufacturing	18,455	18,220	−1.3
Durable goods	10,602	10,360	−2.3
Lumber and wood products	679	685	0.8
Furniture and fixtures	472	468	−1.0
Stone, clay, and glass products	524	520	−0.7
Primary metal industries	726	705	−2.8
Fabricated metal products	1,359	1,337	−1.6
Machinery, except electrical	2,007	1,950	−2.8
Electrical and electronic equip.	1,598	1,545	−3.3
Transportation equipment	1,891	1,834	−3.0
Instruments and related products	980	943	−3.7
Miscellaneous mfg. industries	366	367	0.3
Nondurable goods	7,852	7,870	0.2
Food and kindred products	1,672	1,675	0.2
Tobacco manufacturers	49	49	0.8
Textile mill products	672	679	1.0
Apparel and other textile goods	1,010	1,024	1.3
Paper and allied products	688	689	0.2
Printing and publishing	1,541	1,521	−1.3
Chemicals and allied products	1,072	1,073	0
Petroleum and coal products	159	155	−2.4
Rubber and misc. plastics products	864	880	1.9
Leather and leather products	125	122	−2.1

* Preliminary Estimate
Source: Bureau of Labor Statistics

counted for 7.9% of the gross national product (GNP) in 1992. The industry's record share of GNP was 11.9% in 1966.

International

Industrial countries posted a lackluster record for goods output in 1992. Recoveries were few and weak. At year's end, production gain was the strongest in the Netherlands. Canada and the United States were staging a mild recovery in the final quarter, while Japan, Germany, and Sweden saw production falter. Great Britain faced yet another crisis in its inefficient coal mines as demand for British coal fell sharply. As recently as 1990, the mines in Great Britain produced 80 million tons of coal, a volume that was scheduled to be cut in half in 1992. Industrial production continued to decline in the former Soviet Union and Eastern Europe. Struggling to develop hard-currency exports, Russia found it especially hurtful to have crude oil production decline 15% to a rate of 2.85 million barrels per day.

AGO AMBRE, *U.S. Department of Commerce*

INSURANCE, LIABILITY

The year 1992 brought good and bad news for U.S. liability insurers and their corporate and professional clients. The insurance companies were buoyed in November when the survivors of a woman who allegedly died from smoking cigarettes dropped their case against three cigarette manufacturers. The landmark lawsuit, *Cipollone v. Liggett Group Inc.*, had appeared to open the way for numerous personal injury suits against the makers of cigarettes.

The bad news arose in a Dallas case when a jury decided that a sleeping-pill manufacturer, Upjohn, had failed to adequately warn doctors of a drug's potentially violent side effects. The case involved a former police officer, William Freeman, who claimed that the drug, Halcion, had caused him to murder a friend. Halcion, the world's most widely prescribed sleeping pill, had been criticized widely for its adverse side effects, and the November verdict seemed likely to prompt a wave of suits against the manufacturer and physicians who prescribed the medication.

Tort Reform Debate. Both of these cases fell within the provisions of tort law, which permits citizens to sue for damages arising from faulty products and negligent services. Under the tort system, standards for filing product liability and malpractice suits vary considerably from state to state. After 12 years of debating the merits of federal tort reform legislation, the U.S. Senate in September narrowly rejected a measure that would have set national standards for personal injury lawsuits and upper limits on some awards and settlements.

Support for the measure came from liability insurers and businesses that long had claimed juries grant excessive awards to victims of personal injury, driving up business costs. But the Senate agreed with critics of tort reform, including trial lawyers and consumer groups, who argued that the measure would do little more than curtail the rights of victims to receive compensation for injuries suffered from faulty products and negligent services.

Prospects for Reform. Supporters of federal tort reform enjoyed the Bush administration's unequivocal support. During the presidential election campaign, both the president and Vice-President Dan Quayle repeatedly criticized trial lawyers and their supporters in Congress for blocking passage of federal reform. The November 3 victory of Arkansas Gov. Bill Clinton, who said that the measure would tilt the scales of justice in favor of polluters, manufacturers, and insurance companies, signaled that tort reform advocates would not enjoy the backing of the White House during the coming Democratic administration.

MARY H. COOPER
"CQ (Congressional Quarterly) Researcher"

INTERIOR DESIGN

Retreating from their fast-paced, stress-ridden lives, consumers embraced rustic simplicity in interior design in 1992.

The Rustic Trend. Strong consumer response in 1991 to the rural Southern-style furnishings and accessories shown under "The World of Bob Timberlake" name led to widespread emulation at the Spring 1992 International Home Furnishings Market in High Point, NC. This style was marketed variously as Southwest, Adirondack, Northwest, and country cottage. Similarly, the Mission/Prairie style also continued to generate strong interest.

Several generic American country collections were introduced in April 1992, continuing the 1991 fashion of patriotism-inspired designs. One of the most sophisticated such offerings came from Drexel Heritage Furnishings. Their American Themes collection offered four groupings: New Country Manner, Native Country, Coastal Casual, and Uptown Shaker.

Other Trends. Two of the year's major events—the 500th anniversary of Columbus' arrival in the Americas and the Summer Olympics in Barcelona, Spain—sparked an interest in Spanish styles. Also in vogue in 1992 was the embellishment of case goods with ironwork in a variety of finishes. Often cast with a hand-forged texture, the metal combined with wood, stone, or glass enhanced the predominant rustic mood. Metal details particularly graced the Spanish designs, shaped as scrolls, tassels, vines, and other decorative elements. Pulaski's "Old Barcelona" collection featured such iron work on scrubbed and antique pine finishes.

In a bold move away from the pervasive rustic trend, Pearson presented its exotic Viceroy Collection of 19th-century Anglo-Indian styles by designer Victoria Morland. Additionally, after several years in development, The Biltmore Estate Collection by Drexel Heritage arrived with an eclectic assortment of opulently detailed furnishings true to the legendary George Vanderbilt penchant for grandeur. However, in 1992 the absolute top end belonged to Baker Furniture. Taking inspiration from the Romanovs of Russia, Baker reproduced furniture from the royal family's collection in the State Hermitage Museum in St. Petersburg.

Furniture and Fabrics. Overall, in upholstered furniture, the emphasis was on big, overscaled pieces. Colors were rich and vibrant with a Southwestern flavor. Accessories unveiled at High Point expressed primitive, Southwest, rustic, and contemporary themes. Here, too, wrought-iron looks made a strong showing, often paired with ceramics in earthtone hues, sometimes with antiqued, crackled finishes. Weathered woods were in abundance, as were sunflower and golfing motifs.

In fabrics, plush texture was the watchword. Feel-good finishes like printed velvets and lush chenilles were in demand, with tapestries and overprinted jacquards also strong.

During most of the year, the casual elegance mode continued its appeal, but the fall brought a more contemporary turn. Two influential furniture manufacturers made October introductions inspired by the rounded, nubby, natural California-casual style first defined by Los Angeles' The Kreiss Collection. Another trendsetting company offered a streamlined, contemporized interpretation of Southwest design.

CARLA BREER HOWARD, *"Traditional Home"*

© Baker Furniture

A Russian table desk on massive supports carved in the shape of classical lyres was presented by Baker Furniture as an example of 19th-century Russian detail.

INTERNATIONAL TRADE AND FINANCE

After six years of tough negotiations and a series of crises, the Uruguay Round of world trade talks was nearing conclusion as 1992 came to a close. A trade war between the United States and the European Community (EC) over European farm subsidies narrowly was averted in November, enabling a continuation of negotiations among the 108 nations. These talks, aimed at reducing a broad range of obstacles to international commerce, were sponsored by the General Agreement on Tariffs and Trade (GATT), a body based in Geneva that sets the rules for world trade. Success eventually would boost annual world output by an estimated $100 billion per year.

There were several other notable international trade and financial events in 1992.

Stock Markets. On March 3 the Tokyo Stock Exchange's most widely followed price index sank below the psychologically important 20,000-point barrier, the lowest close in more than five years. It was down nearly half from its peak in late 1989. By mid-November the 225-issue Nikkei Stock Average was even lower—in the 16,370 range. Moreover, Japan's economy was in trouble. National output shrank slightly in 1992 and was expected by some economists to fall further in 1993. It was the worst downturn in Japan since the Organization of Petroleum Exporting Countries (OPEC) sharply hiked oil prices in 1973–74, producing a worldwide recession.

In the United States, stock traders got excited October 5 and sent the Dow Jones industrial average down 104 points in the first two hours. But bargain hunters—perhaps recalling the recovery of stock prices after the 508-point crash in the Dow on Oct. 19, 1987—brought the average back up to a loss of only 21.61 points by the close. By late December, stock prices were up about 3% from January.

In other major stock markets, trends varied greatly. According to Morgan Stanley Capital International Perspective, Geneva, stock prices by mid-November were up 7% in Britain, down 7.1% in Canada, down 25.5% in Japan, up 4.1% in France, down 7.1% in Germany, up 50.8% in Hong Kong, up 15.7% in Switzerland, and down 15% in Australia.

Currency. Europe was shaken by a major currency crisis in early September. British, French, Italian, Spanish, and Swedish central banks together shelled out the equivalent of roughly $100 billion trying vainly to prop up the weaker currencies in the European Exchange Rate Mechanism (ERM). Germany paid out another $50 billion in marks. Their bookkeeping losses on the transactions amounted to an estimated $6 billion, although the actual losses would depend on the exchange rates when the devalued currencies were sold.

The currency crisis was related to a treaty signed in Maastricht, the Netherlands, in late 1991, which was to provide for a common European currency and central bank by 1999 and develop Community-wide defense and foreign policies. French voters approved the treaty in September by such a narrow margin that it took major intervention in foreign-exchange markets by the German and French central banks to avoid devaluation of the franc. It also encouraged the British to delay parliamentary ratification, possibly into 1993, and caused some observers to say that European unity would develop more slowly than had been hoped.

World Economy. The world economy continued to move in slow motion. The Paris-based Organization for Economic Cooperation and Development (OECD) figured economic growth in its 24 industrial member countries would add up to about 1.5% in real terms in 1992, up from a mere 0.8% in 1991.

In the United States, 1992 growth in the gross domestic product (GDP) was estimated at 1.8% after inflation. This recovery was extraordinarily weak compared with the first year or two of other post-World War II economic expansions. Germany's economy was close to shrinking in the last half of 1992, although growth continued positive in the depressed former Communist part of the nation. Germany's central bank, the Bundesbank, eased monetary policy a little in mid-September but remained more concerned about fighting inflation than recession.

The British government of Prime Minister John Major moved November 13 to stimulate Great Britain out of recession by cutting interest rates 1% to 7% and encouraging investment and construction. France's output grew about 2% in 1992, but the economy was weakening. In Italy and Spain, restrictive fiscal policies slowed growth.

Russia. The Russian economy was moving rapidly toward hyperinflation. The Russian central bank still was financing the massive deficits of major state enterprises, swelling the amount of money in circulation and fueling an inflation rate of more than 20% per month. And the country was in massive need of aid. In October the International Monetary Fund (IMF) —which by November had nearly every country in the world represented on its board—said Russia would need $22 billion of loans and aid in 1993 to service its debts and meet other financial needs.

U.S. President George Bush, under pressure from foreign-policy experts and a bipartisan group of congressional leaders, had proposed on April 1 a sweeping plan to help the new regimes in the former Soviet Union. The legislation was part of a $24 billion multilateral-aid package for Russia proposed by the United States and six other leading industrial nations. With an election looming, however, U.S. law-

© AP/Wide World

Amid a European currency crisis in September 1992, a trader at London's Future Exchange Market reacted dramatically as Britain raised its interest rates in an effort to stabilize the value of the pound compared with other currencies.

makers insisted that they could not approve such assistance without providing something to their own constituents. As a result, the final legislation included an extension of unemployment-insurance benefits to the jobless and other increased domestic spending. It also authorized $460 million in bilateral humanitarian, economic, and other assistance for Russia and 11 other republics and $800 million to help dismantle the former Soviet nuclear arsenal, as well as a $12.3 billion increase in the U.S. contribution to the IMF so it could carry out its lending program for these former Soviet nations. President Bush signed the legislation on October 24. Little more than a month earlier the president had offered $900 million in loan guarantees for farm exports and $250 million in food aid to help Russia buy U.S. grain and livestock feed.

The IMF additionally had loaned Russia $1 billion in August for vital imports and the World Bank loaned another $600 million for the same purpose. Previously about $5 billion of loans and loan guarantees had been provided Russia by several governments, much of it from Germany. Prime Minister Yegor Gaidar said late in August that Russia would not be able to pay more than $2 billion in 1992 on its share of the $70 billion in debts owed by Russia and the other former Soviet republics to foreigners.

North American Trade Bloc. Just before the Republican Convention in August, the United States, Mexico, and Canada reached agreement on a free-trade area embracing 360 million people with a total output of nearly $7 trillion —larger than the market of the EC.

The North American Free Trade Agreement (NAFTA), the product of 14 months of negotiations, aims at eliminating tariffs over ten to 15 years, including barriers to agricultural products, manufactured goods, and services. Once the pact is ratified, Mexican import licenses would be abolished immediately. U.S. financial firms would be able to set up wholly owned companies in Mexico and compete on the same terms as Mexican firms for the first time in more than 50 years. The deal also would provide protection for intellectual property rights, such as patents.

Additionally, it would remove restrictions on most investments, although Mexico still would keep a lid on foreign activity in its oil industry. U.S. firms in Mexico would be able to transfer profits home freely and take disputes to binding international arbitration. One difficult issue was the treatment of automobiles. The agreement provides that only vehi-

The "Buy American" Trend

Stimulated by a slow U.S. economy and a surge of nationalism, the "Buy American" movement won greater acceptance in the United States in 1992.

"It is going pretty well," said Joel D. Joseph, who founded the Made in the USA Foundation in 1989 because of his concern about the United States' then-spiraling trade deficits and the erosion of its industrial base. Through a combination of mass mailings and media attention, the organization was adding some 2,000 new members per month in 1992, with its total membership exceeding 50,000. Joseph campaigns for what he calls "fair trade" and promotes goods made in the United States at home and abroad.

Similarly, Robert Swift, executive director of Crafted With Pride in the USA Council Inc., found that his council's television advertisements were getting their highest-ever level of recognition. More important, a larger proportion of Americans were taking the action desired by the New York-based council—looking at labels. The ads talked about the job loss resulting from imported apparel and textiles, and that, according to Swift, proved to be "something that was important to people. The recession is making people more mindful of job issues." In April 1992 an all-time high of 54% of men and 49% of women among the 1,000 consumers surveyed said they looked for the "Made in the USA" labels when shopping for clothing or home textiles.

Crafted With Pride was founded in 1984 by the U.S. textile and apparel industry to strengthen the competitive position of the industry, with its 2 million employees. Its television ads, according to Swift, reach 95% of U.S. women aged 25 to 54 at least 16 times per year. This group purchases more than 80% of the "soft goods" sold in the United States. Though it is clear that the $80 million in TV ads bought since 1984 by Crafted With Pride has boosted awareness of the Buy American issue, the ads have not stopped the erosion of the domestic industry's market share by imports, admits Swift. Some 60% of clothing and textiles was being imported in the summer of 1992.

To some degree, the greater concern with imports manifest in the United States also was a result of the election campaign and the accompanying rhetoric over trade issues. U.S. President George Bush pushed the North American Free Trade Association (NAFTA) with Mexico and Canada to a successful conclusion in the summer. His Democratic opponent, Bill Clinton, waffled on the deal. But many labor leaders charged that the treaty would mean the loss of U.S. jobs to Mexico. Swift held that if NAFTA was approved by Congress and the international Multi Fibre Arrangement was phased out with successful conclusion of the Uruguay Round of trade negotiation under the General Agreement on Tariffs and Trade (GATT), the U.S. industry would be "virtually wiped out." Swift wanted more protection for the domestic industry, not less.

At AFL-CIO headquarters in Washington, DC, Jeffrey Fiedler, secretary-treasurer of the Food & Allied Services Trades department, was trying to see that U.S. retailers lived up to their Buy American claims. He charged that Wal-Mart, the nation's largest retailer, was not truthful when it advertised "We buy American whenever we can." Fiedler attempted to get Wal-Mart's import policy changed through a proxy solicitation, but lost, as he expected, by a huge majority. He did get what he also sought—considerable publicity on the issue. His department represents 3.5 million workers in the food and service industries. Some will be hit by imports built by cheap labor abroad, he argues.

Made in the USA publishes an annual buyer's guide, *Made in the USA: The Complete Guide to America's Finest Products*. Recognizing that it is difficult to find 100% U.S.-made products, it looks for the most "American" that it can find in any given category.

DAVID R. FRANCIS

A Massachusetts car dealer urges prospective customers to purchase U.S. models. A renewed "Buy American" sentiment sprung up during 1992.

cles containing 62.5% North American content would be eligible for free trade. There would be requirements to trace the origin of parts by country so the content could be measured.

The U.S. Congress was expected to consider the pact in the spring of 1993. Although it won the support of President-elect Bill Clinton, he also talked of the need for assurances regarding protection of the environment in Mexico and the provision of assistance to displaced workers in the United States. The Bush administration promised that the deal would create high-paying jobs in the United States. But U.S. organized labor was afraid that low-wage Mexican workers, who often make just $1 per hour, would tempt U.S. companies to build factories in Mexico and would depress the wages of U.S. workers. U.S. exports to Mexico were about $40 billion in 1992, an increase of about 300% since 1987. U.S. officials hoped that increased prosperity in Mexico would stem the flow of illegal immigrants north. Nationwide, 2.1 million U.S. jobs rely on exports to Canada and Mexico. An earlier U.S.-Canadian free-trade deal went into effect in 1989.

World Trade. Because of a 7.5% increase in U.S. export volume, the United States regained its ranking as the largest merchandise exporter in the world during 1991, GATT reported in March 1992. The United States shipped 12%, or $422 billion, of the world's total exports of $3.5 trillion, replacing Germany, which had 11.4%, or $403 billion, as number 1. Japan was third with 8.9%, or $315 billion.

The United States also was the world's largest importer, taking in $509 billion or 13.9% of the world total. It was followed by Germany with $390 billion, or 10.7%, and Japan with $236 billion, or 6.5%. By the third quarter, however, there were signs that growth in U.S. exports was slowing, while demand for imports was rising. The Commerce Department reported an 8.1% increase in the merchandise-trade deficit over the previous quarter. GATT experts anticipated a 4% growth in world trade in 1992, up from 3% in 1991.

GATT Talks. The battle over European farm subsidies reached a crescendo in November when after years of negotiations, the EC still refused to trim the output of its subsidized oilseeds sufficiently to satisfy the United States. As a result, on November 6, U.S. chief negotiator Carla A. Hills announced that in 30 days the United States would begin collecting a 200% import tax on $312 million worth of white wines and other imports from the EC. The measure struck at France, which had sales of $125 million of white wine in the United States in 1991 and was considered a major obstacle. The United States estimated the damage from these subsidies to its own farm interests at $1.6 billion, while the EC said they were at most $400 million.

U.S. officials had been calling on the EC to limit its production of oilseeds to about 8 million metric tons. The EC had offered to reduce acreage devoted to these crops, but not to limit total output. French politicians were afraid of violent protests by French farmers should they give ground, but also were concerned about being isolated from France's European allies, especially Germany. U.S. oilseed farmers were annoyed that subsidized European farm products were winning a larger share of the world market. A compromise deal between the EC and the United States was reached on November 20. The EC agreed to cut back oilseed cultivation by 15%. While agricultural issues overall were dominant ones in the broader GATT talks, a number of other difficult issues lay ahead of the GATT negotiators in late 1992. U.S. law required that a GATT deal be completed before March 2, 1993, if Congress were to take it up under a so-called fast-track procedure, which does not allow amendments. Japan had not agreed to open its market for imported rice. Developing nations were resisting opening their countries to Western service businesses, and the trade negotiations were not made easier by the weakness of the economy in so many nations.

A successful GATT round was expected to reduce tariffs on average by one third and even to eliminate some. Many nontariff barriers to trade also would come down, including some imposed by industrial countries on tropical farm products. Another aim has been to integrate over ten years the textiles and clothing sector into a strengthened GATT. These products, under the 20-year-old Multifibre Arrangement, long have been an exception to normal GATT disciplines, subject to negotiated market-sharing deals.

Third World Debt. Brazil, the largest debtor in the developing world, and its creditor banks agreed July 9 on a series of measures to reduce its $44 billion of debt. The deal was to provide Brazil with lower interest rates and new longer-term loans. Argentina, the next-biggest debtor, reached a deal with its foreign lenders over $31 billion in debt on November 10. It too gave banks various options to swap debt for new securities guaranteed by U.S. Treasury bonds, but this involved forgiveness of as much as 35% of the loans. The Philippines accepted a $5 billion restructuring package with its creditor banks soon after its new President Fidel V. Ramos was sworn into office in the summer of 1992.

Commercial banks have lost an estimated $40 billion to $50 billion on their Third World loans. However, the possibility that default by a major debtor could endanger the world's financial system and the risk of failure of major commercial banks were gone.

DAVID R. FRANCIS
"The Christian Science Monitor"

IOWA

With 65% of the voting-age population participating, Iowa voters cast their seven electoral-college votes for the Democratic presidential team of Bill Clinton and Al Gore in the November 1992 general election. Republican Sen. Charles Grassley easily won his third six-year term over State Sen. Jean Lloyd-Jones. For U.S. House seats, the closest race was in the 2d District, where reapportionment pitted two incumbents—Jim Nussle (R) and Dave Nagle (D)—against each other, with Nussle winning by only 3,200 votes. In the 3d District, incumbent Republican Jim Ross Lightfoot barely defeated Iowa's Secretary of State Elaine Baxter. Other winners were Republican Jim Leach in the 1st District (ninth term); Democrat Neal Smith in the 4th District (18th term); and Republican Fred Grandy, unopposed in the 5th District. State Republicans regained control of the Iowa House of Representatives, but Democrats retained Senate control. In a referendum, an equal-rights amendment again was rejected. The constitution was amended, removing the dueling provision.

The Legislature. Early in the legislative session, the Senate Ethics Committee conducted an investigation of its president, Democratic Sen. Joe Welsh, for his work as a salesman in the $75 million Iowa Trust scandal. He was forced to resign as president and stripped of his major committee assignments but was not removed from the Senate. Because of the scandal, the law regulating public investments was tightened, and tougher franchise regulations were put into place.

The final budget agreement brought an increase of $270 million, with a total expenditure of $3.47 billion. The increase was financed by an increase in the general sales tax from 4% to 5%. One so-called landmark bill limits spending from exceeding revenues beginning on July 1, 1993, and establishes a 5% cash reserve.

Iowa's public-school-aid formula was taken off automatic funding increases, and beginning in 1993, lawmakers and the governor were to set allowable annual spending growth. The 1993 funding was reduced by $39 million for grades K through 12 to a revised increase of $85.7 million. The legislature set 19% of the budget for higher education and student programs.

Other enacted laws included: Iowa's first "stalking" law; permission for cities, counties, and other political subdivisions to seek Chapter 9 bankruptcy protection to restructure a debt that is imposed upon them involuntarily; an increased penalty, from $25 to $50, for illegally parking in a handicapped designated space; a requirement that drivers dim headlights at least 1,000 ft (305 m) from oncoming vehicles; a requirement that massage therapists be licensed

---

IOWA • Information Highlights

Area: 56,275 sq mi (145 753 km²).
Population (July 1, 1991 est.): 2,795,000.
Chief Cities (1990 census): Des Moines, the capital, 193,187; Cedar Rapids, 108,751.
Government (1992): *Chief Officers*—governor, Terry E. Branstad (R); lt. gov., Joy C. Corning (R). *General Assembly*—Senate, 50 members; House of Representatives, 100 members.
State Finances (fiscal year 1991): *Revenue,* $7,137,000,000; *expenditure,* $6,820,000,000.
Personal Income (1991): $48,374,000,000; per capita, $17,296.
Labor Force (June 1992): *Civilian labor force,* 1,531,700; *unemployed,* 78,000 (5.1% of total force).
Education: *Enrollment* (fall 1990)—public elementary schools, 344,874; public secondary, 138,778; colleges and universities, 170,515. *Public school expenditures* (1990), $2,202,260,000.

---

by the Department of Public Health; protection of bats as a nongame species; and subjecting hunters who leave "usable portions" of game in the field to a $100 fine.

A new law banned honoraria and gifts for all public officials and employees, except for food and drink under $3.00. Also banned were campaign contributions from political action committees (PACs) during the legislative session and 30-day gubernatorial bill-signing period. An early-retirement incentive was offered to state employees, and periodic reviews of agencies and programs were mandated.

The Economy. Favorable weather brought record corn and high soybean yields in 1992, but prices were the lowest in recent years. . . . Unemployment was 3.6% in August, in contrast with the national average of 7.4%. . . . The HyVee grocery chain became the state's largest private employer, replacing John Deere. . . . Two riverboat gambling casinos left Iowa for Mississippi, while a third was to leave in May 1993 for Missouri.

RUSSELL M. ROSS, *University of Iowa*

IRAN

The course of events in Iran in 1992 was disappointingly negative and held little promise of improvement, either in internal conditions or in relations with the outside world—the opposite of the trend of the preceding two years. This resulted from a weakening of the moderate and less hard-line anti-Western forces represented, somewhat ambiguously, by President Ali Akbar Hashemi Rafsanjani and a corresponding increase in the power of the supporters of Shia Islam. The latter hold that the legacy of the late Ayatollah Khomeini must not be divorced from his absolutist principles.

Isolation and Economic Distress. The economy exhibited favorable as well as unfavorable symptoms, with a tilt toward the latter as the year progressed. In recent years the economy had shown increased vigor. A number of foreign firms had made investments, some former Iranian exiles had returned with capital to invest, and a construction miniboom had bloomed in Tehran. But uncertainty about the future, and the hostility of many mullahs to any cooperation with the West, discouraged foreign firms and international institutions.

Some observers in 1992 regarded Iran's economic situation as so desperate that they estimated some $50 billion in foreign loans would be needed to shore up the faltering economy. Such sums were unlikely to be forthcoming—and might be rejected if offered. More than 70% of Iranians under 25 were unemployed. Inflation was soaring. In July the government began to default on payments due on its foreign debt, totaling some $40 billion. This was a new situation. Iran had incurred very little foreign debt even during its eight-year war with Iraq, and hitherto had been meticulous in meeting its obligations.

Civil Disorders. There was thus plenty of reason for discontent in Iran, and in 1992 abundant evidence that it existed. However, to attribute the manifestations of discontent to any one group, or to believe that disturbances portended any immediate threat to the existing regime, probably would be a mistake. Still, Iran experienced the worst riots seen there since the establishment of the Islamic theocracy in 1979. The most serious occurred in Mashad, Iran's holiest city, from May 30 to June 2; others broke out in Arak, Shiraz, Khorrambad, and other towns in late April and May. In all cases a minor incident led to stormy protests, and then attacks on public buildings. The rioters reportedly showed some signs of organization and leadership and, particularly in Mashad, their actions had an anti-Islamic character amounting to a demonstration against the regime.

Struggle for Power. The great political drama of the year in Iran was the struggle for power between Rafsanjani and the Ayatollah Khamenei. Rafsanjani, president since August 1989, is a wealthy man—his family are pistachio farmers—and is regarded in the West as a moderate. He was, however, the late Ayatollah Khomeini's closest confidant and his designated successor as head of state, and he and Khamenei sometimes had cooperated. They did so in the preliminaries to the national election to the *Majlis* in the spring, fighting a hard and unscrupulous campaign that was entirely successful. In the preceding *Majlis* elected in April-May 1989, hard-liners, hostile to Rafsanjani and rivals of Khamenei, had won a 60% majority. By using screening committees and the Council of Guardians, Rafsanjani in 1992 had large numbers of his opponents declared ineligible to run.

There were no political parties in any normal sense. The only choice was between

© Greg English/Sygma

A new wave of fundamentalism—as evident in the photo—developed in Iran, even though most of the hard-line opposition was defeated in April 1992 parliamentary elections.

adherents of the Association of Combatant Clergymen, supporters of Rafsanjani, and the radicals put forward by the Association of Militant Clergymen. In Iran's complicated electoral process there was a first round of voting for the 270-seat *Majlis* on April 10, and a second round on May 8. The new *Majlis* was inaugurated on May 28. This time Rafsanjani's supporters had a clear majority—they claimed 70%. Some 66 of the members were clerics, as against 81 earlier, and nine were women, as against four.

Thus in the first five months of the year everything seemed to be going well for Rafsanjani and his reformist policies. He had made a number of foreign visits, which had increased his prestige; the unification of the armed forces announced in February was a victory for him, and now he had a made-to-order parliament. The rest of the year, however, saw a mysterious decline in his power relative to that of Khamenei. No doubt one factor was the riots immediately following the election.

In July a new wave of repression began, aimed at Western fashions, music, and culture. Hundreds of women and youths were arrested. The revived Islamic intolerance was urged on by Khamenei, and Rafsanjani's tone in his rare public appearances became apologetic and defensive. In an apparent personal confrontation

IRAN • Information Highlights

Official Name: Islamic Republic of Iran.
Location: Southwest Asia.
Area: 636,293 sq mi (1 648 000 km²).
Population (mid-1992 est.): 59,700,000.
Chief City (1986 census): Tehran, the capital, 6,042,584.
Government: *Head of state and government,* Ali Akbar Hashemi Rafsanjani, president (took office August 1989). *Legislature* (unicameral)—Islamic Consultative Assembly (*Majlis*).
Monetary Unit: Rial (62.420 rials equal U.S.$1, Aug. 1992).
Gross National Product (1990 est. U.S.$): $80,000,-000,000.
Foreign Trade (1989 U.S.$): *Imports,* $11,600,-000,000; *exports,* $12,300,000,000.

with Khamenei in August the president promised to toe the Islamic line as dictated by Khamenei, and even offered to resign. Thereafter his public pronouncements on economic matters indicated an abandonment of market-oriented policies in favor of more state control. Whether related to these changes or not, a wave of bomb explosions occurred in Tehran at the end of August, with more of the same in the middle of October. On October 16 a spokesman for Khamenei openly scorned the president's policy of encouraging Iranians abroad to return.

The most obvious results of the shift of power from Rafsanjani to Khamenei were, internally, an increase in oppression and diminution of personal freedom and, externally, a mass exodus of would-be lenders. The latter deplored the recent developments, increasingly so as Iran displayed more and more hostile tendencies toward other countries, both in the region and outside.

Foreign Relations. By summer, Iran was behaving as if it was not merely indifferent to growing isolation, but deliberately provoking foreign hostility. While Iran traditionally had enjoyed very good relations with Algeria, it reacted with such vituperation to the crackdown on Islamic fundamentalists there in January that Algeria recalled its ambassador and expelled Iran's. Relations with Switzerland had curdled from December 1991, when Zeyal Sarhadi, an Iranian, was arrested there to face charges in connection with the August 1991 murder in France of former Iranian Prime Minister Shapour Bakhtiar. Iran maintained that Sarhadi had diplomatic immunity, but on May 26 the Swiss Federal Tribunal permitted his extradition to France. Meanwhile, in February, Iran had signed important agreements with the International Red Cross (IRC) to facilitate the repatriation of thousands of prisoners of war taken in the Iran-Iraq war. Only weeks later, on March 21—possibly as a side effect of its grievances against the Swiss—the government tore up the agreement, closed the IRC offices in Tehran, and expelled its staff of 15.

In a more outrageous breach of international norms, Iranian air-force units on April 5 (during the election campaign) bombed a base, deep inside Iraq at Ashraf, of the exiled Iranian opposition group the *Mojahedin-e Khalq* ("People's Fighters"). In yet another rash act with obscure motivation, Iran seized complete control of Abu Musa in the Persian Gulf. This island, along with the Greater and Lesser Tunb, had been ruled solely by the emir of Sharjah until 1971. Iran had stationed troops there since 1971, and administration had been shared, along with oil revenues from offshore wells. The Iranian takeover on April 15 reportedly led to the expulsion of Arab residents from the island. The takeover was an affront to the United Arab Emirates, of which Sharjah is one —a minor but quite unprovoked aggression.

Relations with Britain also were tense. On July 15 the Iranian foreign minister objected to a statement signed by British members of Parliament condemning Iran's bombing of the opposition base in Iraq. In the aftermath a British diplomat was expelled from Iran, and three Iranians were expelled from Britain. Relations between the two countries were poisoned further in November when First Ayatollah Hassan Sane'i renewed threats against the life of the British author Salman Rushdie.

To add insult to injury, Iran fueled growing international concern by continuing its military buildup, purchasing ballistic missiles and a wide variety of sophisticated military hardware from several sources, most notably China. Among its more disconcerting activities, aside from suspected nuclear-weapons development, was the purchase from Russia of at least three "Kilo" class submarines. The first of these arrived at Bandar Abbas in November.

ARTHUR CAMPBELL TURNER
University of California, Riverside

IRAQ

In 1992, in the aftermath of the Persian Gulf war of the previous year, Iraq—and its erstwhile opponents—dealt inconclusively with a great deal of unfinished business. None of the ongoing questions about Iraq's condition and actions, internal and external, reached any kind of decision in 1992. Indeed, they remained throughout the year in a state of suspended animation, as they had been since the end of the war. The most important of these unresolved situations concerned Saddam Hussein's hold on power; living conditions inside Iraq; the rebellious northern and southern areas of the country; Kuwait; and UN attempts to enforce the arms provisions of the cease-fire.

Outlaw State. Defiant and arrogant, Hussein successfully clung to power—in its way, a formidable achievement. The U.S. government clearly had hoped that he would lose his grip on power after Operation Desert Storm, perhaps as a result of the impact of economic sanctions imposed on the Iraqi people.

Various other oblique means had been attempted—and funded—to displace him, but the Iraqi ruler's contempt for the divided counsels and irresolute will of his foreign antagonists proved entirely justified in the event. In any case, bringing about a change of government in Baghdad never had figured in the UN resolutions that had been the formal justification for the war, nor would it have been possible to obtain international agreement on that objective. UN aims had been twofold: to liberate Kuwait, which Iraq had seized; and to neutralize Iraq's military capacity to create future trouble. The first aim had been achieved; the second only partly.

In a nationally televised speech on January 17, the first anniversary of the start of the war, President Hussein claimed that the Iraqi army and people had won a moral victory by standing up to the coalition of Western and Arab states. He also proclaimed his intention to rebuild "an influential military capability." His conduct throughout the year clearly was based on a steely determination to outface, outfox, and outlast his opponents.

Internal Conditions. The international sanctions, which remained in place, certainly created great hardship, though much was done in the way of restoring facilities and rebuilding. Whole sections of the population, formerly fairly prosperous, had been reduced to poverty and desperate scraping from day to day. In an interesting interview in November, Mohammed Mehdi Saleh, the minister of trade, conceded that the inflation rate was running at an annual 3,000%. However, an extremely efficient rationing system delivered basic food supplies at nominal prices; and the main pillars of the regime, notably army officers (mostly Sunni) and the secret police, received handsome pay raises to keep up with the cost of living. The ban on sales of Iraqi oil outside the country was fairly effective, but in many other respects the embargo on foreign trade was something of a sieve.

A ban on the sale of 157 "nonessential luxury items" was imposed on November 20; how far it would be enforced remained uncertain. The purpose was to push traders toward importing food and goods to supply basic needs. Earlier in the year the government had announced the execution of "profiteers."

Iraq had had about $4 billion in overseas holdings before the Kuwait crisis began. These remained blocked, apart from some sums released by Italy and Britain. Imports were financed mostly by the sale of gold reserves. On September 25 the UN Security Council authorized the use by the UN of blocked Iraqi assets to compensate war victims in Kuwait and elsewhere, and to finance relief work.

Since late 1991, Iraq had been offered the possibility of selling oil abroad to the extent of $1.6 billion, provided the funds were used under UN supervision and for approved purposes. The offer was rejected summarily as "infringing Iraqi sovereignty." In November the UN began a large ($200 million) humanitarian effort to aid all parts of Iraq.

Domestic Opposition. An apparent attempted coup against Hussein was crushed at the end of July and resulted in many executions. At the same time, there was no hint of a popular desire to overthrow him; the question of what type of government would come next was too daunting. Also, the heroic mood of "Iraq against the world" evoked by the regime seemed to be shared widely among the people. Not surprisingly, then, the Iraqi opposition was not impressive. In June a meeting of opposition groups in Vienna was attended poorly. Many divergent aims surfaced.

Much more impressive was the four-day opposition conference held in early November at Salahuddin in the Kurdish north. More than 260 delegates from all groups attended. This was the first such meeting of opponents of the regime to be held on Iraqi soil.

The real opposition to Saddam Hussein's rule, in fact, was regional: found in Iraqi Kurdistan and in the Shiite south. Both areas had risen in rebellion in 1991, just after the Iraqi defeat, and both rebellions had been put down ruthlessly. However, the allies later established a "safe haven" in Iraqi Kurdistan, Iraq government military activity being forbidden north of the 36th parallel. Attempts by the two equally important Kurdish leaders, Masoud Barzani and Jalal Talabani, to negotiate a new autonomy agreement with the government had broken down in the fall of 1991, and the government continued to harass the Kurds by a blockade and interdiction of food supplies.

On May 19 an election was held for an Iraqi Kurdistan National Assembly and an executive leader. Barzani's and Talabani's parties each gained 50 seats, and after some delay a compromise was reached on a shared executive. The government in Baghdad refused to recognize the validity of the May 19 election.

IRAQ • Information Highlights

Official Name: Republic of Iraq.
Location: Southwest Asia.
Area: 167,923 sq mi (434 920 km²).
Population (mid-1992 est.): 18,200,000.
Chief City (1987 census): Baghdad, the capital, 3,844,608.
Government: *Head of state and government,* Saddam Hussein, president (took office July 1979).
Monetary Unit: Dinar (0.311 dinar equals U.S.$1, selling rate, August 1992).
Gross National Product (1989 est. U.S.$): $35,000,-000,000.
Foreign Trade (1990 U.S.$): *Imports,* $4,834,-000,000; *exports,* $382,000,000.

In the meantime the government continued to pursue and punish the rebels in the southern marshlands. Few details were known, but clearly there were many executions and much brutality. This led the United States and Britain on August 27 to impose a no-fly zone in southern Iraq south of the 32d parallel. When on December 27 an Iraqi MiG-27 violated the airspace, it was shot down, provoking yet another crisis. Meanwhile Iraqi ground activity against rebels continued.

Expansionist Aims and Weapons. Events in May and June made it quite clear that Iraq's ambition to annex Kuwait was not dead, despite its enforced acceptance of UN Resolution 687 in 1991. The UN commission appointed in 1991 to define the undemarcated boundary made an interim report in April, which in May, Iraq rejected; in June, Iraq began to make references to its "past claims to Kuwait."

A major provision of the cease-fire agreement that ended the 1991 war was the mandated destruction of Iraq's suspected stores of biological and chemical weapons, and also of facilities capable of manufacturing these as well as of developing nuclear weapons. The need was clear, although enforcement of these conditions proved extraordinarily difficult. The visits by inspection teams of the UN's Commission on Iraqi Disarmament and of the International Atomic Energy Agency began in 1991 and continued throughout 1992. The teams faced unremitting Iraqi hostility, prevarication, delays, and occasional physical violence. The process, to be sure, had its successes, notably the destruction in April of the Al-Atheer nuclear-weapons complex near Baghdad. Well-founded doubts remained, however, about simply how much in the way of weapons and facilities had escaped discovery. Twice, in February-March and July-August, there appeared a real possibility that some military steps were about to be taken to enforce compliance, but a face-saving compromise in both cases averted a crisis.

ARTHUR CAMPBELL TURNER
University of California, Riverside

IRELAND

After months of mounting criticism over alleged corruption, Charles J. Haughey, the leader of the Fianna Fail-dominated coalition government, resigned on Feb. 6, 1992. The final blow came when the former minister for justice, Sean Doherty, revealed that Haughey —despite his denials—had known that the phones of two journalists had been tapped in 1982 for political purposes. Led by Desmond O'Malley, the Progressive Democratic Party (six members) withdrew its support from the coalition, forcing the prime minister to resign. A meeting of Fianna Fail members of the Dail

(House of Representatives) then chose Albert Reynolds as their leader. Five days later the Dail endorsed his premiership by a vote of 84 to 78.

Reynolds Government. Reynolds had served as minister for finance in Haughey's government until his dismissal in November for challenging the leadership. A businessman, he was known for his pragmatic politics and grasp of financial matters. In the new government, John Wilson became deputy prime minister; Bertie Ahern continued as minister of finance; David Andrews replaced Gerry Collins as minister of foreign affairs; Padraig Flynn headed the ministry of justice; and Desmond O'Malley stayed at the ministry of industry and commerce.

For the next nine months, Reynolds and his ministers struggled with political and financial problems. Some of the scandals surrounding the Haughey regime also continued to haunt them. Tensions between the Progressive Democrats and Fianna Fail reached a breaking point in October, when Reynolds accused O'Malley of having given "dishonest" testimony at a beef-industry tribunal. Angered by this charge, O'Malley and his supporters deserted the coalition on November 4. A day later the government lost a vote of no confidence by 85 to 77, whereupon Reynolds resigned and the Dail was dissolved pending a general election.

General Election. In the weeks leading up to the election, concerns about the economy vied for attention with a highly charged debate over abortion. On November 25, voters went to the polls to express their views on both issues. When the votes had been counted, the two leading parties each had lost seats. The Labour Party, led by the popular Dick Spring, had more than doubled its seats—from 15 to 33. Fianna Fail emerged with 67 seats, Fine Gael with 45, the Progressive Democrats with ten, and the Democratic Left with five. The Green Party won one seat, the Sinn Fein none—de-

---

IRELAND • Information Highlights

Official Name: Republic of Ireland.
Location: Island in the eastern North Atlantic Ocean.
Area: 27,135 sq mi (70 280 km²).
Population (mid-1992 est.): 3,500,000.
Chief Cities (1986 census): Dublin, the capital, 920,956 (incl. suburbs); Cork, 173,694; Limerick, 76,557.
Government: *Head of state,* Mary Robinson, president (took office Dec. 3, 1990). *Head of government,* Albert Reynolds, prime minister (took office Feb. 11, 1992). *Legislature*—Parliament: House of Representatives (Dail Eireann) and Senate (Seanad Eireann).
Monetary Unit: Pound (0.6116 pound equals U.S.$1, Dec. 30, 1992).
Gross Domestic Product (1990 U.S.$): $33,900,-000,000.
Economic Indexes (1991): *Consumer Prices* (1980 = 100), all items, 216.6; food, 468.1. *Industrial Production* (1980 = 100), 184.
Foreign Trade (1991 U.S.$): *Imports,* $20,760,000,-000; *exports,* $24,232,000,000.

Pro-abortionists rally in Ireland prior to a three-part referendum on the issue on Nov. 25, 1992. Voters decided to permit women to travel abroad for the purpose of obtaining an abortion and gave women the right to seek information about such travel, but defeated a motion to permit abortions in Ireland when a mother's life is threatened.

© Tracie Pierce/Saba

spite contesting more than 36 constituencies. Although these results delighted Labour, the absence of a clear majority for any party resulted in some hard political bargaining before and after the new Dail convened on December 14. Not until Jan. 12, 1993, did Labour cast its lot with Fianna Fail to let Reynolds form a new government.

Economy. The budget introduced on January 29 offered modest tax relief on income, new cars, and gasoline in the hope of stimulating economic growth and moving the unemployment rate below 20%. But increases in the cigarette tax, the value-added tax (VAT), and the vehicle road tax offset these concessions. The scarcity of jobs at home induced many young people to emigrate, and doubtless was a factor at the polls on June 18, when Irish voters approved the Maastricht Treaty for European integration by a two-to-one margin.

Abortion. Within a month of taking office the government had had to deal with the issue of abortion—specifically, a crisis arising out of a court order that prevented a young girl, who had been raped by a friend of her father, from traveling to the United Kingdom to obtain an abortion. Threats of suicide by the 14-year-old victim had moved her parents to consent to the operation; they were in Britain when the attorney general, backed by the court, ordered them to return. On February 17 the Irish High Court upheld this ruling, citing the 1983 constitutional amendment that banned any form of abortion unless the mother's life was in danger. The judges also enjoined the victim—known as "X"—from leaving the country for nine months.

This decision touched off a storm of protest. The girl's lawyers argued that European Community (EC) law guaranteed her right to travel for whatever purpose. A spokesman for the Irish Family Planning Association accused

the state of showing more concern for protecting "the procreative rights of rapists" than the rights of their victims. The case made headlines all over the world; and even the Conference of Irish Bishops made known its opposition to the court order. President Mary Robinson, a longtime champion of women's rights, denounced it and stressed Ireland's need to become "a more compassionate society."

On February 26 the Irish Supreme Court reversed the lower court's decision, clearing the way for the girl's operation in Britain on March 3. While abroad, the family learned that the government would pay their legal fees.

In October the European Court at Strasbourg ruled for the plaintiffs in a case, brought by family-planning agencies in Dublin, that protested the ban on information about abortion.

In the elections on November 25 a majority of voters endorsed two provisions that allowed women access to information about abortion and made it legal for them to seek abortions abroad. But they rejected by a margin of two to one an ambiguously worded constitutional amendment that would have allowed abortion in cases in which the mother's life was at risk.

Northern Ireland. On November 10 the secretary of state for Northern Ireland called a halt to the sporadic talks with representatives of the Irish government, as well as party leaders in the north, about the possibility of ending the conflict there. Earlier, on January 6, in a possibly related event, five armed men had stolen an estimated $4.35 million from a banking center in Waterford. Rumors circulated that the thieves belonged to the Irish Republican Army (IRA). According to British estimates, there were between 375 and 450 active members of the IRA in Northern Ireland and around 250 in the Republic.

L. Perry Curtis, Jr., *Brown University*

ISRAEL

The major event for Israel in 1992 was the defeat of the Likud bloc in the parliamentary elections held in June, as a result of which Yitzhak Rabin (*see* BIOGRAPHY) of the Labor Party became prime minister. Peace talks with the Arab nations begun in 1991 continued, but little progress could be reported. Relations with the Arab population in the occupied territories remained tense, and incidents of violence between the army and Palestinians increased.

Domestic Affairs. In January the right-wing Moledet and Tehiya parties withdrew from the Likud-led governing coalition, charging that Prime Minister Yitzhak Shamir was making too many concessions on Palestinian self-government in the peace negotiations. Their withdrawal left the government without a majority in the Knesset (parliament), and the prime minister decided to hold new elections. With the agreement of the Labor opposition, the balloting was set for June 23.

Meanwhile, in February, Yitzhak Rabin replaced Shimon Peres as leader of the Labor Party. In Likud, squabbling over the election slate led to Foreign Minister David Levy's resignation from the government; he withdrew his resignation after he was guaranteed increased representation within the party and in future official appointments. Levy's departure could have hurt Likud because of his strong following among the Oriental (Sephardi) Jewish population. The left was strengthened in February with the formation of Meretz, a coalition of the Mapam Socialist, Citizens' Rights, and Shinui parties supporting establishment of a Palestinian state alongside Israel. Two ultraorthodox parties, Agudat Israel and Degel HaTorah, also formed a new religious bloc, United Torah Judaism.

By June, 25 parties were approved to contest the 120 Knesset seats; only ten received the 1.5% of the votes required for election. Likud's loss of eight seats ended 15 years of its dominance in Israeli politics; Labor gained five seats to emerge as the strongest party with a total of 44. However, to obtain a parliamentary majority of 61, it had to form a new coalition with Meretz (12 seats) and the ultraorthodox Sephardi Shas party (six seats).

While foreign policy played a major role in the election campaign, bread-and-butter issues were of primary importance. The unexpectedly large vote received by Labor from new Russian immigrants was attributed to their high rate of unemployment and difficulties in adjusting to life in Israel. Labor strongly emphasized the place of Rabin—a hero of the 1967 Arab-Israeli war—as party leader, and his willingness to curtail Jewish settlements in the occupied territories in order to placate the United States.

In July, Rabin formed a new government with Peres as foreign minister; the new coalition was a volatile mix that included the ultraorthodox Shas and the left-of-center, secularly-oriented Meretz. When Rabin appointed Meretz leader Shulamit Aloni minister of education, Shas threatened to abandon the government, which could have led to collapse of the coalition. The coalition held together through the year, but remained threatened by controversy between Shas and Meretz.

As Israel's opposition Labor Party leader, Yitzhak Rabin (right) conferred with Constantine Mitsotakis—the first prime minister of Greece to visit Israel—in May 1992. Rabin returned as Israel's prime minister following the Labor Party's victory in June elections.

Jewish immigration from the former Soviet Union greatly decreased, from the anticipated 200,000 to about half that number. Overall unemployment was above 11%, although it reached 40% among the new immigrants. Government figures showed that more than 10% of the population (562,000 people, 234,000 of them children) were living below the poverty line in 1991, an increase of 4% over 1990. The annual inflation rate during 1991–92 remained stable, at between 17% and 18%. The budget for fiscal year 1992, approved in January after weeks of intense bargaining within the government coalition, included a planned domestic deficit of 6.2% of gross domestic product (GDP).

Among the first measures of the new Rabin government was a cut in publicly financed housing. While units under construction were to be completed, no projects were to be started, resulting in a 50% drop in government housing investments. Rabin's agreement to halt most new housing projects in the occupied territories was a major factor in obtaining support for $10 billion in U.S. loan guarantees.

By the end of the year relations between the government and the Arabs in the territories deteriorated, with increased use of violence by demonstrators opposed to Israel's occupation of the West Bank and Gaza. The fundamentalist Hamas (Islamic Resistance Movement), which opposed the peace negotiations, seemed to be gaining strength, especially in Gaza. Many of its members turned to armed resistance, rather than civil disobedience, which hitherto had been the principal tactic in the five-year-old *intifada* (Palestinian uprising).

Attacks on northern Israel and its "security zone" in south Lebanon also escalated with rocket attacks by Hezbollah (the Party of God, another Islamic fundamentalist group) on Israel's allies and on Jewish settlements in the north. In November the government ordered a massive buildup of Israeli forces along the Lebanese border.

Foreign Affairs. Prior to the formation of the new Labor government, relations with the United States were jeopardized by disputes between the Bush administration and Prime Minister Shamir. The Likud government refused to halt construction of new Jewish settlements in the territories as a condition for the $10 billion U.S. loan guarantee. The United States maintained that continued Jewish settlement was a major obstacle to progress in the peace negotiations. U.S. charges that Israel was reexporting U.S.-supplied Patriot missile technology to China exacerbated the rift, although the charge later was shown to be mistaken. Relations improved when Rabin took office and promised to suspend all new construction in the West Bank and Gaza. Rabin also took other measures to improve relations with the United States and to expedite the peace negotiations: He ordered the release of

ISRAEL • Information Highlights

Official Name: State of Israel.
Location: Southwest Asia.
Area: 8,019 sq mi (20 770 km²).
Population (mid-1992 est.): 5,200,000.
Chief Cities (1989 est.): Jerusalem, the capital, 493,500 (including East Jerusalem); Tel Aviv-Jaffa, 317,800; Haifa, 222,600.
Government: *Head of state,* Chaim Herzog, president (took office May 1983). *Head of government,* Yitzhak Rabin, prime minister (took office July 1992). *Legislature* (unicameral)—Knesset.
Monetary Unit: Shekel (2.6437 shekels equal U.S.$1, Dec. 3, 1992).
Gross National Product (1990 est. U.S.$): $46,500,-000,000.
Economic Indexes (1991): *Consumer Prices* (1980 = 100), all items, 77,838.2; food, 68,518.3. *Industrial Production* (1989, 1980 = 100), 141.
Foreign Trade (1991 U.S.$): *Imports,* $16,906,-000,000; *exports,* $11,889,000,000.

800 Palestinian prisoners, removed army barriers in two Palestinian streets, and canceled the expulsion of 11 Palestinians charged with illegal activities by the Shamir government.

With Labor's appointment of a new Israeli peace-negotiation team, relations with the Syrian, Lebanese, Jordanian, and Palestinian delegations improved somewhat. Rabin's declaration that Israel would consider territorial concessions in the occupied Golan Heights in exchange for a comprehensive peace settlement with Syria led to a more conciliatory tone in statements from Damascus. However, the outbreak of fighting between Israeli and Hezbollah forces in Lebanon threatened to undermine the improved relations with both Syria and Lebanon.

The Labor government was also more forthcoming in negotiations with the Palestinians, offering to permit elections for a 15-member administrative council to carry out day-to-day functions in the territories under Israeli jurisdiction. While this was more than the Likud team was willing to concede, the Palestinians demanded permission to form a 180-member legislative assembly that would take over the authority and functions of the Israeli military administration. On December 17, however, Israel deported some 400 Palestinians, whom the government considered to be militants, to Lebanese territory.

The greatest progress was made in negotiations with Jordan. Israel and Jordan agreed on an agenda aimed at concluding a final comprehensive peace treaty between the two countries. This was the first time Jordan ever had agreed to use the term "peace treaty" in its discussions with Israel.

Rabin also agreed to participate in multilateral meetings on refugees and economic development which Likud had boycotted because of participation by Palestinians from outside the territories.

DON PERETZ
State University of New York, Binghamton

© Stefano Nicozzi/Gamma-Liaison

In Italy during 1992, Oscar Luigi Scalfaro (left), 73-year-old Christian Democrat, was elected to the largely ceremonial post of president and Giuliano Amato (right), 54-year-old deputy leader of the Socialists (PSU), became premier.

ITALY

In 1992, Italy faced mounting crises caused by huge budgetary deficits, pervasive corruption, Mafia terrorism, and a politically splintered Parliament weakened by proportional representation and by the collapse of communism. The results of a parliamentary election held in April showed a decline in support for the hitherto-dominant political parties; following the election a new government under Socialist Giuliano Amato tried to implement an unpopular austerity program.

Election. The country began 1992 under a shaky coalition government—the 50th since World War II—headed by Giulio Andreotti, a Christian Democrat (DC), and composed also of Socialists (PSU), Social Democrats (PSDI), and Liberals (PLI). On February 2, Italian President Francesco Cossiga dissolved Parliament and called a general election for April 5–6. Cossiga, a champion of institutional reforms, explained that the current Parliament had become "politically exhausted." The Andreotti government had been unable to devise structural reforms that Cossiga and others believed were necessary to eliminate Italy's rigid system of proportional representation. The system, which leads to parliaments consisting of a

dozen or more parties, has made it difficult to form stable governments. The election, the first to take place since the collapse of communism, offered voters a chance to change a pattern of government that was perceived widely to have become unresponsive and corrupt.

For 40 years the Christian Democrats, Italy's largest party, had formed the cornerstone of every government, maintaining themselves in office as a bulwark against communism. Then in 1991 the old Italian Communist Party (PCI) disintegrated; most of its supporters began calling themselves the Party of the Democratic Left (PDS), but a hard-line minority formed the separate Communist Refoundation Party (PRC).

The DC's chief coalition partner, the Socialists (PSU), campaigned against the PDS for the number-two spot. Several historic parties of the political center—Social Democrats, Republicans, and Liberals—were also on the ballot. In the north a powerful new regional coalition—the North League (Lega Nord)—argued against further subsidies for the economically backward south. The ballot was cluttered further by special-interest groupings ranging from pensioners, hunters, and automobile drivers to the Party of Love, led by a female pornography star.

On the far right was the neo-fascist Italian Social Movement/National Right (MSI/DN), one of whose new candidates was Alessandra Mussolini, the outspoken 29-year-old granddaughter of Italy's onetime Fascist dictator Benito Mussolini (*see* page 421).

The stormy election campaign was punctuated on March 12 by the killing near Palermo of the top Sicilian Christian Democrat, Salvatore Lima, a former mayor of Palermo and a close ally of Premier Andreotti. The killing reportedly was the work of the Mafia, with which the Christian Democratic Party in Sicily often was accused of having close links. Lima's slaying came one day after Sebastiano Corrado, a leading anti-Mafia local councillor of the Party of the Democratic Left, had been murdered near Naples. In another organized-crime killing, Luciano Carugo, an industrialist known as "the king of asphalt," was kidnapped and found dead near Milan on March 12.

The election on April 5 produced a political "earthquake." Voters' preferences were split so widely that 16 parties won seats in Parliament. Premier Andreotti's DC Party suffered its worst setback in four decades, winning only 29.7% of the vote, down from 34.3% in 1987. His four-party government coalition fell to 48.8% of the popular vote, down from 53.7% in 1987. The Socialist Party, whose leader, Bettino Craxi, had hoped to become the new premier, suffered a setback as a result of financial scandals in his stronghold, the Socialist-run city government of Milan. The Party of the Democratic Left obtained but 16.1% of votes, down from 26.6% for the PCI in 1987. Another 5.6% went to the hard-line Communist PRC.

Among the gainers were the PRI, the PLI, and the Green Party. La Rete, a new anti-Mafia party in Sicily, captured 12 seats in the legislature. Most impressive of all was the performance of the North League, a group clustered around the Liga Lombarda of Umberto Bossi, which increased its representation in Parliament from one seat to 55, and its share of the popular vote from 0.5% to 8.7%.

Resignations of Andreotti and Cossiga. Ten weeks passed before a new government could be cobbled together. Andreotti's government resigned on April 24. The next day, in a surprising move, President Cossiga announced his own resignation, although his term was not due to expire until July 2. In a televised speech, Cossiga spoke disparagingly of Italy's system of government. He declared that his resignation was a response to the results of the election, the disastrous financial situation, and institutional paralysis. The people, he said, had asked for change and reform. This called for strong leadership, and he was a man alone, with no party or other political base. (Cossiga is a former Christian Democrat.) Giovanni Spadolini, as president of the Senate, temporarily assumed Cossiga's powers, and the outgoing Andreotti government continued to exercise its functions until a new president of the republic could be elected by the Parliament and a new government could be formed.

Choice of a New President. After 15 ballots between May 13 and May 23, the legislature still was unable to reach a decision in electing a successor to Cossiga. Further confusion occurred on May 22 when Arnaldo Forlani, an unsuccessful candidate for the presidency, resigned as secretary of the DC, leaving that major party leaderless. On May 23, Judge Giovanni Falcone, one of Italy's senior anti-Mafia investigators, was slain by a car bomb in Sicily. Several others also died in the blast. Falcone had achieved hero status in 1984 by coaxing a confession from a Mafia turncoat that led to the arrest of more than 300 mobsters. In Palermo, 40,000 mourners of Falcone marched in opposition to the Mafia.

Sobered by this assassination, Italy's fractious politicians closed ranks on May 25 and elected Oscar Luigi Scalfaro, a 73-year-old Christian Democrat, as the new president of the republic. Nine parties voted for Scalfaro, with only the North League, the PRI, the MSI/DN, and the PRC in opposition. In his inauguration speech, President Scalfaro, like his predecessor, promoted constitutional reform, and urged the country to get its fiscal house in order so that it could participate as an equal in the new European Community (EC).

The Amato Government. In mid-June, after weeks of political wrangling and spreading scandals that involved key figures in several political parties, President Scalfaro asked Giuliano Amato, the deputy leader of the PSU, to form a coalition government. Amato, a 54-year-old former treasury minister with a reputation for integrity, had been a fellow at the Brookings Institution in Washington and was fluent in English. In recent months he had achieved further distinction by helping to clean up "kickback" scandals in the Socialist Party in Milan.

Amato's cabinet, sworn in on June 28, was composed of the same four parties as the previous government: the Socialists, Christian Democrats, Liberals, and Social Democrats. The new coalition held a slim 16-vote majority in the 630-seat Chamber of Deputies. The government contained some new faces and excluded some prominent former ministers, including Andreotti and Andreotti's foreign minister, Gianni de Michelis. Enzo Scotti, the former interior minister, took over the foreign ministry. The interior ministry, which controlled the country's police forces, was given to Nicola Mancino, who had not served previously in government.

Most of the responsibility for finances and the economy went to outsiders. The managing director of Credito Italiano, Piero Barucci, headed the treasury. Franco Reviglio, who had

ITALY · Information Highlights

Official Name: Italian Republic.
Location: Southern Europe.
Area: 116,305 sq mi (301 230 km²).
Population (mid-1992 est.): 58,000,000.
Chief Cities (Dec. 31, 1990): Rome, the capital, 2,791,354; Milan, 1,432,184; Naples, 1,206,013.
Government: *Head of state,* Oscar Luigi Scalfaro, president (sworn in May 28, 1992). *Head of government,* Giuliano Amato, prime minister (sworn in June 28, 1992). *Legislature*—Parliament: Senate and Chamber of Deputies.
Monetary Unit: Lira (1,354.50 lire equal U.S.$1, Nov. 18, 1992).
Gross Domestic Product (1990 U.S.$): $844,700,000,000.
Economic Indexes (1991): *Consumer Prices* (1984 = 100), all items, 106.4; food, 106.7. *Industrial Production* (1980 = 100), 112.
Foreign Trade (1991 U.S.$): *Imports,* $182,554,-000,000; *exports,* $169,399,000,000.

served in government, industry, and academia, became budget minister—a portfolio that was expanded to include the ministry of the south. Former Premier Giovanni Goria, regarded as a DC reformist, headed the finance ministry. Carlo Ripa di Meana, who had been serving as the European Community's commissioner on the environment, became Italy's environment minister.

Mafia Killing of Palermo Prosecutor. On July 19 the Mafia reportedly sought to upset the new premier's agenda by detonating a car bomb near Palermo that killed Paolo Borsellino, the chief anti-Mafia prosecutor in Sicily, and five bodyguards. The government responded to the car bombing by ordering 7,000 soldiers into Sicily and transferring 55 key mobsters from Palermo's jail to penitentiaries elsewhere in Italy. On July 28 mobsters in Catania gunned down Giovanni Lizzio, head of anti-extortion investigations in that city. He was the first senior police officer to be killed in Catania, a city that long had resisted the Mafia.

Amato's Program. Meanwhile, the Amato government unveiled its austerity plans to curb Italy's huge public sector—which at the time generated 10.5% of the country's gross domestic product (GDP) and was by far the largest in the EC. In addition, Amato called for electoral reform and a new battle against organized crime and corruption. The government also announced plans to privatize a huge and inefficient sector of the economy that for decades had been controlled by politically staffed state holding companies—the IRI (Institute for Industrial Reconstruction); ENI (Hydrocarbons Authority); ENEL (State Electric Authority); and INA (an insurance company). Under the new system, those companies would be converted into joint-stock companies. Another holding company in the manufacturing sector, EFIM, was to be liquidated altogether.

In late July the Amato government called for a vote of confidence on a proposal to reduce the budget deficit of $130 billion by means of tax increases and spending cuts. The government survived the confidence vote, but two senior officials, including Foreign Minister Vincenzo Scotti, quit the cabinet, touching off a new imbroglio. Another Christian Democrat, Emilio Colombo, replaced him.

On August 6, Parliament approved a package of anti-Mafia legislation that gave the police increased powers. In a separate action, Giuseppe Di Gennaro, a supreme-court judge, was named Italy's new "super-magistrate" to investigate the Mafia. And on September 6 police arrested Giuseppe Madonia, one of the nation's most-wanted Mafia leaders.

Currency Crisis. In mid-September, speculative trading and a surge in bank withdrawals pounded the weak lira, which fell 15% against the strong German mark. As a result, Italy had to devalue the lira by 7% and temporarily remove it from the exchange-rate mechanism of the EC's European Monetary System. The currency crisis reflected Italy's high inflation and double-digit interest rates.

Austerity Legislation. On October 10, Premier Amato won a narrow vote of confidence on a key part of his spending-cuts program involving pensions, health and welfare services, and reforms in local governments. The program also would end Italy's indexing of wage increases to inflation. These measures triggered a general strike by the leading trade-union federations. Most union leaders emphasized they did not want to bring down Amato's government; rather, they wanted sacrifices to be distributed more evenly. The strikes forced the government to back off from some of its proposals.

Christian Democratic Renewal? At a big rally held in Rome in October, Mario Segni—a reformist DC member of Parliament and son of former President Antonio Segni—launched the Popular Movement for Reform, which aimed at curbing the power of the DC's old guard. Segni also demanded abolition of proportional representation in Parliament. At about the same time, the DC Party Congress elected a new secretary, Mino Martinazzoli, a northerner who seemed to show sympathy for Segni's populist approach. A woman, Rosa Russo Jervolino, was chosen party president. Meanwhile, the regionalist North League continued to gain strength at the DC's expense. In an election at Mantua it got 33% of the vote, twice as much as the Christian Democrats.

Foreign Affairs. The Maastricht Treaty on European integration, which was the cause of much furor in other EC countries, was ratified by the Italian Parliament with no difficulty. In the Yugoslav crisis, Italy sent naval and air units to help enforce UN-imposed trade sanctions against Serbia, and to support UN/EC peacekeeping operations in Croatia and Bosnia.

CHARLES F. DELZELL, *Vanderbilt University*

JAPAN

In 1992, Japan's long debate over the PKO (Peacekeeping Operations) bill ended with approval of the measure; the country was rocked by a banking crisis and by new revelations of government corruption; and the economy continued to grow at a sluggish rate. In foreign affairs, the Japanese carried on with efforts to settle disputes with the United States and Russia, and to ease frictions with their Asian neighbors dating back to World War II.

Domestic Affairs

On August 15 the nation marked the 47th anniversary of the war's end with ceremonies led by Emperor Akihito at the Nihon Budokan Hall in Tokyo. The observance came in the wake of a vigorous domestic debate over the use of Japanese peacekeeping forces abroad.

The PKO Bill. Late in 1990 a government bill that would have permitted Self-Defense Forces (SDF) to participate in UN peacekeeping operations (for example, in the Persian Gulf war) was defeated in the Diet. Opponents argued that the legislation violated Japan's no-war constitution. In February 1992 a panel headed by Ichiro Ozawa, former secretary-general of the ruling Liberal Democratic Party (LDP), concluded that under the constitution the SDF could join UN forces if provisions were reinterpreted. Somewhat ambiguously, Prime Minister Kiichi Miyazawa told the Diet, "No change is taking place in the government's attitude on the issue." In fact, Miyazawa was prepared to take the next step in peacekeeping operations (dubbed, even by the Japanese media, the PKO dispute).

As of January 15, the 512 seats in the (lower) House of Representatives were distributed as follows: LDP—278, Social Democratic Party of Japan (SDPJ)—138, Komeito —46, Japan Communist Party (JCP)—16, Democratic Socialist Party (DSP)—14, independents and small parties—10, vacancies— 10. The LDP, with 114 in the 252-seat (upper) House of Councillors, lacked a majority. Combined opposition parties—the SDPJ, Komeito, JCP, DSP, and Rengo (a labor federation)— controlled 136 seats (with two vacancies).

Immediately the Diet became involved in a debate over a new LDP-sponsored PKO bill. All parties also were maneuvering toward the triennial House of Councillors election, scheduled for July 26. In February-March the LDP lost two elections for vacancies in the upper house to Rengo candidates who opposed the PKO bill, but won a third by-election in Gunma prefecture. According to a *Kyodo News* poll, by April 1 disapproval of the Miyazawa cabinet had surged to 65.3% (from 41% in December). *Yomiuri Shimbun* reported, however, that nearly 40% of respondents still would vote for the LDP.

After the LDP's PKO proposal was tabled in the lower house, the party chose to win adoption first in the upper house. After days of debate, on June 9 the House of Councillors passed the controversial legislation with a majority vote of 143 in favor (including Komeito and DSP members who supported the LDP).

Marathon sessions in the House of Representatives culminated in a dramatic offer by 141 members (SDPJ and minor parties) to quit, but the ruling party refused to accept the resignations. Finally, after an all-night disruption of procedures, the lower house passed the bill

© AP/Wide World

Japanese farmers stage a rally in Tokyo to oppose the importing of rice. The issue was a trouble spot in international trade discussions during 1992.

by a vote of 329–17 (the SDPJ boycotted the final vote; again, Komeito and DSP members voted for the bill). The PKO bill became law.

The *Asahi Shimbun* editorialized that the PKO bill ignored public opinion, which favored dispatch of civilian but not military personnel. Use of Japanese forces in UN peacekeeping operations became the prime issue in the forthcoming election.

House of Councillors Election. On July 8 the campaign for half the seats in the upper house began. At risk were candidates in the tripartite alliance of the LDP, Komeito, and DSP who had approved the PKO bill. Miyazawa tried to shift focus to the sluggish economy, the need to control corruption, and election reform. However, he was handicapped by a defection from LDP ranks. In 1990, Governor Morihiro Hosokawa of Kumamoto had withdrawn from the party. On the eve of the election, he formed the Japan New Party, and pledged to decentralize the bureaucracy and to revolutionize education. He announced opposition to the PKO.

Chairman Makoto Tanabe of the SDPJ expressed the hope for a socialist coalition to rescind the PKO, despite differences with the DSP over the legislation. All the other opposition parties agreed that UN peacekeeping would remain the single most important election issue.

On July 26 the LDP registered a comeback from three years before by winning 69 of 127 contested seats in the upper house. The SDPJ captured only 22 seats to maintain its preelection total (69). In combination with other opposition parties (total 113), the major opponent of the LDP still could be outvoted by an ad hoc coalition of LDP, Komeito, and DSP (total 139). The Japan New Party won only four seats (in national constituencies). Rengo's future (with only 12 holdovers) was uncertain.

Money Politics. Thoroughly exhausted by the peacekeeping debate, the LDP was weakened further by continuing scandals arising from what Japanese called "money politics." On January 13, Fumio Abe, secretary-general of the Miyazawa faction and ally of the prime minister, was arrested for political misuse of funds contributed by the Kyowa Corporation. In February, in sworn testimony before a Diet committee, former Prime Minister Zenko Suzuki and a former minister, Jun Shiozaki, denied direct involvement in the bribe from the bankrupt steel manufacturer. Shiozaki admitted having received $160,000, but claimed he later returned the funds.

At the time the Kyowa incident broke, prosecutors also had arrested the head of a trucking company, Tokyo Sagawa Kyubin. He allegedly passed more than $4 billion through 58 firms, some linked to a large crime syndicate, Inagawa-kai. The media identified some 100 politicians who had received "donations" from the funds.

On August 27 the main power manipulator behind the LDP screen, Shin Kanemaru, admitted that he had received $4 million from the Sagawa company. He gave up the LDP vice-presidency and quit as head of the largest LDP faction. In October he resigned from the Diet. Meanwhile, Niigata prefecture's Governor Kiyoshi Kaneko resigned, following allegations that he had accepted millions of yen during the 1989 local election.

Economy. The money scandals and the PKO dispute severely hampered the government's management of a battered economy. Even though the House of Councillors voted down the proposal, on April 9 the lower house (with constitutional preference) adopted a $547 billion budget. It was eight days late for fiscal year 1992 and represented the smallest growth in expenditure in five years.

In February the Economic Planning Agency (EPA) estimated the annualized gross national product (GNP) at 423.6 trillion yen ($3.3 trillion at the current rate of exchange). In the period from January through June, inflation-adjusted growth in GNP measured just more than 2% on an annual basis and was projected at 1.8% for 1992 (well below the 3.5% predicted for fiscal 1992 by the EPA).

On March 31 the government adopted a stimulus package, moving up expenditures on public works planned for fiscal 1992. Nonetheless, on the Tokyo Stock Exchange (TSE) the 225-issue Nikkei average dropped to the lowest level in five years. By June the Nikkei had declined almost 60% (to an index of 15,921) from a peak in 1989 (at 38,916). On August 22 the TSE hit bottom, with the Nikkei at the lowest level in 77 months (14,309). Additional government action on the monetary and fiscal fronts resulted in a modest recovery: By October 13 the Nikkei had risen to 17,491.

On July 27, the day after the triennial election, the Bank of Japan lowered the official discount rate to 3.25%. It was the fifth cut since a

---

JAPAN • Information Highlights

Official Name: Japan.
Location: East Asia.
Area: 145,882 sq mi (377 835 km²).
Population (mid-1992 est.): 124,400,000.
Chief Cities (March 31, 1989 est.): Tokyo, the capital, 8,046,160; Yokohama, 3,1759891; Osaka, 2,522,791; Nagoya, 2,100,966.
Government: *Head of state,* Akihito, emperor (acceded Jan. 9, 1989). *Head of government,* Kiichi Miyazawa, prime minister (took office Nov. 6, 1991). *Legislature*—Diet: House of Councillors and House of Representatives.
Monetary Unit: Yen (124.80 yen equal U.S.$1, Nov. 16, 1992).
Gross National Product (1990 U.S.$): $2,115,200,-000,000.
Economic Indexes (1991): *Consumer Prices* (1980 = 100), all items, 126.4; food, 127.5. *Industrial Production* (1980 = 100), 152.
Foreign Trade (1991 U.S.$): *Imports,* $236,744,-000,000; *exports,* $314,525,000,000.

After the Japanese parliament passed a bill permitting Japan to participate in UN peacekeeping operations, Japanese troops took part in the UN Transitional Authority in Cambodia (UNTAC). It was the first time since World War II that Japanese forces had been sent abroad.

© David Portnoy/Black Star

year before, when the rate stood at 6%. On August 28 the Miyazawa cabinet announced expenditures of more than $86 billion to promote recovery. It was the largest stimulative action ever undertaken (2.3% of GNP). Governor Yasushi Mieno of the Bank predicted that these actions would have a "cumulative effect" on the economy.

Banking Crisis. At the same time, the banks themselves began to develop serious problems. Recent declines in property values and stock prices had caused Japan's banking system to become saddled with growing numbers of loan defaults. Bad loans at major banks increased by more than 50% in the period between May and October, reaching a total of 12.3 trillion yen. In August, when the stock market plunged to a six-year low, the government called for a plan to bail out the troubled banks. Leaders of the banking industry came up with such a plan at the end of October, but it was unclear just how much of the cost would have to be borne by the taxpayers.

Demographic Developments. Two demographic trends aroused concern among public officials and business executives. According to the health and welfare ministry, the number of births dropped to 1.22 million in 1991 from a peak of 2.7 million in the baby boom of the late 1950s. The birthrate declined to 1.53 (the average number of babies born to a Japanese woman), well below the 2.08 considered the population-replacement level. Fewer babies meant lower economic demand and a smaller work force in the future.

At the same time, the number of elderly receiving public pensions had exceeded 25 million for the first time in 1989. In 1991, Japan became the world leader in longevity: Life expectancy for women was 82.11; for men, 76.11. The implications for public policy of these two shifts in population occupied all levels of government.

Foreign Affairs

Japan should shift away from "checkbook diplomacy" and play a larger role in multinational efforts to maintain global security, according to the 1991 Diplomatic Blue Book released by the foreign ministry. Action would include participation in UN peacekeeping operations (envisaged in the government's PKO bill). The report added that the Japan-U.S. security alliance is seen by the public as less vital because of the end of the Cold War.

U.S. Relations. In the so-called Strategic Impediments Initiative (SII) begun in 1990, U.S. President George Bush had described the negotiations as a "two-way street." Japanese media, however, noted that most of the pressure was placed on Tokyo. Demands included removal of trade restrictions, breakup of cartels, and increased expenditure on infrastructure. Japanese officials argued that the United States had taken few steps to reduce its budget deficit, to increase private savings, or to improve industrial competitiveness. The U.S. president's postponed and ill-conceived Tokyo visit, January 7–10, reinforced these judgments.

In an unusual move, President Bush arrived in Japan with a delegation which included three automobile chief executives—Robert Stempel (General Motors), Harold Poling (Ford), and Lee Iacocca (Chrysler). Bush and Prime Minister Miyazawa signed the Tokyo Declaration, essentially calling on Japan to aid the ailing U.S. economy. Attached documents included Japanese automakers' "voluntary" pledges to import some 20,000 U.S. vehicles annually and to increase purchases of auto parts from $9 billion (1990) to $19 billion (by 1994).

Minister of International Trade and Industry Kozo Watanabe criticized the agreement as an example of "managed trade." On their return to the United States, the U.S. auto chairmen continued to complain about the unfavorable trade balance. On March 19, however, Watanabe did announce a cut in the self-imposed annual quota on auto exports to the United States, from 2.3 million to 1.6 million.

U.S. Vice-President Dan Quayle sounded a gentler note on May 15, when he attended a ceremony in Tokyo marking the 20th anniversary of the United States' return of Okinawa to Japan's administration. He stressed the "mutual trust" between Tokyo and Washington. Okinawan officials and landowners, however, urged revision of the policy of assigning land and facilities to the U.S. military still based in the southern islands.

Russian Relations. Japan had normalized relations with the USSR in 1956, but a peace treaty to bring a formal end to World War II awaited settlement of a nagging dispute. Tokyo continued to protest Russian military occupation of what Japanese called the "northern territories," four southern Kuril islands.

In July, Prime Minister Miyazawa said he was "not opposed" to financial aid to the new Russian state, but resolution of the territorial problem remained a prerequisite to a treaty. In Washington, on the eve of the Munich summit conference of the G-7 powers (July 6–8), Miyazawa received assurances of support from President Bush. In London, however, British Prime Minister John Major called the problem "a bilateral dispute." Eventually, the G-7 called for settlement as vital for the new world order. In talks held on September 2 in Moscow with Foreign Minister Michio Watanabe, Russian President Boris Yeltsin acknowledged the G-7 call, but warned that excessive pressure from Tokyo could result in gridlock. Finally, in a late-night call to Tokyo on September 9, Yeltsin canceled a trip to Japan. Chief Cabinet Secretary Koichi Kato predicted that Yeltsin's arrival would await achievement of economic and political stability in Russia.

Asia. Another long-expected trip, the first by a Japanese emperor to China, seemed closer to fruition. In August the government announced that Emperor Akihito and Empress Michiko had accepted an official invitation to visit the People's Republic October 23–28. Since 1972, Beijing had issued no less than seven invitations, the latest aimed to mark the 20th anniversary of normalized relations. The proposed trip was highly controversial: Japanese critics on the right wing feared that the emperor would be put in a position of offering an apology for Japan's wartime activities.

The visit went off almost without incident, although there were sporadic demonstrations in Japan. In Beijing, Emperor Akihito expressed "sadness" over the wartime history but stopped short of a direct apology.

In January, Prime Minister Miyazawa visited Seoul, trying to redress a record 1991 trade surplus with South Korea. Japan's Federation of Economic Organizations (Keidanren) offered $40 million to establish foundations for technology transfer, but later, Seoul's trade officials in Tokyo demanded at least $120 million for the project. In June the two sides agreed to leave the matter in the hands of the private sectors in each country.

A more sensitive issue involved the wartime relations between Japan and Korea. On July 6 a foreign ministry spokesman in Seoul welcomed Tokyo's public admission that the Imperial Army officially had supported recruitment of Korean "comfort women" as prostitutes in World War II. The report was, however, "incomplete," according to Seoul.

Although Japan voted with UN members to enable both Koreas to join the international organization in 1991, Tokyo still had no formal relations with Pyongyang. The conversion from informal contacts was made more difficult in September, when North Korea announced its opposition to Japan's quiet campaign to become a permanent member of the United Nations Security Council.

Cambodian Peacekeeping Force. A historic event marked September 17, when Japanese troops were sent abroad for the first time since World War II. (Japanese minesweepers had aided U.S. forces in clearing the Persian Gulf in 1991, but that was after the conflict with Iraq had ended.) On September 3, Tokyo was asked to send SDF components—cease-fire monitors, engineering troops, and police officers—to join the UN Transitional Authority in Cambodia (UNTAC).

As soon as the Miyazawa government succeeded in getting the Diet to enact the PKO bill in June, Yasushi Akashi, the head of UNTAC and highest-ranking Japanese in the UN, stressed the need for Japan to join UN operations in Cambodia. According to LDP compromises with centrist parties, Japanese participation awaited agreement among warring Cambodian factions to accept a cease-fire and the SDF forces as peacekeepers. Such an agreement was obtained in a one-day conference held in Tokyo on June 22.

The dispatch of Japanese troops to Cambodia uncovered mixed feelings among Asians, who recalled Japan's 1910–45 colonial rule of Korea and its invasions of China and of Southeast Asia.

The Olympics. Japan won a record seven medals at the Albertville Winter Olympic Games. The diminutive Midori Ito won a silver in figure skating, despite inordinate pressure from Japanese media. At the Barcelona Summer Games, Japanese athletes won three gold, eight silver, and 11 bronze medals (altogether eight more than were won at the Seoul Games in 1988). The Japanese already were looking forward to the winter games of 1998, to be held in Nagano.

ARDATH W. BURKS, *Rutgers University*

JORDAN

The year 1992 was difficult for Jordan. Both domestic and foreign affairs posed intractable dilemmas for the royal government. Fortunately, King Hussein had proved over many years to be an adroit policymaker, skillful in balancing the many pressures that buffet his kingdom. In 1992 there was some melioration of the great difficulties besetting Jordan in recent years, but new and possibly more fundamental problems were arising.

Liberalization. For two years before 1992, Jordan had been embarked on a program of political liberalization and advance toward democracy. No other Arab country, except Egypt, which is not a monarchy, had gone so far. The extraordinary changes continued in 1992. Jordan, however, was still far short of being a constitutional monarchy on the model of, say, Britain—a country the king and his brother, Crown Prince Hassan, know well. The monarchy retained extensive powers, which it did not hesitate, on occasion, to use. This seemed essential, as it is uncertain whether the Jordanian population provides the materials for a stable political consensus—the majority of the population is now Palestinian. Jordan has both a sophisticated, Western-educated elite and a strong element of resurgent Islamists. In 1992 the Muslim Brotherhood was the largest bloc (22) in the 80-member House of Representatives, freely elected in November 1989. The bloc demonstrated its strength on February 28 when the House passed a resolution recommending (but not implementing) a ban on the manufacture, sale, and consumption of alcohol.

Prime Minister Sherif Zeid bin Shaker, a trusted servant of the crown, shepherded the reforms. In July 1991, King Hussein had issued a decree repealing most of the martial-law regulations that had been in force since 1967; the remaining rules were abolished on April 1, 1992. Also, all security offenses, including espionage and treason, thereafter were to be

© Hanna Farrag/NYT Pictures

Although Jordan's King Hussein was operated on for cancer in 1992, Jordan remained very much under his control. The king's political-liberalization program continued in effect.

dealt with by the state security courts. Similarly, the legalization of political parties (previously banned), which had been foreshadowed in the landmark National Charter of June 1991, was carried out in July 1992 after approval by the House of Representatives (July 5) and Senate (July 23). Certain conditions were included: Every party was required to have at least 50 founding members; a party had to give an undertaking to abide by the constitution; and no party was permitted to receive funding from foreign sources.

The King's Illness. The king was operated on at the Mayo Clinic in Rochester, MN, on August 20. Cancer had been found, and the left kidney and part of the urinary tract were removed. Hussein did not return to Jordan until September 24, after recuperating in London. On his return to Amman he was given a tumultuous welcome, but anxieties about the future remained. Most Jordanians had difficulty imagining a future without Hussein. His reign began in 1953; he had been king for more than half the time Jordan (formerly Transjordan) existed. The presumptive heir, Crown Prince Hassan, although a very able man, was much less known than the king. The king returned to the United States for tests in November.

Financial Matters. Jordan's financial difficulties had increased in recent years, mostly owing to the Persian Gulf war. Some 300,000 Palestinians—most not technically refugees because they held Jordanian passports—had been forced to leave Kuwait and other Gulf

---

JORDAN • Information Highlights

Official Name: Hashemite Kingdom of Jordan.
Location: Southwest Asia.
Area: 35,475 sq mi (91 880 km²).
Population (mid-1992 est.): 3,600,000.
Chief Cities (1989 est.): Amman, the capital, 936,300; Zarqa, 318,055; Irbid, 167,785.
Government: *Head of state,* Hussein I, king (enthroned May 2, 1953). *Head of government,* Sherif Zeid bin Shaker, prime minister (took office November 1991). *Legislature*—Parliament: House of Representatives and Senate.
Monetary Unit: Dinar (.67422 dinar equals U.S.$1, Dec. 30, 1992).
Gross National Product (1990 est. U.S.$): $4,600,000,000.
Economic Index (1991): *Consumer Prices* (1980 = 100), all items, 218.6; food, 206.3.
Foreign Trade (1991 U.S.$): *Imports,* $2,512,000,000; *exports,* $902,000,000.

---

states. Accordingly, they had ceased to send the vitally important expatriate remittances, and had crowded into Jordan's borders; nor were they welcome to return to the Gulf. As a result of Jordan's pro-Iraqi stance during the Gulf war, U.S. and Saudi subsidies were cut off—the former temporarily. In 1992 foreign lenders showed some sympathy with Jordan's difficulties. On January 16 the European Parliament approved $2 billion in aid to Middle Eastern countries, including Jordan.

The U.S. budget sent to Congress in January contained an item of $27 million in military assistance for Jordan in fiscal 1993. (Jordan's total foreign debt was some $7.2 billion.) In early March the "Paris Club" of Western creditor governments agreed to reschedule repayment of about $1.4 billion over 20 years, while the "London Club" of private banks made a similar agreement about $900 million on overdue repayments.

Foreign Affairs. Jordan, placed geographically between Iraq and Israel and culturally between pro-Western and pro-Arab sympathies, continued to follow a careful but vigorously independent foreign policy. In the course of an extensive foreign tour in March that took him to Iceland, Canada, the United States, France, and Germany, the king saw U.S. President George Bush for the first time since the eruption of the Gulf crisis in August 1990. During his period of recuperation in September he saw Bush again, as well as British Prime Minister John Major. It long had been an open, and tacitly tolerated, secret that Jordan was assisting Iraq to circumvent United Nations trade sanctions, in return for cheap supplies of Iraqi oil. In July the United States voiced increasing impatience with this situation. Jordan promised to observe more careful controls, but at the same time flatly turned down the U.S. suggestion that inspectors be established on the Iraq-Jordan border and at the port of Aqaba. Jordan also opposed the creation of the no-fly zone in southern Iraq.

Jordan's partial recovery of Western approval was largely the result of its enthusiastic support of and participation in the ongoing Arab-Israeli negotiations begun in Madrid in October 1991. In a possibly significant breakthrough announced Nov. 1, 1992, Jordanian and Israeli negotiators in Washington drew up an agenda for discussion of common issues in future talks, including water sharing, economic ties, and the final definition of their border.

ARTHUR CAMPBELL TURNER
University of California, Riverside

KANSAS

In the 1992 presidential election, Kansas, following its Republican tradition, supported George Bush with 445,790 votes to Bill Clin-

---

KANSAS • Information Highlights

Area: 82,277 sq mi (213 098 km²).
Population (July 1, 1991 est.): 2,495,000.
Chief Cities (1990 census): Topeka, the capital, 119,883; Wichita, 304,011; Kansas City, 149,767.
Government (1992): *Chief Officers*—governor, Joan Finney (D); lt. gov., James L. Francisco (D). *Legislature*—Senate, 40 members; House of Representatives, 125 members.
State Finances (fiscal year 1991): *Revenue,* $5,249,000,000; *expenditure,* $5,134,000,000.
Personal Income (1991): $45,706,000,000; per capita, $18,322.
Labor Force (June 1992): *Civilian labor force,* 1,310,800; *unemployed,* 56,900 (4.3% of total force).
Education: *Enrollment* (fall 1990)—public elementary schools, 319,697; public secondary, 117,337; colleges and universities, 163,375. *Public school expenditures* (1990), $1,959,200.

---

ton's 387,488. Ross Perot received 27% of the vote. During the year, the state legislature adopted a new method of financing public schools and Democratic Gov. Joan Finney was involved in several controversies.

Election. In 1992, Kansas Republicans succeeded in giving the state's electoral votes to President Bush, reelecting Bob Dole to his fifth term in the U.S. Senate, increasing the Republican majority in the Kansas Senate (26–14), and regaining control of the Kansas House (66–59). Congressional incumbents Pat Roberts (R), Jim Slattery (D), Jan Meyers (R), and Dan Glickman (D) all were reelected. Kansas lost its fifth congressional district due to reapportionment based on 1990 census figures.

Constitutional amendments reclassifying property-tax rates and giving crime victims basic rights during the criminal-justice process were approved. A record number of Kansans —about 1.16 million, comprising 85% of registered voters—participated in the election.

Legislature and Government. In 1992 the Kansas legislature, in an effort to reduce property taxes and in response to a district-court ruling, drastically revised the method of funding public education. While the law decreased property taxes in most districts, residents of several counties in southwest Kansas were upset about their property-tax increases and threatened secession. Primarily because of increased spending on education, the budget of $6.4 billion was the largest in Kansas history.

Other legislation passed in 1992 included uniform sentencing guidelines for a number of crimes, a package of 19 laws known as the Children's Initiative, and an abortion bill keeping abortion legal for women over 18 in early pregnancy while imposing abortion restrictions for those under 18.

Governor Finney was involved in a number of controversies in 1992, ranging from the signing of compacts with Native American tribes to allow casino gambling on their property to several firings and resignations of her cabinet-level appointees. The gambling move was controversial because the legislature had passed a ban on casino gambling that was vetoed by Finney, and the Kansas Supreme Court later ruled that the legislature had to approve the compacts. Among the resignations was that of the secretary of wildlife and parks after it was revealed he had issued hunter-safety certificates to three of Finney's top officials without the required ten hours of instruction.

Agriculture. The wheat crop, hampered by unfavorable weather, totaled 359.7 million bushels harvested from 10.9 million acres (4 411 073 ha). This was down about 1% from the 1991 crop, but it did match the previous year's yield of 33 bushels per acre. However, fall crops set records. Grain sorghum production was expected to set a record yield of 80 bushels per acre with a total of 248 million bushels harvested. Total corn production was estimated to be 243.1 million bushels, the most since 1889, with a yield of 143 bushels per acre. The soybean crop of 64.8 million bushels, 35 bushels per acre, was expected to surpass the previous high yield of 1986. Overall farm income, however, was at its lowest since 1986.

Other. Native Kansan Bill Koch won the America's Cup with his yacht *America*[3]. Monroe School in Topeka—attended by Linda Brown and other plaintiffs when the 1954 Supreme Court landmark desegregation case, *Brown v. the Board of Education of Topeka,* was filed—received national landmark status and was accepted into the National Park Service.

PATRICIA A. MICHAELIS
Kansas State Historical Society

KENTUCKY

Elections, political reform, and a Federal Bureau of Investigation (FBI) sting of the legislature captured headlines in Kentucky during 1992. Other important developments included Kentucky's bicentennial celebration, Gov. Brereton Jones' survival in a helicopter crash, the loss of one congressional seat, state-revenue shortfalls of $136.6 million, the second-year benefits of historic education reform, and a controversial ruling by the Kentucky Supreme Court that the state's sodomy statute was unconstitutional. Economic changes included some plant closings, a downturn in the home-building industry, and the purchase of bankrupt Calumet Farm.

Elections. Garnering 45% of the vote, Bill Clinton narrowly carried Kentucky, defeating President George Bush with 41% and independent Ross Perot with 14%. A near-record 71.7% of registered voters went to the polls.

U.S. Sen. Wendell Ford, the majority whip, easily won a fourth term over an ambitious Republican challenger, with nearly two thirds of the vote. Also reelected were Reps. William

Natcher (D) in the 2d District, Romano Mazzoli (D) in the 3d, Jim Bunning (R) in the 4th, and Hal Rogers (R) in the 5th. Lexington Mayor Scotty Baesler, a Democrat, easily won in the 6th District and Tom Barlow kept the 1st District seat in the Democrats' camp. He had upset nine-term incumbent Carroll Hubbard in the May primary. Hubbard suffered because of 152 House bank overdrafts, heavy political-action-committee (PAC) contributions, and a wife who unsuccessfully ran for a House seat in the 5th District.

Only one incumbent in the General Assembly was ousted in 48 contested races, although the number of women in the legislature dropped from nine to six. Fayette county elected its first black representative, increasing to four the number of minority legislators.

Amendments. By a slim 2% margin voters agreed that future governors and statewide officeholders could succeed themselves in office; made the role of lieutenant governor clearly subservient; and established one election-free year every four years, starting in 1997. Governor Jones helped pave the way for succession by supporting an amendment that would exclude the sitting governor. Kentuckians also adopted by 71% an amendment that legalizes charitable bingo, but rejected by a 3–2 margin an amendment designed to end elections for several of Kentucky's statewide offices.

Corruption. A massive undercover FBI sting operation investigating possible bribery, extortion, and racketeering, involving banking and horse-industry legislation, was revealed in late March. By mid-November ten people had been indicted, including the speaker of the house, seven former legislators, a former powerful lobbyist, and a top aide to former Gov. Wallace Wilkinson. All pleaded guilty except the speaker and the Wilkinson aide.

General Assembly. The legislature passed important measures—in long-term economic-development planning, depoliticizing appointments to university boards, and restricting the

---

KENTUCKY • Information Highlights

Area: 40,410 sq mi (104 660 km²).
Population (July 1, 1991 est.): 3,713,000.
Chief Cities (1990 census): Frankfort, the capital, 25,968; Louisville, 269,063; Lexington-Fayette, 225,366.
Government (1992): *Chief Officers*—governor, Wallace Wilkinson (D); lt. gov., Brereton Jones (D). *General Assembly*—Senate, 38 members; House of Representatives, 100 members.
State Finances (fiscal year 1991): *Revenue,* $9,951,000,000; *expenditure,* $9,048,000,000.
Personal Income (1991): $58,027,000,000; per capita, $15,626.
Labor Force (June 1992): *Civilian labor force,* 1,744,800; *unemployed,* 108,700 (6.2% of total force).
Education: *Enrollment* (fall 1990)—public elementary schools, 459,216; public secondary, 177,185; colleges and universities, 177,852. *Public school expenditures* (1990), $2,499,437,000.

awarding of no-bid government contracts. Path-breaking campaign-finance reform included partial public financing of gubernatorial slates and the slashing of maximum contributions of individuals and PACs from $4,000 to $500 for gubernatorial or legislative candidates.

PENNY M. MILLER, *University of Kentucky*

KENYA

Kenya's first multiparty elections in 25 years took place on Dec. 29, 1992. The election, labeled by a local monitoring group as marred by fraud, resulted in the continuance in power of Kenya President Daniel arap Moi.

Elections and Violence. The year began with Kenya's first legal antigovernment rally in more than two decades. The Forum for the Restoration of Democracy (FORD), the group that led the fight for political pluralism and the first party officially registered, drew more than 100,000 supporters to a January 18 rally and quickly emerged as Kenya's most effective opposition movement.

FORD's leadership included the leading names in Kenya's opposition, but during the year it splintered. Its interim leader, former Vice-President Oginga Odinga, 80, had carried the opposition banner since the time of Kenya's first president, Jomo Kenyatta. In addition to Odinga, however, other FORD leaders announced their candidacy for the presidency, including Kenneth Matiba, a former cabinet minister. Odinga had a strong following among the Luo ethnic group, while Matiba was from the Kikuyu area. To further fracture the opposition, the Kikuyu electorate soon was split by the formation of the Democratic Party, led by former Vice-President Mwai Kibaki, a Kikuyu. (In the December election, he received the most votes after Moi.)

During the year at the local level, members of ethnic groups associated with FORD were attacked by well organized and well armed members of the Kalenjin ethnic group, to which Moi belongs. Under Moi, the Kalenjin had come to dominate Kenya's ruling elite. Reportedly, ethnic unrest led to nearly 2,000 deaths and upward of 20,000 injuries. Moi long had maintained that multiparty politics led to ethnic violence in Africa, and many saw the violence as a catalyst enabling Moi to clamp down on his opponents. In a pastoral letter, the Roman Catholic bishops asserted that the violence was part of "a wider political strategy" to declare certain parts of the country off-limits to the opposition.

Foreign Affairs. En route to the Earth Summit in Rio de Janeiro, Brazil, in June, Moi paid an official visit to South Africa, where he called on President F. W. de Klerk. In protest, Nelson Mandela, head of the African National Congress, canceled a meeting with Moi.

KENYA • Information Highlights

Official Name: Republic of Kenya.
Location: East Coast of Africa.
Area: 224,961 sq mi (582 650 km²).
Population (mid-1992 est.): 26,200,000.
Chief Cities (1989 est.): Nairobi, the capital, 1,286,200; Mombasa (1985 est.), 442,369.
Government: *Head of state and government,* Daniel T. arap Moi, president (took office Oct. 1978). *Legislature* (unicameral)—National Assembly, 188 elected members, 12 appointed by the president.
Monetary Unit: Kenya shilling (32.891 shillings equal U.S.$1, August 1992).
Gross Domestic Product (1990 est. U.S.$): $8,500,-000,000.
Economic Index (1991): *Consumer Prices,* (Nairobi, 1990 = 100), all items, 119.3; food, 123.5.
Foreign Trade (1991 U.S.$): *Imports,* $1,797,000,000; *exports,* $1,107,000,000.

Kenya continued to attract refugees from neighboring Sudan, Somalia, and Ethiopia. The United Nations was prompted to call for more international assistance after Kenya threatened to repatriate some of the refugees, now numbering upward of 300,000.

The Economy. Kenya faced the double shock of the worst drought in history as well as a year-long freeze on international aid because of Kenya's initial resistance to political liberalization. The economy grew at a rate of 2.5% in 1992, down from an average of 5% over the past decade. With a population growth rate of 3.6%, Kenya experienced its first negative per capita growth rate in eight years.

In an effort to increase the production of maize, Kenya raised the producer price by 25%. It also decontrolled the milk price. The lack of rain and increased costs of production, brought on in part by the decline in value of the Kenyan shilling, frustrated farmers. Political unrest also led to a decline in the tourist sector. However, Kenyan coffee and tea continued to draw high international prices.

WILLIAM CYRUS REED
The American University in Cairo

KOREA

With impending political successions in both halves of the divided Korean peninsula, North Korea appeared to yield to strong international pressure in 1992 to throttle back its nuclear-weapons program, which had threatened to become the most destabilizing force in Northeast Asia.

Republic of South Korea (South Korea)

Politics and Government. The political year in South Korea began in March with a defeat for the ruling party in the National Assembly election. The Democratic Liberal Party (DLP) narrowly lost its majority by winning only 149 out of the 299 seats. However, the DLP retained control by allying with ten party members who had run as independents. The Democratic Party, led by South Korea's best-known opposition politician, Kim Dae Jung, won 96 seats. The biggest surprise of the election was the success of the Unification National Party, led by Chung Ju Yung, the founder of the Hyundai conglomerate, which won 32 seats on a platform of less government interference with business.

The election triggered intensified maneuvering for the presidency. Under the constitution, incumbent President Roh Tae Woo could serve only one five-year term and was scheduled to step down in February 1993. Kim Young Sam, a former opposition leader, was clearly Roh's choice as successor. Roh wanted the nominating process to appear democratic and DLP member Lee Jong Chan was set to provide a nominal challenge. Instead, Lee withdrew from the "race" shortly before the DLP convention in May and Kim Young Sam was nominated virtually without opposition, to Roh's visible displeasure. The other two parties held conventions at about the same time and nominated Kim Dae Jung and Chung Ju Yung. For the first time in three decades, none of the presidential candidates was a former military man.

Over the next few months, a major scandal erupted over evidence that the DLP was involved in vote buying during the campaign for the National Assembly. Although nothing new in South Korean politics, the charges were damaging because they raised doubt about the fairness of the upcoming presidential election. DLP presidential candidate Kim Young Sam stood to be hurt most by the affair.

Roh launched a damage-control program in September, announcing he would resign from the DLP. This move had the effect of making Kim the unannounced acting president in the eyes of many Koreans. Within a month, Roh resigned his party membership as promised and replaced Premier Chung Won Shik with an apolitical law professor named Hyun Soong Jong. The idea was to create a "neutral" government that would restore public confidence in the presidential-election process. Like most political maneuvers in South Korea, this move was viewed with considerable public cynicism. Nevertheless, the regard for public opinion was a relatively new and encouraging phenomenon in South Korea and one of many signs that the political system, although still less developed than the economy, was maturing fairly rapidly.

Kim Young Sam was elected president on December 16, receiving 42% of the vote. Kim Dae Jung won 34% and promptly announced his retirement from politics. Chung Ju Yung drew 16%, less than many had expected. The results indicated that voters wanted political stability as the guarantee of continued prosperity. Such an attitude benefited the ruling party.

© Paul Barker/Black Star

In South Korea in December 1992, Kim Young Sam, 65, a former opposition leader, was elected president. The nominee of the Democratic Liberal Party won 42% of the vote.

Economy and Trade. South Korea's per-capita gross national product of $6,253 in 1991 was enough to place it in the World Bank's category of high-income economies. The growth rate had declined slightly in 1991, to 8.6%. Even so, there was overheating and an inflation rate of 9.5%—the highest since 1981. To combat inflation, the government decided to try to hold the growth rate to 7% to 8%, hoping that full employment could be maintained at this level.

South Korea was supposedly in transition from an export-led to a domestic, market-driven economy, but this process had been set back in 1991. Domestic savings and consumption, as well as fixed investment, declined, due largely to a government-initiated reduction of investment in the construction industry. In contrast, foreign trade was up sharply over 1990. Exports rose by 10.6% ($6.8 billion), and imports by 16.8% ($11.7 billion), yielding a record trade deficit of $9.7 billion, roughly twice the level of 1990. The main impetus seems to have been an upsurge in domestic demand, including the demand by Korean firms for the latest equipment to improve their competitive position abroad. About 90% of the deficit was with Japan, with most of the rest with China. Trade with the United States had shown a surplus since 1982, but in 1991 that trend was reversed with a $6 million deficit, mainly because of a sluggish U.S. economy and competition from lower-cost producers in Mexico and Southeast Asia.

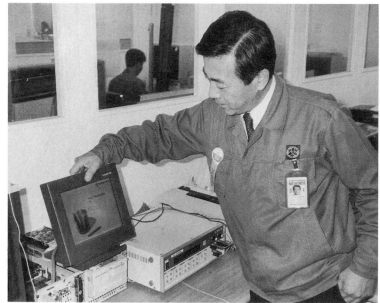

South Korea sought an economic growth rate of 7% to 8% for 1992. The electronics factory (right) serves as a symbol of the nation's recent economic accomplishments and potential.

© Andrew Pollack/NYT Pictures

New direct foreign investment rose 74% over 1990 to $1.4 billion. South Korea's direct investment abroad amounted to $1.6 billion, down 1% from 1990, with most of the money going to Southeast Asia, China, and Mexico, where labor costs were lower.

Foreign Relations. During 1992 there were significant developments in the Republic of Korea's relations with both of its most important Asian neighbors—Japan and China.

In mid-January, Japanese Premier Kiichi Miyazawa paid a visit to Seoul that was clouded by the memories of past colonial occupation and current fears of economic domination. Although Japan has denied any obligation to pay retribution to Korea for its occupation, Miyazawa apologized for the suffering inflicted on the Korean people and promised that compensation would be paid to the 89 surviving "comfort" women forced into prostitution by the Imperial Japanese Army. On the economic front, Miyazawa agreed in principle with President Roh on measures to reduce the trade imbalance, which included a ban on certain Japanese imports such as automobiles, and on freer access to the Japanese market.

Miyazawa insisted, without necessarily convincing his hosts, that there was not and never would be a Japanese threat to the security of the Korean peninsula. This issue surfaced prominently in the middle of the year when the Japanese Diet authorized a peace-keeping mission to send Japanese troops abroad for the first time since 1945. This move helped fuel suspicions that Japan might be planning to acquire such items as an aircraft carrier for a military-strike capability. There were also longer-range concerns that Korea one day might be caught in the middle of a fight between Japan and China, repeating historic precedents. Accordingly, the emphasis of the South Korean military-modernization program shifted from developing ground forces to meet what had been perceived as a sole threat from North Korea, to developing the air force and navy to protect against other possible threats.

South Korea's relations with China were on an entirely different footing than its relations with Japan. Koreans perceived virtually no security threat from China, except perhaps in the distant future. The realization had sunk in that China strongly, if tacitly, opposed the idea of another North Korean attack on South Korea.

Since the early 1980s, an "unofficial" trade had flourished between South Korea and China, with South Korea in the stronger position (by virtue of its technological superiority and relative prosperity), as contrasted to the weaker position it had with Japan. China also figured prominently in Seoul's so-called Nordpolitik, a program of improving ties with Communist (now former Communist) countries to

---

SOUTH KOREA • Information Highlights

Official Name: Republic of Korea.
Location: Northeastern Asia.
Area: 38,023 sq mi (98 480 km^2).
Population (mid-1992 est.): 44,300,000.
Chief City (1990 census, prelim.): Seoul, the capital, 10,627,790.
Government: *Head of state,* Roh Tae Woo, president (formally inaugurated February 1988). *Head of government,* Hyun Soong Jong, prime minister (appointed October 1992). *Legislature*—National Assembly.
Monetary Unit: Won (787.6 won equal U.S.$1, August 1992).
Gross National Product (1991 U.S.$): $242,430,-000,000.
Economic Indexes (1991): *Consumer Prices* (1988 = 100), all items, 124. *Industrial Production* (1988 = 100), 120.
Foreign Trade (1991 U.S.$): *Imports,* $76,800,-000,000; *exports,* $70,000,000,000.

isolate North Korea. China had been the last holdout to establishing diplomatic relations with South Korea, perhaps in deference to its delicate relationship with North Korea. By 1992, however, North Korea's leverage on China had declined to the point where Beijing felt safe in normalizing its relations with Seoul. The initiative took place in late August, to the accompaniment of various agreements designed to enhance the already-booming commercial relationship between the two nations. In view of Beijing's well-known antipathy to "two Chinas," Seoul felt compelled to sever its ties with the Republic of China, on Taiwan. In September, President Roh visited Beijing. In addition to promoting trade, he evidently tried to get Beijing to pressure North Korea to allow mutual inspection of nuclear facilities. China's public response was somewhat vague: The joint communique merely expressed Beijing's general support for the principle of a nonnuclear Korean peninsula and for peaceful unification of the two Koreas, without outside interference.

The United States continued to object to restrictions on access to the South Korean market, and Koreans were shocked at the violence inflicted on Korean businesses during the Los Angeles riots in the spring. However, the Republic of Korea's relations with its sole ally, the United States, centered largely on mutual concerns about North Korea and its nuclear-weapons program. This was the main issue discussed during a visit by U.S. President George Bush to Seoul in early January. Some U.S. officials felt that Seoul might be moving too fast toward reunification, at the expense of near-term mutual inspection of nuclear facilities.

Democratic People's Republic of Korea (North Korea)

Domestic Affairs. On April 15, North Korea's self-proclaimed Great Leader, Kim Il Sung, celebrated his 80th birthday by mobilizing virtually the entire population to join in with huge parades and other kinds of festivities. The considerable expense of the commemoration was financed in part by pro-North Koreans living in Japan.

The milestone was also a reminder that Kim Il Sung soon could be succeeded by his son, the seemingly unstable Dear Leader Kim Jong Il. During the birthday celebrations, the younger Kim was proclaimed a marshal of the armed forces, which like the bureaucracy are believed to be far from enthusiastic about the Dear Leader. This step was merely the latest in a series of clearly designed moves to put the younger Kim in the best possible position to take over from his father. Indeed, Kim Il appeared to have delegated many of the leadership functions to his son, while retaining ultimate decision-making authority.

While North Korea's leaders celebrated, the nation's economy was in poor shape and most of the population was miserable. The only disagreement among foreign observers was how poor and how miserable. Apart from rather scanty natural resources, the main causes for the economic doldrums could be traced to the rigid "socialist" planning and administration of the economy by the Kim regime. This situation was worsened greatly by a virtual cutoff of oil and economic aid from the former Soviet Union and East European countries. Living conditions in most of North Korea appeared to observers to be barely above subsistence level. Under these conditions there was naturally some discontent but no organized public protests. The lack of protests could be explained by the extremely tight network of administrative and police control and an effective propaganda effort aimed at the nation's youth.

Foreign Affairs. Pyongyang was clearly eager to improve its position in the international community, but without endangering its political and economic systems—probably an unattainable goal. The preferred solution to the nation's economic troubles was to attract foreign investment, which would require some improvement of its poor international image. The problem was that the regime had no real enthusiasm for making changes, and really did not know what it needed to do. There was some investment in 1992 from South Korea and Japan, but it was minimal.

Pyongyang's relationship with the United States was warming in 1992, but only at a gradual rate. The relationship did not improve noticeably when North Korea handed over the remains of 30 Americans killed during the Korean War, since 8,000 missing Americans had yet to be accounted for. One perennial diplomatic obstacle was Pyongyang's desire to deal separately with the United States, in contrast to the U.S. preference to include Seoul when possible. Shocked by China's recognition of South Korea, Pyongyang on September 8 proposed a series of high-level talks with the United States intended to lead to a major im-

---

NORTH KOREA • Information Highlights

Official Name: Democratic People's Republic of Korea.
Location: Northeastern Asia.
Area: 46,540 sq mi (120 540 km²).
Population (mid-1992 est.): 22,200,000.
Chief Cities (1986 est.): Pyongyang, the capital, 2,000,000; Hamhung, 670,000.
Government: *Head of state,* Kim Il Sung, president (nominally since Dec. 1972; actually in power since May 1948). *Head of government,* Yon Hyong Muk, premier (appointed Dec. 1988). *Legislature* (unicameral)—Supreme People's Assembly. The Korea Workers' (Communist) Party: General Secretary, Kim Il Sung.
Gross National Product (1990 est. U.S.$): $21.500,-000,000.

provement of relations. In response, U.S. officials repeated the standard insistence on thorough inspections of North Korea's nuclear facilities as a precondition for better relations. Another U.S. concern was North Korea's continued shipment of modern arms, apparently including some ballistic missiles, to unstable and dangerous regimes in the Middle East, notably Syria and Iran.

The Two Koreas

Peaceful Contacts. While committed to the principle of national unification, North Korea and South Korea viewed the possibility of its realization with mixed feelings. The North feared that it might be swallowed by the much more prosperous South, as East Germany had been by West Germany. South Korea, also conscious of the German experience, worried that unification might prove inordinately expensive.

Nevertheless, the two sides had moderated their rhetoric and their behavior toward one another in recent years. On Dec. 31, 1991, they had signed an agreement-in-principle to avoid war and improve relations in all fields. The eighth in a series of meetings between the two premiers was held in September 1992, even though the North had seemed reluctant to make concrete concessions.

One result of this glacial thaw was the recent emergence of bilateral trade: In 1991 it amounted to $190 million. South Korean firms showed an eagerness to trade with and invest in North Korea. While not objecting to this attitude, the South Korean government restricted investment to conserve a bargaining chip with North Korea. It needed all such chips to deal with the most sensitive and dangerous issue—North Korea's nuclear-weapons program.

The North Korean Nuclear Weapons Issue. Despite numerous denials from Pyongyang, overwhelming evidence has indicated that North Korea has been seeking a nuclear weapons capability for years. The idea of a regime with North Korea's record having nuclear weapons was seen widely as an unacceptable threat to the peace and stability of the region and as a possible spur to Japanese rearmament.

The three nations most concerned about the nuclear threat—South Korea, Japan, and the United States—continued to press for a resolution of the issue as a precondition for any substantive improvement in relations and for the trade, aid, and investment that Pyongyang desires. There were differences as to whether North Korea should be required to dismantle its plutonium-reprocessing facilities, or merely to submit them to international inspection.

The United States had withdrawn its nuclear weapons from South Korea late in 1991, and shortly thereafter Seoul offered to open all of the military installations in South Korea to inspection, provided Pyongyang reciprocated. On Dec. 31, 1991, the two Korean premiers issued a joint declaration that allowed for inspection of mutually agreed-upon sites. On March 14, 1992, a joint Nuclear Control Commission was established to initiate inspections by June 10. U.S. officials emphasized, in a series of talks with Pyongyang, that they too expected action by June. However, the inspections never took place, because of various disagreements and what was viewed widely as obstruction on the part of North Korea.

Pyongyang was significantly more cooperative with the International Atomic Energy Agency (IAEA), signing an agreement in January for nuclear-site inspections. There were indications, however, that North Korea might be moving, or hiding, its nuclear technology. In early May, Pyongyang turned over to the IAEA information on some previously unknown nuclear facilities. North Korean officials also admitted to having produced some plutonium, and South Korean officials promptly branded this as a violation of the December 31 accord. An IAEA inspection in June confirmed the existence of a plutonium-reprocessing facility, but yielded no evidence that enough material had been accumulated to make a bomb. Pyongyang announced that it was willing to stop reprocessing plutonium if the West and Japan would supply North Korea with the fuel and technology allegedly needed for a peaceful nuclear-power program. The most plausible explanation for this complex episode appeared to be that Pyongyang indeed had been working to acquire nuclear weapons but had decided under external pressure that their dubious benefits were outweighed by their risks and costs. Accordingly, Pyongyang may have put its nuclear-weapons program on hold, without necessarily abandoning it forever or going so far as to dismantle it.

HAROLD C. HINTON
The George Washington University

KUWAIT

In 1992 recovery from the Iraqi invasion in 1990 and the 1991 war preoccupied Kuwait.

Economic Reconstruction. Production of oil increased to 920,000 barrels per day by April, and Kuwait also was able to refine 310,000 barrels of its own oil per day. Minister of Oil Hamoud al-Raqba announced the goal of pumping 1.5 million barrels per day of oil by the end of 1992. The Organization of Petroleum Exporting Countries (OPEC) on May 22 decided that Kuwait would continue to be exempt from the production-quota system.

On March 31 the Kuwait National Council, an interim parliament, authorized the issuance of $20 billion of government bonds to indem-

© Thomas Hartwell/Sygma

In 1992, Kuwait was rebuilding following the 1990 Iraqi invasion and 1991 war. After Iraqi forces entered contested territory on the Iraqi-Kuwaiti border several times, the U.S.-allied coalition again bombed parts of Iraq early in 1993.

nify commercial banks for their losses during the war. The 1992 budget announced May 10 called for spending of at least $18 billion; the deficit of $17 billion was to be covered by selling foreign assets. About half the contracts for reconstruction went to U.S. firms.

Security and International Relations. Since Iraq maintained its claim to Kuwait despite losing the war, Emir Jabir al-Sabah sought external security guarantees. On January 25, Kuwait took delivery of the first of 40 U.S. military aircraft, and on March 11 the United States announced the sale of $2.5 billion more in air-defense weapons.

Hundreds of resident foreigners were expelled to Iraq by Kuwait as supposed security risks; especially hard hit were Palestinian Arabs. Trials of alleged collaborators with Iraq resumed in April after an eight-month suspension.

When the United Nations delimited the international border between Iraq and Kuwait in April, Kuwait gained additional territory at the expense of Iraq, which refused to accept the new arrangement. Instead, on the second anniversary of the invasion, August 2, Iraqi television again said Kuwait was its "19th province." About 5,000 U.S. troops held joint maneuvers with Kuwaiti troops in early August.

Kuwait also helped the United States—as in the Arab-Israeli peace negotiations. On Nov. 18, 1991, Kuwait eased its boycott of Western firms doing business with Israel. The United States in December 1991 brought about the repeal of the 1975 UN General Assembly resolution equating Zionism with racism; Kuwait's delegate was conveniently absent for the key vote. Kuwait attended the January 1992 talks on Middle Eastern regional peace issues, thereby tacitly recognizing the legitimacy of Israel.

Political Reforms. The emir slowly moved to restore limited political participation by Kuwaiti citizens. An opposition party, the Kuwaiti Democratic Forum, was formed in December 1991. Prepublication newspaper censorship, in effect since 1986, ended on Jan. 12, 1992. However, foreign pressure for increased democracy was resented by some of the ruling elite. On June 4, Abdul-Aziz Masaeed, speaker of the National Council, condemned the United States for interfering in Kuwait's internal affairs by encouraging political opposition.

The opposition scored a victory by electing more than 30 candidates in the October 5 parliamentary elections, as the all-male electorate selected 50 winners from 278 candidates. Most new parliamentarians favored limits on the power of the emir while nevertheless supporting the U.S.-Kuwait alliance.

WILLIAM OCHSENWALD
*Virginia Polytechnic Institute
and State University*

KUWAIT • Information Highlights

Official Name: State of Kuwait.
Location: Southwest Asia.
Area: 6,800 sq mi (17 820 km²).
Population (mid-1992 est.) 1,400,000.
Chief Cities (1985 census): Kuwait, the capital, 44,335; Salmiya, 153,369; Hawalli, 145,126.
Government: *Head of state,* Jabir al-Ahmad al-Sabah, emir (acceded Dec. 1977). *Head of government,* Saad al-Abdallah al-Sabah, prime minister (appointed Feb. 1978). *Legislature—*National Council.
Monetary Unit: Dinar (0.293 dinar equal U.S. $1, May 1992).
Gross Domestic Product (1989 U.S.$): $19,800,-000,000.
Economic Index (1989): *Consumer Prices* (1980 = 100), all items, 132.6; food, 115.0.

© Barry Jarvinen/NYT Pictures

A five-month strike by United Automobile Workers against Caterpillar Inc. ended on April 14, 1992. Workers agreed to return to work without a contract; the construction-machinery company agreed to cease hiring replacement workers.

LABOR

Unemployment continued to be a problem in the United States and much of the rest of the world in 1992.

United States

Presidential Election. For the first time in 16 years, the labor movement in the United States backed the winning candidate in a presidential election. Arkansas Gov. Bill Clinton was not labor's first choice during the primary campaign for the Democratic Party nomination. Once nominated, however, he was supported strongly by the AFL-CIO over incumbent President George Bush and independent Ross Perot. Clinton's main drawback for the labor movement was his conditional support of the North American Free Trade Agreement, which labor opposes because of concern over loss of jobs to Mexico.

Governor Clinton, however, supported many of labor's priorities—expanding jobs and reducing unemployment by government spending on infrastructure and investment-tax credits; a ban on hiring of permanent replacements for striking workers; requiring employers of 50 or more workers to provide unpaid leave to employees to care for sick family members or a newborn or newly adopted child; increasing the minimum wage; overhauling the health-care system to provide universal coverage, while controlling costs; and continuing education and training for workers through a payroll tax on employers. With a Democratic majority in both the House and the Senate, expectations were high that at least some of these measures would be enacted during the Clinton administration.

Employment and Earnings. Employment in the United States during the third quarter of 1992 was 117,737,000, an increase of 1% over the same period in 1991. Unemployment stood at 9,677,000 as compared with 8,477,000 during the previous year, an increase of 1,200,000, or 14%. Long-term unemployment—those idle for 27 weeks or longer—rose by 79% to 2,084,000 in September 1992 as compared with 1991.

The third-quarter unemployment rate of 7.6% represented an increase over the 1991 rate of 6.8%. By November, however, unemployment had decreased for the fifth month in a row, to 7.2%. The percentage of people unemployed rose across the board. The rate for adult men was 7.6%, for adult women, 6.5%, and for teenagers, 20.4%. The unemployment rate was highest for blacks at 14.2%, lowest for white workers at 6.7%, and stood at 11.7% for Hispanic workers.

Average earnings of U.S. families stayed slightly ahead of inflation in 1992. Median earnings of all families with wage and salary workers were $694 per week in the third quarter, up 3.4% from 1991, while the Consumer Price Index increased by 3.0%. However, only white families showed a gain in real earnings. Families of black and Hispanic workers lost ground in terms of real earnings.

Economic Growth and Productivity. The U.S. economy grew at a surprisingly high annual rate of 3.9% in third-quarter 1992. This followed a growth rate of 1.5% in the second quarter. For the first three quarters of 1992, gross domestic product (GDP) grew at an annual rate of 2.75%, a substantial improvement over the 1.25% increase during the last three quarters of 1991.

Productivity in the nonfarm business sector rose at an annual rate of 2.8% during the first three quarters of 1992. The growth in productivity over the five consecutive quarters was regarded by many economists as a sign that the recession was coming to an end and that economic recovery was likely to continue. Some economists, however, took the more cautious view that nothing fundamental, like the pace of technological innovation, has changed and that the spurt in productivity reflected corrections of companies' overoptimistic hiring and sloppy management during the 1980s. Whether the late-1992 rebound in output per worker signaled a permanent turnaround in long-run productivity remained to be seen.

Women in the Labor Force. New research showed that women were big economic winners in the 1980s, and that their gains were likely to continue in the 1990s.

Women gained on men in almost all occupations. While the median annual salary for men slid 8% after inflation between 1979 and 1990 to $28,843 from $31,315, the median salary for women rose 10% to $20,656 from $18,683. In 1990 women earned 70 cents for each dollar earned by men. This compares with 60 cents for each dollar earned by men from 1960 to 1980.

Despite these gains, women's pay is still far below men's, mostly because, on the average, women still are entering lower-paying occupations than men, work fewer hours, are less educated, and have less job experience and fewer skills than men. When women and men with the same skills, backgrounds, and education are compared, there is little difference between their earnings. Thus, women with doctorates in economics earn between 95% and 99% of their male peers' pay.

Women now represent 40% of the work force and, according to the U.S. Bureau of Labor Statistics, will account for half of the work force by the year 2000. A highly signifi-

cant indicator of the acceptance of women employees by employers is the fact that in the early 1990s, for the first time since women joined the labor force in large numbers, the unemployment rate for women, which was standing at 6.5%, was lower than that for men.

Foreign-Owned Companies. Foreign-owned businesses supplied one in every 20 private-sector jobs in the United States in 1990, according to the U.S. Bureau of Labor Statistics. Employment in these companies averaged 4.7 million in the last quarter of 1990, amounting to 5.2% of total private employment. Half of the jobs were in companies owned by British, Japanese, and Canadian investors.

Workers in foreign companies earned an average of $2,500 per month or 22% more than the $2,085 average for U.S. establishments. Among the reasons for such higher earnings was the tendency for foreign companies to invest in higher-paying industries such as mining and manufacturing, which pay higher wages. Foreign-owned firms also have a larger proportion of high-paying positions and locate in areas with relatively high wages.

International

The European Community (EC). Unemployment in EC countries was much worse than in the United States in 1992. As of October, unemployment stood at 9.8% or 14.46 million compared to 9% or 13.3 million in August 1991. Unemployment was highest in Ireland (18.2%) and Spain (18.8%) and lowest in Luxembourg (2%) and Germany (6.7%). Great Britain's rate was 11.2% and in Italy it was 10.6%. As in the United States, unemployment was worst for younger workers. The rate for those under 25 was 18%. Long-term unemployment increased sharply in 1992, with almost half of the unemployed having been out of work for more than a year. Thirty-five percent of the unemployed never had held a job.

Between 1985 and 1990, employment in EC countries grew by 9 million. Job creation slowed and unemployment rose starting in mid-1990. In 1991, EC employment grew by only

U.S. Employment and Unemployment (Armed Forces excluded)		
	1991*	1992*
Labor Force	125,242,000	127,414,000
Participation Rate	65.9%	66.4%
Employed	116,764,000	117,737,000
Unemployed	8,477,000	9,677,000
Unemployment rate	6.8%	7.6%
Adult men	6.5%	7.2%
Adult women	5.5%	6.5%
Teenagers	19.2%	20.4%
White	6.1%	6.7%
Black	12.1%	14.2%
Hispanic	10.2%	11.7%

N.B. Third-quarter average. Source: U.S. Bureau of Labor Statistics. The participation rate is the number of persons in the labor market, whether employed or unemployed, as a percentage of the civilian noninstitutional population.

0.2% compared with 2% in preceding years. The participation rate—the proportion of the working-age population in the labor force—was 60% in 1990, up from 57% in 1985. This compares with a participation rate of 66% in the United States and 72% in Japan.

Japanese Companies in the EC. A survey of 35 Japanese subsidiaries of eight multinational companies in the 12 EC countries found that investment increased from $1,851,000,000 in 1985 to $14,030,000,000 in 1989. By September 1990 the total value of Japanese investment in EC countries was $48,101,000,000. The largest amount of investment was in Great Britain, $18,402,000,000 or 38.3% of the total, followed by the Netherlands with $11,749,000,000 or 24.4%.

The report prepared by the Euro-Japan Institute for Law and Business also noted, among other things, that the top management of Japanese firms doing business in EC countries was overwhelmingly Japanese and predominantly male; that while there was a great deal of autonomy granted subsidiaries in the areas of industrial relations and human resources, manufacturing, product design, and investment decisions were controlled tightly by either European or Japanese headquarters offices; and that unions did not play a major role in most Japanese companies nor did Japanese firms play a major role in employer organization in the EC countries.

Germany. In the former German Democratic Republic (East Germany), global wage developments were determined jointly by the government and the central Free German Trade Union (FDGB) on the basis of national economic plans. After unification with the Federal Republic (West Germany) on July 1, 1990, the concept of free collective bargaining was transferred to the East. By late autumn 1990, basic wages in East Germany had risen from 30% to 35% of West German levels to 40% to 50%. Harmonization of pay and working conditions with the West took a major step forward in the metalworking-industry agreement in spring 1991. This agreement provided for phased harmonization of pay with full parity by April 1994. Similar wage agreements were concluded in iron and steel, glass and ceramics, and roofing. In most other sectors there was no provision for staged increases. Instead, pay was negotiated on an annual basis, which raised basic wages to 60% to 65% of West German levels.

The emphasis on pay harmonization without regard for productivity was criticized by Minister for Economics Jürgen Möllemann. He warned that if pay increases exceed productivity, the competitiveness of East German industry would be undermined, thereby slowing creation of employment and even survival of existing jobs. Both the unions and employers have rejected such criticisms.

The FDGB union confederation contended that a bargaining policy based solely on productivity would cause serious distortions in the labor market. Skilled and qualified workers would continue to flood to the West, thereby undermining the labor potential required for reconstruction. The employers' confederation acknowledged that the pay increases could not be justified by productivity. But it contended that the rapid transition from a command to a market economy had forced the bargaining parties to compromise between securing the competitiveness of East German industry and stemming social unrest and a massive flow of labor to the West.

France. The Labour Inspectorate lodged a complaint with the public prosecutor's office at Créteil alleging infringement of the law by the Euro Disneyland company's rules on employees' appearance at its new theme park outside Paris. The union confederation claimed that the company's dress and appearance code was "an attack on individual liberty." The regulations include a requirement that employees "maintain a weight in harmony with their height"; a ban on mustaches and beards for men; and a prohibition on false eyelashes, eye shadow, eyeliner, and novelty tights or stockings for women.

Norway. The leader of the Norwegian Federation of Trade Unions (LO) issued a strong attack on the minority Labor government in Norway because of a belief that the government was not doing enough to push union policies in parliament. The attack was particularly unusual, coming after a century of close cooperation between the LO and the Labor Party, in that it was made publicly rather than in internal meetings.

The LO claimed that some ministers were not qualified to hold their posts. Though they were not named, it was felt that the attack was directed particularly at the minister of health and social affairs, who had proposed cuts in welfare benefits, and the minister of labor and public administration, who had spoken out in favor of pay reductions for some jobs. An opinion poll conducted prior to the LO attack found that a large majority of LO members favored abandonment of the traditional close cooperation between the trade-union movement and the Labor government.

Sweden. The Swedish government proposed major changes in the 15-year-old code-termination legislation. These changes would move away from collective decision-making and toward more individual relations between employers and employees. Government officials believe that employers would have more freedom to terminate employee contracts without union interference and to hire workers for longer probationary periods than the present six months. A proposed amendment to the 1976 Codetermination Act would remove a provision giving unions veto power over the hiring of subcontractors.

Japan. Seven years after Japan enacted the 1985 equal-opportunity law prohibiting companies from discriminating on the basis of sex in hiring, assignment, or promotion, Japanese women were complaining that the law was not being enforced.

Women make up more than 40% of the work force and more than half of all Japanese women are employed. Japan's largest firms, however, are hiring only a handful each year for career-track positions that carry responsibility comparable to men's jobs. In 1992, Mitsubishi Corporation hired four women and 213 men, C. Itoh & Co. hired five women and 198 men, and Nissho Iwai Corporation hired three women and 127 men. The Recruit Research Company, an affiliate of one of Japan's largest placement firms, reported that in 1992 there were 2.2 job openings for every male seeking employment, and slightly less than one opening for every woman.

Even women graduating from Japan's most elite universities were being forced to scale back their expectations. Many Japanese women echoed the complaints of U.S. women that a "glass ceiling" bars their promotion, that child care is unavailable, and that the executive suite is the province of an all-male power structure. The law, they say, is of little help because companies face no penalty if they fail.

Japanese women generally are considered to be part-time workers even though many actually work more than 40 hours per week. The fact that part-time workers are not figured into Japan's unemployment statistics may explain why, in one of the worst downturns in years, Japan's unemployment rate was reported at about 2.3%.

Switzerland. The cancellation of several important labor agreements, which ultimately could lead to the possibility of strikes in a country where they are anathema, has been the subject of extensive debate in consensus-oriented Switzerland.

Switzerland's virtual strike-free record is due in large part to absolute peace obligations and compulsory arbitration of disputes over rights and interest. Arbitration settlements long have enjoyed considerable credibility, even with the losing party. However, some firms complain that the sectoral awards do not take sufficient account of particular circumstances. Unions have complained that the system of arbitration is too far removed from plants and workers, thus inhibiting the ability of unions to mobilize workers for industrial action.

ILO World Labor Report. The 1992 International Labor Organization (ILO) World Labor report showed that unemployment had been rising in many industrialized countries. For the 24 Organization for Economic Cooperation and Development (OECD) members, 1991 unemployment was 7.1% or 28 million. The 1992 rate was expected to rise to 7.4%. The sharpest increases occurred in Australia, Finland, Great Britain, Ireland, New Zealand, Sweden, and the United States. Adding to the concern over unemployment was the fact that many of the employed are working part-time, and temporary work has increased, allowing companies to adjust output to demand fluctuations without having to bear the cost of a permanent labor force.

Real manufacturing wages in OECD countries fell, on average, 0.3% in 1990. However, in Germany, Japan, and Spain, real hourly earnings grew by more than 2%. In Australia, the United States, and New Zealand, real wages declined by more than 1%.

The ILO also reported that trade-union influence was varying widely among OECD countries. Membership tended to be higher in Europe, with the exceptions of France and Spain, than in the United States. Membership also was higher in smaller countries than in large ones. Unions lost about 5 million members in OECD countries in the 1980s. The average proportion of workers in unions dropped from 37% in 1975 to 28% in 1988. The sharpest declines were in the United States, Great Britain, and France.

While there was a general trend away from bargaining for the entire country and toward bargaining for individual companies, the scope of those benefiting from such agreements was expanding beyond union members. In France, for example, 12% were unionized but 80% benefit from agreements. The ILO also reported that unions were expanding negotiations to include job security, training, and job satisfaction. Employers have been looking for more flexibility in their work force and have tended to link pay to profits.

Employers also have tried to deal with individual workers on issues formerly covered in union agreements. This form of "people" management threatened unions and some unions have entered into consultant arrangements with employers on such subjects as worker motivation and efficiency.

Flexible working time was a matter of concern around the world. In Europe this often had taken the form of negotiations for a shorter workweek. In the United States flexible work patterns often have been introduced to allow more women to enter the labor force. Flexible work time may include part-time work; job-sharing; flextime—allowing employees to choose starting and finishing times; compressed workweeks; hours averaging, which allows for changes in hours worked each week in accordance with demand; and shift work.

See also FEATURE ARTICLE/THE U.S. EMPLOYMENT SCENE, page 48.

JACK STIEBER
Michigan State University

LAOS

Kaysone Phomvihan, the longtime guerrilla leader who led the Communist takeover of Laos in 1975 and took over the nation's presidency in 1991, died in late November 1992. Kaysone was attuned so closely to Hanoi politically that some observers thought the Vietnamese used Laos to test new ideas of economic reform. Yet prior to Kaysone's death, there were indications that his reforms were turning Laos into an economic colony of Thailand, Vietnam's traditional rival.

While Kaysone had trimmed back some of the bureaucracy of his Communist state in 1992, he still made all important decisions as he had for years. Kaysone was also chairman of the ruling Lao People's Revolutionary Party (LPRP), whose dominant position was underscored by the new constitution adopted in 1991.

On November 25, Radio Laos announced that Nouhak Phoumsavan, considered a hardline Communist and ally of Vietnam, had been selected as the new leader of the nation. He had been a member of the Politburo since 1955 and also served as finance minister.

Economics. By opening Laos to foreign investment, Kaysone had attracted enough Western capital to offset the loss of Soviet and East European aid. Inflation fell from 76% in 1989 to about 10% in 1991; the gross national product (GNP) grew by about 4% in 1991 in spite of a severe drought.

Thailand was the largest investor in Laos and the country's main trading partner. Laos was selling hydroelectric power and timber to Thailand and was receiving manufactured goods in return. The Mekong River flows between the two countries and links them economically. In November 1991, Australian engineers began constructing a bridge across the Mekong which would increase trade between the two countries greatly.

Most of the people of Laos live in remote villages and make a bare living by subsistence farming. Their per-capita income is estimated at $180 per year, and their life expectancy is only 42 years.

Foreign Affairs. The Lao government's closest ties were with China and Vietnam, but relations with Thailand have improved steadily since a military clash in 1989. A key problem was that some Lao officials were getting rich by letting their Thai cronies strip the country of its natural wealth. A frequently cited example is Sisavath Keobounphanh, who was ousted from the LPRP Politburo in 1991 but then became minister of agriculture.

Relations between the United States and Laos improved in 1992, and the two countries raised their senior diplomats to the rank of ambassador. Laotian officials were becoming more receptive to U.S. proposals to counter drug trafficking and search for Americans missing in action from the Vietnam war.

PETER A. POOLE
Author, "The Vietnamese in Thailand"

LATIN AMERICA

Latin America's recovery from a decade of debt and depression continued through 1992, as the process of structural reform and economic opening began to bear fruit. Private investment rose in most countries and substantial financial inputs began to flow in from abroad.

Other noteworthy events during the year included a United Nations-sponsored conference on the environment held in Rio de Janeiro (*see also* ENVIRONMENT), the commemoration of the 500th anniversary of Christopher Columbus' arrival in the New World, and the awarding of a Nobel Peace Prize to an Indian woman from Guatemala. Equally striking was the completion of negotiations among Canada, Mexico, and the United States for a North American Free Trade Agreement (NAFTA).

Economy. In a midyear assessment, the United Nations Economic Commission for Latin America and the Caribbean (ECLAC) projected a 1992 economic growth rate of 3.2% for the region, the same as in 1991. Some countries were expected to outperform the regional average. Chile was projected to grow at a rate of 7% during the year; Argentina, Panama, and Venezuela were expected to expand by 6%. Peru, facing an economic slowdown brought on by internal violence and political uncertainty, seemed to be a notable exception. The Latin American recovery was taking place, the ECLAC noted, despite an unfavorable external climate in the rest of the world, including "sluggishness in the industrial economies, slackening world trade, and a steady decline in the prices of commodities exported by Latin America."

Inflation appeared to be receding in virtually all the Latin American economies, with the exception of Brazil. The average inflation rate throughout the region, which had reached 960% in 1990, fell to 49% in 1991 and went down to an annual rate of 23% in the first seven months of 1992.

Debt. The region's external debt essentially remained unchanged in 1992, although the debt-service burden eased. The accumulated Latin American external debt was $432 billion at the end of 1991 and was expected to increase by less than 3% in 1992. Interest payments, on the other hand, were expected to be significantly lower because of aggressive debt-rescheduling negotiations carried out with foreign creditors. Debt repayments were expected to decline to 18% of the region's exports of goods and services.

The region's merchandise trade was expected to remain in surplus in 1992, although at a lower level than in recent years. The value of exports was projected to rise by 5% despite an anticipated decline in the foreign-exchange earnings of oil-exporting countries due to falling prices and a decline in volume. Imports, on the other hand, have been rising sharply, reflecting growing demand as the Latin economies improve. The growth rate of imports in 1992 was expected to reach 18%, bringing total imports in the region to $130 billion.

NAFTA. Canada, Mexico, and the United States completed work on the NAFTA, the North American free-trade pact, on August 12 and President Bush formally notified the U.S. Congress on September 18 of his intent to sign the accord. Under previously adopted rules, December 17 was the earliest the president could sign the agreement. NAFTA provides for a phaseout of customs duties on nearly 10,000 products in five or ten annual stages. For certain sensitive items, the tariffs would be phased out over 15 years. The pact sets rules for the conduct of freer trade in a broad range of sectors from automotive goods and textiles to telecommunications, agriculture, financial services, land transportation, and intellectual property. The pact would not enter into force until implementing legislation is passed by the legislatures of the three signatory countries, which was not expected to occur until mid-1993 or later. Considerable debate—pro and con— was anticipated. Particularly controversial was the potential impact of the agreement on environmental standards and job security.

Free Trade. Whatever the outcome of the NAFTA debate, the free-trade movement appeared to be gathering strength throughout the hemisphere. During the year, Chile and Venezuela began exploring a free-trade arrangement. Chile already has a free-trade pact with Mexico and Argentina, and Venezuela has signed similar agreements with Colombia and with the Caribbean Community. In August, five Central American countries—Costa Rica, El Salvador, Guatemala, Honduras, and Nicaragua—signed a pact establishing the framework for free trade with Mexico. Within Central America, El Salvador, Guatemala, and Honduras agreed to form a free-trade zone by Jan. 1, 1993. Costa Rica, Nicaragua, and Panama were expected to join the regional trade arrangement later. Costa Rica and Chile have explored a liberalized trade arrangement, and Costa Rica has expressed interest in a free-trade accord with the United States.

Free-trade pacts had been entered into by the four countries of the Southern Cone (Mercosur), Argentina, Brazil, Paraguay, and Uruguay, and also by the member countries of the Andean Group—Bolivia, Colombia, Ecuador, Peru, and Venezuela.

U.S. President George Bush earlier had proposed a hemisphere-wide free-trade arrangement called the Enterprise for the Americas Initiative. In September the president said he hoped the arrangement could be implemented within the next four years.

Democracy. As the Latin American economies were recovering, the region's fragile democracies were showing signs of stress. In Venezuela, rebel army units failed in attempts to overthrow the government of President Carlos Andrés Pérez on the night of February 3–4 and on November 27.

In April, President Alberto Fujimori of Peru, in an army-backed coup from the top, disbanded the national Congress and suspended the powers of the judiciary, claiming a state of national emergency. The other hemisphere nations, acting through the Organization of American States (OAS), "deeply deplored" the Peruvian action, but did not impose sanctions. Fujimori's "auto-coup" had widespread popular support in Peru, which increased in September when police captured Abimael Guzman, the leader of the Shining Path, the country's violent rebel guerrilla movement.

Also in September, President Fernando Collor de Mello of Brazil was impeached by the lower house of the Brazilian Congress on charges that his family and friends had accepted bribes in return for government favors. Collor de Mello, Brazil's first elected president in 29 years, was stripped of power for six months and was to stand trial in the Brazilian Senate.

Quincentennial. The commemoration of Columbus' arrival in the New World in 1492 generated considerable controversy around the hemisphere. Indigenous groups across Latin America staged spirited and sometimes destructive demonstrations on October 12 to mark the occasion. Many Indian leaders blamed disease, slavery, and exploitation brought by European colonists for the poverty and misery that plague them today. Perhaps in recognition of the indigenous complaints, Rigoberta Menchú, a 33-year-old Guatemalan Indian woman and an ardent defender of human rights, was awarded the 1992 Nobel Peace Prize on October 16 for more than a decade of denouncing abuses against indigenous people in her country. (*See also* BIOGRAPHY—*Menchú, Rigoberta.*)

RICHARD C. SCHROEDER, *Consultant*
Organization of American States

LAW

The future of abortion rights in the United States dominated the Supreme Court's 1991–92 term despite a host of other high-profile cases. The outcome of a key abortion case from Pennsylvania proved surprising because of the emergence of a three-member moderate conservative bloc on the high court that also was pivotal in other closely watched cases.

The most conservative members of the court, led by Chief Justice William H. Rehnquist, were riding high as the term began. The previous term solidified their control, and the direction of the court appeared even more clear with the 1991 appointment of Justice Clarence Thomas by President George Bush. Thomas began his first term as successor to the retired Justice Thurgood Marshall, who had been an anchor of the dwindling liberal wing of the court. The two most liberal remaining justices were Harry A. Blackmun and John Paul Stevens. Both Midwesterners appointed by Republican presidents, they once were considered in the center of the court.

Most notably at the conclusion of the 1991–92 term, they joined with three others—Justices Anthony M. Kennedy, Sandra Day O'Connor, and David H. Souter—to preserve some abortion rights and to reaffirm the separation of church and state. Justices Kennedy and O'Connor, appointed by former President Ronald Reagan, and Justice Souter, named to the court by President Bush, held the pivotal votes in those cases and in other closely contested issues. The three moderate conservatives exerted a check on the rightward pull of the court. The three expressed reservations about scrapping precedents and voiced concern that the court would be seen as an instrument of politics if it moved too quickly and, for example, permitted states to outlaw abortions.

When the three voted together, they were never on the losing side in any case decided in the term. But some commentators said the more measured pace of the rightward move could be temporary. "It might be too soon to talk about the emerging troika," said Arthur B. Culvahouse, a Washington lawyer and former White House counsel to President Reagan. "It could be case-specific." Added Erwin Chemerinsky, a professor of law at the University of Southern California, It is "impossible to say" whether the alliance "will last beyond one term."

Of the 108 cases decided with full opinions by the court in the 1991–92 term, Justices Kennedy and Souter each dissented only eight times. Justice Souter voted in the majority in 13 of the 14 cases decided by 5–4 votes.

In the lower courts, some of the names in the news were so-called suicide-doctor Jack Kevorkian, underworld boss John Gotti, deposed Panamanian leader Manuel Noriega, and boxer Mike Tyson. A courtroom battle over frozen embryos between a divorced woman and her former husband made headlines.

United States

Supreme Court. The biggest case of the term unquestionably was a dispute over a Pennsylvania law restricting abortion (*Planned Parenthood v. Casey*). But it produced a fragmented ruling that left both "pro-choice" and "pro-life" forces dissatisfied. The court upheld most of the state law, including provisions that doctors must inform women of alternatives to abortion and that women then must wait 24 hours before undergoing the operation. The court also upheld part of the law requiring most teenagers to get parental consent or a judge's permission before having an abortion. But the justices struck down Pennsylvania's attempt to force women to notify their husbands before having an abortion. By a 5–4 vote, the court said women still have a constitutional right to an abortion. But only Justices Stevens and Blackmun voted to reaffirm the court's 1973 ruling in *Roe v. Wade* that made that right predominant over state regulations in the early stages of pregnancy. Instead, Justices O'Connor, Kennedy, and Souter substituted a new standard that states may not impose an "undue burden" or "substantial obstacle" to abortion prior to the time the fetus can survive outside the womb—usually around six months after conception. The new standard was expected to lead to new state laws restricting abortions and new court challenges to those laws. But the high-court ruling makes it clear that laws making abortion a crime would be unconstitutional.

After the court term concluded, the justices also were faced with another abortion issue—the availability of the French-made abortion drug RU486 (*Benten v. Kessler*). The court turned down an emergency request by a California woman seeking to use RU486 pills she brought into the United States from England. The court let the Food and Drug Administration (FDA) ban importation of the pills, which had been confiscated from the woman by customs officials.

In another abortion-related matter, the court deferred until the following term a decision on whether federal judges can use a 19th-century civil-rights law to order anti-abortion protesters, such as Operation Rescue, to stop blocking access to abortion clinics (*Bray v. Alexandria Women's Health Clinic*). (*See also* ABORTION.)

Civil-rights battles were before the court in numerous other cases as well. The court ruled in its first major decision ever on college desegregation that Mississippi failed to prove that by giving blacks and whites freedom of choice it has ended racial segregation in its institutions of higher learning (*U.S. v. Fordice*). The court also said that public secondary schools can be freed gradually from federal-court supervision as they take steps to desegregate various aspects of their operations (*Freeman v. Pitts*).

The court permitted students who say they are victims of sex discrimination or sexual harassment in schools to use a federal law to sue for monetary damages (*Franklin v. Gwinnett County Public Schools*). In a case involving the civil rights of prison inmates, the court said the beating of a prisoner may violate the Constitution even if the inmate's injuries are not serious (*Hudson v. McMillian*). And the justices ruled that defendants in criminal cases may not use their peremptory, or automatic, challenges to exclude potential jurors based on their race (*Georgia v. McCollum*).

Key 1st Amendment cases involving religion and freedom of expression also highlighted the term. The court said nonsectarian prayers at a public middle-school graduation in Providence, RI, violated separation of church and state (*Lee v. Weisman*). The case reaffirmed a ban on state-sponsored prayer in public schools and left intact the court's 20-year-old test for determining when the line between church and state is crossed impermissibly.

In a case that could affect so-called speech codes at public universities, the court said states and communities may not single out for special punishment cross burnings and other "hate crimes" that express racial or religious bigotry (*R.A.V. v. St. Paul*). The court said airports may ban political and religious groups from soliciting donations in terminals but must allow the distribution of literature (*International Society for Krishna Consciousness v. Lee*). The justices said communities may not impose sliding-scale permit fees for parades and rallies, charging more for controversial groups that may require more police protection (*Forsyth County v. Nationalist Movement*). And the court struck down New York's so-called "Son of Sam" law, named for a serial killer there, that was designed to help crime victims by confiscating profits from a criminal's books or movies about his exploits (*Simon & Schuster v. New York Crime Victims Board*). The court rejected free-speech arguments in two election-law cases. It upheld a Tennessee law that barred electioneering within 100 ft (30 m) of polling places (*Burson v. Freeman*). And the court upheld a Hawaii law that banned write-in voting (*Burdick v. Takushi*).

In a major criminal-law case, the court said the U.S. government may kidnap criminal suspects from a foreign country and prosecute them over that nation's objections and despite an extradition treaty between the countries (*U.S. v. Alvarez Machain*). The ruling let the government put on trial in California a Mexican doctor accused in the torture-killing of a Drug Enforcement Administration (DEA) agent. The

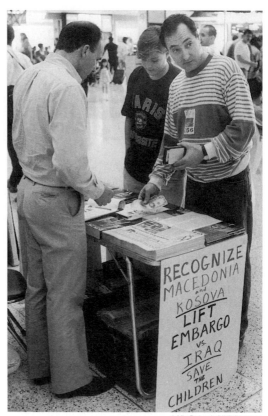

© Vic DeLucia/NYT Pictures

According to a June 1992 U.S. Supreme Court ruling, begging at transportation terminals can be banned but the distribution of literature at such sites is permissible.

court ruled against the government in an undercover operation that resulted in the conviction of a Nebraska farmer on child-pornography charges (*Jacobson v. U.S.*). The justices said the farmer was entrapped in the sting operation into receiving through the mail contraband he otherwise was not predisposed to receive.

The court said insane people acquitted of crimes may not be kept in mental hospitals after regaining their sanity just because they still might be dangerous (*Foucha vs. Louisiana*). The court also said that mentally ill criminal defendants cannot be forced to take antipsychotic medication during trial unless the state can show there is a medical or safety necessity (*Riggins v. Nevada*).

The court limited federal-court review for convicted criminals in one case, ruling inmates can lose the right to a federal-court hearing in such cases if their lawyers fail to present their case properly in state courts (*Keeney v. Tamayo-Reyes*). But the court rejected a more sweeping restriction on such federal review that would have required federal judges to accept state-court findings without further evaluation (*Wright v. West*).

In a case involving the relationship between the states and federal government, the court said cigarette manufacturers may be sued in state courts for allegedly misleading the public

Twelve-year-old Gregory Kingsley, surrounded by his new foster father and his lawyer, shakes hands with Circuit Judge Thomas Kirk after the court ruled that the sixth-grader could divorce his biological parents because of mistreatment and abandonment. The effects of the case caused controversy across the United States.

© Tom Spitz/"The Orlando Sentinel"

over the hazards of smoking (*Cipollone v. Liggett Group*). The court said the federal law requiring warning labels on cigarette packs does not shield the companies from all such suits. But the court said federal law preempts states from regulating airline-fare advertisements (*Morales v. Trans World Airlines*).

The justices were confronted with a number of property-rights and taxation issues. They said government may not automatically deny compensation to a landowner when some regulation to promote public health and safety destroys the property's economic value (*Lucas v. South Carolina Coastal Commission*). The court upheld California's Proposition 13, which results in far higher property taxes for more recent home buyers (*Nordlinger v. Hahn*). And the court continued to ban state taxation of mail-order sales by out-of-state catalogue companies but said Congress has the power to lift the ban (*Quill Corp. v. North Dakota*).

Local Law. In Michigan a judge threw out murder charges against Dr. Jack Kevorkian, who helped two chronically ill women kill themselves in 1991. The judge said the state has no law against assisted suicide and said prosecutors failed to show that Kevorkian actually had triggered the devices used by the women to die. The decision helped spark renewed debate over the ethics of doctor-assisted suicide. (*See also* MEDICINE AND HEALTH—*Medical Ethics.*)

John Gotti, called the head of the nation's most powerful crime family, was convicted in federal court in New York of racketeering and other charges. Gotti was sentenced to life in prison as nearly 1,000 of his supporters protested outside a Brooklyn courthouse.

Manuel Noriega, deposed as Panama's dictator in a bloody 1990 invasion by U.S. forces, was convicted of eight of ten drug and racketeering charges in Miami federal court. He was sentenced to 40 years in prison. President Bush called the conviction "a major victory against the drug lords." Noriega and his lawyer called

the prosecution a politically motivated abuse of power.

In Indianapolis boxer Mike Tyson was found guilty of raping a Miss Black America contestant who said she was lured to his hotel room and overpowered by the former heavyweight champion. He was sentenced to six years in prison. Tyson, in an unusual defense, said he was a crude womanizer whose accuser must have known he wanted sex.

Seven frozen embryos were left in legal limbo after the Tennessee Supreme Court ruled that a divorced woman cannot use them to make her former husband a father against his will. The state court said the woman cannot implant or donate the test-tube embryos that she and her former husband conceived in 1989 before their breakup. The fertility clinic in Knoxville where the embryos were stored said it probably would destroy them.

In Washington former Central Intelligence Agency (CIA) official Clair George was found guilty in December of two counts of lying to Congress, on charges stemming from the Iran-contra affair. George, former director of the CIA's world spying operations, was accused of concealing from Congress the agency's knowledge of the Reagan administration's secret network for sending military supplies to the contras, or Nicaraguan rebels. The support for the rebels was financed by profits from the sale of arms to Iran designed to help gain the release of U.S. hostages there. On December 24, however, President George Bush pardoned George, along with five others involved in the Iran-contra affair.

In a precedent-setting case, Florida Circuit Judge Thomas S. Kirk ruled in Orlando that Gregory Kingsley, 12, may "divorce" the biological parents he said mistreated and abandoned him and may be adopted by his foster parents. Kirk said the boy's biological mother had lied consistently during the legal battle initiated by Gregory to sever his family ties.

JIM RUBIN, *The Associated Press*

International Law

Questions of international law in 1992 centered around three main areas: Yugoslavia, Libya, and the Persian Gulf region.

Yugoslavia. Slovenia and Croatia, the Yugoslav republics that declared their independence in 1991, were recognized at the beginning of the year by the nations of the European Community, soon followed by the United States and other major powers. Subsequently, recognition also was extended to the war-torn republic of Bosnia-Herzegovina. However, the former Yugoslav republic of Macedonia failed to gain recognition, mainly because of Greek fears that its proposed name might imply claims to the portion of historic Macedonia that lies within Greece. This refusal to recognize came about despite the advice given by the Badinder Arbitration Commission—part of the peace conference on former Yugoslavia—and was not meant to imply that Macedonia is not a state. It simply indicated that other states, at that stage, were unwilling to establish diplomatic relations with it.

The United States played a leading role in tightening up sanctions against the new Federal Republic of Yugoslavia (Serbia and Montenegro) and in creating a war-crimes commission at the United Nations to investigate alleged human-rights violations by Serbia and other parties to the Yugoslav conflict. In November, North Atlantic Treaty Organization (NATO) forces began enforcing the anti-Serbian embargo.

Libya and the Lockerbie Incident. The United States and Britain also pursued an action against Libya in the UN Security Council. Libya had refused to surrender two of its nationals charged with involvement in the bombing of a U.S. airliner over Lockerbie, Scotland, in 1988. The Security Council appeared to support the complaint and adopted an air embargo against Libya.

The Libyan government had attempted to avoid UN sanctions and possible Anglo-American hostile measures by seeking the protection of the International Court of Justice. The Libyans relied on the Montreal Convention, which leaves it to the discretion of a state either to extradite terrorist suspects or to try them. Libya argued that it had complied fully with the requirements of the convention by instituting proceedings against the two suspects. But the court refused to grant interim protection to Libya, finding that it was unable to enforce the Montreal Convention in the face of a mandatory resolution adopted by the UN Security Council. The case, however, would proceed beyond this preliminary phase and the ruling was not final.

The Persian Gulf Region. The United States also remained involved in litigation at the World Court over a case brought by Iran in connection with the downing of an Iranian civil airliner by a U.S. warship in 1988. The United States retained its objection to the jurisdiction of the court to hear the case. Iran, on the other hand, brought a second case—this time dealing with the destruction of certain oil installations by U.S. armed forces. No immediate decision could be expected in either case.

The proceedings of the U.S.-Iran claims tribunal, established to process and decide claims resulting from the 1979 revolution in Iran, approached their completion in 1992. The tribunal, which had adjudicated claims worth hundreds of millions of dollars over the past decade, would be disbanded as 1992 ended.

The government of Iraq continued to obstruct the visits of UN weapons inspectors, and failed to compensate those who had suffered direct damages as a result of the 1991 Gulf war. The UN Compensation Commission which had been set up in Geneva therefore was unable to dispense funds to claimants, although it continued to refine guidelines for the registration and disposition of cases. National governments, too, proceeded with the registration of claims to be submitted to the commission.

Iraq also continued to mistreat its own population in violation of international human-rights standards. In August the United States, Britain, and France imposed a "no-fly" zone over southern Iraq to deter attacks by Iraqi airforce planes on the rebellious Shiite minority in that region. The operation was justified by the U.S. government as an act of humanitarian intervention in accordance with UN resolutions.

U.S. Court Actions. U.S. judicial authorities sparked considerable international criticism over their handling of cases that had a bearing on international law. Most notable in this context was the decision of the U.S. Supreme Court in the case of Humberto Alvarez Machain, an individual who had been abducted by U.S. drug-enforcement agents from Mexico. The court refused to hold that the abduction had been unlawful and amounted to a violation of an extradition treaty between the United States and Mexico. Alvarez was ultimately acquitted. On the other hand, the U.S. conviction of former Panamanian strongman Manuel A. Noriega to a prolonged prison sentence for drug-related offenses did not attract significant international condemnation.

Law-Commission Proposals. The International Law Commission drafted a new code dealing with international crimes and proposed the creation of an international tribunal with jurisdiction over crimes against peace, war crimes, acts of genocide, terrorism, and drug-related offenses. The report of the Law Commission was considered at the United Nations General Assembly, but the establishment of the proposed international criminal court remained a distant prospect.

MARC WELLER, *University of Cambridge*

© Bilal Kabalan/Sipa

A group of Lebanese prepare to vote in the nation's first parliamentary elections in 20 years. The results of the balloting were inconclusive, however, as Christians, charging that Syria manipulated the voting, boycotted the polls.

LEBANON

On the surface, Lebanon continued to make progress in 1992 in its recovery from 16 years of civil conflict. The government witnessed the freeing of the last Western hostages, instituted some reforms, recovered government property, held elections, and negotiated with Israel to resolve Lebanese aspects of the Arab-Israeli problem. Far from reassuring the population, however, this apparent progress generally was seen for what it was—a facade for increasing Syrian control over the country. The weight of economic stagnation, crippling inflation, and a collapsed financial system crushed the real advances and dashed public aspirations.

Political Life. Entering 1992, the government of Prime Minister Umar Karami, widely criticized for corruption and unable to agree on any measures to deal with the serious economic problems facing Lebanon, continued to posture rather than govern. It hobbled along until the continuing deterioration of the Lebanese pound produced demonstrations and riots in widely scattered parts of the country. The pound, which traded at less than 1,000 to the U.S. dollar at the beginning of the year, sank to more than 2,000 in early May. On May 6 the Karami government resigned. One week later, President Elias Hrawi asked Rashid Sulh, who last had served as prime minister in 1974, to form a new government. The appointment of Sulh was seen throughout Lebanon as more of the same, and indeed the composition of the government was nearly identical with its predecessor.

The most anticipated political question of the year was not that of a government. In the 1989 Taif accords, which laid the groundwork for Lebanese reconciliation and reconstruction, Syria had pledged to redeploy its forces eastward to the entrance to the Bekaa Valley two years after reforms were implemented. The parliament's adoption of the Taif accords in September 1990 generally was seen as "starting the Taif clock." The majority of Lebanese wondered whether Syria in fact would withdraw its forces from the Beirut area and redeploy them officially eastward—and what this would mean for Lebanon.

The second major political question was related to the first. Due to the civil war, no parliamentary elections had been held in the country since 1972; the prewar legislature automatically renewed itself after each term, pending the restoration of peace. As part of the Taif program, the parliament was expanded from 99 to 108 seats through the appointment of additional members. Historically, the body had had a six-to-five Christian majority. Since one purpose of the expansion was to create a new religious balance, most of the appointees were Muslims. All of the new members were acceptable to Syria. The next step would be to hold the long-deferred parliamentary elections. The most pressing question was, under what circumstances would such elections be held, if at all?

With expectations and apprehension growing, the United States and other foreign powers had made explicit their expectation that Syrian forces would redeploy. There was a general expression that redeployment should precede any national elections. However, if this were to occur, Syria would be less able to ensure its complete control of the outcome. Consequently, by midsummer, senior Syrian officials disputed the timing of the "Taif clock," insisting that not all of the promised reforms had been implemented fully. They also indicated Syrian forces would not redeploy prior to the elections.

The elections were held in several rounds between late August and early October. They were boycotted by the most powerful Christian groups, which argued that they could not be free and fair under existing conditions—especially because of the Syrian presence. In the early stages of the voting the turnout was extremely light, virtually nil in some districts. The speaker of the parliament resigned over irregularities in the voting, which appear to have been widespread. The European Community (EC) and a number of foreign governments criticized various aspects of the elections. Nevertheless, the results—which eliminated some of the traditional Christian parliamentary power centers and created a new Muslim fundamentalist bloc—were accepted by the government.

Following the parliamentary elections, President Hrawi accepted Sulh's resignation and asked Rafiq al-Hariri to form a new government. Hariri, a Lebanese-born businessman who had made a fortune in Saudi Arabia and reputedly was close to the Saudi royal family, was expected to concentrate on the economy, leaving the political sphere to pro-Syrian leaders.

Security. In the areas of Lebanon under nominal government control, security remained acceptable, with violence notably reduced from the war years. Terrorist activity was dormant: Training bases of guerrilla groups were open and active in the Syrian-controlled Bekaa Valley, but one of them, the Kurdish Workers Party (PKK), was forced to leave its Bekaa camp in May, and the remaining two Western hostages—German relief workers Heinrich Struebig and Thomas Kemptner—were freed after three years' captivity in June. There were occasional incidents of harassment, abduction, and assassination, generally directed against critics of Syria or Hezbollah (the Shiite fundamentalist party). Internecine struggles also continued among the various rival Palestinian groups, resulting in a number of assassinations.

The major exception to this improved situation was the southern area, the "Israeli security strip," where incidents and outbreaks of heavy violence occurred intermittently between Hezbollah on the one hand and Israel and the pro-Israeli South Lebanon Army (SLA) on the other. Most began with Hezbollah attacks on the SLA or Israeli patrols. In October, Hezbollah launched rockets into northern Israel. Israel responded with attacks in the southern area, and with occasional aerial and naval strikes elsewhere in Lebanon, since it widely was assumed that the Hezbollah offensive enjoyed Syrian support.

Negotiations With Israel. Israel and Lebanon continued to hold talks as part of the broader Arab-Israeli peace initiative, but the two delegations made little progress in 1992. Since the Lebanese delegation was perceived to be unable to act without Syrian approval, and unable to move substantively in advance of progress on the Syria-Israel front, there was no real possibility of serious discussions until Syria and Israel began themselves to make progress to resolve their differences.

Economy. The collapse of the Lebanese pound reflected both objective realities and psychological factors. Syrian domination frightened off Lebanese (and many foreign) entrepreneurs who feared the gradual imposition of a Syrian-style controlled economy in Lebanon. Continuing political uncertainties were a further deterrent to investment. The objective problems were at least as daunting. Corruption was often flagrant and extreme even by Lebanese standards. The government continued spending money, but was collecting revenues amounting to only a small part of its expenditures. Large numbers of the most skilled and capable people had emigrated during the war years. Modernization in other Middle East countries made Lebanon less necessary as an entrepôt and communications center; indeed, the war-damaged Lebanese communications and transportation infrastructure, once the most advanced in the region, now was among the most backward. Finally, much of the aid that might have gone to Lebanon in the past instead was being directed to the former Soviet republics, the former states of Yugoslavia, Somalia, and other countries where either the need or the consequences of not doing something appeared greater.

As the Lebanese became conscious of these factors, hopes for economic recovery declined, and the fall of the once-proud Lebanese pound followed. Rafiq Hariri's appointment as prime minister in October briefly buoyed the pound, but the underlying causes of its weakness were still in place.

RONALD D. MCLAURIN
Abbott Associates, Inc.

LEBANON • Information Highlights

Official Name: Republic of Lebanon.
Location: Southwest Asia.
Area: 4,015 sq mi (10 400 km²).
Population (mid-1992 est.): 3,400,000.
Chief Cities (1982 est.): Beirut, the capital, 509,000; Tripoli, 198,000.
Government: *President,* Elias Hrawi (took office November 1989); *premier,* Rafiq al-Hariri (named Oct. 22, 1992). *Legislature* (unicameral)—National Assembly.
Monetary Unit: Lebanese pound (1868 pounds equal U.S.$1, Dec. 9, 1992).
Foreign Trade (1989 est. U.S.$): *Imports,* $1,900,000,000; *exports,* $1,000,000,000.

LIBRARIES

Funding and its impact on the ability of libraries to meet society's demand for their services in the information age, coupled with an ever-growing need for literacy programs, challenged libraries in 1992.

Funding Cuts. Like other U.S. institutions which traditionally have depended on government funding for the vast majority of their revenues, most libraries sustained continued budget cuts throughout the late 1980s and 1990s. In 1991 the American Library Association (ALA) emphasized declining support for libraries in its public-relations programs; in 1992 libraries worldwide called attention to their own fights for survival.

Beginning with Freedom of Information Day on March 16, the ALA sponsored a toll-free number through which callers could register their support for library funding. In the four weeks that the number was operational, more than 75,000 callers registered their support for U.S. libraries. More than 100,000 additional li-

brary users signed a petition supporting full funding for libraries. On June 17 the ALA presented these supporters' names and statistics to members of the U.S. Congress.

In such states as Indiana and Pennsylvania, local library associations sponsored similar campaigns. This unprecedented activity was prompted by a series of budget cuts early in 1992. For example, Fairfax (VA) county public libraries had to reduce hours and raise fines; librarians at the Phoenix (AZ) Public Library voluntarily took a three-day unpaid furlough to cushion budget cuts; the Illinois State Library cut funding to state systems by 34%; and the Los Angeles Public Library reduced hours and cut the book budget by half.

The ALA also announced for the first time the nation's "best of the best" and "worst of the worst" stories in library funding. The best award went to San Diego for its investment of $9 million in a Neighborhood Pride and Protection Program that resulted in Sunday hours at the central and 12 branch libraries, rehiring of youth services librarians lost to Proposition 13

With U.S. libraries continuing to face severe budget cuts, Patricia Glass Schuman, the president of the American Libraries Association, and Charles Beard, cochair of the Call for America's Libraries campaign, in June 1992 presented Congress with the names of a group of library supporters.

Library Awards for 1992

Beta Phi Mu Award for distinguished service to education for librarianship: Alice B. Kroeger, Drexel University, Philadelphia

Randolph J. Caldecott Medal for the most distinguished picture book for children: David Wiesner, *Tuesday*

Melvil Dewey Award for recent creative professional achievement of a high order: Michael Gorman, California State University, Fresno

Grolier Award for unique contributions to the stimulation and guidance of reading by children and young people: Effie Lee Morris, San Francisco Public Library

Joseph W. Lippincott Award for distinguished service to the profession of librarianship: John N. Berry III, *Library Journal*

John Newbery Medal for the most distinguished contribution to literature for children: Phyllis Reynolds Naylor, *Shiloh*

in 1978, and the opening of Homework Centers in branches. The worst award went to the state of California, where more than half of all school libraries have closed since the early 1980s.

Across the Atlantic, Great Britain's Library Association held Save our Libraries Day. Library supporters were urged to contact their member of Parliament and arrange rallies or other activities to focus attention on the deterioration of that nation's libraries. One trigger for that event was the closing of 11 of 67 Derbyshire libraries. Book budgets had been cut in half.

New NCLIS Chair. President George Bush appointed J. Michael Farrell, an attorney practicing in Washington, DC, as chair of the National Commission on Libraries and Information Science (NCLIS). Established by Congress in 1970, NCLIS is charged with developing and recommending overall plans to provide library and information services adequate to meet the needs of the public. Farrell has been an NCLIS commissioner since 1990; there is no set limit for the chair's term.

Reading and Literacy. Following Barbara Bush's lead, private foundations and corporations supported reading and literacy programs. The Bell Atlantic Corporation gave $500,000 to the ALA for family literacy programs; the Barbara Bush Foundation awarded more than that amount in 1992–93 alone; and the state librarian of Illinois administered more than $500,000 in 1992 for workplace literacy programs. McDonald's, the fast-food chain, also jumped on the reading bandwagon by using place mats during National Library Week that urged children to "Go Back to the Future at the Library."

Associations. More than 19,000 people attended the ALA's 111th annual conference June 25-July 1 in San Francisco. Presided over by ALA President Patricia Glass Schuman, the conference had as its theme "Your Right to Know: Librarians Make It Happen." Marilyn Miller was inaugurated as the association's new president and Hardy Franklin was welcomed as the president-elect. Peggy Sullivan was present in her new role as executive director, succeeding Linda Crismond, who resigned in May.

"Resource Sharing . . . and the Walls Come Tumbling Down" was the theme of the Canadian Library Association's 47th annual conference held June 11–14 in Winnipeg, Ont. The conference was presided over by President Marnie Swanson, and Françoise Hébert was welcomed as first vice-president/president-elect. Attendance was approximately 800.

CHARLES HARMON, *Headquarters Librarian*
American Library Association

LIBYA

Allegations made late in 1991 of Libyan government complicity in the December 1988 bombing of a U.S. airliner over Lockerbie, Scotland, set the stage for a prolonged dispute that at first pitted Libya against the United States and Great Britain, but ultimately widened to place the country at odds with the United Nations Security Council. Libya's refusal to comply with U.S. and British demands that it extradite two intelligence agents believed to be responsible for the explosion prompted the United Nations to place the country under international sanctions. Although most Arab states sympathized with Libya's reluctance to hand over its citizens, they generally observed the prohibitions ordered by the UN. By the end of the year, the hardships produced by the sanctions had generated some unrest and disillusion with Col. Muammar el-Qaddafi's leadership inside Libya.

UN Action. The confrontation began late in January, when the UN Security Council unanimously passed Resolution 731. While not directly accusing Libya of responsibility for the bombing, the resolution called on it to deliver for trial abroad Libyan agents implicated in the Lockerbie investigation and to cooperate with French authorities in a similar inquiry into the destruction of a French airliner in an explosion over Niger in 1989. When Libya refused to accede to these demands, U.S. President George Bush took the lead in seeking support within the Security Council for the imposition of sanctions on Libya. At the same time, U.S. accusations that Libya was expanding its stockpile of chemical weapons and was acquiring various kinds of equipment with potential nuclear-weapons applications encouraged speculation that the United States was laying the groundwork for a military attack on Libya if it persisted in its noncompliance.

Many Arab states, including several with close ties to the United States—Egypt and Morocco, most notably—and others with a poor record of relations with Colonel Qaddafi urged the United States and Great Britain to reconsider their options. Egyptian President Hosni Mubarak warned that excessive Western pressure on Libya undoubtedly would induce other Arab states to rally to its defense. Such a movement would jeopardize the advances made by the United States in the Middle East as a result of its leadership of the anti-Iraq coalition in 1990–91. Domestic critics of the Bush administration pointed to the absence of precedence for the Security Council resolution and further asserted that it might violate existing international agreements on procedures for combating terrorism and bringing perpetrators to justice.

These arguments in favor of a more cautious policy were enhanced by occasional Libyan efforts to reach a compromise with its antagonists. During February and March, Qaddafi mixed blustering and threats against Great Britain and the United States with conciliatory overtures. Most notable among the latter were an offer to cooperate with the French investigation and a proposal, which the United States rejected, to allow the International Court of Justice to rule on the validity of Resolution 731. As the likelihood that the United Nations would vote in favor of sanctions grew stronger in March, Libyan government officials met with representatives of the Arab League in an attempt to involve the regional organization in the crisis. The collapse of tentative plans to turn over the Lockerbie suspects to the League, however, provided additional ammunition for the supporters of sanctions. France, disturbed by the minimal level of Libyan cooperation in its inquiry, joined Great Britain and the United States in calling for such punitive measures. On March 31 the Security Council voted to ban all air travel to and from Libya, to place an embargo on arms sales to the country, and to reduce the size of Libyan diplomatic missions abroad beginning on April 15 unless Libya surrendered its agents before then.

Colonel Qaddafi rejected the UN ultimatum, which also drew criticism from individual Arab countries and from the Arab League.

Shortly before the sanctions deadline, the International Court of Justice rejected Libya's plea to enjoin Great Britain and the United States from taking action against it. Qaddafi thereupon announced his acceptance, in principle, of the extradition demand. In order to avoid the appearance of yielding completely to the Anglo-U.S. demands, however, he again tried to arrange to hand over the suspects to the Arab League. This plan failed for a second time when mutually agreeable terms could not be reached, and the sanctions took effect as scheduled.

Reaction. Initially, the isolation intended by the sanctions proved more of an inconvenience than a serious problem for Libya. Easy overland access to neighboring Tunisia and Egypt, and to Malta by sea, provided ample alternatives to direct air transportation into and out of the country. Nevertheless, Libyans showed their resentment of these punishments with demonstrations at the Tripoli embassies of Security Council members who had voted in favor of the sanctions. Despite their discomfort with this pressure against a fellow Arab state, governments throughout the Middle East observed the air embargo, at least in part out of fear that similar sanctions would be imposed on any country that defied it.

Several weeks after the imposition of the embargo, some evidence of popular discontent began to appear in Libya. In early June, newspapers featured articles critical of some of Colonel Qaddafi's most cherished policies, including Arab unity. Pointing to Arab participation in the boycott, the articles discounted the possibility of ever achieving Arab unity and suggested that Libya abandon that policy and pursue better relations with the West. But in the absence of any official reaction to these statements, or of any other significant signs of anti-Qaddafi sentiment, most observers dismissed the press campaign as a subterfuge aimed at favorably influencing public opinion in Europe and the United States.

As Libya refused to give ground on the issue of extradition, the possibility of levying more severe penalties, including a ban on oil exports, was raised, but no further steps were taken. By the fall, shortages attributable to the air embargo had begun to spark some disaffection among ordinary Libyans, but the government gave no indication of a willingness to compromise with its Western adversaries. The United States and Great Britain, on the other hand, while able to maintain the existing sanctions, were unable to generate support for any more serious ones, the inevitable result of which would be to deprive their European partners of a relatively cheap and plentiful source of oil. The confrontation remained a stalemate as the year drew to a close.

KENNETH J. PERKINS
University of South Carolina

LIBYA · Information Highlights

Official Name: Socialist People's Libyan Arab Jamahiriya ("state of the masses").
Location: North Africa.
Area: 679,359 sq mi (1 759 540 km²).
Population (mid-1992 est.): 4,500,000.
Chief Cities (1984 census): Tripoli, the capital, 990,697; Benghazi, 435,886.
Government: *Head of state,* Muammar el-Qaddafi (took office 1969). *Legislature*—General People's Congress (met initially Nov. 1976).
Monetary Unit: Dinar (0.277 dinar equals U.S. $1, June 1992).
Gross National Product (1989 est. U.S.$): $24,000,000,000.
Foreign Trade (1988 est. U.S.$): *Imports,* $5,879,000,000; *exports,* $6,683,000,000.

LITERATURE

Overview

In a year that commemorated the 500th anniversary of Columbus' arrival in the Americas and in which multiculturalism influenced the way historic figures and ethnic groups were viewed, the Swedish Academy, in selecting the 1992 Nobelist in literature, chose Derek Walcott, a man who embodies the diverse strands of the New World.

A native of St. Lucia, Walcott is African, English, and Dutch—a descendant of slaves and immigrants. He is a man of the world but also a former subject of a colonial empire; a man educated in the classics but influenced by the folkways of his home; and finally, a man who loves the English language. While acclaimed as a poet, Walcott is, in addition, a playwright, journalist, painter, and a teacher of literature and creative writing at Boston University. He divides his time between the United States and Trinidad, using his Caribbean roots as a source of poetic rhythms and idioms. His poetic works include *Collected Poems 1948–1984* (1986); *The Arkansas Testament* (1987); and the lengthy *Omeros* (1990), influenced by the classic epics, the *Iliad* and the *Odyssey*. Among his plays is the award-winning *Dream on Monkey Mountain* (1970).

Cited by the academy for a "historic vision, the outcome of a multicultural commitment," Walcott, upon learning of his selection, affirmed that vision, saying that "all the races of the world" are found in the Caribbean.

Other Awards. The Brazilian poet and critic Joao Cabral de Melo Neto became the 12th laureate of the Neustadt International Prize for Literature in 1992. The prestigious $40,000 award, which often has foreshadowed a Nobel Prize for its recipient, is given every two years. Poets, playwrights, and novelists are eligible for consideration. Cabral, who also has been a diplomat, is the author of the verse collections *Pedro do Sono, O cao sem plumas,* and *O Rio.*

Controversy surrounded the acceptance of Israel's highest literary honor by the Israeli-Arab novelist Emile Habibi. In accepting the award, Habibi indicated that the award was an "indirect recognition of the Arabs in Israel as a nation. . . . recognition of a national culture." Critics, however, felt that Habibi's acceptance gave legitimacy to Israel and its government.

U.S. Poet Laureate. In June the Pulitzer Prize-winning poet Mona Van Duyn was named the sixth U.S. poet laureate; she is the first woman so honored. Announcing the appointment was James H. Billington, librarian of Congress. Van Duyn had won the Pulitzer in 1991 for her collection *Near Changes.*

Other News. Two literary masters were in the news in 1992. In New York a series of events in the spring commemorated the 100th anniversary of poet Walt Whitman's death. In July a University of Texas scholar linked the voice of Huck Finn in Mark Twain's masterpiece *The Adventures of Huckleberry Finn* (1884) to that of a 10-year-old black servant. Twain had described the boy, Jimmy, in an 1874 article in *The New York Times.* While Twain himself had said that the model for Huck was a poor white boy from Hannibal, MO, others have seized on the notion of multicultural roots inherent in not only Twain's work, but in all American literature.

SAUNDRA FRANCE

Derek Walcott

© Courtesy Farrar, Straus, and Giroux.
Photographer: Virginia Schendler, 1989

Mona Van Duyn

© Library of Congress, Knopf Photo

American Literature

In 1992 the serious historical novel came back to American literature. The notion of setting fiction in the past to show a clash of cultures was made fashionable by Sir Walter Scott's *Waverly* (1814) and established in the United States by James Fenimore Cooper's *Leatherstocking Tales* (1823–1841). Since then, despite novels ranging from Nathaniel Hawthorne's *The Scarlet Letter* (1850) to E. L. Doctorow's *Ragtime* (1975), historical fiction has been considered primarily a popular form devoted to adventure and romance.

Novels. Susan Sontag's *The Volcano Lover,* however, helped revive the historical novel as respectable entertainment. The author of *Against Interpretation* (1966) and other important books of literary criticism turned her considerable imagination and intelligence to a love story set in Naples at the end of the 18th century and involving Sir William Hamilton, the husband of the mistress of Admiral Nelson. Her concern with telling a good story was a reminder that despite contemporary theories on art, traditional narrative may remain our most compelling form.

Other writers turned to the past to reinterpret conventional notions of history, particularly about the settlement of the West. Lawrence Thornton's *Ghost Woman* deals with a Native American woman in the 1800s, a sort of female Robinson Crusoe who, after living ten years alone on an island off the coast of California, is captured and tragically "civilized." Annie Dillard, best known for her meditations on nature, in *The Living* uses the Pacific Northwest for her tale of 19th-century settlers and Native Americans. Janet Burroway's *Cutting Stone,* inspired by an entry in her mother's diary, depicts Arizona in the 1910s with a vivid cast of characters, including Pancho Villa, to portray a West not populated by democratically minded pioneers, but by bigots, racists, and also women and men trying to discover meaning in their lives.

Toni Morrison's *Jazz* moved to a nearer past, to Harlem in the 1920s. Jazz is her metaphor for a sad story of love and violence, involving a married couple whose peace disappears with the husband's passion for a younger woman. William Kennedy's *Very Old Bones,* the fifth novel in his Albany series, focuses on an illegitimate son of Peter Phelan, an artist and younger brother of Francis Phelan of *Ironweed* (1983). Peter's son is himself a writer who uses family history as his subject.

Cormac McCarthy's *All the Pretty Horses* brought attention to a writer who has been called one of the best-kept secrets in American literature. Set in 1948 in a timeless West, it is the first of his projected *Border Trilogy*.

Nanci Kincaid's *Crossing Blood* comes closer to the present in her story of white and black families whose lives cross at a time when Elvis Presley and integration are in the air. Larry Woiwode's *Indian Affairs* describes the strained relations in the 1970s between whites and Native Americans in northern Michigan. John Updike's *Memories of the Ford Administration* is a sort of mock history, since his main character seems to remember far more about personal crises than political events.

The dividing line between fiction and reality long has been of interest to writers. Leonard Michaels' *Sylvia* is a sort of fictional memoir, telling of his years trying to write while living with a disturbed woman, Sylvia Bloch, who, in fact, did the illustrations for this book. Paul West's *Love's Mansion* is the love story of his own parents. Darryl Pinckney's *High Cotton* is a thoughtful and moving autobiographical novel about a young black man, a fourth-generation college graduate and member of the black elite, who feels so estranged from his cultures that he must search for his own reality.

© Annie Leibovitz/Courtesy of Farrar
Straus & Giroux

Courtesy of Farrar Straus & Giroux

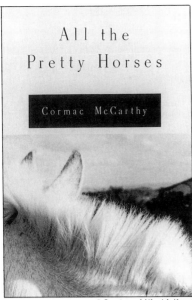

All the
Pretty Horses

Cormac McCarthy

© Courtesy of Alfred A. Knopf

News headlines and research provided the basis for two successful novels. Richard Price's *Clockers*, following the life of New York-area drug dealers, was the result of his spending months with the inhabitants of that world. Rosellen Brown's reality-based *Before and After* tells of idealistic parents who realize their son has killed his girlfriend.

On the other hand, fiction that comments on itself also thrived. Perhaps most spectacular was R. M. Koster's *Carmichael's Dog*, which claims to be an autobiographical novel about a writer and his demons. Mark Leyner's *Et Tu, Babe* is a surrealistic romp by the writer who developed a devoted cult audience with his first book, *My Cousin, My Gastroenterologist* (1990). Eric Kraft continued his delightfully charming, multilevel novel series with *Where Do You Stop? The Personal History, Adventures, Experiences & Observations of Peter Leroy (Continued)*. Kraft's character, Peter Leroy, is a writer who works under a pseudonym to produce the Larry Peters adventures. Leroy is supposed to be writing his memoirs, but he has a tendency to fabricate his own past. Robert Grudin's *Book: A Novel* is a witty self-referential comedy deconstructing academic life. Donna Tartt's well-publicized *The Secret History* uses an unreliable narrator to tell of charismatic professors, overly intense students, and an old-fashioned murder. Nicholson Baker's best-selling *Vox* is devoted entirely to an erotic phone conversation.

In 1992 some very ambitious novels appeared. Leon Forrest's *Divine Days* is an 1,100-page account of a week in the life of the African-American community of a Chicago playwright. Alice Walker's *Possessing the Secret of Joy* exposes the widespread mutilation of women for ritual purposes. Robert Stone's

Outerbridge Reach tells of a man on an around-the-world solo sail, confronting nature and himself.

Short Stories. Anthologies are a form of literary criticism. Joyce Carol Oates' selections for the first *Oxford Book of American Short Stories* implicitly argues for a new landscape in American writing. She rescues a particularly interesting story and writer from oblivion; William Austin's once-popular and now-forgotten "Peter Rugg, the Missing Man" (1824) is a wildly Kafkaesque tale of a man, a child, and a supernatural black horse. Oates omits George Washington Harris, George Washington Cable, Joel Chandler Harris, Bret Harte, Ambrose Bierce, Hamlin Garland, Ring Lardner, James Thurber, John Steinbeck, Truman Capote, and S. J. Perelman; leaving room instead for Sara Orne Jewett, Kate Chopin, Harriet Beecher Stowe, Charlotte Perkins Gilman, Mary Wilkins Freeman, and Zora Neale Hurston. The selections and omissions are not accidental. Oates, in her choices, gives greater voice to women writers and to U.S. multiculturalism. Oates also produced her own collection, *Where Is Here?*

David Shields' *A Handbook for Drowning* reflects the paradoxical nature of the title as his characters struggle to save themselves. Pamela Houston's *Cowboys Are My Weakness* provides penetrating and comic stories of women trying to find ways of surviving their romanticism. Ron Carlson's *Plan B for the Middle Class* captures the incongruities and disappointments of U.S. domestic life in the late 20th century.

History and Biography. Several important political biographies appeared. Blanche Wiesen Cook's *Eleanor Roosevelt: Volume One, 1884–1933* attracted a storm of criticism for its revelations and hypotheses about the private love life of the first lady. Walter Isaacson's thorough *Kissinger: A Biography*, emphasizing Kissinger's personal drive and ambition, was praised by some but attacked by others as inaccurate. David McCullough's *Truman* shows why Harry Truman, little respected in his own time, now is admired.

A good biography can be a rich source of social history. John Loughery's *Alias S. S. Van Dine* recreates the 1910s and 1920s through the eyes of the innovative editor of New York's *Smart Set* magazine, Willard Huntington Wright. Wright published H. L. Mencken and George Jean Nathan before being fired as too controversial; he then created, under the pseudonym S. S. Van Dine, his highly successful Philo Vance detective series. Scott Donaldson's *Archibald MacLeish: An American Life* is an important account of the American poet as public figure. Carol Brightman does a fine job in *Writing Dangerously: Mary McCarthy and Her World*, which covers the 1930s and 1940s, as does Donaldson's book, but from a

AMERICAN LITERATURE: MAJOR WORKS | 1992

NOVELS

Auster, Paul, *Leviathan*
Baker, Nicholson, *Vox*
Bausch, Richard, *Violence*
Berger, Thomas, *Meeting Evil*
Brown, Rosellen, *Before and After*
Burroway, Janet, *Cutting Stone*
Collignon, Jeff, *Her Monster*
Crews, Harry, *Scar Lover*
Dillard, Annie, *The Living*
Dove, Rita, *Through the Ivory Gate*
Edgerton, Clyde, *In Memory of Junior*
Forrest, Leon, *Divine Days*
Fowler, Connie May, *Sugar Cage*
Franzen, Jonathan, *Strong Motion*
Grudin, Robert, *Book: A Novel*
Hoffman, Alice, *Turtle Moon*
Howard, Maureen, *Natural History*
Janowitz, Tama, *The Male Cross-Dresser Support Group*
Kennedy, William, *Very Old Bones*
Kesey, Ken, *Sailor Song*
Kincaid, Nanci, *Crossing Blood*
Koster, R. M., *Carmichael's Dog*
Kraft, Eric, *Where Do You Stop? The Personal History, Adventures, Experiences & Observations of Peter Leroy (Continued)*
Leyner, Mark, *Et Tu, Babe*
McCarthy, Cormac, *All the Pretty Horses*
McDermott, Alice, *At Weddings and Wakes*
McGuane, Thomas, *Nothing But Blue Skies*
McInerney, Jay, *Brightness Falls*
McMillan, Terry, *Waiting to Exhale*
Michaels, Leonard, *Sylvia*
Morrison, Toni, *Jazz*
Naumoff, Lawrence, *Taller Women*
Naylor, Gloria, *Bailey's Cafe*
Nova, Craig, *Trombone*
Pinckney, Darryl, *High Cotton*
Price, Richard, *Clockers*
Prose, Francine, *Primitive People*
Proulx, E. Annie, *Postcards*
Simpson, Mona, *The Lost Father*
Smith, Lee, *The Devil's Dream*
Sontag, Susan, *The Volcano Lover*
Stone, Robert, *Outerbridge Reach*
Tartt, Donna, *The Secret History*
Thornton, Lawrence, *Ghost Woman*
Updike, John, *Memories of the Ford Administration*
Vidal, Gore, *Live From Golgotha*
Walker, Alice, *Possessing the Secret of Joy*
West, Paul, *Love's Mansion*
Woiwode, Larry, *Indian Affairs*

SHORT STORIES

Auchincloss, Louis, *False Gods*
Benedict, Pinckney, *The Wrecking Yard*
Carlson, Ron, *Plan B For the Middle Class*
Chiarella, Tom, *Foley's Luck*
DePew, Alfred, *The Melancholy of Departure*
Eisenberg, Deborah, *Under the 82nd Airborne*
Garrett, George, *Whistling in the Dark: True Stories and Other Fables*
Houston, Pamela, *Cowboys Are My Weakness*
Humphrey, William, *September Song*
Jones, Edward P., *Lost in the City*
Kenan, Randall, *Let the Dead Bury Their Dead*
Maxwell, William, *Billie Dyer and Other Stories*
McCorkle, Jill, *Crash Diet*
McNally, T. M., *Low Flying Aircraft*
Merwin, W. S., *The Lost Upland*
Nelson, Antonya, *In The Land of Men*
Oates, Joyce Carol, *Where is Here?*
Shields, David, *A Handbook for Drowning*
Stern, Daniel, *Twice Upon a Time*
Wideman, John Edgar, *The Stories of John Edgar Wideman*
Williams, Thomas, *Leah, New Hampshire: The Collected Stories of Thomas Williams*

HISTORY AND BIOGRAPHY

Benfey, Christopher, *The Double Life of Stephen Crane*
Bradford, Phillips Verner, and Blume, Harvey, *Ota Benga: The Pygmy in the Zoo*
Brightman, Carol, *Writing Dangerously: Mary McCarthy and Her World*
Cook, Blanche Wiesen, *Eleanor Roosevelt: Volume One, 1884–1933*

Davis, William C., *Jefferson Davis: The Man and His Hour*
de Grazia, Edward, *Girls Lean Back Everywhere: The Law of Obscenity and the Assault on Genius*
Donaldson, Scott, in collaboration with R. H. Winnick, *Archibald MacLeish: An American Life*
Hamilton, Nigel, *JFK: Reckless Youth*
Hulbert, Ann, *The Interior Castle: The Art and Life of Jean Stafford*
Isaacson, Walter, *Kissinger: A Biography*
King, Martin Luther, Jr., *The Papers of Martin Luther King, Jr., Vol. 1: Called to Serve, January 1929-June 1951*, edited by Clayborne Carson et al
Loughery, John, *Alias S. S. Van Dine*
McCarthy, Mary, *Intellectual Memoirs: New York 1936-1938*
McCullough, David, *Truman*
Miller, Edwin Haviland, *Salem Is My Dwelling Place: A Life of Nathaniel Hawthorne*
Pfeiffer, Bruce Brooks, ed., *Frank Lloyd Wright: Collected Writings, Volume One: 1894–1930*
Rubin, Joan Shelley, *The Making of Middlebrow Culture*
Sachar, Howard M., *A History of the Jews in America*
Schwarzkopf, H. Norman, with Peter Petre, *It Doesn't Take a Hero: The Autobiography of H. Norman Schwarzkopf*
Wakefield, Dan, *New York in the Fifties*
Warren, Joyce, *Fanny Fern: An Independent Woman*
Wills, Garry, *Lincoln at Gettysburg: The Words that Remade America*

CULTURE AND CRITICISM

Aldridge, John, *Talents and Technicians: Literary Chic and the New Assembly-Line Fiction*
Aufderheide, Patricia, ed., *Beyond PC: Toward a Politics of Understanding*
Bell, Derrick, *Faces at the Bottom of the Well*
Berman, Paul, ed., *Debating PC: The Controversy Over Political Correctness on College Campuses*
Broyard, Anatole, *Intoxicated by My Illness*
Buckley, William F., Jr., *In Search of Anti-Semitism*
Didion, Joan, *After Henry*
French, Marilyn, *The War Against Women*
Galbraith, John Kenneth, *The Culture of Contentment*
Gates, Henry Louis, Jr., *Loose Canons: Notes on the Culture Wars*
Hentoff, Nat, *Free Speech for Me but not for Thee: How the American Left and Right Relentlessly Censor Each Other*
Kaminer, Wendy, *I'm Dysfunctional, You're Dysfunctional: The Recovery Movement and Other Self-Help Fashions*
Maclean, Norman, *Young Men and Fire*
Medved, Michael, *Hollywood vs. America: Popular Culture and the War on Traditional Values*
Morrison, Toni, *Playing in the Dark: Whiteness and the Literary Imagination*
O'Rourke, P.J., *Give War a Chance: Eyewitness Accounts of Mankind's Struggle Against Tyranny, Injustice, and Alcohol-Free Beer*
Sheehy, Gail, *The Silent Passage*
Thomas, Lewis, *The Fragile Species*
Twitchell, James B., *Carnival Culture: The Trashing of Taste in America*

POETRY

Bly, Robert, *What Have I Ever Lost By Dying?*
Brown, Rosellen, *A Rosellen Brown Reader: Selected Poetry and Prose*
Carruth, Hayden, *Collected Shorter Poems, 1946–1991*
Clifton, Lucille, *Quilting: Poems 1987–1990*
Dickey, James, *The Whole Motion: Collected Poems, 1948–1992*
Gallagher, Tess, *Moon Crossing Bridge*
Garrigue, Jean, *Selected Poems*
Gluck, Louise, *The Wild Iris*
Levertov, Denise, *Evening Train*
Matthews, William, *Selected Poems and Translations, 1969–1991*
Millay, Edna St. Vincent, *Edna St. Vincent Millay: Selected Poems*, edited by Colin Falck
Momaday, N. Scott, *In the Presence of the Sun: Stories and Poems, 1961–1991*
Old, Sharon, *The Father*
Paley, Grace, *New and Collected Poems*
Piercy, Marge, *Mars and Her Children*
Randall, Julia, *The Path to Fairview: New and Selected Poems*
Samaras, Nicholas, *Hands of the Saddlemaker*
Shelnutt, Eve, *First A Long Hesitation*
Simic, Charles, *Hotel Insomnia*
Stern, Gerald, *Bread Without Sugar*
Swenson, May, *The Love Poems of May Swenson*

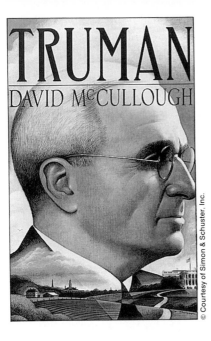

different perspective. McCarthy, married at one time to Edmund Wilson (who wrote a famous parody of a MacLeish poem), belonged to a coterie that believed the artist must remain an oppositional figure, socially rebellious and distrustful of power and government. McCarthy's *Intellectual Memoirs: New York 1936–1938* tells part of the story in her own words. Dan Wakefield's *New York in the Fifties* recalls Greenwich Village and writers like James Baldwin, Norman Mailer, and Gay Talese, a generation then just coming into its own.

Culture and Criticism. The culture wars grew hotter in 1992. American literary critic John Aldridge's *Talents and Technicians: Literary Chic and the New Assembly-Line Fiction* attacks nearly all contemporary writing as superficial and careerist. James B. Twitchell's *Carnival Culture: The Trashing of Taste in America* argues that movies and television encourage vulgarity, violence, and greed to dominate our society. Michael Medved's *Hollywood vs. America: Popular Culture and the War on Traditional Values* takes an even stronger line in condemning the influence of popular culture. More serious and less shrill, John Kenneth Galbraith's *The Culture of Contentment* sees our political life as infected by a complacency that has allowed the powerful to rule at the expense of the common good.

Another battleground was political correctness and censorship. Strong opinions and arguments by various writers on all sides are collected in Patricia Aufderheide's *Beyond PC: Toward a Politics of Understanding* and in *Debating PC: The Controversy Over Political Correctness on College Campuses*, edited by Paul Berman. Nat Hentoff's *Free Speech for Me but not for Thee: How the American Left and Right Relentlessly Censor Each Other* is a spirited attack on those of any political persuasion who put their cause above the protection of the 1st Amendment. Henry Louis Gates, Jr., presented his own thoughtful reflections on these matters in *Loose Canons: Notes on the Culture Wars*.

Social problems were examined by some of our most serious writers in 1992. Derrick Bell's *Faces at the Bottom of the Well* and Toni Morrison's *Playing in the Dark: Whiteness and the Literary Imagination* both seemed to see U.S. culture as defined by an ineradicable racism. Joan Didion's *After Henry* collects her penetrating essays on tensions in the 1980s—from the California writers' strike to New York's Central Park jogger assault. William F. Buckley, Jr.'s *In Search of Anti-Semitism*, inspired by the conservative columnist Pat Buchanan's attacks on the Jewish community, is a thoughtful, reflective essay, followed by contributions by other writers. Marilyn French's *The War Against Women* looks at the history of civilization and finds little progress for women to celebrate.

Poetry. Poetic activity remained lively, with many magazines, independent publications, and public readings gaining new popularity, but no single achievement or debut marked the year. However, there were notable books by Robert Bly, Denise Levertov, Philip Levine, and Grace Paley. Several important collections appeared: James Dickey's *The Whole Motion: Collected Poems, 1948–1992*, Hayden Carruth's *Collected Shorter Poems, 1946–1991*, and N. Scott Momaday's *In the Presence of the Sun: Stories and Poems, 1961–1991*. A chance to reevaluate a poet whose reputation has had its ups and downs was provided by Colin Falck's edition of *Edna St. Vincent Millay: Selected Poems*.

JEROME STERN, *Florida State University*

Children's Literature

The 1992 byword in the children's book field was multiculturalism. After the civil-rights movement picked up steam in the 1960s, there was a concentrated effort to expand children's books past a central cast of white characters, but often the stories were reverential rather than realistic. Today, children's books feature complex, imperfect characters who are rich role models.

Two other trends were the explosion of poetry books for all ages and the growing attention given to artists. As well as several nonfiction series about art, there were several singular individual books, including Pat Cummings' *Talking with Artists* and *Li'l Sis and Uncle Willie*, about black painter William H. Johnson and illustrated with his art.

The 1992 winner of the Newbery Medal was Phyllis Reynolds Naylor for *Shiloh*. David Wiesner won the Caldecott Medal for *Tuesday*.

Multiculturalism. Walter Dean Myers' *Somewhere in the Darkness* is the story of a teenage boy who accompanies his father, recently escaped from prison, on a trip that turns out to be a time of discovery for both of them. *Ajeemah and His Son* by James Berry follows a young West African man and his father after they are captured by slave traders and shipped to the West Indies.

Another aim of multiculturalism is to show that all people share universal experiences. Author/illustrator Patricia Polacco was effective putting forth this idea in 1992 picture books like

The 1992 Newbery Medal winner

Illustration from *Shiloh* by Phyllis Reynolds Naylor.
Illustration copyright © 1992 by Lynne Dennis,
reproduced by permission of Dilys Evans Fine Illustration.

Mrs. Katz and Tush and *Chicken Sunday*. Award-winning adult author Michael Dorris showed readers that the feelings and emotions of a Taino Indian child are not so different from their own in *Morning Girl*.

Picture Books. The explosion in picture books continued, with everything from board books for babies to sophisticated fairy-tale retellings vying for attention. Notable were *The Girl Who Loved Caterpillars*, a story of 12th-century Japan, adapted from a scroll of the period by Jean Merrill and illustrated by Floyd Cooper; Virginia Hamilton's *Drylongso* about a black family on a drought-stricken farm; and *Pancho's Piñata* by Stefan Czernecki and Timothy Rhodes. Trickster tales were also in evidence, most notably *The Fortune-Tellers* by Lloyd Alexander, illustrated by Trina Schart Hyman, and Lois Ehlert's imaginative *Moon Rope*.

Middle-Grade Books. Middle-grade fiction continued to take a less prominent role in children's literature. Series titles such as the Sweet Valley and Babysitters Club books, while continuing to be popular, no longer were glutting the market. Titles by popular authors included Lois Lowry's *Attaboy, Sam!* and Sid Fleischman's *Jim Ugly*, and Cynthia Rylant's *Missing May*, winner of the *Boston Globe*-Horn Book award for fiction.

Nonfiction played a prominent role with books about animals, various cultures, and the environment leading the pack. *I Saw Esau*, a book of childhood rhymes, insults, and riddles, first collected by Peter and Iona Opie in the 1940s, was reillustrated by Maurice Sendak.

Junior High and Young Adult. The young-adult genre continued to produce some of the most praiseworthy titles in 1992. Familiar authors such as Gary Paulsen and Avi were represented. Nonfiction works, handsomely illustrated with photographs, included Russell

The 1992 Caldecott Medal winner

Illustration from *Tuesday* by David Wiesner. Text and illustration copyright © 1991 by David Wiesner. Reprinted by permission of Clarion Books, a Houghton Mifflin Co. imprint. All rights reserved.

SELECTED BOOKS FOR CHILDREN

Picture Books

Aylesworth, Jim. *Old Black Fly*
Carlstrom, Nancy White. *Northern Lullaby*
Cassedy, Sylvia, and Suetake, Kunihiro. *Red Dragonfly on My Shoulder*
Daly, Niki. *Papa Lucky's Shadow*
dePaola, Tomie. *Jingle the Clown*
Heide, Florence Parry, and Gilliland, Judith Heide. *Sami and the Time of the Troubles*
Hepworth, Cathi. *ANTics!*
McDermott, Gerald. *Zomo the Rabbit*
Meddaugh, Susan. *Martha Speaks*
Scieszka, Jon, and Smith, Lane. *The Stinky Cheese Man and Other Fairly Stupid Tales*
Van Allsburg, Chris. *The Widow's Broom*
Young, Ed. *Seven Blind Mice*

The Middle Grades

Avi. *"Who Was That Masked Man, Anyway?"*
Bawden, Nina. *Humbug*
Hurwitz, Johanna. *Roz and Ozzie*
Knight, Margy Burns. *Talking Walls*
Krull, Kathleen. *Gonna Sing My Head Off*
Leverich, Kathleen. *Hilary and the Troublemakers*
Mahy, Margaret. *Underrunners*
Meltzer, Milton. *The Amazing Potato*
Namioka, Lensey. *Yang the Youngest and His Terrible Ear*
Stanley, Diane, and Vennerma, Peter. *The Bard of Avon*
Stanley, Jerry. *Children of the Dust Bowl*
Talbert, Marc. *The Purple Heart*
Taylor, William. *Knitwits*
Vail, Rachel. *Do-Over*

Junior High and High School

Avi. *Blue Heron*
Brooks, Martha. *Two Moons in August*
Doherty, Berlie. *Dear Nobody*
Fine, Anne. *The Book of the Banshee*
Haskins, James. *Thurgood Marshall: A Life for Justice*
Laird, Elizabeth. *Kiss the Dust*
O'Dell, Scott, and Hall, Elizabeth. *Thunder Rolling in the Mountains*
Powell, Randy. *Is Kissing a Girl Who Smokes like Licking an Ashtray?*
Salisbury, Graham. *Blue Skin of the Sea*
Vogel, Ilse-Margret. *Bad Times, Good Friends*
Whitelaw, Nancy. *Theodore Roosevelt Takes Charge*
Wilson, Budge. *The Leaving and Other Stories*

Freedman's *An Indian Winter;* Jim Murphy's *The Long Road to Gettysburg;* and the life of President John F. Kennedy, *A Twilight Struggle* by Barbara Harrison and Daniel Terris.

ILENE COOPER
Editor, Children's Books,"Booklist" magazine

Canadian Literature: English

In a year that saw Canadian book publishers struggling to survive, they welcomed the federal government's promise of C$140 million over five years. But because of a slack economy and the government making its goods and services tax (GST) apply to book sales, some publishers did not survive, and others were forced into cutbacks. However, although profits were weak, the number and quality of new books remained strong. A bright spot in publishing was that Vancouver's small publisher, Talonbooks, celebrated its 25th year of producing mainly literary books.

Nonfiction. Political books were of major interest in 1992. Mordecai Richler's *Oh Canada! Oh Quebec! Requiem for a Divided Country* enraged many Quebec separatists, who favor seceding from Canada. Richler roundly criticized Quebec's banning English signs in that province, yet demanding French as well as English be available in the rest of Canada.

French Canadian writer Laurier LaPierre contributed *Canada, My Canada, What Happened?,* in which he passionately urged both English- and French-speaking Canadians to study their common roots and maintain a united country.

Preston Manning, leader of the new populist Reform Party, contributed his autobiography, *The New Canada.* An evangelical Christian, he wants fiscal responsibility and "no more pandering to Quebec." The Reform Party was also the subject of *Storming Babylon,* by Sydney Sharpe and Don Brai, who discussed Manning's fundamentalist religion and his party's appeal to those unhappy with the federal government.

Another book expressing unhappiness with government was *A Capital Scandal,* by Robert Fife and John Warren. Well-researched, it gives a list of extravagant spending and waste by people in Ottawa with political power.

Popular Pierre Berton once again made history come alive in his *Niagara: A History of the Falls.* The 50th anniversary of the Allies' raid on the German-held French port of Dieppe in World War II was remembered in *Dieppe: Tragedy to Triumph,* by Denis and Shelagh Whitaker. In the self-help category were psychologist Stanley Corey's *The Left-Hander Syndrome,* and Keith Anderson and Roy MacSkimming's *On Your Own Again: The Down-to-Earth Guide to Getting Through a Divorce or Separation and Getting On With Your Life.*

Poetry. Canadian poet bill bissett, who scorns capital letters in his name and in his work, also has his own ideas on spelling, as evidenced by the title of his latest volume, *incorrect thots.* Michael Ondaatje's well crafted *The Cinnamon Peeler,* containing poems from 1963 to 1990, met with praise, as did the memorable characters in J. E. Sorrell's *On the Other Side of the River.*

Fiction. Also well-received in the fiction category was Michael Ondaatje's third novel, *The English Patient,* the compelling tale of an injured World War II English flyer who takes refuge with three companions in a deserted Italian village. *For Art's Sake,* a novel about thieves who steal some priceless pictures, is the latest offering of W. O. Mitchell, one of Canada's favorite storytellers.

Poet John Steffler's first novel, *The Afterlife of George Cartwright,* received exceptionally high praise. Canadian history's real George Cartwright wrote a journal of his experiences

Veteran Canadian author Mordecai Richler wonders why Canadian anglophones and francophones cannot "learn to celebrate what binds them together" in "Oh Canada! Oh Quebec! Requiem for a Divided Country."

© Christopher Morris

Photos, © Courtesy of Alfred A. Knopf

in 18th-century Labrador. Steffler takes off from there to describe the recollections of George Cartwright, ghost, after his death. Janet Turner Hospital's fifth novel, *The Last Magician,* tells how one violent act resonates in the lives of those involved.

Likely Stories: A Postmodern Sampler, edited by George Bowering and Linda Hutcheon, includes short stories by 24 authors, among whom are Alice Munro, Margaret Atwood, and Timothy Findley. *Things As They Are?* is Saskatchewan writer Guy Vanderhaeghe's second award-winning short-story collection. Collected stories by Leon Rooke appeared in *Who Do You Love?* and *The Happiness of Others.*

Barbara Gowdy's stories in *We So Seldom Look on Love* are anything but ordinary, and increase her reputation for shocking tales cleverly told. Editor Robert Caplan's *Cape Breton Book of the Night* gathers tales of mystery and violence. Internationally famous Margaret Atwood's *Good Bones* is a collection of wise and witty short pieces.

DAVID SAVAGE, *Free-lance Writer*

English Literature

English fiction in 1992 displayed in subject matter and imagination, as well as in the cultural origins of the authors, a diversity as far-reaching as the Commonwealth. In that vein, the Pakistan-born Zulfikar Ghose in *The Triple Mirror of the Self* does nothing to diminish his reputation as an author of lyrical, if at times difficult, prose. Ahdaf Soueif's *In the Eye of the Sun* explores the English world of modern Egypt and enjoys a special status as an Arabic novel authentically written in English. Naguib Mahfouz's *Sugar Street: The Cairo Trilogy III* (translated by William Maynard Hutchins and Angele Botros Samaan) joins the previously published *Palace Walk* and *Palace of Desire* to complete the Nobel Prize-winning author's tril-

ogy focusing on a family in Egypt through the two world wars.

In a more traditionally English mode, the prose of Jim Crace's *Arcadia* pulses with a lyricism suggestive of one's associations with his title. Peter Ackroyd's novel, *English Music,* treats the familiar (English gardens, paintings, literature, and music) as the living continuity that constitutes the distinctly English tradition. Among the more familiar names in recent British fiction is Kingsley Amis; his *The Russian Girl* finds the author less interested in plot and character than in a discourse on the nature of art. Peter Costello's novel *The Life of Leopold Bloom* is an example of fiction drawing its subject if not style from a well-known novel. *Serenity House* by Christopher Hope, a comic treatment of the care of the elderly, expands the context of the author's wit by also exposing the absurdities of contemporary social life. In the short-story category, Doris Lessing's 18-story collection, *London Observed: Stories and Sketches,* offers entertainment.

In 1992 two novelists—Michael Ondaatje and Barry Unsworth—shared the Booker Prize, Britain's most prestigious literary honor. *The English Patient* by Michael Ondaatje is set in Tuscany in 1945, where a villa serves to attract several remnants of a once predominantly British world; ruins abound, both spiritual and physical. Barry Unsworth's award-winning novel, *Sacred Hunger,* set in the slave-trade world of 1752, concerns a loss of paradise and the fall of man.

Nonfiction. As though fiction writers led lives more fascinating than those they imagined, dominant again in the expansive category of nonfiction were biography and editions of letters of famous authors. *Robert Bridges: A Biography* by Catherine Phillips and Norman White's *Hopkins: A Literary Biography* should do much to revive interest in two of the great

British novelist Doris Lessing, 72, presented ''The Real Thing,'' a collection of short stories in which the city of London is a character in its own right. The series appeared in Britain under the title ''London Observed: Stories and Sketches.'' Another of her works, ''African Laughter,'' appeared late in 1992.

© Ingrid Von Kruse

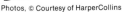

Photos, © Courtesy of HarperCollins

talents of modern English poetry. Of special note for its novel approach to authorship as opposed to writing itself, Michael Millgate's *Testamentary Acts: Browning, Tennyson, James, and Hardy* examines these writers' attempts to assure their literary reputations for posterity. Finally, the awaited second volume of Martin Stannard's biography appeared— *Evelyn Waugh: No Abiding City, 1939–1966.*

For those who favor more intimate, if episodic, glimpses of writers and the chance to form one's own opinion of them, the publication of their letters is particularly welcome. *The Gonne-Yeats Letters, 1893–1938,* edited by Anna McBride White and A. Norman Jeffares, reveals the intensity and complexity of affection between the great poet and his sometime muse, Maud Gonne. However, volume one of *The Selected Letters of Bertrand Russell: The Private Years (1884–1914),* edited by Nicholas Griffin reveals the concerns of the philosopher early in life but little of his thought. And for those still intrigued by the open intimacies of Bloomsbury (which by now must be regarded as a cottage industry), Nigel Nicolson edited *Vita and Harold: The Letters of Vita Sackville-West and Harold Nicolson, 1910–1962.*

Of a more social interest, Mary Louise Pratt's *Imperial Eyes: Travel Writing and Transculturation* examines this sub-genre from a political perspective. Her account includes nature writing as well as travel narratives as early as those of 1750. Hugh Trevor-Roper offers a historical work in his lucid analytical style, *From the Counter-Revolution to Glorious Revolution,* in which he unabashedly focuses on the great thinkers of the times, including Thomas More, Erasmus, Montaigne, and Gibbon. For those who find interest in matters of India, particularly a dark incident of the British presence, Richard Terrell's edition of John Chalmers' *Letters from the Indian Mutiny*

1857–1859 sheds new light on the causes of that tragic affair. And Bruce Palling's *India: A Literary Companion* is testimony to the enduring fascination of the English imagination with that subcontinent.

Poetry. English poetry published during the year exhibits a rich diversity in scene and voice, as though to assert the vitality of the poet's region. *Dark Ages,* a new collection by David Hartnett, is distinguished by its fluency, imagery, and unobtrusive formal quality; it draws its title from a sequence of 15 poems centered on reflections on the landscape of Sussex. William Scammell saw two volumes of his poetry published in 1992. His *Bleeding Heart Yard* and *The Game: Tennis Poems* fuse a Wordsworthian rural sensibility with an urbane wit. *Selected Poetry* of Hugh Mac Diarmid, a Scottish poet of great and diverse inventiveness, appeared to whet the thirst for more. Douglas Dunn, well-known poet in his own right, edited an ample collection, *The Faber Book of Twentieth-Century Scottish Poetry,* complete with a sound introduction entitled ''Language and Liberty.'' Medbh McGuckian's volume of poetry, *Marconi's Cottage,* seeks to affirm a European perspective and influence on contemporary Irish verse. Michael Hamburger, long known as an adroit translator of European poetry into English, saw published his own *Roots in the Air,* poems that subscribe to no set school and exert an uneasy claim on the reader's attention. Ted Hughes, Britain's poet laureate, published *Rain-Charm For the Duchy and Other Laureate Poems,* testimony to the seriousness that he brings to his post. Thom Gunn's *The Man With the Night Sweats,* which appeared ten years after his last book of poems, reveals a stark yet lyrical reality. Other poetic works included Jon Silkin's *The Lens-Breakers* and George Barker's *Street Ballads,* published posthumously.

DONALD L. JENNERMANN
Indiana State University

World Literature*

Several of the major European literatures enjoyed an excellent year in 1992, as did Asia and, to a somewhat lesser extent, Africa and the Near East. Particularly strong among the Europeans were the Germans and the French.

German. Leading the way among German writers were the two towering figures of Günter Grass and the late Heinrich Böll. Despite a vow several years ago to forswear any further fiction writing, Grass issued a new novel in 1992, *Toad Calls.* He again used, as in such earlier novels as *The Rat* and *The Flounder,* a grotesque but fantastically anthropomorphic creature as the centerpiece of a wildly imaginative narrative that decries the current state of the world in matters ecological, political, social, and moral. From Böll came what would have been his first full-fledged novel, had he ignored the advice of older colleagues and published it upon its completion in 1949. *The Angel Fell Silent* paints a grim but open-ended and not wholly pessimistic picture of daily life in Cologne amid the immediate aftermath of World War II, as one family tries to put back together the pieces of their small world and get on with their lives, loves, and careers and rediscover or refashion their ambitions and dreams.

Jurek Becker's latest novel, *Heartless Amanda,* drew raves for its innovative and lively interweaving of three narratives by the heroine's three successive lovers over the last decade: a young newspaper editor; a blacklisted East German writer; and a reporter from the West. Other highlights included the poet-novelist Christoph Meckel's new novel, *Shalamun's Papers,* and such nonfiction works as the essay collection *Fly Torment* by 1981 Nobel Prize recipient Elias Canetti and the wise and witty sketchbook *On Dead Ground* by East German émigré poet and prose writer Günter Kunert.

French. The world beyond France's borders figured large in several of the year's best French books. Emmanuel Roblès' *Grass Among the Ruins* draws from both today's headlines and the annals of 20th-century European history for its tale of love and passion, set against a backdrop of the atrocities of war and totalitarianism. It is written in a sometimes realistic, sometimes allegorical manner vaguely reminiscent of such classics as *The Plague* by Albert Camus. Patrick Grainville's *Anger* immerses its young hero Damien (and the reader) in the colorful and often beautiful but also very dangerous underworld of modern-day Rio as he pursues his elusive object of desire, the lovely and dedicated teacher and social worker Marine. Canadian-born Anne Hébert creates a mystery-laden, fantastic fairy tale in *The Child Full of Dreams,* replete with such archetypal figures as the Valkyrie-like horsewoman (and horse thief) Lydie. The book is set largely within the primeval Canadian forest and on vast landscapes under seemingly endless skies where the natural world blends seamlessly with the supernatural. Pierre-Jean Remy's *Algeria Along the Seine* divides its attention between Paris and France's former North African colony as it presents an account of a younger generation discovering the absurdity and horror of a war which both could have and should have been avoided by their elders. Amin Maalouf's somewhat programmatic novel about women's rights and powers, *The First Century After Beatrice,* looks two decades into the future to a time when a fertility powder has produced such a preponderance of males among all species that the resulting imbalance in nature may soon depopulate the world, unless more people—like the right-thinking narrator—opt for daughters and recapture the feminine and maternal side of their humanity. And the Lebanese-Egyptian native Andrée Chedid gathered 17 of her superb short stories of the last decade under the title *To Death, to Life.*

Russian. Two works of fiction and two of nonfiction highlighted the year in Russian letters. Victor Erofeyev's ambitiously complex postmodernist novel *Russian Beauty,* written a decade ago, tracks the course of a Dostoevskian heroine through a series of affairs, scandals, and atonements in the unabashedly materialistic milieu of "cosmonauts, ambassadors, and underworld millionaires" of the late 1970s and early 1980s. Tatyana Tolstaya's second collection of short stories, *Sleepwalker in a Fog,* garnered praise similar to that enjoyed by her earlier *On the Golden Porch* for the elegant musicality of its prose, the timelessness of its themes, the mordancy of its wit, and the spontaneity and exuberance of its style. Andrei Bitov added the attribute of travel writer to his reputation as one of his country's leading novelists, producing in *A Captive of the Caucasus* an inspired, thoughtful, and engrossing account not only of his extended residence in Armenia but—as in the best travel writing—of his own personal voyage of self-discovery as well. And the 90-year-old Nina Berberova surveyed more than six decades of Russian cultural and sociopolitical life in her memoir *The Italics Are Mine,* ranging in time and place from St. Petersburg of the early 1920s, to Paris of the late 1930s and the war years, to the United States of the 1950s and 1960s. She touches on such greats as Gorky, Pasternak, Bunin, Roman Jakobson, and Nabokov.

Other European Languages. From the rest of Europe and the Americas came several notable new books in 1992. The 1980 Nobel laureate, Polish poet and essayist Czeslaw Milosz, issued two new works during the year. *Provinces* is his first new volume of poetry since *Collected Poems* in 1988 and is a remarkably vigorous and clear-sighted performance by the octogenarian author as he meditates on youth

*Titles translated

and mortality, the redemptive powers of language, the solace of compassion and beauty, and the nature of "the human." In *Beginning with My Streets,* Milosz returns to the Lithuania of his youth in Vilnius and discusses, through essays and letters, a variety of topics including time and ephemerality, nationalism and religion, a number of the author's friends over the years, and several literary figures and authors who in some way have touched his own life and work. The Romanian writer Norman Manea, like Milosz and Berberova now a U.S. resident, made his debut in English with two recent works. *On Clowns,* subtitled "The Dictator and the Artist," comprises a series of essays relating directly to life in Romania under the Ceaușescu regime; *October, Eight O'Clock* is a single narrative loosely divided into several separate tales, all set in the labor camps of Romania and the Ukraine during World War II and possessed of such distinction and linguistic richness as to evoke among European critics comparisons with the likes of Kafka, Musil, and Bruno Schulz. *A Hungarian Romance* by Agnes Hankiss reaches back four centuries in Hungary's turbulent history—to a time when the country's independence had been lost to corrupt foreign powers—to tell a story of love and intrigue that casts a revealing light on recent events in Hungary and challenges age-old assumptions about men and women, language, and history itself. The prolific Brazilian novelist Jorge Amado's 1944 novel *The Golden Harvest* made its long-delayed appearance in English in 1992; set among the cacao boom and bust of the 1930s in the province of Bahia, the book dramatizes the plantation workers' plight and the viciousness of the free-market system in its devastation of so many lives and fortunes, but does so in a remarkably undidactic and vividly entertaining fashion.

Africa. Leading the year's literary harvest from Africa were two works in English and two in French. *Ancestral Voices* by South Africa's Etienne van Heerden traces five generations of an Afrikaner farm family in exhaustive and revealing detail and Old Testament scope and weight. Chenjerai Hove of Zimbabwe followed up his award-winning 1990 novel *Bones* with *Shadows,* the story of two innocent young lovers caught up in a world of poverty and harsh colonial law where people have little or no control over their lives. Tahar Ben Jelloun of Algeria, winner of France's Goncourt Prize in 1987, brought out *The Blind Angel,* a collection of 14 short stories set in southern Italy and Sicily and together constituting chapters of a single "novel about the Mafia" (the working title of the still-uncompleted work) and the group's pervasive reach into every aspect of life in these regions. Henri Lopes of the Congo recounts in *On the Other Shore* the lyric and mysterious tale of a young Caribbean woman's "internal voyage" back to Africa, where she begins to fathom her origins and heritage and to gain some sense of what the future holds.

Middle East. *Sugar Street,* the third and final installment of *The Cairo Trilogy* by Egypt's 1988 Nobel Prize winner Naguib Mahfouz, presents a bitter and pessimistic yet vital and wonderfully readable Dickensian account of the unraveling and decline of the aging patriarch Ahmad Abd al-Jawad's family through the 1940s, its completion coinciding with the coming to power of Gamel Abdel Nasser in 1952. Mahfouz's countrywoman Ahdaf Soueif took the unusual route of writing her massive and extremely impressive novel *In the Eye of the Sun* directly in English, telling an extraordinary tale of sexual politics spanning both the traditional Arab world (Egypt) and the modern-day West (England) and overcoming barriers not only physical and geographic but emotional and existential as well. Lebanese-born Hanan al-Shaykh, rated by many as the Arab world's finest woman writer, brought out *Women of Sand and Myrrh.* The work is a set of four intertwined first-person narratives that paint a poetic yet hard-edged portrait of a wealthy Arab country whose women, even among the rich and privileged, are forced to remain hidden behind veils yet nevertheless find outlets that permit them to survive psychologically. *Mr. Mani* by Israeli novelist Avraham B. Yehoshua made its much-awaited appearance in English, ingeniously and movingly tracing a history of exile and periodic return through six generations of a Jewish family from 1982 back to the mid-18th century.

Asia. Two younger writers led China's literary production in 1992. Han Shaogong's *Homecoming and Other Stories* revealed a mid-1980s shift from social realism to an experimental style heavily indebted to García Márquez and Kundera, among others, yet continued the author's obsession with Chinese history and tradition in his search for the causes of the spiritual void left in his nation by the Cultural Revolution. *Brocade Valley* by Wang Anyi offered a trilogy of lyric, intimate novellas on the shocking (for China) theme of women involved in extramarital affairs; it became a best-seller and effectively exploded the sexual puritanism that has characterized official Chinese writing for decades. Japan's preeminent novelist Kenzaburō Ōe brought out *When I Was Truly Young,* seemingly an autobiographical novel about a college student still only thinking of writing novels, but also an intensely personal probing into the depths of time, memory, guilt, and the unconscious. And lastly, the best of the year's production on the Indian subcontinent was *Cracking India* by Bapsi Sidhwa, a short and apparently simple novel (it is narrated by a little girl from a well-off Parsee family in Lahore, now in Pakistan) about the 1947 partition.

WILLIAM RIGGAN, *"World Literature Today"*

LOS ANGELES

Los Angeles in 1992 experienced a major riot; controversy over its police chief; and tight city, county, and school budgets. Area floods in February also contributed to the tumult. More positive was the end of water rationing in April and a new commuter rail system that began operations in October. In September, Tom Bradley, the city's mayor since July 1973, announced that he would not seek reelection in 1993.

Riot. The trial of four Los Angeles police officers charged with the March 1991 illegal beating of Rodney King, a black motorist, was moved to suburban Ventura county. In April an all-white jury found the men not guilty on all charges, and rioting ensued. Arson, looting, and assaults occurred over a broader area than in the Watts riot of 1965, with thousands of arrests, 2,383 major injuries, and more than 50 riot-related deaths. The Los Angeles Fire Department in mid-May indicated that 623 fires had been set. (Earlier figures had run to more than 5,000.) Factors seen as causing the riot and its spread included: the unexpected verdict; disbelief expressed by some whites; angry remarks by Mayor Bradley; the curious delay in taking action by the police, blamed on Police Chief Daryl F. Gates; and the slow deployment of the National Guard. Much of the looting was carried out by Latinos as well as blacks and was seen as a crime of opportunity, not as a social statement. (*See* SPECIAL REPORT/ CITIES).

Rebuild LA. Recovery was led by the non-profit Rebuild LA group that sought to create jobs, build markets, provide personal safety, and help residents to own their small businesses. But six months after the riot, Rebuild LA was not succeeding in its mission. It had 48 staff members and an unwieldy board of 67 members consisting of many interest groups that bickered over small things. The three co-chairs, including the prominent businessman Peter Ueberroth, faced a frustrating decentralized process.

Critics complained of too few business leaders involved, too little help from state and national governments, and too much government red tape. Study groups found the same riot causes as those that led to unrest in cities during the 1960s, with excessive police aggression and bias as added factors. The primary problems relating to poverty or inadequate education or skills were underplayed. Also, a University of California, Los Angeles opinion survey showed that social attitudes after the riots were unchanged.

Police Chief. At the time of the riot, Mayor Bradley was pressing Gates, police chief since 1978, to retire. After a cat-and-mouse game as

At the request of Los Angeles Mayor Tom Bradley, Peter Ueberroth, chairman of the 1984 Los Angeles Olympic Organizing Committee, served on the Rebuild LA committee, which was organized to bring back the city following the 1992 riots.

to when he would leave, Gates complied on June 30 and was replaced by Willie L. Williams. The former head of the Philadelphia police department was the first outsider in 43 years and the first black ever to be named chief.

Budgets. Since the adoption of Proposition 13 in 1979, California local governments have depended upon state grants-in-aid. In 1992 a state budget shortage compounded local problems. The city's budget of $3.8 billion involved cuts in services for libraries, parks, recreation centers, street resurfacing, and police. More cuts were avoided by delving into redevelopment and airport funds.

The supervisors approved a $13 billion county budget. Sharp cuts were made in almost every department—sparing only welfare, hospitals, and law enforcement. Employee pay and benefits of about $250 million were delayed. Part of the county debt was refinanced, and other funds were taken on a one-time basis. Nonetheless, the county would fall $2.2 billion short of maintaining service levels. Taxes were not to be raised, but some $35 million in service-fee increases were planned.

Schools. The school board had cut more than $1 billion from its budget since 1988. In 1992, with a budget of about $4 billion, it covered a $400 million shortfall through layoffs and pay cuts, with some employees cut by 11.5%. In September, Bill Anton, the first Latino superintendent, resigned after 26 months, criticizing the board for "micro management" and for allowing undue influence by the teachers' union. Sidney Thompson, the first black to head the school system, was named as interim superintendent in October. In 1992, for the first time, all city schools operated on a year-round calendar.

CHARLES R. ADRIAN
University of California, Riverside

LOUISIANA

Louisiana was beginning preparations in late 1992 to open a gambling casino in New Orleans, even as a budget crisis threatened to devastate higher education in the state.

Gambling. Legalized gambling already was flourishing, as hundreds of video poker machines popped up in lounges across the state and the state's weekly multimillion-dollar lottery drawing completed its first full year. But gambling revenue was not expected to be enough to solve a huge state budget deficit that leading university administrators said could ruin higher education in Louisiana.

In spite of some strong local opposition from people who feared a New Orleans casino would cause increased crime, corruption, and traffic, the legislature approved a bill pushed by Gov. Edwin W. Edwards to establish a casino

---

LOUISIANA • Information Highlights

Area: 47,752 sq mi (123 677 km²).
Population (July 1, 1991 est.): 4,252,000.
Chief Cities (1990 census): Baton Rouge, the capital, 219,531; New Orleans, 496,938; Shreveport, 198,525.
Government (1992): *Chief Officers—*governor, Edwin W. Edwards (D); lt. gov., Melina Schwegmann (D). *Legislature—*Senate, 39 members; House of Representatives, 105 members.
State Finances (fiscal year 1991): *Revenue,* $10,764,000,000; *expenditure,* $10,537,000,000.
Personal Income (1991): $ 61,970,000,000; per capita, $15,046.
Labor Force (June 1992): *Civilian labor force,* 1,968,400; *unemployed,* 151,700 (7.7% of total force).
Education: *Enrollment* (fall 1990)—public elementary schools, 586,183; public secondary, 198,574; colleges and universities, 186,599. *Public school expenditures* (1990), $2,872,100,000.

---

in the heart of the city. Even some New Orleans casino proponents were not happy with provisions that give the city no power to license or tax the casino. All public revenue derived from its operations would be funneled directly into state coffers.

Characteristically, the legislature involved itself in several controversies. Transforming themselves from lawmakers to delegates to a special constitutional convention called to deal with tax reform, legislators accomplished nothing. As a result, the state faced a $700 million shortfall for 1993, a state of affairs that could gut the budgets of Louisiana State University and the University of New Orleans. Administrators were trying to rally the support of students and citizens alike to persuade Edwards to call a special legislative session to deal with the crisis.

Legislation. The legislature also weakened one of a number of environmental laws passed during the administration of former Gov. Buddy Roemer, a strong environmentalist, approving a cut in a tax imposed on industries that create hazardous wastes. Legislators rejected an attempt to impose more control on small, church-run day-care centers, some of which use corporal punishment on children.

Lawmakers also dealt a defeat to organized labor, killing a proposal that would have limited the state's right-to-work law, which prohibits a worker's joining a union in order to get a job. The legislature approved the first-ever black-majority district for the state public-service commission and new minority districts for the board of elementary and secondary education and the U.S. Congress. But, because Louisiana did not grow as rapidly as most states in the 1980s, legislative redistricting eliminated one of its eight seats in Congress.

Elections. Democrats profited from the change, because the state went from having an evenly divided delegation in the U.S. House to one of four Democrats and three Republicans. Incumbent Democrats reelected were William

© Alan S. Weiner/NYT Pictures

In the first year of Gov. Edwin Edwards' fourth term, Louisiana agreed to permit casino gambling in New Orleans and approve a constitutional convention to study the tax system.

Jefferson of New Orleans, William Tauzin of Thibodaux, and James Hayes of Lafayette. Former state senator Cleo Fields of Baton Rouge, also a Democrat, was elected in the new black-majority district, which wends its way through many of the state's urban areas outside New Orleans. Incumbent Republicans Bob Livingston of Metairie, Jim McCrery of Shreveport, and Richard Baker of Baton Rouge were reelected. Reapportionment had pitted McCrery and Baker against other incumbent congressmen, with McCrery defeating Democrat Jerry Huckaby of Ringgold and Baker besting fellow Republican Clyde Holloway of Forest Hill.

Sen. John Breaux of Crowley easily won reelection. The state's nine electoral votes went to Gov. Bill Clinton (D).

JOSEPH W. DARBY III
"The Times Picayune," New Orleans

MAINE

Maine voters made headlines in 1992 by showing the depth of their impatience with politics as usual.

Elections. Incumbent President George Bush failed to escape finishing last in the three-way presidential election in the state he often has called home. Maine voters turned out in record numbers to give Arkansas Gov. Bill Clinton 39% of the vote; Bush and Ross Perot split the balance, 30.39% for the president and 30.44% for Perot. The percentage of the vote taken by Perot was about the highest he received in any state.

More than 600,000 persons—close to 74% of Maine's registered voters—cast their ballots as the state's turnout percentage led the nation.

And while Mainers returned incumbents to the state's two U.S. congressional seats, they left no doubt about their wish to send new faces to the Maine legislature.

First District U.S. Rep. Thomas Andrews, a Portland Democrat, handily defeated Linda Bean, a Republican. Bean—a granddaughter of the founder of L. L. Bean, the Freeport retailer and mail-order giant—spent more than $900,000 of her personal funds on a campaign that got her 35% of the 1st District vote. In the 2d District's three-way race, incumbent Republican Olympia Snowe kept her House seat with 48% of the vote; her Democratic opponent, Patrick McGowan, finished with 42%; and Jonathan Carter, the candidate of the newly established Green Party, got 10%.

The 116th Legislature would have more new faces than any in recent history. Angered by the failure of the 115th Legislature's efforts to solve Maine's budgetary and economic problems, voters showed their dissatisfaction with most incumbents. Veteran state Sen. Charles Pray, Senate president for the previous two terms, lost his reelection bid to Republican Stephen Hall; and Senate Majority Leader Nancy Clark of Freeport, a 14-term Democrat, was upset by Phillip Harriman. Although the Democrats' recent large majorities in both the Maine Senate and House were cut severely, the party emerged with control of both.

Another group that wanted change and got it were the 173 citizens of Long Island in Casco Bay, who voted 129–44 to secede from the city of Portland and incorporate as a separate township in July 1993. Other Casco Bay islanders, who long have believed their city taxes were not producing commensurate benefits, were expected to follow suit soon.

Feeling the pinch of Maine's three-year economic malaise, voters defeated several bond issues, among them one that would have raised money to buy up railroad rights-of-way for the hoped-for rebirth of rail passenger service to southern Maine. Voters did approve

---

MAINE • Information Highlights

Area: 33,265 sq mi (86 156 km²).

Population (July 1, 1991 est.): 1,235,000.

Chief Cities (1990 census): Augusta, the capital, 21,325; Portland, 64,358; Lewiston, 39,757; Bangor, 33,181.

Government (1992): *Chief Officers*—governor, John R. McKernan, Jr. (R); secretary of state, G. William Diamond (D). *Legislature*—Senate, 33 members; House of Representatives, 151 members.

State Finances (fiscal year 1991): *Revenue,* $3,222,000,000; *expenditure,* $3,515,000,000.

Personal Income (1991): $21,548,000,000; per capita, $17,454.

Labor Force (June 1992): *Civilian labor force,* 655,100; *unemployed,* 46,600 (7.1% of total force).

Education: *Enrollment* (fall 1990)—public elementary schools, 155,218; public secondary, 59,931; colleges and universities, 57,186. *Public school expenditures* (1990), $1,115,172,000.

a $12 million bond issue for water-pollution-control systems and $10 million to be used as a loan fund for municipal recycling efforts and the cleanup or closing of municipal landfill dumps.

Economy. Heeding the report of a blue-ribbon commission issued in August, a special session of the legislature enacted compromise reforms that were acceptable to those who complained that worker's compensation costs were driving jobs out of the state, and to those who claimed Maine workers were not protected adequately.

In spite of widespread manufacturing layoffs and plant closings, the Maine economic news was not all bad. L. L. Bean reported a 5.2% increase in sales—to $628 million—for the year's first quarter. The city council of Portland approved spending $1.5 million to improve the sports stadium Hadlock Field, soon to be the home of a Double A–Eastern League baseball team.

JOHN N. COLE, *"Maine Times"*

MALAYSIA

In 1992, Malaysia's National Front governing coalition, led by UMNO, the United Malay National Organization, faced a variety of challenges from within and outside the country.

The Monarchy. At home, UMNO took steps to restrict the powers of the monarchy. The position of king is rotated among the hereditary rulers from nine of Malaysia's 13 states. In mid-July the government produced a document forbidding rulers to participate in business except through a trust, and obliging them to accept the advice of the chief minister of their state.

Religious and Ethnic Issues. Islamic extremism continued to be a challenge. The Malacca state government banned *dakwah* (missionary) activities by the Tabliq group, while Kelantan state, controlled by the fundamentalist Parti Islam, planned to implement Islamic criminal law. In August the second Malaysian Chinese Economic Congress adopted a resolution demanding an end to the official distinction between Bumiputras (Malay sons of the soil) and non-Bumis, by which Malays are favored over Chinese. The National Front walks a very fine line trying to control the more extreme Malays, while reassuring the country's Chinese and Indian communities. Malays comprise 59% of the population; Chinese, 32%; and Indians, 9%.

Rain-Forest Destruction. Internationally, Malaysia continued to take criticism over the plight of the displaced Penan people and for the destruction of their rain-forest homeland in the state of Sarawak. In February environmentalist Anderson Mutang was arrested and detained briefly, and in March two German writers from *GEO* magazine were denied entry into the logging area. In April the government took steps to restrict those who could receive logging concessions in the country.

Economy. Malaysia's economy continued to expand in 1992. Gross-domestic-product (GDP) growth was forecast to be 7.5%, while inflation could exceed 5%. Unemployment was down to 5.4%, or near full employment. The government made provisions for the recruitment and registration of foreign laborers to meet the country's employment needs. New and badly needed infrastructure projects include an airport at Johore, continued construction of the national highway system, and a five-year project by Telekom Malaysia for digital phone systems.

Malaysia has decided to speed up its timetable for meeting requirements of the recently established ASEAN (Association of Southeast Asian Nations) Free Trade Area (AFTA). Malaysia will protect only its most strategic industries for a ten-year period, instead of the 15-year AFTA provision, and will protect other industries for no more than three years.

Foreign Relations. Malaysia concluded another active year in its foreign relations. In June, Prime Minister Mahathir bin Mohamad enhanced his own reputation as spokesman for the Third World at the Earth Summit in Rio, where he defended the policies of the developing countries and challenged the developed states to clean up their own environments. Closer to home, Malaysia continued to work with Singapore to settle the ownership of Batu Puteh, and with Indonesia on the issue of Siipadan and Ligitan islands. Malaysia concluded an agreement with Vietnam for cooperative development of jointly claimed parts of the Spratly Islands chain. Partly motivated by the dispute over the Spratlys, the government previously had placed an order for two warships from Britain, and announced the creation of a RDF (Rapid Deployment Force) of brigade strength.

PATRICK M. MAYERCHAK
Virginia Military Institute

MALAYSIA • Information Highlights

Official Name: Malaysia.
Location: Southeast Asia.
Area: 127,317 sq mi (329 750 km²).
Population (mid-1992 est.): 18,700,000.
Chief City (1980 census): Kuala Lumpur, the capital, 919,610.
Government: *Head of state,* Sultan Azlan Shah, king (elected March 1989). *Head of government,* Mahathir bin Mohamad, prime minister (took office July 1981). *Legislature*—Parliament: Dewan Negara (Senate) and Dewan Ra'ayat (House of Representatives).
Monetary Unit: Ringgit (Malaysian dollar) (2.5562 ringgits equal U.S.$1, Dec. 16, 1992).
Economic Indexes (1991): *Consumer Prices* (1990 = 100), all items, 103.8; food, 104.1. *Industrial Production* (1980 = 100), 255.
Foreign Trade (1991 U.S.$): *Imports,* $36,699,-000,000; *exports,* $34,375,000,000.

MANITOBA

Major news stories in Manitoba during 1992 related to the October national referendum on a constitutional-reform plan. Also of interest was the coldest summer on record and the election of Winnipeg's first woman mayor.

The October Referendum. On October 26, Manitoba was one of six provinces to vote "no" to the package of constitutional amendments proposed by the federal government and referred to as the Charlottetown Accord. The vote was 61.6% against the plan, and 37.8% in favor. Premier Gary Filmon, as well as the leader of the official opposition, both supported the "yes" side strongly.

A major issue in the referendum centered on aboriginal self-government, which had the support of the national aboriginal leader, Ovide Mercredi. Many Manitoba chiefs opposed the concept, however, and it was defeated on most Indian reserves.

The Liberal Party was split over the referendum, with the provincial leader, Sharon Carstairs, heading the "no" forces in the province. Her chief lieutenants supported the "yes" side, as did nearly all prominent federal Liberals. Final results of the referendum were not close, except in the Winnipeg South constituency, where Dorothy Dobbie, the Conservative member of Parliament (MP), had headed a task force on national unity.

Shortly after her victory in the referendum campaign, Carstairs announced her resignation as provincial Liberal leader and her retirement from politics.

Weather and Agriculture. Manitoba had its warmest winter in many years, followed by the coldest summer on record. The old record set in 1885 had been an average June-through-August temperature of 61°F (16.1°C). In 1992 the average temperature for the same months was 60°F (15.7°C). Despite the cold summer, there was an extended agricultural growing season

Susan Thompson, 45-year-old retailer and member of the Economic Advisory Board for the government of Manitoba, was the first woman to be elected mayor of Winnipeg.

that lasted until late October, compared with the normal end in early September. As a result, agricultural production was the second highest in Manitoba's history. Prices, however, remained low.

Net farm income in Manitoba was down from C$484 million in 1990 to C$190 million in 1991. The federal government introduced emergency aid packages amounting to roughly C$40 per acre in late 1991.

Elections. Two by-elections for the provincial election were held in September. The governing Progressive Conservatives (PCs) won one seat and the Liberals won the other seat. In terms of voting percentages, the PCs and the Liberals showed declines of 5.3% and 5.5%, respectively. There was a modest increase for the New Democratic Party (NDP), but independents made the largest gains. There was no change in the overall party representation from the 1990 elections—Conservatives (PC), 30; New Democratic Party (NDP), 20; and Liberals, 7. During the by-election campaign, members of the Long Plains Indian band occupied a former air base in one of the constituencies as part of a land claim. The claim remained unresolved as the year drew to a close.

In municipal elections in October, Susan Thompson became the first woman to be elected mayor of Winnipeg. In a closely fought contest, Thompson—the proprietor of a Winnipeg leather-goods store who had no previous political experience—defeated three former councillors, each of whom had the unofficial support of one of the three main political parties in the province.

MICHAEL KINNEAR
University of Manitoba

MANITOBA • Information Highlights

Area: 250,946 sq mi (649 950 km²).
Population (September 1992): 1,097,200.
Chief Cities (1986 census): Winnipeg, the capital, 594,551; Brandon, 38,708; Thompson, 14,701.
Government (1992): *Chief Officers*—lt. gov., George Johnson; premier, Gary Filmon (Progressive Conservative). *Legislature*—Legislative Assembly, 57 members.
Provincial Finances (1992–93 fiscal year budget): *Revenues,* $5,119,000,000; *expenditures,* $5,450,-000,000.
Personal Income (average weekly earnings, July 1992): $489.18.
Labor Force (September 1992, seasonally adjusted): *Employed* workers, 15 years of age and over, 483,000; *Unemployed,* 9.3%.
Education (1992–93): *Enrollment*—elementary and secondary schools, 219,900 pupils; postsecondary—universities, 21,160; community colleges, 4,240.
(All monetary figures are in Canadian dollars.)

MARYLAND

The year 1992 was a year of belt-tightening for the state of Maryland. The economic distress afflicting much of the United States was compounded in Maryland by a Macy's store closing in Cockeysville and temporary layoffs at a General Motors assembly plant in Baltimore during a strike by United Auto Workers.

Budget. A budget shortfall forced Gov. William Donald Schaefer and the legislature to slash spending by about $850 million. The legislature also enacted major tax increases, totaling $450 million annually: a temporary income-tax increase on the wealthy; a nickel-per-gallon gasoline-tax hike, to 23.5 cents; and a 20-cent increase—to 36 cents per pack—in the cigarette tax. At the same time, the 5% sales tax was extended to prepared foods and some services. The state also gave counties the option of increasing local income taxes to make up for cuts in aid to subdivisions.

Elections. Some 50% of Maryland voters cast ballots for Arkansas Gov. Bill Clinton, the Democratic presidential nominee. President George Bush took 36% of the vote; independent Ross Perot received 14%. In the state's U.S. Senate contest, incumbent Democratic Sen. Barbara Mikulski beat Republican challenger Alan L. Keyes 71% to 29%. By a margin of 61% to 39%, voters in the state approved an abortion-rights law assuring wide access to abortion.

For the first time in the state's history the GOP captured half of the state's U.S. congressional seats—four out of eight. In the 1st District, freshman GOP Rep. Wayne Gilchrest defeated Democratic Rep. Tom McMillen 52%

MARYLAND • Information Highlights

Area: 10,460 sq mi (27 092 km²).
Population (July 1, 1991 est.): 4,860,000.
Chief Cities (1990 census): Annapolis, the capital, 33,187; Baltimore, 736,014; Rockville, 44,835.
Government (1992): *Chief Officers*—governor, William Donald Schaefer (D); lt. gov., Melvin A. Steinberg (D). *General Assembly*—Senate, 47 members; House of Delegates, 141 members.
State Finances (fiscal year 1991): *Revenue*, $12,479,000,000; *expenditure*, $12,576,000,000.
Personal Income (1991): $107,836,000,000; per capita, $22,189.
Labor Force (June 1992): *Civilian labor force*, 2,629,800; *unemployed*, 180,900 (6.9% of total force).
Education: *Enrollment* (fall 1990)—public elementary schools, 526,859; public secondary, 188,317; colleges and universities, 260,494. *Public school expenditures* (1990), $4,143,190,000.

---

to 48%. The two incumbents were pitted against each other by congressional redistricting. In the 2d District, incumbent Republican Helen D. Bentley easily defeated Democratic challenger Michael C. Hickey, Jr., 65% to 35%. In Baltimore's 3d District, incumbent Democrat Benjamin L. Cardin dispatched Republican William T. S. Bricker 74% to 26%.

In suburban Washington's newly drawn, minority-dominated 4th District, Democratic state Sen. Albert Wynn defeated Michele Dyson, 76% to 24%. In the 5th District, incumbent Democrat Steny Hoyer beat back a challenge by Republican Lawrence J. Hogan, Jr., winning 53% to 44%, with 3% going to an independent. In the 6th District, GOP nominee Roscoe G. Bartlett defeated Democratic state Rep. Thomas H. Hattery 54% to 46%. Hattery had defeated the incumbent, Beverly J. Byron,

Albert R. Wynn, a 41-year-old lawyer, was one of an increasing number of blacks to be elected to the U.S. House of Representatives in 1992. A member of Maryland's legislature for ten years, he had been chosen in the state's 4th District.

in the March primary. In the 7th District, Democratic incumbent Kweisi Mfume of Baltimore trounced GOP challenger Kenneth Kondner of Baltimore county, winning 85% of the vote. In the 8th District, incumbent Republican Rep. Constance A. Morella beat Democrat Edward J. Heffernan 72% to 28%.

Legislation. The General Assembly reenacted a requirement that motorcyclists wear helmets. For the third year in a row, a bill banning assault weapons was killed in the state Senate. A domestic-violence bill allowing judges to issue longer protective orders for abused spouses passed. A bill requiring reporting of AIDS cases, but not by patients' names, also passed. Legislation requiring stricter emissions controls on cars failed.

Other. A new $105 million stadium for baseball's Baltimore Orioles—Oriole Park at Camden Yards—opened in April. The state's largest health insurer, Blue Cross and Blue Shield of Maryland, came under fire from the U.S. Senate Permanent Subcommittee on Investigations. The subcommittee found that the company inflated its reserves; that subsidiaries lost tens of millions of dollars; and that millions more had been squandered by executives on luxurious perks. Carl Sardegna, chairman of the board and president of the nonprofit insurer, resigned as chairman and later left the company entirely.

DAN CASEY, *"The Annapolis Capital"*

MASSACHUSETTS

Economic stagnation and increased political competition set the stage for 1992 developments in the Bay State.

Economics. Massachusetts continued to experience one of its most severe and protracted recessions. Fifteen banks failed and the state's flagship high-technology industries had persistent troubles. Such giants as Digital Equipment Corporation, whose founding president, Kenneth Olsen, resigned after 35 years, and Prime Computer Corp. had their first-ever large-scale furloughs of employees. The defense industries fared little better, with corporations such as Raytheon, which supplied the Patriot missile used during the 1991 Persian Gulf war, forced into major retrenchments.

Unemployment averaged 8.5%, substantially above the national average. Home foreclosures rose throughout the year. On the plus side, the state's bond rating was raised substantially because of state spending reductions.

Elections. With the bad economy and a 32-year-old tradition of voting Democratic, Republican presidential prospects were dim from the start. Native son and former U.S. Sen. Paul Tsongas won the March Democratic presidential primary. Bill Clinton went on to carry the state in November, handily beating President George Bush 48% to 29%. Independent Ross Perot took 23% of the vote. Voter turnout of more than 2.7 million set a new state record.

There were no U.S. Senate seats on the ballot in 1992. The number of congressional districts fell from 11 to ten following reapportionment as a result of the 1990 census. All districts had been redrawn in a controversial process that was completed at mid year. The state Republican Party organization, with only 13% of registered voters, fielded strong candidates in about half of the congressional races. In the 5th District, incumbent Chester Atkins lost the Democratic primary to former District Attorney Martin Meehan, who, in turn, beat out former Congressman Paul Cronin in November. In the 3d District, longtime Democratic incumbent Joseph D. Early, who was caught up in the House Bank scandal, was beaten by Republican Peter Blute. In the 6th District, seven-term Democrat Nicholas Mavroules, who had been indicted for alleged influence peddling, was defeated by Republican Peter Torkildsen. Incumbent Democrats Gerry Studds and John Olver successfully fended off challenges.

The key state contests were in the 40-member Senate. In 1990, Republicans had picked up a total of 15 seats, giving new Republican Gov. William Weld a "veto-proof" upper house. In 1992, however, voters elected only nine Republicans, thereby restoring Democratic control in the Senate. Especially notable was the defeat of 24-year veteran Republican David Locke, the Senate minority leader. Democrats gained two House seats, giving them a 124–35 majority. One representative is unaffiliated.

Of four ballot referenda, only one passed unchanged. The successful ballot question imposes a 25-cent additional tax on cigarettes, with the proceeds going to antismoking programs. It received 54% of the vote despite vigorous campaigning by tobacco interests.

HARVEY BOULAY, *Rogerson House*

MASSACHUSETTS • Information Highlights

Area: 8,284 sq mi (21 456 km²).

Population (July 1, 1991 est.): 5,996,000.

Chief Cities (1990 census): Boston, the capital, 574,283; Worcester, 169,759; Springfield, 156,983.

Government (1992): *Chief Officer*—governor, William Weld (R); lt. gov., Argeo Paul Celluci (R). *Legislature*—Senate, 40 members; House of Representatives, 160 members.

State Finances (fiscal year 1991): *Revenue,* $18,727,000,000; *expenditure,* $20,349,000,000.

Personal Income (1991): $137,924,000,000; per capita, $23,003.

Labor Force (June 1992): *Civilian labor force,* 3,148,900; *unemployed,* 278,500 (8.8% of total force).

Education: *Enrollment* (fall 1990)—public elementary schools, 604,234; public secondary, 230,080; colleges and universities, 418,874. *Public school expenditures* (1990), $4,897,866,000.

MEDICINE AND HEALTH

Medical headlines during 1992 continued to be dominated by rising health-care costs, ethical dilemmas such as physician-assisted suicide, and the acquired immune deficiency syndrome (AIDS) pandemic. Illnesses that scientists once believed could be eliminated, such as tuberculosis and malaria, were causing renewed problems. On the positive side, there was growing understanding of the relationship between nutrition and health. Also, the development of new technologies and drugs, coupled with a promise of speedier governmental review of new-drug applications, improved prospects for patients.

Overview

Infectious Diseases. In October the Institute of Medicine, which is chartered by the National Academy of Sciences, released "Emerging Infections," a frightening warning that recently emerging infectious diseases such as AIDS, Lassa, and Q fever will be joined by other deadly new diseases: "We can . . . be confident that new diseases will emerge, although it is impossible to predict their individual emergence in time and place." In addition, the institute recognized a growing threat from mutant strains of disease-causing organisms. Among these are tubercular bacteria and malarial protozoans that are resistant to drugs.

The institute found the U.S. public-health system inadequate to deal with these threats. Among its recommendations were the formation of a national and worldwide surveillance system to identify emergences, improved capacity for vaccine development, and better preventive medicine. Today's rapid international travel increases chances of a worldwide epidemic, noted the institute. For example, a cholera outbreak that began in Peru in 1991 has caused an estimated 600,000 cases throughout the Americas. In 1992 the United States recorded a record number of travel-related cholera cases.

A team of scientists at the Centers for Disease Control and Prevention (CDC) reported that the Asian tiger mosquito is a carrier of the virus that causes Eastern equine encephalitis, a form of sleeping sickness that has a fatality rate of up to 80%. The tiger mosquito, which arrived on the U.S. mainland in 1985, has spread to at least 20 states. It is considered to be more dangerous than other mosquitoes that carry the disease because it is very aggressive and often lives near people.

AIDS. Dr. June E. Osborn, chairwoman of the National AIDS Commission, warned in late 1992 that the AIDS epidemic was accelerating; this echoed reports from around the world. Since AIDS first was recognized in 1981, it has claimed the lives of more than 152,000 Americans. More than 230,000 other Americans have developed AIDS and at least 1 million more are infected with HIV, the virus that causes AIDS. Worldwide, an estimated 2 million people have AIDS, with 10 million more infected with HIV.

Heterosexual cases account for the majority of cases worldwide. Even in the United States the greatest rate of increase is among heterosexuals. Behavioral changes have slowed the spread of HIV among homosexual men, who account for the largest number of cases of full-blown AIDS in the United States. A survey of more than 10,000 Americans conducted by Joseph Catania of the University of California, San Francisco, and other researchers found

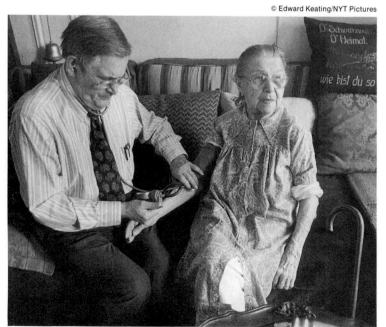

© Edward Keating/NYT Pictures

More and more doctors throughout the United States once again are making house calls as cost factors have restricted hospital stays. Advances in medical equipment, including the home intravenous pump and the portable electrocardiogram machine, encourage the trend.

Living Wills

As medical technology continues to make it increasingly possible for even terminally ill patients to live longer—at least clinically—there has been a surge of interest in what is known as the living will. A living will is a document that specifies that the patient does not wish life-sustaining measures to be used when there is no hope for recovery.

A January 1991 Gallup poll showed that 84% of the respondents would want life-sustaining treatment withheld, but only 20% had living wills. The concept became much more common following enactment of the Patient Determination Act, which went into effect on Dec. 1, 1991. This act requires health-care institutions that receive federal funds to inform patients of their right to fill out a living will and to choose a proxy to act on their behalf should they become incapable of making health-care decisions themselves. Most living wills give patients the option to indicate exactly what treatments they would desire or refuse as death approaches.

In 1992 all states except Nebraska had some form of living-will law. Some laws authorize people to appoint a proxy, while others encourage patients to make their treatment wishes known through a living will.

that among heterosexual adults with two or more sex partners during the past five years, 31% were at some risk of contracting HIV. Only 17% of those with multiple sex partners used condoms all the time.

The U.S. Food and Drug Administration (FDA) approved a new blood test to detect HIV infections. The test can be processed in a physician's office, gives results in ten minutes, and is more than 99% accurate. Previously approved tests have to be processed in a laboratory, which often means a wait of several days or more.

It takes an average of ten and one half years before an HIV-infected person shows symptoms of AIDS. According to a definition used since 1987, infected Americans were not considered to have AIDS until they suffered from one or more of 23 indicator diseases. Responding to pressure from patients and others, the CDC expanded the list of complicating illnesses to include invasive cancer of the cervix, pulmonary tuberculosis, and recurrent bacterial pneumonia. These conditions, while also occurring fairly frequently in otherwise healthy people, are often fatal to HIV-infected women, even though they may not be counted as AIDS patients. The CDC also revised the AIDS definition to include HIV-infected people with CD4 cell counts one fifth the level of a healthy person or less. Expanding the definition of AIDS was expected almost to double the number of cases reported in 1993.

Deoxycytidine (DDC) became the third drug approved by the FDA for treatment of adult AIDS patients. DDC was approved for use in combination with AZT; studies showed that, together, the two drugs tended to raise the CD4 count.

Attendees at the eighth International Conference on AIDS were baffled by reports of AIDS-like symptoms in patients who tested negative for the two known HIV viruses. By October the mysterious illness was known to afflict 68 people in the United States.

Cardiovascular Disorders. Evidence grew in 1992 that vitamins C and E play important roles in preventing heart disease. These vitamins act as antioxidants: They combat oxygen free radicals, molecules believed to play a major role in the development of heart disease and other ailments. A study of 11,348 adults conducted at the University of California, Los Angeles, indicated that people who consumed more than the recommended daily allowance of vitamin C experienced a significantly lower rate of death from cardiovascular disease.

A clinical study at The University of Texas Southwestern Medical Center showed that megadoses of vitamin E may slow the development of atherosclerosis (hardening of the arteries). Volunteers who took daily doses of 800 international units of vitamin E reduced by half the oxidation rate of low-density lipoproteins (LDLs). Scientists believe it is the oxidation of LDLs that triggers the buildup of cholesterol in artery walls, leading to atherosclerosis.

A theory that stored iron in the body may increase the risk of heart disease received support from Finnish researchers, who found that middle-aged men with high concentrations of ferritin (the protein molecule that stores iron) in their blood were more than twice as likely to suffer a heart attack as were men with lower ferritin values. The findings could explain why premenopausal women largely are protected from heart disease: They lose iron during menstruation. After menopause, however, stores of iron build up rapidly in women's bodies, increasing their heart-disease risk.

The American College of Chest Physicians urged people with atrial fibrillation to discuss with their physicians the advisability of drug therapy. Atrial fibrillation indirectly causes 75,000 strokes per year, and the college believes that up to 50% of these strokes could be prevented with more active treatment.

Gynecology and Obstetrics. The FDA approved Depo-Provera, an injectable contraceptive previously approved for use in more than

90 countries. Depo-Provera provides birth control for three months, and is about 99% effective in preventing pregnancy. The drug's most common side effects include weight gain and menstrual irregularities.

Scottish scientists reported that RU486, the "abortion pill" that interrupts pregnancy by preventing the implantation of a fertilized egg on the uterine wall, also is very effective as a "morning-after" birth-control pill when taken within 72 hours of sexual intercourse. RU486 is not available in the United States. Researchers also found evidence that the drug holds promise for treating breast cancer, endometriosis, and other ailments.

Physicians often surgically enlarge a woman's vaginal canal during labor, a procedure called an episiotomy. A Canadian study indicated that episiotomies are usually unnecessary, have no medical benefit, and make recovery more difficult. The researchers recommended that episiotomies be limited to cases in which there is a clear medical need.

Pediatrics. Exposure to even low levels of lead early in life impairs mental development, lowering IQ scores about 5%—a deficit that may last indefinitely, according to Australian researchers, who found that lead-poisoning was as likely to afflict middle-class children as poor children. The major sources of lead are paints, ceramics, water, and soil. The U.S. Environmental Protection Agency said that nearly 20% of the nation's largest cities reported lead levels in drinking water exceeding the federal guideline of 15 parts per billion; Jersey City, NJ, reported levels of 84 parts per billion.

Controversies erupted over the pros and cons of cow's milk. Researchers at the University of Toronto's Hospital for Sick Children reported that a protein in cow's milk may trigger the development of juvenile-onset diabetes in infants genetically susceptible to the disease. Earlier studies had shown that breast-feeding reduces the risk of developing diabetes two- to threefold in infants disposed to the disease.

The Physicians Committee on Responsible Medicine said that "milk should not be required or recommended in government guidelines," asserting that it contains too much fat and causes iron-deficiency anemia, allergies, and other problems in infants and young children. Many physicians disagreed, pointing out the nutritional benefits of milk and the difficulties of planning nutritious diets without dairy products. However, a switch to low-fat milk for children over age 2 was advised by many, particularly after the American Academy of Pediatrics said that children age 2 and older follow the same lower-fat diet recommended for adults to prevent heart disease and obesity.

Although childhood immunization is one of the most effective ways to prevent disease, saving as much as $14 for every $1 invested, the United States continued to have one of the lowest rates in the Western Hemisphere for childhood immunizations against diseases such as measles, mumps, and polio. As a result, there were thousands of preventable hospitalizations. Barriers to increased immunization rates included high vaccine costs and a lack of health insurance in many families.

The World Health Organization suspended use of the high-titer Edmonston-Zagreb vaccine, which over ten years had shown promise in protecting children against measles. Although it did protect children in some developing countries, their risk of dying from other diseases increased. Measles is a major disease in developing countries, infecting 44 million children annually and killing 1.5 million.

© Hank Morgan/Rainbow

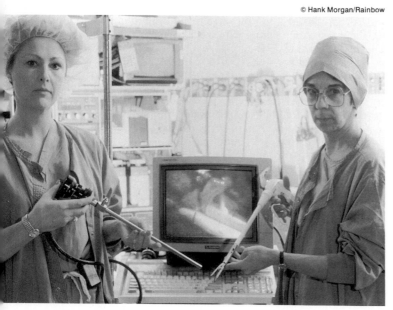

New approaches to surgery replace the traditional scalpel. Slender fiber-optic tubes are inserted into a patient's body through a very small incision. Together with telescopic lenses, a miniature light source, and a tiny video camera, the tubes become videoscopes that project images of the body parts and of the snippers, staplers, and graspers the surgeons must use. The instruments are known as a laparoscope (when used in the abdomen), an arthroscope (when the joints are involved), or a thorascope (when applied to the chest). Correctly performed videoscope surgery is said to be less painful and traumatic than conventional surgery.

Geriatrics. After autopsy studies indicated elevated concentrations of aluminum in the brains of people with Alzheimer's disease, there was widespread debate over the relationship between the metal and the disease, as well as concern that susceptible patients were ingesting aluminum in food, water, or other substances. However, using a new, highly sensitive technique called nuclear microscopy, Dr. Frank Watt and colleagues at Oxford University failed to replicate the earlier findings. They suggested that the aluminum may have been a laboratory contaminant.

The Nutrition Screening Initiative, a national project to promote routine nutrition screening and better nutrition among older Americans, estimated that 6 million of the 30 million older Americans are at high risk of malnutrition; an additional 1 million are malnourished. Factors that contribute to malnutrition include poor eating habits, poverty, isolation, tooth and mouth problems, multiple medications, and physical limitations. Malnutrition causes or worsens numerous illnesses, ranging from heart disease to pneumonia and even dementia. A study by Dr. Howard Filit at New York's Mount Sinai Medical Center indicated that malnutrition is a common problem among elderly people who require hospitalization.

Dr. Ranjit Kumar Chandra, a pediatrician and immunologist at the Memorial University of Newfoundland, reported that taking a daily capsule of 18 vitamins and minerals significantly reduced the number of infections among people 65 years and older. At the end of the yearlong study, Chandra found that people taking the capsule had markedly stronger immune defenses than people taking a placebo.

Sleep disruptions occur in the majority of people aged 65 and over but typically are not a cause for alarm, according to a study conducted by Sonia Ancoli-Israel and colleagues at the University of California, San Diego. Sleep disturbances are among the most common but often unrecognized causes of daytime sleepiness in older persons; other common causes include pain from other illnesses, side effects of medication, and disorders of circadian rhythms.

Surgery. According to the Agency for Health Care Policy and Research, more than half of the 23 million Americans operated on each year suffer unnecessary postoperative pain. "Inadequately managed pain can inhibit recovery, prolong hospitalization, and thus potentially contribute to higher-than-necessary costs," said Dr. Louis W. Sullivan, secretary of Health and Human Services, as he discussed new, voluntary guidelines issued by the agency for the management of postoperative pain. The agency urged physicians to use drugs to prevent the onset of pain, rather than to provide medication only after a patient complains. It recommended morphine as the treatment of choice, noting that it is easier to use for continuous dosage than other drugs. Several studies indicate that the addiction risk from short-term morphine use is less than 0.04%.

Many hospitals were using a new technology for delivering painkilling drugs to postoperative patients. Called Patient Controlled Analgesia (PCA), it involves a pump attached to an intravenous catheter. When the patient pushes a button, the pump sends medication through the IV into the bloodstream. Physicians set a base amount of drugs that may enter the body within a determined time period. Studies show that patients who use PCA need less painkiller, are discharged from hospitals faster, and have less chronic pain problems.

In some procedures the surgeon's traditional tool, the scalpel, is being replaced by a laparoscope. Instead of making a large incision, the surgeon operates through incisions smaller than a dime, manipulating long-handled instruments while watching images of the proceedings on a television screen. Patients suffer less pain and recover faster. Laparoscopy is particularly popular for gallbladder removal. However, health officials reported an increased risk of serious or life-threatening complications when laparoscopic gallbladder surgery was performed by inexperienced or improperly trained surgeons. New York state issued guidelines requiring surgeons to perform at least 15 laparoscopies under supervision before being allowed to perform the procedure independently. Some surgeons believe that laparoscopies are safest when performed by two surgeons, but many insurers do not pay for a second surgeon.

Medications. The FDA warned physicians that Seldane, an antihistamine often prescribed for allergies, can cause lethal heart problems if taken in combination with either ketoconazole (trade name Nizoral), an antifungal drug, or erythromycin, an antibiotic. The action came after 64 cases of serious heart problems, including 15 heart attacks and 4 deaths, had been reported to the FDA.

Although antihistamines have been proven to be effective for allergies, their use in cold remedies has been questioned. Dr. Leslie Hendeles, professor of pharmacy and pediatrics at the University of Florida, told a congressional subcommittee that studies going back to the mid-1970s found that cold sufferers given antihistamines showed no more improvement than people given placebos. Dr. Richard Gorman, medical director of the Maryland Poison Control Center, said that antihistamine overdoses accounted for more than 6% of all calls to poison-control centers. He noted that there is no effective treatment for overdoses.

An advisory committee to the FDA reported that Halcion, a prescription sleeping pill, is safe and effective and should remain on the market. The committee said, however, that

New Tuberculosis Threat

After decades of decline, tuberculosis (TB) again became a serious health problem in the United States in the early 1990s. "Tuberculosis is out of control" in the United States, warned Dr. Dixie Snider, director of the tuberculosis division at the U.S. Centers for Disease Control (CDC). The number of new cases reported to the CDC has risen since reaching a low of 22,201 in 1985—in 1990 there were 25,701 new cases; in 1991, 26,283.

The numbers represent only people with active tuberculosis. Health officials estimate that some 10 million to 15 million Americans carry the tuberculosis-causing organisms in a dormant state, and thus could come down with the disease. Further exacerbating the problem are dangerous, drug-resistant strains of the disease. These strains are causing havoc among health-care workers, who not only find it difficult to treat the afflicted but who themselves are becoming infected.

Background. Tuberculosis is one of the oldest diseases. Written descriptions of the disease date back to Hippocrates in ancient Greece. For centuries, people believed the disease was hereditary. It was not until 1882 that German bacteriologist Robert Koch identified bacteria of the genus *Mycobacterium* as the true cause of the disease. These bacteria can infect almost any organ of the body, but by far the most common form of tuberculosis involves the lungs. Symptoms include coughing, fever, night sweats, weight loss, fatigue, and blood in the sputum. As more and more lung tissue is destroyed, the person becomes weaker and weaker. Without treatment, death commonly results. The bacteria are spread when a person with active tuberculosis coughs or sneezes and another person inhales the contaminated droplets. Infection rarely results from a single exposure to the bacteria. Typically, repeated exposures over a long period of time are needed.

During the 19th century and the first half of the 20th century, tuberculosis was a major cause of death in the United States. In 1930, for example, tuberculosis caused 88,000 deaths. But improved living standards and public hygiene, coupled with the discoveries of streptomycin in 1944 and isoniazid in 1951, led to a decline in both deaths and new cases.

Most people who are infected never come down with the disease. But when people become weakened, it can strike. Today active tuberculosis is most common among the urban poor, the homeless, migrant farm workers, drug abusers, and people with weak immune systems, such as the elderly and persons infected with the virus that causes AIDS. The high incidence of homelessness, drug addiction, and AIDS since the 1980s is responsible for the recent rise in the number of TB cases.

Testing for tuberculosis typically involves injecting protein from the tuberculosis bacterium under the skin of a person's forearm. If the person is infected, a small swelling develops at the site of the injection. Active tuberculosis usually can be detected with chest X rays. However, neither test is reliable for people who also carry the AIDS virus—a problem that has resulted in an increase in the number of full-blown cases of tuberculosis among AIDS patients.

Tuberculosis can be cured if caught. The standard treatment lasts from six to nine months. Unfortunately, in the early 1990s many patients were not completing the treatment. They were not taking the medicine regularly or were taking only enough medicine to suppress the symptoms. Incomplete therapy means that not all the bacteria have been killed. Those that survived the initial doses were drug-resistant strains that can proliferate in the body. Treating such cases is difficult and expensive. The cost of treating a drug-resistant case has been estimated at $180,000—some ten to 15 times the cost of standard therapy. But the greatest concern has been that the drug-resistant strains may supplant susceptible strains as the most common form of TB.

Controlling the Disease. Worldwide, there are some 1.7 billion carriers of tuberculosis, with 8 million new active cases and 3 million deaths annually. Still, much can be done to reverse the upward infection rate and stem the spread of drug-resistant strains in the United States. Health experts have recommended increased testing for tuberculosis, improved diagnosis and compliance with treatment regimens, improved measures to stop the bacteria from spreading, and increased government funding for studying the disease.

On a positive note, scientists announced during the summer of 1992 that they had identified the genetic trick that allows some TB strains to become resistant to drugs. According to Dr. Stewart Cole of the Pasteur Institute in Paris, by knowing how tuberculosis develops resistance to drugs, it might be possible to modify the medicine used to combat it. Dr. Joseph H. Bates, professor of medicine at the University of Arkansas, went on to point out that with such advances, "tests to detect resistant strains quickly are a reasonable expectation within a few years."

JENNY TESAR

the label should contain a stronger warning on possible side effects. Halcion came under attack during 1991 following reports that it caused memory loss, anxiety, depression, and other behavioral problems. In November 1992 the jury in a civil trial found that Halcion had been partly responsible for a man's becoming a murderer; Upjohn, the drug's manufacturer, planned to appeal the decision.

Among the new drugs approved by the FDA in 1992 was Proscar, designed to shrink benign enlargement of the prostate gland, an often-painful condition afflicting about 80% of men middle-aged or older. According to the drug's developer, Proscar gave at least some relief to 71% of a test group of 1,600 patients; 33% experienced "excellent" improvement.

The FDA has been criticized heavily by both patient advocates and pharmaceutical companies for the slow pace of its drug-approval process. U.S. law allows the FDA six months to review new-drug applications, but budget constraints and insufficient staff have prevented the FDA from fulfilling its legal obligations. At the same time, the number of applications is growing rapidly, primarily because of a boom in products developed by biotechnology companies. The logjam was expected to ease as a result of the Prescription Drug User Fee Act of 1992, which requires companies to pay fees to help cover the FDA's cost of reviewing drug safety. In return for collecting an estimated $300 million over five years, the FDA agreed to hire 600 new specialists to work on the reviews.

JENNY TESAR
Free-lance Science Writer

Health Care

The U.S. populace learned a lot more about health-care reform in 1992, but their elected officials again failed to find a prescription to deal with the twin ills plaguing the health-care system. The ills were skyrocketing costs—a total national bill projected to top $800 billion for 1992—and a growing number of Americans without health insurance—35.4 million in 1991, according to the Census Bureau.

The Issue. The year 1992 was the "discussion stage" for the issue of health-care reform. The subject became a favored topic for the media. All the talk was bracketed by two events, both of them elections. It began with the November 1991 upset election of Harris Wofford to fill out the U.S. Senate term of the late John Heinz of Pennsylvania. It ended with the November 1992 election of Gov. Bill Clinton, who made health-care reform a cornerstone of his campaign, as president.

While efforts to reshape the ailing health system had been perking along quietly in Washington, it was Wofford's surprise win that thrust the issue firmly into the national limelight. Wofford, a Democrat who never before had held elected office, was expected to be trounced by his Republican opponent, former Pennsylvania Gov. Dick Thornburgh, who resigned as President Bush's attorney general to make the race. But Wofford beat Thornburgh convincingly, using a platform that included a call for universal health insurance. If criminals have a right to a lawyer, asked Wofford in a now-famous television advertisement, should not sick people have a right to a doctor?

Proposals. Wofford's election delivered a loud wake-up call in Washington, particularly to President Bush, who largely had sidestepped the health-reform issue during his first three years in office. Bush aides had hoped to avoid the divisive issue until the president was reelected to a second term. But Wofford's win forced them to address the issue.

The resulting Bush plan, unveiled in February 1992, was based on the premise that there was nothing fundamentally wrong with the nation's health system that some strategic tinkering could not fix. The centerpiece of the plan was a series of tax credits and deductions aimed at making insurance more affordable to those with low and moderate incomes, as well as a plan to create purchasing groups for small businesses to make coverage more available. The plan was not received warmly, as Democrats and even some Republicans complained that it would not cover all of the uninsured and that it failed to address seriously the issue of rising health costs.

But while Democrats agreed that the Bush plan did not go far enough, that was where the consensus ended. They were split into three main groups. One group of mostly liberal members advocated a single-payer plan, like Canada's, in which the government pays all the bills, although citizens retain free choice of doctors and hospitals. A middle group favored the so-called play-or-pay approach, in which employers would be required either to provide insurance for workers and their dependents or else to pay a tax to the government, which would provide the coverage for them. And a new group of mostly conservatives touted a plan known as "managed competition." Devised by a panel of academics who meet annually in Jackson Hole, WY, managed competition aims to make insurers actively compete for consumers on the basis of both price and quality. The theory is that such an approach can control costs and increase access to insurance simultaneously.

During the Democratic presidential primaries, candidate Clinton stood with the play-or-pay forces, particularly since that appeared to be the position that would capture the support of a majority of the Democrats in Congress. But as 1992 wore on, it increasingly became clear that neither house of Congress would be able to muster a majority for any of the proposals on the table. By late in the campaign season, Clinton had abandoned play-or-pay and endorsed a variation on the managed competition idea. But at the same time he also backed strict national-spending targets for health services, anathema to most Republicans and conservative Democrats.

Outlook. The 1992 elections made it clear that Americans wanted health-care reform. Exit polls showed what other polls throughout the year indicated—that for most Americans, concerns about health insurance ranked only behind worries about jobs and the economy. The trick for 1993 would be for the new president and Congress to find a way to turn those concerns into action.

JULIE ROVNER, *"Congressional Quarterly"*

Medical Ethics

Health-care professionals, the public, and the courts increasingly confront a host of bioethical dilemmas. Two ethical issues of particular importance in 1992 were physician-assisted suicide and HIV-infected health-care professionals.

Physician-Assisted Suicide. A patient's right to refuse medical treatment, even if life-saving, is accepted in law and medicine. Physician-assisted suicide, however, remains controversial. A doctor who provides a patient with the means to end his life is considered to have assisted in the suicide. Such action conflicts with doctors' long-standing ethical obligation to protect life. It also is a crime in most U.S. states. Nevertheless, public-opinion polls consistently indicate majority support and anecdotal evidence suggests that although the practice is not widespread, many doctors have helped patients hasten their death.

During 1992 debate centered on the actions of Dr. Jack Kevorkian, a Michigan pathologist. Since 1990, Kevorkian had assisted in the deaths by suicide of six people. In one such death, a 58-year-old woman with a severe pelvic disorder pushed a button on Kevorkian's homemade "suicide machine," releasing lethal drugs into her veins. Kevorkian's actions were criticized soundly—even by supporters of physician-assisted suicide—on the grounds that his "patients" were not terminally ill. Michigan courts twice dismissed all criminal charges against Kevorkian, however, ruling that his patients had caused their own deaths and that Michigan (unlike most states) had no specific law against assisted suicide. Although his Michigan medical license was suspended in 1991, Kevorkian vowed to continue to assist people seeking to end their own lives.

Other events have rekindled the possibility of the acceptance of physician-assisted suicide. In 1991, Washington state residents narrowly defeated an initiative which would have legalized physician-assisted suicide. A similar initiative was defeated in California in 1992. Bills to legalize physician-assisted suicide also were introduced in four states (including Michigan), although none passed.

HIV-Infected Health-Care Professionals. The December 1991 death of Kimberly Bergalis, 23, of Fort Pierce, FL, increased debate over whether health-care professionals should be tested for HIV infection. Bergalis and four other people were believed to have contracted the human immunodeficiency virus (HIV) from David J. Acer, a Florida dentist who had AIDS while he was treating them. In the ten-year history of the AIDS epidemic, these were the only known cases contracted during a medical procedure.

Despite public and political pressures for mandatory HIV testing of health-care professionals, the U.S. Centers for Disease Control (CDC) has rejected this approach. The CDC instead gave the states until October 1992 to adopt its revised guidelines or to develop their own equivalents. The CDC's guidelines recommend that health-care professionals who perform "exposure-prone" procedures should know their HIV status. The guidelines also recommend that HIV-infected professionals should stop performing such procedures unless they have been advised by an expert review panel under what circumstances, if any, they may continue to perform these procedures, and unless they notify their patients and receive their informed consent. Although the CDC's guidelines were criticized as vague, they were seen by many as striking an appropriate balance between the interests of HIV-infected health-care professionals and of their patients.

Embryos. In a case that addressed issues ranging from the question of when life begins to the procreation rights of individuals, the Tennessee Supreme Court ruled in June that a divorced man could prevent his former wife from using or donating embryos that had been fertilized with his sperm in the laboratory and then frozen for later use.

Other Issues. National attention focused on the case of a Harvard psychiatrist accused of contributing to a patient's suicide by improperly treating him and engaging in sexual relations with him. Margaret Bean-Bayog resigned her medical license in September and thereby avoided a public hearing on the case.

In New York debate continued over whether legislation should be enacted allowing family members to speak for terminally ill patients who no longer can speak for themselves. New York is one of the few states not allowing family members to make a decision on the removal of life support.

REINHARD PRIESTER
Center for Biomedical Ethics
University of Minnesota

Mental Health

New evidence that mental illnesses result from a combination of biological, psychological, and environmental factors was reported in 1992, the third year of the Decade of the Brain, mandated by the U.S. Congress. The findings provide insights that could lead to improved treatments for some of the nation's most disabling afflictions.

Schizophrenia. A research team supported by the National Institute of Mental Health (NIMH) reported evidence linking the chaotic thinking and hallucinations of schizophrenia with shrinkage of tissue in a specific portion of the left side of the brain. Using a new generation of three-dimensional magnetic resonance imaging to produce minutely detailed pictures of the brain, the researchers found a strong correlation between the degree of disordered thought and reduction of brain gray matter in the superior temporal gyrus, a region of the left temporal lobe that is associated with hearing and language. Patients with the greatest brain-volume reduction manifested the severest symptoms of schizophrenia. The tissue loss may reflect damage to a network of nerves important for organizing thoughts and remembering, the researchers suggest.

The study is among the first to relate a clinical symptom of schizophrenia—thought disorder—to a structural brain abnormality and underscores the importance of today's highly sensitive imaging techniques.

Depression in the Elderly. More than 60% of elderly Americans who suffer from depression are not receiving treatment, according to experts at an NIMH-cosponsored consensus-development conference. One reason is that their feelings of sadness and hopelessness, inability to enjoy everyday activities, loss of appetite, and insomnia—all hallmarks of clinical depression—may be viewed erroneously as normal responses to the decline that accompanies aging. Research has shown that nearly 80% of people with clinical depression can be treated successfully with medication, psychotherapy, or both. Electroconvulsive therapy is another effective but underused short-term treatment option for depression in older patients, the panelists concluded.

Maternal Behavior. New evidence from studies of rodents called voles links the brain hormone oxytocin to nurturing maternal behaviors and identifies the hypothalamus as the site of the hormone's action. NIMH scientists found that monogamous species of voles that live in extended family groups and care for their babies have a denser pattern of oxytocin receptors in the hypothalamus than do the species of solitary, polygamous voles that abandon their pups two weeks after birth. The findings suggest that the propensity for nurturing behavior may be hard-wired into the brain. Stud-ies to delineate oxytocin's influence on social behavior in voles may shed light on the neural basis of social behavior in humans.

Eating Disorders. Abnormally high levels of the brain hormone vasopressin have been detected in the cerebrospinal fluid of patients with bulimia nervosa—an eating disorder characterized by recurrent cycles of rigorous dieting, compulsive overeating, and subsequent purging through vomiting or taking large doses of laxatives. Vasopressin normally is released in response to physical and emotional stress. NIMH researchers suggest that excessive vasopressin may lead patients with bulimia nervosa to become conditioned to repeated overeating and purging.

A separate but similar condition—binge-eating disorder—was described in 1992. Preliminary diagnostic criteria for this disorder include recurrent, uncontrolled, excessive eating without the compensatory purging seen in bulimia nervosa. Obese binge eaters may respond to antidepressant medication alone or combined with cognitive-behavioral therapy that helps them recognize and change abnormal eating habits. By distinguishing binge-eating disorder from other causes of obesity, specialists may be better able to devise effective treatment plans.

Chronic Fatigue Syndrome. NIMH scientists and their colleagues have found new evidence that chronic fatigue syndrome—a condition marked by overwhelming, unexplainable fatigue lasting at least six months—is associated with hormonal abnormalities. The researchers found that people with chronic fatigue syndrome have abnormally low levels of cortisol, a hormone the body secretes in response to stress. The scientists believe the cortisol deficiency results from underproduction of a brain chemical called corticotropin releasing hormone (CRH). Even a subtle deficiency in cortisol or CRH could be associated with lethargy and fatigue. Studies were under way in 1992 to determine whether chronic fatigue syndrome can be relieved by correcting the supposed CRH deficiency.

Research Reorganization. Under the Alcohol, Drug Abuse, and Mental Health Administration (ADAMHA) Reorganization Act, signed in 1992, the NIMH's research components, along with those of the institutes on drug abuse and alcohol abuse and alcoholism, were transferred to the National Institutes of Health, the largest U.S. biomedical-research agency. ADAMHA's remaining service components now comprise the new Substance Abuse and Mental Health Services Administration. The reorganization links research in the behavioral sciences more closely with biomedical research and will expedite the transfer of research knowledge into the U.S. health-care system.

FREDERICK K. GOODWIN, M.D.
Director, National Institute of Mental Health

METEOROLOGY

Early snow in Canada and other unusual weather events made the focus on climate-change policy in 1992 especially timely. Also topping the headlines were three tropical storms that battered U.S. territory in late summer.

Earth Summit. At the United Nations Conference on the Environment and Development in Rio de Janeiro, Brazil, 153 nations reached an accord on the first international treaty to address the global-warming issue. Environmentalists and some industrialized nations had hoped for a treaty that would set specific emission limits and timetables to stabilize greenhouse gases, including carbon dioxide (CO_2). The agreement, the Framework Convention on Climate Change, avoided strict limits but required nations to formulate, then update, national programs to address man-made emissions of greenhouse gases. (*See also* SPECIAL REPORT/ENVIRONMENT.)

Climate Change. Implementing the climate-change treaty was considered a challenge. The U.S. Department of Energy released a study concluding that an accelerated program of technology development to cap greenhouse gases was preferable to a crash program of regulation, since the effects of either route will take a number of years to realize.

While policies on climate change were debated, the scientific community continued to seek ways to detect climate change. Even if the greenhouse effect is offset by more cloudiness or different storm tracks, the change still could affect human activities. Thus, detecting climate change might entail much more than simply looking for temperature changes.

Ozone Depletion. The hole in the stratospheric ozone layer made its annual appearance over Antarctica. It was 15% larger and was more persistent than in 1991. Scientists continued to accumulate evidence that the chlorine released from chlorofluorocarbons (CFCs) was the major culprit in ozone depletion. President George Bush announced that the United States had moved up the date for ending CFC production from 2000 to 1995. CFC output in the United States fell to 58% of 1986 levels. CFCs are also a greenhouse gas.

The U.S. Environmental Protection Agency (EPA) took aggressive steps during 1992 to eliminate CFCs and related ozone-depleting chemicals. In 1992, 11 more substitutes were identified by an EPA laboratory, including nine hydrofluorocarbons and two hydrofluoroethers. However, determining the safety and effectiveness of these various substitutes was expected to require another seven to ten years.

Tropical Storms. Tropical storms devastated three areas of the United States within a week of each other. Hurricane Andrew set a new record for damage as it smashed across southeastern Florida in late August and then turned on southern Louisiana. Although Andrew passed close to Miami Beach, FL, the storm was so concentrated that the city was spared major damage. Communities to the south of Miami, such as Homestead, suffered complete destruction. The storm caused 18 deaths and an estimated $10 billion to $20 billion in damage, four

During a time of unusual weather patterns, much of the Middle East experienced a rare winter storm as 1992 began. Snow measuring up to 18 inches (45 cm) and some 2 ft (60 cm) fell in Jerusalem (below) and Amman, Jordan, respectively.

© Esaias Baitel/Gamma-Liaison

times the previous record from Hurricane Hugo in 1990. Nearly 2 million people were evacuated in Florida and Louisiana combined. *(See also* SIDEBAR/FLORIDA.)

On the heels of Hurricane Andrew, Typhoon Omar pounded Guam, forcing almost 3,000 people into shelters. Omar was the strongest storm to strike the U.S. territory in 16 years. A week later Hurricane Iniki caused about $1.6 billion in damage to the western islands of Hawaii, especially Kauai. Nearly every one of the 21,000 homes on Kauai was damaged. In all three cases, modern observing technologies and relatively predictable storm tracks allowed adequate warning that prevented major loss of life.

Despite the notoriety of Hurricane Andrew, the Atlantic hurricane season saw fewer storms than usual for the second straight year. Of the six named storms, four became hurricanes.

Observing Systems. Upgrades to the observing systems in the National Weather Service started to show results in 1992. In particular, the first generation of WSR-88D Doppler weather radars provided significant new forecast information. The accuracy in severe weather warnings by the Oklahoma City forecast office jumped from about 50% to more than 80% after Doppler radar was introduced. At the same time, false alarms dropped from 80% to 30%. A study of the warnings showed essentially equal skill over the area within 150 mi (241.4 km) of the radar, a somewhat larger area than expected.

Satellites. Continued delays in developing a new generation of Geosynchronous Operational Environmental Satellites (GOES) delayed the first of five planned GOES-NEXT launches until December 1993. Geosynchronous weather satellites are a critical tool in predicting the path of hurricanes and tropical storms. At the same time GOES-7, the last of the first generation of GOES, approached the end of its useful life. Ongoing coverage was ensured by moving GOES-7 to view the west coast of the United States and borrowing METEOSAT-3 from the European Space Agency to view the east coast of the United States. Barring sensor failures, GOES-7 was forecast to be useful through late 1994, when its maneuvering fuel will be exhausted.

The National Aeronautics and Space Administration (NASA) announced further changes to the plans for the Earth Observing System (EOS) program in order to save about $3 billion, while preserving essential science objectives and the launch schedule. An additional $1 billion should be saved by deferring certain sensors from the first EOS satellites to those launched later in the program.

Field Experiments. The field phase of the Arctic Leads Dynamic Experiment (LEADEX) was conducted successfully during the winter. "Leads," or openings in the Arctic ice pack, are a major local source of heat and moisture in the Arctic winter, yet relatively little data had been available to describe the interaction.

A more ambitious project aimed at ocean-atmosphere interaction, the Tropical Ocean Global Atmosphere program, started a four-month field campaign in November. The Coupled Ocean-Atmosphere Response Experiment was centered on the western tropical Pacific Ocean, a region with the world's largest expanse of warm ocean temperatures. Ships, aircraft, and satellites collected data showing the interaction of this water with the atmosphere.

Weather Highlights. The lingering effects of the Mount Pinatubo eruption in the Philippines and the large-scale patterns associated with an El Niño combined to help set the weather patterns across the globe. El Niño, a recurring warming in the tropical Pacific Ocean that shifts jet streams and may modify weather patterns, was blamed for some of the globe's more unusual weather events.

Mount Pinatubo's eruption in June 1991 injected massive amounts of aerosols (tiny particles condensed from the volcanic ash) into the stratosphere; these blocked sunlight and slightly cooled the Earth. By May 1992 the global average temperature was about 1° below average and in the Northern Hemisphere it was about 1.5° below average. It will take some four to five years for the effect to end.

Temperatures in many parts of the United States were average or above average during the first several months of 1992, with the National Weather Service reporting the warmest winter in 97 years. But cooling trends set in, making July the third-coolest July on record for the lower 48 states, mostly in the Northeast and Midwest. Precipitation was above average with the fifth-wettest July on record. Then in late August the Canadian prairie provinces experienced early snow that destroyed much of the wheat and barley crops in Alberta.

With an intensity somewhat higher than the event of 1986–87, El Niño was blamed for flooding in coastal Chile, Peru, Argentina, southern Brazil, and Hong Kong, and drought in eastern and southern Africa, Europe, and the Philippines. Some parts of England suffered the worst drought since weather records began in the 1740s. Sri Lanka started with drought, but then in June experienced record rains. Heavy rains or drought also were experienced in Bangladesh, northern India, Pakistan, and parts of Europe.

Tornado activity saw higher-than-normal occurrence and much lower-than-normal deaths. In early October a string of tornadoes across Florida caught forecasters by surprise and prompted calls for an investigation. The most deadly outbreak occurred in mid-November in the Midwest and Gulf states.

GEORGE HUFFMAN
Universities Space Research Association

MEXICO

Mexico experienced a dynamic and controversial year in 1992. In the political arena, opposition parties achieved several major regional victories, but electoral fraud persisted. The government engineered several significant constitutional changes involving church-state relations and land ownership. President Carlos Salinas de Gortari's administration continued to sell off major publicly owned enterprises, including Mexico's leading banks, to domestic investors. Mexico culminated negotiations with Canada and the United States by completing and signing a free-trade agreement. Meanwhile, Mexican-U.S. relations were complicated by a U.S. Supreme Court decision involving the kidnapping of foreign nationals.

Politics. Charges of election fraud during a series of significant state and local elections continued despite the existence of the new Federal Electoral Institute charged with supervising elections. Outside scrutiny was not allowed as government representatives refused to make balloting documents available. A pattern of presidential intervention in elections where there were strong charges of fraud persisted in 1992, making it likely that it will continue in the future.

One such intervention came in January in the gulf state of Tabasco when members of the opposition party, the Democratic Revolutionary Party (PRD), led by Andrés Manuel López Obrador, embarked on a 680-mi (1 094-km)

march to Mexico City where they negotiated PRD victories with government representatives. Salinas also removed Gov. Salvador Neme Castillo.

The year also witnessed the growth of independent political organizations. The Citizens Movement for Democracy, a nonpartisan organization involving dozens of Mexican civic groups, was formed in February. This group described Mexico's most important problems in 1992 as: lack of democracy, lack of respect for human rights, poverty and low salaries, excessive presidential control, poor distribution of wealth, dependency on foreigners, government incompetence, excessive statism, lack of education, public apathy, and government manipulation of the mass media.

Opposition parties nonetheless continued winning local and state elections. In 1992 three gubernatorial elections—Chihuahua, Michoacán, and Durango—were particularly competitive. Francisco Barrio Terrazas, the candidate of the National Action Party (PAN), Mexico's oldest and second-most-influential party, defeated the government's candidate for governor of Chihuahua in a close election, bringing to three the number of opposition governors in office. PAN's victory was marred, however, by the fact that Salinas acknowledged the result before the final vote count was in.

In Michoacán, allegations of electoral fraud persisted even as the winner, the ruling Institutional Revolutionary Party (PRI) candidate, Eduardo Villaseñor, was sworn in on Septem-

The leaders of Canada, the United States, and Mexico— Prime Minister Brian Mulroney (extreme right),President George Bush, and President Carlos Salinas de Gortari—and their trade ministers met in San Antonio, TX, on Oct. 7, 1992, for the initialing of the North American Free Trade Agreement.

ber 15. In October, after intensive opposition from the PRO, Villaseñor resigned and was replaced by an interim appointee. Although PRI candidates were elected in the states of Durango and Tamaulipas, opposition parties were united and issued strong challenges.

Policy Changes. As part of President Salinas' commitment to modernizing Mexico's relationship with the Catholic Church, legislation was passed lifting many of the restrictions against religious organizations, including a previous ban on the clergy's right to vote. This was the first time the legal provisions had been altered significantly since 1917. In September, Mexico and the Vatican established full diplomatic relations.

The president initiated equally bold steps in agricultural policy. One of the unique consequences of the 1910 Revolution in Mexico was the development of an *ejido* land system in which peasants were given rights to use the land but were not allowed to own, rent, or sell it legally. These restrictions prevented peasants from using the land as collateral for bank loans. In February new legislation took effect giving these peasants the ability to enter into contracts involving their farms.

Finally, as the time for the next presidential election (1994) drew nearer, President Salinas shuffled his cabinet, eliminating the powerful ministry of programming and budget, from which he had emerged as presidential nominee in 1987. The president combined it with the finance ministry, strengthening the position of Pedro Aspe, the current finance minister, as a leading contender for the presidential nomination. He also restructured the ministry of urban development and ecology, making it the ministry of social development, and appointed Luis Donaldo Colosio, the former head of the ruling PRI, as its minister.

Economics. Privatization continued in Mexico. Of the 1,155 state-owned companies in 1987, only 286 remained as of early 1992. Nevertheless, as critics pointed out, 12 of the 20 largest firms continued under state tutelage. According to the independent newspaper *El Norte*, 79% of Mexican workers still were employed in state-controlled companies. PEMEX, the government-owned petroleum industry, in an attempt to increase productivity and bring its technology up-to-date following hard times during the 1980s, negotiated its first major loan—$100 million—from a foreign consortium led by Chase Manhattan Bank. But PEMEX came under fire for its role in the April gas explosions which leveled sections of Mexico's second-largest city, Guadalajara, killing more than 180 people, and for its claims that crude reserves stood at 65 billion barrels. Independent analysts estimated the reserves at only half that amount.

The North American Free Trade Agreement negotiations dominated economic news. The pact received the support of President Bush and eventually his Democratic opponent, Bill Clinton. Only Ross Perot, the independent presidential candidate, opposed it. The pact remained to be ratified by the U.S. Congress, where many members feared it might cost U.S. jobs or result in an increase in pollution.

Mexico attracted considerable interest among the international investment community as a popular source for foreign capital. Nonetheless, and despite its foreign-exchange reserves rising to the $20 billion mark, Mexico's projected trade deficit for 1992 stood at about $14 billion. Individual investors were not the only interested parties. Direct investment in Mexico by U.S. corporations jumped 57% from 1989–91, reaching $2.2 billion. One example is U.S. car manufacturers, who by 1992 were producing 425,000 cars in Mexico annually. It was predicted that as many as one out of every six cars made in North America would be made in Mexico by the year 2000.

Social Welfare. President Salinas announced in 1992 that Mexico would pursue a new path of "social liberalism," centering around the controversial Solidarity program. Salinas, who personally emphasized Solidarity by traveling each week to inaugurate public-works projects at the state and local level, said that the program is designed to reject paternalism and encourage local initiative. But critics alleged that the program targets funding to electoral districts where the government party (PRI) is weak. Funds have come primarily from the sale of publicly owned industries. By the end of 1991, the government had disbursed more than $3.4 billion through Solidarity.

Foreign Affairs. Positive relations between Mexico and the United States generally continued except in the area of human rights. International human-rights organizations have not given Mexico high marks in recent years. Both Amnesty International and Americas Watch testified before U.S. congressional committees looking into the free-trade agreement that there

---

MEXICO • Information Highlights

Official Name: United Mexican States.
Location: Southern North America.
Area: 761,602 sq mi (1 972 550 km²).
Population (mid-1992 est.): 87,700,000.
Chief Cities (March 1990 census): Mexico City (Federal District), the capital, 8,236,960; Guadalajara, 1,628,617; Nezahualcóyotl, 1,259,543.
Government: *Head of state and government,* Carlos Salinas de Gortari, president (took office Dec. 1988). *Legislature*—National Congress: Senate and Chamber of Deputies.
Monetary Unit: Peso (3,109.01 pesos equal U.S.$1, floating rate, Oct. 7, 1992).
Gross Domestic Product (1991 U.S.$): $236,000,-000,000.
Economic Indexes: *Consumer Prices* (1991, 1980 = 100), all items, 18,057.9; food, 16,852.9. *Industrial Production* (Nov. 1991, 1980 = 100), 130.
Foreign Trade (1990 U.S.$): *Imports,* $29,993,-000,000; *exports,* $26,524,000,000.

were continued, high levels of violations. Salinas had set up a National Commission on Human Rights in response to earlier criticisms but critics charged that it was unable to enforce its recommendations. By the end of 1991, after 218 months of operation, the commission had received 4,868 complaints, of which only 2,288 were investigated and concluded.

It was a specific case that caused the most controversy. Several years earlier, a U.S. Drug Enforcement Agency (DEA) agent, Enrique "Kiki" Camareno Salazar, was kidnapped, tortured, and murdered by drug traffickers in western Mexico. A Mexican physician, Humberto Alvarez Machain, allegedly helped the drug traffickers. After the DEA offered a sum of money for his delivery, Alvarez was kidnapped by Mexicans and brought to the United States. Although the kidnapping was challenged in the courts, the U.S. Supreme Court ruled that a foreign national may be kidnapped and brought to trial in the United States. Although a U.S. judge acquitted and freed Alvarez in mid-December, the case strained U.S.-Mexican relations.

RODERIC AI CAMP, *Tulane University*

MICHIGAN

Michigan residents were hit hard by cutbacks at General Motors Corp., which was continuing to restructure. Efforts to reduce the size of state government also continued. The Detroit Police Department was rocked by the conviction of its top official and the beating death of a motorist by police.

GM Cutbacks. General Motors announced plans on February 24 to shut down seven Michigan operations as part of a major corporate restructuring. The closing of three more plants was announced in December. In November, John G. Smale, former Procter & Gamble chairman, had become GM chairman in the biggest management shake-up in the company's history. (*See also* AUTOMOBILES.)

State Cutbacks. By Nov. 7, 1992, Gov. John Engler had reduced the number of state employees to 60,413, from 61,734 on Dec. 21, 1991. His program attracted sharp criticism, notably during the closing of Detroit's Lafayette Clinic, the state's only research mental hospital. With television stations broadcasting live, weeping relatives were restrained by police as patients were moved to other facilities.

Police. Two unrelated incidents brought attention to the Detroit Police Department. Four officers were charged—two with second-degree murder—in the November 5 fatal beating of a motorist on a Detroit street. Three other officers were subjected to departmental discipline after Malice Green was beaten with flashlights when his car was stopped near a suspected drug house. The beating touched off

---

MICHIGAN • Information Highlights

Area: 58,527 sq mi (151 586 km²).
Population (July 1, 1991 est.): 9,368,000.
Chief Cities (1990 census): Lansing, the capital, 127,321; Detroit, 1,027,974; Grand Rapids, 189,126; Warren, 144,864; Flint, 140,761; Sterling Heights, 117,810.
Government (1992): *Chief Officers*—governor, John Engler (R); lt. gov., Connie Binsfeld (R). *Legislature*—Senate, 38 members; House of Representatives, 110 members.
State Finances (fiscal year 1991): *Revenue,* $24,505,000,000; *expenditure,* $24,037,000,000.
Personal Income (1991): $174,750,000,000; per capita, $18,655.
Labor Force (June 1992): *Civilian labor force,* 4,586,000; *unemployed,* 404,500 (8.8% of total force).
Education: *Enrollment* (fall 1990)—public elementary schools, 1,145,558; public secondary, 436,367; colleges and universities, 569,803. *Public school expenditures* (1990), $7,653,297,000.

---

several weeks of peaceful demonstrations at the scene of the beating. Fast action in suspending all seven officers without pay immediately after the incident, rapid investigation of Green's death, as well as Mayor Coleman Young's public outrage at the incident, brought praise.

In an unrelated case, Detroit Police Chief William L. Hart was convicted by a federal grand jury of stealing $2.6 million from a police secret-service fund and spending the money on gifts for three girlfriends. He resigned and was sentenced to ten years in federal prison.

Election Results. In the presidential race, Michigan was considered vital to President George Bush. But Bill Clinton won the state with 44% to Bush's 37%. Independent Ross Perot received 19%. The November elections tightened Republican control over the state government, increasing the GOP lead in the state Senate and giving the parties a 55–55 split in the House.

Despite voter rejection of two tax-cut proposals, Governor Engler was expected to push vigorously for property-tax reform and to turn more state jobs, including prison operations, over to private industry. The governor also pledged to continue auto-insurance reform efforts. Voters rejected an American Automobile Association proposal to roll back insurance rates while limiting the amounts for damages resulting from accidents. Voters approved a citizen-initiated proposal to limit the terms of federal and state lawmakers. Opponents, however, planned to challenge the constitutionality of the measure.

Tigers Sale. The Detroit Tigers baseball team was sold by one pizza millionaire—Thomas Monaghan of Domino's—to another—Mike Ilitch of Little Caesars Enterprises, operators of 4,000 restaurants nationwide—for an estimated $85 million.

CHARLES W. THEISEN, *"The Detroit News"*

MICROBIOLOGY

The year 1992 saw new information on the transmission of HIV, the early origin of nucleated cells, the role of papillomavirus in causing cancer, and the different geographical patterns of Lyme disease transmission. The year also brought the successful production of a hepatitis-A vaccine.

Transmission of HIV (AIDS) Virus. Dr. W. Lyman at the Albert Einstein College of Medicine in New York City found a 30% HIV infection rate in second-trimester fetuses carried by HIV-infected mothers. These findings demonstrate clearly that the transfer of HIV can occur during pregnancy. Dr. J. J. Goedert at the National Cancer Institute studied twins born to HIV-infected mothers. He found that 50% of the firstborn twins were infected with HIV, compared with 19% of second-born twins. These cases indicate that, in some pregnancies, the transmission of HIV occurs during birth. If the virus had been passed across the placenta earlier in pregnancy, birth order should make no difference in the incidence of infection of the twins. It was postulated that during the birth of the firstborn, most of the fluid (with its HIV) lining the inside of the birth canal must be expelled, thereby leaving the canal relatively free of the virus.

Dr. P. Van de Perre at the AIDS Reference Laboratory in the African nation of Rwanda studied the children born to a group of 16 women who tested HIV-negative when they delivered but tested HIV-positive 3–18 months later. All 16 women breast-fed their infants. Four of the children tested negative at birth but tested positive within three months of their mothers' positive HIV tests, indicating that breast-feeding can result in HIV transmission.

Eukaryotic Organisms. A dramatic event in cell evolution was the organization of the cell's various activities into separate subcellular structures, called organelles (for example, nucleus, mitochondria, and the chloroplasts of photosynthetic organisms). Organisms whose cells contain organelles are called eukaryotes. They include all animals and most plants. Organisms without this advanced type of cellular organization are called prokaryotes. They include the bacteria and blue-green bacteria.

The time of origin of eukaryotes has been a point of dispute. Drs. T.-M. Han and B. Runnegar at the University of California in Los Angeles studied fossils in rock which had been dated and found to be 2.1 billion years old. In the rock they discovered fossils of the extinct primitive algal species *Grypania spiralis*. All living and well-studied fossil algae have been found to be eukaryotes. The presence of *G. spiralis* in this rock indicates that the eukaryotes must have evolved much before 2.1 billion years ago, which is about 1 billion years earlier than previous estimates.

Human Papillomavirus (HPV) and Cancer. HPV is a virus whose genetic material is in the form of DNA. There are some 60 different strains of HPV, including some that cause harmless "flat warts" on the hands and feet of infected individuals. However, there are other strains that cause flat warts on the genital structures of both males and females. There are about 750,000 new cases of genital warts reported each year. It has been known for some time that females suffering from genital warts have a higher rate of cervical cancer than do uninfected individuals. Cervical cancer kills 4,500 U.S. women annually.

In May 1992, Dr. J. S. Wiener and his colleagues at the Duke University Medical Center in Durham, NC, reported on their study of males suffering from cancer of the penis. Samples of the cancerous tissue were analyzed for the presence of viral DNA. They found HPV-DNA in about one third of the specimens, indicating that the virus infection is most likely the underlying cause of a considerable proportion of U.S. penile-cancer cases.

Lyme-Disease Transmission. Lyme disease is caused by the bacterium *Borrelia burgdorferi*, which is transmitted to humans when they are bitten by an infected tick. The severity of the disease varies, with some individuals experiencing only flu-like symptoms for a short period of time, whereas others develop a chronic arthritis, and still others develop cardiac abnormalities.

The question raised by any insect-borne disease is: Where do the insects pick up the causative agent of the disease? On the U.S. East Coast the tick *Ixodes dammini* feeds on the blood of white-footed mice and, in the process, ingests the bacteria which then can be transmitted to people whenever the tick bites a human. On the West Coast, Drs. R. Brown and R. Lane at the University of California in Berkeley discovered that it is a different tick species, *Ixodes pacificus*, that transmits the Lyme-disease organism, which it ingests when it bites an infected dusky-footed wood rat.

Hepatitis-A Vaccine Development. The hepatitis-A virus (HAV) is the causative agent of about 30,000 cases of liver damage in the United States each year, resulting in approximately 100 deaths. The viral infection is spread by the eating and drinking of contaminated food and water. Dr. D. Nalin of the Merck Sharpe and Dohme Pharmaceutical Company in West Point, PA, developed a vaccine consisting of chemically killed HAV. Injection of 500 children with the vaccine and 500 with a placebo (control group) resulted in 100% protection of the vaccinated children. Unfortunately, there were 25 cases of hepatitis-A disease among those receiving the placebo. The vaccine could result eventually in the complete eradication of HAV.

Louis Levine, *City College of New York*

A Palestinian demonstrates in late 1991 against proposed peace talks with Israel. Although the various Palestinian factions continued in 1992 to debate the issue of their relations with Israel, Arab-Israeli negotiations occurred.

MIDDLE EAST

The Middle East in 1992 saw no events comparable to those witnessed there in the previous two years. There, however, were significant developments and trends—some hopeful, some ominous—that offered indications of how the region's future was being shaped.

Arab-Israeli Peace Process. In at least one respect the year contained events that were unprecedented. For one, Israeli and Arab negotiators actually were meeting throughout the year, though intermittently, in an attempt to further the "peace process" and bring to an end one of the Middle East's great fissures, the unremitting hostility between the Arab neighbors of Israel and the Jewish state. All Israel's neighbors continued to be technically at war with Israel, as they had been since the founding of the Jewish state in 1948—with one exception, Egypt, which made peace in 1979.

The Israeli-Egyptian peace treaty stemmed from the extraordinary gesture of Egyptian President Anwar el-Sadat's going to Jerusalem in 1977; but the Camp David accords and the peace treaty of 1979 came into existence only because both sides were under strong diplomatic pressure from U.S. President Jimmy Carter. Similarly, the Madrid conference of late 1991 and all the 1992 meetings that ensued would not have occurred but for the tireless activity of Secretary of State James Baker, who made eight trips to the Middle East in 1991. U.S. influence got the peace process started in 1991 and applied a forced draft under

it in the first half of 1992 to keep it going; when U.S. interest waned for domestic reasons, the process faltered.

The yearlong series of meetings between Israelis and Arabs was known as the "bilateral" talks on account of their unusual form. There was no general conference. Israeli representatives dealt separately with delegations from Jordan, Syria, Lebanon, and the Palestinians. All the meetings, after Madrid, took place in Washington. Satisfaction that the unprecedented talks were taking place at all had to be tempered by the realization of how little, in substantive terms, actually was accomplished in the whole year.

The first difficulties were procedural. Israel, with U.S. agreement, had been able to insist on its own conditions for joining the peace talks: that is, no separate Palestinian delegation but Palestinians present only as part of the Jordanian delegation; no Palestinian Liberation Organization (PLO) representation; no Palestinians from Jerusalem and none from outside Palestine; and no United Nations role in the negotiations. Then the question of the precise status of the Palestinian negotiators within the joint Jordanian-Palestinian team eluded settlement during the whole of the second round (Dec. 10–18, 1991). However, agreement on it was achieved during the third round (January 13–16), a result somewhat misrepresented by the press as a Palestinian surrender, but which was the outcome of concessions by both sides.

The fourth round of talks took place in Washington in early March, the fifth in late

April. The imminence of the Israeli general election, held in May, then made it impracticable to hold further talks for a considerable period; the opening of the sixth session did not occur until August 24. By that time there had been a considerable change in circumstances.

U.S. Pressure on Israel. It was no secret that in the first months of 1992, as in the second half of the preceding year, the attitude of the U.S. government, and particularly of Secretary Baker, toward Israel had been growing increasingly chilly—this despite Israel's impeccable behavior during the Persian Gulf war, when it had served as a target for Iraqi Scud missiles without retaliating. The basis of the U.S. disapproval was continuation of an energetic Israeli program of settlement in the West Bank (Judea and Samaria), held by Israel since 1967, a policy persisted in by Israel in the face of strong U.S. objections. This led early in the year to rejection (strictly, postponement of consideration) by the U.S. government of an Israeli request for a loan guarantee of $10 billion to assist in constructing housing for the numerous new settlers from the former Soviet Union.

The Israeli election ended the long tenure of the conservative Likud-led coalition and the premiership of Yitzak Shamir. A Labor-led coalition assumed power, with Yitzhak Rabin taking office as prime minister on July 13. The Rabin government was greeted with perhaps undue enthusiasm as improving the prospects for progress in the peace process. In any event the U.S. government moved rapidly to provide the loan guarantees denied to Shamir.

In his first moves as prime minister, Rabin proved conciliatory. He offered to visit Amman, Jordan; Damascus, Syria; or Beirut, Lebanon for informal talks (an offer not taken up), expressed his intention to push forward toward that "autonomy" for Palestinians in the occupied territories envisaged in the Camp David accords as a five-year transitional stage, and halted most of the Jewish settlements in the disputed areas. However, because he drew a distinction between "political" and "strategic" settlements, and firmly declared "Jerusalem is not a negotiable issue," Palestinians and other Arabs saw little cause to cheer.

The talks, then, continued to drag their slow way along in the fall. The sixth round convened on August 24, recessed until September 3, and continued until September 14. The seventh began in late October, recessed until after the U.S. election, and continued to the end of November. An eighth round, begun in early December, ended abruptly when Israel on December 17 expelled 400 Palestinians in retaliation for the kidnap and murder of an Israeli border guard by Palestinian terrorists.

Although it appeared to some that the peace process had ended, some progress had been made, and more perhaps would have been if Baker's constant prodding and supervision had not been lost when he ceased to be secretary of state. The Israelis and Syrians had solved some minor matters amicably. It was significant that in September, Rabin told Israelis that they should not think of holding on to all the land they held, and must abandon dreams of a "Greater Israel." On November 1, Israel and Jordan drew up a most promising agenda for discussing in future talks such basic issues as water sharing and economic ties. Most important and novel of all, Rabin began to speak of the possibility of withdrawal "in the Golan"— though not "from the Golan."

Negotiators' Incompatible Aims. It hardly was surprising that the talks made only creaking progress, as the prime objectives of all the parties were different. The Palestinians' demand was statehood, not an interim period of autonomy on probation; they detest the Camp David scenario, indeed detest Camp David and all its works. The Lebanese wanted complete Israeli withdrawal from southern Lebanon, Syria the same from the Golan Heights. Israel, obsessed (with reason) by security, looked at the map and viewed any withdrawal with apprehension, and particularly from those Golan Heights from which Syrian gunners used to shell northern Israel for years before 1967.

The real prize for Israel would be a separate peace, on the Egyptian model, with any or all of the three states—Syria, Lebanon, and Jordan; but the Arabs' negotiating posture in 1992, at least, was flatly against this. Such agreements would reduce greatly the importance of the Palestinian issue—and so that possibility was a nightmare for the PLO.

Jordan, in fact, has no territorial claims against Israel by virtue of its having given up responsibility for the West Bank; and there is no reason why Jordan should not make a separate peace with Israel, except for the political clout of its own Palestinian population, the fear of seeming to let down the Arab cause. Some observers considered that, in refusing to make any concessions, all of the Arab negotiators were losing a golden opportunity for peace that might never recur.

Multilateral Talks. Virtually unnoticed, but possibly quite as important to the Middle East in the long run as the bilateral talks, some multilateral talks went on. A first round of negotiations on Middle East economic development was held (though boycotted by Israel) in May, and a second round in Paris in November. The presence in Paris of an Israeli delegation and of representatives from some 40 other nations was a triumph for French diplomacy. A quite separate pair of meetings was held on refugees in the Middle East—one in April and one in November, both in Ottawa.

Status of Israel. In some ways the diplomatic position of Israel improved significantly. China, India, and the new Russian state all en-

© J.C. Aunos/Gamma-Liaison

Yitzhak Rabin (left), the newly chosen prime minister of Israel, invited Egypt's President Hosni Mubarak (right) to visit Israel when the two leaders met in Cairo in July 1992.

tered into normal diplomatic relations with Israel early in the year. In December, Japan, beginning to play a larger role in the Middle East, and, in the disarray of the Organization of Petroleum Exporting Countries (OPEC), less fearful than formerly of offending its Arab oil suppliers, issued an official pronouncement that, as Israel had frozen plans to build new settlements in the occupied territories, the Arab side should reciprocate by suspending the boycott on trade with Israel.

Persian Gulf Security. Arab-Israeli relations are one of the two greatest unsolved problems of a region rife with unsolved, and perhaps insoluble, problems; the other is Persian Gulf security. Gulf security has been a dilemma since the shortsighted British withdrawal from the Gulf in 1971, followed by the fall from power in 1979 of the Shah of Iran, who had been friendly to the West and an adequate hegemon of the Gulf. Since 1979 the West has been forced to deal with the fact that the two major local powers—Iran and Iraq—are both aggressive, ambitious, and untrustworthy. No one has been able to devise a better policy—perhaps there is none—than to try to maintain a decent balance between a passionate Islamic theocracy, Iran, intent on furthering Shia Islam everywhere, and Iraq, a secular, semimodernized state led by a clever man hungry for power. Both countries have enormous oil reserves, though Iraq's are the larger. In the long run, Iran is probably the more dangerous because it is much larger than Iraq and has three times the population. In addition, theocracies are not amenable to reason or to any arguments based on practical or expedient considerations.

There was much debate in 1992 on whether the policy toward Iraq of the United States, and of the West generally, had not been simply one of drift, ever since the liberation of Kuwait in 1991. Iraq's President Saddam Hussein remained in power, but it was not easy to imagine policies that would topple him without doing more harm than good. Meanwhile, sanctions against Iraq remained in place.

In particular, there was universal aversion (except in Kuwait) to the idea of destroying the territorial structure of Iraq. Such also was the official view of the United States. Yet Iraq had never existed before the early 1920s, and many political creations of that period had disintegrated recently. If Iraq broke up, it would presumably split into three pieces—the old Ottoman *vilayets* of Mosul, Baghdad, and Basra. But this would imply the emergence in the south of a Shiite political entity wholly or partly under the thumb of Iran—an unwelcome prospect for Saudi Arabia. In the north, it would mean the emergence of an independent Iraqi Kurdistan with power to destabilize the Kurds of Iran as well as of Turkey. In the latter part of 1992, Turkey's long-running fight with the radical independence movement (PKK) among its Kurds erupted into wholesale violence, with fighting between Turkish and Iraqi Kurds, and Turkish troops moving over the Iraqi border (with the consent of the Iraqi Kurdish assembly) to suppress rebels there.

Such considerations led to the convening in Ankara, Turkey, on November 14 of a remarkable meeting of the foreign ministers of Turkey, Iran, and Syria. The ministers were unanimous that an independent Kurdish state should not be encouraged and that the territorial integrity of Iraq was important for all three countries. The ministers meeting in Ankara went even further and condemned the recent meeting in Salahuddin, Iraq, of all the opposition groups opposed to Saddam Hussein.

In the immediate aftermath of the Gulf war, it was thought that a reasonable approach to Gulf security had been made in the Damascus Declaration, initialed (but not ratified) in March 1991 by Egypt, Syria, and the six members of the Gulf Cooperation Council. This declaration envisaged sending Egyptian and Syrian troops to the Gulf to ensure security, with Egypt and Syria being reimbursed financially by the oil-rich but vulnerable Gulf states. However, there were strong Iranian objections, and the Gulf states themselves grew cool to the idea, despite efforts by Egypt's President Hosni Mubarak to keep it alive.

Libya Sanctions. In 1992, Libya joined Iraq in being subject to United Nations sanctions. This was the result of its refusal to hand over for foreign trial the two suspects in the Pan Am Flight 103 bombing disaster. The sanctions were rather nominal, since they did not include any embargo on Libya's export of oil.

ARTHUR CAMPBELL TURNER
University of California, Riverside

MILITARY AFFAIRS

Before losing the national election on Nov. 3, 1992, President George Bush had declared the Cold War over and the United States the winner. Nevertheless, both the United States and the primary successor state to the Soviet Union, Russia, faced unsettling times as each considered downsizing its military forces and making other adjustments to the new realities of the post-Cold War world. Although any violent confrontation between Washington and Moscow had become highly unlikely, concern increased about the arming of smaller nations, including the proliferation of missiles and nuclear weapons.

The Former USSR. The Russian Republic emerged in 1992 as the strongest military unit by far among the 15 republics which formerly had constituted the Soviet Union. Russia retained the bulk of the Red Army; the Navy; and the majority of the strategic nuclear forces, which included long-range bombers, the SLBM-launching nuclear-powered submarines, and the majority of the land-based ICBMs. However, the ICBMs were shared with three other republics —Ukraine, Kazakhstan, and Belarus. Russian troops were engaged in quelling fighting along Russia's borders with the former republics, and in the republics themselves, as ethnic, religious, and nationalistic feelings that had been suppressed by Moscow broke forth into violence.

Social Problems in the U.S. Military. In 1992 the U.S. military wrestled with changing social perspectives in regard to the sexual harassment of women, the possibility of women serving in combat, and gay and lesbian rights.

The services previously had been accused of sexual harassment of their female members. However, it was not until 1992 that the situation received full national attention. It all began in 1991 with the annual convention of naval aviators at the Tailhook Association held in Las Vegas, NV. The name Tailhook is derived from the device on carrier planes that engages arresting cables strung across the deck of an aircraft carrier to bring the planes to a halt.

Rumors of wild goings-on at previous Tailhook Association meetings had circulated before, but it was only after the 1991 meeting that a Navy helicopter pilot, Lt. Paula Coughlin, went public with serious charges about the behavior of male Navy pilots. According to Lieutenant Coughlin, she and 25 other women, half of them officers, were sexually harassed while being pushed along a gauntlet of drunken pilots in a hotel hallway.

Accusations later were made that senior Navy officers had known about the harassment at the 1991 gathering, and at previous ones, and had "looked the other way." In June, Secretary of the Navy Lawrence Garrett stated that he neither had participated in nor seen the al-leged behavior at the 1991 meeting. Still, he resigned, writing: "I hereby tender my resignation as secretary of the navy, effective immediately. In doing so, I accept full responsibility for the post-Tailhook management of my department." President Bush replaced Garrett with Sean O'Keefe as acting secretary.

In September two Navy admirals who were accused of mishandling the Tailhook investigation were retired from the service. Both men claimed that they were being treated unfairly. Additionally, the Navy inspector general, who investigated the Tailhook affair, was reassigned to another position within the Navy, and the position was filled by a civilian.

Less than two years after the Persian Gulf war—a conflict in which 6% of the U.S. forces involved were women, 15 of whom were killed —a special presidential committee wrestled with the question of whether women should participate equally with men in combat roles. The 15-member Presidential Commission on Assignment of Women in the Armed Forces was divided 8–6 in support of the proposition that the current law banning women from serving in combat zones aboard frigates, destroyers, aircraft carriers, and similar surface ships be repealed. According to the panel's recommendations, women would continue to be barred from ground combat, including serving on amphibious vehicles. In addition, the panel felt that women should not serve on submarines or in combat air missions. The panel's report was not binding, but President-elect Bill Clinton indicated that he would give consideration to the recommendations. Changing the ban on combat flying would require action by the Congress.

In November another troubling social conflict arose—for all the military services and in two different contexts. The problem was the traditional position taken by the armed services that homosexuals should be discharged from military service, as 17,000 in the last decade had been.

First, Federal District Judge Terry J. Hatter, Jr., ordered the Navy to reinstate a sailor who had been discharged honorably after he had admitted on a television show that he was a homosexual. The Navy complied with the court's ruling, and Petty Officer Keith Meinhold returned to his duties as a sonar instructor at the Moffett Field Naval Air Station south of San Francisco. Second, in his first press conference as president-elect, Clinton announced that when he became commander-in-chief he would lift the ban against homosexuals in the military, as he had promised he would during the campaign. In making this commitment, however, Clinton indicated that he would consider the views of military leaders on the issue. What the top military leaders thought about the matter was evident from a statement by the

Members of the French and German navies exchange greetings as France and Germany agreed in May 1992 to establish a 35,000-member military force independent of the North Atlantic Treaty Organization.

© Tschaen/Sipa

chairman of the Joint Chiefs of Staff, Gen. Colin L. Powell: "It is difficult in a military setting where there is not privacy, where you don't get choice of association, where you don't get choice of where you live, to introduce a group of individuals who are proud, brave, loyal good Americans but who favor a homosexual life-style." There were rumblings in the services that some individuals would prefer to resign rather than remain in a military required to accept gays and lesbians. Others feared that recruiting would be hurt by lifting the ban against homosexuals.

POWs and MIAs. The nagging question of POWs and MIAs from the Vietnam-war period continued to vex the Pentagon and the White House and to cause grief for friends and families of those servicemen still listed as missing. In the fall the Pentagon released some 30,000 pages of previously classified information concerning Americans listed as missing in action. But against a backdrop of occasional reports of new evidence that Americans still are living in Southeast Asia, the Pentagon and the Bush administration held out little official hope that the missing ever would be returned. Late in the year a team of U.S. senators headed by John Kerry (D-MA) visited Vietnam to discuss the POW/MIA situation with the Hanoi government. The committee reported that they were impressed with the cooperative attitude of the Vietnamese but that no hard evidence was obtained regarding living Americans. In appreciation of Hanoi's increased assistance, President Bush hinted that the trade embargo imposed in 1975 in retaliation for Hanoi's failure to cooperate in the matter of the missing Americans might be lifted.

In a new chapter to the POW/MIA saga, Russian President Boris Yeltsin released startling information to the Senate Select Committee investigating POW/MIA affairs. According to Yeltsin's emissary, former Soviet Gen. Dimitri Volkogonov, U.S. civilians had been jailed in the USSR on phony spy charges in the early 1950s. Of these, some reportedly had been forced to renounce their citizenship, others summarily executed. According to Volkogonov, 730 U.S. pilots and other airmen shot down while making spy flights or otherwise forced to land in the USSR suffered similar fates. However, the committee was told by the Russian general that no Americans captured during the Korean and Vietnamese wars had been transferred to the Soviet Union, but some U.S. researchers remained skeptical.

Downsizing the U.S. Military. Conscious of Republican assertions that Democrats were soft on defense, President-elect Clinton worked after the election to reassure voters of his toughness on national security matters. Noting the end of the Cold War, the president-elect indicated that he would restructure the U.S. military so as to emphasize smaller but highly mobile forces, which would be equipped with advanced technology. His aim, he said, was to enable the U.S. forces to deploy rapidly to world trouble spots rather than being deployed in the relatively stationary fashion used along the old Cold-War, East-West dividing line in central Europe. Such a restructuring would feature the improvement and enlargement of airlift and sealift capabilities.

According to the Clinton national security plan, the military would shrink from 1.8 million men and women to 1.4 million. This would entail a reduction of 200,000 more than envisioned in the Bush administration plan. Further, the Strategic Defense Initiative (SDI), a defense against ballistic missile attack first suggested in 1983 by Ronald Reagan, would be cut back. The antimissile defense advocated by the Clinton administration would emphasize a far less expensive land-based system.

Another emphasis of the new Clinton administration was on accelerating conversion of part of the military-industrial complex to civilian production. "We must rededicate ourselves as a nation to being far more serious than we have been in the last five years with the whole business of conversion," Clinton said. In a gesture of reassurance to mainstream planners, he nominated Rep. Les Aspin (D-WI), the chairman of the House Armed Services Committee, to be his secretary of defense.

The last of the Bush defense-spending bills was signed by the president in October. It called for an expenditure of $274 billion. This was down considerably from the $300 billion-plus defense spending of two years earlier, but the expectation was that the new president would reduce defense spending even more in the new year. The bill cut more than $1 billion from the president's original request of $5.4 billion for the SDI; however, $2.7 billion was included for completing the Air Force's fleet of B-2 stealth bombers, a total of 20 planes.

Nuclear-Arms Control and Disarmament. Both the U.S. Senate and the Russian Parliament finally ratified the START (Strategic Arms Reduction Treaty), which previously had been signed by President Bush and Mikhail Gorbachev in 1991. The nuclear stockpile of the former Soviet Union, held since 1991 by four successor republics—Russia, Ukraine, Kazakhstan, and Belarus—was to be reduced from around 10,000 to about 6,500 warheads. The three smaller republics were to give up all their nuclear weapons, with the balance remaining in Russia. Late in the year a problem developed when Ukrainian leaders linked signing the treaty to receipt of foreign aid, and opposed the signing until the North Atlantic Treaty Organization (NATO) or the United Nations considered the issue of Ukraine's security condition and that of the other two republics when they are without nuclear weapons. Further, although the Congress had approved $800 million for dismantling nuclear arms in the former Soviet Union, Russian and Ukrainian leaders argued over how much assistance each nation should receive. Unfortunately, adherence to START by Russia, Kazakhstan, and Belarus is dependent on ratification by Ukraine.

An agreement reached in June 1992 between President Bush and Boris Yeltsin would cut the warhead totals for both nations to between 3,000 and 3,500 by the year 2003. The pact, known as START II, was signed by the two leaders in Moscow as 1993 began. Of particular interest to the United States was the fact that the agreement would result in the Russians' dismantling their largest ICBM.

Some national-security experts saw the time coming when lessening tensions between the United States and the successor states to the former Soviet Union would result in the abandonment of the strategic nuclear triad. This concept held that each nation had to maintain three separate and independent means of delivering strategic nuclear weapons on the other—land-based ICBMs, submarine-carried SLBMs, and long-range bombers. In a study for the U.S. Government Accounting Office, the suggestion was made that the country in time could eliminate all the ICBMs and place its deterrent faith in the Navy's Trident SLBMs and a mix of B-52 and B-2 bombers.

The reduction in the Soviet threat also resulted in the Pentagon's admitting to the existence of a super-secret agency that played an important intelligence role during the Cold War. Called the National Reconnaissance Office, the clandestine agency handled the nation's "Deep Black" programs, which involved spy satellites and various airborne espionage systems. At roughly the same time, Moscow announced that some of its spy-satellite photos would be available for purchase by the public. The twin announcements led some national-security observers to suggest that the two nations should release their spy-satellite information for dissemination by the United Nations, so the entire world would be better informed regarding threats to the peace. The concept behind the suggestion was that an open world would be a more peaceful one.

Proliferation of Weapons. The breakup of the Soviet Union, combined with the need for hard currency in the former USSR republics, made former Soviet military equipment available on the world market. A primary purchaser was Iran, which had embarked on an impressive rearmament program. The most formidable Soviet equipment to surface in Iran was a Kilo-class submarine, whose purchase could be followed by three or four others, all sold despite U.S. objections. Iran also purchased a nuclear reactor from China, which some experts feared could be used to produced the fissionable material necessary for atomic weapons. Temporarily, at least, Iraq had been removed as a contender for nuclear weapons by the preventive inspection carried out under the terms of the UN-sponsored end to the Gulf war. North Korea was suspected of moving toward a clandestine nuclear-weapons capability, but no hard evidence was found.

While deploring the arms sales by others, the United States remained one of the world's foremost arms merchants, although not of nuclear, chemical, or biological weapons. U.S. weapons sold to allies, ostensibly to contribute to a balance-of-power relationship with "unstable" states, include F-15, F-16, and F-18 jet fighters, Apache attack helicopters, and Patriot antimissile batteries. Purchasing nations were Saudi Arabia, Taiwan, Finland, Greece, South Korea, Germany, and Thailand.

ROBERT LAWRENCE
Colorado State University

MINNESOTA

A financially embattled Northwest Airlines, a distressed farm economy, the nation's second largest voter turnout, a statewide health plan, and a beleaguered senior U.S. senator commanded top attention in Minnesota in 1992.

Economy. Facing the third year of record losses, the Twin Cities-based Northwest Airlines struggled to avoid bankruptcy. It reduced personnel, sought wage concessions from employees, and looked for new capital.

Despite harvesting a record crop, corn growers suffered steep losses because of poor quality and a late harvest. Soybean production was down 3%. The two crops, valued at $2 billion, are the state's largest cash crops.

The Mall of America, the nation's largest shopping and entertainment facility, opened in a Minneapolis suburb. (*See* page 423.)

Elections and Politics. On November 3 the state had a 71% voting-age population turnout, the nation's second largest. Democrat Bill Clinton carried the state with 45%, to President George Bush's 31%. Independent Ross Perot received 24%, drawing strongly from the normally Republican suburban and exurban ring around the Twin Cities. Clinton won absolute majorities in only five counties.

Minnesota's congressional delegation was unchanged with six Democrat-Farmer-Laborites (DFLs) and two Independent-Republicans (IRs). The DFL's Gerry Sikorski lost to political newcomer Rod Grams in a bitter struggle in which Sikorski's banking overdrafts were a major issue. But the DFL won the seat vacated by IR Win Weber when another newcomer, Dave Minge, defeated Cal Ludeman by a scant 521 votes.

Alan Page, a Football Hall of Famer from the Minnesota Vikings, became the first black elected to the state Supreme Court.

Entering the 1993 legislative session, the state faced an $800 million shortfall, promising a struggle between the DFL legislature and IR Gov. Arne Carlson. Despite DFL control of both houses, a majority was believed to be pro-life on the abortion issue. Abortion-rights supporters, however, made sufficient election gains to ensure sustaining a veto of any pro-life measure by the pro-choice governor.

Bipartisan action in the 1992 short session produced MnCare, a health plan designed to cover moderate-and low-income residents. At year's end an implementation plan was being developed.

The state's senior U.S. senator, Dave Durenberger, was rumored to be under indictment on charges growing out of dealings for which he was denounced by the Senate in 1990. In an unrelated matter, the senator was sued by a former client who claimed he had raped her 29 years ago and fathered her son.

Crime. The state witnessed a series of violent crimes. Police linked the slaying of a Minneapolis police officer to gang activity among young blacks. The city council offered a $100,000 reward. A 5-year-old girl was kidnapped and believed murdered. Her body was not found, but a family friend was charged with kidnap and murder.

A socially prominent woman and her boyfriend were murdered by the woman's divorced husband, an heir to the founder of the Twin Cities' leading upscale grocery chain. He committed suicide after being charged. A prominent black leader was killed in his apartment in a struggle during a homosexual encounter. The assailant was convicted and sentenced to life.

ARTHUR NAFTALIN
Professor Emeritus, University of Minnesota

MISSISSIPPI

Elections, dockside gambling, and a stormy legislative session made headlines in Mississippi during 1992, as did legislative redistricting and a landmark higher-education-desegregation lawsuit.

Elections. Voting in record numbers in the November presidential contest, Mississippians gave Republican incumbent George Bush 50% of the nearly 1 million ballots cast—the highest percentage he received in any state. Bill Clinton, the Democratic governor of Arkansas, received 41% of the vote; and Ross Perot, an independent Texas entrepreneur, captured 9%.

In other elections, voters returned the state's five U.S. congressmen, while at the same time approving a term limitation for the lieutenant governor. Elections, ordered by a three-judge federal panel to replace the malapportioned legislature seated in January, resulted in a net gain of 17 blacks, eight Republicans, and six women. Eight constitutional amendments gained approval, including one to lift the ban on lotteries and another to permit voters to propose constitutional amend-

---

MINNESOTA • Information Highlights

Area: 84,402 sq mi (218 601 km²).

Population (July 1, 1991 est.): 4,432,000.

Chief Cities (1990 census): St. Paul, the capital, 272,235; Minneapolis, 368,383; Duluth, 85,493.

Government (1992): *Chief Officers*—governor, Arne Carlson (I-R); lt. gov., Joanell Dyrstad (I-R). *Legislature*—Senate, 67 members; House of Representatives, 134 members.

State Finances (fiscal year 1991): *Revenue,* $13,701,000,000; *expenditure,* $12,730,000,000.

Personal Income (1991): $84,769,000,000; per capita, $19,125.

Labor Force (June 1992): *Civilian labor force,* 2,409,000; *unemployed,* 135,300 (5.6% of total force).

Education: *Enrollment* (fall 1990)—public elementary schools, 545,556; public secondary, 210,818; colleges and universities, 253,789. *Public school expenditures* (1990), $3,800,000,000.

In November 1992, six people died when a tornado tore through a mobile-home park in Brandon, MS (right). The twister was part of a late-season storm system that spawned tornadoes in 12 states.

ments. In 20 of 22 counties, voters opted to retain the unit system rather than return to the old beat system of road administration.

Dockside Gambling. Lured by the promise of easy revenues, Mississippi entered the gambling arena in 1992 with the opening of floating casinos. The first dockside casino began operations August 1 on the Gulf coast; and by year's end, four other such casinos were operational, three on the coast and one in Tunica county, bordering the Mississippi River.

The Legislature. The January-to-May legislative session, the first of Republican Gov. Kirk Fordice's term, was marked by strained legislative-executive relations. The governor vetoed a one-cent sales-tax hike projected to yield $166 million (most of which was earmarked for education) and also a $98 million capital-improvements bill, but both vetoes were overridden. Lawmakers also were suc-

cessful in approving plans that significantly increased the number of legislative districts containing majority black voting-age populations, thereby ending a two-year court fight and setting the stage for November elections.

In September legislators met in a one-day special session called to address an August Mississippi Supreme Court ruling that declared a portion of the state's "sovereign immunity law" unconstitutional. A stopgap bill was enacted to protect state and local governments from civil lawsuits, but much-needed tort reform was deferred to the 1993 legislature.

The Ayers Case. In June the U.S. Supreme Court ruled in a suit—filed 17 years earlier by Jake Ayers in behalf of his son and 21 other black students — that Mississippi had not removed the last vestiges of segregation from its higher- education system. The case was remanded to the Fifth U.S. Circuit Court of Appeals and from there to District Judge Neal Biggers of Oxford to work out an acceptable plan to remedy the situation. Both the plaintiffs and the state submitted proposals, but the year ended with neither agreement nor court resolution of the issue.

Other News. In January lagging revenue collections forced Governor Fordice to cut $76.6 million from state agencies in order to balance the 1992 budget. . . . The economy showed signs of recovery as the year progressed, but many indicators continued to fluctuate. . . . On November 21–22 a series of tornadoes raced through central Mississippi, killing 15 persons and injuring at least 150. Property damage was estimated in the millions of dollars.

DANA B. BRAMMER
University of Mississippi

MISSISSIPPI • Information Highlights

Area: 47,689 sq mi (123 515 km²).
Population (July 1, 1991 est.): 2,592,000.
Chief Cities (1990 census): Jackson, the capital, 196,637; Biloxi, 46,319; Greenville, 45,226.
Government (1992): *Chief Officers*—governor, Raymond Mabus, Jr. (D); lt. gov., Brad Dye (D). *Legislature*—Senate, 52 members; House of Representatives, 122 members.
State Finances (fiscal year 1991): *Revenue,* $5,794,000,000; *expenditure,* $5,171,000,000.
Personal Income (1991): $34,545,000,000; per capita, $13,328.
Labor Force (June 1992): *Civilian labor force,* 1,186,200; *unemployed,* 111,500 (9.% of total force).
Education: *Enrollment* (fall 1990)—public elementary schools, 371,674; public secondary, 130,743; colleges and universities, 122,883. *Public school expenditures* (1990), $1,531,941,000.

MISSOURI

The Democrats' election-day sweep of Missouri's statewide offices, grabbing power from the Republicans for the first time in 12 years, topped 1992 state news. Missouri was a battleground in the presidential race as well, bringing the candidates and their surrogates to the state an unprecedented number of times. Also making headlines were a courthouse shooting spree and a hike in the state gasoline tax.

Politics. Missouri enhanced its status as a presidential bellwether state by favoring Democrat Bill Clinton over President George Bush. Two of the state's U.S. congressional incumbents lost their reelection bids—Republican Tom Coleman of the Kansas City area and Democrat Joan Kelly Horn of suburban St. Louis. The seven other incumbents and U.S. Sen. Christopher "Kit" Bond won new terms.

In state politics, Democratic Lt. Gov. Mel Carnahan easily defeated state Attorney General William Webster to win the governor's office. Webster was plagued by a lingering scandal involving a state fund that his office oversees. A federal grand jury was looking into the fund and other Webster dealings. Democrats also won the offices of lieutenant governor, attorney general, and secretary of state.

Missouri voters approved state and federal term limits and riverboat gambling along the Missouri and Mississippi rivers.

Crime. A man opened fire during a divorce proceeding in May at the St. Louis county courthouse. Kenneth Baumruk killed his estranged wife, injured four people, and terrorized hundreds in the building before being shot by police officers.

Three women mysteriously disappeared and were believed abducted from a Springfield home in June. Massive searches by police and volunteers found no trace of the women.

A federal-court jury convicted two brothers of abducting a southwest Missouri banker and

robbing his bank in 1989. The banker was strapped to a chair and tossed alive into an Oklahoma lake. The brothers would stand trial for murder in Oklahoma in 1993.

St. Louis Circuit Attorney George Peach resigned in August. Peach had pleaded guilty to patronizing prostitutes, then was indicted for stealing cash from the city and from a crime victims' fund.

Rock singer Axl Rose was found guilty of misdemeanor assault and property damage after he lunged for a camera during a St. Louis concert. The action touched off a riot among concertgoers.

Also in 1992, two bank robbers made off with nearly $1 million in a record-setting, daylight hold up in downtown St. Louis; and Kansas City set a record for homicides, breaking the previous high of 140 in 1989.

Business. In Springfield, Zenith Electronics Corp. shut down the last U.S.-owned television-assembly line and moved it to Mexico. About 1,500 workers were laid off. Southwestern Bell announced it was moving its corporate

---

MISSOURI • Information Highlights

Area: 69,697 sq mi (180 516 km²).
Population (July 1, 1991 est.): 5,158,000.
Chief Cities (1990 census): Jefferson City, the capital, 35,481; Kansas City, 435,146; St. Louis, 396,685; Springfield, 140,494; Independence, 112,301.
Government (1992): *Chief Officers—governor,* John Ashcroft (R); lt. gov., Mel Carnahan (R). *General Assembly*—Senate, 34 members; House of Representatives, 163 members.
State Finances (fiscal year 1991): *Revenue,* $10,002,000,000; *expenditure,* $9,254,000,000.
Personal Income (1991): $92,470,000,000; per capita, $17,928.
Labor Force (June 1992): *Civilian labor force,* 2,697,300; *unemployed,* 186,300 (6.9% of total force).
Education: *Enrollment* (fall 1990)—public elementary schools, 584,953; public secondary, 227,281; colleges and universities, 289,407. *Public school expenditures* (1990), $3,214,351,000.

Union Station in Kansas City, MO, is deteriorating rapidly after nearly a decade without maintenance. City officials hoping to renovate the unused railroad station have been unable to raise the estimated $36 million needed to do the job.

headquarters from St. Louis to San Antonio, TX.

Sports. The Kansas City Royals' George Brett became the 18th player in baseball history to reach 3,000 hits (*see* BIOGRAPHY).

Other Developments. The Missouri legislature approved a gasoline-tax increase to pay for statewide highway improvements. . . . Southwest Missouri State University officials fired its president and other top administrators after massive construction-cost overruns and questionable bidding procedures sparked a federal grand-jury investigation. . . . The Missouri Supreme Court pondered a decision in late 1992 on a father's request to remove his brain-damaged daughter's feeding tube.

LANE BEAUCHAMP, *"The Kansas City Star"*

MONGOLIA

In 1992, Mongolia adopted a new constitution, held elections that confirmed the rule of President Punsalmaagiyn Ochirbat's Mongolian People's Revolutionary Party (MPRP), and continued uncertainly along the path to a market economy.

Politics. Approved by the Hural (parliament) in January, the new constitution took effect on February 15. It repudiated the socialist system that had prevailed in Mongolia during the country's long existence as a satellite of the USSR, and established a Western-style parliamentary government with a popularly elected president. The Hural, formerly bicameral, became a unicameral legislature, and the name of the country was changed from the Mongolian People's Republic to the State of Mongolia. The right to private property was recognized, but public ownership of pastureland was continued.

In parliamentary elections held on June 28, the ruling MPRP (former Communists) won a sweeping victory, capturing 70 of the 76 seats in the legislature. A new prime minister, Puntsagiyn Jasray, was elected by the Hural in July. In October the four main opposition parties merged to form a single group, the Mongolian National Democratic Party (MNDP).

Economy. A major step in the process of ending price controls came on March 1, when the government deregulated the prices of most

---

MONGOLIA • Information Highlights

Official Name: State of Mongolia.
Location: East Asia.
Area: 604,247 sq mi (1 565 000 km²).
Population: (mid-1992 est.): 2,300,000.
Chief Cities: (May 1991): Ulan Bator, the capital, 575,000; Darhan, 90,000.
Government: *Head of state*, Punsalmaagiyn Ochirbat (elected September 1990). *Head of government*, Puntsagiyn Jasray, premier (elected July 1992). *Legislature*, Hural.

---

foods except bread and flour. Price deregulation helped fuel Mongolia's rapidly climbing inflation rate (250% in the first nine months of the year). The country's longtime economic dependence on its Russian neighbor has left it ill-equipped to fend for itself at a time when the Russian economy is in crisis, and the radical economic reforms demanded by Western donors in exchange for aid have caused widespread hardship among the more vulnerable sectors of the population. The attempt to convert to a Western-style capitalist economy is fraught with problems in a nation where a large proportion of the people are nomadic herders.

Russian Relations. The last former Soviet troops were withdrawn from Mongolia in September. The following month, Foreign Minister Tserenpilyn Gombosuren visited Moscow for the signing of a treaty on friendly relations and cooperation between Mongolia and Russia.

JOHN ROBINSON

MONTANA

Drought, a decline in the logging industry, and elections were among 1992's news items in Montana.

Elections. Montana voters were forced to choose between their two incumbent congressmen when U.S. Census data showed that the state had too few people to retain two seats in Congress. Democrat Pat Williams beat out Republican Ron Marlenee for the seat. Marc Racicot, a Republican and the state's attorney general, was elected governor, defeating Democratic State Rep. Dorothy Bradley, the first woman to run a general-election campaign for the office. Both candidates called for a state sales tax—a position that previously was supported widely only by Republicans. For health reasons, Gov. Stan Stephens had not sought reelection.

After five years of Democrats running the state House of Representatives, the Republicans became the majority party. For the first time in 22 years, the state House and Senate would be controlled by separate parties. By a margin of fewer than 500 votes, Montanans retained State Supreme Court Chief Justice Jean Turnage, who was challenged by Terry Trieweiler, the newest elected member of the court. Voters also agreed, by a wide margin, to limit the terms of politicians at all levels.

Economy. Balmy winter and spring weather helped the economy by keeping construction workers on the job, but the warmth and lack of snow prompted the governor to declare the state a drought disaster area in June. The eastern part of the state was buoyed a week later by timely rainfall on dry-land grainfields and pastures.

In the western part of the state, blue-collar unemployment remained high as the logging

© Larry Mayer/NYT Pictures

The Crazy Mountains (left) in western Montana have become a battleground of sorts. The Crow Indians who live on a reservation just southeast of Big Timber, MT, consider the mountains sacred. A local lumber company views the area in terms of its valuable stands of timber. Outdoor enthusiasts want to preserve the Crazy Mountains as a pristine playground.

and timber industries continued to decline. The slump was offset, however, by an influx of high-income people from out of state and the resulting rise in home construction in the Gallatin, Flathead, and Yellowstone river valleys. Tourism also fared well as more than 3 million tourists visited Yellowstone National Park, the most ever.

MONTANA • Information Highlights

Area: 147,046 sq mi (380 848 km²).
Population (July 1, 1991 est.): 808,000.
Chief Cities (1990 census): Helena, the capital, 24,569; Billings, 81,151; Great Falls, 55,097.
Government (1992): *Chief Officers*—governor, Stan Stephens (R); lt. gov., Dennis Rehberg (R). *Legislature*—Senate, 50 members; House of Representatives, 100 members.
State Finances (fiscal year 1991): *Revenue,* $2,359,000,000; *expenditure,* $2,384,000,000.
Personal Income (1991): $12,673,000,000; per capita, $15,675.
Labor Force (June 1992): *Civilian labor force,* 411,700; *unemployed,* 30,300 (7.4% of total force).
Education: *Enrollment* (fall 1990)—public elementary schools, 111,172; public secondary, 41,802; colleges and universities, 37,876. *Public school expenditures* (1990), $689,350,000.

Legislation. The Montana legislature met in two special sessions to address a deficit estimated at more than $300 million. In January legislators rejected all significant revenue bills —including those to start a state sales tax— and made cuts too shallow to balance the budget. They voted to borrow $50 million from other state accounts.

In July the legislature cut $6 million from school funding and added a 7% surcharge on taxes already collected in Montana, retroactive to January 1. The surcharge was opposed widely by Republican legislators and was cited frequently by voters as the reason that they voted against Democrats in November.

The legislature approved a Democratic proposal to spend some interest from the state Coal Severance Tax Trust Fund to rebuild roads and other infrastructure.

Wilderness. Federal legislation that would have decided the fate of 6 million acres (2.4 million ha) of roadless public land in Montana died in the final days of the congressional session. The bill was drafted by Montana's senators and passed the Senate with little difficulty. In the House of Representatives, however, it was the target of a celebrity letter-writing campaign and was mired in committees until Congress adjourned.

ROBERT C. GIBSON
"The Billings Gazette"

MOROCCO

Morocco in 1992 continued its efforts to negotiate a settlement on the status of Western Sahara, and took some faltering steps in the direction of political reform; both of these policies helped to improve the international standing of King Hassan II's regime, including promoting better relations with the countries of Western Europe.

Western Sahara. The problem of the Western Sahara, the former Spanish territory claimed by both Morocco and the pro-independence Polisario Front, was to have been settled by a United Nations-sponsored referendum in the territory in January 1993. But by late 1992 the sticky issue of establishing a mutually agreed-upon voting list still was holding up the setting of a referendum date. Polisario wished to use a 1974 census the Spanish carried out before leaving the territory; Morocco insisted on adding 120,000 voters it claimed were bona fide residents who had left the territory before the census. Polisario called this a bold attempt to flood the result with pro-Morocco votes.

Efforts to resolve the conflict suffered a blow in June with the assassination of Algerian President Mohamed Boudiaf, who had been a strong supporter of the peace process.

Morocco and Polisario held indirect talks in New York in August to try to agree on terms for a vote, but failed. With no progress at the negotiating table, the two sides resumed their propaganda war. In October, Polisario threatened at an Algiers press conference to resume its guerrilla war against Morocco, and called on international public opinion to turn up pressure on King Hassan. Rabat won its own public-relations points by focusing international attention on former Polisario leaders who since had defected to Morocco's side. At one September press conference, eight former Polisario leaders called on international humanitarian organizations to ensure that relief supplies were getting to their intended recipients in Sahrawi refugee camps in Algeria. The defectors claimed relief aid was being diverted to Polisario soldiers.

Domestic Politics. On September 4, Moroccans approved a new constitution hailed as a cornerstone in the king's effort to accomplish the country's modernization. Among its innovations, the document outlined new powers for the parliament, called on the prime minister (rather than the king) to name his government, and included in its introduction a reference to the inalienable nature of human rights. But the fact that official figures showed 99.996% of the voters approving the constitution placed a cloud over the positive result and raised doubts about the vote's integrity.

Then on October 16, Moroccans returned to the polls for local elections. Women improved their representation among candidates from 307 in the last elections in 1983 to 1,086 in 1992—still a paltry number compared with the 93,000 total candidates for 22,500 posts. The king had called for "transparency and honesty" in the elections and said they would be a test of Moroccans' "political maturity and intelligence." Against that backdrop, the results were mixed. While progovernment parties took 60% of the seats, several opposition parties showed impressive gains and a number of progovernment former ministers were defeated. On the other hand, the corrupt influence of money was more evident than ever before in Morocco, with widespread reports of vote selling, and even some reported cases of candidates dropping out for a price.

The new local councillors would be responsible for choosing one third of a new parliament that originally was to be elected in December; however, the election was postponed until April 1993. The other two thirds would be elected through universal suffrage.

European Relations. On November 3, Morocco received French Prime Minister Pierre Bérégovoy, who spoke of Morocco as a "precursor" for North African countries seeking to improve economic relations with Europe. After experiencing a falloff in such export sectors as textiles as a result of new competition from Eastern Europe, and with an increase in clandestine emigration from Morocco to Europe across the 16-mi (26-km)-wide Strait of Gibraltar, Morocco found it had both good incentive and good arguments for promoting a European role in its economic development.

HOWARD LAFRANCHI
"The Christian Science Monitor"

MOROCCO • Information Highlights

Official Name: Kingdom of Morocco.
Location: Northwest Africa.
Area: 172,413 sq mi (446 550 km^2).
Population (mid-1992 est.): 26,200,000.
Chief Cities (mid-1990 est., incl. suburbs): Rabat, the capital, 1,427,000; Casablanca, 3,210,000; Fez, 1,012,000; Marrakech, 1,517,000.
Government: *Head of state,* Hassan II, king (acceded 1961). *Head of government,* Azzedine Laraki, prime minister (appointed Sept. 30, 1986). *Legislature* (unicameral)—Chamber of Representatives.
Monetary Unit: Dirham (7.855 dirhams equal U.S.$1, Aug. 1992).
Gross Domestic Product (1990 est. U.S.$): $25,400,000,000.
Economic Indexes : *Consumer Prices* (1991, 1980 = 100), all items, 217.7; food, 217.3. *Industrial Production* (1990, 1980 = 100), 133.
Foreign Trade (1990 U.S.$): *Imports,* $6,919,000,000; *exports,* $4,229,000,000.

MOTION PICTURES

Customary dynamics governed the movie world in 1992, as Hollywood continued its quest for mainstream box-office bonanzas, and intrepid independent filmmakers succeeded in breaking through with more adventurous and often more creative work.

Among the rising directors was Alexandre Rockwell, whose *In the Soup* was highlighted at both Toronto's Festival of Festivals and the New York Film Festival. His freewheeling comedy was an ode to those who persevere and conquer the problems involved in making a first film. Anthony Drazan, another director who attracted attention, presented *Zebrahead*, a moving drama about interracial friendship at a Detroit high school. Presented by Oliver Stone, it also was showcased at the Toronto and New York Festivals.

Newcomer Stacy Cochran satirically looked at the problem of handgun proliferation in *My New Gun*, and Allison Anders' *Gas Food Lodging*, a moving but also humorous film about a mother seeking to raise two daughters on her own at a desert truck stop, was showcased at the prestigious Berlin Film Festival. Hal Hartley, who previously showed his gifts with *Trust*, was back with *Simple Men*, a story about two brothers in search of their long-vanished father. Carl Franklin's taut melo-dramatic crime story *One False Move* was affecting filmmaking.

Domination By Hollywood. Despite examples of widespread if unsung talent, the best distribution efforts for independent films still do not reach the numbers of viewers of expensively promoted Hollywood films. The major box-office successes in 1992 were action films or formula comedies. *Batman Returns* took in more than $162 million, and *Lethal Weapon 3* topped $143 million. *Sister Act*, featuring Whoopi Goldberg in a nun's habit, surpassed $134 million. *Basic Instinct*, a controversial film about a woman killer, benefited from the hype and the marquee value of Michael Douglas and Sharon Stone and took in more than $117 million. Another that passed $100 million was the frivolous comedy *Wayne's World*, a spinoff from television's *Saturday Night Live*. However, one consciousness-raising film that exceeded the $100 million mark was *A League of Their Own*, about the women's baseball teams of the 1940s.

Sometimes intended blockbusters flop. It seemed like a viable idea to come up with a film on the 500th anniversary of Columbus' heralded discovery. In fact, there were two films about Columbus—*Christopher Columbus—The Discovery*, with George Corraface and Marlon Brando; and *1492: Conquest of Paradise*, with Gérard Dépardieu. Both fizzled.

Art and Life. Few films get to open to the kind of publicity that surrounded Woody Allen's *Husbands and Wives*. Audiences went with the intent of finding parallels in the story to the details of Allen's private life permeating the media. Whatever the director's inspiration, he succeeded in drawing incisive characterizations that added up to what many felt ranked among his best work. Commercially, however, the publicity did not draw a bigger audience than usual for an Allen film. Allen's other 1992 release was *Shadows and Fog*, a German expressionist-style comedy.

The most talked-about dramatic film specifically based on a real life was *Malcolm X*, Spike Lee's epic about the renowned slain African American leader, played convincingly by Denzel Washington. Another biographical film, *Hoffa*, starred Jack Nicholson as the vanished labor boss, with a script by David Mamet and direction by Danny DeVito. In a lighter vein, legendary star Charlie Chaplin was played by Robert Downey, Jr., in *Chaplin*, directed by Richard Attenborough.

A two-film combination by director Michael Apted was a most unusual blend of art and real-

In "Unforgiven," Clint Eastwood and Gene Hackman share a bench in Big Whiskey, a fictional no man's town in the U.S. West. Eastwood (left), who also directed and produced the film, stars as an old gunfighter with an unsuccessful hog farm who returns to his former trade in order to collect a $1,000 bounty. Hackman portrays a sadistic sheriff, and Richard Harris (standing) is a former outlaw known as English Bob.

Spike Lee's biographical "Malcolm X," starring Denzel Washington, chronicles the controversial Black Muslim's life from street hustler to spokesman for black power.

© Thomas Hartwell/Sygma

ity. His *Thunderheart* was a fictional treatment of the 1975 shootout at the Pine Ridge reservation in South Dakota. He also directed *Incident at Oglala*, a documentary produced by Robert Redford about the controversial imprisonment of Leonard Peltier following the event.

Personal Bests. On balance the movie year is most likely to be remembered for various high-profile acting performances and directorial achievements. In addition to the performances by Nicholson (also appearing with Tom Cruise in *A Few Good Men*), Washington, and Downey, Jr., numerous other actors also took the spotlight. Anthony Hopkins gave an exquisitely nuanced leading performance in *Howards End*, made by James Ivory and Ismail Merchant from E. M. Forster's book.

Dustin Hoffman gave a sharply etched performance in *Hero*, along with costar Andy Garcia in another worthy performance. Robert De Niro as a sleazy lawyer in *Night and the City*, and Jeremy Irons as a teacher in the throes of a breakdown in *Waterland* and as a father in love with his son's fiancée in *Damage* gave notable performances. Joe Pesci broadened his range in *The Public Eye*, which chronicles the underside of New York life, in a role vastly different from his hilarious performance in *My Cousin Vinny*.

Tim Robbins' stock rose with his impressive performances as the charming but opportunistic producer in *The Player*, Robert Altman's satire on Hollywood, and as the scheming country singer grasping political power in *Bob Roberts*, which he wrote and directed.

Clint Eastwood gave himself one of his best roles as the reformed but still lethal gunfighter in his much-praised western, *Unforgiven*, which he also directed. Eastwood gave full opportunity to Gene Hackman to excel as a villainous lawman, and to Morgan Freeman as Eastwood's buddy. Billy Crystal, playing a self-destructive comedian through various phases of his career, was both funny and endearing in *Mr. Saturday Night*. He added to the tour de force by directing.

Robert Redford starred in the popular action-thriller *Sneakers*, and narrated without credit *A River Runs Through It*, which he skillfully directed, capturing the atmosphere of rural, open-country America in a bygone era. Powerful ensemble acting distinguished *Glengarry Glen Ross*, the adaptation of David Mamet's cynical play depicting real-estate salesmen in a cutthroat atmosphere. Jack Lemmon, Al Pacino, Alec Baldwin, Ed Harris, Alan Arkin, and Kevin Spacey were superb. Gary Sinise and John Malkovich were applauded in *Of Mice and Men*, the latest adaptation of John Steinbeck's classic, with Sinise also directing.

Daniel Day-Lewis was the main reason for seeing the otherwise disappointing *Last of the Mohicans*. James Caan as a tough gambler who deep down is a romantic helped make *Honeymoon in Vegas* enjoyable, as did Nicolas Cage as his rival. One of the year's male performances most likely to be remembered was that of Sydney Pollack as the straying husband in Woody Allen's *Husbands and Wives*, which also featured a noteworthy performance by increasingly popular Liam Neeson. And Steven Seagal, the action favorite, gave his fans more of the same in *Under Siege*. Gary Oldman took his turn at playing the most famous of vampires in Francis Ford Coppola's flamboyant *Bram Stoker's Dracula*. John Lithgow's depiction of a killer with multiple personalities enlivened Brian De Palma's bizarre thriller *Raising Cain*. Ned Beatty gave a glowing portrayal as Irish tenor Josef Locke in the winsome *Hear My Song*.

Women's Roles. There were not nearly as many good roles for women, but Michelle Pfeiffer easily stole *Batman Returns* as Catwoman. Allen's *Husbands and Wives* was brightened by the performances of Judy Davis and Juliette Lewis. A trio of actresses—Emma Thompson, Vanessa Redgrave, and Helena Bonham Carter—brought distinction to *Howard's End*.

Geena Davis boosted her already lively career by playing a baseball player in *A League of Their Own* and the gung-ho television reporter in *Hero*. Marisa Tomei was as memorable as Joe Pesci in *My Cousin Vinny* in her role as his taken-for-granted but smarter girlfriend. Among other rising actresses were Sarah Jessica Parker as the prospective bride in *Honeymoon in Vegas* and Lysette Anthony as the girlfriend in *Husbands and Wives*.

MOTION PICTURES | 1992

ALADDIN. Directors, John Musker and Ron Clements; screenplay by Clements and Musker, Ted Elliott, Terry Rossio. Original score by Alan Menken. (animated)

ALIEN 3. Director, David Fincher; screenplay by David Giler, Walter Hill, Larry Ferguson. With Sigourney Weaver, Charles S. Dutton.

BAD LIEUTENANT. Director, Abel Ferrara; screenplay by Zoe Lund and Ferrara. With Harvey Keitel.

BASIC INSTINCT. Director, Paul Verhoeven; screenplay by Joe Eszterhas. With Michael Douglas, Sharon Stone.

BATMAN RETURNS. Director, Tim Burton; screenplay by Daniel Waters. With Michael Keaton, Danny DeVito, Michelle Pfeiffer, Christopher Walken.

BECOMING COLETTE. Director, Danny Huston; screenplay by Ruth Graham. With Klaus Maria Brandauer, Mathilda May.

BEETHOVEN. Director, Brian Levant; screenplay by Edmond Dantes and Amy Holden Jones. With Charles Grodin.

BEST INTENTIONS, THE. Director, Bille August; screenplay by Ingmar Bergman. With Samuel Froler, Pernilla August, Max von Sydow.

BODYGUARD, THE. Director, Mick Jackson; screenplay by Lawrence Kasdan. With Kevin Costner, Whitney Houston.

BRANCHES OF THE TREE, THE. Written and directed by Satyajit Ray.

BRIEF HISTORY OF TIME, A. Director, Errol Morris, based on the book by Stephen Hawking. (documentary)

BROTHER'S KEEPER. Directors, Joe Berlinger and Bruce Sinofsky. (documentary)

CHAPLIN. Director, Richard Attenborough; screenplay by William Boyd and David Robinson. With Robert Downey, Jr., Dan Aykroyd, Kevin Kline, Geraldine Chaplin.

CHRISTOPHER COLUMBUS: THE DISCOVERY. Director, John Glen; screenplay by John Briley, Cary Bates, and Mario Puzo, based on the story by Puzo. With George Corraface, Marlon Brando, Tom Selleck, Rachel Ward.

CITY OF JOY. Director, Roland Joffé; screenplay by Mark Medoff from the Dominique Lapierre novel. With Patrick Swayze, Pauline Collins.

CRYING GAME, THE. Written and directed by Neil Jordan. With Forest Whitaker, Stephen Rea, Jaye Davidson.

DAMAGE. Director, Louis Malle; screenplay by David Hare. With Jeremy Irons, Miranda Richardson, Juliette Binoche, Rupert Graves.

DEATH BECOMES HER. Director, Robert Zemeckis; screenplay by Martin Donovan and David Koepp. With Meryl Streep, Bruce Willis, Goldie Hawn, Isabella Rossellini.

DIGGSTOWN. Director, Michael Ritchie; based on the novel *The Diggstown Ringers* by Leonard Wise. With James Woods, Louis Gossett, Jr.

DISTINGUISHED GENTLEMAN, THE. Director, Jonathan Lynn; screenplay by Marty Kaplan. With Eddie Murphy.

DOUBLE EDGE. Written and directed by Amos Kollek. With Faye Dunaway, Amos Kollek.

ENCHANTED APRIL. Director, Mike Newell; screenplay by Peter Barnes. With Josie Lawrence, Miranda Richardson, Polly Walker, Joan Plowright.

FAR AND AWAY. Director, Ron Howard; screenplay by Bob Dolman. With Tom Cruise, Nicole Kidman.

FEW GOOD MEN, A. Director, Rob Reiner; screenplay by Aaron Sorkin, from his play. With Tom Cruise, Jack Nicholson, Demi Moore, Kiefer Sutherland, Kevin Bacon.

FINE ROMANCE, A. Director, Gene Saks; screenplay by Ronald Harwood, based on the play *Tchin Tchin* by François Billetdoux. With Julie Andrews, Marcello Mastroianni.

FOREVER YOUNG. Director, Steve Miner; screenplay by J. J. Abrams. With Mel Gibson, Isabel Glasser, Elijah Wood.

1492: CONQUEST OF PARADISE. Director, Ridley Scott; screenplay by Roselyne Bosch. With Gérard Depardieu.

GAS FOOD LODGING. Written and directed by Allison Anders, based on the novel *Don't Look and It Won't Hurt* by Richard Peck. With Brooke Adams, Ione Skye, Fairuza Balk, James Brolin.

HAND THAT ROCKS THE CRADLE, THE. Director, Curtis Hanson; screenplay by Amanda Silver. With Annabella Sciorra, Rebecca De Mornay, Madeline Zima.

HOFFA. Director, Danny DeVito; screenplay by David Mamet. With Jack Nicholson, Danny DeVito, Armand Assante.

HOME ALONE 2: LOST IN NEW YORK. Director, Chris Columbus; screenplay by John Hughes. With Macaulay Culkin, Joe Pesci, Daniel Stern.

HONEY, I BLEW UP THE KID. Director, Randal Kleiser; screenplay by Thom Eberhardt, Peter Elbling, Garry Goodrow. With Rick Moranis, Robert Oliveri.

HOWARDS END. Director, James Ivory; screenplay by Ruth Prawer Jhabvala. With Vanessa Redgrave, Helena Bonham Carter, Emma Thompson, Anthony Hopkins.

HUSBANDS AND WIVES. Written and directed by Woody Allen. With Woody Allen, Mia Farrow, Judy Davis, Juliette Lewis, Liam Neeson, Sydney Pollack.

INCIDENT AT OGLALA. Director, Michael Apted; edited by Susanne Rostock. Narrated by Robert Redford. (documentary)

INDOCHINE. Director, Regis Wargnier; screenplay by Wargnier, Erik Orsenna, Louis Jardel, and Catherine Cohen. With Catherine Deneuve, Vincent Perez.

INTERVISTA. Written and directed by Federico Fellini. With Federico Fellini, Anita Ekberg, Marcello Mastroianni.

IN THE SOUP. Written and directed by Alexandre Rockwell. With Steve Buscemi, Seymour Cassel, Jennifer Beals.

LAST OF THE MOHICANS, THE. Director, Michael Mann; screenplay by Mann and Christopher Crowe, based on the novel by James Fenimore Cooper and the screenplay by Philip Dunne. With Daniel Day-Lewis.

LEAGUE OF THEIR OWN, A. Director, Penny Marshall; screenplay by Lowell Ganz and Babaloo Mandel. With Tom Hanks, Geena Davis, Lori Petty, Madonna.

LEAP OF FAITH. Director, Richard Pearce; screenplay by Janus Cercone. With Steve Martin, Debra Winger.

LETHAL WEAPON 3. Director, Richard Donner; screenplay by Jeffrey Boam and Robert Mark Kamen. With Mel Gibson.

LIGHT SLEEPER. Written and directed by Paul Schrader. With Willem Dafoe, Susan Sarandon, Dana Delany.

LORENZO'S OIL. Written and directed by George Miller. With Nick Nolte, Susan Sarandon, Peter Ustinov.

LOVE FIELD. Director, Jonathan Kaplan; screenplay by Don Roos. With Michelle Pfeiffer, Dennis Haysbert.

LOVER, THE. Director, Jean-Jacques Annaud; screenplay by Gerard Brach, based on the novel by Marguerite Duras. With Jane March, Tony Leung.

MALCOLM X. Director, Spike Lee; screenplay by Arnold Perl and Lee, based on the book *The Autobiography of Malcolm X*, as told to Alex Haley. With Denzel Washington, Angela Bassett, Spike Lee, Kate Vernon.

MAMBO KINGS, THE. Director, Arne Glimcher; screenplay by Cynthia Cidre, based on the novel *The Mambo Kings Play Songs of Love* by Oscar Hijuelos. With Armand Assante, Cathy Moriarty, Antonio Banderas, Desi Arnaz, Jr.

MEDITERRANEO. Director, Gabriele Salvatores; screenplay by Vincenzo Monteleone. With Vanna Barba, Giuseppe Cederna.

MIDNIGHT CLEAR, A. Written and directed by Keith Gordon, based on the novel by William Wharton. With Peter Berg, Ethan Hawke, Frank Whaley, Gary Sinise.

MINDWALK. Director, Bernt Capra; screenplay by Floyd Byars and Fritjof Capra, based on Fritjof Capra's book *The Turning Point*. With Liv Ullmann, Sam Waterston.

MISSISSIPPI MASALA. Director, Mira Nair; screenplay by Sooni Taraporevala. With Denzel Washington.

MISTRESS. Director, Barry Primus; screenplay by Primus and J. F. Lawton. With Robert De Niro, Robert Wuhl, Martin Landau, Eli Wallach, Danny Aiello.

MR. SATURDAY NIGHT. Director, Billy Crystal; screenplay by Crystal, Lowell Ganz, Babaloo Mandel. With Billy Crystal, Helen Hunt, David Paymer, Julie Warner.

MY COUSIN VINNY. Director, Jonathan Lynn; screenplay by Dale Launer. With Joe Pesci, Marisa Tomei.

MY NEW GUN. Written and directed by Stacy Cochran. With Diane Lane, James Le Gros, Stephen Collins, Tess Harper, Bill Raymond, Bruce Altman, Maddie Corman.

NIGHT AND THE CITY. Director, Irwin Winkler; screenplay by Richard Price, from the 1950 Jules Dessin film based on the novel by Gerald Kersh. With Robert De Niro, Jesscia Lange, Cliff Gorman.

NOISES OFF. Director, Peter Bogdanovich; screenplay by

Anthony Hopkins and Emma Thompson are husband and wife in ''Howards End,'' a critically acclaimed, beautifully photographed film from the team of producer Ismail Merchant, director James Ivory, and screenwriter Ruth Prawer Jhabvala. The film, based on an E. M. Forster novel, is a drawing-room drama of the Edwardian era that addresses the English class system and involves two high-minded sisters with a rich acquisitive British family.

© Photofest

Marty Kaplan, based on the play by Michael Frayn. With Carol Burnett, Michael Caine, Denholm Elliott.

OF MICE AND MEN. Director, Gary Sinise; screenplay by Horton Foote, based on the novel by John Steinbeck. With John Malkovich, Gary Sinise.

ONE FALSE MOVE. Director, Carl Franklin; screenplay by Billy Bob Thornton and Tom Epperson.With Bill Paxton.

PASSION FISH. Written and directed by John Sayles. With Mary McDonnel, Alfre Woodard, David Strathairn.

PATRIOT GAMES. Director, Phillip Noyce; screenplay by W. Peter Iliff and Donald Stewart, based on the novel by Tom Clancy. With Harrison Ford.

PETER'S FRIENDS. Director, Kenneth Branagh; screenplay by Martin Bergman, Rita Rudner. With Kenneth Branagh, Emma Thompson, Stephen Fry, Rita Rudner, Imelda Staunton.

PLAYBOYS, THE. Director, Gillies Mackinnon; screenplay by Shane Connaughton and Kerry Crabbe. With Albert Finney, Robin Wright.

PLAYER, THE. Director, Robert Altman; screenplay by Michael Tolkin, based on the novel by Tolkin. With Tim Robbins.

POISON IVY. Director, Katt Shea; screenplay by Shea and Andy Ruben. With Sara Gilbert, Drew Barrymore.

PRELUDE TO A KISS. Director, Norman René; screenplay by Craig Lucas, based on his play. With Alec Baldwin, Meg Ryan, Kathy Bates, Ned Beatty, Patty Duke.

RAISE THE RED LANTERN. Director, Zhang Yimou; screenplay by Ni Zhen, based on a novel by Su Tong. With He Caife, Jin Shuyuan, Gong Li.

RAISING CAIN. Written and directed by Brian De Palma. With John Lithgow.

RESERVOIR DOGS. Written and directed by Quentin Tarantino. With Harvey Keitel, Lawrence Tierney.

RIVER RUNS THROUGH IT, A. Director, Robert Redford; screenplay by Richard Friedenberg. With Tom Skerritt, Craig Sheffer, Brad Pitt, Emily Lloyd.

SCENT OF A WOMAN. Director, Martin Brest; screenplay by Bo Goldman, from Dino Risi's film, *Profumo di Donna*. With Al Pacino, Chris O'Donnell.

SHADOWS AND FOG. Written and directed by Woody Allen. With Woody Allen, Mia Farrow, John Malkovich.

SHINING THROUGH. Written and directed by David Seltzer. With Michael Douglas, Melanie Griffith.

SINGLE WHITE FEMALE. Director, Barbet Schroeder; screenplay by Don Roos, based on the novel *SWF Seeks Same* by John Lutz. With Bridget Fonda, Jennifer Jason Leigh.

SISTER ACT. Director, Emile Ardolino; screenplay by Joseph Howard. With Whoopi Goldberg, Maggie Smith.

SNEAKERS. Director, Phil Alden Robinson; screenplay by Lawrence Lasker, Walter F. Parkes and Robinson. With Robert Redford, Sidney Poitier, Dan Aykroyd, River Phoenix, Ben Kingsley.

STORYVILLE. Director, Mark Frost; screenplay by Frost and Lee Reynolds. With James Spader.

STRAIGHT TALK. Director, Barnet Kellman; screenplay by Craig Bolotin and Patricia Resnick. With Dolly Parton.

STRANGER, THE. Written and directed by Satyajit Ray. With Utpal Dutt, Deepankar De, Mamata Shankar.

STRANGER AMONG US, A. Director, Sidney Lumet; screenplay by Robert J. Avrech. With Melanie Griffith, Eric Thal.

THUNDERHEART. Director, Michael Apted; screenplay by John Fusco. With Val Kilmer, Sam Shepard.

TOUS LES MATINS DU MONDE. Director, Alain Corneau; screenplay by Pascal Quignard and Corneau, based on the novel by Quignard. With Jean-Pierre Marielle, Gérard Départdieu.

TOYS. Director, Barry Levinson; screenplay by Levinson, Valerie Curtin. With Robin Williams.

TRESPASS. Director, Walter Hill; screenplay by Robert Zemeckis, Bob Gale. With Ice-T, Ice Cube.

TWIN PEAKS; FIRE WALK WITH ME. Director, David Lynch; screenplay by Lynch and Robert Engels. With Kyle MacLachlan.

UNDER SIEGE. Director, Andrew Davis; screenplay by J. F. Lawton. With Steven Seagal.

UNFORGIVEN. Director, Clint Eastwood; screenplay by David Webb Peoples. With Clint Eastwood, Gene Hackman.

UNLAWFUL ENTRY. Director, Jonathan Kaplan; screenplay by Lewis Colick. With Kurt Russell, Madeleine Stowe.

USED PEOPLE. Director, Beeban Kidron; screenplay by Todd Graff. With Shirley MacLaine, Jessica Tandy, Kathy Bates, Marcia Gay Harden, Marcello Mastroianni.

VENICE/VENICE. Written and directed by Henry Jaglom. With Henry Jaglom, Nelly Alard.

VOYAGER. Director, Volker Schlöndorff; screenplay by Rudy Wurlitzer, based on the novel *Homo Faber* by Jax Frisch. With Sam Shepard, Julie Delpy.

WATERLAND. Director, Stephen Gyllenhaal; screenplay by Peter Prince, based on the novel by Graham Swift. With Jeremy Irons, Sinead Cusack.

WAYNE'S WORLD. Director, Penelope Spheeris; screenplay by Mike Myers, Bonnie Turner, and Terry Turner. With Mike Myers, Dana Carvey, Rob Lowe, Tia Carrere.

WHISPERS IN THE DARK. Written and directed by Christopher Crowe. With Annabella Sciorra, Jill Clayburgh, Alan Alda.

WHITE MEN CAN'T JUMP. Written and directed by Ron Shelton. With Wesley Snipes, Woody Harrelson.

WIND. Director, Carroll Ballard; screenplay by Rudy Wurlitzer, Mac Gudgeon. With Matthew Modine, Jennifer Grey, Jack Thompson.

WISECRACKS. Director, Gail Singer. (documentary)

WOMAN'S TALE, A. Director, Paul Cox; screenplay by Cox and Barry Dickins. With Sheila Florance.

ZEBRAHEAD. Written and directed by Anthony Drazan. With Michael Rappaport, N'Bushe Wright, Paul Butler, DeShonn Castle, Ron Johnson, Ray Sharkey.

Although *Death Becomes Her* was an ambitious mess in satirizing the effort of actresses to beat the aging process, Meryl Streep and Goldie Hawn went all out in their strange roles bathed in special effects.

Standouts. Overall, the classiest film of the year and one of the best was *Howards End;* director Mike Newall's *Enchanted April* also earned respect for its story of Victorian women broadening their horizons by taking a vacation together. An especially welcome entertainment was *Peter's Friends,* directed by Kenneth Branagh, who appeared in the film as well, along with Emma Thompson. A surprise in the film was the discovery of the acting potential of comedian and cowriter Rita Rudner.

Robert Altman's funny, sophisticated, and thoroughly cynical *The Player,* his merciless take on Hollywood, was hailed as a comeback for the fiercely independent-spirited director, underscoring Hollywood's shortcoming in failing to appreciate some of his worthy but less-heralded efforts.

Candor about sex characterized Jean-Jacques Annaud's film version of Marguerite Duras' novel *The Lover,* set in 1929 colonial Vietnam with Tony Leung and Jane March.

Perhaps the film with the most nerve was the intellectual documentary *A Brief History of Time,* Errol Morris' film of the best-selling book by Stephen Hawking.

Foreign-Language Films. The U.S. market for non-English films continued to be difficult. Among the few that broke through to some extent were Danish filmmaker Bille August's *The Best Intentions,* with Ingmar Bergman's screenplay about the early lives of his parents, and the Russian drama *Adam's Rib.* The New York Film Festival presented numerous foreign-language films, some of which received commercial releases. Foremost among the selections were Agnieszka Holland's *Olivier, Olivier* (French); *Léolo* (French Canadian); the profound and exciting *The Oak* (Romanian); Finnish director Aki Kaurismaki's *La Vie de Bohème* (Finnish/French); and internationally-acclaimed director Zhang Yimou's *The Story of Qiu Ju* (Chinese). Zhang Yimou also won attention for his *Raise the Red Lantern.*

Business. Ismail Merchant and James Ivory (*Howard's End*), whose reputations and careers have thrived on their independence, struck a deal with the Walt Disney Company for a series of films over at least three years. . . . Author and columnist Art Buchwald won his suit against Paramount for taking his idea and turning it into the Eddie Murphy vehicle *Coming to America* (1988), but the award of $150,000 was small by Hollywood standards. . . . The ratings board of the Motion Picture Association of America decided to give in to demands and cite reasons why films have been given their labels.

WILLIAM WOLF, *New York University*

MOZAMBIQUE

After nearly two years of intermittent negotiations, a Mozambique truce was signed in August 1992. Brokered in part by Zimbabwe President Robert Mugabe, Catholic Church leaders, the Italian government, and the head of the British industrial conglomerate Lonrho, the agreement in principle was followed by a peace treaty, signed in Rome on October 4. The agreement ended a 16-year war between the Front for the Liberation of Mozambique (Frelimo) government of President Joaquim Chissano and the Mozambique National Resistance (Renamo) rebel movement, led by Afonso Dhlakama.

The war had claimed an estimated 1 million lives, caused an equal number of people to seek refuge in neighboring countries, and created about 4.5 million refugees in all. Thus, much like war-weary Angolans, Mozambicans greeted the news of a peace agreement with a mixture of cynicism and cautious optimism. The agreement represented a decision by the two leaders to open the way for democratic government. In part, the two leaders were brought to the conference table by a devastating drought, severe economic decline, and international pressures. Before the settlement, Frelimo controlled most of the cities and towns but was cut off from rural areas, many of which were controlled by Renamo.

The Agreement. Under the terms of the agreement, Renamo's organizational structures would remain in place in the areas under its control, but a joint commission would be set up to act as a link between Renamo-controlled areas and the Frelimo government until elections could be held during 1993. The treaty also stipulated that an army of 15,000 members from each side be formed and that major aid donors soon find ways to bring food and water to Mozambique. The groups also agreed to a cease-fire to be monitored by United Nations observers.

While Mozambique's status as a one-party state reportedly ended in March and several political parties had emerged, Frelimo and Renamo were the major contestants for power.

PATRICK O'MEARA and N. BRIAN WINCHESTER
Indiana University

MOZAMBIQUE • Information Highlights

Official Name: Republic of Mozambique.
Location: Southeastern coast of Africa.
Area: 309,494 sq mi (801 590 km²).
Population (mid-1992 est.): 16,600,000.
Chief City (1987 est.): Maputo, the capital, 1,006,765.
Government: *Head of state,* Joaquím A. Chissano, president (took office November 1986). *Head of government,* Mário da Graça Machungo, prime minister (took office July 1986). *Legislature* (unicameral)—People's Assembly.
Gross Domestic Product (1989 est. U.S.$): $1,600,000,000.

© Jack Vartoogian

Marking the 500th anniversary of Columbus' voyage to America, New York's Metropolitan Opera presented the world premiere of Philip Glass' new opera "The Voyage" in 1992. Patricia Schuman, front, sang the role of the Commander in the epic.

MUSIC

Performances honoring the bicentennials of Wolfgang Amadeus Mozart's death (a holdover from 1991) and Gioacchino Rossini's birth, as well as the quincentennial of Columbus' arrival in America, were a running theme in the concert and opera world in 1992. New York City's Lincoln Center continued its survey of Mozart's complete surviving works, wrapping up the series at the end of August. Rossini was the focus of vocal recitals and opera productions, including a new staging of the rarely heard *William Tell* at the San Francisco Opera in June. And Columbus was celebrated in everything from early-instrument concerts devoted to 15th-century Spanish music to works composed on the theme of discovery.

In the pop-music arena, Prince signed a $100 million deal with Warner Brothers records, making him one of the highest-paid pop performers.

Classical

The two major new operas of 1992—John Corigliano's *The Ghosts of Versailles* and Philip Glass' *The Voyage*—both premiered at New York's Metropolitan Opera and in their own ways saluted Mozart, Rossini, and Columbus.

The Corigliano, which had its world-premiere run at the Met at the end of 1991 and in early 1992, was a complex fantasy involving the ghosts of Marie Antoinette and Louis XVI of France, and the playwright Pierre Beaumarchais, whose Figaro plays are now best known through their musical settings by Mozart and Rossini. In a three-hour work in which broad comedy is juxtaposed with elements of tragedy, the Figaro characters are brought back to life, a romance blossoms between Beaumarchais and Marie Antoinette, and the French Revolution is reconsidered.

The production, with Hakan Hagegard, Teresa Stratas, and Marilyn Horne in the large cast, drew mixed critical response but was a tremendous popular success. The critical/popular split was similar with Glass' *The Voyage* (starring Timothy Noble, Tatiana Troyanos, and Patricia Schuman), which had its premiere on Columbus Day. The date was appropriate, since Columbus' voyage was the focus of the second act, and his death was the subject of the epilogue.

It had been assumed that the entire opera was to be about Columbus, following in the footsteps of Jacques Offenbach, Alberto Franchetti, and Daurius Milhaud, but as it turned out, the work was more about exploration and discovery than about specific explorers and discoverers. A prologue shows a wheelchair-bound scientist—clearly meant to be physicist Stephen Hawking; Glass had written the sound-track music for *A Brief History of Time,* the film about Hawking released in the summer. The opera's first act is set in 13,000 B.C., when a band of space travelers crash-lands on Earth, and the third act, set in 2092, shows both earthbound explorers and the crew of a space shot.

Musically, the two works could not have been more different: The lushly scored Corigliano work was eclectic, with everything from 12-tone writing to whistleable melodies; *The Voyage* was the latest expansion of the arpeggiated Minimalist style that Glass helped to create in the late 1960s. Common to both works were noted playwrights as librettists. Corigliano's collaborator was William M. Hoffman, whose best-known play is *As Is.* Glass' partner was David Henry Hwang, author of *M. Butterfly.*

It was unusual for the Met to present two premieres in such close proximity, and altogether there were fewer than usual notable opera premieres in 1992. Outside the Met's pair, the new work that attracted the greatest attention was *McTeague,* William Bolcom's collaboration with Arnold Weinstein and the film director Robert Altman, given its premiere by the Lyric Opera of Chicago in October.

In July the Italian television director Andrea Andermann directed a unique live televised performance of Giacomo Puccini's *Tosca* that was both spectacular and, in an entirely literal way, realistic. With Catherine Malfitano in the title role and Plácido Domingo as Cavaradossi, Andermann staged his *Tosca* at the very settings in Rome where the libretto says that the action took place, and at the appropriate times of day: The first act was broadcast at noon from the Church of Sant'Andrea della Valle; the second act was broadcast that evening from the Palazzo Farnese; and the last act took place on the roof of the Castel Sant'Angelo at six the next morning. Only the singers and the camera crews were present at the locations. Zubin Mehta conducted the orchestra at a studio a few miles away from the performance sites. An estimated 1.5 billion viewers in 107 countries tuned in to the spectacle.

The opera world also had its share of disasters. At Expo '92, the world's fair in Seville, a Paris Opera chorus singer was killed and several others were injured severely when a piece of scenery fell during a rehearsal. And that, in the always volatile world of Parisian cultural politics, led to a shake-up of the Paris Opera's administration. At Munich's Bavarian State Opera House, a hydraulic system, installed during a 1989 renovation and believed to be a state-of-the-art system for operating stage mechanisms, turned out to be a fertile breeding ground for bacteria. In May, when the machinery ground to a halt, the company was forced to cancel several productions and planned to close down for a year.

Another closing—that of England's Glyndebourne, 50 mi (80 km) south of London, at Lewes—was planned and even anticipated: In July, after a gala attended by the Prince of

During the Kirov Opera's first-ever U.S. visit, the company performed Tchaikovsky's opera "Queen of Spades" at the New York Metropolitan Opera House. Valery Gergiev and Oleg Zinogradov were the conductor and choreographer, respectively.

© Halebian/Gamma-Liaison

Wales, Glyndebourne closed its doors, and workmen came to tear down the intimate 830-seat hall. In the summer of 1993 there would be no festival, but in 1994 Glyndebourne was to open a new 1,130-seat theater on the site of the old one.

Also notable in the opera world was the fact that Russian companies, now free to tour at will in the West, found themselves competing against each other for hard currency, with mixed results. Soon after it was announced that the Kirov Opera of St. Petersburg would have a short spring residency at the Met, for example, St. Petersburg's smaller company—once called the Maly Opera and now renamed the St. Petersburg Opera—jumped in for a tour in advance, preempting the Kirov with productions of *Boris Godunov* and *Pique Dame,* which the Kirov also had announced.

It was a bad move. The St. Petersburg productions were threadbare and neither well-staged nor well-sung. In fact, taking those performances together with those the Bolshoi presented in 1991, some critics wondered whether the legends of Soviet musical prowess one heard during the Cold War were merely myth. But the Kirov, led by music director Valery Gergiev, changed all that. With lavish stagings of Sergey Prokofiev's *Fiery Angel* as well as the two works the St. Petersburg Opera earlier had brought over, a polished orchestra, and fine casts, it met expectations of what a great Russian opera company could be.

In October, Ostankino, the Russian Television and Radio Company, announced a joint venture with the Los Angeles-based U.S.S.U. Arts Group to market—through U.S., Asian, and European record companies—its vast archive of concert broadcasts, some 1.2 million tapes.

If opera companies programmed conservatively in 1992, many of the United States' regional companies—including the Virginia Opera, the Houston Grand Opera, and the Seattle Opera—reported better-than-ever ticket sales.

Orchestras. News in the symphony world, over which the recession hung heavily, was gloomier. Virtually all the major U.S. orchestras reported sizable deficits. Contract negotiations upped the ante further at the Chicago Symphony and the New York Philharmonic, where musicians make a minimum salary of between $65,000 and $70,000 per year. At the same time government, corporate, and private sources of the funding on which most orchestras depend have been pressed by other concerns, not to mention a growing pool of applicants. Also, orchestras looked at the lack of musical programs in elementary schools and worried aloud about whether there would be future audiences for symphonic music.

A few regional orchestras, like those of Syracuse, NY, and San Antonio, TX, suspended operations—temporarily in the case of Syracuse.

Some of these concerns were the focus of a report issued by the American Symphony Orchestra League, which celebrated its 50th anniversary in 1992. Using data supplied by orchestras over a 25-year period, the organization presented a report that raised the questions: Has the orchestral world expanded too ambitiously in the last quarter century? Are the year-round seasons that have become common since the early 1970s really supportable? Do tours and recordings help attract recognition and income, or merely deplete the treasuries? And might orchestras better serve their communities and expand their audiences by abandoning their "home" halls and playing at various locations in their cities?

The suggestion inherent in the last of those questions probably would not sit well with orchestras that have spent fortunes either building or renovating their concert halls. In 1992 the San Francisco Symphony tore its ten-year-old hall apart and put it back together in time for its season opening, with encouraging results. And New York City's Avery Fisher Hall, which has been plagued with acoustical problems since it opened in 1972, had its stage area rebuilt, with results more dramatic than when the entire hall was reconfigured in 1976.

Despite the sometimes-grim prognostications of the American Symphony Orchestra League report, orchestras have not forgotten how to celebrate. The New York Philharmonic came through its first season with Kurt Masur on its podium, sounding more cohesive and energized than it had in many years, and in September the orchestra—the oldest in the United States—launched its season-long 150th-birthday party with a schedule of premieres, special exhibitions, a European tour, and several special programs, including a week devoted to the music of Leonard Bernstein.

Thematic programming, in fact, had become a hot trend in the symphonic world. At the Philharmonic, Masur made a point of building programs that brought together works with either musical or historical connections—one, for example, that juxtaposes the Dmitry Shostakovich "Babi Yar" Symphony and Bright Sheng's "H'un," a work about the Chinese Cultural Revolution.

Other conductors thought along similar lines. Leon Botstein, the new music director of the American Symphony Orchestra, announced a season devoted mostly to 20th-century works, with each program devoted to a specific trend in the arts world, and with several related to exhibitions at New York City's museums. And Simon Rattle toured the United States during the year with a concert, lecture, and exhibition series that focused on the musical ferment of the 20th century's first decade.

Allan Kozinn, *"The New York Times"*

Jazz music continued to gain in popularity in 1992, and was brought even more into the public eye when saxophonist Branford Marsalis, far left, was named the Tonight Show's *new bandleader in May.*

Popular and Jazz

It was obvious by 1992 that popular music in the 1990s increasingly had become a patchwork of genres, each of which generally appealed to only one part of the consumer market. That was clear from the charts in the recording industry's primary trade magazine, *Billboard*, which now was tallying its album rankings by actual sales figures gathered from around the United States. One result was that the biggest releases debut high on the chart, many at Number 1. The more telling change, however, was that country and rap artists had come to be equal if not dominant players on a chart that formerly had been dominated by more rock-oriented performers.

The annual Grammy Awards seemed to reflect this diversity by showering awards on a record that belonged to no definite category, Natalie Cole's *Unforgettable*. The album featured songs made famous by the singer's late father, Nat King Cole. The song "Unforgettable," which found the daughter singing a "duet" with her father, was named song of the year despite the fact that it was written 40 years ago. All the same, the success of *Unforgettable* underscored the fact that popular-music fans no longer stop buying music when they reach their 30s and 40s. Insiders were frankly amazed that Bonnie Raitt's *Luck of the Draw* album outsold its phenomenally successful predecessor, *Nick of Time*.

Country. A more general reflection of the broadening of the pop marketplace has been the tremendous surge in popularity of country music. Many older pop-music fans, alienated by rap and loud rock music, have turned to the more tempered style of country music, and are attracted particularly to its emphasis on lyrics.

Garth Brooks struck a country gold mine with a songwriting style that bears the influence of pop artists like James Taylor and Billy Joel, and a stage show that has more to do with rock 'n' roll than traditional country music. Brooks' record sales have been nothing less than spectacular. As of late 1992, his *Garth Brooks* album had sold 3 million; *No Fences*, 8 million; and *Ropin' the Wind*, 7 million. In the last half of 1992, Brooks released two more best-sellers —*The Chase* and a Christmas album called *Beyond the Season*. He also flirted with retirement following the birth of his daughter.

Brooks was not the only one to benefit from the country boom. Reba McEntire had been a country star for years but never had had a million-seller; however, her latest, *For My Broken Heart*, sold more than 2 million by late 1992. The popular mother-daughter duo, the Judds, called it quits, but Wynonna Judd found instant success with her solo debut, *Wynonna*. Among the other performers enjoying banner years were Vince Gill, Trisha Yearwood, Travis Tritt, Alan Jackson, and Marty Stewart.

Meanwhile, the country radio format also surpassed the more pop-oriented Top 40 format. Still, while country acts did well on the album charts, only one scored a huge pop single: Billy Ray Cyrus came out of nowhere to enjoy one of the biggest hits of the year, "Achy Breaky Heart," an uptempo tune that was promoted in part through the invention of the "achy breaky" dance. Cyrus sold 3 million copies of his debut album, *Some Gave All,* and proved that country music can be promoted with the same élan as any other pop product.

© Larry Busacca/Retna Pictures

Country music's sensation of the year was Billy Ray Cyrus with his out-of-nowhere hit, "Achy Breaky Heart." The tremendously popular tune even inspired a dance.

Rap. While country showed tremendous commercial muscle, rap continued to exert great sway on the pop charts and on the culture in general. In the wake of the Los Angeles riots, many scrutinized anew the message offered by the more radical rappers.

Rap is no stranger to controversy, but in 1992 it even emerged as a minor issue in the U.S. presidential campaign. Ice-T, a Los Angeles rapper who also has appeared in movies, took a lot of heat over a song called "Cop Killer" that appeared on an album by Ice-T's group, Body Count. Ironically, Body Count is not even a rap group, but a hard-core heavy-metal band. When police groups in Texas got wind of the song, they gained national publicity with a proposal to boycott Time-Warner, the parent company of Ice-T's record company. U.S. Vice-President Dan Quayle denounced Ice-T. Sales of the album *Body Count* quickly swelled. Ice-T eventually disappointed free-speech advocates by requesting that the song be deleted from future pressings of the album. He also said he would give away free copies of the song at his live concerts. Meanwhile, Democratic candidate Bill Clinton chastised a little-known rapper, Sister Souljah, for allegedly inflammatory remarks she made following the L.A. riots.

The irony in all the controversy was that the biggest rap songs of the year had little to do with politics. Kris Kross, a duo comprised of two young teenagers, shot to the top of the charts with a tune called "Jump," and sold 3 million copies of their debut album, *Totally Krossed Out*. The most radical thing about Kris Kross was their habit of wearing their clothes backwards. And a rapper called Sir Mix-A-Lot had a Number 1 hit, "Baby Got Back," that celebrated a part of the female anatomy.

Rock. The biggest story in rock music in 1992 was the rise of the so-called "grunge" sound, which mostly meant loud guitar bands that owed much to punk rock and Led Zeppelin. Many of these bands hailed from Seattle. Nirvana caused the most excitement, with a dynamic combination of rock bombast and tuneful melodies that powered its *Nevermind* album to sales of more than 3 million. Other bands from Seattle that found a ready audience for brash if not always innovative rock included Soundgarden and Pearl Jam.

U2 received critical kudos for its *Achtung Baby* release, and mounted an ambitious tour that began in arenas and later filled outdoor stadiums. The concert business did well with major names, but continued to have trouble profitably presenting new acts or less popular veterans. One major surprise was the ease with which a concert featuring two rock veterans, Eric Clapton and Elton John, sold out two shows at New York's Shea Stadium. Clapton,

© Porter Gifford/Gamma-Liaison

Eric Clapton, above, and Elton John performed in two shows at Shea Stadium in August 1992. Clapton had a Number 1 hit during the year with "Tears in Heaven."

who had a Number 1 single with "Tears in Heaven," a song about the death of his young son, is now at the peak of a successful career that stretches back to the mid-1960s.

Bruce Springsteen simultaneously released two new collections, *Human Touch* and *Lucky Town,* his first new recordings since 1987, and his first release since disbanding his E Street Band. Though initial sales were brisk, pundits were quick to note that the albums did not remain at the top of the charts. A more realistic assessment might be that the seismic success of Springsteen's *Born in the U.S.A.,* like the even more monumental sales of Michael Jackson's *Thriller,* reflected the serendipity of an artist profitably defining a moment in time. In Springsteen's case, both of his new collections sold more than 1 million copies each even before Springsteen hit the road for a highly successful tour that seemed sure to generate further sales.

Movie soundtracks peppered with rock and rap songs continued to be an effective way to promote movies; sometimes the soundtracks did even better than the films. The oddest soundtrack success came from the hit film *Wayne's World,* which spawned a revival of the old Queen song, "Bohemian Rhapsody." The revived interest in the British rock band was bittersweet, however, as it came after the late 1991 death from AIDS of lead singer Freddie Mercury.

Jazz. The biggest story in jazz continued to be its entrance into mainstream culture. Nineteen ninety-two was the inaugural year of an ambitious program of jazz at New York's Lincoln Center that featured a number of concerts designed to illustrate the jazz repertory. Among the presentations was the debut of the Lincoln Center Jazz Orchestra, a big-band ensemble that includes a principal voice in jazz and the Lincoln Center program, trumpeter Wynton Marsalis. Marsalis himself released albums exploring the relationship between jazz and blues. The Lincoln Center Orchestra toured the country and released its own album, *Portrait of Ellington.*

Saxophonist Branford Marsalis, Wynton's older brother, scored an equally telling milestone: He became the leader of a new "*Tonight Show* Band" when Jay Leno took over the show from Johnny Carson. The Marsalis-led ensemble features a crackerjack band playing songs by Thelonious Monk, John Coltrane, and a host of other jazz composers whose music rarely, if ever, has been featured on network television.

A number of radio stations remained successful with a format featuring groups like the Yellowjackets and the sax player Kenny G—jazz critics called it "jazz lite." At the same time, the purchase of entertainment companies by foreign investors, especially the Japanese, has resulted in better deals for less mainstream artists. Since Sony bought CBS Records, the Japanese branch of the international recording giant has financed recordings by innovators like saxophonist David Murray and the Art Ensemble of Chicago. These musicians typically had recorded for small, independent labels. Now they had major-label distribution in their own country.

The Recording Business. In 1992 the unit sales of compact discs for the first time surpassed those of cassettes, allowing the record industry to record modest growth in spite of the general recession. But there were worries that CD sales might be peaking, with the market penetration of disc players stuck at around 37%. It was no wonder the rollouts were slow for the next round of playback options: the much-anticipated battle between the digital compact cassette from Philips and Sony's Mini Disc. Anticipating the introduction of these recordable machines, labels were looking to improve the quality of their analog tapes in hopes of prolonging the life of the format. One question at least was settled: Six major manufacturers agreed to abandon the longbox and sell compact discs in packaging that adheres to a common 5-inch by 5½-inch (12.7-cm by 13.97-cm) dimension.

JOHN MILWARD
Free-lance Writer and Critic

MYANMAR

In 1992, Myanmar's ruling military junta, the State Law and Order Restoration Committee (SLORC), tried to soften its image as a human-rights violator. Such an effort followed the awarding of the 1991 Nobel Peace Prize to jailed opposition leader Aung San Suu Kyi. Nevertheless, the country remained a pariah in the world community, and was threatened with UN-imposed sanctions. Japan, Myanmar's principal source of foreign aid, also warned the SLORC about its dismal human-rights record.

Conciliatory Measures. In an effort to placate its critics, the SLORC released a number of political prisoners—nearly 350 by late September, including former Prime Minister U Nu. Many of those released were members of the National League for Democracy (NLD), which had won the 1990 elections but was not allowed to govern. In April, Aung San Suu Kyi was permitted to see her husband for the first time in two years, but she remained under house arrest. The regime offered to free her if she would leave the country—a condition she refused to consider. In December a UN General Assembly committee called for the unconditional release of the Nobelist.

The cabinet also was enlarged to include five civilians (some of them former military officers), and the SLORC chairman, Saw Maung, was replaced by another general, Than Shwe. In June the SLORC met with representatives of seven political parties, ostensibly with the aim of drafting a new constitution and holding new elections. However, because the parties all had been purged of their original leadership, the gesture lacked credibility.

The universities, closed for the most part since 1988, were reopened in August. On September 11 the curfew was lifted, but a ban on public assemblies remained in effect. The official end of martial law on September 26 was viewed by most observers as little more than cosmetic.

Ethnic Conflicts and Foreign Relations. The SLORC showed no signs of adopting a more moderate policy toward Myanmar's disaffected minority groups. The year was marked by some particularly savage encounters with insurgents in border areas, which in turn caused problems with neighboring countries.

Trouble erupted with Thailand when the Myanmar army—now more than 300,000 strong and equipped with sophisticated military hardware from China—attacked ethnic Karen rebels just inside the Thai border. In the past, Thailand had ignored such incursions, enjoying as it did lucrative mineral and logging concessions from the SLORC. In October 1991, however, the SLORC abruptly halved the amount of hardwoods Thai companies were allowed to log, and at the same time doubled the price. Environmentally the move was long overdue: Myanmar's teak forests—more than 80% of the world's total—were disappearing at an alarming rate. Politically, however, it meant that Thailand's former indifference to border violations changed to strong opposition, and military clashes resulted.

The most serious dispute, however, was caused by SLORC military action against the Rohingyas, a Muslim people who have lived in northern Myanmar for centuries. During 1992 more than 300,000 Rohingyas fled west into neighboring Bangladesh, reporting incidents of murder, torture, and rape by the rampaging military. Bangladesh, already impoverished and overpopulated, was unable to absorb such large numbers of refugees. In April negotiations between Bangladesh and the SLORC resulted in an end to action against the Rohingyas. Repatriation of the refugees, however, was held up by Rangoon's resistance to UN supervision of the repatriation process.

Economic Conditions. The country continued to struggle with an external debt of nearly $6 billion, a totally unrealistic exchange rate, and a black market that offered goods at one tenth the official rate. The infrastructure continued to decay. Though the government targeted tourism as a priority sector, the political instability, draconian exchange rate, and lack of basic transportation and accommodations suggested that it would be some time before tourism was a significant factor in the economy. Visitors totaled only 10,000 in 1991, less than one quarter the number that came annually before the military crackdown in 1988. Travelers in 1992 had to travel in groups, although they could stay up to two weeks—an increase from the seven-day limit in force for nearly 20 years.

Indictment of the SLORC. Bishop Desmond Tutu and Elie Wiesel, both Nobel peace laureates, charged the SLORC with forcing tens of thousands of juveniles into prostitution in Thailand. They also contended that Myanmar had assumed an enlarged role in the growth, processing, and export of opium and heroin.

LINDA K. RICHTER, *Kansas State University*

MYANMAR · Information Highlights

Official Name: Union of Myanmar.
Location: Southeast Asia.
Area: 261,969 sq mi (678 500 km²).
Population (mid-1992 est.): 42,500,000.
Chief Cities (1983 census): Yangon (Rangoon), the capital, 2,513,023; Mandalay, 532,949.
Government: *Head of government,* Gen. Than Shwe (took power April 23, 1992). *Legislature* (unicameral)—National Assembly.
Monetary Unit: Kyat (5.983 kyats equal U.S.$1, June 1992).
Gross Domestic Product (1990 est. U.S.$): $16,800,-000,000.
Economic Index (1991): *Consumer Prices* (1980 = 100), all items, 386.7; food, 412.3.
Foreign Trade (1991 U.S.$): *Imports,* $616,000,000; *exports,* $412,000,000.

NEBRASKA

Even as Nebraskans in 1992 celebrated the 125th anniversary of statehood, they were concerned with problems reminiscent of 1991. The state continued to wrestle with major tax and budget problems and tried to execute a condemned murderer. Weather extremes again provided almost daily topics for conversation.

Tax Muddle. Problems with Nebraska's tax structure continued to occupy state officials. The state Supreme Court had ruled in 1991 that property-tax exemptions—on seed, grain, livestock, agricultural machinery, and business inventories—violated the clause in the state constitution that required uniformity in taxing. Thus, the effort to create a workable tax system dominated the 1992 legislative session. After much debate, a twofold compromise was reached: LB 1063, a law to tax real and personal property through different formulas, was passed and a constitutional amendment was proposed, authorizing the law to take effect.

Voters ratified the amendment in the May primary election. Then, to avoid possible court challenges to LB 1063, Gov. Ben Nelson called the legislature into special session to reenact it. In the meantime unexpected state expenses had cropped up, and in September the legislature returned to Lincoln for a special budget-cutting session. A package of 16 bills shaved $97.2 million from the state budget over the years 1993–95.

Meanwhile, the state Supreme Court, ruling unconstitutional a stopgap measure passed before the amendment was adopted, ordered the state to refund some $97 million in business and farm taxes. In November the legislature convened for a third special session, passing a one-year tax plan to cover the latest deficit. The measure promptly aroused protests.

Election. There were few surprises in the voting for U.S. president. While choosing three of the state's five electors by congressional districts under a new law that the Democrats hoped would win them at least one electoral vote, the state remained solidly in the Republi-can column. There was no U.S. Senate race in Nebraska; in the House two Republicans and one Democrat, all incumbents, were reelected. Nebraskans also voted for a term-limits law, authorized a state lottery, and gave local governments more control over liquor licenses.

Death Penalty. Harold Lamont Otey, on death row since his conviction for a 1977 murder, again escaped the death penalty when the U.S. Supreme Court upheld a federal judge's order to postpone the execution in order to review claims that Otey received an unfair clemency hearing before the state Pardons Board.

Economy. Though 1992 was hardly a boom year, Nebraskans were fortunate to escape the most severe consequences of the nation's recession. Bankruptcies, while still high, dropped sharply, and the unemployment rate remained among the lowest in the country.

Weather, as always, was a significant factor in the state's agricultural economy, but except for prolonged dry spring weather in western portions, Nebraska experienced one of the wettest years in memory. July temperatures were the lowest on record, and the month's rainfall in Omaha (9.66 inches; 24.5 cm) was the fourth highest ever recorded. Except for areas severely damaged by flooding, farmers enjoyed bumper crops, although at harvesttime prices dropped to their lowest point in years.

WILLIAM E. CHRISTENSEN
Midland Lutheran College

NEBRASKA • Information Highlights

Area: 77,355 sq mi (200 350 km²).
Population (July 1, 1991 est.): 1,593,000.
Chief Cities (1990 census): Lincoln, the capital, 191,972; Omaha, 335,795.
Government (1992): *Chief Officers*—governor, Ben Nelson (D); lt. gov., Maxine Moul (D). *Legislature* (unicameral)—49 members (nonpartisan).
State Finances (fiscal year 1991): *Revenue,* $3,436,000,000; *expenditure,* $2,266,000,000.
Personal Income (1991): $28,220,000,000; per capita, $17,718.
Labor Force (June 1992): *Civilian labor force,* 867,100; *unemployed,* 29,900 (3.5% of total force).
Education: *Enrollment* (fall 1990)—public elementary schools, 198,080; public secondary, 76,001; colleges and universities, 112,831. *Public school expenditures* (1990), $1,116,356,000.

NETHERLANDS

Although 1992 proved to be a quiet political year in the Netherlands, reduction of welfare benefits due to budget pressures brought demands for a rethinking of priorities. Yet the nation tied with Belgium and was behind only Denmark in a ranking of living standards.

Domestic Affairs. In response to a commission report, the education ministry announced that Dutch no longer would be the official language for teaching in the nation's schools and universities; each may teach in the language of its choice. This change was welcomed in some eastern areas, where German immigration has been high in recent years. In February, Prime Minister Ruud Lubbers disbanded the country's foreign intelligence service, following charges of fraud and illegitimate espionage.

Prostitution and Amsterdam's notorious red-light district are well-established institutions in the Netherlands, despite a 1911 law prohibiting brothels. Protests greeted proposals that brothels be legalized so that they could be controlled better and exploitation by pimps could be reduced. Prostitutes resented taxes intended for legal brothels and feared they would have to leave their window parlors for back streets. Social workers warned of the spread of sexual diseases by underground prostitution.

The Netherlands was struck by the worst airline disaster in the nation's history as an El Al cargo plane crashed into a crowded apartment complex in Duivendrecht in October 1992. More than 50 people were killed in the disaster.

© Bernard Bisson/Sygma

The measure legalizing brothels and sex clubs passed, however.

Parliament also approved reporting procedures for voluntary euthanasia, even though euthanasia technically remained a crime. Among other requirements, the terminally ill patient must be suffering extreme pain and have expressed an explicit wish to die. The practice has been growing since the 1970s. Upheld by Supreme Court decisions of 1984 and 1986, euthanasia is endorsed in guidelines issued by the Royal Dutch Society of Medicine.

In April a major earthquake centered in Roermond caused no loss of life in the Netherlands. On October 4, however, many inhabitants of crowded apartments—many of them unregistered immigrants—were killed when an El Al cargo plane crashed in Duivendrecht. The air disaster, the worst in the nation's history, shocked the population deeply.

The Economy. The economy showed slightly increased strength over the previous year, with industrial production, investment, and retail sales (except for autos) rising a few percentage points above 1991 levels. During the first half of the year, the trade surplus and private savings also increased. Nevertheless, the cabinet took prudent steps to ease taxes and to reduce inflation and unemployment, which fell slightly. In September the government released a proposed 1993 budget that cut expenditures for housing and defense and aimed to stimulate economic growth and jobs.

Foreign Affairs. The Dutch took pride in the signing on February 7 of the European Community (EC) treaty negotiated at Maastricht, the Netherlands, in December 1991. Yet there were questions about EC plans: Would required disclosures make Dutch firms susceptible to foreign takeover? Would EC reductions of government shipbuilding subsidies hinder the country's ability to compete? Would fishing quotas threaten that industry? Late in the year, parliament, nevertheless, ratified the Maastricht Treaty.

Killings of demonstrators in East Timor in 1991 brought suspension of Dutch aid to Indonesia. Jakarta responded by demanding that the Netherlands cease all aid and resign from the leadership of the Inter Governmental Group on Indonesia. Despite a desire to increase exports,

---

NETHERLANDS • Information Highlights

Official Name: Kingdom of the Netherlands.
Location: Northwestern Europe.
Area: 14,398 sq mi (37 290 km²).
Population (mid-1992 est.): 15,200,000.
Chief Cities (Jan. 1, 1991): Amsterdam, the capital, 702,444; Rotterdam, 582,266; The Hague, the seat of government, 444,240.
Government: *Head of state,* Beatrix, queen (acceded April 30, 1980). *Head of government,* Ruud Lubbers, prime minister (took office Nov. 1982). *Legislature*—States General: First Chamber and Second Chamber.
Monetary Unit: Guilder (1.6990 guilders equal U.S.$1, Oct. 23, 1992).
Economic Indexes (1991): *Consumer Prices* (1980 = 100), all items, 132.1; food, 122.7. *Industrial Production* (1980 = 100), 120.
Foreign Trade (1991 U.S.$): *Imports,* $125,906,-000,000; *exports,* $133,554,000,000.

the cabinet forbade a sale of four submarines to Taiwan; it conflicted with a 1984 pact with China whereby the Dutch agreed not to sell arms to Taiwan. An open-skies agreement signed with the United States allowed airlines from each country to fly unrestricted to all points in the other.

J. E. HELMREICH
Allegheny College

NEVADA

For Nevada the dominant themes of 1992 were the slumping economy, state governmental budget cuts, and the election. Following the 1990 census, Nevada continued as the fastest-growing U.S. state.

Elections. For the first time since 1964, a Democratic candidate for president, Bill Clinton, won Nevada's electoral votes. Clinton's margin of victory resulted from a strong showing in the Las Vegas area, where two thirds of the state's voters reside. Independent Ross Perot carried an impressive 26% of the vote. In the state Assembly, Democrats increased their control, winning 29 of the 42 seats. Republicans captured control of the state Senate with a bare one-seat majority of its 21 seats. U.S. Sen. Harry Reid, Congresswoman Barbara Vucanovich, and Congressman Jim Bilbray were reelected easily. Miriam Shearing was elected to the State Supreme Court, becoming the first woman on the court in recent history. Voter turnout in the general election was 48%, the lowest in 32 years. A ballot proposal to create an intermediate state court of appeals to lessen the Supreme Court's workload was defeated.

Voters refused to lift the legislators' $60-per-session limit on postage, unchanged since 1865. A constitutional amendment to delete a provision dating from the original constitutional convention that prohibited the state from loaning money to businesses also met defeat. The intent was to allow the offering of loans as an incentive to attract new businesses.

The Economy. The state economy was sluggish throughout 1992, reflecting not only national effects but its dependence on California's economic performance. In August unemployment rose to 7.2%, the highest since December of 1985, and job-rate growth dropped to 1.8%. Nevada's industries were stagnant in the second quarter, with mining showing a decline from the same quarter in 1991. Only the construction industry grew, but that was primarily because of the start of construction on three mega-casinos in Las Vegas, representing a nearly $2 billion investment. In the same quarter, gross gaming revenue dipped to $1.4 billion. The state's two primary sources of revenue, the gaming tax and the sales tax, not only did not increase to the projected 7% but showed declines over several months from the same period in 1991. Nevadans who considered their casino and tourism industries recession-proof learned otherwise in 1992.

Budget Crisis. Gov. Bob Miller was forced to cut government spending because of a potential $12 million deficit. State agencies were cut an average of 20%, public schools received a 6% cut, and higher education an 11% cut. Nearly 500 state employees received layoff notices. An innovative program to reduce class size to 19 students per teacher in the third grade was postponed. Class-size reductions that began in 1990 for the first and second grades remained in place. An additional $17 million deficit remained.

Other. Nevada continued into the seventh year of a drought, with water-use restrictions placed on residents in Reno, Sparks, and Carson City. Las Vegas began negotiations with upstream water users of the Colorado River for additional water for its growing population. . . . Jerry Tarkanian, the highly successful but controversial basketball coach at the University of Nevada, resigned and was replaced by Villanova's coach, Rollie Masamino.

TIMOTHY G. HALLER
Western Nevada Community College

NEW BRUNSWICK

New Brunswickers voted massively in favor of the Charlottetown Accord on the federal constitution, giving it a 61% popular endorsement in the Oct. 26, 1992, national referendum. They were swimming against the tide, however, as more than 54% of Canada's voters cast a "no" ballot.

In other 1992 news, the Question Period returned to the provincial legislature after a four-year absence. The government reduced tobacco and wine taxes, but continued cutting jobs. A C$61.1 million program to raise education standards was introduced.

Question Period. An old institution came back to life in the legislature on February 12,

---

NEVADA · Information Highlights

Area: 110,561 sq mi (286 352 km²).
Population (July 1, 1991 est.): 1,284,000.
Chief Cities (1990 census): Carson City, the capital, 40,443; Las Vegas, 258,295; Reno, 133,850.
Government (1992): *Chief Officer*—governor, Robert J. Miller (D); lt. gov., Sue Wagner (R). *Legislature* —Senate, 21 members; Assembly, 42 members.
State Finances (fiscal year 1991): *Revenue*, $3,553,000,000; *expenditure*, $3,436,000,000.
Personal Income (1991): $25,398,000,000; *per capita*, $19,783.
Labor Force (June 1992): *Civilian labor force*, 666,100; *unemployed*, 44,000 (6.6% of total force).
Education: *Enrollment* (fall 1991)—public elementary schools, 149,882; public secondary, 51,434; colleges and universities, 61,728,471. *Public school expenditures* (1990), $855,675,000.

NEW BRUNSWICK • Information Highlights

Area: 28,355 sq mi (73 440·km²).
Population (September 1992): 728,500.
Chief Cities (1986 census): Fredericton, the capital, 44,352; Saint John, 76,381; Moncton, 55,468.
Government (1992): *Chief Officers*—lt. gov., Gilbert Finn; premier, Frank McKenna (Liberal). *Legislature*—Legislative Assembly, 58 members.
Provincial Finances (1992–93 fiscal year budget): *Revenues,* $3,865,000,000; *expenditures,* $4,000,-000,000.
Personal Income (average weekly earnings, July 1992): $494.03.
Labor Force (September 1992, seasonally adjusted): *Employed* workers, 15 years of age and over, 293,000; *Unemployed,* 12.3%.
Education (1992–93): *Enrollment*—elementary and secondary schools, 141,650 pupils; postsecondary—universities, 19,000; community colleges, 3,450.

(All monetary figures are in Canadian dollars.)

when opposition members put questions to government ministers for the first time in more than four years. In the first Question Period of Liberal Premier Frank McKenna's second term, there were few fireworks. Issues raised by Conservative, New Democrat, and Confederation of Regions members concerned agricultural marketing boards, forest management, and job creation. The Question Period in its traditional, partisan form had been suspended after the Liberals swept all 58 seats in the 1987 provincial election. The Liberals were returned to power in 1991 with 46 seats; the other parties took 12 seats.

Economic News. The provincial budget introduced on March 31 contained a reduction in taxes on cigarettes, wines sold in bars and restaurants, and gasoline. The cuts were intended to discourage U.S. cross-border spending. The budget projected a C$135 million deficit on spending of C$4 billion in the 1992–93 fiscal year. About 750 government jobs were to be axed, mostly through attrition.

Soaring health costs were behind a March 25 government decision to close about 400 hospital beds and eliminate 273 hospital jobs.

Upgrading Education. The McKenna government unveiled a sweeping four-year, C$61.1 million education-reform plan in September, emphasizing more-intensive teaching of students, more testing, and smaller kindergarten classes. Most of the money was to be spent on beefing up curriculum content—especially in math, science, and languages—and on more support for remedial programs, libraries, and technology. The program was in response to a report of a 1991 independent governmental commission. Though the report, published in May 1992, called for a longer school year—200 days—the government retained the present 195-day calendar, but with more actual class time.

Other News. Danny Cameron was elected leader of the Confederation of Regions Party by 16 votes at a September convention in

Campbellton. With his win over Brent Taylor, Cameron became the official opposition leader in the provincial legislature.

Premier McKenna was greeted with an extended ovation when he strode into the legislature on April 14, a day after he endured an emergency landing at the Fredericton airport. McKenna emerged unharmed from the ordeal, which occurred due to a stuck landing gear.

JOHN BEST, *"Canada World News"*

NEWFOUNDLAND

In a nationwide referendum held on Oct. 26, 1992, Newfoundland was one of four provinces to vote "yes" to proposed constitutional amendments, only to see six other provinces reject and thus defeat the so-called Charlottetown Accord. Overall the provincial vote was 62.9% in favor and 36.5% against.

Fishery Concerns. The cod fishery was a cause of great concern in 1992. No matter what the quotas, as the months passed it became clear that there were few fish to be caught in the waters off the northeast coast of Newfoundland. At first the European Community was blamed for overfishing beyond the 200-mile (370-km) limit. To draw public attention, a convoy of seven ships left St. John's on March 29, headed for the Grand Banks. Canada's Prime Minister Brian Mulroney ruled out "gunboat diplomacy" but did condemn the "effective rape of a vital resource." That same month, federal Fisheries Minister John Crosbie announced a five-year ban on commercial salmon fishing. Some 2,600 fishermen were allowed to give up their licenses in return for compensation.

In July, Crosbie announced a two-year moratorium, banning all fishing effort directed at northern cod, in order to allow for the recovery of the stocks. Scientists had advised that the spawning biomass (cod old enough to breed)

NEWFOUNDLAND • Information Highlights

Area: 156,649 sq mi (405 720 km²).
Population (September 1992): 575,900.
Chief Cities (1986 census): St. John's, the capital, 96,216; Corner Brook, 22,719.
Government (1992): *Chief Officers*—lt. gov., Frederick William Russell; premier, Clyde Wells (Liberal). *Legislature*—Legislative Assembly, 52 members.
Provincial Finances (1992–93 fiscal year budget): *Revenues,* $2,759,100,000; *expenditures,* $2,788,-100,000.
Personal Income (average weekly earnings, July 1992): $509.47.
Labor Force (September 1992, seasonally adjusted): *Employed* workers, 15 years of age and over, 189,000. *Unemployed,* 19.2%.
Education (1992–93): *Enrollment*—elementary and secondary schools, 123,050 pupils; postsecondary—universities, 13,200; community colleges, 4,250.

(All monetary figures are in Canadian dollars.)

had declined drastically in the previous 12–18 months and were then at the lowest levels ever observed. Compensation payments for the estimated 20,000 affected plant workers and fishermen were related to earnings and set at a maximum of C$400 per week. The total federal expenditure would amount to more than C$500 million yearly.

An important fishery matter was settled on June 10 when the International Court of Arbitration announced its decision on a boundary dispute between Canada and France concerning the waters surrounding the French islands of St. Pierre and Miquelon. The award favored Canada but reserved important scallop beds for France. By October, negotiations between the two parties to settle individual fishing rights in each other's waters had broken off, and Canada unilaterally announced fishing opportunities for France in Canadian waters.

Hibernia Oilfield. Another blow to the economy centered around the Hibernia oil project. One partner, Gulf Canada Resources Ltd., announced that it would like to pull out of the project. Throughout 1992 the other partners searched for a buyer, but as time passed and none was found, layoffs and the possible mothballing of the construction site were in the offing. At year's end the federal government and Newfoundland's government guaranteed the costs of the work still in progress while the search for a buyer continued.

SUSAN MCCORQUODALE
Memorial University of Newfoundland

NEW HAMPSHIRE

In 1992 politics and the economy dominated the news in New Hampshire. The quadrennial appearances of presidential hopefuls peaked in January and early February as five Democrats and two Republicans bid for votes in tough economic times.

Politics. Both parties had lively primary contests after journalist Pat Buchanan challenged President George Bush in the Republican primary. Although the president received 53% of the vote, Buchanan was perceived as hurting Bush by garnering 37%. Paul Tsongas, with his tough economic message, won the Democratic primary with 33%, followed by Bill Clinton with 25%, Bob Kerry 11%, Tom Harkin 10%, and Jerry Brown 8%.

The state primary results in September gave voters a clear choice in the November gubernatorial contest. Former state Attorney General Steve Merrill (R) faced state Rep. Deborah "Arnie" Arnesen (D). Merrill, a fiscal conservative, advocated the status quo, whereas Arnesen supported a state income tax that would return 75% of the proceeds back to the cities and towns to reduce escalating property taxes. Since the state lacks a general sales or income

tax, the contest for governor was seen as a referendum on the existing tax structure. In the November election, Merrill received 56% of the vote to Arnesen's 40%. Other results demonstrated a clear preference for Republicans as Gov. Judd Gregg (R) won a U.S. Senate seat and two incumbent U.S. representatives, Bill Zeliff (R) and Dick Swett (D), each won reelection with solid majorities. Nonetheless, Clinton took New Hampshire with 39% of the vote. Bush had 38% and Ross Perot 23%. Republicans retained control of the state legislature and the executive council.

The general election undermined long-standing conventional political wisdom about New Hampshire. For the first time since 1952, a winner of the presidential primary did not win the presidency, and a long string of Republican presidential success in the state ended. The March decision of Sen. Warren Rudman (R) not to run for reelection was viewed by many as a loss for the state.

Economics. The economy remained troubled throughout the year. Unemployment through midyear persistently stayed above 7%—from a high of 7.7% in April to a low of 7.1% in February and March. In September a report stated that New Hampshire had lost more than 38,000 jobs between June 1990 and June 1992. Nevertheless, a few positive signs were evident. James River Corp., the north country's largest employer, announced it would keep open its two paper mills. The state's banks did much better than in 1991, and finally, in May, home sales were up from 1991.

Education. During the year the state board of education moved to eliminate mandated minimum standards. In September the board voted to eliminate most standards but decided to retain a limit on class size. The board's actions created an outcry from diverse groups who believed such changes would hurt public education, especially in poorer communities. A final board vote did not occur in 1992.

Other News. The year saw completion of the takeover of the state's largest utility, Public Service Company of New Hampshire, by

Northeast Utilities of Connecticut. . . . When more than 55,000 fans watched an Indianapolis-type auto race at the New Hampshire International Speedway, a state sporting-event attendance record was set.

WILLIAM L. TAYLOR
Plymouth State College

NEW JERSEY

Bickering between a Democratic governor and a Republican legislature, a recession, and election-year politics highlighted affairs in New Jersey in 1992.

Governor and Legislature. With the Republicans having gained control of both the Senate and the Assembly in 1991 elections, the new GOP majority had ambitious plans to modify or eliminate much of Gov. Jim Florio's tax, gun-control, and education programs. A key target was the 7% sales tax enacted in 1990, which the Republicans sought to roll back to 6%.

The governor, meanwhile, sent the legislature a record $15.7 billion budget and was openly skeptical about how the $608 million revenue loss which would result from a sales-tax reduction could be made up without layoffs and service cutbacks. Not surprisingly, the governor vetoed the sales-tax reduction passed by the legislature, and the veto was overridden. Layoffs were announced in August. Regarding gun control, the legislature removed some of the most stringent provisions of the two-year-

old law, but by mid-November had not overridden Florio's veto of the revised legislation.

Recession. A Rutgers University study found that the economic progress made by certain inner-city neighborhoods in the 1980s was gone by 1992.

In midsummer it appeared that there would be a $450 million state-budget deficit. Much was recovered when White House Chief of Staff Samuel Skinner agreed to give New Jersey $412 million in contested Medicaid reimbursement. Nevertheless, Standard and Poor placed the state's bond rating on credit watch. The announcement of 2,300 layoffs of state employees came in late summer. By October the actual number of layoffs had been reduced to about 1,500.

Good news came in late summer when it was announced that Fort Dix, which closed in September as an army training ground for regular troops, might become a federal prison in 1994, thereby creating 500 to 700 permanent new jobs. About 3,100 civilians had lost jobs.

Politics. New Jersey's clout in the U.S. Congress was weakened when three veteran Democrats did not seek reelection and census reapportionment reduced the House of Representatives delegation to 13.

Democrats won their first New Jersey presidential race since 1968 when Gov. Bill Clinton defeated President George Bush by a narrow margin, with some 15% of the vote going to Ross Perot. Statewide there was little change in the party balance of the congressional dele-

People are evacuated from their homes in Highlands, NJ, as a prewinter, hurricane-like storm strikes a 600-mi (966-km) area along the Atlantic Coast in December 1992. The storm hit New Jersey shore communities particularly hard.

NEW JERSEY • Information Highlights

Area: 7,787 sq mi (20 169 km²).
Population (July 1, 1991 est.): 7,760,000.
Chief Cities (1990 census): Trenton, the capital, 88,675; Newark, 275,221; Jersey City, 228,537; Paterson, 140,891; Elizabeth, 110,002.
Government (1992): *Chief Officers*—governor, James J. Florio (D). *Legislature*—Senate, 40 members; General Assembly, 80 members.
State Finances (fiscal year 1991): *Revenue,* $24,743,000,000; *expenditure,* $23,250,000,000.
Personal Income (1991): $199,181,000,000; per capita, $25,666.
Labor Force (June 1992): *Civilian labor force,* 3,998,500; *unemployed,* 367,600 (9.2% of total force).
Education: *Enrollment* (fall 1990)—public elementary schools, 783,558; public secondary, 306,088; colleges and universities, 323,947. *Public school expenditures* (1990), $9,206,952,000.

gation. Seven Democrats—including New Jersey's first Hispanic congressman, Robert Menendez, of the new 13th District—and six Republicans were elected. The expected "throw the rascals out" mentality did not prevail: The ten incumbent members of the House who ran for reelection won.

Locally, Thomas G. Dunn, mayor of Elizabeth since 1965, lost in the Democratic primary and Bret Schundler became the first Republican mayor in Jersey City in 75 years.

Other Issues. In a controversial move in October, New Jersey became the first state to freeze income benefits for women who have additional children while on welfare. . . . In March a federal appeals court reversed a lower-court decision prohibiting a Morristown library from restricting access. Earlier court rulings against the policy had thrown libraries around the nation into a quandary about how to reconcile differences between policies of open access and the homeless' use of libraries as refuges.

HERMANN K. PLATT, *Saint Peter's College*

NEW MEXICO

In 1992, for the first time since 1964, New Mexico gave its electoral votes to a Democratic presidential candidate. The November election saw Arkansas Gov. Bill Clinton win 46% of the state's votes to President George Bush's 38%. Independent candidate Ross Perot took 16%. During the campaign, New Mexico—typically forgotten where national politics is concerned—pulled in both Democratic and Republican leaders, espousing views on the free-trade agreement with Mexico. All three of New Mexico's incumbent U.S. congressmen were reelected.

Legislature. In 1992, New Mexico's focus shifted dramatically to human issues connected with its border with Mexico. The year before, officials had looked at industrial development,

anticipating the opening of a border crossing. Now the focus was the border shantytowns known as Colonias, populated largely by poor migrant workers. The state's congressional delegation fought for funding specifically to take care of waste and water systems in the Colonias. While federal legislators looked for money to clean up problems that already existed, state legislators in 1993 were expected to look at ways to prevent further problems.

The state's public employees gained clout when the legislature approved the Public Employee Bargaining Act, requiring municipalities and other public employers to bargain with public employees within a union.

Environment and Wildlife. Gold in the hills of northern New Mexico took the headlines where environmental issues were concerned. In October, Pegasus Gold, a Canadian mining company, withdrew its effort to mine from a 58,000-acre (23 472-ha) site in the Ortiz Mountains south of Santa Fe. Environmentalists and residents of neighboring towns had opposed the mining because of water contamination associated with extracting trace gold. The mining operation also would use 720,000 gallons (2 725 497 l) of water per day. While the company's withdrawal relieved environmentalists, the threat remained that another company would take up the effort to extract gold. One upshot, however, was that the State Land Office boosted efforts to enact land-reclamation laws requiring mining companies to restore land to the condition it was in before mining took place.

According to a 1991 report by the Western Governor's Association, New Mexico—one of the world's largest producers of copper—was estimated to have 7,222 abandoned mines, 6,335 mine dumps, and 69 mi (111 km) of polluted streams.

New Mexico bird-watchers anguished over the death of a rare yellow-green vireo at the hands of a California ornithologist working near Carlsbad Caverns. The vireo, common in

NEW MEXICO • Information Highlights

Area: 121,593 sq mi (314 925 km²).
Population (July 1, 1991 est.): 1,548,000.
Chief Cities (1990 census): Santa Fe, the capital, 55,859; Albuquerque, 384,736; Las Cruces, 62,126.
Government (1992): *Chief Officers*—governor, Bruce King (D); lt. gov., Casey Luna (D). *Legislature*—Senate, 42 members; House of Representatives, 70 members.
State Finances (fiscal year 1991): *Revenue,* $4,931,000,000; *expenditure,* $4,527,000,000.
Personal Income (1991): $22,665,000,000; per capita, $14,644.
Labor Force (June 1992): *Civilian labor force,* 720,600; *unemployed,* 52,700 (7.3% of total force).
Education: *Enrollment* (fall 1990)—public elementary schools, 209,087; public secondary, 93,794; colleges and universities, 85,596. *Public school expenditures* (1990), $1,132,910,000.

Mexico and Central America, was the second of its kind spotted in New Mexico. The ornithologist killed it to document its presence in the state.

Religious Issues. In March an image of the Virgin Mary was said to appear at a home near Las Cruces. Word spread, and hundreds of people flocked to the home to see the image. Local Catholic Church officials would not confirm the sighting, and discouraged people from visiting the unofficial vision.

The state's Catholic community was shaken when it was discovered that James Porter, a former priest and admitted pedophile who molested dozens of altar boys and students three decades earlier, had served in Jemez Springs, NM, in the late 1960s. Several New Mexico men filed suit against Porter.

Other Matters. State issues not resolved in 1992 included the reintroduction of the Mexican gray wolf to the wild. Also, the Waste Isolation Pilot Plant that was to store nuclear waste in Carlsbad did not receive approval to open. The Santa Teresa border crossing, expected to be an economic boon for the state, failed to open in 1992.

KEITH WHELPLEY, *"Las Cruces Sun-News"*

NEW YORK

The recession continued to hold New York in its grasp in 1992, even as economic problems began to ease in other parts of the country. Entering the final weeks of the year, the jobless rate remained above 8%—more than one percentage point ahead of both the national figure and the level of unemployment in the state in 1991. Economists said by late autumn that they finally were seeing the first signs of impending economic recovery, but they warned that it would come slower to the Empire State than elsewhere in the United States. In other news,

© Porter Gifford/Gamma-Liaison

Following a difficult political campaign against Democrat Robert Abrams, Republican Alfonse D'Amato, New York's junior U.S. senator, captured a third term on Nov. 3, 1992.

government and politics dominated; late in the year New York's chief judge resigned after criminal charges were brought against him.

Government and Politics. The beginning of 1992 saw the state's political landscape somewhat changed. On Dec. 13, 1991, Assembly Speaker Mel Miller, whose influence in state government was second only to that of the governor, was convicted in Manhattan of fraud charges in connection with his private law practice. Also convicted with Miller was his former law partner and chief legislative aide, Jay Adolf. Under the state constitution, Miller automatically forfeited his Assembly seat.

On December 16, Democrats in the New York Assembly voted to name Saul Weprin, a Queens lawyer who had chaired the Ways and Means Committee, to take Miller's place. He joined Senate Majority Leader Ralph J. Marino, a Long Island Republican, and Democratic Gov. Mario Cuomo in three-way negotiations to shape a 1992–93 state budget.

Cuomo's very presence in the budget negotiations in the tenth year of his governorship had been in question until the final days of 1991. Widely viewed for years as a potential Democratic presidential contender, Cuomo announced on Dec. 20, 1991, that he would not be a candidate for his party's 1992 presidential nomination, saying he felt it necessary to devote his energies to resolving New York's persistent fiscal problems, rather than cam-

---

NEW YORK • Information Highlights

Area: 49,108 sq mi (127 190 km²).
Population (July 1, 1991 est.): 18,058,000.
Chief Cities (1990 census): Albany, the capital, 101,082; New York, 7,322,564; Buffalo, 328,123; Rochester, 231,636; Yonkers, 188,082; Syracuse, 163,860.
Government (1992): *Chief Officers*—governor, Mario M. Cuomo (D); lt. gov., Stan Lundine (D). *Legislature*—Senate, 61 members; Assembly, 150 members.
State Finances (fiscal year 1991): *Revenue,* $65,715,000,000; *expenditure,* $64,321,000,000.
Personal Income (1991): $405,765,000,000; per capita, $22,471.
Labor Force (June 1992): *Civilian labor force,* 8,599,300; *unemployed,* 788,400 (9.2% of total force).
Education: *Enrollment* (fall 1990)—public elementary schools, 1,827,936; public secondary, 770,401; colleges and universities, 1,035,323. *Public school expenditures* (1990), $19,515,000,000.

paigning in primaries for the nation's highest office.

Not since 1984 had a state budget been in place by April 1, the beginning of a new fiscal year. But Cuomo, Weprin, and Marino came close, hammering out an agreement that was enacted by legislators only a day late. For the fourth year, a scheduled reduction in the state personal income-tax rate was postponed, and the state imposed various other tax and fee hikes totaling more than $1 billion to put a balanced budget into place.

Bill Clinton won the April presidential primary, then easily carried New York in the November general election on his way to winning the White House, garnering 50% of the vote, to 34% for incumbent George Bush and 16% for independent Ross Perot.

Voters concerned about rising state debt in November turned down a proposal to issue bonds totaling $800 million to raise funds to repair the state's aging infrastructure, a proposal that had been endorsed by Cuomo and legislative leaders as an important stimulus to the economy. The overwhelming Democratic majority in the Assembly and the long-standing Republican hold on the Senate remained in place.

The most hotly contested political race of the year was for the seat of two-term U.S. Sen. Alfonse D'Amato, a Long Island Republican. State Attorney General Robert Abrams squeaked out a hard-fought primary win in September, edging former Rep. Geraldine Ferraro, who in 1984 had been the first woman nominated by a major party for U.S. vice-president. Trailing in the bitter race were the Rev. Al Sharpton, a community activist, and New York City Comptroller Elizabeth Holtzman. D'Amato, whose popularity had sunk in the aftermath of a Senate Ethics Committee probe, seemed politically vulnerable. But he survived a hard-hitting Abrams campaign, winning with barely 51% of the vote.

Another powerful figure disappeared from the official scene, however. Chief Judge Sol Wachtler, who presided over the state's top court and 3,000 other state judges, resigned in November after federal authorities charged him with atempting to extort money from a former lover.

REX SMITH
Editor, "The Record," Troy, NY

NEW YORK CITY

New York City inaugurated 1992 by raising subway and bus fares to $1.25, but, for a change, the budget news got better. In contrast to the state, city officials reached an early accord on a $29.5 billion budget that was lauded by fiscal monitors, although projected gaps, unresolved labor negotiations, and the vagaries of municipal elections in 1993 suggested that financial stability might be short-lived. Not all the euphoria was budgetary. In July the city celebrated the 500th anniversary of Columbus' voyage of discovery with a majestic gathering of tall ships—perhaps the largest such flotilla of the 20th century. The same month, New York again played host to a Democratic National Convention—this time, a virtual love-fest at which Bill Clinton was nominated by the nation's leading might-have-been, Gov. Mario M. Cuomo.

Crime and the Mayor. But much of 1992 in New York was marked by crime, crashes, and contention. The book was closed on two controversial cases. Four young men were sentenced to the maximum 25-years-to-life term in the fatal stabbing of a Utah tourist on a Manhattan subway platform. And, following a sensational trial punctuated by a mob turncoat's gripping testimony, the previously invincible John Gotti was found guilty of murder and racketeering charges that ended his streak of eluding conviction as boss of the Gambino crime family. Gotti was sentenced to life in prison without parole.

The resolution of several other prominent cases seemed inconclusive to many New Yorkers. After an Egyptian immigrant was acquitted of murder in the killing of Meir Kahane, the Jewish Defense League founder, even the judge seemed so surprised that he meted out the maximum sentence for the remaining gun and assault charges on which the defendant was convicted. New York was calm in the aftermath of the Rodney King verdict in California. But in the Washington Heights section of upper Manhattan, a fatal shooting by police sparked several days of disorder. After contradictory testimony, a grand jury cleared the police officer. The neighborhood did not erupt again. Nor, after another jury decision, did violence flare again between blacks and Hasidic Jews in the Crown Heights section of Brooklyn as it had in 1991 after a young black boy was struck and killed by a car driven by a Hasidic man. In the ensuing riot, a rabbinical student was stabbed fatally. The acquittal of his accused assailant a year later prompted expressions of anguish and outrage from Jewish religious and secular leaders and angry complaints that suggested profound cracks in Mayor David N. Dinkins' "gorgeous mosaic."

For Dinkins, the city's first black mayor, 1992 marked another balancing act on a racial tightrope worn further by his frayed relationship with the police force. After the Washington Heights melee, the mayor belatedly moved to fulfill a campaign pledge to create an independent board to review individual complaints of abuse and brutality inflicted by the police. The proposal appeared doomed until a demonstration by angry police officers turned violent and turned the tide. The mayor and City Council compromised on legislation to create a board, all of whose members would be from outside the department. But the internal dissension stung Dinkins, given his role in expanding the force to record numbers and his appointment of a department veteran as police commissioner. A separate mayoral panel also was investigating police corruption and the department's self-policing practices after six officers were arrested for drug-dealing.

Crime was also an issue outside the department. Two students were shot fatally at a Brooklyn high school about an hour before a mayoral visit. And a Hispanic journalist who had been known as a crusader against drugs was shot to death in Queens.

Accidents and the Recession. Two accidents stunned a city seemingly inured to violence. In March a Cleveland-bound U.S. Air jetliner crashed into Flushing Bay on takeoff from La Guardia Airport in a snowstorm. Twenty-seven people were killed. In April the idyllic early-spring calm of Washington Square Park in Greenwich Village was transformed suddenly into chaos when a car careered out of control, killing four people and injuring 24 others.

The recession inflicted heavy social and economic costs. For the first time since the mid-1970s, the number of people on welfare topped 1 million. And, despite a mammoth city commitment to rehabilitate housing, homelessness was rising again—prompting a new response heavy on social services. Also, the city enacted what it hailed as the nation's toughest antismoking law.

SAM ROBERTS, *"The New York Times"*

NEW ZEALAND

In 1992, New Zealand began to experience some recovery from the economic slump of recent years, and voters overwhelmingly approved a change in the electoral system.

The Economy. Although New Zealanders seemed to feel increasing confidence that an export-led recovery was under way, leading indicators continued to give conflicting signals. Inflation for the year ending March 31, 1992, slumped to 0.8%, the lowest since 1950. Three months later it stood at 1%. Interest rates declined correspondingly; the prime lending rate, 13% at the start of 1992, was half that by mid-year.

By contrast, the alarming level of unemployment resisted erosion. In January almost one third of work-force-age Polynesians and one quarter of Maoris were jobless, and new post-World War II records continued to be posted. In June some 15% of the labor-force population was either out of work or employed on subsidized labor schemes. Concern at the inability of government to reverse this trend was reflected in public-opinion polls. In mid-

---

NEW ZEALAND • Information Highlights

Official Name: New Zealand.
Location: Southwest Pacific Ocean.
Area: 103,737 sq mi (268 680 km²).
Population (mid-1992 est.): 3,400,000.
Chief Cities (March 1991 census): Wellington, the capital, 324,792; Auckland, 885,377; Christchurch, 306,856; Napier-Hastings, 109,875.
Government: *Head of state,* Elizabeth II, queen, represented by Dame Catherine Tizard, governor-general (took office November 1990). *Head of government,* James Bolger, prime minister (took office November 1990). *Legislature* (unicameral) —House of Representatives.
Monetary Unit: New Zealand dollar (1.8751 N.Z. dollars equal U.S.$1, Oct. 27, 1992).
Gross Domestic Product (1990 U.S. $): $40,200,-000,000.
Economic Index (1991): *Consumer Prices* (1980 = 100), all items, 282.8; food, 261.4.
Foreign Trade (1991 U.S.$): *Imports,* $8,522,000,000; *exports,* $9,720,000,000.

---

year unemployment was named by 62% of respondents as the most important problem facing New Zealand.

Minister of Finance Ruth Richardson's second budget, presented early in July, announced funding for unemployment projects designed eventually to create 15,500 new jobs, and for a major tree-planting initiative; it also imposed an entertainment tax on business lunches and closed loopholes in the taxing of profits earned abroad.

Despite the prospect of further state assets sales expected to net $1 billion, investors were dissatisfied with the budget deficit of $3.3 billion. Given that two thirds of the budget was allocated to social services, health, and education, this was not surprising. Nevertheless, optimism centered on growth forecasts of 3.1%, and signs that the bitter economic medicine administered since 1985 was having an effect.

Electoral Reform. In September the first of two referendums was held on a proposed reform of the method used to elect members of parliament. Under the present system, all 97 members are elected from single-member constituencies. In a 55% turnout, 85% of the voters voted for a change. Of the four change options, 70% chose the mixed-member proportional (MMP) system. This first referendum was nonbinding; a second, which would be binding, was scheduled to be held in conjunction with the 1993 general election.

Domestic Politics. The ruling National Party's showing in the opinion polls during 1992 afforded it little comfort. At the end of 1991 its support had reached an all-time low, with 80% disapproving of its performance. A month later it just scraped home in a by-election in one of its safest seats. A poll in June revealed an almost even three-way split in support among National, the opposition Labour Party, and the Alliance, a new coalition of five minor parties. A further indication of the National Party's dwindling support was the victory of the Labour Party's candidate in a high-profile December 12 by-election.

Foreign Affairs. Apart from Prime Minister Jim Bolger's success in getting New Zealand a temporary seat on the United Nations Security Council in October, the profile of foreign-policy issues was generally unobtrusive.

GRAHAM BUSH, *University of Auckland*

NIGERIA

Election irregularities and the decision in 1992 by Nigeria's Gen. Ibrahim Babangida, head of the Armed Forces Ruling Council (AFRC), to postpone the transfer of power from military to civilian rule overshadowed problems connected to the rapidly deteriorating economy. Also during 1992, the capital was transferred from Lago to the less-congested Abuja, located in Nigeria's central region, and South Africa's President F. W. de Klerk was welcomed to Nigeria in April on the first visit ever by a South African head of state. Babangida, who also was heading the Organization of African Unity, extended the invitation after South Africa voted in a referendum to support de Klerk's efforts to dismantle the apartheid system.

Political Developments. The transition to a civilian government, begun in 1990, at first seemed on schedule as elections for governors were held in December 1991, followed by elections in July 1992 for a 91-seat Senate and 589-seat House of Representatives. Concurrent with the elections was the work of the National Population Commission (NPC), which was attempting to determine the demographics of Nigeria in order to provide the basis for future allotment of legislative seats. The NPC announced partial results in March, showing Nigeria's population to be only 88.5 million, more than 20 million fewer than previous estimates.

The AFRC and the National Elections Committee (NEC) recognized only two parties —the Social Democratic Party (SDP) and the more-conservative National Republican Convention (NRC). The NRC in the gubernatorial elections won 16 of the 30 vacancies. Despite efforts of the NEC, the legislative elections were marred by vote buying, intimidation, and rigging. Nonetheless, the AFRC accepted the results, which gave the SDP a majority of 15 in the Senate and 88 in the House.

Presidential primary elections, originally scheduled for August 1, were canceled because of irregularities. A new system was established, and three weeks later, elections were held. Of the dozens of candidates, the three most prominent were Gen. Shehu Musa Yar' Adua, who easily won the SDP primary, and Mallan Adamu Ciroma and Alhaji Shinkofi of the NRC, each of whom polled nearly 1 million votes. A runoff election was scheduled, but at this juncture, the AFRC on October 16 moved to halt further elections and dissolved the leadership of the two political parties because of widespread corruption. Caretaker committees were appointed to prepare a convention of the two parties to elect executives at all levels of government. The date for the transition of full authority to civilians, already postponed once, was scheduled for Jan. 2, 1993. In November, however, Babangida delayed the surrender of central authority by the AFRC to civilian rule until August 1993.

Economic Development. In January, Babangida announced that Nigeria could pay only $2.28 billion instead of the promised $5 billion to reduce its external debt. The debt of more than $30 billion forced the AFRC to adopt certain stringent measures suggested by the International Monetary Fund (IMF). This structural-adjustment program, especially the decision in March to float the naira, caused much inflation, with the cost of basic commodities more than doubling. The official exchange rate of the naira moved from 10.5 to 21.5 to the dollar. Revenues from petroleum, once more than $20 billion per year, fell to $7 billion. An added burden was the support given to the military effort of the Economic Community of West African States (ECOWAS) to end the civil war in Liberia. Ten battalions of troops— one half the total deployed—were Nigerian.

Inflation, high urban unemployment, and government corruption led to a series of strikes, and in May there was large-scale rioting in Lagos. The AFRC arrested hundreds of dissidents, banned a number of organizations critical of government actions, and closed most of the nation's universities. Accusations of brutal treatment of prisoners brought condemnation by a number of national and international human-rights organizations.

Nigeria continued to be plagued with endemic religious and ethnic violence. The worst clash—claiming more than 300 lives—was between Christians and Muslims in Kaduna state in May.

HARRY A. GAILEY, *San Jose State University*

NIGERIA • Information Highlights

Official Name: Federal Republic of Nigeria.
Location: West Africa.
Area: 356,668 sq mi (923 770 km²).
Population (mid-1992 est.): 90,100,000.
Chief City: Abuja, the capital.
Government: *Head of state and government,* Maj. Gen. Ibrahim Babangida, president, federal military government (took office Aug. 27, 1985). *Legislature*—Armed Forces Ruling Council; National Council of Ministers and National Council of States.
Monetary Unit: Naira (18.450 naira equal U.S.$1, July 1992).
Economic Index (1991): *Consumer Prices* (1988 = 100), all items, 182.6; food, 177.1.
Foreign Trade (1990 U.S.$): *Imports,* $4,318,000,000; *exports,* $12,912,000,000.

NORTH CAROLINA

Politics dominated the news in North Carolina in 1992.

Elections. North Carolinians maintained their independent habits by voting Republican in presidential and senatorial races and Democratic in state contests. President George Bush narrowly carried the state, and Lauch Faircloth defeated Sen. Terry Sanford by a larger margin. In the governor's race, Jim Hunt, already holding the state's record for gubernatorial service (1977–85), defeated Jim Gardner. Hunt would succeed GOP Gov. Jim Martin, who was constitutionally ineligible for a third term. Democrats also won all seats on the Council of State, an ex-officio panel that advises the governor; maintained a comfortable majority in the legislature; and elected eight of 12 members to the U.S. House of Representatives. As a consequence of partisan redistricting, for the first time since 1901 blacks would hold seats in Congress from North Carolina—Eva Clayton, the state's first black female member, in the 1st District, and Melvin Watt in the new 12th. Ralph Campbell, elected state auditor, would become the first African-American member of the Council of State.

Legislation. Faced with an unprecedented revenue shortfall, the General Assembly, consisting of the Senate and House of Representatives, adopted an $8.3 billion budget for 1992–93 that raised tuition at public colleges but required no general tax increase. Cuts or adjustments were made in a variety of state programs, and laws relating to workplace safety strengthened. The legislature also approved mail-order voter registration.

Crime and Punishment. In the longest and costliest criminal trial in state history, a jury convicted Robert H. Kelly, Jr., on 99 charges of sexual abuse of children in a day-care center in Edenton. He was sentenced to 12 consecutive life terms in prison. In another nationally

© Courtesy of the U.S. Olympic Committee Photo Library

Leroy T. Walker, 74-year-old former track coach and chancellor of North Carolina Central University, became the first black to be named president of the U.S. Olympic Committee.

publicized case, Emmett J. Roe, owner of a Hamlet chicken-processing plant where 25 employees died in a fire in 1991, was sentenced to 20 years in prison for involuntary manslaughter.

In a harbinger of cases to come, the state Supreme Court ruled that the host of a party can be held liable for damages in accidents resulting from a guest's consumption of alcohol. John S. Gardner, executed for a double murder, became the fifth prison inmate to be executed in the state since capital punishment was restored by the U.S. Supreme Court in 1976. Violence, vandalism, drug abuse, and teen pregnancy all increased in 1992. The city of Cary in north-central North Carolina closed its public park, and several school districts in the state instituted body searches for weapons.

People in the News. Julius Chambers, a civil-rights lawyer, was inaugurated as chancellor of North Carolina Central University. . . . Leroy T. Walker, a former chancellor of the same university, was elected president of the United States Olympic Committee, the first black to hold that position. . . . Death claimed William H. Bobbitt, a former chief justice of the state, and Alfreda J. Webb, the first black woman to serve in the North Carolina General Assembly.

Other Events. May 7, with a high of 48° F (9° C), was the coldest May day on record in the Piedmont; on the same day 41 inches (104 cm) of snow fell on Mt. Pisgah in the state's mountainous west. . . . Duke University won the NCAA basketball title for the second successive year.

H. G. JONES
University of North Carolina at Chapel Hill

NORTH CAROLINA · Information Highlights

Area: 52,669 sq mi (136 413 km²).

Population (July 1, 1991 est.): 6,737,000.

Chief Cities (1990 census): Raleigh, the capital, 207,951; Charlotte, 395,934; Greensboro, 183,521; Winston-Salem, 143,485; Durham, 136,611.

Government (1992): *Chief Officers*—governor, James G. Martin (R); lt. gov., Jim Gardner (R). *General Assembly*—Senate, 50 members; House of Representatives, 120 members.

State Finances (fiscal year 1991): *Revenue,* $15,266,000,000; *expenditure,* $15,036,000,000.

Personal Income (1991): $113,536,000,000; per capita, $16,853.

Labor Force (June 1992): *Civilian labor force,* 3,501,300; *unemployed,* 226,500 (6.5% of total force).

Education: *Enrollment* (fall 1990)—public elementary schools, 783,132; public secondary, 303,739; colleges and universities, 351,990. *Public school expenditures* (1990), $4,849,950,000.

NORTH DAKOTA

A political era ended with the death of Democratic U.S. Sen. Quentin Burdick. Despite an abnormally cold summer, farmers reaped a record wheat crop. A young North Dakotan captured the nation's attention with his display of courage following a grisly farm accident.

Burdick. Senator Burdick, 84, died in Fargo, ND, on September 8 of heart failure. A self-described "workhorse, not a show horse," he kept a low profile on Capitol Hill but was an unabashed fan of using committee chairmanships to funnel federal money to projects back home—the pork barrel. Burdick was considered the father of the state's modern Democrat-NPL Party. He was elected to Congress in 1958 and won a Senate seat in 1960. Either Burdick or his father, Usher, had been part of the state's congressional delegation for more than 50 years.

Elections. On November 3, Republicans captured the governorship for only the second time in 32 years. Millionaire businessman Ed Schafer, who promised job creation, defeated Attorney General Nicholas Spaeth, a popular Democrat, 58% to 41%. U.S. Sen. Kent Conrad (D) shocked party leaders with an eleventh-hour announcement that he would honor a 1986 campaign promise and not seek reelection because the federal deficit had not been reined in during his first term. Conrad's announcement allowed several Democrats to leapfrog into higher-profile offices. Rep. Byron Dorgan (D), a 12-year House veteran, won Conrad's Senate seat, topping Republican Steve Sydness 59% to 39%; state Insurance Commissioner Earl Pomeroy (D), who had planned to join the Peace Corps, won the sole U.S. House seat by defeating Republican John Korsmo, 57% to 39%; and Tax Commissioner Heidi Heitkamp (D) was elected attorney general over Republican Warren Albrecht, 62% to 38%.

In presidential balloting, George Bush topped Bill Clinton, 44% to 32%, with 23% for independent Ross Perot. Voters approved by 56% to 44% a measure limiting the state's U.S. senators and congressmen to 12 consecutive years in office. Defeated were limits to police motor-vehicle searches, increased state sales taxes, and Sunday-closing laws. Senator Conrad's political retirement ended before it began; he won a December 4 special election to complete Burdick's Senate term, easily defeating Republican Jack Dalrymple and antiabortionist Darold Larson.

Agriculture. Farmers harvested their biggest-ever wheat crop, an estimated 470 million bushels. A record barley crop also was reaped at 172.5 million bushels.

Accident. John Thompson, an 18-year-old Hurdsfield, ND, youth was working alone on the family farm on January 11 when he became entangled in a tractor's power takeoff shaft.

NORTH DAKOTA · Information Highlights

Area: 70,702 sq mi (183 119 km²).
Population (July 1, 1991 est.): 635,000.
Chief Cities (1990 census): Bismarck, the capital, 49,256; Fargo, 74,111; Grand Forks, 49,425; Minot, 34,544.
Government (1992): *Chief Officers*—governor, Edward Schafer (R); lt. gov., Rosemarie Myrdal (R). *Legislative Assembly*—Senate, 53 members; House of Representatives, 106 members.
State Finances (fiscal year 1991): *Revenue*, $1,998,000,000; *expenditure*, $1,793,000,000.
Personal Income (1991): $9,903,000,000; per capita, $15,605.
Labor Force (June 1992): *Civilian labor force*, 318,100; *unemployed*, 16,800 (5.3% of total force).
Education: *Enrollment* (fall 1990)—public elementary schools, 84,943; public secondary, 32,882; colleges and universities, 37,878. *Public school expenditures* (1990), $416,419,000.

His arms were torn from his body but he walked 100 yds (91 m) to his house, opened the door with his mouth, and called for help by dialing a push-button telephone with a pencil clenched in his teeth. Surgeons at a suburban Minneapolis hospital reattached his arms. On May 17 he graduated from high school.

Crime. State District Judge Lawrence Jahnke of Grand Forks was shot and critically wounded on May 4 in his courtroom while presiding over a child-support hearing. The defendant in the case, former Grand Forks city commissioner Reuben Larson, claimed he fired in self defense. Larson, 43, was convicted in October of attempted murder.

JIM NEUMANN, *Grand Forks, ND*

NORTHWEST TERRITORIES

Residents in the Northwest Territories (NWT) voted in three separate plebiscites during 1992, giving a "yes" to the Nunavut land claim, to an East-West border which would divide the NWT into two territories, and to proposed changes to the Canadian Constitution.

Nunavut Land Claim. The Inuit Federation of Nunavut set itself the strictest of rules for the ratification vote held in November 1992 on the land-claim agreement reached with the government of Canada in 1991. Not voting was considered the same as a "no" vote. Still, almost 70% of the eligible voters supported the agreement. Among those who did vote, about 90% voted "yes." The agreement covers almost 770,000 sq mi (2 000 000 km²) in the Canadian Arctic, generally following the tree-line north of the 60th parallel and extending to the North Pole and east to Baffin Island. The Inuit get full title to 137,000 sq mi (354 830 km²), $580 million in compensation, and a say in wildlife and development issues. It is the largest land-claim settlement in Canadian history. The agreement was subject to ratification by the Canadian Parliament.

NORTHWEST TERRITORIES
· Information Highlights

Area: 1,304,903 sq mi (3 379 700 km2).
Population: (1991 census): 57,649.
Chief Cities (1991 census): Yellowknife, the capital, 15,179; Iqaluit, 3,552; Inuvik, 3,206; Hay River, 3,206.
Government (1992): *Chief Officers*—commissioner, Daniel L. Norris; government leader, Nellie Cournoyea. *Legislature*—Legislative Assembly, 24 elected members.
Public Finances (1991–92 fiscal year): *Revenues,* $1,119,673,000; *expenditures* $1,166,596,000.
Education (1991–92): *Enrollment*—elementary and secondary schools, 14,750 pupils. *Public school expenditures,* $206,374,000.
(All monetary figures are in Canadian dollars.)

While only eligible Inuit voted in the Nunavut agreement plebiscite, all residents of the NWT were eligible to vote on the dividing line that would result in the establishment of two separate territories. In May the division was approved by 54% of those voting.

Constitutional Accord. The Charlottetown Accord—a package of constitutional changes put to the people of Canada in an October national referendum—was supported by 61% of those who voted in the NWT. The NWT was one of only four jurisdictions in the country that voted in favor of the accord, which was defeated by the country as a whole. In the NWT, there was strong backing for the constitutional recognition of aboriginal self-government and improvements in the means by which territories could become provinces.

Mine Strike. An especially bitter strike at the Giant Yellowknife Gold Mine (Royal Oak Mines Inc.) began in May and was continuing at the end of the year. In September a deadly underground explosion took the lives of nine workers. The Royal Canadian Mounted Police (RCMP) stated that it appeared that the blast was deliberate.

Ross M. Harvey
Government of the Northwest Territories

NORWAY

Diplomatic activity dominated 1992 events in Norway. On September 4, Prime Minister Gro Harlem Brundtland of the Labor Party replaced six cabinet ministers and reorganized three other ministries.

Diplomatic and Military Affairs. In 1992, Norway granted diplomatic recognition to the former Yugoslav republics of Slovenia, Croatia, and Bosnia-Herzegovina. On Dec. 16, 1991, the Scandinavian nation had been one of the first nations to recognize the republic of Russia. It later had recognized ten other former Soviet republics, including the Ukraine and Belarus, as well. In March the foreign ministers of Russia and Norway signed a protocol on bilateral cooperation.

In June the foreign ministers of the North Atlantic Treaty Organization (NATO) met in Oslo and addressed the problems raised by the conflicts in the former Yugoslavia. Under consideration were peacemaking efforts by the European Community (EC) and the West European Union, the latter having asked Norway to become a member. During the year Norway sent tons of relief supplies, primarily food and medicine for hospitals serving refugee camps in Sarajevo, to the Balkan war zone. By September 1, Norway had contributed $26 million to help the refugees in the former Yugoslavia and neighboring countries.

In mid-October the Norwegian parliament approved membership in the European Economic Area (EEA) by a vote of 130–35, thus assuring the needed three-quarters majority. The EEA agreement would tie the seven European Free Trade Association nations to the EC but would not give them full access to decision making. In early November a Labor Party convention in Oslo voted 182 to 106 to submit an application for EC membership.

In June the prime minister headed Norway's delegation to the UN Conference on Environment and Development in Rio de Janeiro, Brazil.

As a result of the military and political changes in Europe, the Norwegian parliament (Storting) established a Defense Commission headed by former Prime Minister Kare Willoch. The commission's report, submitted on March 16, called for a number of radical changes. Included were a reduction in the army from 13 to six brigades and a reduction in coast artillery fortifications from 29 to 13. The report also recommended that Norway acquire additional mobile-rocket batteries and submarines as well as 48 late-model fighter planes.

Economic Affairs. Six years after a worldwide moratorium on whaling began, Norway announced that it would resume commercial exploitation of the smaller minke whale. According to Norwegian scientists, the minke ex-

NORWAY · Information Highlights

Official Name: Kingdom of Norway.
Location: Northern Europe.
Area: 125,182 sq mi (324 220 km²).
Population (mid-1992 est.): 4,300,000.
Chief Cities (Jan. 1, 1991): Oslo, the capital, 461,644; Bergen, 213,344; Trondheim, 138,058.
Government: *Head of state,* Harald V, king (acceded January 1991). *Head of government,* Gro Harlem Brundtland, prime minister (took office November 1990). *Legislature*—Storting: Lagting and Odelsting.
Monetary Unit: Krone (6.4255 kroner equal U.S.$1, Nov. 23, 1992).
Gross Domestic Product (1990 U.S.$): $74,200,-000,000.
Economic Indexes (1991): *Consumer Prices* (1980 = 100), all items, 215.6; food, 221.4. *Industrial Production* (1980 = 100), 161.
Foreign Trade (1991 U.S.$): *Imports,* $25,550,-000,000; *exports,* $34,037,000,000.

ists in sufficient numbers not to be threatened by the action. Norway, along with Iceland, Greenland, and the Faroe Islands, formed a North Atlantic Marine Mammal Committee with one of its purposes being the international acknowledgment of their rights to exploit the wealth in the adjacent seas.

Norway's 1993 budget projected an 8.55 billion kroner (about $1.5 billion) deficit and cuts in many areas. Contributing to this record deficit was the rise in social-benefit costs resulting from high unemployment, which in July stood in the 7% range and continued to rise. The unemployment was caused in part by an unprecedented number of mergers and bankruptcies.

Viking Ships. Early in May two of the three replicas of the Viking ships marking the 1000th anniversary of Leif Erikson's reported landing in North America were wrecked in a storm off the coast of Spain.

Erik J. Friis
"The Scandinavian-American Bulletin"

NOVA SCOTIA

During 1992, Nova Scotians were divided sharply over the federal constitutional proposal, frustrated by economic stagnation, and shocked by a major coal-mine disaster.

Legislation and Government. Premier Donald Cameron's Progressive Conservative (PC) government accomplished its 1992 legislative mandate by enacting several controversial laws, including privatization of the Nova Scotia Power Corporation through the initial sale of 76% of its equity followed by the sale of 34% of its stock originally retained by the government. Provincial residents were able to buy a C$10 stock with a down payment of C$6—the balance to be recovered by August 1993. Other legislation tightened loopholes to political-party disclosure laws and streamlined the tenancy-dispute tribunal system.

NOVA SCOTIA • Information Highlights

Area: 21,425 sq mi (55 491 km²).
Population (September 1992): 908,200.
Chief cities (1986 census): Halifax, the capital, 113,577; Dartmouth, 65,243; Sydney, 27,754.
Government (1992): *Chief Officers*—lt. gov., Lloyd R. Crouse; premier, Donald Cameron (Progressive Conservative). *Legislature*—Legislative Assembly, 52 members.
Provincial Finances (1992–93 fiscal year budget): *Revenues,* $4,588,000,000; *expenditures,* $4,741,-000,000.
Personal Income (average weekly earnings, August 1992): $495.57.
Labor Force (September 1992, seasonally adjusted): *Employed* workers, 15 years of age and over, 363,000; *Unemployed,* 12.3%.
Education (1992–93): *Enrollment*—elementary and secondary schools, 168,150 pupils; postsecondary—universities, 30,000; community colleges, 2,750.
(All monetary figures are in Canadian dollars.)

The government also participated in federal-provincial conferences on the Canadian constitution that culminated in the signing of the Charlottetown Accord. This agreement, for the first time in Canadian history, was backed by all provincial premiers. In the October 26 referendum, however, Nova Scotia's "no" side won with 51.1% of the vote.

In March, Liberal leader Vince MacLean resigned after mishandling party trust funds. In June, Dartmouth Mayor John Savage, a physician, was elected to the Liberal leadership.

Economy. The provincial economy in 1992 remained immersed in a pervasive and deep recession. By July, as compared to the first six months of 1991, the values of manufacturing shipments, farm cash receipts, lumber production, and pulp exports had dwindled by 4.6%, 5%, and 5.5%, respectively. Similarly, the construction sector put up a lackluster performance. By July the value of nonresidential permits had fallen 18%, while urban housing starts were down 23% at the end of August. With the exceptions of housing and manufacturing, all sectors recorded reductions in planned public- and private-investment expenditures. The overall impact of such sluggishness was reflected in a double-digit unemployment rate. A glimmer of hope emerged, however, in the retail sector, where a low inflation rate and dwindling interest rates had stimulated sales of household goods. The government, ignoring accusations of a preelection vote-buying gimmick, also unveiled a C$22 million spending plan to jump start the economy.

Mine Disaster. Nova Scotians were shocked by the May 9 Westray mine disaster near Plymouth that killed 26 miners. The government responded by appointing the Westray Mine Inquiry Commission to conduct a judicial probe into the causes of the explosion, but argued for delaying the investigation after police charged Westray mine managers with criminal negligence. Critics, provoked by the possibility of delay, attacked the government's ambivalence of defending the probe while simultaneously suggesting that the investigation be delayed to guarantee the rights of the accused managers to a fair trial. The miners' families, on the other hand, agitated to recover bodies of the dead miners and to investigate the role of the federal and provincial authorities in the tragedy. In November the provincial Supreme Court stopped the provincial inquiry in order to protect the mine managers' rights.

Energy. Nova Scotians were encouraged in June by news that the first offshore oil production had been started by British-owned Lasmo Nova Scotia Ltd. in partnership with a provincial Crown corporation in the reserves near Sable Island.

R. P. Seth
Mount Saint Vincent University, Halifax

OBITUARIES

BEGIN, Menahem Wolfovitch

© UPI/Bettmann

Israeli politician, former prime minister: b. Brest-Litovsk, then a part of Russia, Aug. 16, 1913; d. Tel Aviv, March 9, 1992.

Menahem Begin was the most remarkable of the figures who have led Israel in the 44 years of its existence. Frail physically, he had an indomitable will. Formal in dress and distant in manner, he was yet the most passionate upholder of the rights of his people. An uncompromising Zionist, he nevertheless achieved peace with a major Arab enemy by handing over territory controlled by Israel.

Background. Menahem Wolfovitch Begin was born on Aug. 16, 1913, in Brest-Litovsk, then a part of Russia. He was graduated in law from the University of Warsaw. Early active in politics, he joined Betar, a Zionist youth move-

DIETRICH, Marlene

© AP/Wide World

Motion-picture actress and cabaret performer: b. Berlin, Germany, Dec. 27, 1901; d. Paris, May 6, 1992.

The mystique of Marlene Dietrich, as much an icon as a film star, was easier to savor than to define precisely. She radiated aloof yet naughty sexuality, the free spirit of an independent woman, undying glamour, and a gift for comedy, all sometimes tinged with a cocky suggestion of self-parody. Her talent and beauty, reflected in an array of charismatic screen roles, secured her place as a Hollywood legend.

In the 1950s and 1960s, Dietrich shrewdly parlayed her celebrity into a series of triumphant cabaret and solo theater turns. Whether singing songs for which she was renowned or

McCLINTOCK, Barbara

U.S. geneticist: b. Hartford, CT, June 16, 1902; d. Huntington, NY, Sept. 2, 1992.

When Barbara McClintock was awarded the 1983 Nobel Prize in Physiology or Medicine, it mainly honored work done more than 30 years earlier—work so advanced that it was not confirmed or accepted by other geneticists until the late 1970s.

McClintock established her reputation as a leading geneticist in the 1930s. But when she proposed in 1951 that small fragments of genetic material can "jump," or move from one area on the chromosomes to another, she was ignored or ridiculed. The theory contradicted widely held beliefs that genetic material is arranged in fixed patterns and that all changes in it occur randomly.

© Barton Silverman/NYT Pictures

ment, at age 15, and became its head in 1938. During World War II, Begin joined Irgun Zvai Leumi, an extreme Zionist group. As its commander, for the next several years he conducted a terrorist campaign against the policy of Britain as mandatory power in Palestine.

Shortly after Israeli independence in 1948, Begin founded the Herut (Freedom) Party. In 1973, Herut joined with several other parties to form the rightist Likud group. Begin held cabinet office briefly (1967–70) and tried to become Israel's leader eight times before winning election in May 1977. He won a second election in 1981, staying in office until his retirement in 1983. Likud remained the leading party in the Knesset (parliament) until 1992.

Begin's greatest achievement immediately followed his 1977 victory. He seized on tentative remarks by Egyptian President Anwar Sadat hinting at a readiness to negotiate; the extraordinary outcome was Sadat's visit to Jerusalem in November 1977, followed by the Camp David accords of 1978 and 1979's Israeli-Egyptian peace treaty. The two men shared the Nobel Peace Prize for 1978. The price of normal relations with Egypt was the return of the Sinai Peninsula, occupied by Israel since 1967, and the undertaking to embark on negotiations about Palestinian self-government.

The later years of Begin's premiership were less successful. Inflation ran rampant, and the invasion of Lebanon in 1982 was, most thought, a costly policy error. The crushing blow, however, was the death in November 1982 of Begin's wife of 43 years, Aliza. He retired abruptly in 1983 and became a virtual recluse, except for one brief reemergence in 1991 to point out that his bombing in 1981 of Iraq's nuclear reactor had not been a mistake.

ARTHUR CAMPBELL TURNER

---

dominating the stage in a glittering gown, Dietrich mesmerized adoring audiences.

Background. Maria Magdalene Dietrich, born to a police officer and a merchant's daughter, first coveted a career as a violinist. But when her hand was injured, she turned to acting and singing. Her discovery by film director Josef von Sternberg, who cast her as the leggy seductress Lola-Lola in *The Blue Angel* (1930), set her on the road to international success. He took her to Hollywood and shaped her talent and image as a symbol of sophisticated sex appeal. Their collaboration resulted in such films as *Morocco* (1930), *Shanghai Express* (1932), *The Scarlet Empress* (1934), and *The Devil Is a Woman* (1935).

Working with other directors, Dietrich made many memorable films, including *Desire* (1936), *Destry Rides Again* (1939), *A Foreign Affair* (1948), *Rancho Notorious* (1952), *Witness for the Prosecution* (1957), *Touch of Evil* (1958), and *Judgment at Nuremberg* (1961). A foe of Nazism, she risked her life to entertain front-line Allied troops during World War II.

The actress was married to Rudolph Sieber, a Czech film production assistant and later a chicken farmer, between 1924 and his death in 1975, but they mostly lived apart. Dietrich, who often wore man-tailored clothes, was called the world's most glamorous grandmother after their daughter, Maria Riva, gave birth to the first of four sons in 1948.

In 1972, Dietrich moved from New York to the Paris apartment where she died. Although she kept in touch with friends, she preferred to hide her aging face from the public. While she allowed her voice to be recorded for *Marlene*, Maximilian Schell's 1979 documentary, she would not be photographed.

WILLIAM WOLF

McClintock's revolutionary theory was based on her observations of maize (Indian corn). She saw that as some parts of maize seedlings lost color, other parts gained color. She concluded that mobile genes were responsible for the colors of the kernels. Depending on if and when the genes jumped, the kernels would be dark, pale, or speckled. The implications of her work affected not only genetics but such fields as cancer research and evolution.

Background. Barbara McClintock was born in Hartford, CT, on June 16, 1902. She entered Cornell University in 1919, where she earned a bachelor of science (1923), a master of arts (1925), and a doctorate in plant genetics (1927).

After working at Cornell and the University of Missouri, McClintock moved in 1941 to Cold Spring Harbor Laboratory on Long Island, NY, where she remained until her death. She lived in an apartment on the grounds of the laboratory, a short walk from the building where she worked and which bears her name.

In addition to the Nobel, many other honors and awards were bestowed on McClintock, including the National Medal of Science (1970) and a Lasker Award (1981). In 1981 the MacArthur Foundation chose her as its first Prize Fellow Laureate, guaranteeing her a lifetime tax-free income of $60,000 per year.

McClintock was a reserved woman who valued her solitude and independence. She worked in her laboratory until shortly before her death, putting in six- and seven-day weeks and 12-hour days as she continued to study the genetics of maize. "It might seem unfair," she once said, "to reward a person for having so much pleasure over the years, asking the maize plant to solve specific problems and then watching its responses."

JENNY TESAR

BRANDT, Willy

German politician: b. Lübeck, Germany, Dec. 18, 1913; d. Unkel, Germany, Oct. 8, 1992.

Willy Brandt was one of Germany's and Europe's most important post-World War II statesmen. As mayor of West Berlin (1957–66), foreign minister (1966–69), and chancellor (1969–74), he played a major role in the development of German democracy. After the horrors of the Nazi Third Reich, the visionary and eloquent Brandt came to symbolize "the other Germany," committed to peace, freedom, tolerance, reconciliation, and fair play.

Background. Brandt's original name was Herbert Ernst Karl Frahm. His unmarried mother was a store clerk, and he was raised by his grandfather, an agricultural worker who had moved to Lübeck from Pomerania. At the age of 16, Brandt joined the Social Democratic Party and was forced to flee Germany for Norway and later Sweden after the Nazi takeover in 1933. From then on he used the name Willy Brandt. The Nazis stripped Brandt of his German citizenship in 1938. He thus was the only chancellor not to have lived in Germany during the Third Reich.

Returning to Germany in 1945, Brandt became a Norwegian press attaché with the Norwegian military mission in Berlin in 1946. Soon thereafter he again became active in Social Democratic politics in Berlin, after which he resumed German citizenship. Identified with the party's reformist wing, Brandt quickly rose in the Berlin organization and became governing mayor of the city in 1957. Soviet pressure against this isolated city intensified in the late 1950s and made it a major source of East-West tension. As its mayor, Brandt acquired a reputation as a progressive leader.

In 1961 and again in 1965, Brandt was the Social Democratic Party's unsuccessful candidate for chancellor. During these campaigns, numerous personal attacks regarding his illegitimate birth and wartime activity—which to some Germans made him a traitor—almost caused his retirement from national politics. The formation of a Grand Coalition between the Christian Democrats and Social Democrats in 1966 returned Brandt to the national spotlight as foreign minister. In this post he laid the foundations for the new relationship that the Federal Republic later would develop with the Soviet Union and its East European satellites. After the 1969 national election, Brandt formed a coalition government between his Social Democrats and the smaller Free Democratic Party, becoming the fourth chancellor of the postwar Federal Republic and the first Social Democratic chancellor since 1930.

Between 1969 and 1972, Brandt effected a major transformation of West German foreign

© PhotoWorld

policy through treaties with the Soviet Union, Poland, and East Germany. While in Warsaw in 1970 to sign the Polish treaty, he laid a wreath at a memorial to the destroyed Jewish ghetto, sinking silently to his knees, a gesture that attracted worldwide attention. For his policy of reconciliation with Germany's former enemies in the East, Brandt in 1971 was awarded the Nobel Peace Prize. At the 1972 election—largely a referendum on his *Ostpolitik,* or Eastern foreign policy—he led his party to the greatest victory in its history.

When the focus of German politics after 1972 shifted to domestic issues, Brandt was less successful. His domestic problems grew more acute with the Arab oil embargo in October 1973, and the discovery and arrest of an East German spy on Brandt's personal staff in April 1974 was the final blow. Brandt assumed full responsibility and resigned. As the first chancellor with a record of uncompromising opposition to Nazism, he contributed to the republic's image as a society that had overcome its totalitarian past.

After stepping down as chancellor, Brandt remained the national chairman of the Social Democratic Party until 1987. He also assumed wider responsibilities as president of the Socialist International, an umbrella organization of the world's social democratic political movements, and as the chair of a blue-ribbon panel—the Brandt Commission—which studied North-South relations. With the opening of the Berlin Wall in 1989 and the subsequent collapse of the Communist regime in East Germany, Brandt, although in failing health, became a forceful advocate for German unification.

Brandt was survived by his third wife and four children from previous marriages.

DAVID P. CONRADT

ROSS, Steven J.

U.S. businessman: b. New York City, April 5, 1927; d. Los Angeles, Dec. 20, 1992.

© NYT Pictures

A smooth-talking man with an eye for opportunity, Steven J. Ross liked to tell business associates that if they were not risk takers they did not belong in business. He, of course, saw himself as a risk taker and used that skill to turn a family funeral-parlor business into Time Warner Inc., the largest entertainment and media conglomerate in the world. At the time of Ross' death, Time Warner included music companies, cable systems, publishing houses, magazines, filmed entertainment, and cable programming. Net income for 1991 was nearly $1 billion.

Much to his anger, Ross came to symbolize for many the avarice of the times. The Time Warner merger of 1989 was particularly notable, both for its size and because it was the last major deal of the high-flying decade of the 1980s. Time had bought Warner Communications for $14 billion, incurring $11.4 billion in debt along the way. Ross was criticized resoundingly for the $78.2 million in compensation he received in 1990, $74.9 million of which was for his interest in Warner Communications. He said the payments were his reward for 30 years of work at Warner.

The years immediately after the merger also were troubling as the company struggled under the massive debt load and Ross struggled to work with Nicholas J. Nicholas, Jr., formerly of Time, who was his co-chief executive and whom Ross distrusted. Finally, in February 1992, as Ross was battling prostate cancer, he managed to replace Nicholas with Gerald M. Levin, formerly Time Warner's vice-chairman.

Background. Born Steven Jay Rechnitz, Ross was the son of poor Jewish immigrants. The family name was changed during the Depression when his father sought work. Self-educated, Ross began his business career early —carrying groceries for a nickel a bag when he was 8 years old. He worked for awhile in New York's garment district, but his real break came in 1953 when he married for the first time. His wife, Carol Rosenthal, was the daughter of a successful funeral-parlor operator. As the story goes, Ross took the limousines that his wife's uncle, a partner in the business, provided for funeral services and that sat idle during the evening hours, leasing them to a local limousine company for use in New York's theater district.

In the late 1950s, Ross started Abbey Rent-A-Car, later adding Kinney parking garages and an office-cleaning business. Grouped as Kinney Service, the company—worth about $12.5 million—went public in 1962.

Ross' move into entertainment came in 1967 with the purchase of Ashley Famous Talent Agency. In 1969 he bought the ailing Warner Brothers-Seven Arts studio and record business. In 1972, Kinney was renamed Warner Communications Inc., and over time the old Kinney businesses were sold off.

Ross' knack for spotting trends showed up in the early 1970s when he moved into the cable business even while others doubted its future. He was successful, too, in building loyalty. He picked talented managers and did not interfere with their decisions. Good work was rewarded with lavish financial bonuses.

Nonetheless, perhaps Ross' hands-off management style contributed to the financial setback that Warner experienced in the early 1980s when its Atari video-games business, faced with much competition, collapsed almost overnight, losing more than $1 billion for the company. It also may have been at the root of criticism resulting from the indictments of two Warner officials for their parts in a racketeering scheme that involved a mob-connected Tarrytown, NY, theater. While no charges were brought against Ross, he was the subject of much innuendo involving the case.

Also, despite Ross' proclamation of himself as a risk taker, he was not a true entrepreneur. He never owned more than 1%-2% of the companies he ran. Instead, he obtained elaborate employment contracts filled with stock-option plans, bonuses, and other financial devices that provided great rewards without risks.

At the time of his death, Ross was married to Courtney Sale Ross, his third wife, with whom he had a daughter in 1982. He also had a son and daughter from his first marriage.

KRISTI VAUGHAN

The following is a selected list of prominent persons who died during 1992.
Articles on major figures appear in the preceding pages.

Abolgassem al-Khoei, Grand Ayatollah (95), one of the greatest scholars of Shiite Islam; wrote more than 90 books and manuscripts on Shiite theology: d. Kufa, Iraq, Aug. 8.

Acuff, Roy (89), singer and fiddler; known as the "king of country music," he was elected to the Country Music Hall of Fame in 1962. He joined the Grand Ole Opry in 1938 and in 1942 with Fred Rose founded the Acuff-Rose Publishing Company, the world's leading country-music publisher. His song hits include *Wabash Cannonball:* d. Nashville, TN, Nov. 23.

Albert, Stephen J. (51), composer of symphonic music; won the 1985 Pulitzer Prize in music for his "Symphony Riverrun": d. Truro, MA, Dec. 27.

Allen, James R. (66), U.S. Air Force general; was superintendent of the U.S. Air Force Academy in the 1970s and deputy commander of the U.S. European Command (1979–81): d. Andrews Air Force Base, MD, Aug. 11.

Allen, Peter (48), Australian-born popular concert entertainer and award-winning songwriter; was discovered by Judy Garland in 1964 and used as her opening act. He recorded 11 albums and performed live in nightclubs, on Broadway, and in concerts. He wrote the theme song for the movie *Arthur* (1981) and the Olivia Newton-John hit "I Honestly Love You": d. San Diego, CA, June 18.

Almendros, Nestor (61), Academy Award-winning cinematographer for *Days of Heaven* (1978). He also filmed *Kramer vs. Kramer* (1979), *Sophie's Choice* (1982), and *Billy Bathgate* (1991). Earlier in his career he worked on films with the directors François Truffaut and Eric Rohmer: d. New York City, March 4.

Alzado, Lyle (43), pro football player for the Los Angeles Raiders (1982–86); was drafted by the Denver Broncos in 1971 and was the defensive player of the year in 1977. He later played for the Cleveland Browns (1979–82). He warned of the dangers of steroid abuse, to which he attributed his brain cancer: d. Portland, OR, May 14.

Anderson, Dame Judith (born Frances Margaret Anderson) (93), Australian-born British actress who electrified Broadway audiences in 1947 in the title role of *Medea*. Other notable stage roles were in *Mourning Becomes Electra* (1932), *Old Maid* (1935), and *Hamlet* (1936). As a screen actress she won an Academy Award nomination for her portrayal of the housekeeper Mrs. Danvers in *Rebecca* (1940): d. Santa Barbara, CA, Jan. 3.

Anderson, George W. (85), U.S. admiral; was the chief of naval operations (1961–63) in charge of the U.S. blockade of Cuba during the Soviet missile crisis of 1962: d. McLean, VA, March 20.

Andrews, Dana (83), film actor; noted for leading roles in the 1940s as the young American hero. His films included *The Ox-Bow Incident* (1943), *Wing and a Prayer* (1944), *Laura* (1944), *The Best Years of Our Lives* (1946), *My Foolish Heart* (1950), and *The Last Tycoon* (1976): d. Orange County, CA, Dec. 17.

Arletty (born Léonie Bathiat) (94), French film actress; made more than 50 films. She was a factory worker who became a French cinematic legend; her films include *Hotel du Nord* (1938), *Les Enfants du Paradis* (1945), *Portrait d'un Assassin* (1949), and *The Longest Day* (1962): d. Paris, July 24.

Arnall, Ellis G. (85), Democratic governor of Georgia (1943–47): d. Atlanta, GA, Dec. 13.

Arneson, Robert C. (62), sculptor and ceramicist; noted for whimsical self-portraits: d. Benicia, CA, Nov. 2.

Asimov, Isaac (72), writer of popular science and science fiction; wrote nearly 500 books on many subjects including the Bible, chemistry, physics, biology, humor, Shakespeare, and modern history. His first book was *Pebble in the Sky* (1950). Other books include *I, Robot* (1950) and *Asimov Laughs Again*

(1992). He also taught biochemistry at Boston University (1949–58): d. New York City, April 6.

Attassi, Nureddin al- (63), president of Syria (1966–70): d. Paris, Dec. 3.

Avigad, Nahman (86), Israeli archaeologist and biblical scholar; was a professor at Hebrew University (1951–73) who led excavation of the Herodian "Upper City" of Jerusalem razed by the Romans in A.D. 70 along with the Second Temple. He also worked with the Dead Sea scrolls: d. Jerusalem, Jan. 28.

Bacon, Francis (82), Irish-born painter; known for his macabre abstract images of psychological and physical brutality that critics linked to the surrealist art of Picasso and to German Expressionism. He first gained acclaim in 1945 with his "Three Studies for Figures at the Base of the Crucifixion." Other images included screaming popes, butchered carcasses, and distorted portraits. He did a few landscapes, but primarily was a painter of the human body: d. Madrid, Spain, April 28.

Balfa, Dewey (65), folk fiddler and singer; helped create the U.S. Cajun-music revival: d. Eunice, LA, June 17.

Barber, Walter Lanier (Red) (84), baseball broadcaster for 33 seasons (1934–66); began with the Cincinnati Reds, then broadcast for the Brooklyn Dodgers (1939–53), and ended with the New York Yankees. He had broadcast over National Public Radio since 1981 and wrote seven books. He was a lay minister in the Episcopal Church. In 1978 he was inducted into the Baseball Hall of Fame: d. Tallahassee, FL, Oct. 22.

Barger, Carl (60), president of the Pittsburgh Pirates baseball club (1986–91) and the Florida Marlins (1991–92); he was instrumental in establishing the new Florida Marlins franchise that would begin play in 1993: d. Louisville, KY, Dec. 9.

Bartholomew, Freddie (67), Irish-born Hollywood child film star; noted for playing proper English boys. He made 24 films, including *David Copperfield* (1934), *Little Lord Fauntleroy* (1936), and *Captains Courageous* (1937). For a time he was Hollywood's second-highest-paid child star (after Shirley Temple): d. Sarasota, FL, Jan. 23.

Billotte, Pierre (86), French general and military hero of World War II; was a leader in the French resistance and Free French Movement and a top aide to Charles de Gaulle. After the war, he headed the French delegation at the United Nations and helped to forge the North Atlantic Treaty Organization. He also held the post of defense minister in 1955: d. near Paris, June 29.

Black, Eugene (93), president of the World Bank (1949–62): d. Southampton, NY, Feb. 20.

Blackwood, Easley R., Sr. (89), contract-bridge expert and inventor of a famous bridge convention devised in 1933: d. Indianapolis, IN, March 27.

Bloom, Allan (62), professor of political philosophy; his best-selling book on U.S. universities, *The Closing of the American Mind* (1987), formed an attack on intellectual life that conservatives embraced. He taught at the University of Chicago (1955–60; 1979–92), Yale (1960–63), Cornell (1963–70), and the University of Toronto (1970–79): d. Chicago, IL, Oct. 7.

Blume, Peter (86), Russian immigrant whose dreamlike detailed paintings made him very well known in the United States in the 1930s and 1940s. His "Eternal City" depicted the dictator Mussolini as a green jack-in-the-box: d. New Milford, CT, Nov. 30.

Boe, Nils (78), Republican governor of South Dakota (1965–69): d. Sioux Falls, SD, July 30.

Bohrod, Aaron (84), realist artist; his paintings included Chicago street scenes, rural settings in Wisconsin, and fighting on Omaha Beach in World War II: d. Madison, WI, April 3.

Judith Anderson

Isaac Asimov

Red Barber

Freddie Bartholomew

Eugene R. Black

Shirley Booth

John Cage

Charles "Honi" Coles

Booth, Shirley (born Thelma Booth Ford) (94), actress of stage, screen, and television; perhaps best known for her television portrayal of the title role of the maid in *Hazel* (1961-66). She appeared on stage (1950) and in the film (1952) of *Come Back, Little Sheba*, winning both Tony and Oscar awards. In all, she appeared in some 40 Broadway plays and in several films: d. Chatham, MA, Oct. 16.

Bovet, Daniele (85), Swiss-born Nobel Prize-winning pharmacologist; was the discoverer of the first antihistamine and created muscle-relaxing drugs from curare. The biochemist won the Nobel Prize for Physiology or Medicine in 1957: d. Rome, Italy, April 8.

Boyle, Kay (90), writer of more than four dozen books; noted for her short stories. The collection *White Horses of Vienna* (1936) received critical acclaim; another collection, *Fifty Stories*, was published in 1980. Her 1963 novel *Death of a Man* contained material from her life in Austria in the 1930s: d. Mill Valley, CA, Dec. 27.

Brand, Neville (71), actor; known for his tough-guy roles in films and on television. His best-known films were *Stalag 17* and *The Birdman of Alcatraz*. He also appeared in the televison version of *All the King's Men* in 1958: d. Sacramento, CA, April 16.

Briggs, Frank P. (98), newspaper publisher and state senator from Missouri who was appointed to fill the remainder of Harry Truman's Senate term when he became vice-president in 1944. He served until 1947, running unsuccessfully for election to the seat in 1946: d. Macon, MO, Sept. 23.

Brooks, James (85), abstract expressionist painter; among the most technically accomplished members of the New York school of painting: d. Brookhaven, NY, March 9.

Brooks, Richard (79), film director, screenwriter, and novelist; won an Academy Award for the screenplay of *Elmer Gantry* (1960). Other films for which he wrote the screenplays and also directed were *The Blackboard Jungle* (1955) and *In Cold Blood* (1967). Other directing credits were *Cat on a Hot Tin Roof* (1958) and *Waiting for Mr. Goodbar* (1977): d. Beverly Hills, CA, March 11.

Brown, Georgia (born Lillian Klot) (58), British actress and singer; originated the role of Nancy in *Oliver!* (1960): d. London, July 5.

Buchanan, Buck (51), pro football player, a defensive lineman, for the Kansas City Chiefs (1963–75); inducted into the Hall of Fame (1990): d. Kansas City, MO, July 16.

Burdick, Quentin N. (84), U.S. senator (D-ND, 1960–92); was in the U.S. House (1959–60): d. Fargo, ND, Sept. 8.

Bush, Dorothy (91), mother of U.S. President George Bush: d. Greenwich, CT, Nov. 19.

Cage, John (79), musical composer of minimalist works who involved himself in the worlds of music, dance, and art; he was also a writer and philosopher and was an influence on both the choreographer Merce Cunningham and the artist Jasper Johns. He and they were celebrated in 1989 by a London gallery show called "Dancers on a Plane." His career in music began in the 1930s, and he composed hundreds of works, ranging from music that utilized conventional rules of harmony and thematic development to pieces that broke those rules. He prepared music for conventional and altered musical instruments, worked with electronic and taped music and with spoken texts, and was involved in work with the 12-tone musical system. His compositions include *Europera 5, Eclipticalis with Winter Music, Sonata for Clarinet, Music for Wind Instruments, Metamorphosis, Imaginary Landscape No. 1, Bacchanale, The Seasons, 4' 33"*, and *Hpschd*. He cowrote the book *Virgil Thomson: His Life and Music* (1959) and wrote *Silence* (1961), *A Year From Monday* (1967), and *Empty Words* (1979): d. New York City, Aug. 12.

Carstens, Karl (77), president of West Germany (1979–84). The former Nazi and German Army officer served in the West German parliament (1949–68; 1972–79) and was an architect of the Treaty of Rome, the 1957 pact that became a forerunner of the European Community: d. Meckenheim, Germany, May 30.

Carswell, G. Harrold (72), Richard Nixon nominee to the U.S. Supreme Court in 1970. His nomination brought on a political battle resulting in Carswell's rejection by the Senate. He later made an unsuccessful run for a U.S. Senate seat: d. Tallahassee, FL, July 31.

Chabukiani, Vakhtang (82), Soviet ballet master and choreographer; he was also one of the great dancers of his generation: d. Tbilisi, Georgia, April 5.

Clarke, Mae (born Mary Klotz) (84), actress best remembered for a scene in which James Cagney pushed a grapefruit in her face in *Public Enemy* (1931): d. Woodland Hills, CA, April 29.

Coles, Charles (Honi) (81), tap dancer who was noted for elegance and speed; he won a Tony for his performance in *My One and Only* (1982). A member of the tap duo Coles and Atkins (Cholly Atkins) as well as a soloist, he and Atkins performed a routine that they choreographed in *Gentlemen Prefer Blondes* (1949) on Broadway. Coles appeared solo in Broadway's *Bubbling Brown Sugar* (1976) and appeared in the films *Cotton Club* (1984) and *Dirty Dancing* (1987). He also was a master teacher: d. New York City, Nov. 12.

Connors, Chuck (born Kevin Connors) (71), professional basketball and baseball player and actor; he played for the Boston Celtics and on a Brooklyn Dodgers farm team, later becoming an actor. He gained stardom in the television series *The Rifleman* (1958–63): d. Los Angeles, CA, Nov. 10.

Culliford, Pierre (64), Belgian cartoonist; created the blue dwarves known as Smurfs: d. Brussels, Dec. 24.

Danton, Ray (60), stage and film actor and director; appeared in the films *I'll Cry Tomorrow* (1956) and *The Rise and Fall of Legs Diamond* (1960). From the mid-1960s to the mid-1970s he directed films in Italy and Spain and later directed several popular U.S. television shows: d. Los Angeles, CA, Feb. 11.

d'Aubuisson Arrieta, Roberto (48), far-rightist leader of El Salvador; founded the Nationalist Republican Alliance in 1981 and served as El Salvador's Constituent Assembly president in 1982 and 1983. He ran for but lost the national presidency in 1984. He was thought to be a proponent of the "death squads" during El Salvador's civil war: d. San Salvador, Feb. 20.

David, Elizabeth (78), British cookbook writer, credited with changing cooking in England. Her books include *A Book of Mediterranean Food* (1950), *French Country Cooking* (1951), *Italian Food* (1954), *Summer Cooking* (1955), and *French Provincial Cooking* (1960): d. London, May 22.

Davis, Hallowell (96), director of research at the Central Institute for the Deaf in St. Louis (1946–65), thereafter for 20 years on emeritus status; in the 1930s while at Harvard Medical School, he worked to develop the electroencephalograph, or EEG. He also was noted for his physiological studies of the inner ear: d. St. Louis, MO, Aug. 22.

Dennis, Sandy (54), stage and film actress; made her film debut in *Splendor in the Grass* (1961) and won an Academy Award in 1966 for *Who's Afraid of Virginia Woolf*. She also won two Tony Awards in 1963 for *A Thousand Clowns* and in 1964 for *Any Wednesday*: d. Westport, CT, March 2.

DeRoburt, Hammer (69), president of Nauru (1968-76; 1987–89): d. Melbourne, Australia, July 15.

de Varona, Manuel Antonio (83), prime minister of Cuba (1948–50) and Senate president (1950-52); he was a leading foe of the Castro government: d. Miami, FL, Oct. 29.

Dickens, Monica (77), British author of more than 50 books and a great-granddaughter of Charles Dickens. She lived in the United States for 35 years, opening the first U.S. branch of the Samaritans, a volunteer counseling organization. Her first book was a best-seller entitled *One Pair of Hands* (1939): d. Reading, England, Dec. 25.

Douglas-Home, William (80), British playwright and screenwriter; noted as a light-comedy writer. His works include *The Reluctant Debutante* (1955) and *The King Fisher* (1977). He

Alexander Dubcek

Millicent Fenwick

Philip Habib

Clara "Mother" Hale

was the brother of former British Prime Minister Sir Alec Douglas-Home: d. Winchester, England, Sept. 28.

Drake, Alfred (born Alfredo Capurro) (77), Broadway star of *Oklahoma* (1943), *Kiss Me Kate* (1948), *Kismet* (1953), and in the 1973 revival of *Gigi*. He also was a dramatic actor, appearing in *Hamlet* (1963) and *Much Ado About Nothing* (1957). He won a special Tony Award in 1990 honoring the body of his work: d. New York City, July 25.

Dubcek, Alexander (70), Czechoslovak leader who in 1968 tried to liberalize socialism. This process, known as the "Prague Spring," was crushed by Soviet-led Warsaw Pact troops soon after Dubcek became first secretary of the Communist Party in Czechoslovakia. He was arrested within months, expelled from the party, and given an ambassadorship in 1969 in Turkey and then an obscure forestry job in Bratislava (1970–87). After the fall of communism, he was elected speaker of parliament and was the leader of Slovakia's Social Democrats: d. Prague, Nov. 7.

Dunne, Philip (84), screenwriter and director; founder of the Screen Writers Guild and an opponent of the House Un-American Activities Committee in the 1950s. His screenwriting credits include *How Green Was My Valley*, for which he was nominated for an Academy Award; *Suez; The Count of Monte Cristo; Stanley and Livingston;* and *The Ghost and Mrs. Muir*: d. Malibu, CA, June 2.

Eddleman, Clyde D. (90), U.S. general; was vice chief of staff of the Army (1960–62): d. Washington, DC, Aug. 19.

Elliott, Denholm (70), British character actor; noted as a scene stealer. He appeared in about 80 films, including *Alfie* (1966), *The Apprenticeship of Duddy Kravitz* (1974), and *The Defense of the Realm* (1986). He won an Oscar nomination for his role in *Room with a View* (1986): d. Ibiza, Spain, Oct. 6.

Ellis, John Tracy (87), Roman Catholic priest and historian who in 1955 delivered a speech and essay critical of the church's colleges and universities, "American Catholics and the Intellectual Life." He also wrote more than a dozen books, including the two-volume *Life of James Cardinal Gibbons, Archbishop of Baltimore* (1952), and taught at Catholic University (1938-64; 1977–89): d. Washington, DC, Oct. 16.

Feighan, Michael Aloysius (87), U.S. representative (D-OH, 1943–71): d. Washington, DC, March 19.

Fenwick, Millicent (82), U.S. representative (R-NJ, 1975–83); was known as a champion of women's rights and ethics in government. She ran for a Senate seat in 1982 but was defeated. Later she was associated with the United Nations: d. Bernardsville, NJ, Sept. 16.

Fernandez-Ordoñez, Francisco (Paco) (62), Spanish public official who served in various government posts, including as Spain's foreign minister (1985–92): d. Madrid, Aug. 7.

Ferrer, José (80), actor, writer, director, and producer of plays, films, and television shows. Among his accomplishments was a Tony Award in 1947 for his stage role in *Cyrano de Bergerac*, followed by the 1950 Academy Award for his performance in the screen version. In 1952 he won twin Tony Awards for directing three plays—*Stalag 17, The Fourposter,* and *The Shrike*—and for performing in *The Shrike*. On Broadway he starred in *Man of La Mancha* and directed *The Andersonville Trial*, and on television his work ranged from the serious to light, as in *Gideon's Trumpet* and the series *Magnum P.I.* and *Newhart*: d. Coral Gables, FL, Jan. 26.

Field, Virginia (born Margaret Cynthia Field) (74), actress; often played the "other woman" in movies of the 1930s and 1940s and was in the "Mr. Moto" series of detective films: d. Palm Desert, CA, Jan. 5.

Fisher, M[ary] F[rances] K[ennedy] (83), writer of cookbooks and other works on the art of gastronomy as well as hundreds of articles for *The New Yorker* magazine, a novel, screenplay, a children's book, and travelogues. Among her more important titles are the collected essays *The Gastronomical Me* (1943), *Here Let Us Feast* (1946), *An Alphabet for Gourmets* (1949), and *With Bold Knife and Fork* (1968); the novel *Not*

Now But Now (1947); the English translation of Brillat-Savarin's treatise *The Physiology of Taste* (1949); as well as *A Cordiall Water* (1961), *The Cooking of Provençal France* (1968), and *As They Were* (1982): d. Glen Ellen, CA, June 22.

France, William (82), leading figure in the creation of stock-car racing and the founder of the Daytona 500 competition: d. Ormond Beach, FL, June 7.

Franjieh, Suleiman (82), president of Lebanon (1970–76): d. Beirut, Lebanon, July 23.

Franks, Oliver Shewell (Lord Franks) (87), British diplomat; played a crucial role in putting the post-World War II Marshall Plan into effect: d. Oxford, England, Oct. 15.

Gaines, William (70), founder and publisher of *Mad* magazine with Alfred E. Neuman, the goofy gap-toothed boy on the cover and the "What, me worry?" motto. The first issue came out in 1952: d. New York City, June 3.

Gardenia, Vincent (born Vincent Scognamiglio) (71), Italian-born actor, noted for character roles. His films include *Bang the Drum Slowly* (1973) and *Moonstruck* (1987). He won a Tony award for his stage role in *The Prisoner of Second Avenue* (1971) and a Tony nomination for *Ballroom* (1978). He also appeared on Broadway in *Glengarry Glen Ross*. In 1990 he won an Emmy award for his role in the HBO special *Age-Old Friends*. He also had a regular role in television's *All in the Family*: d. Philadelphia, PA, Dec. 9.

Garrison, Jim (70), New Orleans district attorney who made assertions regarding a widespread conspiracy and cover-up in the 1963 assassination of John F. Kennedy. In 1969 he unsuccessfully prosecuted Clay Shaw as a conspirator. He wrote three books on the case, one of which was *On the Trail of Assassins* (1988), which the Oliver Stone movie *J.F.K.* (1991) drew from. In 1978 he won election to a seat on Louisiana's Court of Appeals for the Fourth Circuit, serving until 1991: d. New Orleans, LA, Oct. 21.

Gleason, Thomas (92), International Longshoremen's Association president (1963–87): d. New York City, Dec. 24.

Goodson, Mark (77), radio and television game-show inventor who produced dozens of game shows, some the longest-running in television history, including *What's My Line?, To Tell the Truth, The Price Is Right, Family Feud, I've Got a Secret, Concentration,* and *The Match Game*: d. New York City, Dec. 18.

Guattari, Felix (62), French psychoanalyst and philosopher; best known abroad for a series of books that he wrote with the philosopher Gulles Deleuze. Their latest was titled *What Is Philosophy* (1991): d. La Borde, France, Aug. 29.

Haack, Robert William (75), president of the New York Stock Exchange (1967–72): d. Potomac, MD, June 14.

Habib, Philip C. (72), Lebanese-American diplomat; served in the foreign service for nearly 30 years and after retirement was a troubleshooter known as a tough and shrewd negotiator. He was credited with aiding in arranging the cease-fire in Lebanon and the withdrawal of the Palestine Liberation Organization in 1982, following the Israeli invasion. He also played a role in persuading Philippine President Ferdinand E. Marcos to go into exile in 1986. A former ambassador to South Korea, he was noted mainly for his expertise in Asia, particularly Vietnam, where he served in the 1960s: d. Puligny-Montrachet, France, May 25.

Hale, Clara M. (87), a pioneer in self-help efforts in poor neighborhoods and the founder of Hale House in Harlem, where about 1,000 drug-addicted babies were cared for over the years. Under her daughter's direction, Hale House also extended help to recovering addicted mothers and had an apprenticeship program for troubled youth and a home for AIDS-infected mothers and babies. The ministry to children began in 1969 when an addict brought her infant to Hale on the advice of Hale's daughter. Earlier, Hale had been a foster parent: d. New York City, Dec. 18.

Haley, Alex (70), author of the Pulitzer Prize-winning *Roots: The Saga of an American Family* (1976), which sold more than

5 million copies and was made into a 1977 television miniseries that became one of television's most popular. A sequel followed in 1979. Among Haley's other works was *The Autobiography of Malcolm X,* written in collaboration with the black nationalist, and the basis of the 1992 film *Malcolm X:* d. Seattle, WA, Feb. 10.

Hanley, Gerald (76), Irish novelist; time in Africa inspired *The Consul at Sunset* and other books on the decline of the British Empire: d. Dan Leaoghaire, Ireland, Sept. 7.

Hare, David (75), sculptor, painter, and photographer; a figure among New York School artists. While he increasingly turned to painting, he was best known for early welded-metal abstract sculptures, influenced by European Surrealism. He also was noted for his works that evoked the Greek god Cronus: d. Jackson Hole, WY, Dec. 21.

Hayakawa, S.I. (85), Canadian-born U.S. scholar on language usage and U.S. senator (R-CA, 1977-83). As an academic, he wrote *Language in Action* (1941). He taught at the University of Chicago (1950–55) and at San Francisco State College, beginning in 1955. During the protest strikes against the Vietnam war, he gained fame by opposing the student movement vigorously. He became acting president of San Francisco State University in 1968 and was its president (1969-73): d. Greenbrae, CA, Feb. 26.

Hayek, Friedrich A. von (92), Austrian-born British Nobel Prize-winning free-market economist; he won the 1974 Nobel for work that included his book *The Road to Serfdom* (1944), which said socialist economics would fail. He influenced Reagan administration advisers: d. Freiburg, Germany, March 23.

Hein, Mel (82), center and linebacker (1931–45) for the New York Giants football team. During his tenure the team won seven division titles and two league championships: d. San Clemente, CA, Jan. 31.

Henreid, Paul (born Paul George Julius von Hernreid) (84), Austrian-born actor; noted for his role as the Nazi-battling resistance leader in *Casablanca* (1942) and as the romantic lead opposite Bette Davis in *Now, Voyager* (1942). In all he appeared in more than 300 film and television dramas: d. Santa Monica, CA, March 29.

Herman, William (Billy) (83), baseball second baseman; played for the Chicago Cubs (1931–41), then joined the Brooklyn Dodgers. He served two years in the Navy during World War II, returning to the Dodgers in 1946. He played a final season with the Pittsburgh Pirates in 1947 and then was a coach and manager. He was elected to the Hall of Fame in 1975: d. Palm Beach, FL, Sept. 5.

Hill, Benny (67), British comedian; had his own television show in Britain by 1955. *The Benny Hill Show,* a collection of skits and naughty jokes, first was broadcast in the United States in 1979: d. London, April 20 (found dead).

Holloway, Sterling (87), actor; provided Winnie the Pooh's voice in several animated films. From 1953 to 1958 he was a regular in the television series *The Life of Riley:* d. Los Angeles, Nov. 22.

Holm, Hanya (born Johanna Eckert) (99), choreographer of modern dance and Broadway musicals. Her musicals included *Kiss Me Kate, Out of this World, My Fair Lady,* and *Camelot.* Her modern dance contributions stemmed from the Central European Expressionist dance tradition in Germany and included *Trend* (1937), a dance of social protest. She taught some of the leading dance choreographers: d. New York City, Nov. 3.

Hopper, Grace M. (85), U.S. Naval rear admiral; served in the Navy as either an active-duty officer or a reservist from 1943 to 1986. She was a mathematician and a pioneer in data processing and earlier taught at Vassar College and was a faculty member at Harvard in the computation laboratory: d. Arlington, VA, Jan. 1.

Hoving, Jane Pickens (83), singer on Broadway, radio, and television; was the musical leader of the Pickens Sisters trio that had its own radio show in the 1930s. In 1972 she challenged then U.S. Rep. Edward Koch in the "Silk Stocking" district on Manhattan's East Side: d. Newport, RI, Feb. 21.

Hughes, Richard Joseph (83), Democratic New Jersey governor (1962–70) and New Jersey chief justice (1974–79): d. Boca Raton, FL, Dec. 7.

Hutchison, Bruce (91), Canadian journalist and columnist; began his career in 1918 as a reporter for the Victoria *Daily Times;* later worked for the *Winnipeg Free Press* and *The Vancouver Sun.* Among other works, he wrote the 1943 best-seller *The Unknown Country* and a 1952 biography of Prime Minister William Lyon Mackenzie King: d. Victoria, B.C., Sept. 14.

Ichord, Richard (66), U.S. representative (D-MO, 1961–81): d. Nevada, MO, Dec. 25.

Ireland, John (78), stage, film, and television actor; nominated for an Academy Award for his role in *All the King's Men* (1949). He also appeared on television in the *Rawhide* series: d. Santa Barbara, CA, March 21.

Irving, K. C. (93), Canadian billionaire; his K. C. Irving Ltd. is one of the largest privately owned conglomerates in North America, owning about 300 private companies—mainly in New Brunswick and Quebec—with interests in oil, timber, mining, shipbuilding, construction, real estate, the information media, and transportation. Since 1972 he had lived in the Bahamas and Bermuda: d. Dec. 13.

Ising, Rudolf (80), cartoonist and creator of "Looney Tunes" and "Merrie Melodies": d. Newport Beach, CA, July 18.

Jacobs, Lou (born Jacob Ludwig) (89), master clown for the Ringling Brothers and Barnum & Bailey Circus for 60 years; he began performing in 1925: d. Sarasota, FL, Sept. 13.

Jaroszewicz, Piotr (82), prime minister of Poland (1970–80): d. Warsaw, Sept. 2 (found dead).

Jones, Allan (84), Hollywood romantic tenor of films of the 1930s and 1940s. His 35 films included *Show Boat* (1936), *The Firefly* (1937), and *A Night at the Opera* (1935). His stage work included the original road company of *Guys and Dolls* in the early 1950s: d. New York City, June 27.

Jones, Walter B. (79), U.S. representative (D-NC, 1966–92): d. Norfolk, VA, Sept. 15.

Joseph, Helen (87), British-born white South African dissident who struggled against apartheid. She was a founder of the Congress of Democrats, the white wing of the African National Congress: d. Johannesburg, Dec. 25.

Kaufman, Irving R. (81), U.S. federal judge; noted for presiding over the Rosenberg espionage case of 1951: d. New York City, Feb. 1.

Kelly, Jack (65), actor; noted for his role as Bart, the brother of Bret, in the *Maverick* television series that ran from 1957 to 1962. Later he was mayor of Huntington Beach, CA (1983–86): d. Huntington Beach, Nov. 7.

Kemeny, John (66), Hungarian-born computer pioneer and mathematician; was president of Dartmouth College (1970–81). He was a co-inventor in 1964 of the Basic computer language: d. Lebanon, NH, Dec. 26.

King, Albert (69), blues guitarist and singer; his important albums included *Born Under a Bad Sign* and *Live Wire/Blues Power.* Later he began recording funk and soul music and became a regular on the rock 'n' roll circuit: d. Memphis, TN, Dec. 21.

Kinison, Sam (38), stand-up comedian; noted for his shrieking, often insulting routines. He appeared in the situation comedy *Charlie Hoover* during 1991–92: d. near Needles, CA, April 10.

Kirk, Andy (94), big-band leader of the 1920s, 1930s, and 1940s; his Clouds of Joy jazz band was noted for its Kansas City sound: d. New York City, Dec. 11.

Kirsten, Dorothy (82), U.S. lyric soprano; sang at New York Metropolitan Opera for 30 years; was noted for her Puccini heroines. In 1945 she debuted at the Met as Mimi in *La Bohème*: d. Los Angeles, CA, Nov. 18.

Knapp, Arthur, Jr. (85), yachtsman; sailed in the America's Cup races of the 1930s and in 1932 helped form the Frostbite Yacht Club: d. Greenwich, CT, June 15.

Alex Haley

Friedrich A. von Hayek

Hanya Holm

Grace Hopper

Krause, Ed (Moose) (79), Notre Dame sportsman who played football under Knute Rockne and who coached under Frank Leahy before succeeding him in 1949 as athletic director; he became athletic director emeritus in 1980. He excelled in basketball, playing center position, and was for a time head basketball coach at Notre Dame. In addition, he competed in baseball and track: d. South Bend, IN, Dec. 3.

La Lupe (53), Cuban-born singer; known during the 1960s as the Queen of Latin Soul: d. New York City, Feb. 28.

Lerner, Max (89), Russian-born writer and educator; was for many years a columnist for the *New York Post*. An unabashed liberal, he called for an antiwar elite and for the rights of Soviet and Eastern European Jews. His books include *Ideas Are Weapons* (1939), *Ideas for the Ice Age* (1941), *The Mind and Faith of Justice Holmes* (1943), *The Unfinished Country* (1959), and *The Age of Overkill* (1962). For a time he was a university teacher as well: d. New York City, June 5.

Lewis, Oscar (99), historian of the American West; one of the early serious writers on the literary, cultural, and social history of the region. His best-known book was *The Big Four* (1938): d. San Francisco, CA, July 11.

Linna, Vaino (71), Finnish author of *The Unknown Soldier* (1954): d. Kangasala, Finland, April 21.

Little, Cleavon (53), actor; best known as the black sheriff in *Blazing Saddles* (1974). He won a Tony Award for best actor in *Purlie* (1970) and also starred in *I'm Not Rappaport* (1986). He appeared in the television series *Temperature's Rising*, *Baghdad Cafe*, and *True Colors* and made some television films: d. Sherman Oaks, CA, Oct. 22.

Li Xiannian (82), president of China (1983–88); a member of the Communist Party central committee for nearly half a century and considered a leading hard-liner and someone whom Deng Xiaoping consulted on crucial decisions. He supported the military suppression of the Tiananmen Square democratic movement in 1989: d. Beijing, June 21.

Lopat, Eddie (born Edmund Walter Lopatynski) (73), baseball pitcher for the New York Yankees during their World Series championship years from 1949 to 1953; in all he had 12 seasons, beginning in 1944, in the major leagues—with the Yankees, the Baltimore Orioles, and the Chicago White Sox. He also managed the Kansas City Athletics in 1963–64: d. Darien, CT, June 15.

Lorentz, Pare (86), writer and film director of such socially conscious documentary films as *The Plow That Broke the Plains* (1936) and *The River* (1938). Both films were made through agencies of the U.S. government and both had a film score by composer Virgil Thomson. Lorentz became head of the U.S. Film Service in 1939 and also worked briefly for RKO. Other films included *The Fight of Life* (1940) and *The Nuremberg Trials* (1946): d. Armonk, NY, March 4.

Louis, Victor (born Vitaly Yevgenyevich Liu) (64), Russian journalist who worked for Western news agencies and gave information that the Communist Party and the KGB wanted in the Western press; he was a part-time correspondent for the *London Evening News* (1951–80): d. London, July 18.

Ludwig, Daniel (95), shipowner and real-estate man; was for many years among the world's richest men: d. New York City, Aug. 27.

Lund, John (81), film actor of the 1940s and 1950s; appeared in *To Each His Own* (1946), *Night Has a Thousand Eyes* (1948), and *A Foreign Affair* (1948). He made two films with Jerry Lewis and Dean Martin, including *My Friend Irma* (1949). Earlier he had written the book and lyrics for the Broadway review *New Faces of 1943* and appeared on Broadway in *The Hasty Heart* (1945): d. Los Angeles, CA, May 10.

MacMillan, Sir Kenneth (62), Scottish resident choreographer and former director (1970–77) of London's Royal Ballet; earlier he also had been a dancer. For the Royal Ballet he created *Noctambules* (1956), *The Burrow* (1958), and *The Invitation* (1960). Later in his career he was noted for evening-length

narrative ballets, including *Romeo and Juliet* (1965), the second version of *Anastasia* (1971), *Manon* (1974), and *Mayerling* (1978). Knighted in 1983, he also was an artistic associate of American Ballet Theatre (1984–90): d. London, Oct. 29.

Maglie, Sal (75), baseball pitcher of the 1950s and the last player to be on all three New York teams—the Giants, Dodgers, and Yankees: d. Niagara Falls, NY, Dec. 28.

Mailliard, William S. (75), U.S. representative (R-CA, 1953–74): d. Reston, VA, June 10.

Man, Evelyn B. (87), biochemist; helped develop the first widely used test to detect low hormone levels in the thyroid gland: d. West Hartford, CT, Sept. 3.

Marshall, James (50), illustrator and author of children's books; best known for his series on George and Martha, the hippopotamuses, for the exploits of the Fox, and for the Stupid Family: d. New York City, Oct. 13.

Martin, Paul (89), Canadian member of Parliament (Liberal Party) for more than 50 years; served in the governments of four Liberal prime ministers and twice sought the party leadership. He wrote much social legislation and was secretary of state in 1945: d. Windsor, Ont., Sept. 14.

McGee, Gale (77), U.S. senator (D-WY, 1959–77): d. Bethesda, MD, April 9.

McGinley, L. J. (86), president of Fordham University (1949–63); Father McGinley was a major figure in the creation of the Lincoln Center for the Performing Arts: d. Rose Hill, Bronx, NY, Aug. 15.

McGowan, William (64), entrepreneur who changed the U.S. telephone industry as chairman of the MCI Communications Corporation when he successfully challenged the monopoly of AT&T in 1974 in federal court. He had bought a part of the fledgling MCI in 1968: d. Washington, DC, June 8.

McIntyre, Thomas J. (77), U.S. senator (D-NH, 1963–79): d. West Palm Beach, FL, Aug. 9.

Megee, Vernon E. (91), U.S. Marine Corps four-star general and a pioneer in combat aviation; was the only person in that branch of service to rise from private to the service's highest rank: d. Albuquerque, NM, Jan. 14.

Messiaen, Olivier (83), French composer; drew inspiration from the natural world and the spiritual world of Roman Catholic mysticism. For the organ he created "Apparition de l'Église Éternelle" (1932) and "Nativité du Seigneur" (1935), and for piano, "Vingt Regards sur l'Enfant Jésus" (1944) and "Catalogue d'Oiseaux" (1959). His orchestral works include "L'Ascension" (1933), "Turangalila-Symphonie" (1949), "Des Canyons aux Étoiles" (1974), and "Éclairs sur l'Au-Delà." He wrote one opera, *St. Francis of Assisi*, which premiered in 1983: d. Paris, April 27.

Miller, Roger (56), country singer and songwriter; his songs include "King of the Road." He wrote the score for the musical *Big River* (1985), winning a Tony Award. He also won 11 Grammy Awards: d. Los Angeles, CA, Oct. 25.

Mills, Wilbur (82), U.S. representative (D-AR, 1939–77); served for many years as chairman of the House Ways and Means Committee. In the 1970s he was stopped by police while driving intoxicated with stripper Fanne Fox. He served one more term following that incident and blamed his struggle with alcoholism for the incident: d. Kensett, AR, May 2.

Mitchell, Joan (66), U.S. abstract expressionist painter and a noted colorist; she lived for many years in France: d. Paris, Oct. 30.

Mitchell, Peter (71), British biochemist; discovered how cells created energy and used it to send nerve signals and move muscles. He received the 1978 Nobel Prize for Chemistry: d. Bodmin, England, April 10.

Morey, Walt (84), author of *Gentle Ben* (1965) and other children's books: d. Wilsonville, OR, Jan. 12.

Morley, Robert (84), British actor of stage and screen; his career spanned more than 50 years. He appeared on stage in *Oscar Wilde* (1936; New York 1938) and on Broadway in *Edward, My*

Dorothy Kirsten

Olivier Messiaen

Wilbur Mills

Robert Morley

Bert Parks

Anthony Perkins

Molly Picon

Satyajit Ray

Son (1948), which he cowrote. His movie credits include *The African Queen* (1951), *Gilbert and Sullivan* (1953), *Beat the Devil* (1954), *Topkapi* (1964), and *The Blue Bird* (1976). He also appeared on television and occasionally directed. He wrote five books of reminiscences, and was made Commander of the British Empire in 1957: d. Reading, England, June 3.

Mott, William P., Jr. (82), director of the U.S. National Park Service (1985–89): d. Orinda, CA, Sept. 21.

Muldoon, Sir Robert (70), prime minister of New Zealand (1975–84); he headed the Conservative National Party. He was knighted in 1983: d. Auckland, New Zealand, Aug. 5.

Murphy, George (89), Hollywood actor and singer; later became a U.S. senator (R-CA, 1965-71). His film career began in the 1930s and from then until the 1950s he appeared in more than 40 movies, including the 1938 film *Little Miss Broadway*, with Shirley Temple: d. Palm Beach, FL, May 3.

Nance, Jim (49), running back for the Boston [now New England] Patriots pro football team (1965–71). He earlier played college football for Syracuse University: d. Quincy, MA, June 15.

Naughton, Bill (81), Irish-born British playwright noted for his 1964 play *Alfie*, which became a successful film for which he wrote the screenplay in 1966. His autobiography, *Saintly Bill: A Catholic Boyhood*, was published in 1988: d. Isle of Man, Jan. 9.

Newell, Allen (65), a founder of the field of artificial intelligence and a leader in the study of human thinking; he was a professor at Carnegie Mellon University (1961–92) and the author of several books, including *Unified Theories of Cognition* (1990): d. Pittsburgh, PA, July 19.

Nie Rongzhen (92), last marshal of China's Communist Revolution; beginning in 1930 he worked in the Red Army. He was a member of China's Communist Party for 69 years and oversaw the development of China's atomic bomb. He was deputy prime minister from 1956 to 1974: d. Beijing, May 14.

Nolan, Sir Sidney (75), Australian painter who was inspired by his country's history, folklore, and landscapes; noted for his Ned Kelly series of paintings of the 1940s and 1950s in which the 19th-century outlaw is depicted with a square black head. He was knighted in 1981: d. London, Nov. 27.

Northrop, F. S. C. (98), Yale University scholar and professor; he was an expert in the fields of philosophy, science, anthropology, and law. His books included *Ideological Differences and World Order* (1949) and *The Meeting of East and West* (1946): d. Exeter, NH, July 22.

Norton, Mary (born Mary Pearson) (88), British writer of children's books; noted for her series about the tiny borrowers. Her award-winning *The Borrowers* (1952) was followed with four sequels. Her *Bedknob and Broomstick* was published in 1957: d. Harland, England, Aug. 29.

O'Neal, Frederick (86), actor noted for character roles and first black president of the Actors' Equity Association (1964–73): d. New York City, Aug. 25.

Oort, Jan H. (92), Dutch astronomer; credited with major discoveries on the movement of the Milky Way galaxy and the origin of comets: d. Leiden, the Netherlands, Nov. 5.

Osborne, Mary (70), jazz guitarist; with her husband, she formed the Osborne Guitar Company (later Osborne Sound Laboratories): d. Bakersfield, CA, March 4.

Page, Robert Morris (88), physicist and a leading figure in the development of radar technology; he was research director of the U.S. Naval Research Laboratory (1957–66). He joined the laboratory in 1927 and began experiments with radar in the early 1930s. His book *The Origin of Radar* was published in 1962: d. Edina, MN, May 15.

Parks, Bert (77), game-show host and the master of ceremonies for the Miss America beauty pageant for 25 years (1955–80). He began in radio and got his big break with *Break the Bank* in 1945; in 1948 he became host of *Stop the Music*. Both shows later went to television. These and other game shows made him a noted television personality: d. La Jolla, CA, Feb. 2.

Parnis, Mollie (90s), fashion designer whose designs were worn by several first ladies, including Mamie Eisenhower and Lady Bird Johnson. She was a friend to actors, journalists, and political figures, mostly of the Democratic Party: d. New York City, July 18.

Parten, Jubal R. (96), independent oil producer and refiner for more than seven decades; he was board chairman of Houston's Parten Oil Company: d. Madisonville, TX, Nov. 8.

Peak, Robert (64), illustrator for magazine covers, movie posters (*West Side Story, Camelot, My Fair Lady*), and postage-stamp designs, including a series of Olympic commemorative stamps (1983–84): d. Scottsdale, AZ, July 31.

Perkins, Anthony (60), actor; best known as the psychopath Norman in *Psycho* (1960). Other films were *The Actress* (1953), *Friendly Persuasion* (1956), *On the Beach* (1959), and *Catch 22* (1970). He also appeared on stage in *Tea and Symphathy, Look Homeward Angel, Equus,* and *Romantic Comedy*: d. Hollywood, CA, Sept. 12.

Phomvihan, Kaysone (71), premier (1975–91) and then president of Laos; he was chairman of the Lao People's Revolutionary Party and was known as a Communist hard-liner: d. Vientiane, Laos, Nov. 21.

Piazzolla, Astor (71), Argentine composer of tango music; wrote some 750 works, including concertos, operas, and film and theatrical scores: d. Buenos Aires, July 5.

Picon, Molly (93), actress of the Yiddish-language theater; appeared in more than 200 Yiddish plays in the 1920s: d. Lancaster, PA, April 5.

Piper, John (88), British painter, printmaker, stage designer, stained-glass artist, and photographer. First gained notice as an abstract painter and then became famous as a watercolor painter of English landscapes. He did 29 paintings of Windsor Castle during World War II, commissioned by Queen Elizabeth, the current Queen mother: d. near Henley-on-Thames, England, June 29.

Poiret, Jean (65), French actor, playwright, and director; wrote the original stage version of *La Cage Aux Folles*. He also appeared in about 40 movies: d. Paris, March 14.

Polk, James H. (80), U.S. four-star general; held U.S. military commands in Berlin and West Germany during the post-World War II Cold War. A graduate of West Point in 1933, he was an armor commander in Europe during World War II. He retired in 1971: d. El Paso, TX, Feb. 18.

Pousette-Dart, Richard (76), abstract expressionist painter; linked with New York School artists like Jackson Pollock and Willem de Kooning: d. New York City, Oct. 25.

Price, Sammy (83), jazz pianist whose career began in the 1920s: d. New York City, April 14.

Pucci, Emilio (78), Italian fashion designer; noted for his brilliantly colored prints that first became popular in the 1960s: d. Florence, Italy, Nov. 29.

Quadros, Janio da Silva (75), president of Brazil; elected in 1960 and resigned in 1961 after seven months. His resignation touched off a process that culminated in a military takeover in 1964: d. Sao Paulo, Brazil, Feb. 16.

Rauh, Joseph, Jr. (81), civil-liberties lawyer; championed civil rights and liberal causes and helped found Americans for Democratic Action in 1947: d. Washington, DC, Sept. 3.

Ray, Satyajit (70), award-winning Indian director; noted for his "Apu" film trilogy—*Pather Panchali* (1955), *Aparajito* (1956), *The World of Apu* (1959)—of childhood, youth, and manhood in Bengal. He received an honorary Academy Award in March 1992 for lifetime achievement in cinema. A second series, the "Calcutta Series," also was notable. Other works by the self-taught director included *Distant Thunder* (1973), *The Home of the World* (1984), and *Branches of the Trees* (1990): d. Calcutta, April 23.

Reed, Robert (born John Robert Rietz, Jr.) (59), actor; perhaps best known for his role as the father on television's *Brady Bunch* (1969-74): d. Pasadena, CA, May 12.

Reisman, Philip (87), social-realist painter and printmaker;

Lee Salk

William Schuman

Eric Sevareid

William Shawn

known for his views of New York City street life: d. New York City, June 17.

Reshevsky, Samuel (born Samuel Rzeszewski) (80), Polish-born chess prodigy and grand master. He won the U.S. Chess Championship seven times: d. Suffern, NY, April 4.

Roach, Hal (Harold Eugene) (100), writer, producer, and director who pioneered U.S. film comedy, originating the *Our Gang* comedies; he was chief of Hal Roach Studios for almost 40 years. He introduced the comedy team of Stan Laurel and Oliver Hardy to his film audiences and also produced the acclaimed *Of Mice and Men* (1939). After World War II, his studios produced some television series: d. Los Angeles, CA, Nov. 2.

Roberts, (Herbert) Ray (79), U.S. representative (D-TX, 1962–81): d. Denton, TX, April 13.

Robertson, Durant Waite, Jr. (77), Princeton University professor (1946–80); widely regarded as the century's most influential Chaucer scholar: d. Chapel Hill, NC, July 26.

Rockefeller, Blanchette (83), philanthropist and widow of John D. Rockefeller 3d; was a benefactor of New York's Museum of Modern Art: d. Briarcliff Manor, NY, Nov. 29.

Romanov, Grand Duke Vladimir Kirillovich (74), a direct descendant of Czar Alexander II of Russia, he was born in exile in Finland and was a resident of France: d. Miami, FL, April 21.

St. Aubin, Helen C. (69), Canadian-born baseball player of the All-American Girls Professional Baseball League. She was a subject of two films—a documentary made in part by her son that inspired a 1992 Hollywood film—both called *A League of Their Own*: d. Santa Barbara, CA, Dec. 8.

Salk, Lee (65), child psychologist and author of eight books on family relationships; he made frequent television appearances and wrote a monthly column for *McCall's* magazine. He came to national attention in 1965, when he published research relating to the calming effect of a mother's heartbeat on a newborn infant: d. New York City, May 2.

Schueler, Jon (75), abstract expressionist painter; noted for his evocations of nature: d. New York City, Aug. 5.

Schuman, William (81), composer and president of Lincoln Center (1962–69) and of the Juilliard School (1945–62). He incorporated jazz and folk traditions in his music, writing ten symphonies; five ballet scores, piano, violin, viola, and cello concertos; four string quartets; as well as chorus works, band scores, and operas. For his compositions he won two Pulitzer Prizes—in 1943 for the cantata "A Free Song" and in 1985 for his composition and work as a educator and administrator: d. New York City, Feb. 15.

Segal, Vivienne (95), musical-comedy stage and film actress; appeared on Broadway in *The Desert Song, No, no, Nanette*, and *Pal Joey*. She also made some films, debuting in 1927, and appeared on television: d. Los Angeles, CA, Dec. 29.

Selikoff, Irving J. (77), codiscoverer of a treatment for tuberculosis in 1952; he went on to fight for discontinuing the use of asbestos. He was affiliated with New York City's Mount Sinai Medical Center and School of Medicine for 51 years: d. Ridgewood, NJ, May 20.

Sergeyev, Konstantin (82), artistic director of the Kirov Ballet (1951–56; 1960–70) as well as a leading male dancer of the Soviet Ballet and choreographer: d. St. Petersburg, Russia, April 1.

Sevareid, Eric (79), journalist and radio and television correspondent; his commentaries were featured regularly on the *CBS Evening News With Walter Cronkite* (1964–77). During his career he was in several European and South American countries, in Washington and New York, and in Vietnam. He covered World War II as a correspondent and associate of Edward R. Murrow and early in his career had worked as a reporter in Minneapolis and for the Paris edition of the *New York Herald Tribune* and for United Press, the wire service. His books include *Canoeing with the Cree* (1935), *Not So Wild*

a Dream (1946), *In One Ear* (1952), and *Small Sounds in the Night* (1956): d. Washington, DC, July 9.

Shawn, William (85), chief editor of *The New Yorker* magazine (1952–87); known as a "gentle despot," he exerted through the pages of the magazine a powerful influence on U.S. writers and also on public opinion. During his tenure the magazine provided reports and commentaries on such matters as the environment, poverty, racial strife, the Vietnam war, and nuclear disarmament. Also, Truman Capote's 1965 best-seller *In Cold Blood* appeared first in *The New Yorker*. In the post-*New Yorker* years, he was a consulting editor for the book publisher Farrar, Straus, and Giroux: d. New York City, Dec. 8.

Sheehan, John Clark (76), chemist and professor at the Massachusetts Institute of Technology (1946–77); pioneered synthetic penicillin in 1957: d. Key Biscayne, FL, March 21.

Shurr, Gertrude (88), pioneer in modern dance who performed in the 1920s and 1930s with such dance companies as Denishawn (1925–27), the Humphrey Weidman Concert Company (1927–29), and the early Martha Graham Company (1930–38). She also taught dance: d. Tucson, AZ, Jan. 2.

Shuster, Joseph (78), cartoonist; cocreator of Superman who sold the rights to the character for $130 after syndicators repeatedly rejected the comic strip. In 1975 he and his collaborator finally received pensions of $20,000 annually, raised to $30,000 in 1981, plus a $15,000 bonus after the first film in the *Superman* series grossed $275 million: d. Los Angeles, CA, July 30.

Sirica, John Joseph (88), U.S. federal judge; presided over the Watergate break-in trials—including the original trial of the burglars. He ordered President Richard Nixon to turn over White House tape recordings to a House Judiciary Committee considering Nixon's impeachment and presided over the trial of Nixon's chief aides. His career as a lawyer and judge spanned 60 years: d. Washington, DC, Aug. 14.

Souez, Ina (born Ina Rains) (89), soprano who appeared in Britain's Glyndebourne Festival during the 1930s and later did slapstick comedy with Spike Jones and his City Slickers in the 1950s: d. Santa Monica, CA, Dec. 7.

Spencer, Eighth Earl (born Edward John Spencer) (68), father of Diana, Princess of Wales: d. London, March 29.

Springer, William L. (83), U.S. representative (R-IL, 1951–73): d. Champaign, IL, Sept. 20.

Stang, Gunnar (85), Swedish finance minister (1955–76) and one of the leading architects of Sweden's social-welfare system. He remained in Parliament until 1985: d. Stockholm, March 6.

Stern, Philip M. (66), political journalist, writer, and philanthropist; wrote *The Great Treasury Raid* (1964), *The Rape of the Taxpayer* (1973), *The Best Congress Money Can Buy* (1988). In the 1980s he founded two political organizations intended to draw attention to the influence of money on politics. As a philanthropist he directed the Stern Fund that worked to end poverty and promote social change: d. Washington, June 1.

Stirling, Sir James Frazer (66), British architect and 1981 Pritzker Architecture Prize winner; noted during the post-World War II years as a leader of an unorthodox movement away from stylistic uniformity of modern architecture, he rejected the term postmodern and instead called himself post-International. His buildings had color, historic reference, and quirkiness and can be found in Rome, Berlin, Stuttgart, Tokyo, and Tehran and at several U.S. universities. In 1986 he designed Clore Gallery, an addition to the Tate Gallery in London. He was knighted days before his death: d. London, June 25.

Stotz, Carl (82), founder of Little League baseball in 1939, now played by more than 2.5 million young people in more than 30 countries: d. Williamsport, PA, June 4.

Sturges, John (81), film director of action films like *Gunfight at OK Corral* (1956), *The Magnificent Seven* (1960), and *The Great Escape* (1963); he won an Oscar nomination in 1955 for *Bad Day at Black Rock*: d. near San Luis Obispo, CA, Aug. 18.

Summerson, Sir John (87), British architectural historian; he was a trained architect and a journalist. His books include *Georgian London* (1945) and *Heavenly Mansions* (1949). He was curator of Sir John Soane's Museum in London from 1945 to 1984. He was knighted in 1958: d. London, Nov. 10.

Swanberg, William A. (84), biographer; won a Pulitzer Prize in 1973 for his biography of Henry Luce, *Luce and His Empire*: d. Southbury, CT, Sept. 17.

Syms, Sylvia (74), pop-jazz singer and a legendary cabaret performer; she recorded 15 albums and had one popular hit, "I Could Have Danced All Night," in 1956: d. New York City, May 10.

Tal, Mikhail (55), Latvian chess grand master; held the world chess championship in 1960–61: d. Moscow, June 28.

Temianka, Henri (85), British-born violinist and conductor; founded the Paganini string quartet (1946–66), and the California symphony orchestra, begun in 1961. He was concertmaster of the Pittsburgh symphony (1940–41): d. Los Angeles, CA, Nov. 7.

Ter-Arutunian, Rouben (72), Georgian-born (Soviet) designer for dance, opera, theater, and television; well noted for his designs for George Balanchine's *Nutcracker* for the New York City Ballet: d. New York City, Oct. 17.

Thorp, Willard L. (92), economist who served three U.S. presidents—Franklin Roosevelt, Harry Truman, and John Kennedy—and who helped draft the Marshall Plan. In the 1950s and 1960s he returned to academia, mainly at Amherst College, where he had taught in the 1920s: d. Pelham, MA, May 10.

Tomasek, Cardinal Frantisek (93), head of the Roman Catholic church in Czechoslovakia; he secretly was elevated to cardinal in 1976. For much of his career he pursued a delicate policy between confrontation and compromise with Communist authorities: d. Prague, Aug. 4.

Tully, Paul (48), political director of the Democratic National Committee; he had worked in every presidential election since 1968: d. Little Rock, AR, Sept. 24.

Uri, Pierre (80), French economist; one of the chief architects of the European Community: d. Paris, July 22.

Van Fleet, James A. (100), four-star U.S. Army general who was a machine-gunner in World War I; his command participated in the D-day landings of World War II. He was involved in the Allied intervention in Greece during the post-World War II Communist threat and later was a field commander in Korea. He retired in 1953: d. Polk City, FL, Sept. 23.

Varsi, Diane (54), actress; received an Oscar nomination for *Peyton Place* (1957), her first film: d. Los Angeles, CA, Nov. 19.

Ventura, Charlie (born Charles Venturo) (75), jazz tenor saxophonist during the big-band era of the 1940s: d. Pleasantville, NY, Jan. 17.

Vieira da Silva, Maria-Helena (83), Portuguese-born painter; her semi-abstractions include landscapes, games, city streets, and atmospheric effects. During World War II her painting reflected the grim European scene: d. Paris, March 6.

Voorhees, Arthur B., Jr. (70), developer of the first successful artificial arteries; the doctor's pioneering work began in the late 1940s, and his first implant in a human patient occurred in 1952: d. Albuquerque, NM, May 12.

Walker, Nancy (born Anna Myrtle Swoyer) (69), actress; known for her television roles as the mother on *Rhoda* (1973–78) and as *McMillan and Wife*'s housekeeper (1971–76), as well as for her television commercials. She also appeared on Broadway and made some movies: d. Studio City, CA, March 25.

Walton, Samuel Moore (Sam) (74), founder of Wal-Mart Stores, Inc.: d. Little Rock, AR, April 5. (*See also* page 457.)

Watson, William W. (92), physicist; chairman of the physics department at Yale (1940–61) who helped develop the atomic bomb during World War II: d. Hamden, CT, Aug. 3.

Wang Hongwen (58), deputy chairman of the Chinese Communist Party (1973–76) and one of the "gang of four" who presided over the Cultural Revolution: d. China, Aug. 3.

Weatherby, William J. (62), British journalist and novelist; during a long career in the United States he was a columnist and feature writer for *The Guardian*. His books include *Love in the Shadows, Conversations with Marilyn, James Baldwin, Artist on Fire*, and *Salman Rushdie, Sentenced to Death*: d. Poughkeepsie, NY, Aug. 5.

Webb, James (85), administrator of the National Aeronautics and Space Administration (1961–69); was credited with guiding the U.S. space program to man's first walk on the Moon: d. Washington, DC, March 27.

Weiss, Theodore (Ted) (64), Hungarian-born U.S. representative (D-NY, 1977–92): d. New York City, Sept. 14.

Welk, Lawrence (89), folksy band leader who played "Champagne music" and shaped one of the longest-running television shows in history. The show ran from 1955 to 1971 on network television, then 11 more years on independent stations, and more recently on public television. He was reportedly the wealthiest show-business performer after Bob Hope and had a huge music library and lucrative royalty rights: d. Santa Monica, CA, May 17.

Wells, Mary (49), pop singer of the 1960s; her songs "The One Who Really Loves You," "You Beat Me to the Punch," "Two Loves," and "My Guy" were top-20 songs on the pop chart: d. Los Angeles, CA, July 26.

Weltner, Charles L. (64), chief justice of the Georgia Supreme Court (1992); earlier had been a U.S. representative (1963–67). He was a moderate Democrat who supported the civil-rights legislation of the 1960s and withdrew from the 1966 race rather than take a party pledge of loyalty. He had been associate justice of the Georgia Supreme Court since 1981: d. Atlanta, GA, Aug. 31.

Whitehead, Edwin C. (Jack) (72), developer of scientific and clinical equipment; in the early 1980s he created Whitehead Institute, one of the world's foremost biomedical-research centers: d. Greenwich, CT, Feb. 2.

Whitney, Cornelius Vanderbilt (93), heir to oil and rail fortunes; he was also a cofounder of Pan American Airways, serving as its chairman from 1931 until 1941. In another venture, he took control in 1931 of Hudson Bay Mining and Smelting Company in Canada, remaining chairman of the board until 1964. He was also a sportsman who maintained a horse farm and racing stable, and he saw service during World Wars I and II: d. Saratoga Springs, NY, Dec. 13.

Williams, Bill (born William Katt) (77), actor; played the title role in the television series *The Adventures of Kit Carson* in the early 1950s. He later was in the series *Date With an Angel*: d. Burbank, CA, Sept. 21.

Wojciechowicz, Alex (76), football lineman; played pro football (1938–51) with such teams as the Detroit Lions and Philadelphia Eagles. He entered the pro-football Hall of Fame in 1968. In college he had played at Fordham University: d. South River, NJ, July 13.

Wojnarowicz, David (37), artist who worked in many media, including painting, photography, performance, and writing; his work about AIDS put him at the center of a debate involving the National Endowment for the Arts in 1989. His books included *Close to the Knives* (1990): d. New York City, July 22.

Yates, Richard (66), novelist; wrote *Revolutionary Road* (1961) and other books dealing with themes of self-deception, disappointment, and grief: d. Birmingham, AL, Nov. 7.

Yawkey, Jean (83), Boston Red Sox baseball owner and a major Boston philanthropist; she also had been director of the National Baseball Museum and Hall of Fame since 1984. Her husband, who died in 1976, had bought the team in 1938. She later owned the team in association with others: d. Boston, MA, Feb. 26.

York, Dick (63), actor; was the original actor who played the role of Darrin, the husband of the witch Samantha, in *Bewitched* (1964–69). His films include *My Sister Eileen* (1955) and *Inherit the Wind* (1960): d. Grand Rapids, MI, Feb. 20.

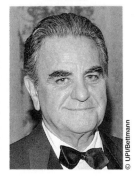

John Sirica

James Stirling

James Van Fleet

Lawrence Welk

OCEANOGRAPHY

Signs of the development of an El Niño in the Pacific Ocean early in 1992 were confirmed by mid-spring with sea-surface temperatures 1° C to 4° C (34° F to 39° F) above normal along the entire west coast of the United States. This trend persisted during May until coastal waters were 5° C to 6° C (41° F to 43° F) above normal in a band extending 100 mi to 200 mi (160 km to 322 km) offshore from central California to the Columbia River. Sea-surface temperature increases also were seen off South America, where the El Niño was named originally from its occurrence near Christmas about every five to seven years due to the interaction of ocean and atmosphere in the tropical Pacific.

ENSO and TOGA. The El Niño/Southern Oscillation, or ENSO, plays an important role in the redistribution of solar energy by the equatorial ocean, replacing normally cold coastal currents of upwelled water and displacing fish populations. The effects on fisheries in 1992 included reports of sardines caught off southern California and a decline in the availability of anchovy, along with a northern extension of the range of several subtropical species. Weather systems in continental North America also are affected by an ENSO, since the shift of Pacific Ocean winds and currents changes worldwide weather patterns. Early in the winter of 1991, temperatures were 3° C to 7° C (37° F to 45° F) above normal from central Alaska through western Canada to Lake Superior and precipitation was at least 200% above normal across Texas.

Under the Tropical Ocean/Global Atmosphere (TOGA) program, interest focused on the physical processes in the western Pacific pool of warm surface waters in the area north of New Guinea, where the highest open ocean temperatures in the world ocean are found. The early stages of ENSO events are thought to originate in this area as anomalies of the westerly winds that then alter the dynamics of the eastern Pacific. Satellite remote sensing gives well-resolved synoptic pictures of the ocean-surface temperature; the atmospheric circulation cells are shown to be coupled tightly with the dynamics of these warm surface pools. Continued monitoring should correlate these observations still better with the computer forecast models that successfully gave a prediction for the present ENSO event.

An ENSO event may give a reduction in carbon dioxide (CO_2) brought from ocean depths to the surface, with some resultant lowering of the atmospheric carbon-dioxide level that contributes to global warming. The Joint Global Ocean Flux Study (JGOFS)—a three-year effort by many research institutions—surveyed the equatorial Pacific to evaluate the CO_2 balance in detail. The World Ocean Circulation Experiment (WOCE)—an international program that has occupied scientists from some 40 nations for more than five years—also is collecting measurements to describe the ocean circulation of heat, water, and chemical tracers, as well as the formation and modification of water masses and the statistics of ocean variability. The programs are to develop information useful in predicting future climate change.

ODP. In 1992 the Ocean Drilling Program (ODP) concluded a series of drilling transects at active and remnant island arc/backarc basin systems that rim the western Pacific. Details of the tectonic and geologic processes associated with sediment accretion at convergent plate margins were obtained near the Tonga trench. Sites were selected to give a sedimentary and stratigraphic sequence over time and a sample of magma variations as the basin opened. Rock and sediment ages were determined by a combination of fossil data and paleomagnetic reversals. An eastward-moving wave of volcanic events within the basin, toward the trench, is postulated. In later studies in the eastern equatorial Pacific near the Galápagos Islands, ODP sought paleoclimatic records from the deep-sea sediments beneath the upwelling system of the near-surface waters. Altogether, 18,169 ft (5 538 m) of sediment were recovered from below 13,123 ft (4 000 m) of water, with sedimentary data achieved by precision overlapping of the separate drill sections.

Sewage Sludge. Since 1987, an estimated 40 million tons of processed sewage sludge were dumped into the sea at a site 106 mi (171 km) off the mid-Atlantic coast. This disposal method ended on June 30, 1992, when the last barge load departed New York harbor; New Jersey already had switched to landside disposal six months earlier. Because of the considerable depth and the strong currents in the dump area, it was thought that dispersal would eliminate any hazardous accumulations. Studies show, however, that sludge particles were reaching the seafloor in measurable quantities and entering the food chain for some animals such as sea urchins. The long-term impact of the sludge dumping would be seen in restructuring of the seafloor community in favor of opportunistic species, such as the sea urchin, that can exploit the organic material.

In 1992 some scientists were advocating conveying the sludge still further offshore to a new site halfway between the United States and Bermuda, so that any accumulation would be at depths where the water circulation is reduced greatly. The sludge would be lowered through the water on powerful hoists with leak-proof buckets larger than a house, then dumped on the ocean bottom near 13,123 ft (4 000 m) for bacterial decomposition. The proposal raises many concerns about the potential of the untouched undersea abyssal plains.

DAVID A. McGILL
U.S. Coast Guard Academy

OHIO

Politics dominated news events in Ohio in 1992. Both George Bush and Bill Clinton visited the state repeatedly in their quest for the state's electoral votes. Above-average rainfall and below-average summer temperatures in much of the state helped to alleviate serious drought conditions.

Elections. Democrats generally fared well in Ohio in 1992. Bill Clinton won the state with 40% of the vote, to 39% for George Bush and 21% for independent candidate Ross Perot. Democrat John Glenn became the first Ohio senator to be elected to a fourth consecutive term, beating back a challenge from Lt. Gov. Michael DeWine, 55%-45%. DeWine tried to make issues of Glenn's involvement with convicted savings-and-loan executive Charles Keating and his lingering debt from a 1984 presidential bid. Two congressional incumbents implicated in the House banking scandal—Mary Rose Oakar (D-Cleveland) and Bob McEwen (R-Hillsboro)—were defeated. The state's U.S. congressional delegation would include six new members.

In state elections, Democrats retained their 20-year hold on the state House, but by a reduced margin, 53 to 46. Republicans maintained control of the Senate and the Supreme Court. Term limitations of 12 years for U.S. senators, eight years for U.S. congressmen, and eight years for state legislators and elected officials passed. But voters rejected a proposed state constitutional convention, an issue required to be on the ballot every 20 years. And they turned down by a wide margin a controversial measure requiring warning labels on many products containing chemicals con-

sidered to be potential causes of cancer or birth defects. The latter issue was backed by some environmentalists and consumer activists, but vigorously opposed by a coalition of business, labor, and agricultural groups and most of the state's large newspapers.

Government. A sluggish economy and lagging tax receipts forced Gov. George Voinovich to impose significant budget cuts—in some cases up to 19%—on state agencies and programs in July, in order to keep the budget in balance. Annual welfare benefits to certain recipients were cut in half, forcing city, county, and private agencies to provide additional assistance. In October the head of the state human-services department resigned amid questions about its management and expenditures. Fourteen current or former technical- and community-college presidents agreed to perform community service for their involve-

Despite having been investigated by the U.S. Senate Ethics Committee for involvement with convicted savings-and-loan executive Charles Keating, Jr., former astronaut John Glenn, 71, easily captured a fourth term in the U.S. Senate.

© Ira Wyman/Sygma

ment in illegal contributions of public funds to political candidates. Four other current or former presidents pleaded innocent to the charges and were to stand trial.

A report on public higher education issued by the Board of Regents recommended more effective coordination of the 60-campus system, with most research funding to be concentrated at The Ohio State University and the University of Cincinnati.

Quincentenary. Columbus, the largest city in the world named in honor of the famous explorer, celebrated the 500th anniversary of his voyage with AmeriFlora, a six-month-long international flower show and exhibition. Some 15 nations presented exhibits ranging from "Seeds of Change"—the biological transfer between the Old World and the New—to simulated tropical rain forests and deserts. Total attendance of approximately 2 million was less than projected, however, and ticket sales and other revenue failed to cover the $95 million cost.

JOHN B. WEAVER
Sinclair Community College

OKLAHOMA

Dominating Oklahoma's news in 1992 were stories about a major tax-limitation measure, the legislature's struggle over the financing of welfare costs, the general election, and Gov. David Walters' 1990 campaign contributions.

Government and Politics. Elections began early with a vote in March on State Question 640, a constitutional amendment to limit legislative power to increase taxes. The controversy arose initially from passage in 1990 of HB1017, a law that substantially increased taxes and mandated education reforms. In 1991 state voters opposed repeal of HB1017. But in 1992 voters passed SQ640, which required that the legislature pass revenue-raising measures by a three-fourths vote in each house or by a

vote of the people in the next general election. State leaders read passage of SQ640 to mean that all future tax increases were to be submitted to a vote of the people. Oklahoma was not the first state to pass such a measure, but its amendment was among the most stringent.

Passage of SQ640 influenced the legislature in its annual session. Common education, welfare, and higher education received 35%, 20%, and 16%, respectively, of appropriated funds. For common education this share was enough to keep abreast of reforms mandated by HB1017. But welfare advocates argued for the need for additional funding for the elderly indigent in nursing homes. The legislators then formulated a providers tax to fall on nursing homes and other health-care operators, to be voted upon in the fall elections as required by SQ640.

Further legislative controversy arose from state Ethics Commission rules, forwarded to the legislature and governor for approval. The legislature adopted a diluted set of rules, causing objection from some commission members who contested them through the courts.

In the fall elections, President George Bush carried Oklahoma with 43% of the vote; Bill Clinton was second with 34%; and Ross Perot received an impressive 23%. Incumbent U.S. Sen. Don Nickles, a Republican, beat Democrat Steve Lewis with 59% of the vote. The state's congressional delegation remained four Democrats and two Republicans. Republican incumbent Rep. Mickey Edwards, implicated in overdrafts at the House bank, lost out in the primaries to Ernest Istook, who won the general election.

Seven State Questions were also on the ballot. SQ647, the provider tax formulated to fund the shortfall in welfare costs, failed. SQ649 and SQ650 passed; together they authorized the issuance of $350 million in bonds, mostly to fund higher-education improvements, a proposed museum of natural history, and a system of bond financing dependent chiefly upon taxes on bingo games.

Governor Walters, who won election as the vice-chairman of the Democratic Governors Association, attracted media attention regarding questionable campaign contributions made during his 1990 election run. Federal officials late in 1991 cleared him of violating federal law. In an ongoing inquiry, however, the Oklahoma attorney general convened a multicounty grand jury to probe violations of state laws. In September the jurors indicted a major contributor who was, before resigning, the civil-defense director. The former adjutant general of the National Guard, another contributor, publicly admitted defrauding an insurance company of more than $300,000 in claims filed on behalf of members of the Guard.

HARRY HOLLOWAY
University of Oklahoma (emeritus)

OKLAHOMA • Information Highlights

Area: 69,956 sq mi (181 186 km²).
Population (July 1, 1991 est.): 3,175,000.
Chief Cities (1990 census): Oklahoma City, the capital, 444,719; Tulsa, 376,302; Lawton, 80,561.
Government (1992): *Chief Officers*—governor, David Walters (D); lt. gov., Jack Mildren (D). *Legislature*—Senate, 48 members; House of Representatives, 101 members.
State Finances (fiscal year 1991): *Revenue,* $7,819,000,000; *expenditure,* $7,267,000,000.
Personal Income (1991): $49,340,000,000; per capita, $15,541.
Labor Force (June 1992): *Civilian labor force,* 1,524,300; *unemployed,* 107,600 (7.1% of total force).
Education: *Enrollment* (fall 1990)—public elementary schools, 424,901; public secondary, 154,186; colleges and universities, 173,221. *Public school expenditures* (1990), $2,042,530,000.

ONTARIO

Ontario, Canada's most populous and industrialized province, was hit badly by the recession in 1992, and Premier Bob Rae's New Democratic Party (NDP) government was forced to abandon several of its policies.

Governmental and Economic Affairs. In January, Premier Rae made an unprecedented television broadcast on the provincial economy. He announced cuts in most public services and promised municipal, hospital, school, and university grant increases of only 1%, leaving an unacceptable deficit of C$14.3 billion. The budget of April 30 tried to keep the deficit below C$10 billion, hold social spending, and stimulate the economy. Personal income tax was raised 1.5%, with an additional 14% surcharge for incomes more than C$53,000 (effectively siphoning off 1992's federal tax cut) and 20% for incomes over C$69,000. To aid business, corporate taxes were cut from 14.5% to 13.5% and small-business taxes from 10% to 9.5%, but a surcharge was introduced on banks. Liquor taxes were raised, but cigarette and gasoline taxes were not increased for fear of aggravating U.S. cross-border shopping. As an environmental measure, the tax was raised on canned but not bottled beer. Revenue was also to be raised by selling assets (including C$150 million for the Skydome), cutting civil-service jobs, and restraining health and education spending. Total expenditure (operating and

ONTARIO · Information Highlights

Area: 412,580 sq mi (1 068 580 km²).
Population (September 1992): 10,114,200.
Chief Cities (1986 census): Toronto, the provincial capital, 612,289; Ottawa, the federal capital, 300,763; Scarborough, 484,676; Mississauga, 374,005; Hamilton, 306,728; London, 269,140.
Government (1992): *Chief Officers*—lt. gov., Hal Jackman; premier, Robert Keith Rae (New Democrat). *Legislature*—Legislative Assembly, 130 members.
Provincial Finances (1992–93 fiscal year budget): *Revenues,* $44,900,000,000; *expenditures,* $54,800,000,000.
Personal Income (average weekly earnings, July 1992): $579.84.
Labor Force (September 1992, seasonally adjusted): *Employed* workers, 15 years of age and over, 4,698,000; *Unemployed,* 11.3%.
Education (1992–93): *Enrollment*—elementary and secondary schools, 2,084,600 pupils; postsecondary—universities, 223,700; community colleges, 105,700.
(All monetary figures are in Canadian dollars.)

capital) was estimated at C$54.847 billion, with revenue of C$44.925 billion for a C$9.992 billion deficit. To provide jobs and stimulate the economy, funds were set up for construction, transportation, and environmental projects, as well as job-training schemes and 20,000 units of public housing.

Despite the budget, unemployment continued to rise, hitting 11.3% in August (the highest level since May 1983). Ontario accounts for 40% of Canada's gross domestic product, and its manufacturing base was hit hard. Since September 1989, 18% of Ontario's manufacturing jobs (189,000) had been lost. High wage rates and real-estate prices were blamed by some.

Despite vocal opposition from business groups, the NDP government pressed ahead with changes in provincial labor legislation that would ban the use of replacement workers during strikes and increase the powers of unions. Although the bill was modified after legislative hearings in the fall, a negative media campaign by business groups was launched.

In June, Premier Rae announced the government had abandoned its long held position against Sunday shopping. Rae indicated that the public wanted Sunday shopping, but that no one would be forced to work on Sunday.

In a search for additional revenue, the government took the highly controversial step of legalizing casino gambling and was to introduce legislation to allow sports lotteries and off-track betting. Consumer Minister Marilyn Churley announced in October that the site of the first casino would be the border city of Windsor.

October Referendum. Ontario's vote in the October 26 referendum on the Charlottetown Accord was a virtual dead heat: The "yes" side won by less than 0.05%. Premier Rae, who had campaigned vigorously for the "yes" side, interpreted the result as a rejection. The "yes"

Ontario's Premier Bob Rae campaigns for the Charlottetown Accord. In the October 26 referendum, the province voted in favor of the constitutional changes by less than 0.05%.

© Ryan Remiorz/Canapress Photo Service

415

vote was strong in metropolitan Toronto and Ottawa, but the rest of the province voted "no."

Energy. The financially troubled Ontario Hydro, North America's largest electricity utility, announced plans to trim its capital spending by C$7 billion in the coming decade to reduce prices. With rates the second highest in Canada, domestic consumers were switching to cheaper natural gas, and large purchasers like Falconbridge Inc. (its largest customer) and some municipalities were thinking of building their own generating plants.

PETER J. KING, *Carleton University*

OREGON

For the sixth consecutive year, Oregon's population growth outpaced that of the nation. Much of the increase was from Californians moving north. The controversy over the spotted owl continued as federal judge Helen Frye in January halted all logging under the jurisdiction of the U.S. Bureau of Land Management in western Oregon that might affect owl habitat, and a 1991 federal injunction closing 66,000 acres (26 709 ha) of U.S. Forest Service lands remained in effect. Oregon's unemployment rate peaked at 8% in March, then fell to 7.2% by the fall, just below the national average. Only two sectors of the economy—wholesale trade and finance, and insurance and real estate —showed any strength as the fourth quarter got under way. Manufacturing was weak throughout 1992. A drought and the elections also made news in Oregon in 1992.

Drought. During the year, Oregon experienced a historic drought. Unlike the one-year record drought of 1977, this one represented an accumulation of six successive dry years. The Cascade snowpack in July amounted to less than half that of 1977. In September, Democratic Gov. Barbara Roberts declared a statewide drought emergency. Many cities, including Portland, already had imposed severe water restrictions. The drought, insect infestation, and salvage restrictions combined to present the state with its greatest wildfire danger in years. While not reaching record proportions, thousands of acres of forest were destroyed in the Winema and Rogue River national forests.

Governmental Affairs. Two attempts to recall Governor Roberts fell short of gathering the signatures necessary to place a petition on the ballot. Governor Roberts, in anticipation of a more than $1 billion revenue shortfall because of property-tax limitation, called a special session of the legislature. She asked for a sales-tax referendum coupled with belt-tightening. The session ended in a fiasco when the governor and the Republican speaker of the House could not agree upon a date for the ref-

OREGON · Information Highlights

Area: 97,073 sq mi (251 419 km²).
Population (July 1, 1991 est.): 2,922,000.
Chief Cities (1990 census): Salem, the capital,107,786; Portland, 437,319; Eugene, 112,669.
Government (1992): *Chief Officers*—governor, Barbara Roberts (D); secretary of state, Phil Keisling (D); *Legislative Assembly*—Senate, 30 members; House of Representatives, 60 members.
State Finances (fiscal year 1991): *Revenue,* $8,201,000,000; *expenditure,* $7,249,000,000.
Personal Income (1991): $51,353,000,000; per capita, $17,575.
Labor Force (June 1992): *Civilian labor force,* 1,540,300; *unemployed,* 109,700 (7.1% of total force).
Education: *Enrollment* (fall 1990)—public elementary schools, 350,748; public secondary, 133,904; colleges and universities, 166,641. *Public school expenditures* (1990), $2,371,300,000.

erendum. It then fell to the legislature to deal with the budget uncertainties. In the absence of any permanent solution, observers expected an income-tax surcharge and a patchwork of fee and tax increases.

Elections. Easily the most controversial of 1992's initiatives was a measure that sought a constitutional amendment declaring homosexuality, pedophilia, sadism, and masochism to be "abnormal, wrong, unnatural, and perverse" behaviors that are to be discouraged and avoided. The amendment would have prevented recognition of any categorical provision such as sexual orientation. The measure was defeated, along with other measures that would have closed Oregon's only nuclear generator; permitted the state to issue bonds for state parks; permitted the use of gasoline taxes for park purposes; banned triple-trailer trucks from state highways; introduced a two-tiered property tax; and restricted gill net salmon fishing on the Oregon side of the lower Columbia River. The only measure to pass involved term limitations.

The most hotly contested statewide race was that between Democrat Les AuCoin, who gave up his 1st District U.S. House seat, and incumbent Bob Packwood for the U.S. Senate. Packwood won the race, but soon after was accused of several instances of sexual misconduct. AuCoin's seat was won by a political novice, Democrat Elizabeth Furse. She defeated state Treasurer Tony Meeker. Abortion rights were a key campaign issue, as Meeker took a strong antiabortion stand. All other incumbent U.S. congressmen—Republican Robert F. Smith, Democrat Ron Wyden, Democrat Peter A. DeFazio, and Democrat Mike Kopetski—won reelection. In the presidential race, Democrat Bill Clinton carried the state with 43% of the vote, compared with 32% for President George Bush (R) and 25% for independent candidate Ross Perot.

L. CARL and JOANN C. BRANDHORST
Western Oregon State College

OTTAWA

In 1992, Ottawa's concerns centered on its youth, the city center, and its sports teams. Budget cutting under newly elected and budget conscious Mayor Jacqueline Holtzman saw the elimination of three top departmental positions at City Hall.

Health Concern. An outbreak of meningococcal disease in January caused five teenage deaths in the Ottawa-Hull region and great public alarm. Because of the virulence of the strain and the teenage deaths, medical authorities reversed an earlier decision and launched a mass immunization program for schoolchildren and teenagers in the Ottawa region, western Quebec, and Prince Edward Island. They denied, however, that there was an actual epidemic.

Education. In March and April the region was hit by a series of teachers' strikes. Ottawa public high-school teachers, seeking a 9% pay raise, struck on March 23 after the school board, faced with a budget crisis requiring it to trim C$21 million or raise taxes by 22%, proposed eliminating 300 teaching and 78 other jobs. With the provincial government considering public demands for back-to-work legislation, a new contract was signed and classes resumed on April 27. In early April the suburban public high-school teachers of the Carleton Board also struck, the major issue being job security. At one point 27,000 high-school students were out of class.

City Center. The character of the city center attracted attention during the year. The demolition of the Daly building in the very heart of the city opened up new and pleasing prospects for the area and generated pressure on the National Capital Commission (NCC) to forgo rebuilding and develop the site as an open space. The city finally decided to dismantle the adjacent Rideau Street Mall, long a complaint of shoppers and store owners alike. Concern was expressed over the historic Byward Market area (a leading tourist attraction); rising taxes and rents were driving out the local produce vendors and food stores that give the area its distinctive flavor.

In September, Marcel Beaudry, a former mayor of Hull, succeeded Jean Piggot as chairman of the NCC. The NCC, a federal agency, controls about 135,908 acres (55 000 ha) of land in the capital region, and some feared that the appointment may be an indication of the federal government's agenda to privatize large amounts of federally held assets, particularly in the Greenbelt area.

Sports. The Ottawa Roughriders of the Candian Football League were bought by a Detroit businessman and enjoyed a successful season. . . . The Ottawa Senators, the city's new National Hockey League team, played their first game in September.

PETER J. KING, *Carleton University*

PAKISTAN

In 1992, Pakistan's prime minister, Nawaz Sharif, was weakened by splits in his ruling coalition, but pressed forward with his privatization program. In foreign affairs, Pakistan was strengthened by the victory of its *mujahidin* allies in neighboring Afghanistan, and established ties with the Muslim republics of the former USSR.

Politics. Nawaz Sharif completed his second year in power despite erosion of his political base, challenges from the opposition, and serious law-and-order problems. The ruling Islami Jamhoori Ittehad (IJI)—in English, Islamic Democratic Alliance (IDA)—suffered several splits, but managed to hold on to power. The Jamaati Islami party left the alliance largely over differences on Afghanistan policy. In March, Pakistan Muslim League (PML) leader Pir Pagara pulled out and created a new party, the Functional Muslim League (FML). A few weeks later Nawaz expelled the National People's Party (NPP). Both Nawaz and President Ghulam Ishaq Khan came under repeated attack from opposition leaders, especially former Premier Benazir Bhutto, leader of the Pakistan People's Party (PPP). Bhutto and large numbers of her supporters were arrested during a protest demonstration against the government in November.

Sindh continued to be Pakistan's most volatile province. Robbery, kidnapping, armed attacks on trains, and other violence finally resulted in army intervention. The crackdown began in PPP-dominated Sindh, but later spread to Karachi, Hyderabad, and other cities.

The army's involvement in the urban areas further alienated Altaf Hussein's Mohajir Qaumi Movement (MQM), erstwhile political ally of Nawaz Sharif's IJI. The MQM itself suffered a serious split. Altaf Hussein went into exile in London early in 1992.

Crimes against women have become a more frequent feature of political news in Pakistan.

PAKISTAN • Information Highlights

Official Name: Islamic Republic of Pakistan.
Location: South Asia.
Area: 310,402 sq mi (803 940 km²).
Population (mid-1992 est.): 121,700,000.
Chief Cities (1981 census): Islamabad, the capital, 204,364; Karachi, 5,180,562.
Government: Head of state, Ghulam Ishaq Khan, president (elected Dec. 12, 1988). Head of government, Nawaz Sharif, prime minister (took office Nov. 6, 1990). Legislature—Parliament: Senate and National Assembly.
Monetary Unit: Rupee (25.47 rupees equal U.S.$1, Nov. 23, 1992).
Gross National Product (1990 est. U.S.$): $43,300,000,000.
Economic Index (1991): Consumer Prices (1982 = 100), all items, 184.8; food, 187.5.
Foreign Trade (1991 U.S.$): Imports, $8,427,000,000; exports, $6,471,000,000.

Former Pakistan Prime Minister Benazir Bhutto and other leaders of Pakistan's People's Party were arrested on Nov. 19, 1992, for leading demonstrations against the government.

© Panjiar/India Today/Sipa

A rally of women in Lahore protested the widespread incidence of rape and other violence against women, including alleged incidents involving politicians, police, and other public figures.

In response to charges that the plane crash in which former President Mohammed Zia ul-Haq lost his life in 1988 had been caused by military sabotage, Nawaz Sharif established a new judicial commission to reinvestigate the crash.

Economy. The Nawaz Sharif government continued its economic-restructuring program, including denationalization of state-owned enterprises, deregulation, liberalization of currency-exchange rules, and export promotion.

By some measures, the reforms were succeeding. With a growth rate of 6.4% in 1991, Pakistan was ranked by the Asian Development Bank as the fastest-growing economy in South Asia. Exports grew by 21% during the first quarter of fiscal year (FY) 1992. Booming equities markets indicated strong investor confidence.

However, the process of privatization itself came in for considerable criticism, with issues raised over both the pace of the government sell-off and the fairness of the competition among possible bidders.

Adding uncertainty to the economic equation was the potential impact of judicial decisions concerning the Islamic proscription against interest. The deadline for terminating the use of interest within the economic system initially had been set for the end of June 1992, but impending difficulties in implementation forced a postponement.

Heavy flooding in Punjab and Sindh during August and September left more than 1,100 people dead and more than 6 million displaced from their homes. More than 3 million acres (1.2 million ha) of farmland were destroyed by the floods.

Foreign Affairs. The victory of the Afghan *mujahidin* over the Marxist Najibullah regime in Kabul did not end factional fighting between the *mujahidin* groups, but the dramatic change in Kabul opened the door for the return of large numbers of the nearly 3 million Afghan refugees still in Pakistan. Nawaz visited Kabul in April, on the heels of the *mujahidin* victory.

In the wake of events in Kabul and in the former Soviet Union, Pakistan moved in 1992 to establish diplomatic, economic, and cultural relations with the former Soviet Central Asian republics. All five of the predominantly Muslim republics joined the Pakistan-Iran-Turkey Economic Cooperation Organization (ECO). Pakistan International Airways began direct flights to Tashkent, capital of Uzbekistan.

Pakistan also continued to build relations with other Muslim countries in Asia. Khaleda Zia, prime minister of Bangladesh, visited Pakistan in August and formed with Pakistan a joint ministerial committee to expand trade. A joint economic commission also was formed with the United Arab Emirates. Pakistan also was asked to represent the interests of Iran in the United States. A small contingent of Pakistani troops went to Somalia under UN auspices.

Visiting India and Pakistan in January, U.S. Sen. Larry Pressler (R-SD) bluntly criticized Pakistan's nuclear-weapons program, and U.S. opposition to the program continued to limit U.S. aid to Pakistan. Nevertheless, the United States did show some flexibility on the issue. In March, USAID released $135 million for the support of Pakistan's National Development Finance Corporation, and the direct sale of spare parts for F-16 aircraft and other equipment also was permitted. Later in the year the

U.S. Congress agreed to allow aid for social programs such as narcotics control, child welfare, and food distribution. Joint U.S.-Pakistan naval exercises in August also signaled improved relations.

In June, Nawaz Sharif attended the Rio Conference on Development and Environment as chair of the Group of 77.

WILLIAM L. RICHTER
Kansas State University

PARAGUAY

Major changes in the political process took effect in Paraguay in 1992 as the first new constitution in 25 years was approved.

1992 Constitution. Under the 291-article charter, future presidents now only need to win a plurality of votes but cannot be reelected immediately. On the military side, the president can delegate his role as commander-in-chief, so that the military would not have to serve under a civilian. Military personnel can no longer join a political party but those who already have done so do not have to resign.

New controls on the media met a mixed reaction from journalists. Newspaper owners opposed limitations on media ownership. Labor leaders rejoiced over legalization of the right to strike and bargain collectively and over the granting of permission for public-sector employees to organize.

Politics and Government. Despite controlling half of the 198 constitutional convention delegates, President Andrés Rodríguez and the Colorado Party failed to block approval of the reelection provision because of defections. Nonetheless, Rodríguez swore to uphold the new constitution. The Colorado Party's interim leader, Luis María Argaña, known for his presidential ambitions, had been among the defectors and was ousted as party leader. He was replaced by Blas Riquelme, a brewery executive.

Tight control by Colorado militants over the political process led other parties to join with the main opposition group, the Authentic Radical Liberal Party (PLRA), and form a united front for the May 1993 presidential election. Coalition groups include Asuncion for All and Paraguay for All, and factions of the Revolutionary Febreristas and Christian Democrats.

Economy. Cotton production in 1992, which had comprised 45% of the previous year's export earnings, was projected to be down by 40%, due to drought and heavy rains. Growers were given an extra 60 days in which to pay back their loans. The agriculture ministry encouraged farmers to limit cotton cultivation in favor of vegetables, fruit, and small livestock.

Paraguay obtained a $54 million loan from the Inter-American Development Bank in June for low-income housing. In April the World

---

PARAGUAY · Information Highlights

Official Name: Republic of Paraguay.
Location: Central South America.
Area: 157,046 sq mi (406 750 km²).
Population (mid-1992 est.): 4,500,000.
Chief City (1985 est.): Asunción, the capital, 477,100.
Government: *Head of state and government,* Gen. Andrés Rodríguez, president (took office 1989). *Legislature*—Congress: Senate and Chamber of Deputies.
Monetary Unit: Guaraní (1,452.0 guaraníes equal U.S.$1, selling rate, June 1992).
Gross Domestic Product (1990 est. U.S.$): $4,600,-000,000.
Foreign Trade (1990 U.S.$): *Imports*, $1,400,000,000; *exports*, $980,000,000.

Bank, in its first lending to Paraguay since 1984, extended $29 million to strengthen the agricultural sector. Paraguay failed, for the third time, to reach an agreement with the International Monetary Fund (IMF) on rescheduling its foreign debt. Paraguayans rejected conditions that included increasing the fiscal surplus and curbing inflation—projected to reach 15% in 1992.

In February, Paraguay resumed interest payments on debts due in 1992, but not on some $500 million of arrears accumulated since payments were suspended four years earlier. About $300 million was owed to members of the Paris Club. Assets of $24 million, belonging to the Central Bank of Paraguay on deposit in New York, had been frozen temporarily in December 1991 under a court order obtained by five European financial entities.

Foreign Relations. President Patricio Aylwin of Chile paid a three-day official visit to Paraguay and signed bilateral-cooperation agreements. Rodríguez attended presidential-level meetings of the Mercosur common market's council in December 1991 and June. The market is to be functional by the end of 1994.

LARRY L. PIPPIN
University of the Pacific

PENNSYLVANIA

The fall election dominated the news from Pennsylvania in 1992. Both President George Bush and Gov. Bill Clinton targeted Pennsylvania, making numerous visits to the state. Although pro-life Gov. Robert P. Casey, a Democrat, never endorsed Clinton because of the latter's pro-choice position, Clinton became the first Democrat to carry the state since Jimmy Carter in 1976. Clinton won easily with 45% of the vote over Bush's 36% and H. Ross Perot's 19%.

Politics. The sharply contested race for the U.S. Senate seat of Republican incumbent Arlen Specter received national attention. Lynn H. Yeakel was the surprise winner of the Democratic primary. With the strong support of women voters, Yeakel defeated Lt. Gov.

Mark S. Singel and Allegheny county District Attorney Robert Colville in the primary. A political newcomer who was director of a charity that provides help to battered women, Yeakel said she ran because of her anger at Senator Specter's questioning of Anita Hill during the Clarence Thomas confirmation hearings in 1991. Specter set up a fall contest against Yeakel by winning 65% of the vote in a bitter Republican primary against Stephen F. Friend, author of Pennsylvania's controversial anti-abortion statute. Although both Specter and Yeakel took a pro-choice stance, they argued heatedly about other issues, including character, the value of experience, economic growth, and, of course, Specter's role in the Thomas hearings. Specter won with just more than half of the vote. Each candidate ran unusually well among some groups in which their party's candidates generally fare poorly: Yeakel among Republican women and Specter with blacks.

Former TV reporter Marjorie Margolies Mezvinsky, a Democrat, became the first Pennsylvania woman to win a U.S. House seat without succeeding her husband. Her victory helped the Democrats maintain their 11 seats, the number they had before redistricting cost the state two seats. The Republican delegation dropped from 12 to ten.

Although 1992 campaigns had many words about change, few incumbents in state legislative races lost their seats. The Democrats retained control of the House. Only four of the 170 state House members who sought reelection lost. In the state Senate, the Democrats gained a one-vote majority, although not a single challenger defeated an incumbent. State Sen. James G. Greenwood resigned after winning a U.S. House seat and Republican Sen. Frank A. Pecora shifted parties after redistricting.

Economy. Unemployment in Pennsylvania stood at 7.4% in late fall, a figure above the national average. Continued weakness in manufacturing, particularly in western industrial

© Robert Trippett/Sipa

In Pennsylvania's closely watched U.S. Senate race, incumbent Arlen Specter (R) edged Lynn Hardy Yeakel, executive director of the charity Women's Way, to win a third term.

communities, accounted for much of the rise in unemployment. Better news in 1992 was the steady condition of Pennsylvania's Index of Leading Indicators. The lack of either rising or falling scores on this measure of future expectations suggested that the state was unlikely to fall into a deep recession, but that economic growth would be slow well into 1993.

Environment. The U.S. Environmental Protection Agency (EPA) became involved with air-pollution issues in Pennsylvania. In January, EPA completed a survey of more than 100,000 houses in the Philadelphia suburbs. The agency found that 25 homes had high indoor radon levels and relocated 13 families. The houses, built between 1910 and 1920, had plaster and concrete tainted with radium-contaminated sand. In March, EPA fined Bethlehem Steel Corporation some $6.7 million for air-pollution violations in Bethlehem and Johnstown. The company agreed to install $32 million in emission-control equipment.

Pittsburgh. On June 28 doctors at the University of Pittsburgh transplanted a baboon's liver to a 35-year-old man whose life was threatened by hepatitis B. They chose the liver of a baboon, who had been raised for this purpose, because a human liver, unlike an animal liver, still would have been susceptible to hepatitis B. After 71 days the man died from a stroke, not rejection of the liver. Pittsburgh residents read little about this controversial procedure, however, because their two daily newspapers had been shut down since May 17, the result of a strike of delivery drivers. By year's end plans were advancing for new ownership of the papers and a settlement.

ROBERT E. O'CONNOR
Pennsylvania State University

PENNSYLVANIA • Information Highlights

Area: 45,308 sq mi (117 348 km²).

Population (July 1, 1991 est.): 11,961,643.

Chief Cities (1990 census): Harrisburg, the capital, 52,376; Philadelphia, 1,585,577; Pittsburgh, 369,379; Erie, 108,718; Allentown, 105,090.

Government (1992): *Chief Officers*—governor, Robert P. Casey (D); lt. gov., Mark A. Singel (D). *Legislature*—Senate, 50 members; House of Representatives, 203 members.

State Finances (fiscal year 1991): *Revenue,* $27,086,000,000; *expenditure,* $26,710,000,000.

Personal Income (1991): $230,917,000,000; per capita, $19,306.

Labor Force (June 1992): *Civilian labor force,* 5,968,400; *unemployed,* 454,200 (7.6% of total force).

Education: *Enrollment* (fall 1990)—public elementary schools, 1,172,164; public secondary, 495,670; colleges and universities, 604,060. *Public school expenditures* (1990), $9,934,398,000.

People, Places, and Things

The following four pages recount the stories behind a selection of people, places, and things that may not have made the headlines in 1992 but drew attention and created interest.

© Geoff Franklin/Sygma

© Gouverneur/Gamma-Liaison

Former track star Sebastian Coe, left, and actress Glenda Jackson, above, threw their hats into Britain's political ring in 1992. In April parliamentary elections, the 36-year-old former Olympian was elected as a Conservative from a district in southwest England. The 56-year-old actress, a member of the Labour Party, was chosen from a north London district. Meanwhile in Italy, Alessandra Mussolini, below, the 29-year-old granddaughter of the World War II dictator Benito Mussolini, won a parliamentary seat from Naples. She ran as a neo-Fascist Italian Social Movement candidate.

© Antonello Nusca/Gamma-Liaison

In 1992, Dagwood resigned from the J. C. Dithers Company. He returned, however, after Blondie fired him from her catering business for "eating up all her profits." Manon Rheaume, left, 20, was the first woman to play in the National Hockey League as she tended goal in a preseason game for the Tampa Bay Lightning. She later joined the team's top minor-league club. Bible Lands Museum, founded by Dr. Elie Borowsky, below with his wife, opened in Jerusalem in May. Its aim is to "illuminate the life and times of the Bible in its ancient environment."

© Markel/Gamma-Liaison

© Brooks Karft/Sygma

The National Air and Space Museum of the Smithsonian Institution presented " 'Star Trek': The Exhibition," above left, from Feb. 28 through Sept. 7, 1992. It featured more than 80 original props, costumes, and models from the successful television series of the 1960s. The director pointed out that the show had inspired many people to enter the field of space exploration. In 1946, Harold Russell, above right, was the first disabled actor to win an Oscar—for his supporting performance as a wounded veteran in William Wyler's "The Best Years of Our Lives." In 1992, Russell became the first Academy Award winner to sell his prize. The statue earned $55,000 at an auction. The biggest U.S. shopping establishment, the 78-acre (32-ha) Mall of America, below, located in Bloomington, MN, opened in August 1992. The grandiose "megamall" has more than 300 stores as well as the largest indoor amusement park—Knott's Berry Farm's 7-acre (2.8-ha) Camp Snoopy. The center's developer, Melvin Simon & Associates Inc., hoped that the Mall of America would become a tourist mecca.

© Greg Ryan-Sally Beyer

© Jon Levy/Gamma-Liaison

© Bob East/"The News Times," Danbury

Some officials felt that the best-selling Super Soaker water gun, above, should be banned because of its connection with urban violence. The Norwalk (CT) Museum under curator Ralph C. Bloom, right, honored the Raggedy Ann doll on its 75th birthday. With much media publicity, Woody Allen sued Mia Farrow for custody of their three children; allegations arose that Allen had sexually abused one of their children; and reports of a romance between Allen, 56, and a young adopted daughter of Farrow came to light.

© Angie Coqueran

PERU

During 1992 events in Peru were dominated by President Alberto Fujimori's coup on April 5 and the September 12 capture of Abimael Guzmán, the founder of Shining Path, a Maoist guerrilla group that had led a 12-year insurrection against the Peruvian government.

Coup. The "self coup" took place when Fujimori shut down the Congress, arrested several opposition leaders, imposed censorship, and announced that he would rule as a dictator backed by the military until a new constitution was approved in a plebiscite. Fujimori justified the action as an offensive against guerrillas and drug traffickers. He said that the coup would lead to authentic democracy in Peru, claiming the judiciary was tainted by corruption and the legislature was dominated by elitist, unrepresentative parties. Fujimori dismissed the attorney general, 13 of the 30 Supreme Court justices, and 135 more judges and prosecutors.

Despite a decree imposing jail terms on purged officials who challenged the coup, Vice-President Maximo San Román was sworn in as president before 200 of the 240 legislators. Although this act was supported by former President Alan García—who had fled to exile in Colombia—and most of the political establishment, polls taken after the coup showed that Fujimori's popularity had risen to more than 80% and the opposition soon had to treat Fujimori as the *de facto* president.

The international community at first condemned the coup, with Germany, Japan, and the United States freezing millions of dollars in aid. Argentina and Venezuela recalled their ambassadors. Peru retaliated against Venezuela by suspending its membership in the Andean Pact. At a May 17 meeting of the Organization of American States (OAS) in the Bahamas, however, Fujimori won grudging tolerance for his actions by promising that elections for a constituent assembly would be held within five months and that basic rights would be reinstituted within days. This 80-member Democratic Constituent Congress was a concession to the opposition, which had rejected the president's initial plan to have his rule ratified by a July plebiscite. The pro-Fujimori Nueva Mayoría and Cambio 90 parties won a slight majority of the seats in Congress in November 22 elections. The opposition parties—APRA and Accion Popular, whose legislators were banned as candidates—boycotted both the negotiations over the composition of the Congress and the elections themselves.

Terrorism. In some ways the government was losing its battle against terrorism in 1992. The Shining Path terrorist group continued its new strategy of infiltrating grass-roots self-help organizations in the shantytowns surrounding Lima and gaining control through intimidation and violence or by running candidates openly. The group's new presence in Lima was underscored in mid-July as a string of car-bomb explosions rocked the upper-class neighborhood of Miraflores.

On the positive side, however, at least 400 guerrillas surrendered in response to a government promise of reduced penalties or pardons for terrorists who turned themselves in, complemented by lengthened minimum prison terms of 25–30 years. Peru also set up anonymous tribunals to try cases involving terrorism in order to protect judges from intimidation. The government's greatest success, however, was the capture of Guzmán. In an ingenious raid on a Lima residence, police captured the elusive Shining Path founder and other leaders comprising 70% of the group's national leadership. Guzmán's logistical planner in Lima, Alberto Arana Franco, had been captured earlier.

Victor Polay Campos, leader of the MRTA terrorists, also was returned to prison two years after his escape. However, these successes did not put an end to terrorist attacks, and experts believed that Guzmán was replaced quickly by third-ranking leader Oscar Alberto Ramírez Durand. In fact, violence intensified as a new terrorist group, the Ayacucho AntiTerrorist Movement (MATA), issued death threats against 190 alleged Shining Path collaborators. Hundreds of *rondas campesinas,* or peasant militias, emerged to protect their villages and their coca fields in the Apurimac Valley.

The Economy. The liberalization program of Economy Minister Carlos Boloña—together with the cholera epidemic and power blackouts caused by terrorist bombings—depressed production—especially in agriculture, fishing, and manufacturing—and led to the closure of many small mining companies, 90% of Peru's textile exporters, and many insolvent banks. Eighty percent of Peruvians could find work only in

Peruvian troops were on guard in Lima in April 1992 as President Alberto Fujimori dissolved Congress, suspended civil liberties, and established government by decree.

© Patrick Chavel/Sygma

PERU · Information Highlights

Official Name: Republic of Peru.
Location: West coast of South America.
Area: 496,224 sq mi (1 285 220 km²).
Population (mid-1992 est.): 22,500,000.
Chief Cities (mid-1989 est.): Lima, the capital, 6,233,800; Arequipa, 612,100; Callao (mid-1985 est.), 515,200.
Government: *Head of state,* Alberto Fujimori, president (took office July 28, 1990). *Head of government,* Alfonso de los Heros, prime minister (took office November 1991). *Legislature*—Congress: Senate and Chamber of Deputies.
Monetary Unit: new sol (1.510 new sols equal U.S.$1, official rate, Nov. 2, 1992).
Gross Domestic Product (1990 est. U.S.$): $19,300,-000,000.
Economic Index (Lima, 1991): *Consumer Prices* (1990 = 100), all items, 509.2.
Foreign Trade (1991 U.S.$): *Imports,* $2,955,000,000; *exports,* $3,379,000,000.

the informal sector. The ambitious privatization program also got off to a disappointing start as the sale of 80% of the profitable Condestable copper mine brought in only 68% of the company's nominal value.

Nevertheless, Boloña's plan brought the 1992 inflation rate down to about 50% from more than 7,500% in 1990. The country's reserves rose to $2 billion, and a budget surplus estimated at $400 million made it possible for Fujimori to announce a series of economic-reactivation programs even while cutting the consumption tax from 15% to 10%. The reactivation programs included an emergency agriculture program for small farmers, wage increases for health and education workers, a program to build new housing and repair homes destroyed by terrorism, and funding for road building, sanitation, and electricity distribution.

MICHAEL COPPEDGE
Johns Hopkins University

PHILANTHROPY

Charities suffered a double blow in 1992, as the lingering recession and a scandal involving the United Way of America prompted many Americans to tighten their purse strings.

Recession. The recession worked against philanthropy in two ways. First, because many Americans were either out of work or fearful of losing their jobs, charities were unable to raise as much money as they could in more prosperous times. Second, the poor economic conditions that reduced charities' incomes also drove up demand for their services. Homeless shelters, soup kitchens, and social-service agencies across the United States found that they had more clients displaced by joblessness than they could serve.

United Way. Perhaps even more devastating to U.S. charities than the economic downturn was the scandal that erupted in early 1992 at

the United Way of America, the national umbrella group representing 2,200 United Way chapters around the country. The United Way agencies raise funds through local employers and channel funds to area charities. By allowing for direct payroll deductions, employers offer a convenient way for workers to donate funds to a broad range of worthy causes in their communities.

But this traditionally broad support for the United Way suffered a severe blow in January and February 1992 amid reports that William Aramony, president of the United Way of America since 1970, had enjoyed an extravagant life-style—including a $463,000 salary-and-benefits package—at the organization's expense. Aramony was forced to step down in February, but the revelations posed a serious threat to the entire organization's credibility. United Way officials tried to minimize damage from the adverse publicity and restore public confidence in its operations with a series of staff reductions, salary freezes, and voluntary resignations at national headquarters. Local chapters tried to distance themselves from the national organization, based in Alexandria, VA, by assuring donors that their money would be used for local services only and would not end up at national headquarters. In August, Elaine Chao, a former Peace Corps director and transportation official in the Bush administration, was named as the organization's new president and chief executive officer.

Because the United Way chapters act as fund-raisers for thousands of nonprofit organizations, many of which are too small to raise funds on their own, any drop in contributions would mean a loss of funds for the actual providers of social and health services. With less funding, they could help fewer people in need. And this unfortunate situation came at a time when financially strapped state and local governments were being forced to cut back on public services.

The scandal's impact on charities across the country was expected to be enormous. Although the final tally was not in by year's end, analysts expected a drop in charitable giving in 1993—the sharpest decline in 40 years.

Other. According to a Gallup poll, the typical U.S. household gave about $650 to charities, churches, and other nonprofit groups in 1991, down from about $800 the year before. And bigger paychecks did not appear to make most Americans more generous. Another Gallup poll revealed that the poorest households gave a bigger percentage of their incomes to charities than did wealthier households and that black families donated a bigger portion of their incomes than did white families. Similar patterns were found in volunteering for charitable organizations.

MARY H. COOPER
"CQ [Congressional Quarterly] Researcher"

After the Philippine Senate in 1991 rejected a treaty permitting a continued U.S. military presence in the Philippines, U.S. military personnel were withdrawn from the Subic Bay Naval Base, some 50 mi (80 km) northwest of Manila, in 1992.

PHILIPPINES

In several ways, 1992 was a critical year of transition for the Philippines. The election of a new president, the completed phaseout of the U.S. air-force and naval presence, and the relative increase in the importance of other Asian powers in the Philippines' economy—all seemed to indicate the beginning of a new era in the country's political and economic development.

The Economy. The Philippines remained desperately poor, with approximately 60% of the population living below the poverty line. Contributing to the poverty was the fact that more than 20% of all revenues was needed to service the country's massive external debt, which skyrocketed during the free-spending days of the Ferdinand Marcos presidency (1965-86). The World Bank took steps to restructure $5 billion of the debt in March to ease the credit crunch, but the problem remained serious.

The official unemployment figure for the year was approximately 7.6%, but underemployment in the countryside, which provided 44% of the nation's jobs, was as high as 38%, and underemployment topped 21.3% in the urban areas. This situation was not helped by massive dislocations of the population resulting from eruptions of the Mount Pinatubo volcano and subsequent mudslides in 1991. Southern Luzon also was affected by the closure of Clark Air Force Base (1991) and Subic Bay Naval Base (1992)—two huge U.S. installations that once employed more than 60,000 people.

Negligence and poor planning added to the economic woes during 1992, as the nation found itself critically short of power. Rain that provides water to power generators was in short supply. The power crisis first emerged in Mindanao in the southern Philippines in January. By April extensive brownouts and blackouts for up to 12 hours per day were paralyzing production and services throughout Luzon, especially in Manila. Layoffs, shop closures, unfilled production orders, and a crisis of confidence on the part of foreign investors were the result. Only the beginning of the monsoon in July eased the crisis. A failure to plan for spiraling power needs, aggravated by major technical flaws in a new nuclear plant in Bataan, left the country unprepared.

Under the administration of President Corazon Aquino (1986–92), some progress was made on another economic issue—tax collection. The Philippines has relatively fair and progressive tax laws, but the tax base is very small—fewer than 4 million of the 62 million in the nation. Those that actually pay taxes are only about 1.4 million. Tax evasion is a way of life for the majority of people and businesses who should be contributing. The Aquino government managed to make some improvements in this area, but the Philippines still lagged well behind other nations in the region in collection of taxes. Moreover, unless salaries are raised significantly for the bureaucracy, it is unrealistic to expect more successful enforcement of the laws.

Environmental concerns also threatened the long-term viability of several industries. "Red tide" created by dangerous microorganisms ruined the fishing in several parts of the country, killed some people, and destroyed the livelihood of many thousands. Studies also found 70% of the Philippine reefs in threatened or critical condition. Some reefs were damaged from methods for harvesting fish or dynamiting coral to improve beaches for tourists.

Particularly frightening was the discovery that nearly 10% of the vegetable producers in Benguet were using cyanide in the raising of their produce. Since Benguet produces nearly 76% of the nation's vegetables, there was growing concern that this deadly agricultural shortcut soon might result in thousands of victims. No deaths had been reported by year's end, however.

The first major oil find in nearly 15 years was made off Palawan in the southern Philippines. It was expected to result in more than $100 million annually in badly needed oil. The discovery occurred just at the time when the country's existing petroleum reserves were about to be exhausted.

Plans were going forward for the reconversion of Subic Bay Naval Base into an economic free port. The process, which began in March, was expected to be completed in phases over two to three years. Money for the reconversion was supposed to come from the sale of military-held land in Manila, a process that likely would not be implemented easily. The Subic Bay leasing process, the building of a number of new hotels, and other infrastructure projects were expected to signal a new boom in foreign investment. Currently, Japan has only 5% of the investment in the Philippines that it has in Indonesia, but hopes were high that major foreign investment would surge. Since the early 1980s political instability, power shortages, lawlessness, labor militancy, and an overvalued peso have kept investment flowing in fits and starts.

The Presidential Election. The first half of the year was dominated by the prospects of the first presidential election since the fall of Ferdinand Marcos in 1986. The May 11 election was unusual in several respects. It was the first held under the new 1987 constitution, which limits the president to a single six-year term. It also was unusual in that the presidential race was running at the same time as the ones for all

---

PHILIPPINES • Information Highlights

Official Name: Republic of the Philippines.
Location: Southeast Asia.
Area: 115,830 sq mi (300 000 km²).
Population: (mid-1992 est.): 53,700,000.
Chief Cities (1990 census): Manila, the capital, 1,598,918; Quezon, 1,666,766; Davao, 849,947; Caloocan, 761,011.
Government: *Head of state and government,* Fidel V. Ramos, president (sworn in June 30, 1992). *Legislature* (bicameral)—Senate and House of Representatives.
Monetary Unit: Peso (25.50 pesos equal U.S. $1, floating rate, Nov. 23, 1992).
Gross National Product (1990 est. U.S.$): $45,200,-000,000.
Economic Index (1991): *Consumer Prices* (1980 = 100), all items, 423.4; food, 405.9.
Foreign Trade (1990 U.S.$): *Imports,* $13,042,000,000; *exports,* $8,186,000,000.

---

the members of Congress and all provincial and local offices. More than 17,000 elected posts were being contested. This convergence of national and local races had the effect of greatly weakening the impact of the traditional power brokers—large clans with vertical networks of followers—who historically have shifted supporters between two conventional nonideological parties. In 1992 such alliances were more apt to concentrate on the local and provincial races, leaving the presidential aspirants to put their own coalitions together.

By March the number of candidates had been reduced to seven. They included Miriam Defensor Santiago, former chief of customs and unconfirmed secretary of agrarian reform. She was known as a feisty, no-nonsense individual, devoid of traditional party links, but with a strong following among the poor and those disillusioned with politics as usual. She ran much stronger than anyone could have predicted. Ramon Mitra, former speaker of the house, was expected to run very strongly, but he made a lackluster showing when the votes of May 11th finally were tallied in mid-June. Eduardo Cojuanco, distant and feuding relative of President Aquino and former crony of Ferdinand Marcos, was considered a major threat, given his economic assets and network of influence around the country. He lost, but his running mate, movie actor Joseph Estrada, won the vice presidency. Imelda Marcos, in a dazzling display of chutzpah, ran for president of the country that she and her husband reportedly had looted so thoroughly. She was reputed to have made the bid to keep those attempting to prosecute her from doing so. She retained some support in her home base of Leyte and in her husband's home province of Illocos Norte —two regions that did quite well during the Marcos years. Had she and Eduardo Cojuanco teamed up in a bid to consolidate former Marcos support, they well could have been formidable. Salvador Laurel, incumbent vice-president and perpetual thorn in the side of President Aquino for more than five years, made a poor showing despite his virtual non-stop campaign for the presidency for much of the previous six years. Jovito Salonga, considered one of the most honest and courageous of the traditional leaders to compete for power, did not do well except in the areas of the country which are the poorest and where insurgents are the strongest. His age and failing health well may explain his failure to do better.

Gen. Fidel Ramos was considered to be a long shot because he had lost his party's endorsement to Ramon Mitra; his major base of support was the backing he got from President Aquino, whose own fortunes had been tarnished badly by her perceived weak control over the nation's economy. As Aquino's secretary of defense, Ramos repeatedly had rallied troops to defeat attempts to overthrow her. Her endorsement was seen in Philippine terms as *utang na loob*, a debt she was repaying gratefully. He was not a charismatic figure; he is a Protestant in a country that is 85% Catholic. He, in fact, had been a loyal supporter of President Marcos until his timely defection shortly after the corrupt 1986 election that led to Marcos' downfall. (*See also* BIOGRAPHY.)

Philippine elections have not been known for their penetrating discussion of the issues. This one was no exception, but it was noteworthy for what was missing almost totally from the campaign rhetoric—discussions of land reform, Muslim autonomy, or the U.S. role in the Philippine economy. This suggested that the chronic insurgencies that have plagued the Philippines for decades may be ebbing and with them the perceived urgency of reform. Meanwhile, the decision of the United States to withdraw its forces quietly after the Philippine Senate refused to renew the bases agreement left nationalists without their most enduring issue.

The election was a major landmark in Philippine history because it broke from the unhealthy tradition of being dominated by "guns, goons, and gold." A ban on guns that went into force in January helped control the violence that so often accompanied past elections. Aquino's national budget was austere and apparently little of it became diverted into the type of pork barrel projects that so often caused widespread inflation during past campaigns. Aquino, herself the target of more than seven coup attempts during her time in office, also was determined to make this the first peaceful transfer of power in the history of the independent Philippines. That she did so despite a seven-way race for the presidency and despite the fact that her successor, Fidel Ramos, received less than one quarter of the votes, was a testament to the positive transitional role she played.

The Ramos Presidency. Fidel Ramos, who took the oath of office in June, announced that his priorities would be reform, change, and growth. He immediately got off to a rocky start with the powerful Catholic Church by appointing a population-control activist to a key post in his cabinet. His proposals to grant amnesty to Communist and Muslim rebels and legalize the Communist Party, however, were seen as positive moves toward reconciliation with old foes. He was not expected to advance the cause of agrarian reform, despite provisions guaranteeing such reforms in the new constitution. He seemed more concerned with a restructuring of the bureaucracy that would include a significant increase in the powers of the provincial administrations. This commitment was a marked departure from the strong centralized control that had characterized Philippine politics and government in the past. Encouraging more foreign investment, particularly in tourism, was another thrust of his growth strategy. By late 1992 he had disappointed many in his inability to forge an effective and united cabinet and in his highly profiled but ineffective war on crime.

International Affairs. Philippine-U.S. relations entered a new phase with the closure of the bases. Both sides were hoping for continued strong relations as shared interests remained substantial. Nearly 3 million Filipinos live in the United States, and more than 200,000 Americans live in the Philippines. Financial linkages are also important. Clearly, however, the Philippines was concerned that U.S. aid to the nation would be reduced sharply without the threat of Soviet expansion in Asia, and in the absence of the Clark and Subic Bay installations. U.S. aid was down already in 1992, and further cuts were expected in the future. The United States was talking about a friendship treaty, however, and the Philippines was seeking an extradition treaty with the Americans.

Kidnappings. Major Asian investors were poised to become involved in the Philippine economy once they could be assured of security and infrastructural improvements. But a rash of kidnappings involving wealthy Chinese families did nothing to reassure investors that the timing was as yet auspicious. Between January and October, more than 50 kidnap-for-ransom incidents were reported by the Philippines' Chinese community. In one case, two abducted college students were slain by the kidnappers even after the ransom had been paid. Fidel Ramos' Presidential Anti-Crime Commission (PACC), created in July to try to deal with the problem and headed by Vice-President Estrada, was unable to halt the crimes terrorizing the ethnic Chinese population. Particularly disturbing were the widespread rumors of links between the kidnap gangs and members of the Philippine army and police.

LINDA K. RICHTER
Kansas State University

PHOTOGRAPHY

By late 1992, the simple word photography was no longer sufficient to describe the medium. Imaging—as used in *Popular Photography*'s new cover line, ''world's largest imaging magazine''—more aptly described the ongoing expansion in electronic technology, still and motion video equipment, and photography's interface with computers.

Notable was the August 1992 introduction of Kodak's Photo CD system which, at a minimum, will allow family photo albums to be stored on a compact disc and shown on a television screen and, in a much more sophisticated sense, will allow those with powerful computers to manipulate images.

The traditional photograph, however, was far from gone. Despite an ongoing recession that caused a decline in sales of single-lens reflex (SLR) cameras, film and photofinishing sales continued strong with 17 billion pictures expected to be snapped before year's end, mostly with 35mm auto-everything cameras. In the art market, the medium was still a relatively bright spot. Auction returns at Sotheby's in New York went down, but not drastically. The top price, $88,000, was paid for Tina Modatti's ''Telephone Wires.''

© Collection of the Smithsonian Institution, National Anthropological Archives
The photographs of Alexander Gardner (1821–82), including the 1872 portrait of Medicine Bear, above, were shown at New York City's International Center of Photography.

Hardware and Software. Point-and-shoot 35mm fully automatic cameras were the largest segment of the market, continuing to replace the SLR as the photographer's primary camera. Trends included further miniaturization, with almost all companies producing a true shirt-pocket-size model; dual-lens cameras and those with true zooms; high-end cameras costing $200 to $300 for pros and advanced amateurs; very feature-laden models with longer and wider zooms; waterproof and sandproof cameras; and dual-format cameras, which could be changed from regular to panoramic effect in midroll.

Single-use, 24-exposure, disposable cameras from Fuji, Kodak, and Konica were increasingly popular, with expected sales at least as great as the 15 million sold in 1991. Capturing an estimated 2% of the film market and costing only $10 to $20, the disposable cameras came in a myriad of variations from fish-eye to telephoto. There were panoramics for indoor use and cameras in plastic housing to use while snorkeling, some with ISO 1600 film, and even some for microphotography.

Among SLRs, models were becoming quieter and far more electronic. Nikon's N90 was the first to connect directly to a personal computer, Sharp's Wizard, and the first to examine and determine flash and regular exposure in three dimensions with auto fill-in. And Canon introduced the EOS A2E, which autofocuses wherever one looks in the viewfinder.

In the video arena the big news was an image-stabilization system, developed jointly by Sony and Canon, which optically compensates for vibration. This makes it possible to shoot jiggleless movies at any focal length without a tripod. Sony's TR101 Hi 8, for instance, can be handheld with its 10:1 lens zoomed to 62mm.

Kodak, which was basing the future of its snapshot business on electronics, finally made available its Photo CD system, which allows conventional photos to be recorded on optical compact discs in digital form. A flat golden disc just less than 5 inches (13 cm) in diameter can hold the equivalent of more than 100 35mm images. These then can be displayed on television using a special CD player or used to produce photographic-quality prints at a photo finisher. The system is an attempt to combine the high clarity of conventional silver-halide film with the ease of editing and transmission of electronic images. The professional versions also can record text, sound, and other format films.

In the silver-halide-film arena, viable ISO 400 slide films were introduced by Kodak and 3M, and electromagnetic information was added to color print film, allowing higher quality prints without a skilled operator.

A five-year legal battle over patented autofocus technology ended when Honeywell reached settlements of $124.1 million with six camera makers—including Canon, Kodak, and Nikon—shortly after Minolta agreed to pay $127.5 million.

"Projet Patrimoine 2001"

On March 4, 1992, the United Nations Educational, Scientific and Cultural Organization (UNESCO) inaugurated "Projet Patrimoine 2001," a five-year plan to photograph the world's cultural and natural wonders before they are harmed further by war or environmental causes. Many of the sites have been photographed numerous times by tourists but not by photographic experts. The project is to be conducted by UNESCO, supported financially by the Caixa Foundation of Barcelona, Spain, and implemented by the Gamma photo agency in Paris, France. In addition, the Kodak Company is to supply its digital expertise and the French national communications corporation would transmit the project's images. The initial goal was to photograph 200 sites between 1992 and 1996.

This photo of a monk at the Temple of Bayon in the ancient Cambodian city of Angkor Thom was taken for "Projet Patrimoine 2001," a five-year plan to photograph the world's cultural and natural treasures.

© Patrimoine 2001/Photo, Julio Donoso

Exhibitions and Publications. In New York City the Metropolitan Museum announced the formation of a separate photography department, headed by Dr. Maria Morris Hambourg, and the Whitney Museum of Art said it would begin acquiring photos for its permanent collection. In Daytona Beach, FL, the Southeast Museum of Photography opened its doors.

Extensively traveling shows originated from New York City and Washington, DC, respectively. At the American Museum of Natural History the Sierra Club celebrated its 100th anniversary by remounting the influential (1955) multiphotographer show "This is the American Earth," featuring the work of Ansel Adams. The 1960 book by the same title also was reissued. At the Corcoran Gallery of Art, "Songs of My People," a diversified look at African Americans through the eyes of 50 prominent black photojournalists, started its lengthy tour, with a book and video special.

Another significant new book was *Ernst Haas, in Black and White*. This is a view of Haas' largely unknown black-and-white images done before and while he produced the pioneering color work for which he is renowned.

BARBARA LOBRON
Writer, Editor, Photographer

PHYSICS

In 1992 the future of the Superconducting Super Collider (SSC) was questioned; important results were obtained on the solar-neutrino puzzle, and progress was made in fusion power.

Superconducting Super Collider. As proposed, the Superconducting Super Collider (SSC)—with a tunnel some 50 mi (80 km) long with two 20 TeV (1 TeV = 10^{12} electron volts) colliding proton beams—would be the world's largest scientific instrument. In 1992 the question arose whether the SSC would be completed. The original estimated cost of the SSC, which was to be built in Waxahatchie, TX, was $4.5 billion but 1992 estimates by the U.S. Department of Energy (DOE) put the cost at $8 billion, while other government estimates exceeded $10 billion. Efforts to obtain major international scientific and financial partners for the project had failed, and opposition to the SSC was significant. Nevertheless, contracts had been awarded by the SSC laboratory in more than 40 states and grants and contracts were given by the DOE to some 100 universities and institutes.

Lightning struck the SSC in June 1992 when the U.S. House of Representatives voted to stop funding the project, leaving only a small amount of funds to shut it down. Many scientific groups and science-oriented legislators had felt that the project absorbed too large a fraction of the U.S. research budget. Many legislators simply said that such megaprojects could not be afforded in difficult financial times. The issue did not end with the House vote, however, as an August vote in the Senate—calling for the spending of $550 million on the project during fiscal year 1993—strongly supported the SSC. Joint Senate-House action in September resolved the difference, allocating $517 million for the super collider.

Solar Neutrinos. Several experiments were under way in 1992 to resolve the discrepancy between the number of neutrinos expected to be emitted by the Sun and the number actually observed. Remarkably, 25 years after the first observation of this difference—the solar-neutrino puzzle—the issue remained in doubt.

Until the early 1990s, the only data came from neutrino detectors at the Homestake Gold Mine near Lead, SD, and from the Japanese detector Kamiokande II. Giant liquid detectors are used to detect the neutral neutrinos which interact only very weakly with matter, with chemical separation of the very few radioactive nuclei which are the end products of the neutrino interaction. The Homestake results were less than predicted—the original solar neutrino puzzle—as were the Kamiokande results. Two new systems, the Soviet-American Gallium Experiment (SAGE) in the former Soviet Caucasus and the Gallex experiment at Gran Sasso, Italy, were designed to be sensitive to low-energy neutrinos which were not detected in the earlier experiments. The SAGE and Gallex groups reported preliminary results in 1992. Very few solar neutrinos were observed in the first SAGE results; some have suggested that even these very few events were false and that the data were consistent with zero. One possible solution is that the predicted number of neutrinos are created in the Sun but that these ordinary neutrinos are transformed into another type of neutrino during passage to Earth.

Gallex presented its first results, indicating that neutrinos were observed at a far higher rate than previously but at a lower rate than predicted by theory. More extensive data and careful analysis may resolve the issue, either to confirm the standard model or to agree with the early experiments, which seem to require new physics. However, the issue may not be resolved until the next-generation neutrino detector—the Sudbury Neutrino Observatory (SNO), near Sudbury, Ont.—is available in 1995. The SNO should be able to detect 20 times as many neutrinos as any present system.

Fusion Power. Of the thermonuclear-fusion processes which fuel the stars, the favored nuclear reaction for application on Earth is the fusion of the nuclei of deuterium and tritium (the isotopes of hydrogen with masses two and three). For fusion to occur, the nuclei must have temperatures of millions of degrees. Since no material can withstand such temperatures, the particles must be contained indirectly by magnetic fields. The combination of choice for the magnetic fields is called tokamak. The quality factor for such a system is the product of the temperature, density, and confinement time. The goal is to maximize this factor so that much more energy is released than inputted.

During 1992 at the Joint European Torus (JET) in Abingdon, England, scientists produced more than 1 million watts for two seconds, more than 100 times the largest energy amount obtained in previous experiments. The promising result has helped to spur enthusiasm for the planned International Thermonuclear Experimental Reactor (ITER), with more than 1,000 times the power of current fusion reactors. ITER would be the first controlled fusion reactor to achieve energy break-even. The project was expected to take a decade and cost an estimated $7.5 billion. ITER involves members of the European Community (EC), Japan, the Commonwealth of Independent States (the former USSR), and the United States.

Although progress in fusion has been striking in the last decade, U.S. government support for fusion has been erratic. For economic reasons, the DOE canceled the next planned tokamak in the fusion program, the $1.8 billion Burning Plasma Experiment.

Gary Mitchell
North Carolina State University

POLAND

The year was characterized by economic difficulties, even as Poland continued to move in the direction of a market economy. Politically, 1992 was marked by squabbles and government instability.

Economy. High unemployment and inflation combined to take their toll in 1992 even as signs of improvement were becoming evident. Official statistics released in April indicated a degree of economic recovery. Industrial production rose by about 17% in the first quarter of the year. Unemployment was still at 2.2 million but slightly less than in February—the first such decline since the beginning of economic reforms in 1990. The rate of inflation at the end of the quarter was estimated at 38%. This was about half of the rate for the equivalent period of 1991. The number of private firms had increased by 39% over the comparable period in 1991. The National Bank of Poland was keeping its prime interest rate at 40% in 1992.

According to the official data, at the beginning of 1992 the private sector in Poland—including agriculture—employed 25% of the work force. The public sector still accounted for 62% and cooperatives for approximately 13%. Most of the public-sector firms were doing very poorly, losing money and frequently failing to deliver tax revenues to the government. Polish exports had grown by 18% in 1991 but imports rose by 72%.

There were numerous instances of strikes and threatened strikes throughout Poland in response to difficult economic conditions during the year. On February 19 there was a nationwide "warning strike" by railroad workers protesting cuts in public-sector wages. As an austerity measure, the government had announced the intention of cutting wages by 5% in 1992.

Some 70,000 members of the Solidarity trade-union organization marched on Warsaw on April 24, threatening a general strike unless the government acted to help public-sector employees. They also called for an end to partisan bickering in the Sejm. The most serious strikes occurred in December in the coal fields. Toward the end of the month a three-week stoppage by several hundred thousand mine workers was ended formally.

In early February the Polish ministry of finance, confronted with widespread tax evasion, announced a controversial scheme that would reward tax informers, i.e., those turning in their neighbors or acquaintances. Chocolates and flowers were to be offered to "snitchers" for turning in private individuals who failed to pay their taxes and cash rewards were to be offered for those turning in delinquent business firms.

In early March the government considered easing its austerity policies by relaxing interest rates and reintroducing public-sector subsidies. On March 5 the Sejm rejected this plan by a vote of 171 to 138 with 38 abstentions. The Democratic Union, the Liberal Democrats, and the PPP (Polish Beer Lovers' Party), among others, opposed the plan. The Christian National Union, the Confederation of Independent Poland, and other smaller groups supported it. The former Communists—Alliance of the Democratic Left—thought the plan did not change the course of economic policy sufficiently. Parliamentary debates on amending the original Olszewski proposals were heated but ultimately unproductive. Nevertheless, the cabinet was willing to continue in existence with the old policies in effect.

The largest foreign-investment agreement in post-Communist Poland was concluded on May 20 between the government and the Italian car manufacturer, Fiat, which pledged to invest about $2 billion in the modernization of the Polish automobile-manufacturing facilities in Tychy. The Polish government was to retain 10% of the profits from this new venture.

On June 5 the Sejm approved a new state budget which had been drafted after consultation with the International Monetary Fund (IMF). The latter had suspended aid to Poland in 1991 because of the lack of financial discipline shown by previous Polish governments and excessive deficit spending. Through higher taxes and some spending cuts, the Sejm now brought the new budget somewhat closer to a balance between revenues and expenditures.

Government and Politics. On April 6, Defense Minister Jan Parys caused a sensation by charging that a military coup was being planned by certain unidentified generals in a series of secret meetings with top aides to President Walesa. The president called on Premier Olszewski to fire Parys. Parys was put on leave by the premier and resigned on May 18.

Warsaw's *Gazeta Wyborcza* published a front-page attack on Walesa in late April charging him with incompetence, shielding former

---

POLAND • Information Highlights

Official Name: Republic of Poland.
Location: Eastern Europe.
Area: 120,726 sq mi (312 680 km²).
Population (mid-1992 est.): 38,400,000.
Chief Cities (Dec. 31, 1990 est.): Warsaw, the capital, 1,655,700; Lodz, 848,200; Krakow, 750,500.
Government: *Head of state,* Lech Walesa, president (inaugurated Dec. 22, 1990). *Head of government,* Hanna Suchocka, premier (confirmed July 10, 1992). *Legislature* (bicameral)—Sejm and Senate.
Monetary Unit: Zloty (14,706 zlotys equal U.S.$1, Dec. 16, 1992).
Gross National Product (1990 est. U.S.$): $158,500,-000,000.
Economic Indexes (1991): *Consumer Prices* (1980 = 100), all items, 38,082.3; food, 37,727.0. *Industrial Production* (1980 = 100), 70.
Foreign Trade (1991 U.S.$): *Imports,* $14,261,-000,000; *exports,* $14,460,000,000.

© Wojick/Gamma-Liaison

On July 10, 1992, Hanna Suchocka became the premier of Poland—the first woman to hold that post in the country's history. Suchocka, 46, holds a doctorate in law from Poland's University of Poznan, and has studied in Germany, France, and the United States. Shortly after she assumed power, the Sejm, the lower house of Poland's parliament, gave Suchocka something of an inaugural gift: the power to carry out economic reforms by decree. By bypassing the Sejm, Suchocka would be able to avoid the political infighting that typically has stalled economic legislation.

Sejm's failure to support the cabinet's financial policies. The specific issue concerned a court decision which forbade the government from cutting salaries, pensions, and benefits of workers employed in the state sector. The court action put the Polish budget beyond the limits demanded by the IMF and thus jeopardized further international financial aid. Olechowski's predecessor, Karol Lutkowski, had resigned on February 17 in protest of the government's own failure to support tough economic reforms.

On June 5 the Sejm ousted Premier Jan Olszewski's cabinet on a no-confidence vote with 273 deputies voting against Olszewski, 119 for, and 33 abstaining. On the next day, the Sejm voted to approve Walesa's nominee, Waldemar Pawlak, as premier with a majority of 261 to 149, with seven abstentions. The 33-year-old Pawlak, a Peasant Party leader, became the fourth premier of Poland since the fall of communism. Unlike his predecessors, he had not been affiliated with the Solidarity movement. The main cause of the fall of the Olszewski cabinet was the scandal of the so-called "informers" list distributed on June 4 by the government to various parliamentary leaders. The list allegedly contained 60 names of former secret-police collaborators, now in high political offices. According to some accounts, Lech Walesa's own name was among these. In any event, Walesa called for Olszewski's dismissal in the wake of the controversial distribution, and the Sejm vote followed within 24 hours.

Acting Interior Minister Andrzej Milczanowski in a statement on June 12 indicated that an unnamed official in Prime Minister Jan Olszewski's cabinet unsuccessfully tried to get a military alert put on throughout Poland as a way of preventing the cabinet's dismissal by the Sejm.

Despite a month of frantic effort, Pawlak proved unable to put together a coalition cabinet from the several parties required to give the new government majority support in the 460-member Sejm. Finally, on July 10, agreement was reached to try a new government under a new premier: 46-year-old Hanna Suchocka, a constitutional lawyer and member of the Democratic Union Party. She was the fifth premier in Poland since 1989 and the first woman to hold that office. The vote for Suchocka was 233 to 61, with 113 abstentions. Her 22-member cabinet was supported by seven political parties from the right to moderate left. Suchocka pledged herself to a continuation of economic reforms, with more austerity and privatization. She also identified Poland's integration in the European Community (EC) as a key foreign-policy task.

In early September, former Communist Prime Minister Piotr Jaroszewicz, 82, and his wife were found murdered in their suburban Warsaw home. Jaroszewicz had served as pre-

Communists, and with appointment of largely ineffectual executive assistants. In a televised speech on April 26, President Walesa called for constitutional changes which would give him new powers, similar to those exercised by the president of France. He repeated these demands publicly in May and in June. Walesa argued that Poland could not be ruled effectively by fragmented and bickering party coalitions as apparently had been the case thus far. In a speech to the Sejm on May 9, Walesa claimed that the Polish public was sick of the "condition of permanent crisis" which in recent months had characterized parliamentary governments, unable to pursue decisive policies amid the discord of 29 political groupings represented in the Sejm. Walesa asked for the power to appoint, not merely nominate, the premier and the cabinet.

Polish Minister of Finance Andrzej Olechowski resigned on May 6 in protest of the

mier from 1970 to 1980 and was expelled from the Communist Party in 1981. There were no apparent suspects in the case.

Church-State Relations. The leadership of the Roman Catholic Church continued to exert its efforts in shaping social and political relations in Poland. A notable achievement with 1992 effects had been the adoption of an antiabortion stance by the Congress of Physicians in December 1991. Poland's main organization of medical practitioners, the Congress adopted a code of ethics which called for revocation of medical licenses for those performing state-financed abortions. According to press reports, the decision was having a significant impact on halting abortion procedures throughout the country in 1992.

There was continuing discussion in Poland and abroad of the role of the Church in support of the Solidarity movement during the 1980s, and of the role of the Vatican in support of anticommunist causes in pre-1989 Poland. Allegations of close Church cooperation with the Reagan administration in the United States during those years were being denied by the Vatican and the Polish episcopate.

By the end of the year, parliament shelved a very stringent antiabortion law supported by the Church and its political allies. It did pass a measure calling for the maintenance of "Christian values" in radio and television programming.

Foreign Relations. The year was marked by wide-ranging diplomatic activity. In mid-January, Poland extended official diplomatic recognition to Croatia and Slovenia. This action was taken in concert with Germany and several other European states. South Africa's President F. W. de Klerk visited Poland in early February, presumably to explore renewed economic-cooperation possibilities with Warsaw. Also in February, President Walesa in a speech to the Council of Europe in Strasbourg, France, criticized Western nations for failing to make long-term investments in Poland and instead exploiting the Polish economy for quick profits. He warned of a rich-versus-poor conflict in the emergent post-Communist Europe.

On February 19 the German government announced that it would forgive half of Poland's $5.5 billion debt to the Federal Republic. On March 25, Poland joined with 24 other states representing Europe, the former USSR, and North America in signing the so-called open-skies treaty in Helsinki, Finland. The treaty provided for mutual airborne inspections to monitor arms-control agreements. At the end of March, President Walesa visited Germany and met with President Richard von Weizsäcker. In mid-April, Premier Olszewski visited U.S. President George Bush at the White House and was given pledges of new initiatives to increase private U.S. investment in the Polish economy.

In late May, British Prime Minister John Major visited Warsaw on a trip to Eastern Europe. Major announced that Britain no longer would require visas of Poles traveling to Great Britain. But Polish attempts to get British support for the integration of Poland in the Western defense system proved unavailing. On May 22 in Moscow, President Walesa and Russian President Boris Yeltsin signed a treaty of friendship and cooperation. They agreed also to the withdrawal of the remaining 40,000 troops of the former Soviet Union still on Polish soil, most of them by Nov. 15, 1992. Some noncombat units would be allowed to remain in Poland to help with the logistics of the Red Army's withdrawal from the former East Germany.

On his return from Moscow, President Walesa stopped at the site of the Katyn forest massacre in Belarus, where the bodies of more than 4,000 Polish officers killed by the Soviets had been found in 1943. In early October the document condemning the Polish officers to death, signed by Joseph Stalin on March 5, 1940, was made public in Moscow, thus finally resolving a longtime mystery regarding the precise nature of Soviet responsibility for the massacre. Poland, along with 29 other states, participated in the signing of a revised version of the 1990 Conventional Forces Agreement in Oslo, Norway, on June 5. A planned reduction in the size and quality of former Soviet forces deployed in Europe was a feature of principal interest to Poland.

ALEXANDER J. GROTH
University of California, Davis

POLAR RESEARCH

Antarctic. During 1992 paleobotanists found a 260-million-year-old deciduous forest in the TransAntarctic Mountains, about 370 mi (595 km) from the South Pole. This discovery supported the view that, between 250 million and 280 million years ago, Antarctica enjoyed a climate much warmer than today's. The fossils were found at about 82° south—the furthest from the equator that a forest ever has been found.

At McMurdo and South Pole stations, U.S. and Italian researchers used balloon-borne and lidar (laser infrared radar) probes to examine ozone-destroying chemistry in the stratosphere. In October they noted a record-breaking low in ozone abundance above the continent, found a 2.5-mi (4-km)-thick region between 8.5 and 11 mi (13.7 and 17.7 km) altitude where all ozone was destroyed, and recorded significant losses at lower altitudes. The extent of the damage was greater than in previous years and may be related to the eruption during 1991 of Mount Pinatubo in the Philippines.

From February to June 1992, U.S. and Russian marine scientists worked on an ice floe in the western Weddell Sea. The scientists found multiple sources of Antarctic bottom water, with subtle differences in salinity and temperature, along the track of their drifting camp. Further north, these waters mix and become the characteristic Antarctic bottom water that spreads out globally.

U.S. astronomers pioneered a new use for the South Pole's ice sheet—as a neutrino detector. In early 1992 a University of California at Berkeley group tested a detector made of tubes frozen into the ice 2,600 ft (792.5 m) below the surface. Their success shows that the ice is free of radioactivity and close to optically perfect—making it a perfect medium for detecting the flashes caused by collisions in the ice as neutrinos pass through the Earth.

Biologists monitoring Weddell seal populations near McMurdo Station believed they could correlate changes in seal birthrates with the climate phenomenon El Niño, which alters weather in temperate and tropical regions. Until now there was no evidence that the phenomenon had effects so far south, but University of Alaska researchers noted a decline in the number of births among these seals every four to six years—a cycle that matches El Niño's. The lower birthrate probably is tied to changes in fish populations caused when El Niño makes ocean currents shift. British scientists working near the Antarctic Peninsula recorded a similar pattern.

In December 1992, Dante, an eight-legged, 8-ft (2.4-m)-tall robotic rover, attempted to descend into the crater of the active volcano Mount Erebus on Ross Island. One of 120 projects supported by the National Science Foundation (NSF) in Antarctica during the 1992-93 austral summer, Dante was to observe activity and sample lava in the volcano's inner crater, where temperatures can reach more than 1,000° F (542° C). Although cold weather and an unexpected minor eruption thwarted the spiderlike robot's first attempt, the scientists who designed Dante hoped the experiment would aid in the design of similar robots to be used for extraterrestrial research.

Arctic. In Greenland, U.S. and European earth scientists continued to drill through the ice sheet to collect ice cores for research. In July 1992 the European group reached its goal —the bottom of the ice sheet—and retrieved a 9,937-ft (3 029-m)-long ice core. A faulty cable impeded U.S. efforts, stopping operations in mid-July at 7,382 ft (2 250 m). Analysis of the U.S.-obtained ice core has revealed that between 20,000 and 40,000 years ago, the Earth's climate often shifted in as few as one or two years between glacial conditions to warm weather.

WINIFRED REUNING
National Science Foundation

PORTUGAL

Portugal's presidency of the European Community (EC), from January to June 1992, put the Social Democratic (PSD) regime of Prime Minister Anibal Cavaco Silva into the forefront of continental affairs. International affairs eclipsed much of Portugal's own policy agenda, but its handling of the EC presidency drew praise throughout Europe.

Politics. Fresh from victory in the October 1991 parliamentary contests, Cavaco Silva maintained his party's firm grasp on power, while internal strife racked the opposition. In February, 43-year-old engineer Antonio Guterres ousted Jorge Sampaio as general secretary of the Portuguese Socialist Party (PSP), the Social Democrats' main rival in the 230-member parliament. Guterres then launched an aggressive campaign to revitalize his party for the December 1993 local elections.

Portugal's Communist Party (PCP), which rapidly was losing its status as the largest Communist Party in Western Europe suffered internal discord of its own as PCP dissidents seceded from the party and formed the Platform of the Left, designed to fill the political void between the old-line PCP and centrist Socialists. Leaders of the small center-right Christian Democratic Party (CDS) raised a battle cry against EC bureaucrats in Brussels but were disappointed to find pro-European attitudes even within their own party's ranks.

In a protracted feud, Portugal's popular head of state, President Alberto Mário Soares, clashed with Prime Minister Cavaco Silva over the planned restructuring of the armed forces. Many suspected that the PSD provoked and prolonged the dispute to divert attention from the flagging national economy or to clear the way for an eventual Cavaco Silva presidential candidacy. On June 11, Soares announced that he would not seek reelection in 1996.

Economics. Cavaco Silva's economic policy continued to focus on financially aligning Portugal with its EC partners in preparation for potential European Monetary Union in 1997. Modernizing the agricultural system and privatizing state-owned industries were priorities. The government sold a 60% stake in the huge Banco Espirito Santo and a sizable share (eventually to comprise 51%) of Petrogal, the country's largest enterprise.

The 9% inflation rate, however, was almost twice the EC average. Silva did hold wage increases to 10%, down 4% from the previous year but government spending increased. Silva's April decision to align the escudo with the European Monetary System (EMS) drastically reduced Lisbon's control over monetary policy.

Entry into the EMS strengthened the national currency and boosted the influx of foreign investment. Gross domestic product

(GDP) expanded 2.3%, but was below the 2.5% and 4.1% levels of 1991 and 1990. Unemployment remained low at 5% but so did productivity and earnings.

Foreign Relations. Bloody civil war in Yugoslavia and potential chaos in the old Soviet Union, as well as the rejection of the Maastricht Treaty on the EC in Denmark, made for a tumultuous EC presidency for Portugal. The EC did sign a historic, 19-nation European Economic Area free-trade agreement during Lisbon's stewardship, but the presidency produced few other concrete results. Portugal neither convinced the body to approve the initiative to increase EC aid to the four poorest Community nations (including Portugal) nor did it succeed in raising the salience of Third World problems of concern to Lisbon.

The Cavaco government, nonetheless, proved to Europe and the world that a mature, democratic Portugal had committed itself to the new European order. Lisbon did not waiver in that commitment despite the currency upheaval that drove Great Britain and Italy from the EMS. Portugal's parliament was on course to ratify the Maastricht Treaty by Christmas.

GEORGE W. GRAYSON
College of William and Mary

POSTAL SERVICE

The challenges that the United States Postal Service (USPS) faced during the 1992 fiscal year (FY) ending September 30 promised to continue into 1993. Operating under three different postmasters general (PMG), the service further expanded its automation program while also undergoing a major reorganization and downsizing.

After four years in office, PMG Anthony Frank resigned effective March 9, 1992. During his tenure the USPS had moved from processing 28% of its letter mail by automated equipment in 1988 to 71% in 1992, accompanied by a work-force reduction of more than 20,000, to about 750,000. The comprehensive decentralization planned by his predecessors largely was completed, and during 1990–91, he had negotiated four-year labor contracts highly favorable to the USPS. While large deficits existed three out of Frank's four years, these mainly were caused by congressional assessments on the service—averaging nearly $1 billion yearly from 1988—to help ease the federal deficit. Also, Postal Rate Commission (PRC) decisions in 1991 resulted in less first-class and third-class revenues than planned.

Deputy PMG Michael Coughlin became acting PMG upon Frank's departure and continued the cost-cutting efforts. By the summer, volume began to improve, but when the FY 1992 accounts were closed in September, the USPS showed a deficit of $536 million. Further congressional assessments in the fall of 1992 plus increasing personnel-related costs led to an early projection for FY 1993 of a $2 billion deficit.

In May 1992 the USPS Board of Governors named Marvin T. Runyon the 70th PMG, effective July 6. A former executive with the Ford and Nissan auto companies, Runyon had gained a national reputation as chairman of the Tennessee Valley Authority (TVA). There he had stabilized rising rates by overseeing cuts of 40% in the work force and $400 million in expenses.

Within a month, "Carvin' Marvin," as he was nicknamed at the TVA, announced a 25% cut in postal managerial positions (30,000 to 40,000 jobs out of 130,000). Also, 42 assistant postmasters general were to be replaced by 22 vice-presidents. A further overhaul of the system's top-heavy hierarchy was in the works. Other cost-cutting moves, such as debt restructuring, as well as ways to increase income, were under review, according to Runyon. To minimize layoffs, redundant managers were offered retirement incentives, and by late fall it appeared that the downsizing largely would be accomplished by early winter, along with the consolidation of 73 divisions into ten regional units. Runyon hoped that these and other actions would permit the delay of any rate increase from 1993 to 1994.

Canada. After three years in the black, the Canada Post Corporation had a deficit of $121 million in FY 1992, ending March 30. Declining economic conditions plus a costly strike were held responsible. Revenues of $3.7 billion were based on a volume of about 10 billion pieces. The domestic first-class rate was 42 cents (Canadian) plus three cents of goods and services tax in 1992. Based on comparative exchange rates, the Canadian postal rate is the world's third-lowest, behind Australia and the United States, respectively.

PAUL P. VAN RIPER
Texas A&M University

PRINCE EDWARD ISLAND

A new but inconclusive chapter in the history of Canadian confederation was written in 1992 where it all began 128 years earlier—in Charlottetown.

Renewal Undone. Charlottetown, the cradle of confederation, in 1992 became the site of its renewal—temporarily. Applause greeted Canada's political leaders on August 28, when they emerged from two days of meetings in the Prince Edward Island (PEI) capital with a new constitutional deal. Premier Ghiz announced "the rebirth of our nation," in a glare of flashing cameras and television floodlights.

The locale was fitting since it was in Charlottetown in 1864 that the first intercolonial meetings leading to the 1867 creation of Canada had taken place. On October 26, however, despite the support of about 74% of PEI voters, Canadians overall rejected the Charlottetown Accord in a national referendum.

Four days after the referendum, Ghiz suddenly announced his resignation as premier, effective early in 1993. He insisted that the decision had nothing to do with the failure of the constitutional compact, having been made well before the vote.

Road to the Isle. The federal government announced on July 17 its intention to enter into negotiations with Strait Crossing Inc. of Calgary for construction of the long-debated "fixed link" across Northumberland Strait. Work was expected to begin on the bridge in 1993, providing that a deal could be struck and the PEI and New Brunswick governments gave their approval. The target year for completing the project, which could cost C$900 million, was 1997. Strait Crossing was one of three consortiums that sought the contract, and it offered the lowest bid for an annual operating subsidy: C$40.6 million. The company envisaged a span rising 131 ft (40 m) above the water, supported by 44 octagonal pillars.

© Gord Johnston

George Ramsay, the mayor of the Prince Edward Island town of Borden, is opposed to the federal government's plan to build a bridge linking P.E.I. and New Brunswick.

Under an industrial-benefits agreement signed in Charlottetown on December 17 by Premier Ghiz and Paul Giannelia, president of Strait Crossing, 70% of the materials and services for the bridge will be purchased in economically depressed Atlantic Canada.

Economic News. The Speech from the Throne opening the PEI legislature on March 23 had recession written into it. The speech called for a variety of measures to deal with the economic realities, and set the 1991–92 provincial deficit at a high C$51.8 million. Ghiz blamed falling transfer payments from Ottawa for economically squeezing the province. His government pledged to pursue industrial opportunities in aerospace and communications.

The stimulative April 7 budget froze personal-income taxes while reducing provincial corporate taxes. The budget forecast a 1992–93 operating deficit of C$26.8 million. Provincial government employment rolls and social-welfare programs were left untouched.

Base Closing. The Canadian Forces base at Summerside officially closed on April 1, three years after its demise was foretold in the 1989 federal budget. When the shutdown came, only 23 military personnel remained, where once there had been 1,500.

JOHN BEST
"Canada World News"

PRINCE EDWARD ISLAND
• Information Highlights

Area: 2,185 sq mi (5 660 km²).

Population (September 1992): 130,200.

Chief Cities (1986 census): Charlottetown, the capital, 15,776; Summerside, 8,020.

Government (1992): *Chief Officers*—lt. gov., Marion Reid; premier, Joe Ghiz (Liberal). *Legislature*—Legislative Assembly, 32 members.

Provincial Finances (1992–93 fiscal year budget): *Revenues,* $723,000,000; *expenditures,* $749,838,000.

Personal Income (average weekly earnings, July 1992): $446.91.

Labor Force (September 1992, seasonally adjusted): *Employed* workers, 15 years of age and over, 53,000; *Unemployed,* 17.9%.

Education (1992–93): *Enrollment*—elementary and secondary schools, 24,950 pupils; postsecondary—universities, 2,740; community colleges, 1,250.

(All monetary figures are in Canadian dollars.)

PRISONS

The number of U.S. citizens in prison, following a decades-long trend, continued to rise to record levels. The additional prison cells constructed since the early 1960s continued to be filled and overfilled. Federal and state prisons, numbering 1,037, held 698,570 inmates as 1992 began. Jails, designed to hold persons for more than 48 hours but less than one year, number more than 3,000 and contain a daily average of more than 425,000 inmates.

The Sentencing Project, a private research and advocacy group based in Washington, DC, which gathers international prison statistics, reported that the U.S. lead among all nations of the world in the number of citizens under arrest had increased. Imprisonment in South Africa, the country with the second-highest rate of incarceration, had declined by 6.6%. The rate of incarceration per 100,000 citizens rose to 455 in the United States, while it was 311 in South Africa. The U.S. rate was more than ten times higher than those of Japan, Sweden, Ireland, and the Netherlands. The U.S. prison population has tripled since 1970, doubled since 1980, and federal and state estimates called for an increase of 30% by 1995.

In response to those statistics, one critic of the criminal-justice system, Rep. John Conyers, Jr. (D-MI), chair of the House Committee on Government Operations, said: "We are not stopping crime. We are not curbing drugs. We are not helping victims, and we are not rehabilitating criminals. The only beneficiary of our distorted 'lock 'em up' criminal-justice policies is prison construction, not crime control or prevention." Professor Mark H. Moore of the John F. Kennedy School of Government at Harvard University was more guarded in his assessment of the meaning of these figures. He called attention to the disproportionate numbers of poor and black among those imprisoned, and the "large waste of lives and talent, and a failure of the society." But rather than blaming the criminal-justice system itself, he cautioned that the high rate of incarceration "may be a sign of the success of the criminal-justice system."

In fact, the increases in prison construction over the past decades have been more than matched by increases in the number of police officers making arrests and particularly those with full-time responsibilities for enforcement of drug laws. More arrests as well as higher rates of prosecution and mandatory-sentencing laws, as well as longer terms of imprisonment, have created the present system of overcrowding and strained conditions in the nation's jails and prisons. The latest figures available put the federal prisons at 165% of capacity. Almost all state prisons are overcrowded severely.

Members of many black and Hispanic communities have known firsthand that minorities are represented disproportionately in U.S. prisons. One in four black men from the ages of 20 to 29 is behind bars, on parole, or probation. A study in Baltimore, MD, showed that on any given day, 56% of the city's black men between the ages of 18 and 35 were either behind bars, on probation, on parole, or were being sought on warrants.

AIDS and TB. In recent years the high incidence of AIDS among prisoners and even its spread among those confined have posed a special burden for those who work or are kept behind bars. Precautions against AIDS transmission have been taken in most state prisons. New evidence that tuberculosis (TB), an airborne infection which is especially hard to control in poorly ventilated places, has become a new danger in prisons and jails. Thorough studies of the prevalence of TB were undertaken in New York state after a guard and more than 20 prisoners died from an antibiotic-resistant form of the disease. The results of the testing, published in March, showed that of the 55,000 inmates tested, 12,530 or 23% had been exposed to the disease. Preventive drugs were administered to reduce the threat, but medical authorities became alarmed that the forms of TB that remain often are resistant to treatment. No other states undertook such thorough investigations and the possibility of widespread epidemics among people behind bars alarmed many groups who monitor prison conditions.

Capital Punishment. With the execution in a gas chamber of Robert Alton Harris on April 21, California joined 19 states that actually had resumed capital punishment since it was revalidated by the Supreme Court in 1976. With 328 prisoners on death row in California—second behind Texas with almost 350—the state's decision to proceed with Harris' execution followed a long and extensive debate on the issue of capital punishment. Although more than 150 prisoners have been executed since 1976, the procedure has been limited overwhelmingly to southern states. These are the same states that performed most of the executions before the Supreme Court in 1972 ruled in a Georgia case that the death penalty had been used unequally along racial lines. Since that decision some 36 states have rewritten their laws to conform to the Supreme Court guidelines, although 16 states have not used those laws. Lawyers representing Harris filed a class-action suit on behalf of all of California's death-row inmates, charging that the use of the gas chamber was cruel and unusual punishment in violation of the U.S. Constitution. Arguing that the use of gas was similar to choking or drowning, lawyers received last-minute permission to videotape Harris' execution. The video was sealed under court order, only to be used in deciding the lawsuit.

DONALD GOODMAN
John Jay College of Criminal Justice

PRIZES AND AWARDS

NOBEL PRIZES[1]

Chemistry: Rudolph Marcus, California Institute of Technology, for work on the transfer of electrons between molecules

Economics: Gary Becker, University of Chicago, for research on how economics affects individuals' and families' life decisions

Literature: Derek Walcott, St. Lucia, for writing encompassing a "historic vision, the outcome of a multicultural commitment" (*See* LITERATURE—*Overview.*)

Peace: Rigoberta Menchú, Guatemala, "in recognition of her work for social justice and ethno-cultural reconciliation" (*See* BIOGRAPHY.)

Physics: Georges Charpak, European Laboratory for Particle Physics, for the invention of devices that monitor the smallest particles

Physiology or Medicine: Edmond Fischer and Edwin Krebs, University of Washington, Seattle, for pioneering breakthroughs in understanding cellular processes

[1] $1.2 million in each category.

ART

American Academy and Institute of Arts and Letters Awards
  Academy-Institute Awards ($5,000 ea.): architecture—Thom Mayne, Michael Rotondi; music—Charles C. Fussell, Eugene Kurtz, Peter Lieberson, Tobias Picker
  Award for Distinguished Service to the Arts: W. McNeil Lowry
  Arnold W. Brunner Memorial Prize in Architecture: Sir Norman Foster
  Jimmy Ernst Award: Hans Burkhardt
  Gold Medal for Graphic Art: David Levine
  Walter Hinrichson Award: Hi Kyung Kim
  Charles Ives Fellowship ($10,000): Geoffrey Stanton
  Goddard Lieberson Fellowships ($10,000): Laura Clayton, Cindy McTee
  Louise Nevelson Award in Art: Peter Voulkos
  Richard and Hinda Rosenthal Foundation Award ($5,000): Laura Newman

Capezio Dance Awards: Frederic Franklin (lifetime achievement); Tina Ramirez (citation of honor)

Carlsberg Architectural Prize ($235,000): Tadao Ando

Grawemeyer Award for musical composition ($150,000): Krzysztof Penderecki, Poland

John F. Kennedy Center Honors for career achievement in the performing arts: Lionel Hampton, Paul Newman, Ginger Rogers, Mstislav Rostropovich, Paul Taylor, Joanne Woodward

National Academy of Recording Arts and Sciences Grammy Awards for excellence in phonograph records

Album of the year: *Unforgettable,* Natalie Cole
Classical album: *Bernstein: Candide,* London Symphony Orchestra, Leonard Bernstein conducting; Hans Weber, producer
Country music song: "Love Can Build a Bridge," Naomi Judd, John Jarvis, Paul Overstreet (songwriters)
Country vocal performance: (female) "Down at the Twist and Shout," Mary-Chapin Carpenter; (male) *Ropin' the Wind,* Garth Brooks
Jazz vocal performance: *He Is Christmas,* Take 6
New artist: Marc Cohn
Pop vocal performance: (female) "Something to Talk About," Bonnie Raitt; (male) "When a Man Loves a Woman," Michael Bolton
Record of the year: "Unforgettable," Natalie Cole; David Foster, producer
Rock vocal performance, solo: *Luck of the Draw,* Bonnie Raitt
Song of the year: "Unforgettable," Irving Gordon (songwriter)

National Medal of Arts: Marilyn Horne, Allan Houser, James Earl Jones, Minnie Pearl, Robert Saudek, Earl Scruggs, Robert Shaw, Billy Taylor, Robert Venturi and Denise Scott Brown, Robert Wise, The AT&T Foundation, Lila Wallace-Reader's Digest Fund

Praemium Imperiale for lifetime achievement in the arts ($115,000 ea.): Frank O. Gehry, United States (architecture); Akira Kurosawa, Japan (theater and film); Pierre Soulages, France (painting); Anthony Caro, England (sculpture); Alfred Schnittke, Germany and Russia (music)

Pritzker Architecture Prize ($100,000): Alvaro Siza

Pulitzer Prize for Music: Wayne Peterson, *The Face of the Night, The Heart of the Dark*

Samuel H. Scripps/American Dance Festival Award ($25,000): Donald McKayle

Richard Tucker Award for Voice ($30,000): Deborah Voigt

JOURNALISM

Maria Moors Cabot Prizes ($1,000 ea.): Danilo Arbilla, editor and director, *Semanario Busqueda,* Montevideo, Uruguay; Sam Dillon, former South American correspondent, *The Miami Herald;* John Dinges, managing director for news and information, National Public Radio, Washington, DC; Gustavo Gorriti, journalist and author, Lima, Peru

National Magazine Awards
  Design: *Vanity Fair*
  Essays and criticism: *The Nation*
  Feature writing: *Sports Illustrated*
  General excellence: *National Geographic, Mirabella, Texas Monthly, The New Republic*
  Photography: *National Geographic*
  Public-interest: *Glamour*
  Reporting: *The New Republic*

© Carol T. Powers/The White House

As Barbara Bush looked on, violinist Isaac Stern (center) received the Presidential Medal of Freedom from President George Bush in 1992.

Single-topic issue: *Business Week*
Special-interest: *Sports Afield*

Overseas Press Club Awards

Book on foreign affairs: Sam Dillon, *Commandos: The CIA and Nicaragua's Contra Rebels*

Business or economic reporting from abroad: (magazines)—Bill Powell, *Newsweek*, "Japan as an Economic Power"; (newspapers and wire services)—Jonathan Peterson, *The Los Angeles Times*, "The Collapse of the Soviet Union"; (radio and television)—Brian Ross and Rhonda Schwartz, NBC News *Expose*, "French Spies"

Cartoon on foreign affairs: Tony Auth, *The Philadelphia Inquirer*, "Editorial Cartoons"

Daily newspaper or wire-service interpretation of foreign affairs: Carol Williams, *The Los Angeles Times*, "The Last Days of Yugoslavia"

Daily newspaper or wire-service reporting from abroad: Peter Gumbel, *The Wall Street Journal*, "The Vodka Putsch"

Magazine reporting from abroad: Michael Kelly, *The New Republic*, "The Rape & Rescue of Kuwait City," "Highway to Hell," and "Back to the Hills"

Photographic reporting from abroad (magazines and books)—Steve McCurry, *National Geographic*, "Persian Gulf: After the Storm"; (newspapers and wire services—Associated Press photographers, "A New Russia Emerges" and David Turnley, *The Detroit Free Press*, "The Soviet Journal"

Radio interpretation or documentary of foreign affairs: Tom Gjelten and Julie McCarthy, National Public Radio, "Two Villages"

Radio spot news from abroad: Lou Millano, WCBS Radio New York, "Lou Millano in the Gulf War"

Reporting or interpretation in print by a foreign correspondent or reporter in the United States for publication outside the United States: Andrew Stephen, *The Observer*, London, "Reporting on the USA Government and Politics"

Television interpretation or documentary of foreign affairs: Artyom Borovik and George Crile, *60 Minutes*, CBS, "Room 19"

Television spot news reporting from abroad: Jim Maceda, NBC News, "Attempted Coup in the Soviet Union"; Bill Blakemore, ABC News, "From Baghdad During the Gulf War"

Eric and Amy Burger Award (for best entry dealing with human rights): John Quinones and Robert Campos, *ABC Prime Time Live*, "Bitter Harvest"; Dinah Lee, Amy Borrus, Joyce Barnathan, *Business Week*, "China's Ugly Export: Secret Prison Labor"

Robert Capa Gold Medal (photographic reporting from abroad requiring exceptional courage and enterprise): Christopher Morris, Black Star, for *Time* magazine, "Slaughter in Vukovar"

Madeline Dane Ross Award (for foreign correspondent in any medium showing a concern for the human condition): Philip Dine, *St. Louis Post-Dispatch*, "Tyranny's Children"

George Polk Memorial Awards

Career award: Claude Sitton, *The News and Observer*, Raleigh, NC (retired), and *The New York Times* (retired)

Cultural reporting: Konstantin Akinsha and Grigory Kozlov, "The Soviet's Stolen Art," *Art News*

Economics reporting: Donald L. Barlett and James B. Steele, *The Philadelphia Inquirer*, "America: What Went Wrong?"

Education reporting: Jeff Gottlieb, *The San Jose Mercury News*

Foreign reporting: Francis X. Clines, Moscow bureau chief, *The New York Times*; Barbara Crossette, New Delhi bureau chief, *The New York Times*; Patrick Sloyan, *Newsday*

Local reporting: Holly A. Taylor, *The Berkshire* (MA) *Eagle*

Local television reporting: Christopher Scholl, KWWL-TV, Waterloo, IA

National reporting: Jeff Taylor and Mike McGraw, *The Kansas City Star*

National television reporting: "The Great American Bailout," *Frontline*

Radio reporting: Nina Totenberg, National Public Radio

Regional reporting: Dan Barry, John Sullivan, Ira Chinoy, *The Providence* (RI) *Journal-Bulletin*, "The Ruin of the Central Credit Union"

Special award: Andrew Schneider and Mary Pat Flaherty, *The Pittsburgh Press*

Pulitzer Prizes

Beat reporting: Deborah Blum, *The Sacramento* (CA) *Bee*
Commentary: Anna Quindlen, *The New York Times*
Editorial cartooning: Signe Wilkinson, *The Philadelphia Daily News*
Editorial writing: Maria Henson, *The Lexington* (MA) *Herald-Leader*
Explanatory journalism: Robert S. Capers and Eric Lipton, *The Hartford* (CT) *Courant*
Feature photography: John Kaplan, *The Herald* (Monterey, CA), and *The Pittsburgh Post-Gazette*
Feature writing: Howell Raines, *The New York Times*
International reporting: Patrick J. Sloyan, *Newsday*
Investigative reporting: Lorraine Adams and Dan Malone, *The Dallas Morning News*
National reporting: Jeff Taylor and Mike McGraw, *The Kansas City Star*
Public service: *The Sacramento* (CA) *Bee* for "The Sierra in Peril" by Tom Knudson
Spot news photography: The Associated Press staff
Spot news reporting: New York *Newsday* staff

LITERATURE

American Academy and Institute of Arts and Letters Awards

Academy-Institute Awards ($5,000 ea.): Alice Adams, John Crowley, Richard Foreman, Vicki Hearne, Ruth Prawer Jhabvala, Tim O'Brien, Simon Schama, August Wilson
Award of Merit for Poetry: Charles Wright
Witter Bynner Prize for Poetry ($1,500): George Bradley
E.M. Forster Award: Timothy Mo
Sue Kaufman Prize for First Fiction ($2,500): Alex Ullmann
Richard and Hinda Rosenthal Foundation Award ($5,000): Douglas Hobbie
Jean Stein Award ($5,000): James Applewhite
Harold D. Vursell Memorial Award ($5,000): Angus Fletcher
Morton Dauwen Zabel Award ($2,500): Jorie Graham

Bancroft Prizes in American history: William Cronon, *Nature's Metropolis: Chicago and the Great West*; Charles Royster, *The Destructive War: William Tecumseh Sherman, Stonewall Jackson, and the Americans*

Canada's Governor-General Literary Awards ($10,000 ea.)
English-language awards
Drama—John Mighton, *Possible Worlds* and *A Short History of Night*
Fiction—Michael Ondaatje, *The English Patient*
Nonfiction—Maggie Siggins, *Revenge of the Land: A Century of Greed, Tragedy and Murder on a Saskatchewan Farm*
Poetry—Lorna Crozier, *Inventing the Hawk*
French-language awards
Drama—no award
Fiction—Anne Hébert, *L'enfant chargé de songes*
Nonfiction—Pierre Turgeon, *La Radissonie. Le pays de la baie James*
Poetry—Gilles Cyr, *Andromè attendra*

Ruth Lilly Poetry Prize ($25,000): John Ashbery

Mystery Writers of America/Edgar Allan Poe Awards
First novel: Peter Blauner, *Slow Motion Riot*
Novel: Lawrence Block, *A Dance at the Slaughterhouse*
Grandmaster award: Elmore Leonard

National Book Awards ($10,000 ea.):
Fiction: Cormac McCarthy, *All the Pretty Horses*
Nonfiction: Paul Monette, *Becoming a Man: Half a Life Story*
Poetry: Mary Oliver, *New and Selected Poems*

National Book Critics Circle Awards
Biography/autobiography: Philip Roth, *Patrimony: A True Story*
Criticism: Lawrence L. Langer, *Holocaust Testimonies: The Ruins of Memory*
Fiction: Jane Smiley, *A Thousand Acres*
Nonfiction: Susan Faludi, *Backlash: The Undeclared War Against American Women*
Poetry: Albert Goldbarth, *Heaven and Earth: A Cosmology*
Award for criticism: George Scialabba

National Book Foundation Medal for distinguished contribution to American letters ($10,000): James Laughlin

Neustadt International Prize for Literature ($40,000): Joao Cabral de Melo Neto, Brazil

PEN/Faulkner Award ($7,500): Don DeLillo, *Mao II*

Pulitzer Prizes
Biography: Lewis B. Puller, Jr., *Fortunate Son: The Healing of a Vietnam Vet*
Fiction: Jane Smiley, *A Thousand Acres*

General nonfiction: Daniel Yergin, *The Prize: The Epic Quest for Oil, Money and Power*
History: Mark E. Neely, Jr., *The Fate of Liberty: Abraham Lincoln and Civil Liberties*
Poetry: James Tate, *Selected Poems*
Special award: Art Spiegelman, *Maus*
Rea Award for the Short Story ($25,000): Eudora Welty

MOTION PICTURES

Academy of Motion Pictures Arts and Sciences ("Oscar") Awards
Actor—leading: Anthony Hopkins, *The Silence of the Lambs*
Actor—supporting: Jack Palance, *City Slickers*
Actress—leading: Jodie Foster, *The Silence of the Lambs*
Actress—supporting: Mercedes Ruehl, *The Fisher King*
Cinematography: Robert Richardson, *JFK*
Costume design: Albert Wolsky, *Bugsy*
Director: Jonathan Demme, *The Silence of the Lambs*
Film: *The Silence of the Lambs*
Foreign-language film: *Mediterraneo* (Italy)
Music—original score: Alan Menken, *Beauty and the Beast*
Music—original song: Alan Menken and Howard Ashman, "Beauty and the Beast" (from *Beauty and the Beast*)
Screenplay—original: Callie Khouri, *Thelma and Louise*
Screenplay—adaptation: Ted Tally, *The Silence of the Lambs*
Cannes Film Festival Awards
Palme d'Or (best film): Bille August, *The Best Intentions* (Sweden)
Grand Jury Prize: Gianni Amelio, *Stolen Children* (Italy)
Jury Prize (shared): Victor Erice, *El Sol del Membrillo* (Spain); Vitaly Kanevsky, *An Independent Life* (Russia)
Best actor: Tim Robbins, *The Player*
Best actress: Pernilla August, *The Best Intentions* (Sweden)
Best director: Robert Altman, *The Player*
Camera d'Or (best first-time director): John Turturro, *Mac*
45th-anniversary award: James Ivory, *Howard's End* (England)
National Society of Film Critics Awards
Film: *Life Is Sweet*
Actor: River Phoenix, *My Own Private Idaho*
Actress: Alison Steadman, *Life Is Sweet*
Director: David Cronenberg, *Naked Lunch*

PUBLIC SERVICE

Africa Prize for Leadership for the Sustainable End of Hunger ($100,000 shared): Graça Simbine Machel, president, National Organization of Children of Mozambique; Ebrahim M. Samba, director, West African Onchocerciasis (River Blindness) Control Progam

Charles A. Dana Foundation Awards for pioneering achievements in health and higher education ($50,000 ea.): health—Masakazu Konishi, Fernando Nottebohm, Stanley B. Prusiner; education—Gary B. Keller, Henry M. Levin; distinguished achievement award—Bernadine P. Healy
Four Freedoms Awards of the Franklin and Eleanor Roosevelt Institute
Four Freedoms award: Javier Pérez de Cuéllar
Freedom from Fear award: Lord Carrington
Freedom from Want award: Jan Tinbergen
Freedom of Speech award: Mstislav Rostropovich
Freedom of Worship award: Terry Waite
American Institute for Public Service Jefferson Awards
National Awards ($5,000 ea.):
Benefiting Disadvantaged: Eunice Shriver
Public Official: Hon. Thurgood Marshall
Private Citizen: Faye Wattleton
Citizen under 35 (shared): Michael Brown, Alan Khazei
National Endowment for the Humanities' Frankel Prize:
Allan Bloom, Shelby Foote, Richard Rodriguez, Harold J. Skramstad, Jr., Eudora Welty
Templeton Prize for Progress in Religion ($800,000): Dr. Kyung-Chik Han, Young Nak Presbyterian Church, Seoul, South Korea
U.S. Presidential Medal of Freedom (awarded by President George Bush on March 17, 1992): Sam Walton; (awarded Dec. 11, 1992): David Brinkley, Johnny Carson, Ella Fitzgerald, Audrey Hepburn, I.M. Pei, Richard Petty, Harry W. Shlaudeman, Isaac Stern, John W. Vessey, Elie Wiesel

SCIENCE

Charles Stark Draper Prize for lifetime achievement in engineering ($375,000 ea.): Sir Frank Whittle, Hans J. P. von Ohain
Bristol-Myers Squibb Award for distinguished achievement in cancer research ($50,000): Thomas A. Waldmann
General Motors Cancer Research Foundation Awards ($100,000 ea.)
Kettering Award: Lawrence H. Einhorn
Mott Award: Brian MacMahon
Sloan Award: Christiane Nusslein-Bolhard
National Medal of Technology (presented by President George Bush on June 23, 1992): Norman Joseph Woodland

TELEVISION AND RADIO

Academy of Television Arts and Sciences ("Emmy") Awards
Actor—comedy series: Craig T. Nelson, *Coach* (ABC)
Actor—drama series: Christopher Lloyd, *Avonlea* (Disney Channel)

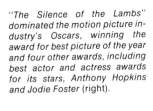

"The Silence of the Lambs" dominated the motion picture industry's Oscars, winning the award for best picture of the year and four other awards, including best actor and actress awards for its stars, Anthony Hopkins and Jodie Foster (right).

Tony Award winners honored for their performances on Broadway included (left to right) Gregory Hines, Glenn Close, Faith Prince, and Judd Hirsch. Hines and Prince were honored as best actor and actress in musicals, while Close and Hirsch garnered their awards for top-notch performances in dramas.

© Fame/Gamma-Liaison

Actor—miniseries or a special: Beau Bridges, *Without Warning: The James Brady Story* (HBO)

Actress—comedy series: Candice Bergen, *Murphy Brown* (CBS)

Actress—drama series: Dana Delany, *China Beach* (ABC)

Actress—miniseries or a special: Gena Rowlands, *Face of a Stranger* (CBS)

Comedy series: *Murphy Brown* (CBS)

Directing—comedy series: Barnet Kellman, *Murphy Brown* (CBS)

Directing—drama series: Eric Laneuville, *I'll Fly Away* (NBC)

Directing—miniseries or a special: Joseph Sargent, "Miss Rose White," *Hallmark Hall of Fame* (NBC)

Directing—variety or music program: Patricia Birch, *Unforgettable, with Love: Natalie Cole Sings the Songs of Nat King Cole* (PBS)

Drama series: *Northern Exposure* (CBS)

Miniseries: *A Woman Named Jackie* (NBC)

Supporting actor—comedy series: Michael Jeter, *Evening Shade* (CBS)

Supporting actor—drama series: Richard Dysart, *L.A. Law* (NBC)

Supporting actor—miniseries or a special: Hume Cronyn, *Neil Simon's Broadway Bound* (ABC)

Supporting actress—comedy series: Laurie Metcalf, *Roseanne* (ABC)

Supporting actress—drama series: Valerie Mahaffey, *Northern Exposure* (CBS)

Supporting actress—miniseries or a special: Amanda Plummer, "Miss Rose White," *Hallmark Hall of Fame* (NBC)

Variety, music, or comedy program: *The Tonight Show Starring Johnny Carson* (NBC)

George Foster Peabody Awards

Radio: National Public Radio, for coverage of Supreme Court confirmation hearings of Clarence Thomas; KCRW, Santa Monica, CA (distributed by National Public Radio), *Joe Frank: Work in Progress;* Armed Forces Radio and Television Service, in honor of its 50th anniversary of broadcasting; Zouk Production, Philadelphia, PA (broadcast on American Public Radio), *The Miles Davis Radio Project;* National Public Radio, *N.P.R.'s Horizons,* "The Case Against Women: Sexism in the Courts" (Helen Borten, New York, producer); WNCN-FM, New York, *New York City Musicbox;* Caedmon Audio, a division of HarperAudio, HarperCollins, New York, for "preserving our rich oral tradition"

Television: KTLA-TV, Los Angeles, for reporting on the Rodney King beating; Falahey-Austin Street Productions, Los Angeles, for *I'll Fly Away,* NBC, and *Northern Exposure,* CBS; Shukovsky-English Productions in association with Warner Brothers Television, *Murphy Brown* (CBS); WRAL-TV, Raleigh, NC, *WRAL Environmental Reporting;* KSTP-TV, St. Paul, MN, *Who's Watching the Store?;* NBC News, New York, *Brian Ross Reports on B.C.C.I.;* CBS News, New York, *60 Minutes,* "Friendly Fire"; Cable News Network, Atlanta, GA, for coverage of the Soviet coup attempt; HBO Sports, New York, and Black Canyon Productions, *When It Was a Game;* Channel 13, New York, *Dance in America: Everybody Dance Now!;* NBC Productions Inc. in association with Carson Productions and Cardboard Shoe Productions, Inc., *Late Night with David Letterman;* Home Box Office, New York, *America Undercover,* "Heil Hitler! Confessions of a Hitler Youth"; MTV Networks, New York City (a Lucky Duck Production for Nickelodeon), *Nickelodeon Special Edition: It's Only Television;* Turner Multimedia, Atlanta, GA, *Coup d'État: The Week That Changed the World;* Central Independent Television, Nottingham, England (Public Broadcasting System version by WETA-TV, Washington, DC, *Soviets: Red Hot;* ABC News, New York, and NHK, Japan, *Pearl Harbor: Two Hours That Changed the World;* Discovery Channel, Bethesda, MD, *People of the Forest: The Chimps of Gombe;* KARK-TV, Little Rock, AR, and the Arkansas Department of Health, *Arkansas' Time Bomb: Teen Pregnancy;* CBS Sports, New York, *The Masters;* Peggy Charren, founder of Action for Children's Television, for her "commitment to improving children's television"

THEATER

New York Drama Critics Circle Awards

Best new play ($1,000): *Dancing at Lughnasa,* by Brian Friel

Best American play: *Two Trains Running,* by August Wilson

Antoinette Perry ("Tony") Awards

Actor—play: Judd Hirsch, *Conversations with My Father*

Actor—musical: Gregory Hines, *Jelly's Last Jam*

Actress—play: Glenn Close, *Death and the Maiden*

Actress—musical: Faith Prince, *Guys and Dolls*

Choreography: Susan Stroman, *Crazy for You*

Director—play: Patrick Mason, *Dancing at Lughnasa*

Director—musical: Jerry Zaks, *Guys and Dolls*

Featured actor—play: Larry Fishburne, *Two Trains Running*

Featured actor—musical: Scott Waara, *The Most Happy Fella*

Featured actress—play: Brid Brennan, *Dancing at Lughnasa*

Featured actress—musical: Tonya Pinkins, *Jelly's Last Jam*

Musical: *Crazy for You*

Musical—book: William Finn and James Lapine, *Falsettos*

Musical—score: William Finn, *Falsettos*

Play: *Dancing at Lughnasa*

Reproduction of a play or musical: *Guys and Dolls*

Pulitzer Prize for Drama: Robert Schenkkan, *The Kentucky Cycle*

PUBLISHING

Some observers blamed segments of the publishing industry for a general and over-blown sense of malaise among the U.S. public during 1992, as the economy rebounded slowly from a protracted recession. In some ways, magazines and newspapers suffered more than many segments of the economy, and the numbers of people employed by them hit multiyear lows. Perhaps as a result, the tone of their contents at times seemed to exaggerate general difficulties. As the year unfolded, hopes for a strong advertising rebound were slow to materialize in the magazine and newspaper industries. Sales of books, however, continued to be comparatively immune to economic troubles.

Books. For 1991 the U.S. Commerce Department reported that book shipments increased by 2%. After a weak start, as audiences focused on news reports from the Persian Gulf, book sales finished 1991 with a strong holiday season. At the start of 1992, the Commerce Department predicted 3% annual growth in shipments through 1996. More evidence of continuing strength appeared as 1992 developed. By midyear, consumer spending on books was expected to reach $21.6 billion for 1992, a 7.2% increase from 1991. Net dollar sales in all categories of books were growing faster than in 1990 or 1991. Investment bankers Veronis, Suhler and Associates, a firm specializing in the publishing industry, predicted a 7.6% annual growth in consumer spending on books, from $20.3 billion for 1991 to $29.9 billion in 1996.

Despite the lingering problems with the U.S. economy, publishers continued paying successful and celebrity authors multimillion-dollar advances for books. In May, Barbara Taylor Bradford signed with HarperCollins for more than $20 million to deliver three books. The deal perhaps was the highest-priced multiple-book contract in history. Others receiving multimillion-dollar contracts included basketball great Earvin "Magic" Johnson and Gen. Norman Schwarzkopf. Book exports also continued to grow, increasing by 10% from a year earlier. Reflecting the economic downturn, however, publishers continued to produce fewer titles than in the recent past. Preliminary data for 1991 indicated that U.S. publishers issued only about 47,000 titles, about 15% fewer than in 1988.

In January, André Schiffrin, formerly the managing director of Pantheon Books, launched the New Press, a not-for-profit endeavor devoted to publishing books with political and social themes that commercial houses may avoid. He compared the New Press, which operates on grants from major foundations, to public television. Among its first titles was former Pantheon author Studs Terkel's *Race: How Blacks and Whites Think and Feel*

© Rick Maiman/Sygma

Gen. Norman Schwarzkopf signs a copy of his new autobiography "It Doesn't Take A Hero." Publishers continued in 1992 to pay record sums to famous and celebrity authors.

about the American Obsession. Schiffrin's removal at Pantheon in 1990, following reports of substantial financial losses in 1989, set off widespread protests among authors, editors, and agents. Pantheon long had had a reputation as a publisher that emphasized literary merit.

British media magnate Robert Maxwell's death in November 1991 preceded the collapse of his communications empire, which included Macmillan, a major U.S. book publisher he acquired in 1988. In March, Time Warner acquired publisher MacDonald & Co. Ltd. of London from Maxwell Communications Corporation. In June the British accounting firm named to administer the insolvent Maxwell Communications Corp. proposed selling off its U.S. publishing interests to relieve debt.

During the second quarter of 1992, the presidents of two prominent publishers replaced each other. First, Peter Jovanovich resigned at Harcourt Brace Jovanovich to move to the joint Macmillan/McGraw-Hill School Publishing Company. Jovanovich's resignation surprised General Cinema, which in late 1991 had purchased HBJ for $1.3 billion. Richard T. Morgan then moved to HBJ.

In August, Fukutake of Japan offered to purchase the majority of shares of Berlitz International, the largest Macmillan subsidiary. Whether the sale would occur was questionable because of a continuing dispute about ownership of the shares following the collapse of Maxwell's financial empire. Maxwell's sons, Ian and Kevin, faced charges of misappropriating shares of Berlitz, along with other assets.

In September, Reed International PLC of the United Kingdom and Elsevier NV of the Netherlands agreed in principle to merge. The merger, subject to approval by stockholders of each company, would create one of the world's six largest publishing and information groups, with 7,500 employees in North America. Combined market capitalization would be estimated at $9.3 billion. That same month, the Times Mirror Co. agreed to purchase college text publisher William C. Brown. In October, K Mart acquired Borders, owners of numerous book superstores.

Many in the publishing industry expressed concern about proposed U.S. legislation that would allow victims of sex crimes to sue publishers whose products were linked to the crimes. On the other hand, the industry cheered an August ruling by a federal judge that single-copy photocopying of scientific journals violates fair use copyright laws.

Magazines. The U.S. magazine industry opened 1992 amid depressing developments. Total advertising pages for 1991 fell 8.7%, the largest decline since 1961. The number of employees at non-newspaper periodicals stood at about 122,000, having declined by 4.5% during the previous year to the lowest level in more than 50 months. As 1992 developed, some modestly hopeful developments occurred. Through July, advertising pages increased 2.5% among consumer magazines tracked by LNA/*Magazine Week,* in comparison to the first seven months of 1991. Trade magazines showed similar growth. In addition, observers reported the appearance of healthy numbers of new titles. By mid-1992, Veronis, Suhler and Associates predicted that total advertiser and reader spending on consumer and business magazines would increase 6.4% annually, from $18.3 billion in 1991 to $25.1 billion in 1996.

Nonetheless, the lingering economic problems resulted in some noteworthy casualties. In January, Hearst announced the merger of *Connoisseur* into *Town & Country.* Both titles had seen their advertising pages drop by almost 30% in 1991. In August an attempt to resuscitate the *National Lampoon* failed. The once-trendy humor magazine had lost most of its circulation during the previous decade.

Early 1992 also saw the birth of some potentially significant titles. As a joint venture, Dow Jones Co. and Hearst launched *Smart Money: The Wall Street Journal Magazine of Personal Business,* and Fidelity Investments launched *Worth.* Both represented attempts to compete with *Kiplinger's Personal Finance Magazine* and *Money.* One important merger occurred in September. McFadden's consumer magazines, including *True Confessions,* and Sterling's Magazines, owner of *Daytime TV,* merged to form the Sterling's/McFadden Partnership. The new company has total annual revenues of more than $50 million.

A number of magazines underwent changes and development during the year. *Time* unveiled the most radical redesign in its 69-year history. *New Woman* also was redesigned. Makeovers were done at *Elle* and *Reader's Di-*

gest. At the start of the year, *Newsweek* and *People* came out with audiocassettes based on their magazines. An April issue of *Forbes* included a computer disc containing advertisements. Editor Tina Brown moved from *Vanity Fair* to *The New Yorker* and attempted to make the traditionally well-written but stuffy publication more vivacious. Her inaugural issue appeared in October. In response to recent and future increases in postal rates, many magazines examined the possibility of delivering copies by means other than the mail.

Concern with legal issues continued during 1992. A federal appeals court upheld a $4.37 million award against *Soldier of Fortune* magazine. The court held that the publication was liable for the contract murder of an Atlanta businessman that was arranged through a gun-for-hire ad that it printed.

Newspapers. Profitability generally increased among publicly traded newspaper companies during the first half of 1992, even as advertising volume remained flat and few daily newspapers reported circulation increases. Smaller payrolls, increased ad rates, and very low prices for newsprint contributed. By 1992, newsprint costs amounted to only about 20% of newspaper expenditures, instead of 30% as during the early 1980s.

The improvements came in the wake of perhaps the worst year in decades. Advertising expenditures for newspapers tumbled 6% in 1991, with classified advertising, the most profitable, showing the largest decrease. Daily circulation slipped an estimated 2%. By early 1992, newspaper employment reached a six-year low of about 454,000. Analysts expected circulation to remain flat during 1992.

By late 1991, about 1,586 dailies, 25 fewer than a year earlier, were being published in the United States. The dailies had a combined circulation of about 60.7 million. Chains continued to own about 75%. The number of Sunday newspapers, however, reached an all-time high of 875 in 1991. They had a combined circulation of about 62 million. *The Wall Street Journal,* with a circulation of about 1.85 million, continued to lead all dailies, followed by *USA Today* and *The New York Times.* By early 1992, the number of weeklies totaled about 7,417, with a combined circulation of about 54.5 million.

During late 1991 and early 1992, economic troubles continued to take a toll as newspapers, especially afternoon dailies, died at a historically rapid rate. In December 1991 the *Dallas Times-Herald* folded, resulting in 900 lost jobs and making Dallas the largest U.S. city with only one daily. The *Arkansas Gazette* also died, and the *Knoxville Journal* stopped publishing as a daily. On Jan. 3, 1992, the Elizabeth (N.J.) *Daily Journal* became the first casualty of the new year, closing after 213 years. The *Fort Lauderdale News* folded in March. In July the *Spokane Chronicle* published its final edi-

News-staff members of "The Pittsburgh Press" watched as the E. W. Scripp Company announced on Oct. 2, 1992, that it would try to sell the paper, which had been on strike since May. The walkout also idled "The Pittsburgh Post-Gazette."

tion. The *Gwinnett Daily News,* published in suburban Atlanta, and the *Tulsa Tribune* both closed in September.

During the year, large metropolitan newspapers increasingly tried to compete outside their traditional markets against relatively distant rivals. This led observers to predict that small papers near a major city would face especially difficult times during the coming years.

In general, few publications changed hands as 1992 developed, as owners generally refused to sell at depressed prices. On the other hand, in early October, Scripps-Howard announced its intention to sell the *Pittsburgh Press,* shortly after an indefinite suspension in talks between the Teamsters and the Pittsburgh Press Co. A strike, begun in May, had shut down both major Pittsburgh dailies. Troubles at the *New York Daily News* also continued during 1992. The paper, which Robert Maxwell acquired in early 1991 after a lengthy strike and which went bankrupt after his death, lost millions of dollars during the first half of 1992. Two prominent prospective buyers, *U.S. News & World Report* owner Mortimer Zuckerman and Canadian media baron Conrad Black, negotiated to purchase it during the summer. In September, Zuckerman emerged as the apparent front-runner when he reached a tentative agreement with most of the nine unions at the paper. Black shelved his attempt to buy it after negotiations with the unions broke down. In late October a federal bankruptcy judge cleared the way for the sale of the *News,* once the largest U.S. daily, to Zuckerman. Also in October the nation's only black-owned newspaper, *The Oakland Tribune,* was sold to the Alameda Newspaper Group.

In June, United Press International was sold at a bankruptcy auction to a Saudi-con-trolled, London-based television production company. The company represented the fifth owner in ten years for the wire service, which once competed on almost equal footing with The Associated Press in supplying national and international news to newspapers and other media organizations. In January the boards of the American Newspaper Publishers Association and the Newspaper Advertising Bureau agreed to merge, thus creating the Newspaper Association of America on June 1. The merger also involved five other newspaper organizations.

The number of newspapers offering audiotex services continued to grow. By early 1992, about 1,200 publications offered information via the telephone, and the number was expected to increase to 2,000 by 1993. Increasingly, newspapers used audiotex systems to enable customers to request specific information for facsimile delivery. This provided a source of revenue from audiotex services.

Legal issues continued to attract the attention of the newspaper industry. Many in it supported proposed federal legislation that would keep regional telephone companies from competing with publishing companies in the delivery of information services. Some in the industry, however, spoke against the proposed legislation. Evidence appeared of increasing difficulties with libel law. The Libel Defense Resource Center reported that in 1990 and 1991, jury awards to successful libel plaintiffs averaged about $9 million, roughly six times as much as during the 1980s. Of this amount, punitive damages accounted for more than $8 million. Publishers won only 27% of cases involving jury trials during the two years.

DAVID K. PERRY
The University of Alabama

PUERTO RICO

In 1992, Puerto Rico elected a new governor, experienced its second straight year of record-breaking homicides, and was pounded by torrential rains.

The Elections. Puerto Rican voters elected pediatric surgeon Pedro Rosselló of the pro-statehood New Progressive Party (NPP) as governor on Nov. 3, 1992. With 1,881,872 or 84.5% of eligible voters casting their ballots, Rosselló—a relative newcomer on the political scene who in 1988 lost a bid for resident commissioner—beat the pro-commonwealth Popular Democratic Party (PDP) candidate Victoria Muñoz Mendoza by almost 76,000 votes. Muñoz, daughter of former Gov. Luis Muñoz Marín, was the first woman ever to run for governor in Puerto Rico. Earlier in the year, Gov. Rafael Hernández Colón had announced his decision to retire from public office after serving three terms as governor and 23 years as PDP president.

An apparent crossing of party lines by disgruntled PDP voters handed the NPP its largest margin of victory since the party was established in 1968. The NPP claimed overwhelming control of the Senate and House, and controlled 54 of the island's 78 mayoral seats.

During the campaign, Rosselló vowed to hold a status referendum in 1993. Puerto Rico has been a U.S. commonwealth since 1952. After his victory, Rosselló prepared to introduce legislation to reinstate English as Puerto Rico's official second language. English was repealed as an official language in 1991; it had been the official second language since 1902.

The elections also saw the resurgence of former Gov. Carlos Romero Barcelo, who was picked as resident commissioner. It was believed widely, however, that Romero would not survive the Senate investigation of the planning and cover-up of the 1978 slayings of two young supporters of independence for Puerto Rico. An initial Senate probe revealed that the two men were killed by police agents. A report released on December 31 by Senate investigator Edgardo Pérez Viera charged Romero with violating the Puerto Rican constitution by failing to enforce the law when he did not seek to identify and punish those involved.

Crime. Nineteen ninety-two marked the second consecutive year that Puerto Rico had a record-breaking number of homicides. Preliminary police reports indicated that 862 people were murdered in 1992; the total number of murders in 1991 was 817. That year, Puerto Rico had the highest per-capita rate of murders in the country, with 23.2 per 100,000 population.

Other News. Torrential rains pounded the central mountain region of the island with a record-breaking 20 inches (50.8 cm) of precipitation over a 24-hour period January 5-6. Flooding claimed the lives of 23 people and caused more than $100 million in damage. President George Bush declared 35 of the island's municipalities disaster areas, paving the way for relief assistance from the Federal Emergency Management Agency, which provided $88 million in funds.

In an unprecedented move led and sponsored by the U.S. Department of Housing and Urban Development, 332 of the island's government-run housing projects were turned over to private management firms. Hundreds of the residents were hired by the management companies to do various general repairs of the buildings and their surroundings. Providing these jobs to residents would motivate them to take better care of their community, officials maintained.

PETER J. ORTIZ, *"The San Juan Star"*

QUEBEC

Reconciliation between Quebec and English-speaking Canada—constitutionally speaking—seemed almost within reach for a time in 1992. Then it faded again. Government finances continued to be squeezed by the recession. Hydro-Quebec lost a major power contract.

Constitutional Referendum. One event overshadowed all others in Quebec in 1992—the October 26 referendum, where voters turned down a constitutional-reform plan aimed mostly at resolving a decade-long schism between Quebec and the rest of Canada. More than 55% of Quebecers voted to reject the deal concluded by Premier Robert Bourassa and Canada's other political leaders at Charlottetown in August.

However, in this case Quebec was not isolated, as it had been in 1981 when the Constitution was brought home from Britain under a formula the province found unacceptable. All but four of the other nine provinces renounced the Charlottetown Accord that, among other things, would have recognized Quebec's cultural distinctness and devolved some additional powers to the Canadian provinces.

Nevertheless, Quebec's two most prominent separatists, Jacques Parizeau, leader of the Parti Québécois (PQ), and Lucien Bouchard, head of the Bloc Québécois in the federal Parliament, both hailed the result as a step toward independence for the province. For his

---

PUERTO RICO · Information Highlights

Area: 3,515 sq mi (9 104 km²).
Population (mid-1992 est.): 3,700,000.
Chief Cities (1990 census): San Juan, the capital, 437,745; Bayamon, 220,262; Ponce, 187,749.
Government (1992): *Chief Officer*—governor, Rafael Hernández Colón (Popular Democratic Party). *Legislature*—Senate, 27 members; House of Representatives, 51 members.

In June 1992, Premier Robert Bourassa (right) discussed Quebec's position regarding Canada's constitution with Saskatchewan's Premier Roy Romanow in Regina. Bourassa was on his first trip to western Canada in more than two years.

© Canapress Photo Service

part, Bourassa, who had returned to the constitutional bargaining table in early August after a two-year boycott, appeared more than ever a committed federalist. It was clear, however, that he had some fence-mending to do before the next provincial election in 1993 or 1994, considered virtually certain to be another battle over Quebec independence.

Election in Anjou. PQ continued to shake off its parliamentary by-election jinx, winning for the second time in a row with a triumph in the Montreal east-end riding of Anjou on January 20. The PQ candidate, Pierre Belanger, defeated his Liberal opponent, Charlotte Goudreault, by more than 1,000 votes. PQ had scored its first-ever by-election victory in August 1991 after losing 35 times in a row. Parizeau immediately proclaimed the latest win as evidence that "Quebec is ready for sovereignty."

Financial Squeeze. Treasury Board President Daniel Johnson released estimates on March 24 that projected record 1992–93 expenditures of C$41.09 billion. The figure represented a 5.8% increase over 1991–92 and reflected the continuing burdens imposed by the recession. Welfare and other social pro-

grams were expected to cost C$547 million, up 15.3%. With health and social services accounting for 30.9% of government expenditures, Johnson underlined the need to find alternative means of financing health care.

Health Minister Marc-Yvan Cote followed up on May 8 with a plan to reduce the projected cost of medical services by C$135 million in 1992–93 and by C$211 million in 1993–94. For example, people aged 18 to 40 henceforth would have to pay for routine eye examinations, and children over age 10 for dental care. Some senior citizens would have to pay a $2 user fee for drug prescriptions, and hospitals were asked to trim $50 million from their operating budgets in 1992 and 1993.

Finance Minister Gérard-D. Levesque, by contrast, brought down a budget on May 14 that was relatively painless for consumers. Because of an anticipated 17% increase in federal transfer payments, the minister was able to predict that the deficit would drop to C$3.8 billion in 1992–93, down C$405 million from 1991–92, without boosting income, gasoline, alcohol, and tobacco taxes. The new services sales tax was set at 4%, instead of the 8% charged for goods. However, business was hit by a new 2% surtax on most income, accompanied by a tightening of corporate tax laws.

Power Sale Lost. The timetable for building the huge—and hugely controversial—Great Whale hydroelectric project in northern Quebec was upset by New York state's decision on March 27 to pull out of a $17 billion deal to purchase power from Quebec.

Energy Minister Lise Bacon said in Montreal on March 31 that the C$13.1 billion energy project would have to be broken into three parts, with construction of the first phase beginning in 1993 and ending by the year 2000 (when the entire development originally was set for completion). The second phase was to be completed by 2005 and the third in 2008. Bacon blamed agitation by Cree Indians for New York's withdrawal, although Gov. Mario Cuomo said that the state's need for additional

---

QUEBEC · Information Highlights

Area: 594,857 sq mi (1 540 680 km²).
Population (September 1992): 6,931,700.
Chief Cities (1986 census): Quebec, the capital, 164,580; Montreal, 1,015,420; Laval, 284,164.
Government (1992): *Chief Officers*—lt. gov., Gilles Lamontagne; premier, Robert Bourassa (Liberal). *Legislature*—National Assembly, 125 members.
Provincial Finances (1992–93 fiscal year budget): *Revenues,* $34,900,000,000; *expenditures,* $38,400,000,000.
Personal Income (average weekly earnings, July 1992): $538.13.
Labor Force (September 1992, seasonally adjusted): *Employed* workers, 15 years of age and over, 2,964,000; *Unemployed,* 12.5%.
Education (1992–93): *Enrollment*—elementary and secondary schools, 1,149,600 pupils; postsecondary—universities, 134,800; community colleges, 165,900.
(All monetary figures are in Canadian dollars.)

power had diminished due to conservation measures and independent production. Bacon vowed that the project would be pushed to completion despite the Cree opposition.

Racism on the Rise. A prominent Quebec civil-rights group, *Ligue des droits et libertés*, called for an all-out effort to curb racial intolerance in the province. A 115-page report released by the group in Montreal on July 7 cited more than 30 incidents and listed a number of active racist organizations, many with Ku Klux Klan and Aryan-supremacy affiliations. The group's recommendations were relatively mild, however, and included better education, a broad debate on racism, and greater media awareness of the problem.

Language Acquittals. Twelve merchants charged with violating Quebec's French-only law governing outdoor advertising signs were acquitted on a technicality in Montreal on September 14. Judge Monique Dubreuil found that the defendants had been denied the benefit of a two-year grace period established under the law.

JOHN BEST, *"Canada World News"*

REFUGEES AND IMMIGRATION

During 1992 refugee and migration crises continued to dominate the international political agenda of the early post-Cold War era, with most of the 17 million exiles the victims of Cold War conflicts. In the republics of what were formerly Yugoslavia and the USSR, the Horn of Africa and southern Africa, and in numerous other locations, war and mass displacements of peoples contributed to the disintegration of nations. These refugee exoduses commanded the attention of high-level policymakers, not only for humanitarian reasons and because of the numbers involved, but also because of the serious consequences that mass displacements had for international stability and the functioning of international and regional organizations.

Post-Cold War Refugee Emergencies. Disintegration, civil war, and the redrawing of boundaries created both massive internal hemorrhaging in the former Yugoslavia and Soviet Union and large numbers of refugees in neighboring European states. Conflict and "ethnic cleansing" in Bosnia-Herzegovina killed thousands and drove more than 2 million people from their homes. During the year, more than 200,000 former Yugoslavs applied for political asylum in Germany and 50,000 more fled to neighboring Hungary. Smaller but significant displacements also occurred in parts of the former Soviet Union, including Azerbaijan, Moldova, the Caucasus region, and Central Asia. Throughout 1992, Western European governments feared a mass influx of refugees arising from chaos and conflict in former Yugoslavia. Central European states feared similar refugee influxes should events spin out of control in the former USSR. How governments should respond to the political confrontations between majority and minority groups, and to pogroms and other forms of violent persecution causing refugee problems in Europe, became a matter of growing political importance. These events undoubtedly would influence the formulation of future political and security policies in Europe.

The most acute refugee crises in other parts of the world occurred in Africa, where millions of people were at risk from widespread famine. In the wake of the overthrow of Siad Barre in 1991, Somalia degenerated into anarchy and fierce interclan conflict. Thousands of Somalians were killed and hundreds of thousands were uprooted. International efforts to distribute food to starving Somalians were disrupted by the killing and looting of rival clans and warlords. In September 1992 aid agencies warned of similar refugee and famine emergencies in southern Africa—particularly in Mozambique, Zimbabwe, and Malawi—unless urgent relief measures were initiated.

Asylum Crises in the West. Internal conflicts in former Communist states and the developing world produced not only an increasing number of refugees, but also an increasing number of these uprooted people who sought asylum in Western Europe and North America during the year. In a time of recession and economic embattlement, the increase in asylum-seekers led to a resurgence of xenophobic and racist attitudes among Western populations and an increase in violent attacks in nearly every country hosting immigrant communities. Throughout Europe, anti-immigrant feeling was exploited by extreme right-wing political parties, leading to tighter restrictions on entry of refugees.

The most serious events took place in Germany. In the summer of 1992 outbreaks of violence against foreigners erupted first in Rostock in former East Germany and then quickly spread throughout other parts of Germany. During the year about 400,000 foreigners sought political asylum. The growing number of asylum-seekers, the high rate of unemployment, and the shortage of affordable housing in the eastern half of the country contributed to the growing resentment. The response of the German government was to focus on deterrence and the containment of migration from Eastern Europe and the developing countries. In September, Germany reached an agreement with Romania to return tens of thousands of gypsies and considered revising the liberal provisions for asylum contained in its constitution.

In the United States there was a major controversy over the government's handling of refugees from Haiti. The outflow of refugees from Haiti increased after the military coup d'état against the democratically elected President Jean-Bertrand Aristide in September 1991. The

In the wake of the disintegration of the Soviet Union and Yugoslavia, long-suppressed ethnic animosities have resurfaced. The resulting conflicts have produced millions of refugees, many of whom fled to Western Europe during 1992.

Organization of American States ordered economic sanctions against the Haitian military junta that illegally had seized power. Unfortunately, these sanctions had a crushing impact on the poorest Haitians and generated yet more refugees. Between October 1991 and August 1992, more than 37,000 Haitians fled their country to seek refuge in the United States. Throughout the year, the status of Haitian boat people was the focus of litigation in the U.S. courts. On May 24, 1992, U.S. President George Bush issued an executive order which denied Haitians intercepted at sea the right to immigration interviews to determine their eligibility for U.S. political asylum. On Aug. 1, 1992, the U.S. Supreme Court temporarily upheld the legality of the executive order, pending a full review.

During 1992 smaller but significant numbers of Cuban boat people also arrived in the United States and were allowed to apply for political asylum, thus raising questions about the fairness of U.S. procedures.

Long-standing Refugee Crises. Alongside new refugee exoduses, continuing problems involving refugees from Cambodia, Afghanistan, Vietnam, Mozambique, Angola, and Central America posed a threat to regional security. Although several of these conflicts were in the process of being resolved and refugee populations had started to return home in 1992, significant political and security problems remained, making the safe return and full reintegration of these people impossible. Most of the countries to which refugees returned had been devastated by years of war, including the leveling of entire villages, the destruction of irrigation systems and other infrastructure, and the loss of homes and land. In addition, economies had been brought to a virtual standstill, and vast amounts of territory had been mined. During 1992 the international community showed little willingness to provide the resources for comprehensive programs for reconstruction.

Future Needs. The mass refugee movements of 1992 demonstrated the inadequacy of present international and national policies and the need for a more comprehensive approach to the refugee problem. In the early part of the year, the office of the United Nations (UN) Emergency Relief Coordinator was established in order to strengthen and expedite international action in humanitarian emergencies, especially in cases where governments refused to cooperate. While this development should lead to some improvements in the response capacity of the UN, the refugee crises in former Yugoslavia and Somalia revealed the inadequacy of the UN and regional organizations to intervene politically in internal and ethnic conflicts. Given the nature, size, and complexity of the contemporary refugee problem, no overall permanent solution can be expected. However, there is much need for the development of a stronger and more rapid UN response system for internal conflicts and refugee emergencies.

GIL LOESCHER
University of Notre Dame

RELIGION

Overview

The Rev. Konrad Raiser, a member of the Evangelical (Lutheran) Church in Germany, was elected general secretary of the World Council of Churches in August 1992, succeeding the Rev. Emilio Castro, a Methodist from Uruguay.

A rift in the ecumenical movement in the United States was healed in March when five Orthodox churches decided to "provisionally resume" membership in the National Council of Churches, which they had suspended in 1991. The rift involved Orthodox complaints that their views often were ignored in the council's statements. Under the new agreement, the 32-member council will publicize both majority and minority views when it makes statements with which some member churches disagree.

A study titled "Churches and Church Membership in the United States," compiled by the Association of Statisticians of American Religious Bodies, found that 137 million Americans, or 55.1% of the population, are affiliated with a religious group in the Judeo-Christian tradition. Among other things, the study found large areas west of the Rocky Mountains in the United States where less than one fourth of the residents are claimed by a Christian or Jewish religious group.

A milestone in religious publishing was reached in July with the issuing of the six-volume Anchor Bible Dictionary, the work of an international team of 1,000 scholars who labored on the project for six years. The dictionary contains about 6,200 entries and was described by the publisher, Doubleday, as the largest, most comprehensive English-language Bible dictionary in history.

The Rev. Dr. Kyung-Chik Han, founder and pastor emeritus of the Young Nak Church in Seoul, South Korea—the world's largest Presbyterian church—was awarded the 1992 Templeton Prize for Progress in Religion.

Christian Science. One of the most publicized religious controversies in 1992 involved the usually quiet Christian Science Church. The dispute dated to 1991, when the church's board of directors decided to publish a book about Christian Science founder Mary Baker Eddy that was declared heretical when it first was issued in 1947. Publication of the book, *The Destiny of the Mother Church,* could make the church eligible for a $98 million bequest from the estates of the family of the author, the late Bliss Knapp.

The church's bid for the bequest came at a time when administrators were borrowing more than $40 million from the church pension fund to help eliminate deficits in the Monitor Channel, a 24-hour-per-day cable service that finally closed in June.

© Susan Lapides

With the Christian Science Church facing financial difficulties and a publication's controversy, Harvey Wood resigned as board chairman of the Mother Church in Boston (above).

Publication of the Knapp book was delayed because of legal proceedings involving competing bids for the Knapp estates. Christian Science officials called for unity at the church's annual meeting in Boston in June, but the controversy led to the resignation of dozens of members of the church's administrative staff and a restructuring of the headquarters operation.

DARRELL J. TURNER, *Religious News Service*

Far Eastern

Hindu attempts to maintain dominance over Muslims in India led to the worst sectarian rioting in decades, leaving more than 1,000 people dead. The violence erupted on Dec. 6, 1992, when fundamentalist Hindus destroyed a 16th-century mosque in Ayodhya that they said was built on the site where the Hindu god Rama was born. Some Hindus claimed that Muslims had torn down a shrine to Rama at Ayodhya before building the Babri Masjid mosque. The structure had been a focus of strife for years between Hindus, who make up more than 80% of India's population and Muslims, who comprise about 11%. Hindus built a provisional temple at the site, but the Indian government announced plans to buy land for both a mosque and temple there. The cabinet of Prime Minister P. V. Narasimha Rao also asked the Indian Supreme Court to resolve the historical dispute.

The presence of Hindu gods and priests at a Buddhist temple in Bodh Gaya, India, led 2,000 outraged Buddhist pilgrims to break several idols and slap Hindu holy men in May. The site is administered by a committee of five Hindus and four Buddhists. Buddhist priests demanded complete control of the temple, but Hindus who maintained that the Buddha was an incarnation of a Hindu god insisted that the site should be open to Hindu idols and ceremonies as well as those of Buddhists.

The Dalai Lama, Tibet's chief Buddhist leader, sent off the first of a series of monthly contingents of Tibetan refugees to the United States from Dharamsala, India, in April. The displaced Tibetans had fled their homeland to escape China's claims of sovereignty.

During July and August, two representatives of the Dalai Lama visited eight Jewish summer camps in the United States to observe how a religious culture is preserved outside the group's homeland. One of the Buddhist representatives said he learned from the camps that reenactments of crucial incidents in religious history—in the campers' case, an escape from the Holocaust—can have a greater impact than books, which are scarce in Tibetan Buddhist schools in India.

In June an 8-year-old boy was recognized and confirmed as the new leader of the Kagyu sect, one of the four branches of Tibetan Buddhism. The enthronement of the leader, known as the Gyalwa Karmapa, was the first time the Chinese government had permitted such a ceremony to take place in Tibet. The new Kagyu leader has the given name of Ugyen Tinley. He is the 17th in a line of Buddhists that began in the 12th century.

DARRELL J. TURNER

Islam

The struggle to define the appropriate status of Islam in the modern state continued to unfold during 1992. Organizations committed to giving Islamic values and practices the central role in the management of the state found themselves at odds with governments of a more secular orientation in several Muslim countries. In others, however, official attempts to require the rigid observance of traditional Islamic prescriptions met with opposition from Muslims who preferred to limit Islam to a more exclusively spiritual function. Non-Muslim citizens' resentment of such policies occasionally sparked clashes with their Muslim neighbors. Conversely, minority Muslim populations in Asia and Europe experienced persecution and displacement at the hands of governments bent on establishing ethnic and religious homogeneity in their lands.

Algeria. A victory by the Islamic Salvation Front (FIS) in an initial round of parliamentary elections in Algeria in December 1991 appeared to ensure that the nation would be the first country in which a political party devoted to Islamic ideals achieved power through elections. But in January 1992 army leaders forced President Chadli Benjedid to resign and canceled the final round of voting. For the next months, the FIS' supporters battled security forces, with the most violent demonstrations usually following the noon prayers on Friday, the Muslim day of communal worship. According to government figures, more than 100 protesters were killed and another 9,000 arrested.

A new government headed by Mohammed Boudiaf ordered the arrest of key FIS leaders. In March the organization was banned. Although partisans of the FIS came under suspicion when Boudiaf was assassinated in June, no conclusive evidence linked them to his murder. Deprived of legal outlets for their activities, some militant supporters of the FIS launched a terrorist campaign that took the lives of more than 100 government officials and agents of the security forces by late summer.

Other Turmoil. In several of the predominantly Muslim Central Asian republics of the former USSR, new Islamic parties also competed for political influence. They achieved their greatest success in Tajikistan where, in September, the Islamic Renaissance Party led a successful campaign to depose the country's formerly Communist president as a prelude to the establishment of an Islamic state.

Reacting to the turmoil in Algeria, Tunisia clamped down on its Islamic organizations. Strict enforcement or censorship laws curbed the Islamic press and the government's assumption of sweeping powers led to the arrest of thousands suspected of involvement in the activities of an illegal Islamic political party. In August a military court sentenced 46 of the party's sympathizers, some of them accused of plotting to assassinate President Zine El Abidine Ben Ali, to life imprisonment and imposed lesser punishments on another 200.

Elsewhere, the Sudanese government pressed on with its campaign to impose Islamic law throughout the country, including in the heavily non-Muslim south, despite that area's rejection of this and other intrusions by Khartoum through a prolonged civil war. Similarly, Afghanistan's *mujahidin* commanders, for whom the fall of Kabul in April capped a campaign to supplant a regime installed by the USSR in 1986, quickly instituted an Islamic government. Although virtually all Afghanis are Muslims, uncertainties about the *mujahidins'* interpretation and application of Islamic law created an uneasiness among some citizens. Their discomfort mounted as the new leaders demanded adherence to traditional practices and meted out Koranic punishments.

In Egypt, Muslims and Christians clashed in several Nile Valley towns, reviving a pattern of violence stemming from local rivalries and economic competition that had lain dormant for almost a year. In June, Faruq Fuda, a political commentator whose writings criticized Islamic extremism, was assassinated in Cairo.

Muslims in Bosnia-Herzegovina, a historically Islamic region of the Balkans, endured a ruthless campaign of "ethnic cleansing" at the hands of Serbs intent on driving other ethnic groups from areas of the former Yugoslavia that they hoped to dominate. The plight of Bosnia's Muslims aroused world sympathy.

(*See also* THE BREAKUP OF YUGOSLAVIA.)
KENNETH J. PERKINS
University of South Carolina

Judaism

World political events were of unusual concern to Jews in 1992.

The Former USSR and Eastern Europe. The difficulties experienced by the new non-Communist governments in the former Soviet Union and its erstwhile satellites in Eastern Europe evoked renewed anxiety about the fate of Jews living in these countries. The movement to separate Slovakia from the Czechoslovak Federation raised the specter of extreme Slovakian nationalists attaining power and possibly undermining the status of Jews. The outbreak of war in Bosnia endangered the Jewish community there, although, for the time being, there were no signs of overt anti-Semitism. While agitation against Jews in the former USSR did not lead to violence, many observers felt that further deterioration of the economy could encourage those opposed to free-market reforms to blame Jews. Meanwhile, Jews in several former Soviet republics organized federations to reconstruct their cultural and religious institutions.

U.S. Developments. Jews in the United States had to deal with threats to their interests connected with the presidential campaign. Patrick J. Buchanan, challenging President George Bush for the Republican nomination, had made several remarks over the years that Jews considered hostile, including the claim that only Israel and its supporters favored U.S. intervention against Iraq in 1991's Persian Gulf crisis. Even more alarming was the Republican candidacy of David Duke, former Ku Klux Klan leader and Nazi sympathizer. Neither man did well, however: Duke quit the race in April, and Buchanan won few delegates.

U.S. Jews had a stake in two 1992 U.S. Supreme Court decisions. As proponents of separation of church and state, most Jewish organizations hailed a ruling barring, at public-school graduations, prayers that mentioned God or contained biblical passages. And as advocates of a woman's right to abortion, most Jews were dissatisfied with the court ruling that, although states might not curtail that right, they did have the power to enact abortion regulations.

The prospect of demographic erosion, highlighted by a national survey of the U.S. Jewish population, was a vexing issue. The knowledge that more than half of Jews were choosing non-Jewish mates, and that relatively few of the offspring were likely to identify as Jews, dominated the agendas of Jewish religious organizations. Accepting that high intermarriage rates were unavoidable in an open society, the Reform and Conservative movements sought to devise new ways of reaching out to mixed-religion couples so they would not be lost to Judaism. Even Orthodox Judaism, the most insular denomination and the least likely to experience mixed marriage, began to adjust: Despite vehement protests from many colleagues, a small group of Orthodox rabbis suggested welcoming intermarried Jews into the synagogue.

Two research reports released during the year gave further grounds for pessimism about U.S. Jewish life. A survey of the Jewish communal involvement of U.S. Jews indicated that, while many Jews affiliated with Jewish organizations, they were more likely to devote time and money to nonsectarian causes. And a study of the costs involved in living a Jewish life showed that many Jews who would like to affiliate lacked the means to do so.

The most explosive religious issue of the year was the question of the role of homosexuals in Judaism. The small Reconstructionist movement issued an official declaration of unconditional equality regardless of sexual preference. But the more traditionalist Conservative branch went through an agonizing struggle over the matter. The Conservative rabbinical organization voted to allow its members to accept pulpits in gay synagogues. But the movement's Committee on Law and Standards, made up of academic scholars as well as pulpit rabbis, was unable to reach a consensus over whether gays and lesbians should be accepted as rabbis. It established a panel that would wrestle with the issue and report to the committee in 1994.

Lubavitch Messianism. The phenomenon of Lubavitch messianism, which attracted considerable attention in 1991, did not abate. Under the leadership of Menachem Mendel Schneerson, the Lubavitch Hasidic sect continued to argue that the downfall of communism, the mass migration of Soviet Jews to Israel, the Gulf war, and other world events clearly foreshadowed the imminent emergence of the messiah, who would bring world peace. Even the hospitalization of Rabbi Schneerson after a stroke did not dampen the enthusiasm of his followers.

LAWRENCE GROSSMAN
The American Jewish Committee

Orthodox Eastern

Bartholomeos I, the newly elected ecumenical patriarch of Constantinople, called the primates of the world's Orthodox churches to Istanbul in March 1992. Fourteen church leaders participated in this first such meeting in more than a millennium. In their joint statement the patriarchs and archbishops affirmed Orthodox church unity and blessed ecumenical efforts for greater unity among Christians and all peoples. They celebrated the downfall of Communist regimes and decried bloodshed and war, especially in former Yugoslavia. They lamented moves of Western Christians—particularly Roman Catholics of Latin and Eastern rites, Protestant fundamentalists, schismatic Orthodox sectarians, and others—to treat former Marxist countries as missionary territories, distinguishing between respectable evangelism and unscrupulous proselytism. And they decried the corruption of social life on the planet through wicked uses of technological and economic power.

Albania. Attempts made by the ecumenical patriarchate to reestablish the Orthodox church in Albania met with opposition from Albanian nationalists, both Muslim and Christian, within the country and abroad. Led by Metropolitan Anastasios Yannoulatis, a missionary bishop and professor, the renewed church planned to consecrate suffragan bishops, open seminaries, ordain priests, and carry on missionary and renewal activities.

Russia and Ukraine. In the former USSR, the Moscow patriarchate under the leadership of Alexei II experienced grave internal difficulties, including economic problems, while continuing to receive and renovate church properties; open monasteries, schools, and hospitals; and baptize thousands of people. The finding of several bishops' names on lists of KGB activists brought serious criticism to the patriarchate, long charged with cooperation with the Soviets. Patriarch Alexei repented for the shameful behavior of many churchmen under Marxism and vowed to take action in cases where concrete criminal or antichurch action harmful to humans could be proved.

Metropolitan Philaret of Kiev, among those charged, was unfrocked by the patriarchate. He created an independent church in addition to the Ukrainian church group led by Patriarch Mystislav I. About two thirds of the Orthodox in Ukraine remained faithful to the Moscow patriarchate. Millions of Ukrainians had returned to union with Rome.

Serbia. Serbian Orthodox Patriarch Pavle visited the United States in October. He called for an end to bloodshed in former Yugoslavia; collected humanitarian aid for all the suffering, including that of Albanians and Croatians, Catholics and Muslims; and celebrated the reunion of divided Serbian Orthodox groups in the United States and Canada. The patriarch also presided over the centennial of Orthodoxy in Chicago and received an honorary doctorate from St. Vladimir's Seminary in Crestwood, NY.

Obituary. On July 22 the dean of St. Vladimir's, Protopresbyter John Meyendorff, unexpectedly died of cancer. Among Orthodoxy's leading theologians, Father Meyendorff was born (1926) in France and went to the United States in 1959, where he joined the seminary faculty and Harvard's Byzantine Research Center, Dumbarton Oaks, Washington, DC. He was a Fordham University professor from 1967, wrote many books on church history and patristics, and edited *The Orthodox Church* newspaper.

THOMAS HOPKO, *St. Vladimir's Seminary*

Protestantism

Questions regarding homosexuality and the ordination of women continued to generate controversy in the world of Protestantism during 1992.

Issues. The 15-million-member Southern Baptist Convention, the largest Protestant denomination in the United States, expelled two North Carolina congregations from membership in June for taking stands approving the practice of homosexuality. It was the first time any local churches had been removed for a reason other than lack of financial support, and the action generated opposition even from many Baptists who opposed the positions taken by the two churches. In contrast, the General Board of American Baptist Churches rejected a proposal to condemn the practice of homosexuality. The denomination stressed that in so doing, it was taking a position of neutrality on the issue.

The United Methodist Church reaffirmed its stance that homosexuality is incompatible with Christian teaching at its quadrennial General Conference in May. But the margin of the vote to retain the 20-year-old position, 710 to 238, was about 5% smaller than the previous vote, taken in 1988.

The General Board of the National Council of Churches voted in November against giving observer status to the Universal Fellowship of Metropolitan Community Churches, a largely homosexual denomination. At the same time, the council decided to maintain contacts with the fellowship. About 12 of the council's 32 Protestant and orthodox members had threatened to leave if observer status was given.

The Permanent Judicial Commission of the Presbyterian Church (U.S.A.) ruled against the appointment of a practicing lesbian, the Rev. Jane Spahr, as copastor of a congregation in Rochester, NY, in early November. In so doing, it cited a 1978 statement by the denomination's General Assembly that barred "unrepentant homosexuals" from ordination.

The Rev. Maria Jepsen of Hamburg, Germany, made history in April when she became the first woman ever to be elected a Lutheran bishop. Two months later, the Rev. April Ulring Larson became the first woman to attain that distinction in the United States. Larson was chosen to head the La Crosse (WI) Area Synod of the Evangelical Lutheran Church in America.

The General Synod of the Church of England approved the ordination of women to the priesthood in November following years of bitter debate. The measure received the required two-third majorities in each of the synod's three houses—bishops, clergy, and laity. Earlier in 1992, women priests were ordained by Anglican bodies in Australia and southern Africa.

One setback for women clergy came in the Christian Reformed Church, which voted in June against giving final approval to a 1990 resolution to open the ordained ministry to women. The issue severely had divided the 225,000-member denomination, with people on both sides quoting the Bible to support their positions. The 1992 synod said women should be allowed to preach, teach, and provide pastoral care without being ordained.

Conventions. Another conflict-ridden body, the Lutheran Church-Missouri Synod, chose a new president and ended a bitter dispute over the leadership of one of its seminaries at its triennial convention in Pittsburgh in July. The Rev. Alvin Barry, president of the Synod's Iowa District East, defeated 11-year incumbent Ralph A. Bohlmann to win the presidency of the 2.6-million-member denomination. Many of Barry's supporters had faulted Bohlmann for taking sides with opponents of the Rev. Robert Preus, who was "honorably retired" from the presidency of the synod's Concordia Seminary in Fort Wayne, IN, against his will in 1989. The synod's highest court ruled that Preus had been removed improperly from both the seminary presidency and the church's clergy roster, but the seminary regents defied the rulings. The convention resolved the dispute by restoring Preus to the presidency of the seminary until May 1993 or until a successor was chosen, whichever happened first.

The Presbyterian Church (U.S.A.), whose 1991 General Assembly had a divisive debate on human sexuality, had a relatively quieter meeting in 1992. Representatives replaced a strongly worded abortion-rights position adopted in 1983 with a statement that views abortion as an "option of last resort" and stresses that the denomination does not advocate the procedure. The biggest surprise at the Presbyterian meeting came when the Rev. W. Clark Chamberlain III of Houston was chosen for stated clerk, the denomination's highest

Photographer, Peter Williams/© Courtesy, World Council of Churches

Konrad Raiser, 54, an ordained Lutheran pastor and professor of systematic theology and ecumenics in the Protestant theological faculty of Ruhr University in Bochum, Germany, was chosen general secretary of the World Council of churches in August 1992. He would take office in January.

elected position, and then resigned less than a day later. He explained that he turned down the post because he was about to be charged with sexual misconduct. A church committee cleared him of the charges in mid-September. After Chamberlain resigned, delegates took another vote and reinstated the Rev. James Andrews, who earlier was ousted from the post.

The Rev. Ed Young, pastor of the 18,000-member Second Baptist Church of Houston, was elected president of the Southern Baptist Convention in June, defeating two other fundamentalists. Moderates in the denomination elected the Rev. Cecil Sherman to head their Cooperative Baptist Fellowship in Atlanta.

DARRELL J. TURNER

Roman Catholicism

Pope John Paul II underwent four-hour colon surgery to remove a moderate-sized tumor July 15, 1992, at Rome's Gemelli Polyclinic. Doctors said they caught the tumor before it turned cancerous. After a 17-day hospital stay, the 72-year-old pope's long-term prospects were declared "absolutely good."

Concerns about the pope's health forced Vatican planners to drop Mexico, Jamaica, and Nicaragua from a trip to Latin America marking the 500th anniversary of Christianity in the Americas. The only stop left on the itinerary

Roman Catholic clergymen peruse the new universal catechism which was issued in 1992. The catechism not only reinstates traditional Catholic beliefs but also identifies a list of sins associated with today's society, including tax evasion, drug abuse, and damaging the environment. The work was drafted in the French language and 1,000 copies went on sale in Paris in November. The English-language edition was to be released in the spring of 1993.

© Cham/Sipa

was the Dominican Republic, the site of Christopher Columbus' landing in the New World. The Vatican published two volumes of papal documents on the good and bad of Catholicism's arrival in the Americas. The documents revealed an emphasis on evangelization and attempts by popes to separate church activity from the colonial policies of Spain and Portugal, including strong papal condemnations of slavery and a defense of Native Americans as human beings entitled to equal rights, especially after conversion—a view questioned in Europe at the time.

In 1992 the pope also traveled to Senegal, Gambia, and Guinea in February and to Angola and São Tomé in June. By late 1992 the pontiff had made 56 trips outside Italy during his 14-year pontificate.

A New Catechism. After six years of preparation, the Vatican released a new universal catechism in November. Aimed at promoting interculturation—the effort to announce the gospel through local cultures—the 580-page document reflects the teaching of the Second Vatican Council and presents the Christian message about sin in modern language. Drunken driving, drug dealing, tax evasion, wasting resources, excessive spending, and embezzling all are on the Catholic Church's updated list of immoral acts.

Homosexual and Women's Issues. Gay groups reacted angrily to a Vatican document asking U.S. bishops to oppose laws intended to protect homosexuals if the laws also promote acceptance of homosexual conduct. The document argued that "there are areas in which it is not unjust discrimination to take sexual orientation into account" in civil laws and policies. These included adoption or foster care, employment of teachers and athletic coaches, and in military recruitment. Cincinnati Archbishop Daniel Pilarczyk, president of the U.S. bishops, said the document "rightly warns against legislation designed more to legitimate homosexual behavior than to secure basic civil rights." However, he added that U.S. bishops "will continue to look for ways in which those

people who have a homosexual orientation will not suffer unjust discrimination."

Ending nine years of work, the U.S. bishops defeated a controversial pastoral letter on women's concerns at their annual meeting in November but then voted to send the document to their executive committee for further action. It was the first time in history the bishops defeated a pastoral letter proposed for a final vote. The final draft of the pastoral condemned sexism. It also vigorously defended the church position that it cannot ordain women priests. Several U.S. bishops openly said they were not satisfied with the Roman Catholic rationale for barring women from the priesthood. A Gallup poll showed that two thirds of U.S. Catholics think women should be ordained priests and nearly three fourths favor expanding the priesthood to include married priests.

The Vatican called the Church of England's decision to ordain women to the priesthood a "new and grave obstacle" to unity between the churches but Catholic and Anglican leaders vowed to continue talks.

The Clergy and Sexual Abuse. With many dioceses reporting payment of millions of dollars to victims of sex abuse by former members of the clergy, U.S. bishops discussed pedophilia at their annual meeting for the fifth time in recent years. Archbishop Pilarczyk said "the protection of the child is and will continue to be our first concern." The bishops also met with experts to discuss pastoral, canonical, and legal aspects of child sex abuse by priests.

Statistics. Vatican statistics showed the first annual increase in the number of priests under Pope John Paul II. The 403,173 priests recorded showed an increase of 1,694 over the previous year. Also, the number of seminarians was up 13% over the previous five years. The biggest gains were in Africa and Asia.

The world's total Catholic population was 928.5 million, nearly 18% of the world's population. Some 44 million students were educated in 160,000 Catholic schools worldwide.

DANIEL MEDINGER
Editor, "The Catholic Review," Baltimore

RETAILING

Conservatism ruled in U.S. retailing circles in 1992 as buyers searched for value.

Retail Sales. General-merchandise sales were better than in 1991 (when sales rose only 0.76%, the flattest rate in 30 years) but remained sluggish, rising at an annual rate of only about 4% during the first half of 1992. A slightly improved rate of 5.5% to 6% was expected for the rest of the year.

Although some well-known names struggled to stay alive, strong increases were reported at other retailers. August sales at J. C. Penney, for example, were 12.4% higher than in August 1991, and Wal-Mart Stores had a 10% increase in sales over the same period of time. Christmastime was a roller-coaster season for many retailers as sales started strong, dropped off, and skyrocketed as the holiday neared. Initial estimates for the season indicated a 5% increase in sales compared with 1991. Christmastime sales exceeded expectations at several large department stores.

Bankruptcies. High debt continued to be a problem, with a number of retailers choosing to close their doors or reorganize under court protection. In January the New York-based department store R. H. Macy & Company, struggling under about $3.6 billion of debt, filed Chapter 11 bankruptcy, a form of bankruptcy that puts creditors on hold while executives draw up a plan to better balance cash flow and costs. Sales dropped during the year, and by September, Macy acknowledged problems far beyond its debt and offered a preliminary plan to its creditors that addressed the way the company merchandised and marketed itself. One strategy prescribed by the company was a renewed dedication to the moderate costumer base that it had ignored while pursuing more-affluent shoppers.

Other 1992 casualties included Seaman's, the largest furniture retailer in the Northeast, and the McCrory Corporation, one of the nation's largest operators of dime stores. Both filed for Chapter 11 protection. Zale, the Dallas-based jewelry retailer, closed 400 of its stores; Hartmarx consolidated its specialty and discount stores; and Alexander's, a New York department-store chain, closed its 11 stores.

Changing Times. In an effort to survive, many retailers reined in expanded operations. Sears, Roebuck & Co. announced in September that it was returning to its original retailing focus, putting its securities business, Discover credit card, real-estate operations, and up to 20% of its Allstate Insurance subsidiary up for sale. The debt associated with these acquisitions hindered Sears' ability to overhaul its catalogue and department-store business.

With department-store sales stagnating, Seattle-based Nordstrom Inc. also moved into off-price stores—stores selling brand-name

---

The Legacy of Samuel M. Walton

Samuel Moore Walton died at the age of 74 on April 5, 1992, 30 years after he set in motion a merchandising strategy that would change forever the face of small-town America. Walton, founder of Wal-Mart Stores Inc., and the most successful merchant of his time, long had struggled against two types of cancer. Only one month earlier, President George Bush had awarded Walton the Presidential Medal of Freedom for his service to the nation.

Beginning with the 1962 opening of that first Wal-Mart Discount City in Rogers, AR, and continuing into 1992, the Walton strategy has been simple: Keep prices low, put the customer first, and listen to everyone's ideas. The pricing concept, in particular, may not have been new—K Mart and Sears also had tried it—but Walton found growth in places others passed by—small towns and cities.

Wal-Mart today is the largest U.S. retailer and one of the nation's biggest companies of any sort with 425,000 employees and projected sales for 1992 of $54 billion. By the end of the third quarter of 1992, there were 1,804 Wal-Mart Stores in 44 states as well as more than 200 Sam's Clubs (wholesale outlets) and four Hypermarts—large grocery stores. Growth plans called for another 160 stores in each of the next several years and a major expansion into Mexico.

Scouting out new real estate in airplanes he frequently piloted himself, Walton found locations for new stores on the fringes of town and then waited for the town to come to him. Downtown retailers found it hard to compete with his prices and service. Across the South and Midwest—prime Wal-Mart territory—many a downtown store now is empty, its owners resentful.

Stockholders, meanwhile, have made Wal-Mart one of the most sought-after companies on Wall Street. From 1981 to 1991, Wal-Mart shares produced an average yearly return of 46.8%, meaning that a $3,000 investment in Wal-Mart stock in January 1981 would have been worth about $170,000 at the time of Walton's death. Not just outside investors got wealthy. The Walton family controls 39% of the common stock and employees have benefited through profit-sharing plans.

Following Sam Walton's death, his oldest son, S. Robson Walton, became the company's chairman. He planned no major changes but was opting instead to leave untouched the successful philosophy of encouraging innovation and risk-taking by managers and employees.

KRISTI VAUGHAN

The Franchising Trend

Franchising, a method of distributing products or services, has undergone a steady increase in recent years. According to an industry survey, franchising companies and their franchisees accounted for more than $757.8 billion in the sale of retail goods and services in 1991, with a new franchise opening every 16 minutes. At least two levels of people are involved in the franchise system—the franchisor, who lends his trademark or trade name; and the franchisee, who pays a royalty and often an initial fee for the right to do business under the franchisor's name and system. Technically, the contract binding the two parties is the franchise, but the term often is used to mean the actual business that the franchisee buys from the franchisor.

The majority of franchise sales are generated by product and trade-name franchise chains—e.g., automobile and truck dealerships, gasoline service stations, and soft-drink bottlers. However, the fastest-growing segment in franchising is the "business-format" franchise—where the franchisor prescribes for the franchisee a complete plan, or format, for managing and operating his or her establishment. The plan provides step-by-step procedures for every aspect of the business and provides a complete matrix for management decisions confronted by the franchisee.

Growth. As the U.S. economy becomes more service-oriented, as more women enter the workplace, and as a larger percentage of the population grows older, growth areas in franchising are responding to these demographic changes. The industry categories that were expected to continue to experience rapid growth for the 1990s were service-related fields such as maid services, home repair and remodeling, carpet cleaning, household furnishings, and various other maintenance and cleaning services; all business-support services, including accounting, mail processing, advertising services, package wrapping and shipping, and personnel services; automotive repairs and services, such as quick lube and tune-up; and such areas as weight-control centers, hair-styling salons, temporary-employment services, printing and copying services, medical centers, and computers.

As an economic and social force, franchises—with their trademarks, systematic business formats, and global marketing power—will help make the world an even smaller place. Many new types of franchised businesses will join the ranks of the widely recognized fast-food restaurants, hotels, and rental-car agencies that rose to dominance in the 1970s and 1980s.

Two major factors account for the rapid growth and success of franchising—the quest for opportunity and the desire for security. Franchised businesses offer both opportunity and security for the entrepreneur who develops the franchise system, for the business owners and investors who "buy into" the system, and for the consumers who shop for familiar quality products and services. For the entrepreneur, the franchising method provides the opportunity to develop a business at a much more rapid pace than otherwise might be possible with one person's limited capital. And it provides the entrepreneur with the security of sharing with many individual franchise-business owners a vested interest in the success of the business. The individual franchise investor or owner has the unique opportunity to be in business *for* himself but not *by* himself. Franchises provide the business owner with the security of a proven, systematic way of operating the business and the expertise and marketing clout of the franchise company.

For job seekers, the explosive growth of new franchised businesses and new companies embarking on franchising has added hundreds of thousands of new jobs to the U.S. work force. By the early 1990s, franchising was employing 7.2 million people in more than 60 industries, and more than 100,000 new jobs were being created by franchises annually. By the turn of the century, more than 10 million people will work in franchised businesses in the United States.

MICHAEL W. TIERNEY

---

merchandise at discounts of up to 75%. Liz Claiborne Inc. joined the discount movement when it bought Russ Togs.

Expansion and Recovery. All was not bleak, however. Privately owned Saks Fifth Avenue, which reportedly suffered big losses in 1991, received a $300 million equity infusion and announced plans to open several new stores and renovate older locations. Massachusetts-based Bradlees Inc. and K Mart planned to expand, and Federated Department Stores Inc.

emerged from two years of Chapter 11 protection.

Groceries. Technology continued to change supermarket shopping. The Turner Broadcasting System Inc. created the Checkout Channel, a network of supermarket television monitors that display news, weather, and advertising at the checkout counter. The venture, called place-based or out-of-home media, was designed to reach people as they shop.

KRISTI VAUGHAN

RHODE ISLAND

The year began with vivid reminders of the state's traumatic year of 1991. Unpaid depositors in credit unions that had been closed the previous January packed the galleries of the House and Senate on January 7, the first day of the new session.

Lingering Recession. Rhode Island continued in the throes of the worst recession since the 1930s. Unemployment was at 8% in January, would rise to nearly 10% by June, and decline to between 8% and 9% in the fall. Defense cutbacks threatened the state's largest employer, submarine builder Electric Boat, located in Groton, CT, but cancellation of the "Seawolf" project was averted by a midyear compromise. The 4,000 layoffs threatened in February became only 2,188 by June, with no more planned.

All economic indices showed continuing deep recession with little sign of improvement. Rhode Island had the sixth-highest bankruptcy rate and the highest level of consumer-loan delinquencies in the United States as of June. Its two-year loss of jobs, 8.9%, was the worst of any of the hard-hit New England states, and compared with a 2.2% loss in the nation. Midyear figures showed a flat income-growth rate. The housing market improved some but median prices were at a five-year low.

Confronting the Damage. This grim picture faced the General Assembly when it convened. Legislation was introduced early to pay the remaining credit-union depositors 90% of their deposits by June 30, and the remaining 10% over 20 years. This bill, signed by Gov. Bruce Sundlun on March 11, together with a deal for Northeast Savings Bank of Hartford, CT, to take over seven of the still-closed credit unions in May, would end most of the depositors' pain. State taxpayers, however, would be repaying the money required for the settlement—up to $36 million per year for 30 years, according to one study. By fall polls found the credit-union problem had ceased to be a political issue, reducing a major threat to Governor Sundlun's reelection bid.

Legislative Retrenchment. The 1992 session was the longest since 1971, and difficult. The governor's budget proposed a reduction in total spending of $318 million from the current year, asked no income-tax increase, but included a package of other needed revenue hikes. It finally was passed two weeks into the fiscal year after adjustments in some cuts and tax proposals, and insertion of an income surcharge on the wealthy. Other major legislation included curbs on abuses in the state-pension system, a new legislative-districting plan, major overhaul of the state's expensive worker-compensation system, and ethics legislation to tighten campaign-finance regulation and bar former legislators from state jobs for one year.

The Assembly also proposed a constitutional amendment providing for four-year terms for the governor and other state officers with a recall and two-term limit. It passed comfortably in November, as did an amendment for a budget-reserve fund.

Fall Elections. The state voted for Democratic presidential candidate Bill Clinton and easily reelected Governor Sundlun, a Democrat, over a weak opponent. State Rep. Robert Weygand, also a Democrat, was elected lieutenant governor. Republican newcomer Nancy Mayer won the vacated general treasurership, while Republicans Jeffrey Pine and Barbara M. Leonard ousted Democrats James E. O'Neil and Kathleen S. Connell from the offices of attorney general and secretary of state. The General Assembly, battered by criticism, would include an unprecedented one third new members come January 1993.

ELMER E. CORNWELL, JR., *Brown University*

RHODE ISLAND • Information Highlights

Area: 1,212 sq mi (3 140 km²).
Population (July 1, 1991 est.): 1,004,000.
Chief Cities (1990 census): Providence, the capital, 160,728; Warwick, 85,427.
Government (1992): *Chief Officers*—governor, Bruce G. Sundlun (D); lt. gov., Roger N. Begin (D). *General Assembly*—Senate, 50 members; House of Representatives, 100 members.
State Finances (fiscal year 1991): *Revenue,* $3,305,000,000; *expenditure,* $3,465,000,000.
Personal Income (1991): $19,291,000,000; per capita, $19,207.
Labor Force (June 1992): *Civilian labor force,* 520,200; *unemployed,* 50,700 (9.8% of total force).
Education: *Enrollment* (fall 1990)—public elementary schools, 101,797; public secondary, 37,016; colleges and universities, 78,273. *Public school expenditures* (1990), $828,109,000.

ROMANIA

Romania began 1992 under a new constitution, approved by national referendum in early December 1991. The year was marked by continued conflict over the pace of economic change, which led to a split in the ruling National Salvation Front (NSF). The reelection of President Ion Iliescu in October strengthened those who favored putting a brake on market-oriented reforms.

Political Affairs. In mid-January the Romanian Senate established a special commission of inquiry to investigate alleged corruption and mismanagement in the government of former Prime Minister Petre Roman, who was forced out of office in September 1991. Critics claimed the move was a politically motivated effort by followers of President Iliescu to discredit Roman. Roman and Iliescu represented opposing factions in the NSF, Roman being the party's leader and Iliescu being the former party leader.

ROMANIA • Information Highlights

Official Name: Romania.
Location: Southeastern Europe.
Area: 91,699 sq mi (237 500 km²).
Population (mid-1992 est.): 22,400,000.
Chief Cities (Dec. 31, 1989 est.): Bucharest, the capital, 2,325,037; Braçsov, 352,260; Constanta, 312,504.
Government: *Head of state,* Ion Iliescu, president (took office December 1989). *Head of government,* Nicolae Vacaroiu, prime minister (named Nov. 4, 1992). *Legislature* (unicameral)—Grand National Assembly.
Monetary Unit: Leu (383.000 lei equal U.S.$1, August 1992).
Gross National Product (1990 est. U.S.$): $69,900,-000,000.
Foreign Trade (1991 U.S.$): *Imports,* $5,600,000,-000; *exports,* $4,124,000,000.

NSF infighting intensified following a dramatic loss of support in large urban areas in the mayoral contests in early February. In March, when the party held its third national convention in Bucharest, tensions ran high between Roman's reformist wing and the conservatives loyal to Iliescu. On the last day of the convention, Roman successfully blocked an attempt to restore the NSF leadership to Iliescu, prompting a walkout by conservatives. Roman then was reelected by 64% of the remaining delegates, and was awarded the new title of NSF president. Iliescu's supporters subsequently seceded and formed a new party, the Democratic National Salvation Front (DNSF).

In late April, 21 former Communist officials previously acquitted by military courts were found guilty of "aggravated murder" by the Supreme Court in connection with their attempts to suppress the 1989 revolt that unseated Romanian dictator Nicolae Ceauşescu. They were sentenced to lengthy prison terms. One of those convicted, former Foreign Minister Ion Totu, committed suicide following the sentencing.

Also in April former King Michael, an exile for 45 years, visited the country to observe Orthodox Easter. The former king, granted a four-day visa by Romanian authorities under the name Michael von Hohenzollern, was cheered by tens of thousands of royalist supporters in the streets of Bucharest.

President Iliescu won reelection in a runoff against Democratic Convention candidate Emil Constantinescu, a dean at Bucharest University, on October 11. Iliescu received nearly 61% of the vote, with more than 73% of the nation's 16.5 million eligible voters casting ballots. Constantinescu did well in urban areas, but was unable to counter Iliescu's support in the politically conservative rural areas and towns. However, support for Iliescu fell far short of the 85% he won in the presidential election of 1990, and showed that the opposition was no longer an unorganized minority. In parliamentary elections held on September 27,

Iliescu's DNSF had won 28% of the seats, the Democratic Convention 20%, and the NSF only 10%.

Following the election, the president postponed a planned elimination of some $100 million in state subsidies and pledged to follow a more leisurely pace in the transition to capitalism. In November, Nicolae Vacaroiu, an economist who supported Iliescu's policy, was appointed prime minister.

Economic Affairs. Unemployment continued to grow throughout the year, affecting about 9% of the work force in November. The inflation rate was a major problem. It was in an effort to curb the mounting increase in the cost of living (prices rose by 12% in the month of July alone) that President Iliescu slowed the phasing out of state subsidies in October. Romania also faced a massive decline in tourism, due mainly to the rising price of hotel accommodations.

Romania's foreign debt increased by $916 million (to $3.2 billion) in the first six months of 1992. In June the International Monetary Fund (IMF) approved a loan of $108 million to cover excess costs of 1991 oil imports due to decreased flow of Soviet oil and the Persian Gulf war. The IMF also approved a standby credit of $440 million for Romania's economic-reform program. Also in June, the World Bank approved a $100 million loan for the support of private farms and rural enterprises and a $400 million loan for structural adjustments to the economic-reform program.

In May the Romanian National Bank began a policy of allowing Romanian companies to hold hard-currency accounts, rather than requiring them to convert all currency to lei, in the hope of encouraging exports and speeding reform. In June new foreign-exchange rules were introduced to liberalize the leu through bank auctions, with the intention of equating the official exchange rate and that of licensed foreign offices.

By mid-June 152 companies from 106 countries were participating in the Romanian economy. European Community (EC) countries accounted for 87% of foreign investment in the first half of 1992 (up from 5% in 1991). However, most of the investments were quite small, averaging $1,500. Remaining convertibility restrictions on the leu were seen as the greatest obstacles for foreign investors.

A conflict arose concerning the status of hundreds of thousands of homes confiscated by the former Communist regime. The present tenants wished to buy the houses from the government, while the former owners wanted ownership restored and the present tenants to pay them rent. In mid-July the Senate passed a bill suspending all lawsuits on the matter until legislative action could be taken.

Foreign Affairs. The conflict in neighboring Moldova, where a Romanian-speaking majority was at war with a Russian-Ukrainian minority, dominated Romania's diplomatic relations in 1992. Moldova, formerly the Soviet republic of Moldavia, became independent in 1991; this immediately raised the possibility of its reunion with Romania, which had controlled most of the region prior to World War II. Officially, however, the Romanian government supported Moldova's independence while objecting to Russian interference in its civil war. In May, President Iliescu paid an extremely low-profile visit to Moldova, and in October, Romania and Moldova set up a joint committee to coordinate relations between their parliaments.

VLADIMIR TISMANEANU
Foreign Policy Research Institute

RWANDA

Rwanda's President Juvénal Habyarimana, pressured by the foreign governments which provide much of the financial support for the African nation's shattered economy, agreed in July 1992 to peace talks with representatives of the Tutsi-dominated rebel Rwandan Patriotic Front (RPF). These meetings resulted in an agreement that promised an end to the civil war that had devastated northern Rwanda.

During Belgian hegemony the Tutsi were recognized as the ruling aristocracy. Hutu political leaders even before independence deposed the Tutsi king, and in the ensuing violence approximately 20,000 Tutsi were killed. An additional 130,000 were driven into exile, many settling along the border in Uganda. This orgy of killing was duplicated a decade later in 1973, driving more from the country. An estimated 500,000 Tutsi today live in exile. The Tutsi who remained were brutalized by the police and army. Soon after independence the government was dominated by one party, the Republican Movement for Democracy and Development (MRND), led by Grégoire Kayibanda. In 1973, Habyarimana led a coup that established an even more dictatorial regime. Until 1990 no other political party was allowed and all opponents were kept in line by a 6,000-member army.

The civil war began in October 1990 when RPF elements attacked from Uganda. Many were deserters from the Ugandan army and their modern weapons assured local success against the ill-trained national army. Habyarimana's regime soon was bolstered by the arrival of Zairian, Belgian, and French troops relieving Rwandan forces near the capital, Kigali. A small contingent of French soldiers remained. The Rwandan army expanded sixfold since 1990 to counter the insurgents who made progress in the north. Mass arrests were made and violence against Tutsi escalated. More than 300 civilians were slain at Kibirira and even more at Bugogwe village. Pressure from France and the United States forced the government and the RPF in March 1991 to agree to a cease-fire. Neither side adhered to this agreement.

The more definitive agreement of July 1992 also did not halt endemic violence. Incongruously, the war hastened the pace of political reform. Habyarimana, threatened by a failing economy and growing criticism even from Hutu, promised a return to democracy. A new constitution was adopted and political parties other than the MRND were allowed. In April a transitional cabinet was formed; 11 of the 20 ministers were members from the four opposition parties, although the MRND still held the key positions. Political competition introduced another cause for violence and this spread even to Kigali, where a number of deadly clashes occurred in the wake of the government reorganization.

HARRY A. GAILEY
San Jose State University

SASKATCHEWAN

An austerity budget, a campaign over nuclear power, a controversial murder case, and a sex scandal dominated news in Saskatchewan during 1992. In addition, more than 55% of the province's voters cast "no" ballots in the October national referendum on the Charlottetown Accord, a plan on constitutional reform. Former Premier Grant Devine resigned in November as leader of the Progressive Conservative (PC) Party, which was expected to pick a new leader in 1993.

The Budget. Following its return to power in late 1991, the socialist New Democratic Party (NDP) presented its first budget in May. The C$5 billion budget contained C$344 million in spending cuts and C$312 million in increases in taxes or user fees. New taxes included a 1% hike, to 8%, in the provincial sales tax and a 10% surtax, and made residents the highest personal provincial taxpayers in Canada. Cuts included the abolition of 500 civil-service jobs and C$10 million less for physicians' fees. Even with the cuts, the province expected to

---

RWANDA • Information Highlights

Official Name: Republic of Rwanda.
Location: East Africa.
Area: 10,170 sq mi (26 340 km²).
Population (mid-1992 est.): 42,500,000.
Chief City: Kigali, the capital.
Government: *Head of government,* Juvénal Habyarimana, Maj. Gen. (took power 1973). *Legislature* (unicameral)—National Development Council.
Monetary Unit: Rwandan franc (139.780 francs equal U.S.$1, July 1992).
Gross Domestic Product (1989 est. U.S.$): $2,200,-000,000.
Foreign Trade (1989 est. U.S.$): *Imports,* $293,000,000; *exports,* $117,000,000.

SASKATCHEWAN · Information Highlights

Area: 251,865 sq mi (652 330 km²).
Population (September 1992): 994,200.
Chief Cities (1986 census): Regina, the capital,
175,064; Saskatoon, 177,641; Moose Jaw, 35,073.
Government (1992): *Chief Officers*—lt. gov., F. W.
Johnson; premier, Roy Romanow (New Demo-
crat). *Legislature*—Legislative Assembly, 64
members.
Provincial Finances (1992–93 fiscal year budget):
Revenues, $4,483,000,000; *expenditures,*
$5,000,000,000.
Personal Income (average weekly earnings, July
1992): $472.10.
Labor Force (September 1992): *Employed* workers,
15 years of age and over, 436,000; *Unemployed,*
8.4%.
Education (1992–93): *Enrollment*—elementary and
secondary schools, 207,500 pupils; postsecondary—universities, 23,100; community colleges,
3,500.
(All monetary figures are in Canadian dollars.)

run a C$517 million deficit in 1992–93. Sas-
katchewan continued to fund health care from
general revenues and was the only province
that did not require its residents to pay health-
care-insurance premiums.

Finance. In an effort to ease the C$14 billion
accumulated debt, Finance Minister Ed Tchor-
zewski unveiled a provincial savings-bond plan
for financing its deficit and suggested that it
would be a patriotic deed for residents to buy
provincial savings bonds rather than invest in
the rest of Canada, the United States, or Europe. In 1992–93 alone, Saskatchewan would
have to borrow C$1.7 billion, including rolling
over old debt and the 1992–93 deficit of C$571
million.

Nuclear Power. The NDP government vetoed an agreement signed by the previous PC
government that could have seen the construction of a C$1 billion Candu-3 nuclear reactor
and made the province the manufacturing base
for several more such reactors to be sold overseas. Proponents of the project claimed that
Saskatchewan had thrown away its best chance
in decades for industrial development.

Justice. The Supreme Court of Canada in
April freed David Milgaard, age 39, after he
had spent 23 years in prison for a murder he
always claimed he did not commit. Milgaard
was found guilty in 1970 of the 1969 slaying of
Saskatoon nurse Gail Miller. Milgaard, his
mother, and friends had campaigned continu-
ously to prove his innocence. The Supreme
Court actually ordered a new trial for Milgaard,
but Saskatchewan Justice Minister Robert
Mitchell declined to mount it, and Milgaard
was freed from a Manitoba prison. Milgaard's
mother claimed, however, that she had evidence that as long ago as 1971, Premier Roy
Romanow, then justice minister, and others
knew there were doubts about her son's guilt
but did nothing.

Scandals. An investigation into an unli-
censed day-care center in Martensville, a small
community just outside Saskatoon, resulted in
more than 120 charges brought against nine individuals relating to sexual abuse against some
30 children from the ages of 2 to 12. Some of
the accused were current and former police officers. The case was caught up in legal squabbles and issues as the year closed.

In Regina the Rev. Lucien Larre, a Roman
Catholic priest once hailed as the "saint of Saskatchewan," was found guilty on two charges
of abusing youngsters in his care.

PAUL JACKSON, *"Saskatoon Star-Phoenix"*

SAUDI ARABIA

The military, political, and economic ramifications of the 1991 Persian Gulf war continued to dominate Saudi Arabia during 1992.

International Relations and the Military.
While Iraq had been defeated in the war, Saudi
Arabia feared that if President Saddam Hussein
persisted in power he could pose a threat to the
kingdom's security. As a result, Saudi Arabia
sought to increase its own military strength,
work closely with the United States and Middle
Eastern allies, decrease tensions in other parts
of the region, and encourage opponents of Hussein to overthrow him.

The United States and Saudi Arabia had
planned on an arms deal in November 1991, but
when 67 U.S. senators opposed the Saudi purchase of defensive weapons systems, U.S.
President George Bush had to delay the sale.
New attempts were made on three occasions in
1992, but each time they met with opposition
from Congressional leaders, who feared Israel
would lose some of its military superiority
should such a sale take place. Finally on Sept.
11, 1992, Saudi Arabia arranged to obtain from
the United States a weapons and training package costing about $9 billion; at the same time
U.S. assistance was offered to Israel.

The United States wanted to position large
quantities of weapons in Saudi Arabia in the
event of another war, but Saudi opinion opposed this. Instead, the two sides agreed on
May 31 to expand the 1977 Military Training
Mission Treaty to permit closer military cooperation. On August 27, Britain, France, and the
United States declared a "no-fly zone" in
southern Iraq to stop Iraqi planes from destroying Shiite opponents. Many of the U.S. airplanes used were based in Saudi Arabia while
others flew off U.S. war vessels in the Gulf.

Saudi Arabia attended the Arab-Israel
peace talks held in Moscow in January, thereby
publicly participating in negotiations with Israel. The Saudi government assisted the nearly
bankrupt Russian Republic in paying for the
talks. King Fahd also encouraged Syria and the
Palestinian Arabs toward compromise with Israel in the bilateral series of talks held in Washington, DC. Although on Dec. 16, 1991, Saudi

Arabia had voted to maintain the 1975 UN General Assembly resolution that proclaimed Zionism to be a form of racism, the Saudis still welcomed an American Jewish Congress delegation January 19–22 and informed them that Saudi Arabia now recognized Israel's right to exist.

Iraqis opposing Saddam Hussein met in Riyadh February 24, and the Iraqi government on May 6 charged that Saudi Arabia brought smuggled counterfeit Iraqi money into Iraq to help overthrow Hussein. Nearly 33,000 Iraqi refugees remained in Saudi camps in 1992 despite the strong desire of many to find another country that would receive them.

Saudi Arabia sought closer cooperation against Iraq from members of the Gulf Cooperation Council, but this became more difficult following a Saudi border clash with Qatar on September 30 in which at least two persons were killed. The Saudi ambassador to Yemen, which had opposed Saudi policy during the Gulf war, was held briefly for ransom.

Political Changes. Saudi monarchs had promised political reforms for many years, but it was only after the Persian Gulf war that they became a reality. King Fahd announced March 1 the most far-reaching political changes in the history of modern Saudi Arabia. In three royal decrees that collectively formed a kind of constitution—the first ever for the kingdom—Fahd changed the system of choosing the heir to the throne, established a Consultative Council to advise the government, and guaranteed some civil liberties to his subjects. Future kings were to be chosen from the grandsons and not just the sons of former King Abd al-Aziz, and kings could remove as well as choose the crown prince (heir apparent). The 61-member national Consultative Council was to be appointed by the king, who also permanently would hold the post of prime minister. The powers of the Consultative Council would include reviewing "laws, agreements, alliances, international accords and concessions"; proposing new laws to the cabinet; questioning any official; and subpoenaing documents. Provincial ten-member Consultative Councils with more limited

powers also would be established. New limits were placed on governmental power; for instance, entering a private residence or arresting someone would be permitted only with due cause. The right to privacy in phone calls and postal service also was to be protected.

Despite these changes, the royal government retained all real power. King Fahd declared on March 29 that since "Islam is our social and political law," Saudi Arabia would not adopt a democratic system and competitive elections.

Economy and Oil. As the price of oil fell on the world market from October 1991 to January 1992, Saudi Oil Minister Hisham Nazer said that the kingdom wanted a new balance between supply and demand for oil. Nevertheless, the Saudi government for the moment opposed the reimposition of strict country-by-country oil quotas. Saudi oil production in late 1991 was about 8.5 million barrels per day, and Saudi Arabia at that time provided about 10% of all the oil used in the United States and one third of the oil coming from the Organization of Petroleum Exporting Countries (OPEC). Under Saudi leadership, OPEC in early 1992 did reimpose country quotas. Mild reductions were made in member oil quotas for production. On March 4, Kuwait and Saudi Arabia began anew production from the Neutral Zone oil fields between the two countries, which had been disrupted by the Persian Gulf war.

The role of oil in environmental pollution was a major topic for the 153 nations that met in June in Brazil. In cooperation with other oil-producing countries, Saudi Arabia secured the deletion from the Rio Declaration of passages urging less use of fossil fuels.

Saudi Arabia had not issued official budgets during the Persian Gulf war, but on January 2, King Fahd issued a budget calling for $48.1 billion in spending and a deficit of about $8 billion.

The worldwide scandal concerning the Bank of Credit and Commerce International (BCCI) affected Saudi Arabia as well. Khalid bin Mahfouz, head of the National Commercial Bank of Saudi Arabia, was indicted July 1 in New York for fraud and was assessed a fine of $170 million. The former head of the Saudi government's intelligence service, Kamal Adham, also was accused of extensive involvement with BCCI.

WILLIAM OCHSENWALD
*Virginia Polytechnic Institute
and State University*

SAUDI ARABIA · Information Highlights

Official Name: Kingdom of Saudi Arabia.
Location: Arabian peninsula in southwest Asia.
Area: 829,996 sq mi (2 149 690 km²).
Population (mid-1992 est.): 16,100,000.
Capital (1981 est.): Riyadh, 1,000,000.
Government: *Head of state and government,* Fahd bin 'Abd al-'Aziz Al Sa'ud, king and prime minister (acceded June 1982).
Monetary Unit: Riyal (3.7495 riyals equal U.S.$1, Oct.27, 1992).
Gross Domestic Product (1989 est. U.S.$): $79,000,-000,000.
Economic Index (1991): *Consumer Prices* (1980 = 100), all items, 100.1; food, 107.2.
Foreign Trade (1990 U.S.$): *Imports,* $24,069,-000,000; *exports,* $44,417,000,000.

SINGAPORE

In 1992, Singapore experienced another good year in terms of its economy, while maintaining a stable, if at times Orwellian, political environment. U.S. economist Lester Thurow predicted that in the coming century the small

Asian nation would be among the world's 20 richest economies. It was the first choice among international businessmen as a site for international corporate headquarters, and was the world's busiest container port. Singapore also was judged number 1 among the Southeast Asian countries in environmental management, according to a Business International study, and was lauded for its plan to create a model "green city" by the year 2000.

Domestic Politics. Social constraints were tightened in June when the government banned the sale and importation of chewing gum. But most citizens were relieved by the government's action to introduce a number of tax cuts affecting corporations, reservists, low-income families, and other groups. Greater diversity in the media was achieved with the launching of a second English-language newspaper operated by the government-sponsored National Trade Union Congress (NTUC). In April a 24-hour news channel began broadcasting and in June two pay-TV channels went on the air.

On the other hand, three reporters who reported the June gross-domestic-product (GDP) growth rate were detained and questioned under the Official Secrets Act. At year's end approximately 1,000 individuals were being detained under the country's Internal Security Act (ISA), which provides for detention without trial or charges being filed.

Politics was interjected into a taxpayer-funded housing-refurbishment scheme when Prime Minister Goh Chok Tong announced that in cases where there were competing constituencies, demonstrated electoral support for the ruling Peoples Action Party (PAP) would be the tiebreaker.

Defense. Singapore's defense industries were beginning to establish themselves outside of Southeast Asia. One local product, the thermal imager, was used extensively by allied troops against Iraq in the Persian Gulf war. In 1992, Singapore was the host of Asian Aerospace 92, one of the three largest and most important aerospace shows in the world. Deputy

© Reuters/Bettmann

Singapore's Prime Minister Goh Chok Tong accompanied U.S. President George Bush and Mrs. Bush on a tour of the city-state during Bush's Asian tour in January 1992.

Prime Minister Lee Hsien Loong announced that Singapore would build the Changi Aviation Industrial Complex in order to establish the country as a "one-stop" center for aerospace activities in the region. Aerospace industries should account for about S$2 billion (about $1.25 billion) by 1995. In January, Singapore and Malaysia carried out a cooperative air-defense exercise, Minor ADEX 92–1.

Economy. Singapore's economy flourished in 1992. The GDP grew by 5.0%, and the inflation rate was only 2.7%, down from 3.5% for 1991. The country's savings rate, 47% of GDP, is the highest in the world.

Singapore took a giant step in decreasing its oil dependence when a new natural-gas pipeline from Malaysia was opened in January. The pipeline will supply enough natural gas to produce about 700 megawatts of electricity, about 30% of the country's daily needs.

Foreign Relations. Also in January, Singapore was the site of the fourth summit meeting of the Association of Southeast Asian Nations (ASEAN), consisting of Brunei, Indonesia, Malaysia, the Philippines, Singapore, and Thailand. Accomplishments of the summit included the creation of an ASEAN Free Trade Area (AFTA) and a system of Common Effective Preferential Tariffs (CEPT).

U.S. President George Bush, visiting Singapore on January 4, announced that the United States would move a naval-logistics facility from the Philippines to Singapore.

PATRICK M. MAYERCHAK
Virginia Military Institute

SINGAPORE • Information Highlights

Official Name: Republic of Singapore.
Location: Southeast Asia.
Area: 244 sq mi (632.6 km²).
Population (mid-1992 est.): 2,800,000.
Capital: Singapore City.
Government: *Head of state,* Wee Kim Wee, president (took office September 1985). *Head of government,* Goh Chok Tong, prime minister (took office November 1990). *Legislature* (unicameral)—Parliament.
Monetary Unit: Singapore dollar (1.6385 S. dollars equal U.S. $1, Dec. 16, 1992).
Gross Domestic Product (1990 U.S.$): $34,600,-000,000.
Economic Index (1991): *Consumer Prices* (1980 = 100), all items, 129.3; food, 119.8.
Foreign Trade (1991 U.S.$): *Imports,* $66,108,-000,000; *exports,* $59,046,000,000.

In 1992 homeless people in Boston, MA, began writing and selling "Spare Change," a "journal of the street—by, of, and for the people." With homelessness continuing as a major problem, similar newspapers could be found in other urban areas.

SOCIAL WELFARE

The uninspiring state of the U.S. economy and its impact on the social well-being of Americans took center stage in the 1992 presidential-election campaign. The year also was marked by widespread social upheaval throughout the world brought on most significantly by drought, famine, and regional armed conflicts.

In the United States, the annual Census Bureau report on family income and poverty reported the highest number of Americans living below the poverty line since 1964. The report, released September 3, found that in 1991 some 35.7 million Americans—about 14.2% of the population—lived below the poverty line, which was defined as a total cash income of $13,924 for a family of four and $6,932 for a single person. For the second consecutive year the poverty rate rose by some 0.7%, and the number of those living in poverty increased by some 2.1 million. After increasing for seven consecutive years, real (after adjusting for inflation) per-capita income declined in 1991, the report found, to $14,617.

The report also estimated that real median household income dropped by nearly $1,100, a 5.1% decrease since 1989 when adjusted for inflation. The poverty rate among blacks was 32.7%; for Hispanics, 28.7%; for Asian Americans, 13.8%; for whites, 11.3%; for the elderly, 12.4%; and for children, 21.8%.

Measuring Poverty. Some observers, primarily conservatives, questioned the accuracy of the Census Bureau's annual poverty statistics, contending that they exaggerated poverty because they do not count noncash benefits such as food stamps, Medicaid, and housing assistance. The poverty statistics "systematically exaggerate the extent of income inequity and poverty by ignoring almost 75% of all government assistance to the poor," said Rep. Dick Armey (R-TX).

Nevertheless, other data released during 1992 seemed to buttress arguments that growing numbers of Americans were being affected adversely by the continuing recession. For example, the annual "Index of Social Health"—issued on October 5 by social scientists at Fordham University in New York and measuring 16 American social problems, including unemployment, poverty rates, homicides, and child abuse—reported that in 1990 overall social well-being was at its lowest point since the study began in 1970.

The U.S. Department of Agriculture reported in July that a record 25.8 million Americans—about 10% of the population—were receiving food stamps, an increase of some 7 million compared with 1989. Families and individuals are eligible to receive food stamps—a maximum of $370 per month for a family of four —if their net incomes fall below the poverty line and their liquid assets are under $2,000.

The national unemployment rate reached a yearly high of 7.7% in June before decreasing slightly during the rest of the year. For most of 1992, the U.S. Labor Department reported, nearly 10 million American adults were looking for work. A Census Bureau report, issued May 11, found that the proportion of Americans working at low-paying full-time jobs (those with wages below the official federal poverty line) increased from about 12% in 1979 to some 18% in 1990. (*See also* FEATURE ARTICLE/THE U.S. EMPLOYMENT SCENE.)

© Mario Ruiz/*Time* Magazine

Homeless advocate Richard Kreimer sued the Morristown, NJ, public library for evicting him. Although he reached a financial settlement in the case, a U.S. District Court in Newark ruled in favor of the library in an appeal.

The nonprofit Community Service Society of New York reported in June that, based on an analysis of 1991 Census Bureau data, more than 25% of New York City's residents in 1990 had incomes below the federal poverty line. Officials in New York announced in July that the number of the city's residents receiving welfare reached 1,005,210—a 22% increase compared with January 1990 and the largest number since New York City's fiscal crisis in the 1970s.

Poverty among blacks remained a significant problem in 1992. While the black middle and upper classes have grown in recent years, the proportion of black families living in poverty increased by 50% from 1967 to 1990, according to a report issued by the Census Bureau in September. The annual "State of Black America" report by the National Urban League, released in January 1992, contained statistics indicating that blacks trailed whites in every economic indicator of well-being. African Americans "were in a recession before this recession hit," Urban League President John Jacob said when the report was issued, "and now we are in a deep economic depression."

A report by the U.S. House of Representatives' Select Committee on Hunger, issued in September, estimated that hunger had grown by about 50% since the mid-1980s and that some 30 million Americans in 1992 were malnourished. "When we see increasing poverty and decreasing incomes, it's not at all surprising that hunger has increased," said J. Larry

Brown, director of Tufts University's Center on Hunger, Poverty, and Nutrition Policy.

Welfare Reform. In 1992 more Americans than ever before were receiving some form of government welfare. In midyear a record 4.8 million families, accounting for about 13.7 million people, for example, were collecting benefits under the federal government's main welfare program, Aid for Families with Dependent Children (AFDC). Welfare itself became a prominent issue in the 1992 presidential campaign. Both President George Bush and Arkansas Gov. Bill Clinton advanced proposals to change the nation's welfare system. President Bush called for giving states more incentives to experiment with programs that drastically would cut welfare rolls. Governor Clinton, who instituted a program in Arkansas that helped welfare parents (90% of whom were single mothers) find work and get off welfare, called for a $6 billion federal tax credit and a job-training program for welfare mothers.

Welfare reform also gained momentum on the state level. Many states—including California, Massachusetts, New Jersey, Oregon, and Wisconsin—considered sweeping proposals designed to encourage work and education and reduce welfare rolls. In New Jersey, Democratic Gov. Jim Florio signed a controversial bill in January that had been passed by the state legislature in 1991 barring automatic increases in aid to welfare mothers who had more children after joining the state- and federally-funded AFDC program. U.S. Secretary of Health and Human Services Louis W. Sullivan approved the change in July.

In 1988, Congress passed the Family Welfare Reform Act, a sweeping overhaul of the welfare system designed primarily to encourage welfare parents to get off welfare by requiring states to run education programs for those on welfare. The first report on the law's effect, released in April by the Manpower Demonstration Research Corporation, a New York-based nonprofit research group, looked at welfare recipients in six California counties. The report found that welfare parents who went through California's education program earned 17% more than those who did not, and those in the program received 5% less in welfare payments.

The Disabled. In 1990 the federal Americans With Disabilities Act for the first time prohibited private employers from denying jobs to the nation's physically and mentally disabled persons and gave protection to the disabled from discrimination in public accommodations, transportation, and telecommunications. The law set up a timetable for all businesses that deal with the public to make their facilities accessible to the disabled. The first major phases of the law went into effect on Jan. 26 and July 26, 1992.

The law's public-accommodations provisions for existing buildings and businesses with more than 25 employees—which require all commercial establishments to undertake "readily achievable reasonable accommodations" for the disabled—took effect on January 26. The law did not spell out specific changes, but typical alterations included grocery and other stores installing wider doors and lower sales counters to accommodate persons in wheelchairs, and putting Braille signs in elevators and restrooms for the blind.

Businesses with 25 or fewer employees and annual revenue of $1 million or more came under the law's public-accommodations provisions on July 26. In addition, on that date those businesses with 25 or more employees had to conform with the law's employment regulations, which mandated that employers not discriminate against qualified disabled persons in hiring, advancement, compensation, or training. The employment regulations were designed to bring millions of disabled Americans into the workplace; an estimated 70% of the nation's 14 million working-age disabled persons were unemployed.

Advocates for the disabled and many businesses praised the law, saying it gave much-needed legal protection to disabled persons without placing undue fiscal burdens on businesses. On the other hand, many businesses worried about the law's long-term fiscal and legal ramifications.

International Social Crises

While North America faced significant problems with poverty and unemployment, the situation there once again paled in comparison with the social conditions faced by hundreds of millions of people in Africa, Asia, Latin America, and even in Europe. Social upheaval was most widespread in Africa, where drought and civil war brought death and social disintegration in the sub-Saharan countries of Angola, Malawi, Mozambique, Swaziland, Zambia, and Zimbabwe, and in the nations of Ethiopia, Kenya, Somalia, and Sudan located on the Horn of Africa.

Africa. About 110 million people lived in the southern African countries that were being hit by what was believed to be the most severe drought in the region in the 20th century. "The UN estimates that 30 million of them will suffer in some way—18 million are at risk and could die if we don't intervene," Andrew Natsios of the U.S. Agency for International Development said in September.

Most of the world's attention focused on what relief officials termed 1992's most daunting worldwide humanitarian crisis—the disastrous famine in the East African nation of Somalia brought on by a drought and severely exacerbated by virtual anarchy caused by a civil war among warring Somali clan chiefs. The International Committee of the Red Cross

estimated in August that 2.5 million Somalis had been forced to flee and 2 million of the nation's 7 million people were at risk of starvation before the end of 1992. The Red Cross, mounting the largest humanitarian relief effort in its history, was joined by the United States, other countries, and the United Nations in an airlift of tons of food to Somalia. But, with no functioning national government, a large portion of the relief supplies was stolen by armed gangs before reaching the starving population.

In Sudan an intensification of a prolonged civil war between the nation's fundamentalist Islamic government and the rebellious Sudan People's Liberation Army forced the evacuation of more than 1 million people in the first six months of the year, according to the United Nations. That brought to 3 million the number of Sudanese, most of them from the southern part of the country, displaced by the civil war. As was the case in Somalia, the warring factions in Sudan deliberately kept relief supplies and food from the civilian population.

Latin America. Social conditions were particularly bleak in 1992 among the tens of millions of poor people who in recent years had flocked to the large cities of Latin America. According to UN statistics, nearly three quarters of Latin America's population lived in megacities such as Buenos Aires, Argentina; Rio de Janeiro, Brazil; Santiago, Chile; Lima, Peru; and Mexico City, which, with more than 20 million residents, is the world's largest city. Many of the residents lived in rudimentary shantytowns or on the streets in conditions of extreme poverty, rampant crime, and virtually uncontrolled pollution. Unchecked population growth in the overcrowded cities is "the worst problem in Latin America," said Alfredo Gastal, director of the United Nations Office of Environment and Human Settlement in Santiago.

Europe. Another widely reported instance of social upheaval in 1992 was the continued civil war in the former nation of Yugoslavia, where an estimated 200,000 people were killed or wounded in fighting among Bosnians, Croatians, Serbs, and Muslims. There also were sporadic outbreaks of civil violence in several former republics of the Soviet Union, primarily in Georgia, Azerbaijan, and Tajikistan.

The largest cities in Western Europe—particularly London, Paris, Rome, Madrid, and Berlin—for the first time in recent years faced significant problems with homelessness. Many of those living on the streets were refugees from Eastern Europe, but the homeless also included large numbers of indigenous poor and the mentally ill. Many of the homeless in France "now have mental problems even if they didn't start off that way," said Jean-Marie Ederer, a director of Emmaus, a relief agency. "They are trapped in a vicious circle which completely excludes them from society."

MARC LEEPSON, *Free-lance Writer*

SOMALIA

It was a bleak year for Somalia as civil war, death, famine, and terror led to the almost total dismemberment of the African nation.

Civil War and Famine. In November 1991 the ruling United Somali Congress (USC) had split apart as Gen. Mohamed Farah Aidid disputed the leadership of Ali Mahdi Mohamed. Throughout 1992 both sides struggled for power in the capital city of Mogadishu, using heavy artillery and antiaircraft weapons. By late 1992, Mogadishu was in shambles with more than 100,000 civilians killed or starved to death.

There also was fighting among different clans. Both the north, which had seceded in 1991, and the south were caught up in the maelstrom that pitted clan against clan. The International Committee of the Red Cross estimated in August that 2.5 million Somalis had been forced to flee their traditional lands, while as many as 10,000 people a month were starving to death. Up to 2 million people were likely to die of famine by the end of 1992, according to the Red Cross. Planting was impossible under

As civil war and famine continued to devastate Somalia, residents of all ages lined up to receive whatever food aid they could. The Red Cross and the UN were prime suppliers.

© Mark Peters/Sipa

SOMALIA · Information Highlights

Official Name: Somali Democratic Republic.
Location: Eastern Africa.
Area: 471,776 sq mi (637 660 km²).
Population (mid-1992 est.): 8,300,000.
Chief City (1984 est.): Mogadishu, the capital, 600,000.
Government: *Head of government,* Ali Mahdi Mohamed, interim president (took office 1991). *Head of state,* Omar Arteh Ghalib, interim prime minister (appointed 1991).
Monetary Unit: Shilling (3,800 shillings equal U.S. $1, December 1990).
Gross Domestic Product (1988 U.S. $): $1,700,-000,000.

---

anarchic conditions, the nation's camel and cattle stocks had declined by 25%, and the sale of stolen relief food had become big business. More than 500,000 refugees had fled the country, most often to Kenya, but also to Ethiopia, Djibouti, and Yemen.

The United Nations Position. Although the United Nations obtained a cease-fire in February, the agreement was not applied. In April the UN Security Council agreed to dispatch 50 military observers to enforce the cease-fire, but because Aidid refused to sanction their arrival they did not move into the country until August. That same month, UN Secretary-General Boutros Boutros-Ghali, angered by what he considered the Security Council's neglect of Africa, proposed the deployment of 3,500 UN personnel to secure the country within four separate zones and to help feed the population with donated food. The Security Council approved but the agreement of the clan leaders was required.

Earlier, the UN Security Council and all factions in Mogadishu agreed upon the deployment of 500 armed UN troops from Pakistan to protect the delivery of relief supplies. In early December the United Nations approved a U.S.-led military intervention—Operation Restore Hope—in Somalia. Its purpose was to open the harbor at Mogadishu and protect the delivery of relief supplies to residents in the city and inland. The initial response in Somalia to the mission was positive and there was little resistance from the fighting warlords. The presence of U.S. forces also helped reduce the number of guns visible on the nation's streets. The year ended with U.S. President George Bush visiting U.S. troops in Somalia. It, however, was unclear how long the U.S. force would remain there.

The United States earlier had announced it would initiate an emergency airlift of 145,000 tons of food to the hinterland of the country after already having donated $77 million in food and humanitarian aid. By the end of 1992, the UN and the Red Cross had shipped 400,000 tons of food to Somalia.

PETER SCHWAB
State University of New York at Purchase

SOUTH AFRICA

South Africa's attempts at negotiating a constitutional settlement and an end to the internecine violence that has plagued the country for so long met with mixed success in 1992. In a referendum held in March, white voters gave President F. W. de Klerk an overwhelming mandate to continue the reform process and to negotiate a new constitution. However, the multiracial, multiparty Convention for a Democratic South Africa (CODESA) which was seeking to negotiate the new constitutional and political future for the country subsequently ended in a stalemate. After several months of uncertainty, the National Party (NP) government and the African National Congress (ANC) agreed to resume negotiations. In December, President de Klerk corroborated allegations of the subversive activities by members of the South Africa Defense Force by firing 23 military officers found to have been involved in illegal activities aimed at undermining the reform process. All the while, racial, ethnic, and political violence continued.

Historic Referendum Supports Reform. After his Nationalist Party was defeated badly by right-wing forces opposed to change, President de Klerk felt compelled to go to the white electorate for a mandate to continue to pursue constitutional reform. On February 24 he called for a national, whites-only referendum to decide whether to continue the reform process and negotiate a new constitution. De Klerk added that a clear majority in favor of the reform process would make it unnecessary to return to the white electorate for approval of binding agreements. The opposition Democratic Party and the 19 major groups taking part in the CODESA forum announced their support for a ''yes'' vote; the ANC, although it opposed the racially exclusive nature of the process of the referendum, also urged support for a ''yes'' vote, and endorsed safeguards for minority interests as a way to reassure white voters. Dr. Andries Treurnicht, the leader of the pro-apartheid Conservative Party indicated that his party would participate in the referendum and work to defeat it. A remarkable 85% turnout of the white electorate was testimonial to the implications of one of the most important decisions in South Africa's history. Cognizant of the likely domestic violence and international hostility that a rejection of reform would cause, nearly 70% voted on March 17 to continue that process and end white minority rule. Only one out of 15 electoral regions recorded a majority ''no'' vote. President de Klerk, who had staked his political future on the outcome, said: ''Today we closed the book on apartheid. We have changed, and we will change, the face of South Africa.''

Budget. In March the then finance minister, Barend du Plessis, presented a national budget that reflected South Africa's weak economy and escalating demands for social programs. Revenue for these new programs was to be generated by a tax increase of more than 27% on individual taxpayers, and by a hike in the price of gasoline. There were large new allocations for education, health, and a special injection of funds for black housing. Funds were also allocated to narrow the gap between white and black pensions. Because of increased crime and violence in the country, some funds from the military budget were reallocated to the police budget, which was increased by 21.8%; the defense budget received only a modest increase of 5.6%.

Cabinet Reshuffle. In May, following the April resignation of Barend du Plessis, President de Klerk announced a cabinet reshuffle. Du Plessis was replaced by Derek Keys, who came into the cabinet with extensive experience in the business sector. Roelf Meyer replaced Gerrit Viljoen as minister of constitutional development. Du Plessis and Viljoen claimed to be exhausted from their arduous duties in the constitutional process and in running their ministries at the same time. Viljoen, however, remained in the cabinet as a minister of state and continued to assist the president in the constitutional negotiating process. Roelf Meyer was replaced as minister of defense by Gene Louw. Foreign Minister R. F. ''Pik'' Botha retained his portfolio.

CODESA. In May the second full session of CODESA collapsed in a deadlock. CODESA was created at the end of 1991 to act as a multiracial, multiparty forum for South Africa's transition to democracy. Its constitutional committee, one of five working groups, was unable to reach an agreement over the form of national assembly that would draw up a new constitution. The National Party insisted that all constitutional decisions should require a 75% majority, while the ANC insisted on 70%.

SOUTH AFRICA • Information highlights

Official Name: Republic of South Africa.
Location: Southern tip of Africa.
Area: 471,444 sq mi (1 221 040 km²).
Population (mid-1992 est.): 41,700,000.
Chief Cities (1985 census, city proper): Pretoria, the administrative capital, 443,059; Cape Town, the legislative capital, 776,617; Durban, 634,301; Johannesburg, 632,369.
Government: *Head of state and government,* Frederik W. de Klerk, state president (took office Sept. 1989). *Legislature*—Parliament (tricameral): House of Assembly, House of Representatives (Coloured), and House of Delegates (Indians).
Monetary Unit: Rand (2.99 rands equal U.S. $1, Dec. 16, 1992).
Gross Domestic Product (1990 U.S.$): $101,700,-000,000.
Economic Index (1991): *Consumer Prices* (1980 = 100), all items, 452.2; food, 496.3.
Foreign Trade (1991 U.S.$): *Imports,* $17,607,-000,000; *exports,* excluding exports of gold, $17,146,000,000.

Although efforts to bring peace and a constitutional settlement were under way in South Africa in 1992, violence and mass murder continued. After at least 43 persons were massacred in the town of Boipatong in June, members of the African National Congress (ANC) rallied (right), demanding revenge against the rival Inkatha movement and the white-ruled government they claimed supported the attack.

© Juhan Kuus/Sipa

Both sides agreed that a Bill of Rights should require a 75% majority. The NP also favored the creation of an upper house or senate that would allow it, in effect, to block constitutional proposals it opposed. Commenting on the breakdown, President de Klerk denied that his government was trying to entrench white rule through these proposals; Nelson Mandela maintained that the ANC was unable to save CODESA because of NP intransigence.

The impasse remained until a Record of Understanding between the government and the ANC was signed on September 26, specifying a democratically elected single chamber legislature, and a constituent assembly that would serve as an interim parliament and which would draft and adopt a new constitution. President de Klerk's decision to reenter negotiations with the ANC marked a victory for moderates in the National Party who advocated moving away from support for Zulu Chief Mangosuthu Buthelezi's Inkatha Freedom Party (IFP). At the same time, Nelson Mandela's participation indicated that he successfully had navigated between conservative and militant wings of the ANC. Chief Buthelezi denounced the agreement because decisions which affected the IFP were made without his involvement, including a national ban on the carrying of Zulu traditional weapons. In defiance of the weapons ban, Buthelezi led a march of armed IFP supporters through downtown Johannesburg on October 17.

A resumption of talks was scheduled for late November, to begin to address the remaining major differences on constitutional issues between the ANC and the National Party. In December, just before the ANC and the National Party were about to resume talks, Chief Mangosuthu Buthelezi introduced a constitutional plan to establish Natal province and KwaZulu as a semiautonomous state within a federal framework. This clearly was aimed at giving Buthelezi new visibility and leverage at a time when he essentially had been excluded from constitutional discussions.

Mass Action. According to Nelson Mandela, the week of mass protests that began on August 3 sought to ". . . pressure the government into accepting an interim government and democratic elections." The Inkatha Freedom Party and the Pan African Congress declined to participate in the protests. The two-day work strike resulted in a stay-at-home of nearly 4 million workers, including an estimated 90% of the work force in the Johannesburg area. More than 50,000 protesters led by Nelson Mandela marched to the Union Buildings in Pretoria, site of the offices of President de Klerk. A team of ten United Nations observers monitored the protests.

Continuing Violence. South Africa has become a country in which mass murder has become appallingly commonplace; since 1990 there have been more than four dozen incidents in which more than ten people were killed. There were almost daily killings in the townships as a result of the violent rivalry between members of the ANC and the IFP. One of the worst such incidents occurred on June 17, in the town of Boipatong, south of Johannesburg, in the Transvaal, where at least 43 men, women, and children were killed, allegedly by a mob of Zulus sympathetic to the IFP. The Boipatong massacre was horrifying, not only because of the large number of people killed, but because of allegations that members of the South African police assisted IFP supporters in the killings. The government denied complicity and charged 78 residents of a steel workers' hostel—an IFP stronghold—with murder or public violence. Several days after the incident, President de Klerk attempted to tour the scene of the massacre, but was accosted by angry residents. Police officers accompanying the president fired into the hostile crowd, forcing de Klerk's motorcade to flee the township and thereby escalating the violence.

On September 7 in Ciskei, one of South Africa's black homelands, between 50,000 and 80,000 ANC supporters marched on Bisho, the homeland's capital, in a protest against the rule of Ciskei leader Joshua "Oupa" Gqozo. The march could be seen as part of the ANC's larger strategy of undermining the legitimacy of allegedly progovernment and "undemocratic" homeland leaders in the constitutional negotiating process. The ANC's expectation was that the unpopular Gqozo would be an easy target, and that his successful overthrow would send a message to leaders in other homelands such as Bophuthatswana and KwaZulu. During the march, a group led by Communist Party member Ronnie Kasrils found a gap in the fence surrounding the stadium where the ANC rally was to be held, and started to move into an area that had been declared off limits to the marchers. Ciskei troops fired on the crowd, and in the ensuing melee 28 people were killed and 188 were wounded.

While the ANC blamed President de Klerk for the massacre because "the Ciskei is the creation of the apartheid regime and they are responsible for the atrocities committed in its name," the South African government blamed the ANC for bringing its supporters into a dangerous situation in which there had been prior warnings that people might get killed. In late November, members of the Azanian People's Liberation Army (APLA), the military wing of the Pan-Africanist Congress (PAC), claimed responsibility for an attack on a King William's Town all-white golf club, which resulted in four deaths and 17 injuries. This event, as well as subsequent attacks on white farmers in the Queenstown area, was condemned by the ANC and the government and signaled renewed attacks aimed at whites who largely had been excluded from the political violence that dominated the country.

Proposed Political Amnesty. In September, in an effort to draw the ANC back into talks, President de Klerk began freeing political prisoners convicted of murder and other major crimes. Later in the month the NP's Further Indemnity Bill was defeated in a joint session of the parliamentary houses. The central purpose of the bill had been to release several hundred ANC prisoners not covered by previous legislation. The bill also would have allowed for indemnity applications from any political offenders. In October the National Party introduced legislation in a special parliamentary session that in effect would have given President de Klerk the power to protect state officials from prosecution for past political crimes. The applications would be heard by a national council on indemnity appointed by the president. The ANC opposed this measure, believing that amnesty should only be granted by a multiparty interim government. De Klerk denied that the main purpose of the bill was to grant amnesty to white officials who might be prosecuted for actions in the future. The opposition Democratic Party referred to the bill as "unilateral, illiberal, and open to serious abuse." De Klerk referred the bill to the President's Council, a "rubber-stamp" body where it was likely to receive ratification. This was the first time since he took office that de Klerk found it necessary to turn to the Council. He maintained that he was using this constitutional remedy on the advice of his cabinet, and that the Record of Understanding agreed to with the ANC in September would be threatened if the bill were not passed.

ANC Torture Revelations. In March 1991, Nelson Mandela had ordered an internal investigation into allegations of torture by the ANC. In October 1992 the ANC admitted that it had tortured dissident members while it was in exile. In announcing the findings of the investigation he said that ANC leaders accepted collective responsibility for the actions. While he agreed that acts of torture were "inexcusable" he emphasized that they had to be understood in the context in which they occurred.

Foreign Relations. Despite great difficulties surrounding constitutional talks and the increasing violence throughout the country, South Africa's international stature greatly improved in 1992, a recognition of the significance that international actors attach to recent reforms and to the white referendum supporting those reforms. Throughout the year African and non-African nations moved to establish diplomatic ties, signaling an end to South Africa's pariah status. In January the European Community formally lifted remaining economic sanctions, Japan restored diplomatic links, and Angola established formal diplomatic ties for the first time. President de Klerk's state visit to Nigeria and Kenyan President Daniel Arap Moi's visit to South Africa opened the way to formal ties just short of full diplomatic relations. The new Russian Federation, Ukraine, Lesotho, the Ivory Coast, and Mexico all established full diplomatic relations. The Seychelles announced the opening of a consulate in South Africa and Djibouti lifted all trade and travel restrictions. For the first time since 1960 South Africa was allowed to participate in the Summer Olympic Games.

Mandela Separation. On April 13, Nelson Mandela announced that he was separating from his wife Winnie. In his statement he recognized his wife's courage in the struggle against apartheid, but acknowledged that ". . . owing to differences between ourselves on a number of issues in recent months we have mutually agreed that a separation would be the best for each of us." In May the ANC's Women's League in the Johannesburg area suspended Mrs. Mandela as its president.

PATRICK O'MEARA and BRIAN WINCHESTER
Indiana University

SOUTH CAROLINA

In South Carolina political changes—including congressional redistricting, revisions in the state's election law, and passage of local-government consolidation legislation—dominated 1992 events.

Legislature. Republican Gov. Carroll A. Campbell, Jr., made three major proposals for legislative consideration but only one succeeded. Campbell strongly advocated restructuring state government during the year, partially in response to major scandals involving legislators. He suggested a cabinet system to replace a fragmented state system dominated by semiautonomous boards and commissions. Gridlock occurred in the Democrat-dominated legislature, however, and no action on the issue was taken. The governor also failed to see his no-fault auto-insurance proposal enacted, but the issue likely would return in 1993.

Governor Campbell did convince the legislature to extend the life of the Barnwell county low-level nuclear-waste-disposal site until 1996. The concession made by supporters of the site was a ban on nuclear waste from anywhere but the eight states of the Southeast Nuclear Waste Compact after July 1, 1994.

Landmark legislation was passed when the legislature voted to allow local governments to consolidate if their voters approved. A complicated bill, the legislation was invoked in the latter part of the year by Richland county, which includes the state capital of Columbia, when it moved to establish a Consolidation Charter Study Commission. The commission was due to report in 1993.

SOUTH CAROLINA · Information Highlights

Area: 31,113 sq mi (80 582 km²).
Population (July 1, 1991 est.): 3,560,000.
Chief Cities (1990 census): Columbia, the capital, 98,052; Charleston, 80,414; North Charleston, 70,218.
Government (1992): *Chief Officers*—governor, Carroll A. Campbell, Jr. (R); lt. gov., Nick A. Theodore (D). *General Assembly*—Senate, 46 members; House of Representatives, 124 members.
State Finances (fiscal year 1991): *Revenue,* $9,413,000,000; *expenditure,* $8,970,000,000.
Personal Income (1991): $55,005,000,000; per capita, $15,467.
Labor Force (June 1992): *Civilian labor force,* 1,759,100; *unemployed,* 111,700 (6.3% of total force).
Education: *Enrollment* (fall 1990)—public elementary schools, 452,033; public secondary, 170,079; colleges and universities, 159,302. *Public school expenditures* (1990), $2,480,244,000.

Redistricting and Elections. With state officials unable to agree on a congressional-redistricting format, a three-judge federal panel prepared the state's redistricting plan. Six districts were retained with little significant change occurring in five of them. In the sixth, however, a black-majority congressional district was created for the first time in the 20th century. Not surprisingly, Democrat James Clyburn easily won the seat in November and became the first black from South Carolina to go to Congress since 1897. The state's only woman in Congress, Elizabeth J. Patterson, a Democrat, was defeated, however, by Bob Inglis, a Republican, while the remaining four incumbents were reelected. George Bush won the presidential race, continuing the state's recent tendency to vote Republican on that level. U.S. Sen. Ernest Hollings (D) was reelected.

Tim Dominick/"The State Record"

James E. Clyburn, a 52-year-old Democrat who had served as South Carolina's human affairs commissioner since 1974, was the first black to be elected to the U.S. House of Representatives from South Carolina since 1897. He won in the 6th District.

The major political parties lost control over the state's primary elections when the state legislature passed a bill turning over responsibility for conducting the Democratic and Republican primary elections to the state's Election Commission.

Economy. A slowdown in the state's economy resulted in reduced state revenues and state budget cuts. A midyear shortfall of $200 million resulted in deep cuts across the board following a court challenge of selective reductions proposed by the governor and the state's Budget and Control Board. Since 1989 state budget cuts had reduced appropriations by more than $800 million.

On a brighter note, BMW, the German automaker, was expected to invest $300 million in and near Spartanburg county in 1993. A $30 million package of tax breaks, facilities, and other incentives for the auto giant generated considerable debate over the wisdom of using such extensive incentives to lure economic development.

CHARLIE TYER
University of South Carolina

SOUTH DAKOTA

South Dakota Democrats made substantial gains in the 1992 elections. While urban residents employed in the public sector and service industries enjoyed economic stability, rural South Dakotans endured a sagging economy and voted accordingly. Sioux tribes, meanwhile, sought to achieve economic self-sufficiency and political self-determination.

Elections. South Dakotans voted to cast their three presidential electoral votes for George Bush by a narrow margin: President Bush, 41%; Bill Clinton, 37%; Ross Perot, 22%. Yet for the first time in 16 years they gave Democrats a majority of seats in the state Senate (20D-15R) and several additional seats in the state House of Representatives (29D-41R).

They also reelected the two Democrats in their three-member congressional delegation by strong majorities—U.S. Sen. Tom Daschle by 66%, and U.S. Rep. Tim Johnson by 73% of the vote.

Nevertheless, 69% of the voters cast ballots in favor of a state constitutional amendment to limit the terms of elected officials to 12 consecutive years in any federal office and eight years in any state office. On referendum ballots, voters rejected the operation of a new state waste-dumping site and placed stricter controls on surface mining. They also voted down a proposal for a corporate and personal income tax, which included no guarantee for corresponding reductions in sales and property taxes; and, to sustain the flow of funds into the state treasury, they voted to allow the continued operation of a profitable video-lottery network.

Legislation. The state legislature appropriated for fiscal year 1993 some $1,499,816,839, of which $592,213,816 (39.5%) came from federal funds. The most substantial amounts were extended to the Department of Social Services (20.4%), the Board of Regents of Higher Education (16.7%), the Department of Education and Cultural Affairs (16.5%), and the Department of Human Services (7%).

Indian Affairs. In 1992 casino gambling on the tribal lands of the Yankton, Flandreau, Sisseton-Wahpeton, and Lower Brule Sioux helped to lift their reservation societies from conditions of financial distress to middle-class standards. Tribal leaders worked to strengthen reservation economies as well as to nurture cultural survival through educational facilities, including five tribally controlled community colleges. Critical to both economic improvement and cultural survival was litigation in federal courts to defend the jurisdictional prerogatives of tribal governments against state encroachment. Overall, reservation leadership groups demonstrated growing expertise and determination to achieve for the tribes of South Dakota both economic self-sufficiency and political self-determination.

The Economy. In mid-1992 unemployment in South Dakota stood at approximately 3.5%, and average personal income rose by 6.1% from a year earlier, but the improvement occurred mainly in urban areas. Agricultural incomes declined because of reductions in federal price supports, especially among wheat producers; the curtailment of hay production; and a decline in livestock prices.

Death Penalty. A change in mood about law and order evident across the United States was reflected in South Dakota when a jury of seven women and five men found Donald Moeller guilty of rape and murder and recommended the death penalty by lethal injection. The last execution in the state had been in 1947.

HERBERT T. HOOVER
University of South Dakota

SOUTH DAKOTA • Information Highlights

Area: 77,116 sq mi (199 730 km²).
Population (July 1, 1991 est.): 703,000.
Chief Cities (1990 census): Pierre, the capital, 12,906; Sioux Falls, 100,814; Rapid City, 54,523.
Government (1992): *Chief Officers*—governor, George S. Mickelson (R); lt. gov., Walter D. Miller (R). *Legislature*—Senate, 35 members; House of Representatives, 70 members.
State Finances (fiscal year 1991): *Revenue,* $1,597,000,000; *expenditure,* $1,417,000,000.
Personal Income (1991): $11,303,000,000; per capita, $16,071.
Labor Force (June 1992): *Civilian labor force,* 357,800; *unemployed,* 12,700 (3.5% of total force).
Education: *Enrollment* (fall 1990)—public elementary schools, 95,169; public secondary, 33,995; colleges and universities, 34,208. *Public school expenditures* (1990), $494,765,000.

SPACE EXPLORATION

Space exploration in 1992 centered on dramatic observations concerning the universe, relayed primarily by U.S. spacecraft orbited in previous years. Several countries launched environmental survey satellites to examine changes to the global climate. A growing number of communications satellites put into orbit would link more and more nations together electronically. Throughout the year, eight U.S. shuttle flights demonstrated satellite servicing, with one spectacular repair of an Intelsat communications satellite.

The year was marked by major organizational changes within the National Aeronautics and Space Administration (NASA) engineered by the new administrator, Daniel Goldin. His predecessor, Richard Truly—a former astronaut—reportedly was ousted for policy disputes with the White House. Fueled by budget shortfalls, NASA adopted a cheaper, better, and faster approach to its space planning.

Despite economic and political hardships in the former Soviet Union, cosmonauts continued to live aboard the *Mir* space station as it circled Earth, gaining more operational experience in human spaceflight.

Shuttle Program. NASA flew eight shuttle flights during 1992, the second-highest number of missions flown in one year (in 1985 there were nine shuttle missions).

The seven-person crew of space shuttle *Discovery* STS-42 (January 22–30) conducted experiments in life sciences and materials science. The crew of the first International Microgravity Laboratory mission was made up of one researcher from Canada, a representative of the European Space Agency, and five U.S. crew members. The eight-day flight enabled the international team to study the human nervous system's adaptation to low gravity and the effects of microgravity on other life forms, such as shrimp eggs, lentil seedlings, fruit-fly eggs, and bacteria.

The seven-person crew of the *Atlantis* STS-45 mission (March 24-April 2) conducted the first space-shuttle mission to focus on the Earth's atmosphere and its electromagnetic and solar environment in space. By recording atmospheric conditions during an 11-year solar cycle, scientists hope to see how variations in solar energy may affect the atmosphere and global climate. *Atlantis'* orbit took it over high northern and southern latitudes, enabling the crew to observe brilliant auroral displays, including the first artificial auroras ever produced in space.

The maiden flight of shuttle *Endeavour* on its STS-49 mission (May 7–16) resulted in the cliffhanger mission of the year. The primary duty of the seven-person crew was to rendezvous with an INTELSAT VI F-3 communications satellite stranded in an unusable orbit due to a faulty boost by a Titan launch vehicle in March 1990.

First attempts by two spacewalking astronauts to grapple the errant satellite with an $800 million capture bar were unsuccessful. Despite intensive training with the device on Earth, the zero-gravity conditions amplified even the slightest movement, making it difficult to handle. The crew improvised a satellite-rescue plan. The first three-person space walk in history enabled the astronauts to ''catch'' the spinning 8,960-lb (4 064-kg) satellite by hand and steady it to make the capture bar work. The threesome then attached a grapple fixture

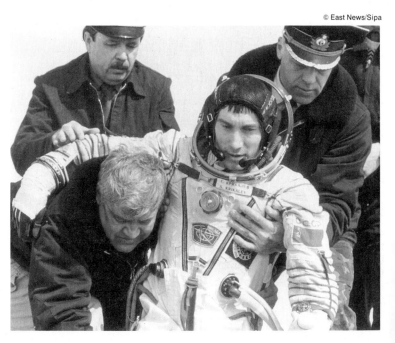

Sergei Krikalev returned to Earth on March 25, 1992, after ten months in space. While he circled the Earth, the Soviet Union fell, a Commonwealth of Independent States was formed in its place, and Soviet President Mikhail Gorbachev left the national and world scenes.

to the spacecraft, eventually lowering it gently atop a new rocket motor. The INTELSAT satellite then was ejected from the shuttle and the newly attached rocket motor boosted the spacecraft into a correct, geostationary orbit. Yet another space walk allowed two astronauts to practice methods for building the U.S. space station *Freedom* toward the close of the decade. This first flight of *Endeavour* yielded the longest space walk in history (8 hours, 29 minutes) and the longest space walk by a woman (7 hours, 45 minutes).

Columbia's STS-50 13-day marathon mission, the longest shuttle flight to date, carried the first U.S. Microgravity Laboratory. More than 30 experiments focused on medical and materials-science research, including materials processing, the effect of microgravity on body fluids, and experiments with HIV-related protein crystals for AIDS research.

The shuttle *Atlantis* from July 31 to August 6 conducted the first trial of a Tethered Satellite System (TSS-1). A joint project of the United States and Italy, the 1,139-lb (517.7-kg) satellite is designed to reel out on a 12-mi (19.3-km)-long tether that contains electrically conducting metal strands in its core. The purpose of the tether experiment was to convert the mechanical energy of the shuttle's more than 17,000-mph (2 753-km/h) orbital motion into 5,000 volts of electrical energy by passing a conductor through the Earth's magnetic field lines. Use of tethers to generate electrical power in space is one potential application. However, the experiment never was conducted because of a snag and the TSS-1 never reached more than 850 ft (256 m) from the shuttle. An investigation of the $379 million experiment revealed that a bolt had prevented the TSS-1 from properly unreeling.

The *Endeavour* STS-47 mission (September 12–20) marked NASA's 50th shuttle flight since the first shuttle mission in 1981. Free of prelaunch difficulties, it was also the first shuttle flight since 1985 to lift off at the precise time planned. The eight-day flight carried seven astronauts into space, including the first professional Japanese astronaut, the first female black astronaut, and the first married couple. STS-47's primary objective was to haul a Spacelab for materials-processing and life-sciences experiments. The National Space Development Agency (NASDA) of Japan paid $90 million to participate in the joint venture with NASA. Four female frogs, two Japanese carp, 30 chicken eggs, 180 oriental hornets, and some 400 adult fruit flies, along with 7,200 fly larvae, turned the Spacelab into a near Noah's ark for biological research in microgravity. During the flight, the crew induced the fertilization of frog eggs, resulting in the first tadpoles conceived and developed in weightlessness.

A ten-day journey by the shuttle *Columbia* on its STS-52 mission (October 22–November 1) placed five U.S. astronauts and one Canadian into orbit. *Columbia*'s primary objective was to leave in space a Laser Geodynamics Satellite (LAGEOS II). The small, $4 million, Italian-built LAGEOS II is covered with 426 retroreflectors, each a small prism, that can reflect a burst of laser light beamed from Earth back to its source. By recording the round-trip travel time of the laser beam to the satellite and back to Earth, the slow movement of the planet's crustal plates can be measured. *Columbia* astronauts also took measurements of the Earth's stratosphere during the flight, melted samples of metals in two small furnaces, and tested a new television/computer system that controlled the shuttle's Canadian-built robot arm.

The last shuttle flight of 1992 was STS-53 (December 2–9), with the last major military payload planned for the shuttle fleet. The dedicated Department of Defense (DoD) mission tasked shuttle *Discovery* to leave in space a secret DoD payload. This was the tenth and final planned Pentagon-chartered flight for the NASA shuttle program.

Space Station. In spite of tight budgets, Congress approved $2.1 billion for the space station Freedom and defeated a vote to kill the project. The purpose of the yet-to-orbit facility —escalating in cost from a projected tally of $8 billion in 1984 to $40 billion in 1992—triggered numerous debates in Congress. While its merits as a scientific research outpost largely were valued, the project's employment of thousands of aerospace workers, already impacted by defense cutbacks, helped to shore up the political go-ahead.

Throughout 1992 the Russian *Mir* space station was occupied on a continuing basis by cosmonaut crews. Automatic Progress spacecraft docked on several occasions with *Mir*, supplying station personnel with fresh supplies of food, water, mail, and equipment. Starting in January, the economic troubles facing the breakup of the former Soviet Union crept into the ground-control facilities of the *Mir* space station and controllers threatened to strike for wage increases.

Two cosmonauts replaced Alexander Volkov and Sergei Krikalev, who returned to Earth March 25. Rocketed to *Mir* in 1991, Krikalev had spent ten months in space, leaving the planet and returning to Earth over a period of time that saw the collapse of his government. Krikalev had been asked to extend his space voyage by nearly five months due to the government change.

Space Science. Over the course of the year, the U.S. Hubble Space Telescope delivered many new findings, including support for the existence of black holes and the photography of the core of the most distant known galaxy, 10 billion light-years from Earth. The orbiting observatory also peered into the core of a galaxy in the Virgo Cluster, 45 million light-years from Earth, detecting a disk of material being pulled into a suspected black hole. Similarly, the telescope viewed an immense ring of dust which is believed to be fueling a massive black hole at the heart of the spiral galaxy M51, located 20 million light-years away. In addition to a host of distant observations, Hubble produced the first ultraviolet image of the northern aurora of Jupiter, and explored Jupiter's volcanic moon, Io.

En route to the Sun, the European Space Agency's Ulysses spacecraft encountered Jupiter in February. Scientists later reported Ulysses had found that the solar wind exerts a much stronger influence on Jupiter's magnetic field than was thought previously.

On June 7, NASA orbited from Cape Canaveral, FL, the Extreme Ultraviolet Explorer (EUVE). The EUVE is the first satellite to make both spectroscopic and wide-band observations of astronomical objects over the entire ultraviolet part of the electromagnetic spectrum. During its first several months in orbit, the EUVE detected an entirely new source of extreme ultraviolet radiation from the corona of a star some 16 light-years from Earth. Associated with volcanism, corona are large circular features. The EUVE satellite also observed an exotic object 2 billion light-years beyond the Milky Way galaxy, an elliptical galaxy theorized to perhaps contain at its center a super-sized black hole.

On July 10 the European Space Agency's Giotto spacecraft encountered comet Grigg-Skjellerup. Passing within 124 mi (200 km) of the celestial body, it was the closest flyby ever achieved.

A Solar, Anomalous and Magnetospheric Particle Explorer (SAMPEX) satellite was lofted July 3. The NASA spacecraft was the first of a low-cost breed of Explorer, sporting a price tag of a modest $75 million to $80 million to build and operate. SAMPEX instruments focused on studying the energetic particles from the Milky Way galaxy and solar energetic particles from the Sun.

On July 24 a Delta booster placed the Geotail satellite into space on a four-year mission, a joint effort between Japan's Institute of Space and Astronautical Science and NASA. Geotail used flybys of the Moon to alter its trajectory for deep space surveys of how particles from the Sun interact with Earth's magnetic field.

The first U.S. Mars mission in 17 years lifted off from Cape Canaveral, FL, on September 25. The Mars Observer rode a Titan III rocket into Earth orbit, after which a privately built Transfer Orbit Stage propelled the 5,672-lb (2 572-kg) satellite on its Mars trajectory. Mars Observer would reach its target after an 11-month trek, arriving at the red planet in August 1993.

© CNES/Sygma

A Soyuz rocket, 160 ft (49 m) high, carried a Frenchman and two Russians into space on July 27. It was the first of four joint French-Russian missions to be completed by 1996.

Sinking into the Venusian clouds and burning up, the U.S. Pioneer 12 spacecraft expired after 14 years of gathering data around the cloud-veiled planet on October 8. As the planet's gravity pulled the probe toward its fiery destruction, Pioneer continued to relay data as it sampled the high atmosphere of Venus.

Meanwhile, the U.S. Magellan spacecraft transmitted back to Earth impressive sets of radar images of the Venusian surface. Magellan data bolstered the theory that some forces on Venus which shape its surface are like those on Earth. A large landslide was detected using Magellan images, possibly triggered by seismic activity or quakes on the planet. Because of budget cutbacks, the probe's mission would end in September 1993 with 99% of the surface mapped by radar image.

A Swedish Freja satellite was placed into orbit by a Chinese-Long March rocket on October 6. The Freja research satellite was built to study the Earth's upper atmosphere and near space, training its sensors on electromagnetic fields that create auroras.

On October 12, making use of radio telescopes in Arecibo, Puerto Rico, and Goldstone, CA, NASA began the most comprehensive search for extraterrestrial intelligence. The ten-year search will use advanced computer technology that enables a dedicated and all-sky search for radio signals emitted by intelligent life living on distant planets circling other stars.

Applications Satellites. Several nations orbited satellites during the year that scan the Earth's environment and gauge reserves of precious resources on the planet. Japan launched its first Earth remote-sensing satellite for resource-mapping purposes on February 11. The satellite provides day/night scanning of the planet and can observe through dense cloud cover.

The Topex-Poseidon, a joint oceanographic satellite developed by the United States and France, was orbited on August 10 on a French Ariane rocket, marking the first time a NASA satellite rode into space on an Ariane rocket. Using its radar and laser reflecting system, the Topex-Poseidon can measure precisely the heights of ocean waves, as well as ocean wind speeds, thus helping scientists better to measure the circulation patterns of the Earth's oceans. One early test of the satellite involved ocean waves kicked up by Hurricane Iniki as it raced toward the Hawaiian island of Kauai in September.

A Scout rocket toted into orbit on November 21 the Miniature Seeker Technology Integration-1 satellite (MSTI). Rocketed from the Vandenberg Air Force Base in California, the 330-lb (150-kg) satellite carried high-tech camera equipment to image target sites on Earth. MSTI was to orbit Earth for a short six months, evaluating techniques to detect missile exhaust plumes as part of the Pentagon's Strategic Defense Initiative, or "Star Wars" program.

Communications Satellites. The lofting of communications satellites, and the services they render, served as the most profitable space business in 1992. France's Arianespace racked up an impressive set of launches throughout 1992. All Ariane rockets were launched from Kourou, French Guiana. On February 26 the Arab League's Arabsat 1C satellite and a Superbird B1 satellite for the Space Communications Corporation of Japan were orbited by France's Ariane launcher. Ariane also launched satellites for the United States, the Arab League, Europe, Japan, and Spain.

The U.S. launch companies lofted an array of satellites including the DFS Kopernikus 3 satellite for a German consortium, a powerful Intelsat K telecommunications satellite, and a military Defense Satellite Communication System (DSCS). China used its Long March 2-E rocket on August 13 to orbit an Australian Optus B1 satellite. A follow-up Optus B2 satellite also was rocketed spaceward for Australia by China on December 21. The satellite, however, apparently exploded prior to reaching orbit.

See also ASTRONOMY.

LEONARD DAVID
Space Data Resources & Information

SPAIN

Hosting the Summer Olympics in Barcelona and Expo '92, a world's fair, in Seville made 1992 the "Year of Spain." (*See also* FEATURE SECTION, page 64.) Constant political and economic headaches gave Prime Minister Felipe González Márquez and his Socialist Workers Party (PSOE) little reason to celebrate.

Politics. Allegations of corruption continued to haunt González as a real-estate scandal forced the resignation of his health minister in January. In May, Mariano Rubio Jimenez, governor of the Bank of Spain, and former Finance Minister Miguel Boyer were charged with regulatory fraud and share-price manipulation.

There also was dissension as the PSOE's left wing pushed for statist policies. This hope was dashed by Spain's need for close ties with the European Community (EC), but Alfonso Guerra, the prime minister's longtime confidant, warned that "difficult times for the party are coming."

José Maria Aznar also had trouble unifying his conservative Popular Party (PP). Constant maneuvering by Manuel Fraga, his predecessor as PP head, and opposition from regional-based rightist groups combined to undermine his leadership. González and Aznar, meanwhile, were watching Mario Conde, a wealthy Madrid banker who flirted with a run for national office. Conde purchased several Spanish media enterprises and basked in a highly publicized audience with Pope John Paul II. His political intentions and party affiliation were unclear.

Catalonian elections in March returned veteran incumbent Jordi Pujol and his moderate-nationalist Convergence and Union Party (CiU) to power in the 135-seat regional parliament. The CiU's 71 total seats dwarfed the performance of González' Socialists, whose 39 seats comprised the worst-ever showing. The most surprising election result was the rise

---

SPAIN • Information Highlights

Official Name: Kingdom of Spain.
Location: Iberian Peninsula in southwestern Europe.
Area: 194,884 sq mi (504 750 km²).
Population (mid-1992 est.): 38,600,000.
Chief Cities (March 1991 est.): Madrid, the capital, 2,984,576; Barcelona, 1,653,175; Valencia, 777,427.
Government: *Head of state,* Juan Carlos I, king (took office Nov. 1975). *Head of government,* Felipe González Márquez, prime minister (took office Dec. 1982). *Legislature*—Cortés Generales: Senate and Congress of Deputies.
Monetary Unit: Peseta (111.95 pesetas equal U.S.$1, Dec. 14, 1992).
Gross Domestic Product (1990 U.S.$): $435,900,-000,000.
Economic Indexes (1991): *Consumer Prices* (1980 = 100), all items, 258.1; food, 255.0. *Industrial Production* (1980 = 100), 119.
Foreign Trade (1991 U.S.$): *Imports,* $93,314,-000,000; *exports,* $60,182,000,000.

The Greek oil tanker "Aegean Sea" ran aground in bad weather near La Coruña, Spain, on Dec. 3, 1992. The ship then split in two, creating an oil slick that spread along 60 mi (100 km) of Spain's Atlantic coastline.

© Antonio Ribeiro/Gamma-Liaison

from six to 11 seats by the radical, proindependence Republican Left of Catalonia.

A drop in Communist support in Catalonia reflected the turmoil besetting the Spanish Communist Party (PCE) nationwide. Many PCE members advocated the organization's outright dissolution and sought to transform the United Left (IU) electoral coalition into a cohesive new social-democratic political party. PCE leader Julio Anguita fought successfully to preserve the Communist Party.

González said he would seek a fourth term in the 1993 general elections, but was almost certain to resign his post by 1995. Rumors abounded that he wanted to succeed Jacques Delors at the EC helm in Brussels.

Economy. Spain's determination to join the EC economic and monetary union by 1997 was reflected in its economic targets, which included such unattainable goals as reduced inflation, diminished public spending, higher economic growth, and a stable peseta. González insisted on curbing government spending, even as he pumped billions of dollars into the Olympics and Expo '92. Strikes early in the year failed to break the austerity plan.

González' anti-inflation program was thwarted by wage settlements that exceeded the cost of living, higher social spending, a boom in both government outlays and consumer prices in Barcelona and Seville, and fiscal irresponsibility by the autonomous regional governments. Inflation, originally forecast at 5%, came in at 6.5%, making foreign investment in Spain and Spanish exports less attractive. Despite tax increases, the budget deficit also shot up. Spain recorded an anemic 1.5%

growth rate—far lower than the 4% average annual rate recorded between 1986 and 1991. The 17% unemployment rate was among the EC's highest.

On the bright side was the September announcement by the Ford Motor Company that it would build a $773.9 million engine plant in the country. General Motors also showed interest in operating a Basque sports-car plant, and González laid the groundwork for privatization in such areas as securities, energy, mining, and manufacturing.

The September currency machinations in Europe caught Spain off-guard and resulted in a 5% devaluation of the peseta. Yet, unlike Italy and Great Britain, Spain remained in the EMS and it appeared likely to ratify the Maastricht Treaty.

Foreign Affairs. International intelligence cooperation helped Spain prevent Basque terrorists from disrupting its 1992 festivities. On the diplomatic front, Spain in July hosted the second annual 18-nation Iberian-Latin American summit, where leaders pledged to deepen ties, particularly in technology, education, economic development, and human rights. Following the meeting, Cuban President Fidel Castro was greeted as a prodigal son by the people of Lancara, his father's hometown.

Immigration was a problem as thousands of illegal immigrants, mostly Moroccans, sought entrance to a better life in Europe through Spain. González championed development of North Africa's Maghreb economic union in an effort to stem the influx.

GEORGE W. GRAYSON
College of William and Mary

© John Iacono/"Sports Illustrated"

© Duomo

SPORTS

Overview

The 1992 sports year was highlighted by the Toronto Blue Jays becoming the first team from outside the United States to win baseball's World Series; Riddick Bowe (*right*) defeating Evander Holyfield for the world heavyweight boxing crown; the Alabama Crimson Tide football team winning their first national championship since the 1970s; and repeat championship performances by Duke's basketball team, the Chicago Bulls of the NBA, and the Pittsburgh Penguins of the NHL. In addition, Fred Couples was judged the year's best golfer; Monica Seles and Jim Courier were Number 1 in tennis; AP Indy was in the running for horse-of-the-year honors; the Indianapolis 500 was historically close; and the United States retained the America's Cup. Meanwhile, Martin Buser, a native of Switzerland, set a record in the Iditarod Trail Sled Dog Race, and cyclist Miguel Indurain of Spain captured a second consecutive Tour de France.

Sports fans were saddened by the news that Arthur Ashe, a classy former tennis star, had contracted the AIDS virus and watched attentively as Magic Johnson attempted a comeback. . . . Former heavyweight boxing champ Mike Tyson was convicted of rape. . . . Baltimore baseball fans welcomed a new, cozy, open-air home for their Orioles—Oriole Park at Camden Yards (*above*). . . . Free agency was the topic. . . . Marge Schott, owner of the Cincinnati Reds, apologized for her alleged racial slurs. . . . Larry Bird of the Boston Celtics retired. . . . Legendary announcer Red Barber died in October.

The year also was an Olympic one, with the Winter Games being played in Albertville, France, and Barcelona, Spain, hosting the Summer competition. Jackie Joyner-Kersee's performance at the latter gave her the right to challenge the late Babe Didrikson for the laurel of greatest woman athlete ever.

See also FEATURE ARTICLE/ THE PRO ATHLETE TODAY.

Auto Racing

In 1992 the closest finish in the 76-year history of the Indianapolis 500 saw Al Unser, Jr., of Albuquerque, NM, beat Scott Goodyear of Toronto, Ont., by .043 of a second. It was the first Indianapolis victory for the 30-year-old Unser, whose father is a four-time champion. Goodyear bounced back to win the Marlboro 500 at Brooklyn, MI, the only other 500-mi (804.7-km) race in the Championship Auto Racing Teams (CART) Indy Car World Series.

CART's season championship was won by Bobby Rahal of Dublin, OH, the series' fifth champion in five years. In securing his third CART title, the 39-year-old Rahal won four races and earned $2,235,298 in the 16-race series. He edged Michael Andretti of Nazareth, PA, by four points (196–192) and clinched the championship by capturing the final race at Monterey, CA. Andretti won five races and seven pole positions while leading 54% of the laps. Unser was the most consistent driver, scoring points in every race and completing 99% of his laps.

Nigel Mansell of Great Britain won the Formula One championship with 108 points, outdistancing Riccardo Patrese's 56 points. Mansell won the first five races of the season. He announced that he would drive Indy cars in 1993 and take over the Newman-Haas car previously driven by Michael Andretti, the son of former Formula One champion Mario Andretti.

Alan Kulwicki of Concord, NC, won the Winston Cup stock-car championship. Kul-

AUTO RACING

Major Race Winners, 1992

Indianapolis 500: Al Unser, Jr., United States
Marlboro 500: Scott Goodyear, Canada
Daytona 500: Davey Allison, United States

1992 Champions

World Championship: Nigel Mansell, Great Britain
CART: Bobby Rahal
NASCAR: Alan Kulwicki

Grand Prix for Formula One Cars, 1992

South African: Nigel Mansell, Great Britain
Mexican: Mansell
Brazilian: Mansell
Spanish: Mansell
San Marino: Mansell
Monaco: Ayrton Senna, Brazil
Canadian: Gerhard Berger, Austria
French: Mansell
British: Mansell
German: Mansell
Hungarian: Senna
Belgian: Michael Schumacher, Germany
Italian: Senna
Portuguese: Mansell
Japanese: Riccardo Patrese, Italy
Australian: Berger

wicki trailed Davey Allison and Bill Elliott entering the season's final race, the Hooters 500 at Hampton, GA, but emerged with a 4,078–4,068 points margin over Elliott. Kulwicki finished second to Elliott in the race; Allison crashed, finishing 27th. Also in 1992, Richard Petty of Level Cross, NC, ended a 35-year career in which he won 200 races—a Winston Cup record.

STAN SUTTON
"Louisville Courier-Journal"

© IMS Photo by Bill Watson/Sportschrome East West

Al Unser, Jr., 30, of Albuquerque, NM, wins the 1992 Indianapolis 500 by defeating Scott Goodyear of Canada by 0.43 seconds. It was the closest finish in 76 runnings of the race.

Baseball

Baseball in 1992 was marked by milestones, millionaires, and mayhem. A commissioner was deposed, three teams were sold, and the average player salary reached seven figures. Eighteen of the existing 26 clubs reported declining attendance but recouped some revenue from the postseason expansion draft that stocked new National League (NL) teams in Miami and Denver.

Play-offs and World Series. Three of the four teams that advanced to postseason play in 1991 won repeat divisional titles in 1992. The Pittsburgh Pirates, fending off a surprise late-season challenge from the Montreal Expos, won their third consecutive NL East crown with a 96–66 record, nine games ahead of the Expos. The Toronto Blue Jays and Oakland Athletics, winners of the American League East and West, respectively, matched that mark, while the Atlanta Braves, champions of the NL West, led the majors with a 98–64 record and a .605 winning percentage. After jumping from last in 1990 to first in 1991, the Braves won more convincingly, spotting the Cincinnati Reds a first-half lead of two games before a powerful pitching staff permitted the Atlanta team to pull away from the pack.

The Braves then won three of the first four games in the best-of-seven NL Championship Series (NLCS), taking 5–1 and 13–5 victories at home on October 6 and 7 and winning Game 4 in Pittsburgh by a 6–4 score on October 10. But surprise starter Bob Walk went all the way in Game 5 to give Pittsburgh a 7–1 victory and send the series back to Atlanta. Rookie knuckleballer Tim Wakefield, coming off a 3–2 win in Game 3 on October 9, followed Walk's three-hitter with his second straight complete-game win on October 13. That 13–4 game, featuring an eight-run, second-inning explosion against Atlanta ace Tom Glavine, forced a seventh game the following night. Star Pirate starter Doug Drabek, defeated by John Smoltz in the first and fourth games, took a 2–0 lead into the bottom of the ninth inning but could not hold it. After Atlanta loaded the bases with nobody out, Ron Gant greeted reliever Stan Belinda with a long sacrifice fly that was nearly his second grand slam of the NLCS. One out later, seldom-used Francisco Cabrera lined a two-run single to left for a 3–2 Atlanta victory. It was the most stunning comeback in the 24-year history of the NLCS. Smoltz, the starting pitcher in Game 7, was named most valuable player (MVP) of the NL play-offs.

Toronto earned its fourth trip to postseason play when it wrapped up the American League (AL) East crown on the next-to-last day of the season, finishing with a four-game lead over the late-charging Milwaukee Brewers. Oakland overtook Minnesota in August and crossed the finish line with a lead of six lengths.

© Jim Gund/Allsport

With two out in the top of the 11th inning in Game 6, veteran star Dave Winfield doubled home two runs to give the Toronto Blue Jays their first World Series championship.

In the AL Championship Series (ALCS), however, Toronto's combination of pitching and power proved too formidable for the Athletics. A ninth-inning homer by Harold Baines gave Oakland a 4–3 win in the opener October 7 but Toronto rebounded with three consecutive victories, 3–1, 7–5, and 7–6 in 11 innings. The turning point came on October 11, when the Jays overcame a 6–1 deficit against Oakland relief ace Dennis Eckersley in Game 4. Roberto Alomar, later named ALCS most valuable player, delivered the key hit: a game-tying, two-run homer in the ninth. After the Athletics got a complete-game win from long-time ace Dave Stewart in Game 5, Toronto rode the right arm of Game 3 winner Juan Guzman to a 9–2 victory in Game 6 on October 14.

The Blue Jays, who hit a record ten home runs in the ALCS, also used their power to win the World Series in six games. Toronto out-homered the Braves, six to three, and became the first team to homer at least once in ten consecutive postseason games.

Atlanta got a complete game from Glavine and a three-run homer from Damon Berryhill to win a 3–1 opener on October 17. But Toronto's Ed Sprague hit a two-run, pinch homer against Atlanta closer Jeff Reardon in the ninth inning of Game 2 for a 5–4 edge that evened the series. Toronto took 3–2 and 2–1 wins at home before Lonnie Smith's grand slam gave the Braves a 7–2 victory in Game 5 on October 22. A two-out, two-run double by Dave Winfield off Charlie Leibrandt in the 11th inning of Game 6 two nights later gave Canada its first world championship. For the second straight year, Atlanta outscored its World Series opponent but lost. Toronto's bullpen contributed a record 15⅓ scoreless innings, while the Jays scored eight of their 17 runs after the sixth inning. Over the same span, Atlanta plated only four of its 20 runs. Pat Borders, the little-known Toronto catcher, hit .450 to win World Series MVP honors and extended his postseason hitting streak to 14 games.

Regular Season. Economic concerns continued to threaten the health of the game. Attendance dropped nearly 2% and two teams with payrolls of $40 million plus—the Los Angeles Dodgers and New York Mets—finished last and next-to-last, respectively. Economics figured in numerous player transactions, including an August 31 blockbuster that sent longtime Oakland Athletics slugger Jose Canseco to the Texas Rangers for Ruben Sierra and Jeff Russell, a pair of potential free agents, plus Bobby Witt. Several other clubs conceded that they could not afford to retain the services of established stars who later became free agents.

One week after the Canseco trade, Baseball Commissioner Francis T. (Fay) Vincent, Jr., resigned in the wake of a no-confidence vote from team owners. He was replaced temporarily by a ten-man executive council consisting of eight owners plus the league presidents. Bud Selig of the Milwaukee Brewers was chosen as the council's chairman.

Vincent had intervened to end the 32-day lockout that delayed the start of the 1990 season and owners—gearing for another potential work stoppage in 1993—did not want history to repeat. The owners also were troubled by Vincent's history of making executive decisions without consulting them first. He made controversial rulings on expansion money and National League realignment, handed lifetime suspensions to owner George Steinbrenner and pitcher Steve Howe of the New York Yankees, and was an outspoken opponent of TV superstations—the chief revenue source of several powerful club owners. He also became involved directly in the sale of the Seattle Mariners to Japanese interests and the attempted sale and transfer of the San Francisco Giants to a syndicate from Tampa-St. Petersburg, FL. (The latter move fell through.) Removing Vincent from forthcoming talks on new labor and television agreements and reducing the powers of the commissioner to make arbitrary decisions "in the best interests of baseball" became a top priority for a majority of owners.

On September 9, Robin Yount of the Milwaukee Brewers became the 17th player—and the first since 1985—to reach 3,000 hits. George Brett of the Kansas City Royals became the 18th player with 3,000 when he collected four hits against the California Angels on September 30. (*See also* BIOGRAPHY.)

When Detroit's Cecil Fielder finished the year with 124 runs batted in (RBIs), he became the first player to lead the American League in that department three years in a row since Babe Ruth did it (1919–21). Sixteen other players from both leagues reached 100 RBIs, including 40-year-old Dave Winfield (Blue Jays), the oldest player to reach that plateau. Another unexpected 100-RBI man was Gary Sheffield, who made a serious bid for the National League's first Triple Crown since 1937. In his first year with the San Diego Padres after an unhappy tenure in Milwaukee, Sheffield finished first in batting (.330), third in home runs (33), and fifth in RBIs (100). A broken finger that kept him sidelined for the last six games crippled his bid for the rare trifecta.

Teammate Fred McGriff led the league with 35 homers, while Darren Daulton (Phillies) finished first with 109 RBIs. The only big-leaguers with 40 homers were Juan Gonzalez (Rangers) and Mark McGwire (Athletics), with 43 and 42, respectively. Another slugger, Barry Bonds of the Pittsburgh Pirates, was named National League MVP for the second time in three seasons. He led the majors with a .624 slugging percentage and .456 on-base average, led the league with 109 runs scored, and ranked second in the NL with 34 homers and fourth with 103 RBIs. Bonds received 127 walks, most in the National League, and finished with a .311 average, tied for sixth in the circuit.

Edgar Martinez of the Seattle Mariners led the American League with a .343 batting average, while Frank Thomas (White Sox) led with a .439 on-base average and McGwire had the best slugging percentage (.585). Lance Johnson, Thomas' teammate in Chicago, had base-

With a .330 batting average, 33 home runs, and 100 RBIs, San Diego's Gary Sheffield made a serious bid to become the National League's first Triple Crown winner in 55 years.

© Stephen Dunn/Allsport

ball's best hitting streak, 25 games, while Kirby Puckett (Twins) had the most hits: 210.

Marquis Grissom (Expos) led both leagues with 78 stolen bases, while two rookies—Kenny Lofton (Indians) and Pat Listach (Brewers)—finished first and second in the American League with 66 and 54, respectively. Both broke John Cangelosi's 1986 rookie record of 50 steals. Listach later defeated Lofton and pitchers Dave Fleming (Mariners) and Cal Eldred (Brewers) in a close vote for AL rookie-of-the-year honors. For the first time since 1984 and the third time in baseball history, a relief pitcher received MVP honors as well as the Cy Young Memorial Award for pitching excellence. Dennis Eckersley of the Oakland Athletics won after converting 51 of 54 save opportunities (a .944 percentage) and finishing 65 games. Eckersley, who also won seven of eight decisions, averaged 10.5 strikeouts and 1.2 walks per nine innings. Oakland went 66–3 in games Eckersley pitched. Lee Smith (Cardinals) led the National League in saves (43) for the second year in a row. He finished the year with 355 career saves, two behind Jeff Reardon on the lifetime list. Reardon had passed Rollie Fingers to take first place when he saved Boston's 1–0 victory over the New York Yankees on June 15.

Among starting pitchers, Kevin Brown (Rangers) and Jack Morris (Blue Jays) led the majors with 21 wins, while Tom Glavine (Braves) and Greg Maddux (Cubs) shared NL leadership with 20 victories each. Jack McDowell (White Sox) also won 20 games. Maddux, the Cy Young winner, led the league with 268 innings pitched, tied for first with 35 starts, and finished third with a 2.18 ERA. Bill Swift (Giants) led the majors with a 2.08 earned run average (ERA), while Roger Clemens (Red Sox) won the American League ERA title for the third straight year with a 2.41 mark. Although David Cone struck out 261 batters in a season split between the two leagues, he did not lead either. John Smoltz (Braves) finished with 215, one more than Cone, to lead the NL, while Randy Johnson (Mariners) led AL pitchers with 241. Kevin Gross (Dodgers) pitched the year's only no-hitter, a 2–0 win over the San Francisco Giants, on August 17.

The American League notched its fifth consecutive win in the All-Star game by defeating the Nationals, 13–6, at San Diego on July 14. Ken Griffey, Jr., had three hits, including a home run, in three at-bats to win MVP honors. Ken Griffey, Sr., had won the same award in 1980, when he also hit an All-Star homer.

On August 2, three former pitchers were inducted into the Baseball Hall of Fame at Cooperstown, NY, along with the late umpire Bill McGowan. Left-hander Hal Newhouser, the only pitcher to win consecutive MVP awards (1944–45), was accompanied by 311-game winner Tom Seaver and reliever Rollie Fingers,

BASEBALL

Professional—Major Leagues

Final Standings, 1992

AMERICAN LEAGUE

Eastern Division	W	L	Pct.	Western Division	W	L	Pct.
Toronto	96	66	.593	Oakland	96	66	.593
Milwaukee	92	70	.568	Minnesota	90	72	.556
Baltimore	89	73	.549	Chicago	86	76	.531
Cleveland	76	86	.469	Texas	77	85	.475
New York	76	86	.469	California	72	90	.444
Detroit	75	87	.463	Kansas City	72	90	.444
Boston	73	89	.451	Seattle	64	98	.395

NATIONAL LEAGUE

Eastern Division	W	L	Pct.	Western Division	W	L	Pct.
Pittsburgh	96	66	.593	Atlanta	98	64	.605
Montreal	87	75	.537	Cincinnati	90	72	.556
St. Louis	83	79	.512	San Diego	82	80	.506
Chicago	78	84	.481	Houston	81	81	.500
New York	72	90	.444	San Francisco	72	90	.444
Philadelphia	70	92	.432	Los Angeles	63	99	.389

Play-offs—American League: Toronto defeated Oakland, 4 games to 2; National League: Atlanta defeated Pittsburgh, 4 games to 3.

World Series—Toronto defeated Atlanta, 4 games to 2. First Game (Atlanta-Fulton County Stadium, Atlanta, Oct. 17, attendance 51,763): Atlanta 3, Toronto 1; Second Game (Atlanta-Fulton County Stadium, Oct. 18, attendance 51,763): Toronto 5, Atlanta 4; Third Game (SkyDome, Toronto, Oct. 20, attendance 51,813): Toronto 3, Atlanta 2; Fourth Game (SkyDome, Oct. 22, attendance 52,268): Toronto 2, Atlanta 1; Fifth Game (SkyDome, Oct. 22, attendance 52,268): Atlanta 7, Toronto 2; Sixth Game (Atlanta-Fulton County Stadium, Oct. 24, attendance 51,763): Toronto 4, Atlanta 3.

All-Star Game (Jack Murphy Stadium, San Diego, July 14, attendance 59,372): American League 13, National League 6.

Most Valuable Players—American League: Dennis Eckersley, Oakland. National League: Barry Bonds, Pittsburgh.

Cy Young Memorial Awards (outstanding pitchers)—American League: Dennis Eckersley, Oakland; National League: Greg Maddux, Chicago.

Managers of the Year—American League: Tony LaRusso, Oakland; National League: Jim Leyland, Pittsburgh.

Rookies of the Year—American League: Pat Listach, Milwaukee; National League: Eric Karros, Los Angeles.

Leading Hitters—(Percentage) American League: Edgar Martinez, Seattle, .343; National League: Gary Sheffield, San Diego, .330. (Runs Batted In) American League: Cecil Fielder, Detroit, 124; National League: Darren Daulton, Philadelphia, 109. (Home Runs) American League: Juan Gonzalez, Texas, 43; National League: Fred McGriff, San Diego, 35. (Hits) American League: Kirby Puckett, Minnesota, 210; National League: Terry Pendleton, Atlanta, and Andy Van Slyke, Pittsburgh, 199. (Runs) American League: Tony Phillips, Detroit, 114; National League: Barry Bonds, Pittsburgh, 109. (Slugging Percentage) American League: Mark McGwire, Oakland, .585; National League: Bonds, .624.

Leading Pitchers—(Earned Run Average) American League: Roger Clemens, Boston, 2.41; National League: Bill Swift, San Francisco, 2.08. (Victories) American League: Jack Morris, Toronto, and Kevin Brown, Texas, 21; National League: Tom Glavine, Atlanta, and Greg Maddux, Chicago, 20. (Strikeouts) American League: Randy Johnson, Seattle, 241; National League: John Smoltz, Atlanta, 215. (Shutouts) American League: Clemens, 5; National League: David Cone, New York, and Glavine, 5. (Saves) American League: Dennis Eckersley, Oakland, 51; National League: Lee Smith, St. Louis, 43. (Innings) American League, Brown, 265.2; National League, Maddux, 286.0.

Professional—Minor Leagues, Class AAA

American Association: Oklahoma City
International League: Columbus
Pacific Coast League: Colorado Springs

Amateur

NCAA: Pepperdine
Little League World Series: Long Beach, California

whose 341 saves ranked first on the career list before 1992. Seaver received a record 98.8% of the vote and became the 23d player elected in his first year of eligibility.

DAN SCHLOSSBERG, *Baseball Writer*

Basketball

The Chicago Bulls became only the fourth franchise in National Basketball Association (NBA) history to win back-to-back championships when they defeated the Portland Trail Blazers, four games to two, to take the 1992 title. The previous season, the Bulls had beaten the Los Angeles Lakers in five games to capture the championship, the first in their history. But the season was dominated by another story: Earvin (Magic) Johnson, star guard of the Los Angeles Lakers, announced his retirement in the early days of the season after testing positive for the HIV virus.

The National Collegiate Athletic Association (NCAA) men's basketball championship went to Duke University, which beat Michigan, 71–51, in the tournament's final game. Duke became the first college team to win two straight titles since UCLA in the early 1970s. The Blue Devils had won the 1991 crown by downing Kansas. Virginia took the National Invitation Tournament (NIT), while Stanford beat Western Kentucky to capture the women's NCAA championship. In a major off-the-court development, controversial Jerry Tarkanian retired as coach of Nevada-Las Vegas (UNLV) after 19 stormy years and one national title.

The Professional Season

The most compelling story of the 1991–92 NBA season concerned Magic Johnson, whose stunning retirement announcement cast a shadow over the ensuing months of the schedule. Johnson left as one of the great players of all time after leading the Lakers to five titles. He was the league's career leader in assists and one of its most celebrated spokesmen and statesmen. In a truly dramatic moment, he returned to play in the midseason All-Star Game, eventually being selected as the contest's most valuable player (MVP). He also was selected to play on the 1992 U.S. Olympic basketball team.

The most intriguing story of the season concerned the Chicago Bulls and their brilliant star, Michael Jordan. The question was: Could the Bulls repeat as champions? In response, they put together an impressive regular season, leading the league with 67 victories, while winning the Central Division title by ten games over the Cleveland Cavaliers. In the Atlantic Division, the Boston Celtics and New York Knicks battled throughout the winter for first place, eventually finishing in a tie with 51–31 records. It was an especially pleasing season for the Knicks under new coach Pat Riley, who had directed the Lakers to four NBA titles. The

© Focus on Sports

Portland's Danny Ainge tries to guard Chicago superstar Michael Jordan (23) during the 1992 NBA play-off finals. The Bulls defeated the Trail Blazers, four games to two, for back-to-back championships. Jordan was voted the most valuable player of the title series.

Celtics were successful despite the struggles of star forward Larry Bird, who spent much of the season sidelined by a back injury. He retired as a player following the Olympics.

Young Golden State made a strong bid to win the Pacific Division, only to be turned away by the veteran Portland Trail Blazers. Phoenix also was a solid challenger, and the Seattle Supersonics finished strongly under new coach George Karl. San Antonio and Utah were locked in a close battle for the Midwest title until Spurs center David Robinson hurt his right thumb in the final weeks. Utah then won the division championship by eight games. Miami became the first of the recent NBA expansion teams to qualify for the play-offs, as did perennial also-rans the Los Angeles Clippers and New Jersey Nets. But the performances of the Milwaukee Bucks (31–51), Philadelphia 76ers (35–47), and Dallas Mavericks (22–60) were disappointing. Coaches who either resigned or were fired included Bill Fitch of New Jersey, Del Harris of Milwaukee, Dick Motta of Sacramento, Paul Westhead of Denver, Don Chaney of Houston, Chuck Daly of Detroit, and Cotton Fitzsimmons of Phoenix. Philadelphia star Charles Barkley was traded in the off-season to Phoenix for three players.

Michael Jordan, the league's best player, won a sixth straight scoring title, averaging 30.1 points. Only Wilt Chamberlain had won more in a row (seven). Second to Jordan was Karl Malone of Utah, who averaged 28.0, and third was Golden State's Chris Mullin (25.6). Jordan easily was the league's most valuable player, with Portland's Clyde Drexler finishing second in the voting. Until he was hurt, Robinson was a serious MVP challenger. He still wound up among the leaders in five major statistical categories, only the third player in NBA history to pull off that feat. Utah's John Stockton led in both assists (13.7) and steals (2.98). But perhaps the most impressive achievement belonged to Detroit's Dennis Rodman, who grabbed 1,530 rebounds to average 18.7 per game, both league highs since Wilt Chamberlain's 1,572 and 19.2 in 1972.

Jordan, Mullin, Malone, Robinson, and Drexler were named first-team All-NBA. Rodman, Jordan, Robinson, Chicago's Scottie Pippen, and Detroit's Joe Dumars made the all-defensive team. Golden State's Don Nelson was selected coach of the year; Indiana's Detlef Schrempf won the Sixth Man award; and Robinson was chosen defensive player of the year. Charlotte's Larry Johnson easily beat out Denver's Dikembe Mutombo for rookie of the year.

The Play-offs. Based on regular-season results, the Chicago Bulls and Portland Trail Blazers were expected to meet for the league championship. That is how it eventually worked out, but not before the Bulls had to struggle through earlier play-off rounds.

PROFESSIONAL BASKETBALL

National Basketball Association
(Final Standings, 1991–92)

Eastern Conference

Atlantic Division	W	L	Pct.	Games Behind
*Boston	51	31	.622	—
*New York	51	31	.622	—
*New Jersey	40	42	.488	11
*Miami	38	44	.463	13
Philadelphia	35	47	.427	16
Washington	25	57	.305	26
Orlando	21	61	.256	30

Central Division	W	L	Pct.	Games Behind
*Chicago	67	15	.817	—
*Cleveland	57	25	.695	10
*Detroit	48	34	.585	19
*Indiana	40	42	.488	27
Atlanta	38	44	.463	29
Charlotte	31	51	.378	36
Milwaukee	31	51	.378	36

Western Conference

Midwest Division	W	L	Pct.	Games Behind
*Utah	55	27	.671	—
*San Antonio	47	35	.573	8
Houston	42	40	.512	13
Denver	24	58	.293	31
Dallas	22	60	.268	33
Minnesota	15	67	.183	40

Pacific Division	W	L	Pct.	Games Behind
*Portland	57	25	.695	—
*Golden State	55	27	.671	2
*Phoenix	53	29	.646	4
*Seattle	47	35	.573	10
*Los Angeles Clippers	45	37	.549	12
*Los Angeles Lakers	43	39	.524	14
Sacramento	29	53	.354	28

*In play-offs

Play-offs
Eastern Conference

First Round	Boston	3 games	Indiana	0
	Chicago	3 games	Miami	0
	Cleveland	3 games	New Jersey	1
	New York	3 games	Detroit	2
Second Round	Chicago	4 games	New York	3
	Cleveland	4 games	Boston	3
Finals	Chicago	4 games	Cleveland	2

Western Conference

First Round	Phoenix	3 games	San Antonio	0
	Portland	3 games	L.A. Lakers	1
	Seattle	3 games	Golden State	1
	Utah	3 games	L.A. Clippers	2
Second Round	Portland	4 games	Phoenix	1
	Utah	4 games	Seattle	1
Finals	Portland	4 games	Utah	2
Championship	Chicago	4 games	Portland	2
All-Star Game	West 153, East 113			

Individual Honors

Most Valuable Player: Michael Jordan, Chicago
Most Valuable Player (championship): Michael Jordan
Most Valuable Player (All-Star Game): Earvin (Magic) Johnson
Rookie of the Year: Larry Johnson, Charlotte
Coach of the Year: Don Nelson, Golden State
Defensive Player of the Year: David Robinson, San Antonio
Leader in Scoring: Michael Jordan, 30.1 points per game
Leader in Assists: John Stockton, Utah, 13.7 per game
Leader in Rebounds: Dennis Rodman, Detroit, 18.7 per game
Leader in Field-Goal Percentage: Buck Williams, Portland, .604
Leader in Free-Throw Percentage: Mark Price, Cleveland, .947
Leader in Steals: John Stockton, 2.98 per game
Leader in Blocked Shots: David Robinson, 4.49 per game

After breezing past Miami in the first round, Chicago was extended to seven games in a conference semifinal-round series by the Knicks.

Then the Bulls had to overcome a strong bid by the Cleveland Cavaliers in the Eastern Conference finals to win the title in six games. That set up the championship showdown with Portland, which had tied with Cleveland for the league's second-best record. The Trail Blazers had a relatively easy time advancing to the final round, beating the Los Angeles Lakers, Phoenix, and Utah in convincing fashion during early play-off series.

Portland had lost to Detroit in five games for the 1990 championship. But the Trail Blazers were convinced they had improved enough to win the 1992 title. They were wrong, mostly because they could not control Jordan. The teams split the first two games in Chicago. Jordan was sensational in the first contest. He scored 35 of his 39 points in the first half—a final-round record—and made six three-point shots during the first 24 minutes, tying another record. But Portland came back to take the second game, 115–104, in overtime behind guard Danny Ainge, who scored nine points in the extra period.

The series resumed in Portland, where the Trail Blazers had lost three straight to Detroit two years before. Jordan scored 26 points and Scottie Pippen added 18 in game three as the Bulls took a 2–1 lead in the series with a 94–84 victory. But Portland, needing a win to have a chance for the title, rallied in the fourth period of game four and won, 93–88. Drexler and forward Jerome Kersey each had 21 points. That set up the pivotal fifth game and again Jordan dominated, scoring 46 points. Pippen's play also was important in the 119–106 Chicago victory. He scored 24 points and had 11 rebounds and nine assists. In game six in Chicago, Portland led by as many as 17 points late in the third quarter. But the Bulls rallied in the fourth. Jordan and Pippen combined for their team's last 19 points and Chicago finished off the series with a 97–93 win. Jordan, who averaged 35.8 points, was selected as the most valuable player, the only man to win two straight final-round MVP awards. Besides Chicago, the only other franchises to win back-to-back titles were Boston; Los Angeles, which also accomplished the feat when it was located in Minneapolis; and Detroit.

The College Season

The 1991–92 college basketball season had two major stories: the quest of Duke University for a second straight NCAA-tournament title and the ongoing controversy involving the NCAA, Nevada-Las Vegas, and its basketball coach, Jerry Tarkanian. Tarkanian had been involved in a long-running dispute with the NCAA that began when he coached at Long Beach State. In 1977 the NCAA put Nevada-Las Vegas on probation for violation of NCAA rules and told the school to suspend Tarkanian

for a year. The coach took the NCAA to court; the disagreement was not settled until 1990. As part of that settlement, the Rebels played in the 1991 NCAA tournament—they won the 1990 title—but were suspended for the 1992 tournament. Tarkanian agreed to resign his job at UNLV after the 1992 season, but then tried to change his mind. The school held firm and he was replaced by Rollie Massimino, longtime coach at Villanova. Tarkanian's final team finished with a 26–2 record. After the season, St. John's popular coach, Lou Carnesecca, retired after 24 seasons. Earlier, Carnesecca had been elected to the Basketball Hall of Fame.

Duke, which had the majority of the players returning from its 1990–91 team, was favored to win a second national title. It was expected to be challenged by such teams as Arkansas, Arizona, Ohio State, UCLA, Indiana, Seton Hall, and LSU. Duke more than lived up to expectations. The Blue Devils won their first 17 games and finished the regular season with a 25–2 record, winning the Atlantic Coast Conference championship and staying atop the polls the entire season. By season's end, challengers for the national title included Big Eight champion Kansas, Pacific-10 power Arizona, Big Ten champion Ohio State, Indiana, and Ar-

---

COLLEGE BASKETBALL

Conference Champions

Atlantic Coast: Duke[r,t]
Atlantic 10: Massachusetts[r,t]
Big East: Seton Hall, Georgetown, St. John's (tied) [r]; Syracuse[t]
Big Eight: Kansas[r,t]
Big Sky: Montana[r,t]
Big South: Radford [r], Campbell [t]
Big Ten: Ohio State
Big West: UNLV[r], New Mexico State[t]
Colonial Athletic: Richmond, James Madison (tied) [r]; Old Dominion[t]
East Coast: Hofstra[r], Towson State[t]
Great Midwest: DePaul, Cincinnati (tied) [r]; Cincinnati[t]
Ivy League: Princeton
Metro: Tulane[r], North Carolina-Charlotte[t]
Metro Atlantic Athletic: Manhattan[r]; LaSalle[t]
Mid-American: Miami, Ohio[r,t]
Mid-Continent: Wisconsin-Green Bay[r], E. Illinois[t]
Mid-Eastern Athletic: Howard[r,t]
Midwestern Collegiate: Evansville[r,t]
Missouri Valley: Illinois State, Southern Illinois (tied) [r]; S.W. Missouri State[t]
North Atlantic: Delaware[r,t]
Northeast: Robert Morris[r,t]
Ohio Valley: Murray State[r,t]
Pacific-10: UCLA
Patriot League: Fordham[r,t]
Southeastern: Kentucky (eastern division), Arkanas (western division) [r]; Kentucky[t]
Southern: East Tennessee State, Tennessee-Chattanooga (tied) [r]; East Tennessee State[t]
Southland: Texas-San Antonio[r], Northeast Louisiana[t]
Southwest: Houston and Texas (tied) [r]; Houston[t]
Southwestern Athletic: Mississippi Valley State[r,t]
Sun Belt: Louisiana Tech and Southwestern Louisiana (tied) [r]; Southwestern Louisiana[t]
Trans America Athletic: Georgia Southern[r,t]
West Coast: Pepperdine[r,t]
Western Athletic: Brigham Young and Texas-El Paso (tied) [r]; Brigham Young[t]
[r]regular-season winner; [t]conference-tournament winner

Tournaments

NCAA Division I: Duke
NCAA Division II: Virginia Union
NCAA Division III: Calvin
NIT: Virginia
NAIA: Oklahoma City
NCAA Division I (women): Stanford

© Focus on Sports

Guard Bobby Hurley (11) of Jersey City, NJ, was named most valuable player of the NCAA championship as he directed the Duke Blue Devils to a 71–51 win over Michigan for a second consecutive title.

kansas. Among the most disappointing teams were Georgetown, Oklahoma, and LSU, which had center Shaquille O'Neal, the most dominating player in the country. The strongest conferences were the Big Eight, the Pacific-10, and the Big Ten.

The best player in the United States was Duke center Christian Laettner, who was a consensus All-American. O'Neal was another consensus choice, along with Ohio State guard Jimmy Jackson. Other selections on most All-American teams included Georgetown center Alonzo Mourning and Southern California guard Harold Miner. Other standout players included Walt Williams of Maryland, Byron Houston of Oklahoma State, Don MacLean of UCLA, Anthony Peeler of Missouri, Adam Keefe of Stanford, Todd Day and Lee Mayberry of Arkansas, Calbert Cheaney of Indiana, Bobby Hurley of Duke, and Malik Sealy of St. John's. O'Neal, Jackson, and Miner all decided to join the professional ranks after their junior seasons.

The Tournaments. Along with Duke, the top seeds in the NCAA tournament were Kansas, Ohio State, and UCLA. But those ratings did not hold up once the tournament began. While Duke won the East Regional, beating Kentucky in overtime on a last-second shot by Laettner, Ohio State fell to Michigan in the Southeast. UCLA lost to Indiana in the West, and Kansas was eliminated in an early round of the Midwest by Texas-El Paso. Cincinnati eventually won the Midwest.

In the final four at the Metrodome in Minneapolis, Duke played Indiana in one semifinal and Cincinnati met Michigan in the other. Duke pulled away from the Hoosiers in the second half and finished with an 81–78 victory. Michigan, which started five freshmen, used its height advantage to wear out Cincinnati eventually, 76-72. That set up a final between the experienced Blue Devils and the young Wolverines. After a close first half, in which Duke committed more errors than usual, the Blue Devils rallied behind Laettner and Grant Hill to come away with a 71-51 victory. Guard Bobby Hurley was selected most valuable player of the final four. It was Duke's fifth straight appearance in the final four and sixth in seven years. No school had won back-to-back championships since UCLA won the last of its seven straight in 1973.

In the NIT, Virginia forward Bryant Stith made five free throws in overtime as the Cavaliers beat Notre Dame, 81–76, in New York's Madison Square Garden. Elmer Bennett scored 39 for the Irish. In the women's NCAA tournament, favored Virginia was upset in the semifinal by Stanford, 66-65. In the final, Stanford met Western Kentucky, which defeated Southwest Missouri State, 84-72, in the other semifinal. Stanford won the championship, 78-62. Stanford's Molly Goodenbour was chosen MVP of the final four.

See also SPORTS—*Olympic Games.*

PAUL ATTNER
Senior Writer, "The Sporting News"

Boxing

The world heavyweight boxing championship changed hands for the third time in three years in 1992, but an event outside the ring involving former heavyweight champion Mike Tyson attracted worldwide attention.

The Tyson Case. Tyson, in his prime considered to be one of the most dominant of heavyweight champions, was sentenced on March 26, 1992, to six years in prison after being convicted of rape. Tyson was charged with raping an 18-year-old woman, Desiree Washington, in Indianapolis, IN. The case was publicized highly, and the verdict brought a quick demise to Tyson's ring fortunes.

The Heavyweights. On November 13 at Las Vegas, NV, Evander Holyfield, a well-liked champion who had not truly proved his mettle, was outpunched and overpowered by Riddick Bowe, like Tyson a product of the mean streets of Brooklyn, NY. Bowe took the title from Holyfield, who had taken it from James (Buster) Douglas on Oct. 25, 1990. Douglas had dethroned Tyson on Feb. 10, 1990, in Tokyo in one of boxing's biggest upsets. After a long layoff, an overweight and undertrained Douglas lost decisively to Holyfield.

Holyfield's tenure as heavyweight champion had left much to be desired: He defeated an over-the-hill former champion, George Foreman; a journeyman battler, Bert Cooper, who knocked Holyfield down; and another overweight and over-the-hill former champion, Larry Holmes. He was unable to knock down either Foreman or Holmes; and in all five fights involving the title, he failed to show the authority of a champion. Holyfield's loss to Bowe was his first in 29 bouts and ended his reign at two years, 19 days.

In the 25-year-old Bowe, a strapping 6′5″ (1.95 m) and 235 lbs (107 kg), boxing fans thought they had at last the kind of champion who could restore luster to the heavyweight title. Bowe floored Holyfield in the 11th round of their 12-round bout. But Holyfield, who fought back gallantly in the 11th, in some measure regained stature. He won new respect by his refusal to quit as the fighters staged one of the fiercest slugfests in the heavyweight division in many years. Bowe had earned his shot at Holyfield earlier in the year when he knocked out 6′4″ (1.93-m), 230-lb (104-kg) Pierre Coetzer of South Africa in the seventh round at Las Vegas for his 32d straight victory. Toward year's end, Bowe resigned his World Boxing Council (WBC) title; the Council declared Briton Lennox Lewis the champ.

The Lighter Divisions. The fight most boxing fans wanted in 1992 was the Julio César Chávez-Hector (Macho) Camacho bout for the WBC junior-welterweight title. That came about on September 13 at Las Vegas. Chávez, often called "the best fighter in the world

pound for pound," scored a lopsided 12-round decision. The decision was unanimous, with one judge giving Chávez every round. With this fight, Chávez lifted his record to an astounding 82–0 with 70 knockouts. Camacho (41–1, 18 knockouts, one no contest), a former champion, showed tremendous courage in weathering the barrage Chávez threw at him, and won respect from fans for his gameness and endurance. Chávez had tuned up for the Camacho bout in April with a fifth-round knockout of Angel Hernandez of Puerto Rico in a bout in Mexico City.

There were other outstanding performances in the lighter divisions. Terry Norris, 24, the WBC junior-middleweight champion and another nominee for best fighter "pound for pound," took four rounds to stop Meldrick Taylor, the World Boxing Association (WBA) welterweight champion and a superlative boxer who had held two world titles and had lost only once, to Chávez, in 31 previous fights. Norris had made the match, wanting to prove himself against the best. Both fighters got the biggest paydays of their careers—$1.3 million for Norris, and almost twice that for Taylor.

GEORGE DE GREGORIO, *"The New York Times"*

WORLD BOXING CHAMPIONS[1]

Heavyweight: World Boxing Council (WBC)—Lennox Lewis, Great Britain, 1992; World Boxing Association (WBA)—Riddick Bowe, United States, 1992; International Boxing Federation (IBF)—Bowe, 1992.

Cruiserweight: WBC—Anaclet Wamba, France, 1991; WBA—Bobby Czyz, United States, 1991; IBF—Alfred Cole, United States, 1992.

Light Heavyweight: WBC—Jeff Harding, Australia, 1991; WBA—Virgil Hill, United States, 1992; IBF—Charles Williams, United States, 1990.

Super Middleweight: WBC—Nigel Benn, Great Britain, 1992; WBA—Michael Nunn, United States, 1992; IBF—Iran Barkley, United States, 1992.

Middleweight: WBC—Julian Jackson, Virgin Islands, 1990; WBA—Reggie Johnson, United States, 1992; IBF—James Toney, United States, 1991.

Junior Middleweight: WBC—Terry Norris, United States, 1990; WBA—Julio Cesar Vasquez, Argentina, 1992; IBF—Gianfranco Rosi, Italy, 1989.

Welterweight: WBC—James McGirt, United States, 1991; WBA—Crisanto Espana, Ireland, 1992; IBF—Maurice Blocker, United States, 1991.

Junior Welterweight: WBC—Julio César Chávez, Mexico, 1989; WBA—Morris East, Philippines, 1992; IBF—Pernell Whitaker, United States, 1992.

Lightweight: WBC—Miguel Angel Gonzalez, Mexico, 1992; WBA—Tony Lopez, United States, 1992; IBF—Vacant.

Junior Lightweight: WBC—Azumah Nelson, Ghana, 1988; WBA—Genaro Hernandez, United States, 1991; IBF—Juan Molina, Puerto Rico, 1992.

Featherweight: WBC—Paul Hodkinson, Great Britain, 1991; WBA—Yung-kyun Park, South Korea, 1991; IBF—Manuel Medina, Mexico, 1991.

Junior Featherweight: WBC—Tracy Harris Patterson, United States, 1992; WBA—Wilfredo Vazquez, Mexico, 1992; IBF—Kennedy McKinney, United States, 1992.

Bantamweight: WBC—Victor Manuel Rabanales, Mexico, 1992; WBA—Jorge Eliecer Julio, Colombia, 1992; IBF—Orlando Canizales, United States, 1988.

Junior Bantamweight: WBC—Sunkil Moon, South Korea, 1990; WBA—Katzuya Onizuka, Japan, 1992; IBF—Robert Quiroga, United States, 1990.

Flyweight: WBC—Yuri Arvachakov, Russia, 1992; WBA—Aquiles Guzmán, Venezuela, 1992; IBF—Pichit Sitbangphacan, Thailand, 1992.

Junior Flyweight: WBC—Humberto Gonzalez, Mexico, 1989; WBA—Myung Woo Yuh, South Korea, 1992; IBF—Michael Carbajal, United States, 1990.

Strawweight: WBC—Ricardo Lopez, Mexico, 1990; WBA—Choi Hi-Yong, South Korea, 1991; IBF—Manny Melchor, Philippines, 1992.

[1]As of Dec. 22, 1992; date indicates year title was won.

Football

The most important event of the 1992–93 pro football season happened off the field, not on. After several years of turmoil and debate, the National Football League (NFL) and its labor union reached agreement on a new collective-bargaining contract. The new contract established, for the first time in NFL history, a liberalized form of free agency. On the field, the San Francisco 49ers, who had won four Super Bowls during the 1980s, finished with the league's best record (14-2) but nevertheless lost in the National Football Conference (NFC) championship game to the revitalized Dallas Cowboys. The Cowboys' opponent in the Super Bowl was the Buffalo Bills, who were making their third straight appearance in the title game.

Super Bowl XXVII, which was played on Jan. 31, 1993, before 98,374 fans in the Rose Bowl in Pasadena, turned out to be a major disappointment for the Bills, however. They were overwhelmed by Dallas, 52-17. Nine turnovers by the Bills were a major reason for their defeat. Charles Haley and Ken Norton led the Dallas defense. Cowboys' quarterback Troy Aikman completed 22 of 30 passes, threw for four touchdowns, and was voted the game's most valuable player. Jim Kelly, the quarterback of the Bills, left the game in the second quarter with a knee injury. It was the ninth straight time that an NFC team took the title and the third consecutive year that a team from its Eastern Division emerged as Super Bowl champs.

In college competition, the Alabama Crimson Tide won their first national championship since the late 1970s by defeating the previously unbeaten Miami Hurricanes, 34-13, in the Sugar Bowl. The Heisman Trophy, however, went to Miami quarterback Gino Torretta, who became the second Hurricane quarterback to win that award.

In the Canadian Football League (CFL), the Calgary Stampeders won the Grey Cup, defeating the Winnipeg Blue Bombers by a score of 24-10. Calgary's Doug Flutie, a former Heisman Trophy winner, won most valuable player (MVP) honors for the regular season and for the championship game. He became the first CFL player to win both MVP awards since 1969.

The Professional Season

NFL Developments. The decision by the NFL and the NFL Players Association (NFLPA) to agree on a new labor contract was greeted with relief by both players and team executives. The two groups had been without a contract since 1987, and the failure to reach an agreement had held up plans for expansion. The main stumbling block had been the subject of free agency. The owners did not want it;

PROFESSIONAL FOOTBALL

National Football League

Final Standings, 1992

AMERICAN CONFERENCE

Eastern Division	W	L	T	Pct.	Points For	Points Against
Miami	11	5	0	.688	340	281
Buffalo	11	5	0	.688	381	283
Indianapolis	9	7	0	.563	216	302
N.Y. Jets	4	12	0	.250	220	315
New England	2	14	0	.125	205	363
Central Division						
Pittsburgh	11	5	0	.688	299	225
Houston	10	6	0	.625	352	258
Cleveland	7	9	0	.438	272	275
Cincinnati	5	11	0	.313	274	364
Western Division						
San Diego	11	5	0	.688	335	241
Kansas City	10	6	0	.625	348	282
Denver	8	8	0	.500	262	329
L.A. Raiders	7	9	0	.438	249	281
Seattle	2	14	0	.125	140	312

PLAY-OFFS
San Diego 17, Kansas City 0
Buffalo 41, Houston 38
Buffalo 24, Pittsburgh 3
Miami 31, San Diego 0
Buffalo 29, Miami 10

NATIONAL CONFERENCE

Eastern Division	W	L	T	Pct.	Points For	Points Against
Dallas	13	3	0	.813	409	243
Philadelphia	11	5	0	.688	354	245
Washington	9	7	0	.563	300	255
N.Y. Giants	6	10	0	.375	306	367
Phoenix	4	12	0	.250	243	332
Central Division						
Minnesota	11	5	0	.688	374	249
Green Bay	9	7	0	.563	276	296
Tampa Bay	5	11	0	.313	267	365
Chicago	5	11	0	.313	295	361
Detroit	5	11	0	.313	273	332
Western Division						
San Francisco	14	2	0	.875	431	236
New Orleans	12	4	0	.750	330	202
Atlanta	6	10	0	.375	327	414
L.A. Rams	6	10	0	.375	313	383

PLAY-OFFS
Washington 24, Minnesota 7
Philadelphia 36, New Orleans 20
San Francisco 20, Washington 13
Dallas 34, Philadelphia 10
Dallas 30, San Francisco 20

SUPER BOWL XXVII: Dallas 52, Buffalo 17

however, the players did. The sides finally reached a compromise, allowing most five-year players to become free agents after their existing contracts expire. The agreement was given further impetus by a jury verdict in September 1992 which found that the NFL had violated antitrust laws regarding its existing free-agency system, called Plan B. The NFL was the last major sports league lacking liberalized free-agency rules.

After six years of controversy, the NFL's instant-replay rule was reversed in March 1992. The rule—which called for booth officials to view a videotape of a specific play and then confirm or reverse the on-field officials' ruling on the play—had received much criticism, primarily for slowing down the game unnecessarily.

Play-offs. The Washington Redskins had hoped to repeat as world champions, but suffered a string of major injuries and barely made the play-offs. Instead, the NFC East was dominated by the upstart Dallas Cowboys, who had been a dismal 1-15 in 1989. But a new owner, Jerry Jones, and a new coach, Jimmy Johnson —both of whom had joined the organization before the 1989 debacle—quickly rebuilt the team through a series of great trades and fine draft choices. The Cowboys finished with a 13–3 record, the most wins in the history of the storied franchise, which already had been to five Super Bowls and was known as ''America's team.''

The NFC Central title went to the Minnesota Vikings, one of a handful of teams that exceeded expectations under a new coach. In this case, the Vikings were guided expertly by Dennis Green, only the second black head coach in NFL history. The Vikings won the title on the last day of the regular season by beating the Green Bay Packers, who made great strides under new coach Mike Holmgren. The Chicago Bears, longtime division power, played poorly, and their coach Mike Ditka was fired after the season ended.

The Buffalo Bills, led by quarterback Jim Kelly, clinched the AFC championship — and a third consecutive Super Bowl appearance — with a 29-10 win over the Miami Dolphins.

© AP/Wide World

San Francisco was considered the league's best team in the regular season. The 49ers were led by quarterback Steve Young, who replaced injured star Joe Montana and wound up being named the league's most valuable player. Young's team won the NFC West, beating out the New Orleans Saints, who qualified for the play-offs as a wild-card team along with Washington.

In the American Football Conference (AFC), Pittsburgh and its new coach, Bill Cowher, were the surprise winners of the Central title. Cowher, who grew up near Pittsburgh, had replaced Chuck Noll, coach of five Steeler Super Bowl-winning teams. Denver and Kansas City had been expected to fight for the AFC West crown. Instead, San Diego, long a doormat in the division, overcame a 0-4 start to win the title, thanks in part to the play of quarterback Stan Humphries. The biggest shock, though, came in the AFC East, when Buffalo —favored to win the AFC championship—lost to Houston on the final weekend and was beaten out by the Miami Dolphins, thus failing to finish with the best record in the AFC. The Dolphins' coach, Don Shula, became the second coach in NFL history to win 300 regular-season games. (Chicago's George Halas was the first.) Houston and Buffalo became the wild-card teams. Indianapolis did not make the play-offs, but improved considerably under new coach Ted Marchibroda after being the worst team in the league in 1991–92.

In the play-offs, Buffalo and Houston played in what became a historic game. The Bills overcame a record-breaking 32-point second-half deficit to pull out the victory. San Diego shut out Kansas City in the other AFC wild-card game, while Washington overpowered Minnesota and Philadelphia rallied in the second half to down the New Orleans Saints. In the semifinals, San Francisco held off a last-quarter surge by the Redskins and Dallas overwhelmed Philadelphia to set up the NFC title game. Meanwhile, in the AFC, Buffalo ran past the Steelers and the Dolphins shut out the San Diego Chargers.

Miami was a slight favorite to beat Buffalo in the AFC championship game, but the Dolphins made too many turnovers to overcome the more-talented Bills, who got five field goals from Steve Christie. Buffalo became only the second team in history to appear in three consecutive Super Bowls. Quarterback Jim Kelly, who missed the first play-off game because of a bad knee, played against Miami.

Dallas and San Francisco put on a dramatic performance at Candlestick Park. The 49ers, the NFL's Number 1-ranked offense, committed four turnovers to Dallas' Number 1 defense. The teams combined for a total of almost 850 yards, but it was the running of Dallas' Emmitt Smith, who gained 114 yards, and the passing of quarterback Troy Aikman, with two

The College Season

The undefeated Alabama Crimson Tide won the national championship for the 12th time in school history by overwhelming previously unbeaten Miami on New Year's night in the Sugar Bowl. Miami, which entered the game as the nation's Number 1-ranked team, had been trying to win its fifth national title in ten years, an unprecedented achievement in college-football history.

Miami had been a sound favorite to beat Alabama, which had won the first Southeastern Conference championship play-off game over Florida to secure a spot in the Sugar Bowl. But the Crimson Tide, who last had won the national title in 1979 under legendary coach Paul (Bear) Bryant, proved to be far too strong for Miami, winning 34-13. The Hurricanes were limited to just 48 rushing yards, and Alabama —which had the nation's top-ranked defense— intercepted three passes thrown by Miami quarterback Gino Torretta, who earlier had won the Heisman Trophy as the nation's outstanding player. Two of those interceptions came in the third quarter. One led to an Alabama field goal, and the other was returned 31 yards for a touchdown by George Teague to

© AP/Wide World

The outstanding running of Emmitt Smith (22) helped the Dallas Cowboys defeat the San Francisco 49ers, 30-20, to win the NFC championship and gain a Super Bowl berth.

touchdown passes, that led the Cowboys to a 30–20 victory.

Individual Performances. Emmitt Smith of Dallas won his second straight rushing title (1,713 yards), while Buffalo's Thurman Thomas led the league in combined yards (2,113) for a record fourth straight year. Green Bay's Sterling Sharpe caught a league-record 108 passes. Steve Young of San Francisco was the most accurate passer for the second straight season, while the Dolphins' Pete Stoyanovich led in scoring with 124 points. Other standouts included defensive end Bruce Smith of Buffalo, defensive tackle Cortez Kennedy of Seattle, linebackers Junior Seau of San Diego and Wilbur Marshall of Washington, defensive backs Rod Woodson of Pittsburgh and Steve Atwater of Denver, running back Barry Foster of Pittsburgh, and receiver Jerry Rice of the 49ers.

Off the Field. Besides Ditka, other coaches who were fired during the season included Dan Reeves of Denver, Dick MacPherson of New England, and Ray Handley of the New York Giants. Admitted to the Pro Football Hall of Fame were running back John Riggins, owner Al Davis, tight end John Mackey and cornerback Lem Barney. The season once again was marred with numerous injuries to players, particularly quarterbacks. Defensive lineman Dennis Byrd of the New York Jets was left partially paralyzed after a collision.

COLLEGE FOOTBALL

Conference Champions	Atlantic Coast—Florida State Big Eight—Nebraska Big Ten—Michigan Big West—Nevada Pacific Ten—(tie) Washington, Stanford Southeastern—Alabama Southwest—Texas A&M Western Athletic—(tie) Brigham Young, Fresno State, Hawaii
NCAA Champions	Division I-AA—Marshall Division II—Jacksonville State Division III—Wisconsin-La Crosse
NAIA Champions	Division I—Central State University (Ohio) Division II—Findlay University (Ohio)
Individual Honors	Heisman Trophy—Gino Torretta, Miami Lombardi Award—Marvin Jones, Florida Outland Trophy—Will Shields, Nebraska

Major Bowl Games

Aloha Bowl (Honolulu, HI, Dec. 25)—Kansas 23, Brigham Young 20
Blockbuster Bowl (Fort Lauderdale, FL, Jan. 1)—Stanford 24, Penn State 3
Blue-Gray Classic (Montgomery, AL, Dec. 25)—Gray 27, Blue 17
Citrus Bowl (Orlando, FL, Jan. 1)—Georgia 21, Ohio State 14
Copper Bowl (Tucson, AZ, Dec. 29)—Washington State 31, Utah 28
Cotton Bowl (Dallas, TX, Jan. 1)—Notre Dame 28, Texas A&M 3
Fiesta Bowl (Tempe, AZ, Jan. 1)—Syracuse 26, Colorado 22
Freedom Bowl (Anaheim, CA, Dec. 29)—Fresno State 24, Southern Cal 7
Gator Bowl (Jacksonville, FL, Dec. 31)—Florida 27, North Carolina State 10
Hall of Fame Bowl (Tampa, FL, Jan. 1)—Tennessee 38, Boston College 23
John Hancock Bowl (El Paso, TX, Dec. 31)—Baylor 20, Arizona 15
Holiday Bowl (San Diego, CA, Dec. 30)—Hawaii 27, Illinois 17
Independence Bowl (Shreveport, LA, Dec. 31)—Wake Forest 39, Oregon 35
Las Vegas Bowl (Las Vegas, NV, Dec. 18)—Bowling Green 35, Nevada 34
Liberty Bowl (Memphis, TN, Dec. 31)—Mississippi 13, Air Force 0
Orange Bowl (Miami, FL, Jan. 1)—Florida State 27, Nebraska 14
Peach Bowl (Atlanta, GA, Jan. 2)—North Carolina 21, Mississippi State 17
Rose Bowl (Pasadena, CA, Jan. 1)—Michigan 38, Washington 31
Sugar Bowl (New Orleans, LA, Jan. 1)—Alabama 34, Miami 13

Senior quarterback Gino Torretta (13) of the Miami Hurricanes was named the 1992 Heisman Trophy winner. Torretta led his team to an almost-perfect 1992 season, and racked up a 26-1 career record as Miami's starting quarterback.

© Damion Strohmeyer/Allspor

give the Crimson Tide a 27-6 lead. Halfback Derrick Lessic gained 143 rushing yards for Alabama, which extended its winning streak to 23 games under veteran coach Gene Stallings and ended Miami's streak at 29 in a row.

With the loss, Miami dropped to Number 3 in the final Associated Press (AP) poll. Florida State, which was playing as well as any team in the nation by the end of the season, finished with the Number 2 ranking. The Seminoles were led by quarterback Charlie Ward, who also was a starter on the school's highly regarded basketball team. Behind Ward's two touchdown passes, the Seminoles secured their Number 2 rating by defeating Big Eight champion Nebraska, 27-14, in the Orange Bowl. It was their eighth straight bowl victory, a college record.

Texas A&M had finished the regular season undefeated and won the Southwest Conference championship. But its national-title aspirations were doused by a powerful Notre Dame team, which overwhelmed the Aggies, 28-3. Notre Dame scored 21 points in the second half to secure the triumph. The Irish were particularly effective running the ball, with tailback Reggie Brooks gaining 115 yards. Notre Dame finished ranked fourth while Texas A & M slipped to seventh.

In the Rose Bowl, Michigan was much more successful in keeping its undefeated record intact, defeating Washington, 38-31. The Wolverines relied on the running of halfback Tyrone Wheatley, who carried just 15 times but still gained 247 yards and scored touchdowns on runs of 88, 56, and 24 yards. Michigan won the game with five and one half minutes left on a pass from quarterback Elvis Grbac to Tony

McGee. The Wolverines had won nine games but also had three ties, which prevented them from challenging for the national title. Washington had been ranked Number 1 earlier in the season but wound up losing three games, amid stories which charged financial misconduct by some players and alumni. Michigan ended the season ranked fifth.

The race for the Heisman Trophy was one of the most publicized in history. The major contenders were Torretta, who broke most of Miami's major career passing records; San Diego State's Marshall Faulk, who led the nation in rushing despite a series of injuries; and Georgia's Garrison Hearst, who was another standout running back. Faulk was trying to become the first sophomore ever to win this prestigious award. However, he injured a knee toward the end of the season and finished second in the voting to Torretta, who lost only one regular-season game as Miami's starting quarterback.

Florida State's Marvin Jones emerged as the nation's outstanding defensive player. He was named winner of the Lombardi Trophy, which honors the top lineman or linebacker, and the Butkus Award, which goes to the top linebacker. Nebraska's Will Shields won the Outland Trophy, which is awarded to the top interior lineman.

Marshall won the Division I-AA title by defeating Youngstown State, 31-28, on a last-second field goal. Jacksonville State took the Division II championship with a 17-13 victory over Pittsburgh State while Wisconsin La Crosse downed Washington and Jefferson, 16-12, for the Division III title.

PAUL ATTNER, *"The Sporting News"*

Golf

Raymond Floyd, a 30-year PGA tour veteran, was golf's story of the year in 1992.

Floyd, winner of 22 tournaments and four major championships during his career on the tour, was 49 when he won the Doral Ryder Open in March. Soon thereafter he finished second in the Masters and went on to rank 13th on the regular tour's money list with $741,918. In September, Floyd turned 50 and went part-time to the Senior PGA tour. In seven tournaments, he won only three, including the season-ending Senior Tour Championship at Dorado Beach with a record-tying 19-under-par 197. Floyd became the first player to win events on both tours in the same year. He won $436,991 to rank 14th on the Senior tour, but

GOLF

PGA Tour

Infiniti Tournament of Champions: Steve Elkington (279)
Bob Hope Chrysler Classic: John Cook (336)
Phoenix Open: Mark Calcavecchia (264)
AT&T Pebble Beach National Pro-Am: Mark O'Meara (275)
United Airlines Hawaiian Open: John Cook (265)
Northern Telecom Open: Lee Janzen (270)
Buick Invitational of California: Steve Pate (200)
Nissan Los Angeles Open: Fred Couples (269)
Doral Ryder Open: Ray Floyd (271)
Honda Classic: Corey Pavin (273)
Nestle Invitational: Fred Couples (269)
The Players Championship: Davis Love III (273)
Freeport-McMoran Classic: Chip Beck (276)
Masters: Fred Couples (275)
Deposit Guaranty Golf Classic: Richard Zokol (267)
MCI Heritage Classic: Davis Love III (269)
K Mart Greater Greensboro Open: Davis Love III (272)
Shell Houston Open: Fred Funk (272)
BellSouth Classic: Tom Kite (272)
GTE Byron Nelson Classic: Billy Ray Brown (199)
Southwestern Bell Colonial: Bruce Lietzke (267)
Kemper Open: Bill Glasson (276)
Memorial: David Edwards (273
Federal Express St. Jude Classic: Jay Haas (263)
U.S. Open: Tom Kite (285)
Buick Classic: David Frost (268)
Centel Western Open: Ben Crenshaw (276)
Anheuser-Busch Classic: David Peoples (271)
Chattanooga Classic: Mark Calcavecchia (269)
New England Classic: Brad Faxon (268)
Canon Greater Hartford Open: Lanny Wadkins (274)
Buick Open: Dan Forsman (276)
PGA Championship: Nick Price (278)
The International: Brad Faxon (+14)
NEC World Series of Golf: Craig Stadler (273)
Greater Milwaukee Open: Richard Zokol (269)
Canadian Open: Greg Norman (280)
Hardee's Golf Classic: David Frost (266)
B.C. Open: John Daly (266)
Buick Southern Open: Gary Hallberg (206)
Las Vegas Invitational: John Cook (334)
Walt Disney World/Oldsmobile Classic: John Huston (262)
H.E.B. Texas Open: Nick Price (263)
Tour Championship: Paul Azinger (276)
Amoco Centel Championship: Don Pooley (268)
Lincoln-Mercury Kapalua International: Davis Love III (275)
Franklin Funds Shark Shootout: David Love III/Tom Kite (191)
Skins Game: Payne Stewart ($220,000)

LPGA Tour

Oldsmobile LPGA Classic: Colleen Walker (279)
The Phar-Mor at Inverrary: Shelley Hamlin (206)
Itoki Hawaiian Ladies Open: Lisa Walters (208)
Women's Kemper Open: Dawn Coe (275)
Inamori Classic: Judy Dickinson (277)
Ping/Welch's Championship: Brandie Burton (277)
Standard Register Ping: Danielle Ammaccapane (279)
Nabisco Dinah Shore: Dottie Mochrie (279)
Las Vegas LPGA International: Dana Lofland (212)
Sega Women's Championship: Dottie Mochrie (277)
Sara Lee Classic: Maggie Will (207)
Centel Classic: Danielle Ammaccapane (275)
Crestar Farm Fresh Classic: Jennifer Wyatt (208)
Mazda LPGA Classic Championship: Betsy King (267)
LPGA Corning Classic: Colleen Walker (276)
JC Penney/LPGA Skins Game: Pat Bradley (8 Skins)
Oldsmobile Classic: Barb Mucha (276)
McDonald's Championship: Ayako Okamoto (205)
ShopRite LPGA Classic: Anne-Marie Palli (207)
Lady Keystone Open: Danielle Ammaccapane (208)
Rochester International: Patty Sheehan (269)
Jamie Farr Toledo Classic: Patty Sheehan (209)
The Phar-Mor in Youngstown: Betsy King (209)
JAL Big Apple Classic: Juli Inkster (273)
U.S. Women's Open: Patty Sheehan (280)
Welch's Classic: Dottie Mochrie (278)
McCall's LPGA Classic at Stratton Mountain: Florence Descampe (278)
du Maurier Ltd. Classic: Sherri Steinhauer (277)
Northgate Computer Classic: Kris Tschetter (211)
Sun-Times Challenge: Dottie Mochrie (216)
Rail Charity Golf Classic: Nancy Lopez (199)
Ping-Cellular One LPGA Championship: Nancy Lopez (209)

Safecon Classic: Colleen Walker (277)
Los Coyotes LPGA Classic: Nancy Scranton (279)
Solheim Cup: Europe 11 1/2, United States 6 1/2
Nichirei International: USA 21 1/2 points, Japan 10
Mazda Japan Classic: Betsy King (205)
JC Penney Classic: Dottie Mochrie/Dan Forsman (264)
JBP Cup LPGA Match Play Championship: Dawn Coe-Jones

Senior PGA Tour

Infiniti Tournament of Champions: Al Geiberger (282)
Senior Skins Game: Arnold Palmer ($205,000)
Royal Caribbean Classic: Don Massengale (205)
Aetna Challenge: Jimmy Powell (197)
GTE Suncoast Classic: Jim Colbert (200)
Chrysler Cup: United States
GTE West Classic: Bruce Crampton (195)
Vantage at the Dominion: Lee Trevino (201)
The Vintage Arco Invitational: Mike Hill (203)
Fuji Grand Slam: Ray Floyd (197)
The Tradition at Desert Mountain: Lee Trevino (274)
PGA Seniors Championship: Lee Trevino (278)
Liberty Mutual Legends of Golf: Trevino-Hill (251)
Las Vegas Senior Classic: Lee Trevino (206)
Murata Reunion Pro-Am: George Archer (211)
Doug Sanders Kingwood Celebrity Classic: Mike Hill (134)
Bell Atlantic Classic: Lee Trevino (205)
NYNEX Commemorative: Dale Douglass (133)
PaineWebber Invitational: Don Pies (203)
Mazda Presents SR Players Championship: Dave Stockton (277)
Southwestern Bell Classic: Gibby Gilbert (193)
Kroger Senior Classic: Gibby Gilbert (198)
U.S. Senior Open: Larry Laoretti (275)
Ameritech Senior Open: Dale Douglass (201)
Newport Cup: Jim Dent (204)
Northville Long Island Classic: George Archer (205)
Digital Seniors Classic: Mike Hill (136)
Bruno's Memorial Classic: George Archer (208)
GTE Northwest Classic: Mike Joyce (204)
Franklin Showdown Classic: Orville Moody (137)
First of America Classic: Gibby Gilbert (202)
Bank One Classic: Terry Dill (203)
GTE North Classic: Ray Floyd (199)
Nationwide Championship: Isao Aoki (136)
Vantage Championship: Jim Colbert (132)
Raley's Senior Gold Rush: Bob Charles (201)
Transamerica Senior Golf Championship: Bob Charles (200)
Ralph's Senior Classic: Ray Floyd (195)
Kaanapali Classic: Tommy Aaron (198)
Ko Olina Senior Invitational: Chi Chi Rodriguez (206)
Du Pont Cup: United States 22, Japan 10
Senior PGA Tour National Qualifying Tournament: Larry Gilbert (276)
PGA Seniors Championship: Ray Floyd (197)

Other Tournaments

British Open: Nick Faldo (272)
Toyota World Match Play; Nick Faldo
Team: United States
Curtis Cup: Great Britain 10, United States 8
U.S. Men's Amateur: Justin Leonard
U.S. Women's Amateur: Vicki Goetze
U.S. Men's Public Links: Warren Schutte
U.S. Women's Public Links: Amy Fruhwirth
U.S. Mid-Amateur: Danny Yates
U.S. Women's Mid-Amateur: Marion Maney-McInerney
U.S. Senior Men's Amateur: Clarence More
U.S. Senior Women's Amateur: Rosemary Thompson
U.S. Junior Boys: Eldrick Woods
U.S. Junior Girls: Fuma Jamie Koizumi
NCAA Men: Individual: Phil Mickelson; Teams: Arizona
NCAA Women: Individual: Vicki Goetze; Team: San Jose State
Women's World Amateur Team: Spain (588)
World Amateur Team: New Zealand (823)
British Amateur: Stephen Dundas
British Senior Open: John Fourie
Seniors British Amateur: Cliff Hartland (221)
Dunhill Cup: England
Grand Slam of Golf: Nick Price (137)
Sun City Million Dollar Challenge: David Frost (276)

his combined winnings of $1,178,909 on both tours put him third among all money-winners in U.S. golf. His scoring average of 69.69 on the regular tour was tied for third-best, and his Senior scoring average of 67.95 was far and away the best, although he was not eligible for the official title.

On the PGA tour, Fred Couples won the Masters and two other tournaments and led the money list with $1,344,188. He also won the Vardon trophy for scoring average at 69.38 and was named Player of the Year by the Professional Golfers Association and the Golf Writers Association of America (GWAA).

Tom Kite, golf's all-time leading money-winner and heretofore "the best player never to win a major," took care of that problem by overcoming fierce winds in the final round at Pebble Beach to win the U.S. Open at the age of 42. Nick Faldo recovered from a semicollapse in the last round to beat John Cook in the British Open at Muirfield in Scotland, and Nick Price outlasted the field with a final-round 70 to win the PGA Championship at Bellerive by three strokes. Cook—who tied for second in the PGA, won three other tournaments, and finished third on the money list with $1,165,606 —was named Comeback Player of the Year by *Golf Digest* after recovering from hand surgery.

Davis Love III also won three tournaments early in the year, finished as second-leading money-winner with $1,191,630, and was named *Golf Digest*'s Most Improved Professional. Mark Carnavale was named Rookie of the Year by *Golf Digest*. And the magazine named Faldo World Player of the Year.

Senior Tour. Lee Trevino won the PGA Senior Championship and four other tournaments on the Senior PGA tour before the end of May. Despite an injury to his left thumb that required surgery after the season, he held on to win the money title with $1,027,002 and the Byron Nelson scoring-average award with 69.46.

LPGA Tour. Dottie Mochrie won four tournaments, including the Nabisco Dinah Shore, and swept the honors on the LPGA tour. She was the leading money-winner with $693,336 and won the Vare Trophy with a scoring average of 70.8, the fifth-lowest in history. She was named Player of the Year by the LPGA and the GWAA.

In the other women's majors, Patty Sheehan won the U.S. Women's Open in a play-off over Juli Inkster at Oakmont, Betsy King won the LPGA, and Sherri Steinhauer won the du Maurier Limited Classic. For that feat, Steinhauer was named Most Improved on the LPGA Tour by *Golf Digest*. The magazine named Florence Descampe its Rookie of the Year, while the LPGA gave the same honor to Helen Alfredsseon.

LARRY DENNIS, *Creative Communications*

Horse Racing

A.P. Indy, a three-year-old colt trained by Neil Drysdale and ridden by Eddie Delahoussaye, won the $3 million Breeders' Cup Classic on Oct. 31, 1992, at Gulfstream Park in Hallandale, FL. A.P. Indy finished two lengths ahead of five-year-old Pleasant Tap, as Jolypha placed third. The winning time over 1.25 mi (2 km) was 2:00⅕. A.P. Indy, owned by Japan's Tomonori Tsurumaki and others, also won the Santa Anita Derby in Arcadia, CA, and the Belmont Stakes at Elmont, NY.

The highly touted French horse, Arazi, faded badly and finished 11th in the $1 million Breeders' Cup Mile. Lure led wire-to-wire for a three-length victory over long shot Paradise Creek in 1:32⅘. Gilded Time won the 1.06-mi (1.7-km) Breeders' Cup Juvenile in 1:43⅗ to become the early favorite for the 1993 Kentucky Derby. The Breeders' Cup Sprint was marred by a spill in which Lester Piggott, a 56-year-old English jockey, sustained multiple

© Focus on Sports

Fred Couples took the 1992 Masters (left), the Nissan Los Angeles Open, and the Nestle Invitation; won the Vardon trophy for scoring average at 69.38; and was voted Player of the Year by the Professional Golfers Association and the Golf Writers Association of America.

A. P. Indy, a powerful bay with a white stripe on his face, captured the $3 million Breeder's Cup Classic and put himself in the contest for being named Horse of the Year.

© Bill Frakes/"Sports Illustrated"

fractures when Mr Brooks tumbled and rolled onto the rider. Mr Brooks was destroyed.

Lil E. Tee, a 16–1 long shot, outran Casual Lies down the stretch to win the 1.25-mi (2-km) Kentucky Derby in Louisville, KY. It was the first Derby victory for the colt's 82-year-old owner, W. Cal Partee, and for jockey Pat Day, who was making his tenth attempt. Arazi finished eighth, the worst ever for an odds-on favorite. Lil E. Tee was timed in 2:03. A.P. Indy held off a challenge by Preakness Stakes winner Pine Bluff to win the 124th Belmont, the last of the Triple Crown races that include the Kentucky Derby and the Preakness in Baltimore, MD. The winning time in the 124th Belmont Stakes, run over 1.5 mi (2.4 km), was 2:26.

Pine Bluff won the 1.19-mi (1.9-km) Preakness in 1:55⅗ as Alydeed placed second.

Harness Racing. Alf Palema gave trainer Per Eriksson his second straight victory in the 67th Hambletonian for 3-year-old trotters at East Rutherford, NJ. Alf Palema had won only three of 18 previous starts but beat King Conch by a head. Alf Palema trotted the mile in 2:56¾ and was driven by Mickey McNichol.

Fake Left won the Little Brown Jug for 3-year-old pacers at Delaware, OH, by a nose over Western Hanover in the first four-horse raceoff in the race's 47-year history. Western Hanover won the Cane Pace at Yonkers, NY, and the Messenger Stakes at East Rutherford.

STAN SUTTON

HORSE RACING

Major U.S. Thoroughbred Races

Arkansas Derby: Pine Bluff, $500,000 (total purse)
Arlington Million: Dear Doctor, $1 million
Belmont Stakes: A.P. Indy, $500,000
Blue Grass Stakes: Pistols and Roses, $500,000
Breeders' Cup Classic: A.P. Indy, $3 million
Breeders' Cup Turf: Fraise, $2 million
Breeders' Cup Juvenile: Gilded Time, $1 million
Breeders' Cup Juvenile Fillies: Eliza, $1 million
Breeders' Cup Mile: Lure, $1 million
Breeders' Cup Distaff: Paseana, $1 million
Breeders' Cup Sprint: Thirty Slews, $1 million
Budweiser International: Zoman, $750,000
Florida Derby: Technology, $500,000
Donn Handicap: Sea Cadet, $500,000
Haskell Invitational Handicap: Technology, $500,000
Hollywood Gold Cup: Sultry Song, $1 million
Jim Beam Stakes: Lil E. Tee, $500,000
Jockey Club Gold Cup: Pleasant Tap, $2.5 million
Iselin Handicap: Jolie's Halo, $500,000
Kentucky Derby: Lil E. Tee, $974,800
Kentucky Oaks: Luv Me Luv Me Not, $280,700
Mother Goose Stakes: Turnback the Alarm, $200,000
Nassau County Handicap: Strike the Gold, $500,000
Pimlico Special: Strike the Gold, $700,000
Preakness Stakes: Pine Bluff, $744,800
Santa Anita Derby: A.P. Indy, $500,000
Santa Anita Handicap: Best Pal, $1 million
Strub Stakes: Best Pal, $500,000
Suburban Handicap: Pleasant Tap, $500,000

Super Derby: Señor Thomas, $750,000
Rothman's International: Snurge, $1 million
Travers Stakes: Thunder Rumble, $1 million
Turf Classic: Sky Classic, $500,000
Whitney Handicap: Sultry Song, $250,000
Wood Memorial: Devil His Due, $500,000
Woodward Stakes: Sultry Song, $500,000

Major North American Harness Races

Breeders Crown Horse and Gelding Pace: Artsplace, $368,100
Breeders Crown Horse and Gelding Trot: No Sex Please, $468,100
Breeders Crown Mare Pace: Shady Daisy, $306,750
Breeders Crown Mare Trot: Peace Corps, $288,958
Cane Pace: Western Hanover, $364,350
Hambletonian: Alf Palema, $1,382,000
Kentucky Futurity: Armbro Keepsake, $172,000
Little Brown Jug: Fake Left, $575,150
Meadowlands Pace: Carlsbad Cam, $1 million
Messenger Stakes: Western Hanover, $366,750
Metro: Presidential Ball, $719,000
Peter Haughton Memorial: Giant Chill, $526,000
Sweetheart Pace: Immortality, $668,750
U.S. Pacing Championship: Artsplace, $137,000
Woodrow Wilson Pace: America's Pastime, $889,000
World Trotting Derby: Alf Palema, $665,000

Ice Hockey

The Pittsburgh Penguins overcame the death of their coach Bob Johnson from cancer in November 1991 and won their second consecutive Stanley Cup title in a year that almost saw the play-offs wiped out by a strike. The National Hockey League's (NHL's) first-ever strike was called April 1, 1992, with less than one week of the regular-season schedule left, and lasted nine days before play resumed. The stumbling points were revenue to the players for the sale of trading cards, loosening of player free-agency movement, and the length of the new contract. The new collective-bargaining agreement would run through the 1992–93 season; the NHL owners want some form of revenue-sharing among the teams as well as a cap on skyrocketing salaries. In June, NHL president John Ziegler resigned under pressure from several league owners after 15 years at the helm.

The Penguins struggled to make the play-offs in a troubled season that not only included Johnson's death but also the sale of the team and a subsequent trade of Paul Coffey—the highest-scoring defenseman in history. They made the play-offs in the last ten games of the season and were one loss from being eliminated in the first round by Washington when they rallied to win the next three games in the best-of-seven series. Once again, captain Mario Lemieux led the way; he bounced back from a broken hand in the Patrick Division final series against the New York Rangers to win the play-off MVP award.

Regular Season. The Rangers, spearheaded by Hart Trophy (MVP) winner Mark Messier, won the overall points title with 105 points. They finished seven points ahead of Washington in the Patrick Division. The Capitals tied Detroit, who won the Norris Division, for second in total points with 98. The Vancouver Canucks, who had not had a winning season in 15 years, surprisingly won the Smythe Division with 96 points. The Montreal Canadiens took the Adams with 93.

Lemieux, who only played 26 games in 1990–91 because of a disc problem in his back, won his third Art Ross award as the Number 1 point producer with 131. Lemieux reached 1,000 points in only his eighth year; only Wayne Gretzky got to that plateau in fewer games. Pittsburgh linemate Kevin Stevens was next with 123. Stevens, who had 54 goals, finished two points ahead of nine-time scoring champion, Los Angeles center Wayne Gretzky. The 121 points for Gretzky, now aged 31, were the fewest in his 13-year NHL career, prompting him to suggest that he might not play too much longer. Gretzky only had 31 goals but he moved past Marcel Dionne into the second spot (749) on the all-time list. Gordie Howe (801) is first. St. Louis winger Brett Hull led in

goals (70) for the third year in a row and was fourth with 109 points. Hull now had scored 70 goals or more three times; only Gretzky's record is better (four).

The Play-offs. The Minnesota North Stars, who had made it to the Stanley Cup final against Pittsburgh in 1991, were ousted in the seventh game of the opening round by Detroit.

ICE HOCKEY

National Hockey League
(Final Standings, 1991–92)

Wales Conference

Adams Division	W	L	T	Pts.	Goals For	Goals Against
*Montreal	41	28	11	93	267	207
*Boston	36	32	12	84	270	275
*Buffalo	31	37	12	74	289	299
*Hartford	26	41	13	65	247	283
Quebec	20	48	12	52	255	318
Patrick Division						
*N.Y. Rangers	50	25	5	105	321	246
*Washington	45	27	8	98	330	275
*Pittsburgh	39	32	9	87	343	308
*New Jersey	38	31	11	87	289	259
N.Y. Islanders	34	35	11	79	291	299
Philadelphia	32	37	11	75	252	273

Campbell Conference

Norris Division	W	L	T	Pts.	Goals For	Goals Against
*Detroit	43	25	12	98	320	256
*Chicago	36	29	15	87	257	236
*St. Louis	36	33	11	83	279	266
*Minnesota	32	42	6	70	246	278
Toronto	30	43	7	67	234	294
Smythe Division						
*Vancouver	42	26	12	96	285	250
*Los Angeles	35	31	14	84	287	296
*Edmonton	36	34	10	82	295	297
*Winnipeg	33	32	15	81	251	244
Calgary	31	37	12	74	296	305
San Jose	17	58	5	39	219	359

*In play-offs

Stanley Cup Play-offs
Wales Conference

First Round	Boston	4 games	Buffalo	3
	Montreal	4 games	Hartford	3
	New York	4 games	New Jersey	3
	Pittsburgh	4 games	Washington	3
Second Round	Boston	4 games	Montreal	0
	Pittsburgh	4 games	New York	2
Finals	Pittsburgh	4 games	Boston	0

Campbell Conference

First Round	Chicago	4 games	St. Louis	2
	Detroit	4 games	Minnesota	3
	Edmonton	4 games	Los Angeles	2
	Vancouver	4 games	Winnipeg	3
Second Round	Chicago	4 games	Detroit	0
	Edmonton	4 games	Vancouver	2
Finals	Chicago	4 games	Edmonton	0

Stanley Cup Finals

Pittsburgh	4 games	Chicago	0

Individual Honors

Hart Trophy (most valuable player): Mark Messier, New York Rangers
Ross Trophy (leading scorer): Mario Lemieux, Pittsburgh
Vezina Trophy (top goaltender): Patrick Roy, Montreal
Norris Trophy (best defenseman): Brian Leetch, New York Rangers
Selke Trophy (best defensive forward): Guy Carbonneau, Montreal
Calder Trophy (rookie of the year): Pavel Bure, Vancouver
Lady Byng Trophy (sportsmanship): Wayne Gretzky, Los Angeles
Conn Smythe Trophy (most valuable in play-offs): Mario Lemieux
Adams Trophy (coach of the year): Patrick Quinn, Vancouver
King Clancy Trophy (humanitarian service): Ray Bourque, Boston
Masterton Trophy (sportsmanship-dedication to hockey): Mark Fitzpatrick, New York Islanders

NCAA: Lake Superior State

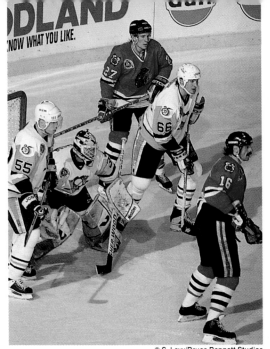

© S. Levy/Bruce Bennett Studios

Mario Lemieux (66), the NHL's leading scorer during the season, led Pittsburgh to a second consecutive Stanley Cup. The Penguins overpowered Chicago in the Cup finals.

They led the Red Wings, three games to one, but could not hold on. Chicago, who was second in the Norris Division, beat St. Louis in six games, then the Red Wings in four. The Blackhawks thereby gained a measure of revenge after the 1990–91 season when they had the NHL's best point total (106) but went out in the first play-off round.

The Edmonton Oilers, who had traded their captain, Messier, to New York in October and premier goalie Grant Fuhr to Toronto in September, had a rebuilt team but still took the Smythe Division. The Oilers knocked off Gretzky's Kings for the third straight year, in six games, setting up a meeting with Vancouver. The Canucks had rallied from being down three games to one to beat Winnipeg in seven games, outscoring them 21-5. The Oilers won their eighth Smythe title in ten years with a six-game win over Vancouver.

In the Patrick Division final the Penguins rallied to beat New York, who had outlasted New Jersey in the opening round. Pittsburgh played without its captain, Lemieux, for the final five games. Montreal had an easy time winning the regular-season Adams title but crashed in the play-offs to second-place Boston. The Bruins crushed the Canadiens, 4-0, in their series after getting great goaltending from Andy Moog to beat Buffalo in seven games in the first round. Montreal had needed an overtime goal by Russ Courtnall in game seven to beat Hartford in their opening series.

The Blackhawks, who had lost three Campbell Conference finals to the Oilers, clobbered them in four straight to reach the matchup with the Penguins. Pittsburgh got an overtime win-

ner from Jaromir Jagr to beat Boston, 4-3, in the opener of the Wales Conference championship, then swept the next three.

Stanley Cup Finals. Lemieux scored a power-play goal with 12 seconds left to give the Penguins a come-from-behind 5-4 victory in the first game in Pittsburgh. Jagr had tied it late in the third on a brilliant individual stick-handling effort as the Penguins overcame a 4-1 second-period deficit. Lemieux scored two goals 2½ minutes apart on Chicago goalie Ed Belfour in the second game in Pittsburgh to key a 3-1 victory.

In Chicago, Pittsburgh goalie Tom Barrasso stymied the Blackhawks in a 1-0 win in game three. In game four, Lemieux and Rick Tocchet helped subdue Chicago, 6-5. Each player had a goal and an assist in the shootout that saw Belfour replaced early in the first period after giving up two goals in four shots.

JIM MATHESON, *"Edmonton Journal"*

Ice Skating

In March 1992, Kristi Yamaguchi became the first American woman since Peggy Fleming in 1968 to defend her world figure-skating title. The 20-year-old Californian also finished first in the women's singles at the U.S. Figure Skating Championships and took the gold medal at the Winter Olympics in Albertville, France.

At the European figure-skating championships in Lausanne, Switzerland, in January, France's Surya Bonaly successfully defended her singles title and Petr Barna of Czechoslovakia outpointed the favored Petrenko for the men's crown.

Speed Skating. Roberto Sighel was the first Italian to win the men's all-around speed-skating championship and Germany's Gunda Kleeman Niemann defended her all-around title among the women.

See also SPORTS—*Olympic Games.*

ICE SKATING

World Figure-Skating Championships

Men: Viktor Petrenko, Commonwealth of Independent States
Women: Kristi Yamaguchi, United States
Pairs: Natalya Mishkutienok and Artur Dmitriev, Commonwealth of Independent States
Dance: Marina Klimova and Sergei Ponomarenko, Commonwealth of Independent States

U.S. Figure-Skating Championships

Men: Christopher Bowman, United States
Women: Kristi Yamaguchi
Pairs: Calla Urbanski and Rocky Marval, United States
Dance: April Sargent-Thomas and Russ Witherby, United States

World All-Around Speed-Skating Championships

Men's Overall: Roberto Sighel, Italy
Men's 500 meters: Peter Adeberg, Germany
Men's 1,500 meters: Falko Zandstra, Netherlands
Men's 5,000 meters: Johann Olav Koss, Norway
Men's 10,000 meters: Falko Zandstra
Women's Overall: Gunda Niemann, Germany
Women's 500 meters: Ye Qiaobo, China
Women's 1,500 meters: Emese Nemeth Hunyady, Austria
Women's 3,000 meters: Gunda Niemann
Women's 5,000 meters: Gunda Niemann

Olympic Games

More than anything else, the quadrennial renewal of the Olympic Games during 1992 will be remembered as the first Games to reflect a new athletic—and world—order. Following closely after political upheaval had restructured Europe, the Winter Games, staged during February in Albertville, France, and the Summer Games, held during late July and early August in Barcelona, Spain, were unlike any other in modern history.

Most of the athletes from the former Soviet Union competed as the Unified Team, which was represented by the Olympic flag and the Olympic anthem for team gold medals. When individual members of the Unified Team won a gold medal, the anthem and flag of their respective Soviet republics were played and displayed. Other former Soviet states—such as Estonia, Latvia, and Lithuania—competed as independent nations. For the next Olympics, starting with the 1994 Winter Games in Lillehammer, Norway, the Unified Team will be broken into 12 independent states. Athletes of the former German Democratic Republic (East Germany) joined the West Germans on a single German team. For the Summer Games, South Africa returned to Olympic competition for the first time in 32 years. The nation that once was Yugoslavia was represented by three flags—Croatia, Slovenia, and Bosnia-Herzegovina. Athletes from the former Yugoslav republics of Serbia, Macedonia, and Montenegro were grouped as Independent Olympic Participants (IOP). In all, a record 172 nations and territories participated in the Summer Games.

Just as significantly, both the Winter and Summer Games were not marred by boycotts. In 1988, five nations had stayed away from the Seoul Games. But this time around, the Summer Olympics were free of political stains for the first time since 1972. On a more somber note, both of the 1992 Games were characterized by a growing intrusion of commercialism and professionalism. For the first time, players from the National Basketball Association (NBA) were allowed to play in the Summer Games. It is expected that other sports, such as soccer and baseball, eventually will be open to all athletes, amateur and professional, perhaps as early as the 1996 Summer Games in Atlanta, GA.

The XXV Summer Games

The city of Barcelona invested more than $4 billion to prepare for the Summer Olympics, resulting in an improved road system, a revitalized airport and beachfront, and impressive athletic facilities. Organizers also produced one of the most efficient and beautiful Olympics ever staged, despite the overwhelming presence of 10,000 athletes and a total Olympic family of more than 20,000. But there also was some political tension. Barcelona is located within Catalonia, a maverick region within Spain that has its own language and yearning for independence. But any signs of political problems were confined to an open display of the flag of Catalonia hanging outside most apartment balconies throughout Barcelona. *See also* FEATURE ARTICLE/THE YEAR OF SPAIN, page 64.

© John Biever/"Sports Illustrated"

Cuba's Javier Sotomayor, 24, missed only once as he took the gold in the high jump at the 1992 Summer Olympics in Barcelona, Spain. He was particularly proud of his accomplishment since his homeland was making its first appearance at the Summer Olympics since 1980.

After a disappointing performance at the U.S. Olympic Trials, Carl Lewis (arms extended) *returned to his old form, anchoring the U.S. team to a gold and a world record in the 4x100-m relay. He also captured a gold in the long jump.*

With the former Soviet Union represented by the fragmented Unified Team, it was expected that the United States would dominate the Games. However, the Unified Team put on a heroic showing and came away with both the most medals (112) and the most gold medals (45). The United States was second in both categories, with 108 and 37. The combined German team won a disappointing 82 medals, four years after the East German squad finished second in the medal count at Seoul with 102. The top individual winner was gymnast Vitaly Scherbo of the Unified Team, who won an amazing six gold medals.

Basketball. The presence of the U.S. Dream Team, a group of 11 National Basketball Association players and one recent collegian, elevated basketball to the glamour sport of these Summer Olympics. The team members, including three of the greatest players of all time—Earvin "Magic" Johnson, Larry Bird, and Michael Jordan—were treated as celebrities by fans and fellow athletes alike. Considered the greatest team of all time, the Americans coasted to a gold medal, winning their games by an average of 44 points. The team defeated Croatia, 117-85, in the final. The Games marked the last competition for Bird of the Boston Celtics, who retired soon after he returned to the United States. The Olympics also were the first significant competition for Johnson since he announced nine months earlier that he had tested HIV-positive.

The U.S. women's team also was favored heavily to win a gold but was upset in a semifinal game by the Unified Team and finished third. The Americans had not lost a game in the Olympics since 1976, when women's basketball was introduced to Olympic competition.

Track and Field. Less than two months after his wonderful track career appeared to be over,

Carl Lewis of the United States swept to two gold medals to emerge as the star of the track competition. Lewis, the world record holder in the 100-m dash, failed to qualify in both that event and the 200-m dash at the U.S. Olympic Trials in June. But in Barcelona, he won the long jump, beating world record holder Mike Powell by 1¼". Running as a substitute, he also anchored the U.S. 4x100-meter relay team to a gold medal in world-record time. Lewis now had won eight gold medals during the last three Olympics, and he did not rule out the possibility that he would enter the 1996 Games.

Jackie Joyner-Kersee (*see* BIOGRAPHY) stamped herself as perhaps the greatest woman athlete in history by winning her second straight Olympic heptathlon, although she failed to break her own world record. She also tried to repeat as long-jump champion but was beaten out by longtime rival, Germany's Heike Drechsler, who prevailed on her last try. The most disappointing performance was turned in by pole vaulter Sergei Bubka of the Unified Team, who was considered a virtual shoo-in for a gold. Instead, he failed to clear any height and did not take a medal.

There ultimately were few memorable efforts in the track and field competition. The only individual world record was set by Kevin Young of the United States, who broke Edwin Moses' 1983 mark in the 400-m hurdles. Quincy Watts of the United States nearly broke the world record in winning the 400-m dash, and Mike Marsh of the United States missed a world record in the 200-m dash by one tenth of a second. But the U.S. 4x400-m and 4x100-m relay teams did break world marks in winning their events.

Perhaps the most emotional victory was registered by Gail Devers of the United States, who took the 100-m dash. She had suffered

499

from Graves' disease and, at one point, doctors had talked about amputating one of her feet. She also was leading in the 100-m hurdles, only to hit the final hurdle and finish fifth, losing to Paraskevi Patoulidou of Greece. Fellow American Gwen Torrence, who won the 200-m dash, indicated that she suspected Devers of using steroids but later admitted she had no proof. Two Americans, Jud Logan and Bonnie Dasse, failed drug tests and were sent home. In another controversy, Khalid Skah of Morocco won the 10,000-m run, only to lose his gold when it was ruled that a teammate interfered with second-place finisher Richard Chelimo of Kenya. But the decision later was reversed and Skah was given back the gold.

Swimming and Diving. With the breakup of the powerful East German women's swim team, which had won eight individual gold medals in 1988 and dominated the competition, the United States was favored to sweep the events. Although the U.S. women swimmers came away with 14 medals overall, they won only three individual events, a major disappointment. But one bright spot for the United States was Janet Evans, who had won two individual golds in 1988, in the 400-m and 800-m freestyles. This time, she finished second in the 400 but first in the 800. The individual woman star was Krisztina Egerszegi of Hungary, who won both the 100-m and the 200-m backstrokes and the 400-m individual medley.

Matt Biondi won three medals, including two golds as a member of the U.S. 4x100-m freestyle and 4x100 medley relay teams. That gave him 11 Olympic medals, tying him with swimmer Mark Spitz and shooter Carl Osburn for the most in U.S. history. But Biondi failed to win any individual events. Strong performances were turned in by Melvin Stewart of the United States in the 200-m butterfly; Mike Barrowman of the United States, who set a world record in winning the 200-m breaststroke; and Aleksandr Popov of the Unified Team, who won the 50-m and 100-m freestyles.

The Chinese dominated the diving competition. Gao Min (springboard) and Fu Mingxia (platform) won the women's events and Sun Shuwei took the men's platform. But Mark Lenzi of the United States prevented a Chinese sweep by capturing the men's springboard.

Gymnastics. Vitaly Scherbo emerged as the most successful of the Summer Games competitors after his stunning performances in men's gymnastics. He won the all-around event and added individual gold medals in pommel horse, vault, rings, and parallel bars in addition to sharing the team gold with his Unified squad. The U.S. men's team had hoped to challenge for a medal but finished a disappointing sixth, although Trent Dimas won the gold on the horizontal bar. The women's all-around went to Tatiana Gutsu of the Unified Team, who edged Shannon Miller of the United States, wrapping up the title on her last vault of the competition. The Unified Team also won the women's team gold, with Romania second and the United States third. U.S. star Kim Zmeskal, who had been favored to win the all-around, had a poor competition and had to be satisfied with only a team medal. Miller finished with two individual silver and two individual bronze medals.

Boxing. Cuba marked its return to the Olympics by nearly sweeping the boxing events, which once again were marred by controversy. In these Olympics, judges scored by using a computer to mark every time they decided that one of the boxers landed a punch. But some of the judges used the computer faster than others and ultimately not all the legitimate punches were recorded officially. U.S. boxers, especially, thought they lost some fights because of improper scoring. Cuba won seven of the 12 weight classes. The lone U.S. gold medalist was lightweight (60-kg/132-lb) Oscar De La Hoya.

Among the women swimmers, Hungary's Krisztina Egerszegi was the star at Barcelona, winning golds in the 100-m and 200-m backstrokes as well as the 400-m individual medley.

© Sichov/Sipa Sport © Bob Martin/Allsport

Romania's Lavinia Corina Milosovici, left, and Vitaly Scherbo of the Unified Team dominated women's and men's gymnastics, respectively, at the 1992 Games. Milosovici took four medals; Scherbo won the all-around and five other golds.

Baseball. A veteran Cuba team, which long has been the strongest in international baseball competition, easily won the gold medal by beating Taiwan, 11-1, in the championship game. But the baseball event was disappointing for the United States, which had hoped to challenge the older Cubans for first place. Instead, the Americans could not generate enough good pitching during the tournament and wound up finishing fourth, behind bronze-medal winners Japan.

Other Sports. Tennis produced one of the more surprising results when U.S. teenager Jennifer Capriati defeated Steffi Graf, the world's Number 2 ranked player, 3-6, 6-3, 6-4, in the gold-medal final. It was Capriati's first win over Graf. Marc Rosset of Switzerland defeated Jordi Arrese of Spain in the men's bracket. Weight lifter Naim Suleymanoglu of Turkey, who retired after winning a gold medal in 1988, when he was considered pound for pound the strongest man in the world, came back in this Olympics to win once again the 60-kg (132-lb) class.

The Unified Team showed its strength in weight lifting, where it won five gold medals, and in wrestling, where it recorded six first places in freestyle and Greco-Roman. John Smith of the United States, probably the greatest wrestler in U.S. history, took the gold in the featherweight (62-kg/137-lb) freestyle division. The German team dominated canoeing and rowing, winning seven gold medals in canoeing and four in rowing. In a major upset, the U.S. water polo team finished fourth, behind Italy, Spain, and the Unified Team. The U.S. volleyball team, which won gold medals in 1984 and 1988, had to settle for a bronze this time around, finishing behind Brazil and the Netherlands. Early in the competition, a victory by the United States over Japan was reversed on a rule technicality and the U.S. players shaved their heads in protest. In addition to baseball, badminton and women's judo made their debuts at the 1992 Summer Games as medal-winning sports.

Overall. Despite all the sudden political changes in the world during the months preceding the competition, the 1992 Summer Olympics were conducted with hardly a hitch, with a record 62 nations and territories plus the Unified Team and the IOP winning medals. Free of protests and major controversies, the Games were a happy affair, highlighted by the impressive beauty of Barcelona. Juan Antonio Samaranch, president of the International Olympic Committee, was especially proud of the competition. A resident of Barcelona, Samaranch was mainly responsible for the Games winding up in his city.

XXV SUMMER OLYMPICS—Gold Medalists

Archery
Men's 70-m Individual: Sebastien Flute, France
Men's Team: Spain
Women's 70-m Individual: Cho Youn-Jeong, South Korea
Women's Team: South Korea

Badminton
Men's Singles: Alan Budi Kusuma, Indonesia
Men's Doubles: South Korea
Women's Singles: Susi Susanti, Indonesia
Women's Doubles: South Korea

Baseball
Cuba

Basketball
Men: United States
Women: Unified Team

Boxing
48-kg (106-lb): Rogelio Marcelo, Cuba
51-kg (112-lb): Su Choi-Chol, North Korea
54-kg (119-lb): Joel Casamayor, Cuba
57-kg (126-lb): Andreas Tews, Germany
60-kg (132-lb): Oscar De La Hoya, United States
63.5-kg (140-lb): Hector Vinent, Cuba
67-kg (148-lb): Michael Carruth, Ireland
71-kg (157-lb): Juan Lemus, Cuba
75-kg (165-lb): Ariel Hernández, Cuba
81-kg (179-kg): Torsten May, Germany
91-kg (201-lb): Felix Savón, Cuba
Over 91-kg (Over 201-lb): Roberto Balado, Cuba

Canoeing
Men's 500-m Kayak Singles: Mikko Yrjoe Kolehmainen, Finland
Men's 500-m Kayak Doubles: Germany
Men's 1,000-m Kayak Singles: Clint Robinson, Australia
Men's 1,000-m Kayak Doubles: Germany
Men's 1,000-m Kayak Fours: Germany
Men's Single Kayak Slalom: Pierpaolo Ferrazzi, Italy
Men's 500-m Canoe Singles: Nikolai Boukhalov, Bulgaria
Men's 500-m Canoe Doubles: Unified Tean
Men's 1,000-m Canoe Singles: Nikolai Boukhalov
Men's 1,000-m Canoe Doubles: Germany
Men's Single Canoe Slalom: Lukas Pollert, Czechoslovakia
Men's Doubles Canoe Slalom: United States
Women's Single Kayak Slalom: Elisabeth Micheler, Germany
Women's 500-m Kayak Singles: Birgit Schmidt, Germany
Women's 500-m Kayak Doubles: Germany
Women's 500-m Kayak Fours: Hungary

Cycling
Men's 1-km Time Trial: José Moreno, Spain
Men's 4-km Individual Pursuit: Chris Boardman, Great Britain
Men's 4,000-m Team Pursuit: Germany
Men's Individual Sprint: Jens Fiedler, Germany
Men's Individual Road Race: Fabio Casartelli, Italy
Men's Team Road Race: Germany
Men's Individual Points Race: Giovanni Lombardi, Italy
Women's 3,000-m Individual Pursuit: Petra Rossner, Germany
Women's Individual Sprint: Erika Salumae, Estonia
Women's Individual Road Race: Kathryn Watt, Australia

Equestrian
Individual 3-Day Event: Matthew Ryan, Australia
Team 3-Day Event: Australia
Individual Dressage: Nicole Uphoff, Germany
Team Dressage: Germany
Individual Jumping: Ludger Beerbaum, Germany
Team Jumping: Netherlands

Fencing
Men's Individual Foil: Philippe Omnes, France
Men's Team Foil: Germany
Men's Individual Sabre: Bence Szabo, Hungary
Men's Team Sabre: Unified Team
Men's Individual Epée: Eric Srecki, France
Men's Team Epée: Germany
Women's Individual Foil: Giovanna Trillini, Italy
Women's Team Foil: Italy

Field Hockey
Men: Germany
Women: Spain

Gymnastics
Men's All-Around: Vitaly Scherbo, Unified Team
Men's Floor Exercises: Li Xiaoshuang, China
Men's Horizontal Bar: Trent Dimas, United States
Men's Pommel Horse: Vitaly Scherbo and Pae Gil-Su, North Korea
Men's Vault: Vitaly Scherbo
Men's Parallel Bars: Vitaly Scherbo
Men's Rings: Vitaly Scherbo
Men's Team: Unified Team
Women's All-Around: Tatiana Gutsu, Unified Team
Women's Balance Beam: Tatiana Lisenko, Unified Team

Women's Floor Exercises: Lavinia Corina Milosovici, Romania
Women's Uneven Bars: Lu Li, China
Women's Vault: Lavinia Corina Milosovici and Henrietta Onodi, Hungary
Women's Team: Unified Team
Women's Rhythmic Gymnastics: Alexandra Timoshenko, Unified Team

Handball
Men: Unified Team
Women: South Korea

Judo
Men's Under 60-kg (132-lb): Nazim Gousseinov, Unified Team
Men's 65-kg (143-lb): Rogerio Sampaio Cardoso, Brazil
Men's 71-kg (157-lb): Toshihiko Koga, Japan
Men's 78-kg (172-lb): Hidehiko Yoshida, Japan
Men's 86-kg (190-lb): Waldemar Legien, Poland
Men's 95-kg (209-lb): Antal Kovacs, Hungary
Men's 95-plus-kg (209-plus-lb): David Khakhaleichvili, Unified Team
Women's Under 48-kg (106-lb): Cécile Nowak, France
Women's 52-kg (115-lb): Almudena Muñoz Martínez, Spain
Women's 56-kg (123-lb): Miriam Blasco Soto, Spain
Women's 61-kg (134-lb): Catherine Fleury, France
Women's 66-kg (146-lb): Odalis Reve Jiménez, Cuba
Women's 72-kg (159-lb): Kim Mi-Jung, South Korea
Women's 72-plus-lb (159-plus-lb): Zhuang Xiaoyan, China

Modern Pentathlon
Individual: Arkadiusz Skrzypaszek, Poland
Team: Poland

Rowing
Men's Single Sculls: Thomas Lange, Germany
Men's Double Sculls: Australia
Men's Quadruple Sculls: Germany
Men's Pairs With Coxswain: Great Britain
Men's Pairs Without Coxswain: Great Britain
Men's Fours With Coxswain: Romania
Men's Fours Without Coxswain: Australia
Men's Eights With Coxswain: Canada
Women's Single Sculls: Elisabeta Lipa, Romania
Women's Double Sculls: Germany
Women's Quadruple Sculls: Germany
Women's Pairs Without Coxswain: Canada
Women's Four Without Coxswain: Canada
Women's Eights With Coxswain: Canada

Shooting
Men's Rapid-Fire Pistol: Ralf Schumann, Germany
Men's Free Pistol: Konstantine Loukachik, Unified Team
Men's Running Game Target: Michael Jakosits, Germany
Men's Free Rifle: Lee Eun-Chul, South Korea
Men's Three-Position Rifle: Gratchia Petikiane, Unified Team
Men's Air Rifle: Iouri Fedkine, Unified Team
Men's Air Pistol: Wang Yifu, China
Women's Air Rifle: Yeo Kab-Soon, South Korea
Women's Air Pistol: Marina Logvinenko, Unified Team
Women's Three-Position Rifle: Launi Meili, United States
Women's Sport Pistol: Marina Logvinenko
Open Skeet: Zhang Shan, China
Open Trap: Petr Hrdlicka, Czechoslovakia

Soccer
Spain

Swimming and Diving
Men's 100-m Backstroke: Mark Tewksbury, Canada
Men's 200-m Backstroke: Martin López-Zubero, Spain
Men's 100-m Breaststroke: Nelson Diebel, United States
Men's 200-m Breaststroke: Mike Barrowman, United States
Men's 100-m Butterfly: Pablo Morales, United States
Men's 200-m Butterfly: Melvin Stewart, United States
Men's 50-m Freestyle: Aleksandr Popov, Unified Team
Men's 100-m Freestyle: Aleksandr Popov
Men's 200-m Freestyle: Evgueni Sadovyi, Unified Team
Men's 400-m Freestyle: Evgueni Sadovyi
Men's 1,500-m Freestyle: Kieren Perkins, Australia
Men's 400-m Freestyle Relay: United States
Men's 800-m Freestyle Relay: Unified Team
Men's 200-m Individual Medley: Tamas Darnyi, Hungary
Men's 400-m Individual Medley: Tamas Darnyi
Men's 400-m Medley Relay: United States
Men's Platform Diving: Sun Shuwei, China
Men's Springboard Diving: Mark Lenzi, United States
Women's 100-m Backstroke: Krisztina Egerszegi, Hungary
Women's 200-m Backstroke: Krisztina Egerszegi
Women's 100-m Breaststroke: Yelena Roudkovskaia, Unified Team
Women's 200-m Breaststroke: Kyoko Iwasaki, Japan
Women's 100-m Butterfly: Qian Hong, China
Women's 200-m Butterfly: Summer Sanders, United States
Women's 50-m Freestyle: Yang Wenyi, China
Women's 100-m Freestyle: Zhuang Yong, China
Women's 200-m Freestyle: Nicole Haislett, United States
Women's 400-m Freestyle: Dagmar Hase, Germany
Women's 800-m Freestyle: Janet Evans, United States

Women's 400-m Freestyle Relay: United States
Women's 200-m Individual Medley: Lin Li, China
Women's 400-m Individual Medley: Krisztina Egerszegi
Women's 400-m Medley Relay: United States
Women's Platform Diving: Fu Mingxia, China
Women's Springboard Diving: Gao Min, China

Synchronized Swimming
Solo: Kristen Babb-Sprague, United States
Duet: Karen Josephson and Sarah Josephson, United States

Table Tennis
Men's Singles: Jan Waldner, Sweden
Men's Doubles: China
Women's Singles: Deng Yaping, China
Women's Doubles: China

Tennis
Men's Singles: Marc Rosset, Switzerland
Men's Doubles: Boris Becker and Michael Stich, Germany
Women's Singles: Jennifer Capriati, United States
Women's Doubles: Gigi Fernandez and Mary Joe Fernandez, United
   States

Track and Field
Men's 100-m: Linford Christie, Great Britain
Men's 200-m: Mike Marsh, United States
Men's 400-m: Quincy Watts, United States
Men's 800-m: William Tanui, Kenya
Men's 1,500-m: Fermin Cacho Ruiz, Spain
Men's 5,000-m: Dieter Baumann, Germany
Men's 10,000-m: Khalid Skah, Morocco
Men's Marathon: Hwang Young-Cho, South Korea
Men's 110-m Hurdles: Mark McKoy, Canada
Men's 400-m Hurdles: Kevin Young, United States
Men's 3,000-m Steeplechase: Mathew Birir, Kenya
Men's 400-m Relay: United States
Men's 1,600-m Relay: United States
Men's 20-km Walk: Daniel Plaza Montero, Spain
Men's 50-km Walk: Andrei Perlov, Unified Team
Men's Decathlon: Robert Zmelik, Czechoslovakia
Men's High Jump: Javier Sotomayor, Cuba
Men's Long Jump: Carl Lewis, United States
Men's Triple Jump: Mike Conley, United States
Men's Discus: Romas Ubartas, Lithuania
Men's Shot Put: Mike Stulce, United States
Men's Hammer Throw: Andrei Abduvaliyev, Unified Team
Men's Javelin: Jan Zelezny, Czechoslovakia
Men's Pole Vault: Maksim Tarassov, Unified Team
Women's 100-m: Gail Devers, United States
Women's 200-m: Gwen Torrence, United States
Women's 400-m: Marie-Jose Perec, France
Women's 800-m: Ellen Van Langen, Netherlands
Women's 1,500-m: Hassiba Boulmerka, Algeria
Women's 3,000-m: Yelina Romanova, Unified Team
Women's 10,000-m: Derartu Tulu, Ethiopia
Women's Marathon: Valentina Yegorova, Unified Team
Women's 400-m Relay: United States
Women's 1,600-m Relay: Unified Team
Women's 100-m Hurdles: Paraskevi Patoulidou, Greece
Women's 400-m Hurdles: Sally Gunnell, Great Britain
Women's 10-km Walk: Chen Yueling, China
Women's Heptathlon: Jackie Joyner-Kersee, United States
Women's High Jump: Heike Henkel, Germany
Women's Long Jump: Heike Drechsler, Germany
Women's Discus: Maritza Marten García, Cuba
Women's Shot Put: Svetlana Kriveleva, Unified Team
Women's Javelin: Silke Renk, Germany

Volleyball
Men: Brazil
Women: Cuba

Water Polo
Italy

Weight Lifting:
52-kg (115-lb): Ivan Ivanov, Bulgaria
56-kg (123-lb): Chun Byung-Kwan, South Korea
60-kg (132-lb): Naim Suleymanoglu, Turkey
67.5-kg (148-lb): Israel Militossian, Unified Team
75-kg (165-lb): Fedor Kassapu, Unified Team
82.5-kg (181-lb): Pyrros Dimas, Greece
90-kg (198-lb): Kakhi Kakhiachvili, Unified Team
100-kg (220-lb): Viktor Tregoubov, Unified Team
110-kg (243-lb): Ronny Weller, Germany
110-plus-kg (243-plus-lb): Aleksandr Kourlovitch, Unified Team

Wrestling, Freestyle
48-kg (106-lb): Kim Il, North Korea
52-kg (115-lb): Li Hak-Son, South Korea
57-kg (126-lb): Alejandro Puerto Díaz, Cuba
62-kg (137-lb): John Smith, United States
68-kg (150-lb): Arsen Fadzaev, Unified Team
74-kg (163-lb): Park Jang-Soon, South Korea

82-kg (181-lb): Kevin Jackson, United States
90-kg (198-lb): Makharbek Khadartsev, Unified Team
100-kg (220-lb): Leri Khabelov, Unified Team
130-kg (287-lb): Bruce Baumgartner, United States

Wrestling, Greco-Roman
48-kg (106-lb): Oleg Koutherenko, Unified Team
52-kg (115-lb): Jon Ronningen, Norway
57-kg (126-lb): An Han Bong, South Korea
62-kg (137-lb): M. Akif Pirim, Turkey
68-kg (150-lb): Attila Repka, Hungary
74-kg (163-lb): Mnatsakan Iskandarian, Unified Team
82-kg (181-lb): Peter Farkas, Hungary
90-kg (198-lb): Maik Bullmann, Germany
100-kg (220-lb): Hector Milian Pérez, Cuba
130-kg (287-lb): Aleksandr Karelin, Unified Team

Yachting
Soling: Denmark
Flying Dutchman: Spain
Star: United States
Finn: José Van Der Ploeg, Spain
Tornado: France
Europe: Linda Anderson, Norway
Men's Sailboard: Franck David, France
Women's Sailboard: Barbara Kendall, New Zealand
Men's 470: Spain
Women's 470: Spain

Final Medal Standings

	Gold	Silver	Bronze
Unified Team*	45	38	29
United States	37	34	37
Germany	33	21	28
China	16	22	16
Cuba		6	11
Spain	13	7	2
South Korea	12	5	12
Hungary	11	12	7
France	8	5	16
Australia	7	9	11
Italy	6	5	8
Canada	6	5	7
Great Britain	5	3	12
Romania	4	6	8
Czechoslovakia	4	2	1
North Korea	4	0	5
Japan	3	8	11
Bulgaria	3	7	6
Poland	3	6	10
Netherlands	2	6	7
Kenya	2	4	2
Norway	2	4	1
Turkey	2	2	2
Indonesia	2	2	
Brazil	2	1	0
Greece	2	0	0
Sweden	1	7	4
New Zealand	1	4	5
Finland	1	2	2
Denmark	1	1	4
Morocco	1	1	1
Ireland	1	1	0
Ethiopia	1	0	2
Algeria	1	0	1
Estonia	1	0	1
Lithuania	1	0	1
Switzerland	1	0	0
Jamaica	0	3	1
Nigeria	0	3	1
Latvia	0	2	1
Austria	0	2	0
Namibia	0	2	0
South Africa	0	2	0
Belgium	0	1	2
Croatia	0	1	2
I.O.P.**	0	1	2
Iran	0	1	2
Israel	0	1	1
Mexico	0	1	0
Peru	0	1	0
Taiwan	0	1	0
Mongolia	0	0	2
Slovenia	0	0	2
Argentina	0	0	1
Bahamas	0	0	1
Colombia	0	0	1
Ghana	0	0	1
Malaysia	0	0	1
Pakistan	0	0	1
Philippines	0	0	1
Puerto Rico	0	0	1
Qatar	0	0	1
Suriname	0	0	1
Thailand	0	0	1

*Athletes from former Soviet republics. **Independent Olympic Participants (athletes from Serbia, Montenegro, and Macedonia).

The XVI Winter Games

For all the turmoil and the concern about potential severe weather problems in the French Alps, the XVI Winter Olympics turned out to be exciting and smoothly run. A record number of athletes, 2,174, participated in a total of 57 events. Medal competition was introduced in freestyle skiing and short-track speed skating. Americans won gold medals in two of the new events. Donna Weinbrecht took first in women's freestyle skiing and Cathy Turner was first in the 500-meter race of the women's short-track speed skating. In all, Germany won the most medals at Albertville, 26, followed by the Unified Team with 23, and Austria with 21. The United States picked up 11, equaling its highest Winter total ever on foreign soil.

Alpine Skiing. Even though he won just one gold medal, the Alpine skiing star once again was Italy's Alberto Tomba, who had dominated the Calgary Winter Games in 1988 with gold medals in the giant slalom and slalom. Under intense pressure to repeat, the flamboyant Tomba raced to a first-place finish in the giant slalom and barely missed out on a second gold in the slalom, finishing second to Norway's Finn Christian Jagge. Otherwise, injuries and upsets highlighted the skiing competition. Patrick Ortlieb of Austria was the surprise winner of the men's downhill, while Norway's Kjetil Andre Aamodt upset veteran Marc Girardelli of Luxembourg in the super-giant competition. Girardelli, a longtime skiing star who did not win a medal in Calgary, wound up with two silvers this time.

Petra Kronberger of Austria dominated the women's events. She won two gold medals, taking both the slalom and the combined events. But she had to share the spotlight with two surprising winners, Canada's Kerrin Lee-Gartner in the downhill and Italy's Deborah Compagnoni in the super-giant slalom. Hilary Lindh of the United States picked up an unexpected second-place finish in the downhill, while teammate Diann Roffe tied for the silver in the giant slalom.

Figure Skating. Midori Ito of Japan, the greatest leaper in the history of women's figure skating, was favored to win the gold medal. But she was upset by graceful Kristi Yamaguchi of

© Bob Martin/Allsport

Kristi Yamaguchi, 20-year-old defending world figure-skating champion, became the first U.S. woman since Dorothy Hamill in 1976 to take the gold medal.

XVI WINTER OLYMPICS—Gold Medalists

Alpine Skiing
Men's Combined: Josef Polig, Italy
Men's Downhill: Patrick Ortlieb, Austria
Men's Giant Slalom: Alberto Tomba, Italy
Men's Slalom: Finn Christian Jagge, Norway
Men's Super-Giant Slalom: Kjetil Andre Aamodt, Norway
Women's Combined: Petra Kronberger, Austria
Women's Downhill: Kerrin Lee-Gartner, Canada
Women's Giant Slalom: Pernilla Wiberg, Sweden
Women's Slalom: Petra Kronberger
Women's Super-Giant Slalom: Deborah Compagnoni, Italy

Biathlon
Men's 10-km: Mark Kirchner, Germany
Men's 20-km: Yevgeny Redkine, Unified Team
Men's Relay: Germany
Women's 7.5-km: Anfissa Restzova, Unified Team
Women's 15-km: Antje Misersky, Germany
Women's Relay: France

Bobsled
2-Man: Switzerland
4-Man: Austria

Figure Skating
Men's Singles: Viktor Petrenko, Unified Team
Women's Singles: Kristi Yamaguchi, United States
Pairs: Artur Dmitriev and Natalya Mishkutienok, Unified Team
Dance: Sergei Ponomarenko and Marina Klimova, Unified Team

Freestyle Skiing
Men's Moguls: Edgar Grospiron, France
Women's Moguls: Donna Weinbrecht, United States

Ice Hockey
Unified Team

Luge
Men's Singles: Georg Hackl, Germany
Men's Pairs: Stefan Krausse and Jan Behrendt, Germany
Women's Singles: Doris Neuner, Austria

Nordic Skiing
Men's 10-km: Vegard Ulvang, Norway
Men's 15-km: Bjorn Dahlie, Norway
Men's 30-km: Vegard Ulvang
Men's 50-km: Bjorn Dahlie
Men's 40-km Relay: Norway
Men's 90-m Ski Jump: Ernst Vettori, Austria
Men's 120-m Ski Jump: Toni Nieminen, Finland
Men's 120-m Ski Jump Team: Finland
Men's Individual Combined: Fabrice Guy, France
Men's Team Combined: Japan

Women's 5-km: Marjut Lukkarinen, Finland
Women's 10-km: Lyubov Yegorova, Unified Team
Women's 15-km: Lyubov Yegorova
Women's 30-km: Stefania Belmondo, Italy
Women's 20-km Relay: Unified Team

Speed Skating
Long Track
Men's 500-m: Uwe-Jens Mey, Germany
Men's 1,000-m: Olaf Zinke, Germany
Men's 1,500-m: Johann Koss, Norway
Men's 5,000-m: Geir Karlstad, Norway
Men's 10,000-m: Bart Veldkamp, Netherlands
Women's 500-m: Bonnie Blair, United States
Women's 1,000-m: Bonnie Blair
Women's 1,500-m: Jacqueline Börner, Germany
Women's 3,000-m: Gunda Kleeman Niemann, Germany
Women's 5,000-m: Gunda Kleeman Niemann

Short Track
Men's 1,000-m: Kim Ki Hoon, South Korea
Men's 5,000-m Relay: South Korea
Women's 500-m: Cathy Turner, United States
Women's 3,000-m Relay: Canada

Medal Standings

	Gold	Silver	Bronze
Germany	10	10	6
Unified Team*	9	6	8
Norway	9	6	5
Austria	6	7	8
United States	5	4	2
Italy	4	6	4
France	3	5	1
Finland	3	1	3
Canada	2	3	2
South Korea	2	1	1
Japan	1	2	4
Netherlands	1	1	2
Sweden	1	0	3
Switzerland	1	0	2
China	0	3	0
Luxembourg	0	2	0
New Zealand	0	1	0
Czechoslovakia	0	0	3
North Korea	0	0	1
Spain	0	0	1

Note: A tie caused two silver medals and no bronze to be awarded in the women's Alpine skiing giant slalom.
*Represented the former Soviet republics of Belarus, Kazakhstan, Russia, Ukraine, and Uzbekistan.

Italy's Alberto Tomba repeated as the gold medalist in the giant slalom. The popular 25-year-old skier barely missed winning a second consecutive gold in the slalom.

© Bernard Asset/Vandystadt/Allsport

the United States, one of the few competitors to hold up under the great pressure. Yamaguchi, the defending world champion, showed off wonderful artistry and composition. Ito kept falling on her most difficult jumps and barely was able to beat out Nancy Kerrigan of the United States for second place.

The men's competition also was marred by unsteady performances. One of the favorites, Canada's Kurt Browning, skated so poorly that he finished sixth. That opened the way for unheralded Paul Wylie of the United States, whose spectacular performances earned him a silver medal behind Viktor Petrenko of the Unified Team.

Home-country favorites Isabelle and Paul Duchesnay of France were unable to win the gold medal in ice dancing. They were outskated by Marina Klimova and Sergei Ponomarenko of the Unified Team, the most impressive pair in the skating competition. Another Unified pair, Natalya Mishkutienok and Artur Dmitriev, easily won the pairs competition.

Speed Skating. Bonnie Blair (*see* BIOGRAPHY), who had won the women's 500 meters at

© Richard Martin/Vandystadt/Allsport

As a member of Finland's gold-winning ski-jumping team, Toni Nieminen, nearly 17, became the youngest athlete to capture a gold medal in Winter competition. He also won gold and bronze medals in individual jumping.

Calgary, successfully handled the pressure of trying to repeat her performance in Albertville. Not only did she win the 500, but she also added a second gold by taking the 1,000 meters, making her the dominant U.S. athlete at these Games. Her two medals were matched by Germany's Gunda Kleeman Niemann, who won both the 3,000 and 5,000 meters.

Another American, Dan Jansen, had a second heartbreaking Olympics. A favorite to win two medals in 1988, he fell twice in those

The Unified Team's Lyubov Yegorova, 25, dominated women's cross-country skiing, taking the gold in the 10-k, 15-k, and relay and the silver in the 5-k and 30-k.

© Gromik/Sipa Sport

Games and also lost his sister to leukemia during the competition. In Albertville, the best he could do was a fourth-place finish in the 500.

Hockey and Other Events. There was speculation that the political unrest in the former Soviet Union would end that country's domination of Olympic hockey. But the Unified Team proved otherwise by winning the gold medal. Canada finished second and the United States, which had been one of the most impressive teams in the early stages of the competition, wound up fourth behind bronze-winning Czechoslovakia.

Norway's Vegard Ulvang won three gold medals in cross-country skiing, as did teammate Bjorn Dahlie. Lyubov Yegorova of the Unified Team was a superstar among the women. The 25-year-old was the recipient of medals in all the women's cross-country events, taking three gold and two silver medals.

Toni Nieminen, a 16-year-old Finn who captured two gold medals and a bronze in ski jumping, became the youngest male gold medalist in Winter competition. In contrast, Raisa Smetanina of the Unified Team was awarded a record tenth Winter Olympics medal as she approached her 40th birthday. She took a gold skiing in the second lap of the 20-km cross-country relay race.

Overall. U.S. television ratings for the Games were unexpectedly high, in part because of the American success in figure skating. In a departure from traditional scheduling, the next Winter Games would be held in 1994, not 1996, in Lillehammer, Norway.

PAUL ATTNER, *"The Sporting News"*

Skiing

Austria's Petra Kronberger enhanced her reputation as the world's best woman skier by taking her third consecutive overall World Cup title in March 1992. She thereby became second to her fellow countrywoman Annemarie Moser-Proell, who won five consecutive overall World Cup crowns (1971–75). On the men's side, Switzerland's Paul Accola captured the overall World Cup title as well as the World Cup's super-giant slalom.

Diann Roffe-Steinrotter of Potsdam, NY, became the first woman since Canada's Nancy Greene in 1965 to win three events at the U.S. Alpine Championships. Roffe-Steinrotter, 24, captured the slalom, giant slalom, and super giant slalom in Winter Park, CO, in late March. She did not participate in the downhill. Erik Schlopy of Stowe, VT, was a dominating force in the men's events, winning the giant and super-giant slaloms.

See also SPORTS—*Olympic Games.*

SKIING

World Cup

Men's Downhill: Franz Heinzer, Switzerland
Men's Slalom: Alberto Tomba, Italy
Men's Giant Slalom: Alberto Tomba
Men's Super-Giant Slalom: Paul Accola, Switzerland
Men's Overall: Paul Accola
Women's Downhill: Katja Seizinger, Germany
Women's Slalom: Vreni Schneider, Switzerland
Women's Giant Slalom: Carol Merle, France
Women's Super-Giant Slalom: Carol Merle
Women's Overall: Petra Kronberger, Austria

U.S. Alpine Championships

Men's Combined: Toni Standteiner, United States
Men's Downhill: Jeff Olson, United States
Men's Slalom: Matt Grosjean, United States
Men's Giant Slalom: Erik Schlopy, United States
Men's Super-Giant Slalom: Erik Schlopy
Women's Combined: Hilary Lindh, United States
Women's Downhill: Kate Pace, Canada
Women's Slalom: Diann Roffe-Steinrotter, United States
Women's Giant Slalom: Diann Roffe-Steinrotter
Women's Super-Giant Slalom: Diann Roffe-Steinrotter

NCAA: University of Vermont

Soccer

Nine U.S. cities were selected in 1992 as host sites for the 1994 World Cup, which will be held for the first time in the United States. The cities chosen were Washington, DC; Chicago, IL; Dallas, TX; East Rutherford, NJ; Foxboro, MA; Orlando, FL; Pasadena, CA; Pontiac, MI; and Palo Alto, CA. Giants Stadium in New Jersey would host seven games, including one of the two semifinals; Pasadena's Rose Bowl would host the other semifinal and the championship game. Games in Pontiac's Silverdome would be the first in cup history played indoors. World Cup organizers were expecting to spend in excess of $80 million providing security at the tournament's nine venues. The World Cup competition was expected to attract 1 million visitors.

In NCAA Division I play, the University of Virginia defeated the University of San Diego, 2-0, for the championship.

World. In a stunning upset, Denmark defeated reigning World Cup champion Germany, 2-0, to win the European Championship held in Sweden. The Danes came into the tournament as an added starter, replacing banned Yugoslavia in the eight-team, quadrennial event. After only nine days of preparation, the Danes eventually upset France, 2-1, in the quarterfinals and then beat defending champion the Netherlands, 5-4, on penalty kicks to reach the final. It was Denmark's first major soccer championship.

Ronald Koeman scored with eight minutes left to give Barcelona a 1-0 victory over Sampdoria of Genoa for the European Cup. It was Barcelona's first cup championship in its 93-year history. Koeman's winning goal came off a free kick. He earlier had a free kick saved by Sampdorian goalie Gianluca Pagliuca.

Liverpool won the Football Association Cup in England by defeating Sunderland, a Second Division team, 2-0, in Wembley Stadium. Michael Thomas and Ian Rush scored goals for Liverpool, which won the trophy for the fifth time. A. C. Milan took the Italian League championship for the 12th time, and Ajax Amsterdam ended Italy's three-year hold on the Union of European Football Associations (UEFA) Cup, getting the edge over Torino through a complicated tiebreaking system.

Diego Maradona, the world's most celebrated soccer player, moved from Naples to Seville for a $7.5 million transfer fee. In June, Maradona finished a 15-month suspension for testing positive for cocaine following an Italian League match.

United States. The U.S. national team recorded a meaningful international victory by winning the U.S. Cup, defeating a strong field which included Italy and Portugal. One of the U.S. heroes was Roy Wegerle, an international star from South Africa who became a U.S. citizen in 1991.

In the Major Indoor Soccer League, San Diego defeated Dallas, four games to two, to wrap up its third straight title. However, the league suspended operations after 14 seasons when only five franchises remained in operation.

PAUL ATTNER

Swimming

Some of the best and brightest young world-class swimmers set records in 1992. The Summer Olympics in Barcelona, Spain, were the highlight of the year for the swimming world, as only one world record was set anywhere except at the U.S. Olympic trials or at Barcelona. The exception was the achievement of Kieren

Perkins of Australia, who broke the record in the 800-m freestyle at a meet in Sydney with a time of 7:46.60.

At the U.S. Olympic trials at the Indiana University Natatorium in Indianapolis in March, two world records were shattered by two U.S. teenagers in the space of two days. Nineteen-year-old Jenny Thompson of Dover, NH, broke the eight-year-old record of 54.73 seconds set by former East German star Kristin Otto in the 100-m freestyle, becoming the first American to shatter that mark since Helene Madison in 1931. Thompson's time of 54.48 seconds won the semifinal event. She also won the final, qualifying for the Olympics with a 54.63 effort—the second-fastest time ever.

The second record breaker, 15-year-old Anita Nall of Towson, MD, broke the 200-m breaststroke record twice in one day as she became one of the youngest swimmers, men or women, to lower a world standard. Nall broke the 200-m mark in the morning heats with a time of 2:25.92, then came back eight hours later in the evening final to do it in 2:25.35. Her earlier mark lowered the 1988 record held by Silke Hörner, then an East German, in the Olympics at Seoul, South Korea.

Although Mike Barrowman, the world-record holder and U.S. swimmer of the year three years in a row, qualified for the Olympics, he was edged out in the 200-m breaststroke final by Roque Santos, to whom he never had lost. The margin was .04 seconds in a winning clocking of 2:13.50, well off Barrowman's world mark of 2:10.60. Barrowman had lowered the world mark in the 200-m five times in the preceding 31 months.

The trials threw a scare into Matt Biondi, who had won five gold medals, one silver, and one bronze in the 1988 Seoul Olympics. In the 100-m butterfly, the 26-year-old Biondi finished sixth, and he was nervous about his chances of qualifying. But the next day he took the 100-m freestyle to garner a berth at Barcelona.

Other outstanding performances in the trials were by 20-year-old Janet Evans, who took the women's 400-m and 800-m freestyles; Summer Sanders, 19, who qualified for five events and won the 200-m and 400-m individual medleys; Nelson Diebel, a 21-year-old Princeton swimmer, whose 1:01.40 in the 100-m breaststroke set a U.S. record; and the grand old man of the sport, Pablo Morales, who at 27 qualified by winning the 100-m butterfly after failing to make the 1988 Olympics in any of the three events he tried.

GEORGE DE GREGORIO

Tennis

While her homeland, Yugoslavia, was disintegrating, Monica Seles was firmer than ever

TENNIS

Davis Cup: United States
Federation Cup: Germany

Major Tournaments

Australian Open—men's singles: Jim Courier; men's doubles: Todd Woodbridge (Australia) and Mark Woodforde (Australia); women's singles: Monica Seles (Yugoslavia); women's doubles: Arantxa Sanchez Vicario (Spain) and Helena Sukova (Czechoslovakia); mixed doubles: Mark Woodforde (Australia) and Nicole Provis (Australia).
International Players Championships—men's singles: Michael Chang; men's doubles: Ken Flach and Todd Witsken; women's singles: Arantxa Sanchez Vicario (Spain); women's doubles: Arantxa Sanchez Vicario (Spain) and Larisa Savchenko-Neiland (Latvia).
Italian Open—men's singles: Jim Courier; men's doubles: Jakob Hlasek (Switzerland) and Marc Rosset (Switzerland); women's singles: Gabriela Sabatini (Argentina); women's doubles: Monica Seles (Yugoslavia) and Helena Sukova (Czechoslovakia).
French Open—men's singles: Jim Courier; men's doubles: Jakob Hlasek (Switzerland) and Marc Rosset (Switzerland); women's singles: Monica Seles (Yugoslavia); women's doubles: Gigi Fernandez and Natalia Zvereva (Belarus); mixed doubles: Arantxa Sanchez Vicario (Spain) and Todd Woodbridge (Australia).
Wimbledon—men's singles: Andre Agassi; men's doubles: John McEnroe and Michael Stich (Germany); women's singles: Steffi Graf (Germany); women's doubles: Gigi Fernandez and Natalia Zvereva (Belarus); mixed doubles: Cyril Suk (Czechoslovakia) and Larisa Savchenko-Neiland (Latvia).
U.S. Open—men's singles: Stefan Edberg (Sweden); men's doubles: Jim Grabb and Richey Reneberg; women's singles: Monica Seles (Yugoslavia); women's doubles: Gigi Fernandez and Natalia Zvereva (Belarus); mixed doubles: Nicole Provis (Australia) and Mark Woodforde (Australia); masters men's singles: Hank Pfister; masters men's doubles: Paul McNamee (Australia) and Tomas Smid (Czechoslovakia); masters women's doubles: Wendy Turnbull (Australia) and Virginia Wade (Great Britain); senior mixed doubles: Wendy Turnbull (Australia) and Marty Riessen; boys' singles: Brian Dunn; boys' doubles: J. J. Jackson and Eric Taino; girls' singles: Lindsay Davenport; girls' doubles: Lindsay Davenport and Nicole London.
A.T.P. Finals—singles: Boris Becker, (Germany); doubles: Mark Woodforde (Australia) and Todd Woodbridge (Australia).
Virginia Slims Championship—singles: Monica Seles (Yugoslavia); doubles: Arantxa Sanchez Vicaro (Spain) and Helena Sukova (Czechoslovakia).
NCAA (Division I)—men's singles: Alex O'Brien, Stanford; men's team: Stanford; women's singles: Lisa Raymond, Florida; women's team: Florida.

N.B. All players are from the United States, unless otherwise noted.

in her domination of the game of tennis. U.S. men players, in the persons of Jim Courier and Andre Agassi, reached an 18-year high point. And Martina Navratilova gilded her legend by becoming the player with the most wins of all time. Those were the saliences of the 1992 tennis season, which concluded with unlikely Switzerland led by only two players of note, Jakob Hlasek and Marc Rosset, in the Davis Cup finals for the first time. Its final opponent, the United States, took the Cup, 3-1, for a record 30th time, however.

By winning three majors—the Australian, the French, and the United States—for the second consecutive year, Seles, a U.S. resident, who turned 19 in December, retained her Number 1 ranking. She took ten titles in 15 tournaments on a 70-5 match record. A unique stylist among history's major champs—two-fisted on both forehand and backhand sides—she was the youngest ever to pocket seven majors (also having won the French in 1990). Only the final-round verve of Germany's Steffi Graf, who won her fourth Wimbledon, 6-2, 6-1, cost Seles a rare Grand Slam. But she became only the eighth person to play in all four finals in a calendar year.

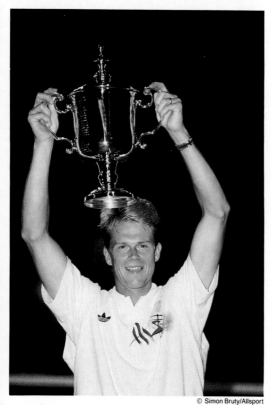
© Simon Bruty/Allsport

© Bob Martin/Allsport

In September 1992, Sweden's Stefan Edberg (left) won his second consecutive U.S. Open men's singles crown. Earlier, Andre Agassi of the United States was overjoyed to win his first grand-slam tennis title — the men's singles at Wimbledon.

Seles had defended her Australian title successfully, 7-6, 6-3, over Mary Joe Fernandez of the United States. She hung on grittily to top Graf at the French, the best of the major women's finals, 6-2, 3-6, 10-8. In one of the more one-sided charges to the U.S. title, Seles permitted her foes a total of 27 games, no sets, and beat Spain's Arantxa Sanchez Vicario for the title, 6-3, 6-3.

By winning the Australian and French and three other titles, Courier, at 22, seized the Number 1 ranking from Sweden's Stefan Edberg. Courier won five of 20 tournaments on a 72-17 match record. He beat Edberg at Melbourne, 6-3, 3-6, 6-4, 6-2, and Czech Petr Korda to successfully defend at Paris, 7-5, 6-2, 6-1. Then when Andre Agassi, 22, playing only his second Wimbledon and seeded only 12th, beat Croatia's 8th seeded Goran Ivanisevic, 6-7, 6-4, 6-4, 1-6, 6-4, for the oldest of all titles, U.S. men had won three majors. That had not happened since Jimmy Connors took the Australian, Wimbledon, and U.S. Open in 1974.

Pete Sampras appeared on his way to taking a fourth major for the United States at Flushing Meadow, but Edberg rebounded as he had throughout the U.S. Open to win that title a second straight time, 4-6, 6-4, 7-6, 6-2. Edberg's win in the semis over Michael Chang of the United States, 6-7, 7-5, 7-6, 5-7, 6-4, lasted 5 hours 26 minutes and was the longest match ever played in a major.

Saving two match points, 35-year-old Navratilova beat Jana Novotna, 7-6, 4-6, 7-5, in the finals of the Virginia Slims of Chicago. In her 20th professional season she had won her 158th career singles title, eclipsing the United States' Chris Evert's monumental standard fashioned over 19 seasons. Martina added three more titles and, after turning 36, made it to the final of the season-climaxing Virginia Slims Championships for the 14th time. However, Seles was too strong, winning it for a third successive year, 7-5, 6-3, 6-1. Another former Czech, Ivan Lendl, joined Navratilova as a U.S. citizen and celebrated by beating Henrik Holm of Sweden, 7-6, 6-4 to win a Tokyo match, his 92nd career title.

In high heat on slow clay at Barcelona unseeded, Marc Rosset, a 6'5" (1.9 m) flame-throwing server, and 16-year-old Jennifer Capriati of the United States were surprise Olympic gold medalists in singles. . . . In winning the season-climaxing ATP Championships (formerly the Masters) in Frankfurt, Germany's Boris Becker not only beat Courier in the final, 6-4, 6-3, 7-5, but also took his fifth title for the year. This tied him with Courier and Sampras for the season high. . . . Seles set a single season prize money record of $2,622,352 while Navratilova increased her career record to $18,396,526. Edberg led the men's money chase with $2,341,804.

BUD COLLINS, *"The Boston Globe/NBC"*

© Michael Kullen/"Sports Illustrated"

With snow on the ground and temperatures nearing freezing, 126 of the world's best female runners took part in the 1992 world cross-country championship in Boston. Lynn Jennings (352) won the event for the third consecutive time.

Track and Field

The 1992 Summer Olympics in Barcelona, Spain, were the focal point of the season in track and field, but there were surprising developments in the sport that, in some cases, proved as dramatic as the events in Barcelona.

Field Events. Dan O'Brien, the much-heralded U.S. decathlon star, incredibly knocked himself out of contention for an Olympic berth when he missed his first three attempts in the pole vault at the U.S. Olympic trials in New Orleans, LA, on June 27. In the first five decathlon events, O'Brien had set a first-day world record of 4,698 points and seemed well on his way to breaking the ten-event world record of 8,847 set by Daley Thompson of Great Britain in the 1984 Olympics. However, O'Brien, recovering from a stress fracture in his right leg and a sprained left ankle, hit the crossbar on his first two vault attempts and went under the bar on his third, scoring no points when he expected 900. Nevertheless, a month after the Olympics, O'Brien broke Thompson's mark, scoring 8,891 points at Talence, France. He became the first American to hold the decathlon world record since Bruce Jenner in 1976.

Sergei Bubka of Ukraine, the 1988 Olympic and 1991 world champion in the pole vault, shocked fans at Barcelona when he failed to clear any height. But on September 19, at an international meet in Tokyo, Bubka set a world record of 20′ 1¼″ (6.13 m), bettering his mark of 20′ 1″ (6.12 m), which he had cleared in Padua, Italy, on August 30. It was the 32d time that Bubka, 28, set a world pole-vault mark since 1984. Bubka's best indoor mark is also 20′ 1¼″ (6.13 m).

Running Events. Carl Lewis, the world-record holder in the 100-m dash (9.86 seconds), failed to qualify for the Olympics in his specialties—the 100-m and 200-m dashes—but did qualify in the long jump and relay. But at Zurich, Switzerland, two weeks after the Olympics, Lewis won the 100-m in 10.07 seconds. At a later meet in Copenhagen, Denmark, Lewis lost to Dennis Mitchell, a bronze medalist at the Olympics and the winner of the 100-m in the 1992 U.S. trials. Mitchell's margin was .03 seconds, as he recorded a wind-aided 9.92. The crowd of 11,999 jeered when a replay of the start indicated that Mitchell had moved out of the blocks too early. An attempt to disqualify Mitchell, however, fell through.

In the Copenhagen meet, Moses Kiptanui, the world champion who missed qualifying for the Olympics because of a foot injury, broke the world record in the 3,000-m steeplechase. The 20-year-old Kenyan finished in 8:02.08—well under the 1989 record of countryman Peter Koech (8:05.35). Three days earlier, on August 16, Kiptanui had set a world record in the 3,000-m at Cologne, Germany, becoming the first runner since 1978 to set two records over 3,000 meters in the same year. Henry Rono of Kenya also accomplished that feat. At Rieti, Italy, on September 6, Algerian runner Noureddine Morceli smashed the world record for the 1,500-m run, clocking 3:28.86. Morceli's time broke the 1985 record of 3:29.46 set by Said Aouita of Morocco.

Litigation. Butch Reynolds, the 400-m world-record holder—who was banned by The Athletics Congress (TAC) from competing in the Olympic trials because of alleged steroid use—won a U.S. Supreme Court reversal barring TAC from enforcing an international ban by the world governing body. Reynolds competed, but the litigation became academic as he finished fourth in the final, not qualifying for the Olympics.

Marathons. The winners of the Boston Marathon were Ibrahim Hussein of Kenya and Olga Markova of Russia. Willie Mtolo of South Africa and Lisa Ondieki of Australia took the New York City Marathon.

GEORGE DE GREGORIO

Yachting

For the 27th time in 28 challenges in the 141-year history of the America's Cup, the United States again won the cup in 1992. This time, however, the U.S. helmsman was Bill Koch, a 52-year-old oil heir and multimillionaire from Wichita, KS.

The 6'5" (1.8-m) Koch, with only eight years of racing experience, had his detractors. Among yachting's experts, few thought he could defend the cup. Koch put up $10 million personally and $44 million from his private foundations to back the $64 million campaign of *America³*, and he won the right to defend the cup over Dennis Conner, considered by many to be the top cup sailor in the United States for more than a decade. Koch eliminated Conner, sailing in *Stars & Stripes*, in the series to determine the defender.

Conner had established a popular reputation as a cup sailor and in 1987 his stock zoomed when he won back the cup from Australia with *Stars & Stripes*. In 1983, Australia had become the first and only nation to take the cup out of the United States in the history of the yachting event.

The challenge in the finals came from an Italian entry, *Il Moro di Venezia*, which had eliminated New Zealand in the challenger trials. However, the European boat proved no match for the sleek, 75-ft (22-m) *America³* as the Koch syndicate retained the cup for the San Diego Yacht Club, four races to one.

The Italian vessel, whose syndicate was headed by Raul Gardini, a wealthy Italian businessman, was skippered by Paul Cayard, a 33-year-old San Franciscan who lived in Venice. Virtually from the first race, the pattern of the series was established. Cayard made a tactical mistake from which he and *Il Moro di Venezia* never recovered fully. At the start of the opening race on May 9, Cayard misjudged the current and jumped the gun. By the time he could bring his yacht back to the starting line, *America³* had a 30-second lead and, in 30-knot winds, was sailing along in conditions much to her liking.

The next day, *Il Moro di Venezia* captured her only race of the series, registering the closest victory in the history of cup racing. *Il Moro* crossed the finish line three seconds ahead of *America³*. The call was so close that a team of on-the-water umpires took several minutes to decide who had won. The previous closest margin was 26 seconds in 1962 when *Weatherly*, the U.S. defender, beat *Gretel*, the Australian challenger. The triumph by the Italians was the first by a European entry since 1934.

Although *America³* lost the second race, she had established a pattern of superior speed at almost every sail point, and carried over this superiority to subsequent races. She made quick work of her opponent in the next three races, winning by large margins in each—1 minute 58 seconds, 1 minute 4 seconds, and 44 seconds, respectively.

GEORGE DE GREGORIO

© Stephen Dunn/Allsport

"America³," the U.S. entry, defeats Italy's *"Il Moro di Venezia,"* four races to one, to retain the America's Cup. Helmsman Bill Koch called his victory *"a triumph for America, for American technology, and for American teamwork."*

SPORTS SUMMARIES[1]

ARCHERY—World Champions: men: barebow: A. Rosenberg, Sweden; freestyle: Jay Barrs, United States; combined: Morgan Lundin, Sweden; women: barebow: Nadine Visconti, France; freestyle: Carol Ferriou, France; combined: Susanne Kessler, Denmark. **U.S. Champions:** men's freestyle: Allen Rasor, Jr., Los Angeles; women's freestyle: Sherry Block, Colorado Springs, CO.

BADMINTON—World Champions: men's singles: Zhao Jianhua, China; women's singles: Tang Jiuhong, China. **U.S. Champions:** men's singles: Chris Jogis, Palo Alto, CA; women's singles: Joy Kitzmiller, Manhattan Beach, CA.

BIATHLON—U.S. Champions: men: 10k: Josh Thompson, Gunnison, CO; 20k: Josh Thompson; women: 7.5k: Joan Guestchow, Minnetonka, MN; 15k: Angie Stevenson, Bend, OR.

BILLIARDS—World Champions: men's 9-ball: J. Archer, Twin Cities, GA; women's 9-ball: F. Stark, Germany.

BOBSLEDDING—World Champions: 2-man World Cup: Gunther Huber, Italy; 4-man World Cup: Wolf Hoppe, Germany.

BOWLING—Professional Bowlers Association Tour: BPAA U.S. Open: Robert Lawrence, Austin, TX; Firestone Tournament of Champions: Marc McDowell, Madison, WI; Bud Light PBA National Championship: Eric Forkel, Chatsworth, CA; Bud Light Touring Players Championship: Pete Weber. St. Louis. **Ladies Professional Bowlers Tour:** BPAA U.S. Open: Tish Johnson, Panorama City, CA; Sam's Town Invitational: Tish Johnson.

CANOEING—U.S. Sprint National Champions: Men: Canoe: 500 m: Jim Terrell, Milford, OH; 1,000 m: Greg Steward, Williamsburg, OH; 10,000 m: James Ross, Bethesda, MD; Kayak: 1,000 m: Greg Barton, Bellingham, WA. Women: Kayak: 500 m: Sheila Conover, Newport Beach, CA; 5,000 m: Sheila Conover.

CASTING—U.S. Champions: Men's all-around: Steve Rajeff, Poulsbo, WA.

CRICKET—World Cup: Pakistan.

CURLING—World Champions: men: Markus Eggler, Switzerland; women: Elisabet Johansson, Sweden. **U.S. Champions:** men: Doug Jones, Seattle, WA; women: Lisa Schoeneberg, Madison, WI.

CYCLING—World Champions: men's pro road: Gianni Bugno, Italy; men's pro sprint: Michael Huebner, Germany; Men's pro pursuit: Mike McCarthy, New York City; women's points race: Ingrid Haringa, Netherlands; World Cup: Olaf Ludwig, Germany; Tour de France: men: Miguel Indurain, Spain.

DOG SHOWS—Westminster: best in show: Ch. Registry's Lonesome Dove, wire fox terrier, owned by Marion and Samuel Lawrence, Orlando, FL.

EQUESTRIAN—World Champions: World Cup Jumping: Thomas Fruhmann, Genius, Austria; World Cup Dressage: Isabell Werth, Sabienne, Germany.

FENCING—USFA Champions: men's foil: Nick Bravin, Los Angeles, CA; men's épée: Rob Stull, Austin, TX; men's saber: Michael Lofton, New York City; women's foil: Caitlin Bilodeaux, Concorde, MA; women's épée: Barbara Turpin, Minneapolis, MN.

FIELD HOCKEY—NCAA Division I: women: Old Dominion.

GYMNASTICS—World Champions: men's floor exercise: Igor Korobchinski, Unified Team (parts of the former USSR); men's parallel bars—2-way tie: 1) Li Jing, China; 2) Alexei Voropaev, Unified Team; men's pommel horse—3-way tie: 1) Pae Gil Fu, Korea; 2) Vitaly Scherbo, Unified Team; 3) Li Jing; men's still rings: Vitaly Scherbo; men's vault: You Ok Youl, Korea; men's high bar: Grigori Misutin, Unified Team; women's floor exercise: Kim Zmeskal, United States; women's uneven bars: Lavinia Milosovici, Romania; women's balance beam: Kim Zmeskal; women's vault: Henrietta Onodi, Hungary.

HANDBALL—U.S. Handball Association: men's one-wall: Joe Durso, Brooklyn, NY; men's four-wall: Octavio Silveyra, Commerce, CA; women's one-wall: Dori Ten, Brooklyn, NY; women's four-wall: Lisa Fraser, Winnipeg, Ont.

HORSESHOE PITCHING—World Champions: men: Kevin Cone, IA; women: Sue Snyder, IN.

JUDO—U.S. Champions: men's open: Christophe Leininger, Colorado Springs, CO; women's open: D'Anaya Bierria, Colorado Springs, CO.

KARATE—U.S. Champions: men: Advanced Kumite: Carlos Quintero, Hialeah, FL; Advanced 80+ kg: Jay Farell, Beaverton,

OR; Advanced 75 kg: Chris Nicholas, Akron, OH; Advanced -80 kg: Doug Selchon, North Huntington, PA; Advanced -70 kg: Ferdie Allas, Ironton, OH; Advanced -65 kg: William Chadrow, Redmond, WA; Advanced -60 kg: Bismark Leon, NY; women: Advanced 60+ kg: Tina Franks, Florence, KY; Advanced -60 kg: Tracey Day, Coram, NY; Advanced -53 kg: Christina Mucini, Douglastown, NY; Advanced: Edna Loeber, NY.

LACROSSE—NCAA Division I: men: Princeton; women: Maryland.

LUGE—U.S. Champions: men: Duncan Kennedy, Lake Placid, NY; women: Cammy Myler, Lake Placid, NY. **World Cup Champions:** men: Markus Prock, Austria; women: Susi Erdmann, Germany.

MODERN PENTATHLON—United States: men: Mike Gostigian, Newtown Square, PA; women: Terry Lewis, San Antonio, TX.

PADDLE TENNIS—U.S. Champions: men's singles: Scott Freedman, Culver City, CA; women's singles: Nicole Marois, Los Angeles, CA.

PLATFORM TENNIS—U.S. Champions: men's singles: Andrew Kinney, Rowayton, CT; women's doubles: Sue Aery, Denville, NJ, and Gerri Viant, Nyack, NY.

POLO—Regina World Cup: Rolex A&K. **U.S. Open:** Hana Lei Bay, CA.

RACQUETBALL—U.S. Champions: men's amateur singles: Chris Cole, Flint, MI; women's amateur singles: Michelle Gilman-Gould, Ontario, OR; men's pro singles: Mike Ray, Hilton Head, SC; women's pro singles: Jackie Paraiso-Gibson, San Diego, CA.

SHOOTING—Amateur Trapshooting Association: Men's clay target championship: William Godschalk, Hartford City, IN; men's grand American Handicap: Mark T. Wade, Kenilworth, NJ; men's doubles championship: Larry Bumstead, Conrad, IA; men's high all-around championships: Leo Harrison III, Hannibal, MO; women's clay target championship: Janet Loebs, Shore Wood, IL; women's grand American handicap: Kelly Doll, Hanover, PA; women's doubles championship: Cathy Wehinger, Monroe, WI; women's high all-around championship: Nora Martin, Midway, KY.

SLED DOG RACING: Iditarod (Anchorage to Nome): Martin Buser, Two Rivers, AK.

SOFTBALL—U.S. Champions: men's fast pitch: National Health Care Discount, Sioux City, IA; women's fast pitch: Raybestos Brakettes, Stratford, CT.

VOLLEYBALL—National Championship: U.S. Open: men: Creole Six Pack, Elmhurst, NY; women: Nick's Kronies, Chicago, IL.

WEIGHT LIFTING—U.S. Weightlifting Federation: men: 52 kg: Brian Okada, Wailuku, HI; 56 kg: Robert (Gene) Gilsdorf, Onaga, KA; 60 kg: Bryan Jacob, Norcross, GA; 67.5 kg: Vernon Patao, Kahului, HI; 75 kg: David Santillo, Runnemede, NJ; 82.5 kg: R. Urrutia, Hollywood, FL; 90 kg: Bret Brian, Baton Rouge, LA; 100 kg: Wesley Barnett, St. Joseph, MO; 110 kg: Rich Schutz, Mt. Prospect, IL; Plus 110: Mario Martinez, South San Francisco, CA; women: 44 kg: Sibby Flowers, Carollton, GA; 48 kg: Misha Utley, Lawrenceburg, IN; 52 kg: Robin Byrd, Newnan, GA; 56 kg: Ursula Garza, Austin, TX; 60 kg: Giselle Shepatin, San Francisco, CA; 67.5 kg: Dianna Fuhrman, Simi Valley, CA; 75 kg: Arlys Johnson, Seattle, WA; 82.5 kg: Mary Hyder, Dallas, TX; Plus 82.5 kg: Carla Garrett, Tucson, AZ.

WRESTLING—National Champions: freestyle: 105.5 lbs: Rob Eiter, Scottsdale, AZ; 114.5 lbs: Jack Griffin, Iowa City, IA; 125.5 lbs: Kendall Cross, Stillwater, OK; 136.5 lbs: John Fisher, Ann Arbor, MI; 149.5 lbs: Matt Demaray, Madison, WI; 163 lbs: Greg Elinsky, Philadelphia, PA; 180.5 lbs: Royce Alger, Iowa City, IA; 198 lbs: Dan Chaid, Newtown Square, PA; 220 lbs: Bill Scherr, Evanston, IL; 286 lbs: Bruce Baumgartner, Cambridge Springs, PA; Div. I team: Sunkist Kids; Div. II team: Foxcatcher; Greco-Roman: 105.5 lbs: Eric Wetzel, Quantico, VA; 114.5 lbs: Mark Fuller, Gilert, AZ; 125.5 lbs: Dennis Hall, Neosho, WI; 136.5 lbs: Buddy Lee, Woodbridge, VA; 149.5 lbs: Rodney Smith, Fort Benning, GA; 163 lbs: Travis West, Portland, OR; 180.5 lbs: John Morgan, Minneapolis, MN; 198 lbs: Michial Foy, Brooklyn Park, MN; 220 lbs: D. Koslowski, St. Louis Park, MN; 286 lbs: Matt Ghaffari, Chandler, AZ; Div. I team: N.Y. Athletic Club; Div. II team: Sunkist Kids; women's freestyle: 97 lbs: Cheryl Meyer, Morrill, KS; 103.5 lbs: Afsoon Roshanzimir, Davis, CA; 110 lbs: Tricia Saunders, Phoenix, AZ; 116.5 lbs: Jennifer Ottiano, Orelo, CT; 125.5 lbs: Lee Ann Gonzalez, Hanford, CA; 134 lbs: Diana Wesendunk, Hillsbrough, CA; 143 lbs: Grace Jividen, Colorado Springs, CO.

[1]Sports for which articles do not appear in pages 479–511.

SRI LANKA

In Sri Lanka the year 1992 ended as it began —with a mixture of hope and anxiety. The bloody civil war that had raged intermittently between government forces and Tamil militants in the north and northeast for nearly a decade showed some signs of ebbing, but severe fighting flared up at least five times during the year. The economy continued to be hurt by the civil strife, and also by such natural disasters as floods, drought, and cyclones. Accelerating trends toward liberalization of the economy offered some hope for economic recovery. The United National Party (UNP) government of President Ranasinghe Premadasa remained firmly in power, in spite of evidence of waning support.

Continuing Civil Strife. Military actions against the leading Tamil militant group, the Liberation Tigers of Tamil Eelam (LTTE), in the first two months of the year proved inconclusive. After a lull in fighting of nearly three months, the Sri Lankan government on May 28 launched a massive offensive known as Operation Balaregaya II in an attempt to seal off the Jaffna Peninsula, the main LTTE stronghold. In the first eight days of battle, 300 rebels and 70 government soldiers lost their lives. Although the offensive seemed to weaken the Tigers early on, the government's campaign bogged down well short of its objective. Reports also had surfaced about an alleged government atrocity in May—the shelling of a Hindu temple in which 23 Tamil worshipers were killed.

On August 8 government forces suffered a major reversal when ten senior army and navy officers—including the commander of the campaign against the LTTE and the senior commander of forces in Jaffna—were killed by a mine explosion on Kayts Island off the Jaffna Peninsula. This killing shocked the entire island nation.

On November 16 a suicide bomber detonated explosives near a car carrying Vice-Admiral Clancy Fernando in Colombo, killing the admiral and three aides. Authorities believed that a 22-year-old member of the LTTE, who was killed in the incident, threw the bomb. Meanwhile, it was reported that the government had issued a decree requiring all Sri Lankans to register their home addresses with the police.

As the year ended, both the government forces and the LTTE seemed to be suffering from low morale and near-exhaustion. More than 17,000 people had died in the civil war, with an estimated 7,000 perishing since 1990.

The prolonged civil conflict continued to exacerbate a massive refugee problem. By 1992 more than 600,000 Tamil, Muslim, and Sinhalese refugees were sheltered in camps across the island. Nearly 200,000 Tamil refugees were housed in camps in India's southern state of Tamil Nadu, and thousands more were living in other countries.

The Economy. The most encouraging aspects of the economy were related to continued liberalization, with the growing private sector accounting for much of the progress. This hopeful trend, however, was offset, at least temporarily, by continuing internal instability, an increase in the trade gap, a decline in foreign-exchange earnings, a fall in the production of basic export commodities—notably tea, and declining prices for these commodities on international markets.

Politics. There was some speculation that the Premadasa government would hold a "snap" parliamentary election in the near future, but Premadasa insisted that elections would not be held until close to the end of his term in early 1995. Most of the opposition parties agreed to campaign in the next presidential election on the demand to abolish the executive presidency and to restore parliamentary democracy of the Westminster model. Opposition to the UNP and President Premadasa was weakened by a split in the leading opposition party, the Sri Lanka Freedom Party (SLFP), which was headed by former Prime Minister Sirimavo Bandaranaike.

Foreign Policy. Sri Lanka continued to be active in foreign affairs, with special attention aimed at obtaining international economic assistance and investment. In early September, President Premadasa led Sri Lanka's delegation to the nonaligned summit in Jakarta. During the year, he visited all the South Asian nations in his capacity as chairman of the South Asian Association for Regional Cooperation (SAARC). During an official two-day visit to India in early October—his first since assuming the presidency of Sri Lanka—he had frank discussions with top Indian officials on issues that had caused long-standing disputes between the two nations.

NORMAN D. PALMER, *Professor Emeritus*
University of Pennsylvania

SRI LANKA • Information Highlights

Official Name: Democratic Socialist Republic of Sri Lanka.
Location: South Asia.
Area: 25,332 sq mi (65 610 km²).
Population (mid-1992 est.): 17,400,000.
Chief Cities (mid-1990 est.): Colombo, the capital, 615,000; Dehiwala-Mount Lavinia, 196,000.
Government: *Head of state,* R. Premadasa, president (took office Jan. 1989). *Head of government,* D. B. Wijetunga, prime minister (appointed March 3, 1989). *Legislature* (unicameral)—Parliament.
Monetary Unit: Rupee (44.08 rupees equal U.S.$1, July 1992).
Gross Domestic Product (1990 U.S.$): $6,600,-000,000.
Economic Index (Colombo, 1991): *Consumer Prices* (1980 = 100), all items, 355.6; food, 359.2.
Foreign Trade (1991 U.S.$): *Imports,* $3,083,000,000; *exports,* $1,965,000,000.

STAMPS AND STAMP COLLECTING

The philatelic world rediscovered Christopher Columbus in 1992, 500 years after his arrival in the New World. Postage stamps galore from the United States and other countries honored the quincentenary celebration. The first Columbus issue by the United States Postal Service (USPS), on January 24, was dedicated to the World Columbian Stamp Expo '92, the international stamp show held in Rosemont, IL. Then, on April 24, a block of four stamps honored Columbus' first voyage. This was a joint issue with Italy.

For the first time ever, the United States issued stamps jointly with three other countries—Italy, Portugal, and Spain. The USPS reissued the entire Columbian Exposition Series of 1893 as souvenir sheets. The sheets reproduce, as exactly as possible, the designs and colors of the originals, considered by most philatelists to be the first U.S. commemorative stamps. The only design change was in the date—from 1892 to 1992. The 16 stamps range in value from 1¢ to $5. The designs for all four countries' sheets are the same, with the only difference in the language of the text. Another explorer receiving accolades was Juan Rodríguez Cabrillo, who visited the entire California coast and discovered San Diego Bay.

The year 1992 was an Olympic year also, and two sets of U.S. stamps were issued for the occasion: a strip of five for the Winter Olympics and five for the Summer Games, plus a special stamp for Olympic baseball.

Early in the year, the USPS issued another "Love" stamp in the long and popular series. And in continuation of its 50th-anniversary series for World War II, the Postal Service issued its second sheet of ten commemoratives, featuring key 1942 events. For each year of the war (1941–45), ten stamps would be released.

In the Black Heritage Series, a 29¢ stamp honored W. E. B. DuBois, a pioneer civil-rights leader. Writer and poet Dorothy Parker was hailed in the Literary Arts Series. Wild animals were tamed on a set of five stamps, and tiny hummingbirds, too, were highlighted in a booklet pane of five. Also issued was a pane of

The Elvis Stamp

The late Elvis Presley, recognized worldwide as the "King of Rock 'n' Roll," made philatelic history in 1992 when the United States Postal Service (USPS) announced it would issue a postage stamp to honor him. The stamp is one of a series called "Legends of American Music," to be released in 1993 to commemorate rock 'n' roll musicians. A problem arose, however, as to the stamp's design. Should the illustration depict a young, slender Elvis or the performer in his later, heavier years? More than 50 artists' conceptions were reviewed and two were chosen—one of the singer as a young man and one of the older Presley. The USPS then held the first-ever public vote on the design of a U.S. stamp. The results were emphatic: The young Elvis was the winner in a landslide.

The Postal Service hoped to come out a winner too with the issue of the Presley stamp. It expected at least half the stamps issued to be kept by collectors rather than used as postage, therefore garnering a profit of 29¢ for each stamp without having to provide a service. It was estimated that profits on the stamp could reach $20 million or more.

Stamp Design © 1992 U.S. Postal Service. Reproduced With Permission.

50 stamps depicting wildflowers. In a patriotic mood, the USPS issued a "Flag Over the White House" stamp and an "Eagle and Shield" design for its self-adhesive stamp. A joint issue with Russia resulted in a block of four portraying space achievements and envisioning future cooperation.

The traditional U.S. Christmas stamp for 1992 portrayed Madonna and Child, while the contemporary stamp featured a set of four, each illustrating a Christmas toy of the past. At year's end, the United States scheduled a "Happy New Year" stamp as a tribute to the Chinese New Year.

SYD KRONISH, *The Associated Press*

Selected U.S. Stamps for 1992

Subject	Denomination	Date	Subject	Denomination	Date	Subject	Denomination	Date
Winter Olympics	29¢	Jan. 11	Space Adventures	29¢	May 29	Theodore von Karman	29¢	Aug. 31
World Columbian Stamp Expo	29¢	Jan. 24	Alaska Highway	29¢	May 30	Pledge of Allegiance	29¢	Sept. 8
W. E. B. DuBois	29¢	Jan. 31	Kentucky Statehood	29¢	June 1	Minerals	29¢	Sept. 17
Love	29¢	Feb. 6	Summer Olympics	29¢	June 11	Eagle and Shield	29¢	Sept. 25
Olympics Baseball	29¢	April 3	Hummingbirds	29¢	June 15	Juan Rodríguez Cabrillo	29¢	Sept. 28
Flag over the White House	29¢	April 23	Wildflowers	29¢	July 24	Wild Animals	29¢	Oct. 1
First Voyage of Columbus	29¢	April 24	World War II	29¢	Aug. 17	Christmas (traditional)	29¢	Oct. 22
New York Stock Exchange	29¢	May 17	Dorothy Parker	29¢	Aug. 22	Christmas (contemporary)	29¢	Oct. 22
Columbus Souvenir Sheet	various	May 22				Happy New Year	29¢	Dec. 30

STOCKS AND BONDS

The U.S. stock market rose to record highs in 1992 as the nation elected a new president and the economy made a tortuous transition from recession toward recovery. Bond prices also rose, on balance, as interest rates continued their descent of the previous several years. But progress in both markets was restrained by uncertainties over such matters as political change at home and economic setbacks elsewhere in the industrialized world.

Trends. The Dow Jones average of 30 industrials, the oldest and best-known indicator of stock-price trends, reached a new peak of 3,413.21 on June 1, then wavered in a relatively narrow range just below that level for the rest of the year. It closed December 31 at 3,301.11, up 132.28 points, or 4.17% from the end of 1991. Most of the broader market indexes, considered better gauges of the overall market, were at new highs.

In the credit markets, interest rates continued a decline to some of the lowest levels in a generation or more. The short-term money-market yields declined on such popular savings vehicles as bank certificates of deposit (CDs) and money-market mutual funds to practically negligible levels. Yields on Treasury bills of three-month to one-year duration, which had fallen from about 7% to less than 4.5% in 1991, tumbled further to less than 3% in 1992 before turning upward slightly late in the year. Yields on long-term Treasury bonds, with maturities as long as 30 years, took a zigzag route from about 7.75% in late 1991 to a little less than 7.5% a year later.

Bond-market interest rates hit their 1992 low in late summer, and then bounced upward as it became increasingly evident that Gov. Bill Clinton of Arkansas, the Democratic nominee, was likely to deny President George Bush a second term in the White House. Fears on traditionally Republican Wall Street focused on expectations that Democratic moves to stimulate the economy also might aggravate the government's severe budget problems and increase inflationary pressures. The stock market, along with bonds, sank on those misgivings, with the Dow Jones industrials hitting a low for the year of 3,316.58 on October 9. The market recovered as analysts described the political anxieties as overdrawn.

Economic Upturn. When Governor Clinton swept to a decisive victory in the November 3 election, much was made of the rallying cry his campaigners had used: "It's the economy, stupid!" Though economic conditions, viewed purely in statistical terms, apparently had been in a recovery since the spring of 1991, the progress of that recovery was the source of widespread dissatisfaction and frustration among the electorate. Through the spring and summer, the economic news—notably statistics on employment—produced one disappointment after another.

In a strange twist, the reports on business conditions took an abrupt turn for the better just after the election. For instance, the estimated growth rate for the economy in the third quarter was revised upward to 3.9%—its best reading in four years—and the civilian unemployment rate fell from 7.4% in October to 7.2% in November. These developments were greeted warmly by both stock and bond traders, on the assumption that they would encourage the President-elect to moderate his plans for economic stimulus.

Funds Shift. Visions of a stronger economy may have come too late to the voting public but they abounded among stock-market investors throughout the early months of the year. This prompted a much-heralded shift of funds from the growth stocks that had paced the market in 1991 to cyclical stocks of companies in basic industries like paper, metals, and chemicals, and other businesses with close links to the ups and downs of the business cycle. Thus, even though the promise of a strong economy was slow to be fulfilled, and little change occurred meanwhile in the fundamentals of most growth companies, it was not at all uncommon for stocks in growth arenas such as pharmaceuticals and food processing to suffer setbacks of 20% to 30% or more. In an extreme example, shares of United States Surgical, a growth favorite, fell from a record high of $134.50 in the early days of 1992 to $53.50 by late summer before rallying into the 60s.

A stock with even more celebrated problems was International Business Machines (IBM), the longtime Number 1 holding of investing institutions. IBM shares, battered by intense competition in the market for mainframe computers and other business woes, sagged to below $50, their lowest price in a decade and less than one third of their 1987 peak of $175.87.

The health-care stocks, besides carrying the out-of-favor "growth" label, also came in for selling as prospective targets of a promised effort by Clinton to reform the nation's health-care system. Investors, meanwhile, scrambled after potential Clinton-era beneficiaries—among them engineering firms likely to participate in a rebuilding of the nation's roads, bridges, and other infrastructure. Clinton's ascendancy also helped touch off a brisk rally in small growth stocks, encouraged by studies that asserted a historical tendency for smaller companies to prosper in Democratic administrations. That catapulted the NASDAQ composite index for the over-the-counter market—home to many "junior growth" stocks—to new highs in the late stages of the year.

Junk bonds—which appeared to be all but dead after some of the fiascoes of the 1980s—made a comeback, with junk-bond sales for the

DOW JONES
INDUSTRIAL AVERAGE

Weekly Close

3,500

3,000

2,500

2,000

0

JAN   FEB   MAR   APR   MAY   JUNE   JULY   AUG   SEPT   OCT   NOV   DEC

Designed by George Stewart

year expected to surpass the $31.9 billion record set in 1986. Unlike the 1980s, however, when junk bonds were used largely for corporate takeovers, they now were being used more often for working capital.

Securities Business. Given rising stock and bond prices, Wall Street's own securities industry enjoyed a prosperity that helped ease memories of its lean years in the late 1980s. For the first nine months of 1992, the New York Stock Exchange said its member firms doing business with the public achieved record after-tax income of $3.31 billion.

The money-management business, meanwhile, extended a long run of rapid expansion. Assets of the nation's mutual funds, as reported by the Investment Company Institute, a trade group, stood at $1,556,000,000,000 at the end of October, up from about $1,300,000,000,000 a year earlier. Over that interval, bond-fund assets swelled from $417.3 billion to $551.1 billion, and stock-fund assets from $337.6 billion to $429.8 billion. By all accounts, the funds were magnets for money that flowed out of CDs and other short-term vehicles, as yields in the money markets continued to shrivel.

Questions for the Future. A prime question for 1993 and beyond was whether stocks and bonds would continue to benefit from this kind of shift, especially if the Federal Reserve Board no longer was pushing short-term interest rates lower. From late 1990 to mid-1992, the central bank lowered its discount rate, or charge on loans to private financial institutions,

seven times, bringing it from 7% to a 30-year low of 3%. Plainly, this trend came closer to its end the nearer the rate got to zero. Increasing numbers of analysts believed a bottom had been reached as 1992 came to a close, as stronger economic statistics and the prospect of stimulus through fiscal policy reduced the incentives for the Fed to pump up the economy further. Indeed, most analysts cited the possibility of an upturn in short-term interest rates as the biggest visible risk facing investors in stocks and bonds for 1993.

World Markets. Troubling questions existed about the depressed or uncertain status of economies in other leading industrialized nations. An economic slump in Japan and currency turmoil in Europe helped keep many overseas stock markets off-balance. In early December, a world index compiled by Morgan Stanley Capital International Perspective showed a loss of 7.4% since the end of 1991.

Japan was the biggest individual loser among seven major overseas markets, down 22.6% as the Tokyo market continued to tumble from its highs at the end of the 1980s. Japanese stocks showed signs of steadying in the second half of the year, however, after the government announced a sweeping program aimed at shoring up the markets and the economy. Other nations in the negative column included Australia, down 11.2%; Canada, down 6.7%; and Germany, down 6.1%. On the plus side stood Hong Kong, up 20.7%; Switzerland, up 16.4%; and Britain, up 10.2%.

CHET CURRIER, *The Associated Press*

SUDAN

Sudan faced continuing civil conflict and economic difficulties in 1992, the third year of rule by Omar Hassan al-Bashir.

Political Affairs. The formal transition to a new political system based on an Islamic populism began in 1992. A Transitional National Assembly was appointed by the Revolutionary Command Council for National Salvation (RCCNS) in February to serve as a temporary parliament, while local "popular committees" were to be created by consultative conferences. Security problems hindered the formation of committees in many areas, and the country remained firmly under the control of the RCCNS. All formal political parties remained illegal, while the National Islamic Front (NIF), under its leader, Hasan al-Turabi, provided the ideological and popular civilian foundations for the state. Turabi was injured seriously when he was attacked by a Sudanese exile during a trip to North America in May, but recovered from his injuries.

The government's position appeared more secure in 1992, with fewer coup attempts reported. Human-rights violations continued to be reported in the treatment of opposition and minority groups. Non-Muslim Sudanese opposed the implementation of Islamic law. Late in 1991 the Sudan Catholic Bishops' Conference issued a letter criticizing government actions, and throughout 1992 there was a continuous exchange of charges between the government and church officials.

The civil war continued in the southern region despite some mediation efforts. Formal negotiations took place in February between the government and the two major factions of the Sudan People's Liberation Movement (SPLM) in Abuja, Nigeria, but little progress was made toward a settlement. By late in 1992, government forces had captured the major SPLM centers of Kapoeta and Torit, and observers were predicting the end of effective military opposition by the SPLM. SPLM problems were exacerbated by internal conflicts between the faction led by John Garang and the "Nasir group." Antigovernment insurgents were also active in the Nuba Mountains and Darfur.

The major opposition group in exile, the National Democratic Alliance (NDA), met in February in London and issued a program emphasizing the need for Sudan to return to a multiparty and secular political system. The leader of a major traditional group, Muhammad Uthman al-Mirghani, became more active in opposition after the assets of his Khatmiyya organization were taken over by the government in midyear. Sadiq al-Mahdi, leader of the other major traditional group, remained in Sudan where he continued to speak out against the government while being restricted in his movements by security forces.

Economic Affairs. The government took drastic measures to resolve the economic issues facing the country, including floating the currency and removing subsidies on many basic commodities. Despite major price increases, there was little public resistance to measures which in past years had caused major riots. Shortages continued in some goods, but the best harvest since 1970 meant that food was available, although expensive. The government also began a major privatization effort involving the sale of many large publicly owned enterprises.

International Affairs. Sudan remained at odds with many of its former allies, while consolidating further its relations with both Iran and Iraq. The Sudanese government supported Iraq during the Persian Gulf war of 1991, and continued that support in 1992. Relations with Iran were strengthened through trade and military-aid agreements.

Sudanese relations with Tunisia and Egypt were affected by charges, denied by the Sudanese, that Sudan was supporting terrorists in those two countries. Relations with Egypt were strained further when Egypt reasserted claims to the Halaib region on the Red Sea coast at the end of 1991. Discussions continued throughout the year on the Halaib issue. Relations with Saudi Arabia were also antagonistic because of Sudanese support for Iraq. These tensions resulted in Sudan's suspending its membership in the Islamic Conference Organization.

The execution in August of a Sudanese citizen employed by the U.S. aid organization created problems in Sudan's relations with the United States.

JOHN O. VOLL
University of New Hampshire

SUDAN · Information Highlights

Official Name: Republic of the Sudan.
Location: Northeast Africa.
Area: 967,494 sq mi (2 505 810 km²).
Population (mid-1992 est.): 26,500,000.
Chief Cities (1983 census): Khartoum, the capital, 476,218; Omdurman, 526,287; Khartoum North, 341,146.
Government: *Head of government,* Omar Hassan Ahmed al-Bashir, prime minister (took over June 30, 1989). A 15-member Revolutionary Command Council for National Salvation serves as the supreme executive, legislative, and judicial body.
Monetary Unit: Pound (99.010 pounds equal U.S.$1, April 1992).
Foreign Trade (1990 est. U.S.$): *Imports,* $1,000,000,000; exports, $465,000,000.

SWEDEN

The demise of the Soviet Union in late 1991 and Sweden's anticipated membership in the Economic Community (EC) affected diplo-

SWEDEN • Information Highlights

Official Name: Kingdom of Sweden.
Location: Northern Europe.
Area: 173,732 sq mi (449 964 km²).
Population (mid-1992 est.): 8,700,000.
Chief Cities (Dec. 31, 1991 est.): Stockholm, the capital, 679,364; Göteborg, 432,112; Malmö, 234,796; Uppsala, 170,743.
Government: *Head of state,* Carl XVI Gustaf, king (acceded Sept. 1973). *Head of government,* Carl Bildt, prime minister (took office Oct. 4, 1991). *Legislature* (unicameral)—Riksdag.
Monetary Unit: Krona (5.8140 kronor equal U.S.$1, Oct. 27, 1992).
Gross Domestic Product (1989 est. U.S.$): $132,700,-000,000.
Economic Indexes (1991): *Consumer Prices* (1980 = 100), all items, 227.2; food, 239.1. *Industrial Production* (1980 = 100), 106.
Foreign Trade (1991 U.S.$): *Imports,* $49,759,-000,000; *exports,* $55,129,000,000.

matic and economic affairs in Sweden throughout 1992.

Foreign Affairs. Sweden, which had recognized the new state of Russia on Dec. 19, 1991, granted full recognition to the former Yugoslavian republics of Croatia and Slovenia as well as to the former Soviet republics of Armenia, Azerbaijan, Kazakhstan, Kyrgyzstan, Moldova, Tajikistan, and Uzbekistan on Jan. 16, 1992. Georgia was recognized later.

Sweden also signed trade agreements with the three Baltic republics—Estonia, Latvia, and Lithuania—which it had recognized in August 1991. Demonstrating Sweden's close relations with the Baltic states, King Carl XVI Gustaf and Queen Silvia paid a state visit to Estonia in April. Visits were made to Latvia in September and to Lithuania in mid-October.

A decision was made to lift gradually the economic sanctions that Sweden, along with many other nations, had instituted against South Africa some years earlier. The sanctions would be lifted as the apartheid system is replaced by true democracy in South Africa.

Prime Minister Carl Bildt met with U.S. President George Bush at the White House in February. Bush used the occasion to point out that U.S.-Swedish cooperation for freedom and democracy is not new, as Sweden was one of the first countries to recognize the fledgling United States more than 200 years ago.

Refugees. Sweden long has been a favorite destination for refugees and immigrants from Africa, Asia, and nations of the formerly Communist Eastern Europe. In 1992, Sweden was flooded with refugees from war-torn Yugoslavia. At midsummer, Sweden was host to no less than 41,000 refugees from that disintegrating country in addition to 40,000 permanent residents of Yugoslav origin. The United Nations Refugee Commission requested that the Swedish government keep its borders open for additional people.

Economic Affairs. In May a poll of 9,300 Swedish voters showed that 36% were opposed to joining the EC, while 31% were in favor and 32% indicated no preference. Along party lines, some 65% of the Moderates and 55% of the Liberals voted yes, respectively. Social Democrats and Center Party members indicated that 20% to 25% were in favor, 45% were opposed, and 30% to 35% had no preference.

The July unemployment rate was 6.5%—Sweden's highest in 50 years. An estimated 307,000 people were out of work. This was up 100% from the July 1991 rate and there were predictions that more than 500,000 Swedes would be jobless in 1993.

On September 20 the nonsocialist government and the opposition Social Democrats concluded an economic agreement to prevent speculation against the krona, while safeguarding welfare and employment and preventing runaway inflation. It was a historic political deal in the wake of Finland's decision to float the markka and uncertainty about ratification of the Maastricht treaty regarding the EC. The Swedish Central Bank had raised the short-term marginal lending rate to a staggering 500% five days earlier but lowered it on September 21 to 50%. The agreement was to be accompanied by slashes in public spending and tax increases that would reinforce the budget by 40.6 billion kronor (about $7 billion) over five years.

Politics. At the beginning of the new parliamentary session in October, the government's most serious problem was the high budget deficit of more than 100 billion krona ($18 billion). The government's expectations for the future rested on the belief that the international business cycle would turn upward in 1993 or certainly before parliamentary elections in 1994.

In early fall the government issued a White Paper detailing the work done during its first year in power. The signing of the European Economic Area Treaty—instituting economic cooperation between the countries of the European Free Trade Association (EFTA) and the EC—was seen as the first step toward Sweden's full membership in the EC by 1995. The government claimed that inflation had been brought under control and that abolition or reduction of certain taxes was revitalizing the economy.

ERIK J. FRIIS
"The Scandinavian-American Bulletin"

SWITZERLAND

Decisions pointing toward ending Switzerland's traditional policy of supranational nonalignment dominated political and economic concerns in 1992.

European Economic Integration. In a national referendum on May 17, voters endorsed Switzerland's application for membership in the International Monetary Fund (IMF) and the

Swiss voters in a December 6 referendum rejected membership in a 19-nation European free-trade zone that had been negotiated earlier by the European Community and the European Free Trade Association, to which Switzerland belongs.

World Bank. Encouraged by this, the Swiss Federal Council announced on May 18 that Switzerland would seek full membership in the European Community (EC), targeting 1995–96 as the entry date. Since all decisions in Switzerland are subject to approval in a national referendum, skeptics, remembering the overwhelming rejection of United Nations membership by Swiss voters in 1986, remained dubious regarding the eventual success of this initiative.

The first test came on September 27, when voters approved the building of two major rail tunnels that greatly will improve commercial and passenger rail capacity between northern and southern Europe, while significantly reducing transit time. Passage of this measure was mandated if Switzerland were to join the new European Economic Area (EEA), scheduled to go into effect on Jan. 1, 1993. In return the EEA nations had agreed that Switzerland could maintain lower weight limits on trucks than

those standard in other countries, as well as its days. In a December 6 referendum, however, voters rejected EEA membership that would have established a free-trade zone among the 19-member nations. Negotiations regarding EC membership had not been concluded yet.

Domestic Issues. Also approved in the May 17 referendum was a reduction in the age of consent for sexual relations from 16 to 13, if the partner was no more than three years older; in addition, voters endorsed regulations establishing a civilian alternative to required military service for conscientious objectors.

During January and February, the Zurich city government ended a five-year, controversial experiment in drug-use regulation and control when they ordered a small park, the *Platzspitz,* shut down and enclosed with a 10-ft (3-m) fence. In a country with stringent anti-drug laws, the *Platzspitz* had served as an area where drug use and trafficking were tolerated openly, with health officials providing medical assistance along with a ready supply of clean syringes. Originally attracting a few hundred persons in 1987, the park's population had swelled to nearly 20,000, 25% of whom, it was estimated, came from outside Switzerland. While recognizing that the matter had gotten out of hand, health authorities asserted that the program had done much to curtail the spread of the AIDS epidemic.

Davis Cup Success. The Swiss rejoiced on September 27, when their team advanced for the first time to the Davis Cup tennis finals by defeating Brazil, thus earning the right to contest the United States for the Cup in December. The Swiss lost to the U.S. team in the finals.

PAUL C. HELMREICH
Wheaton College, MA

SWITZERLAND • Information Highlights

Official Name: Swiss Confederation.
Location: Central Europe.
Area: 15,942 sq mi (41 290 km²).
Population (mid-1991 est.): 6,800,000.
Chief Cities (Dec. 31, 1989 est.): Bern, the capital, 134,393; Zurich, 342,861; Basel, 169,587.
Government: *Head of state,* Arnold Koller, president (took office Jan. 1990). *Legislature*—Council of States and National Council.
Monetary Unit: Franc (1.3890 francs equal U.S.$1, Dec. 10, 1991).
Gross Domestic Product (1989 est. U.S.$): $119,500,-000,000.
Economic Indexes (1990): *Consumer Prices* (1980 = 100), all items, 139.6; food, 145.1. *Industrial Production* (1980 = 100), 122.
Foreign Trade (1990 U.S.$): *Imports,* $69,869,-000,000; *exports,* $63,884,000,000.

SYRIA

Of all the states involved in the Persian Gulf war of 1991, Syria had the most reason to view the results with satisfaction; it was not a chance outcome, but one testifying to the political and diplomatic skills of the country's wily, long-term president, Hafiz al-Assad. Lining up with the anti-Iraqi coalition had gained Syria Western approval. Participation in the war was minimal and pain-free: Syrian troops suffered no casualties. Syria further capitalized by agreeing to take part in Middle East peace talks. All this achieved not only the cachet of respectability but also tangible benefits in foreign aid.

According to an authoritative report released in March, the Syrian economy grew substantially in 1991; gross domestic product (GDP) increased 27%, and there was a large trade surplus. Oil production was growing steadily, averaging 470,000 barrels per day in 1991, an improvement that continued in 1992. The growth surge resulted from increased foreign aid and some lessening of government controls.

Human Rights. In late March the government announced release of 600 "mostly political" prisoners. This was in addition to the more than 2,800 it claimed to have released in December 1991. However, in early April a human-rights group in New York reported that 17 Syrian human-rights activists recently had been sentenced to prison terms of from three to ten years; and the parliament of the European Community on June 16, while voting aid to various Middle East countries, banned aid to Syria, citing human-rights abuses.

On the positive side, perhaps as a result of foreign pressure, Syria on April 17 announced that it was lifting restrictions on travel abroad by Syrian Jews, and also easing restrictions on their transferring property. The Syrian Jewish community of some 4,000, one of the oldest in the Middle East, actually had been prosperous and little subject to discrimination since previous severe regulations were lifted in 1976. However, Syrian Jews still were not permitted to move to Israel.

Armaments. Like other Middle East states, Syria hastened to upgrade its weapons in the aftermath of the Gulf war. Despite U.S. disapproval, China and other states welcomed the opportunity to supply Syria with advanced technology and missiles. In an embarrassing incident in February, the U.S. Navy failed to keep track of a North Korean freighter carrying a cargo of Chinese Scud-C missiles to Syria. Scud-Cs have a longer range than the Scud-Bs that Syria already had. Syria also announced purchase from China of two small nuclear reactors for peaceful purposes. Hans Blix, director-general of the International Atomic Energy Agency (IAEA), visited Damascus in February,

ary, and on March 25 in Vienna, Syria and the IAEA signed accords allowing inspection of all Syrian nuclear facilities.

Foreign Relations. On March 12, in Assad's fourth inaugural address, he abruptly criticized both Israel and the United States. From that point on, also, Syrian policy toward Iraq became less hostile. Telephone links were reopened, and despite sanctions, some trade recommenced. The anti-U.S. tilt may have been provoked by U.S. refusal, on February 16, to remove Syria from the list of states sponsoring terrorism (the others being Cuba, Iraq, Iran, North Korea, and Libya). U.S. aid thus continued to be banned. However, French Foreign Minister Roland Dumas, while visiting Damascus from February 12 to 14, had promised more financial aid despite Syria's virtual default on earlier loans. Turkish Foreign Minister Hikmet Cetin visited in August, and some progress was made on the vital issue of water sharing, as well as on trade matters.

On March 17 and 18, President Assad visited Cairo to see Egypt's President Hosni Mubarak, and between April 19 and 22 he visited all six member states of the Gulf Cooperation Council (Saudi Arabia, Kuwait, Bahrain, Qatar, the United Arab Emirates, and Oman). Little had come of the Damascus Declaration of March 1991, under which Syria and Egypt were to station troops in the Gulf. Assad and Mubarak agreed on opposing any further military moves against Iraq.

Syrian negotiators and their Lebanese clients met with Israelis intermittently throughout the year, but no substantive agreement emerged despite concord on an agenda. Syria's public position was that no agreement was possible without total Israeli withdrawal from the Golan Heights. However, Assad, the region's greatest pragmatist, probably would make peace with Israel whenever he considered it to be, on balance, advantageous.

ARTHUR CAMPBELL TURNER
University of California, Riverside

TAIWAN

Significant changes were effected in the political system of the Republic of China on Taiwan in 1992 as a result of the National Assembly elections in December 1991, which produced a threefold political mandate. In the first place, the very substantial majority obtained by the Kuomintang (KMT), or Nationalist Party, reflected voter dissatisfaction with the strong stand of the opposition Democratic Progressive Party (DPP) in favor of an independent Republic of Taiwan. At the same time, however, there was an equally clear mandate for reform and change of the outdated political system controlled by the Kuomintang. Finally, voters found it difficult to vote against an administration under whose auspices Taiwan had enjoyed unprecedented prosperity.

Rewriting the Constitution. The newly elected National Assembly met for two months beginning at the end of February to start the process of reconstitution. Among the most controversial questions to be taken up was whether the president should be elected directly by the people or indirectly by delegates to the National Assembly. Indeed, so heated did the debate become that the issue was tabled for the time being. In any case, the issue was moot until the next presidential election, which would not be held until 1996.

The DPP was surprised by the outcome of the 1991 elections. They believed that their independence platform reflected the views of the majority. In fact, many on Taiwan did disfavor strongly reunification with the mainland provinces under the aegis of the government in Beijing. Moreover, they regarded as no more than a nostalgic myth the long-standing claim of the KMT that it one day would reclaim the mainland under its own control. Nevertheless, voters appeared reluctant to entrust the future of

Taiwan to a political party committed to transforming these widely held private views into public policy. They took seriously Beijing's threats to use force to prevent Taiwan from declaring its independence.

Despite the very substantial liberalization of the political system on Taiwan, advocating independence for the island was technically still illegal. Conservatives within the KMT pressed to have the opposition party disbanded because of its preelection stance. Cooler heads within the party prevailed, however, and the issue was dropped.

Based on its experience, then, the DPP decided to change its approach in the run-up to the December 1992 legislative elections. While not renouncing its pro-independence stance, the party played down the issue and focused its platform on domestic issues.

Election Fever. The December 1992 election was one of the most hotly contested ever on the island. Since 1947 the Legislative Yuan had consisted mostly of delegates elected on the mainland prior to the withdrawal of the KMT to Taiwan. These elders were finally forced to retire at the end of 1991 under arrangements put forward by the KMT to bring the political system into line with political reality. The 1992 legislative elections were thus the first in which all of the candidates were elected on Taiwan.

Not only was there sharp rivalry between the KMT and the DPP, but there also was a division within the KMT itself—between the older conservatives, many of whom had come to Taiwan at the end of the civil war on the mainland in 1949, and the younger, more liberal party members, many of whose families had lived on Taiwan for generations. This division within the KMT sharpened as the election drew near, and a number of KMT members, failing to acquire the endorsement of the party, ran and were elected as independent candidates.

A military parade in Taiwan bears testimony to the importance the island nation places on its defensive capability. In a much-publicized 1992 purchase, Taiwan paid $4 billion for F-16 fighter jets from the United States.

The outcome of the election showed a significant gain for the DPP, which took 31% of the vote. The KMT received a majority of only 53%—its lowest figure in any election on Taiwan. A shakeup of the government was anticipated following the election.

Economic Integration, Political Isolation. Unlike the election of a year earlier, the election of 1992 hurt the ruling party even though the economy had manifested signs of strength throughout the year. Overall growth for the year was projected at 7%. Per-capita income stood at about $10,000—nearly 30 times that on the mainland—and unemployment stayed under 2%. (These facts alone accounted for much of the opposition on Taiwan to the idea of reunification with the mainland on Beijing's terms.) The increase in foreign trade was projected at more than 12%, with a trade surplus at year's end amounting to some $11 billion. Taiwan in 1992 was the 13th-largest trading nation in the world—ranking ahead of mainland China despite the difference in size of the two economies—and its foreign-exchange reserves amounted to a hefty $90 billion.

Despite these statistics, Taiwan suffered what it took to be a major setback on the international front when, without prior notification, South Korea in August withdrew its recognition of the government in Taipei and established formal diplomatic ties with Beijing. South Korea had been the last major state in Asia to maintain diplomatic ties with Taiwan, and their loss, coupled with what was taken to be the sly way they were broken, produced an angry reaction in Taipei.

Taiwan's international isolation stood in sharp contrast to its firm economic ties with the world economy. The government capitalized on its economic prowess during 1992 to help remedy this contradiction. With the ostensible purpose of increasing international trade and investment, it hosted visits by officials of France, Germany, Russia, and the United States. In addition, the Taiwan government pursued and, in several instances, concluded deals to purchase military equipment to upgrade the defensive capability of its navy and air force. Under consideration for purchase were German submarines, French aircraft, and the long-awaited F-16 fighter jets from the United States—the $4 billion sale of which was approved by U.S. President George Bush during his unsuccessful reelection campaign.

Who Is Our Friend, Who Is Our Enemy? Efforts to upgrade Taiwan's defensive ability clearly were directed against Taiwan's only likely adversary, which, paradoxically, was the very mainland nation that had become the principal locus of Taiwan's new business opportunities. Trade with the Chinese mainland in 1992 amounted to more than $7 billion. In addition, Taiwan investors set up more than 3,000 enterprises on the mainland, with many located in Fujian, the province that faces Taiwan across the Strait. More than 1 million Taiwan citizens were visiting the mainland each year, many of them businessmen carrying on the management of mainland-based factories and enterprises.

JOHN BRYAN STARR, *Yale-China Association*

TANZANIA

Tanzanians have been discussing the establishment of a multiparty system since 1990, when former President Julius Nyerere stepped down as head of the ruling Chama Cha Mapinduzi (CCM) Party; the process reached a new stage in 1992, as the country took the first steps toward ending a period of one-party rule that has lasted for more than 20 years.

Multiparty Politics. In May both the Tanzanian and Zanzibari parliaments unanimously approved constitutional amendments legalizing a multiparty political system and set 1995, the end of President Ali Hassan Mwinyi's current term, as the target date for Tanzania's first multiparty elections. The move followed a report by a presidential commission which, despite lukewarm domestic support for political change, called for an end to one-party rule. The report was endorsed by the executive committee of the CCM in January and by a special conference of the CCM in February.

The first phase of the transition would include separating the ruling party from the state and establishing the necessary legal framework for competitive elections. No political party would be permitted to have branches in any workplace or the civil service. During the transition period the CCM would continue to rule and members of parliament who joined the opposition would have to defend their seats in by-elections.

Economic Reform. Political change in Tanzania comes on the heels of an internationally supported economic reform program. The World Bank Consultative Group, commonly known as the Paris Club, agreed on an aid package of $900 million—two thirds of which would be grants and the rest concessional

---

TAIWAN • Information Highlights

Official Name: Taiwan.
Location: Island off the southeastern coast of mainland China.
Area: 13,892 sq mi (35 980 km²).
Population (mid-1992 est.): 20,800,000.
Chief Cities (Dec. 31, 1989 est.): Taipei, the capital, 2,702,678; Kaohsiung, 1,374,231; Taichung, 746,780; Tainan, 675,685.
Government: *Head of state,* Lee Teng-hui, president (installed Jan. 1988). *Head of government* Hau Pei-tsun, prime minister (appointed March 1990). *Legislature* (unicameral)—Legislative Yuan.
Monetary Unit: New Taiwan dollar (25.43 NT dollars equal U.S.$1, Dec. 30, 1992).
Gross National Product (1990 U.S.$): $150,800,-000,000.

TANZANIA • Information Highlights

Official Name: United Republic of Tanzania.
Location: East coast of Africa.
Area: 364,900 sq mi (945 090 km²).
Population (mid-1992 est.): 27,400,000.
Chief City (1985 est.): Dar es Salaam, the capital, 1,096,000.
Government: *Head of state,* Ali Hassan Mwinyi, president (took office November 1985). *First Vice President,* John Malecela (took office November 1990). *Legislature* (unicameral)—National Assembly, 233 members.
Monetary Unit: Tanzanian shilling (300 shillings equal U.S.$1, June 1992).
Gross Domestic Product (1989 est. U.S.$): $5,920,-000,000.
Foreign Trade (1988 U.S.$): *Imports,* $1,495,000,000; *exports,* $337,000,000.

loans. Approximately 37% of the aid would finance Tanzania's imports. In spite of a record cotton crop, the collapse in the prices of coffee, tea, and sisal had led to a crisis situation in which the country's foreign-exchange earnings covered only 29% of its import needs. The Club also granted 50% relief on Tanzania's $5 billion external debt, and Belgium agreed to write off 2.58 billion Tanzanian shillings (about $11 million) in bilateral debt.

In an effort to continue the reform process, Tanzania opened up its foreign-currency markets and reduced taxes. In addition, the government announced that it was planning to lay off 50,000 civil servants over three years. Tanzania also came under pressure from Sweden, one of its most consistent supporters, which threatened to stop all aid if Tanzania did not account for the $36 million it received in 1991.

WILLIAM CYRUS REED
The American University in Cairo

TAXATION

U.S. tax policy during fiscal year (FY) 1992 —Oct. 1, 1991-Sept. 30, 1992—was influenced heavily by the 1992 presidential-election campaign. The Omnibus Budget Reconciliation Act of 1990 (OBRA-90), agreed to by President George Bush and Congress, was cited as one factor in President Bush's reelection loss to Gov. Bill Clinton of Arkansas. The agreement, which broke a Bush 1988 presidential-campaign pledge of "no new taxes," raised income and excise taxes by more than $140 billion over five years. Consequently, although record budget deficits still were expected, no new tax legislation was passed in the United States in FY 1992.

In the face of significant fiscal hardships and past federal-aid cutbacks, many of the states raised taxes to fund growing expenditure responsibilities and to cover declining state-tax revenues.

On the international scene, the European Community imposed minimum business-tax rates on its member countries, and Russia instituted a new tax on oil and gas producers to encourage exploration and development.

United States

While tax reforms of the 1980s continued to benefit some federal taxpayers in 1992, their federal tax savings in many cases were offset by rising state and local taxes.

Federal. Federal-tax collections in FY 1992 were estimated at $1,075,738,000,000. An estimated $478.78 billion in individual income taxes made up about 45% of the total tax revenue; $410.88 billion in social-insurance taxes and contributions (for Social Security) accounted for 38% of collections; and $89 billion in corporation income taxes totaled about 8% of collections. The remaining 9% of federal-tax collections were composed of excise taxes, estate and gift taxes, and customs duties and fees. While the fraction of tax revenue collected through the individual income tax has remained fairly constant in recent years, corporate-tax revenues continued to decline as a percentage of total federal-tax revenues, and social-insurance taxes represented an increasingly important portion of total taxes.

During FY 1992, U.S. tax law continued to be governed by the Tax Reform Act of 1986 (TRA-86). The TRA-86 reduced the number of tax brackets from 14 to four, lowered the highest income-tax bracket from 50% to 33%, eliminated many personal deductions ("loopholes") for those itemizing deductions, and increased the personal exemption and standard deduction—the fixed deduction from gross income available as an option to all taxpayers—from $3,670 to $5,700 in 1991. The act also removed the favored tax treatment for capital gains, which thereafter were taxed at the same rate as regular income, and it reduced the tax rate on corporate profits from 45% to 34%, while removing the investment-tax credit. In addition, it rescinded accelerated depreciation accounting, which had enabled corporations to lower or eliminate their tax burden.

This arrangement was modified in the fall of 1990 when the administration and Congress agreed to OBRA-90, which among other things reduced the number of marginal tax rates from four to three (15%, 28%, and 31% on taxable family income of $1 to $34,000, $34,000 to $82,150, and more than $82,150, respectively). It also further reduced the availability of itemized deductions and, by simplifying and refining the marginal rate structure, eliminated an unintended provision that had enabled the wealthiest Americans to escape the top rate. Thus, even with the significant reduction in the number of marginal tax rates, the federal income tax remained progressive.

On the other hand, the growing portion of total federal taxes—the social-insurance tax (payroll taxes)—in 1992 was a flat statutory tax of 6.2% applied to all labor income. (Interest and capital gains are not covered by this tax.) No tax is paid on income above $53,400. In addition to the employee's share, the employer also was responsible for 6.2% of the employee's labor income. An additional flat tax on the employer and employee of 1.45% of labor income is designated for the medical-insurance program (Medicare) for the elderly. The OBRA-90 increased the cap on employee wages subject to the Medicare portion of the payroll tax to $125,000 from $53,400. Since the tax rate does not vary by income level and it goes to zero beyond $53,400, the social-insurance tax is regressive. The regressivity of this tax is reduced, however, when the payments from these taxes (Social Security, Medicare, and unemployment insurance) are taken into consideration.

Notwithstanding these changes in the tax code, the Bush administration and Congress continued to entertain tax-reform proposals because of the lack of economic growth. Both presidential candidates and many members of Congress favored new tax measures designed to stimulate private investment, but the executive and legislative branches could not agree on a package of incentives. The president proposed economic stimulus in his State of the Union address, including capital-gains-tax relief, and he challenged Congress to enact a bill by March. Congressional Democrats complied, but included a measure to raise the marginal rate on the wealthiest Americans from 31% to 35%. The president vetoed the bill on March 20.

In July, House Democrats introduced another bill, the centerpiece of which was to be urban enterprise zones—blighted neighborhoods to which potential investors would be drawn by tax breaks. The bill in its final form would have cost $27 billion in lost revenues over five years and spent only $7 billion on cities, while granting tax breaks to yacht buyers, real-estate developers, and wealthy investors. It too would have raised the income taxes of the richest citizens. The president vetoed the bill on November 4 on grounds that it included tax increases and favored special interests over urban aid.

State and Local. State-and local-government revenues were about $750 billion in FY 1991. States obtained about 75% of their revenue from income taxes on individuals and corporations, sales taxes, and federal grants. Local governments received the bulk of their revenue from property taxes, state grants, and, in a few localities, income taxes.

Most states are required constitutionally to balance their budgets. Moreover, as the major sources of tax revenue for the states (income and sales taxes) are based on economic activity, the economic slowdown in FY 1992 imposed severe constraints on states at a time of increased expenditure responsibilities, notably for welfare and Medicaid, which rise during an economic recession. Even though they were reluctant to increase major taxes because policymakers were concerned about the migration of individuals and corporations out of state in response to relatively high tax burdens, many states raised income, sales, and excise taxes in FY 1992.

Tax initiatives appeared on November ballots in several states. While voters in Massachusetts approved an increase in the cigarette tax of 25 cents a pack, sales-tax hikes were defeated in Colorado and North Dakota. South Dakota voters defeated efforts to create personal and corporate state income taxes.

On May 26 the U.S. Supreme Court overturned a ruling allowing the state of North Dakota to make out-of-state mail-order companies collect state sales taxes. The decision was a blow to revenue-starved states, and may prompt Congress to lift the court's ban by legislation.

International

Several countries modified their tax systems in response to changing world political and economic events. Denmark raised its value-added tax on goods and services, and Belgium raised its retail gasoline tax. Savings and investment activity changed in Germany in response to increased taxes on savings to help finance the unification of East and West Germany.

European Community. With significant legislated freedoms in capital movement within the proposed European Community, member states with relatively high tax rates were concerned about capital flight to escape high tax burdens. In 1992, European Community ministers agreed on minimum value-added-tax and excise-tax rates, the major taxes on business activity in the European countries. These minimum rates would preclude member countries' decreasing business-tax rates significantly in order to attract business from neighboring countries.

Russia. Countries of the former USSR continued to suffer severe fiscal hardships in 1992. Russia's deficit was about 20% of gross national product. In a continuing effort to encourage domestic production activity, President Boris Yeltsin approved a new tax on oil and gas producers. The tax was designed to encourage exploration and development of energy resources by taxing producers working in the harsher regions of Russia at lower rates or not at all. Consequently, the tax would fall mostly on producers in areas considered geologically and geographically superior.

THOMAS A. HUSTED
The American University

Real-life anchorwomen (r-l) Katie Couric, Paula Zahn, Joan Lunden, Faith Daniels, and Mary Alice Williams (extreme left) *joined Corky (Faith Ford, second from left) and Murphy Brown (Candice Bergen) for Murphy's 1992 baby shower.*

TELEVISION AND RADIO

It was hard to tell in 1992 whether real life was becoming more like television or vice versa. In any case, the American people were kept vividly aware of the blurring boundaries between the two.

Vice-President Dan Quayle denounced the fictional title anchorwoman of *Murphy Brown* (Candice Bergen) for her decision to have a baby out of wedlock on the Columbia Broadcasting System (CBS) comedy series. Murphy responded by mocking the vice-president in a subsequent episode. Then, while collecting the Emmy Award for best comedy series, *Murphy Brown* creator Diane English told the single mothers in the awards' television audience, "Don't let anybody tell you you're not a family"—which Quayle, among others, termed a misinterpretation of what he had said. It was one of the trigger controversies in the public debate about "family values" in which news and entertainment, election-year politics, and ratings ploys all dizzyingly became merged.

And it was the year when Mariel Hemingway bared her breasts and buttocks on American Broadcasting Companies' (ABC's) *Civil Wars* (a "first" for the networks). In sum, it was a weird year made even weirder by TV.

Independent presidential candidate Ross Perot scorned the old rules of television campaigning, dodging the tougher and less manageable questioners on the evening network news shows in order to make his appearances on

Cable News Network's (CNN's) *Larry King Live;* the National Broadcasting Company's (NBC's) *Today;* CBS' *CBS This Morning;* and ABC's *Good Morning America.* President George Bush and his Democratic rival, Arkansas Gov. Bill Clinton, followed suit in what *The New York Times* called "breakfast television politics."

On the side of good old-fashioned hardball journalism, meanwhile, Governor and Mrs. Clinton were questioned bluntly about the rumors of his extramarital affair on CBS' *60 Minutes.* The Clintons (especially wife Hillary) were perceived as handling the interview so well that it helped put the candidate back on the track that led to the Democratic nomination and the presidency.

The widespread criticism of liberal bias in the news media was dramatized during coverage of the Republican Convention in August, when the usually benign Barbara Bush gave a surprisingly confrontational interview to Judy Woodruff, saying she would be "monitoring" the anchorwoman for fairness. Also responding to such criticism was the Corporation for Public Broadcasting (CPB), which set up a toll-free hotline and invited comment from viewers on all programming on National Public Radio and the Public Broadcasting Service (PBS). The move was in part in response to the congressional reauthorization bill of 1991, which required a system of "accountability" for the taste and political tone of CPB programming.

A hybrid of reality and entertainment was the baby-shower episode of *Murphy Brown*, in which the fictional Murphy played hostess to her "professional peers," real-life network anchorwomen Katie Couric, Joan Lunden, Paula Zahn, Faith Daniels, and Mary Alice Williams.

The 1991–92 Season. It was the symbolic end of an era of NBC prime-time dominance that had emerged with *The Cosby Show* in the mid-1980s when Bill Cosby and the rest of his Huxtable clan bade farewell to 44 million Americans on the series' final episode on April 30. It was CBS, instead, that won the 1991–92 ratings crown, coming back from third place among the three major networks in 1991. It was CBS' first ratings victory in seven years. A key to CBS' dominance was its success on Sunday, when the "big three" run movies directly against each other. CBS TV movies were six of the seven top-rated shows in that slot, the top two being *A Woman Scorned: The Betty Broderick Story*, starring Meredith Baxter as a killer, and a classy adaptation of Willa Cathers' *O Pioneers*, featuring Jessica Lange.

A glamour event was the arrival of filmland producer-director George Lucas (*Star Wars* and *Indiana Jones* series) with a new ABC series, *The Young Indiana Jones Chronicles*.

Among standout shows were CBS' fresh and witty *Northern Exposure*, which won the 1992 Emmy Award for best drama series; and NBC's *Seinfeld* (featuring Jerry Seinfeld as a stand-up comic exactly like himself, as he told Barbara Walters on her interview special), which won the Emmy for best comedy writers for Elaine Pope and Larry Charles. NBC's *I'll*

Fly Away and CBS' *Brooklyn Bridge* also garnered high marks among critics. As befalls so many such classy programs, *Bridge* was canceled for low ratings at year's end, and *Fly Away* reportedly was next in line for termination.

The Fox Network's *The Simpsons*, with its Matt Groening cartoon family of lovable underachievers, continued to be a beacon of wit in a network often associated with lowbrow entertainment. One episode, in which Bart is trapped for days down in a well, was packed with satire. Krusty the Clown's invitation to his "showbiz friends" (including rock star Sting as his cartoon self) to make a music video on Bart's behalf hilariously spoofed the *We Are the World* crusade.

After experiencing up-and-down ratings in an effort to find a suitable replacement for Jane Pauley, NBC's *Today* found one in Katie Couric. Her combination of journalistic savvy and perky persona helped buoy *Today* ratings. (Also, she reportedly got along with the large talent and ego of coanchor Bryant Gumbel).

With news documentaries about current affairs becoming an endangered species because of their inability to attract high ratings, it was the cable service Home Box Office (HBO)—not known for documentaries—which made news with *Abortion: Desperate Choices*. HBO further explored the topic of abortion with its original film *A Private Matter*, starring Sissy Spacek.

(Continued on page 529.)

"The Cosby Show," which became the most-watched sitcom in TV history, concluded on April 30, 1992. Its producer, director, and star (l-r)—Gordon Gartrelle, Jay Sandrich, and Bill Cosby—took a break during the taping of the finale.

© Lee Romero/NYT Pictures

© Alice S. Hall, NBC/Globe Photos

Good-bye, Johnny

With his unique brand of low-key yet sometimes biting humor and his comfortable Midwestern persona, Johnny Carson, host of NBC's *The Tonight Show,* was a fixture in the late-night lives of Americans for 30 years. After taking over *Tonight* on Oct. 1, 1962, from Jack Paar, Carson proceeded to win over the viewing audience with a witty monologue, celebrity guests, and hilarious skits in which he played various original characters. On May 22, 1992, Carson bid good-bye to America with one last show *(photo above)*—which had an estimated audience of 55 million.

Johnny Carson, born in Iowa and raised in Nebraska, started his life in show business as the host of a morning radio show in Los Angeles. After a brief (39-week) stint as host of *The Johnny Carson Show* on ABC in 1955–56, Carson headed for New York and served as host of the quiz show *Who Do You Trust?* (1957–62). As host of *The Tonight Show,* he was an almost immediate hit, and maintained his popularity through three decades simply by being himself and not changing his format with each new trend. *Tonight* became the standard against which all other variety/talk shows were judged, and any similar new show scheduled against it was almost sure to fail.

Ed McMahon *(above center),* Carson's sidekick since 1962, and Doc Severinsen *(above left),* bandleader since 1967, became as important parts of *Tonight* as Carson himself.

His easy onstage banter with the two was a familiar ritual, as were frequent sketches featuring original characters like Carnac the Magnificent and Floyd R. Turbo.

Carson's gift for tapping the political feelings of Americans and reflecting them in his nightly monologues was such that it was said that President Richard Nixon's political demise was inevitable once Carson began making jokes about Nixon's role in Watergate. However, he usually was fair, targeting conservatives and liberals, Republicans and Democrats, equally. Despite his pointed barbs, the wisecracks seemed to be without malice for the most part—a trait that further endeared him to viewers.

Although many television fans considered Carson almost a family member, it seems that no one, even close friends, really knows him well. An intensely private man, Carson is rumored to be kind and generous with his friends, although often inexpressive, but unforgiving of those he believes have hurt him.

In his final monologue, Carson quipped that even the breakup of the USSR was not so well-covered in the media as was his impending retirement; he may have been right. The outpouring of public interest, however, was simply a sign that U.S. television viewers would sincerely miss the man who had "tucked America in at night" for 30 years.

MEGHAN O'REILLY LeBLANC

TELEVISION | 1992

Some Sample Programs

Adam Bede—A *Masterpiece Theatre* two-part presentation of George Eliot's classic novel. PBS, March 1.

The Best of Friends—A *Masterpiece Theatre* dramatization of the correspondence and friendship between George Bernard Shaw and two of his intellectual acquaintances. With John Gielgud, Wendy Hiller, Patrick McGoohan. PBS, Oct. 18.

The Burden of Proof—A two-part TV movie, based on the Scott Turow novel. With Hector Elizondo, Brian Dennehy. ABC, Feb. 9.

Cabeza de Vaca—An *American Playhouse* docudrama set in America in the 1500s, based on the true story of explorer Álvar Núñez Cabeza de Vaca. PBS, Dec. 2.

Capriccio—A *Great Performances* telecast of the Richard Strauss opera. With Anna Tomowa-Sintow, Eberhard Buchner. PBS, Aug. 7.

Celebrating Creativity, American Style—A *Great Performances* 20th-anniversary show. PBS, Oct. 9.

Charlton Heston Presents the Bible—A four-part series of stories from the Bible. Arts & Entertainment (A&E), Dec. 20.

Clarissa—A three-part *Masterpiece Theatre* presentation of Samuel Richardson's 1748 novel. PBS, April 5.

The Cloning of Joanna May—A TV movie adaptation of the Fay Weldon novel in which a former husband has his wife cloned. With Patricia Hodge, Brian Cox. A&E, March 1.

Comedy Store's 20th Birthday—A tribute to the Los Angeles comedy club. With David Letterman, Garry Shandling, Richard Pryor, Damon Wayans, Bob Saget, Sandra Bernhard. NBC, Sept. 24.

A Doll's House—A *Masterpiece Theatre* adaptation of the Ibsen play. With Juliet Stevenson. PBS, March 29.

Donahue: The 25th Anniversary—A tribute to Phil Donahue, a pioneer of the audience-participation show. NBC, Nov. 15.

Elvis—The Great Performances—A nostalgic retrospective focusing on the singer's music, film clips, television appearances, and home movies. CBS, April 24.

Emmylou Harris—Musical hour filmed at the Grand Ole Opry in Nashville. TNN, Jan. 15.

Empire of the Air: The Men Who Made Radio—A Ken Burns documentary on radio pioneers Lee de Forest, Edwin Howard Armstrong, and David Sarnoff. PBS, Jan. 29.

Fonda on Fonda—Jane Fonda's tribute to her father through film clips and reminiscences. TNT, Jan. 13.

For Richer, for Poorer—A made-for-cable movie about a prosperous businessman who gives away his money. With Jack Lemmon. HBO, Feb. 29.

The Ghost of Versailles—A *Metropolitan Opera Presents* telecast of John Corigliano's comic opera on the French revolution. With Hakan Hagegard, Teresa Stratas, Marilyn Horne. PBS, Sept. 14.

The Glory and the Power—Three-part series on religious fundamentalism in Christianity, Judaism, and Islam. PBS, June 15.

Grass Roots—A two-part TV movie about a murder in Georgia and a parallel story involving the tracking of a white supremacist. With Corbin Bernsen, Raymond Burr, John Glover, James Wilder. NBC, Feb. 24.

Gunsmoke: To the Last Man—A TV movie returns James Arness to his Matt Dillon role. CBS, Jan. 10.

In the Deep Woods—A TV movie about a serial-murder case. With Anthony Perkins. NBC, Oct. 26.

The Jacksons: An American Dream—A two-part TV movie biography of the performing Jackson family. With Lawrence Hilton-Jacobs, Angela Bassett, Jason Weaver, Alex Burrall. ABC, Nov. 15.

The Kennedys—An *American Experience* two-part documentary on a political dynasty. PBS, Sept. 20.

The Last of His Tribe—A made-for-cable movie about the relationship between an anthropologist and a Yahi Indian. With Jon Voight, Graham Greene. HBO, March 28.

Last Wish—A fact-based TV movie that struggles with the right-to-die issue. With Patty Duke, Maureen Stapleton. ABC, Jan. 12.

Legacy—Six-part documentary series exploring the world's first civilizations. PBS, Feb. 2.

Live from Lincoln Center—The New York Philharmonic marks its 150th anniversary. With Kurt Masur, Zubin Mehta, Pierre Boulez. PBS, Dec. 7.

Lodz Ghetto—A 1989 documentary depicting life in the Polish ghetto during World War II. PBS, April 30.

The Man Upstairs—A TV movie about a lonely woman who takes in an escaped convict. With Katharine Hepburn, Ryan O'Neal. CBS, Dec. 6.

Metropolitan Opera Silver Anniversary Gala—A *Great Performances* telecast celebrating the Met's 25 years at New York's Lincoln Center. With Plácido Domingo, Mirella Freni, Luciano Pavarotti. PBS, March 9.

Michael Bolton—Concert footage from a performance at Chicago's historic Arie Crown Theatre. NBC, Oct. 28.

Millennium—A ten-hour anthropology series on the "tribal wisdom" of indigenous peoples. PBS, May 11.

Miss Rose White—A TV movie about the daughter of a New York Polish Jewish immigrant trying to bridge the gap between the old and new worlds. With Kyra Sedgewick, Maureen Stapleton, Maximilian Schell. NBC, April 26.

The Missiles of October: What the World Didn't Know—An *ABC News Special* chronicling the 1962 Cuban missile crisis. ABC, Oct. 15.

A Mother's Right: The Elizabeth Morgan Story—A docudrama recounting the case of divorced doctors who fight for child custody amid charges of sexual abuse. With Bonnie Bedelia, Caroline Dollar. ABC, Nov. 29.

Mrs. 'arris Goes to Paris—A TV movie about an English charwoman in Paris to buy a Dior dress. With Angela Lansbury, Omar Sharif, Diana Rigg. CBS, Dec. 27.

Mrs. Cage—An *American Playhouse* presentation about a neglected wife who says she has murdered someone. With Anne Bancroft, Hector Elizondo. PBS, May 20.

Murder without Motive: The Edmund Perry Story—A fact-based TV movie about the murder of a Harlem scholar by a policeman. With Curtis McClarin. NBC, Jan. 6.

Neil Simon's Broadway Bound—TV adaptation of the 1986 play, part of an autobiographical trilogy. With Corey Parker, Anne Bancroft, Jerry Orbach, Hume Cronyn, Jonathan Silverman. ABC, March 23.

O Pioneers!—A TV movie dramatizing the Willa Cather novel about a turn-of-the-century Nebraska farm family. With Jessica Lange. CBS, Feb. 2.

Portrait of a Marriage—Fact-based, three-part *Masterpiece Theatre* telecast on the relationship of writers Vita Sackville-West and Harold Nicolson. With Janet McTeer, David Haig, Cathryn Harrison. PBS, July 19.

Prime Suspect—A three-part *Mystery* telecast about a female detective who gets a chance to head a murder investigation. With Helen Mirren. PBS, Jan. 23.

The Railway Station Man—A made-for-cable movie set against Ireland's sectarian strife. With Julie Christie, Donald Sutherland. TNT, Oct. 18.

Riccardo Muti Salute—A salute to the conductor as he steps down as the music director of the Philadelphia Orchestra. With Luciano Pavarotti. A&E, April 22.

The Secret Agent—A three-part *Masterpiece Theatre* adaptation of Joseph Conrad's novel that also marks the final appearance on the series of host Alistair Cook. With David Suchet. PBS, Nov. 15.

Sinatra—A two-part TV movie biography of Frank Sinatra. With Philip Casnoff, Olympia Dukakis, Gina Gershon, Marcia Gay Harden. CBS, Nov. 8.

Stalin—A made-for-cable movie biography of the Soviet dictator. With Robert Duvall. HBO, Nov. 21.

Taking Back My Life: The Nancy Ziegenmeyer Story—A fact-based TV movie about a rape victim's struggle for justice. With Patricia Wettig. CBS, March 15.

Tales from Hollywood—An *American Playhouse* presentation. With Jeremy Irons, Alec Guinness. PBS, Oct. 19.

Three Dances by Martha Graham—A *Great Performances* telecast of Graham choreography. PBS, Dec. 28.

Today at 40—Prime-time reunion show marking the 40th anniversary of the morning *Today* show. NBC, Jan. 14.

Tonight—Final show with regular guests for host Johnny Carson, with Bette Midler, Robin Williams; final show with members of the *Tonight* family. NBC, May 21–22.

Trial: The Price of Passion—Two-part TV movie about a tarnished lawyer defending an indigent Hispanic. With Peter Strauss, Jill Clayburgh. NBC, May 3.

Unforgettable, with Love—A *Great Performances* telecast of Natalie Cole in concert, singing the songs made popular by her father. PBS, March 7.

Unplugged—Paul Simon special in which the singer performs with an 11-piece acoustic band. MTV, June 3.

A Woman Scorned: The Betty Broderick Story—A TV docudrama based on a famous California murder case. With Meredith Baxter, Stephen Collins. CBS, March 1.

Regulating Cable

Like so many businesses that rode high in the 1980s, the ever-burgeoning (but oft-criticized) cable-television industry may have been brought down to earth in the 1990s. New federal regulatory legislation, three years in the making and finally passed by Congress in October over the veto of President George Bush, was designed to curb cable's runaway rate increases and to make the industry more competitive and accountable.

"Think of it as a $6 billion tax cut for consumers," said Rep. Edward Markey (D-MA), a sponsor of the bill. The congressman was using his widely disputed estimate of how much viewers could save collectively on their monthly cable bills. Some critics, including the president, feared that the new regulation could discourage technological improvements and slow the growth of cable—in about 60% of U.S. households in 1992—to areas not yet served.

The main provisions of the bill were:
• Ordering the Federal Communications Commission (FCC) to write guidelines by which local governments can set "reasonable" prices on a tier of basic cable service, consisting of local over-the-air stations, public-access and educational channels, and government-access channels such as C-SPAN.
• Ordering the FCC to set guidelines by which consumers and local governments can appeal "unreasonable" prices for additional, optional services, such as Cable News Network, movie channels such as HBO, and special-interest channels such as ESPN, Nickelodeon, and the Discovery Channel.
• Discouraging cable operators from charging extra for special sporting events.

• Prohibiting operators from requiring subscribers to buy unwanted program packages in order to obtain premium channels.
• Prohibiting local governments from granting exclusive cable franchises, which has led to the creation of cable monopolies in nearly all markets.
• Requiring cable-programming producers to offer their programs at "reasonable" prices to rival technologies (microwave frequencies, satellites, telephone companies) that claimed they might distribute the programs more cheaply than cable operators.
• Allowing over-the-air stations to demand royalties from cable operators for the right to carry their signals or to forfeit that option and force cable operators to carry their signal for free. (The nation's largest cable operator, Tele-Communications Inc. of Denver, immediately announced that it would refuse to pay any such fees.)

It was considered doubtful that the regulation would lead directly to the entry of many new companies to make the cable market more competitive because of the huge financial risks of starting up against the original, well-established franchises. As a *New York Times* analysis observed, "The cable television law undoubtedly will make life more difficult for cable-television companies. But supporters view the cable law as an imperfect measure that provides limited rate regulation and that will only chip away at the fundamental cause of soaring cable prices, which is the absence of competition. Yet the law is likely to restrain price increases in the future."

DAN HULBERT

One of the new specialty services on cable was the Sci-Fi Channel, which brought a renewed "camp" appreciation of the 1960s series, *Lost in Space*. For an even more specialized audience there was Trucker TV, beamed from Washington by satellite to highway truck stops across the country.

Late Night. Johnny Carson got his largest audience ever—55 million—on a May 22 farewell program of *The Tonight Show* that was hailed for its low-key simplicity and heartfelt sincerity. To mark the end of his 30-year, 4,500-telecast reign, Carson offered a behind-the-scenes look at the show's preparation, generously shifting the spotlight from himself to many never-before-seen staffers. (*See* SPECIAL REPORT, page 527.)

Jay Leno's retooled edition of *Tonight* (a new band fronted by Branford Marsalis, a hipper guest card) had high ratings initially, but

interest then leveled off. To add to Leno's concern, a longtime associate, Helen Kushnick, was dismissed by NBC as a *Tonight* producer for reportedly pressuring guests not to appear on such rival programs as the syndicated *Arsenio Hall Show*.

Hall, whose ratings had dipped below Leno's after a hot start at the beginning of the decade, regarded the new host as a threat to his share of the hip, young, racially mixed audience, and made public a letter in which he accused Leno of "the most vicious and unethical business behavior I've ever observed."

David Letterman no sooner had celebrated his triumphant tenth anniversary on NBC's *Late Night* when he let it be known that he was unhappy at being passed over for Carson's job and was negotiating with other networks. Speculation finally ended in December when CBS offered the comedian $16 million per year.

Coach Hayden Fox, played by Craig T. Nelson, confronts his long-time girlfriend (Shelley Fabares) in a scene from "Coach," the popular sitcom that first was aired in 1989.

© Photofest

The New Season. The 1992–93 lineup was touted widely as the "20-something season." But in this youth movement, few of the programming ideas were as fresh as their stars' complexions. As a spinoff to *Beverly Hills 90210* (the ratings champ among teenage viewers, with current heartthrob Jason Priestley), Fox introduced the critically panned *Melrose Place*.

On NBC especially, the move toward hipper fashions was combined with higher visibility of black stars. *Here and Now* starred Malcolm-Jamal Warner as an inner-city youth counselor; *Up All Night* featured pop singer Patti LaBelle as a dance-club owner; *Rhythm and Blues* was set in a Detroit soul-music radio station. None of these programs had made a strong ratings showing by year's end.

CBS, which has specialized in older target audiences for decades, was less anxious to board the "20s" bandwagon. Bob Newhart returned in yet another incarnation (a cartoonist) in the network's *Bob*. Diane English, writer on *Murphy Brown*, weighed in with an adult-style romantic comedy, *Love and War*, about a grouchy newspaper columnist (Jay Thomas) and a sophisticated restaurant owner (Susan Dey, defecting from NBC's *L.A. Law*). A feisty romance between characters played by John Ritter and Markie Post was at the heart of *Hearts Afire,* which appeared to be shaping up as one of the fall's few new hits.

ABC grafted a young, black-white cast onto a script of above-average intelligence in *Going to Extremes*. The tales of U.S. students at a Caribbean-island medical school was a new creation from *Northern Exposure* whizzes Joshua Brand and John Falsey. A late-starting sitcom, *The Jackie Thomas Show,* starring Roseanne Arnold's husband Tom Arnold, was launched with hit-level ratings, while the established *Coach* received a dramatic ratings boost when it moved to a new time slot. Together they fueled a resurgence of ABC.

A highlight of the probing PBS series, *The American Experience,* was "The Kennedys," a multipart documentary on the political dynasty. No less a success was Barney, the purple roly-poly *Tyrannosaurus rex* of PBS' *Barney and Friends.*

Stalin, HBO's three-hour drama of the Soviet despot's life starring Robert Duvall, was perhaps the most ambitious project ever for the cable station, although it was deemed stilted.

Atlanta-based Turner Broadcasting System (TBS), parent of CNN and the TNT movie network, added the 24-hour Cartoon Network as its newest cable service. It features such animated classics as "The Flintstones."

Radio. *Billboard* magazine reported the most popular radio formats in 1992 (percentage of listeners, 6 A.M. to midnight): adult contemporary (18.1%); news/talk (13.8%); country (12.1%); top 40 (10.8%); album rock (9.9%).

Howard Stern, dubiously famed as the king of the "shock jocks" (radio talk-show deejays with a provocative or outrageous style), drew the largest fine of its kind ($600,000) from the Federal Communications Commission (FCC) for "indecent" language. Another controversial radio personality was the politically conservative Rush Limbaugh, whose listenership had grown to 13 million on 529 stations.

A *New York Times* article described an increasingly lopsided industry, where the 50 biggest of the 11,000-odd radio stations generated 50% of the profits. With very few stations under the $1 million-revenue mark generating any profit, one of the areas hit hardest by cutbacks was active gathering of news.

DAN HULBERT
"The Atlanta Journal and Constitution"

TENNESSEE

Except for the Nixon-Kennedy race of 1960, Tennesseans have voted for the winning ticket in every presidential contest since the 1920s. The year 1992 was no exception, as the Clinton-Gore ticket amassed 47% of the popular vote. All incumbent U.S. congressmen were reelected; the only close race was in the 3d District, where Democrat Marilyn Lloyd emerged the victor. Republican Don Sundquist, who already had announced that he would run for governor in 1994, was reelected by nearly 65% in the 7th District, where media predictions had called a much closer contest. Democrats remained in solid control of the legislature. A record 72% of registered voters went to the polls.

The election of Albert Gore, Jr., of Tennessee to the vice-presidency left his Senate seat to be filled; Gov. Ned McWherter, also a Democrat, appointed his chief aide, Harlan Mathews, to the post. Mathews, a prominent figure in state politics for 20 years, would serve until a special election in 1994.

Legislature. Earlier in the year legislators met in a three-week special session to consider tax and education reform, but traditional fear of an income tax resulted in no action at all. Later, when legislators assembled in regular session, they added one-half cent to the sales tax, which would provide $230 million for educational reform—an amount less than half that required to fund the governor's recommended program. The tax increase, which was to expire after 12 months, boosted the levy to 8.75% and made it one of the highest in the country.

Other taxes included a levy of $200 on professionals—including doctors and lawyers, a tax on legal documents, and a tax on hospitals earmarked to supplement the state's Medicaid program. The election of county school superintendents was taken from the voters and placed in the hands of elected school boards.

Economy. Adequate rains, which fell throughout the spring and summer months, brought about record major-crop yields. Tobacco, which had declined for a decade, was making a comeback in the 1990s and was the highest-valued crop in 1992. Cotton production also continued to increase and was expected to be more than double that of a decade earlier. The production of corn, soybeans, and sorghum also continued to rise. Cattle prices remained steady during the year, but hog prices declined. The number of small farms increased, as part-time farmers began to make their land holdings more profitable. The number of large commercial farms remained steady. About 53% of farm income came from livestock and livestock products, the remainder from crops.

The state's economy was predicted to grow faster than that of the nation in 1993, owing in large measure to expanding automotive manufacture. Nissan Motors of Smyrna unveiled the new Altima, which would sell in the medium-price range, and General Motors' Saturn plant at Spring Hill was poised to unveil a new "entry-level" sports coupe in 1993. Airbags were planned for all 1993 Saturns, and a price increase of 2.5% was projected.

Late in the year the state's unemployment rate was at 6.5%, a full point below the national jobless rate. Tax collections were up more than 16% over those of the year before, prompting state officials to announce in November plans for a pay raise for all state employees as of January 1. Officials as late as November would not make a definite commitment as to the amount of the raise but had stated that each 1% would cost $27 million.

ROBERT E. CORLEW
Middle Tennessee State University

TEXAS

One of U.S. President George Bush's consolations in losing the November 1992 election was winning the 32 electoral votes of his adopted home state by about 3% of the vote. In so doing, however, he accorded his opponent, Bill Clinton, the negative distinction of being the only Democrat in U.S. history to win the presidency without carrying Texas. Clinton selected Texas' senior U.S. senator, Lloyd Bentsen, to be secretary of the treasury in the new administration. Gov. Ann Richards said she would appoint an interim successor to Bentsen in early 1993. A special election to fill the unexpired term would be held in the spring. Except for the election, the chief political news in Texas was the Republican National Convention, held in Houston in August.

Politics. Bush's victory in Texas was impressive in light of a sluggish economy and widespread unemployment. After rosy forecasts early in 1992, Texas economic indicators

---

TENNESSEE • Information Highlights

Area: 42,144 sq mi (109 152 km²).
Population (July 1, 1991 est.): 4,953,000.
Chief Cities (1990 census): Nashville-Davidson, the capital, 510,784; Memphis, 610,337; Knoxville, 165,121; Chattanooga, 152,466; Clarksville, 75,494.
Government (1992): *Chief Officer*—governor, Ned McWherter (D). *General Assembly*—Senate, 33 members; House of Representatives, 99 members.
State Finances (fiscal year 1991): *Revenue,* $9,544,000,000; *expenditure,* $9,238,000,000.
Personal Income (1991): $81,651,000,000; per capita, $16,486.
Labor Force (June 1992): *Civilian labor force,* 2,435,300; *unemployed,* 160,400 (6.6% of total force).
Education: *Enrollment* (fall 1990)—public elementary schools, 598,111; public secondary, 226,484; colleges and universities, 226,238. *Public school expenditures* (1990), $2,827,839,000.

© Paul Hosefros/NYT Pictures

In December 1992, President-elect Bill Clinton (rear left) named U.S. Senate Finance Committee Chairman Lloyd Bentsen (D-TX), 71, as his secretary of the treasury.

began to sag. Unemployment, for example, increased nearly a percentage point from August to September, from 6.7% to 7.5%. Five days before the election, moreover, federal regulators took over the insolvent First City Bancorporation of Texas, a statewide banking empire.

The presidential candidacy of Dallas businessman H. Ross Perot also drew substantial support. His native state gave him 22% of the vote compared with about 19% nationally.

Only one incumbent congressman in Texas failed to be returned to office, despite several

hotly contested races. Democratic U.S. Rep. Albert Bustamante of San Antonio, whose constituency was altered radically by redistricting, lost by a 21% margin to Republican Henry Bonilla. In the new 30th District in Dallas, Democratic state Sen. Eddie Bernice Johnson, a black, became the first woman elected to Congress from Texas since Barbara Jordan, who left office in 1979.

In the new 29th District in Harris county (Houston), the majority Hispanic population preferred State Sen. Gene Green, an Anglo and a Democrat, over Clark Kent Ervin, a black and a Republican. The victor in a third new district, the predominantly Hispanic 28th in south Texas, was Democrat Frank Tejeda.

Rose Spector, a state district judge from San Antonio, became the first woman elected to the Texas Supreme Court. Fort Worth's Lawrence Meyers was the first Republican elected to the Texas Court of Criminal Appeals.

In 1991, Governor Richards had selected fellow Democrat Lena Guerrero of Austin to fill a vacancy on the powerful Texas Railroad Commission, which regulates the oil and gas industries and the transportation business in Texas. Guerrero thus became the first Hispanic woman in Texas history to hold statewide elective office. Obliged to stand for election in 1992, Guerrero seemed headed for victory until it was revealed that she had misrepresented her educational background. She subsequently lost to Barry Williamson of Dallas.

In the Texas Senate, Republicans increased their numbers by four for a total of 13 to the Democrats' 18. Democrats maintained a comfortable majority in the Texas House.

Education. Texas lawmakers returned late in the year for another attempt at producing a plan for financing public-school districts that would meet constitutional criteria. Governor Richards proposed to shift about $400 million in local property-tax money from wealthy school districts to poor districts. A $1.9 billion plan to upgrade state-university education along the Texas-Mexico border was proposed in hopes of settling a lawsuit filed by Hispanic organizations that prompted a federal judge to rule that the current system denied Hispanics equal educational opportunity.

Other News. Within six months of the May 29, 1992, start of a state lottery, Texans had spent $737 million, netting the state more than $250 million. Horse and dog racing in 1992 took in $248 million, adding about $3 million to the state's coffers.

A federal court allowed an Oklahoma firm to proceed with its plan to transfer 100 tons of sewage sludge a day from New York City to part of the firm's ranch in Texas' Hudspeth county.

LYNWOOD ABRAM
Free-lance Writer, El Paso

TEXAS • Information Highlights

Area: 266,807 sq mi (691 030 km²).
Population (July 1, 1991 est.): 17,349,000.
Chief Cities (1990 census): Austin, the capital, 465,622; Houston, 1,630,553; Dallas, 1,006,877; San Antonio, 935,933; El Paso, 515,342; Fort Worth, 447,619; Corpus Christi, 257,453.
Government (1992): *Chief Officers*—governor, Ann Richards (D); lt. gov., Bob Bullock (D). *Legislature*—Senate, 31 members; House of Representatives, 150 members.
State Finances (fiscal year 1991): *Revenue,* $33,773,000,000; *expenditure,* $29,532,000,000.
Personal Income (1991): $298,928,000,000; per capita, $17,230.
Labor Force (June 1992): *Civilian labor force,* 8,821,600; *unemployed,* 720,600 (8.2% of total force).
Education: *Enrollment* (fall 1990)—public elementary schools, 2,510,955; public secondary, 871,932269; colleges and universities, 901,437. *Public school expenditures* (1990), $13,665,821,000.

THAILAND

Thailand returned to democractic consitutional rule in 1992, after two elections separated by a bloody confrontation in Bangkok's streets between prodemocracy demonstrators and the Thai Army. The Thai economy continued on its course toward making Thailand Asia's next industrialized nation.

Politics. The military junta that seized power in 1991, now organized as the National Peacekeeping Council (NPC), fulfilled its pledge to hold elections for a new parliament; at the same time, it succeeded in forcing a new constitution on the country that promised to guarantee continued military dominance through a Senate appointed by the chairman of the NPC. When the elections were held on March 22, three promilitary parties emerged with 190 (53%) of the parliamentary seats. Together with two smaller parties, they set out to form a government with close ties to the military leadership. The Palang Dharma was the largest opposition party with 42 seats. A crisis developed, however, when it was disclosed that the prime minister-designate, leader of the Unity Party, was suspected of drug trafficking. At that point, Gen. Suchinda Kraprayoon, head of the junta, stepped forward and had himself sworn in as prime minister on April 7.

Opposition to Suchinda mounted daily as tens of thousands of Thais from all walks of life demanded his resignation. Bangkok's popularly elected Gov. Maj. Gen. Chamlong Srimuang began a hunger strike. In May open battles between protesters and police led to a declaration of a state of emergency and the calling in of troops, who fired into the waves of young protesters, killing some 300 of them. The military's resort to deadly force shocked the Thai citizenry, particularly the growing middle class on whom Thailand's economic success is founded. On the evening of May 20, King Bhumibol Adulyadej intervened; meeting with Suchinda and Chamlong, he urged them to compromise their differences, work in the best interests of the Thai people, and to amend the constitution to make it more democratic. After Suchinda arranged an executive amnesty for himself and his military supporters, he resigned on May 24. In order to restore public confidence in the democratic process, former Prime Minister Anan Panyarachun came back to head an interim government, and quickly removed the military leaders who had turned the troops on their own people.

The Anan government organized a second election on September 13. The contest was fought between five parties who were viewed as promilitary, characterized by the Thai press as the "devils," and four prodemocracy "angels." This was Thailand's 19th election and the turnout (62%) was the highest ever. The "angels" won a bare majority of the parlia-

THAILAND · Information Highlights

Official Name: Kingdom of Thailand (conventional); Prathet Thai (Thai).
Location: Southeast Asia.
Area: 198,456 sq mi (514 000 km²).
Population (mid-1992 est.): 56,300,000.
Chief City (June 30, 1989 est.): Bangkok, the capital, 5,845,152.
Government: *Head of state,* Bhumibol Adulyadej, king (acceded June 1946). *Head of government,* Chuan Leekpai, prime minister (took power Feb. 1991).
Monetary Unit: Baht (25.46 baht equal U.S.$1, December 16, 1992).
Gross National Product (1990 est. U.S.$): $79,000,000,000.
Economic Index (Bangkok, 1991): *Consumer Prices* (1980 = 100), all items, 166.3; food, 160.1.
Foreign Trade (1991 U.S.$): *Imports,* $37,188,000,000; *exports,* $28,395,000,000.

ment's 360 seats. Chuan Leekpai's Democracy Party led the field with 79 seats, and Chuan became Thailand's 20th prime minister. In order to ensure a stable majority, he included one of the "devil" parties in his coalition.

Economy. The Thai economy continued to be one of the most buoyant in Asia. The temporary drop in tourism resulting from the year's political upheavals was offset by record export growth of 15% above the 1991 level. At the end of the third quarter the annual growth figure was projected to be between 7.6% and 7.8%, with the expectation of more than 8% in 1993. The inflation rate slowed to just under 5%, down from 5.7% in 1991.

As part of the effort to restrict the military's role in society, the post-Suchinda governments moved to displace senior officers from leadership of state enterprises. It was hoped that professional management control would clean up corruption in the enterprises. At the same time, it would deny the military important sources of off-budget funds for political and personal enrichment.

Foreign Relations. Thailand's foreign-policy concerns in 1992 centered around its borders with its troubled Cambodian and Myanmar (Burmese) neighbors. Although Thailand supported the recent United Nations-brokered peace settlement in Cambodia, some businessmen and military continued to be active in the economic exploitation of Khmer Rouge-controlled western Cambodia. International pressure was put on Thailand to help isolate the Khmer Rouge so as to force them to comply with the terms of the United Nation's peacekeeping mandate. The deep involvement of the Thai political and military elite in Myanmar affairs was at the heart of the Chuan government's first cabinet crisis: The opposition demanded the resignation of Minister of Finance Boonchu Thritong, who was accused of having made payoffs to Karen rebels in Myanmar in return for logging rights in their territory.

DONALD E. WEATHERBEE
University of South Carolina

THEATER

For one sudden springtime blaze, at least—beginning around St. Patrick's Day, expiring by Memorial Day—Broadway was back in its old glory in 1992. The 37 openings of new productions in 1991–92 (up from 28 the previous season) was the highest mark in five years. The ice-cold autumn of 1991, however, held down the overall attendance to 7.35 million, barely surpassing the disappointing levels of recent seasons. Fortunately, a quartet of first-class musicals (*Jelly's Last Jam, Falsettos,* the brilliant revival of *Guys and Dolls,* and the Tony Award winner *Crazy for You*) beat the odds by surviving the year.

The autumn of 1992 was another matter, as deathly still as have been most of the Broadway falls since the 1980s, with no outstanding new entry until Lincoln Center's *My Favorite Year* (lovingly musicalized from the 1982 film) opened in December. It was clear that Broadway was settling into a cycle of stunted seasons: Producers were holding back their shows until the warmer months. At that time, tourists begin to pour into New York, and the Tony Awards are imminent (presented around June 1) to boost the winners' box office.

A Star-Struck Spring—Broadway Awakens. One reason for the spring surge was the rare concentration of stars. *Death and the Maiden* had three of them: Glenn Close, Gene Hackman, and Richard Dreyfuss (or four, counting ace director Mike Nichols). Nichols was the main culprit for not capitalizing on this talent and a promising Ariel Dorfman script about political terror in an unnamed Latin American country, but Close's performance won a Tony.

Unfortunately, there was not such a saving performance in *A Streetcar Named Desire* (except perhaps Alec Baldwin's respectable Stanley Kowalski). Jessica Lange's fragile Blanche DuBois might have been fine for a film of the Tennessee Williams classic, but her muted portrayal lacked Broadway-caliber punch. Once again a prominent director (Greg Mosher, fresh from his six-year resuscitation of Lincoln Center Theater) squandered an opportunity.

Also slightly disappointing was *Four Baboons Adoring the Sun.* Set against an archaeological dig in the tropics, it was John Guare's return to the Lincoln Center scene of his great 1990 success, *Six Degrees of Separation.* But even director Sir Peter Hall (*Amadeus*), stars Stockard Channing (*Six Degrees*) and James Naughton (*City of Angels*), and a cast of appealing children (as the two stars' large, combined brood) could not focus Guare's ambiguous drama about the ancient pulls of sexuality and mysticism.

Others on the soaring '92 star roster were Alan Alda in *Jake's Women* (a so-so play by Neil Simon standards); Judd Hirsch in *Conversations with My Father* (so-so by Herb Gardner standards); classic specialist Brian Bedford in *Two Shakespearean Actors* (so-so by Richard Nelson standards); and Al Pacino as an arrestingly decadent King Herod in *Salome* (middling Oscar Wilde).

Joan Collins in Noel Coward's *Private Lives* did not shine by anyone's standards—except fans of Collins' television temptress roles, who packed the limited-run revival.

© Martha Swope

Glenn Close (right) *was awarded a Tony for her performance in Ariel Dorfman's "Death and the Maiden." The Broadway play also featured Gene Hackman and Richard Dreyfuss* (center) *as the costars and Mike Nichols as the director.*

"Crazy for You," a *"new Gershwin musical"* featuring songs from the 1930 work *"Girl Crazy,"* took the 1992 Tony Award for best musical and was one of Broadway's biggest hits of the year. Ken Ludwig rewrote the book for the new production.

There were absolutely no stars in *Two Trains Running.* That was the main reason August Wilson's flavorful group portrait of Pittsburgh diner patrons—seemingly becalmed amid the black-power 1960s—closed early. It was also the least focused in Wilson's cycle of plays about black history.

The lack of stars, fortunately, did not hurt *Dancing at Lughnasa,* the Irish comedy-drama that arrived in the fall of 1991 from London. Brian Friel's glowing but haunting, heartbreaking memory play about growing up in a colorful household of an unmarried grown sister managed to hold onto most of its superb original cast from the Abbey Theatre of Dublin to take the 1992 Tony for best play. Among the most noteworthy off-Broadway plays was *Sight Unseen,* Donald Margulies' breakthrough exposé of misplaced values in the art world.

Musicals. While *Dancing* was the dominant class act among the plays, there were several new entries that had that distinction among the musicals. Foremost was *Guys and Dolls.* Jerry Zak's staging of Frank Loesser's 1950 classic musical was—in two words—on fire. It was breathlessly swift (thanks to Christopher Chadman's choreography), devastatingly funny (thanks to Faith Prince's star-maker turn as Miss Adelaide), and thrillingly eye-filling (thanks to Tony Walton's sets). It won the Tony for best revival and could have won for perfect revival: A completely new vision, yet

with a vintage style that made it a homage to the great artists of the original production.

Best musical went to a new work that also had strong roots in a grand Broadway tradition, *Crazy for You.* It was duly billed "the new Gershwin musical." For even though it featured the Gershwin score (*I Got Rhythm, The Man I Love*) from the 1930s *Girl Crazy,* the forgettable book of that musical was completely rewritten by playwright Ken Ludwig into a charming let's-put-on-a-show tale set in a dusty Western town. Newcomer Susan Stroman's dances were a godsend for a Broadway scene desperate for new choreographer talent.

Contrasting with these sunny, all-American productions were outstanding musicals with a sharper edge, set in worlds of the disenfranchised (blacks, gays). In the dark but entertaining *Jelly's Last Jam,* featuring a Jelly Roll Morton score, author-playwright George C. Wolfe looked at the jazz composer (dazzlingly acted and danced by Tony winner Gregory Hines) torn between his racial identity and his struggle for success in a white world. *Falsettos,* based on two William Finn one-act musicals previously produced off-Broadway (1981's *March of the Falsettos* and 1990's *Falsettoland*), was a breakthrough in Broadway subject matter. The tale of a man who leaves his wife and son for a male lover had more wit and whimsy—and broader audience appeal—than its synopsis might suggest.

© Martha Swope

Broadway audiences welcomed the return of Frank Loesser's "Guys and Dolls," starring Nathan Lane and Faith Prince (above). The musical was presented a Tony as best revival.

With four long-runners—*Cats, Les Miserables, Phantom of the Opera,* and *Miss Saigon* —still dominating the Broadway box office, British producer Cameron Mackintosh sent a small, spunky show from London in 1992. *Five Guys Named Moe* was a quick-footed revue of songs by 1940s jazz legend Louis Jordan.

Overshadowed, but quietly triumphant, was the too-short-lived revival of *The Most Happy Fella* that originated at the Goodspeed Opera House in Connecticut. The burnished production of the neglected 1956 work, with a classic Frank Loesser score, starred Spiro Malas as the aging California vineyard owner who despairs of wooing a much younger woman. The risky use of just two pianos for accompaniment (Loesser's original intention) gave the show a uniquely warm, intimate tone.

The Fall—Broadway Sleeps. From Labor Day through Thanksgiving, Broadway seemed to be in suspended animation in the area of new productions. Reality—the crushing economic pressures facing commercial-theater production—was returning. Pummeled by pans in its first season, Tony Randall's National Actors Theatre returned for a slate of classics. Although many cheered the selection of the opener—*The Seagull,* the first Chekhov on Broadway in 15 years—reviews were mixed for the production that starred Tyne Daly and Jon Voight.

Lincoln Center, beginning its first full season under artistic director Andre Bishop, helped to fill the production void with two appealing new entries. In the Center's smaller Mitzi Newhouse Theater, Wendy Wasserstein offered *The Sisters Rosensweig,* her first play since her 1989 Pulitzer Prize-winner *The Heidi Chronicles.* The play, in a limited run, was a portrait of three Jewish-American sisters reunited—among friends and romantic interests —at the London townhouse of the eldest (Jane Alexander as an international investment banker). Although slightly tainted by a smug, aren't-we-rich-and-wonderful air (*The New York Times* devoted a full-length article to the play's name-dropping of expensive clothing and goods), *Sisters* sparkled with wittily, affectionately drawn characters, including Robert Klein's self-deprecating "faux furrier" and Madeline Kahn's ditsy-but-wise Westchester housewife, Gorgeous.

My Favorite Year, on the Center's Beaumont stage, was captivatingly giddy. With Tim Curry standing in for the film version's irreplaceable Peter O'Toole, the musical wisely downplayed that role of the perpetually soused former matinee idol, Swann. It focused instead on the cub television-comedy writer Benjy (a winning Evan Pappas) and the heady, frantic days of live television. Lainie Kazan recreated her hilarious screen role as Benjy's ultimate Jewish mother, Belle.

The all-too-brief New York engagement of France's Théâtre du Soleil, only its second in the United States, could not be considered an official Broadway entry because of its eccentric venue—an armory. But under the sponsorship of the Brooklyn Academy of Music, the fabled troupe under brilliant director Ariane Mnouchkine was more dazzling than anything on Broadway in the fall of 1992, bringing its unique blend of European and Middle Eastern styles to *Les Atrides,* an adaptation of four connected Greek tragedies.

The liveliest responses of the fall—including controversy, delight, and apoplectic ire— were provoked off-Broadway by David Mamet's *Oleanna.* Its relationship between a professor (William H. Macy) and a female student (Rebecca Pidgeon, the playwright's wife) revealed a primal male-female power struggle in which the seemingly timid student ruthlessly exploits a questionable interpretation of sexual harassment. While stacked in favor of the male, Mamet's disturbing work struck chords of recognition—in the wake of the controversy concerning the confirmation of Supreme Court Justice Clarence Thomas—and became New York's most talked-about play.

The Resident Theaters. For perhaps the first time in a decade, the financial and attendance problems of the nonprofit resident theaters overshadowed even the perennial woes of Broadway. The ravages of the recession upon the pocketbook—of both the audience and corporate supporters—bore down upon a theater

BROADWAY OPENINGS | 1992

MUSICALS

Anna Karenina, music by Daniel Levine; book and lyrics by Peter Kellogg; directed by Theodore Mann; with Anne Crumb; Aug. 26-Oct. 4.

Crazy for You, music by George Gershwin; lyrics by Ira Gershwin; book by Ken Ludwig; directed by Mike Ockrent; with Harry Groener, Jodi Benson; Feb. 19-.

Falsettos, music and lyrics by William Finn; book by Finn and James Lapine; directed by Lapine; with Michael Rupert, Chip Zien; April 29-.

Five Guys Named Moe, by Clarke Peters; music by Jordan; directed by Charles Augins; with Jerry Dixon, Doug Eskew; April 8-.

Four Baboons Adoring the Sun, by John Guare; music by Stephen Edwards; directed by Sir Peter Hall; with Stockard Channing, James Naughton; March 18-April 19.

Guys and Dolls, music and lyrics by Frank Loesser; book by Jo Swerling and Abe Burrows; directed by Jerry Zaks; with Nathan Lane, Faith Prince; April 14-.

The High Rollers Social and Pleasure Club, by Allen Toussaint; directed by Alan Weeks; with Vivian Reed, Deborah Burrell-Cleveland, Nikki Rene; April 21-May 2.

Jelly's Last Jam, by George C. Wolfe; music by Wolfe and Luther Henderson; lyrics by Susan Birkenhead; directed by Wolfe; with Gregory Hines; April 26-.

Man of La Mancha, music by Mitch Leigh; lyrics by Joe Darion; book by Dale Wasserman; directed by Albert Marre; with Raul Julia, Sheena Easton; April 24-July 26.

Metro, music by Janusz Stoklosa; English lyrics by Mary Bracken Phillips; English book by Phillips and Janusz Jozefowicz; directed by Jozefowicz; with Katarzyna Groniec, Robert Janowski; April 16-April 26.

The Most Happy Fella, book, music, and lyrics by Frank Loesser; directed by Gerald Gutierrez; with Spiro Malas; Feb. 13-Aug. 30.

My Favorite Year, music by Stephen Flaherty; lyrics by Lynn Ahrens; book by Joseph Dougherty; directed by Ron Lagomarsino; with Evan Pappas, Tim Curry, Lainie Kazan; Dec. 10-.

3 From Brooklyn, by Sal Richards; directed by Jay Harvey; with Sal Richards; Nov. 19-.

PLAYS

Chinese Coffee, by Ira Lewis; directed by Arvin Brown; with Al Pacino; June 29-Aug. 1.

A Christmas Carol, by Charles Dickens; with Patrick Stewart; Dec. 17-.

Conversations With My Father, by Herb Gardner; directed by Daniel Sullivan; with Judd Hirsch; March 22-.

Crazy He Calls Me, by Abraham Tetenbaum; directed by John Ferraro; with Barry Miller, Polly Draper; Feb. 19-March 1.

Death and the Maiden, by Ariel Dorfman; directed by Mike Nichols; with Glenn Close, Richard Dreyfuss, Gene Hackman; March 17-Aug. 2.

Hamlet, by William Shakespeare; directed by Paul Weidner; with Elizabeth McGovern; April 2-May 10.

Jake's Women, by Neil Simon; directed by Gene Saks; with Alan Alda, Helen Shaver; March 24-Oct. 25.

A Little Hotel on the Side, by Georges Feydeau and Maurice Desvallieres; directed by Tom Moore; with Tony Randall, Lynn Redgrave, Rob Lowe; Jan. 26-March 1.

The Master Builder, by Henrik Ibsen; directed by Tony Randall; with Earle Hyman, Madeleine Potter; March 19-April 26.

The Price, by Arthur Miller; directed by John Tillinger; with Hector Elizondo, Debra Mooney; June 10-July 19.

Private Lives, by Noel Coward; directed by Arvin Brown; with Joan Collins, Simon Jones; Feb. 20-March 22.

The Real Inspector Hound and **Fifteen-Minute Hamlet,** by Tom Stoppard; directed by Gloria Muzio; Aug. 13-Oct. 4.

Salome, by Oscar Wilde; directed by Robert Allan Ackerman; with Al Pacino; June 29-July 29.

The Seagull, by Anton Chekhov; directed by Marshall W. Mason; with Tyne Daly, Jon Voight; Nov. 29-.

Search and Destroy, by Howard Korder; directed by David Chambers; with Griffin Dunne; Feb. 26-April 5.

Shimada, by Jill Shearer; directed by Simon Phillips; with Ben Gazzara, Ellen Burstyn, Mako, Estelle Parsons; April 23-April 25.

The Show-Off, by George Kelly; directed by Brian Murray; with Pat Carroll, Boyd Gaines; Nov. 5-Dec. 13.

A Small Family Business, by Alan Ayckbourn; directed by Lynne Meadow; with Jane Carr, Anthony Heald; April 27-June 7.

Solitary Confinement, by Rupert Holmes; directed by Kenneth Frankel; with Stacy Keach; Nov. 8-Nov. 29.

Someone Who'll Watch Over Me, by Frank McGuinness; directed by Robin Lefèvre; with Alec McCowen, Stephen Rea, James McDaniel; Nov. 23-.

A Streetcar Named Desire, by Tennessee Williams; directed by Gregory Mosher; with Jessica Lange, Alec Baldwin, Amy Madigan; April 12-Aug. 9.

Two Shakespearean Actors, by Richard Nelson; directed by Jack O'Brien; with Brian Bedford, Victor Garber; Jan. 16-Feb. 9.

Two Trains Running, by August Wilson; directed by Lloyd Richards; with Larry Fishburne, Roscoe Lee Brown; April 13-Aug. 30.

The Visit, by Friedrich Durrenmatt; adapted by Maurice Valency; directed by Edwin Sherin; with Jane Alexander, Harris Yulin; Jan. 23-March 1.

OTHER ENTERTAINMENT

Gypsy Passion, a flamenco revue; with Antonio El Pipa and Sara Baras; Nov. 17-.

Tommy Tune Tonite!, directed by Jeff Calhoun; with Tommy Tune, Robert Fowler, Frantz Hall; Dec. 27-.

---

community already suffering defections of talent to the worlds of film and television. The closures continued, bringing to about 25 the number of professional theaters that had shut down since 1987. And for the first time in 18 years of statistical surveys, the Theatre Communications Group in New York reported a decline in the combined audience of the nation's nonprofit resident theaters. Against this backdrop of gloom and uncertainty, attention was galvanized on the reportedly thrilling *Angels in America,* which shattered the 25-year boxoffice records of the Mark Taper Forum in Los Angeles. Tony Kushner's epic, two-evening event, subtitled *A Gay Fantasia on National Themes*—encompassing AIDS, Mormon mythology, and the villainy of gay-hating AIDS

victim Roy Cohn—was a 1991 smash at Britain's Royal National Theatre.

Actors Theatre of Louisville's 16th Annual Humana Festival of New American Plays recaptured some of the headiness of the festival's early days. Marsha Norman (1983 Pulitzer Prize winner for *'night, Mother*) showed a gift for expansive comedy with *D. Boone,* about a cleaning lady in a Louisville museum who takes a whimsical myth-debunking trip through time to visit the frontiersman. José Rivera made a stunning entrance onto the national stage with *Marisol,* which scanned for the existence of a compassionate divinity over the rubble of a surrealistically devastated Bronx.

Three Atlanta theaters joined forces to mount *Athol Fugard's 60th Birthday Celebra-*

Stephen Spinella and Cynthia Mace performed in "Perestroika," part two of Tony Kushner's "Angels in America." The epic set box-office records at Los Angeles' Mark Taper Forum.

tion, a festival of plays including a month-long residency by the great South African playwright. The centerpiece was the Alliance Theatre's U.S. premiere (in collaboration with the La Jolla Playhouse) of Fugard's *Playland,* directed by the author.

La Jolla had another noteworthy collaboration—this time with the commercial music/theater tour producer, the Pace Group of Houston and Broadway's Dodger Productions—to create a dazzling stage musical of *Tommy* at the theater in the San Diego suburbs. Working with British composer Peter Townshend of The Who, La Jolla artistic director Des McAnuff opened the 1969 rock opera into an impressive high-tech spectacle that took on a new resonance of concern for abused children.

Perhaps the hottest resident theater in New York continued to be the resurgent Manhattan Theatre Club, thanks partly to its regularly featured playwright, Terrence McNally. His 1991 play, *Lips Together, Teeth Apart,* reopened in early 1992 and captured the national moment and mood of uncertainty and apprehension, while also providing a generous dose of witty comedy.

There was also apprehension with regard to the troubled in-transition New York Shakespeare Festival (NYSF). Under new iconoclastic artistic director JoAnne Akalaitis (*'Tis Pity She's a Whore*), there was a sharp drop in the rate of production at the festival's six-stage newly named Joseph Papp Public Theater and in the star power the late producer Joseph Papp delighted in. An exception was Elizabeth McGovern's turn as Rosalind in a pleasant Central Park production of *As You Like It.* One

new NYSF work to achieve both critical acclaim and a long run was Anna Deavere Smith's *Fires in the Mirror.* The talents of Bill Irwin, the consummate actor-clown, underlined the comedy behind the dark pathos of Samuel Beckett in NYSF's *Texts for Nothing,* adaptations of rare prose works by the late 20th-century Irish dramatist.

Women were represented as never before in the ranks of artistic directors. In addition to Akalaitis, women newly appointed to lead resident theaters in 1992 included playwright-director Emily Mann, whose challenging but stylish fare (a *Three Sisters* with Linda Hunt), quickly revived the flagging box office of the McCarter Theatre of Princeton, NJ. Libby Appel brought a similar maverick image to the conservative Indiana Repertory Theatre of Indianapolis. Irene Lewis took the reins of Center Stage of Baltimore, where she already was favored for her classics. Carey Perloff quickly generated a lively San Francisco news-media controversy with a Dario Fo spoof of Vatican politics to jolt the long-becalmed American Conservatory Theatre.

The Goodman Theatre won the 1992 Special Tony Award for achievement in regional theater. Among the many outstanding plays that the Chicago flagship theater developed was *Marvin's Room,* a play of dark comedy—but glowing humanity—about a housewife heroically struggling to be a caregiver to a family with catastrophic illnesses. Scott McPherson's work went on to an acclaimed run off-Broadway.

DAN HULBERT
"The Atlanta Journal and Constitution"

TRANSPORTATION

Transportation showed mixed results in 1992. Some carriers achieved strong traffic and earnings, but most reported poor performance in the face of slow recovery from recession in the United States and slowing economies in Japan, Germany, and elsewhere.

Airlines. The U.S. airline industry entered 1992 hoping to increase traffic, regain profitability, and begin recouping the $5.8 billion in losses suffered the two previous years. Traffic did rebound; the total number of passengers carried by the ten major U.S. airlines during January-July rose to 673.3 million, an increase of 7.81% over the same period in 1991. Revenue passenger-kilometers grew 13%, while freight-ton kilometers increased 8.98%. Summer traffic reached all-time highs. Unfortunately, this surge did not restore profitability. Losses between January and June totaled $1.2 billion, and preliminary data for July-December indicated 1992 would mark the third consecutive annual aggregate deficit. Among the ten largest U.S. carriers, only Southwest Airlines reported profits.

Foreign airlines' results were similar. Both Air Canada and Canadian Airlines reported deficits, as did Air France, Lufthansa, and other European carriers. Although British Airways remained profitable, its earnings declined from 1991 levels. European carriers' deficits, like U.S. carriers', occurred despite favorable trends in traffic.

Root causes of the industry's deficits included capacity in excess of demand, inadequate labor productivity, and ruinous pricing tactics. During the first quarter, the intense fare competition that had wracked airline profits in 1991 abated. Yields (average revenue per passenger kilometer) increased, and the percentage of total passenger revenue generated by discount fares declined. In April, however, American Airlines tried to simplify its pricing structure by curtailing the wide array of discounted fares created by the industry practice of so-called yield management. Other carriers chose not to emulate American. This sparked a succession of retaliatory fare reductions which enveloped the industry through the summer and fall. As a result, it appeared that aggregate losses suffered by U.S. airlines since 1990 would reach $7 billion by year's end.

The negative impact of these factors on the airlines' already inadequate cash inflow sparked additional cost-cutting efforts. USAir suffered a short strike in October as it sought changes in work rules and other labor-contract provisions affecting operating efficiency. Several carriers announced layoffs or terminations for management and union employees. Delta, long known for employment stability, announced its first cuts of pilots in 35 years. Just after year's end, on Jan. 5, 1993, United—cit-

ing huge losses for 1992—announced a package of layoffs, salary cuts, fewer flights, and route closures designed to cut operating expenses by $400 million per year.

Cancellations and stretch-outs in the delivery of on-order aircraft were made by both airlines and GPA Group PLC, the world's largest aircraft leasing company. Early in the year, Trans World Airlines (TWA) filed for voluntary protection under Chapter 11 of the federal bankruptcy law in an effort to reduce its interest expense and debt-repayment burdens while continuing to operate. This was the sequel to a leveraged buyout in 1988, which imposed more debt than TWA could support from operating revenues, thus forcing it to sell valuable international route assets and handicapping modernization of its aging fleet.

The year also saw continuing steps toward the evolution of global carriers. Air France acquired ownership stakes in CSA, the Czechoslovak airline, and Sabena, the Belgian airline, and opened discussions on a marketing alliance with United Airlines. Italy's national carrier, Alitalia, purchased a 35% share in Hungary's Malev on December 15. Air Canada and Canadian Airlines explored a merger but could not reach an agreement. Air Canada then moved to acquire control of Continental Airlines and form a large North American network that also could feed traffic to Air Canada's transoceanic routes. On December 29, American Airlines announced a conditional agreement to invest $195 million in Canadian Airlines and provide it with certain technical services.

The most dramatic steps toward multinational expansion were taken by British Airways. In midyear it announced a proposal to acquire a 44% equity stake in USAir, along with 21% voting control of USAir shares, representation on an expanded USAir board (through appointment of four of 16 directors), and veto power over key USAir board decisions. However, British Airways withdrew the proposal on December 22, in expectation that it would not receive necessary approval from the U.S. Department of Transportation. The proposal had drawn strong opposition from American, United, Delta, and Federal Express, which contended that its approval should be made contingent on liberalized access to British airports—access the British government appeared unwilling to grant. Withdrawal of the proposal was a blow to financially strapped USAir, which needed a strong international partner to compete more effectively with larger U.S.-based carriers.

British Airways did succeed in buying portions of three other carriers: a 25% stake in Qantas, the Australian national airline; a 49% share in TAT European Airways, with an option to buy the remaining shares in 1997; and a 49% interest in Deutsche BA, a German domestic carrier established during the year in

© Jeff Jacobson

Local, state, and federal funds are being used to repair and upgrade the interstate highway system. In California (above), several new highway projects should help relieve some of the state's perennial traffic-congestion problems.

collaboration with three German banks. It also acquired total ownership of Scandinavian Airline System's (SAS') subsidiary Danair, a regional European airline on the verge of financial failure, by agreeing to pay off Danair's debt, employ about 600 Danair personnel, and provide severance compensation to approximately 1,500 other Danair employees. In still another move, British Airways entered into a joint venture agreement with Aeroflot to develop Air Russia, a new airline intended to link Moscow with points in Europe, Asia, and the United States, beginning in 1993.

Bus. Class I motor carriers of passengers also experienced difficulties, caused in part by the competitive impact of airline-fare reductions, as revealed by comparative data for the first halves of 1991 and 1992. Total revenue passengers declined 6.3%, from 14.7 million to 13.7 million, while operating revenues fell 6.3%, from $405.9 million to $379.6 million. However, cost reductions through such actions as discontinuance of service in unprofitable markets resulted in improved profitability. Net operating income rose from $1.9 million to $8.6 million, and the net deficit (the negative balance after deduction of interest and other fixed charges, income taxes, and various types of extraordinary income and expense elements) fell from $15 million to $11.4 million.

Major hostilities broke out between Greyhound Lines, Inc. and the smaller regional carriers that make up the remainder of the industry. The regionals alleged that charges for their shared use of Greyhound terminal facilities, typically imposed as a percentage of ticket sales, had been raised to unaffordable levels. For example, Blue Ridge Trailways reduced westbound departures from Asheville, NC, by 50% and discontinued all service to several smaller communities in that state after Greyhound more than doubled Blue Ridge's rent in the Charlotte terminal. American Bus Company removed its operations from five of the 16 Greyhound terminals it had used after an expected 75% hike in rental payments.

The regional carriers also contended that Greyhound had moved to discourage the interchange of passengers with them by limiting joint ticketing and changing scheduled arrival and departure times so as to require long waiting times for interline transfers. As a result, several regional carriers demanded that the Interstate Commerce Commission (ICC) reopen its 1987 Greyhound-Trailways merger case and impose conditions protective of the regional carriers on Greyhound. In addition, some regionals began to discuss banding together to make a new national bus system competitive with Greyhound.

Rail. Total carload shipments (excluding intermodal traffic) on major U.S. freight railways during the 50 weeks beginning January 1 increased 1.1% from the same period in 1991. Intermodal traffic moved in trailers and containers increased 7.4%, reflecting continuing strong growth in so-called double-stack service and new partnerships with trucking companies. Revenue ton-miles increased 2.8%. Aggregate gross operating revenue for these carriers for the 12 months ended June 30 totaled $28.1 billion, up $559 million from the previous 12 months; net income from railway operation (excluding large extraordinary expenses, such as the costs of implementing labor-force reductions and write-downs of lines to be sold or abandoned) rose 16.5%, to $2.6 billion.

A labor dispute between the freight railways and the International Association of Machinists resulted in a nationwide stoppage starting at 12:01 A.M. on June 24. Union members began returning to work shortly after 1:00 A.M. on June 26, when President George Bush signed legislation ending the stoppage and providing procedures for settling the dispute. In addition to blocking freight service, the incident stopped Amtrak operations in all areas but the Northeast, and commuter service in some places.

Several large carriers continued efforts to sell light- and medium-density line segments to short-line and regional railways and commuter authorities. Most notable was Southern Pacific's announcement in December of plans to offer for sale or lease nearly 3,000 mi (4 840 km) of low-density branches and secondary mainlines. Santa Fe announced in October that it had found a buyer for approximately 830 mi (1 339 km) of light-density lines in Oklahoma and Kansas. This was the last major spin-off in Santa Fe's plan to reduce itself to a core system of 7,500 mi (12 094 km).

In contrast to these transactions, two regional carriers acted to increase their size by announcing proposals to acquire smaller railways spun off in years past from larger systems. The 2,500-mi (3 630-km) Kansas City Southern sought ICC approval to acquire about 1,200 mi (1 935 km) of line owned by Mid-South Corporation. Wisconsin Central received ICC approval for expansion of its 2,029-mi (3 305-km) system through purchase of the 227-mi (366-km) Green Bay & Western and the 208-mi (335-km) Fox River Valley Corporation.

On November 18, Consolidated Rail Corporation (Conrail) and Norfolk Southern (NS) announced plans to convert NS' Triple Crown intermodal service unit into a jointly owned venture. The announcement represented cooperation between two carriers that have competed against each other in numerous markets, and the proposed agreement involves use of RoadRailer vans, which run on either rails or highway, as well as more conventional truck-rail intermodal technology.

Canada's two major freight railways suffered losses stemming from the recession and changing trade patterns. In November, CP Rail System announced that it would seek regulatory authority to abandon or sell all of its rail operations in Canada's maritime provinces and Maine. Purchase of the Delaware & Hudson Railway in 1991 enabled CP to participate in international rail-ocean traffic more economically through New York and Philadelphia than through Saint John, N.B.

In the passenger sector, National Railroad Passenger Corporation (Amtrak) carried 21.3 million passengers from October 1991 through September 1992, a decline of 3.1% from the 22 million level achieved in the same period in 1990–91.

Amtrak ordered 50 new-design, single-level "Viewliner" sleeping cars to replace existing single-level sleepers 40 or more years in age. Delivery was expected within 24–33 months. Amtrak also began testing the X2000, a high-speed passenger train on loan from Swedish State Railways. The train uses tilt technology and self-steering radial-axle trucks to take curves at speeds up to 40% higher than conventional Amtrak equipment, thus offering a means for reducing travel time without the heavy investments in infrastructure required for operation of such high-speed equipment as the French TGV and German Inter-City Express (ICE).

Trucking. Gross operating revenues for the 100 largest Class I motor freight carriers increased 8.7%, from $10.7 billion to almost $11.7 billion, for the six months ended June 30, as compared with the same period in 1991. Net operating income (before fixed charges, non-operating income, income taxes, special charges, etc.) grew 48.8%, from $336.1 million to $500.3 million. Revenue tons hauled rose 10.4%, from 44.1 million to 48.7 million. The greatly improved profitability reflected aggressive cost-control efforts.

Intermodal-service agreements also increased significantly. J. B. Hunt added Conrail, Union Pacific, and Wisconsin Central to its list of intermodal partners. Hunt raised $95.8 million in additional capital to acquire 10,000 new containers and related trucking equipment designed specifically for intermodal operation. Another motor carrier entering the intermodal-service arena was KLLM Inc., which specializes in hauling temperature-controlled freight.

U.S. truckers also made strides in forging international links. Yellow Freight System and Netherlands-based Frans Maas launched joint transatlantic less-than-truckload freight service in September, enabling movement of freight between all points in Yellow's North American network and Frans Maas' European system. ABF Freight System on June 1 began less-than-containerload service between the United States and Europe in alliance with Votainer International, a nonvessel-operating carrier headquartered in the Netherlands. United Parcel Service (UPS) completed its 16-year effort to assemble a network in Western Europe with the purchase of Carryfast, Ltd., an express parcel-service firm in Great Britain. UPS now provides European as well as transatlantic and North American service.

See also AUTOMOBILES.

JOHN C. SPYCHALSKI
The Pennsylvania State University

TRAVEL

Despite hurricanes, political uncertainties, and lingering economic woes, the U.S. travel-industry picture was brighter in 1992. Both domestic and international travel rebounded from 1991 lows. Business travel remained constant for the year, with corporate spending levels falling slightly, but leisure travel was on the rise. Most U.S. travelers opted for shorter, less expensive vacations, taking advantage of summer airfare wars to pick up bargain flights. But 45 million others, undaunted by the weak dollar abroad, vacationed outside the United States.

Domestic Travel. U.S. travelers seeking less expensive alternatives flocked to amusement parks. Responding to this trend, parks throughout the United States introduced an array of new attractions, such as Disneyland's wildly successful Fantasmic! experience and the *Backdraft* show at Universal Studios Hollywood. Minnesota's Mall of America, which opened in August, includes a 7-acre (2.8-ha) theme park in the middle of its gigantic shopping complex (*see also* page 423).

Hurricanes devastated southern Florida and the Hawaiian island of Kauai, dampening area tourism. But the appeal of Orlando's Disney World was cited as the main reason that more Americans vacationed in the South than in any other region of the country. Already depressed from downturns in mainland travel, Hawaiian tour operators rerouted vacationers to neighboring islands and put together tour packages priced as low as $369 for one-week stays.

Thanks to a wave of discounted fares, leading U.S. carriers posted the busiest June in airline history—and projected a 5% growth in traffic for the year. Motor-vehicle travel also rose a few percentage points. Rail travel sagged below 1991 totals, but Amtrak still planned to add high-speed equipment to the Boston-New York route and extend Sunset Limited service as far as Miami.

International Travel. U.S. tour volume to foreign countries was close to 1990 records. Thanks to their proximity, Canada and Mexico accounted for 65% of outbound travel. Nearly 16 million Americans headed overseas, 8% more than in 1991. Some 7 million went to Europe, lured in part by the Olympic Games in Barcelona and a world's fair in Seville. This was a 10% increase over 1991 and the second-best year ever. The resulting demand for passports created a backlog in issuing offices.

The Caribbean and Bermuda, Asia, the South Pacific, Central and South America, and the Middle East accounted for 19% of total overseas travel. Egypt, in particular, soared above pre-Persian Gulf war levels. Travelers visited the Balkans, but political unrest hurt tourism to other former Soviet Union sites.

Regardless of destination, U.S. citizens booked shorter stays and bought packaged tours to control costs and eliminate fears of the unknown. Surprisingly, the high end of the escorted tour market did well. Particularly popular were regional tours of Great Britain, Greece, and other Western European sites.

Favorable exchange rates continued to attract large numbers of foreign visitors to the United States. According to U.S. Travel & Tourism Administration projections, 46 million inbound travelers came to the United States in 1992, spending an estimated $70 billion—$21 billion more than U.S. travelers spent overseas.

Cruising. Cruise sales were strong for 1992, although revenues failed to match the double-digit growth seen in the past few years. Steep discounts and two-for-one offers attracted first-time and repeat passengers. Popular itineraries included the Mediterranean, Alaska, and the Caribbean. Banking on continued growth, cruise lines added a dozen newly built cruise ships to their fleets.

BARBARA J. BRAASCH
Free-lance Travel Writer

Japanese tourists enjoy the sights at New York City's Rockefeller Center. With favorable exchange rates, a large number of foreigners visited the United States in 1992, giving a boost to U.S. commerce.

TUNISIA

Tunisia in 1992 marked the fifth anniversary of President Zine El Abidine Ben Ali's rise to power. On Nov. 7, 1987, then General and Interior Minister Ben Ali had stripped Habib Bourguiba of the "presidency for life." By Nov. 7, 1992, Ben Ali had become the "man of change" to his supporters, while November 7 had eclipsed even the country's independence day as the symbol of the country's "new era."

Fundamentalism and Human Rights. The "new era" was supposed to lead unhesitatingly to democracy, but the country's battle with Islamic fundamentalism and the lack of a mature political opposition had stalled the democratization process. After thousands of fundamentalists were arrested and hundreds tried in the summer for terrorism and acts against the state, however, Ben Ali told the central committee of his ruling Constitutional Democratic Rally (RCD) that "we have definitively turned the page of extremism" and that Tunisia could turn to the "concretisation of pluralism." On December 27, President Ben Ali announced before the National Assembly an electoral-reform program designed to open the country to genuine pluralism and to end the international embarrassment of a single-party parliament.

The importance that the issue of human rights would hold throughout 1992 first became evident in March, when Amnesty International issued a severe report on human-rights applications in Tunisia. Instead of condemning the report as foreign interference, however, the government responded by asking a recently created High Committee on Human Rights and Fundamental Freedoms to provide a full accounting of the human-rights situation. The resulting report, issued on July 13, won points both inside and outside the country for openly calling attention to a number of problem areas, such as conditions during prison detentions and interrogations. Most spectacular of all, the report documented seven cases of death, in "obscure and suspect circumstances," of Islamic fundamentalist activists while in the hands of the police or military. Until that report was issued, rumors of torture and deaths at the hands of the state had been dismissed as lies designed to smudge Tunisia's international standing.

Nevertheless the country's attempt to improve its human-rights image, especially in the eyes of international opinion, suffered an important setback in June when a new law on associations forced the dissolution of the Tunisian Human Rights League, the oldest such organization in the Arab world. In September, Ben Ali authorized the League to reorganize in conformity with the new law, but damage to both the League and Tunisia's reputation already was deep.

The July report of the High Committee was issued just as the summer's trials of hundreds

---

TUNISIA • Information Highlights

Official Name: Republic of Tunisia.
Location: North Africa.
Area: 63,170 sq mi (163 610 km²).
Population (mid-1992 est.): 8,400,000.
Chief City (1987 est.): Tunis, the capital, 1,600,000, district population.
Government: *Head of state,* Zine El Abidine Ben Ali, president (took office Nov. 7, 1987). *Head of government,* Hamed Karoui, prime minister (took office Sept. 27, 1989). *Legislature* (unicameral)—National Assembly.
Monetary Unit: Dinar (0.803 dinar equals U.S.$1, August 1992).
Gross Domestic Product (1990 est. U.S.$): $10,000,000,000.
Economic Index (1991): *Consumer Prices* (1980 = 100), all items, 236.5; food, 244.6.
Foreign Trade (1991 U.S.$): *Imports,* $5,189,000,000; *exports,* $3,713,000,000.

---

of supporters of Ennahda, the outlawed Islamic fundamentalist party, got under way. The state sought penalties ranging up to death. But when sentences were handed down by a Tunis military tribunal August 28 and 30, 41 of the 265 militants found guilty were condemned to life imprisonment, but none to death.

The antifundamentalist crackdown appeared to enjoy widespread support, and the relative clemency of the Ennahda trial sentences was accepted as a sign that Tunisia wished not to be at war with any faction of its population. But as the year ended, Ben Ali continued to warn that "foreign powers" still were fomenting Islamic extremism throughout the region.

Economy. Tunisia's economic performance brightened considerably in 1992, with the country registering something above 8% in gross-national-product (GNP) growth. The upswing resulted in part from better days for the country's tourist trade after the Persian Gulf war, and from a return to weather conditions favorable to the country's agricultural sector after three years of drought. But the growing economy also attested to Tunisia's development as an offshore assembly site for European industries.

HOWARD LaFRANCHI
"The Christian Science Monitor"

TURKEY

Turkish concerns in 1992 were dominated by the Kurdish problem at home, and by regional conflicts in the Persian Gulf area, the former USSR, Bosnia-Herzegovina, and Cyprus.

The Kurdish Problem and Iraq. The resurgence of Kurdish nationalism in Iraq created difficulties for Turkey, which has a large Kurdish population of its own. After Iraq's defeat in the 1991 Gulf war, a safe haven was established for the Iraqi Kurdish population north of the 36th parallel, protected by U.S., French, and British aircraft based in Incirlik, Turkey. With Turkey's cooperation, the Allies excluded Iraqi government forces from the protected zone, where a Kurdish autonomous government was established in May 1992.

Although Turkey collaborated with its Western allies in this endeavor, the Turks worried that it might lead to the dismemberment of Iraq, which would enable Iran to dominate the Gulf region. Even worse, they feared it would encourage a nationalist movement seeking to incorporate the 20 million Kurds of Iraq, Iran, Turkey, and Syria, thereby threatening the territorial integrity of all of Iraq's northern neighbors and the very foundations of the Turkish state. Approximately 20% of Turkey's 59 million people are Kurdish, with approximately half of the Kurds living in southeastern Turkey.

The separatist Kurdish Workers' Party (PKK) in Turkey had been waging guerrilla warfare against the Turkish government since 1984. It has attempted to create a region-wide insurrection and has attempted to use the safe haven in Iraq for sanctuary. Leaders of the Iraqi Kurds, who rely on Turkish support for the safe haven in Iraq, have condemned PKK terrorism and collaborated with the Turks in suppressing the PKK in Iraq. In Turkey, meanwhile, more than 4,500 people — more than 1,300 in 1992 alone — are estimated to have been killed in the eight-year separatist movement.

The Suleyman Demirel government, seeking to improve its human-rights record and join the European Community (EC), has been increasingly responsive to the minority rights of Kurds. It belatedly recognized their cultural identity and spent billions of dollars on the Southeast Anatolia Project—the fifth-largest hydroelectric and irrigation project in the world. The project promises to meet half of Turkey's energy needs, and at the same time raise the standard of living in southeastern Turkey.

But the government's determination to crush the relatively small yet violent separatist movement with military means has resulted in harsh tactics and collateral damage that has killed innocent victims and gained the PKK some sympathy among Turkey's Kurdish population. It also has created another obstacle to Turkey's membership in the EC. To complicate matters further, in October 1992 the Iraqi Kurds, responding to Turkish pressure, expelled PKK forces that had sought refuge in their territory. Fighting broke out between the two Kurdish factions, and Turkish forces became involved as well. Ethnic Turks believe that the root of this problem stems from the activities of foreign-supported terrorists, while Turks of Kurdish origin blame current problems on various "repressive policies" of the government in Ankara.

In addition, the PKK has been supported by Iraq, Syria, and Iran, whose assistance has fueled ongoing differences with the Turks over a number of issues, not the least of which concerns control over the waters of the Tigris and Euphrates rivers.

External Affairs. The end of the Cold War unleashed regional conflicts throughout the region surrounding Turkey: in Nagorno-Karabakh between Armenians and Azerbaijanis (with whom the Turks share religious and ethnic ties); in Georgia between Georgians, Ossetians, and Abkhazians; and in Bosnia-Herzegovina between Serbs and Bosnians (2 million Turks are of Bosnian descent). Coupled with these difficulties were the 18-year standoff between Greek and Turkish Cypriots on Cyprus—where the United Nations was making a concerted effort to complete an agreement unifying the island—and the unsettled situation in Iraq and Iran. In the face of this unrest, Prime Minister Demirel's primary foreign-policy objective was to create "a circle of peace" around Turkey by improving relations with its neighbors.

On June 25, 1992, the heads of state of Turkey, Romania, Bulgaria, Albania, Greece, Russia, Ukraine, Moldova, Georgia, Azerbaijan, and Armenia met in Istanbul to establish the Black Sea Economic Cooperation Zone. Its aim was to develop the region's economies, raise living standards, and make effective use of economic resources by promoting the free circulation of people, capital, services, and goods.

With the collapse of the Soviet Union, the emergence of Turkic-speaking republics in the Transcaucasus and Central Asia reinvigorated Turkey's interest in the world's 180 million Turkic-speaking population, 50 million of whom live in the new republics of Azerbaijan, Kazakhstan, Kyrgyzstan, Turkmenistan, and Uzbekistan. Turkish leaders denied any desires for expansion and emphasized commonalities of civilization, culture, belief, and language.

TURKEY • Information Highlights

Official Name: Republic of Turkey.
Location: Southeastern Europe and southwestern Asia.
Area: 301,382 sq mi (780 580 km²).
Population (mid-1992 est.): 59,200,000.
Chief Cities (1990 census): Ankara, the capital, 2,559,471; Istanbul, 6,620,241; Izmir, 1,757,414.
Government: Head of state, Turgut Özal, president (took office November 1989). Head of government, Suleyman Demirel, prime minister (took office November 1991). Legislature—Grand National Assembly.
Monetary Unit: Lira (7,975.00 liras equal U.S. $1, Nov. 9, 1992).
Gross Domestic Product (1990 U.S.$): $178,000,-000,000.
Economic Index (1991): Consumer Prices (1987 = 100), all items, 754.4; food, 851.7.
Foreign Trade (1991 U.S.$): Imports, $20,091,-000,000; exports, $13,603,000,000.

They were broadcasting, in the Turkish language, 82 hours per week of news, entertainment, and cultural programming via Intelsat VI satellite into the former Soviet regions, and the new republics agreed to institute a common Turkish language. Turkey also extended $750 million in credits and signed economic, political, and technical agreements—including an $11.7 billion protocol to operate and develop oil fields in Kazakhstan. The Turks were constituting a secular, democratic model for their Turkish and Muslim brothers in the former USSR.

Missile Accident. While U.S. and Turkish ships were participating in NATO naval exercises in the Aegean Sea on October 2, the U.S. aircraft carrier *Saratoga* accidentally fired two Sea Sparrow missiles that struck the Turkish destroyer *Muavenet,* killing the Turkish vessel's captain and four seamen and injuring 15 others. U.S. President George Bush telephoned Turkey's President Turgut Özal to apologize for the tragic incident.

See also MIDDLE EAST.

BRUCE R. KUNIHOLM
Duke University

UGANDA

After six years in power, Uganda's President Yoweri Museveni in 1992 faced increasing pressure to establish a timetable for a return to multiparty politics which, according to him, would aggravate regional and religious tension. Although international donors continued to fund Uganda's structural-adjustment program, the country was confronted with a mounting list of problems.

Political Affairs. International donors, including the European Commission, Denmark, Germany, and the United States, all indicated that their aid to Uganda could be cut if political reform was not forthcoming. A constitutional commission appointed in 1989 was scheduled to issue its report in December, but the military indicated that it expected a formal role in parliament.

In spite of his own personal popularity, Museveni had yet to establish a firm political base outside of the military, though he hoped to do so through the newly created Uganda Democratic Congress (UDC). With his allies in the Democratic Party, whose traditional base is among the Buganda in the south, Museveni hoped to expand his support beyond the western regions, and win any upcoming election.

In the bandit-plagued north the security situation complicated matters. The military was attempting to limit the inflow of refugees from southern Sudan and in the process was amassing a long record of human-rights abuses. Furthermore, economic reforms have required Museveni's government to make dramatic reductions in military spending, which only can decrease his popularity among his principal supporters.

Economic Reforms. With its most austere budget since 1986, Uganda continued to implement a policy of structural adjustment. The budget included reductions in government spending—including laying off almost 6,500 civil servants and reducing the size of the military—and establishing a new taxation system that promised to increase government revenue by 350% and at the same time make it possible to reduce taxes on imports and exports. The government also began to return property expropriated by former Ugandan President Idi Amin from the country's Asian population, which he drove into exile. That move created friction between returning Asians and those Ugandans who had occupied the property for the past 20 years.

In recognition of these reform efforts, the Paris Club of international donors recommended that Uganda's external debt of $3 billion be waived by 50%, and that the remainder be rescheduled over 25 years. In addition, donors pledged $850 million in new aid, slightly less than the $1 billion Uganda requested.

Uganda's biggest challenge was the international collapse in the value of coffee, which had been providing some 70% of its export earnings. Coffee was slated to earn $120 million in 1992, compared with more than $400 million in previous years. Uganda liberalized the marketing of coffee to speed up payments to farmers and sought to diversify its exports to include food and tea. The production of the latter jumped by 50% in 1991, although it remained at just half its 1972 level. Over the long term, the government encouraged coffee producers to replace aging trees with higher-yielding varieties of higher-value Arabic coffee.

WILLIAM CYRUS REED
The American University in Cairo

UGANDA • Information Highlights

Official Name: Republic of Uganda.
Location: Interior of East Africa.
Area: 91,135 sq mi (236 040 km²).
Population: (mid-1992 est.): 17,500,000.
Chief Cities (1982 est.): Kampala, the capital, 460,000; Jinja, 55,000.
Government: *Head of state,* Yoweri Museveni, president (took office Jan. 29, 1986). *Head of government,* George Adyebo, prime minister (took office Jan. 22, 1991). *Legislature* (unicameral)—National Assembly.
Monetary Unit: Uganda shilling (1,168.6 shillings equal U.S. $1, May 1992).
Foreign Trade (1988 U.S.$): *Imports,* $544,000,000; *exports,* $274,000,000.

USSR. *See* BALTIC STATES; COMMONWEALTH OF INDEPENDENT STATES; GEORGIA, REPUBLIC OF.

UNITED NATIONS

The United Nations started four new peace-keeping operations in 1992, for a total of 13. With its resources stretched thin, the organization found its authority flouted by recalcitrant warring factions around the globe, prompting it to try more aggressive peacekeeping tactics than it traditionally had used.

Former-Yugoslavia Imbroglio. At the first-ever summit-level Security Council meeting on January 31, the five heads of state, seven heads of government, one king, and two foreign ministers who attended pledged their commitment to international law and the UN Charter and urged the secretary-general to find ways to make the organization a more effective peacekeeper and peacemaker.

In their first test, however, the Council and secretary-general's efforts to halt the war in the former Yugoslavia were thwarted. On February 21 the Council voted unanimously to deploy in Croatia the UN Protection Force (UNPROFOR) to keep Croatian forces separated from Serbian and Yugoslavian National Army forces, as provided for in the cease-fire agreement signed in Geneva in November 1991. By year's end the multinational force stood at 22,500 military and civilian members, costing about $650 million that year.

No peacekeeping operation was authorized for blood-drenched Bosnia-Herzegovina because UN negotiators were unable to obtain a cooperation agreement from the warring factions. But on June 9—after UN humanitarian convoys and airlifts were delayed repeatedly by cease-fire violations, attacks, and harassment—the Council authorized UN peacekeepers to operate Sarajevo's airport.

On May 19 the Council imposed wide-ranging trade sanctions against Yugoslavia in retaliation for its military support of Bosnian-Serb forces, who by year's end had seized 70% of Bosnia-Herzegovina. In November, when it became clear the sanctions were being ignored, the Council asked neighboring countries to intercept Yugoslavia-bound shipments.

On October 6 the Council asked the secretary-general to investigate reports of Serbian atrocities, for a possible war-crimes tribunal. By year's end, with the war threatening to spread throughout the region, the Council was considering military action to enforce the no-fly zone it had declared over Bosnia-Herzegovina on October 9. It also was considering partially lifting a 1991 arms embargo on Yugoslavia to allow Bosnian Muslims to obtain weapons.

Intervention in Somalia. Meanwhile, in April the UN had deployed a battalion of 655 Pakistani peacekeepers in civil war-torn Somalia to ensure that humanitarian aid from UN and nongovernmental organizations reached more than 1 million starving Somalis. But the initial dispatch of a planned 3,500 troops was not authorized to use force and so could not stop clans from fighting; nor could it prevent armed bandits from stealing food aid.

Thus on December 3, calling Somalia's human tragedy "a threat to international peace and security," the Security Council approved Secretary-General Boutros Boutros-Ghali's recommendation to send a U.S.-led military force to secure ports and airfields and ensure delivery of food. The initial force of 28,000 U.S. and 2,000 French troops began arriving on December 9. Some 34 other nations planned to contribute troops.

Because many nations, especially in the developing world, opposed giving the United States the kind of absolute control it had had over the prosecution of the Persian Gulf war, the United States agreed to consult the secretary-general and Council regularly during the operation. A key disagreement surfaced early. Boutros-Ghali insisted U.S. troops would have to disarm the warring clans before UN peacekeepers could take over operations. U.S. officials said disarmament was not the United States' mission. In practice, U.S. forces first seized weapons aimed at them and, later, in January 1993, raided a main arsenal.

Other Peacekeeping Operations. In Cambodia cease-fire violations by the Khmer Rouge and the government threatened efforts by the UN Transitional Authority in Cambodia (UNTAC) to hold elections in spring 1993, ending 13 years of civil war.

The Khmer Rouge, the most powerful force in the Cambodian civil war, kidnapped 27 UN peacekeepers during December, releasing only some of them. The rebels refused to disarm until the Supreme National Council—which represents the Khmer, two other rebel groups, and the Vietnamese-backed government—assumed powers held exclusively by the government, led by Prime Minister Hun Sen.

On December 2 the Council had voted to ban imports of oil to Khmer Rouge territory in Cambodia and to block exports of lumber. But it urged UNTAC to hold elections with or without the rebels. Deployed since March, UNTAC had more than 22,000 soldiers and civilian officials and, at no less than $2 billion, was the costliest operation in UN history.

The Council expanded its role in Africa in 1992, spurred by criticism that millions were dying on the continent while it concentrated its attention and resources on Yugoslavia.

On December 16 the Council voted to dispatch 7,500 UN peacekeepers to war-scarred Mozambique to monitor a cease-fire agreement signed in Rome on October 4 by the government of President Joaquím Chissano and the Mozambique National Resistance, the rebel force known as Renamo. The UN operation, costing about $330 million, was to disarm the rival armies and organize elections.

ORGANIZATION OF THE UNITED NATIONS

THE SECRETARIAT

Secretary-General: Boutros Boutros-Ghali (until Dec. 31, 1996)

THE GENERAL ASSEMBLY (1992) *President:* Stoyan Ganev, Bulgaria

The 179 member nations were as follows:

Afghanistan	Central African	Ghana	Lesotho	Pakistan	Spain
Albania	Republic	Greece	Liberia	Panama	Sri Lanka
Algeria	Chad	Grenada	Libya	Papua New	Sudan
Angola	Chile	Guatemala	Liechtenstein	Guinea	Suriname
Antigua and	China, People's	Guinea	Lithuania	Paraguay	Swaziland
Barbuda	Republic of	Guinea-Bissau	Luxembourg	Peru	Sweden
Argentina	Colombia	Guyana	Madagascar	Philippines	Syria
Armenia	Comoros	Haiti	Malawi	Poland	Tajikistan
Australia	Congo	Honduras	Malaysia	Portugal	Tanzania
Austria	Costa Rica	Hungary	Maldives	Qatar	Thailand
Azerbaijan	Croatia	Iceland	Mali	Romania	Togo
Bahamas	Cuba	India	Malta	Russia	Trinidad and Tobago
Bahrain	Cyprus	Indonesia	Marshall Islands	Rwanda	Tunisia
Bangladesh	Czechoslovakia	Iran	Mauritania	Saint Kitts	Turkey
Barbados	Denmark	Iraq	Mauritius	and Nevis	Turkmenistan
Belarus	Djibouti	Ireland	Mexico	Saint Lucia	Uganda
Belgium	Dominica	Israel	Micronesia	Saint Vincent and	Ukraine
Belize	Dominican	Italy	Moldova	The Grenadines	United Arab Emirates
Benin	Republic	Ivory Coast	Mongolia	Samoa	United Kingdom
Bhutan	Ecuador	Jamaica	Morocco	San Marino	United States
Bolivia	Egypt	Japan	Mozambique	Sao Tomé and	Uruguay
Bosnia-Herzegovina	El Salvador	Jordan	Myanmar	Príncipe	Uzbekistan
Botswana	Equatorial Guinea	Kazakhstan	Namibia	Saudi Arabia	Vanuatu
Brazil	Estonia	Kenya	Nepal	Senegal	Venezuela
Brunei Darussalam	Ethiopia	Korea, Democratic	Netherlands	Seychelles	Vietnam
Bulgaria	Fiji	People's Republic of	New Zealand	Sierra Leone	Yemen
Burkina Faso	Finland	Korea, Republic of	Nicaragua	Singapore	Yugoslavia
Burundi	France	Kuwait	Niger	Slovenia	Zaire
Cambodia	Gabon	Kyrgyzstan	Nigeria	Solomon Islands	Zambia
Cameroon	Gambia	Laos	Norway	Somalia	Zimbabwe
Canada	Georgia	Latvia	Oman	South Africa	
Cape Verde	Germany	Lebanon			

COMMITTEES

General. Composed of 29 members as follows: The General Assembly president; the 21 General Assembly vice-presidents (heads of delegations or their deputies of Afghanistan, Belize, Benin, Cape Verde, China, Comoros, France, Gabon, Ireland, Kuwait, Lesotho, Libyan Arab Jamahiriya, Nicaragua, Philippines, Russian Federation, Sri Lanka, Suriname, Turkey, United Kingdom of Great Britain and Northern Ireland, United States of America, and Yemen); and the chairmen of the main committees below, which are composed of all 179 member countries.

First (Political and Security): Nabil Elaraby (Egypt)
Special Political: Hamadi Khouini (Tunisia)
Second (Economic and Financial): Ramiro Piriz Ballon (Uruguay)
Third (Social, Humanitarian and Cultural): Florian Krenkel (Austria)
Fourth (Decolonization): Guillermo Melendez Barahona (El Salvador)
Fifth (Administrative and Budgetary): Marian-George Dinu (Romania)
Sixth (Legal): Javad Zarif (Iran)

THE ECONOMIC AND SOCIAL COUNCIL

President: Robert Mroziewicz (Poland)
Membership ends on December 31 of the year noted.

Angola (1994)	France (1993)	Poland (1994)
Argentina (1993)	Gabon (1995)	Romania (1995)
Australia (1994)	Germany (1993)	Russia (1995)
Austria (1993)	Guinea (1993)	Somalia (1993)
Bahamas (1995)	India (1994)	Spain (1993)
Bangladesh (1994)	Japan (1993)	Sri Lanka (1995)
Belarus (1994)	Korea, Republic of	Suriname (1994)
Belgium (1994)	(1995)	Swaziland (1994)
Benin (1994)	Kuwait (1994)	Syria (1993)
Bhutan (1995)	Libyan Arab Jamahiriya	Togo (1993)
Botswana (1993)	(1995)	Trinidad and Tobago
Brazil (1994)	Madagascar (1994)	(1993)
Canada (1995)	Malaysia (1993)	Turkey (1993)
Chile (1993)	Mexico (1995)	Ukraine (1995)
China (1995)	Morocco (1993)	United Kingdom (1995)
Colombia (1994)	Nigeria (1995)	United States (1994)
Cuba (1995)	Norway (1995)	Yugoslavia (1993)
Denmark (1995)	Peru (1993)	Zaire (1995)
Ethiopia (1994)	Philippines (1994)	

THE SECURITY COUNCIL

Membership ends on December 31 of the year noted; asterisks indicate permanent membership.

Brazil (1994)	Hungary (1993)	Russia*
Cape Verde (1993)	Japan (1993)	Spain (1994)
China*	Morocco (1993)	United Kingdom*
Djibouti (1994)	New Zealand (1994)	United States*
France*	Pakistan (1994)	Venezuela (1993)

THE TRUSTEESHIP COUNCIL

President: (to be elected in 1993)

China[2] France[2] Russia[2] United Kingdom[2] United States[1]

[1] Administers Trust Territory. [2] Permanent member of Security Council not administering Trust Territory.

THE INTERNATIONAL COURT OF JUSTICE

Membership ends on February 5 of the year noted.

President: Sir Robert Y. Jennings (United Kingdom, 2000)
Vice-President: Shigeru Oda (Japan, 1994)

Roberto Ago (Italy, 1997)	Ni Zhengyu (China, 1994)
Andres Aguilar Mawdsley (Venezuela, 2000)	Raymond Ranjeva (Madagascar, 2000)
Bola Ajibola (Nigeria, 1994)	Stephen Schwebel (United States, 1997)
Mohammed Bedjaoui (Algeria, 1995)	Mohamed Shahabuddeen (Guyana, 1997)
Jens Evensen (Norway, 1994)	
Gilbert Guillaume (France, 2000)	Nikolai Konstantinovich Tarassov (Russia, 1997)
Manfred Lachs (Poland, 1994)	Christopher G. Weeramantry (Sri Lanka, 2000)

INTERGOVERNMENTAL AGENCIES

Food and Agricultural Organization (FAO); General Agreement on Tariffs and Trade (GATT); International Atomic Energy Agency (IAEA); International Bank for Reconstruction and Development (World Bank); International Civil Aviation Organization (ICAO); International Fund for Agricultural Development (IFAD); International Labor Organization (ILO); International Maritime Organization (IMO); International Monetary Fund (IMF); International Telecommunication Union (ITU); United Nations Educational, Scientific and Cultural Organization (UNESCO); United Nations Industrial Development Organization (UNIDO); Universal Postal Union (UPU); World Health Organization (WHO); World Intellectual Property Organization (WIPO); World Meteorological Organization (WMO).

New Opportunities and New Crises, Too

The Cold War's end and the collapse of communism have released the United Nations from nearly a half century of paralysis, giving it a chance to become the powerful force for world peace its founders envisioned. At the same time, the organization faces new crises, along with demands that it be restructured to reflect today's political realities.

Boosted by a host of newly independent former Soviet republics, the United Nations is bigger than ever, with 179 members, up from 159 in 1990. And it is busier and more prestigious than ever, too, as the world increasingly looks to it to resolve disputes.

Peacekeeping. From 1988 through 1992, the United Nations started 12 peacekeeping operations, compared with 12 in the previous 40 years. From 1991 to 1992 alone the number of blue-helmeted soldiers deployed soared from 11,000 to about 45,000, in areas ranging from Central America to Africa, the Balkans to Cambodia.

But the splintering of Communist blocs also has spawned an epidemic of ethnic and tribal conflicts that threaten to overwhelm already-strained UN resources. In places such as Bosnia-Herzegovina and Somalia, tens of thousands of civilians, perhaps more, have been killed in civil wars and by starvation as UN peacekeepers stand by helplessly. The Security Council has been unable or unwilling to intervene militarily.

In a June report to the Council, titled "Agenda for Peace," UN Secretary-General Boutros Boutros-Ghali said the United Nations must make bold changes to be able to respond to those crises or a great opportunity for world peace will be lost. He proposed creating a UN army, under joint command, to enforce Council measures and heavily armed quick-strike units to restore and maintain cease-fire agreements that have broken down. He wants member states to supply him with intelligence that would allow deployment of peacekeeping forces within the borders of threatened countries before the bullets start flying and innocent people start dying.

Funding. The idea of putting military forces under a joint command is sure to face opposition from countries, including the United States, that are unwilling to give up authority over their soldiers. But none of these grand plans will be realized if the United Nations,

which frequently flirts with bankruptcy, is not better funded. As of Aug. 31, 1992, UN members were $1.6 billion in arrears on their dues, with the financially wracked former Soviet republics owing more than $500 million. The United States, which withheld dues during the Reagan era because it disagreed with UN policies, was the number-one deadbeat, owing $733 million.

To improve UN finances, Boutros-Ghali asked for the authority to borrow commercially and to charge interest on back dues to give countries an incentive to pay on time. He proposed a $50 million revolving fund, so new peacekeeping operations can be mounted quickly, and a $1 billion peace-endowment fund. He also wants defense ministries to pay for peacekeeping because their budgets tend to get approved faster than those of foreign ministries.

© United Nations Photo

Bureaucracy. Since taking office on Jan. 1, 1992, Boutros-Ghali also was trying to trim the unwieldy Secretariat bureaucracy so as to cut costs and give himself more time for peacekeeping. He reduced to eight the number of top officials reporting to him, down from 30 under the old system.

The 15-member Security Council itself may not be immune to change. Many countries believe the Council, which was formed with the post-World War II world in mind, should be expanded. As of 1992 the Council had five permanent members—the United States, Britain, France, China, and Russia, which assumed the Soviet Union's seat—who had veto power. Ten rotating members were serving two-year terms on the Council.

Germany and Japan believe their economic might warrants permanent Council seats. Several of the world's poor, populous countries believe their sheer size merits representation. One plan would combine the seats of France and Britain (whose power has diminished since World War II), into one European seat to be shared with Germany. Another plan would give Germany and Japan permanent nonveto seats, along with such countries as Brazil, India, Egypt, and Nigeria. Because changes in the Council's membership are almost certain to engender disputes and complications, diplomats say it could be years before any changes are made in the long-established structure of this body.

RICK MITCHELL

By insisting on full disarmament in Mozambique (and Somalia), the UN was attempting to avoid repeating the blunder it had made in Angola, where it had arranged a cease-fire and sent peacekeepers to end a long civil war, but had not disarmed the warring parties. Though certified free and fair by the UN Angola Election Verification Mission, September elections were contested by Jonas Savimbi, leader of the rebel force UNITA, and his forces captured key towns from the government. At year's end the UN still was trying to reestablish peace so that a runoff election could be held.

On November 23, in a comprehensive review of Iraq's compliance with resolutions passed following the U.S.-led forces' expulsion of Iraq from Kuwait in 1991, the Council voted to maintain economic sanctions against that country. The Council said Iraq continued "grave human-rights abuses" against its population and had not provided full, final, and complete disclosure of all aspects of its programs for weapons of mass destruction and ballistic missiles.

On March 31 the Council voted to impose mandatory sanctions against Libya for its failure to surrender two Libyan nationals believed responsible for the bombing of Pan Am flight 103 and UTA (of France) flight 772, both of which killed hundreds. The sanctions included an air and arms embargo. The vote was ten in favor, none opposed; China, Cape Verde, India, Morocco, and Zimbabwe abstained.

El Salvador provided one of the year's few UN-peacekeeping successes, formally ending its 12-year civil war. The Council also extended the mandate of the UN Peacekeeping Force in Cyprus (UNFICYP), despite a budget shortfall of $197 million.

General Assembly. During the resumed 46th General Assembly, which began in 1991, the Assembly admitted to UN membership 13 new nations—Moldova, Kazakhstan, Kyrgyzstan, Azerbaijan, Uzbekistan, Tajikistan, Turkmenistan, Armenia, San Marino, Bosnia-Herzegovina, Croatia, Slovenia, and Georgia—for a record 179 members. Later, on September 22, it voted to expel the rump Yugoslavia, the first time it had removed a member-state.

The 47th Assembly, which began on September 15, elected as its president Bulgarian Foreign Minister Stoyan Ganev, who succeeded Samir S. Shihabi of Saudi Arabia. The Assembly, on October 28, also elected five new nonpermanent members of the 15-nation Security Council—Brazil, Djibouti, New Zealand, Pakistan, and Spain—to begin two-year terms beginning Jan. 1, 1993. They replaced Austria, Belgium, Ecuador, India, and Zimbabwe.

In a minor setback for the United States, on November 24 the Assembly approved a resolution urging the United States to end its 30-year trade embargo against Cuba. It also protested the U.S. Cuban Democracy Act of 1992, which makes it illegal for foreign subsidiaries of U.S. companies to trade with Cuba and punishes those who do. The vote on the resolution was 59 in favor—including Canada, Belgium, and France—three against, and 71 abstentions, including Britain.

On December 23 the Assembly adopted a zero-growth budget of $2.468 billion for the 1992-93 biennium. The UN spent $2.8 billion on peacekeeping during 1992, a fourfold increase over 1991.

Agencies and Conferences. From June 3 to June 14 the UN Conference on Environment and Development, or Earth Summit, convened in Rio de Janeiro, Brazil. Some 118 heads of state, including U.S. President George Bush, attended. Delegates from more than 170 countries approved by consensus a Declaration on Environment and Development, containing principles and policies; Agenda 21, a plan for environmental action through the 21st century; and a statement to guide forestry practices. A negotiating process was mandated for a Convention on Desertification. Also, some 153 countries, including the United States, by then had signed the Convention on Climate Change. The United States refused to sign the Convention on Biological Diversity, saying it threatened U.S.-held patents. (*See* SPECIAL REPORT/ ENVIRONMENT.)

Appealing for funds from the international community, the UN High Commissioner for Refugees, Sadako Ogata, said that in 1992 some 3 million people were forced to flee their homes by various calamities, for a worldwide total of 18 million refugees. That figure did not include an estimated 20 million people displaced in their own countries, she said.

In November, at a three-day conference of parties to the 1987 Montreal Treaty organized by the United Nations Environment Program, ministers and high government officials from 74 countries and the European Community agreed to a complete phaseout of ozone-depleting chlorofluorocarbons (CFCs) by Jan. 1, 1996, four years ahead of schedule.

Secretary-General. Boutros Boutros-Ghali (*see* BIOGRAPHY), former foreign minister of Egypt, became the UN's sixth secretary-general on January 1. He replaced Javier Pérez de Cuéllar of Peru, who retired after two terms.

With smoldering ethnic tensions threatening to graduate to civil war in several republics of the former Soviet Union, the secretary-general sent fact-finding missions to several republics and sent former U.S. Secretary of State Cyrus Vance to Nagorno Karabakh to coax peace talks between Armenians and Azerbaijanis. In March he decided to establish UN Interim Offices in the region, for distributing UN development and public information. The first opened in Armenia on October 24.

RICK MITCHELL
"U.N. Observer & International Report"

© Trippett/Sipa

The 41st U.S. chief executive, George Bush, welcomed the president-elect, Bill Clinton, to the White House on Nov. 18, 1992. Two weeks earlier, the president had lost to the Arkansas governor by an electoral-vote margin of 370 to 168.

UNITED STATES

When President George Bush journeyed to the Capitol on Jan. 28, 1992, to deliver his annual State of the Union address, expectations were high. In the face of the prolonged economic slowdown, the president had been under mounting pressure from leaders of his own party as well as from the opposition Democrats to spur economic recovery and also to meet the increasing demand for health reform. But for months the White House had put off any significant response, by promising bold new initiatives in the State of the Union address.

Striving to live up to his word, President Bush announced three actions to revive the economy—a 90-day moratorium on new government regulations, a reduction in federal income-tax withholding, and a speedup in government spending. He then challenged Congress to enact other measures, including a variety of tax breaks—notably a cut in the capital-gains-tax rate—along with a proposal for extending of unemployment benefits.

On the health front, Bush rejected ideas offered by Democrats for health-care reform, which he argued would restrict patient choice and lead to rationing of care. Instead the president called for a $3,750 tax credit for low-income families combined with reforms in the health-insurance industry. Setting a March 20 deadline for the legislative branch to approve his economic proposals, President Bush

warned: "From the day after that, if it must be, the battle is joined."

With the use of such martial terms, President Bush sought to evoke recollections of his leadership of the Persian Gulf war. "We can bring the same courage and sense of common purpose to the economy that we brought to Desert Storm," he declared.

Domestic Affairs

Ironically, as the year progressed, Bush's critics would seek to turn the events that led up to the Desert Storm triumph against the president. In the third and final debate among 1992's three candidates for the White House—the president, Democrat Bill Clinton of Arkansas, and independent Ross Perot—in East Lansing, MI, on October 19, Perot accused Bush of temporizing in his dealings with Iraqi ruler Saddam Hussein prior to Saddam's invasion of Kuwait in August of 1990. And charges that the Bush administration had mishandled a $5 billion bank-fraud case involving loans to Iraq by the Atlanta branch of Italy's Banca Nazionale del Lavoro (BNL) forced the appointment on October 16 of a special prosecutor. Among the allegations, lumped together under the rubric "Iraqgate" by the press, was the contention that the Justice Department had withheld evidence in the case from government prosecutors. But setting aside such allegations, the challenge Bush faced in striving to restore public confidence in his stewardship of the economy confronted him with obstacles and opponents who, unlike Hussein, could not be overwhelmed with armed might.

The most direct opposition came from the Democratic majorities in Congress. Shrugging off Bush's deadline for action, the Democrats dismissed most of his tax-cutting economic proposals as simply another variation of what they labeled Republican "trickle-down" economics. But even tougher for Bush to overcome were the obstacles created by the economy. For most of the year the recovery from the slump was so weak that it was hard to convince Americans that the recession had ended. On November 25 the Commerce Department reported that growth in the third quarter had reached a vigorous pace of 3.9%. But this hopeful news was too late to save Bush from defeat in his bid for reelection. (*See* FEATURE ARTICLE/THE 1992 ELECTION, page 26.)

A disturbing postscript to the election campaign was the disclosure on December 17 that Attorney General William Barr had arranged the appointment of a special prosecutor to investigate the circumstances surrounding the search of President-elect Clinton's passport files during the campaign. The probe was aimed at determining responsibility for the passport search, which apparently was aimed at getting negative information to be used to damage Clinton's candidacy.

In an effort to put another troublesome controversy—the Iran-contra case—behind him, on Christmas Eve, President Bush granted full pardons to former Defense Secretary Caspar Weinberger and five other former officials of the Reagan administration who had been linked to the Iran-contra case. This affair, which first came to light in 1986, involved the sale of U.S. arms to Iran in exchange for release of U.S. hostages, with proceeds from the sales going to help finance the anticommunist contra rebels in Nicaragua.

Weinberger, who Bush described as "a true American patriot," had been indicted on October 30 for perjury. At that time, Lawrence Walsh, the independent prosecutor in charge of the case, released a 1986 note written by Weinberger that contradicted Bush's long-maintained claim that he was "out of the loop" on the arms-for-hostages transaction. The others pardoned, whose actions Bush contended had been motivated by "patriotism," not "profit," were: Duane R. Clarridge, a former Central Intelligence Agency (CIA) official, who was awaiting trial; Elliott Abrams, former Reagan administration assistant secretary of state, and Robert C. McFarlane, Reagan's former national security adviser—both of whom had pleaded guilty to withholding information from Congress; and former CIA officials Clair George, who was found guilty of lying to Congress, and Alan D. Fiers, Jr., who pleaded guilty of withholding information from Congress. Prosecutor Walsh called the president's action part of a "cover-up" of the case and said that he would pursue the investigation by focusing on whether Bush himself improperly had withheld his personal diary from the investigators in order to impede the probe.

Congress. The 102d Congress, which began on a high note of history in 1991 when it authorized the desert war against Iraq, ended its life in 1992 near the depths of frustration. Hindered by partisan confrontations with the White House and squabbling in its own ranks, the 102d probably would be remembered less for what it accomplished than for the embarrassment it brought on itself as a result of misjudg-

President-elect Clinton and Vice-President-elect Al Gore meet with their transition team—headed by Warren Christopher and Vernon Jordan—in Little Rock, AR. The Clinton administration would be the first Democratic one in 12 years.

ments and misbehavior. (*See* FEATURE ARTICLE/CONGRESS—A STORM CENTER IN 1992, page 32.)

The year's final congressional controversy flared after the election, on November 22, when *The Washington Post* in a well-documented story reported that during his 24 years of service on Capitol Hill, Republican Sen. Bob Packwood of Oregon, who just had been reelected, had made uninvited sexual advances to a number of women who worked for him or with him. On December 10, faced with calls for his resignation, Packwood—a longtime champion of feminist causes—admitted that his behavior had been "just plain wrong," but insisted he would stay on in the Senate. A Senate ethics-committee inquiry into his behavior went forward. Earlier in the year, Democratic Sen. Brock Adams of Washington dropped his plans to seek reelection after the *Seattle Times* reported that he had sexually abused female associates.

Though Democrats controlled both the Senate and House, their leaders insisted that President Bush and his vetoes should bear at least some of the blame for the low productivity on Capitol Hill. The president's vetoes in 1992 brought the total for his term in the White House to 37. Only once was Congress able to override—on October 5, when both House and Senate mustered the more than two-thirds majorities needed to overturn Bush's rejection of a new law to reregulate the cable-television industry in order to curb price increases and stimulate competition.

Here is what the Congress achieved, and where it fell short in key issue areas in 1992:

• *Economic Policy.* After much haggling, Congress produced a budget that cut defense spending $11 billion below the spending limits set in the 1990 budget agreement, with all the savings going to reduce the deficit. The most dramatic battle on the fiscal front came over a proposed constitutional amendment requiring a balanced budget. Democrat House leaders and interest groups mustered enough opposition to leave proponents nine votes short of the two-thirds majority required for approval by the House of Representatives.

Late in the session both houses passed legislation embodying $27 billion in tax relief along with an urban-aid package. But President Bush vetoed the bill November 4, the day after losing the presidential election, complaining that the measure contained "numerous tax increases" that "would destroy jobs and undermine small business."

• *Energy and Environment.* Congress enacted a far-reaching revision of energy laws aimed at promoting energy conservation and developing alternative energy sources. Major provisions included restructuring of the electric-utility industry to promote competition; easing of licensing for nuclear-energy plants; and tax breaks for independent oil and gas drillers and also for efforts to foster renewable energy production, promote mass transit, and develop autos driven by nongasoline fuels.

Another wide-ranging new law affected water policy in the West. It authorized water projects in 17 states and provided for water from California's Central Valley project to be diverted to wildlife habitats and also made available to cities and industries.

On the negative side, Congress failed to reauthorize the Endangered Species Act and the Resource Conservation and Recovery Act —the nation's main solid- and hazardous-waste law.

• *Social Policy.* The list of unmet goals in the area of social policy was far longer than what was accomplished. Democratic leaders could not line up enough support behind any single approach to health-care reform to pass promised legislation. And Congress was unable to override presidential vetoes of family-leave legislation and of a measure overturning the administration's ban on abortion counseling in

© Brad Markel/Gamma-Liaison

Sen. John F. Kerry (D-MA), center, chairman of the U.S. Senate Select Committee on POW-MIA Affairs, and committee members —Sen. Hank Brown (R-CO) and Sen. Tom Daschle (D-SD), right —report on their November 1992 trip to Southeast Asia in search of information regarding the servicemen missing as a result of the Vietnam war.

In early December 1992, soldiers at Fort Drum, NY, prepared to participate in "Operation Restore Hope"—a U.S.-led mission under UN auspices to help deliver supplies to the starving people of Somalia.

© Rick Falco/Sipa

federally funded abortion clinics. Congress did enact the higher-education bill, which greatly expanded student access to loans regardless of family income. (*See also* page 590.)

Race Relations. In March of 1991, when the 81-second videotape of four white Los Angeles police officers beating black motorist Rodney King repeatedly was shown around the country, most Americans were shocked. Most black Americans saw the incident as illustrating the pervasiveness of race discrimination and injustice. They looked to the legal system to punish King's assailants. But on April 29, when the jury considering the charges against the four police officers involved handed down its verdict clearing them of all but one minor charge, for many Americans, particularly blacks, it was as great a shock as was the King beating itself. The result was that Los Angeles was engulfed in a wave of violence, which took the highest toll of lives of any race riot in U.S. history.

Blacks were incensed that the six-man, six-woman jury that acquitted the officers of all the serious charges against them had no black members, although one juror was Hispanic and another an Asian American. The makeup of the jury reflected the fact that to avoid the influence of the intense publicity given to the King incident in Los Angeles, the trial had been shifted to the mostly white bedroom community of Simi Valley in Ventura county, about 45 mi (72 km) northwest of Los Angeles. Another factor contributing to the anger in the streets was a long history of tension between the black community in Los Angeles and the Los Angeles police department under controversial chief Daryl Gates.

Soon after the violence erupted, Los Angeles Mayor Tom Bradley declared a local state of emergency and California Gov. Pete Wilson ordered the National Guard to assist local police. But these forces could not cope with the mobs that swept through predominantly black and Hispanic south central Los Angeles, burning and looting. It took more than four days and the help of 1,500 Marines and 3,000 Army troops to restore order. The death toll exceeded 50, with damage totaling more than $1 billion. Violence on a smaller scale erupted in a number of other cities, including San Francisco, Atlanta, Seattle, Las Vegas, and Miami.

In the wake of the rioting a retrial to be held in Los Angeles was ordered for one of the officers, Lawrence M. Powell, on charges of using excessive force under color of police authority. The jury in the initial trial had been unable to reach agreement on that charge. Then on August 5 a federal grand jury in Los Angeles indicted Powell and three other white officers on charges of violating Rodney King's civil rights. Conviction could mean a maximum sentence of ten years in prison.

Both President Bush and his Democratic challenger Bill Clinton visited the city in the days immediately following the rioting. White House Press Secretary Marlin Fitzwater sought to put part of the blame for violence on what he called the "failed" social-welfare programs of the 1960s and 1970s. And independent presidential contender Ross Perot used the riots to underline his claim to be a man of action. "If I were home watching (the rioting)," he said, "I'd head for the airport, and on the way to the airport I'd call the attorney general and tell him to file a federal case."

After a five-month inquiry, a commission headed by former FBI Director William H. Webster issued a report on October 21. It said that city officials had been unprepared for any disorder and described their response "as marked by uncertainty, some confusion, and an almost total lack of coordination."

But whatever the faults of Los Angeles' leaders, the roots of racial tension in the nation clearly reached far deeper and over a wider area. In New York City, for example, once considered the paradigm of U.S. status as an ethnic and racial melting pot, friction between Hasidic Jews and blacks in the Crown Heights section of Brooklyn, which had led to violence in 1991, continued to roil the city; the city's black Mayor David Dinkins called on all New

---

UNITED STATES • Information Highlights

Official Name: United States of America.
Location: Central North America.
Area: 3,618,768 sq mi (9 372 610 km²).
Population (Jan. 1, 1993 est.): 256,600,000.
Chief Cities (1990 census): Washington, DC, the capital, 606,900; New York, 7,322,564; Los Angeles, 3,485,398; Chicago, 2,783,726; Houston, 1,630,-553; Philadelphia, 1,585,577; San Diego, 1,110,549.
Government: *Head of state and government,* George Bush, president (took office Jan. 20, 1989). *Legislature*—Congress: Senate and House of Representatives.
Monetary Unit: Dollar.
Gross National Product (1990): $5,465,300,000,000.
Merchandise Trade (1991): *Imports,* $509,320,-000,000; *exports,* $421,730,000,000.

Yorkers to reject "the poisonous philosophy" of bigotry. (*See* SPECIAL REPORT/CITIES.)

MIA Controversy. The prolonged dispute over whether U.S. servicemen reported as missing in action (MIA) in the Vietnam war still were alive and being held prisoner by Hanoi flared again in 1992, despite official assurances that such beliefs were unfounded.

Seeking to allay suspicions that the government had failed to investigate adequately the fate of the MIAs by addressing a group of their relatives in suburban Virginia on July 24, President Bush was heckled by some in the audience at the meeting. Bush shouted back at one persistent heckler: "Would you please shut up and sit down?"

A more serious episode in the continuing drama took place at a hearing before a special Senate committee investigating the controversy. On September 21 the committee was told by key Nixon administration officials, including former Defense Secretaries Melvin Laird and James Schlesinger, that the Nixon administration had private doubts, never made public, about North Vietnam's claim in March 1973 when fighting stopped in Vietnam that it had released all U.S. prisoners of war. But the next day, Henry M. Kissinger—who served Nixon as national security adviser and then secretary of state—asserted that no firm evidence ever had been produced to show that prisoners of war had been left behind.

Another long-smoldering controversy, over the 1963 assassination of President John Kennedy, was revived by the late 1991 release of the motion picture *JFK*, which dramatized purported evidence of a conspiracy to kill the president. Congress established a commission to review and then release still-secret government records on the case.

Clinton's Team. The appointments a president-elect makes during the transition period following his election and preceding his inauguration always are watched closely for clues to the policies the new chief executive will pursue in office. In the case of President-elect Clinton, his choices took on a an added note of drama and urgency because he was the first Democrat to win the White House in 12 years and also because it was clear that he would be challenged seriously at the start of his tenure by the nation's economic problems.

Reflecting his awareness of the economy's importance, Clinton announced his choices of economic advisers first—at a Little Rock press conference on December 10. The top three were: Democratic Sen. Lloyd Bentsen of Texas for secretary of the treasury, Democratic Rep. Leon Panetta of California as director of the Office of Management and Budget, and investment banker Robert E. Rubin to the new post of chairman of the National Economic Council. All were regarded as having the centrist backgrounds and outlooks that would reassure the business community. By contrast, in the social-policy field, Clinton's major appointees seemed more likely to try the sort of innovative policies his campaign had promised. They were Carol M. Browner, Florida's top environmental regulator, as head of the Environmental Protection Agency; Donna E. Shalala, chancellor of the University of Wisconsin, as secretary of health and human services; and Harvard economist Robert Reich as labor secretary.

In a December 21 press conference near the end of the selection process, Clinton openly expressed his irritation at pressure from feminist groups to choose women appointees. He likened the groups to "bean counters" and accused them of playing "quota games." Nevertheless, Clinton assured them that women would play a prominent role in his administration by naming Zoe Baird as his choice for attorney general; former Carter aide Madeleine Albright as UN ambassador; Hazel O'Leary as secretary of energy; and Laura D'Andrea Tyson, professor of economics at the University of California at Berkeley, as chair of the Council of Economic Advisers, in addition to picking Shalala and Browner.

The president-elect also chose his campaign chairman, Los Angeles lawyer Mickey Kantor, as U.S. trade representative, and for White House chief of staff he named a childhood friend, the head of an Arkansas natural-gas conglomerate, Thomas F. "Mack" McLarty.

In the fields of foreign policy and national security, in which he himself had little background, Clinton chose people who had been seasoned by experience. As secretary of state he named Warren Christopher, for secretary of defense he picked Democratic Rep. Les Aspin of Wisconsin, as national security adviser he selected Anthony Lake, and for director of the Central Intelligence Agency he picked James Woolsey, who had served both Presidents Bush and Carter. (*See also* SIDEBAR.)

ROBERT SHOGAN
Washington Bureau, "Los Angeles Times"

THE CLINTON CABINET

As promised, President-elect Bill Clinton completed his cabinet appointments by Dec. 24, 1992. His 14 nominees—still to be confirmed by the Senate—included four blacks, three women, and two Hispanics (both men). Clinton selected several former Carter administration officials and also some longtime associates.

Department of Agriculture: First elected to Congress in 1986, Mike Espy was Mississippi's first black representative in more than a century. Born in Yazoo City on Nov. 30, 1953, Espy was graduated from Howard University in 1975 and earned his law degree from the University of Santa Clara Law School. He worked with Central Mississippi Legal Services and various state agencies. A member of the House Agriculture Committee, he has worked to represent the interests of farmers.

Department of Commerce: Ronald H. Brown—chairman of the Democratic National Committee and a partner at Patton, Boggs, & Blow, a law firm in Washington, DC—would become the first black to head the Commerce Department. Brown is a native Washingtonian, born Aug. 1, 1941. Brown worked as general counsel, deputy executive officer, and vice-president of operations at the Urban League (1971–79). He was chief counsel to the Senate Judiciary Committee (1980), and general counsel for Sen. Edward Kennedy (1981).

Department of Defense: Les Aspin first was elected to Congress in 1970 and has chaired the House Armed Services Committee since 1985. He has built a reputation for expertise in military affairs by exposing Pentagon waste. The secretary-designate worked as an economist under Secretary of Defense Robert McNamara. He advised Clinton on defense matters during the campaign. Born on July 21, 1938, in Milwaukee, WI, Aspin holds a bachelor's degree from Yale University and a master's from Oxford University.

Department of Education: Richard W. Riley is known for his efforts to improve the education system in South Carolina during his two terms as governor (1979–87). Born on Jan. 2, 1933, Riley was a member of the Illinois General Assembly (1963–66) and the Illinois Senate (1966–76). He worked with Clinton on education issues at the National Governors' Association and was assistant director for personnel matters for Clinton's transition team. The position put him in charge of hundreds of appointments.

Department of Energy: Hazel R. O'Leary would be the first energy secretary to have worked for an energy company. As vice-president at Northern States Power Company of Minnesota, the former energy consultant oversaw public relations, legal affairs, and environmental and personnel matters at the company. O'Leary, who is known to be an expert on nuclear-waste disposal, served in both the Ford and Carter administrations. Born on May 17, 1937, she holds a law degree from Rutgers University.

Department of Health and Human Services: Chancellor of the University of Wisconsin at the time of her nomination, Donna E. Shalala is known as an advocate for children's issues. She succeeded Hillary Clinton as chairwoman of the Children's Defense Fund and served on the board of the National Institutes of Health. Shalala was a housing official in the Carter administration and is known as an expert on urban finance. Born on May 17, 1937, she holds a doctorate from Syracuse University.

Department of Housing and Urban Development: Former San Antonio Mayor Henry G. Cisneros is credited with turning that city into a major business center. Born on June 11, 1947, the Texas native was graduated from Texas A&M University with bachelor's and master's degrees. He earned a master's in urban affairs from Harvard University and a doctorate from George Washington University. Cisneros was elected mayor in 1981, but declined to run for reelection in 1989. He then started his own investment firm.

Department of the Interior: After his unsuccessful bid for the Democratic presidential nomination in 1988, former Arizona Gov. Bruce Babbitt became a partner at the law firm of Steptoe & Johnson in Phoenix and Washington, DC. Babbitt, born on June 27, 1938, was graduated from the University of Notre Dame and earned his law degree from Harvard University in 1965. An ardent environmentalist, Babbitt is president of the League of Conservation Voters. He has written several books on the southwestern landscape.

Department of Justice: Corporate lawyer Zoe Baird served in the Justice Department's Office of Legal Counsel in the Carter administration. When nominated, she was senior vice-president and general counsel at Aetna Life and Casualty Co., based in Hartford, CT. Baird would be the first woman attorney general. She earned both her undergraduate and law degrees from the University of California at Berkeley. Although she was born in Brooklyn, NY, Baird has lived most of her life in Seattle, WA.[1]

Department of Labor: Robert B. Reich, born on June 24, 1946, is a longtime Clinton associate, having met him as a Rhodes scholar at Oxford University. A professor at Harvard's John F. Kennedy School of Government since 1981, Reich earned his law degree from Yale University and his undergraduate degree from Dartmouth College. He served as assistant solicitor general at the U.S. Department of Justice (1974–76) and at the Federal Trade Commission (1976-81).

Secretary of State: Warren M. Christopher is best-known for his role in negotiating the release of U.S. hostages from Iran. Born on Oct. 27, 1925, in Scranton, PA, he later moved to California. He was graduated from the University of Southern California in 1945 and earned his law degree from Stanford University. A law clerk under Justice William O. Douglas, he has served as deputy attorney general (1967–69) and deputy secretary of state (1977–81). He headed up Clinton's transition team.

Department of Transportation: Federico F. Peña was Denver's first Hispanic mayor (1983–91). Born on March 15, 1947, and originally from Texas, Peña served in the Colorado House of Representatives (1979–83). While mayor, he successfully forged complex agreements to make way for a new airport, to be the world's largest. He also gained approval for a major new convention center and an oxygenated-fuels program. Peña declined to run for reelection in 1991 and formed a pension-management company.

Department of the Treasury: A native of Texas, Lloyd Bentsen was born on Feb. 11, 1921, and was graduated from the University of Texas with a law degree. He enlisted in the U.S. Army, and was awarded the Distinguished Flying Cross for his service in the Air Force Reserve. He has served in the U.S. Senate since 1970 and was chairman of the Senate Finance Committee and a member of the Joint Economic Committee. An expert on tax law, Bentsen was Michael Dukakis' running mate in 1988.

Department of Veterans Affairs: Jesse Brown, 48, is executive director of the Disabled American Veterans Association. Brown received the Purple Heart for his tour of duty in Vietnam and has a paralyzed right arm. After the war, he worked as a service officer in Chicago, helping veterans through the regulatory maze so they could receive benefits. As a veterans' advocate, he has fought for VA recognition of such disabilities stress disorder and diseases said to result from exposure to Agent Orange.

[1]Nomination withdrawn in January 1993.

The Economy

The U.S. economy in 1992 puzzled the economic and political leadership, exasperated business and industry, and disappointed almost everyone. Throughout the year, it teetered between growth and malaise. Many businesses raised their profits, but business failures grew still more; exports showed more strength, but manufacturing continued weak; new business formation was vigorous, but large companies found themselves forced to terminate tens of thousands of workers, close plants, and otherwise cut costs in an attempt to adjust to an economic world marked by change and little respect for the old ways of doing things.

The inconsistencies were reflected psychologically also, with one month's optimism followed by a new month's despair. Economic arrows that had pointed up one month were snapped the next by the release of the latest official economic statistics. It was that way until late in the year when the numbers finally seemed to confirm a consistent upturn, although the weakest of any recovery in the post-World War II period.

Differing Economic Views. Perhaps the biggest division of opinion was between ordinary people and the administration of George Bush. It amounted to a schism, with neither side seeming to understand the other and with the disharmony gradually but relentlessly developing into bitterness. Based on the president's criteria, including a small increase in gross domestic product (GDP), the recession was over and the economy was growing. Relying on such figures, Bush attempted to convince voters they were better off than they realized, but many voters were using different criteria. With unemployment of about 9.2 million workers—a 7.2% rate that did not include 1 million who had given up looking and therefore were not counted, and another 6 million involuntarily working only part-time—the president's message was unconvincing, and he too lost his job.

Even those who had jobs seemed to experience difficulties. According to the Tax Foundation, an independent researcher, real income growth, inflation, and accelerating taxes made the typical family $214 poorer in 1992 than in 1991; it was the fourth straight year of losses, bringing the total to $1,444. In explaining the plight of the typical family, the foundation also provided insight into reasons for the insistent voter demand for change. After stating that the two-earner family—it now had become the norm—that made $33,492 in 1982 now was earning an estimated $53,984, it explained that when federal, state, and local taxes and inflation were taken into account, this sizable $20,492 increase resulted in a mere $4,021 net gain. Lest the point be missed, it reiterated that "over 80% of the family's income growth in the past decade has been eroded by taxes and inflation." Even those whose income was too low to be taxed were affected by the languishing economy. The latest official poverty-level figures (for 1989) showed a rise to 35.7 million people, or 12.8 % of the population. The high level was explained as a consequence of low-skill, low-wage immigrants and the persistence of an underclass that perpetuated itself through the welfare system. The estimate was questioned widely and vigorously for various reasons—one being that income from noncash benefits, including food stamps and housing subsidies, was excluded from income calculations.

Laura D'Andrea Tyson addresses the conference of some 300 economists, business and community leaders, and representatives of labor that assembled in Little Rock, AR, in mid-December 1992 under the direction of President-elect Bill Clinton. The 45-year-old economist from the University of California, Berkeley, had been designated chairman of the Council of Economic Advisers in the new Clinton administration.

GROSS DOMESTIC PRODUCT
Percent Change from Preceding Quarter

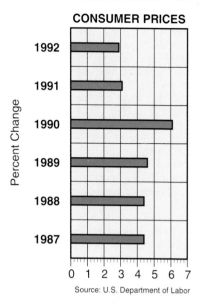

| | 1990 | | | | 1991 | | | | 1992 | | |

(seasonally adjusted at annual rate—constant dollars)

Source: U.S. Department of Commerce

CONSUMER PRICES

Percent Change

1992
1991
1990
1989
1988
1987

0 1 2 3 4 5 6 7

Source: U.S. Department of Labor

Attempting to explain the wide gap between professional economic interpretations and those of working families, economists argued that the malaise and recession were created not solely by a cyclical downturn. Instead, they said, structural problems impervious to the usual fiscal and monetary remedies were involved. Low interest rates, they said, hardly would spur a commercial real-estate market that had built sufficient capacity for the next five years.

Economic Restraints. Besides such impediments, there also were the spending restraints imposed by household business and governmental debt that had been amassed during the 1980s. Debtors in all categories seemed intent on paying down their bills rather than buying additional goods and services.

Still another structural difficulty involved the need of large corporations to adjust to a more competitive global environment and stiffer competition. Prestigious companies felt compelled to downsize—to radically cut their employee rolls and physical plant. It was rumored that among the reasons they did so was the startling and seemingly uncontrollable rise in health-care-benefit costs, generally in the double-digit range. Many companies also cut such benefits and changed the rules, requiring employees to contribute more to premiums. IBM, an icon of the U.S. economic surge over the previous four decades, terminated 40,000 jobs during the year, announced plans in December to cut 25,000 more, and reduced its plant capacity drastically. General Motors was forced repeatedly to close plants and cut payrolls. Among those also downsizing were top defense contractors, such as United Technologies and General Dynamics, forced to do so by cutbacks in defense spending.

Atop these problems, the financial system remained stressed. Banks still failed and, more-over, in an attempt to correct that problem, regulators sternly looked over the shoulders of lenders. According to Federal Reserve Chairman Alan Greenspan, this probably contributed to what many called a credit crunch for small businesses.

Changing Habits. The news was not all bad. There was evidence that economic problems were being corrected. People watched their use of credit and the total of installment credit outstanding fell for seven straight months before rising again late in the year.

Shoppers looked for bargains—the chic new attitude was to brag about discounts obtained rather than money spent, to seek quality rather than style or fad—thus putting pressure on producers and retailers to hold the price line. *Vogue* magazine, a showcase of fashions costing in the high four figures, announced plans for an issue devoted exclusively to fashions under $500. In part, economizing was forced on consumers by the slow growth or stagnation of real disposable income. Retailers and producers instituted more efficient methods in order to remain competitive.

Inflation and Interest Rates. Consumer prices remained within bounds all year long; the Consumer Price Index for the year averaged just over 3%, a full percentage point below the year-earlier figure, and the producer price index was even lower. Interest rates also remained low, at least in comparison to those that had existed during the previous few years. The prime interest rate as the year ended was 6%, compared with 6.5% a year earlier.

With mortgage rates at their lowest since the early 1970s, homeowners refinanced their properties, exchanging the high fixed rates they had held for a decade for lower variable rates. In the process, many cut their monthly payments by hundreds of dollars. For the first time in several years, young couples seemed eager to go house hunting. Existing home sales exceeded 3 million, and sales of new single-family homes rose sharply. The big exception to the housing recovery was the collapse of multifamily construction, another hangover from the overproduction of the mid and late 1980s, a splurge that left the commercial real-estate market nearly dead. With an oversupply of commercial structures, speculative construction all but ceased. So product-heavy was the market that the value of many structures declined, threatening the financial well-being of the big insurance firms that had financed them.

Signs of Improvement. Despite the sometimes despairingly low level of consumer and business confidence, evidence accumulated that the economy was righting itself. Corporate profits, which came in surprisingly strong, supplied additional documentation. After five quarters of declines, corporate net income rose throughout 1992. More importantly for the future, if not for the present, the results of the companies making up the Standard and Poor's 500-stock index rose 16%, while sales were estimated to have risen by less than one-half that percentage. Even more heartening was the fact that the gains covered most industries.

Not all fared so well, of course. Dun & Bradstreet counted 50,582 business failures in the first half of the year alone, more than 7,000 greater than in the like period of 1992.

The good news, surprising in view of the downcast attitude of many economy watchers, was reflected in the official GDP figures. At first the government announced that third-quarter GDP, the total domestic production of all goods and services, had risen 2.7%. The news was greeted with incredulity by many but viewed as confirmation by those who supported the Bush administration's claim that things were getting better. Almost incredibly, the gain later was revised upward to 3.9%, making the total nearly $5 trillion (1987 dollars), indicating a far more vigorous recovery than had been realized. The new figures compelled a new perspective, and Michael J. Boskin, chairman of the President's Council of Economic Advisers, expressed it. He reminded the economic naysayers that the economy had grown at a rate averaging 2.75% over the first three quarters of 1992, double the percentage increase that had occurred in the comparable period of 1991. Still, it was too late to help the president. The figures came out two weeks after the election.

Problems Persist. Meanwhile, a laundry list of challenges seemed to grow rather than diminish. Such challenges included the merchandise-trade and budget deficits. The merchandise deficit ran at an average of more than $6 billion per month in the first nine months—a rate that would exceed 1991's $65.4 billion. The budget deficit rose to $292 billion from $210 billion one year earlier.

© AP/Wide World

Investment banker Robert H. Rubin, 54, was named by President-elect Clinton to the Economic Security Council, a new department intended to coordinate economic policy.

Were such problems beyond the abilities of government to resolve? Sometimes it seemed so, since programs to affect positive change so often had undesirable consequences. Efforts of the Federal Reserve to spur the economy with lower interest rates, for example, caused havoc in the budgets of many retired people. While interest expenses fell as a consequence of the Fed's moves, and thereby lowered the burdens on debtors, interest income also shrank, serving to undermine and delay the goal of greater economic activity.

It was this sense of frustration that lay behind the insistent demands from the public for new ideas and approaches, and which were reflected politically by cries for change—unspecified change—just change. Many people had lost faith in government's ability to correct the problems it had helped create, and saw its efforts as mere promises seldom fulfilled and inevitably postponed.

Nothing illustrated the feeling more sharply than repeated failures to deal with the budget deficits. Scholars at the Institute for Policy Innovation, a Texas-based think tank, observed that of six so-called deficit-reduction agreements between Congress and the White House in the previous ten years, none had reduced the deficit. Its studies also showed that real (adjusted for equal buying power) government spending per person had grown from $2,899 in 1959 to $6,519 at the beginning of 1992, and that real taxes per person had risen from $2,831 in 1959 to $5,870. And, suggested Stephen Moore, director of fiscal policy studies for the Cato Institute in Washington, DC, the ability to deal with deficits seemed to be waning.

See also FEATURE ARTICLE/THE U.S. EMPLOYMENT SCENE, page 48; BUSINESS AND CORPORATE AFFAIRS.

JOHN CUNNIFF, *The Associated Press*

Foreign Affairs

As in most presidential-election years, U.S. foreign policy in 1992 became entangled in campaign issues, especially as President George Bush's opponents accused him of paying too little attention to domestic matters. Moreover, despite its vaunted prior foreign policy successes, the administration was charged with inconsistencies and indiscretions, such as propping up Iraqi President Saddam Hussein before the Persian Gulf conflict of 1990–91, covering up international banking scandals and the Iran-contra affair, failing to take firm action regarding trouble spots in Eastern Europe and Africa, making mistakes in trade policy and environmental talks, and neglecting to secure control over international arms traffic and arms-control verification.

Interestingly timed administration announcements of jet-fighter and tank sales to the Middle East and Asia punctuated campaign stops in defense-dependent communities like St. Louis, Detroit, and Fort Worth; farm export subsidies were raised even as Washington opposed those in Europe; U.S. sugar-import quotas were sustained, even as Japan's rice-import quotas were criticized. In the end, the Bush defeat probably had far more to do with the economy than with foreign policy, but the two in many respects were interrelated.

Middle East Negotiations. Perhaps the clearest signal of election-year priorities was the late summer departure of James Baker as secretary of state to head the White House staff. Certain of his initiatives, such as the Middle East peace talks, nevertheless continued, with some indication of progress in Israeli-Syrian dialogue on the Golan Heights issue. Palestinian autonomy plans also were discussed, but with no clear meeting of the minds on the extent of Arab self-determination in the occupied territories. U.S.

leaders plainly were pleased at the June Israeli Labor Party election victory, in view of Labor's promises to limit the building of new settlements in these territories and move forward on the peace front. Thus, the long-delayed U.S. loan guarantees to Israel finally were approved. However, the talks ended inconclusively in December.

The Bush administration also pressured Iraq into accepting UN inspection of weapons facilities, and by summer's end a "no-fly" area was enforced by U.S. jets to protect Shiite Arab zones in southern Iraq from Baghdad's repression. Some U.S.-Turkish friction resulted from Washington's similar protection of Kurdish zones in northern Iraq, however. As in the Gulf war itself, Saddam Hussein did not appear to challenge these moves, but rather to delay and hinder full implementation of UN resolutions. Washington was even less successful in efforts to persuade Libya's Muammar el-Qaddafi to extradite two suspects in the 1988 Pan American Flight 103 bombing.

Arms Talks. Presidents Bush and Boris Yeltsin of Russia agreed in June to cut strategic nuclear forces by an additional 50% beyond the levels set by the Strategic Arms Reduction (START) treaty, though uncertainty persisted about the pace and verification of reductions. START itself finally was ratified by the Senate late in its term—both to encourage the Russians and as a precondition for negotiations to renew the global nuclear nonproliferation (NPT) treaty later in the decade. By year's end, alarming though perhaps somewhat exaggerated reports were surfacing of Russian nuclear-fuel smuggling across European borders.

The Bush administration strenuously objected to continued Russian, East European, Chinese, and Korean weapons sales to Iran and other hot spots. However, the force of its objections was blunted because Washington itself

© Brad Markel/Gamma-Liaison

An additional reduction in U.S.-Russian strategic nuclear weapons resulted from talks between Russia's President Boris Yeltsin (extreme left) and President George Bush at the White House in June 1992. As 1993 began, President Bush was in Moscow to join President Yeltsin in signing the arms agreement, which had become known as START II.

set new arms export records, in the process removing requirements for repayment of government subsidies by exporters. The five-power agreement of 1991 to restrain weapons sales to volatile regions largely disintegrated, and though there was still a near-consensus opposing export of weapons of mass destruction (nuclear, chemical, and biological), the administration moved to weaken some provisions in nuclear-export legislation in July. The administration also continued to resist congressional pressure for a comprehensive nuclear-test ban.

Defense Cuts. The overall U.S. defense budget again was lowered in 1992, to the $270 billion range, and foreign-assistance programs, many of which had military components, remained around $13 billion (of which about $3 billion went to Israel). Defense cuts involved gradual reduction of personnel and bases (including 1992 base closings in the Philippines) with some curtailment of various weapons systems, among them the B-2 bomber, MX and Midgetman missiles, and the Strategic Defense Initiative. Nevertheless, U.S. military spending for forces in Europe remained at about $150 billion per year. The two main presidential candidates largely agreed on the substance of defense cuts, with Gov. Bill Clinton placing somewhat greater emphasis than President Bush on economic security, industrial conversion to peacetime production, and a leaner, more mobile military.

Russian Aid and Chinese Trade. At a summer summit of the G-7 economic powers, a $24 billion multinational Russian assistance and debt-relief package was assembled in an effort to shore up Russia's fragile democratic institutions. Another $20 billion in aid to the 14 other former Soviet republics was considered. By year's end, though, except for some humanitarian relief, agricultural credits, and assistance in dismantling nuclear forces and employing nuclear engineers (for fear of their migration to the Third World), little aid had been delivered. Notwithstanding about $1 billion in immediate International Monetary Fund (IMF) credits (pushed by Washington), hopes for Moscow's inclusion in the organization dimmed as clear indications of improvement in the Russian (and Ukrainian) economy or effective measures to strengthen its currency failed to appear.

Among the contrasting election-campaign themes was support, or lack of it, for human rights and democracy, particularly regarding China. Rights groups criticized the administration's grant of most-favored-nation trade status to China, and the administration countered that it best could encourage reform by continuing contact. To ease pressure about missing POWs from the Vietnam war, an agreement with Vietnam for a final full accounting was announced in late October, and on December 14 the administration eased trade curbs, allowing U.S. firms to do business with Vietnam.

Problems of European Security. The ethnic strife in the former Yugoslavia verged on genocide in 1992, and U.S. policymakers had little success in efforts to stop the bloodshed. After hoping the Europeans would devise their own solution, Washington in May finally backed UN and North Atlantic Treaty Organization (NATO) initiatives to embargo trade with Belgrade and arms shipments to all sides, and protect relief convoys with force if necessary. Later in the year this outside intervention was extended to a naval blockade and a Serbian "no-fly" zone was discussed. However, given uncertainties about the terrain and guerrilla war, actual deployment of UN forces was slow and hesitant, with no U.S. contingents. Governor Clinton criticized the administration's hesitancy, though less emphatically as the election approached. On December 15, NATO and the UN agreed to coordinate their efforts to end the fighting.

Because of other potential national and ethnic explosions in the former Soviet sphere, the Balkans, and in Cyprus, NATO and a new North Atlantic Cooperation Council (including Eastern European countries, Russia, and other former Soviet republics) prepared possible strategies for conflict management and peacekeeping. Tension nevertheless persisted between the United States and some of its key allies in both Europe and Asia.

With no visible superpower threat, NATO planning revolved around the proper role of the alliance vis-à-vis European institutions, such as the European Community (EC), in devising security policy for smaller threats both inside and outside Europe. The new but unratified EC Maastricht accords—themselves very controversial—regarding a common Euro-defense and currency caused worries in Washington and London that the Western European Union (WEU) or a joint French-German military force might signal a more independent European military doctrine.

Trade Negotiations. Further difficulties with Europe burst into the open in the autumn as U.S. negotiators protested the long-stalled General Agreement on Tariffs and Trade (GATT) tariff-reduction talks, citing French opposition to reducing European farm subsidies. At length, and ultimately successful, the United States brought pressure on France's EC partners through threatened higher tariffs on wine and edible-oil imports; the specter of a trade war loomed at a time of acute global recession. A highly publicized "get tough" trade trip to Japan in January during which the president was accompanied by U.S. auto executives, also ended without clear results. Japanese rice imports remained the last key issue in the way of a new GATT agreement.

U.S.-African Affairs. As bad as were the effects of unemployment in the Northern Hemisphere, however, they did not begin to rival the

On December 4, Chairman of the Joint Chiefs of Staff Colin Powell (right) and Secretary of Defense Dick Cheney discussed the ordering of U.S. military forces to help deliver relief supplies to war-torn Somalia.

© Jeffrey Markowitz/Sygma

rigors of famine and destitution in some African regions, notably war-torn Somalia. Under pressure from critics who termed the imbroglio in Yugoslavia a "rich man's war" and derided the West's focus on it, Washington joined stepped-up UN and private relief efforts to flood Somalia with food and supplies, much of which was stolen by bandits and warring factions. Finally, in December, Bush ordered some 30,000 U.S. troops to Somalia to ensure the safe delivery of relief supplies.

In South Africa, after the Bush administration had removed economic (though not military) sanctions against the white-minority regime, civil violence in 1992 threatened to unravel the frail progress toward a new constitution and majority rule. At the same time, in neighboring Angola former U.S. client Jonas Savimbi refused to abide by the outcome of free elections. Notwithstanding a growing demand for UN peacekeeping troops in various African, Asian, European, and Latin American trouble spots, the United States continued in arrears in its UN financial assessments.

Problems of East Asian Security. As the United States reduced its direct Asian military presence, a corresponding buildup of Asian arms began. Moreover, the Japanese-Russian territorial (Kuril Islands) dispute and China's future naval role in contesting its claims to the Spratly Islands and other territories caused nagging concern. However, tension over possible North Korean nuclear developments seemed to abate with negotiation and mutual assurances, even though no effective inspection agreement could be reached.

Inter-American Affairs. In Western Hemispheric affairs, a key debate emerged about the prospective costs and benefits of the North American Free Trade Agreement (NAFTA), signed by the United States, Canada, and Mexico in December. Organized labor and environmentalists in the United States accused the Bush administration of selling out thousands of U.S. manufacturing jobs to corporate interests seeking cheaper labor south of the border. Defenders pointed to a potential boom in export-oriented jobs in the United States. Governor Clinton supported NAFTA, but with stipulations about U.S. worker retraining and environmental reform in Mexico.

The environment was the theme of an unprecedented worldwide gathering of governmental and nongovernmental organizations in Rio de Janeiro in June. After agreeing to certain environmental cleanup provisions regarding the ozone layer, the Bush administration insisted on weakening a treaty to cut emissions of "greenhouse" gases supposedly causing global warming, and it opposed action to preserve "biodiversity" of species. The administration, which did agree to somewhat increased environmental aid (but not to an aid target level), cited economic costs as well as lack of convincing scientific evidence on climate change for its opposition to stringent limits. Although the Bush administration quietly increased spending on global population control by 30%, it was branded by critics as having reneged on promises of an "environmental presidency."

Global Concerns. All in all, issues of trade and economic competition dominated the news and public dialogue in the United States in 1992, while military and traditional security policy took second place. Still, there was little in-depth consideration of the realities of a global economy: debt relief (75% of El Salvador's debt was forgiven), capital movements, poverty, global monetary pressures, and the implications of regional economic pacts. The Bush administration would leave office with a set of achievements including the anti-Iraqi coalition, nuclear demobilization, the NAFTA agreement, and Arab-Israeli peace talks, inconclusive though they were. But unmet problems remained.

FREDERIC S. PEARSON, *Wayne State University*

URUGUAY

President Luis Alberto Lacalle's battle to get a privatization program in place dominated events in Uruguay in 1992.

Privatization. In a mid-December referendum, Uruguayans overwhelmingly threw out President LaCalle's privatization program. The battle had started in January when, rejecting labor demands, Lacalle declared he would not modify his neoliberal privatization programs. By decree, rather than awaiting legislative action, the government in February offered to sell the nation's printing plant; administration of several ports, air terminals, and grain silos; and a navy oil tanker.

The Uruguayan electorate rejected Lacalle's program in a midyear advisory vote but the president disregarded the electorate's position because of low voter turnout. On October 1, 30% of the country's electors voted in favor of a national referendum on the issue. As President Lacalle's plan was not approved, privatization of much of ANTEL, the telephone company, was blocked. At least eight bids for a 49% share of the state-owned phone company had been received from Europe and the United States.

Politics. Dissatisfied that the legislature had enacted only two of the five programs he promised when elected in late 1989, Lacalle on January 30 called for his 13-member cabinet to resign. New ministers were named for economy and finance, industry and energy, housing, and environment. The others were reconfirmed.

Economics. The new cabinet contained a special component—the ministers of economy and finance, industry and energy, and agriculture, and the president of the Banco de la República—charged with making the industrial sector competitive with those of Uruguay's trading partners in the new regional trade bloc, Mercosur. The agreement forming Mercosur—comprising Argentina, Uruguay, Brazil, and Paraguay—was signed in June and was scheduled to be fully effective by the end of 1994. The first benefit from the new common market was a jump in Uruguayan trade with its Mercosur neighbors.

Meanwhile, two major integration projects involving Uruguay were approved, to be financed in part by private capital. Competitive bidding was scheduled on a 33.3-mi (53.6-km) toll bridge across the River Plate Estuary connecting Colonia, Uruguay, and Buenos Aires, Argentina. In June preliminary studies on a $1 billion Paraná-Paraguay Waterway project were authorized. The 2,065-mi (3 323-km) inland waterway for barge traffic would increase greatly the activity at Uruguay's port of Nueva Palmira. Financing also was approved in February for a privately owned free-trade zone in Montevideo.

Foreign Relations. Uruguay signed an accord with the United States and ten Latin American and Caribbean countries in June that called for continued progress toward free trade and strengthening of democracy.

President Lacalle rejected a June 15 decision by the U.S. Supreme Court that made it legal to kidnap fugitives from U.S. justice in foreign countries. He joined the chief executives of Chile, Argentina, Brazil, Bolivia, and Paraguay in saying the action was contrary to the region's tradition of judicial protection.

Treasure. The Lacalle government on June 30 issued its plan for distribution of its 50% share of whatever is retrieved from a reputed $500 million treasure aboard the *Preciado,* which was sunk in 1792 by English pirates near the port of Montevideo. Disregarding claims by several of the continent's indigenous groups to the gold, silver, and jewels, Lacalle indicated that they would be sold and the proceeds devoted to funding social programs. Half of the treasure recovered from the wreckage, in 26 ft (8 m) of water, was to go to the salvage operators.

LARRY L. PIPPIN
University of the Pacific

UTAH

Unprecedented voter turnout, a unique presidential-election result, conservative victories in state elections—with only two notable exceptions—and controversial initiatives marked the 1992 elections in Utah.

Voter Turnout. More Utah voters went to the polls in 1992 than ever before. Approximately half of those registered voted in the September primary, and a record 741,076 cast ballots for president in November—a 13.2% increase over the previous high, set four years earlier. Nearly two thirds of the almost 1.1 million voting-age residents of the state voted.

National Elections. Presidential-election results indicated that Utah is one of the most conservative states in the nation. Traditional voting patterns gave George Bush Utah's five

UTAH • Information Highlights

Area: 84,899 sq mi (219 889 km²).
Population (July 1, 1991 est.): 1,770,000.
Chief Cities (1990 census): Salt Lake City, the capital, 159,936; West Valley City, 86,976; Provo, 86,835.
Government (1992): *Chief Officers*—governor, Norman H. Bangerter (R); lt. gov., W. Val Oveson (R). *Legislature*—Senate, 29 members; House of Representatives, 75 members.
State Finances (fiscal year 1991): *Revenue,* $4,344,000,000; *expenditure,* $4,108,000,000.
Personal Income (1991): $25,890,000,000; per capita, $14,625.
Labor Force (June 1992): *Civilian labor force,* 818,200; *unemployed,* 39,600 (4.8% of total force).
Education: *Enrollment* (fall 1990)—public elementary schools, 326,266; public secondary, 121,625; colleges and universities, 121,303. *Public school expenditures* (1990), $1,245,652,000.

electoral votes with 43% of the popular vote. Ross Perot came in second with 27%, and Bill Clinton, the national victor, was third with 25%. Only 182,850 Utah voters cast ballots for the president-elect. James "Bo" Gritz, an ultraconservative, captured 4% of the vote.

Utah's 1993 congressional delegation would have two new faces, but the political makeup would be the same. Republicans would continue to hold both Senate seats. Sen. Orrin Hatch would be joined by Robert Bennett, who defeated Democratic Rep. Wayne Owens by a wide margin to replace retiring Jake Garn.

In the race to replace Congressman Owens in Utah's 2d District, Democrat Karen Shepherd defeated Republican Enid Greene in a close race, winning by just more than 9,000 votes. This was an anomaly in Utah politics. Shepherd, a businesswoman and state senator, favors abortion rights, whereas the Mormon Church and most of Utah's citizens oppose abortion rights. In the state's rural districts both congressional incumbents won easily. In the 1st District, James Hansen won a seventh term by a 65%-to-28% margin over Democrat Ron Holt. In another, biennial anomaly, Democrat Bill Orton was reelected in the 3d District, considered one of the country's GOP strongholds, defeating Republican Richard Harrington 59% to 37%.

State Elections. Utah voters mostly stayed with status-quo Republicans in statewide races. GOP candidate Mike Leavitt was elected governor with 43% of the vote. Independent candidate Merrill Cook garnered an impressive 34%, followed by the Democratic candidate, Stewart Hanson, with only 23%. The only Democrat to win a state office was Jan Graham, a woman, who narrowly defeated Republican Scott Burns to become attorney general. Utah Republicans also kept a firm hold on the legislature—securing a 49–26 majority in the House and an 18–11 advantage in the Senate.

Initiatives. An initiative that would have allowed Utah counties to institute pari-mutuel betting by local option was defeated soundly. Proponents had no difficulty collecting the 100,000 signatures needed to get the proposal on the ballot, but they failed to take account of the Mormon Church, whose leaders denounced pari-mutuel betting as gambling and said it would open the state to casino gambling and immorality. The antibetting group eventually raised more than $530,000 to launch a major campaign to defeat the measure. Proponents raised only $130,000. The final result was that 40% voted for the initiative; 60% voted against.

In a second initiative, Salt Lake county voters were asked to vote for or against a proposal to add one fourth of one percent to the sales tax charged in the county for the purpose of funding an expanded transportation system in the Salt Lake valley, including a light rail, expanded bus system, and additional lanes on Interstate I-15 to alleviate traffic gridlock. This also was defeated—57% to 43%.

LORENZO K. KIMBALL, *University of Utah*

VENEZUELA

Confidence in Venezuelan democracy was shaken on Feb. 4, 1992, when the country experienced its first coup attempt in nearly 30 years. A group of young officers, led by members of the 1976 class of the Venezuelan military academy, took over the downtown airstrip in Caracas and attacked the presidential residence. Another contingent assaulted the Miraflores presidential palace and came within yards of capturing or assassinating the president, Carlos Andrés Pérez. Pérez evaded the rebels, however, and made his way to a television studio where he made a series of speeches asking for army loyalty. After heavy fighting, loyal troops defeated the coup and its leader—Lt. Col. Hugo Chávez Frías—was arrested along with his surviving fellow plotters. An estimated 80 soldiers and civilians died in the uprising and 1,130 soldiers were arrested.

VENEZUELA • Information Highlights

Official Name: Republic of Venezuela.
Location: Northern coast of South America.
Area: 352,143 sq mi (912 050 km²).
Population (mid-1992 est.): 18,900,000.
Chief Cities (June 30, 1990 est., incl. suburbs): Caracas, the capital, 3,435,795; Maracaibo, 1,400,643; Valencia, 1,274,354.
Government: *Head of state and government,* Carlos Andrés Pérez, president (took office February 1989). *Legislature*—National Congress: Senate and Chamber of Deputies.
Monetary Unit: Bolívar (76.90 bolívares equal U.S.$1, floating rate, Nov. 2, 1992).
Gross Domestic Product (1990 est. U.S.$): $42,400,000,000.
Economic Index (Caracas, 1990): *Consumer Prices* (1984 = 100), all items, 534.8; food, 960.8.
Foreign Trade (1990 U.S.$): *Imports,* $6,365,000,000; *exports,* $17,586,000,000.

© Felipe Amilibia/Gamma-Liaison

A dusk-to-dawn curfew was imposed in Venezuela in late November during the second unsuccessful coup attempt of 1992. The rebels decried President Carlos Andrés Pérez for presiding over an economic system that ignored the nation's poor.

The conspirators involved appear to have been concentrated in a single army battalion of paratroopers. However, fears for democracy were not assuaged by their defeat because many Venezuelans, both outside the military and within it, shared some of the rebels' aims, if not their methods. In the days following the failed attempt, there were demonstrations calling for the release of and amnesty for Chávez, who was regarded as a hero by many. When former President Rafael Caldera of the opposition Social Christian Party (COPEI) argued that the coup attempt should be understood as a signal of the population's frustrations, his presidential prospects blossomed overnight. According to polls, however, even Caldera was eclipsed in popularity for a time by Chávez.

The Economy and Discontent. The coup attempt was baffling to outsiders because the Pérez government was regarded as an economic success story. Venezuela's gross domestic product (GDP) had grown by 9.2% in 1991 and continued to rise at a similar pace in the first half of 1992. Inflation peaked at 80% in 1989 and since had fallen to about 30%. Growth was expected to slow to 4% for 1992 due to falling oil prices, but private-sector growth in construction, manufacturing, and services was high. Reserves were strong at $13.5 billion, and unemployment was falling. Furthermore, with new free-trade arrangements in force with Colombia, the Andean Pact, and Mexico, nontraditional exports were expected to expand, and foreign investment was flowing in.

While the benefits of this recovery and expansion had not yet trickled down to much of the population, the economic roots of the crisis were not as strong as the political roots. Venezuelans were upset about deteriorating public services, growing crime, and especially corruption. All three problems, as well as past economic troubles, were blamed on a political "establishment," staffed by the leaders of the two largest parties, Pérez' Acción Democrática (AD) and COPEI, that had become unaccountable to the people.

The government responded to this discontent by seeking elite consensus and promoting constitutional reforms. Pérez invited COPEI to join his cabinet, but a coalition was made impossible by tensions within the opposition party between Caldera, who strongly opposed the government's economic policies, and party Secretary-General Eduardo Fernández, who largely supported them. Two COPEI leaders were allowed to join the cabinet without formal party backing, but they were forced to resign when Pérez announced his intention to attend the Earth Summit in Rio de Janeiro. The only concrete result of the drive for consensus was an agreement between AD and the Fernández wing of COPEI to support a tax increase, budget cuts, and accelerated privatization to close a budget deficit in the second half of the year caused by falling oil prices.

Reforms. Although calls for a new constitution were rejected by AD and COPEI, many possible reforms were discussed, including shortening Pérez' term to four years, using single-member districts in congressional elections, banning presidential reelection, and prohibiting simultaneous ownership of newspapers and broadcast media. The Chamber of Deputies passed more than 100 amendments but the Senate defeated them all in September. Corruption charges were leveled against former President Jaime Lusinchi and AD union leader Antonio Ríos but Lusinchi proved hard to locate. After Ríos was released from detention, Lusinchi's house was bombed and Ríos was wounded critically in a drive-by shooting. A new group called the Bolivarian Liberation Forces, echoing the rhetoric of the coup plotters, claimed responsibility.

The inadequacy of the government's response to the political crisis became plain on November 27, when a second coup—involving 1,200 troops led by air-force and navy officers—was attempted. After 12 hours of intense fighting, which included aerial bombardment of the presidential palace in downtown Caracas, loyal troops defeated the rebels, but at a cost of more than 200 dead and much property damage due to civilian looting.

MICHAEL COPPEDGE
Johns Hopkins University

VERMONT

In Vermont during 1992, hopes for a rapid recovery from the economic recession were dashed by IBM's downsizing, Digital's decision to leave the area, and General Electric's layoffs in Rutland and Burlington.

Elections. Vermont followed the nation in the November election by voting for the second time in its history for the Democratic candidate for president, giving Bill Clinton a margin of 46% to 32% for George Bush and 22% for Ross Perot. The percentage turnout was the largest since 1964. Democratic Gov. Howard Dean was elected to a full term; and U.S. Sen. Patrick Leahy, also a Democrat, together with Vermont's lone congressman, Independent (and self-styled socialist) Bernard Sanders, handily won reelection. Democrats prevailed in the lower house of the state legislature as well, with their largest majority ever.

The Republican candidate for lieutenant-governor, Barbara Snelling—widow of Governor Dean's predecessor, Richard A. Snelling—was one of the two Republicans to win state-wide office. She would preside over a Senate that would include 16 Republicans and 14 Democrats—the first Republican-controlled Senate in almost a decade. A record number of women were elected to the state legislature.

Events in the Capital. The 1992 legislature, almost evenly divided between the parties, saw much acrimony over the budget deficit and taxes. Responding to a troubled economy and lagging state revenues, the legislators passed a $600 million budget that reflected cuts in welfare benefits and state education aid but retained property-tax relief. The legislature also created a Health Care Authority to select among alternative systems of universal access to health care; included homosexuals in the state's antidiscrimination law; provided a family-leave law; took initial action on a constitutional amendment to ease denial of bail to dangerous criminals; and passed a series of bills to stimulate business. Welfare reform and measures to weaken the state's environmental controls failed.

Vermont's state capital of Montpelier saw more than political excitement when an ice jam on the Winooski River in March backed floodwaters up into the business section of the city. Although the flood abated within the day, it left more than $5 million in damage.

In June the state Supreme Court rejected Abenaki Indian claims to lands in northwestern Vermont, saying those claims had been extinguished "by the increasing weight of history." The decision overruled a lower court ruling that had recognized "aboriginal rights" for Abenakis to fish in their ancestral homes without state licenses.

Campus Developments. In April, John M. McCardle, interim president of Middlebury College, was named president and within the month confronted students condemning the college for inadequate progress toward the goal of a graduating class with 10% minorities. In August the University of Vermont, also the scene of demands for greater minority representation, accepted the resignation of its provost, the university's highest-ranking black official. Generating even greater public protest than minority concerns, however, was the fact that the provost had received a substantial severance payment from the financially strapped

---

VERMONT • Information Highlights

Area: 9,614 sq mi (24 900 km²).

Population (July 1, 1991 est.): 567,000.

Chief Cities (1990 census): Montpelier, the capital, 8,247; Burlington, 39,127; Rutland, 18,230.

Government (1992): *Chief Officer*—governor, Howard B. Dean (D). *General Assembly*—Senate, 30 members; House of Representatives, 150 members.

State Finances (fiscal year 1991): *Revenue,* $1,703,000,000; *expenditure,* $1,736,000,000.

Personal Income (1991): $10,198,000,000; per capita, $17,997.

Labor Force (June 1992): *Civilian labor force,* 312,400; *unemployed,* 21,900 (7.0% of total force).

Education: *Enrollment* (fall 1990)—public elementary schools, 70,860; public secondary, 24,902; colleges and universities, 36,398. *Public school expenditures* (1990), $506,685,000.

university. This was the third "golden parachute" awarded in a year to a top administrator who had been with the university less than two years.

ROBERT V. DANIELS and
SAMUEL B. HAND
University of Vermont

VIETNAM

A new Vietnamese constitution was approved in March 1992, but a Communist Party leader was quoted in the press as saying that it would not change much. The party retained the right to play a leading role in all aspects of Vietnamese society.

Politics. Premier Vo Van Kiet, a leading advocate of reform, was reelected to head the government, but he was not appointed to the politburo's standing committee, which included party chief Do Muoi, President Le Duc Ahn, and ideology chief Dao Duy Tung. Thus, Kiet was excluded from the most important decision-making body. His old mentor, former party leader Nguyen Van Linh, openly accused Kiet and his wife of corruption.

The vast majority of the Vietnamese people are peasant farmers. For them, the most important feature of the new constitution was that it allowed them to hold land under a form of contract with the government, and they even could pass the land on to their children. But the state also could take back the land if it decided it was not being put to good use.

The last of some 100,000 people who were taken prisoner when the Communists conquered South Vietnam in 1975 were released in 1992. But the amnesty did not apply to some 2,000 people jailed for political offenses after 1975. Vietnamese newspapers still were controlled directly or indirectly by the state, but they were becoming somewhat more daring in exposing corruption and mismanagement by the ruling party.

Economics. Vietnam's Communist leaders thought they could have economic growth by allowing some scope for private enterprise while keeping a monopoly on political power. They passed laws to attract foreign business

people to come and invest in joint-venture operations with Vietnamese private and state-owned companies. Since 1986 about $3 billion had been invested by foreigners. But a leading Vietnamese economist estimated that Vietnam would have to attract $2.5 billion per year for ten years in order to reach self-sustaining growth.

The largest group of foreign investors was Taiwanese, who often had family ties among the remaining ethnic Chinese living in Vietnam. (Many Chinese were driven out of Vietnam after 1975.) Taiwan and Vietnam each created new airlines in 1992 for the purpose of flying between the two countries. China had objected to Vietnam's plans to use its national airlines.

Of the 2 million ethnic Vietnamese living abroad—half in the United States—a few had returned to their native land and set up private businesses, often to help family members who remained in Vietnam. The overseas Vietnamese also were sending $500 million per year to help their families in Vietnam, a sum equal to about one quarter of Vietnam's export earnings. About 60,000 overseas Vietnamese went to Vietnam for brief visits in 1992. Many were doctors, lawyers, and teachers who spent time giving seminars and spreading new ideas in a country that long has been isolated by war and its rigid political system.

Vietnam's state-owned telecommunications company was modernizing its equipment rapidly with the $15 million to $20 million profits it earned each year from overseas Vietnamese calling home. Australia had installed three satellite earth stations, while France and Germany installed digital switching systems.

Vietnam was believed to have up to 3 billion barrels of oil reserves, and it had begun auctioning off concessions in some of the richest areas. The Hanoi government also wanted to build an oil refinery as a prestige item and to guarantee its fuel supply.

Foreign Relations. A U.S. economic embargo of Vietnam had been in effect since the Vietnamese invasion of Cambodia in 1978. But few countries honored it after Vietnam withdrew its forces from Cambodia. Japan resumed economic aid to Vietnam after the 1992 U.S. election. The United States itself began to ease restrictions on economic contacts in return for Hanoi's cooperation in accounting for U.S. MIAs lost in the Vietnam war. Hanoi was eager for the United States to end its ban on aid by the World Bank.

In July the Association of Southeast Asian Nations (ASEAN), which includes most of Vietnam's non-Communist neighbors, signed a treaty of friendship and cooperation with Vietnam, which eventually would be granted full membership in the association.

PETER A. POOLE
Author
"Eight Presidents and Indochina"

VIETNAM • Information Highlights

Official Name: Socialist Republic of Vietnam.
Location: Southeast Asia.
Area: 127,243 sq mi (329 560 km²).
Population (mid-1992 est.): 69,200,000.
Chief Cities (April 1, 1989 census): Hanoi, the capital, 3,056,146; Ho Chi Minh City, 3,169,135.
Government: Communist Party secretary, Do Muoi.
Monetary Unit: Dong (9,200 dongs equal U.S.$1, March 1992).
Gross National Product (1990 est. U.S.$): $15,200,-000,000.

VIRGINIA

Crime, tragedies in transportation, and politics made headlines in Virginia in 1992.

Elections. The political campaigns resulted in two historic elections and one historic debate. In October the three presidential candidates—George Bush, Bill Clinton, and Ross Perot—went to the University of Richmond for the first presidential debate in which the public did the questioning. On November 3, Democrat Leslie L. Byrne became the first woman from the state to be elected to the U.S. Congress and Democrat Robert C. Scott became the first black from Virginia to be chosen a U.S. congressman in a century. Overall, eight incumbent U.S. congressmen were reelected, with Republican Robert W. Goodlatte winning the third open seat. The results divided the state's U.S. House delegation seven to four in favor of Democrats.

In the presidential race, the big news came when Gov. L. Douglas Wilder dropped out early in the year. On election day the state fought the national tide and favored President Bush over Governor Clinton, 45% to 41%, with independent Ross Perot capturing 14%. The voters also approved three bond issues, totaling $613 million, and gave up Virginia's status as the last state to eschew the election of school-board members.

Crime. Former coal miner Roger Keith Coleman was executed in May for the rape-murder of his sister-in-law in 1981. Although he complained that archaic court rules barred evidence that could exonerate him, he failed a lie-detector test on his execution day.

In a case suitable for a TV miniseries, Beverly Anne Monroe was convicted in November of murdering her millionaire lover, Robert de la Burde. The 60-year-old land speculator, art collector, and self-proclaimed French count was shot with his own gun in a scene staged to look like a suicide. Four days before the shoot-

© Richmond Newspapers

In 1992, Leslie L. Byrne, a 46-year-old Democratic member of the Virginia House of Delegates since 1986, became the first woman from the state to be elected to the U.S. House.

ing, Monroe discovered that de la Burde had conceived a child with another woman in a quest for a male heir.

Marshall Honaker, sheriff of Bristol for almost 20 years and head of the National Sheriffs' Association, shot himself when a federal grand-jury investigation showed that he had pilfered almost $700,000 in city money over six years.

U.S. Sen. Charles S. Robb also was a federal grand-jury target. A jury in Norfolk began investigating Robb's office in June after he said his staff possessed a tape made secretly from Governor Wilder's car telephone. Three of Robb's aides resigned and pleaded guilty to violating federal election and wiretapping laws.

Legislature and Other Headlines. The legislature passed a $28 billion two-year budget and made stalking a crime. In October, Governor Wilder and Jack Kent Cooke, millionaire owner of professional football's Washington Redskins, abandoned a plan announced in July to move the Redskins to a proposed stadium in Alexandria.

The *Richmond News-Leader*, the capital's 100-year-old afternoon newspaper, died. An Australian syndicate that spent $5 million on chances for a state lottery drawing won $27 million.

Tragedies. Seven Navy reserve fliers were killed in June when a Navy helicopter exploded in midair and crashed into Lynnhaven Bay at Virginia Beach. Less than one month later, three Marines and four civilians were killed when an experimental military aircraft crashed

---

VIRGINIA • Information Highlights

Area: 40,767 sq mi (105 586 km²).

Population (July 1, 1991 est.): 6,286,000.

Chief Cities (1990 census): Richmond, the capital, 203,056; Virginia Beach, 393,069; Norfolk, 261,229; Newport News, 170,045; Chesapeake, 151,976.

Government (1992): *Chief Officers*—governor, L. Douglas Wilder (D); lt. gov., Donald S. Beyer, Jr. (D). *General Assembly*—Senate, 40 members; House of Delegates, 100 members.

State Finances (fiscal year 1991): *Revenue,* $14,523,000,000; *expenditure,* $13,352,000,000.

Personal Income (1991): $126,237,000,000; per capita, $20,082.

Labor Force (June 1992): *Civilian labor force,* 3,391,100; *unemployed,* 216,800 (6.4% of total force).

Education: *Enrollment* (fall 1990)—public elementary schools, 728,282; public secondary, 270,319; colleges and universities, 353,284. *Public school expenditures* (1990), $5,048,423,000.

into the Potomac River at the Quantico Marine Base.

Two people were killed and 44 were injured in a chain-reaction accident involving more than 60 cars on fog-shrouded Afton Mountain in April. In August, 77 people were injured when an Amtrak train derailed in Newport News at the same place an April derailment killed one person and injured 53.

ED NEWLAND, *"Richmond Times-Dispatch"*

WASHINGTON

An employment cut at Boeing, the highest state unemployment rate in more than five years (7.7% in March 1992), and the closure of two major Northwest retail chains were signs that the national economic slowdown was being felt in Washington state in 1992.

Elections. Democrats made major gains in Washington's 1992 elections. The state contributed its 11 electoral votes to Arkansas Gov. Bill Clinton's presidential victory and sent state Sen. Patty Murray (D-Seattle) to the U.S. Senate. Murray won the seat vacated by Sen. Brock Adams, who dropped his reelection effort after published allegations of sexual misconduct with women staffers. Democrats took eight of the state's nine congressional seats, won six of eight partisan state offices, increased their majority in the state House of Representatives, and gained a majority in the state Senate. Democrat Mike Lowry, a former congressman, was elected governor, defeating Republican Attorney General Ken Eikenberry.

State voters passed initiatives limiting terms of state and congressional officials and restricting political contributions.

Business. A sluggish airline industry caused the Boeing Company to cut its state work force from 104,700 to 98,000. At the same time, the company began preliminary production work on the model 777, to be the world's largest

WASHINGTON • Information Highlights

Area: 68,139 sq mi (176 479 km²).
Population (July 1, 1991 est.): 5,018,000.
Chief Cities (1990 census): Olympia, the capital, 33,840; Seattle, 516,259; Spokane, 177,196; Tacoma, 176,664.
Government (1992): *Chief Officers—governor,* Booth Gardner (D); lt. gov., Joel Pritchard (R). *Legislature*—Senate, 49 members; House of Representatives, 98 members.
State Finances (fiscal year 1991): *Revenue,* $16,394,000,000; *expenditure,* $15,666,000,000.
Personal Income (1991): $97,766,000,000; per capita, $19,484.
Labor Force (June 1992): *Civilian labor force,* 2,598,400; *unemployed,* 176,300 (6.8% of total force).
Education: *Enrollment* (fall 1990)—public elementary schools, 612,597; public secondary, 227,112; colleges and universities, 263,278. *Public school expenditures* (1990), $3,922,541,000.

twin-engine jetliner, with a capacity of more than 400 passengers.

A difficult year for retailers was marked by the bankruptcy and closure of Frederick & Nelson, a 63-year-old Seattle-based department-store chain, and Pay 'N Pak, a Kent-based hardware chain. But strong sales and new products fueled the continued success of software giant Microsoft, whose chairman, Bill Gates, was named by *Forbes* magazine in October as the richest person in the United States, worth an estimated $6.3 billion.

Environment. Dissatisfied with a timber-harvest plan submitted by the U.S. Forest Service, U.S. District Judge William Dwyer renewed his restrictions on timber sales in Northwest old-growth forests to protect the habitat of the spotted owl. Industry sources said the restrictions threatened tens of thousands of jobs in Washington, Oregon, and northern California.

Crime. Joseph Meling, an Olympia-area insurance agent, was arrested by the Federal Bureau of Investigation (FBI) and charged in a

© Steve Schneider/Sipa

Washington state Sen. Patty Murray campaigned for the U.S. Senate as a "mom in tennis shoes." Running as a political outsider, the 42-year-old Democrat defeated Rod Chandler for the seat vacated by Sen. Brock Adams, who retired. Murray had been elected to the state Senate in 1988 and became its Democratic whip in 1990. She was one of four women newly elected to the U.S. Senate in 1992.

1991 product-tampering case that resulted in two deaths and caused a nationwide recall of Sudafed cold capsules. In Wenatchee three boys admitted starting a campfire that got out of control due to high winds and destroyed 18 homes and 17 apartment units, causing more than $5 million in damage. In the Seattle-Everett area, more than 80 arson fires set over a three-month period caused about $10 million in damage.

Weather. A drought in the usually moist Puget Sound area prompted mandatory water-use restrictions. Seattle residents were banned from watering their lawns all summer. By November regular rainfall had resumed.

Science. Two University of Washington scientists, Edmond Fischer and Edwin Krebs, received the Nobel Prize in Physiology or Medicine for research that advanced knowledge about cellular processes, aiding in the understanding of diabetes, Alzheimer's disease, and organ transplantation.

Sports. With the approval of major-league baseball owners, the Seattle Mariners were sold to a largely Japanese-financed group of local buyers.

JACK BROOM
"Seattle Times"

WASHINGTON, DC

With the highest murder rate in the United States, the nation's capital in 1992 appeared to some observers to be a house divided, a community split into warring camps. Officials of the federal government, and especially of the House of Representatives' oversight District of Columbia Committee, called for restoring the city's death penalty. At the same time, local government officials, jealous of their recently won prerogatives under the limited home rule granted them by the U.S. Congress, deplored the failure of the central government to help the nation's beleaguered cities in general, as well as Washington, DC, in particular.

Crime. Nowhere was the divide between white and black, rich and poor, national and local more flagrant than in the historic precinct of Capitol Hill. A neighborhood of 19th-century row houses and well-kept gardens lately gentrified by affluent, mostly white, urban homesteaders, usually at the expense of evicted black tenants, the Hill overlooks the Capitol building and Library of Congress to the west and the ravaged, crime-ridden slum of Anacostia to the east. Street crime on the Hill had become a subject of heated argument after several highly publicized crimes involving prominent victims took place there; among them was the mugging of the wife of Sen. Kent Conrad (D-ND) in December 1991. Then, on Jan. 11, 1992, Tom Barnes—a 25-year-old legislative assistant to Democratic Sen. Richard Shelby of Alabama—was shot and killed in the area by a mugger.

The Barnes killing brought the problem to a head. The situation prompted vehement demands, most notably from Senator Shelby himself, for a restoration of capital punishment in the city. Meanwhile, according to a study undertaken by the National Center on Institutions and Alternatives released in April, some 42% of black men in the capital aged 18 through 35 were caught in the workings of the criminal-justice system on any given day of the year. In September, fighting back tears of frustration, Police Chief Isaac Fulwood, Jr., resigned, to be replaced only in November by Fred Thomas, a former city patrolman.

Finances. In July the House passed a fiscal 1993 spending bill for the city providing for $714 million in federal funds. Included was a one-time grant of $30.8 million to fight crime. The bill also authorized the city to spend $3.95 billion in locally raised revenue. Initially vetoed by President George Bush because it failed to prohibit spending for abortions, the bill was redrafted with the prohibition and duly passed. The bill's final version also prohibited the city from using federal money to implement its "domestic partnership" law, enacted by the City Council earlier in the year. The law would permit homosexual and unmarried companions of city employees to receive city health-care benefits as do spouses of employees.

Elections. The September Democratic primary yielded two altogether expected results: landslides for both Arkansas Gov. Bill Clinton in the race for the presidential nomination (74% of the vote) and former Mayor Marion Barry (70%) in a race for the City Council seat from Anacostia's Eighth Ward (the city's poorest). Barry recently had completed a six-month prison term for cocaine possession, and his triumphant victory was unsettling to many, perhaps including Democratic Mayor Sharon Pratt Kelly, who was not up for reelection.

In November's general election all of the Democrats on the ballot swept into office in a landslide. Clinton received 86% of the vote to President Bush's 9% and independent candidate Ross Perot's 4%. Eleanor Holmes Norton, also a Democrat, won a second term as the city's nonvoting delegate to the U.S. House of Representatives.

A referendum on the death penalty, placed on the ballot by Congress in its July authorization bill, was defeated soundly by a two-to-one margin.

Sports. Professional football's Washington Redskins, after triumphing over the Buffalo Bills in Super Bowl XXVI, were denied a shot at Super Bowl XXVII. The team weathered a series of late-season defeats to qualify for the play-offs again, but ultimately were defeated by the San Francisco 49ers.

JOHN S. COX

WEST VIRGINIA

Politics and economic struggles marked much of the year in West Virginia.

Elections. The majority of registered Democrats went to the polls in record numbers on Nov. 3, 1992, giving the state's five electoral votes to Bill Clinton and Al Gore. Voters also elected Gov. Gaston Caperton to a second four-year term and returned the three incumbents to the U.S. House of Representatives. On the state level Democrats gained five seats in the House of Delegates, making their majority 79 to 21. Only in the state Senate was there any GOP gain. There now would be two Republicans instead of one, making the margin 32D-2R.

Voters approved two amendments to the state constitution, one authorizing a bonus for veterans of all conflicts since Korea, the other clarifying and strengthening the rights of owners of tax-delinquent property.

Economy. In an apparent statement that voters still are suffering financially, they soundly defeated a third amendment which would have allowed local lawmakers to institute new taxes with a 50% majority vote. Currently it takes a 60% vote to approve new levies. The defeat came at a time when the state's unemployment still was the nation's highest. In July, for example, when the national average was 7.6%, the unemployment rate in West Virginia was about 12%.

An independent survey in April ranked the state 48th (out of 50 states plus the District of Columbia) for fiscal strength. In addition to the unemployment rate, the poll specified the lack of any "rainy day" funds, a pension system funded at only 26.9% (the lowest in the nation), and the 13th-highest per-capita debt as special concerns for the state.

Legislature. Governor Caperton and the legislature struggled with major issues, most of them fiscal, during the year. Included were programs to provide new jobs, improve public-health services, and reorganize key administrative agencies. Lawmakers provided low-interest loans for those who wished to set up rural health clinics; stiffened penalties for domestic violence; approved tougher child-abuse statutes; and gave voters the right to approve or reject the existence of hazardous-waste dumps in their counties.

Although public-school salaries were up to 40th in the nation when the fall term began (compared with 50th two years earlier), higher-education salaries continued to lag. A task force formed to study the matter was due to issue a report before the opening of the 1993 legislative session. Skeptical professors in colleges and universities expressed strong dissatisfaction not only with substandard salaries and benefits but with general working conditions.

Much of the legislature's time was spent working on court-ordered changes in the penal institutions. This was spurred by the February escape of three convicted murderers from the high-security prison at Moundsville. The three prisoners were recaptured by mid-March but their flight led to the revelation of antiquated facilities that promoted the resignation of the corrections commissioner, the prison's warden, and the chairman of the parole board.

DONOVAN H. BOND
West Virginia University

WISCONSIN

The defeat of a Republican senator, protests at abortion clinics, and a welfare experiment highlighted 1992 in Wisconsin.

Elections. Wisconsin voters, in an independent mood, chose Democrat Russell F. Feingold as their new U.S. senator and favored Bill Clinton for president, but gave Republicans seven more seats in the state legislature.

Feingold, a state senator from Middleton, won a brutal Democratic primary by staying above the mud-slinging campaigns conducted by two opponents, 5th District Rep. Jim Moody and businessman Joseph Checota. He continued his humorous campaign, defeating two-term Republican Sen. Robert W. Kasten, Jr., in November.

Another Democratic state senator, Thomas Barrett, succeeded Moody in the U.S. House, while all other members of the congressional delegation were reelected. In the state legislature, the new Senate had 16 Democrats and 15 Republicans, with two vacancies, and the new Assembly had 52 Democrats and 47 Republicans.

Abortion Protests. Following demonstrations in other cities, Milwaukee was targeted for massive antiabortion protests. Thousands gathered for six weeks of protests beginning in June, then stayed on. Some 1,000 arrests were made, and the city's costs for policing and courts exceeded $1 million.

A humorous and coincidental moment in Wisconsin's U.S. Senate race: As Russell D. Feingold, a Democratic state senator, pounds the pavement looking for votes, the campaign bus of his opponent, incumbent Sen. Robert W. Kasten, Jr., passes by. The 39-year-old Feingold won by a margin of 53% to 47%.

© Morry Gash/NYT Pictures

Legislative Action. Facing fall elections, legislators passed a balanced budget bill but watered down or avoided proposals on gambling, juvenile crime, property-tax relief, and other key issues. A part of the $6.9 billion state budget was a $6 million package that included new standardized testing, teacher training, and incentives for more neighborhood control of schools. Republican Gov. Tommy G. Thompson angered Milwaukee Mayor John O. Norquist by vetoing the legislature's plan to add $22 million to $319 million in property-tax credits. He also vetoed a more equitable way to distribute the credits.

One of the most hotly contested issues was a plan proposed by Thompson for two-tier welfare experiments. The legislature finally approved a plan that would test whether the state's higher-than-average benefits under Aid for Families with Dependent Children (AFDC) attracted welfare families from other states. Under the plan, people who had lived in Wisconsin for less than six months and who applied for AFDC would receive welfare benefits equal to the AFDC benefits paid in their home state. A pilot program was to start on July 1, 1994.

After more heated debate, legislators approved a bill requiring parental consent for a minor's abortion, but allowed adult family members to substitute for the parent. Abortion foes opposed the latter provision.

Economy. While the state's economy continued to improve, the transition was slower than in past recoveries. Total nonfarm employment of 2,327,100 was expected to be 1.6% above the average level of 1991, and total personal income of $93.3 billion was expected to be 4.6% more than in 1991. Durable-goods-manufacturing employment was expected to languish at its current level for several years.

Dahmer Sentenced. Bringing an end to the criminal proceedings against Jeffrey L. Dahmer, a Milwaukee judge sentenced the serial killer to consecutive life sentences for each of the 15 murders committed in Wisconsin, a total of 957 years. A jury rejected Dahmer's plea of insanity, and Dahmer was committed to the Columbus Correctional Institution.

PAUL SALSINI
"Milwaukee Journal"

WISCONSIN • Information Highlights

Area: 56,153 sq mi (145 436 km²).
Population (July 1, 1991 est.): 4,955,000.
Chief Cities (1990 census): Madison, the capital, 191,262; Milwaukee, 628,088; Green Bay, 96,466.
Government (1992): *Chief Officers*—governor, Tommy G. Thompson (R); lt. gov., Scott McCallum (R). *Legislature*—Senate, 33 members; Assembly, 99 members.
State Finances (fiscal year 1991): *Revenue,* $14,137,000,000; *expenditure,* $12,448,000,000.
Personal Income (1991): $88,891,000,000; per capita, $17,939.
Labor Force (June 1992): *Civilian labor force,* 2,686,400; *unemployed,* 139,800 (5.2% of total force).
Education: *Enrollment* (fall 1990)—public elementary schools, 565,520; public secondary, 232,101; colleges and universities, 299,774. *Public school expenditures* (1990), $4,159,292,000.

WOMEN

The year 1992 was billed as "The Year of the Woman" and in U.S. politics at least, that proved to be true, as the number of women in elected jobs reached an all-time high. But while women made gains politically, they still faced discrimination in other areas, notably wages and career advancement.

Politics. Results of the November 3 election brought to six the number of women in the U.S. Senate, up from two. The 103d Congress also would see 47 women in the House of Representatives, an increase of 19. Additionally, there were now 71 women holding statewide elected offices at the executive level, according to the Center for American Women and Politics at Rutgers University. Most of the women candidates were Democrats, a fact many analysts attributed to the Republican Party's alienation of some women with its anti-abortion stance.

California became the first state ever to send two women to the U.S. Senate when voters there elected former San Francisco Mayor Dianne Feinstein and U.S. Rep. Barbara Boxer, both Democrats. Also elected to the Senate were Carol Moseley Braun, a Cook county, IL, Democrat (*see* BIOGRAPHY), and Patty Murray, a Washington state Democrat.

Women's political presence expanded in 1992 partly in reaction to the Senate's 1991 handling of Anita Hill's allegations of sexual harassment and other gender issues, but also because voters agreed with the women candidates' stance on the economy, the environment, and health care and were seeking change.

Business. Gains for women in the business world were not as apparent. In 1990 women earned 71 cents for every dollar earned by men, according to recent statistics. That indicated a gain of only 11 cents over 1980, showing women still to be years away from equality.

Women's gain or loss was a hot topic of discussion for much of the year following the late-1991 publication of Susan Faludi's bestseller, *Backlash: The Undeclared War Against American Women.* Faludi pointed to the novelty of a woman being promoted to an executive level as one example of women's failure to progress. In 1991 only 3% of all senior executives were women, compared with 46% of the labor force.

Nonetheless, analyses of U.S. women's gain in the workplace showed that they made greater economic advances during the 1980s than did men, with median annual salaries rising 10% while men's salaries during the same period slid 8% after inflation. Studies also showed that women have been earning more bachelor of arts degrees than have men; a business degree is women's first choice. More than one third of all professional degrees now were being earned by women, up from 6% in 1971.

Faced with "glass ceilings" in the corporate world, however, many women have quit to go out on their own. Many succeed, but not without overcoming obstacles, such as reluctance by some banks to lend to woman-owned businesses. The nation's 5.4 million women business owners now employ more than 11 million people, according to the National Foundation for Women Business Owners. The U.S. Census Bureau and Small Business Adminis-

Marking "The Year of the Woman," a large group of women officeholders and candidates assembled at the Democratic National Convention in July 1992. Women candidates scored major gains at both the federal and local levels in November.
© Wesley Bocxe/Sipa

Members of the Movement for the Ordination of Women, left, welcomed the November 1992 decision of the General Synod of the Church of England approving the ordination of women. The issue of whether women should be ordained remained a controversial one and a topic of debate in many religious circles.

tration project that women could own 48% of all U.S. businesses by the year 2000.

Sexual Discrimination and Harassment. Issues of sexual discrimination and harassment continued to capture attention in the United States in the wake of Clarence Thomas' confirmation hearings and Anita Hill's allegations that he had sexually harassed her. By mid-1992, 4,754 complaints of sexual harassment had been filed with the Equal Employment Opportunity Commission (EEOC), up from the 3,135 filed by the same time in 1991. It was estimated that 9,500 complaints could be filed by year's end.

Employers responded to new awareness of sexual harassment by hiring sensitivity trainers to talk with employees about behavior constituting harassment. Perceptions of insensitivity were heightened further by the revelation of a 1991 scandal in the U.S. Navy in which a group of aviators was accused of manhandling 26 women. An admiral who ignored his aide's complaints—she was one of those mistreated—was reassigned, and Secretary of the Navy H. Lawrence Garrett 3d resigned.

In its fight against discrimination, the federal EEOC filed suit against Sundstrand Corporation of Rockford, IL, claiming it illegally had a policy of excluding pregnant women from certain jobs. The case was based on a 1991 U.S. Supreme Court ruling that said employers who exclude women from certain jobs in which a fetus might be harmed are guilty of sex discrimination. At the University of California at Berkeley, Herma Hill Kay, long a fighter against sex-based discrimination, was named dean of the school of law. She was the first woman to hold the position.

Women's Groups. The National Organization for Women marked its 25th anniversary in 1992 with a new president, Patricia Ireland, who took office in late 1991. The group faced a changing role as the fights of the 1960s and 1970s against sexual discrimination in employment, education, credit, and public accommodation largely had been won. Efforts now were expected to concentrate on holding those gains.

At Planned Parenthood, President Faye Wattleton resigned. She had been president for 14 years. Pamela J. Maraldo was named as her successor in November.

Other Issues. The role of women in the military had been an issue since the Persian Gulf conflict. In November a presidential commission recommended that women should continue to be barred from flying combat planes and from ground combat. It, however, voted to allow women to serve on most warships.

On the medical front, a move was under way to develop a new medical specialty in women's medicine. Proponents said women would benefit from having doctors trained specifically in women's health.

International. Feminism was on the rise in some countries, including Japan. The number of unmarried women in Japan has been increasing steadily, with a number of successful businesswomen saying they do not want to lower their standard of living by getting married.

In Canada, Judy Rebick, president of the Toronto-based National Action Committee on the Status of Women, was heading a fight against sexual discrimination, poverty, racism, and violence against women. Women gained in that country when the Canadian Supreme Court in February upheld the obscenity provision of the criminal code, ruling that it was needed to suppress materials that harm women.

KRISTI VAUGHAN

WYOMING

Wyoming's news for 1992 focused on the legislature, general election, economy, and personalities.

Legislature. Confronted with tough issues regarding the state's sluggish economy and a federal mandate to reapportion the state's legislative districts before a February 21 deadline, Wyoming's 51st budget session proved one of the bitterest in history. During a February presession to address the issue of reapportionment, the legislature drafted a redistricting plan which Gov. Mike Sullivan (D) promptly vetoed for lack of "clarity, consistency, rationality, or fairness." In a highly partisan atmosphere that included closed caucuses, shouting matches, and charges of gerrymandering, the legislature drafted another plan that was signed by Governor Sullivan.

Under the new plan, the old county-based system of multimember districts gave way to nearly equally populated single-member districts. The new plan reduced the number of members in the state House to 60; the number of senators remained 30. Besides pitting incumbents against each other in the general election, the new plan also created 15 House districts and four Senate districts for which there were no incumbents. In short, the new plan guaranteed the biggest change in the legislature since Wyoming's creation in 1890.

Other highlights of the budget session included the adoption of a 1993–94 biennial budget of $780 million in general-fund spending. Public schools were funded completely through fiscal 1993 but were left with a $68 million deficit for 1994. At the conclusion of the session, Governor Sullivan admonished the House and Senate for their failure to deal with the state's tax system and its "indefensible dependence" upon "extractive industries for our tax revenues." The legislature's failure to broaden the tax base to provide for the state's traditional commitments to education, health, and human services practically assured that the 1994 legislature would have to raise taxes.

General Election. With a 61% turnout of its voting-age population in the November election, Wyoming favored incumbent George Bush over Bill Clinton in the presidential race by a margin of 40% to 34%. Independent presidential candidate Ross Perot took 26% of the state's vote. Incumbent Republican Craig Thomas won handily over challenger Jon Herschler (D), of Sheridan, for the state's lone seat in the U.S. House of Representatives. As expected, Republicans strengthened their control in the state legislature, gaining enough seats to override any veto by Governor Sullivan.

Wyoming voters passed three initiatives: (1) to ban triple trailers on Wyoming highways; (2) to impose term limits on state and federal officials; and (3) to regulate railroad transportation of hazardous waste. They also voted against retaining state Supreme Court Justice Walter Urbikit.

Economy. Modest gains in oil and gas industries, along with the state's strong showing in coal, trona, and tourism, were not enough to offset projected deficits fueled in part by declining revenues from the minerals sector. Balancing the state's economic and environmental needs remained a great challenge.

Personalities. Mark Hopkinson was executed by lethal injection on January 22, bringing to an end 12 years of legal controversy. . . . Former U.S. ambassador and three-term U.S. senator Gale McGee died on April 9 in Bethesda, MD.

ROBERT A. CAMPBELL
University of Wyoming

YUGOSLAVIA. *See* FEATURE ARTICLE, page 38.

YUKON

The general economic recession in the Yukon Territory was cushioned somewhat by large federal financial contributions, although employment was weak during 1991 and early 1992. Indian land claims made significant advances toward a final agreement, and major changes were seen on the political scene. Yukon's population rose by more than 2%.

Politics. A general election, based on 17 legislative seats—one more than before redistribution and major constituency boundary changes—was held on October 19. Although candidates from all three political parties—the ruling New Democrats (NDP), Liberals, and the Yukons (formerly the Progressive Conservatives, or PCs)—and several independents staged a long campaign, the Yukon Party was the winner. Its leader, John Ostashek, took over the premiership in November.

WYOMING • Information Highlights

Area: 97,809 sq mi (253 326 km²).
Population (July 1, 1991 est.): 460,000.
Chief Cities (1990 census): Cheyenne, the capital, 50,008; Casper, 46,742; Laramie, 26,687.
Government (1992): *Chief Officers*—governor, Michael J. Sullivan (D); secretary of state, Kathy Karpan (D). *Legislature*—Senate, 30 members; House of Representatives, 64 members.
State Finances (fiscal year 1991): *Revenue,* $1,979,000,000; *expenditure,* $1,813,000,000.
Personal Income (1991): $7,783,000,000; per capita, $16,937.
Labor Force (June 1992): *Civilian labor force,* 240,400; *unemployed,* 13,600 (5.7% of total force).
Education: *Enrollment* (fall 1990)—public elementary schools, 70,941; public secondary, 27,285; colleges and universities, 31,326. *Public school expenditures* (1990), $515,595,000.

Less than one week after the election, Yukon residents went to the polls again and joined voters in the four western provinces, Nova Scotia, and Quebec in rejecting the proposed changes in the federal constitution which would have recognized Quebec's distinct culture. (*See also* CANADA.)

Economy. Low world metal prices along with increasingly tighter environmental controls by the government began to tell on mining and exploration development in 1992. Yukon had two operating lead-zinc mines—the largest at Faro, 250 mi (402 km) northeast of Whitehorse, and the other north of Watson Lake in southeastern Yukon. However, exploration expenditures during the summer were only about C$10 million, considered to be the lowest in Yukon's mining history. A nine-week strike at Faro in mid-1991 had added to the economic disruption.

Indian Land Claims. After two decades of negotiations over Indian land claims, Yukon Indians and representatives of the federal and territorial governments had signed a historic "umbrella agreement" in late 1991. The agreement paved the way for the control of 8.6% of the territorial landmass and led to a prototype agreement on Indian self-government. Individual tribal negotiations on specific grounds continued in 1992.

DON SAWATSKY, *Whitehorse*

ZAIRE

Zaire—possessing great timber, agricultural resources, and much of the world's supply of cobalt, copper, and industrial diamonds—nevertheless remained one of the poorest countries in the world in 1992.

Economy. Zaire's 20-year history of economic distress reached a peak in September 1991 when soldiers seeking the overthrow of President Mobutu Sese Seko's regime set off rioting throughout the country. Arson and looting eliminated most of what remained of the modern productive sector. A total of 20,000 expatriates including teachers, health workers, managers, and aid workers fled the country. The effects of those events were multiplied in 1992. Exports of diamonds and cobalt stood at only half of 1990 levels. Copper exports, which amount to almost half the export earnings, had fallen by 40% since 1986.

A general strike in February further paralyzed the moribund economy; soldiers were

Zaire, one of the world's poorest nations, remained under the autocratic rule of Mobutu Sese Seko in 1992. Western nations sought to pressure Mobutu to democratize. The president spent much of his time aboard his yacht (below).

© François-Laurent/Figarzai/Gamma-Liaison

ZAIRE • Information Highlights

Official Name: Republic of Zaire.
Location: Central equatorial Africa.
Area: 905,564 sq mi (2 345 410 km²).
Population (mid-1992 est.): 37,900,000.
Chief City (1987 est.): Kinshasa, the capital, 2,500,000.
Government: *Head of state,* Mobutu Sese Seko, president (took office 1965). *Head of government,* Étienne Tshisekedi, prime minister (appointed Aug. 15, 1992). *Legislature* (unicameral)—National Legislative Council.
Monetary Unit: Zaire (383,064 zaires equal U.S.$1, June 1992).
Foreign Trade (1991 U.S.$): *Imports,* $713,000,000; *exports,* $832,000,000.

pressed into service to unload ships at Matadi. In April all banks closed because of a shortage of funds. There was mass unemployment in all the cities and civil servants, except those in the 100,000-member army, went months without pay. The inflation rate since the September 1991 riots reached a staggering 23,000%. The zaire, the basic currency, rated then at 300 to one against the dollar, by mid-1992 was 250,000 to one. In May the government issued a 500,000-zaire note to facilitate large transactions in cash. The note was worth only $2.00.

Gasoline shortages in the capital and differences between the government and the petroleum companies led to the seizure of all foreign oil companies on May 29 and this promptly stopped production of crude oil. Zaire's economic situation grew more desperate because of the end of the Cold War. The United States and the European Community (EC) cut off most of the aid to the stricken state until there was significant movement toward establishing a democratic system.

Foreign Pressure. Foreign pressure centered on stripping much of the power from Mobutu, the autocrat who had ruled Zaire for 27 years. The Belgian and French governments conditioned a resumption of economic aid to his complete removal, while the United States, fearing anarchy if Mobutu was overthrown, supported a greater sharing of power with an elected legislature. Despite riots, threats of rebellion, and a shattered economy, Mobutu remained in control largely because of divisions within the opposition.

The National Conference forced upon Mobutu proved unable to unite to create a new constitution after a year of deliberation. The onetime leader of the Sacred Coalition of Parties, Étienne Tshisekedi, who was to be prime minister in late 1991, was shunted aside and ultimately Nguza Karl-I-Bond was selected. Nguza, a onetime close associate of Mobutu as foreign minister, proved to be ineffective in curbing the economic decline and in forwarding political reform. The National Convention was suspended in late January by Nguza, who wanted instead a roundtable conference of par-

ties with fewer delegates. Opposition to this caused the reconvening of the convention in April, and in August it returned Tshisekedi to the prime ministership. Meanwhile, Mobutu's ability to influence political decisions in the last analysis rested with his control of the army, particularly the elite. This was shown in the crushing of a coup led by some disaffected army members who in January seized and briefly held the radio station in Kinshasa.

HARRY A. GAILEY
San Jose State University

ZIMBABWE

Zimbabwe, as it entered its second year of economic structural adjustment in 1992, suffered severe shortages of some basic commodities and price hikes for many others. To make matters worse, the country was devastated by perhaps the worst drought of the 20th century.

Land Acquisition Bill. White commercial farmers were angered and dismayed by the Land Acquisition Bill, which was introduced in February and passed into law on March 19. The main purpose of the bill was to nationalize, as part of the government's resettlement program, 12.4 million acres (5 million ha) of the 28 million acres (11.4 million ha) presently used for large-scale commercial farming. The bill provided for compulsory acquisition of land with compensation to be staggered during a five-year period and with no recourse to the courts. The Commercial Farmers Union, which represents about 4,500 white farmers, maintained that the legislation threatened Zimbabwe's position as one of the few food exporters on the continent, was contrary to the country's economic structural-adjustment program, and did not provide fair compensation for the land taken over. Supporters of the bill maintained that there was a deepening land crisis and that the promises of land redistribution made at independence in 1980 had not been met. Furthermore, whites—who represent 1% of the country's population of 10 million—owned more than one third of the land.

ZIMBABWE • Information Highlights

Official Name: Republic of Zimbabwe.
Location: Southern Africa.
Area: 150,803 sq mi (390 580 km²).
Population (mid-1992 est.): 10,300,000.
Chief Cities (1983 est.): Harare (formerly Salisbury), the capital, 681,000; Bulawayo, 429,000; Chitungwiza, 202,000.
Government: *Head of state and government,* Robert Mugabe, executive president (sworn in Dec. 31, 1987). *Legislature*—unicameral Parliament.
Monetary Unit: Zimbabwe dollar (5.076 Z dollars equal U.S.$1, May 1992).
Economic Index (1990): *Industrial Production* (1980 = 100), 134.
Foreign Trade (1990 U.S.$): *Imports,* $1,850,000,000; *exports,* $1,723,000,000.

© Howard Burditt/NYT Pictures
Southern Africa was devastated by a severe drought in 1992, forcing Zimbabwe's wildlife authorities to kill animals for food for starving humans and other animals.

Devastating Drought. In March, President Robert Mugabe declared the drought a national disaster and thus opened the way for the government to provide local financial aid and for donor organizations to launch relief efforts. In addition, each of Zimbabwe's eight administrative regions, or provinces, were assigned a cabinet minister to help coordinate and supervise drought-relief efforts. Water rationing was introduced in parts of the country hardest hit by the drought; large numbers of farm workers lost their jobs; and thousands of cattle were sold for slaughter.

Cabinet Reshuffle. On July 3, in response to economic structural-adjustment pressures from the World Bank and other donors, President Mugabe reduced his cabinet from 32 ministers, vice-presidents, ministers of state, and the attorney general to 26 appointments. He also reshuffled many of the portfolios and reduced the number of deputy ministers from 13 to nine. Among the ministers dropped was the controversial Minister of Energy and Water Resources, Herbert Ushewokunze, who had been accused of corrupt practices. Chris Anderson was dropped from the cabinet and replaced as minister of mines by Eddison Zvobgo. Denis Norman, the minister of transport, assumed the additional assignment of minister of energy. Minister of Health Timothy Stamps took on the additional portfolio of child welfare. The ministry of political affairs was renamed national affairs, employment creation, and cooperatives. Didymus Mutasa remained the senior minister and Fay Chung, former minister of education and culture, was appointed as a minister of state in this new cabinet office. Nathan Shamuyarira and Bernard Chidzero remained ministers of foreign affairs and finance, respectively.

Opposition Group. In May the Forum for Democratic Reform was formed by a group of Zimbabwean business leaders, former judges, lawyers, and others. The participants claimed that they hoped to open debate on Zimbabwe's political and economic future and hoped that political parties might emerge that transcended ethnic allegiances. They emphasized that their group was a think tank and not a political party but that it might become "the source of a new party."

In July a number of Zimbabweans, including former Prime Minister Ian Smith; the Rev. Ndabaningi Sithole, once a leader of the Zimbabwe African National Union (ZANU); and others came together to form a united front aimed at removing the Mugabe government from office.

University Students Expelled. In June the University of Zimbabwe expelled 10,000 students after a month of protests, demonstrations, and boycotts. The demonstrators were demanding higher grants because of substantial increases in fees. Subsequently, students had to reapply for admission.

National Budgets. The government described the August budget as an effort to stabilize the economy by reducing public spending at a time of rapid inflation and declining output. The budget included tax increases on wine, spirits, and cigarettes and a special short-term 10% tax as a drought levy.

The inflation rate increased to more than 36% from nearly 28% in 1991. In part, the rise was a result of the country's structural-adjustment program, which led to higher prices for imports and the removal of price controls on a number of commodities. Food prices were said to have increased by nearly 50% from June 1991 to July 1992 and the cost of living rose by as much as 45% for the same period. The government considered that the high rate of inflation was to be expected because of the move from a highly centralized economy to a more liberal one in which prices were determined by the market.

In October, Christiaan Poortman, the World Bank's representative in Zimbabwe, indicated that because of the drought some of the targets of the economic structural-adjustment program would not be met.

Death of First Lady. Sally Mugabe, wife of President Mugabe, died on January 27 after a long kidney illness. After five days of mourning, the 60-year-old Ghanaian-born first lady was buried at the National Heroes Acre, the first woman to be so honored.

PATRICK O'MEARA, *Indiana University*

ZOOS AND ZOOLOGY

A major urban-renewal project was completed with the June 1992 opening of the Queens Zoo in New York City's Flushing Meadows Park. Refurbished exhibits feature North American wildlife, bison, elk, prairie dogs, mountain lions, bobcats, and coyotes. The Queens Zoo is the second facility jointly renovated by the New York Zoological Society and the city; the first project, Central Park Zoo, reopened in 1988.

Visitors to the Henry Doorly Zoo in Omaha, NE, leave civilization behind when they enter Lied Jungle, which opened in April. The largest indoor tropical rain forest in the United States, Lied Jungle is home to white-handed gibbons, pygmy hippos and antelopes from Africa, and the dramatic Danger Point—which overlooks a 50-ft (15.2-m)-high waterfall and provides a view of tapirs and woolly monkeys in the South American rain forest.

At the Tennessee Aquarium, which opened in 1992, the world's largest freshwater tank, below, *explores the underwater terrain of the Tennessee River's Nickajack Lake.*
© Courtesy of the Tennessee Aquarium, photographer R. T. Bryant.

Also in April, the Fort Worth Zoo (TX) opened the World of Primates, a 2.5-acre (1-ha) tropical rain forest with indoor displays of lowland gorillas, colobus monkeys, and free-flying Asian and African birds; it also features outdoor exhibits with chimpanzees, bonobos (pygmy chimps), gibbons, orangutans, and mandrill baboons. The Asian Falls, another new exhibit, is a natural habitat with Sumatran tigers and Malayan sun bears.

On May 1, 1992, the Tennessee Aquarium made its debut in Chattanooga. The largest building in the world dedicated to freshwater wildlife, the new 130,000-sq-ft (12 077-m²), $45 million facility has five major galleries: the Rivers of the World, the Tennessee River Gallery, the Mississippi Delta, the Appalachian Cove Forest, and Discovery Falls.

Exhibits. The Milwaukee County Zoo opened its Apes of Africa exhibit on May 9, 1992. The new exhibit is part of a $10.7 million Primate Complex and features western lowland gorillas and bonobos in West African rain-forest habitats. In the second half of the project, the zoo was renovating the Primates Building for orangutans, siamang gibbons, and mandrills; it was scheduled to open in early 1993.

On June 17, Busch Gardens in Tampa, FL, unveiled Myombe Reserve: The Great Ape Domain. Three acres (1.2 ha) of forest, waterfalls, and open grassy plains provide homes for six lowland gorillas and nine common chimpanzees.

The San Diego Zoo completed its new Hummingbird Pavilion in July. The pavilion features small jewels of the animal and plant kingdom. Visitors can view native hummers such as the Anna's hummingbird as well as orchids, cycads, and anthuriums.

Endangered Species. Among the remarkable wildlife births of 1992 was the April 6 appearance of a baby aye-aye at Duke University's Primate Center in North Carolina. The aye-aye, a type of lemur found only on the island of Madagascar, is one of the most endangered primates in the world. The local people believe the aye-aye is demonic and fear the primate's long middle finger.

The two clouded leopard cubs born at the Nashville Zoo on May 27 were the first of their kind produced through artificial insemination. Reproductive specialists JoGayle Howard and Onnie Byers at the National Zoo's New Opportunities in Animal Health Sciences Center in Washington, DC, developed the procedure, called laparoscopic intrauterine artificial insemination. In August, with Dr. William Karesh, the international field veterinarian of the New York Zoological Society, Howard collected fresh semen samples from wild leopard cats in Sabah and Sarawak, Indonesia. The semen will be used to artificially inseminate animals of this species in North American zoos—the first time the genetic pool of captive small

The Eastern U.S. Rabies Epidemic

As of Aug. 31, 1992, the number of confirmed rabid animals in New York state alone was 1,181, according to the state's Department of Health officials. That figure surpassed the 1,030 confirmed cases in New York for all of 1991. An epidemic of raccoon rabies has been spreading up the eastern coast of the United States since the 1950s. The incidence of rabid animals really began to multiply in the late 1970s, probably because clubs in Virginia started to import animals from Florida to hunt from horseback. Together with foxes, skunks, and bats, raccoons account for 87% of the reported cases of animal rabies in the United States.

The rabies virus is transmitted in saliva through bites from infected animals or from contact with infected brain or nerve tissue. If left untreated, rabies attacks the victim's nervous system and leads to convulsions, paralysis, and ultimately, death. Prompt vaccination after exposure can prevent the disease in humans. Routine immunization of pet dogs and cats with vaccine almost has stopped the transmission of pet rabies in the United States. But until recently, mass inoculations of wildlife such as raccoons and skunks required that each animal be trapped and injected individually—a costly and impractical task.

An oral vaccine created in 1984 by the Wistar Institute in Philadelphia, PA, is a promising development in the battle against rabies. During field tests conducted in 1991 and early in 1992, in which the vaccine was spread out in bait, it appeared to be effective in immunizing individual raccoons. Testing was continuing at year's end, and final approvals for commercial use of the oral vaccine may be forthcoming.

This "magic bullet" may not be the complete answer to the raccoon rabies problem, however. Raccoons are widespread in the eastern U.S. region and are highly adaptable. They seem to thrive wherever people are. Perhaps the most important tool in rabies prevention is public education. People should be aware of the dangers in attracting and feeding wild animals, should make sure garbage cans are covered securely, and never should provide handouts for raccoons. Pets and livestock should be inoculated against rabies; and farmers, veterinarians, and other people who regularly work with domestic and wild animals also should be vaccinated. Children should be instructed not to touch or pick up any wild animals.

If someone is bitten by a potentially rabid animal, he or she should wash the wound thoroughly and seek medical attention immediately. The animal in question should be captured, or killed if necessary, without damaging the head, which is needed for positive laboratory diagnosis. Local or state health officials should be contacted as soon as possible.

DEBORAH A. BEHLER

---

wild cats will be increased while leaving the donors to roam free in the wild.

On July 13, wildlife biologists sighted a female black-footed ferret and two kits in south central Wyoming. Probably the most appealing of wildlife success stories in the United States, black-footed ferrets nearly became extinct in the 1980s. The last remaining group of 18 was taken into captivity in a recovery plan overseen by the U.S. Fish and Wildlife Service and Wyoming Game and Fish Department. By 1991 the ferrets had multiplied to 325 and that fall, 49 were released in an area with a high density of prairie dogs, ferrets' favorite food. By late summer 1992 the biologists had found another three adults and a second litter with four kits. In September another 80 captive-bred ferrets were released at the same site.

Zoological Research. Zoologists have known for some time that the blue-throated macaw existed in Bolivia because dealers were selling the birds in the pet market. But no one seemed to know where they lived until Aug. 7, 1992, when Charles A. Munn, a research zoologist with Wildlife Conservation International (WCI), found a pair apparently excavating a nest in northeastern Bolivia. WCI launched a study of the pair, hoping to learn if there are other sites where the birds live and what effect hunting has on the species' numbers.

Researchers in Florida are trying to discover why so many manatees, or sea cows, are hurt and killed in collisions with boats. Nine hundred of these large marine mammals have been identified by their distinctive scar patterns; one animal appeared to have been hit 12 times. Many people think the animals are too dim-witted or just move too slowly to get out of the way. But Geoffrey Patton, of Sarasota's Mote Marine Laboratory, believes the animals may not be able to hear the boats' engines. Patton and Edmund Gerstein of Florida Atlantic University began a project to determine the hearing abilities of manatees at Tampa's Lowry Park Zoo. Once the species' hearing range has been determined, it may be possible to outfit boats with warning devices alerting the manatees to danger.

DEBORAH A. BEHLER
"Wildlife Conservation" Magazine

Statistical and Tabular Data

NATIONS OF THE WORLD [1]

A Profile and Synopsis of Major 1992 Developments

Nation, Region	Population in millions	Capital	Area Sq mi (km²)	Head of State/Government
Antigua and Barbuda, Caribbean	0.1	St. John's	170 (440)	Sir Wilfred E. Jacobs, governor-general Vere C. Bird, prime minister

The government released a scaled-back budget in 1992 that led to several weeks of civil unrest. Accused of misappropriation of funds, Prime Minister Vere C. Bird survived demands for his resignation. Gross Domestic Product (GDP) (1989 est.): $350 million. Foreign Trade (1989 est.): Imports, $347.8 million; exports, $31.6 million.

Bahamas, Caribbean	0.3	Nassau	5,382 (13 940)	Clifford Darling, governor-general Hurbert A. Ingraham, prime minister

Parliamentary elections on August 19 ended the rule of Sir Lyndon O. Pindling of the Progressive Liberal Party. Pindling had served as prime minister since the Bahamas gained independence from Great Britain in 1973. Newly elected Prime Minister Hurbert Ingraham of the Free National Movement pledged greater cooperation with the United States to step up drug-interdiction efforts and to liberalize laws on foreign investment. GDP (1989 est.): $2.4 billion. Foreign Trade (1989): Imports, $1.15 billion; exports, $259 million.

Bahrain, W. Asia	0.5	Manama	239 (620)	Isa bin Salman Al Khalifa, emir Khalifa bin Salman Al Khalifa, prime minister

Faced with shrinking oil reserves, Bahrain planned to build 50 shallow oil wells. Some predict the nation, the smallest of Persian Gulf oil producers, could exhaust its oil supply within a decade. GDP (1988): $3.4 billion. Foreign Trade (1991): Imports, $4.0 billion; exports, $3.4 billion.

Barbados, Caribbean	0.3	Bridgetown	166 (430)	Dame Nita Barrow, governor-general L. Erskine Sandiford, prime minister

GDP (1989 est.): $1.7 billion. Foreign Trade (1991): Imports, $695 million; exports, $202 million.

Benin, W. Africa	5.0	Porto Novo	43,483 (112 620)	Nicephore Soglo, president

Prime Minister Nicephore Soglo, Benin's first freely elected leader in almost 30 years, successfully faced several tests of his democratic regime, including a student protest, a civil strike, and a failed military rebellion. GDP (1989 est.): $1.8 billion. Foreign Trade (1989 est.): Imports, $413 million; exports, $226 million.

Bhutan, S. Asia	0.7	Thimphu	18,147 (47 000)	Jigme Singye Wangchuck, king

Bhutan and Bangladesh signed an accord on March 11 to expand bilateral trade and economic cooperation. GDP (1988 est.): $273 million. Foreign Trade (1989 est.): Imports, $138.3 million; exports, $70.9 million.

Botswana, S. Africa	1.4	Gaborone	231,803 (600 370)	Quett Masire, president

France announced it would provide $478 million to Botswana for the construction of a contovorsial military air base. In addition, France would supply military aircraft and equipment. GDP (1990 est.): $3.1 billion. Foreign Trade (1988): Imports, $1.7 billion; exports, $1.8 billion.

Brunei Darussalam, S.E. Asia	0.3	Bandar Seri Begawan	2,288 (5 770)	Sir Muda Hassanal Bolkiah, sultan and prime minister

Brunei established diplomatic relations with Vietnam and Czechoslovakia. GDP (1989 est.): $3.3 billion. Foreign Trade (1989): Imports, $1.2 billion; exports, $1.9 billion.

Burkina Faso, W. Africa	9.6	Ouagadougou	105,869 (274 200)	Blaise Compaoré, president

On May 24 the first legislative elections in 14 years brought an overwhelming victory for President Blaise Compaoré's party, the Organization for Popular Democracy. Compaoré named Youssouf Ouedraogo as his prime minister. GDP (1989): $1.75 billion. Foreign Trade (1989): Imports, $619 million; exports, $262 million.

Burundi, E. Africa	5.8	Bujumbura	10,745 (27 830)	Pierre Buyoya, president Adrien Sibomana, prime minister

Amnesty International reported that at least 1,000 rebels were executed. A Burundi spokesman condemned the report. GDP (1989): $1.1 billion. Foreign Trade (1991): Imports, $248 million; exports, $91 million.

Cameroon, Cen. Africa	12.7	Yaoundé	183,568 (475 440)	Paul Biya, president Simon Achidi Achu, prime minister

The first free parliamentary elections in decades were held on March 1, but three main opposition groups boycotted the polls. Paul Biya was reelected president in the first multiparty presidential elections on October 11 amid reports of voting irregularities. On December 28 police used tear gas to disperse demonstrators protesting the detention of opposition leader Fru Ndi. GDP (1990 est.): $11.5 billion. Foreign Trade (1990 est.): Imports, $2.1 billion; exports, $2.1 billion.

Cape Verde, W. Africa	0.4	Praia	1,556 (4 030)	Antonio Monteiro Mascarenhas, president Carlos Alberto Wahnon de Carvalho Veiga, prime minister

Cape Verde on March 12 joined other nations that hold a rotating seat on the UN Security Council in voting not to relax sanctions against Iraq for failure to comply with the terms of the 1991 cease-fire agreement. GDP (1988): $262 million. Foreign Trade (1989): Imports, $112 million; exports, $7.0 million.

[1] Independent nations not covered separately in alphabetical section.

Nation, Region	Population in millions	Capital	Area Sq mi (km²)	Head of State/Government
Central African Republic, Cen. Africa	3.2	Bangui	240,533 (622 980)	André-Dieudonné Kolingba, president Edouard Franck, prime minister

A national forum was convened in August to discuss the country's political, economic, and social directions. Attendees drafted a revised constitution to establish a semipresidential system with separation of powers. But the "Great National Debate" was boycotted by a majority of the opposition parties. GDP (1990 est.): $1.3 billion. Foreign Trade (1989): Imports, $150 million; exports, $134 million.

Chad, Cen. Africa	5.1	Ndjamena	495,753 (1 284 000)	Gen. Idriss Déby, president Joseph Yodoyman, prime minister

In January rebels loyal to former President Hissein Habré captured briefly two towns 90 mi (144 km) northwest of the capital but later were overcome by government military forces. France sent some 450 paratroopers to the former French territory to protect property and French nationals. GDP (1989 est.): $1.02 billion. Foreign Trade (1990 est.): Imports, $264 million; exports, $174 million.

Comoros, E. Africa	0.5	Moroni	838 (2 170)	Said Mohammed Djohar, president

On June 7 delegates approved a new constitution which sets a presidential term of five years, renewable for a second term. Senatorial and Assembly members would hold terms for six and four years, respectively. Djohar survived a coup attempt on September 26 carried out by junior officers. The Comoros held legislative elections from mid-November through early December. The Assembly has numerous parties with roughly half progovernment and half opposition parties. GDP (1990 est.): $245 million. Foreign Trade (1990 est.): Imports, $41 million; exports, $16 million.

Congo, Cen. Africa	2.4	Brazzaville	132,046 (342 000)	Pascal Lissouba, president Stephane Maurice Bongho-Nourra, prime minister

After 27 years of military rule, Congo held its first multiparty elections since independence in 1960. Pascal Lissouba's Pan-American Union for Social Democracy party won 23 out of 60 seats in Senate elections and 31 out of 67 seats in the National Assembly vote. Lissouba had replaced President Denis Sassou Nguesso, who in 1991 conceded to calls for pluralism. (See also AFRICA.) GDP (1989 est.): $2.26 billion. Foreign Trade (1990): Imports, $600 million; exports, $976 million.

Djibouti, E. Africa	0.4	Djibouti	8,494 (22 000)	Hassan Gouled Aptidon, president Barkat Gourad Hamadou, premier

A UN-observed referendum to approve a new constitution was held on September 4. The adoption paved the way for a multiparty, democratic system. It also would establish a guarantee of certain liberties and makes a distinction among executive, legislative, and judicial powers. Gross National Product (GNP) (1989): $340 million. Foreign Trade (1986): Imports, $215 million; exports, $25 million.

Dominica, Caribbean	0.1	Roseau	290 (750)	Clarence A. Seignoret, president Eugenia Charles, prime minister

GDP (1989 est.): $153 million. Foreign Trade (1990): Imports, $118 million; exports, $55 million.

Dominican Republic, Caribbean	7.5	Santo Domingo	18,815 (48 730)	Joaquín Balaguer Ricardo, president

GDP (1989): $6.68 billion. Foreign Trade (1990 est.): Imports, $1.9 billion; exports, $922 million.

Equatorial Guinea, Cen. Africa	0.4	Malabo	10,830 (28 050)	Obiang Nguema Mbasogo, president Silvester Siale Bileka, prime minister

Throughout 1992, members of several opposition groups were reported arrested or missing, including supporters from the Convergence for Social Democracy and the Union for Democracy and Social Development. GNP (1988 est.): $144 million. Foreign Trade (1988 est.): Imports, $50 million; exports, $30 million.

Fiji, Oceania	0.8	Suva	7,054 (18 270)	Kamisese Mara, acting president Sitiveni Rabuka, prime minister

On May 29–30, Fiji held its first general election since two 1987 coups. The Fijian Political Party (FPP) took 30 seats in the new 70-seat Parliament. The Fiji Labour Party and the National Federation Party won 13 and 14 seats respectively. GDP (1990 est.) $1.36 billion. Foreign Trade (1990): Imports, $738 million; exports, $435 million.

Gabon, Cen. Africa	1.1	Libreville	103,348 (267 670)	El Hadj Omar Bongo, president Casimir Oye Mba, premier

The opposition party, the African Forum for Reconstruction, in July resigned from various councils of the National Assembly to protest the adoption of a new electoral code it termed antidemocratic. GDP (1990): $3.3 billion. Foreign Trade (1989): Imports, $0.78 billion; exports, $1.16 billion.

Gambia, W. Africa	0.9	Banjul	4,363 (11 300)	Sir Dawda Kairaba Jawara, president

Dawda Jawara on April 29 was reelected to his fourth consecutive term as president of Gambia. Jawara, leader of the People's Progressive Party (PPP), won 58.4% of the vote. General elections, held on the same day, left the majority PPP with 31 fewer seats in parliament. GDP (1990 est.): $195 million. Foreign Trade (1990): Imports, $155.2 million; exports, $122.2 million.

Ghana, W. Africa	16.0	Accra	92,100 (238 540)	Jerry Rawlings, president

Voters approved a new constitution which provided for legislative and presidential elections. Military leader Jerry Rawlings, who seized power in 1981, was elected civilian president by 58.5% of the vote on November 4. Trading partners praised Rawlings' economic-austerity program that included trade-liberalization policies. GNP (1990 est.): $5.8 billion. Foreign Trade (1990): Imports, $1.2 billion; exports, $826 million.

Grenada, Caribbean	0.1	St. George's	131 (340)	Sir Paul Scoon, governor-general Sir Nicholas Brathwaite, prime minister

GDP (1990): $200.7 million. Foreign Trade (1989 est.): Imports, $115.6 million; exports, $27.9 million.

Guinea, W. Africa	7.8	Conakry	94,927 (245 860)	Lansana Conté, president

President Lansana Conté took several steps toward his promised democratization by releasing some basic laws based on a constitution approved in December 1991. They form the framework for executive, judicial, and legislative institutions and include guidelines for certain civil liberties. Presidential elections were promised for late 1992. Guinea was one of ten countries with the highest misery ratings in 1992, according to the Washington-based Population Crisis Committee. GDP (1989 est.): $2.7 billion. Foreign Trade (1989 est.): Imports, $551 million; exports, $645 million.

Nation, Region	Population in millions	Capital	Area Sq mi (km²)	Head of State/Government
Guinea-Bissau, W. Africa	1.0	Bissau	13,946 (36 120)	João Bernardo Vieira, president

The Party for Social Renovation and the Party for Renovation and Development were legalized in Guinea-Bissau, bringing to ten the number of opposition parties. GDP (1989): $154 million. Foreign Trade (1989 est): Imports, $68.9 million; exports, $14.2 million.

Guyana, N.E. South America	0.8	Georgetown	83,000 (214 970)	Cheddi Jagan, president Samuel Hinds, prime minister

Guyana's October 5 presidential elections were characterized by former U.S. President Jimmy Carter, part of an observer delegation, as the first fair elections since 1964. Former President Hugh Desmond Hoyt lost to former Marxist Cheddi Jagan of the People's Progressive Party (PPP). The People's National Congress (PNC) got 41% of the vote as compared with the PPP's 54%. GDP (1989 est.): $287.2 million. Foreign Trade (1989 est.): Imports, $257 million; exports, $224 million.

Ivory Coast, W. Africa	13.0	Yamoussoukro	124,502 (322 460)	Félix Houphouët-Boigny, president Alassane Ouattara, prime minister

Hundreds of political prisoners imprisoned for antigovernment protests were pardoned under a law passed by parliament on June 29. GDP (1989): $9.5 billion. Foreign Trade (1989): Imports, $1.4 billion; exports, $2.5 billion.

Jamaica, Caribbean	2.5	Kingston	4,243 (10 990)	Howard Cooke governor general P.J. Patterson, prime minister

On March 28 the People's National Party (PNP) elected P.J. Patterson as party leader, automatically making him prime minister. Former Prime Minister Michael Manley resigned due to ill health. The PNP elected Patterson by almost three to one over Portia Simpson, the other candidate. GDP (1990): $3.9 billion. Foreign Trade (1990): Imports, $1.02 billion; exports, $1.83 billion.

Kiribati, Oceania	0.07	Tarawa	277 (717)	Teatao Teannaki, president

GDP (1990 est.): $36.8 million. Foreign Trade (1990 est.): Imports, $26.7 million; exports, $5.8 million.

Lesotho, S. Africa	1.9	Maseru	11,718 (30 350)	Letsie III, king Elias Phisoana Ramaema, chairman, military council

King Moshoeshoe II was allowed to return to the country from his two-year exile in London. His son, Letsie III, elected king by a tribal assembly, stated he would abdicate the throne for his father, an action opposed by Ramaema. GDP (1990 est.): $420 million. Foreign Trade (1989 est.): Imports, $499 million; exports, $66 million.

Liberia, W. Africa	2.7	Monrovia	43,000 (111 370)	Amos Sawyer, president

Liberia's civil war flared as rebel soldiers led by Charles Taylor advanced toward the capital of Monrovia in 1992. According to UN reports, at least 3,000 people have died since the siege began. En route to the capital, rebels captured a U.S.-owned rubber plant. An October 21 attack on the capital was stymied by a Western African peacekeeping force. Roman Catholic officials also reported the killing of five U.S. nuns. GDP (1988): $988 million. Foreign Trade (1989 est.): Imports, $394 million; exports, $505 million.

Liechtenstein, Cen. Europe	0.03	Vaduz	62 (160)	Hans Adam II, prince Hans Brunhart, prime minister

GDP (1990 est.): $630 million.

Luxembourg, W. Europe	0.4	Luxembourg	998 (2 586)	Jean, grand duke Jacques Santer, prime minister

A court in Luxembourg, headquarters of the defunct Bank of Commerce and Credit International (BCCI), on October 22 settled on a liquidation plan that would give 40 cents on the dollar of $10 billion lost to creditors. GDP (1990 est.): $6.9 billion. (Luxembourg's foreign trade is recorded with Belgium's.)

Madagascar, E. Africa	11.9	Antananarivo	226,656 (587 040)	Didier Ratsiraka, president Guy Razanamasy, prime minister

The first round of presidential elections held in November gave incumbent Didier Ratsiraka only 29% of the vote, but Albert Zafy with 46% of the vote failed to win a majority. A runoff was scheduled for January or February of 1993, with legislative elections to be held two months thereafter. GDP (1990): $2.4 billion. Foreign Trade (1990): Imports, $436 million; exports, $290 million.

Malawi, E. Africa	8.7	Lilongwe	45,745 (118 480)	Hastings Kamuzu Banda, president

Malawi citizens, after 28 years of peaceful autocratic rule by Hastings Kamuzu Banda, demanded for themselves the democratization sweeping other parts of Africa. On May 9, Banda witnessed the first antigovernment demonstration since he took office in 1964. Western donor nations suspended aid to the nation, one of the five poorest on the African continent, in response to its poor human-rights record. GDP (1990 est.): $1.6 billion. Foreign Trade (1990): Imports, $560 million; exports, $390 million.

Maldives, S. Asia	0.2	Malé	116 (300)	Maumoon Abdul Gayoom, president

GDP (1988): $136 million. Foreign Trade (1988 est.): Imports, $90.0 million; exports, $47.0 million.

Mali, W. Africa	8.5	Bamako	478,764 (1 240 000)	Alpha Omar Konare, chief of state Younoussi Toure, prime minister

In Mali's first democratic election since independence from France in 1960, Alpha Omar Konare was chosen as president. A runoff on April 26 between Konare and another presidential contender, Tieoule Mamadoure Konate, gave the victor 70% of the vote. GDP (1989 est.): $2.0 billion. Foreign Trade (1989): Imports, $513 million; exports, $285 million.

Malta, S. Europe	0.4	Valletta	124 (320)	Vincent Tabone, president Edward Fenech Adami, prime minister

Prime Minister Edward Adami was reelected by an absolute majority in the nation's parliament. Adami said his top priority would be admittance to the European Community by 1995. GDP (1988): $1.9 billion. Foreign Trade (1989): Imports, $1.51 billion; exports, $858 million.

Mauritania, W. Africa	2.1	Nouakchott	397,954 (1 030 700)	Maaouiya Ould Sid Ahmed Taya, president

On January 24, President Maaouiya Ould Sid Ahmed Taya won overwhelmingly in the country's first multiparty elections. Despite voting irregularities, outside observers considered the victory legitimate. Coming in second to Taya was

Nation, Region	Population in millions	Capital	Area Sq mi (km²)	Head of State/Government

Ahmed Ould Daddah, with about 33% of the vote. Ethnic tensions between Arab-Berbers and Negro-Africans flared in the latter half of 1992. At least five people were killed. Mauritania joined Senegal in creating a committee to promote peace between the two nations. The two countries have been at odds since April 1989. GDP (1989 est.): $942 million. Foreign Trade (1989 est.): Imports, $567 million; exports, $519 million.

Mauritius, E. Africa	1.1	Port Louis	718 (1 860)	Cassam Uteem, president Rabindranath Ghurburren, vice-president

On June 30 parliament designated Cassam Uteem as the new president of Mauritius. President Uteem named Rabindranath Ghurburren as his vice-president. GDP (1989): $2.1 billion. Foreign Trade (1991): Imports, $1.5 billion; exports, $1.1 billion.

Monaco, S. Europe	0.03	Monaco-Ville	0.7 (1.9)	Rainier III, prince Jacques Dupont, minister of state
Nauru, Oceania	0.009	Nauru	8 (21)	Bernard Dowiyogo, president

Foreign Trade (1984): Imports, $73 million; exports, $93 million.

Namibia, W. Africa	1.5	Windhoek	318,259 (824 290)	Sam Nujoma, president

GNP (1990 est.): $1.8 billion. Foreign Trade (1989): Imports, $894 million; exports, $1,021 million.

Nepal, S. Asia	19.9	Katmandu	54,363 (140 800)	Birendra Bir Bikram, king Girija Prasad Koirala, prime minister

Morrison Knudsen Corporation announced that it would lead an international group that will build a $233 million hydroelectric project on the Kali Gandaki River in south central Nepal. GDP (1990): $3.0 billion. Imports, $454.3 million; exports, $124 million.

Niger, W. Africa	8.3	Niamey	489,189 (1 267 000)	Ali Saibou, president

Mutinous soldiers seized the airwaves in Niger on February 28 to demand back pay and government reforms. Elections scheduled for the end of 1992 were postponed until January 1993. GDP (1989 est.): $2.0 billion. Foreign Trade (1989 est.): Imports, $386 million; exports, $308 million.

Oman, W. Asia	1.6	Muscat	82,031 (212 460)	Qaboos bin Said, sultan and prime minister

Oman on January 28 joined a host of other Arab states in their first peace talks with Israel. GDP (1987 est.): $8.5 billion. Foreign Trade (1990): Imports, $2.7 billion; exports, $5.2 billion.

Papua New Guinea, Oceania	3.9	Port Moresby	178,259 (461 690)	Wiwa Korowi, governor-general Paias Wingti, prime minister

Papua New Guinea warned Australian officials worried about the environmental damage caused by its gold and copper mines to mind their own business. A team of U.S. biologists studying in the country in October discovered the first known instance of a poisonous bird. GDP (1989 est.): $2.7 billion. Foreign Trade (1991): Imports, $1.4 billion; exports, $1.3 billion.

Qatar, W. Asia	0.5	Doha	4,247 (11 000)	Khalifa bin Hamad Al Thani, emir and prime minister

A group of 54 prominent citizens presented the leader of Qatar with a petition on May 12, demanding parliamentary elections, a constitution, and other democratic institutions. A number of petitioners, including university professors and senior officials, were arrested or had passports confiscated. GDP (1988): $6.6 billion. Foreign Trade (1989 est.): Imports, $1.4 billion; exports, $2.6 billion.

Saint Kitts and Nevis, Caribbean	0.04	Basseterre	139 (360)	Clement A. Arrindell, governor-general Kennedy A. Simmonds, prime minister

GDP (1988): $97.5 million. Foreign Trade (1989): Imports, $89.6 million; exports, $32.8 million.

Saint Lucia, Caribbean	0.2	Castries	239 (620)	Sir Stanislaus A. James, governor-general John Compton, prime minister

A general election on April 27 gave John Compton of the United Worker's Party a third consecutive five-year term as prime minister. (1989 est.): $273 million. Foreign Trade (1989): Imports, $265.9 million; exports, $111.9 million.

Saint Vincent and the Grenadines, Caribbean	0.1	Kingstown	131 (340)	David Jack, governor-general James F. Mitchell, prime minister

GDP (1989 est.): $146 million. Foreign Trade (1989): Imports, $127.5 million; exports, $74.6 million.

San Marino, S. Europe	0.023	San Marino	23 (60)	Coregents appointed semiannually

The UN Security Council voted on February 25 to accept San Marino's application to change from observer status at the United Nations to full membership.

São Tomé and Príncipe, W. Africa	0.1	São Tomé	371 (960)	Miguel Trovoada, president Norberto Costa Alegre, prime minister

President Miguel Trovoada on April 22 dismissed the government of Prime Minister Daniel Lima dos Santos Daio. Demonstrating citizens blamed Daio for the country's economic difficulties. Norberto Costa Alegre was appointed the new prime minister on May 11. GDP (1989): $46.0 million. Foreign Trade (1989 est.): Imports, $26.8 million; exports, $5.9 million.

Senegal, W. Africa	7.9	Dakar	75,749 (196 190)	Abdou Diouf, president Habib Thiam, prime minister

Senegal and Mauritania established a committee to promote tolerance and peace between the two nations. GDP (1989 est.): $4.6 billion. Foreign Trade (1989 est.): Imports, $1.0 billion; exports, $801 million.

Seychelles, E. Africa	0.1	Victoria	176 (455)	France Albert René, president

President Albert René's ruling party was given 58.4% of the vote to elect representatives of a constitutional committee. On October 1 the 20-member group drafted a new constitution. GDP (1989 est.): $283 million. Foreign Trade (1991): Imports, $173 million; exports, $48 million.

Nation, Region	Population in millions	Capital	Area Sq mi (km²)	Head of State/Government
Sierra Leone, W. Africa	4.4	Freetown	27,699 (71 740)	Valentine Strasser, president

Joseph Momoh, president since 1985, was ousted by a military coup on April 29 and reportedly went into hiding in Guinea. Rebel soldiers said they had been fighting near the Liberian border without pay, ammunition, or food. An interim government, the National Provisional Defense Council, was headed up by Capt. Valentine Strasser, a junta leader. About 1,000 Americans were flown out of the country on May 4. GDP (1989): $1.3 billion. Foreign Trade (1991): Imports, $162 million; exports, $145 million.

Nation, Region	Population in millions	Capital	Area Sq mi (km²)	Head of State/Government
Solomon Islands, Oceania	0.4	Honiara	10,985 (28 450)	Sir George Lepping, governor-general Solomon Mamaloni, prime minister

GDP (1989 est.): $156 million. Foreign Trade (1990): Imports, $92 million; exports, $70 million.

Nation, Region	Population in millions	Capital	Area Sq mi (km²)	Head of State/Government
Suriname, S. America	0.4	Paramaribo	63,039 (163 270)	Ronald Venetiaan, president

GDP (1989 est.): $1.35 billion. Foreign Trade (1988 est.): Imports, $370 million; exports, $425 million.

Nation, Region	Population in millions	Capital	Area Sq mi (km²)	Head of State/Government
Swaziland, S. Africa	0.8	Mbabane	6,703 (17 360)	Mswati III, king Obed Mfanyana Dlamini, prime minister

On October 9, King Mswati III dissolved parliament and elections scheduled for November were postponed until 1993. The monarchy took steps to introduce political reforms slowly, including the introduction of multiparty politics. GNP (1990 est.): $563 million. Foreign Trade (1990): Imports, $651 million; exports, $543 million.

Nation, Region	Population in millions	Capital	Area Sq mi (km²)	Head of State/Government
Togo, W. Africa	3.8	Lomé	21,927 (56 790)	Gnassingbé Eyadéma, president Joseph Kokou Koffigoh, prime minister

After at least three transitional governments in 1992, Joseph Kokou Koffigoh remained premier of an interim government. Soldiers loyal to President Gnassingbé Eyadéma, who was stripped of all but ceremonial duties in 1991, made several attempts to disrupt the interim government. The European Community decided not to resume aid to the nation until an election timetable was observed. GDP (1989 est.): $1.4 billion. Foreign Trade (1989 est.): Imports, $344 million; exports, $331 million.

Nation, Region	Population in millions	Capital	Area Sq mi (km²)	Head of State/Government
Tonga, Oceania	0.1	Nuku'alofa	289 (748)	Taufa'ahau Tupou IV, king Baron Vaea, prime minister

GDP (1989 est.): $86 million. Foreign Trade (1991): Imports, $62 million; exports, $14 million.

Nation, Region	Population in millions	Capital	Area Sq mi (km²)	Head of State/Government
Trinidad and Tobago, Caribbean	1.3	Port-of-Spain	1,981 (5 130)	Noor Hassanali, president Patrick Manning, prime minister

Rebels from a 1990 attempted coup were released from a Trinidad and Tobago prison by order of a court there. The rebels had been promised amnesty if captives were released safely but the government reneged on its promise. GDP (1989 est.): $4.05 billion. Foreign Trade (1991): Imports, $1.65 billion; exports, $1.96 billion.

Nation, Region	Population in millions	Capital	Area Sq mi (km²)	Head of State/Government
Tuvalu, Oceania	0.009	Funafuti	10 (26)	Sir Tupua Leupena, governor-general Bikenibeu Paeniu, prime minister

GNP (1989 est.): $4.6 million. Foreign Trade (1983 est.): Imports, $2.8 million; exports, $1 million.

Nation, Region	Population in millions	Capital	Area Sq mi (km²)	Head of State/Government
United Arab Emirates, W. Asia	2.4	Abu Dhabi	32,278 (83 600)	Zayid bin Sultan Al Nuhayyan, president Rashid bin Said Al Maktum, prime minister

The government of Abu Dhabi of the United Arab Emirates agreed to pay creditors $2.2 billion for its role as the main shareholder in the defunct Bank of Credit and Commerce International. GDP (1989 est.): $27.3 billion. Foreign Trade (1989 est.): Imports, $9.0 billion; exports, $15 billion.

Nation, Region	Population in millions	Capital	Area Sq mi (km²)	Head of State/Government
Vanuatu, Oceania	0.2	Port-Vila	5,699 (14 760)	Frederick Timakata, president Donald Kalpokas, prime minister

GDP (1989 est.): $137 million. Foreign Trade (1989 est.): Imports, $58.4 million; exports, $14.5 million.

Nation, Region	Population in millions	Capital	Area Sq mi (km²)	Head of State/Government
Vatican City, S. Europe	0.001	Vatican City	0.17 (0.438)	John Paul II, pope

On January 13 the Vatican recognized the independence of Croatia and Slovenia, two predominantly Roman Catholic republics.

Nation, Region	Population in millions	Capital	Area Sq mi (km²)	Head of State/Government
Western Samoa, Oceania	0.2	Apia	1,104 (2 860)	Tanumafili II Malietoa, head of state

GDP (1990 est.): $115 million. Foreign Trade (1990 est.): Imports, $87 million; exports, $9.4 million.

Nation, Region	Population in millions	Capital	Area Sq mi (km²)	Head of State/Government
Yemen, S. Asia	10.4	San'a	203,850 (527 970)	Ali Abdullah Saleh, president

Yemen and Saudi Arabia held talks on July 20 and September 29 to resolve a long-standing border dispute. On October 1, Yemen signed a border-demarcation agreement with Oman. In June, Yemen allowed hundreds of refugees from Somalia to enter its port in Aden. Elections scheduled for November 1992 were postponed until April 1993. GDP (1990 est.): $5.3 billion. Foreign Trade (North—1988): Imports, $1.3 billion; exports, $606 million; (South—1989 est.): Imports, $553.9 million; exports, $113.8 million.

Nation, Region	Population in millions	Capital	Area Sq mi (km²)	Head of State/Government
Zambia, E. Africa	8.4	Lusaka	290,583 (752 610)	Frederick Chiluba, president Levy Mwanawsa, vice president

Zambia, which in 1991 had a new democratic government, struggled to keep order in 1992 amidst strikes, political clashes, and a drought that wiped out one third of the country's corn crop. GDP (1990): $4.7 billion. Foreign Trade (1990): Imports, $1.1 million; exports, $1.1 million.

POPULATION Vital Statistics of Selected Countries

	Estimated population mid-1992 (millions)	Birthrate per 1,000 population	Death rate per 1,000 population	Infant mortality [1]	Life expectancy at birth [2]	Urban population [3]
World	5,420.0	26	9	68	63/67	43
Afghanistan	16.9	48	22	172	41/42	18
Albania	3.3	25	6	30.8	70/76	36
Algeria	26.0	35	7	61	65/67	50
Argentina	33.1	21	8	25.7	66/73	86
Armenia	3.5	24	7	35	69/75	68
Austria	7.9	12	11	7.4	73/79	55
Azerbaijan	7.1	26	6	45	67/74	53
Bangladesh	111.4	37	13	120	54/53	14
Belarus	10.3	14	11	20	67/76	67
Belgium	10.0	13	11	7.9	72/79	95
Bolivia	7.8	36	10	89	58/64	51
Brazil	150.8	26	7	69	62/68	74
Cambodia	9.1	38	16	127	47/50	13
Canada	27.4	15	7	7.1	73/80	78
Cen. Afr. Republic	3.2	44	18	141	45/48	43
Chile	13.6	23	6	17.1	71/76	85
China	1,165.8	20	7	34	68/71	26
Colombia	34.3	26	6	37	68/73	68
Cuba	10.8	18	6	11.1	74/78	73
Cyprus	0.7	19	9	11	74/78	62
Denmark	5.2	13	12	7.5	72/78	85
Ecuador	10.0	31	7	57	65/69	55
Egypt	55.7	32	7	73	58/61	45
El Salvador	5.6	36	8	55	61/68	48
Ethiopia	54.3	47	20	139	46/48	12
Finland	5.0	13	10	5.8	71/79	62
France	56.9	13	9	7.3	73/81	73
Georgia	5.5	17	9	33	68/76	56
Germany	80.6	11	11	7.5	72/78	90
Ghana	16.0	44	13	86	52/56	32
Greece	10.3	10	9	10.0	73/78	58
Guatemala	9.7	39	7	61	60/65	39
Haiti	6.4	45	16	106	53/56	29
Hungary	10.3	12	14	15.4	65/74	63
India	882.6	30	10	91	58/59	26
Indonesia	184.5	26	8	70	58/63	31
Iran	59.7	41	8	43	63/66	54
Iraq	18.2	45	8	67	66/68	73
Ireland	3.5	15	9	8.0	71/77	56
Israel	5.2	21	6	8.7	75/78	91
Italy	58.0	10	9	8.6	73/80	72
Japan	124.4	10	7	4.6	76/82	77
Jordan	3.6	39	5	39	69/73	70
Kazakhstan	16.9	22	8	44	64/73	58
Kenya	26.2	45	9	62	59/63	22
Korea, North	22.2	24	6	31	66/72	64
Korea, South	44.3	16	6	15	67/75	74
Kyrgyzstan	4.5	29	7	35	64/72	38
Laos	4.4	46	17	112	48/51	16
Lebanon	3.4	28	7	46	66/70	84
Liberia	2.8	47	15	144	53/56	44
Libya	4.5	37	7	64	65/70	76
Malaysia	18.7	30	5	29	69/73	35
Mexico	87.7	29	6	47	66/72	71
Moldova	4.4	18	10	35	66/72	48
Morocco	26.2	33	8	73	62/65	46
Myanmar (Burma)	42.5	30	11	72	56/60	24
Netherlands	15.2	13	9	6.8	74/80	89
New Zealand	3.4	18	8	7.6	72/78	84
Nigeria	90.1	46	16	114	48/49	16
Norway	4.3	14	11	6.9	73/80	71
Pakistan	121.7	44	13	109	56/57	28
Panama	2.4	24	5	21	71/75	53
Paraguay	4.5	34	7	34	65/69	43
Peru	22.5	31	9	76	60/63	70
Philippines	63.7	32	7	54	63/66	43
Poland	38.4	14	11	15.9	67/76	61
Romania	23.2	12	11	25.7	67/73	54
Russia	149.3	14	11	30	64/75	74
Saudi Arabia	16.1	42	7	65	63/66	77
South Africa	41.7	34	8	52	61/67	56
Spain	38.6	10	9	7.6	73/80	91
Sweden	8.7	14	11	6.0	75/80	83
Syria	13.7	45	7	48	64/66	50
Taiwan	20.8	16	5	6.2	71/76	71
Tajikistan	5.5	38	6	73	67/72	31
Tanzania	27.4	50	15	105	49/54	21
Thailand	56.3	20	6	39	64/69	18
Tunisia	8.4	27	6	44	65/66	53
Turkey	59.2	29	7	59	64/69	59
Turkmenistan	3.9	34	7	93	62/68	45
Uganda	17.5	52	15	96	50/52	10
Ukraine	52.1	13	12	22	66/75	68
United Kingdom	57.8	14	11	7.9	73/79	90
United States	255.6	16	9	9.0	72/79	75
Uruguay	3.1	18	10	20.4	68/75	89
Uzbekistan	21.3	33	6	64	66/72	40
Venezuela	18.9	30	5	24.2	67/73	84
Vietnam	69.2	30	8	45	62/66	20
Zaire	37.9	46	14	83	50/54	40
Zambia	8.4	51	13	76	51/54	49
Zimbabwe	10.3	41	10	61	58/61	26

[1] Deaths under age one per 1,000 live births
[2] Male/female
[3] Percentage of the total population

Source: 1992 World Population Data Sheet, Population Reference Bureau, Inc., Washington, DC

WORLD MINERAL AND METAL PRODUCTION

ALUMINUM, primary smelter (thousand metric tons)
	1990	1991
United States	4,048	4,121
USSR[e]	2,200	2,000
Canada	1,567	1,830
Australia	1,234	1,235
Brazil	931	1,140
China[e]	850	860
Norway	845	833
Germany	736	690
Venezuela	594	610
India	433	504
Spain	355	355
United Kingdom	290	294
France	326	286
Netherlands	270	264
Other countries[a]	3,302	3,246
Total	17,981	18,268

ANTIMONY, mine[b] (metric tons)
	1990	1991
China[e]	35,000	35,000
USSR[e]	9,000	8,500
Bolivia	8,454	7,532
South Africa	4,815	4,500[e]
Mexico	2,614	2,900
Australia	1,420	1,500[e]
Czechoslovakia	1,270	1,000[e]
Guatemala	1,050	1,000[e]
Peru	560	600[e]
Canada	653	525
Thailand	537	500[e]
Other countries[a]	1,510	1,098
Total	66,883	62,655

ASBESTOS[c] (thousand metric tons)
	1990	1991
USSR[e]	2,400	2,000
Canada	686	687
Brazil	210[e]	210[e]
Zimbabwe	161	161[e]
China[e]	160	150
South Africa	146	149
Greece	66[e]	60
Other countries[a]	90	73
Total	3,919	3,490

BARITE[c] (thousand metric tons)
	1990	1991
China[e]	1,750	1,800
India	707	500[e]
USSR[e]	500	450
United States	439	448
Morocco	364	360[e]
Turkey	271	275[e]
Mexico	305	211
Germany	173	168[e]
France	93	90[e]
Other countries[a]	993	969
Total	5,595	5,271

BAUXITE[d] (thousand metric tons)
	1990	1991
Australia	41,391	40,503
Guinea	17,524	17,054
Jamaica	10,921	11,552
Brazil	9,678	10,310
China[e]	4,200	5,200
India	4,852	4,835
USSR[e]	5,294	4,795
Suriname	3,267	3,198
Yugoslavia	2,952	2,700[e]
Guyana	1,424	2,204
Greece	2,504	2,130
Hungary	2,559	2,037
Sierra Leone	1,430	1,288
Indonesia	1,206	1,242
Other countries[a]	3,293	3,719
Total	112,495	112,767

CEMENT[c] (thousand metric tons)
	1990	1991
China	209,712	244,656
USSR	137,322	122,400
Japan	80,445	89,200
United States	71,310	65,052
India	44,720	49,788
Germany	40,435	42,002
Italy	39,500	40,000[e]
South Korea	33,600	39,168
Spain	28,092	27,576
Brazil	25,900	27,492
Turkey	24,408	26,028[e]
France	26,388	25,020
Mexico	23,900	24,648
Other countries[a]	350,705	367,471
Total	1,141,437	1,190,501

CHROMITE[c] (thousand metric tons)
	1990	1991
South Africa	4,618	5,078
USSR[e]	3,800	3,800
India	939	900[e]
Albania[e]	910	800
Turkey	730[e]	800[e]
Zimbabwe	573	600[e]
Finland	489	475[e]
Brazil	267	275[e]
Philippines	183	200[e]
Other countries[a]	339	309
Total	12,848	13,237

COAL, anthracite and bituminous[c] (million metric tons)
	1990	1991
China	1,080	1,059
United States	861	823
USSR	471	405
India	209	220[e]
South Africa	175	175[e]
Australia	159	165[e]
Poland	148	140
United Kingdom	89	96
Germany	76	73
Canada	59	62
North Korea[e]	55	55
Other countries[a]	195	198
Total	3,577	3,471

COAL, lignite[c f] (million metric tons)
	1990	1991
Germany	387	279
USSR	157	152
Czechoslovakia	86	79
United States	83	79
Poland	68	69
Yugoslavia	76	58
Greece	52	52[e]
Turkey	44	46
Australia	46	41
Romania	34	28
Other countries[a]	105	100
Total	1,138	983

COPPER, mine[b] (thousand metric tons)
	1990	1991
Chile	1,588	1,814
United States	1,588	1,631
Canada	802	777
USSR[e]	600	550
Zambia	496	412
Peru	334	399
Poland	329	390
China[e]	375	375
Australia	330	311
Mexico	321	297
Zaire	356	292
Papua New Guinea	170	204
South Africa	197	200
Philippines	182	147
Other countries[a]	1,154	1,153
Total	8,822	8,952

COPPER, refined, primary and secondary (thousand metric tons)
	1990	1991
United States	2,017	1,995
Chile	1,192	1,238
Japan	1,008	1,076
USSR[e]	930	870
China[e]	560	560
Canada	516	538
Germany	533	523
Zambia	438	430
Poland	352	378
Belgium	361	287
Australia	274	282
Peru	182	246
South Korea	186	201
Spain	171	190
Zaire	173	140
Other countries[a]	1,630	1,047
Total	10,523	10,001

DIAMOND, natural (thousand carats)
	1990	1991
Australia	34,662	35,965
Zaire	19,427	20,000[e]
Botswana	17,352	18,000[e]
USSR[e]	15,000	15,000
South Africa	8,708	8,412
Angola	1,300	1,300[e]
Namibia	761	1,194
China[e]	1,000	1,000
Other countries[a]	3,356	3,515
Total	101,566	104,386

FLUORSPAR[g] (thousand metric tons)
	1990	1991
China[e]	1,700	1,600
Mongolia[e]	614	520
Mexico	634	352
USSR[e]	380	350
South Africa	311	270
France[e]	201	200[e]
Germany	155	135[e]
Italy	123	100[e]
Other countries[a]	907	827
Total	5,025	4,354

GAS, natural[n] (billion cubic meters)
	1990	1991
USSR	850	841
United States	497	506
Canada	100	109
Netherlands	76	77[e]
Algeria	64	65[e]
Indonesia	43	48[e]
United Kingdom	42	43
Mexico	36	38[e]
Norway	28	31[e]
Romania	28	29
Other countries[a]	350	360
Total	2,114	2,147

GOLD, mine[b] (kilograms)
	1990	1991
South Africa	605,400	601,013
United States	294,527	289.885
USSR[e]	302,000	240,000
Australia	244,137	234,218
Canada	167,373	172,708
China[e]	100,000	120,000
Brazil[e]	85,000	80,000
Papua New Guinea	31,035	60,780
Poland[e]	29,400	31,500
Colombia	29,352	30,000[e]
Chile	27,503	28,000[e]
Ghana	16,840	26,310
Philippines	24,591	24,938
Other countries[a]	199,640	203,670
Total	2,156,798	2,143,022

GYPSUM[c] (thousand metric tons)
	1990	1991
United States	14,883	14,021
China[e]	8,000	8,200
Canada	8,202	8,000[e]
Iran[e]	7,724	8,000[e]
Thailand	5,753	7,196
Japan[e]	6,400	6,300
France	5,796	5,600[e]
Mexico	5,434	5,500
Spain[e]	5,000	5,000
USSR[e]	4,500	4,000
United Kingdom[e]	4,000	3,500
Australia[e]	1,800	2,000
Germany[e]	2,100	1,950
Other countries[a]	15,378	14,768
Total	94,970	94,035

IRON ORE, marketable equivalent[c] (thousand metric tons)
	1990	1991
USSR	236,160	200,000
Brazil	155,200	155,000
China[e]	117,000	119,000
Australia	110,508	117,134
India	54,579	57,638
United States	56,408	55,616
Canada	35,670	35,961
South Africa	30,291	29,069
Venezuela	20,365	21,222
Sweden	19,812	19,284
Mauritania	11,420	11,000[e]
North Korea[e]	9,500	10,000
France	8,729	7,472
Other countries[a]	62,785	58,817
Total	928,427	897,213

IRON, crude steel (thousand metric tons)
	1990	1991
USSR	154,414	132,666
Japan	110,339	109,649
United States	89,726	79,738
China	64,656	70,560
Germany	44,022	42,169
South Korea	23,125	26,001
Italy	25,439	25,007
Brazil	20,572	22,617
France	19,032	18,437
United Kingdom	17,908	16,511
India	14,963	16,394
Canada	12,281	12,987
Spain	12,705	12,700[e]
Czechoslovakia	14,877	12,133
Belgium	11,426	11,332
Taiwan	9,747	10,957
Poland	13,625	10,439
Other countries[a]	110,337	103,366
Total	769,194	733,663

LEAD, mine[b] (thousand metric tons)
	1990	1991
Australia	565	571
United States	497	477
USSR[e]	420	400
China[e]	364	380
Canada	232	235
Peru	189	203
Mexico	180	158
North Korea[e]	120	120
Sweden	84	79
Yugoslavia	83	77
Other countries[a]	640	605
Total	3,374	3,305

LEAD, refined, primary and secondary[i] (thousand metric tons)
	1990	1991
United States	1,327	1,229
USSR[e]	700	630
Germany	394	403
China[e]	296	330
Japan	329	328
United Kingdom	329	301
France	260	283
Australia	229	230
Canada	192	211
Italy	173	208
Mexico	202	195
Belgium	92	99
Other countries[a]	1,317	1,182
Total	5,840	5,629

	1990	1991
MAGNESIUM, primary (thousand metric tons)		
United States	139	131
USSR[e]	88	80
Norway	48	44
Canada	27	36[e]
France	15	14[e]
Japan	13	12
Brazil	7	8
Other countries[a]	17	14
Total	354	339
MANGANESE ORE[c] (thousand metric tons)		
USSR[e]	8,500	8,000
China[e]	3,300	3,400
South Africa	4,402	3,144
Gabon	2,540[e]	2,125
Brazil	2,000[e]	2,000[e]
Australia	1,988	1,482
India	1,363	1,300[e]
Other countries[a]	1,120	1,185
Total	25,213	22,636
MERCURY, mine (metric tons)		
USSR[e]	2,100	1,900
Mexico	735	720[e]
China[e]	800	700
Spain	425	450[e]
Algeria	637	431
United States	40[e]	40[e]
Other countries[a]	364	335
Total	5,101	4,576
MOLYBDENUM, mine[b] (metric tons)		
United States	61,611	53,364
China[e]	15,700	16,000
Chile	13,830	14,540
Canada	12,188	11,000[e]
USSR[e]	11,000	10,000
Peru	2,410	3,000[e]
Mexico	3,200[e]	2,550[e]
Other countries[a]	2,293	1,770
Total	122,232	112,224
NATURAL GAS LIQUIDS (million barrels)		
United States	569	575[e]
USSR[e]	250	245
Saudi Arabia	195	200[e]
Mexico	156	165[e]
Canada	156	158
United Arab Emirates	58	60[e]
Other countries[a]	387	395
Total	1,771	1,798
NICKEL, mine[b] (thousand metric tons)		
USSR[e]	260	250
Canada	199	193
New Caledonia	89	92
Indonesia	68	69[e]
Australia	67	69
Cuba[e]	40	35
South Africa	30	30[e]
China[e]	27	28
Dominican Republic	29	25[e]
Other countries[a]	128	132
Total	937	923
NITROGEN, content of ammonia (thousand metric tons)		
China[e]	17,500	18,000
USSR[e]	18,200	17,100
United States	12,524	12,692
India	7,022	7,043
Canada	3,054	3,016
Netherlands	3,194	3,000
Indonesia	2,600[e]	2,500[e]
Germany	2,671	2,348
Mexico	2,164	2,221
Poland[e]	2,006	1,669
France	1,586	1,604
Other countries[a]	25,074	22,518
Total	97,595	93,711
PETROLEUM, crude (million barrels)		
USSR	3,911	3,484
Saudi Arabia	2,354	2,986
United States	2,685	2,707
Iran	1,127	1,217
China	1,009	1,021
Mexico	932	977

	1990	1991
PETROLEUM, crude (cont'd)		
United Arab Emirates	773	890
Venezuela	780	865
Nigeria	669	710
United Kingdom	662	656
Indonesia	534	589
Canada	565	563
Libya	502	541
Algeria	440	442
Iraq	745	109
Kuwait	428	68
Other countries[a]	3,916	4,026
Total	22,032	21,851
PHOSPHATE ROCK[c] (thousand metric tons)		
United States	46,343	48,096
USSR[e]	33,500	30,000
China[e]	19,000	20,000
Morocco	21,396	17,900
Tunisia	6,259	6,000[e]
Jordan	5,925	4,000[e]
Israel	3,516	3,370
Brazil	2,968	3,309
South Africa	3,165	3,050
Togo	2,314	2,965
Senegal	2,147	1,700
Other countries[a]	7,823	6,469
Total	154,356	146,859
POTASH, K$_2$O equivalent basis (thousand metric tons)		
USSR	9,000	8,400
Canada	7,345	7,012
Germany	4,865	3,868
United States	1,713	1,749
Israel	1,311	1,270
France	1,230	1,129
Other countries[a]	2,221	2,120
Total	27,685	25,548
SALT[c] (thousand metric tons)		
United States	36,959	35,943
China[e]	20,000	25,500
USSR	14,700	14,000
Germany	14,288	13,785
Canada	11,097	11,000
India	9,503	9,500[e]
Australia[e]	7,227	7,791
Mexico	7,135	7,595
Romania	6,500[e]	6,500[e]
France	6,450	6,500[e]
United Kingdom	6,434	5,200[e]
Brazil	5,203	5,000[e]
Poland[e]	4,065	3,900[e]
Other countries[a]	32,792	32,645
Total	182,353	184,859
SILVER, mine[b] (metric tons)		
Mexico	2,346	2,196
United States	2,125	1,848
Peru	1,725	1,770
USSR[e]	1,400	1,300
Canada	1,466	1,274
Australia	1,138	1,180
Poland	832	870[e]
Chile	633	655
Bolivia	311	337
Spain	270	270[e]
Sweden	185	211
Morocco	235	178
South Africa	181	172
Other countries[a]	2,092	2,026
Total	14,939	14,287
SULFUR, all forms[j] (thousand metric tons)		
United States	11,560	10,816
USSR[e]	9,025	8,100
Canada	6,849	7,100[e]
China[e]	5,370	5,470
Poland	4,834	4,820[e]
Japan	2,657	2,754
Germany	2,018	1,990
Mexico	2,342	1,980
Saudi Arabia[e]	1,435	1,450[e]
France	1,049	1,199
Spain	858	910[e]
Iran	680	700
Other countries[a]	9,477	8,303
Total	58,154	55,592

	1990	1991
TIN, mine[b] (metric tons)		
China[e]	42,000	43,000
Indonesia	30,200	30,061
Brazil	39,149	29,300
Malaysia	28,468	20,710
Bolivia	17,249	16,863
Thailand	14,635	14,937
USSR[e]	15,000	13,500
Peru	5,134	6,559
Australia	7,425	5,630
Other countries[a]	19,258	16,135
Total	218,518	196,695
TITANIUM MINERALS[c k] (thousand metric tons)		
ILMENITE		
Australia	1,621	1,381
Norway	814	800[e]
USSR[e]	430	400
Malaysia	530	336
India[e]	160	160
China[e]	150	150
Brazil	114	120[e]
Other countries[a]	133	139
Total	3,952	3,486
RUTILE		
Australia	245	201
Sierra Leone	144	155
South Africa[e]	64	75[e]
Other countries[a]	22	19
Total	475	450
TITANIFEROUS SLAG		
South Africa[e]	840	900
Canada	760	600
Total	1,600	1,500
TUNGSTEN, mine[b] (metric tons)		
China[e]	20,000	20,000
USSR[e]	8,800	8,000
Peru	1,536	1,600[e]
Austria	1,378	1,400[e]
Portugal	1,405	1,400[e]
Bolivia	1,014	1,060
South Korea	1,361	1,037
Other countries[a]	4,382	3,454
Total	39,876	37,951
URANIUM OXIDE (U$_3$O$_8$)[l] (metric tons)		
Canada	10,342	9,124
Australia	4,162	4,453
United States	2,658	3,585
Niger	3,340	3,495
France	3,461	2,907
Namibia	3,921	2,889
South Africa	2,875	1,974
Other countries[a]	1,573	1,430
Total	32,332	29,857
ZINC, mine[b] (thousand metric tons)		
Canada	1,203	1,148
Australia	933	1,048
USSR[e]	750	650
China[e]	619	650
Peru	577	623
United States	543	547
Mexico	322	301
Spain	258	260
Ireland	167	188
Sweden	157	155
Poland	178	144
Other countries[a]	1,613	1,568
Total	7,320	7,282
ZINC, smelter, primary and secondary (thousand metric tons)		
USSR[e]	890	800
Japan	688	731
Canada	592	661
China[e]	550	526
United States	358	377
Germany	350	347
Australia	310	330
France	264	300
Belgium	290	298
Spain	253	273
Italy	264	265
South Korea	248	250
Netherlands	208	201
Mexico	199	189
Other countries[a]	1,589	1,534
Total	7,053	7,082

GENERAL NOTES: In the foregoing table, "USSR" includes the area that constituted the Soviet Union of midyear 1991, including all of the 15 individual republics. "Yugoslavia" includes Bosnia-Herzegovina, Croatia, Macedonia, Montenegro, Serbia, and Slovenia. [a] Estimated in part. [b] Content of concentrates. [c] Gross weight. [d] Includes calculated bauxite equivalent of estimated output of aluminum ores other than bauxite (nepheline concentrate and alunite ores) that are produced for the recovery of aluminum only in the USSR. [e] Estimate. [f] Includes coal classified as brown coal in some countries. [g] Gross weight of marketable product. [h] Marketable production (includes gas sold or used by producers as fuel, but excludes gas reinjected to reservoirs for pressure maintenance, as well as that flared or vented to the atmosphere, and hence not used either as a fuel or as an industrial raw material, and thus having no economic value). [i] Data for each country exclude bullion produced for refining elsewhere. [j] Includes: (1) Frasch process sulfur; (2) elemental sulfur mined by conventional means; (3) by-product recovered elemental sulfur; and (4) elemental sulfur equivalent of sulfur recovered in the form of sulfuric acid or other chemicals from pyrite and other materials. [k] Excludes output in the United States, which cannot be disclosed because it is company proprietary information. [l] Excludes output, if any, by Albania, Bulgaria, China, Cuba, Czechoslovakia, Hungary, North Korea, Mongolia, Poland, Romania, USSR, and Vietnam.

UNITED STATES: 103d CONGRESS
First Session

SENATE MEMBERSHIP

(As of January 1993: 57 Democrats, 43 Republicans.) Letters after names refer to party affiliation—D for Democrat, R for Republican, I for Independent. Single asterisk (*) denotes term expiring in January 1995; double asterisk (**), term expiring in January 1997; triple asterisk (***), term expiring in January 1999. [1]Elected in 1992 to fill unexpired term. [2]Appointed to fill vacancy.

Alabama
** H. Heflin, D
*** R. C. Shelby, D

Alaska
** T. Stevens, R
*** F. H. Murkowski, R

Arizona
* D. DeConcini, D
*** J. McCain, R

Arkansas
*** D. Bumpers, D
** D. H. Pryor, D

California
* D. Feinstein, D[1]
*** B. Boxer, D

Colorado
** H. Brown, R
*** B. Nighthorse Campbell, D

Connecticut
*** C. J. Dodd, D
* J. I. Lieberman, D

Delaware
* W. V. Roth, Jr., R
* J. R. Biden, Jr., D

Florida
*** B. Graham, D
* C. Mack, R

Georgia
** S. Nunn, D
*** P. Coverdell, R

Hawaii
*** D. K. Inouye, D
* D. K. Akaka, D

Idaho
** L. E. Craig, R
*** D. Kempthorne, R

Illinois
** P. Simon, D
*** C. Moseley Braun, D

Indiana
* R. G. Lugar, R
*** D. Coats, R

Iowa
*** C. E. Grassley, R
** T. Harkin, D

Kansas
*** R. Dole, R
** N. L. Kassebaum, R

Kentucky
*** W. H. Ford, D
** M. McConnell, R

Louisiana
** J. B. Johnston, D
*** J. B. Breaux, D

Maine
** W. S. Cohen, R
* G. J. Mitchell, D

Maryland
* P. S. Sarbanes, D
*** B. A. Mikulski, D

Massachusetts
* E. M. Kennedy, D
** J. F. Kerry, D

Michigan
* D. W. Riegle, Jr., D
** C. Levin, D

Minnesota
* D. F. Durenberger, R
** P. Wellstone, D

Mississippi
** T. Cochran, R
* T. Lott, R

Missouri
* J. C. Danforth, R
*** C. S. Bond, R

Montana
** M. Baucus, D
* C. Burns, R

Nebraska
** J. J. Exon, Jr., D
* J. R. Kerrey, D

Nevada
*** H. Reid, D
* R. H. Bryan, D

New Hampshire
** R. C. Smith, R
*** J. Gregg, R

New Jersey
** B. Bradley, D
* F. R. Lautenberg, D

New Mexico
** P. V. Domenici, R
* J. Bingaman, D

New York
* D. P. Moynihan, D
*** A. M. D'Amato, R

North Carolina
** J. Helms, R
*** L. Faircloth, R

North Dakota
*** B. L. Dorgan, D
* K. Conrad, D[1]

Ohio
*** J. H. Glenn, Jr., D
* H. M. Metzenbaum, D

Oklahoma
** D. L. Boren, D
*** D. L. Nickles, R

Oregon
** M. O. Hatfield, R
*** B. Packwood, R

Pennsylvania
*** A. Specter, R
* H. Wofford, D[1]

Rhode Island
** C. Pell, D
* J. H. Chafee, R

South Carolina
** S. Thurmond, R
*** E. F. Hollings, D

South Dakota
** L. Pressler, R
*** T. A. Daschle, D

Tennessee
* J. R. Sasser, D
** Harlan Mathews, D[2]

Texas
* R. Krueger, D[2]
** P. Gramm, R

Utah
* O. Hatch, R
*** R. F. Bennett, R

Vermont
*** P. J. Leahy, D
* J. M. Jeffords, R

Virginia
** J. W. Warner, R
* C. S. Robb, D

Washington
* S. Gorton, R
*** P. Murray, D

West Virginia
* R. C. Byrd, D
** J. D. Rockefeller IV, D

Wisconsin
* H. Kohl, D
*** R. D. Feingold, D

Wyoming
* M. Wallop, R
** A. K. Simpson, R

HOUSE MEMBERSHIP

(As of January 1993, 255 Democrats, 176 Republicans, 1 independent, 3 vacant.) "At-L." in place of congressional district number means "representative at large."

Alabama
1. S. Callahan, R
2. T. Everett, R
3. G. Browder, D
4. T. Bevill, D
5. B. Cramer, D
6. S. Bachus, R
7. E. F. Hilliard, D

Alaska
At-L. D. Young, R

Arizona
1. S. Coppersmith, D
2. E. Pastor, D
3. B. Stump, R
4. J. L. Kyl, R
5. J. Kolbe, R
6. K. English, D

Arkansas
1. B. Lambert, D
2. R. Thornton, D
3. T. Hutchinson, R
4. J. Dickey, R

California
1. D. Hamburg, D
2. W. W. Herger, R
3. V. Fazio, D
4. J. Doolittle, R
5. R. T. Matsui, D
6. L. Woolsey, D
7. G. Miller, D
8. N. Pelosi, D
9. R. V. Dellums, D
10. B. Baker, R
11. R. W. Pombo, R
12. T. Lantos, D

13. F. H. Stark, D
14. A. G. Eshoo, D
15. N. Y. Mineta, D
16. D. Edwards, D
17. vacant
18. G. Condit, D
19. R. H. Lehman, D
20. C. Dooley, D
21. B. M. Thomas, R
22. M. Huffington, R
23. E. Gallegly, R
24. A. Beilenson, D
25. H. P. McKeon, R
26. H. L. Berman, D
27. C. J. Moorhead, R
28. D. Dreier, R
29. H. A. Waxman, D
30. X. Becerra, D
31. M. G. Martinez, Jr., D
32. J. C. Dixon, D
33. L. Roybal-Allard, D
34. E. E. Torres, D
35. M. Waters, D
36. J. Harman, D
37. W. R. Tucker, D
38. S. Horn, R
39. E. Royce, R
40. J. Lewis, R
41. J. C. Kim, R
42. G. E. Brown, Jr., D
43. K. Calvert, R
44. A. A. McCandless, R
45. D. Rohrabacher, R
46. R. K. Dornan, R
47. C. C. Cox, R
48. R. Packard, R
49. L. Schenk, D.
50. B. Filner, D

51. R. Cunningham, R
52. D. Hunter, R

Colorado
1. P. Schroeder, D
2. D. Skaggs, D
3. S. McInnis, R
4. W. Allard, R
5. J. Hefley, R
6. D. Schaefer, R

Connecticut
1. B. B. Kennelly, D
2. S. Gejdenson, D
3. R. DeLauro, D
4. C. Shays, R
5. G. Franks, R
6. N. L. Johnson, R

Delaware
At-L. T. M. Castle, R

Florida
1. E. Hutto, D
2. P. Peterson, D
3. C. Brown, D
4. T. Fowler, R
5. K. Thurman, D
6. C. B. Stearns, R
7. J. L. Mica, R
8. B. McCollum, R
9. M. Bilirakis, R
10. C. W. Young, R
11. S. Gibbons, D
12. C. T. Canady, R
13. D. Miller, R

14. P. J. Goss, R
15. J. Bacchus, D
16. T. Lewis, R
17. C. Meek, D
18. I. Ros-Lehtinen, R
19. H. A. Johnston, D
20. P. Deutsch, D
21. L. Diaz-Balart, R
22. E. C. Shaw, Jr., R
23. A. L. Hastings, D

Georgia
1. J. Kingston, R
2. S. Bishop, D
3. M. Collins, R
4. J. Linder, R
5. J. Lewis, D
6. N. Gingrich, R
7. G. Darden, D
8. J. R. Rowland, D
9. N. Deal, D
10. D. Johnson, D
11. C. McKinney, D

Hawaii
1. N. Abercrombie, D
2. P. Mink, D

Idaho
1. L. LaRocco, D
2. M. D. Crapo, R

Illinois
1. B.L. Rush, D
2. M. Reynolds, D
3. W. O. Lipinski, D
4. L. V. Gutierrez, D

5. D. Rostenkowski, D
6. H. J. Hyde, R
7. C. Collins, D
8. P. M. Crane, R
9. S. R. Yates, D
10. J. E. Porter, R
11. G. E. Sangmeister, D
12. J. F. Costello, D
13. H. W. Fawell, R
14. J. D. Hastert, R
15. T. W. Ewing, R
16. D. Manzullo, R
17. L. Evans, D
18. R. H. Michel, R
19. G. Poshard, D
20. R. J. Durbin, D

Indiana
1. P. J. Visclosky, D
2. P. R. Sharp, D
3. T. Roemer, D
4. J. Long, D
5. S. Buyer, R
6. D. Burton, R
7. J. T. Myers, R
8. F. McCloskey, D
9. L. H. Hamilton, D
10. A. Jacobs, Jr., D

Iowa
1. J. Leach, R
2. J. Nussle, R
3. J. Lightfoot, R
4. N. Smith, D
5. F. L. Grandy, R

Kansas
1. P. Roberts, R
2. J. Slattery, D
3. J. Meyers, R
4. D. Glickman, D

Kentucky
1. T. Barlow, D
2. W. H. Natcher, D
3. R. L. Mazzoli, D
4. J. Bunning, R
5. H. Rogers, R
6. S. Baesler, D

Louisiana
1. B. Livingston, R
2. W. J. Jefferson, D
3. W. J. Tauzin, D
4. C. Fields, D
5. J. McCrery, R
6. R. H. Baker, R
7. J. A. Hayes, D

Maine
1. T. H. Andrews, D
2. O. J. Snowe, R

Maryland
1. W. T. Gilchrest, R
2. H. D. Bentley, R
3. B. L. Cardin, D
4. A. R. Wynn, D
5. S. H. Hoyer, D
6. R. G. Bartlett, R
7. K. Mfume, D
8. C. A. Morella, R

Massachusetts
1. J. Olver, D
2. R. E. Neal, D
3. P. I. Blute, R
4. B. Frank, D
5. M. T. Meehan, D
6. P. G. Torkildsen, R
7. E. J. Markey, D
8. J. P. Kennedy II, D
9. J. J. Moakley, D
10. G. E. Studds, D

Michigan
1. B. Stupak, D
2. P. Hoekstra, R
3. P. B. Henry, R
4. D. Camp, R
5. J. Barcia, D
6. F. S. Upton, R
7. N. Smith, R
8. B. Carr, D
9. D. E. Kildee, D
10. D. E. Bonior, D
11. J. Knollenberg, R
12. S. M. Levin, D
13. W. D. Ford, D
14. J. Conyers, Jr., D
15. B. R. Collins, D
16. J. D. Dingell, D

Minnesota
1. T. J. Penny, D
2. D. Minge, D
3. J. Ramstad, R
4. B. F. Vento, D
5. M. O. Sabo, D
6. R. Grams, R
7. C. C. Peterson, D
8. J. L. Oberstar, D

Mississippi
1. J. L. Whitten, D
2. vacant
3. G. V. Montgomery, D
4. M. Parker, D
5. G. Taylor, D

Missouri
1. W. Clay, D
2. J. M. Talent, R
3. R. A. Gephardt, D
4. I. Skelton, D
5. A. Wheat, D
6. P. Danner, D
7. M. D. Hancock, R
8. B. Emerson, R
9. H. L. Volkmer, D

Montana
P. Williams, D

Nebraska
1. D. Bereuter, R
2. P. Hoagland, D
3. B. E. Barrett, R

Nevada
1. J. H. Bilbray, D
2. B. F. Vucanovich, R

New Hampshire
1. B. Zeliff, Jr., R
2. D. Swett, D

New Jersey
1. R. E. Andrews, D
2. W. J. Hughes, D
3. H. J. Saxton, R
4. C. H. Smith, R
5. M. Roukema, R
6. F. Pallone, Jr., D
7. B. Franks, R
8. H. C. Klein, D
9. R. G. Torricelli, D
10. D. M. Payne, D
11. D. A. Gallo, R
12. D. Zimmer, R
13. R. Menendez, D

New Mexico
1. S. Schiff, R
2. J. Skeen, R
3. B. Richardson, D

New York
1. G. J. Hochbrueckner, D
2. R. A. Lazio, R
3. P. T. King, R
4. D. A. Levy, R
5. G. L. Ackerman, D
6. F. H. Flake, D
7. T. J. Manton, D
8. J. Nadler, D
9. C. E. Schumer, D
10. E. Towns, D
11. M. R. Owens, D
12. N. M. Velazquez, D
13. S. Molinari, R
14. C. B. Maloney, D
15. C. B. Rangel, D
16. J. Serrano, D
17. E. L. Engel, D
18. N. Lowey, D
19. H. Fish, Jr., R
20. B. A. Gilman, R
21. M. R. McNulty, D
22. G. B. H. Solomon, R
23. S. L. Boehlert, R
24. J. M. McHugh, R
25. J. T. Walsh, R
26. M. D. Hinchey, D
27. B. Paxon, R
28. L. M. Slaughter, D
29. J. J. LaFalce, D
30. J. Quinn, R
31. A. Houghton, R

North Carolina
1. E. Clayton, D
2. T. Valentine, D
3. H. M. Lancaster, D
4. D. E. Price, D
5. S. L. Neal, D
6. H. Coble, R
7. C. Rose, D
8. W. G. Hefner, D
9. J. A. McMillan, R
10. C. Ballenger, R
11. C. H. Taylor, R
12. M. Watt, D

North Dakota
At-L. E. Pomeroy, D

Ohio
1. D. Mann, D
2. W. D. Gradison, Jr., R
3. T. P. Hall, D
4. M. G. Oxley, R
5. P. E. Gillmor, R
6. T. Strickland, D
7. D. L. Hobson, R
8. J. A. Boehner, R
9. M. Kaptur, D
10. M. R. Hoke, R
11. L. Stokes, D
12. J. R. Kasich, R
13. S. Brown, D
14. T. C. Sawyer, D
15. D. Pryce, R
16. R. Regula, R
17. J. A. Traficant, Jr., D
18. D. Applegate, D
19. E. Fingerhut, D

Oklahoma
1. J. M. Inhofe, R
2. M. Synar, D
3. B. K. Brewster, D
4. D. McCurdy, D
5. E. J. Istook, R
6. G. English, D

Oregon
1. E. Furse, D
2. R. F. Smith, R
3. R. Wyden, D
4. P. A. DeFazio, D
5. M. Kopetski, D

Pennsylvania
1. T. M. Foglietta, D
2. L. E. Blackwell, D
3. R. A. Borski, Jr., D
4. R. Klink, D
5. W. F. Clinger, R
6. T. Holden, D
7. C. Weldon, R
8. J. Greenwood, R
9. B. Shuster, R
10. J. M. McDade, R
11. P. E. Kanjorski, D
12. J. P. Murtha, D
13. M. M. Mezvinsky, D
14. W. J. Coyne, D
15. P. McHale, D
16. R. S. Walker, R
17. G. Gekas, R
18. R. Santorum, R
19. W. F. Goodling, R
20. A. J. Murphy, D
21. T. J. Ridge, R

Rhode Island
1. R. K. Machtley, R
2. J. F. Reed, D

South Carolina
1. A. Ravenel, Jr., R
2. F. D. Spence, R
3. B. C. Derrick, Jr., D
4. B. Inglis, R
5. J. M. Spratt, Jr., D
6. J. E. Clyburn, D

South Dakota
At-L. T. Johnson, D

Tennessee
1. J. H. Quillen, R
2. J. J. Duncan, Jr., R
3. M. Lloyd, D
4. J. Cooper, D
5. B. Clement, D
6. B. Gordon, D
7. D. K. Sundquist, R
8. J. S. Tanner, D
9. H. E. Ford, D

Texas
1. J. Chapman, D
2. C. Wilson, D
3. S. Johnson, R
4. R. M. Hall, D
5. J. Bryant, D
6. J. L. Barton, R
7. B. Archer, R
8. J. M. Fields, Jr., R
9. J. Brooks, D
10. J. J. Pickle, D
11. C. Edwards, D
12. P. Geren, D
13. B. Sarpalius, D
14. G. Laughlin, D
15. K. de la Garza, D
16. R. D. Coleman, D
17. C. W. Stenholm, D
18. C. Washington, D
19. L. Combest, R
20. H. B. Gonzalez, D
21. L. S. Smith, R
22. T. DeLay, R
23. H. Bonilla, R
24. M. Frost, D
25. M. A. Andrews, D
26. R. K. Armey, R
27. S. P. Ortiz, D
28. F. Tejeda, D
29. G. Green, D
30. E. B. Johnson, D

Utah
1. J. V. Hansen, R
2. K. Shepherd, D
3. B. Orton, D

Vermont
At-L. B. Sanders, I

Virginia
1. H. H. Bateman, R
2. O. B. Pickett, D
3. R. C. Scott, D
4. N. Sisisky, D
5. L. F. Payne, Jr., D
6. R. W. Goodlatte, R
7. T. J. Bliley, Jr., R
8. J. P. Moran, D
9. R. Boucher, D
10. F. R. Wolf, R
11. L. L. Byrne, D

Washington
1. M. Cantwell, D
2. A. Swift, D
3. J. Unsoeld, D
4. J. Inslee, D
5. T. S. Foley, D
6. N. D. Dicks, D
7. J. McDermott, D
8. J. Dunn, R
9. M. Kreidler, D

West Virginia
1. A. B. Mollohan, D
2. R. E. Wise, Jr., D
3. N. J. Rahall II, D

Wisconsin
1. vacant
2. S. Klug, R
3. S. Gunderson, R
4. G. D. Kleczka, D
5. T. M. Barrett, D
6. T. E. Petri, R
7. D. R. Obey, D
8. T. Roth, R
9. F. J. Sensenbrenner, Jr., R

Wyoming
At-L. C. Thomas, R

AMERICAN SAMOA
Delegate, E. F. H. Faleomavaega, D

DISTRICT OF COLUMBIA
Delegate, Eleanor Holmes Norton, D

GUAM
Delegate, Ben Blaz, R

PUERTO RICO
Resident Commissioner
J. B. Fuster, D

VIRGIN ISLANDS
Delegate, Ron de Lugo, D

UNITED STATES: Major Legislation Enacted During the Second Session of the 102d Congress

SUBJECT	PURPOSE
Unemployment	Extends unemployment benefits for the long-term unemployed by 13 weeks beyond the 26 weeks of regular state benefits and 13–20 weeks of emergency federal benefits. Signed February 7. Public Law 102–244.
Insular Areas	Establishes the Salt River Bay National Historical Park and Ecological Preserve on the island of St. Croix, U.S. Virgin Islands. Signed February 24. Public Law 102–247.
Historical Site	Establishes the Manzanar National Historical Site in the state of California. Signed March 3. Public Law 102–248.
Drought	Gives the secretary of the interior the authority to take action to protect and preserve fish and wildlife habitats and assist in combating drought conditions in the Western states for a ten-year period. Signed March 5. Public Law 102–250.
Congressional Pay Amendment	Congress passes resolutions recognizing the 27th amendment to the U.S. Constitution, proposed by James Madison in 1789 and ratified by the required number of states in 1992. The amendment delays any congressional pay increase until after an election has occurred. Resolutions were enacted May 20. No presidential action required.
Cities	Authorizes dire emergency supplemental appropriations for disaster assistance to meet urgent needs because of calamities such as those that occurred in Los Angeles and Chicago for fiscal year 1992. Signed June 22. Public law 102–302.
National Historic Site	Establishes the Palo Alto Battlefield National Historic Site in the state of Texas. Signed June 23. Public Law 102–303.
Unemployment	Provides $5.5 billion to extend until March 6, 1993, the temporary extension of unemployment benefits for workers who exhaust their normal unemployment benefits. Signed July 3. Public Law 102–318.
Higher Education	Expands the student-loan program. Signed July 23. Public Law 102–325. (*See* page 219).
Animal Research Laboratories	Makes it a federal crime to vandalize animal research laboratories or farms. Signed August 26. Public Law 102–346.
Television	Reauthorizes the nonprofit Corporation for Public Broadcasting (CPB) for three years. Signed August 26. Public Law 102–356.
Job Training	Reauthorizes the 1982 Job Training Partnership Act (JTPA). Signed September 7. Public Law 102–367.
Older Americans	Reauthorizes for four years the 1965 Older Americans Act without provision for the so-called Social Security earning test that would remove the limits on how much older Americans can earn without losing Social Security benefits. Signed September 30. Public Law 102–375.
Physics	Approves funding to continue the building of the superconducting super collider, an underground atom smasher under construction in Waxahachie, TX. Signed October 2. Public Law 102–377.
Cable Television	Imposes new regulations on the cable-television industry. Congress overrode presidential veto on October 5. Public Law 102–385. (*See* page 529).
Foreign Aid	Appropriates funds for foreign aid, including a five-year program of guarantees for $10 billion in loans for Israel. Signed October 6. Public Law 102–391. (*See* page 243.)
Global Warming	Senate ratifies a UN treaty requiring countries to try to limit emission of heat-trapping "greenhouse gases" believed to contribute to global warming. Ratified October 7.
Energy	Signed October 24. Public Law 102–486. (*See* page 221).
Crime	Makes carjacking a federal crime. Signed October 25. Public Law 102–519. (*See* page 202).
Drift Nets for Fishing	Authorizes the administration to implement an international agreement to establish a global moratorium on tuna-fishing practices using purse seine nets, which trap and kill dolphins. Signed October 26. Public Law 102–523.
John F. Kennedy Assassination	Authorizes a special commission to review still-secret documents regarding President Kennedy's assassination in 1963 and to make public all those documents, except those that compromise national security or a person's privacy. Signed October 26. Public Law 102–526.
Housing	Provides for a $66.5 billion reauthorization of federal housing programs. Puts new controls on the Federal National Mortgage Association (Fannie Mae) and the Federal Home Loan Mortgage Corp. (Freddie Mae). Creates new rules to reduce and eliminate lead-based paint poisoning hazards in private and federal housing. Signed October 28. Public Law 102–550.
Farming	Establishes a new loan program for farmers, requiring the Farmers Home Administration (FmHA) to help support new farmers for ten years and limits the number of years a farmer can receive FmHA loans for operating expenses. Signed October 28. Public Law 102–554.
Telephone Consumer Protection	Protects consumers from unscrupulous 900-number phone services by requiring that callers be warned of the cost and terms of such calls. Signed October 28. Public Law 102–557.
Prescription Drugs	Requires prescription-drug manufacturers to pay "user fees" to help offset the cost of federal safety and efficacy reviews. Signed October 29. Public Law 102–571.
Western Water Policy	Revamps the operations of the Bureau of Reclamation's Central Valley Project in California, protects the shores of the Grand Canyon from damaging water releases from the Glen Canyon Dam, and authorizes $922 million for completion of the Central Utah Project. Signed October 30. Public Law 102–575.

Contributors

ABRAM, LYNWOOD, Free-lance Writer and Newspaper Correspondent, El Paso, TX: TEXAS

ADRIAN, CHARLES R., Professor of Political Science, University of California, Riverside; Author, *A History of City Government: The Emergence of the Metropolis 1920–1945;* Coauthor, *State and Local Politics, A History of American City Government: The Formation of Traditions, 1775–1870, Governing Urban America:* CALIFORNIA; LOS ANGELES

AMBRE, AGO, Economist, Office of Economic Affairs, U.S. Department of Commerce: INDUSTRIAL PRODUCTION

ARNOLD, ANTHONY, Author, *Afghanistan: The Soviet Invasion in Perspective, Afghanistan's Two-Party Communism: Parcham and Khalq, The Fateful Pebble: Afghanistan's Role in the Fall of the Soviet Empire:* AFGHANISTAN

ATTNER, PAUL, Senior Writer, *The Sporting News:* SPORTS —Basketball, Football, Olympic Games, Soccer

AUSTIN, TERESA, Free-lance Writer: ENGINEERING, CIVIL

BATRA, PREM P., Professor of Biochemistry, Wright State University: BIOCHEMISTRY

BEAUCHAMP, LANE, *The Kansas City Star:* MISSOURI

BECK, KAY, Department of Communications, Georgia State University: GEORGIA

BEHLER, DEBORAH A., Executive Editor, *Wildlife Conservation* magazine: ZOOS AND ZOOLOGY; ZOOS AND ZOOLOGY —The Eastern U.S. Rabies Epidemic

BEST, JOHN, Chief, *Canada World News,* Ottawa: NEW BRUNSWICK; PRINCE EDWARD ISLAND; QUEBEC

BOND, DONOVAN H., Professor Emeritus of Journalism, West Virginia University: WEST VIRGINIA

BOULAY, HARVEY, Director of Development, Rogerson House; Author, *The Twilight Cities:* MASSACHUSETTS

BOWER, BRUCE, Behavioral Sciences Editor, *Science News:* ANTHROPOLOGY; ARCHAEOLOGY

BRAASCH, BARBARA, Free-lance Travel Writer: DISNEY GOES PARISIAN; TRAVEL

BRAMMER, DANA B., Director, Public Policy Research Center, University of Mississippi: MISSISSIPPI

BRANDHORST, L. CARL, and JoANN C., Department of Geography, Western Oregon State College: OREGON

BROOM, JACK, Reporter, *The Seattle Times:* WASHINGTON

BUGAJSKI, JANUSZ, Associate Director of East European Studies, Center for Strategic and International Studies; Author, *Nations in Turmoil: Conflict and Cooperation in Eastern Europe, East European Fault Lines: Dissent, Opposition, and Social Activism:* ALBANIA

BURKS, ARDATH W., Professor Emeritus Asian Studies, Rutgers University; Author, *Third Order of the Rising Sun, Japan: A Postindustrial Power:* JAPAN

BUSH, GRAHAM W. A., Associate Professor of Political Studies, University of Auckland; Author, *Governing Big Cities, Advance in Order: The Auckland City Council 1971–89:* NEW ZEALAND

CAMP, RODERIC AI, Tulane University; Author, *Generals in the Palacio, Entrepreneurs and Politics in Twentieth Century Mexico:* MEXICO

CAMPBELL, ROBERT, University of Wyoming; Coauthor, *Discovering Wyoming:* WYOMING

CASEY, DAN, Staff Writer, *The (Annapolis) Capital:* MARYLAND

CASSIDY, SUZANNE, Free-lance U.S. Journalist, London: BIOGRAPHY—*John Major;* GREAT BRITAIN; GREAT BRITAIN —The Arts, Spotlight on Scotland

CHRISTENSEN, WILLIAM E., Professor of History, Midland Lutheran College; Author, *Saga of the Tower: A History of Dana College and Trinity Seminary, New Song to the Lord: A History of First Lutheran Church, Fremont, Nebraska:* NEBRASKA

COLE, JOHN N., Maine Journalist; Founder, *Maine Times;* Author, *Fishing Came First, In Maine, Striper, Salmon:* MAINE

COLLINS, BUD, Sports Columnist, *The Boston Globe;* Author, *My Life With The Pros:* SPORTS—*Tennis*

COLTON, KENT W., Executive Vice-President and Chief Executive Officer, National Association of Home Builders, Washington, DC: HOUSING

CONRADT, DAVID P., Professor of Political Science, University of Florida; Visiting Professor, University of Dresden, Germany; Author, *The German Polity, West European Politics;* GERMANY; OBITUARIES—*Willy Brandt*

COOPER, ILENE, Children's Book Editor, *Booklist Magazine:* LITERATURE—*Children's*

COOPER, MARY H., Staff Writer, *CQ Researcher,* Congressional Quarterly; Author, *The Business of Drugs:* ABORTION; ENERGY; FOREIGN AID; INSURANCE, LIABILITY; PHILANTHROPY

COPPEDGE, MICHAEL, Assistant Professor, Latin American Studies Program, Paul H. Nitze School of Advanced International Studies, Johns Hopkins University: ECUADOR; PERU; VENEZUELA

CORLEW, ROBERT E., Dean, Middle Tennessee State University: TENNESSEE

CORNWELL, ELMER E., JR., Professor of Political Science, Brown University: RHODE ISLAND

CUNNIFF, JOHN, Business News Analyst, The Associated Press; Author, *How to Stretch Your Dollar:* BUSINESS AND CORPORATE AFFAIRS; UNITED STATES—*The Economy*

CURRIER, CHET, Financial Writer, The Associated Press; Author, *The Investor's Encyclopedia, The 15-Minute*

Investor; Coauthor, *No-Cost/Low-Cost Investing:* STOCKS AND BONDS

CURTIS, L. PERRY, JR., Professor of History, Brown University: IRELAND

DANIELS, ROBERT V., Professor of History, University of Vermont; former Vermont state senator; Author, *Russia: The Roots of Confrontation:* VERMONT

DARBY, JOSEPH W., III, Reporter, *The Times-Picayune,* New Orleans: LOUISIANA

DAVID, LEONARD, Director, Space Data Resources and Information: SPACE EXPLORATION

De GREGORIO, GEORGE, Sports Department, *The New York Times;* Author, *Joe DiMaggio, An Informal Biography:* SPORTS—*Boxing, Swimming, Track and Field, Yachting*

DELZELL, CHARLES F., Professor of History Emeritus and Adjunct Professor, Vanderbilt University; Author, *Italy in the Twentieth Century, Mediterranean Fascism, Mussolini's Enemies:* ITALY

DENNIS, LARRY, Golf Writer, Creative Communications: SPORTS—*Golf*

DUFF, ERNEST A., Professor of Politics, Randolph-Macon Woman's College; Author, *Agrarian Reform in Colombia, Violence and Repression in Latin America, Leader and Party in Latin America:* COLOMBIA

ELKINS, ANN M., Fashion Director, *Good Housekeeping Magazine:* FASHION

ENSTAD, ROBERT H., Writer, *Chicago Tribune:* CHICAGO; ILLINOIS

EWEGEN, ROBERT D., Editorial Writer, *The Denver Post:* COLORADO

FAGEN, MORTON D., Formerly, AT&T Bell Laboratories; Editor, *A History of Engineering and Science in the Bell System,* Vol. 1, *The Early Years, 1875–1925,* and Vol. II, *National Security in War and Peace, 1925–1975:* COMMUNICATION TECHNOLOGY

FISHER, JIM, Editorial Writer and Columnist, *Lewiston Morning Tribune:* IDAHO

FRANCIS, DAVID R., Economy Page Editor, *The Christian Science Monitor:* INTERNATIONAL TRADE AND FINANCE; INTERNATIONAL TRADE AND FINANCE—*The "Buy American" Trend*

FRIIS, ERIK J., Editor and Publisher, *The Scandinavian-American Bulletin;* Coauthor and translator, *Nordic Democracy:* DENMARK; FINLAND; NORWAY; SWEDEN

GAILEY, HARRY A., Professor of History, San Jose State University; Author, *History of the Gambia, History of Africa, Road to Aba:* NIGERIA; RWANDA; ZAIRE

GEORGE, PAUL S., Assistant Professor, Miami-Dade Community College; Author, *Florida: Yesterday and Today, A Guide to the History of Florida:* FLORIDA

GIBSON, ROBERT C., Associate Editor, *The Billings Gazette;* Coauthor, *The Big Drive;* Editor, *Yellowstone on Fire, Wagons Across Wyoming:* MONTANA

GOODMAN, DONALD, Associate Professor of Sociology, John Jay College of Criminal Justice, City University of New York: PRISONS

GOODWIN, FREDERICK K., Director, National Institute of Mental Health: MEDICINE AND HEALTH—*Mental Health*

GORDON, MAYNARD M., Detroit Bureau Chief, *Dealer Business* magazine; Author, *The Iacocca Management Technique:* AUTOMOBILES

GOUDINOFF, PETER, Professor, Department of Political Science, University of Arizona; Author, *People's Guide to National Defense:* ARIZONA

GRAYSON, GEORGE W., Class of 1938 Professor of Government, College of William and Mary; Author, *The Politics of Mexican Oil, The United States and Mexico: Patterns of Influence, Oil and Mexican Foreign Policy:* THE YEAR OF SPAIN; BRAZIL; PORTUGAL; SPAIN

GROSSMAN, LAWRENCE, Director of Publications, The American Jewish Committee: RELIGION—*Judaism*

GROTH, ALEXANDER J., Professor of Political Science, University of California, Davis; Author, *People's Poland, Contemporary Politics: Europe, Comparative Resource Allocation, Public Policy Across Nations:* POLAND

HALLER, TIMOTHY G., Department of Political Science, Western Nevada Community College: NEVADA

HALSEY, MARGARET BROWN, Professor of Art History, New York City Technical College of the City University of New York: ART

HAND, SAMUEL B., Professor of History, University of Vermont: VERMONT

HARMON, CHARLES, American Library Association: LIBRARIES

HARVEY, ROSS M., Director, Policy and Planning, Department of Culture and Communications, Government of the Northwest Territories: NORTHWEST TERRITORIES

HELMREICH, ERNST C., Professor Emeritus of History, Bowdoin College; Author, *The German Churches under Hitler: Background, Struggle, and Epilogue:* AUSTRIA

HELMREICH, JONATHAN E., Professor of History, Allegheny College; Author, *Belgium and Europe: A Study in Small Power Diplomacy, Gathering Rare Ores: The Diplomacy of Uranium Acquisition, 1943–54;* Coauthor, *Rebirth: A History of Europe Since World War II:* BELGIUM; NETHERLANDS

HELMREICH, PAUL C., Professor of History, Wheaton College; Author, *Wheaton College: The Seminary Years, 1834–1912; From Paris to Sèvres: The Partition of the Ottoman Empire at the Peace Conference of 1919–1920;* Coauthor, *Rebirth: A History of Europe Since World War II:* SWITZERLAND

HINTON, HAROLD C., Professor Emeritus, The George Washington University; Author, *Korea under New Leadership: The Fifth Republic, Communist China in World Politics, The China Sea: The American Stake in Its Future:* KOREA

HOLLOWAY, HARRY, Professor Emeritus, Department of Political Science, University of Oklahoma; Coauthor, *Public Opinion: Coalitions, Elites, and Masses, Party and Factional Division in Texas:* OKLAHOMA

HOOVER, HERBERT T., Professor of History, University of South Dakota; Author, *South Dakota Leaders, The Yankton Sioux, To Be an Indian, The Chitimacha People, Higher Education in South Dakota:* SOUTH DAKOTA

HOPKO, THE REV. THOMAS, Assistant Professor, St. Vladimir's Orthodox Theological Seminary: RELIGION—*Orthodox Eastern*

HOWARD, CARLA BREER, Furnishings and Antiques Editor, *Traditional Home:* INTERIOR DESIGN

HOYT, CHARLES K., Senior Editor, *Architectural Record;* Author, *More Places for People, Building for Commerce and Industry:* ARCHITECTURE

HUFFMAN, GEORGE J., Universities Space Research Association: METEOROLOGY

HULBERT, DAN, *Atlanta Journal & Constitution:* TELEVISION AND RADIO; TELEVISION AND RADIO—*Regulating Cable;* THEATER

HUSTED, THOMAS A., Assistant Professor, Department of Economics, The American University: TAXATION

JACKSON, PAUL CONRAD, Editor, *The Calgary Sun;* Columnist, *Saskatoon Star-Phoenix;* Author, *Battleground: The Socialist Assault on Grant Devine's Canadian Dream:* ALBERTA; SASKATCHEWAN

JENNERMANN, DONALD, Director, University Honors Program, Indiana State University; Author, *Born of a Cretan Spring, Literature for Living:* LITERATURE—*English*

JONES, H. G., Curator, North Carolina Collection, University of North Carolina at Chapel Hill; Author, *North Carolina Illustrated, 1524–1984:* NORTH CAROLINA

JUDD, DENNIS R., Professor and Chair, Department of Political Science, University of Missouri-St. Louis; Coauthor, *The Development of American Public Policy, Leadership and Urban Regeneration;* Coeditor, *Urban Affairs Quarterly:* CITIES AND URBAN AFFAIRS; CITIES AND URBAN AFFAIRS—*The Los Angeles Riots*

KARNES, THOMAS L., Professor of History Emeritus, Arizona State University; Author, *Latin American Policy of the United States, Failure of Union: Central America 1824–1960:* CENTRAL AMERICA

KIMBALL, LORENZO K., Professor Emeritus, Department of Political Science, University of Utah: UTAH

KIMBELL, CHARLES L., Senior Foreign Mineral Specialist, U.S. Bureau of Mines: STATISTICAL AND TABULAR DATA—*Mineral and Metal Production*

KING, PETER J., Professor of History, Carleton University, Ottawa; Author, *Utilitarian Jurisprudence in America:* ONTARIO; OTTAWA

KINNEAR, MICHAEL, Professor of History, University of Manitoba; Author, *The Fall of Lloyd George, The British Voter:* MANITOBA

KISSELGOFF, ANNA, Chief Dance Critic, *The New York Times:* DANCE

KOBILINSKY, LAWRENCE, Professor, John Jay College of Criminal Justice, City University of New York: CRIME—*DNA "Fingerprinting"*

KOZINN, ALLAN, Music Critic, *The New York Times;* Author, *Mischa Elman and the Romantic Style, The Guitar: The History, The Music, The Players:* MUSIC—*Classical*

KRONISH, SYD, Stamp Editor, The Associated Press: STAMPS AND STAMP COLLECTING; STAMPS AND STAMP COLLECTING—*The Elvis Stamp*

KUNIHOLM, BRUCE R., Director, Terry Sanford Institute of Public Policy, Duke University: TURKEY

KUNZ, KENEVA, University of Iceland: ICELAND

LABATON, STEPHEN, Washington Bureau, *The New York Times*: BANKING AND FINANCE

LaFRANCHI, HOWARD, Staff Correspondent, *The Christian Science Monitor*: FRANCE; MOROCCO; TUNISIA

LAI, DAVID CHUENYAN, Professor of Geography, University of Victoria, British Columbia; Author, *The Forbidden City Within Victoria: Myth, Symbol and Streetscape of Canada's Earliest Chinatown*: HONG KONG

LANCASTER, CAROL, Director, African Studies Program, Georgetown University; Coeditor, *African Debt and Financing*: AFRICA

LAPCHICK, RICHARD E., Director, Center for the Study of Sports in Society, Northeastern University: THE PRO ATHLETE TODAY

LAWRENCE, ROBERT M., Professor of Political Science, Colorado State University; Author, *The Strategic Defense Initiative*: MILITARY AFFAIRS

LEE, STEWART M., Professor of Economics, Geneva College; Coauthor, *Consumer Economics: The Consumer in Our Society*: CONSUMER AFFAIRS

LEEPSON, MARC, Free-lance Writer: DRUGS AND ALCOHOL; SOCIAL WELFARE

LEVINE, LOUIS, Professor, Department of Biology, City College of New York; Author, *Biology of the Gene, Biology for a Modern Society*: BIOTECHNOLOGY; GENETICS; MICROBIOLOGY

LEWIS, ANNE C., Education Policy Writer: EDUCATION

LEWIS, JEROME R., Director for Public Administration, College of Urban Affairs and Public Policy, University of Delaware: DELAWARE

LOBRON, BARBARA L., Editor, Photographer, Writer: PHOTOGRAPHY

LOESCHER, GIL, Professor of International Relations, University of Notre Dame; Author, *Calculated Kindness: Refugees and America's Half-Open Door, Refugees and International Relations*: REFUGEES AND IMMIGRATION

MARCOPOULOS, GEORGE J., Professor of History, Tufts University: CYPRUS; GREECE

MATHESON, JIM, Sportswriter, *Edmonton Journal*: SPORTS—*Ice Hockey*

MAYERCHAK, PATRICK M., Professor of Political Science, Virginia Military Institute; Author, *Scholar's Guide to Southeast Asia*; Coauthor, *Linkage or Bondage: US-ASEAN Economic Relations*: MALAYSIA; SINGAPORE

McCORQUODALE, SUSAN, Professor of Political Science, Memorial University of Newfoundland: NEWFOUNDLAND

McGILL, DAVID A., Professor of Marine Science, U.S. Coast Guard Academy: OCEANOGRAPHY

McLAURIN, RONALD D., President, Abbott Associates, Inc.; Author, *The Emergence of a New Lebanon: Fantasy or Reality?, Lebanon and the World in the 1980s*: LEBANON

MEDINGER, DANIEL, Editor, *The Catholic Review*: RELIGION—*Roman Catholicism*

MICHAELIS, PATRICIA A., Curator of Manuscripts, Kansas State Historical Society: KANSAS

MICHIE, ARUNA NAYYAR, Associate Professor of Political Science, Kansas State University: BANGLADESH

MILLER, PENNY M., Professor, Department of Political Science, University of Kentucky; Coauthor, *Political Parties and Primaries in Kentucky, The Kentucky Legislature: Two Decades of Change*: KENTUCKY

MILLER, RANDALL M., Department of History, St. Joseph's University; Author, *Immigration to New York, "Dear Master": Letters of a Slave Family, Shades of the Sunbelt: Essays on Race, Ethnicity and the Urban South*: ETHNIC GROUPS, U.S.

MILWARD, JOHN, Free-lance Writer and Critic: MUSIC—*Popular and Jazz*

MITCHELL, G. E., Professor of Physics, North Carolina State University: PHYSICS

MITCHELL, RICK, U.N. Observer and Reporter: BIOGRAPHY—*Boutros Boutros-Ghali*; UNITED NATIONS; UNITED NATIONS—*The New UN*

MONASTERSKY, RICHARD, Earth Sciences Editor, *Science News*: GEOLOGY

MORTIMER, ROBERT A., Professor, Department of Political Science, Haverford College; Author, *The Third World Coalition in International Politics*; Coauthor, *Politics and Society in Contemporary Africa*: ALGERIA

MORTON, DESMOND, Professor of History and Principal, Erindale College, University of Toronto; Author, *Working People: An Illustrated History of the Canadian Labour Movement, A Military History of Canada*: CANADA

MURPHY, ROBERT F., Editorial Writer, *The Hartford Courant*: CONNECTICUT

NAFTALIN, ARTHUR, Professor Emeritus of Public Affairs, University of Minnesota: MINNESOTA

NEUMANN, JAMES, Free-lance Writer, Grand Forks, ND: NORTH DAKOTA

NEWLAND, ED, Assistant City Editor, *Richmond Times-Dispatch*: VIRGINIA

OCHSENWALD, WILLIAM, Professor of History, Virginia Polytechnic Institute and State University; Author, *The Middle East: A History, The Hijaz Railroad, Religion, Society, and the State in Arabia*: KUWAIT; SAUDI ARABIA

O'CONNOR, ROBERT E., Associate Professor of Political Science, The Pennsylvania State University; Coauthor, *Politics and Structure: Essentials of American National Government*: PENNSYLVANIA

O'MEARA, PATRICK, Director, African Studies Program, Indiana University; Coeditor, *Africa, International Politics in Southern Africa, Southern Africa, The Continuing Crisis*: ANGOLA; MOZAMBIQUE; SOUTH AFRICA; ZIMBABWE

ORTIZ, PETER J., The San Juan Star: PUERTO RICO

PALMER, NORMAN D., Professor Emeritus of Political Science and South Asian Studies, University of Pennsylvania; Author, *Westward Watch: The United States and the Changing Western Pacific, The United States and India: The Dimensions of Influence, Elections and Political Development: The South Asian Experience, The New Regionalism in Asia and the Pacific*: INDIA; SRI LANKA

PEARSON, FREDERIC S., Director, Center for Peace and Conflict Studies, Wayne State University, Detroit; Coauthor, *International Relations: The Global Condition, Fuel on the Fire? Effects of Armament During Warfare*: UNITED STATES—*Foreign Affairs*

PERETZ, DON, Professor of Political Science, State University of New York at Binghamton; Author, *The West Bank—History, Politics, Society & Economy, Government and Politics of Israel, The Middle East Today*: EGYPT; ISRAEL

PERKINS, KENNETH J., Assistant Professor of History, University of South Carolina: LIBYA; RELIGION—*Islam*

PERRY, DAVID K., Associate Professor, Department of Journalism, The University of Alabama: PUBLISHING

PIPPIN, LARRY L., Professor of Political Science, University of the Pacific; Author, *The Remón Era*: ARGENTINA; PARAGUAY; URUGUAY

PLATT, HERMANN K., Professor of History, Saint Peter's College: NEW JERSEY

POOLE, PETER A., Author, *The Vietnamese in Thailand, Eight Presidents and Indochina*; Coauthor, *American Diplomacy*: CAMBODIA; LAOS; VIETNAM

PRIESTER, REINHARD, Center for Biomedical Ethics, University of Minnesota: MEDICINE AND HEALTH—*Medical Ethics*

RALOFF, JANET, Senior Editor, *Science News*: ENVIRONMENT; ENVIRONMENT—*Earth Summit*

REBACK, MARILYN, Associate Editor, *The Numismatist*: COINS AND COIN COLLECTING

REED, WILLIAM CYRUS, Director of African Studies, The American University in Cairo (Egypt): KENYA; TANZANIA; UGANDA

REMINGTON, ROBIN ALISON, Frederick A. Middlebush Professor of Political Science, University of Missouri-Columbia: THE BREAKUP OF YUGOSLAVIA

REUNING, WINIFRED, Writer, Polar Program, National Science Foundation: POLAR RESEARCH

RICHTER, LINDA K., Professor of Political Science, Kansas State University; Author, *Land Reform and Tourism Development: Policy-Making in the Philippines, The Politics of Tourism in Asia*: BIOGRAPHY—*Fidel Ramos*; MYANMAR; PHILIPPINES

RICHTER, WILLIAM L., Professor and Head, Department of Political Science, Kansas State University: PAKISTAN

RIGGAN, WILLIAM, Associate Editor, *World Literature Today*, University of Oklahoma; Author, *Picaros, Madmen, Naifs, and Clowns, Comparative Literature and Literary Theory*: LITERATURE—*World*

ROBERTS, SAM, Urban Affairs Columnist, *The New York Times*: NEW YORK CITY

ROBINSON, LEIF J., Editor, *Sky & Telescope*; Author, *Outdoor Optics*: ASTRONOMY

RODGERS, THOMAS E., University of Southern Indiana: INDIANA

ROSS, RUSSELL M., Professor of Political Science, University of Iowa; Author, *State and Local Government and Administration, Iowa Government and Administration:* IOWA

ROVNER, JULIE, *Congressional Quarterly:* MEDICINE AND HEALTH—*Health Care*

RUBIN, JIM, Supreme Court Correspondent, The Associated Press: CRIME; LAW

RUFF, NORMAN J., Assistant Professor, Department of Political Science, University of Victoria, B.C.; Coauthor, *The Reins of Power: Governing British Columbia:* BRITISH COLUMBIA

SALSINI, PAUL, Staff Development Director, *The Milwaukee Journal:* WISCONSIN

SAVAGE, DAVID, Free-lance Writer: CANADA—*The Arts;* LITERATURE—*Canadian*

SAWATSKY, DON, Free-lance Writer/Broadcaster; Author, *Ghost Town Trails of the Yukon:* YUKON

SCHLOSSBERG, DAN, Baseball Writer; Author, *The Baseball IQ Challenge, The Baseball Catalog, The Baseball Book of Why, Cooperstown: Baseball's Hall of Fame Players:* BIOGRAPHY—*George Howard Brett, Robin Yount;* SPORTS—*Baseball*

SCHROEDER, RICHARD, Consultant, Organization of American States: BIOGRAPHY—*Rigoberta Menchú;* BOLIVIA; CARIBBEAN; CHILE; HAITI; LATIN AMERICA

SCHWAB, PETER, Professor of Political Science, State University of New York at Purchase; Author, *Ethiopia: Politics, Economics, and Society, Human Rights: Cultural and Ideological Perspectives:* ETHIOPIA, SOMALIA

SEIDERS, DAVID F., Chief Economist and Senior Staff Vice-President, National Association of Home Builders, Washington, DC: HOUSING

SENSER, ROBERT A., Free-lance Writer, Washington, DC: THE U.S. EMPLOYMENT SCENE; EXECUTIVE COMPENSATION—*A Discordant Trend;* HUMAN RIGHTS

SETH, R. P., Chairman, Department of Economics, Mount Saint Vincent University, Halifax: CANADA—*The Economy;* NOVA SCOTIA

SEYBOLD, PAUL G., Professor, Department of Chemistry, Wright State University: CHEMISTRY

SHARLET, ROBERT, Professor of Political Science, Union College; Author, *Soviet Constitutional Crisis:* BALTIC REPUBLICS; COMMONWEALTH OF INDEPENDENT STATES; GEORGIA, REPUBLIC OF

SHEPRO, CARL E., Professor of Political Science, University of Alaska-Anchorage: ALASKA

SHOGAN, ROBERT, National Political Correspondent, Washington Bureau, *Los Angeles Times;* Author, *A Question of Judgment, Promises to Keep:* THE 1992 ELECTION: THE DEMOCRATS TAKE BACK THE PRESIDENCY; CONGRESS: A STORM CENTER IN 1992; BIOGRAPHY—*Patrick Joseph Buchanan, George Herbert Walker Bush, Bill Clinton, Albert Gore, Jr., James Danforth Quayle, Ross Perot;* UNITED STATES—*Domestic Affairs*

SIMON, SHELDON W., Professor of Political Science, Arizona State University-Tempe; Author, *The Future of Asian-Pacific Security Collaboration:* ASIA

SMITH, REX, Editor, *The* (Troy, NY) *Record:* NEW YORK

SNODSMITH, RALPH L., Ornamental Horticulturist; Author, *Ralph Snodsmith's Tips from the Garden Hotline:* GARDENING AND HORTICULTURE

SPYCHALSKI, JOHN C., Chairman, Department of Business Logistics, College of Business Administration, The Pennsylvania State University: TRANSPORTATION

STARR, JOHN BRYAN, President, Yale-China Association; Author, *Continuing the Revolution: The Political Thought of Mao;* Editor, *The Future of U.S.-China Relations:* CHINA; TAIWAN

STERN, JEROME H., Professor of English, Florida State University; Author, *Making Shapely Fiction:* LITERATURE—*American*

STEWART, WILLIAM H., Professor of Political Science, The University of Alabama; Coauthor, *Alabama Government and Politics;* Author, *Leadership in the Public Service, The Alabama Constitution:* ALABAMA

STIEBER, JACK, Professor Emeritus, School of Labor and Industrial Relations and Department of Economics, Michigan State University; Author, *U.S. Industrial Relations: The Next Twenty Years, Governing the UAW, Public Employee Unionism:* LABOR

SUTTON, STAN, Sportswriter, *The Courier-Journal,* Louisville, KY: SPORTS—*Auto Racing, Horse Racing*

TABORSKY, EDWARD, Professor of Government, University of Texas at Austin; Author, *Communism in Czechoslovakia, 1948–1960, Communist Penetration of the Third World:* CZECHOSLOVAKIA

TAYLOR, WILLIAM L., Professor of History, Plymouth State College: NEW HAMPSHIRE

TESAR, JENNY, Science and Medicine Writer; Author, *Introduction to Animals, Parents as Teachers:* A GROWING INTEREST IN ALTERNATIVE MEDICINE; COMPUTERS; COMPUTERS—*The Tiny Personal Computer;* MEDICINE AND HEALTH; MEDICINE AND HEALTH—*New Tuberculosis Threat;* OBITUARIES—*Barbara McClintock*

THEISEN, CHARLES W., Assistant News Editor, *The Detroit News:* MICHIGAN

TIERNEY, MICHAEL W., International Franchise Association: RETAILING—*Franchising*

TISMANEANU, VLADIMIR, Associate Professor, Department of Government and Politics, University of Maryland (College Park); Author, *Reinventing Politics: Eastern Europe from Stalin to Havel:* BULGARIA; HUNGARY; ROMANIA

TURNER, ARTHUR CAMPBELL, Professor of Political Science, University of California, Riverside; Coauthor, *Ideology and Power in the Middle East:* IRAN; IRAQ; JORDAN; MIDDLE EAST; OBITUARIES—*Menahem Begin;* SYRIA

TURNER, CHARLES H., Free-lance Writer: HAWAII

TURNER, DARRELL J., Associate Editor, Religious News Service, New York, NY: RELIGION—*Overview, Far Eastern, Protestantism*

TYER, CHARLIE B., Associate Professor, Department of Government and International Studies, University of South Carolina; Coeditor, *Local Government in South Carolina, Government in the Palmetto State:* SOUTH CAROLINA

VAN RIPER, PAUL P., Professor Emeritus and Head, Department of Political Science, Texas A&M University; Editor and Coauthor, *The Wilson Influence on Public Administration:* POSTAL SERVICE

VOLL, JOHN O., Professor of History, University of New Hampshire; Author, *Islam: Continuity and Change in the Modern World;* Coauthor, *Sudan: Unity and Diversity in a Multicultural Society;* Editor, *Sudan: State and Society in Crisis:* SUDAN

VOLSKY, GEORGE, Center for Advanced International Studies, University of Miami: CUBA

WEATHERBEE, DONALD E., Department of Government, University of South Carolina: INDONESIA; THAILAND

WEAVER, JOHN B., Department of History, Sinclair Community College (Dayton, OH): OHIO

WELLER, MARC, Lecturer, University of Cambridge Research Centre for International Law; Coeditor, *The Kuwait Crisis, Volumes I and III:* LAW—*International*

WHELPLEY, KEITH, Writer, *Las Cruces Sun-News:* NEW MEXICO

WILLIAMS, C. FRED, Professor of History, University of Arkansas at Little Rock; Author, *Arkansas: An Illustrated History of the Land of Opportunity, Arkansas: A Documentary History:* ARKANSAS

WILLIS, F. ROY, Professor of History, University of California, Davis; Author, *France, Germany and the New Europe, 1945–1968, Italy Chooses Europe, The French Paradox:* EUROPE

WISNER, ROBERT N., Professor, Iowa State University; Coeditor, *Marketing for Farmers;* Author, *World Food Trade and U.S. Agriculture:* AGRICULTURE; FOOD

WOLF, WILLIAM, New York University; Author, *The Marx Brothers, Landmark Films, The Cinema and Our Century:* MOTION PICTURES; OBITUARIES—*Marlene Dietrich*

WOLFE, JOHN, New York Bureau Chief, *Advertising Age:* ADVERTISING

YOUNGER, R. M., Journalist and Author; Author, *Australia and the Australians, Australia! Australia! A Bicentennial Record:* AUSTRALIA; BIOGRAPHY—*Paul John Keating*

Acknowledgments

We also wish to thank the following for their services: typesetting, Dix Type Inc.; color separations, Gamma One, Inc. and Colotone Graphics; test stock printed on Champion's 60# Courtland Matte; covers printed by Mid-City Lithographers; cover materials provided by Holliston Mills, Inc. and Decorative Specialties International, Inc.; and printing and binding by R. R. Donnelley & Sons, Co.

Index

Main article headings appear in this index as bold-faced capitals; subjects within articles appear as lower-case entries. Both the general references and the subentries should be consulted for maximum usefulness of this index. Illustrations are indexed herein. Cross references are to the entries in this index.